FINANCIAL ACCOUNTING

THE IMPACT ON DECISION MAKERS

GARY A. PORTER

LOYOLA UNIVERSITY CHICAGO

CURTIS L. NORTON

NORTHERN ILLINOIS UNIVERSITY

THE DRYDEN PRESS

HARCOURT BRACE COLLEGE PUBLISHERS

Fort Worth   Philadelphia   San Diego   New York   Orlando   Austin   San Antonio
Toronto   Montreal   London   Sydney   Tokyo

Editor-in-Chief: Lyn Keeney Hastert
Acquisitions Editors: Bill Teague, Elizabeth Storey
Developmental Editor: Craig Avery
Project Editor: Jim Patterson
Designer: Linda Wooton Miller
Production Managers: Kelly Cordes, Mandy Manzano
Photo Permissions Editor: Elizabeth Banks
Director of Marketing: Diana Farrell
Product Manager: Annie Todd
Marketing Coordinator: Kipp Murray

Copy Editor: JaNoel Lowe
Indexer: Sylvia Coates
Compositor: Monotype
Text Type: 11/12 Adobe Garamond

Cover photo: © 1994 Ben Britt

Some material in this work previously appeared in FINANCIAL ACCOUNTING: The Impact on Decision Makers, Preliminary Edition.

Address for orders:
The Dryden Press
6277 Sea Harbor Drive
Orlando, FL 32887-6777
1-800-782-4479, or 1-800-433-0001 (in Florida)

Address for editorial correspondence:
The Dryden Press
301 Commerce Street, Suite 3700
Fort Worth, TX 76102

ISBN: 0-15-500192-2

Library of Congress Catalog Card Number: 94-70134

Printed in the United States of America

4 5 6 7 8 9 0 1 2 3 0 3 2 10 9 8 7 6 5 4 3 1

The Dryden Press
Harcourt Brace College Publishers

To those who really "count":
Melissa
Kathy, Amy, Andrew

The Dryden Series in Accounting

Introductory

BISCHOFF
Introduction to College Accounting
Third Edition

Principles

HANSON, HAMRE, AND WALGENBACH
Principles of Accounting
Sixth Edition

Computerized

BISCHOFF AND WANLASS
*The Computer Connection: General Ledger and Practice Sets
to accompany Introductory Accounting*
Second Edition

WANLASS
Computer Resource Guide: Principles of Accounting
Fourth Edition

Financial

PORTER AND NORTON
Financial Accounting: The Impact on Decision Makers

STICKNEY AND WEIL
Financial Accounting: An Introduction to Concepts, Methods, and Uses
Seventh Edition

BEIRNE AND DAUDERIS
Financial Accounting: An Introduction to Decision Making

BACKER, ELGERS, AND ASEBROOK
Financial Accounting: Concepts and Practices

Managerial

MAHER, STICKNEY, AND WEIL
*Managerial Accounting: An Introduction to Concepts, Methods,
and Uses*
Fifth Edition

KETZ, CAMPBELL, AND BAXENDALE
Management Accounting

Intermediate

WILLIAMS, STANGA, AND HOLDER
Intermediate Accounting
Fifth Edition

Advanced

PAHLER AND MORI
Advanced Accounting: Concepts and Practice
Fifth Edition

HUEFNER AND LARGAY
Advanced Financial Accounting
Third Edition

Financial Statement Analysis

STICKNEY
Financial Statement Analysis: A Strategic Perspective
Second Edition

Auditing

RITTENBERG AND SCHWIEGER
Auditing: Concepts for a Changing Environment

GUY, ALDERMAN, AND WINTERS
Auditing
Third Edition

Theory

BLOOM AND ELGERS
Foundations in Accounting Theory and Policy: A Reader

BLOOM AND ELGERS
Issues in Accounting Theory and Policy: A Reader

BELKAOUI
Accounting Theory
Third Edition

Taxation

EVERETT, RAABE, AND FORTIN
1995 Income Tax Fundamentals

DUNCAN
Essentials of U.S. Taxation
Second Edition

Reference

MILLER AND BAILEY
Miller Comprehensive GAAS Guide
College Edition

WILLIAMS AND MILLER
Miller Comprehensive GAAP Guide
College Edition

Governmental and Not-for-Profit

DOUGLAS
Governmental and Nonprofit Accounting: Theory and Practice
Second Edition

ZIEBELL AND DECOSTER
Management Control Systems in Nonprofit Organizations

The Harcourt Brace College Outline Series

CAMPBELL, GRIERSON, AND TAYLOR
Principles of Accounting I
Revised Edition

EMERY
Principles of Accounting II

EMERY
Intermediate Accounting I
Second Edition

EMERY
Intermediate Accounting II

FRIGO
Cost Accounting

POTEAU
Advanced Accounting

Preface

We are all conscious of the dynamic and increasingly complex nature of the business world. Students are under ever-increasing pressure to obtain both functional and analytical skills in order to compete in this very competitive environment. As accounting educators, we must meet the call for the way we teach our students to give them every advantage in their post-academic careers. Because of these external pressures the Accounting Education Change Commission and others have mandated that we must begin by teaching our students to "learn to learn," emphasizing the development of critical thinking skills necessary to make and understand decisions in the world of business. Much of the reform effort to date has, for good reason, centered on the introductory courses. As authors, our mission in writing this introduction to financial accounting was to address the needs of today's students as they enter the changing business world and to give them the skills necessary to "learn to learn."

Throughout the writing and development of this book, four basic philosophies guided our efforts to fulfill this mission:

■ **Most students in the first course will be users, not preparers, of accounting information in their careers.** Does this mean that students in a first accounting course should not be asked to record transactions and prepare financial statements? Not necessarily. We feel that the guiding principle should be that preparation of accounting information should be used as a learning tool if it will enhance the student's understanding of how the information is used.

Although many instructors continue to rely on preparing journal entries as one major route to accounting understanding, we have chosen to adopt a more conceptual approach: linking all journal entries and transactions to the financial statements with the use of the accounting equation. This forces students to think about the impact each transaction has on the financial statements. It also allows flexibility for the instructor who chooses not to cover the debit/credit mechanism and would rather simply present all transactions in terms of the accounting equation.

The design and pedagogical framework of this book were carefully constructed to support the theme that understanding rather than preparation of accounting information is the goal. This includes *integration of ratio analysis* throughout. For example, we present receivable turnover in the chapter on cash and receivables. Meticulous attention to the *integration of conceptual learning objectives* throughout the text material reinforces the decision orientation of the book. **Accounting for Your Decisions** is a unique feature that places the student in a business situation where he or she is asked to role-play as a banker, broker, stockholder, or other real user of accounting information. **Linkages** at the beginning of each chapter draw the student's attention to the relationships among various topics and concepts in previous, current, and upcoming chapters. In addition, *all exhibits, statements, and business documents are presented in the most clear, real-world fashion possible.*

■ **A course emphasizing the use of accounting information should stress financial statements throughout—and whenever possible, the statements of real companies.** It is our hope that when students have completed this textbook they can read and understand the financial statements of real companies and make business decisions based on those statements. In addition, they should appreciate the value of the information contained in other parts of an annual report. We have used the innovative and entertaining *annual report of Ben & Jerry's Homemade, Inc. in every chapter,* as well as the reports of numerous other highly recognizable corporations, to enhance student interest and learning. A copy of the entire **Ben & Jerry's Annual Report** is packaged with new copies of the textbook, and Appendix 1 features the financial statements and notes from that annual report.

From Concept to Practice marginal assignments, using Ben & Jerry's Annual Report, appear within the chapter as additional references to the statements under discussion. (An index of these assignments appears at the end of this book.) **Reading and Interpreting Financial Statements** cases are at the end of each chapter to apply the concepts therein.

■ **The emphasis should be on concepts rather than procedures** in a course aimed at users of financial statements. After many months of intensive market research with almost 300 accounting instructors, we found that most of you have shifted the focus of your course to emphasize the conceptual framework of accounting from the more traditional method of teaching and learning mechanics. In general, highly procedural topics such as specialized journals and subsidiary ledgers are simply not covered. Certain other relatively procedural topics like reversing entries and payroll accounting are placed in appendixes at the end of the chapters to allow instructors the flexibility to cover as they see fit.

The first four chapters set the tone for the balance of concepts and procedures. Important accounting concepts such as the nature of business activities, as well as accounting's role within the firm, are introduced in Chapter 1. The conceptual framework of accounting is presented in Chapter 2 as an overview of financial statements (both hypothetical and real) found in the remainder of the chapter. Adjusting entries are illustrated in Chapter 4, but only after a thorough discussion of the accrual accounting system. *This theme—presenting traditional methods and procedures within a conceptual context—recurs throughout the book.*

The conceptual focus of the book is evident in the treatment of two important topics in a course aimed at users: *cash flows* and *statement analysis*. Both are covered, where appropriate, throughout the book as each major category of assets, liabilities, and owners' equity is discussed. The final two chapters of the book (Chapter 14 on cash flows and Chapter 15 on financial statement analysis) then serve to draw together many of these ideas introduced earlier.

■ **"Why" is more important than "how" if the focus is on using accounting information to make decisions.** An emphasis on the use rather than the preparation of accounting information, and a focus on concepts as opposed to procedure, demands a book that stresses the why rather than the how. A number of elements through out the book give the reader an appreciation of why accounting is important in decision making. Every chapter opens with a **Focus on Financial Results,** which highlights the role of accounting information in a real company. **Accounting for Your Decisions** boxes are placed strategically throughout all chapters and require the reader to think about why accounting information is important in making decisions. The end-of-chapter material goes beyond the how and requires analysis, thought, and response.

Supplements and Teaching Materials That Emphasize Integration and Flexibility

It is critical to the success of any accounting textbook that it be accompanied by a supplements and teaching package as functional and innovative as the narrative and problems in the book. It is also critical that all of these components are thoroughly integrated, both conceptually and practically, for the enhancement of the student and the ease of use for the instructor. With these goals in mind, The Dryden Press introduces a package to accompany our textbook that is just as strongly researched and developed—and just as flexible—as the book itself.

Planning for the package began with rigorous market research and concept testing of each component. Authors were chosen generally from among those who had reviewed and understood the aims of the textbook, and we benefited from their synergies during a special supplements author team meeting held for final concept approval and to verify plans for articulation among the package components.

Supplements authors continue to communicate with one another to refine their common goals of maximum integration, enhancement of learning, and teaching flexibility. For students we provide traditional supplements (study guides, working papers, and practice sets); however, the student and instructor may want to innovate in how they use these materials, depending on the instructor's focus in the course. For the instructor, we provide new and exciting software and visual supplements that complement all of the more traditional items.

For the Instructor

Instructor's Resource Kit, by Patricia Doherty (Boston University) is a complete toolbox for easing the instructor's transition to a less procedural, more financial statement-oriented and interactive course. The Package Integrator is a roadmap of the entire textbook and supplement package. Other key components of the kit include the Financial Statement Resource (also available in the Student Resource Kit), Chapter Outlines (with Integrated Lecture Suggestions), Projects and Activities (including In-Class Discussions, Outside Assignments, Food for Thought, and Ethical Dilemmas), and a Bibliography of Readings. Together, these components will provide ideas, suggestions, and resources for a variety of classroom styles across the spectrum of instructors within a department. *Available printed and on a computer diskette.*

Financial Statement Resource, a component of the Instructor's Resource Kit, gives instructors and students access to the financial statements of the companies discussed in the textbook. The complete annual reports of three of the companies are reprinted in the Instructor's Resource Kit and the remaining eleven reports are available on disk.

Solutions Manual, prepared by the textbook authors for complete consistency with the textbook, has been carefully reviewed and exhaustively checked for accuracy. Over 50 class test sites have also used the Solutions Manual successfully, along with the Test Bank and the textbook, as a further validation of the authors' efforts.

Electronic Lectures in Powerpoint, by Jay LaGregs (Tyler Junior College), provides visual enhancement for a course that stresses the impact of accounting practices on financial statements. It is designed in a Windows environment for schools with access to computer screens projected with an LCD monitor. Included here are detailed lecture outlines of every chapter in the textbook. Also included are many of the projected images in the Teaching Transparencies. Electronic Lectures in Power point makes it easier for instructors to create an interactive presentation focusing on what-if analysis and decision-making. Although use with Powerpoint allows instructors to customize and even create their own lecture enhancements, viewer files are included for non-Powerpoint classrooms.

Teaching and Solutions Transparencies, by Jay LaGregs (Tyler Junior College), Kathy Horton (University of Illinois at Chicago), and the textbook authors, enhance classroom presentations with acetates of approximately 100 of the Electronic Lectures as well as solutions to end-of-chapter material. Teaching Transparencies, selected by Patricia Doherty (Boston University), are available in electronic format as well as in these overhead acetates. Solutions Transparencies for selected exercises, problems, and cases have been chosen by Kathy Horton for maximum classroom usefulness. Specially designed enlarged-type transparency masters are included for all remaining end-of-chapter exercises, problems, and cases.

Test Bank, by David Fetyko (Kent State University) and Jane Park (California State University at Los Angeles), includes questions that reflect the changes in the course focus. Test items focus on real financial statements provided as data. Procedural problems are followed by a few multiple-choice, short answer and/or essay questions that test understanding, require analysis and interpretation, or ask "why" or "what if." All short problems and several other questions in each chapter are based on *real-company financial statements.*

All problems have been carefully reviewed for consistency with the textbook—both the narrative and end-of-chapter material. Each solution was checked by at least two instructors. The Test Bank has also been used successfully at class test sites along with the textbook and Solutions Manual.

EXAMASTER+ Computerized Test Bank, the computerized testing software, is almost as important as the bank of test items itself. By way of its easy-to-use editing and scrambling functions, EXAMASTER+ software allows instructors to customize their tests by selecting items according to criteria meaningful to the changing course focus. In addition, Dryden's **RequesTest** service allows instructors to call a toll-free number to order custom test masters. A fax service is also available. RequesTest service and software support are available Monday through Friday, 9 AM to 4 PM (Central Time) for questions, guidance, or other help.

Lecture Launching Videos are based on the chapter-opening vignettes. These brief clips (ten minutes or less) use real-company examples to show why accounting is needed, how accounting decisions are made, and the business implications of these decisions. Many of the videos are based on material that is culled from CBS News reports, some are shot on location. These videos can be used as mini-cases or ethical dilemmas to provoke classroom discussion. Notes and suggestions on using the videos appear in the Package Integrator portion of the Instructor's Resource Kit.

For the Student

Student Resource Kit, by Diana Adcox (University of North Florida), Kathy Horton (University of Illinois at Chicago), and Mary Nisbet (University of California at Santa Barbara), allows an instructor to design student support material for his or her specific course by providing an array of options for either limited or complete review of each concept and procedure discussed in the textbook. All of the materials in the kit will enable instructors to focus on the "how to," the "why," or both. The potential components of the Student Resource Kit include the Procedural Review, Study Guide, Working Papers, Checklist of Key Figures, and Financial Statement Resource.

Study Guide, by Mary Nisbet (University of California—Santa Barbara), mirrors the text in style and presentation. The Study Guide focuses on helping students set priorities (focusing on the key concepts), review terms and concepts, and practice for taking tests.

Procedural Review, by Diana Adcox (University of North Florida), allows instructors to concentrate less on procedures in lectures and discussion while assigning students to practice procedures outside of class. Based on a procedural audit of the textbook by the authors, the Procedural Review guides students through procedures applicable to each textbook chapter. Each procedure is clearly labeled and keyed by Learning Objective; then an exercise-style example provides annotated steps for the calculations. Solutions and approaches to each example are provided, along with useful tips and student exercises with solutions. Flexible custom options allow the instructor to choose the procedures that will be included in the Procedural Review for his or her own classes. The Procedural Review does not duplicate the Study Guide.

Working Papers, selected by Kathy Horton (University of Illinois at Chicago), allow instructors to select from among partially filled-out or blank working papers for every procedural problem in the book for inclusion in the Student Resource Kit.

Computerized Study Guide, based on the Test Bank and the Study Guide, prepares students to take tests and drills them on concepts and procedures.

FS/CASE (Financial Statement Case) Software, by Tom McLaughlin (Monmouth College), consists of a series of mini-cases, with real financial statements, that enable students to review both the procedural and conceptual aspects of the course. Students perform an analysis in a case format, interacting with computerized data to strengthen their understanding of the text by Learning Objectives. For example, a unit on inventories would ask students to use the LIFO method with company data. It would query them on what the data tells them, how it impacts financial statements, and whether it would have been more appropriate to use FIFO (and why). The package will include master disks to be provided to schools with a file for each textbook chapter and a separate instructor's disk with solutions to all problems.

Spreadsheet Templates Problem Solver (STPS), by Paul Bayes (East Tennessee State University), consists of Lotus templates for relevant textbook problems and exercises. Many templates include separate what-if questions that ask students about financial statement relationships. Separate "instructor-only" templates provide a fresh source for template test assignments or classroom demonstration material.

General Ledger Problem Solver (GLPS) by Leon Hanouille (Syracuse University) and Jay Joseph Cappy, is a computerized general ledger program to help students solve selected exercises and problems in the textbook. The graphical user interface, pull-down menus, context-sensitive help, and program tour make this DOS-based program easy to use. Special computerized instructions replace the manual requirements for each problem included here. Available in network and stand-alone versions.

Tamije Garden Supply, Inc.: A Service and Merchandising Practice Set by Leon Hanouille (Syracuse University), is a service and merchandising corporate practice set covering one month of operations and focusing on the accounting cycle. The emphasis is on analyzing transactions and preparing financial statements, including the statement of cash flows. Transactions are representative of those in actual situations, and excess clerical detail has been eliminated to concentrate on the entire cycle. Useful coaching tips and techniques follow selected transactions. Optional requirements for thought and analysis are included in the manual version. Estimated completion time is 18 hours.

Tamije Garden Supply, Computerized Version by Leon Hanouille (Syracuse University) and Jay Joseph Cappy. This computerized version of Tamije Garden Supply uses the same DOS-based graphical user interface software that drives the General Ledger Problem Solver.

Introduction to Business, by Louis E. Boone (University of South Alabama) and David L. Kurtz (University of Arkansas). This booklet, available to adopters, provides background in business concepts, activities, and terminology for business and nonbusiness majors alike to give students a springboard for this first business course. Dryden's research among financial accounting instructors indicates that many schools do not offer any introduction to business courses. Thus the authors of Dryden's best-selling business book help make the introductory accounting course doubly meaningful to business and nonbusiness majors alike.

Acknowledgments

To develop, write, and publish a book to meet the changing needs of students and instructors in the 1990s truly requires a team effort. We recognize the sincere and devoted work of these individuals.

From initial concept to finished book, exhaustive research has been the hallmark of our efforts. Professionally conducted regional focus groups were a major factor in identifying the key goals of instructors as they face the transition. We are grateful to these participants for sharing their vision for the future with us: Mark Bettner, Bucknell University; Frank Biegbeder, Rancho Santiago Community College; John Blahnik, Lorain County Community College; Jim Cashell, Miami University; Mayer Chapman, California State University at Long Beach; Judith Cook, Grossmont College; Henry H. Davis, Eastern Illinois University; Kathy Dunne, Rider College; Alan Falcon, Loyola Marymount University; Charles Fazzi, Robert Morris College; Howard Felt, Temple Univerity; David Fetyko, Kent State University; J. Patrick Forrest, Western Michigan University; Veronique Frucot, Rutgers University—Camden; Don E. Giacomino, Marquette University; Marilyn Greenstein, Lehigh University; Robert E. Holtfreter, Ft. Hays State University; William Jones, Seton Hall University; Lucille E. Lammers, Illinois State University; Susan Lightle, Wright State University; Margaret McCrory, Marist College; Thomas D. McLaughlin, Monmouth College; E. James Meddaugh, Ohio University; Priscilla O'Clock, Xavier University; Joseph Ragan, St. Joseph's University; Mary Rolfes, Mankato State University; Edward Schwan, Susquehanna University; Don Schwartz, National University; Anita Stellenwerf, Ramapo College; Linda Sugarman, University of Akron; Vicki Vorell, Cuyahoga Community College; Robert Zahary, California State University at Los Angeles.

Based on the responses from these focus groups, we conducted follow-up telephone surveys that tracked national trends in content, procedures, software, and supplement needs among financial accounting instructors across the spectrum of change. We relied on their input, and that of the focus groups, when we developed the topical approaches and pedagogical features in the book and package. We continue to rely on individual respondents in a number of important ways. Thanks go to these respondents for the invaluable information they provided:

Diana Adcox
University of North Florida

David Angelovich
San Francisco State University

Maj. Curt Barry
U.S. Military Academy

Karen Bird
University of Michigan

Michelle Bissonnette
California State Univ.—Fresno

Saul Ahiaria
SUNY at Buffalo

Alana Baier
Marquette University

Peter Battell
University of Vermont

Francis Bird
University of Richmond

Ed Bresnahan
American River College

Marcia Anderson
University of Cincinnati

Amelia A. Baldwin-Morgan
Eastern Michigan University

Paul Bayes
East Tennessee State University

Eddy Birrer
Gonzaga University

David C. Coffee
Western Carolina University

David Collins
Eastern Kentucky University

Patricia Doherty
Boston University

Anita Feller
University of Illinois

Gary Freeman
University of Tulsa

Claudia Gilbertston
Anoka Ramsey Community Coll.

Paul Griffin
University of California—Davis

Robert Hartwig
Worcester State College

Danny Ivancevich
University of Nevada—Las Vegas

Randy Johnston
Pennsylvania State University

Jean Killey
Midlands Tech. College

Michael Lagrone
Clemson University

Patsy Lund
Lakewood Community College

Janice Mardon
Green River Community College

Christine McKeag
University of Evansville

William Mister
Colorado State University

Howard Mount
Seattle Pacific University

Beau Parent
Tulane University

Mitchell Raiborn
Bradley University

Victoria Rymer
University of Maryland

Richard Scott
University of Virginia

Catherine Staples
Virginia Commonwealth Univ.

Jeanie Sumner
Pacific Luthern University

Judy Wenzel
Gustavus Adolphus College

T. Sterling Wetzel
Oklahoma State University

Carol Wolk
University of Tennessee

Alan Davis
Community College of Philadelphia

Margaret Douglas
University of Arkansas

Richard File
University of Nebraska—Omaha

Michelle Gannon
Western Connecticut State Univ.

Larry Godwin
University of Montana

Leon Hanouille
Syracuse University

Jean Hatcher
Univ. of South Carolina at Sumner

Janet Jackson
Wichita State University

Naida Kaen
University of New Hampshire

Marcia Kertz
San Jose State University

Kris Lawyer
North Carolina State University

Raymond D. MacFee
University of Colorado

Al Maypers
University of North Texas

Laura McNally
Black Hills State College

Perry Moore
David Lipscomb University

Michael O'Neill
Gannon University

Paul Parkison
Ball State University

Ann Riley
American University

Warren Schlesinger
Ithaca College

Amy Spielbauer
St. Norbert College

Stephen Strange
Indiana University at Kokomo

Judy Swingen
Rochester Institute of Technology

Michael Werner
University of Miami

Jack Wilkerson
Wake Forest University

Lyle Dehning
Metropolitan State College—Denver

Kenneth Elvik
Iowa State University

Ed Finkhauser
University of Utah

Linda Genduso
Nova University

Lynn Grace
Edison Community College

Joseph Hargadon
Widener University

Thomas F. Hilgeman
St. Louis Community Coll.—Meramec

Sharon Jackson
Auburn University at Montgomery

Jane Kapral
Clark University

Ronald King
Washington University

Tom Linsmeier
University of Iowa

David Malone
University of Idaho

Nancy McClure
Lock Haven University

Cynthia Miller
GM Institute

Barbara Morris
Angelo State University

Rimona Palas
William Paterson Coll. of New Jersey

Donna Philbrick
Portland State University

Leo A. Ruggle
Mankato State University

Edward S. Schwan
Susquehanna University

Charles Stanley
Baylor University

Kathy Sullivan
George Washington University

Ann Watkins
Louisiana State University

Shari Wescott
Houston Baptist University

Lyle Wimmergren
Worcester Polytechnic Institute

Reviewers played a central role in influencing the chapter-by-chapter development of the book. The manuscript underwent two full rounds of reviews among instructors at a variety of schools across the country. We also conducted single-issue reviews, as well as background interviews with selected accounting educators on pedagogy and topical coverage. Their insights have informed the writing of every draft, and many reviewers continue to serve as touchstones on through publication. To them we are grateful:

Diana Adcox
University of North Florida

Bobbe M. Barnes
University of Colorado at Denver

Eddy Birrer
Gonzaga University

John C. Corless
California State University—Sacramento

Patricia Doherty
Boston University

Alan Falcon
Loyola Marymount University

Gary Freeman
University of Tulsa

Leon Hanouille
Syracuse University

Kathy Horton
University of Illinois, Chicago

Jay LaGregs
Tyler Junior College

Bruce Lubich
Syracuse University

David Malone
University of Idaho

Thomas D. McLaughlin
Monmouth College

Ron Pawliczek
Boston College

Mary Rolfes
Mankato State University

Edward S. Schwan
Susquehanna University

Charles Stanley
Baylor University

Steven D. White
Western Kentucky University

David Angelovich
San Francisco State University

Paul Bayes
East Tennessee State University

Gyan Chandra
Miami University

Shirley J. Daniel
University of Hawaii at Manoa

Margaret Douglas
University of Arkansas

David Fetyko
Kent State University

Will Garland
Coastal Carolina University

Robert Hartwig
Worcester State College

Sharon Jackson
Auburn University at Montgomery

Michael Lagrone
Clemson University

Catherine Lumbattis
Southern Illinois University

John C. McCabe
Ball State University

Howard E. Mount
Seattle Pacific University

Harry V. Poynter
Central Missouri State Univ.

Leo A. Ruggle
Mankato State University

Don Schwartz
National University

Phil Walter
Bellevue Community College

Steve Wong
San Jose City College

Amelia A. Baldwin-Morgan
Eastern Michigan University

Mark Bettner
Bucknell University

Judith Cook
Grossmont College

Lyle E. Dehning
Metropolitan State College, Denver

Anette Estrada
Grand Valley State University

Jeannie M. Folk
College of DuPage

Roger Gee
San Diego Mesa College

Robert E. Holtfreter
Fort Hays State University

Manu Kai'ama
University of Hawaii at Manoa

Kristine Lawyer
North Carolina State University

Raymond D. MacFee, Jr.
University of Colorado

Margaret McCrory
Marist College

Phil Olds
Virginia Commonwealth Univ.

Mitchell Raiborn
Bradley University

George Sanderson
Moorhead State University

Richard Sherman
St. Joseph's University

T. Sterling Wetzel
Oklahoma State University

The textbook, Solutions Manual, and Test Bank benefitted greatly from the comments and advice of instructors and students who have been using these three core elements in ongoing class testing and evaluation. By their selection and continuing use of the book and its package, they have helped establish *Financial Accounting: The Impact on Decision Makers* as the guidepost for the transition in accounting education. Among these instructors, we especially wish to thank the following:

Mike Akers
Marquette University

Linda Campbell
University of Toledo

Judy Cook
Grossmont College

Alan Falcon
Loyola Marymount Univ.

Patrick Fort
Univ. of Alaska—Fairbanks

Joe Gallo
Cuyahoga Comm. College

Lorraine Glascock
University of Alabama

Bruce Ikawa
Loyola Marymount Univ.

Ellen Landgraf
Loyola University Chicago

Chao-Shin Liu
Univ. of Notre Dame

Mary D. Maury
St. John's University

Rafael Munoz
Univ. of Notre Dame

Janet O'tousa
Univ. of Notre Dame

Karen Saurlander
Univ. of Toledo

Bente Villadsen
Washington University

Charles Werner
Loyola University Chicago

Sarah Brown
Univ. of North Alabama

Charles Caufield
Loyola University Chicago

Dean Crawford
University of Toledo

Richard File
Univ. of Nebraska—Omaha

Diane Franz
University of Toledo

John Gartska
Loyola Marymount Univ.

Leon Hanouille
Syracuse University

William Kinsella
Loyola Marymount Univ.

Horace Landry
Syracuse University

Bruce Lubich
Syracuse University

Tami Mittelstaedt
Univ. of Notre Dame

Mary J. Nisbet
Univ. of Cal—Santa Barbara

Sue Pattillo
Univ. of Notre Dame

Ray Slager
Calvin College

Alan K. Vogel
Cuyahoga Comm. Coll.—Western

Samuel Wild
Loyola Marymount Univ.

Carolyn Callahan
Univ. of Notre Dame

Alan Cherry
Loyola Marymount Univ.

Ed Etter
Syracuse University

J. Patrick Forrest
Western Michigan Univ.

Tom Frecka
Univ. of Notre Dame

Cynthia Van Gelderen
Aquinas College

Donna Sue Hetzel
Western Michigan Univ.

Jay LaGregs
Tyler Junior College

Terry Lease
Loyola Marymount Univ.

Janice Mardon
Green River Comm. College

Mike Morris
Univ. of Notre Dame

Curtis L. Norton
Northern Illinois University

Gary A. Porter
Loyola University Chicago

Tim Tancy
Univ. of Notre Dame

Vicki Vorell
Cuyahoga Comm. Coll.—Western

Steve Wong
San Jose City College

We would like to extend our thanks to the fine team of academicians who prepared the various supplements to our book. Without their dedication to quality, innovation, and accuracy, we would not have been able to fulfill our mission: Diana Adcox, University of North Florida; Paul Bayes, East Tennessee State University; Jay Cappy; Patricia Doherty, Boston University; David Fetyko, Kent State University; Leon Hanouille, Syracuse University; Kathy Horton, University of Illinois at Chicago; Jay LaGregs, Tyler Junior College; Mary Nisbet, University of California at Santa Barbara; Tom McLaughlin, Monmouth College; and Jane Park, California State University at Los Angeles.

We wish to thank the following team of reviewers who have helped us develop the supplements package. Combined with the efforts of the ancillary author team, their insights have made this the most useful, intuitive, flexible, and integrated package available. They include Amelia Baldwin-Morgan, Eastern Michigan University; Mark Bettner, Bucknell University; Philip Buchanan, George Washington University; Rosie Bukics, Lafayette College, Mike Claire, College of San Mateo; Judith Cook, Grossmont College; Alan Falcon, Loyola Marymount University; Gary Freeman, University of Tulsa; Will Garland, Coastal Carolina University; Robert Hartwig, Worcester State College; Kathy Horton, University of Illinois at Chicago; Raymond

D. MacFee, Jr., University of Colorado; David Malone, University of Idaho; Mallory McWilliams, San Jose State University; Theodore D. Morrison, Valparaiso University; Leo A. Ruggle, Mankato State University; Richard Sherman, St. Joseph's University; Charles Stanley, Baylor University; Paul Wertheim, Pepperdine University; Steve Wong, San Jose City College; Robert Zahary, California State University—Los Angeles; and Thomas L. Zeller, Loyola University Chicago.

We are grateful to Kathy Horton, Judy Cook, Donna Hetzel, Brenda Hartman (Tomball College), and Robbie Sheffy (Tarrant County Junior College) for their untiring devotion to accuracy. We are indebted as well to Stuart Weiss, Jeannie Folk, and Sandra Bitenc for their special contributions. And to Carrie O'Donnell, Karen Misler, and Claire Hunter, all of O'Donnell & Associates, we owe more than we can express for their efforts.

We as authors are fortunate to work with a publisher as committed to accounting education as The Dryden Press. The following Dryden team members have left their imprint on the book: Bill Teague and Elizabeth Storey, acquisitions editors, and Craig Avery, senior developmental editor, for their tireless devotion to the text and package; Lyn Keeney Hastert, editor-in-chief, Diana Farrell, director of marketing, and Annie Todd, product manager, for their overall involvement and marketing savvy. Last but not least, we thank the very dedicated and creative members of our book team: Jim Patterson, project editor; Linda Miller, senior designer; Kelly Cordes and Mandy Manzano, production managers; Elizabeth Banks, picture developmental editor; Kipp Murray, marketing coordinator; and Yvette Rubio and Becky Miller, editorial assistants.

The unique and innovative annual reports of Ben & Jerry's Homemade, Inc., have been an inspiration to us. We are indebted to Alan Parker and Fran Rathke for their cooperation in what we view as an exciting partnership between education and the real world.

We are grateful to our colleagues at Loyola University Chicago and at Northern Illinois University for their many comments and suggestions in the preparation of this book, as well as to our own students who participated in a class test of the manuscript.

We especially appreciate the efforts of John Everett, Virginia Commonwealth University, for his role in developing the book's tax appendix, and K.K. Raman, University of North Texas, for the governmental and not-for-profit appendix. We are indebted to a former student, Jack Trierweiler, for his valuable insights into the merchandising business. Finally, a special thanks to Jack McHugh and Tim Vertovec for their guidance and commitment to the project.

Gary A. Porter
Curtis L. Norton

About the Authors

Gary A. Porter, CPA, is Professor and Chairman of the Accounting Department at Loyola University Chicago. He earned Ph.D. and M.B.A. degrees from the University of Colorado and his B.S.B.A. from Drake University. He is co-author of a textbook in management accounting and has published in the *Journal of Accounting Education, Journal of Accounting, Auditing & Finance,* and *Journal of Accountancy,* among others.

Dr. Porter's professional activities include membership on the Illinois CPA Society's 150 Hour Implementation Task Force, experience as a staff accountant with Deloitte & Touche in Denver, and a participant in KPMG Peat Marwick Foundation's Faculty Development Program.

He has won an Excellence in Teaching award from the University of Colorado and an Outstanding Professor award from San Diego State University. Dr. Porter is on the steering committee of the midwest region of the American Accounting Association and is also on the board of directors of the Chicago chapter of the Financial Executives Institute.

Curtis L. Norton is Deloitte & Touche Professor of Accountancy at Northern Illinois University in DeKalb, Illinois. He earned his Ph.D. from Arizona State University and his M.B.A. from the University of South Dakota. His extensive list of publications includes articles in *Accounting Horizons, The Journal of Accounting Education, Journal of Accountancy, Journal of the American Taxation Association, Real Estate Review, The Accounting Review, CPA Journal,* and many others. In 1988–89, Dr. Norton received the University Excellence in Teaching Award, the highest university-wide teaching recognition at NIU. He is also a consultant and has conducted training programs for government authorities, banks, utilities, and other entities.

Dr. Norton is a member of the American Accounting Association and the Financial Executives Institute.

Brief Contents

Contents

Each chapter contains the following material:
Review Problem, Solution to Review Problem, Guidance Answers to Accounting
for Your Decisions, Chapter Highlights, Key Terms Quiz, Alternate Terms,
Questions, Exercises, Problems, Alternate Problems, Cases, Solutions to Key
Terms Quiz

Part 1
The Accounting Model 1

Chapter 1 presents the business
context of accounting and basic
business terminology first, using
the Ben & Jerry's story to show
how a real business starts up.

A rich mix of end-of-chapter exercises
and problems, with few clones, makes
for fewer closed-ended, preparer-only
quizzes and exams. Nearly all
procedural end-of-chapter items
contain at least one conceptual,
thought-based, extended, open-ended,
or communication requirement.

Chapter 2
Financial Statements and the Annual Report 52

Chapter 2 introduces the financial statements and annual reports early, using two real companies—UAL Corp. and Quaker Oats—and a hypothetical merchandiser for simplicity.

Accounting for Your Decisions boxes (two per chapter) promote active and cooperative learning by asking students to put themselves in the user's shoes—to reflect on the accounting and financial statement issues just presented in the text, role play as bankers, investors, or other statement users, and then make and defend business decisions based on that information. (Guidance Answers follow the solution to the review problem.)

Focus on the Financial Results
← chapter-opening vignettes concentrate on the end results first—introducing the chapter with the story of a real company and an aspect of its financial statement related to the chapter.

The accounting cycle is covered in two chapters so the instructor can focus more on concepts and less on procedures.

The accounting cycle worksheet is in an appendix to let instructors decide whether to teach preparation or not.

**Part II
Accounting for
Assets 249**

**Chapter 5
Merchandise Accounting and Internal Control 250**

Placing control with merchandising and before inventories and cash lets students see that control covers all assets.

The merchandising worksheet is appendicized to let instructors emphasize process over procedures.

Chapter 6
Inventories and Cost of Goods Sold 312

Chapter 6, emphasizing inventory costing methods, is a natural extension of the COGS model and the two inventory systems introduced in Chapter 5.

Chapter 7
Cash and Receivables 370

Chapters 5, 6, and 7 are organized to show students how businesses operate. Chapter 5 introduces buying and selling and the internal control necessary for managing a business. Chapter 6 expands on the inventory issues. Chapter 7 covers the outputs of buying and selling: cash and receivables.

Chapter 8
Operating Assets: Property, Plant, and Equipment, Natural Resources, and Intangibles 422

Chapter 9
Current Liabilities, Contingent Liabilities, and the Time Value of Money 472

Understanding and using ratios is important for a basic business understanding among accounting majors and nonmajors alike. Financial ratios are integrated into chapter discussions where relevant—concepts, uses, and analysis—as well as completely discussed in Chapter 15.

An **Integrative Problem** at the end of each part in the book is a comprehensive test of skills and concepts gained in that part.

Part III
Accounting for Liabilities and Owners' Equity 471

Time value of money is covered here so students will understand this concept before studying long-term liabilities in Chapter 10.

To read financial statements, students need to be able to understand the difficult topics of pensions, leases, and deferred taxes in an easy-to-read user perspective.

← **Focus on Users** boxes, one per chapter, bring the viewpoints and backgrounds of actual financial statement users into the classroom. Come into the offices of investment bankers, stockbrokers, and others who evaluate companies for a living; listen to them explain their work through interviews with a professional financial writer.

Chapter 12 shows students how to read and understand complex corporate income statements.

**Part IV
Additional Topics
in Financial
Reporting 671**

Using actual company examples, Chapter 13 focuses on the real challenges of the global corporation.

Preparation of the statement of cash flows is shown using T-accounts and a skeleton statement, rather than a preparer-oriented worksheet which is covered in a chapter appendix.

FINANCIAL ACCOUNTING
THE IMPACT ON DECISION MAKERS

A WORD TO STUDENTS ABOUT THIS COURSE

Knowing accounting is just smart for everyone in today's job market. Thus this book is not just for accounting majors—it's for anyone who wants to learn how to read and understand financial information. You'll manipulate numbers in this course. But at every turn, this book and its study aids—not to mention your instructor—will walk you through the details. You'll write some memorandums backing up your calculations, pitting your analytical skills against real financial statements and problems. And you'll have the chance to put yourself in different business roles. In fact, **this book will help you think, talk, and write skillfully about accounting information.**

Part I

The Accounting Model

Chapter 1
Accounting as a Form of Communication

Chapter 1 is an **introduction to business** and illustrates how accounting and accountants play a role in defining and communicating business activities as financial information. Study the chapter, of course, but along the way, **make a loan decision based on Ben & Jerry's cash flows** (p. 19), **play the role of supplier to Kmart** (p. 21), and **meet a journalist who studied accounting** (p. 27). In every chapter, you'll also analyze Ben & Jerry's financial statements in **From Concept to Practice boxes.**

Chapter 2
Financial Statements and the Annual Report

Here we cut to the real business reasons why studying financial statements is important— it forces you to see financial information as bankers, managers, brokers, and stockholders see them. Along the way, you'll **become a concerned supplier to United Airlines** (p. 70), **make an investor's decision about Quaker Oats** based on the income statement (p. 78), and **meet a spare-time investor** (p. 87).

Chapter 3
Processing Accounting Information

Chapters 3 and 4 cover the accounting cycle—the process of turning economic events into useful financial information. Chapter 3 focuses on the **basic concepts and tools** of this accounting model. Along the way, you'll **envision General Motors' chart of accounts** (p. 122), **become a manager looking at the books** (p. 133), and **see transactions from an auditor's viewpoint** (p. 136).

Chapter 4
Income Measurement and Accrual Accounting
Appendix 4A:
Accounting Tools: Work Sheets and Reversing Entries

In Chapter 3 you mastered recognizing economic events as transactions. In Chapter 4 you must grasp exciting new concepts of **accrual accounting** that form the basis of understanding and preparing financial statements. Along the way, you'll **investigate a franchise investment** (p. 174), **consider granting a loan based on income information** (p. 181), and **get career advice from a bank vice president** (p. 198).

Integrative Problem for Part I

Focus on Financial Results

Ben & Jerry's Home-made, Inc., is one of the few companies to recognize in its annual report that many people do not know how to read a financial statement. They have not had the opportunity to take this accounting course, yet there they are, on the phone to their stockbroker, buying and selling shares of stock.

Perhaps you are one of them. You like ice cream, you like Ben & Jerry's, so you buy the stock. Or maybe you like Nike shoes so you buy Nike's stock. Or Snapple. Or McDonald's hamburgers. To be sure, some investment pros think your familiarity—and comfort with a product—should be a factor in your investment decision.

But what Ben & Jerry's is trying to get across in its coloring book style annual report is that you should not buy the stock unless you understand the financials. That is why it has tried to teach its readers a little bit about accounting throughout the financial section of the report. Of course, the reader would discover all sorts of tidbits like this one from page 19: since 1988, net income has more than tripled from $0.31 to $1.07 per share. This suggests not only that Ben & Jerry's sells popular products but that it is successful financially as well.

FIVE YEAR FINANCIAL HIGHLIGHTS
(In thousands except per share data)

			Year Ended		
Summary of Operations:	12/26/92	12/28/91	12/29/90	12/30/89	12/31/88
Net sales	$ 131,969	$ 96,997	$ 77,024	$ 58,464	$ 47,561
Cost of sales	94,389	68,500	54,203	41,660	33,935
Gross profit	37,580	28,497	22,821	16,804	13,627
Selling, general and administrative expenses	26,243	21,264	17,639	13,009	10,655
Operating income	11,337	7,233	5,182	3,795	2,972
Other income (expense)- net	(23)	(729)	(709)	(362)	(274)
Income before taxes	11,314	6,504	4,473	3,433	2,698
Income taxes	4,639	2,765	1,864	1,380	1,079
Net income	6,675	3,739	2,609	2,053	1,618
Net income per common share[1]	$ 1.07	$ 0.67	$ 0.50	$ 0.40	$ 0.31
Weighted average common shares outstanding[1]	6,254,000	5,572,000	5,225,000	5,199,000	5,157,000
			Year Ended		
Balance Sheet Data:	12/26/92	12/28/91	12/29/90	12/30/89	12/31/88
Working capital	$ 18,053	$ 11,035	$ 8,202	$ 5,829	$ 5,614
Total assets	88,207	43,056	34,299	28,139	26,307
Long-term debt	2,641	2,787	8,948	9,328	9,670
Stockholders' equity[2]	66,760	26,269	16,101	13,405	11,245

[1] The per share amounts and average shares outstanding have been adjusted for the effects of all stock splits, including stock splits in the form of stock dividends.

[2] No cash dividends have been declared or paid by the Company on its capital stock since the Company's organization. The Company intends to reinvest earnings for use in its business and to finance future growth. Accordingly, the Board of Directors does not anticipate declaring any cash dividends in the foreseeable future.

Chapter 1

Accounting as a Form of Communication

LEARNING OBJECTIVES

After studying this chapter, you should be able to

1. Explain why financial information is important in making decisions.
2. Distinguish among the forms of organization.
3. Describe the various types of business activity.
4. Identify the primary users of accounting information and their needs.
5. Explain the purpose of each of the financial statements and the relationships among them and prepare a set of simple statements.
6. Identify and explain the primary assumptions made in preparing financial statements.
7. Describe the process of setting standards in financial accounting and the various groups involved in the process.
8. Describe the various roles played by accountants in organizations.

Linkages

A LOOK AT THIS CHAPTER

We begin the study of accounting by considering why financial information is important in making decisions and who uses this information. This will require us to examine the various forms that organizations take and the types of activities in which they engage. We will see that accounting is an important form of communication and that financial statements are the medium that accountants use to communicate with those who in some way have an interest in the financial affairs of a company.

A LOOK AT UPCOMING CHAPTERS

Chapter 1 introduces you to accounting and financial statements. In Chapter 2, we look in more detail at the composition of each of the statements and the conceptual framework of accounting that supports the work of the accountant. Chapter 3 steps back from financial statements, the end result, and examines how companies process economic events as a basis for preparing the statements. Chapter 4 completes our introduction to the accounting model by considering the importance of accrual accounting in this communication process.

Ben & Jerry's: The Need to Make Financial Decisions

LO   1

Explain why financial information is important in making decisions.

Ben & Jerry's, Vermont's Finest All Natural Ice Cream & Frozen Yogurt, was founded in 1978 in a renovated gas station in Burlington, Vermont by childhood friends Ben Cohen and Jerry Greenfield with a $12,000 investment ($4,000 of which was borrowed). With the help of an old-fashioned rock salt ice cream maker and a then-$5 correspondence course in ice cream-making from Penn State under their belt, they soon became popular for their funky, chunky, flavors, made from fresh Vermont milk and cream. A year later they were delivering Ben & Jerry's ice cream to grocery stores and restaurants.[1]

Today Ben & Jerry's is a highly successful corporation. Sales in 1992 exceeded $130 million. Numerous reasons account for the company's phenomenal success. From its beginning, the company has taken an extremely active role in promoting social responsibility. It has some of the most far-reaching and liberal employment policies in U.S. business. However, any company owes a major part of its success to its ability to make *financial decisions*. Initially, Ben Cohen and Jerry Greenfield made the decision to invest $8,000 of their own money and to borrow $4,000 to start their ice cream–making business. Would *you* have been willing to risk your savings to start a new business? Would you have been willing to sign a note agreeing to repay a loan in the future? Both of these were financial decisions the two had to make.

In 1980, after two years in business, Ben and Jerry decided to rent space in an old mill and to begin packing ice cream in pints. Once again, they were faced with a financial decision: Could they make enough money from selling pints of ice cream to pay the rent? More decisions, each one involving higher stakes, faced the young

[1] *The History of Ben & Jerry's Homemade, Inc.,* Statement of Mission, 1988.

Ben & Jerry's Homemade, Inc.'s ice cream factory in Waterbury, Vermont. From the first scoops served in 1978 to a thriving firm with multiple plants and numerous franchises, the company has grown as a result of sound financial and business decisions.

entrepreneurs during the 1980s. In 1984 Ben and Jerry decided to sell stock to the public for the first time (staying loyal to their adopted state, the stock was available only to Vermonters). What prompted them to make this financial decision? On the basis of record sales of $4 million in 1984, they realized that their current production facilities were inadequate to handle the increased volume. They needed money to build a new plant. The sale of stock that year netted the company about $700,000. The company made an even larger decision that same year, however: it borrowed more than $2 million. At that point, major financial decisions about the company were being made not only by the original owners but also by outsiders. Given the opportunity back then, would you have bought stock in this company? Would you have been willing to loan money to it that year, as many people and organizations actually did?

In 1985 the company borrowed more money and sold stock to people outside Vermont for the first time. It was the first year the stock of Ben & Jerry's was traded on an organized stock exchange. Then there were more decisions for Ben & Jerry's and those who loaned money to the company and bought stock in it. Construction on the new manufacturing plant and company headquarters began in 1985 and was completed the following year. Was it a wise decision to sell stock and borrow money to build the new facility? Sales in 1986 were double those of the prior year, reaching almost $20 million. By 1992 the company was so successful that it began construction on its *third* manufacturing plant, at an estimated cost of $25 million.

All of us use financial information in making decisions. For example, when you made a decision to enroll at your present school, you needed information on the tuition and room and board costs at the different schools under consideration. When a labor union asks for a cost-of-living increase, it needs information on the profitability of the company. When trying to decide whether to loan money to a company, a banker must consider the company's current debts.

In this book, we explore how accounting can help all of us in making informed financial decisions. Before we turn to the role played by accounting in decision making, we need to explore business in more detail. What forms of organizations carry on business activity? In what types of business activity do those organizations engage?

Forms of Organization

There are many different types of organizations in our society. One convenient way to categorize the myriad types is to distinguish between those that are organized to earn money and those that exist for some other purpose. Although the lines can become blurred, generally speaking, business entities are organized to earn a profit while nonbusiness entities exist to serve various segments of society. Both types are summarized in Exhibit 1-1.

LO 2
Distinguish among the forms of organization.

Business Entities

Business entities are organized to earn a profit. Legally, profit-oriented companies are one of three types: proprietorships, partnerships, and corporations.

Sole Proprietorships   This form of organization is characterized by a single owner. Many small businesses are organized as **sole proprietorships.** Very often the business is owned and operated by the same person. Because of the close relationship between the owner and the business, it is imperative that the affairs of the two be kept separate. This is one example in accounting of the **economic entity concept,**

EXHIBIT 1-1   Forms of Organization

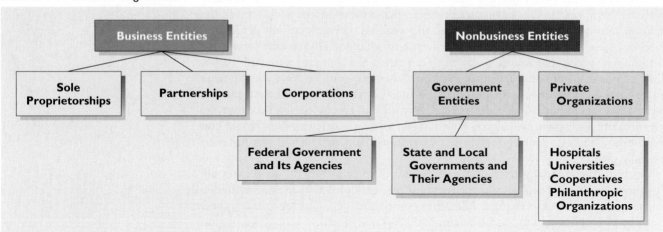

which requires that a single, identifiable unit of organization be accounted for in all situations. For example, assume that Bernie Berg owns a neighborhood grocery store. In paying the monthly bills, such as utilities and supplies, Bernie must separate his personal costs from those associated with the grocery business. In turn, financial statements prepared for the business must not intermingle Bernie's personal affairs with those of the company.

Unlike the distinction made for accounting purposes between an individual's personal and business affairs, the IRS does not recognize the separate existence of a proprietorship from its owner. That is, a sole proprietorship is not a taxable entity, and any profits earned by the business are taxed on the return of the individual.

Partnerships   A **partnership** is a business owned by two or more individuals. Ben & Jerry's began as a partnership. When the two partners started selling ice cream, they needed some sort of agreement as to how much each would contribute to the business and how they would divide any profits. In many small partnerships, the agreement is often just an oral understanding between the partners. In large businesses, the partnership agreement is formalized in a written document.

Although Ben & Jerry's involved just two owners, some partnerships have thousands of partners. Public accounting firms, law firms, and other types of service companies are often organized as partnerships. Like a sole proprietorship, a partnership is not a taxable entity. The individual partners pay taxes on their proportionate share of the profits of the business.

Corporations   Although proprietorships and partnerships dominate in sheer number, corporations control an overwhelming majority of the private resources in this country. A **corporation** is an entity organized under the laws of a particular state. Each of the 50 states is empowered to regulate the creation and operation of businesses organized as corporations in it.

To start a corporation, articles of incorporation must be filed with the state. If the articles are approved by the state, a corporate charter is issued, and the corporation can begin to issue stock. A **share of stock** is a certificate that acts as evidence of ownership in a corporation. Although not always the case, stocks of many corporations are traded on organized stock exchanges, such as the New York and American Stock Exchanges.

What are the advantages of running a business as a corporation rather than a partnership? This was the question Ben and Jerry had to ask themselves. The company enjoyed early success in the market and to capitalize on that success, it needed to grow. To grow meant that it would need a larger production facility, more equipment, and a larger staff. All of these things cost money. Where would the money come from?

One of the primary advantages of the corporate form of organization is the ability to raise large amounts of money in a relatively brief period of time. This is what prompted Ben & Jerry's to "go public" in 1984. To raise money, the company sold two different types of securities: stocks and bonds. As stated earlier, a share of stock is simply a certificate that evidences ownership in a corporation. A **bond** is similar in that it is a certificate or piece of paper issued to someone. However, it is different from a share of stock in that a bond represents a promise by the company selling it to repay a certain amount of money at a future date. Interest on the bond is usually paid semiannually. In other words, if you were to buy a bond from Ben & Jerry's, you would be loaning it money. We will have more to say about stocks and bonds when we discuss financing activities later in the chapter.

The ease of transfer of ownership in a corporation is another advantage of this form of organization. If you hold shares of stock in a corporation and decide that you want out, you simply call your broker and put in an order to sell. Another distinct advantage is the limited liability of the stockholder. Generally speaking, a stockholder is liable only for the amount contributed to the business. That is, if a company goes out of business, the most the stockholder stands to lose is the amount invested. On the other hand, both proprietors and general partners usually can be held personally liable for the debts of the business.

Nonbusiness Entities

Most **nonbusiness entities** are organized for a purpose other than to earn a profit. They exist to serve the needs of various segments of society. For example, a hospital is organized to provide health care to its patients. A municipal government is operated for the benefit of its citizens. A local school district exists to meet the educational needs of the youth in the community.

All of these entities are distinguished by the lack of an identifiable owner. The lack of an identifiable owner and the profit motive changes to some extent the type of accounting used by nonbusiness entities. It is called *fund accounting* and is discussed in advanced accounting courses. Regardless of the lack of a profit motive in nonbusiness entities, there is still a demand for the information provided by an accounting system. For example, a local government needs detailed cost breakdowns in order to levy taxes. A hospital may want to borrow money and will need financial statements to present to the prospective lender.

Organizations and Social Responsibility

Although nonbusiness entities are organized specifically to serve members of society, U.S. businesses have become more and more sensitive to their broader social responsibilities. Because they touch the lives of so many members of society, most large corporations recognize the societal aspects of their overall mission. For example, Ben & Jerry's statement of mission consists of three parts: a product mission, a social mission, and an economic mission. Its social mission is as follows:

> To operate the company in a way that actively recognizes the central role that business plays in the structure of society by initiating ways to improve the quality of life of a broad community—local, national and international.

Ben & Jerry's has done more than just pay lip service to its social mission. Each year it donates 7.5 percent of its pre-tax earnings to a foundation that in turn awards monies to charities. Most other large corporations have established similar charitable foundations to foster their goals in this area.

The Nature of Business Activity

LO   3

Describe the various types of business activity.

Because corporations dominate business activity in the United States, we will focus our attention in this book on this form of organization. Corporations engage in a multitude of different types of activities. It is possible to categorize all of them into one of three types, however: financing, investing, and operating.

Financing Activities

All businesses must start with financing. Simply put, money is needed to start a business. Ben and Jerry needed $12,000 to start their business. They came up with $8,000 of their own funds and borrowed the other $4,000. As described earlier, the company found itself in need of additional financing in 1984 when it started construction on the new manufacturing plant. At that point, it obtained approximately $2 million from the sale of bonds and another $700,000 from the sale of stock to citizens of Vermont. In 1985 the company continued to look for sources of financing. For the first time, it issued stock to investors outside the state of Vermont and raised more than $5 million. In that same year, Ben & Jerry's borrowed another $600,000 on a long-term basis.

As you will see throughout this book, accounting has its own unique set of terminology. In fact, accounting is often referred to as *the language of business.* The discussion of financing activities brings up two important accounting terms: liabilities and capital stock. A **liability** is an obligation of a business; it can take many different forms. When a company borrows money at a bank, the liability is called a *note payable.* When a company sells bonds, the obligation is termed *bonds payable.* Amounts owed to the government for taxes are called *taxes payable.* Ben & Jerry's happens to buy the milk it needs to produce ice cream from the St. Albans Cooperative Creamery. Assume that St. Albans gives the company 30 days to pay for purchases. During this 30-day period, Ben & Jerry's has an obligation called *accounts payable.*

Capital stock is the term used by accountants to indicate the dollar amount of stock sold to the public. Capital stock differs from liabilities in one very important respect. Those who buy stock in a corporation are not loaning money to the business, as are those who buy bonds in the company or make a loan in some other form to the company. Someone who buys stock in a company is called a **stockholder,** and that person is providing a *permanent* form of financing to the business. In other words, there is not a due date at which time the stockholder will be repaid. Normally, the only way for a stockholder to get back his or her original investment from buying stock is to sell it to someone else on the stock exchange. On occasion, a corporation buys back the stock of one of its stockholders. Someone who buys bonds in a company or in some other way makes a loan to it is called a **creditor.** A creditor does *not* provide a permanent form of financing to the business. That is, the creditor expects repayment of the amount loaned and, in many instances, payment of interest for the use of the money as well.

Investing Activities

There is a natural progression in a business from financing activities to investing activities. That is, once funds are generated from creditors and stockholders, money is available to invest. Ben & Jerry's used the cash obtained from selling stock and bonds to build its manufacturing plant and to add to its equipment, in particular its storage freezer. More than $3 million was spent in 1985 on additions to property, plant, and equipment and almost $3 million in 1986.

An **asset** is a future economic benefit to a business. For example, cash is an asset to a company. Ben & Jerry's buildings are assets to it, as are its storage freezers and its other equipment. At any point in time, Ben & Jerry's has a supply of ice cream awaiting sale, as well as supplies of raw materials such as milk and other ingredients to be used in the production of ice cream. The finished products and the raw materials are called *inventory* and are another valuable asset of a company.

An asset represents the right to receive some sort of benefit in the future. The point is that not all assets are tangible in nature as are inventories and plant and equipment. For example, assume that Ben & Jerry's sells ice cream to one of its distributors and allows this customer to pay for its purchase at the end of 30 days. At the time of the sale, Ben & Jerry's doesn't have cash yet, but it has another valuable asset. The right to collect the amount due from the customer in 30 days is an asset called an *account receivable.* As a second example, assume that a company acquires from an inventor a patent that will allow the company the exclusive right to manufacture a certain product. The right to the future economic benefits from the patent is an asset. In summary, an asset is a valuable resource to the company that controls it.

At this point, you should notice the inherent tie between assets and liabilities. How does a company satisfy its liabilities, that is, its obligations? Although we will find out that there are some exceptions, most liabilities are settled by transferring assets. The asset most often used to settle a liability is cash.

Operating Activities

Once funds are obtained from financing and investments are made in productive assets, a business is ready to begin operations. Every business is organized with a *purpose* in mind. The purpose of some businesses is to sell a *product*. Ben and Jerry organized to sell ice cream. Other companies are organized to provide *services*. Service-oriented businesses are becoming an increasingly important sector of the U.S. economy. Some of the largest corporations in this country, such as banks and airlines, sell services rather than products. Some companies sell both products and services.

Accountants have a name for the sale of products and services. **Revenue** is the inflow of assets resulting from the sale of products and services. When a company makes a cash sale, the asset it receives is cash. When a sale is made on credit, the asset received is an account receivable. For now, you should understand that revenue is a *representation*. That is, it represents the dollar amount of sales of products and services for a specific period of time.

We have thus far identified one important operating activity: the sale of products and services. However, on the other side, costs must be incurred to operate a business. Employees must be paid salaries and wages. Suppliers must be paid for purchases of inventory, and the utility company has to be paid for heat and electricity. The government must be paid the taxes owed it. All of these are examples of important operating activities to a business. As you might expect by now, accountants use a

EXHIBIT 1-2   A Model of Business Activities

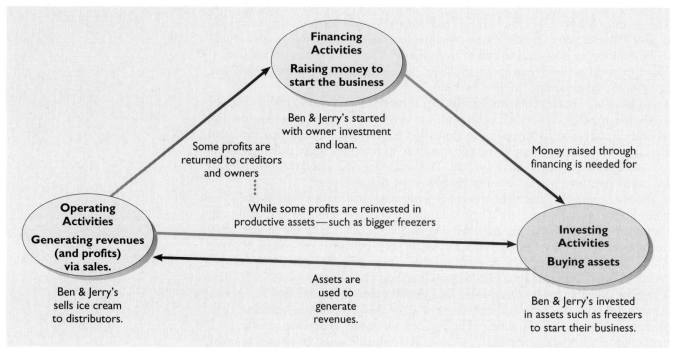

specific name for the costs incurred in operating a business. An **expense** is the outflow of assets resulting from the sale of goods and services.

Exhibit 1-2 summarizes the three types of activities conducted by a business. Our discussion and the exhibit present a simplification of business activity, but actual businesses are in a constant state of motion with many different financing, investing, and operating activities going on at any one time. The model as portrayed in Exhibit 1-2 should be helpful as you begin the study of accounting, however. To summarize, a company obtains money from various types of financing activities, uses the money raised to invest in productive assets, and then provides goods and services to its customers.

What Is Accounting?

Many people have preconceived notions about what accounting is. They think of it as a highly procedural activity practiced by people who are "good in math." This notion of accounting is very narrow and focuses only on the *record-keeping* or *bookkeeping* aspects of the discipline. Accounting is in fact much broader than this in its scope. Specifically, **accounting** is "the process of identifying, measuring, and communicating economic information to permit informed judgments and decisions by users of the information."[2]

Each of the three activities in this definition—*identifying, measuring,* and *communicating*—require the judgment of a trained professional. We will return later in this

[2] American Accounting Association, *A Statement of Basic Accounting Theory* (Evanston, Ill.: American Accounting Association, 1966), p. 1.

chapter to accounting as a profession and the various roles of accountants in our society. Note that the definition refers to the users of economic information. Who *are* the users of accounting information? We turn our attention now to this important question.

Users of Accounting Information and Their Needs

It is helpful to categorize users of accounting information on the basis of their relationship to the organization. Internal users, primarily the managers of a company, are involved in the daily affairs of the business. All other groups are external users.

LO 4

Identify the primary users of accounting information and their needs.

Internal Users

Internal users are in a position to obtain financial information in a way that best suits their needs. For example, if a production manager at Ben & Jerry's needs to know how much it costs to produce a pint of Chunky–Monkey ice cream, this information exists in the accounting system and can be reported. If a department supervisor wants to find out if monthly expenditures are more or less than the budgeted amount, a report can be generated to provide the answer. **Management accounting** is the branch of accounting concerned with providing internal users (management) with information to facilitate the planning and control functions. The ability to produce management accounting reports is limited only by the extent of the data available and the cost involved in generating the relevant information.

External Users

External users, those not involved directly in the operations of a business, need information that differs from that needed by internal users. In addition, the ability of external users to obtain the information is more limited. Without the day-to-day contact with the affairs of the business, outsiders must rely on the information presented to them by the management of the company.

Certain external users, such as the Internal Revenue Service, require that information be presented in a very specific manner and have the authority of the law to ensure that they get the required information. Stockholders, bondholders, and other creditors must rely on general-purpose financial statements for their information.[3] **Financial accounting** is the branch of accounting concerned with the preparation of general-purpose financial statements for use by both management and outsiders.

Stockholders and Potential Stockholders   Both existing and potential stockholders need financial information about a business. If you currently own stock in a company, you need information that will aid in your decision either to continue to hold the stock or to sell it. If you are considering buying stock in a company, you need financial information that will help in choosing among competing alternative investments. What has been the recent performance of the company in the stock market? What were its profits for the most recent year? How do they compare with those of the prior year? How much did the company pay in dividends? One source for much of this information is the company's financial statements.

---

[3] Technically, stockholders are insiders because they own stock in the business. In most large corporations, however, it is not practical for them to be involved in the daily affairs of the business. Thus, they are better categorized here as external users because they normally rely on general-purpose financial statements as do creditors.

Bondholders, Bankers, and Other Creditors Before buying a bond in a company (remember you are loaning money to the company), you need to feel comfortable that the company will be able to pay you the amount owed at maturity and the periodic interest payments. Financial statements can help you to decide whether to purchase a bond. Similarly, before lending money, a bank needs information that will help it to determine the company's ability to repay both the amount of the loan and interest. Therefore, a set of financial statements is a key ingredient in a loan proposal.

Government Agencies Numerous government agencies have information needs specified by law. For example, the Internal Revenue Service (IRS) is empowered to collect a tax on income from both individuals and corporations. Every year a company prepares a tax return to report to the IRS the amount of income it earned. Another government agency, the Securities and Exchange Commission (SEC), was created in the aftermath of the Great Depression. This regulatory agency is empowered to set the rules under which financial statements must be prepared for corporations that sell their stock to the public on organized stock exchanges. Similar to the IRS, the SEC has the authority to prescribe the manner in which financial information is presented to it. Companies operating in specialized industries submit financial reports to other regulatory agencies, such as the Interstate Commerce Commission and the Federal Trade Commission.

Other External Users Many other individuals and groups rely on financial information given to them by businesses. A supplier of raw material needs to know the creditworthiness of a company before selling it a product on credit. As part of its negotiations for a cost-of-living raise, a labor union needs information on the profitability of a company. To promote its industry, a trade association must gather financial information on the various companies in the industry. Other important users are financial intermediaries, such as stockbrokers and financial analysts. They use financial reports in advising their clients on investment decisions. In reaching their decisions, all of these users rely to a large extent on accounting information provided by management.

Financial Statements: How Accountants Communicate

LO 5
Explain the purpose of each of the financial statements and the relationships among them and prepare a set of simple statements.

The primary concern of this book is financial accounting. As we noted earlier, this branch of accounting is concerned with the preparation of general-purpose financial statements. We turn our attention now to the composition of each of the major statements: the balance sheet, the income statement, the statement of retained earnings, and the statement of cash flows.

The Accounting Equation and the Balance Sheet

The *accounting equation* is the foundation for the entire accounting system:

$$\text{Assets} = \text{Liabilities} + \text{Owners' Equity}.$$

The left side of the accounting equation refers to the valuable economic resources controlled by a company—that is, its assets. The logic of the equation is that assets come from somewhere. In other words, what are the *sources* of these assets? Who has a *claim* on these assets? This is what the right side of the equation tells us. It tells us that some of the company's assets were provided by creditors. To them we have an obligation, or a liability. Other assets were provided by the owners of the business. Their claim to the assets of the business is represented by **owners' equity** in the accounting equation.

The term *stockholders' equity* is used to refer to the owners' equity of a corporation. **Stockholders' equity** is the mathematical difference between a corporation's assets and its obligations or liabilities. That is, after taking into account the amounts owed to bondholders, banks, suppliers, and other creditors, stockholders' equity is the amount of interest or claim that the owners have on the assets of the business.

Stockholders' equity arises in two distinct ways. First, it is created when a company issues stock to an investor. As we noted earlier, capital stock is a representation of ownership in a corporation in the form of a certificate. It represents the amounts contributed by the owners to the company. Second, stockholders have a claim on the assets of a business when it is profitable. **Retained earnings** represents the owners' claims on the assets of the company that result from its earnings that have not been paid out in dividends. It is the earnings retained by the company.

The **balance sheet** is the financial statement that summarizes, as of a specific point in time, the assets, liabilities, and owners' equity of a company. It is a "snapshot" of the business at a certain date. A balance sheet can be prepared on any day of the year, although it is most commonly prepared on the last day of a month, quarter, or year. At any point in time, the balance sheet must be "in balance." That is, assets must equal liabilities and owners' equity.

An alternative title for the balance sheet is the statement of financial position. Although this title is more descriptive than the title "balance sheet," it has not achieved widespread popularity. We will refer to the statement that summarizes assets, liabilities, and owners' equity as the *balance sheet.*

Comparative balance sheets for Ben & Jerry's as of the end of two recent years are shown in Exhibit 1-3. When a balance sheet is presented, it is common to present the balance sheet as of the end of the prior period as well. This allows the user to make comparisons from one period to the next. Note the date of each of the two balance sheets. Unlike many companies, Ben & Jerry's does not end its fiscal or accounting year on December 31. Instead, the date on each of these balance sheets corresponds with the last Saturday in the calendar year.

One of the purposes of this book is to enhance your understanding of the balance sheet. Note for now the types of items that appear on the balance sheet. *Property, plant, and equipment* is Ben & Jerry's largest asset, which is typical for a company that produces a product. Because it sells a product, *inventories* are another significant asset to the company. *Accounts receivable* arise from selling ice cream products to distributors on credit. Similarly, Ben & Jerry's purchases supplies and other items on credit, as indicated by the significant balance in *accounts payable and accrued expenses.*

The Income Statement

An **income statement,** or statement of income, as it is sometimes called, summarizes the revenues and expenses of a company for a period of time. Comparative income statements for Ben & Jerry's for three recent years are shown in Exhibit 1-4. Unlike the balance sheet, an income statement is a *flow* statement. That is, it summarizes the flow of revenues and expenses for the year. As was the case for the balance sheet, you are not expected at this point to understand fully all of the complexities involved in preparing an income statement. For now, refer to the descriptions given at the bottom of the income statement. These will give you an appreciation of the various items on the statement.

FROM CONCEPT TO PRACTICE

READING BEN & JERRY'S BALANCE SHEET

Note the large increase at the end of 1992 in inventories. What liability increased by a large amount and how is it related to inventories?

FROM CONCEPT TO PRACTICE

READING BEN & JERRY'S INCOME STATEMENT

Compute the percentage increase in net sales for 1991 and 1992. Did the company hold the line on the costs to make the products? What was the percentage increase in cost of sales each year?

EXHIBIT 1-3 Ben & Jerry's Balance Sheet

	December 26, 1992	December 28, 1991
Current assets:		
Cash and cash equivalents	$ 7,356,133	$ 6,704,006
Accounts receivable, less allowance for doubtful accounts:		
$350,000 in 1992 and 1991	8,849,326	6,939,975
Income taxes receivable	306,193	
Inventories	17,089,857	8,999,666
Deferred income taxes	1,730,000	984,000
Prepaid expenses	208,996	107,325
Total current assets	35,540,505	23,734,972
Property, plant and equipment	39,312,513	28,496,080
Less accumulated depreciation	12,575,088	9,196,551
	26,737,425	19,299,529
Investments	25,200,000	
Other assets	728,885	21,598
	$ 88,206,815	$ 43,056,099

CONSOLIDATED BALANCE SHEET ASSETS

ASSETS ~ THINGS THE COMPANY OWNS.

~ CASH
~ ACCOUNTS RECEIVABLE · MONEY OWED TO THE COMPANY
~ INVENTORY · MANUFACTURED PRODUCTS WAITING TO BE SOLD, ALSO INGREDIENTS, PACKAGING & SUPPLIES
~ PROPERTY, PLANT & EQUIPMENT · BUILDINGS, MACHINERY, TRUCKS ETC. DEPRECIATION IS THE PART OF THE VALUE OF THESE ASSETS THAT HAS BEEN USED UP, BASED ON HOW LONG IT IS EXPECTED TO LAST.
~ PREPAID EXPENSES, DEFERRED INCOME TAXES, OTHER ASSETS · THESE ARE MISCELLANEOUS OTHER PURCHASED ASSETS THE COMPANY HAS THAT HAVE VALUE.

	December 26, 1992	December 28, 1991
Current liabilities:		
Accounts payable and accrued expenses	$16,858,919	$11,951,308
Income taxes payable		233,853
Current portion of long-term debt and obligations under capital lease	628,098	514,905
Total current liabilities	17,487,017	12,700,066
Long-term debt and obligations under capital lease	2,640,982	2,786,659
Deferred income taxes	1,319,000	1,300,000
Commitments and contingencies		
Stockholders' equity:		
$1.20 noncumulative Class A preferred stock – $1.00 par value, redeemable at $12.00 per share; 900 shares authorized, issued and outstanding, aggregate preference on voluntary or involuntary liquidation – $9,000	900	900
Class A common stock – $.033 par value; authorized 10,000,000 shares; issued: 6,239,575 shares at December 26, 1992 and 5,033,917 shares at December 28, 1991	206,327	166,541
Class B common stock – $.033 par value; authorized 3,000,000 shares; issued: 962,008 shares at December 26, 1992 and 986,888 shares at December 28, 1991	31,746	32,565
Additional paid-in capital	47,941,134	14,261,484
Retained earnings	19,984,461	13,309,121
Unearned compensation	(38,014)	(134,588)
Treasury stock, at cost: 66,453 Class A and 1,092 Class B shares at December 26, 1992 and 66,419 Class A and 1,075 Class B shares at December 28, 1991	(1,366,738)	(1,366,649)
Total stockholders' equity	66,759,816	26,269,374
	$88,206,815	$43,056,099

LIABILITIES AND STOCKHOLDERS' EQUITY

See accompanying notes.

LIABILITIES ~ WHAT THE COMPANY OWES.
~ CURRENT LIABILITIES ~ BILLS, PAYROLL DUE, TAXES & OTHER OBLIGATIONS THAT HAVE TO BE PAID WITHIN A YEAR.
~ LONG TERM DEBT & OBLIGATIONS UNDER CAPITAL LEASES ~ LOANS OR AGREEMENTS TO PAY FOR USE OF EQUIPMENT A YEAR OR MORE FROM NOW.
~ OTHER LIABILITIES ~ MISCELLANEOUS OTHER FINANCIAL COMMITMENTS.

STOCKHOLDERS' EQUITY
THIS IS CALLED THE "BOOK VALUE" OF THE OWNERS' STAKE IN THE COMPANY. IT INCLUDES PROCEEDS THE COMPANY RECEIVED FROM THE INITIAL AND SUBSEQUENT SALES OF STOCK TO THE PUBLIC, PLUS ACCUMULATED PROFITS, CALLED RETAINED EARNINGS.
THIS BOOK VALUE IS NOT THE SAME AS THE VALUE OF STOCK ON THE PUBLIC STOCK MARKET WHICH IS CALLED THE "MARKET VALUE". THE STOCK MARKET DETERMINES IN ITS OWN WAYS WHETHER THE COMPANY IS WORTH MORE THAN THE BOOK VALUE OF WHAT IT OWNS MINUS WHAT IT OWES. FOR EXAMPLE, A COMPANY'S STOCK PRICE CHANGES REGULARLY WITHOUT REGARD TO THE VALUE OF THE ASSETS & LIABILITIES IT USES TO RUN ITS BUSINESS.

EXHIBIT 1-4 Ben & Jerry's Income Statement

CONSOLIDATED STATEMENT OF INCOME

	December 26, 1992	Years Ended December 28, 1991	December 29, 1990
Net sales	$ 131,968,814	$ 96,997,339	$ 77,024,037
Cost of sales	94,389,391	68,500,402	54,202,387
Gross profit	37,579,423	28,496,937	22,821,650
Selling, general and administrative expenses	26,242,761	21,264,214	17,639,357
Operating income	11,336,662	7,232,723	5,182,293
Other income (expenses):			
Interest income	394,817	147,058	296,329
Interest expense	(181,577)	(736,248)	(868,736)
Other	(235,765)	(139,627)	(136,578)
	(22,525)	(728,817)	(708,985)
Income before income taxes	11,314,137	6,503,906	4,473,308
Income taxes	4,638,797	2,764,523	1,864,063
Net income	$ 6,675,340	$ 3,739,383	$ 2,609,245
Net income per common share	$ 1.07	$ 0.67	$ 0.50
Weighted average number of common shares outstanding	6,253,825	5,572,368	5,224,667

See accompanying notes.

STATEMENT OF INCOME

- NET SALES - THIS IS THE TOTAL SALES OF THE COMPANY MINUS THE VALUE OF PRODUCT DISCOUNTED OR RETURNED.
- COST OF SALES - WHAT IT COST TO MAKE & STORE THE PRODUCTS UNTIL THEY ARE SOLD. INCLUDES INGREDIENTS, PACKAGING, LABOR COSTS, & THE COST TO RUN PRODUCTION & STORAGE MACHINERY.
- GROSS PROFIT - NET SALES MINUS COST OF SALES.
- SELLING & ADMINISTRATIVE EXPENSES - THESE ARE THE COSTS OF MARKETING & SELLING THE PRODUCT AFTER IT HAS BEEN MADE, PLUS ALL OF THE ADMINISTRATIVE COSTS TO RUN THE COMPANY.

- OPERATING INCOME - GROSS PROFIT MINUS SELLING, GENERAL & ADMINISTRATIVE EXPENSES. THIS MEASURES HOW MUCH A COMPANY EARNS (BEFORE TAXES) FROM THE CORE BUSINESS IT IS IN.
- INCOME BEFORE TAXES, INCOME TAXES & NET INCOME - INCOME TAXES ARE THE AMOUNT OF FEDERAL & STATE TAXES PAID OR DUE BASED ON THE COMPANY'S BOOK INCOME. SUBTRACTING THOSE TAXES FROM INCOME BEFORE TAXES RESULTS IN NET INCOME OR THE "BOTTOM LINE." CONTINUED → (REMEMBER, BEN & JERRY'S HAS TWO "BOTTOM LINES.")

The Statement of Retained Earnings

As discussed earlier, retained earnings represents the accumulated earnings of a business less the amount paid in dividends to stockholders. **Dividends** are distributions of the net income or profits of a business to its stockholders. Not all businesses pay cash dividends. Ben & Jerry's rationale for not paying dividends to stockholders is stated in its annual report:

The Company has never paid any cash dividends on the Class A Common Stock or the Class B Common Stock and the Company presently intends to reinvest earnings for use in its business and to finance future growth. Accordingly, the Board of Directors does not anticipate declaring any cash dividends in the foreseeable future.

A **statement of retained earnings** explains the change in retained earnings during the period. The basic format for the statement is as follows:

Beginning balance	$xxx,xxx
Add: Net income for the period	xxx,xxx
Deduct: Dividends for the period	xxx,xxx
Ending balance	$xxx,xxx

Revenues minus expenses, or net income, is an increase in retained earnings, and dividends are a decrease in the balance. Why are dividends shown on a statement of retained earnings instead of on an income statement? Dividends are not an expense and thus are *not a determinant of* net income as are expenses. Instead, they are a *distribution of* the income of the business to its stockholders.

Recall that stockholders' equity consists of two parts: capital stock and retained earnings. Some corporations prepare a comprehensive statement to explain the changes both in the various capital stock accounts and in retained earnings during the period. A statement of stockholders' equity for Ben & Jerry's is presented in Exhibit 1-5.

EXHIBIT 1-5 Ben & Jerry's Statement of Stockholders' Equity

CONSOLIDATED STATEMENT OF STOCKHOLDERS' EQUITY

	Preferred Stock Par Value	Common Stock Class A Par Value	Common Stock Class B Par Value
Balance at December 30, 1989	$ 900	$131,909	$38,383
Net income			
Common Stock forfeited under restricted stock plan (306 Class A shares and 150 Class B shares)			
Common Stock issued under stock purchase plan (12,462 shares)		411	
Conversion of Class B shares to Class A shares (78,048 shares)		2,576	(2,576)
Conversion of subordinated debentures to Class A shares (644 shares)		21	
Balance at December 29, 1990	900	134,917	35,807
Net income			
Common stock issued under restricted stock plan (53,450 Class A shares)			
Amortization of unearned compensation			
Conversion of Class B shares to Class A shares (98,230 shares)		3,242	(3,242)
Conversion of subordinated debentures to Class A shares (847,804 shares)		27,976	
Common stock forfeited under restricted stock plan (40 Class A shares and 20 Class B shares)			
Common stock issued under stock purchase plan (12,292 Class A shares)		406	
Common stock contributed (89,624 Class A shares)			
Balance at December 28, 1991	900	166,541	32,565
Net income			
Common stock issued through public offering (1,170,000 Class A shares)		38,610	
Common stock issued under stock purchase plan (8,778 Class A shares)		291	
Common stock issued under restricted stock plan (2,000 Class A shares)		66	
Common stock forfeited under restricted stock plan (34 Class A shares and 17 Class B shares)			
Conversion of Class B to Class A shares (24,880 shares)		819	(819)
Amortization of unearned compensation			
Balance at December 26, 1992	$ 900	$ 206,327	$ 31,746

(STATEMENT OF INCOME CONTINUED)

– NET INCOME PER COMMON SHARE – USING THE WEIGHTED AVERAGE NUMBER OF SHARES "OUTSTANDING" THIS IS A CALCULATION OF HOW MUCH OF THE COMPANY'S NET INCOME CAN BE ASSIGNED TO INDIVIDUAL'S SHARES. SOMETIMES CALLED "EARNINGS PER SHARE", THIS IS AN IMPORTANT YARDSTICK FOR COMPARING A COMPANY'S PERFORMANCE IN THE CURRENT PERIOD (A YEAR OR A QUARTER) TO PERFORMANCE IN A PREVIOUS PERIOD.

BEN&JERRY'S HOMEMADE INC.
CLASS A
CHER HOULDER
CERTIFICATE OF STOCK
CORPORATE SEAL

Note the way in which the statement is presented. The various elements of stockholders' equity are presented across the top of the statement in columns (Retained Earnings is the fifth column). The activity in each of the elements is described down the left side of the statement. For example, for each of the three years presented in the statement, net income is added in the Retained Earnings column. If dividends had been paid, they would be reflected as a deduction in this column.

The Statement of Cash Flows

We talked earlier in the chapter about the types of business activities conducted by organizations. The purpose of the **statement of cash flows** is to summarize the cash effects of a company's operating, investing, and financing activities for a period of time. Because it summarizes flows for a period of time, the statement of cash flows is similar to the income statement. It differs from the income statement in two important respects, however. First, the income statement reports only on the operating activities during the period. The statement of cash flows is broader in that it reports

EXHIBIT 1-5 *(continued)*

Additional Paid-in Capital	Retained Earnings	Unearned Compensation	Treasury Stock Class A Cost	Treasury Stock Class B Cost
$6,302,851	$6,960,493	$ 0	($24,729)	($4,413)
	2,609,245			
			(534)	(264)
82,149				
4,978				
6,389,978	9,569,738	0	(25,263)	(4,677)
	3,739,383			
(53,450)		(211,750)	567,907	
		77,162		
5,925,527				
94,919			(71)	(35)
1,904,510			(1,904,510)	
14,261,484	13,309,121	(134,588)	(1,361,937)	(4,712)
	6,675,340			
33,467,490				
155,226				
56,934				
			(59)	(30)
	96,574			
$47,941,134	$19,984,461	$ (38,014)	$ (1,361,996)	$ (4,742)

See accompanying notes.

EXHIBIT 1-6 Ben & Jerry's Statement of Cash Flows

Years Ended	12/26/92	12/28/91	12/29/90
Cash flows from operating activities:			
Net income	$ 6,675,340	$ 3,739,383	$ 2,609,245
Adjustments to reconcile net income to net cash provided by operating activities:			
Depreciation and amortization	3,455,720	2,980,826	2,320,666
Provision for doubtful accounts receivable		100,000	88,000
Deferred income taxes	(727,000)	(294,000)	91,000
Amortization of unearned compensation	96,574	77,162	
(Gain) Loss on disposition of assets	(14,232)	13,250	3,666
Stock awards	57,000	302,601	
Changes in assets and liabilities:			
Accounts receivable	(1,909,351)	(1,995,530)	(1,462,567)
Income tax receivable/payable	(540,046)	(98,441)	390,413
Inventories	(8,090,191)	1,083,476	(6,086,592)
Prepaid expenses	(101,671)	10,601	72,363
Other assets	93,656		
Accounts payable and accrued expenses	4,907,611	4,399,156	3,198,786
Net cash provided by operating activities	3,903,410	10,318,484	1,224,980
Cash flows from investing activities:			
Additions to property, plant and equipment	(10,447,007)	(4,034,124)	(2,597,635)
Proceeds from sale of property, plant and equipment	105,084	70,000	42,500
Increase in investments	(25,200,000)		
Changes in other assets	(836,657)		
Net cash used for investing activities	(36,378,580)	(3,964,124)	(2,555,135)
Cash flows from financing activities:			
Borrowings on short-term debt		8,900,000	
Repayments of short-term debt		(8,900,000)	
Repayments of long-term debt and capital leases	(534,231)	(439,002)	(348,731)
Net proceeds from issuance of common stock	33,661,528	95,325	81,763
Payment of bond redemption costs		(102,867)	
Net cash provided by (used for) financing activities	33,127,297	(446,544)	(266,968)
Increase (decrease) in cash and cash equivalents	652,127	5,907,816	(1,597,123)
Cash and cash equivalents at beginning of year	6,704,006	796,190	2,393,313
Cash and cash equivalents at end of year	$ 7,356,133	$6,704,006	$ 796,190

CONSOLIDATED STATEMENT OF CASH FLOWS

29

See accompanying notes.

financing and investing activities as well as operating activities. Second, an income statement is prepared on an *accrual* basis. This means that revenues are recognized when they are earned and expenses when they are incurred, regardless of when cash is received or paid. Alternatively, a statement of cash flows reflects the cash effects from buying and selling products and services.

A statement of cash flows for Ben & Jerry's is shown in Exhibit 1-6. Note the three major categories on the statement: operating, investing, and financing. We will return to the preparation of this important statement later in the book. For now, note that net income is the first item in the operating activities section of the statement. Adjustments are made to this number to convert it to net cash provided by operating activities.

A brief look at Ben & Jerry's statement of cash flows for 1992 tells an interesting story. Slightly less than $4 million in cash was provided by operating activities. Another $33 million was provided by financing activities, specifically from the issuance of stock. In turn, nearly all of the cash generated from operating and financing activities was needed to pay for the investing activities of the period. The net cash used for investing activities in 1992 was approximately $36 million. The end result was that the net increase in cash for the period, as shown at the bottom of the statement, was less than $1 million.

■ **ACCOUNTING FOR YOUR DECISIONS**   **You Are the Banker**

Assume Ben & Jerry's comes to your bank and wants to borrow $1 million. Which sections of its statement of cash flows would you look at most closely before making the loan, and what would you be concerned with in each of these sections?

Relationships among Ben & Jerry's Financial Statements

Because the statements of a real-world company such as Ben & Jerry's are complex, it may not be easy at this point to see the important *links* among them. The relationships among the statements are summarized for you in Exhibit 1-7. Five important relationships are seen by examining the exhibit (the numbers that follow correspond to the highlighted numbers in the exhibit):

1 The 1992 income statement reports net income of $6,675,340. Net income increases retained earnings as reported on the statement of stockholders' equity.

2 The ending balance of $19,984,461 in retained earnings, as reported on the statement of stockholders' equity for 1992, is transferred to the balance sheet at the end of 1992.

3 Net income appears in the operating activities section of the statement of cash flows. Adjustments are made to convert net income to net cash from operating activities.

4 The cash balance on the balance sheet at the end of 1991 is $6,704,006. This amount appears at the bottom of the statement of cash flows for 1992. When this balance is added to the increase in cash of $652,127 for 1992, the result is the ending balance in cash of $7,356,133.

5 The ending cash balance of $7,356,133 appears as an asset on the balance sheet at the end of 1992.

The Conceptual Framework: Foundation for Financial Statements

The task of preparing financial statements for Ben & Jerry's or any other business may appear at first glance to be procedural in nature. As noted previously, many observers of the accounting profession perceive the work of an accountant as being routine. In reality, accounting is anything but routine and requires a great deal of judgment on the part of the accountant. The record-keeping aspect of accounting—what we normally think of as bookkeeping—is the routine part of the accountant's work, and only a small part of it. Most of the job deals with communicating relevant information to financial statement users.

The accounting profession has worked in recent years to develop a *conceptual framework for accounting*. The purpose of the framework is to act as a foundation for the specific principles and standards needed by the profession. An important part of the conceptual framework is a set of assumptions we make in preparing financial statements. We will briefly consider these assumptions and return to a more detailed discussion of them in later chapters.

LO 6

Identify and explain the primary assumptions made in preparing financial statements.

EXHIBIT 1-7   The Relationships among Ben & Jerry's Financial Statements

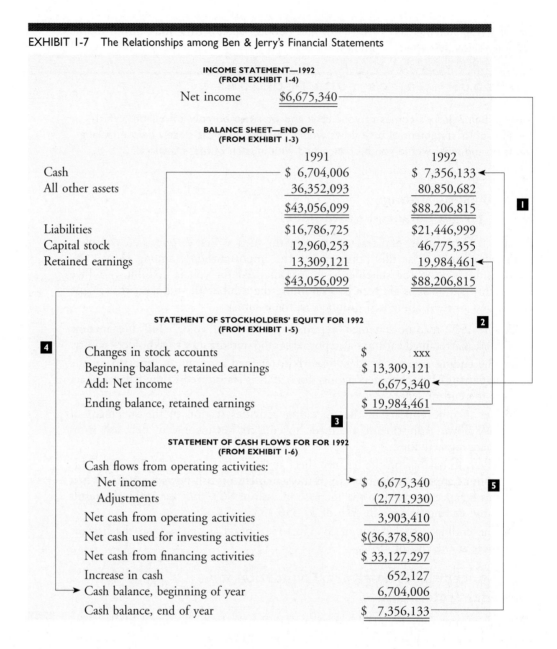

INCOME STATEMENT—1992
(FROM EXHIBIT 1-4)

Net income $6,675,340

BALANCE SHEET—END OF:
(FROM EXHIBIT 1-3)

	1991	1992
Cash	$ 6,704,006	$ 7,356,133
All other assets	36,352,093	80,850,682
	$43,056,099	$88,206,815
Liabilities	$16,786,725	$21,446,999
Capital stock	12,960,253	46,775,355
Retained earnings	13,309,121	19,984,461
	$43,056,099	$88,206,815

STATEMENT OF STOCKHOLDERS' EQUITY FOR 1992
(FROM EXHIBIT 1-5)

Changes in stock accounts	$ xxx
Beginning balance, retained earnings	$ 13,309,121
Add: Net income	6,675,340
Ending balance, retained earnings	$ 19,984,461

STATEMENT OF CASH FLOWS FOR FOR 1992
(FROM EXHIBIT 1-6)

Cash flows from operating activities:	
Net income	$ 6,675,340
Adjustments	(2,771,930)
Net cash from operating activities	3,903,410
Net cash used for investing activities	$(36,378,580)
Net cash from financing activities	$ 33,127,297
Increase in cash	652,127
Cash balance, beginning of year	6,704,006
Cash balance, end of year	$ 7,356,133

The *economic entity concept,* as discussed earlier in the chapter relative to a sole proprietorship, has just as much relevance to a partnership or corporation. The economic entity concept or assumption requires that an identifiable, specific entity be the subject of a set of financial statements. For example, even though Ben Cohen and Jerry Greenfield are stockholders and therefore own part of Ben & Jerry's, it is important that their personal affairs be kept separate from those of the business. When we look at a balance sheet for the ice cream business, we need assurance that it shows the financial position of that entity only and does not intermingle the personal assets and liabilities of Ben, Jerry, or any of the other stockholders.

What is the basis for recording assets on a balance sheet? For example, what amount should appear on a balance sheet for inventory or for land? The **cost principle** requires that we record assets at the cost to acquire them and to continue to show

One firm goes out of business, another thrives in the same location. The difference may lie simply in the natural abilities of the owner or manager. More often, success comes from setting goals, working hard to reach them, and making the best decisions possible based on high-quality financial information.

this amount on all balance sheets until we dispose of them. With a few exceptions, companies do not carry assets at their market value but at original cost. Accountants use the term *historical cost* to refer to the original cost of an asset. Why not show an asset such as land at market value? This might seem appropriate in certain instances, but the *subjectivity* inherent in determining market values is a major reason for the practice of carrying assets at their historical cost. The cost of an asset is subject to verification by an independent observer and is much more *objective* than market value.

We assume in accounting that the entity being accounted for is a **going concern.** That is, we assume that Ben & Jerry's is not in the process of liquidation and that it will continue indefinitely into the future. Another important justification for the use of historical cost rather than market value to report assets is the going concern assumption. If we assume that a business is *not* a going concern, then we assume that it is in the process of liquidation. If this is the case, market value might be more relevant than cost as a basis for recognizing the assets. But if we are able to assume that a business will continue indefinitely, cost can be more easily justified as a basis for valuation. The **monetary unit** used in preparing the statements of Ben & Jerry's was the dollar. The reason for using the dollar as the monetary unit is that it is the recognized medium of exchange in the United States. It provides a convenient yardstick to measure the position and earnings of the business. As a yardstick, however, the dollar, like the currencies of all countries, is subject to instability. We are all well aware that a dollar will not buy as much today as it did 10 years ago.

■ ACCOUNTING FOR YOUR DECISIONS   You Are the Supplier

Assume your company manufactures appliances and sells them to a number of mass merchandisers, such as Kmart, Wal-Mart, and Sears. In reading the financial statements for these customers, why would the going concern assumption be important to you?

Inflation is evidenced by a general rise in the level of prices in an economy. Its effect on the measuring unit used in preparing financial statements is an important concern to the accounting profession. Although accountants have experimented with financial statements adjusted for the changing value of the measuring unit, the financial statements now prepared by corporations are prepared under the assumption that the monetary unit is relatively stable. At various times in the past, this has been a reasonable assumption and at other times not so reasonable.

One final assumption made in preparing financial statements is the **time period** assumption. We assume that it is possible to prepare an income statement that accurately reflects net income or earnings for a specific time period. In the case of Ben & Jerry's, this time period was one year. It is somewhat artificial to measure the earnings of a business for a period of time indicated on a calendar, whether it be a month, a quarter, or a year. Of course, the most accurate point in time to measure the earnings of a business would be at the end of its life. We prepare periodic statements, however, because the users of the statements demand information about the entity on a regular basis. We will see in later chapters that the time-period assumption requires the accountant to make a number of estimates.

An important concept regarding financial statements is **generally accepted accounting principles** (GAAP). This term refers to the various methods, rules, practices, and other procedures that have evolved over time in response to the need for some form of regulation over the preparation of financial statements. For example, the cost principle, mentioned earlier, is an important part of GAAP. As changes have taken place in the business environment over time, GAAP have developed in response to these changes.

Accounting as a Social Science

Accounting is a service activity. As we have seen, its purpose is to provide financial information to decision makers. Thus, accounting is a *social* science. Accounting principles are much different from the rules that govern the *physical* sciences. For example, it is a rule of nature that an object dropped from your hand will eventually hit the ground rather than be suspended in air. There are no rules comparable to this in accounting. The principles that govern financial reporting are not governed by nature but instead develop in response to changing business conditions. For example, consider the lease of an office building. Leasing has developed in response to the need to have access to valuable assets, such as office space, without the large outlay necessary to buy the asset. As leasing has increased in popularity, it has been left to the accounting profession to develop guidelines, some of which are quite complex, to be followed in accounting for leases. Those guidelines are now part of generally accepted accounting principles.

Who Determines the Rules of the Game?

LO   7

Describe the process of setting standards in financial accounting and the various groups involved in the process.

Who determines the rules to be followed in preparing an income statement or a balance sheet? We know that the government, through the Internal Revenue Service, dictates the requirements in preparing a tax return. However, neither the government nor any one group in the private sector is totally responsible for setting the standards or principles to be followed in preparing financial statements. The process is a joint effort. We will briefly consider the groups that have been involved in setting generally accepted accounting principles.

The Securities and Exchange Commission The federal government, through the **Securities and Exchange Commission** (SEC), has the ultimate authority to determine the rules to be followed in preparing financial statements by companies whose securities are sold to the general public. This authority was given to the Commission when Congress established it in 1934. The SEC requires that companies file both annual and quarterly financial statements, as well as other types of reports, with it on a timely basis. Although the SEC has the authority to set accounting principles, it has to a large extent allowed the accounting profession to establish its own rules. The Commission has on occasion intervened and dictated certain rules when it has believed that the profession was not responding quickly enough or in the correct manner.

The Financial Accounting Standards Board The **Financial Accounting Standards Board** (FASB) currently has the authority to set accounting standards in the United States. Although the FASB receives funding from various sources, it exists as an independent group with seven full-time members supported by a large staff. The Board has issued more than 100 financial accounting standards since its creation in the early 1970s. These standards deal with a variety of financial reporting issues, such as the proper accounting for lease arrangements and pension plans. In addition, the FASB has issued six statements of financial accounting concepts, which are used to guide the Board in setting accounting standards.

American Institute of Certified Public Accountants The **American Institute of Certified Public Accountants** (AICPA) has taken an active role in setting accounting standards. Prior to the establishment of the FASB, the AICPA had the primary responsibility for setting GAAP through its Accounting Principles Board. With the creation of the FASB, the AICPA has acted in a more advisory role. The AICPA does, however, set the *auditing* standards to be followed by public accounting firms in performing these services for their clients. We will consider the work of public accounting firms in the next section.

The AICPA is the professional organization of certified public accountants. The title **certified public accountant** (CPA) is the professional designation for accountants who have passed a rigorous exam and met certain other requirements. Each of the 50 states regulates the requirements to become a CPA in a particular state. However, all candidates for the certificate take a uniform exam prepared and graded by the American Institute of Certified Public Accountants. Although many CPAs are in public practice, accountants with the professional certification are also employed in business and nonbusiness entities, as well as in the academic community.

The Accounting Profession

Accountants play many different roles in society. Understanding what the various roles are will help you to more fully appreciate the importance of accounting in organizations.

LO **8**

Describe the various roles played by accountants in organizations.

Employment by Private Business

Many accountants work for business entities. Regardless of the types of activities a company engages in, accountants perform a number of important functions for them. A partial organization chart for a corporation is shown in Exhibit 1-8. The chart indicates that three individuals report directly to the chief financial officer: the controller, the treasurer, and the director of internal auditing.

EXHIBIT 1-8 Partial Organization Chart

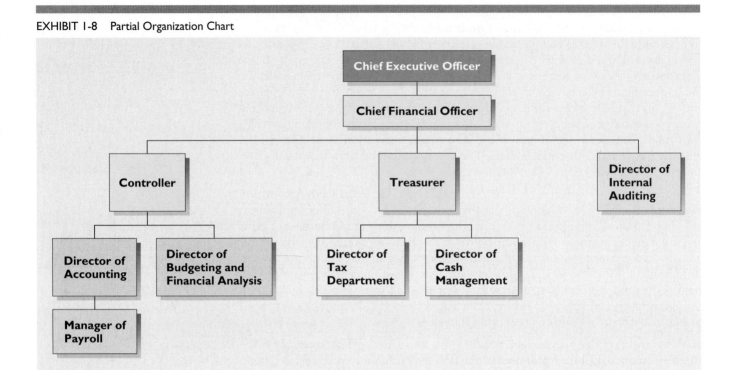

This partial organization chart does not show the other departments in the company—such as marketing, sales, production, and so on. That does not mean they are unimportant to the flow of accounting information. In fact, accounting information for internal decision making forms a complex system of reporting, responsibility, and control collectively known as management accounting.

The **controller** is the chief accounting officer for a company and typically has responsibility for the overall operation of the accounting system. Accountants working for the controller record the company's activities and prepare periodic financial statements. In this organization, the payroll function is assigned to the controller's office, as is responsibility for the preparation of budgets.

The **treasurer** of an organization is typically responsible for the safeguarding, as well as efficient use of, the company's liquid resources, such as cash. Note that the director of the tax department in this corporation reports to the treasurer. Accountants in the tax department are responsible for both preparing the company's tax returns and planning transactions in such a way that the company pays the least amount of taxes possible within the confines of the Internal Revenue Code.

Internal auditing is the department in a company responsible for the review and appraisal of accounting and administrative controls. The department must determine whether the company's assets are properly accounted for and protected from losses. Recommendations are made periodically to management for improvements in the various controls.

Employment by Nonbusiness Entities

Nonbusiness organizations, such as hospitals, universities, and various branches of the government, have as much need for accountants as do companies organized to earn a profit. Although the profit motive is not paramount to nonbusiness entities, all organizations must have financial information to operate efficiently. A county government needs detailed cost information in determining the taxes to levy on its constituents. A university must pay close attention to its various operating costs in setting the annual tuition rates. Accountants working for nonbusiness entities perform most of the same tasks as their counterparts in the business sector. In fact, many of the job titles in business entities, such as controller and treasurer, are also used by nonbusiness entities.

Employment in Public Accounting

Public accounting firms provide valuable services in much the same way as do law firms or architectural firms. They provide a professional service for their clients in return for a fee. The usual services provided by public accounting firms include auditing and tax and management consulting services.

Auditing Services   The auditing services rendered by public accounting firms are similar in certain respects to the work performed by internal auditors. However, there are key differences between the two. Internal auditors are more concerned with the efficient operation of the various segments of the business, and therefore, the work they do is often called *operational auditing*. On the other hand, the primary objective of the external auditor, or public accountant, is to provide assurance to stockholders and other users that the statements are fairly presented. In this respect, **auditing** is the process of examining the financial statements and the underlying records of a company in order to render an opinion as to whether the statements are fairly presented.

As we discussed earlier, the financial statements are prepared by the company's accountants. The external auditor performs various tests and procedures to be able to render his or her opinion. The public accountant has a responsibility to the company's stockholders and any other users of the statements. Because most stockholders are not actively involved in the daily affairs of the business, they must rely on the auditors to ensure that management is fairly presenting the financial statements of the business.

Note that the auditors' report is an *opinion,* not a statement of fact. For example, one important procedure performed by the auditor to obtain assurance as to the validity of a company's inventory is to observe the year-end physical count of inventory by the company's employees. However, this is done on a sample basis. It would be too costly for the auditors to make an independent count of every single item of inventory.

The auditors' report on the financial statements for Ben & Jerry's is shown in Exhibit 1-9. Note first that the report is directed to the company's stockholders and board of directors. The company is audited by Ernst & Young, a large international accounting firm. Public accounting firms range in size from those with a single owner to others such as Ernst & Young that have thousands of partners. The opinion given by Ernst & Young on the company's financial statements is the *standard auditors' report.* The first paragraph indicates that the firm has examined the company's balance sheet and the related statements of income, stockholders' equity, and cash flows. Note that the second paragraph of the report indicates that evidence supporting the amounts and disclosures in the statements was examined on a *test* basis. The third paragraph states the firm's *opinion* that the financial statements are fairly presented in conformity with generally accepted accounting principles.

Tax Services   In addition to auditing, public accounting firms provide a variety of tax services. Firms often prepare the tax return for the companies they audit. They also usually work throughout the year with management to plan acquisitions and other transactions to take full advantage of the tax laws. For example, if tax rates are scheduled to decline next year, a public accounting firm would advise its client to accelerate certain expenditures this year as much as possible to receive a higher tax deduction than would be possible by waiting until next year.

FROM CONCEPT TO PRACTICE

READING BEN & JERRY'S AUDITORS' REPORT

Note the date at the bottom of the report. Why do you think it takes two months after the end of the year to release this report?

EXHIBIT 1-9 Ben & Jerry's Auditors' Report

The Board of Directors and Stockholders
Ben & Jerry's Homemade, Inc.

REPORT OF
INDEPENDENT
AUDITORS

We have audited the accompanying balance sheets of Ben & Jerry's Homemade, Inc. as of December 26, 1992 and December 28, 1991, and the related statements of income, stockholders' equity and cash flows for each of the three years in the period ended December 26, 1992. These financial statements are the responsibility of the Company's management. Our responsibility is to express an opinion on these financial statements based on our audits.

We conducted our audits in accordance with generally accepted auditing standards. Those standards require that we plan and perform the audit to obtain reasonable assurance about whether the financial statements are free of material misstatement. An audit includes examining, on a test basis, evidence supporting the amounts and disclosures in the financial statements. An audit also includes assessing the accounting principles used and significant estimates made by management, as well as evaluating the overall financial statement presentation. We believe that our audits provide a reasonable basis for our opinion.

In our opinion, the financial statements referred to above present fairly, in all material respects, the financial position of Ben & Jerry's Homemade, Inc. at December 26, 1992 and December 28, 1991, and the results of its operations and its cash flows for each of the three years in the period ended December 26, 1992 in conformity with generally accepted accounting principles.

Ernst & Young

ERNST & YOUNG

March 8, 1993

Management Consulting Services   By working closely with management to provide auditing and tax services, a public accounting firm becomes very familiar with various aspects of a company's business. This vantage point allows the firm to provide expert advice to the company to improve its operations. The management consulting services rendered by public accounting firms to their clients take a variety of forms. For example, the firm might advise the company on the design and installation of a computer system to fill its needs. The services provided in this area have grown dramatically to include such diverse activities as advice on selection of a new plant site or an investment opportunity.

Accountants in Education

Some accountants choose a career in education. As the demand for accountants in business entities, nonbusiness organizations, and public accounting has increased, so has the need for qualified professors to teach this discipline. Accounting programs range from two years of study at community colleges to doctoral programs at some universities. All of these programs require the services of knowledgeable instructors. In addition to their teaching duties, many accounting educators are actively involved in research. The **American Accounting Association** is a professional organization of accounting educators and others interested in the future of the profession. The group advances its ideas through its many committees and the publication of a number of journals.

HOW USEFUL IS AN ACCOUNTING COURSE? ASK THIS JOURNALIST

Name: Jeffrey M. Laderman
Profession: Magazine Journalist
College Major: History

You never know when you're going to need accounting knowledge. It was the last thing on Jeff Laderman's mind as he earned his bachelor's degree in liberal arts from Rutgers University and his Master's in Journalism from Columbia. Why would a journalist need to study accounting?

After working for a small daily paper in New Jersey, Jeff joined the *Detroit News,* where he spent seven years. "I didn't start doing business and financial reporting until the latter half of my time there." But after joining *Business Week* in 1982, "I soon discovered that there were gaps in my knowledge, and while I was a quick study, I wanted to know more and have a better grasp."

So, at the age of 37, Jeff began a study of accounting through the Chartered Financial Analyst program, a three-year course of study in accounting as well as finance and economics culminating in the CFA designation. One goal: to be able to read a company's financial statements. "If you're reporting on a company, you want to know about its sales and earnings growth and what's its cash flow—because the earnings might look good but the cash flow isn't and that's a danger

sign. Or, the cash flow might be strong but the earnings look spotty, so it might be undervalued."

When he is going to do an article about a company, the first thing he gets is its annual report—so he can ask intelligent questions of management as well as securities analysts who follow it. "I like to look at the footnotes to the financial statements," he says. "You can find out if there are material lawsuits against the company. Sometimes you find that the company has made big loans to key people."

Laderman covers finance for the magazine and sometimes writes the "Inside Wall Street" column, in which he tries to make a case for a stock. True, the lets experts on Wall Street make the arguments, but his own analysis is relevant also: Here's a company that's doing well in one line of business but not another. That could be a sign that the company may sell the lagging business—which could be a positive for the stock if you buy it at the right time. There's a company that is building up inventory quarter after quarter. What's the matter? Is the product not selling?

Even if you intend a career that seems far afield from accounting, don't be surprised to look back and be glad you took this course. You never know when you'll need it.

Accountants and Ethical Judgments

Remember the primary goal of accounting: to provide useful information to aid in the decision-making process. As we discussed, the work of the accountant in providing useful information is anything but routine and requires the accountant to make subjective judgments about what information to present and how to present it. The latitude given accountants in this respect is one of the major reasons accounting is a profession and its members are considered professionals. Along with this designation as a professional, however, comes a serious responsibility. As we noted, general-purpose financial statements are prepared for external parties who must rely on these statements to provide information on which to base important decisions.

Cases appear at the end of each chapter titled "Accounting and Ethics: What Would You Do?" The cases require you to evaluate difficult issues and make a decision. Judgment is needed in deciding which accounting method to select or how to report a certain item in the statements. As you are faced with these decisions, keep in mind the trust placed in the accountant by various financial statement users. This is central to reaching an ethical decision.

REVIEW PROBLEM

Note to the student: At the end of each chapter is a problem to test your understanding of some of the major ideas presented in the chapter. Try to solve the problem before turning to the solution that follows it.

Clipper Corporation is organized on June 1, 1995. The company will provide lawn care and tree-trimming services on a contract basis. Following is an alphabetical list of the items that should appear on its income statement for the first month and its balance sheet at the end of the first month (you will need to determine on *which* statement each should appear).

Accounts payable	$ 800
Accounts receivable	500
Building	2,000
Capital stock	5,000
Cash	3,300
Gas, utilities, and other expenses	300
Land	4,000
Lawn care revenue	1,500
Notes payable	6,000
Salaries and wages expense	900
Retained earnings (beginning balance)	–0–
Tree-trimming revenue	500
Truck	2,000
Tools	800

■ REQUIRED

1. Prepare an income statement for the month of June.

2. Prepare a balance sheet at June 30, 1995. *Note:* You will need to determine the balance in Retained Earnings at the end of the month.

■ SOLUTION TO REVIEW PROBLEM

1.

THE CLIPPER CORPORATION
INCOME STATEMENT
FOR THE MONTH ENDED JUNE 30, 1995

Revenues:		
Lawn care	$1,500	
Tree trimming	500	$2,000
Expenses:		
Salaries and wages	$ 900	
Gas, utilities, and other expenses	300	1,200
Net income		$ 800

2.

THE CLIPPER CORPORATION
BALANCE SHEET
AT JUNE 30, 1995

ASSETS		LIABILITIES AND OWNERS' EQUITY	
Cash	$ 3,300	Accounts payable	$ 800
Accounts receivable	500	Notes payable	6,000
Truck	2,000	Capital stock	5,000
Tools	800	Retained earnings	800
Building	2,000		
Land	4,000		
Total	$12,600	Total	$12,600

GUIDANCE ANSWERS TO ACCOUNTING FOR YOUR DECISIONS

YOU ARE THE BANKER

A banker must be concerned with the *operating* cash flow of a business. This is the lifeblood of a business and it is necessary that sufficient cash be generated from a company's operations to repay debts and any interest on these debts. In addition, the banker needs to know what additional borrowing the company has done lately. This can be found by looking at the financing activities section of the statement of cash flows.

YOU ARE THE SUPPLIER

As the supplier of merchandise to these companies, you are primarily concerned with the ability to pay their accounts on time. (It is likely that you will need to grant each of them credit in order to secure their business.) If there is any question about the ability of the customers to stay in business, this information could have a significant effect on your decision to sell to them.

CHAPTER HIGHLIGHTS

1. **(LO 1)** All organizations rely on financial information in making decisions. It is not the only type of information that must be considered in making decisions, but it is certainly one of the most important.

2. **(LO 2)** The information needed for making decisions depends on the organization form of an entity. Business entities are organized to earn a profit whereas nonbusiness organizations exist for some other purpose, such as providing health care or municipal services. Business entities are organized as either sole proprietorships, partnerships, or corporations.

3. **(LO 3)** All businesses carry on three basic types of activities. These are financing, investing, and operating activities. Financing activities are necessary to provide

the funds to start a business and to expand it in the future. Investing activities are needed to provide the valuable assets required to run it. Operating activities focus on the sale of products and services.

4. **(LO 4)** Both individuals external to a business, as well as those involved in the internal management of the company, use accounting information. External users include present and potential stockholders, bankers and other creditors, government agencies, suppliers, trade associations, labor unions, and other interested groups.

5. **(LO 5)** The accounting equation is the basis for the entire accounting system: Assets = Liabilities + Owners' Equity. Assets are future economic benefits. Liabilities are future sacrifices of economic benefits. Owners'

equity is the residual interest that remains after deducting liabilities from the assets.

6. **(LO 5)** A balance sheet summarizes the financial position of a company at a specific point in time. An income statement reports on its revenues and expenses for a period of time. The statement of cash flows summarizes the operating, financing, and investing activities of a company for a period of time. A statement of retained earnings explains the changes in retained earnings during a particular period.

7. **(LO 6,7)** A number of assumptions are made in preparing financial statements. Accounting is not an exact science, and judgment must be used in deciding what

to report on financial statements and how to report the information. Generally accepted accounting principles (GAAP) have evolved over time and are based on a conceptual framework. The Securities and Exchange Commission in the public sector and the Financial Accounting Standards Board in the private sector have the most responsibility for developing GAAP at the present time.

8. **(LO 8)** Accountants are employed by business entities, nonbusiness entities, public accounting firms, and educational institutions. Public accounting firms provide audit services for their clients, as well as tax and management consulting services.

KEY TERMS QUIZ

Note to the student: We conclude each chapter with a quiz on the key terms, which are in **boldface** print where they appear in the chapter. Because of the large number of terms introduced in this chapter, it has two key terms quizzes. Select from the following list of key terms used in the chapter and fill in the appropriate blank to the left of each description. The solution appears at the end of the chapter.

Quiz 1

Sole proprietorship
Partnership
Share of stock
Nonbusiness entity
Capital stock
Creditor
Revenue
Accounting
Financial accounting
Stockholders' equity
Balance sheet
Dividends
Statement of cash flows

Economic entity concept
Corporation
Bond
Liability
Stockholder
Asset
Expense
Management accounting
Owners' equity
Retained earnings
Income statement
Statement of retained
   earnings

_____   **1.** A future economic benefit.

_____   **2.** A statement that summarizes revenues and expenses.

_____   **3.** The statement that summarizes the income earned and dividends paid over the life of a business.

_____   **4.** The owners' equity in a corporation.

_____   **5.** The process of identifying, measuring, and communicating economic information to various users.

_____ **6.** A business owned by two or more individuals; organization form often used by accounting firms and law firms.

_____ **7.** The branch of accounting concerned with the preparation of general-purpose financial statements for both management and outsider use.

_____ **8.** The owners' claim on the assets of an entity.

_____ **9.** The statement that summarizes the cash effects of the operating, investing, and financing activities for a period of time.

_____ **10.** The financial statement that summarizes the assets, liabilities, and owners' equity at a specific point in time.

_____ **11.** An inflow of assets resulting from the sale of goods and services.

_____ **12.** A form of entity organized under the laws of a particular state; ownership evidenced by shares of stock.

_____ **13.** Organization operated for some purpose other than to earn a profit.

_____ **14.** The part of owners' equity that represents the income earned less dividends paid over the life of an entity.

_____ **15.** An outflow of assets resulting from the sale of goods and services.

_____ **16.** An obligation of a business.

_____ **17.** The branch of accounting concerned with providing management with information to facilitate the planning and control functions.

_____ **18.** A certificate that acts as ownership in a corporation.

_____ **19.** A certificate issued by corporations representing a promise to repay a certain amount of money and interest in the future.

_____ **20.** One of the owners of a corporation.

_____ **21.** Someone to whom a company has a debt.

_____ **22.** The assumption that requires that a single, identifiable unit be accounted for in all situations.

_____ **23.** Form of organization with a single owner.

_____ **24.** A category on the balance sheet to indicate amounts contributed by the owners to a corporation.

_____ **25.** A distribution of the net income of a business to its owners.

Quiz 2

Cost principle	Going concern
Monetary unit	Time period
Generally accepted accounting principles	Securities and Exchange Commission
Financial Accounting Standards Board	Certified Public Accountant
American Institute of Certified Public Accountants	Controller
	Internal auditing
Treasurer	Auditing
American Accounting Association	

_____ **1.** The various methods, rules, practices, and other procedures that have evolved over time in response to the need to regulate the preparation of financial statements.

_____ 2. Assets recorded at the cost to acquire them.

_____ 3. The federal agency with ultimate authority to determine the rules in preparing statements for companies whose stock is sold to the public.

_____ 4. The professional designation for public accountants who have passed a rigorous exam and met certain requirements determined by the state.

_____ 5. The professional organization for accounting educators.

_____ 6. The officer of an organization responsible for the safeguarding and efficient use of a company's liquid assets.

_____ 7. The assumption that an entity is not in the process of liquidation and that it will continue indefinitely.

_____ 8. The group in the private sector with authority to set accounting standards.

_____ 9. The yardstick used to measure amounts in financial statements; the dollar in the United States.

_____ 10. The professional organization for certified public accountants.

_____ 11. The department in a company responsible for the review and appraisal of a company's accounting and administrative controls.

_____ 12. Artificial segment on the calendar used as the basis for preparing financial statements.

_____ 13. The chief accounting officer for a company.

_____ 14. The process of examining the financial statements and the underlying records of a company in order to render an opinion as to whether the statements are fairly presented.

ALTERNATE TERMS

BALANCE SHEET Statement of financial position.

COST PRINCIPLE Original cost; historical cost.

CREDITOR Lender.

INCOME STATEMENT Statement of income.

NET INCOME Profits or earnings.

REPORT OF INDEPENDENT ACCOUNTANTS Auditors' report.

STOCKHOLDER Shareholder.

QUESTIONS

1. What is accounting? Define it in terms understandable to someone without a business background.
2. How do financial accounting and management accounting differ?
3. What are five different groups of users of accounting information? Briefly describe the types of decisions each group must make.
4. What are the three forms of business organization? Briefly describe each form.
5. What is an asset? Give three examples.

6. What is a liability? How does the definition of *liability* relate to the definition of *asset?*
7. How does owners' equity fit in to the accounting equation?
8. What are the two distinct elements of owners' equity in a corporation? Define each element.
9. What is the purpose of a balance sheet?
10. How should a balance sheet be dated: as of a particular day or for a particular period of time? Explain your answer.
11. What does the term *cost principle* mean?
12. What is the purpose of an income statement?
13. How should an income statement be dated: as of a particular day or for a particular period of time? Explain your answer.
14. Rogers Corporation starts the year with a Retained Earnings balance of $55,000. Net income for the year is $27,000. The ending balance in Retained Earnings is $70,000. What was the amount of dividends for the year?
15. What is the purpose of a statement of cash flows?
16. How do an income statement and a statement of cash flows differ? How are they similar?
17. How do the duties of the controller of a corporation typically differ from those of the treasurer?
18. What are the three basic types of services performed by public accounting firms?
19. How would you evaluate the following statement: "The auditors are in the best position to evaluate a company because they have prepared the financial statements"?
20. Why is the economic entity assumption important in preparing a set of financial statements?
21. What is the relationship between the cost principle and the going concern assumption?
22. Why does inflation present a challenge to the accountant? Relate your answer to the monetary unit assumption.
23. What is meant by the phrase *generally accepted accounting principles?*
24. What role has the Securities and Exchange Commission played in setting accounting standards? Contrast its role with that played by the Financial Accounting Standards Board.

EXERCISES

(LO 7) EXERCISE 1-1 ORGANIZATIONS AND ACCOUNTING

Match each of the organizations listed below with the statement that most adequately describes the role of the group.
Securities and Exchange Commission
Financial Accounting Standards Board
American Institute of Certified Public Accountants
American Accounting Association

_____ 1. Federal agency with ultimate authority to determine rules used in preparing financial statements for companies whose stock is sold to the public.

_____ 2. Professional organization for accounting educators.

_____ 3. Group in the private sector with authority to set accounting standards.

_____ 4. Professional organization for certified public accountants.

(LO 5) EXERCISE 1-2 THE ACCOUNTING EQUATION

Based on your understanding of the accounting equation, answer each of the following independent questions:

1. Blue Company starts the year with $100,000 in assets and $80,000 in liabilities. Net income for the year is $25,000, and no dividends are paid. How much is owners' equity at the end of the year?

2. Red Corporation doubles the amount of its assets from the beginning to the end of the year. Liabilities at the end of the year amount to $40,000, and owners' equity is $20,000. What is the amount of Red's assets at the beginning of the year?

3. During the year, the liabilities of Brown Enterprises triple in amount. Assets at the beginning of the year amount to $30,000, and owners' equity is $10,000. What is the amount of liabilities at the end of the year?

(LO 5) EXERCISE 1-3 CLASSIFICATION OF FINANCIAL STATEMENT ITEMS

Classify each of the following items according to (1) whether it belongs on the income statement (IS) or balance sheet (BS) and (2) whether it is a revenue (R), expense (E), asset (A), liability (L), or owners' equity (OE) item.

ITEM	APPEARS ON THE	CLASSIFIED AS
Example: Cash	BS	A
1. Salaries expense	_____	_____
2. Equipment	_____	_____
3. Accounts payable	_____	_____
4. Membership fees earned	_____	_____
5. Common stock	_____	_____
6. Accounts receivable	_____	_____
7. Buildings	_____	_____
8. Advertising expense	_____	_____
9. Retained earnings	_____	_____

(LO 4) EXERCISE 1-4 USERS OF ACCOUNTING INFORMATION AND THEIR NEEDS

Listed below are a number of the important users of accounting information. Below the list are descriptions of a major need of each of these various users. Fill in the blank with the one user group that is most likely to have the need described to the right of the blank.

Company management   **Banker**
Stockholder   **Supplier**
Securities and Exchange Commission   **Labor union**
Internal Revenue Service

USER GROUP   **NEEDS INFORMATION ABOUT**

_____   1. The profitability of each division in the company.

_____   2. The prospects for future dividend payments.

_____   3. The profitability of the company since the last contract with the workforce was signed.

_____   4. The financial status of a company issuing securities to the public for the first time.

_____   5. The prospects that a company will be able to meet its interest payments on time.

—————————————— **6.** The prospects that a company will be able to pay for its purchases on time.

—————————————— **7.** The profitability of the company based on the tax code.

(LO 6) EXERCISE 1-5 ACCOUNTING PRINCIPLES AND ASSUMPTIONS

The following basic accounting principles and assumptions were discussed in the chapter:

Economic entity   Going concern
Monetary unit   Time period
Cost principle

Fill in each of the blanks below with the accounting principle or assumption that is relevant to the situation described.

—————————————— **1.** Timberland Corporation is now in its 30th year of business. The founder of the company is planning to retire at the end of the year and turn the business over to his daughter.

—————————————— **2.** Winchester Company purchased a 20-acre parcel of property on which to build a new factory. The company recorded the property on the records at the amount of cash given to acquire it.

—————————————— **3.** Jim Barnes enters into an agreement to operate a new law firm in partnership with a friend. Each partner will make an initial cash investment of $10,000. Jim opens a checking account in the name of the partnership and transfers $10,000 from his personal account into the new account.

—————————————— **4.** International Corp. has a division in Japan. Prior to preparing the financial statements for the company and all of its foreign divisions, International translates the financial statements of its Japanese division from yen to U.S. dollars.

—————————————— **5.** Huntley Company has always prepared financial statements annually, with a year end of June 30. Because the company is going to sell its stock to the public for the first time, the Securities and Exchange Commission requires that Huntley also prepare quarterly financial reports.

(LO 5) EXERCISE 1-6 THE ACCOUNTING EQUATION

For each of the following independent cases, fill in the blank with the appropriate dollar amount.

	CASE 1	CASE 2	CASE 3	CASE 4
Total assets, end of period	$40,000	$_____	$75,000	$50,000
Total liabilities, end of period	_____	15,000	25,000	10,000
Capital stock, end of period	10,000	5,000	20,000	15,000
Retained earnings, beginning of period	15,000	8,000	10,000	20,000
Net income for the period	8,000	7,000	_____	9,000
Dividends for the period	2,000	1,000	3,000	_____

(LO 5) EXERCISE 1-7 STATEMENT OF RETAINED EARNINGS

Ace Corporation has been in business for many years. Retained earnings on January 1, 1995, is $235,800. The following information is available for the first two months of 1995:

	JANUARY	FEBRUARY
Revenues	$83,000	$96,000
Expenses	89,000	82,000
Dividends paid	–0–	5,000

Prepare a statement of retained earnings for the month ended February 28, 1995.

(LO 1) EXERCISE 1-8 ANNUAL REPORT INFORMATION

Critics of financial reporting have said that accounting information, specifically an annual report, is not useful for decision making because it is published three or more months after the end of the company's fiscal year. Therefore, it does not contain any real news. Besides, *all* information you need about a company can be found in the business section of newspapers or trade and news periodicals.

Look at the annual report for Ben & Jerry's. What information is usually available in detail *only* in the annual report? What advantages or disadvantages are involved in relying on annual reports for making financial decisions about investing in or lending to a company?

(LO 2) EXERCISE 1-9 FORMS OF ORGANIZATION

A university is an entity that requires an accounting system. What kind of entity is a university, business or nonbusiness? What type of accounting system do universities use? Within large entities, such as a university, are smaller entities. Food service is often a separate entity within a university, and it operates as a business entity. Identify some other entities that may exist within a university and therefore require separate accounting records. Identify each as business or nonbusiness entities.

MULTI-CONCEPT EXERCISES

(LO 4, 8) EXERCISE 1-10 ROLES OF ACCOUNTANTS

One day on campus, you overhear two nonbusiness majors discussing the reasons each did not major in accounting. "Accountants are bean counters. They just sit in a room and play with the books all day. They do not have people skills, but I suppose it really doesn't matter because no one ever looks at the statements they prepare," said the first student. The second student replied, "Oh, they are very intelligent, though, because they must know all about the tax laws, and that's too complicated for me."

Comment on the students' perceptions of the roles of accountants in society. Do you agree that no one ever looks at the statements they prepare? If not, identify who the primary users are.

(LO 3, 5) EXERCISE 1-11 CASH FLOWS

The operating activities of Glendale Corporation generated $50,000 of cash during the year. Net income for the year was $75,000, and $45,000 was paid in dividends. Glendale spent $35,000 to acquire a piece of real estate. The company borrowed $25,000 from the bank during the year. Glendale had cash at the end of the year of $220,000.

Was enough cash generated from operating activities to pay for Glendale's acquisitions and its dividends? Where did the rest of the money come from? Compute the amount of cash at the beginning of the year.

PROBLEMS

(LO 5) PROBLEM 1-1 BALANCE SHEET

The following items are available from records of Illinois Corporation at the end of the 1995 calendar year:

Accounts payable	$12,550
Accounts receivable	23,920
Advertising expense	2,100
Buildings	85,000
Capital stock	25,000
Cash	4,220
Office equipment	12,000
Notes payable	50,000
Retained earnings, end of year	37,590
Salary and wage expense	8,230
Sales revenue	14,220

■ REQUIRED

Prepare a balance sheet. *Hint:* Not all of the items listed should appear on a balance sheet. For each of these items, indicate where they should appear.

(LO 5) PROBLEM 1-2 INCOME STATEMENT, STATEMENT OF RETAINED EARNINGS, AND BALANCE SHEET

Shown below, in alphabetical order, is a list of the various items that regularly appear on the financial statements of Maple Park Theatres Corp. The amounts shown for balance sheet items are balances as of September 30, 1995 (with the exception of retained earnings, which is the balance on September 1, 1995), and the amounts shown for income statement items are balances for the month ended September 30, 1995:

Accounts payable	$17,600
Accounts receivable	6,410
Advertising expense	14,500
Buildings	60,000
Capital stock	50,000
Cash	15,230
Concessions revenue	60,300
Cost of concessions sold	23,450
Dividends paid during the month	8,400
Furniture and fixtures	34,000
Land	26,000
Notes payable	20,000
Projection equipment	25,000
Rent expense—movies	50,600
Retained earnings	73,780
Salaries and wages expense	46,490
Ticket sales	95,100
Water, gas, and electricity	6,700

■ REQUIRED

1. Prepare an income statement for the month ended September 30, 1995.
2. Prepare a statement of retained earnings for the month ended September 30, 1995.
3. Prepare a balance sheet at September 30, 1995.
4. You have $1,000 to invest. On the basis of the statements you prepared, would you use it to buy stock in Maple Park? What other information would you want before making a final decision?

(LO 5) PROBLEM 1-3 INCOME STATEMENT AND BALANCE SHEET

Green Bay Corporation began business in July 1995 as a commercial fishing operation and passenger service between islands. Shares of stock were issued to the owners in exchange for cash. Boats were purchased by making a down payment in cash and signing a note payable for the balance. Fish are sold to local restaurants on open account, and customers are given 15 days to pay their account. Cash fares are collected for all passenger traffic. Rent for the dock facilities is paid at the beginning of each month. Salaries and wages are paid at the end of the month. The following amounts are from the records of Green Bay Corporation at the end of its first month of operations:

Accounts receivable	$18,500
Boats	80,000
Capital stock	40,000
Cash	7,730
Dividends	5,400
Fishing revenue	21,300
Notes payable	60,000
Passenger service revenue	12,560
Rent expense	4,000
Retained earnings	???
Salary and wage expense	18,230

■ REQUIRED

1. Prepare an income statement for the month of July.
2. Prepare a balance sheet at July 31, 1995.
3. What information would you need about the Notes Payable to fully assess Green Bay's long-term viability? Explain your answer.

(LO 5) PROBLEM 1-4 CORRECTED FINANCIAL STATEMENTS

Nowrinkles, Inc., operates a small dry cleaning business. The company has always maintained a complete and accurate set of records. Unfortunately, the company's accountant left in a dispute with the president and took the records with him. The balance sheet and the income statement shown below were prepared by the president at the end of the first year after the departure of the accountant.

NOWRINKLES, INC.
INCOME STATEMENT
FOR THE YEAR ENDED DECEMBER 31, 1995

Revenues:		
Accounts receivable	$15,200	
Cleaning revenue—cash sales	32,500	$47,700
Expenses:		
Dividends	$ 4,000	
Accounts payable	4,500	
Utilities	12,200	
Salaries and wages	17,100	37,800
Net income		$ 9,900

NOWRINKLES, INC.
BALANCE SHEET
DECEMBER 31, 1995

ASSETS		LIABILITIES AND OWNERS' EQUITY	
Cash	$ 7,400	Cleaning revenue—	
Building and equipment	80,000	credit sales	$26,200
Less: Notes payable	(50,000)	Capital stock	20,000
Land	40,000	Net income	9,900
		Retained earnings	21,300
		Total liabilities and	
Total assets	$77,400	owners' equity	$77,400

The president is very disappointed with the net income for the year because it has averaged $25,000 over the last 10 years. She has asked for your help in determining whether the reported net income accurately reflects the profitability of the company and whether the balance sheet is prepared correctly. You are able to determine that all amounts reported on the two statements are correct (this does *not* mean that they are classified properly) with the exception of Retained Earnings. The president simply "plugged" this amount in order to make the balance sheet balance.

1. Prepare a corrected income statement for the year.

2. Prepare a statement of retained earnings for the year. Assume that you are able to determine that the correct balance in Retained Earnings on January 1, 1995, is $42,700.

3. Prepare a corrected balance sheet at December 31, 1995.

4. Draft a memo to the president explaining the major differences between the income statement she prepared and the one you prepared.

■ REQUIRED

(LO 1) PROBLEM 1-5 YOU WON THE LOTTERY

You have won a lottery! You will receive $200,000, after taxes, each year for the next five years.

Describe the process you will go through in determining how to invest your winnings. Consider at least two options and make a choice. You may consider the stock of a certain company, bonds, real estate investments, bank deposits, and so on. Be specific. Identify how much risk you are willing to take, and why. What information did you need to make a final decision? How was your decision affected by the fact that you will receive the winnings over a five-year period rather than in one lump sum? Would you prefer one payment? Explain.

■ REQUIRED

(LO 4) PROBLEM 1-6 USERS OF ACCOUNTING INFORMATION AND THEIR NEEDS

Courtland Company would like to buy a building and equipment to produce a new product line. Some information about Courtland is more useful to some people involved in the project than to others.

Complete the following chart by identifying the information listed on the right with the user's need to know the information. Identify the information as

■ REQUIRED

a. *Need* to know.

b. *Helpful* to know.

c. *Not necessary* to know.

INFORMATION

1. Amount of current debt, repayment schedule, and interest rate
2. Fair market value of the building
3. Condition of the roof and heating and cooling, electrical, and plumbing systems
4. Total cost of the building, improvements, and equipment to set up production
5. Expected sales from the new product, variable production costs, related selling costs

(LO 2) PROBLEM 1-7 EFFECT OF FORMS OF ORGANIZATION ON ACCOUNTING FOR THE ENTITY

Entities can be organized as proprietorships, partnerships, or corporations. The following is a list of entities:

a. A snow cone stand, open for the summer only, in a leased space, owned and operated by a college student.

b. A chain of snow cone stands that owns the portable kiosks, located across the state, owned and operated by two brothers.

c. An accounting firm organized by two accountants, one experienced, the other a new college graduate, and two bookkeepers, that operates in leased space.

d. A real estate office with one broker and five agents, operating in a small converted gas station owned by the broker.

e. A bridge and road construction company started by 10 investors and operated by a hired manager.

■ REQUIRED   For each of the entities, recommend the type of organization you believe suits it best. Write a sentence or two explaining your reason for the choice. The reason is just as important as the choice.

(LO 7) PROBLEM 1-8 SETTING NEW STANDARDS

As the financial environment changes, so do accounting standards. In recent years, many companies have been "right sizing," which usually means that they close offices and lay off employees. The companies incur severance pay, retraining costs, and gains and losses on the sale of investments. Currently, these items are expensed in the year in which the changes occur.

■ REQUIRED   Write clear, concise answers to the following questions:

1. If the company will benefit from these changes in future years, do you think that the cost of "right sizing" should be matched with future years when the benefit will be realized?

2. What could you do to have an accounting practice changed? Which organizations would you write? Choose a position either for or against changing the way "right sizing" costs are handled and write a letter to the organization that you believe would be most effective in acting on your recommendation.

MULTI-CONCEPT PROBLEMS

(LO 2, 8) PROBLEM 1-9 ROLE OF THE ACCOUNTANT IN VARIOUS ORGANIZATIONS

The following positions in various entities require a knowledge of accounting practices:

a. Chief financial officer for the subsidiary of a large company

b. Tax adviser to a consolidated group of entities

c. Independent computer consultant

d. Financial planner in a bank

e. Real estate broker in an independent office

f. Production planner in a manufacturing facility

g. Quality control adviser

h. Superintendent of a school district

i. Manager of one store in a retail clothing chain

j. Salesperson for a company that offers subcontract services to hospitals, such as food service and maintenance

For each position listed above, identify the entity in which it occurs as business or nonbusiness, and describe the kind of accounting knowledge (such as financial, managerial, taxes, not for profit) required by each position.   ■ REQUIRED

(LO 5, 6) PROBLEM 1-10 PRIMARY ASSUMPTIONS MADE IN PREPARING FINANCIAL STATEMENTS

Joe Hale opened a machine repair business in leased retail space, paying the first month's rent of $300 and a $1,000 deposit with a check on his personal account. He took the tools and equipment, worth about $7,500, from his garage to the shop. He also bought some more equipment to get started. The new equipment had a list price of $5,000, but Joe was able to purchase it on sale at Sears for only $4,200. He charged the new equipment on his personal Sears charge card. Joe's first customer paid $400 for services rendered, so Joe opened a checking account for the company. He completed a second job, but the customer has not paid Joe the $2,500 for his work. At the end of the first month, Joe prepared the following balance sheet and income statement.

JOE'S MACHINE REPAIR SHOP
BALANCE SHEET
JULY 31, 1995

Cash	$ 400		
Tools	5,000	Equity	$5,400
Total	$5,400	Total	$5,400

JOE'S MACHINE REPAIR SHOP
INCOME STATEMENT
FOR MONTH ENDED JULY 31, 1995

Sales		$2,900
Rent	$ 300	
Tools	4,200	4,500
Loss		($1,600)

Joe believes that he should show a greater profit next month because he won't have large expenses for items such as tools.

Identify the assumptions that Joe has violated and explain how each event should   ■ REQUIRED
have been handled. Prepare a corrected balance sheet and income statement.

ALTERNATE PROBLEMS

(LO 5) PROBLEM 1-1A BALANCE SHEET

The following items are available from the records of Wisconsin Corporation at the end of its fiscal year ended July 31, 1995:

Accounts payable	$16,900
Accounts receivable	5,700
Butter and cheese inventory	12,100
Buildings	35,000
Capital stock	25,000
Cash	21,800
Computerized mixers	25,800
Delivery expense	4,600
Office equipment	12,000
Notes payable	50,000
Retained earnings, end of year	26,300
Salary and wage expense	8,230
Sales revenue	14,220
Tools	5,800

■ REQUIRED

Prepare a balance sheet. *Hint:* Not all of the items listed should appear on a balance sheet. For each of these items, indicate where they should appear.

(LO 5) PROBLEM 1-2A INCOME STATEMENT, STATEMENT OF RETAINED EARNINGS, AND BALANCE SHEET

Shown below, in alphabetical order, is a list of the various items that regularly appear on the financial statements of Sterns Audio Book Rental Corp. The amounts shown for balance sheet items are balances as of December 31, 1995 (with the exception of retained earnings, which is the balance on January 1, 1995), and the amounts shown for income statement items are balances for the year ended December 31, 1995:

Accounts payable	$ 4,500
Accounts receivable	300
Advertising expense	14,500
Audio tape inventory	70,000
Capital stock	50,000
Cash	2,490
Display fixtures	45,000
Dividends paid during the year	12,000
Notes payable	10,000
Rental revenue	125,900
Rent paid on building	60,000
Retained earnings	35,390
Salaries and wages expense	17,900
Water, gas, and electricity	3,600

■ REQUIRED

1. Prepare an income statement for the year ended December 31, 1995.
2. Prepare a statement of retained earnings for the year ended December 31, 1995.

3. Prepare a balance sheet at December 31, 1995.

4. You have $1,000 to invest. On the basis of the statements you prepared, would you use it to buy stock in this company? What other information would you want before making a final decision?

(LO 5) PROBLEM 1-3A INCOME STATEMENT AND BALANCE SHEET

Fort Worth Corporation began business in January 1995 as a commercial carpet cleaning and drying service. Shares of stock were issued to the owners in exchange for cash. Equipment was purchased by making a down payment in cash and signing a note payable for the balance. Services are performed for local restaurants and office buildings on open account, and customers are given 15 days to pay their account. Rent for office and storage facilities is paid at the beginning of each month. Salaries and wages are paid at the end of the month. The following amounts are from the records of Fort Worth Corporation at the end of its first month of operations:

Accounts receivable	$24,750
Equipment	62,000
Capital stock	80,000
Cash	51,650
Dividends	5,500
Cleaning revenue	45,900
Notes payable	30,000
Rent expense	3,600
Retained earnings	???
Salary and wage expense	8,400

1. Prepare an income statement for the month of January.

REQUIRED

2. Prepare a balance sheet at January 31, 1995.

3. What information would you need about the Notes Payable to fully assess Fort Worth's long-term viability? Explain your answer.

(LO 5) PROBLEM 1-4A CORRECTED FINANCIAL STATEMENTS

SmoothasSilk, Inc., operates a small pastry business. The company has always maintained a complete and accurate set of records. Unfortunately, the company's accountant left in a dispute with the president and took the records with her. The balance sheet and the income statement shown below were prepared by the president at the end of the first year after the departure of the accountant.

SMOOTHASSILK, INC.
INCOME STATEMENT
FOR THE YEAR ENDED DECEMBER 31, 1995

Revenues:		
Accounts receivable	$15,500	
Pastry revenue—cash sales	23,700	$39,200
Expenses:		
Dividends	$ 5,600	
Accounts payable	6,800	
Utilities	9,500	
Salaries and wages	18,200	40,100
Net loss		$ (900)

SMOOTHASSILK, INC.
BALANCE SHEET
DECEMBER 31, 1995

ASSETS		LIABILITIES AND OWNERS' EQUITY	
Cash	$ 3,700	Pastry revenue—	
Building and equipment	60,000	Credit sales	$22,100
Less: Notes payable	(40,000)	Capital stock	30,000
Land	50,000	Net loss	(900)
		Retained earnings	22,500
		Total liabilities and	
Total assets	$73,700	owners' equity	$73,700

The president is very disappointed with the net loss for the year because net income has averaged $21,000 over the last 10 years. He has asked for your help in determining whether the reported net loss accurately reflects the profitability of the company and whether the balance sheet is prepared correctly. You are able to determine that all amounts reported on the two statements are correct (this does not mean that they are classified properly) with the exception of Retained Earnings. The president simply "plugged" this amount in order to make the balance sheet balance.

■ REQUIRED

1. Prepare a corrected income statement for the year.

2. Prepare a statement of retained earnings for the year. Assume that you are able to determine that the correct balance in Retained Earnings on January 1, 1995, is $39,900.

3. Prepare a corrected balance sheet at December 31, 1995.

4. Draft a memo to the president explaining the major differences between the income statement he prepared and the one you prepared.

(LO 1) PROBLEM 1-5A WHAT TO DO WITH A MILLION DOLLARS

You have inherited $1 million!

■ REQUIRED

Describe the process you will go through in determining how to invest your inheritance. Consider at least two options and choose one. You may consider the stock of a certain company, bonds, real estate investments, bank deposits, and so on. Be specific. Identify how much risk you are willing to take and why. What information did you need to make a final decision? Where did you find the information you needed? What additional information will you need to determine if you want to make a change in your investment?

(LO 4) PROBLEM 1-6A USERS OF ACCOUNTING INFORMATION AND THEIR NEEDS

Palmer, Inc., would like to buy a franchise to provide a specialized service. Some information about Palmer is more useful to some people involved in the project than to others.

■ REQUIRED

Complete the following chart by identifying the information listed on the left with the user's need to know the information. Identify the information as

a. *Need* to know

b. *Helpful* to know

c. *Not necessary* to know

1. Expected revenue from the new service
2. Cost of the franchise fee and recurring fees to be paid to the franchisor
3. Cash available to Palmer, the franchisee, to operate the business after the franchise is purchased
4. Expected overhead costs of the service outlet
5. Palmer's required return on its investment

(LO 2) PROBLEM 1-7A EFFECT OF FORMS OF ORGANIZATION ON ACCOUNTING FOR THE ENTITY

Entities can be organized as proprietorships, partnerships, or corporations. The following is a list of entities:

a. A snow cone stand, open for the summer only, in a leased space, owned and operated by a college student.

b. A chain of snow cone stands that owns the portable kiosks, located across the state, owned and operated by two brothers.

c. An accounting firm organized by two accountants, one experienced, the other a new college graduate, and two bookkeepers, in leased space.

d. A real estate office with one broker and five agents, operating in a small converted gas station owned by the broker.

e. A bridge and road construction company started by 10 investors and operated by a hired manager.

For each of the entities, recommend the type of organization you believe suits it best. Each company will have financial statement items that are unique to its business. List at least 5 items, other than cash, that might be found on their individual statements.

■ REQUIRED

(LO 7) PROBLEM 1-8A SETTING NEW STANDARDS

As the financial environment changes, so do accounting standards. In recent years, many companies have been expanding their operations into underdeveloped countries. Many of these countries have unstable economies and governments. As a user of financial statements, you are concerned that the assets invested in these countries are commingled with other company assets.

Write clear, concise answers to the following questions:

■ REQUIRED

1. Why would this accounting practice cause concern?
2. To which accounting assumption would you refer if you wanted the profession to consider a change in the way these assets are reported? Which organizations would you write? Write a letter to the organization that you believe would be most effective in acting on your recommendation to report assets invested in underdeveloped countries in a different manner.

ALTERNATE MULTI-CONCEPT PROBLEMS

(LO 2, 8) PROBLEM 1-9A ROLE OF ACCOUNTANT IN VARIOUS ORGANIZATIONS

The following positions in various entities require a knowledge of accounting practices.

a. Chief financial officer for the subsidiary of a large company
b. Tax adviser to a consolidated group of entities
c. Accounts receivable computer analyst

d. Financial planner in a bank

e. Budget analyst in a real estate office

f. Production planner in a manufacturing facility

g. Quality control adviser

h. Manager of the team conducting an audit on a state lottery

i. Assistant superintendent of a school district

j. Manager of one store in a retail clothing chain

k. Controller in a company that offers subcontract services to hospitals, such as food service and maintenance

l. Staff accountant in a large audit firm

■ **REQUIRED** For each position listed above, classify the position as one of the general categories of accountants listed below.

1. Financial accountant

2. Managerial accountant

3. Tax accountant

4. Accountant for not-for-profit organization

5. Auditor

6. Not an accounting position

(LO 5, 6) PROBLEM 1-10A PRIMARY ASSUMPTIONS MADE IN PREPARING FINANCIAL STATEMENTS

Millie Abrams opened a ceramic studio in leased retail space, paying the first month's rent of $300 and a $1,000 deposit with a check on her personal account. She took molds and paint, worth about $7,500, from her home to the studio. She also bought a new firing kiln to start the business. The new kiln had a list price of $5,000, but Millie was able to trade in her old kiln, worth $500 at the time of trade, on the new kiln, and therefore she paid only $4,500 cash. She wrote a check on her personal checking account. Millie's first customers paid a total of $1,400 to attend classes for the next two months. She opened a checking account in the company's name with the $1,400. She has conducted classes for one month and has sold for $3,000 unfinished ceramic pieces called *greenware*. Greenware sales are all cash. Millie incurred $1,000 of personal cost in making the greenware. At the end of the first month, Millie prepared the following balance sheet and income statement.

MILLIE'S CERAMIC STUDIO
BALANCE SHEET
JULY 31, 1995

Cash	$1,400		
Kiln	5,000	Equity	$6,400
Total	$6,400	Total	$6,400

MILLIE'S CERAMIC STUDIO
INCOME STATEMENT
FOR THE MONTH ENDED JULY 31, 1995

Sales		$4,400
Rent	$300	
Supplies	600	900
Income		$3,500

Millie needs to earn at least $3,000 each month for the business to be worth her time. She is pleased with the results.

Identify the assumptions that Millie has violated and explain how each event should have been handled. Prepare a corrected balance sheet and income statement.

■ REQUIRED

CASES

READING AND INTERPRETING FINANCIAL STATEMENTS

(LO 5) CASE 1-1 READING AND INTERPRETING BEN & JERRY'S FINANCIAL STATEMENTS

Refer to the financial statements for Ben & Jerry's reproduced in the chapter and answer the following questions:

1. What was the company's net income for 1992?

2. What was the company's net cash provided by operating activities for 1992?

3. What are some of the reasons that the amounts in (1) and (2) above are different?

4. State Ben & Jerry's financial position on December 26, 1992, in terms of the accounting equation.

5. Explain the reason for the change in retained earnings from a balance of $13,309,121 on December 28, 1991, to a balance of $19,984,461 on December 26, 1992. Also, what amount of dividends did the company pay in 1992?

(LO 4) CASE 1-2 AN ANNUAL REPORT AS READY REFERENCE

Refer to the Ben & Jerry's annual report, and identify where each of the following users of accounting information would first look to answer their respective questions about Ben & Jerry's.

1. Investors: How much did the company earn for each share of stock I own? How much of that earnings did I receive and how much was reinvested in the company?

2. Potential Investors: What amount of earnings can I expect to see from Ben & Jerry's in the near future?

3. Bankers and creditors: Should I extend the short-term borrowing limit to Ben & Jerry's? Do they have sufficient cash or cash-like assets to repay short-term loans?

4. Internal Revenue Service: How much does Ben & Jerry's owe for taxes?

5. Employees: How much money did the president and vice presidents earn? Should I ask for a raise?

MAKING FINANCIAL DECISIONS

(LO 1, 5) CASE 1-3 PREPARATION OF PROJECTED STATEMENTS FOR A NEW BUSINESS

Upon graduation from MegaState University, you and your roommate decide to start your respective careers in accounting and salmon fishing in Remote, Alaska. Your career as a CPA in Remote is going well, as is your roommate's job as a commercial fisher. After one year in Remote, he approaches you with a business opportunity.

As we are well aware, the video rental business has yet to reach Remote, and the nearest rental facility is 250 miles away. We each put up our first year's savings of $5,000 and file for articles of incorporation with the State of Alaska to do business as Remote Video World. In return for our investment of $5,000, we will each receive equal shares of capital stock in the corporation. Then we go to the Corner National Bank and apply for a $10,000 loan. We take the total cash of $20,000 we have now raised and buy 2,000 videos at $10 each from a mail-order supplier. We rent the movies for $3 per title and sell monthly memberships for $25, allowing a member to check out an unlimited number of movies during the month. Individual rentals would be a cash-and-carry business, but we would give customers until the 10th of the following month to pay for a monthly membership. My most conservative estimate is that during the first month alone, we will rent 800 movies and sell 200 memberships. As far as I see it, we will have only two expenses. First, we will hire two high school students to run the store for 30 hours each per week and pay them $5 per hour. Second, the landlord of a vacant store in town will rent us space in the building for $1,000 per month.

■ REQUIRED

1. Prepare a projected income statement for the first month of operations.

2. Prepare a balance sheet as it would appear at the end of the first month of operations.

3. Assume that the bank is willing to make the $10,000 loan. Would you be willing to join your roommate in this business? Explain your response. Also, indicate any information other than that he has provided that you would like to have before making a final decision.

(LO I) CASE I-4 AN INVESTMENT OPPORTUNITY

You have saved enough money to pay for your college tuition for the next three years when a high school friend comes to you with a deal. He is an artist who has spent most of the past two years drawing on the walls of old buildings. The buildings are about to be demolished and your friend thinks you should buy the walls before the buildings are demolished and open a gallery featuring his work. Of course, you are level headed and would say "No!" Recently, however, your friend has been featured on several local radio and television shows and is talking to some national networks about doing a feature on a well-known news show. To set up the gallery would take all of your savings, but your friend feels that you will be able to sell his artwork for 10 times the cost of your investment. Describe the relationship between risk and potential return as it relates to these two investments—college education and the art gallery. What kind of profit split would you suggest to your friend if you decide to open the gallery?

ACCOUNTING AND ETHICS: WHAT WOULD YOU DO?

(LO I, 4, 5) CASE I-5 IDENTIFICATION OF ERRORS IN FINANCIAL STATEMENTS AND PREPARATION OF REVISED STATEMENTS

Bay City Bombers, Inc., is a minor league baseball organization that has just completed its first season. You and three other investors organized the corporation; each put up $10,000 in cash for shares of capital stock. Because you live out of state, you have not been actively involved in the daily affairs of the club. However, you are thrilled to receive a dividend check for $10,000 at the end of the season—an amount equal to your original investment! Included with the check are the following financial statements, along with supporting explanations:

BAY CITY BOMBERS, INC.
INCOME STATEMENT
FOR THE YEAR ENDED DECEMBER 31, 1995

Revenues:

Single game ticket revenue	$420,000	
Season ticket revenue	140,000	
Concessions revenue	280,000	
Advertising revenue	100,000	$940,000

Expenses:

Cost of concessions sold	$110,000	
Salary expense—players	225,000	
Salary and wage expense—staff	150,000	
Rent expense	210,000	695,000
Net Income		$245,000

BAY CITY BOMBERS, INC.
STATEMENT OF RETAINED EARNINGS
FOR THE YEAR ENDED DECEMBER 31, 1995

Beginning balance, January 1, 1995	$ –0–
Add: Net income for 1995	245,000
Deduct: Cash dividends paid in 1995	(40,000)
Ending balance, December 31, 1995	$205,000

BAY CITY BOMBERS, INC.
BALANCE SHEET
AT DECEMBER 31, 1995

ASSETS		LIABILITIES AND OWNERS' EQUITY	
Cash	$ 5,000	Notes payable	$ 50,000
Accounts receivable		Capital stock	40,000
Season tickets	140,000	Additional owners' capital	80,000
Advertisers	100,000	Parent club's equity	125,000
Auxiliary assets	80,000	Retained earnings	205,000
Equipment	50,000		
Player contracts	125,000	Total liabilities and	
Total assets	$500,000	owners' equity	$500,000

Additional information:

1. Single game tickets sold for $4 per game. The team averaged 1,500 fans per game. With 70 home games × $4 per game × 1,500 fans, single game ticket revenue amounted to $420,000.

2. No season tickets were sold during the first season. During the last three months of 1995, however, an aggressive sales campaign resulted in the sale of 500 season tickets for the 1996 season. Therefore, the controller (who is also one of the owners) chose to record an Account Receivable—Season Tickets and corresponding revenue for 500 tickets × $4 per game × 70 games or $140,000.

3. Advertising revenue of $100,000 resulted from the sale of the 40 signs on the outfield wall at $2,500 each for the season. However, none of the advertisers have paid their bill yet (thus, an account receivable of $100,000 on the balance sheet) because the contract with Bay City required them to pay only if the team

averaged 2,000 fans per game during the 1995 season. The controller believes that the advertisers will be sympathetic to the difficulties of starting a new franchise and be willing to overlook the slight deficiency in the attendance requirement.

4. Bay City has a working agreement with one of the major league franchises. The minor league team is required to pay $5,000 *every* year to the major league team for each of the 25 players on its roster. The controller believes that each of the players is certainly an asset to the organization and has therefore recorded $5,000 × 25, or $125,000, as an asset called Player Contracts. The item on the right side of the balance sheet entitled Parent Club's Equity is the amount owed to the major league team by February 1, 1996, as payment for the players for the 1995 season.

5. In addition to the cost described in part 4, Bay City directly pays each of its 25 players a $9,000 salary for the season. This amount—$225,000—has already been paid for the 1995 season and is reported on the income statement.

6. The items on the balance sheet entitled Auxiliary Assets on the left side and Additional Owners' Capital on the right side represent the value of the controller's personal residence. She has a mortgage with the bank for the full value of the house.

7. The $50,000 note payable resulted from a loan that was taken out at the beginning of the year to finance the purchase of bats, balls, uniforms, lawn mowers, and other miscellaneous supplies needed to operate the team (equipment is reported as an asset for the same amount). The loan, with interest, is due on January 15, 1996. Even though the team had a very successful first year, Bay City is a little short of cash at the end of 1995 and has therefore asked the bank for a three-month extension of the loan. The controller reasons that "by the due date of April 15, 1996, the cash due from the new season ticket holders will be available, things will be cleared up with the advertisers, and the loan can be easily repaid."

■ **REQUIRED**

1. Identify any errors that you think the controller has made in preparing the financial statements.

2. On the basis of your answer in part 1, prepare a revised income statement, statement of retained earnings, and balance sheet.

3. On the basis of your revised financial statements, identify any ethical dilemma you now face. Do you have a responsibility to share these revisions with the other three owners? What is your responsibility to the bank?

(LO 1, 4) CASE 1-6 REPORTING THE COMPANY PRESIDENT'S DECISIONS

As the controller, you are responsible for the preparation of financial statements and the annual report. Some areas of reporting are not as straightforward as others. For example, a customer has filed a lawsuit against the company for $1 million. The president considers the suit to be frivolous, but the corporate attorneys have been spending a great deal of time preparing their case for the preliminary hearing.

Another situation involves a customer who has a substantial balance on his account with the company. You have heard, through the grapevine, that the customer is planning to file for bankruptcy protection after the first of the year. The president is a personal friend of the customer and has assured you that "we'll get our money eventually." The account is currently on the books as an asset, accounts receivable.

Finally, the president has mentioned to you that he would like the board to vote for an unusually large dividend after the first of the year, because his daughter is getting married in the spring. The President owns 25% of the company stock and could be persuasive enough to swing the vote.

How would you report each of these items on the financial statements? What information is relevant to investors?

ANALYTICAL SOFTWARE CASE

To the Student: Your instructor may assign one or more parts of the analytical software case that is designed to accompany this chapter. This multi-part case gives you a chance to work with real financial statement data using software that stimulates, guides, and hones your analytical and problem-solving skills. It was created especially to support and strengthen your understanding of the chapter's Learning Objectives.

SOLUTIONS TO KEY TERMS QUIZ

Quiz 1

1. Asset (p. 9)
2. Income statement (p. 13)
3. Statement of retained earnings (p. 16)
4. Stockholders' equity (p. 13)
5. Accounting (p. 10)
6. Partnership (p. 6)
7. Financial accounting (p. 11)
8. Owners' equity (p. 13)
9. Statement of cash flows (p. 17)
10. Balance sheet (p. 13)
11. Revenue (p. 9)
12. Corporation (p. 6)
13. Nonbusiness entity (p. 7)
14. Retained earnings (p. 13)
15. Expense (p. 10)
16. Liability (p. 8)
17. Management accounting (p. 11)
18. Share of stock (p. 6)
19. Bond (p. 7)
20. Stockholder (p. 8)
21. Creditor (p. 8)
22. Economic entity concept (p. 5)
23. Sole proprietorship (p. 5)
24. Capital stock (p. 8)
25. Dividends (p. 15)

Quiz 2

1. Generally accepted accounting principles (p. 22)
2. Cost principle (p. 20)
3. Securities and Exchange Commission (p. 23)
4. Certified public accountant (p. 23)
5. American Accounting Association (p. 26)
6. Treasurer (p. 24)
7. Going concern (p. 21)
8. Financial Accounting Standards Board (p. 23)
9. Monetary unit (p. 21)
10. American Institute of Certified Public Accountants (p. 23)
11. Internal auditing (p. 24)
12. Time period (p. 22)
13. Controller (p. 24)
14. Auditing (p. 25)

Focus on Financial Results

For thousands of companies, the annual report is nothing more than a dry chairman's letter followed by the numbers. But another group views the annual report as a showcase. For this group, it also becomes the company's premier marketing document—to be handed out to suppliers, customers, and employees as well as to stockholders and investment brokers.

Nike, Inc., is one such company. Of course, its flashy report would have little impact if the company's numbers weren't so impressive: sales have quadrupled from $1 billion to $4 billion between 1988 and 1993. Earnings have more than tripled from $102 million to $365 million in the same time period.

But in addition to stellar numbers, Nike uses action photographs of its growing list of athletic endorsers such as Gail Devers (shown here) and Charles Barkley. The chairman's letter is written in five languages—English, French, German, Spanish, and Japanese—to convey the company's growing international business. And, unlike so many annual reports, Nike's is written in a tone consistent with its public persona. Here's a quote from the chairman's letter: "So let's sum up the year of this report thusly: Fiscal '93: Great job. End of discussion."

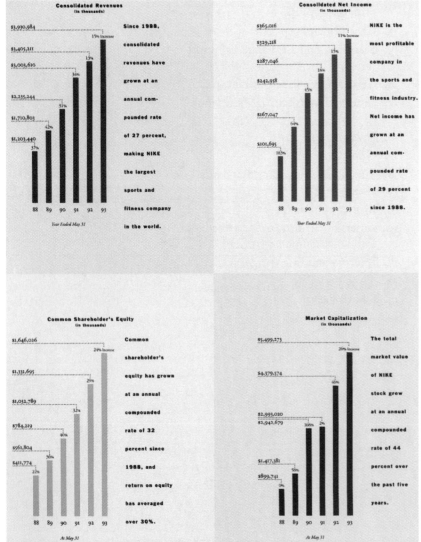

Consolidated Revenues
(in thousands)

$3,930,984 — 15% increase
$3,405,211 — 13%
$3,003,610 — 34%
$2,235,244 — 31%
$1,710,803 — 42%
$1,203,440 — 37%

88 89 90 91 92 93
Year Ended May 31

Since 1988, consolidated revenues have grown at an annual compounded rate of 27 percent, making NIKE the largest sports and fitness company in the world.

Consolidated Net Income
(in thousands)

$365,016 — 11% increase
$329,218 — 15%
$287,046 — 18%
$242,958 — 45%
$167,047 — 64%
$101,695 — 183%

88 89 90 91 92 93
Year Ended May 31

NIKE is the most profitable company in the sports and fitness industry. Net income has grown at an annual compounded rate of 29 percent since 1988.

Common Shareholder's Equity
(in thousands)

$1,646,026 — 24% increase
$1,331,695 — 29%
$1,032,789 — 32%
$784,219 — 40%
$561,804 — 36%
$411,774 — 22%

88 89 90 91 92 93
At May 31

Common shareholder's equity has grown at an annual compounded rate of 32 percent since 1988, and return on equity has averaged over 30%.

Market Capitalization
(in thousands)

$5,499,273 — 26% increase
$4,379,574 — 46%
$2,993,020 — 2%
$2,942,679 — 108%
$1,417,381 — 58%
$899,741 — 0%

88 89 90 91 92 93
At May 31

The total market value of NIKE stock grew at an annual compounded rate of 44 percent over the past five years.

Chapter 2

Financial Statements and the Annual Report

LEARNING OBJECTIVES

After studying this chapter, you should be able to

1. Describe the objectives of financial reporting.
2. Describe the qualitative characteristics of accounting information.
3. Explain the concept and purpose of a classified balance sheet and prepare the statement.
4. Use a classified balance sheet to analyze a company's financial position.
5. Explain the difference between a single-step and a multiple-step income statement and prepare each type of income statement.
6. Use a multiple-step income statement to analyze a company's operations.
7. Identify the components of the statement of retained earnings and the statement of stockholders' equity and prepare each statement.
8. Identify the components of the statement of cash flows and prepare the statement.
9. Describe the various elements in the annual report of a publicly held company.

Linkages

A LOOK AT THE PREVIOUS CHAPTER

Chapter 1 introduced the role of accounting in our society. We explored how investors, creditors, and others use accounting and the outputs of an accounting system, financial statements, in reaching informed decisions.

A LOOK AT THIS CHAPTER

In this chapter, we take a closer look at the financial statements, as well as the other elements that make up an annual report. In the first part of the chapter, we explore the underlying *conceptual framework of accounting*. Every discipline has a set of interrelated concepts, principles, and conventions that guide daily practice. In the second part of the chapter, we will see how the concepts introduced in the first part of the chapter are used in the development of financial statements.

A LOOK AT UPCOMING CHAPTERS

Chapter 2 focuses on the end result by examining the outputs of an accounting system, the financial statements. We will take a step back in Chapters 3 and 4 to consider how economic events are processed in an accounting system and are then summarized in the financial statements.

Objectives of Financial Reporting

LO   I

Describe the objectives of financial reporting.

Financial reporting has one overall objective and a set of related objectives that follow from it. We will first examine the primary objective and then turn our attention to the related ones.

The Primary Objective: Provide Information for Decision Making

The primary objective of financial reporting is to *provide economic information to permit users of the information to make informed decisions.* Users include both the management of a company (internal users) and others not involved in the daily operations of the business (external users). Without access to the detailed records of the business and without the benefit of daily involvement in the affairs of the company, external users rely on *general-purpose financial statements* prepared by management to make their decisions. According to the Financial Accounting Standards Board (FASB)

> Financial reporting should provide information that is useful to present and potential investors and creditors and other users in making rational investment, credit, and similar decisions.[1]

We see from this statement how closely the objective of financial reporting is tied to decision making. The purpose of financial reporting is to help the users reach their decisions in an informed manner.

Reflect Prospective Cash Receipts to Investors and Creditors

Present stockholders must decide whether to hold their stock in a company or sell it. For potential stockholders, the decision is whether to buy the stock in the first place. Bankers, suppliers, and other types of creditors must decide whether to loan money to a company. All of these groups rely *partially* on the information provided in financial statements in making their decisions. Other sources of information are sometimes as important, or more important, in reaching a decision. For example, the most recent income statement may report the highest profits in the history of a company. However, a potential investor may choose not to buy stock in the company if *The Wall Street Journal* or *Business Week* were to report that a strike is likely to shut down operations for an indeterminable period of time.

If you buy stock in a company, your primary concern is the *future cash to be received from the investment.* First, how much, if any, will you periodically receive in *cash dividends?* Second, how much cash will you receive from the *sale of the stock?* The interests of a creditor, such as a banker, are similar. The banker is concerned with the receipt of the original amount of money loaned and interest on the loan. In summary, another objective of financial reporting is to

> provide information to help present and potential investors and creditors and other users in assessing the amounts, timing, and uncertainty of prospective cash receipts from dividends or interest and the proceeds from the sale, redemption, or maturity of securities or loans.[2]

---

[1] *Statement of Financial Accounting Concepts [SFAC], No. 1,* "Objectives of Financial Reporting by Business Enterprises" (Stamford, Conn.: Financial Accounting Standards Board, November 1978), par. 34.
[2] *SFAC No. 1,* par. 37.

Reflect Prospective Cash Flows to the Enterprise

Thus, the two ultimate concerns of the investor or creditor are the cash received from sale of the stock, or maturity of the loan, and cash received from dividends, or interest. Note that it is not the *company's* cash flows but the cash *you* receive from an investment that is your ultimate concern. It is generally acknowledged, however, that a relationship exists between the cash flows to the company and those to the investor:

> Thus, since an enterprise's ability to generate favorable cash flows affects both its ability to pay dividends and interest and the market prices of its securities, expected cash flows to investors and creditors are related to expected cash flows to the enterprise in which they have invested or to which they have loaned funds.[3]

Therefore, another objective of accounting is to provide information that will allow users to make decisions about the cash flows of a company. This does *not* mean, however, that a company should use a *cash basis* of accounting to attain this objective. Certainly, the cash flow statement provides useful information in making decisions about the cash flows of a company in the future. However, income statements and balance sheets prepared using the accrual basis of accounting are better indicators of the ability to generate favorable cash flows than statements limited to the effects of cash inflows and outflows.

Reflect Resources and Claims to Resources

The FASB has emphasized the roles of the balance sheet and income statement in providing useful information:

> Financial reporting should provide information about the economic resources of an enterprise, the claims to those resources (obligations of the enterprise to transfer resources to other entities and owner's equity), and the effects of transactions, events, and circumstances that change resources and claims to those resources.[4]

Exhibit 2-1 summarizes the objectives of financial reporting as they pertain to the decision of a potential investor. The exhibit should help you to understand how something as abstract as a set of financial reporting objectives can be applied to a decision-making situation.

What Makes Accounting Information Useful? Qualitative Characteristics

Quantitative considerations, such as tuition costs, certainly were a concern in choosing your current school. In addition, your decision required you to make subjective judgments about the *qualitative characteristics* you were looking for in a college. Similarly, there are certain qualities that make accounting information useful.

LO **2**

Describe the qualitative characteristics of accounting information.

Understandability

For anything to be useful, it must be understandable. Usefulness and understandability go hand in hand. However, **understandability** of financial information varies considerably, depending on the background of the user. For example, should financial

[3] *SFAC No. 1,* par. 39.
[4] *SFAC No. 1,* par. 40.

EXHIBIT 2-1   The Application of Financial Reporting Objectives

FINANCIAL REPORTING OBJECTIVE	POTENTIAL INVESTOR'S QUESTIONS
1. Provide information useful to present and potential investors, creditors, and other users in making investment, credit, and similar decisions.	"Should I buy a share of stock in the ABC Corporation?"
2. Provide information to help present and potential investors, creditors, and other users in assessing the amounts, timing, and uncertainty of prospective cash receipts from dividends or interest and the proceeds from the sale, redemption, or maturity of securities or loans.	"How much cash will I receive in dividends each year and from the sale of the stock of ABC Corporation in the future?"
3. Provide information to help investors, creditors, and others assess the amounts, timing, and uncertainty of prospective net cash inflows to the related enterprise.	"What will be the prospective net cash inflows of the ABC Corporation during the time I hold the stock as an investment?"
4. Provide information about the economic resources, the claims to those resources, and the effects of transactions that change resources and the claims to those resources.	"What can the balance sheet, income statement, and statement of cash flows of ABC Corporation tell me about my investment in the stock of the company?"

statements be prepared so that they are understandable by anyone with a college education? Or should it be assumed that all readers of financial statements have completed at least one accounting course? Is a background in business necessary for a good understanding of financial reports, regardless of one's formal training? As you might expect, there are no simple answers to these questions. However, the FASB believes that financial information should be comprehensible to *those who are willing to spend the time to understand it:*

> Financial information is a tool and, like most tools, cannot be of much direct help to those who are unable or unwilling to use it or who misuse it. Its use can be learned, however, and financial reporting should provide information that can be used by all—nonprofessionals as well as professionals—who are willing to learn to use it properly.[5]

Relevance

Understandability alone is certainly not enough to render information useful. To be useful, information must be *relevant.* **Relevance** is the capacity of information to make a difference in a decision.[6] For example, assume that in your role as a banker, Palmer Company has presented you with its most recent annual report as the basis for a loan. The comparative income statements show a very profitable company over the past several years, and the balance sheet indicates a sound financial position. According to a report you read in yesterday's newspaper, however, the company has been named as the defendant in a multimillion-dollar antitrust lawsuit filed by the federal government. Undoubtedly, this information will be relevant to your decision. Disclosure of the lawsuit in the financial statements will add to their relevancy.

[5] *SFAC No. 1,* par. 36.
[6] *Statement of Financial Accounting Concepts, No. 2,* "Qualitative Characteristics of Accounting Information" (Stamford, Conn.: Financial Accounting Standards Board, May 1980), par. 47.

Reliability

What makes accounting information *reliable?* According to the FASB,

> Accounting information is reliable to the extent that users can depend on it to represent the economic conditions or events that it purports to represent.[7]

Three individual characteristics are involved in the concept of **reliability:** verifiability, representational faithfulness, and neutrality. To illustrate these qualities, consider historical cost. It is often defended as a basis of measuring value because of its high degree of reliability.

Assume that a company buys a parcel of land for $100,000. The historical cost, or amount paid, for the land is *verifiable,* or free from error, because we can simply look at the contract to determine cost. Information is a *faithful representation* when it is valid, that is, when there is agreement between the underlying data and the events represented. Again, the use of historical cost is defended on the basis that it provides a valid representation of the transaction that resulted in the acquisition of the land. Finally, accounting information is *neutral* when it is not slanted to portray a company's position in a light any worse or any better than the *actual* circumstances would dictate. Whether or not the historical cost of the land is a neutral measurement of its value today is questionable. For example, what if the land has a market value of $500,000? Is neutrality violated if the accountant continues to report the asset on the balance sheet at only $100,000? Does this portray the company's position in a *worse* light than circumstances would dictate? There are no easy answers to these questions, and the issue of whether historical cost or current market value is a better measuring unit remains unsettled.

It is interesting to note that other countries have experimented with the use of current values in reporting property, plant, and equipment. Although there is a strict prohibition in the United States on the valuation of long-term assets in an amount in excess of cost, the practice is acceptable for certain types of assets in the United Kingdom, Australia, Canada, and South Africa.

Comparability and Consistency

Comparability is the quality of accounting information that allows comparisons to be made *between or among companies.* Generally accepted accounting principles (GAAP) allow a certain amount of freedom in choosing among competing alternative treatments for certain transactions.

One of the choices a company must make is the method of depreciation it uses. **Depreciation** is the process of *allocating* the cost of a long-term tangible asset such as a building or equipment over its useful life. One approach to allocating the cost of an asset over its useful life is the straight-line method. *Straight-line depreciation* assigns an equal amount of expense to each year in the useful life of the asset. An alternative is the use of an accelerated method. *Accelerated depreciation* results in the assignment of more depreciation to the earlier years in the useful life of the asset and less depreciation to the later years. GAAP allow a company to choose between the straight-line method and one of the accelerated methods. How does this freedom of choice in selecting a depreciation method affect the ability of an investor to make comparisons between companies?

Assume that at the end of 1992, an investor was considering buying stock in one of the Big Three auto manufacturers. According to the 1992 annual reports of these companies, Ford and General Motors used accelerated methods of depreciation while

[7] *SFAC No. 2,* par. 62.

Chrysler used the straight-line method. Does this lack of a common depreciation method make it impossible for the investor to compare the performance of the three auto makers?

Obviously, comparisons among Chrysler, Ford, and GM would be easier and more meaningful if all three used the same depreciation method. However, comparisons are not rendered impossible just because companies use different methods. The accounting profession continues to debate the relative merits of comparability and *uniformity*. Certainly, the more alike—that is, uniform—statements are in terms of the principles used to prepare them, the more comparable they will be. However, the profession has felt it necessary to allow a certain freedom of choice in selecting from among alternative generally accepted accounting principles.

To render statements of companies using different methods more meaningful, *disclosure* assumes a very important role. For example, we will see later in this chapter that the first footnote in the annual report of a publicly traded company is the disclosure of its accounting policies. The reader of this footnote for the Big Three is made aware that the companies do not use the same depreciation method. Disclosure of accounting policies allows the reader to make some sort of subjective adjustment to the statements of one or more of the companies to compensate for the different depreciation method being used.

Consistency is closely related to the concept of comparability. Both involve the relationship between two numbers. *However, comparability is the quality of information that allows for comparisons to be made between two or more companies whereas consistency is the quality that allows for comparisons to be made within a single company from one accounting period to the next.*

Consider again our depreciation example. We concluded that the use of different depreciation methods makes comparisons between the three companies difficult but not impossible. Interestingly, Ford Motor Co. disclosed in its 1992 annual report that for assets placed in service after January 1, 1993, the straight-line method would be used. Will it be possible to compare the company's earnings in 1993 with those for 1992? As was the case with comparability, changes in accounting methods from one period to the next do not make comparisons impossible, only more difficult. To help the reader evaluate the impact of the change, Ford provided the following estimate in the 1992 report:

> Although the effect on net income of this change will be based on the level of future capital spending, the change is expected to improve 1993 after-tax results by $80 to $100 million.[8]

Accounting changes are covered in more detail in Chapter 12.

Materiality

We have concluded that to be useful, accounting information must be relevant to a decision. The concept of **materiality** is closely related to relevance. Consider the following example. A company pays cash for two separate purchases: one for a $5 pencil sharpener and the other for a $50,000 computer. Theoretically, each expenditure results in the acquisition of an asset that should be depreciated over its useful life. However, what if the company decides to account for the $5 as an expense of the period rather than treat it in the theoretically correct manner? *Will this error affect in any way the judgment of someone relying on the financial statements?* Because such a slight error will not affect any decisions, minor expenditures of this nature are considered *immaterial* and are accounted for as an expense of the period.

[8] *Ford Motor Co. 1992 Annual Report,* p. 29.

The *threshold* for determining materiality will vary from one company to the next, depending to a large extent on the size of the company. Many companies establish policies that *any* expenditure under a certain dollar amount should be accounted for as an expense of the period. The threshold might be $50 for the corner grocery store but $1,000 for a large corporation.

Conservatism

The concept of **conservatism** is a holdover from earlier days when the primary financial statement was the balance sheet and the primary user of this statement was the banker. It was customary to deliberately understate assets in the balance sheet because this resulted in an even larger margin of safety that the assets provided as collateral for a loan were sufficient.

Today the balance sheet is not the only financial statement, and *deliberate* understatement of assets is no longer considered desirable. The practice of conservatism is reserved for those situations in which there is *uncertainty* about how to account for a particular item or transaction:

> Thus, if two estimates of amounts to be received or paid in the future are about equally likely, conservatism dictates using the less optimistic estimate; however, if two amounts are not equally likely, conservatism does not necessarily dictate using the more pessimistic amount rather than the more likely one.[9]

Various accounting rules are based on the concept of conservatism. For example, inventory held for resale is reported on a balance sheet at *the lower of cost or market.* This rule requires a company to compare the cost of its inventory with the market price, or current cost to replace that inventory, and report the lower of the two amounts on the balance sheet at the end of the year. We will explore the lower of cost or market rule as it pertains to inventory more fully in Chapter 6.

Exhibit 2-2 summarizes the qualities that make accounting information useful as they pertain to a banker's decision as to whether to loan money to a company.

The Classified Balance Sheet

Now that we have learned about the conceptual framework of accounting, we turn our attention to the outputs of the system: the financial statements. First, we will consider the significance of a *classified balance sheet.* We will then examine the *income statement,* the *statement of stockholders' equity,* and the *statement of cash flows.* The chapter concludes with a brief look at other elements in an annual report.

LO **3**

Explain the concept and purpose of a classified balance sheet and prepare the statement.

What Are the Parts of the Balance Sheet?
Understanding the Operating Cycle

In the first part of this chapter, we stressed the importance of *cash flow.* For a company that sells a product, the **operating cycle** begins with the investment of cash in inventory and ends when cash is collected by the enterprise from its customers.

Assume that on August 1 a retailer, Ace Computer Sales, buys a computer for $50,000 from the manufacturer, MBI Corp. At this point, Ace has merely substituted one asset, cash, for another, inventory. On August 20, 20 days after buying the computer, Ace sells it to an accounting firm, Brown & Company, for $60,000.

[9] *SFAC No. 2,* par. 95.

EXHIBIT 2-2   Qualitative Characteristics of Accounting Information

SITUATION   A bank is trying to decide whether to extend a $1 million loan to Holmes Corporation. Holmes presents the bank with its most recent balance sheet, showing its financial position on an historical cost basis. Each quality of the information is summarized in the form of a question.

QUALITY	QUESTION
Understandability	Can the information be used by those willing to learn to use it properly?
Relevance	Would the information be useful in deciding whether or not to loan money to Holmes?
Reliability	
Verifiability	Can the information be verified?
	Is the information free from error?
Representational faithfulness	Is there agreement between the information and the events represented?
Neutrality	Is the information slanted in any way to present the company more favorably than is warranted?
Comparability	Are the methods used in assigning amounts to assets the same as those used by other companies?
Consistency	Are the methods used in assigning amounts to assets the same as those used in prior years?
Materiality	Will a specific error affect in any way the judgment of someone relying on the financial statements?
Conservatism	If there is any uncertainty about any of the amounts assigned to items in the balance sheet, are they recognized using the least optimistic estimate?

Under the purchase agreement, Brown will pay for the computer within the next 30 days. At this point, both the form of the asset and the amount have changed. The form of the asset held by Ace has changed from inventory to accounts receivable. Also, because the inventory has been sold for $10,000 more than its cost of $50,000, the size of the asset held, the account receivable, is now $60,000. Finally, on September 20, Brown pays $60,000 to Ace, and the operating cycle is complete. Ace can now take the cash and buy another computer for resale.

Ace's operating cycle is summarized in Exhibit 2-3. The length of the company's operating cycle was 50 days. The operating cycle consisted of two distinct parts. From the time Ace purchased the inventory, 20 days elapsed before it sold the computer. Another 30 days passed before the account receivable was collected. The length of the operating cycle depends to a large extent on the nature of a company's business. For example, in our illustration, the manufacturer of the computer, MBI Corp., received cash immediately from Ace and did not have to wait to collect a receivable. However, additional time is added to the operating cycle of MBI Corp. to *manufacture* the computer.

The operating cycle of the accounting firm in our example, Brown & Company, differs from that of either the manufacturer or the retailer. Brown sells a service rather than a product. Its operating cycle is determined by two factors: the length of time involved in providing a service to the client and the amount of time required to collect any account receivable.

Current Assets

The basic distinction on a classified balance sheet is between current and noncurrent items. **Current assets** are

EXHIBIT 2-3   The Operating Cycle for a Retailer

DATE	TRANSACTION	ASSET FORM
		Cash of $50,000
		↓
August 1	Ace Computer Sales buys a computer from the manufacturer, MBI Corp., for $50,000 in cash.	Inventory of $50,000
		↓
August 20	Ace sells the computer to Brown & Company for $60,000; customer has 30 days to pay.	Accounts Receivable of $60,000
		↓
September 20	Ace collects $60,000 from Brown.	Cash of $60,000

cash and other assets that are reasonably expected to be realized in cash or sold or consumed during the normal operating cycle of a business or within one year if the operating cycle is shorter than one year.[10]

Most businesses have an operating cycle shorter than one year. The operating cycle for Ace Computer Sales in our illustration was 50 days. Therefore, cash, accounts receivable, and inventory are classified as current assets because they either *are* cash, will be *realized* in (converted to) cash (accounts receivable), or will be *sold* (inventory) within one year.

Can you think of a situation in which a company's operating cycle is longer than one year? A construction company is a good example. A construction company essentially builds an item of inventory, such as an office building, to a customer's specifications. The entire process, including construction of the building and collection of the sales price from the customer, may take three years to complete. According to our earlier definition, because the inventory will be sold and the account receivable will be collected within the operating cycle, they will still qualify as current assets.

In addition to cash, accounts receivable, and inventory, the two other most common types of current assets are marketable securities and prepaid expenses. Excess cash is often invested in the stocks and bonds of other companies, as well as in various government instruments. If the investments are made for the short term, they are classified as current and are typically called either *short-term investments* or *marketable securities.* Alternatively, some investments are made for the purpose of exercising influence over another company and thus are made for the long term. These investments are classified as noncurrent assets. Various prepayments, such as office supplies, rent, and insurance, are classified as *prepaid expenses* and thus are current assets. These assets qualify as current because they will usually be *consumed* within one year.

[10] Accounting Principles Board, *Statement of the Accounting Principles Board, No. 4,* "Basic Concepts and Accounting Principles Underlying Financial Statements of Business Enterprises" (New York: American Institute of Certified Public Accountants, 1970), par. 198.

Noncurrent Assets

All assets that do not meet the definition of a current asset are classified as *long-term* or *noncurrent assets*. Three common categories of long-term assets are (1) investments, (2) property, plant, and equipment, and (3) intangibles.

Investments Recall from the discussion of current assets that stocks and bonds that we expect to sell within the next year are classified as current assets. Securities that are *not* expected to be sold within the next year are classified as *investments*. In many cases, the investment is in the common stock of another company. The purpose of the investment is either to exercise some influence or actually to control the operation of the other company. Other types of assets classified as investments are land held for future use and buildings and equipment not currently used in operations. Finally, a special fund held for the retirement of debt or for the construction of new facilities is also classified as an investment.

Property, Plant, and Equipment This category consists of the various *tangible, productive assets* used in the operation of a business. Land, buildings, equipment, machinery, furniture and fixtures, trucks, and tools are all examples of assets held for use in the *operation* of a business rather than for *resale*. The distinction between inventory and equipment, for example, depends on the company's *intent* in acquiring the asset. For example, IBM classifies a *computer system* as *inventory* because its intent in manufacturing the asset is to offer it for resale. However, this same computer in the hands of a law firm would be classified as *equipment* because its intent in buying the asset from IBM is to use it in the long-term operation of the business.

The relative size of property, plant, and equipment on the balance sheet depends largely on a company's business. A company such as Inland Steel, in the capital-intensive steel industry, has approximately 50% of its total assets in property, plant, and equipment. On the other hand, property, plant, and equipment represents only about 1% of the total assets of many banks. Regardless of the relative size of property,

The Quaker Oats man is a product image that helps make Quaker Oats different from other such products on store shelves. But is he an intangible asset? Only if some costs can be identified as having been incurred in developing him.

plant, and equipment, all assets in this category are subject to depreciation, with the exception of *land*. A separate accumulated depreciation account is used to account for the depreciation recorded on each of these assets over its life.

Intangibles   Intangible assets are similar to property, plant, and equipment in that they provide benefits to the firm over the long term. The distinction, however, is in the *form* of the asset. *Intangible assets lack physical substance.* Trademarks, copyrights, franchise rights, patents, and goodwill are examples of intangible assets. The cost principle governs the accounting for intangibles, just as it does for tangible assets. For example, the amount paid to an inventor for the patent rights to a new product is recorded as an intangible asset. Similarly, the amount paid to a franchisor of a fast-food restaurant for the exclusive right to operate in a certain geographic area is recorded as an intangible asset. Similar to tangible assets, intangibles are written off to expense over their useful life. *Depreciation* is the name given to the process of writing off tangible assets; the same process for intangible assets is called *amortization*. Depreciation and amortization are both explained more fully in Chapter 8.

Current Liabilities

The definition of a current liability is closely tied to that of a current asset. A **current liability** is an obligation that will be satisfied within the next operating cycle, or within one year if the cycle is shorter than one year. For example, the classification of a note payable on the balance sheet depends on its maturity date. If the note will be paid within the next year, it is classified as current; otherwise, it is classified as a long-term liability. On the other hand, by their nature, accounts payable, wages payable, and income taxes payable are all short-term or current liabilities.

Most liabilities, such as those for purchases of merchandise on credit, are satisfied by the payment of cash. However, certain liabilities are eliminated from the balance sheet when the company performs services. For example, the liability, Subscriptions Received in Advance, which would appear on the balance sheet of a publisher, is satisfied not by the payment of any cash but by the delivery of the magazine to the customer. Finally, it is possible to satisfy one liability by substituting another in its place. For example, a supplier might ask a customer to sign a written promissory note to replace an existing account payable if the customer is unable to pay at the present time.

Long-Term Liabilities

Any obligation that will not be paid or otherwise satisfied within the next year or the operating cycle, whichever is longer, is classified as a long-term liability. Notes payable and bonds payable, both promises to pay money in the future, are two common forms of long-term debt. Some bonds have a life as long as 25 or 30 years. Companies that enter into long-term leases for the use of various types of property are required in certain cases to recognize a liability for the future cash payments required by the contract.

Stockholders' Equity

Recall that stockholders' equity represents the owners' claims on the assets of the business. These claims arise from two sources: *contributed capital* and *earned capital*. Contributed capital appears on the balance sheet in the form of capital stock and earned capital takes the form of retained earnings. *Capital stock* indicates the amount of capital contributed by the owners of the business. *Retained earnings* represents the accumulated earnings, or net income, of the business since its inception less all dividends paid during that time.

A majority of companies have a single class of capital stock called *common stock.* It is the most basic form of ownership in a business. All other claims against the company, such as those of *creditors* and *preferred stockholders,* take priority. *Preferred stock* is a form of capital stock that, as the name implies, carries with it certain preferences. For example, the company must pay dividends on preferred stock before it makes any distribution of dividends on common stock. In the event of liquidation, preferred stockholders have priority over common stockholders in the distribution of the entity's assets.

Capital stock may appear as two separate items on the balance sheet. The two items are *Par Value* and *Paid-in Capital in Excess of Par Value.* The addition of these two items tells us the total amount that has been paid by the owners for the stock. We will take a closer look at these items in Chapter 11.

Using a Classified Balance Sheet

LO   4

Use a classified balance sheet to analyze a company's financial position.

A classified balance sheet is different from the type presented in the previous chapter in that the line items are grouped under the various headings just discussed. An example of a classified balance sheet for a hypothetical company, Dixon Sporting Goods, Inc., is shown in Exhibit 2-4. After examining each of Dixon's financial statements, we will compare each of them to the same statements for actual companies.

Working Capital

One important use of a balance sheet is in evaluating the **liquidity** of a business. *Liquidity* is a relative term and deals with the ability of a company to pay its debts as they come due. As you might expect, bankers and other creditors are particularly interested in the liquidity of businesses to which they have loaned money. A comparison of current assets and current liabilities is a starting point in evaluating the ability of a company to meet its obligations. **Working capital** is the difference between current assets and current liabilities at a point in time. The working capital for Dixon Sporting Goods on December 31, 1993, is

WORKING CAPITAL

FORMULA	FOR DIXON SPORTING GOODS
Current Assets − Current Liabilities	$118,000 − $59,900 = $58,100

The *management* of working capital is an important task for any business. A company must continually strive for a *balance* in managing its working capital. For example, too little working capital—or in the extreme, negative working capital—may signal the inability to pay creditors on a timely basis. However, an overabundance of working capital could indicate that the company is not investing enough of its available funds in productive resources, such as new machinery and equipment.

Current Ratio

Because it is an absolute dollar amount, working capital is limited in its informational value. For example, $1 million may be an inadequate amount of working capital for a large corporation but far too much for a smaller company. In addition, a certain dollar amount of working capital may have been adequate for a company earlier in its life but is inadequate now. A related measure of liquidity, the **current ratio,** allows us to compare the liquidity of companies of different sizes and a single company

EXHIBIT 2-4   Balance Sheet for Dixon Sporting Goods, Inc.

DIXON SPORTING GOODS, INC.
BALANCE SHEET
AT DECEMBER 31, 1993

ASSETS

Current assets			
Cash		$ 5,000	
Marketable equity securities		11,000	
Accounts receivable		23,000	
Merchandise inventory		73,500	
Prepaid insurance		4,800	
Store supplies		700	
Total current assets			$118,000
Investments			
Land held for future office site			150,000
Property, plant, and equipment			
Land		100,000	
Buildings	$150,000		
Less: Accumulated depreciation	60,000	90,000	
Store furniture and fixtures	$ 42,000		
Less: Accumulated depreciation	12,600	29,400	
Total property, plant, and equipment			219,400
Intangible assets			
Franchise agreement			55,000
Total assets			$542,400

LIABILITIES

Current liabilities			
Accounts payable		$ 15,700	
Salaries and wages payable		9,500	
Income taxes payable		7,200	
Interest payable		2,500	
Bank loan payable		25,000	
Total current liabilities			$ 59,900
Long-term debt			
Notes payable, due December 31, 2003			120,000
Total liabilities			$179,900

STOCKHOLDERS' EQUITY

Contributed capital			
Capital stock, $10 par, 5,000 shares			
issued and outstanding		$ 50,000	
Paid-in capital in excess of par value		25,000	
Total contributed capital		$ 75,000	
Retained earnings		287,500	
Total stockholders' equity			362,500
Total liabilities and stockholders' equity			$542,400

over time. The ratio is computed by dividing current assets by current liabilities. Dixon Sporting Goods has a current ratio of just under 2 to 1:

CURRENT RATIO

FORMULA	FOR DIXON SPORTING GOODS

$$\frac{\text{Current Assets}}{\text{Current Liabilities}} \qquad \frac{\$118,000}{\$59,900} = \underline{\underline{1.97 \text{ to } 1}}$$

Some analysts use a rule of thumb of 2 to 1 for the current ratio as a sign of short-term financial health. However, as is always the case, rules of thumb can be dangerous. Historically, companies in certain industries have operated quite efficiently with a current ratio of less than 2 to 1, whereas a ratio much higher than this is necessary to survive in other industries. For example, department stores such as J.C. Penney and Neiman-Marcus typically report current ratios of 2 to 1 or higher. On the other hand, companies in the telephone communication business, such as Ameritech and Bell Atlantic, routinely have current ratios well under 1 to 1.

Unfortunately, neither the amount of working capital nor the current ratio tells us anything about the *composition* of current assets and current liabilities. For example, assume two companies each have total current assets equal to $100,000. Company A has cash of $10,000, accounts receivable of $50,000, and inventory of $40,000. Company B also has cash of $10,000 but accounts receivable of $20,000 and inventory of $70,000. All other things being equal, Company A is more liquid than Company B because more of its total current assets are in receivables than inventory. Receivables are only one step away from being cash, whereas inventory must be sold and then the receivable collected. Note that Dixon's inventory of $73,500 makes up a large portion of its total current assets of $118,000. An examination of the *relative* size of the various current assets for a company may reveal certain strengths and weaknesses not evident in the current ratio.

In addition to the composition of the current assets, the *frequency* with which they are "turned over" is important. For instance, how long does it take to sell an item of inventory? How long is required to collect an account receivable? Many companies could not exist with the current ratio of .56 reported by McDonald's Corporation at the end of 1992. However, think about the nature of the fast-food business. The frequency of its sales, and thus the numerous operating cycles within a single year, mean that it can operate with a much lower current ratio than a manufacturing company, for example.

Debt-to-Equity Ratio

Investors and creditors are interested in not only the short-run liquidity of a company but also its *solvency* or ability to remain in business over the long run. The *capital structure* of a company is the focal point in making this determination. This refers to the right side of the balance sheet and the mix between liabilities and stockholders' equity. All companies need a minimum investment by the owners to start a new business. Many businesses benefit by incurring debt, however. Finding the right mix of debt and equity is as important to a business in the long run as managing working capital is in the short run. One common measure of long-run viability is the **debt-to-equity ratio.** Dixon's ratio at the end of the year is computed as follows:

DEBT-TO-EQUITY RATIO

FORMULA	FOR DIXON SPORTING GOODS

$$\frac{\text{Total Liabilities}}{\text{Total Stockholders' Equity}} \qquad \frac{\$179,900}{\$362,500} = \underline{\underline{.5 \text{ to } 1}}$$

The debt-to-equity ratio tells us that for every $1 of stockholders' equity, Dixon has $.50 of liabilities or debt. Recall the accounting equation: Total Assets = Total Liabilities + Total Stockholders' Equity. An alternative way to assess the long-run solvency of a business is to compare debt to *total assets* rather than to stockholders' equity. Because Dixon has $.50 of liabilities for every $1 of stockholders' equity, we would expect to find that it has a **debt-to-total assets ratio** of .50/(.50 + 1.00), or .33 to 1:

DEBT-TO-TOTAL ASSETS RATIO

FORMULA	FOR DIXON SPORTING GOODS
$\dfrac{\text{Total Liabilities}}{\text{Total Assets}}$	$\dfrac{\$179{,}900}{\$542{,}400} = \underline{.33 \text{ to } 1}$

Based on its debt-to-total assets ratio, Dixon does not appear to be too reliant on creditors for funds. Two-thirds of the existing assets have been funded through stock and retained earnings. Whether Dixon could profit by borrowing additional money to invest in inventories and various types of plant and equipment is a question requiring much more analysis. Financial statement analysis is explored in more detail in Chapter 15.

Examples of Classified Balance Sheets

The balance sheet for our hypothetical company, Dixon Sporting Goods, Inc., introduced the components of a classified balance sheet. We now turn our attention to the balance sheets of two actual companies. These statements are more complex and require additional analysis and a better understanding of accounting to fully appreciate them. However, we will concentrate our attention on certain elements on each of these statements. At this stage in your study of accounting, you should look for the similarities rather than the differences between these statements and those of Dixon.

The Balance Sheet for a Manufacturer: The Quaker Oats Company

The balance sheets for Quaker Oats Company at the end of each of three years are shown in Exhibit 2-5. First, note Quaker's choice for its accounting or *fiscal year*. Its fiscal year ends on June 30. A majority of companies choose an accounting year that corresponds to the calendar, that is, beginning on January 1 and ending on December 31. However, some companies choose a fiscal year that ends at a point when sales are at their lowest in the annual cycle. For example, Wal-Mart ends its fiscal year on January 31, after the busy holiday season. Quaker chooses June 30 because sales of many of its products, such as hot cereals, are at their lowest during the summer.

Quaker Oats releases what are called *consolidated financial statements,* which reflect the position and results of all operations that are controlled by a single entity. For example, in addition to its traditional line of food products, Quaker is a leading manufacturer of dog food through its Pet Foods Division. Sometimes, as is the case with Pet Foods, various units of a company are organized as divisions. In other cases, the units are separate corporations, called *subsidiaries.* Any division, branch, or subsidiary controlled by another entity is included in the financial statements of that entity.

EXHIBIT 2-5 Quaker Oats' Comparative Balance Sheets

The Quaker Oats Company and Subsidiaries

Consolidated Balance Sheets	June 30	1993	1992	1991
	Assets			
	Current Assets:			
	Cash and cash equivalents	$ **61.0**	$ 95.2	$ 74.6
	Trade accounts receivable—net of allowances	**478.9**	575.3	655.6
	Inventories:			
	Finished goods	**241.5**	302.8	309.1
	Grains and raw materials	**73.1**	93.7	86.7
	Packaging materials and supplies	**39.4**	38.8	26.5
	Total inventories	**354.0**	435.3	422.3
	Other current assets	**173.7**	150.4	150.0
	Total Current Assets	**1,067.6**	1,256.2	1,302.5
	Other Receivables and Investments	**88.8**	83.0	79.1
	Property, plant and equipment	**2,059.2**	2,066.1	1,914.6
	Less accumulated depreciation	**831.0**	792.8	681.9
	Property—Net	**1,228.2**	1,273.3	1,232.7
	Intangible Assets—Net of Amortization	**431.3**	427.4	446.2
	Total Assets	$ **2,815.9**	$3,039.9	$3,060.5

See accompanying notes to the consolidated financial statements.

Quaker presents *comparative* balance sheets to indicate its financial position on June 30 of each of the last three years. As a minimum standard, the Securities and Exchange Commission requires that the annual report include balance sheets as of the two most recent years and income statements for each of the three most recent years. Note that all amounts on the balance sheet are stated in millions of dollars. This type of rounding is a common practice in the financial statements of large corporations and is justified under the materiality concept. Knowing the exact dollar amount of each asset would not change a decision made by an investor.

The presentation of comparative balance sheets allows the reader to make comparisons between years. For example, Quaker's *working capital* decreased between June 30, 1992, and June 30, 1993, and is a *negative* amount on the latter date:

WORKING CAPITAL

	JUNE 30, 1993	JUNE 30, 1992
Current Assets − Current Liabilities	$1,067.6 − 1,105.1	$1,256.2 − 1,087.5
	= $(37.5)	= $168.7

EXHIBIT 2-5 *(continued)*

Dollars in Millions

June 30	**1993**	1992	1991
Liabilities and Shareholders' Equity			
Current Liabilities:			
Short-term debt	**$ 128.0**	$ 61.0	$ 80.6
Current portion of long-term debt	**48.9**	57.9	32.9
Trade accounts payable	**391.6**	420.2	395.3
Accrued payroll, pension and bonus	**161.3**	147.0	116.3
Accrued advertising and merchandising	**130.6**	120.2	105.7
Income taxes payable	**33.7**	82.6	58.5
Payable to Fisher-Price	**—**	—	29.6
Other accrued liabilities	**211.0**	198.6	165.8
Total Current Liabilities	**1,105.1**	1,087.5	984.7
Long-term Debt	**632.6**	688.7	701.2
Other Liabilities	**426.2**	171.7	231.9
Deferred Income Taxes	**89.5**	242.0	236.9
Preferred Stock, no par value, authorized 1,750,000 shares; issued 1,282,051 of $5.46 cumulative convertible shares (liquidating preference $78 per share)	**100.0**	100.0	100.0
Deferred Compensation	**(85.9)**	(90.5)	(94.5)
Treasury Preferred Stock, at cost, 34,447 shares; 21,315 shares; and 10,089 shares, respectively	**(2.7)**	(1.6)	(0.7)
Common Shareholders' Equity:			
Common stock, $5 par value, authorized 200,000,000 shares; issued 83,989,396 shares	**420.0**	420.0	420.0
Additional paid-in capital	**—**	2.9	7.2
Reinvested earnings	**1,190.1**	1,162.3	1,047.5
Cumulative translation adjustment	**(65.4)**	(24.5)	(52.9)
Deferred compensation	**(154.0)**	(160.4)	(168.0)
Treasury common stock, at cost, 14,533,157 shares; 10,586,091 shares; and 7,660,675 shares, respectively	**(839.6)**	(558.2)	(352.8)
Total Common Shareholders' Equity	**551.1**	842.1	901.0
Total Liabilities and Shareholders' Equity	**$2,815.9**	$3,039.9	$3,060.5

Quaker's *current ratio* at each of the two dates follows:

CURRENT RATIO

	JUNE 30, 1993	JUNE 30, 1992
$\dfrac{\text{Current Assets}}{\text{Current Liabilities}}$	$\dfrac{\$1,067.6}{1,105.1} = \underline{\underline{.97 \text{ to } 1}}$	$\dfrac{\$1,256.2}{1,087.5} = \underline{\underline{1.16 \text{ to } 1}}$

Both the amount of working capital and the current ratio decreased between 1992 and 1993. The largest change in the current assets is the decrease in trade accounts receivable—net of allowances.

On the liability side of its balance sheet, Quaker lists three noncurrent liabilities: long-term debt, other liabilities, and deferred income taxes. Quaker does not report an amount for total liabilities, so we need to add these three amounts to the total current liabilities to find total liabilities. To find total stockholders' equity, it is necessary to add the balances in three items to common shareholders' equity. These three items are Preferred Stock, Deferred Compensation, and Treasury Preferred

Stock. Note that the balance in two of these accounts is negative. Quaker's *debt-to-equity ratio* at the end of each of the two years is as follows:

DEBT-TO-EQUITY RATIO

	JUNE 30, 1993	JUNE 30, 1992
$\dfrac{\text{Total Liabilities}}{\text{Total Shareholders' Equity}}$	$\dfrac{\$2,253.4}{562.5} = 4.01 \text{ to } 1$	$\dfrac{\$2,189.9}{850.0} = 2.58 \text{ to } 1$

The Balance Sheet for a Service Company: United Airlines

Service companies are becoming an increasingly important sector of our economy. As a future user of financial information, you are just as likely to need to analyze the statements of a company that sells a service as one that sells a product. Service companies take many different forms in our economy. Companies in the transportation, communication, and banking industries all rely on the sale of services to earn a profit. The balance sheet for a company in the transportation business, UAL Corporation (the holding company for United Airlines), is presented in Exhibit 2-6. Note that UAL uses the title statement of consolidated financial position rather than balance sheet.

   The most striking difference between the balance sheet of a service company such as United compared to that of a product-oriented company such as Quaker Oats is the former's lack of an inventory account on the balance sheet. On the other hand, noncurrent assets, particularly property, plant, and equipment, represent a large percentage of the total assets on the balance sheet of most service companies. United's net operating property and equipment at the end of 1992 of nearly $6.4 billion (note that all amounts are stated in millions of dollars) represents 52% of its total assets of $12.3 billion. Quaker's ratio of properties to total assets is only 44%. As you might expect, a majority of United's property and equipment consists of its flight equipment.

■ ACCOUNTING FOR YOUR DECISIONS   **You Are the Supplier**

Assume your company sells aircraft fuel to United Airlines on credit.

1. Compute United's current ratio at the end of 1992 and 1991.
2. On the basis of United's current ratio, would you be concerned about selling them fuel on a credit basis?

The Income Statement

The *income statement* is used to summarize the results of *operations* of an entity for a *period of time.* As a minimum, all companies prepare income statements at least once a year. Companies that must report to the Securities and Exchange Commission prepare financial statements, including an income statement, every three months. Monthly income statements are usually prepared for internal use by management.

What Appears on the Income Statement?

From an accounting perspective, it is important to understand what transactions of an entity should appear on the income statement. The makeup of the income

EXHIBIT 2-6   UAL Corporation Comparative Balance Sheets

STATEMENT OF CONSOLIDATED
FINANCIAL POSITION

(In Millions)	December 31 1992	1991
ASSETS		
Current assets:		
Cash and cash equivalents	$ 522.2	$ 449.0
Short-term investments	960.6	727.4
Receivables, less allowance for doubtful accounts		
(1992 – $11.9; 1991 – $13.1)	1,066.3	912.2
Aircraft fuel, spare parts and supplies, less obsolescence allowance		
(1992 – $46.4; 1991 – $67.3)	324.3	336.2
Refundable income taxes	63.6	166.9
Deferred income taxes	33.2	–
Prepaid expenses	328.1	290.2
	3,298.3	2,881.9
Operating property and equipment:		
Flight equipment	7,790.1	6,710.1
Advances on flight equipment	710.3	784.6
Other property and equipment	2,099.2	1,906.8
	10,599.6	9,401.5
Accumulated depreciation and amortization	(4,205.0)	(3,887.5)
	6,394.6	5,514.0
Operating property and equipment under capital leases:		
Flight equipment	959.2	682.3
Other property and equipment	100.7	100.3
	1,059.9	782.6
Accumulated amortization	(343.6)	(301.2)
	716.3	481.4
Other assets:		
Intangibles, less accumulated amortization		
(1992 – $146.0; 1991 – $91.4)	907.4	666.3
Deferred income taxes	588.8	27.2
Other	352.0	305.5
	1,848.2	999.0
	$12,257.4	$ 9,876.3

The accompanying notes to consolidated financial statements are an integral part of these statements.

STATEMENT OF CONSOLIDATED
FINANCIAL POSITION

(In Millions, Except Share Data)	December 31 1992	1991
LIABILITIES AND SHAREHOLDERS' EQUITY		
Current liabilities:		
Short-term borrowings	$ 449.8	$ 448.6
Long-term debt maturing within one year	116.2	68.7
Current obligations under capital leases	53.7	39.3
Advance ticket sales	1,067.6	882.6
Accounts payable	645.9	580.1
Accrued salaries, wages and benefits	910.9	775.0
Accrued aircraft rent	715.0	526.3
Other accrued liabilities	885.9	762.7
	4,845.0	4,083.3
Long-term debt	2,800.7	1,826.6
Long-term obligations under capital leases	812.4	596.6
Other liabilities and deferred credits:		
Deferred pension liability	576.1	622.8
Postretirement benefit liability	960.0	–
Deferred gains	1,430.4	1,126.7
Other	127.2	22.4
	3,093.7	1,771.9
Redeemable preferred stock:		
5-1/2% cumulative prior preferred stock, $100 par value	–	1.1
Common shareholders' equity:		
Common stock, $5 par value; authorized, 125,000,000 shares; issued, 25,284,670 shares in 1992 and 25,244,206 shares in 1991	126.4	126.2
Additional capital invested	340.4	304.0
Retained earnings	332.1	1,288.9
Unearned compensation	(11.4)	(17.2)
Pension liability adjustment	(7.9)	–
Common stock held in treasury — 1,046,188 shares in 1992 and 1,486,100 shares in 1991	(74.0)	(105.1)
	705.6	1,596.8
Commitments and contingent liabilities (See Note 15)		
	$12,257.4	$9,876.3

statement has in fact been a subject of considerable debate by the profession. The FASB introduced the concept of **comprehensive income** and has defined it as the change in equity of a business enterprise during a

period from transactions and other events and circumstances from nonowner sources. It includes all changes in equity during a period except those resulting from investments by owners and distributions to owners.[11]

The accounting equation is the key to understanding this definition of income:

$$\text{Assets} = \text{Liabilities} + \text{Owners' Equity}$$

[11] *Statement of Financial Accounting Concepts, No. 6,* "Elements of Financial Statements" (Stamford, Conn.: Financial Accounting Standards Board, December 1985), par. 70.

If we rearrange the equation so that liabilities are on the left side,

$$\text{Assets} - \text{Liabilities} = \text{Owners' Equity}$$

According to the definition, other than changes in the equity in a business that result from either investments and withdrawals by the owners, income is the *cause* for the change in owners' equity during a period. At this stage, you should be aware that net income as shown on the income statement in most companies is not in total agreement with comprehensive income as defined earlier. Certain items are included in comprehensive income but are presently excluded from the income statement. These items are covered in Chapter 12.

In general, the income statement reports the excess of *revenue over expense,* that is, *net income,* or in the event of an excess of *expense over revenue,* the *net loss* of the period. As a reference to the "bottom line" on an income statement, it is common to use the terms *profits* or *earnings* as synonyms for *net income.*

Certain special types of revenues, called *gains,* are sometimes reported on the income statement, as are certain special types of expenses, called *losses.* For example, assume that Stevenson Company holds a parcel of land for a future building site. The company paid $50,000 for the land 10 years ago. The state pays Stevenson $60,000 for the property to use in a new highway project. Stevenson has a special type of revenue from the condemnation of its property. It will recognize a *gain* of $10,000: the excess of the cash received from the state, $60,000, over the cost of the land, $50,000.

Format of the Income Statement

LO   5

Explain the difference between a single-step and a multiple-step income statement and prepare each type of income statement.

Although we said earlier that the purpose of the income statement is to present the results of operations of the entity for a period of time, different formats are used by corporations to present their results. The major choice a company makes is whether to prepare the income statement in a single-step or a multiple-step form. Both are generally accepted, as indicated by a recent survey of the number of companies using each format. Exhibit 2-7 presents the results of that survey. Next, we'll explain what the differences are between the two forms and their variations.

Single-Step Format for the Income Statement   In a **single-step income statement,** all expenses are added together and then are deducted *in a single step* from all revenues to arrive at net income. As indicated from the survey, in practice there are two variations on the single-step format. In 1992, 206 of the 211 companies using the single-step format reported income taxes separately. Only five companies reported income tax among the operating items. A single-step format for the income statement of Dixon Sporting Goods is presented in Exhibit 2-8. The primary advantage of the single-step form is its simplicity. No attempt is made to classify either revenues or expenses or to associate any of the expenses with any of the revenues.

Multiple-Step Format for the Income Statement   The survey indicates that nearly two-thirds of the companies use the **multiple-step income statement.** The purpose of this format is to subdivide the income statement into specific sections and provide the reader with important subtotals. As was the case with the single-step format, two variations on the multiple-step approach are found in practice. One approach deducts both cost of sales and other types of expense from sales to show operating income. The survey indicates that for 1992, 230 companies followed this approach. Alternatively, 159 companies deducted only the cost of sales from sales

EXHIBIT 2-7   Income Statement Format: A Survey

	NUMBER OF CORPORATIONS IN			
	1992	1991	1990	1989
Single-step Form				
Federal income tax shown as separate last item	206	213	206	229
Federal income tax listed among operating items	5	3	9	3
Multi-step Form				
Costs and expenses deducted from sales to show operating income	230	222	229	220
Costs deducted from sales to show gross margin	159	162	156	148
Total Companies	600	600	600	600

SOURCE: *Accounting Trends & Techniques,* 47th ed. (New York: American Institute of Certified Public Accountants, 1993).

EXHIBIT 2-8   Income Statement (Single-Step Format) for Dixon Sporting Goods, Inc.

DIXON SPORTING GOODS, INC.
INCOME STATEMENT (SINGLE-STEP FORMAT)
FOR THE YEAR ENDED DECEMBER 31, 1993

Revenues		
Sales	$357,500	
Dividends	1,500	
Total revenues		$359,000
Expenses		
Cost of goods sold	$218,300	
Depreciation on store furniture and fixtures	4,200	
Advertising	13,750	
Salaries and wages for sales staff	22,000	
Depreciation on buildings and amortization of trademark	6,000	
Salaries and wages for office staff	15,000	
Insurance	3,600	
Supplies	1,050	
Interest	16,900	
Income taxes	17,200	
Total expenses		318,000
Net income		$ 41,000
Earnings per share		$ 8.20

to show gross margin, or gross profit as it is also called. This format is illustrated for Dixon Sporting Goods in Exhibit 2-9.

The multiple-step income statement for Dixon indicates three important subtotals. First, cost of goods sold is deducted from sales to arrive at **gross profit:**

$$\text{Gross profit} = \text{Sales} - \text{Cost of goods sold}$$

Sales	$357,500
Cost of goods sold	218,300
Gross profit	$139,200

Cost of goods sold, as the name implies, is the cost of the units of inventory sold during the year. It is logical to associate cost of goods sold with the sales revenue

EXHIBIT 2-9   Income Statement (Multiple-Step Format) for Dixon Sporting Goods, Inc.

DIXON SPORTING GOODS, INC.
INCOME STATEMENT (MULTIPLE-STEP FORMAT)
FOR THE YEAR ENDED DECEMBER 31, 1993

Sales		$357,500	
Cost of goods sold		218,300	
Gross profit			$139,200
Operating expenses			
Selling expenses			
Depreciation on store furniture and fixtures	$ 4,200		
Advertising	13,750		
Salaries and wages	22,000		
Total selling expense		$ 39,950	
General and administrative expenses			
Depreciation on buildings and amortization of trademark	$ 6,000		
Salaries and wages	15,000		
Insurance	3,600		
Supplies	1,050		
Total general and administrative expense		25,650	
Total operating expenses			65,600
Income from operations			$ 73,600
Other revenues and expenses			
Dividend revenue		$ 1,500	
Interest expense		16,900	
Excess of other expenses over other revenue			15,400
Income before taxes			$ 58,200
Income tax expense			17,200
Net income			$ 41,000
Earnings per share			$ 8.20

for the year because the latter represents the *selling price* of the inventory sold during the period.

The second important subtotal on Dixon's income statement is *income from operations* of $73,600. This is found by subtracting *operating expenses* of $65,600 from the gross profit of $139,200. Operating expenses are further subdivided between *selling expenses* and *general and administrative expenses*. For example, note that two depreciation amounts are included in operating expenses. Depreciation on store furniture and fixtures is classified as a selling expense because the store is where sales take place. Alternatively, we will assume that the buildings are offices for the administrative staff and thus depreciation on the buildings is classified as a general and administrative expense.

The third important subtotal on the income statement is *income before taxes* of $58,200. Dividend revenue and interest expense, neither of which is an operating item, are included in other revenues and expenses. The *excess* of *interest expense* of $16,900 over *dividend revenue* of $1,500, which equals $15,400, is subtracted from *income from operations* to arrive at *income before taxes*. Finally, *income tax expense* of $17,200 is deducted to arrive at *net income* of $41,000.

Using a Multiple-Step Income Statement

The distinct advantage of the multiple-step income statement is that it provides additional information to the reader. Although all of the amounts needed to calculate certain ratios are available on a single-step statement, such calculations are easier with a multiple-step statement. For example, the deduction of cost of goods sold from sales to arrive at gross profit allows us to quickly calculate the **gross profit ratio.** The ratio of Dixon's gross profit to its sales, rounded to the nearest percent, is

LO   6
Use a multiple-step income statement to analyze a company's operations.

GROSS PROFIT RATIO

FORMULA	FOR DIXON SPORTING GOODS
$\dfrac{\text{Gross Profit}}{\text{Sales}}$	$\dfrac{139,200}{357,500} = \underline{\underline{39\%}}$

The gross profit ratio tells us that after paying for the product, for every dollar of sales, 39 cents is available to cover other expenses and earn a profit. The complement of the gross profit ratio is the ratio of cost of goods sold to sales. For Dixon, this ratio is $1 - .39 = .61$, or 61%. For every dollar of sales, Dixon spends 61 cents on the cost of the product.

An important use of the income statement is to evaluate the *profitability* of a business. For example, a company's **profit margin** is the ratio of its net income to its sales. Dixon's profit margin is as follows:

PROFIT MARGIN

FORMULA	FOR DIXON SPORTING GOODS
$\dfrac{\text{Net Income}}{\text{Sales}}$	$\dfrac{41,000}{357,500} = \underline{\underline{11\%}}$

For every dollar of sales, Dixon has 11 cents in net income.

Two important factors should be kept in mind in evaluating any financial statement ratio. First, how does this year's ratio differ from that of prior years? For example, a decrease in the profit margin may indicate that the company is having trouble this year controlling certain costs. Second, how does the ratio compare with industry

FROM CONCEPT TO PRACTICE

READING BEN & JERRY'S INCOME STATEMENT
Refer to the income statements in Ben & Jerry's annual report. Does it use the single-step or multiple-step approach? Compute the profit margin for the last two years. Did it go up or down from the prior year to the current year?

norms? It is always helpful to compare key ratios, such as the profit margin, with an industry average, or with the same ratio for a close competitor of the company.

All publicly held companies are required to report **earnings per share** on the face of the income statement. This ratio translates an entity's net income from an absolute dollar amount to an amount per share of common stock:

EARNINGS PER SHARE

$$\frac{\text{Net Income}}{\text{Average Number of Common Shares Outstanding}}$$

Dixon's earnings per share of $8.20 was calculated by dividing its net income of $41,000 by the 5,000 shares of common stock, as indicated on the balance sheet in Exhibit 2-4.

DIXON'S EARNINGS PER SHARE

$$\frac{\$41,000}{5,000 \text{ shares}} = \underline{\underline{\$8.20}}$$

One important advantage of earnings per share over net income as a measure of profitability is that this ratio itself can be related to the market price of a company's stock. Many investors pay close attention to a company's *price-earnings ratio,* which is simply the ratio of market price per share of the stock to earnings per share. For example, a low price-earnings ratio may be an indication of an undervalued stock. That is, it can be bought at a low price, relative to its earnings.

Knowing a company's profit margin has limited informational value to investors. The ratio indicates profitability but does not relate it to the size of the investment. The **return on stockholders' equity** ratio measures the relationship between profitability and the investment made by the stockholders:

RETURN ON STOCKHOLDERS' EQUITY

$$\frac{\text{Net Income}}{\text{Average Stockholders' Equity}}$$

We will look in much more detail in Chapter 15 at the analysis of financial statements. For now, however, it is worth noting that because net income is a measure of profitability *for the year,* it is necessary to use *average* stockholders' equity in calculating return on equity. If we assume that Dixon's stockholders' equity at the beginning of the year was $346,500, its return on equity ratio is as follows:

DIXON'S RETURN ON STOCKHOLDERS' EQUITY

$$\frac{41,000}{(346,500 + 362,500)/2} = \underline{\underline{12\%}}$$

The ratio indicates that for every dollar invested by the stockholders, the company has earned a return for them of 12 cents.

Examples of Income Statements

We have examined two basic formats for the income statement: the single-step format and the multiple-step format. In practice, numerous variations on these two basic formats exist, depending to a large extent on the nature of a company's business.

For example, the multiple-step form, with its presentation of gross profit, is not used by service businesses because they do not sell a product. (Remember that gross profit is sales less cost of goods sold.) As we will see in the following examples, the form of the income statement is a reflection of a company's operations.

Quaker Oats' Income Statement

Multiple-step income statements for Quaker Oats Company for a three-year period are presented in Exhibit 2-10. "Statement of income," as used by Quaker, is an acceptable name for the income statement. The condensed nature of Quaker's statement is typical of many published income statements. For example, note that a single line is used to indicate the total for selling, general, and administrative expenses. "Provision for income taxes" is a title often used for income tax expense.

Two items on Quaker's comparative income statements deserve special mention. In 1991 Quaker reported a loss of $30 million from discontinued operations. A discontinued operation is a segment of the business that has been either sold or discontinued. In 1991 Quaker completed a plan to dispose of its Fisher-Price toy division. Because any income or loss from segments of a business that has been discontinued will not by nature arise in the future, these amounts are separated from the income from continuing operations. Another unusual item on Quaker's income

EXHIBIT 2-10   Quaker Oats' Comparative Income Statements

The Quaker Oats Company and Subsidiaries

Dollars in Millions (Except Per Share Data)

Consolidated Statements of Income	Year Ended June 30	1993	1992	1991
	Net Sales	**$5,730.6**	$5,576.4	$5,491.2
	Cost of goods sold	**2,858.4**	2,817.7	2,839.7
	Gross profit	**2,872.2**	2,758.7	2,651.5
	Selling, general and administrative expenses	**2,279.4**	2,213.0	2,121.2
	Interest expense—net of $10.5, $9.6 and $9.0 interest income, respectively	**55.1**	67.4	86.2
	Other expense—net	**70.1**	56.8	32.6
	Income from Continuing Operations Before Income Taxes and Cumulative Effect of Accounting Changes	**467.6**	421.5	411.5
	Provision for income taxes	**180.8**	173.9	175.7
	Income from Continuing Operations Before Cumulative Effect of Accounting Changes	**286.8**	247.6	235.8
	(Loss) from discontinued operations—net of tax	**—**	—	(30.0)
	Income Before Cumulative Effect of Accounting Changes	**286.8**	247.6	205.8
	Cumulative effect of accounting changes—net of tax	**(115.5)**	—	—
	Net Income	**171.3**	247.6	205.8
	Preferred dividends—net of tax	**4.2**	4.2	4.3
	Net Income Available for Common	**$ 167.1**	$ 243.4	$ 201.5
	Per Common Share:			
	Income from Continuing Operations Before Cumulative Effect of Accounting Changes	**$ 3.93**	$ 3.25	$ 3.05
	(Loss) from discontinued operations	**—**	—	(0.40)
	Income Before Cumulative Effect of Accounting Changes	**3.93**	3.25	2.65
	Cumulative effect of accounting changes	**(1.59)**	—	—
	Net Income	**$ 2.34**	$ 3.25	$ 2.65
	Dividends declared	**$ 1.92**	$ 1.72	$ 1.56
	Average Number of Common Shares Outstanding (in thousands)	**71,974**	74,881	75,904

See accompanying notes to the consolidated financial statements.

statement is the "Cumulative effect of accounting changes—net of tax" of ($115.5) in 1993. This represents the effect on income of changing the method Quaker uses to account for health and life insurance benefits paid to retirees. Because the effect is significant, it is reported separately on the income statement. Accounting for discontinued operations and for accounting changes is covered more fully in Chapter 12.

■ ACCOUNTING FOR YOUR DECISIONS   You Are the Investor

You are considering buying Quaker Oats stock. On the basis of the income statements presented in Exhibit 2-10 would you be interested in buying any stock, given the decrease in income from 1992 to 1993?

The Income Statement for a Service Company: United Airlines

Comparative income statements for a three-year period for UAL Corporation are presented in Exhibit 2-11. The most obvious difference between the income statement

Federal Express is another example of a service company. It obtains most of its revenues from the delivery of packages, much of it delivered by aircraft. Thus cargo in the form of bulk packages would account for a large part of its total operating revenues.

EXHIBIT 2-11   UAL Corporation Comparative Income Statements

STATEMENT OF CONSOLIDATED OPERATIONS

(In Millions, Except Per Share)	1992	1991	1990
		Year ended December 31	
Operating revenues:			
Passenger	$11,523.6	$10,295.8	$ 9,633.6
Cargo	795.8	704.1	592.9
Contract services and other	570.3	662.7	811.0
	12,889.7	11,662.6	11,037.5
Operating expenses:			
Salaries and related costs	4,562.5	4,056.7	3,549.9
Commissions	2,231.3	2,046.5	1,718.9
Aircraft fuel	1,699.5	1,674.1	1,811.4
Rentals and landing fees	1,342.3	1,084.6	829.3
Purchased services	936.1	783.8	658.8
Depreciation and amortization	725.6	603.8	559.6
Food and beverages	341.9	291.6	241.6
Aircraft maintenance	330.3	362.9	388.1
Personnel expenses	270.6	238.9	202.2
Advertising and promotion	214.9	208.4	203.2
Other	772.5	805.4	910.8
	13,427.5	12,156.7	11,073.8
Loss from operations	(537.8)	(494.1)	(36.3)
Other income (expense):			
Interest expense	(327.8)	(209.9)	(192.2)
Interest capitalized	92.2	91.2	71.3
Interest income	68.6	85.4	122.6
Equity in earnings of Covia Partnership	41.6	7.3	16.2
Net gains on disposition of property	31.6	48.7	285.8
Other, net	(24.4)	(36.2)	(103.0)
	(118.2)	(13.5)	200.7
Earnings (loss) before income taxes and cumulative effect of accounting changes	(656.0)	(507.6)	164.4
Provision (credit) for income taxes	(238.8)	(175.7)	69.9
Earnings (loss) before cumulative effect of accounting changes	(417.2)	(331.9)	94.5
Cumulative effect of accounting changes:			
Accounting for postretirement benefits, net of tax	(580.0)	–	–
Accounting for income taxes	40.4	–	–
Net earnings (loss)	$ (956.8)	$ (331.9)	$ 94.5
Per share:			
Earnings (loss) before cumulative effect of accounting changes	$ (17.34)	$ (14.31)	$ 4.33
Cumulative effect of accounting changes	(22.41)	–	–
Net earnings (loss)	$ (39.75)	$ (14.31)	$ 4.33

The accompanying notes to consolidated financial statements are an integral part of these statements.

of a product-oriented company and that of a service company, such as an airline, is the lack of cost of goods sold and gross profit on the income statement of the latter. From the statements, it is obvious that the airline generates most of its revenue from passenger flights. Cargo accounts for a minor part of the total operating revenue each year. It is also worth noting that salaries and related costs are the largest expense for the airline, amounting to 34% of the total operating expenses in 1992. Commissions and aircraft fuel are the second- and third-largest operating expenses.

The Statements of Retained Earnings and Stockholders' Equity

LO 7

Identify the components of the statement of retained earnings and the statement of stockholders' equity and prepare each statement.

The purpose of a statement of stockholders' equity is to explain the changes in the components of owners' equity during the period. Retained earnings and capital stock are the two primary components of stockholders' equity. If there are no changes during the period in a company's capital stock, it may choose to present a statement of retained earnings instead of a statement of stockholders' equity. A statement of retained earnings for Dixon Sporting Goods is shown in Exhibit 2-12.

The statement of retained earnings provides an important link between the income statement and the balance sheet. Dixon's *net income* of $41,000, as detailed on the income statement, is an *addition* to retained earnings. Note that the *dividends* declared and paid of $25,000 do not appear on the income statement because they are a payout or *distribution* of net income to stockholders, rather than one of the expenses deducted to arrive at net income. Accordingly, they appear as a direct deduction on the statement of retained earnings. The beginning balance in retained earnings is carried forward from last year's statement of retained earnings.

To emphasize the relationship between the two, some companies *combine* the statement of retained earnings with the income statement. A combined statement follows the general format:

Revenues	$xxx
Less: Expenses	xxx
Net income	$xxx
Add: Retained earnings at beginning of year	xxx
Subtotal	$xxx
Less: Dividends declared during the year	xxx
Retained earnings at end of year	$xxx

As indicated in the survey reported in Exhibit 2-13, most corporations (481 of the 600 companies in the 1992 survey) present a statement of stockholders' equity. A separate statement of retained earnings was used by 48 of the companies, and 27 combined the statements of income and retained earnings.

EXHIBIT 2-12   Statement of Retained Earnings for Dixon Sporting Goods, Inc.

DIXON SPORTING GOODS, INC.
STATEMENT OF RETAINED EARNINGS
FOR THE YEAR ENDED DECEMBER 31, 1993

Retained earnings, January 1, 1993	$271,500
Add: Net income for 1993	41,000
	$312,500
Less: Dividends declared and paid in 1993	(25,000)
Retained earnings, December 31, 1993	$287,500

EXHIBIT 2-13   Presentation of Changes in Stockholders' Equity: A Survey

	NUMBER OF CORPORATIONS IN			
	1992	1991	1990	1989
Statement of stockholders' equity	481	473	461	456
Separate statement of retained earnings	48	47	56	60
Combined statement of income and retained earnings	27	27	30	35
Changes shown in notes	44	53	53	49
Total Companies	600	600	600	600

SOURCE: *Accounting Trends & Techniques,* 47th ed. (New York: American Institute of Certified Public Accountants, 1993).

A statement of changes in stockholders' equity for UAL Corporation is shown in Exhibit 2-14. United lists the components of stockholders' equity across the top of the statement and the explanations for the changes in each of them down the side. At this point, you might want to trace the December 31, 1992, balance in each of the accounts to the balance sheet in Exhibit 2-6.

The Statement of Cash Flows

The statement of cash flows was introduced in Chapter 1, and we will return to a detailed discussion of how to prepare the statement in Chapter 14. For now, however, recall the purpose of the statement: to summarize the cash flow effects of a company's operating, investing, and financing activities for the period. All publicly held corporations are required to present a statement of cash flows in their annual report.

LO **8**

Identify the components of the statement of cash flows and prepare the statement.

The Cash Flow Statement for Dixon Sporting Goods

The statement for Dixon Sporting Goods is shown in Exhibit 2-15. The statement consists of three categories: operating activities, investing activities, and financing activities. Each of these three categories can result in a net inflow of cash or a net outflow of cash.

Dixon's *operating activities* generated $56,100 of cash during the period. As the name implies, operating activities have to do with the purchase and sale of a product, in this case the acquisition of sporting goods from distributors and the subsequent sale of those goods. An income statement summarizes a company's operations for the period, and, thus, net income is listed as the first item in this section of the statement. However, net income reflects revenues when they are earned, not necessarily when cash is received. Expenses are reflected when they are incurred, not necessarily when cash is paid. We will discuss the statement of cash flows in detail in Chapter 14 and the preparation of this section of the statement. For now, it is enough to know that adjustments are necessary to convert net income to a cash basis.

The one *investing activity,* the purchase of land for a future office site, required the use of cash and thus is shown as a net outflow of $150,000. Dixon had two *financing activities:* dividends of $25,000 required the use of cash, and the proceeds

EXHIBIT 2-14 UAL Corporation Comparative Statements of Changes in Stockholders' Equity

STATEMENT OF CONSOLIDATED COMMON SHAREHOLDERS' EQUITY

(In Millions, Except Per Share)	Common Stock	Additional Capital Invested	Retained Earnings	Unearned Compensation	Pension Liability Adjustment	Treasury Stock	Total
Balance at December 31, 1989	$ 117.1	$ 47.3	$1,526.5	$(14.5)	$ −	$(112.1)	$1,564.3
Year ended December 31, 1990:							
Net earnings			94.5				94.5
Cash dividends declared on prior preferred stock ($5.50 per share)			(0.1)				(0.1)
Exercises of stock options	0.2	5.0					5.2
Issuance of treasury stock under restricted stock plan		0.1		(0.3)		0.2	−
Amortization of unearned compensation under restricted stock plan				6.8			6.8
Balance at December 31, 1990	117.3	52.4	1,620.9	(8.0)	−	(111.9)	1,670.7
Year ended December 31, 1991:							
Net loss			(331.9)				(331.9)
Cash dividends declared on prior preferred stock ($5.50 per share)			(0.1)				(0.1)
Issuance of common stock	8.6	238.5					247.1
Exercises of stock options	0.3	4.9					5.2
Issuance of treasury stock under restricted stock plan		8.2		(15.0)		6.8	−
Amortization of unearned compensation under restricted stock plan				5.8			5.8
Balance at December 31, 1991	126.2	304.0	1,288.9	(17.2)	−	(105.1)	1,596.8
Year ended December 31, 1992:							
Net loss			(956.8)				(956.8)
Exercises of stock options	0.2	4.2					4.4
Issuance of treasury stock pursuant to Air Wis acquisition		32.6				31.4	64.0
Forfeiture of restricted stock . . .		(0.5)		1.0		(0.5)	−
Adjustment required to recognize minimum pension liability . . .					(7.9)		(7.9)
Amortization of unearned compensation under restricted stock plan				4.8			4.8
Other treasury stock issuances . . .		0.1				0.2	0.3
Balance at December 31, 1992	$126.4	$340.4	$ 332.1	$(11.4)	$(7.9)	$ (74.0)	$ 705.6

The accompanying notes to consolidated financial statements are an integral part of these statements.

EXHIBIT 2-15   Statement of Cash Flows for Dixon Sporting Goods, Inc.

DIXON SPORTING GOODS, INC.
STATEMENT OF CASH FLOWS
FOR THE YEAR ENDED DECEMBER 31, 1993

Cash flows from operating activities		
Net income	$ 41,000	
Adjustments to reconcile net income to net cash provided by operations:		
Depreciation expense	10,200	
Decrease in accounts receivable	5,000	
Increase in inventory	(3,000)	
Increase in prepaid insurance	(1,200)	
Decrease in store supplies	200	
Increase in accounts payable	4,100	
Decrease in salaries and wages payable	(1,500)	
Increase in income taxes payable	1,300	
Net cash provided by operating activities		$ 56,100
Cash flows from investing activities		
Purchase of land for future office site		(150,000)
Cash flows from financing activities		
Dividends declared and paid	$ (25,000)	
Proceeds from issuance of long-term note	120,000	
Net cash provided by financing activities		95,000
Net increase in cash		$ 1,100
Cash at beginning of year		3,900
Cash at end of year		$ 5,000

from the issuance of a long-term note generated cash of $120,000. The balance in cash on the bottom of the statement of $5,000 must agree with the balance for this item as shown on the balance sheet in Exhibit 2-4.

The Statement of Cash Flows for Quaker Oats

A statement of cash flows for Quaker Oats is shown in Exhibit 2-16. A quick overview of the 1993 statement indicates that Quaker generated more than $558 million of cash from operations. Investing activities were a large drain on cash; the company bought property, plant, and equipment requiring $172.3 million of cash. However, financing activities were an even larger drain on cash; Quaker purchased its own common stock, requiring $323.1 million in cash. As we will see in Chapter 11, companies repurchase their own stock for a variety of reasons. In Quaker's case, the repurchased shares are used for stock option and incentive plans.

In summary, Quaker generated a very sizable amount of cash from the manufacture and sale of its products during 1993. However, a slightly larger amount of cash was used to add to property, plant, and equipment and for various financing activities, such as payment of cash dividends and the repurchase of the company's own stock on the market. The result was a net decrease in cash of $34.2 million. At this point, you should verify that the bottom line on the cash flow statement, the amount of

EXHIBIT 2-16 Quaker Oats' Comparative Statements of Cash Flows

Dollars in Millions

Consolidated Statements of Cash Flows	Year Ended June 30	1993	1992	1991
	Cash Flows from Operating Activities:			
	Net income	**$171.3**	$247.6	$205.8
	Adjustments to reconcile net income to net cash provided by operating activities:			
	Cumulative effect of accounting changes	**115.5**	—	—
	Depreciation and amortization	**156.9**	155.9	177.7
	Deferred income taxes and other items	**(46.4)**	—	14.0
	Restructuring charges and gains on divestitures—net	**20.5**	(1.0)	10.0
	Loss on disposition of property and equipment	**23.8**	23.1	17.9
	Decrease (Increase) in trade accounts receivable	**59.1**	84.7	(116.6)
	Decrease (Increase) in inventories	**41.9**	(14.3)	30.7
	(Increase) Decrease in other current assets	**(25.8)**	(10.1)	5.1
	(Decrease) Increase in trade accounts payable	**(7.6)**	24.0	19.2
	(Decrease) Increase in other current liabilities	**(6.4)**	132.5	56.6
	Change in deferred compensation	**11.0**	11.6	(0.2)
	Other items	**44.4**	(43.1)	27.4
	Change in payable to Fisher-Price	**—**	(29.6)	29.6
	Change in net current assets of discontinued operations	**—**	—	66.0
	Net Cash Provided by Operating Activities	**558.2**	581.3	543.2
	Cash Flows from Investing Activities:			
	Additions to property, plant and equipment	**(172.3)**	(176.4)	(240.6)
	Change in other receivables and investments	**(25.6)**	(20.0)	(10.7)
	Purchases and sales of property and businesses, net	**1.2**	16.5	—
	Discontinued operations	**—**	—	(19.8)
	Net Cash Used in Investing Activities	**(196.7)**	(179.9)	(271.1)
	Cash Flows from Financing Activities:			
	Cash dividends	**(140.3)**	(132.8)	(123.0)
	Change in short-term debt	**67.0**	(19.6)	(265.6)
	Proceeds from long-term debt	**0.5**	1.1	1.8
	Reduction of long-term debt	**(59.0)**	(46.2)	(39.7)
	Proceeds from short-term debt to be refinanced	**—**	50.0	—
	Proceeds from issuance of debt for Fisher-Price spin-off	**—**	—	141.1
	Issuance of common treasury stock	**23.3**	20.3	25.6
	Repurchases of common stock	**(323.1)**	(235.1)	—
	Repurchases of preferred stock	**(1.1)**	(0.9)	(0.7)
	Net Cash Used in Financing Activities	**(432.7)**	(363.2)	(260.5)
	Effect of Exchange Rate Changes on Cash and Cash Equivalents	**37.0**	(17.6)	(6.0)
	Net (Decrease) Increase in Cash and Cash Equivalents	**(34.2)**	20.6	5.6
	Cash and Cash Equivalents—Beginning of Year	**95.2**	74.6	69.0
	Cash and Cash Equivalents—End of Year	**$ 61.0**	$ 95.2	$ 74.6

See accompanying notes to the consolidated financial statements.

FROM CONCEPT TO PRACTICE

READING BEN & JERRY'S STATEMENT OF CASH FLOWS

Refer to the statement of cash flows in Ben & Jerry's annual report. What was the largest cash inflow for the current year? The largest cash outflow?

LO 9

Describe the various elements in the annual report of a publicly held company.

cash and cash equivalents at the end of the period, $61.0 million, agrees with the amount of cash and cash equivalents as shown on the balance sheet for Quaker in Exhibit 2-5.

Other Elements of an Annual Report

No two annual reports look the same. The appearance of an annual report depends not only on the size of a company but also on the budget devoted to the preparation of the report. Some companies publish "bare-bones" annual reports, whereas others issue a glossy report complete with pictures of company products and employees. In recent years, many companies have scaled back the amount spent on the annual report as a cost-cutting measure. For example, General Motors printed a recent annual report on plain paper. The creativity in annual reports varies as well. McDonald's 1991 annual report looked like an issue of *The Wall Street Journal,* and its 1992 report was available with a video. Ben & Jerry's stitched the cover of its annual report one year as a way to support the sewing industry in central Vermont.

Privately held companies tend to distribute only financial statements, without the additional information normally included in the annual reports of public companies. For the annual reports of public companies, however, certain basic elements are considered standard. A letter to the stockholders from either the president or the chairman of the board of directors appears in the first few pages of most annual reports. A section describing the company's products and markets is usually included. At the heart of any annual report is the financial report or review, which consists of the financial statements accompanied by certain other basic elements. We will now consider these other elements as presented in the 1992 annual report of McDonald's Corporation.

Report of Management and Report of Independent Auditors

The first page in McDonald's Financial Review consists of two important statements. These are titled "Management's report" and "Report of independent auditors." Each of these reports sets out the responsibilities of each group for the financial statements. These two reports are reproduced in Exhibit 2-17.

The first sentence in management's report clearly states its responsibility for the information in the annual report. The first paragraph also refers to generally accepted accounting principles. There are also references in the report to the company's independent auditors and to the audit committee of the board of directors.

Two key phrases should be noted in the first sentence of the last paragraph of the report of independent auditors, or auditors' report as it is commonly called: *in our opinion* and *present fairly.* The report indicates that responsibility for the statements rests with McDonald's and that the auditors' job is to *express an opinion* on the statements based on certain tests. It would be impossible for an auditing firm to spend the time or money to retrace and verify every single transaction entered into during the year by McDonald's. Instead, the firm performs various tests of the accounting records to be able to assure itself that the statements are free of *material misstatement.* Auditors do not "certify" the total accuracy of a set of financial statements but render an opinion as to the reasonableness of those statements.

The Ethical Responsibility of Management and the Auditors

Management of a company and its auditors share a common purpose: to protect the interests of stockholders. In large corporations, the stockholders are normally removed from the daily affairs of the business. The need for a professional management team to run the business is a practical necessity, as is the need for a periodic audit of the company's records. Because stockholders cannot run the business themselves, they need assurances that the business is being operated effectively and efficiently and that the financial statements presented by management are a fair representation of the company's operations and financial position. Management and the auditors have a very important ethical responsibility to their constituents, the stockholders of the company.

EXHIBIT 2-17 McDonald's 1992 Report of Management and Report of Independent Auditors

FINANCIAL REVIEW

Management's report

Management is responsible for the preparation and integrity of the consolidated financial statements and Financial Comments appearing in this annual report. The financial statements were prepared in accordance with generally accepted accounting principles and include certain amounts based on management's best estimates and judgments. Other financial information presented in the annual report is consistent with the financial statements.

The Company maintains a system of internal accounting controls designed to provide reasonable assurance that assets are safeguarded, and that transactions are executed as authorized and are recorded and reported properly. This system of controls is based upon written policies and procedures, appropriate divisions of responsibility and authority, careful selection and training of personnel and utilization of an internal audit program. Policies and procedures prescribe that the Company and all employees are to maintain the highest ethical standards and that business practices throughout the world are to be conducted in a manner which is above reproach.

Ernst & Young, independent auditors, has audited the Company's financial statements and their report is presented herein.

The Board of Directors has an Audit Committee composed entirely of outside Directors. Ernst & Young has direct access to the Audit Committee and periodically meets with the Committee to discuss accounting, auditing and financial reporting matters.

McDONALD'S CORPORATION

Oak Brook, Illinois
January 27, 1993

Report of independent auditors

The Board of Directors and Shareholders
McDonald's Corporation

We have audited the accompanying consolidated balance sheet of McDonald's Corporation as of December 31, 1992 and 1991, and the related consolidated statements of income, shareholders' equity and cash flows for each of the three years in the period ended December 31, 1992. These financial statements are the responsibility of McDonald's Corporation's management. Our responsibility is to express an opinion on these financial statements based on our audits.

We conducted our audits in accordance with generally accepted auditing standards. Those standards require that we plan and perform the audit to obtain reasonable assurance about whether the financial statements are free of material misstatement. An audit includes examining, on a test basis, evidence supporting the amounts and disclosures in the financial statements. An audit also includes assessing the accounting principles used and significant estimates made by management, as well as evaluating the overall financial statement presentation. We believe that our audits provide a reasonable basis for our opinion.

In our opinion, the financial statements referred to above present fairly, in all material respects, the consolidated financial position of McDonald's Corporation at December 31, 1992 and 1991, and the consolidated results of its operations and its cash flows for each of the three years in the period ended December 31, 1992, in conformity with generally accepted accounting principles.

ERNST & YOUNG

Chicago, Illinois
January 27, 1993

Management Discussion and Analysis

Preceding the financial review is a section of McDonald's annual report titled "Year in Review." This report, commonly called *management discussion and analysis,* gives management the opportunity to discuss the financial statements and provide the stockholders with explanations for certain amounts reported in the statements. For

A SMALL INVESTOR

Name: Rick Boettcher
Profession: Pharmacist
College Major: Pharmacy

Four days a week, Rick Boettcher is a practicing pharmacist. But his true love is the stock market. His home office is equipped with the latest investment software and databases. He can get the latest news on the 20 stocks he owns, mostly small companies that aren't well known. But even though he's instantly updated on the numbers, Boettcher doesn't like to buy a stock until he reads the company's annual report.

Sure, the annual report has the income statement and balance sheet—critical data for investors. But it also has some intangibles that the numbers can't convey. The chairman's letter is very important to him, especially if the company has had a rough time. "I'll look at the CEO's reasoning," says Boettcher. "If he or she says 'We didn't do so well. Because the economy failed to improve,' then that's a red flag that they're not being aggressive in improving the company's prospects."

Since he invests primarily in small companies, he'd rather the company not spend a lot of money on the annual report. For one thing, he doesn't have time to read a 100-page document. And he would look askance at a company that obviously spent lavishly on the annual report—but wasn't very profitable.

"I place great emphasis on growth in revenues and growth in earnings," says Boettcher, describing the kind of companies that interest him. "You may have had a real good year in earnings but if your revenues are flat, then your earnings are from cost cutting. Once you've cut costs, what are you going to do next to increase profits?" The annual report may explain the company's marketing strategy and prospects for growth.

On the balance sheet, Boettcher focuses on the current ratio. "If the ratio is low, they may be facing a cash squeeze and can't take advantage of opportunities as they arise," he says. He also checks to make sure that inventory isn't piling up—and that long-term debt as a percentage of stockholders' equity is declining.

Still, it's the annual report's written words—and sometimes the message conveyed "between the lines" that Boettcher says he can't get anywhere else. The chairman's message. The corporate strategy. Even the footnotes to the financials. "It's the qualitative factor that I'm interested in," says Boettcher. "I can get a lot of the numbers that I need from the computer."

example, management explains the increase in general, administrative, and selling expenses as follows:

The 1992 increase was due to higher employee costs associated with expansion, partially offset by a reduction in U.S. marketing costs associated with the value program. The 1991 increase was due to higher advertising costs on a worldwide basis, and higher employee costs outside of the U.S. resulting from expansion. These expenses—as a percent of Systemwide sales—have remained relatively constant over the past five years and were 3.9% in 1992 and 4.0% in 1991.[12]

[12] *McDonald's 1992 Annual Report,* Year in Review, p. 12.

Notes to Consolidated Financial Statements

The following appears at the bottom of each of McDonald's four financial statements: "The accompanying Financial Comments are an integral part of the consolidated financial statements." These comments, or *footnotes,* as they are commonly called, are necessary to satisfy the need for *full disclosure* of all the facts relevant to a company's results and financial position. The first footnote in all annual reports is a summary of *significant accounting policies.* A company's policies for valuing inventories, depreciating assets, and recognizing revenue are among the important items contained in this footnote. For example, McDonald's describes its policy for depreciating assets as follows:

> Property and equipment are stated at cost with depreciation and amortization provided on the straight-line method over the following estimated useful lives: buildings—up to 40 years; leasehold improvements—lesser of useful lives of assets or lease terms including option periods; and equipment—3 to 12 years.[13]

In addition to the summary of significant accounting policies, other footnotes discuss such areas as long-term debt and taxes. One of McDonald's footnotes lists all of the company's debt obligations, with the amounts maturing in each year.

Summary of Selected Financial Data

It is common to include in an annual report a summary of selected data, such as revenue, net income, and total assets, for the current year and a number of prior years. McDonald's report includes an 11-year summary. These summaries allow the reader to look for trends in the data and, the company hopes, will aid him or her in predicting future sales and earnings for the company.

This completes our discussion of the makeup of the annual report. By now you should appreciate the flexibility companies have in assembling the report, aside from the need to follow generally accepted accounting principles in preparing the statements. It should be noted that the accounting standards followed in preparing the statements, as well as the appearance of the annual report itself, differ in other countries. As has been noted elsewhere, although many corporations operate internationally, accounting principles are far from being standardized.

The following review problem will give you the opportunity to apply what you have learned by preparing two of the financial statements for an actual company.

REVIEW PROBLEM

Shown below, in alphabetical order, are items taken from the 1992 financial statements of Wm. Wrigley Jr. Company, the well-known manufacturer of chewing gums. You are to use the items to prepare two statements. First, prepare a *combined statement of income and retained earnings* for the year ended December 31, 1992. The income statement should be in *single-step form.* Second, prepare a *classified balance sheet* at December 31, 1992. The descriptions in parentheses are *not* part of the items but have been added to provide you with certain hints. The solution that follows is a reprint of the two actual statements published by Wrigley.

---

[13] *McDonald's 1992 Annual Report,* Financial Comments, p. 24.

ITEMS
(ALL AMOUNTS ARE IN THOUSANDS OF DOLLARS)

Accounts payable	$ 53,761
Accounts receivable	95,939
Accrued expenses (current liability)	50,912
Accumulated depreciation (deduct from total property, plant, and equipment)	291,280
Additional paid-in capital	1,568
Buildings and building equipment	166,342
Cash and cash equivalents	84,144
Class B common stock—convertible (show after common stock)	3,457
Common stock	12,121
Cost of sales	572,468
Cumulative effect of an accounting change (show as last item before net income as a deduction)	7,278
Deferred income taxes—current asset	4,217
Deferred income taxes—noncurrent asset	13,942
Deferred income taxes—current liability	634
Deferred income taxes—noncurrent liability	13,220
Dividends declared	74,409
Dividends payable	11,683
Foreign currency translation adjustment (show as the last line in stockholders' equity as a deduction)	9,692
Income and other taxes payable	32,500
Income taxes (expense)	83,730
Interest (expense)	1,173
Inventories—Finished goods	38,352
Raw materials and supplies	117,403
Investment and other income	14,346
Land	17,010
Machinery and equipment	330,065
Marketable equity securities (noncurrent asset)	2,539
Net sales	1,286,921
Other assets and deferred charge (noncurrent asset)	24,115
Other current assets	10,270
Other noncurrent liabilities	49,727
Retained earnings at beginning of the year	579,665
Selling, distribution, and general administrative (expense)	495,323
Short-term investments	98,314
Treasury stock retirement (show as a deduction on the statement of retained earnings)	155,070

■ SOLUTION TO REVIEW PROBLEM

STATEMENT OF
CONSOLIDATED EARNINGS AND RETAINED EARNINGS

WM. WRIGLEY JR. COMPANY AND WHOLLY OWNED ASSOCIATED COMPANIES

YEAR ENDED DECEMBER 31	1992	1991	1990
	In thousands of dollars except for per share amounts		
EARNINGS			
Revenues:			
Net sales	$1,286,921	1,148,875	1,110,639
Investment and other income	14,346	10,888	12,869
Total revenues	1,301,267	1,159,763	1,123,508
Costs and expenses:			
Cost of sales	572,468	507,795	508,957
Selling, distribution and general administrative	495,323	442,575	425,175
Interest	1,173	1,379	1,117
Total costs and expenses	1,068,964	951,749	935,249
Earnings before income taxes and cumulative effect of accounting changes	232,303	208,014	188,259
Income taxes	83,730	79,362	70,897
Earnings before cumulative effect of accounting changes	148,573	128,652	117,362
Cumulative effect of accounting changes for:			
Postretirement benefits — net of income tax effect	(10,143)	—	—
Income taxes	2,865	—	—
Net earnings	141,295	128,652	117,362
RETAINED EARNINGS			
Retained earnings at beginning of the year	$ 579,665	515,615	458,247
Dividends declared (per share: 1992—$.63; 1991—$.55; 1990—$.51)	(74,409)	(64,602)	(59,994)
Treasury stock retirement	(155,070)	—	—
Retained earnings at end of the year	$ 491,481	579,665	515,615
PER SHARE AMOUNTS			
Earnings before cumulative effect of accounting changes	$ 1.27	1.09	1.00
Cumulative effect of accounting changes, net	(.06)	—	—
Net earnings per average share of common stock	$ 1.21	1.09	1.00
Dividends paid per share of common stock	$ .62	.55	.49

See accompanying accounting policies and notes.

CONSOLIDATED BALANCE SHEET

WM. WRIGLEY JR. COMPANY AND WHOLLY OWNED ASSOCIATED COMPANIES

As of December 31	1992	1991
	In thousands of dollars	

ASSETS

	1992	1991
Current assets:		
Cash and cash equivalents	$ 84,144	73,335
Short-term investments, at cost which approximates market	98,314	71,575
Accounts receivable		
(less allowance for doubtful accounts: **1992—$2,357;** 1991—$2,454)	95,939	92,527
Inventories—		
Finished goods	38,352	37,736
Raw materials and supplies	117,403	117,770
	155,755	155,506
Other current assets	10,270	10,415
Deferred income taxes - current	4,217	—
Total current assets	448,639	403,358
Marketable equity securities, at cost		
(market value: **1992—$29,501;** 1991—$28,553)	$ 2,539	2,540
Other assets and deferred charges	24,115	17,790
Deferred income taxes—noncurrent	13,942	—
Property, plant and equipment, at cost:		
Land	17,010	16,629
Buildings and building equipment	166,342	157,044
Machinery and equipment	330,065	312,848
	513,417	486,521
Less accumulated depreciation	291,280	285,135
	222,137	201,386
Total assets	$711,372	625,074

(continued)

Balance Sheet (*continued*)

AS OF DECEMBER 31	1992	1991
	In thousands of dollars and shares	

LIABILITIES AND STOCKHOLDERS' EQUITY

Current liabilities:

	1992	1991
Accounts payable	$ 53,761	48,034
Accrued expenses	50,912	43,224
Dividends payable	11,683	9,785
Income and other taxes payable	32,500	26,268
Deferred income taxes—current	634	—
Total current liabilities	149,490	127,311
Deferred income taxes—noncurrent	13,220	7,763
Other noncurrent liabilities	49,727	26,601

Stockholders' equity:

Preferred stock—no par value
  Authorized: 2,000 shares
  Issued: None

Common stock—no par value
  Common stock
    Authorized: 150,000 shares

	1992	1991
Issued: **1992—90,411 shares;** 1991—116,862 shares	$ 12,121	15,582

Class B common stock—convertible
  Authorized: 45,000 shares

	1992	1991
Issued and outstanding: **1992—26,423 shares;** 1991—27,138 shares	3,457	3,618
Additional paid-in capital	1,568	2,504
Retained earnings	491,481	579,665
Foreign currency translation adjustment	(9,692)	5,719
Common stock in treasury, at cost (1991—26,582 shares)	—	(143,689)
Total stockholders' equity	498,935	463,399
Total liabilities and stockholders' equity	$711,372	625,074

See accompanying accounting policies and notes.

GUIDANCE ANSWERS TO ACCOUNTING FOR YOUR DECISIONS

YOU ARE THE SUPPLIER

1. United's current ratio is approximately .68 and .71 at the end of 1992 and 1991, respectively.

2. The slight decrease in the current ratio between these two years should not be a major concern, unless this is a trend that has been in process for many years. You may want to compare United's current ratio with that of some of the other major airlines.

YOU ARE THE INVESTOR

It is true that Quaker's net income decreased significantly from 1992 to 1993. However, income from continuing operations increased rather than decreased. The decrease in the bottom-line net income was caused by a line called "cumulative effect of accounting changes." Assuming that this item is not expected to recur in the future, the potential stockholder should look favorably on the picture portrayed on Quaker's comparative income statements.

CHAPTER HIGHLIGHTS

1. **(LO 1)** The primary objective of financial reporting is to provide information that is useful in making investment, credit, and similar decisions.

2. **(LO 1)** Investors and creditors are ultimately interested in their own prospective cash receipts from dividends or interest and the proceeds from the sale, redemption, or maturity of loans. Because these expected cash flows are related to the expected cash flows to the company, its cash flows are of interest to investors and creditors. Information about the entity's economic resources, claims to them, and the effects of transactions that change resources and claims to those resources are also of interest.

3. **(LO 2)** Financial information should be understandable to those who are willing to spend the time to understand it. To be useful, the information should be relevant and reliable. Relevant information has the capacity to make a difference in a decision. Reliable information can be depended on to represent the economic events that it purports to represent.

4. **(LO 2)** Comparability is the quality that allows for comparisons to be made between two or more companies whereas consistency is the quality that allows for

comparisons to be made within a single company from one period to the next. These two qualities of useful accounting information are aided by full disclosure in the footnotes to the financial statements of all relevant information.

5. **(LO 3)** The operating cycle depends to a large extent on the nature of a company's business. For a retailer, it encompasses the period of time from the investment of cash in inventory to the collection of any account receivable from sale of the product. The operating cycle for a manufacturer is expanded to include the period of time required to convert raw materials into finished products.

6. **(LO 3)** Current assets will be realized in cash or sold or consumed during the operating cycle or within one year if the cycle is shorter than one year. Because most businesses have numerous operating cycles within a year, the cut-off for classification as a current asset is usually one year. Cash, accounts receivable, inventory, and prepaid expenses are all examples of current assets.

7. **(LO 3)** The definition of *current liability* is related to that of *current asset*. A current liability is an obligation that will be satisfied within the operating cycle or within one year if the cycle is shorter than one year. Many liabilities are satisfied by making a cash payment. However, some obligations are settled by rendering a service.

8. **(LO 4)** A classified balance sheet is helpful in evaluating the liquidity of a business. Working capital is the difference between current assets and current liabilities, and it indicates the buffer of protection for creditors. The current ratio, current assets divided by current liabilities, provides the reader with a relative measure of liquidity. The debt-to-equity ratio is a useful measure of the long-run solvency of a company.

9. **(LO 5)** All expenses are added together and subtracted from all revenues in a single-step income statement. The multiple-step income statement provides the reader with classifications of revenues and expenses as well as with important subtotals. Cost of goods sold is subtracted from sales revenue on a multiple-step statement, with the result reported as gross profit.

10. **(LO 6)** Profitability analysis includes such measures as the gross profit ratio—the ratio of gross profit to sales—and the profit margin—the ratio of net income to sales. A combination of information from the balance sheet and the income statement is useful in assessing profitability. The return on stockholders' equity ratio indicates net income relative to the investment made by the stockholders.

11. **(LO 7,8)** A statement of stockholders' equity summarizes the changes in owners' equity during the period. If there are no changes in the capital stock accounts, some companies present a statement of retained earnings or a combined statement of income and retained earnings. The statement of cash flows summarizes the operating, investing, and financing activities of an entity for the period.

12. **(LO 9)** No two annual reports are the same. However, certain basic elements are included in most of them. In addition to the financial statements, annual reports include the reports of management and the independent auditors, management's discussion of the amounts appearing in the statements, footnotes to the statements, and a summary of selected financial data over a period of years.

KEY TERMS QUIZ

Select from the following list of key terms used in the chapter and fill in the appropriate blank to the left of each description. The solution appears at the end of the chapter.

Understandability	**Relevance**
Reliability	**Comparability**
Depreciation	**Consistency**
Materiality	**Conservatism**
Operating cycle	**Current asset**
Current liability	**Liquidity**
Working capital	**Current ratio**
Debt-to-equity ratio	**Debt-to-total assets ratio**
Comprehensive income	**Single-step income statement**
Multiple-step income statement	**Gross profit**
Gross profit ratio	**Profit margin**
Earnings per share	**Return on stockholders' equity**

_____ **1.** An income statement in which all expenses are added together and subtracted from all revenues.

_____ **2.** The magnitude of an omission or misstatement in accounting information that will affect the judgment of someone relying on the information.

_____ **3.** The capacity of information to make a difference in a decision.

——————————————————   **4.** An income statement that provides the reader with classifications of revenues and expenses as well as with important subtotals.

——————————————————   **5.** The practice of using the least optimistic estimate when two estimates of amounts are about equally likely.

——————————————————   **6.** The change in equity during a period from transactions and other events from nonowner sources.

——————————————————   **7.** The quality of accounting information that makes it comprehensible to those willing to spend the necessary time.

——————————————————   **8.** Net income divided by number of common shares outstanding.

——————————————————   **9.** Gross profit divided by sales.

——————————————————   **10.** Current assets divided by current liabilities.

——————————————————   **11.** The quality of accounting information that makes it dependable in representing the events that it purports to represent.

——————————————————   **12.** An obligation that will be satisfied within the next operating cycle or within one year if the cycle is shorter than one year.

——————————————————   **13.** The period of time between the purchase of inventory and the collection of any receivable from the sale of the inventory.

——————————————————   **14.** Total liabilities divided by total stockholders' equity.

——————————————————   **15.** Current assets minus current liabilities.

——————————————————   **16.** Net income divided by sales.

——————————————————   **17.** The quality of accounting information that allows a user to analyze two or more companies and look for similarities and differences.

——————————————————   **18.** Total liabilities divided by total assets.

——————————————————   **19.** An asset that is expected to be realized in cash or sold or consumed during the operating cycle or within one year if the cycle is shorter than one year.

——————————————————   **20.** The ability of a company to pay its debts as they come due.

——————————————————   **21.** The quality of accounting information that allows a user to compare two or more accounting periods for a single company.

——————————————————   **22.** Sales less cost of goods sold.

——————————————————   **23.** Net income divided by average stockholders' equity.

——————————————————   **24.** The allocation of the cost of a tangible, long-term asset over its useful life.

ALTERNATE TERMS

BALANCE SHEET Statement of financial position or condition.

CAPITAL STOCK Contributed capital.

GROSS PROFIT Gross margin.

INCOME STATEMENT Statement of income.

INCOME TAX EXPENSE Provision for income taxes.

LONG-TERM ASSETS Noncurrent assets.

NET INCOME Profits or earnings.

REPORT OF INDEPENDENT AUDITORS Auditors' report.

REPORT OF MANAGEMENT Management's report.

RETAINED EARNINGS Earned capital.

QUESTIONS

1. How would you evaluate the following statement: "The cash flows to a company are irrelevant to an investor. All the investor cares about is the potential for receiving dividends on the investment"?

2. A key characteristic of useful financial information is understandability. How does this qualitative characteristic relate to the background of the user of the information?

3. What does *relevance* mean with regard to the use of accounting information?

4. What is the qualitative characteristic of comparability and why is it important in preparing financial statements?

5. What is the difference between comparability and consistency as they relate to the use of accounting information?

6. How does the concept of materiality relate to the size of a company?

7. How does the operating cycle of a retailer differ from that of a service company?

8. How does the concept of the operating cycle relate to the definition of a current asset?

9. What are two examples of the way the intent of a company in using an asset affects its classification on the balance sheet?

10. How would you evaluate the following statement: "A note payable with an original maturity of five years will be classified on the balance sheet as a long-term liability until it matures"?

11. How do the two basic forms of owners' equity items for a corporation, capital stock and retained earnings, differ?

12. What are the limitations of working capital as a measure of the liquidity of a business as opposed to the current ratio?

13. What is meant by a company's capital structure?

14. How would you evaluate the following statement: "The debt-to-total assets ratio is a better indicator of a company's solvency than is the debt-to-equity ratio"?

15. What is the major weakness of the single-step form for the income statement?

16. Why might a company's gross profit ratio increase from one year to the next but its profit margin ratio decrease?

17. What advantage does the return on stockholders' equity ratio have over the profit margin ratio as a measure of profitability?

18. Why should *average* stockholders' equity be used in calculating return on stockholders' equity?

19. How does a statement of retained earnings act as a link between an income statement and a balance sheet?

20. How would you evaluate the following statement: "A statement of cash flows is unnecessary, and actually redundant, because the increase or decrease in cash for the period can be easily calculated by looking at the cash account on two successive balance sheets"?

21. In auditing the financial statements of a company, does a certified public accountant *certify* that the statements are totally accurate and without errors of any size or variety?

22. What is the first footnote in the annual report of all publicly held companies and what is its purpose?

EXERCISES

(LO 2) **EXERCISE 2-1 CHARACTERISTICS OF USEFUL ACCOUNTING INFORMATION**

Fill in the blank with the qualitative characteristic for each of the following descriptions:

————————————— **1.** Information that users can depend on to represent the events that it purports to represent.

————————————— **2.** Information that has the capacity to make a difference in a decision.

————————————— **3.** Information that is valid, that indicates that there is agreement between the underlying data and the events represented.

————————————— **4.** Information that allows for comparisons to be made from one accounting period to the next.

————————————— **5.** Information that is free from error.

————————————— **6.** Information that is meaningful to those who are willing to learn to use it properly.

————————————— **7.** Information that is not slanted to portray a company's position any better or worse than the circumstances warrant.

————————————— **8.** Information that allows for comparisons to be made between or among companies.

(LO 3) **EXERCISE 2-2 CLASSIFICATION OF ASSETS AND LIABILITIES**

Indicate the appropriate classification of each of the following as either a current asset (CA), noncurrent asset (NCA), current liability (CL), or long-term liability (LTL):

————————————— **1.** Inventory

————————————— **2.** Accounts payable

————————————— **3.** Cash

————————————— **4.** Patents

————————————— **5.** Notes payable, due in six months

————————————— **6.** Taxes payable

————————————— **7.** Prepaid rent (for the next nine months)

————————————— **8.** Bonds payable, due in 10 years

————————————— **9.** Machinery

(LO 7) **EXERCISE 2-3 STATEMENT OF RETAINED EARNINGS**

Birch Corporation was organized on January 2, 1993, with the investment of $100,000 by each of its two stockholders. Net income for its first year of business was $85,200. It increased during 1994 to $125,320 and to $145,480 during 1995. Birch paid $20,000 in dividends to each of the two stockholders in each of the three years.

Prepare, in good form, a statement of retained earnings for the year ended December 31, 1995.

(LO 4) **EXERCISE 2-4 RELATIONSHIP BETWEEN THE DEBT-TO-EQUITY RATIO AND THE DEBT-TO-TOTAL ASSETS RATIO**

Denver Corporation has a debt-to-total assets ratio of .40 to 1. Total debt or liabilities amount to $64,000. What is the dollar amount of total assets? What is the company's debt-to-equity ratio? Is the *information* provided by these two ratios different? Explain your answer.

(LO 8) **EXERCISE 2-5 COMPONENTS OF THE STATEMENT OF CASH FLOWS**

From the following list, identify each item as operating (O), investing (I), financing (F), or not on the statement of cash flows (N).

_____ Paid for supplies

_____ Sold products

_____ Purchased land (held for resale)

_____ Purchase land (for construction of new building)

_____ Paid dividend

_____ Issued stock

_____ Purchased computers

_____ Sold old equipment

(LO 9) **EXERCISE 2-6 BASIC ELEMENTS OF FINANCIAL STATEMENTS**

Most financial reports contain the following list of basic elements. For each element, identify the person(s) who prepared the element and describe the information a user would expect to find in each element. Some information is verifiable; other information is subjectively chosen by management. Comment on the verifiability of information in each element.

Management's report

Product/markets of company

Financial statements

Notes to financial statements

Auditors' opinion

MULTI-CONCEPT EXERCISES

(LO 1, 3, 6, 7) **EXERCISE 2-7 FINANCIAL STATEMENT ANALYSIS**

Potential stockholders and lenders are interested in a company's financial statements. From the list below, identify the statement (balance sheet, income statement, retained earnings statement) on which each item would appear. Which items are of the most interest to stockholders and lenders? Why?

Accounts receivable	Accounts payable
Advertising expense	Bad debt expense
Bonds payable	Buildings
Cash	Depreciation expense
Deferred income taxes	Dividends
Common stock	Land held for future expansion
Loss on the sale of equipment	Organizational costs
Office supplies	Patent amortization expense
Retained earnings	Sales
Unearned revenue	Utilities expense

(LO 5, 6) **EXERCISE 2-8 SINGLE- AND MULTIPLE-STEP INCOME STATEMENT**

Some headings and/or items are used on either the single-step or the multiple step income statements. Some are used on both. For the list below, indicate the following: single-step (S), multi-step (M), both formats (B), or not used on either income statement (N).

_____ Sales

_____ Cost of goods sold

_____ Selling expenses

_____ Total revenues

_____ Utilities expense

_____ Administrative expense

_____ Net loss

_____ Supplies on hand

_____ Accumulated depreciation

_____ Gross profit

(LO 5, 6) EXERCISE 2-9 MULTIPLE-STEP INCOME STATEMENT

Annie Bell's partial income statement follows:

Sales	$1,200,000
Cost of sales	450,000
Selling expenses	60,800
General and admin. expenses	75,000

Determine the gross profit ratio, profit margin, earnings per share (1,000,000 shares outstanding), and price-earnings ratio (the market price is $7.50). Would you consider investing in Annie Bell? Explain your answer.

PROBLEMS

(LO 4) PROBLEM 2-1 FINANCIAL STATEMENT RATIOS

The following items, in alphabetical order, are available from the records of Marshall Corporation as of December 31, 1995 and 1994:

	DECEMBER 31, 1995	DECEMBER 31, 1994
Accounts payable	$ 8,400	$ 5,200
Accounts receivable	13,230	19,570
Cash	10,200	9,450
Cleaning supplies	450	700
Interest payable	–0–	1,200
Inventory	24,600	26,200
Marketable securities	6,250	5,020
Note payable, due in six months	–0–	12,000
Prepaid rent	3,600	4,800
Taxes payable	1,450	1,230
Wages payable	1,200	1,600

1. Calculate the following ratios, as of December 31, 1995, and December 31, 1994:   ■ REQUIRED

   a. Working capital

   b. Current ratio

2. On the basis of your answers in part 1, comment on the relative liquidity of the company at the beginning and end of the year. As part of your answer, explain the change in the company's liquidity from the beginning to the end of the year.

(LO 3) PROBLEM 2-2 CLASSIFIED BALANCE SHEET

The following balance sheet items, listed in alphabetical order, are available from the records of Ruth Corporation at December 31, 1995.

Accounts payable	$ 18,255
Accounts receivable	23,450
Accumulated depreciation—buildings	40,000
Accumulated depreciation—automobiles	22,500
Automobiles	112,500
Bonds payable, due December 31, 1999	160,000
Buildings	200,000
Capital stock, $10 par value	150,000
Cash	13,230
Income taxes payable	6,200
Interest payable	1,500
Inventory	45,730
Land	250,000
Long-term investments	85,000
Notes payable, due June 30, 1996	10,000
Office supplies	2,340
Paid-in capital in excess of par value	50,000
Patents	40,000
Prepaid rent	1,500
Retained earnings	311,095
Salaries and wages payable	4,200

■ **REQUIRED**

1. Prepare in good form a classified balance sheet as of December 31, 1995.

2. Compute Ruth's current ratio.

3. On the basis of your answer to requirement 2, does Ruth appear to be *liquid?* What other information do you need to fully answer this question?

(LO 5) PROBLEM 2-3 SINGLE-STEP INCOME STATEMENT

The following income statement items, arranged in alphabetical order, are taken from the records of Oak Corporation for the year ended December 31, 1995.

Advertising expense	$ 1,500
Commissions expense	2,415
Cost of goods sold	29,200
Depreciation expense—office building	2,900
Income tax expense	1,540
Insurance expense—salespersons' autos	2,250
Interest expense	1,400
Interest revenue	1,340
Rent revenue	6,700
Salaries and wages expense—office	12,560
Sales revenue	48,300
Supplies expense—office	890

■ **REQUIRED**

1. Prepare in good form a single-step income statement for the year.

2. What weaknesses do you see in this form for the income statement?

(LO 5) PROBLEM 2-4 MULTIPLE-STEP INCOME STATEMENT

Refer to the list of income statement items in Problem 2-3. Assume that Oak Corporation classifies all operating expenses into two categories, (1) selling and (2) general and administrative.

1. Prepare in good form a multiple-step income statement for the year.

2. Compute Oak's gross profit percentage.

3. What does this percentage tell you about Oak's mark-up on its products?

■ REQUIRED

(LO 8) PROBLEM 2-5 STATEMENT OF CASH FLOWS

Colorado Corporation was organized on January 1, 1995, with the investment of $250,000 in cash by its stockholders. The company immediately purchased an office building for $300,000, paying $210,000 in cash and signing a three-year promissory note for the balance. Colorado signed a five-year, $60,000 promissory note at a local bank during 1995 and received cash in the same amount. During its first year, Colorado generated $4,870 in cash from operations and paid $5,600 in cash dividends.

1. Prepare in good form a statement of cash flows for the year ended December 31, 1995.

2. What does this statement tell you that an income statement doesn't?

■ REQUIRED

(LO 2) PROBLEM 2-6 DEPRECIATION

A salesperson is expected to use his new car for the next three years and during that period he expects to drive 150,000 miles. The car costs $36,000 and is expected to be sold for $6,000 at the end of three years. The company knows that it must depreciate the car, which means that it will match the cost of the car with the benefit derived from its use. The company is uncertain, however, about which of the following methods to use.

a. Depreciate a higher amount in the first year because the car loses more market value in the early years.

b. Depreciate the same amount every year.

c. Use either miles driven or sales dollars as the basis of allocation.

1. Rank the options in order of most appropriate to least appropriate.

2. Make a recommendation to the company and be prepared to support it.

■ REQUIRED

(LO 2) PROBLEM 2-7 MATERIALITY

Jenny Bee, a newly hired accountant, wanted to impress her boss, so she stayed late one night to analyze the office supplies expense. She determined the cost by month, for the past 12 months, of each of the following: computer paper, copy paper, fax paper, pencils and pens, note pads, postage, corrections supplies, stationery, and miscellaneous items.

1. What did Jenny think her boss would learn from this information? What action might be taken as a result of knowing it?

2. Would this information be more relevant if Jenny worked for a hardware store or for a real estate company? Discuss.

■ REQUIRED

(LO 2) PROBLEM 2-8 COSTS AND EXPENSES

The following costs are incurred by a retailer:

Display fixtures in a retail store
Advertising
Merchandise for sale
Incorporation (i.e., legal costs, stock issue costs)
Cost of a franchise
Office supplies
Wages in a restaurant
Computer software
Computer hardware

■ REQUIRED   For each of these costs, explain whether all of the cost or only a portion of the cost would appear as an expense on the income statement for the period in which the cost was incurred. If not all of the cost would appear on the income statement for that period, explain why.

(LO 4) PROBLEM 2-9 WORKING CAPITAL AND CURRENT RATIO

The balance sheet of Stevenson, Inc., includes the following items:

Cash	$ 23,000
Accounts receivable	13,000
Inventory	45,000
Prepaid insurance	800
Land	80,000
Accounts payable	54,900
Salaries payable	1,200
Capital stock	100,000
Retained earnings	5,700

■ REQUIRED   **1.** Determine the current ratio and working capital.

2. Beyond the information provided in your answers to 1, what does the composition of the current assets tell you about Stevenson's liquidity?

3. What other information do you need to fully assess Stevenson's liquidity?

(LO 7) PROBLEM 2-10 STATEMENT OF STOCKHOLDERS' EQUITY AND RETAINED EARNINGS

Timeshare, Inc., includes the changes in retained earnings in a statement that combines retained earnings and stockholders' equity. Use the following information to complete the statement for the years 1992, 1993, and 1994.

1992	Net income, $5,000,000
	Dividends, $1,000,000
1993	Net income, $12,000,000
	Dividends, $1,100,000
	Issued 100,000 shares of stock for $2 each
1994	Net income, $18,000,000
	Dividends, $1,650,000
	Stock split, 2 for 1 (the number of shares outstanding doubled and the par value per share reduced by one-half)

	NUMBER OF SHARES	COMMON STOCK, PAR	PAID-IN CAPITAL	RETAINED EARNINGS	TOTAL
Jan. 1, 1992	1,000,000	$1,000,000	$500,000	$462,000	$1,962,000
Dec. 31, 1992					
Dec. 31, 1993					
Dec. 31, 1994					

(LO 9) PROBLEM 2-11 BASIC ELEMENTS OF FINANCIAL REPORTS

Comparative income statements for Grammar, Inc., are presented below.

	1995	1994
Sales	$1,000,000	$500,000
Cost of sales	500,000	300,000
Gross margin	$ 500,000	$200,000
Operating expenses	120,000	100,000
Operating income	$ 380,000	$100,000
Loss on sale of subsidiary	(400,000)	—
Net income	$ (20,000)	$100,000

■ REQUIRED

The president and management believe that the company is in better financial condition at the end of 1995 than it was at the beginning of the year. Write the letter from the president to be included in the 1995 annual report. Explain why the company is financially sound and shareholders should not be alarmed by the $20,000 loss in a year when sales have doubled.

MULTI-CONCEPT PROBLEMS

(LO 2, 5) PROBLEM 2-12 COMPARABILITY AND CONSISTENCY IN INCOME STATEMENTS

The following income statements were provided by Munuz Company, a retailer:

1994 INCOME STATEMENT		1993 INCOME STATEMENT	
Sales	$1,700,000	Sales	$1,500,000
Cost of sales	520,000	Cost of sales	450,000
Gross profit	$1,180,000	Sales salaries	398,000
Selling expense	702,000	Advertising	175,000
Administrative expense	95,000	Office supplies	54,000
Total selling and administrative expense	$ 797,000	Depreciation—building	40,000
		Delivery expense	20,000
		Total expenses	$1,137,000
Net income	$ 383,000	Net income	$ 363,000

■ REQUIRED

1. Identify each income statement as either single-step or multiple-step format.
2. Convert the 1993 income statement to the same format as the 1994 income statement.

(LO 1, 4, 8) PROBLEM 2-13 CASH FLOW

Franklin Co., a specialty retailer, has a history of paying quarterly dividends of $.50 per share. Management is trying to determine whether the company will have adequate cash on December 31, 1995, to pay a dividend if one is declared by the board of directors. The following additional information is available:

■ All sales are on account, and accounts receivable are collected one month after the sale. Sales volume has been increasing 5% each month.

■ All purchases of merchandise are on account, and accounts payable are paid one month after the purchase. Cost of sales is 40% of the sales price. Inventory levels are maintained at $75,000.

- Operating expenses in addition to the mortgage are paid in cash. They amount to $3,000 per month and are paid as they are incurred.

FRANKLIN CO.
BALANCE SHEET
SEPTEMBER 30, 1995

Cash	$ 5,000	Accounts payable	$ 5,000
Accounts receivable	12,500	Mortgage note†	150,000
Inventory	75,000	Common stock—$1 par	50,000
Note receivable*	10,000	Retained earnings	66,500
Building/Land	169,000	Total liabilities	
Total assets	$271,500	and stockholders' equity	$271,500

*Notes Receivable represents a one-year, 5% interest-bearing note, due November 1.
†Mortgage note is 30-year, 7% note due in monthly installments of $1,200.

■ REQUIRED Determine the cash that Franklin will have available to pay a dividend on December 31, 1995. Round all amounts to the nearest dollar. What can Franklin's management do to increase the cash available? Should management recommend that the board of directors declare a dividend?

ALTERNATE PROBLEMS

(LO 4) PROBLEM 2-1A FINANCIAL STATEMENT RATIOS

The following items, in alphabetical order, are available from the records of Jenkins Corporation as of December 31, 1995 and 1994:

	DECEMBER 31, 1995	DECEMBER 31, 1994
Accounts payable	$10,500	$ 6,500
Accounts receivable	16,500	26,000
Cash	12,750	11,800
Office supplies	900	1,100
Interest receivable	200	–0–
Note receivable, due 12/31/97	12,000	12,000
Prepaid insurance	400	250
Taxes payable	10,000	5,800
Salaries payable	1,800	800

■ REQUIRED
1. Calculate the following ratios, as of December 31, 1995, and December 31, 1994:
   a. Working capital
   b. Current ratio

2. On the basis of your answers in part 1, comment on the relative liquidity of the company at the beginning and end of the year. As part of your answer, explain the change in the company's liquidity from the beginning to the end of 1995.

(LO 3) PROBLEM 2-2A CLASSIFIED BALANCE SHEET

The following balance sheet items, listed in alphabetical order, are available from the records of Singer Company at December 31, 1995.

Accounts payable	$ 34,280
Accounts receivable	26,700
Accumulated depreciation—buildings	40,000
Accumulated depreciation—equipment	12,500
Bonds payable, due December 31, 2001	250,000
Buildings	150,000
Capital stock, $1 par value	200,000
Cash	60,790
Equipment	84,500
Income taxes payable	7,500
Interest payable	2,200
Land	250,000
Merchandise inventory	112,900
Marketable securities	15,000
Notes payable, due April 15, 1996	6,500
Office supplies	400
Paid-in capital in excess of par value	75,000
Patents	45,000
Prepaid rent	3,600
Retained earnings	113,510
Salaries payable	7,400

REQUIRED

1. Prepare in good form a classified balance sheet as of December 31, 1995.

2. Compute Singer's current ratio.

3. On the basis of your answer to requirement 2, does Singer appear to be *liquid?* What other information do you need to fully answer this question?

(LO 5) PROBLEM 2-3A SINGLE-STEP INCOME STATEMENT

The following income statement items, arranged in alphabetical order, are taken from the records of Lucky Enterprises, a software sales firm, for the year ended December 31, 1995.

Advertising expense	$ 9,000
Cost of goods sold	150,000
Depreciation expense—computer	4,500
Dividend revenue	2,700
Income tax expense	30,700
Interest expense	1,900
Rent expense—salesperson's car	18,000
Rent expense—office	26,400
Sales revenue	350,000
Supplies expense—office	1,300
Utilities expense	6,750
Wages expense—office	45,600

REQUIRED

1. Prepare in good form a single-step income statement for the year.

2. What weaknesses do you see in this form for the income statement?

(LO 5) PROBLEM 2-4A MULTIPLE-STEP INCOME STATEMENT

Refer to the list of income statement items in Problem 2-3A. Assume that Lucky Enterprises classifies all operating expenses into two categories, (1) selling and (2) general and administrative.

■ REQUIRED

1. Prepare in good form a multiple-step income statement for the year.

2. Compute Lucky's gross profit percentage.

3. What does this percentage tell you about Lucky's mark-up on its products?

(LO 8) PROBLEM 2-5A STATEMENT OF CASH FLOWS

Wisconsin Corporation was organized on January 1, 1995, with the investment of $400,000 in cash by its stockholders. The company immediately purchased a manufacturing facility for $300,000, paying $150,000 in cash and signing a five-year promissory note for the balance. Wisconsin signed another five-year note at the bank for $50,000 and received cash for the same amount. During its first year, Wisconsin generated $54,900 in cash from operations and paid $4,000 in dividends.

■ REQUIRED

1. Prepare in good form a statement of cash flows for the year ended December 31, 1995.

2. What does this statement tell you that an income statement doesn't?

(LO 2) PROBLEM 2-6A DEPRECIATION

A new restaurant is expected to use a broasting oven for the next three years and during that period expects to prepare 150,000 meals from the oven. The oven costs $8,500 and is expected to be sold for $400 at the end of three years. The company knows that it must depreciate the oven, which means that it will match the cost with the benefit derived from its use. The company is uncertain, however, about which of the following methods to use.

a. Depreciate a higher amount in the first year because the oven loses more market value in the early years.

b. Depreciate the same amount every year.

c. Use either meals prepared or sales dollars as the basis of allocation.

■ REQUIRED

1. Rank the options in order of most appropriate to least appropriate.

2. Make a recommendation to the company and be prepared to support it.

(LO 2) PROBLEM 2-7A MATERIALITY

Sara Barkley, a newly hired accountant, wanted to impress her boss, so she stayed late one night to analyze the long distance calls by area codes and time of day placed. She determined the cost by month, for the past 12 months, by hour, and area code called.

■ REQUIRED

1. What did Sara think her boss would learn from this information? What action might be taken as a result of knowing it?

2. Would this information be more relevant if Sara worked for a hardware store or for a real estate company? Discuss.

(LO 2) PROBLEM 2-8A COSTS AND EXPENSES

The following costs are incurred by a retailer:

Point-of-sale systems in a retail store

An ad in the yellow pages

An inventory control computer software system

Shipping merchandise for resale to our chain outlets

For each of these costs, explain whether all of the cost or only a portion of the cost would appear as an expense on the income statement for the period in which the cost is incurred. If not all of the cost would appear on the income statement for that period, explain why.

■ REQUIRED

(LO 4) PROBLEM 2-9A WORKING CAPITAL AND CURRENT RATIO

The balance sheet of Kapinski, Inc., includes the following items:

Cash	$ 23,000
Accounts receivable	43,000
Inventory	75,000
Prepaid insurance	2,800
Land	80,000
Accounts payable	84,900
Salaries payable	3,200
Capital stock	100,000
Retained earnings	35,700

1. Determine the current ratio and working capital.

■ REQUIRED

2. Kapinski appears to have a positive current ratio and a large net working capital. Why would it have trouble paying bills as they come due?

3. Suggest three things that Kapinski can do to help it pay bills on time.

(LO 7) PROBLEM 2-10A STATEMENT OF STOCKHOLDERS' EQUITY AND RETAINED EARNINGS

Texas Two-step, Inc., includes the changes in retained earnings in a statement that combines retained earnings and stockholders' equity. Use the following information to complete the statement for the years 1992, 1993, and 1994.

1992	Net income, $45,000
	Dividends, $21,000
1993	Net loss, ($15,000)
	Dividends, $11,000
	Issued 100,000 shares of stock for $6 each
1994	Net income, $15,000
	Dividends, $11,650

TEXAS TWO-STEP, INC.
STATEMENT OF STOCKHOLDERS' EQUITY AND RETAINED EARNINGS

	NUMBER OF SHARES	COMMON STOCK, PAR	PAID-IN CAPITAL	RETAINED EARNINGS	TOTAL
Jan.1, 1992	7,000,000	$7,000,000	$900,000	$162,000	$8,062,000
Dec. 31, 1992					
Dec. 31, 1993					
Dec. 31, 1994					

(LO 9) PROBLEM 2-11A BASIC ELEMENTS OF FINANCIAL REPORTS

Comparative income statements for Thesaurus, Inc., are presented below.

	1995	1994
Sales	$1,000,000	$500,000
Cost of sales	500,000	300,000
Gross margin	$ 500,000	$200,000
Operating expenses	120,000	100,000
Operating income	$ 380,000	$100,000
Gain on the sale of subsidiary	—	400,000
Net income	$ 380,000	$500,000

■ **REQUIRED** The president and management believe that the company is in better financial condition at the end of 1995 than it was at the beginning of the year. Write the letter from the president to be included in the 1995 annual report. Explain why the company is financially sound and shareholders should not be alarmed by the reduction in income in a year when sales have doubled.

ALTERNATE MULTI-CONCEPT PROBLEMS

(LO 2,5) PROBLEM 2-12A COMPARABILITY AND CONSISTENCY IN INCOME STATEMENTS

The following income statements were provided by Sweeny Company, a wholesale food distributor:

	1994	1993
Sales	$1,700,000	$1,500,000
Cost of sales	612,000	450,000
Sales salaries	427,000	398,000
Delivery expense	180,000	175,000
Office supplies	55,000	54,000
Depreciation—truck	40,000	40,000
Computer line expense	23,000	20,000
Total expenses	$1,137,000	$1,337,000
Net income	$ 363,000	$ 363,000

■ **REQUIRED** 1. Identify the income statements as either single-step or multiple-step format.

2. Restate each item in the income statements as a percentage of sales. Why did net income remain unchanged when sales increased?

(LO 1, 4, 8) PROBLEM 2-13A CASH FLOW

Roosevelt, Inc., a consulting service, has a history of paying annual dividends of $1 per share. Management is trying to determine whether the company will have adequate cash on December 31, 1995, to pay a dividend if one is declared by the board of directors. The following additional information is available:

- All sales are on account, and accounts receivable are collected one month after the sale. Sales volume has been decreasing 5% each month.

- Operating expenses are paid in cash in the month incurred. Average monthly expenses are $10,000 (exluding the biweekly payroll).

- Biweekly payroll is $4,500 and it will be paid December 15 and December 31.

- Unearned revenue is expected to be earned in December. This amount was taken into consideration in the expected sales volume.

ROOSEVELT, INC.
BALANCE SHEET
DECEMBER 1, 1995

Cash	$ 15,000	Unearned revenue	$ 2,000
Accounts receivable	40,000	Notes payable*	30,000
Computer equipment	120,000	Common stock—$2 par	50,000
		Retained earnings	$ 93,000
		Total liabilities and	
Total assets	$175,000	stockholders' equities	$175,000

*The note payable plus 3% interest for six months is due January 15, 1996.

■ **REQUIRED**

Determine the cash that Roosevelt will have available to pay a dividend on December 31, 1995. Should management recommend that the board of directors declare a dividend?

CASES

READING AND INTERPRETING FINANCIAL STATEMENTS

(LO 9) CASE 2-1 INTERPRETATION OF AN AUDITORS' REPORT

The following is an excerpt from a retailer's 1993 annual report. Explain the significance of each of the words or phrases in italics. Why does the board of directors contract with an accounting firm to perform an audit?

> We have *audited* the accompanying consolidated balance sheets . . . as of January 31, 1993 and 1992, and the related consolidated statements of income, shareholders' equity, and cash flows for each of the three years in the period ended January 31, 1993. The *financial statements are the responsibility of the Company's management.* Our responsibility is to *express an opinion* on these financial statements based on our audits.
>   We conducted our audits in accordance with generally accepted auditing standards. Those standards require that we plan and perform the audit to *obtain reasonable assurance* about whether the financial statements are free of *material misstatement.**

*Wal-Mart annual report, 1993, p. 18.

(LO 5, 6) CASE 2-2 PROFITABILITY ANALYSIS

The income statements for a specialty retailer are presented below in a condensed form, rounded to the nearest million except for the shares outstanding.

	1993	1992	1991
Sales	$629	$587	$563
Cost of sales	383	358	352
Selling expenses	180	173	170
Depreciation	15	15	14
Interest	15	16	12
Loss on sale of subsidiary	6	—	—
Taxes	9	9	5
Loss from subsidiary	4	4	2
Income	$ 17	$ 12	$ 8

Shares outstanding each year:
37,500,000 shares

For each year, compute the gross profit ratio, profit margin, and earnings per share. Why did the income go up so much in 1993? To compare operating results from one year to the next, it is sometimes helpful to take out nonrecurring items and subsidiary income (loss). After doing this, what statement can you make about 1993 that was not evident before? Would you recommend investing in this company? What other information would you want to know first?

MAKING FINANCIAL DECISIONS

(LO 8) CASE 2-3 ANALYSIS OF CASH FLOW FOR A SMALL BUSINESS

Charles, a financial consultant, has been self-employed for two years. His list of clients has grown, and he is earning a reputation as a shrewd investor. Charles rents a small office, uses the pool secretarial services, and has purchased a car that he is depreciating over three years. The following income statements cover Charles's first two years of business:

	YEAR 1	YEAR 2
Commissions revenue	$ 25,000	$65,000
Rent	12,000	12,000
Secretarial services	3,000	9,000
Car expenses, gas, insurance	6,000	6,500
Depreciation	15,000	15,000
Net income	$(11,000)	$22,500

Charles believes that he should earn more than $11,500 for working very hard for two years. He is thinking about going to work for an investment firm where he can earn $40,000 each year. What would you advise Charles to do?

(LO 9) CASE 2-4 FACTORS INVOLVED IN AN INVESTMENT DECISION

As an investor, you are considering purchasing stock in a fast-food restaurant chain. The annual reports of several companies are available for comparison.

Prepare an outline of the steps you would follow to make your comparison. Start by listing the first section on the financial reports that you would read. What would you expect to find there and why did you choose that section first? Continue with the other sections of the financial report.

Many fast-food chains are owned by large conglomerates (i.e., PepsiCo owns Taco Bell, KFC, and Pizza Hut). What limitation does this create in your comparison? How would you solve it?

ACCOUNTING AND ETHICS: WHAT WOULD YOU DO?

(LO 4, 6) CASE 2-5 BARBARA APPLIES FOR A LOAN

Barbara Bites, owner of Bites of Bagels, a drive-through bagel shop, would like to expand her business from its current one location to a chain of bagel shops. Sales in the bagel shop have been increasing an average of 8% each quarter. Profits have been increasing accordingly. Barbara is conservative in spending and a very hard worker. She has an appointment with a banker to apply for a loan to expand the business. To prepare for the appointment, she instructs you, as the chief financial officer and payroll clerk, to copy the quarterly income statements for the past two years but not to include a balance sheet. Barbara already has a substantial loan from another bank on the books. In fact, she has very little of her own money invested in the business.

What should you do? Do you think the banker will lend Barbara more money?

(LO 2) CASE 2-6 THE EXPENDITURE APPROVAL PROCESS

Roberto is the plant superintendent of a small manufacturing company that is owned by a large corporation. The corporation has a policy that any expenditure over $1,000 must be approved by the chief financial officer in the corporate headquarters. The approval process takes a minimum of three weeks. Roberto would like to order a new labeling machine that is expected to reduce costs and pay for itself in six months. The machine costs $2,200, but Roberto can buy the sales rep's demo for $1,800. Roberto has asked the sales rep to send two separate bills for $900 each.

What would you do if you were the sales rep? Do you agree or disagree with Roberto's actions? What do you think about the corporate policy?

ANALYTICAL SOFTWARE CASE

To the Student: Your instructor may assign one or more parts of the analytical software case that is designed to accompany this chapter. This multi-part case gives you a chance to work with real financial statement data using software that stimulates, guides, and hones your analytical and problem-solving skills. It was created especially to support and strengthen your understanding of the chapter's Learning Objectives.

SOLUTION TO KEY TERMS QUIZ

1. Single-step income statement (p. 72)
2. Materiality (p. 58)
3. Relevance (p. 56)
4. Multiple-step income statement (p. 72)
5. Conservatism (p. 59)
6. Comprehensive income (p. 71)
7. Understandability (p. 55)
8. Earnings per share (p. 76)
9. Gross profit ratio (p. 75)
10. Current ratio (p. 64)
11. Reliability (p. 57)
12. Current liability (p. 63)
13. Operating cycle (p. 59)
14. Debt-to-equity ratio (p. 66)
15. Working capital (p. 64)
16. Profit margin (p. 75)
17. Comparability (p. 57)
18. Debt-to-total assets ratio (p. 67)
19. Current asset (p. 60)
20. Liquidity (p. 64)
21. Consistency (p. 58)
22. Gross profit (p. 74)
23. Return on stockholders' equity (p. 76)
24. Depreciation (p. 57)

Focus on Financial Results

Magazines, recording artists, theme parks, movies, HBO, and Cinemax are all part of **Time Warner, Inc.,** one of the world's largest entertainment and publishing conglomerates. And Time Warner believes its future lies with its cable segment's Full Service Network™, "the world's first interactive electronic superhighway to the home."

Time Warner was once two separate companies: Time Inc. and Warner Bros. The

Time Warner's strength comes from the global distribution of our unmatched, ever-expanding libraries of journalistic and artistic expression.

two merged in the late 1980s, and the combined entity took on more than $10 billion in debt. Since that time, Wall Street analysts could not evaluate the company using their normal standards—earnings per share, price-earnings ratios, and so forth. The reason was that interest charges made the bottom line negative, even though each component business—Time, HBO, and the others—was highly profitable. Today, the investment community analyzes Time Warner by looking at its "EBITDA"—earnings before interest, taxes, depreciation, and amortization. EBITDA is a measure of cash flow—and separates operating performance from the company's debt load. Indeed, the stock rose steadily and split 4:1 in 1993 as investors focused on the company's improving operating cash flows in each core business.

FINANCIAL HIGHLIGHTS

Years Ended December 31, (millions, except per share amounts)	1993(a)	Restated 1992(a)
EBITDA (b)		
TIME WARNER		
Publishing	$ 372	$ 328
Music	643	585
ENTERTAINMENT GROUP		
Filmed Entertainment	549	520
Programming–HBO	230	215
Cable	1,035	977
Combined EBITDA	$ 2,829	$ 2,625
Combined Revenues	$14,544	$13,560
Income (loss) before unusual and extraordinary items	$ (94)	$ 86
Net income (loss) (c)	$ (221)	$ 86
Loss per common share, after preferred dividend requirements:		
Loss before unusual and extraordinary items	$ (.56)	$ (1.46)
Net loss (c)	$ (.90)	$ (1.46)

(a) The 1993 operating results of Time Warner reflect the deconsolidation of the Entertainment Group effective January 1, 1993. Within the Entertainment Group, the operating results of Filmed Entertainment reflect the consolidation of Six Flags effective January 1, 1993. Prior period results have been restated for comparability.

(b) EBITDA (Earnings Before Interest, Taxes, Depreciation and Amortization) presents business segment operating income before depreciation and amortization expense, including amortization relating to the $14 billion acquisition of Warner Communications Inc. in 1989, the $1.3 billion acquisition of the minority interest in American Television and Communications Corporation in 1992 and other business combinations accounted for by the purchase method. Although it is one way Wall Street measures cash flow, EBITDA is not adjusted for all noncash expenses or for working capital, capital expenditures and other investment requirements.

(c) The net loss for the year ended December 31, 1993 includes an extraordinary loss on the retirement of debt of $57 million ($.15 per common share) and an unusual charge of $70 million ($.19 per common share) for the effect of the new income tax law on Time Warner's deferred income tax liability.

Chapter 3

Processing Accounting
Information

LEARNING OBJECTIVES

After studying this chapter, you should be able to

1. Explain the difference between an external and an internal event.
2. Explain the role of source documents in an accounting system.
3. Analyze the effects of transactions on the accounting equation.
4. Define the concept of a general ledger and use the T account as a method for analyzing transactions.
5. Explain the rules of debits and credits.
6. Record journal entries.
7. Explain how journal entries are transferred to the general ledger.
8. Explain the purpose of a trial balance.

Linkages

⚙ A LOOK AT PREVIOUS CHAPTERS

Up to this point, we have focused our attention on the role of accounting in decision making and the way accountants use financial statements to communicate useful information to the various users of the statements.

⚙ A LOOK AT THIS CHAPTER

In this chapter, we consider how accounting information is *processed*. We begin by considering the *inputs* to an accounting system, that is, the transactions entered into by a business. We look at how transactions are analyzed and then turn to a number of accounting tools and procedures designed to facilitate the preparation of the *outputs* of the system, the financial statements. Ledger accounts, journal entries, and trial balances are tools that allow a company to process vast amounts of data efficiently.

⚙ A LOOK AT UPCOMING CHAPTERS

Chapter 4 concludes our overview of the accounting model. We will examine the accrual basis of accounting and its effect on the measurement of income. Adjusting entries, which are the focus of the accrual basis, will be discussed in detail in Chapter 4, along with the other steps in the accounting cycle.

Economic Events—The Basis for Recording Transactions

Many different types of economic events affect an entity during the year. A sale is made to a customer. Inventory is purchased from a supplier. A loan is taken out at the bank. A fire destroys a warehouse. A new contract is signed with the union. In short, "An **event** is a happening of consequence to an entity."[1]

External and Internal Events

Two types of events affect an entity: internal and external. An **external event** "involves interaction between the entity and its environment."[2] For example, the *purchase* of raw material from a supplier is an external event, as is the *sale* of inventory to a customer. An **internal event** occurs entirely within the entity. The *transfer* of raw material into production is an internal event as is the use of a piece of equipment. We will use the term **transaction** to refer to any event, external or internal, that is recognized in a set of financial statements.[3]

What is necessary to recognize an event in the records? Are all economic events recognized as transactions by the accountant? The answers to these questions involve the concept of *measurement.* An event must be measured to be recognized. Certain events are relatively easy to measure: the payroll for the week, the amount of inventory destroyed by an earthquake, or the sales for the day. Not all events that affect an entity can be measured *reliably,* however. For example, how does a manufacturer of breakfast cereal measure the effect of a drought on the price of wheat? A company hires a new chief executive. How can it reliably measure the value of the new officer to the company? There is no definitive answer to the measurement problem in accounting. It is a continuing challenge to the accounting profession and something we will return to throughout the text.

The Role of Source Documents in Recording Transactions

The initial step in the recording process is one of *identification.* A business needs a systematic method for recognizing events as transactions. A **source document** provides the evidence needed in an accounting system to record a transaction. Source documents take many different forms. An invoice received from the supplier is the source document for a purchase of inventory on credit. A cash register tape is the source document used by a retailer to recognize a cash sale. The payroll department forwards the time cards for the week to the accountant as the necessary documentation to record wages.

Not all recognizable events are supported by a standard source document. For certain events, it is necessary to generate some form of documentation. For example, no standard source document exists to recognize the financial consequences from a fire or the settlement of a lawsuit. Documentation is just as important for these types of events as it is for standard, recurring transactions.

---

[1] *Statement of Financial Accounting Concepts No. 3,* "Elements of Financial Statements of Business Enterprises" (Stamford, Conn.: Financial Accounting Standards Board, 1982), par. 65.
[2] *SFAS No. 3.*
[3] Technically, a transaction is defined by the Financial Accounting Standards Board as a special kind of external event in which the entity exchanges something of value with an outsider. Because the term *transaction* is used in practice to refer to any event that is recognized in the statements, we will use this broader definition.

Analyzing the Effects of Transactions on the Accounting Equation

Economic events are the basis for recording transactions in an accounting system. For every transaction it is essential to analyze its effect on the accounting equation

Assets = Liabilities + Owners' Equity

We will now consider a series of events and their recognition as transactions for a hypothetical corporation, Glengarry Health Club.

(**1**) *Issuance of capital stock.* The company is started when Mary-Jo Kovach and Irene McGuinness file articles of incorporation with the state to obtain a charter. Each invests $50,000 in the business. In return, each receives 5,000 shares of capital stock. Thus, at this point, each of them owns 50 percent of the outstanding stock of the company and has a claim to 50 percent of its assets. The effect of this transaction on the accounting equation is to increase both assets and owners' equity:

LO 3
Analyze the effects of transactions on the accounting equation.

			Assets			=	Liabilities	+	Owners' Equity	
NUMBER	CASH	ACCOUNTS RECEIVABLE	EQUIPMENT	BUILDING	LAND		ACCOUNTS PAYABLE	NOTES PAYABLE	CAPITAL STOCK	RETAINED EARNINGS
1	$100,000								$100,000	
Totals:			$100,000						$100,000	

As you see, each side of the accounting equation increases by $100,000. Cash is increased and because the owners contributed this amount, their claim to the assets is increased in the form of capital stock.

The start-up of a new business can consist of hundreds or thousands of details: Finding and leasing the right retail space, searching for an architect, the approval of logo and interior designs, the construction of a store interior, conceiving and paying for an advertising campaign for the new store, ordering and delivery of goods for resale, depositing the first day's sales revenues. These details, if they are measurable, are economic events *that must be accounted for in transactions identified by source documents like lease agreements, contracts, invoices, delivery vouchers, and deposit slips.*

(**2**) *Acquisition of property in exchange for a note.* The company buys a piece of property for $200,000. The seller agrees to accept a five-year promissory note. The note is given by the health club to the seller and is a written promise to repay the principal amount of the loan at the end of five years. To the company, the promissory note is a liability. The property consists of land valued at $50,000 and a newly constructed building valued at $150,000. The effect of this transaction on the accounting equation is to increase both assets and liabilities by $200,000:

| | | | Assets | | | = | Liabilities | + | Owners' Equity | |
| | | | | | | | | | | |
NUMBER	CASH	ACCOUNTS RECEIVABLE	EQUIPMENT	BUILDING	LAND		ACCOUNTS PAYABLE	NOTES PAYABLE	CAPITAL STOCK	RETAINED EARNINGS
Bal.	$100,000								$100,000	
2				$150,000	$50,000			$200,000		
Bal.	$100,000			$150,000	$50,000			$200,000	$100,000	
	Totals:		$300,000					$300,000		

(**3**) *Acquisition of equipment on an open account.* Mary-Jo and Irene contact an equipment supplier and buy $20,000 of exercise equipment: treadmills, barbells, and stationary bicycles. The supplier agrees to accept payment in full in 30 days. The health club has acquired an asset and at the same time incurred a liability:

| | | | Assets | | | = | Liabilities | + | Owners' Equity | |
| | | | | | | | | | | |
NUMBER	CASH	ACCOUNTS RECEIVABLE	EQUIPMENT	BUILDING	LAND		ACCOUNTS PAYABLE	NOTES PAYABLE	CAPITAL STOCK	RETAINED EARNINGS
Bal.	$100,000			$150,000	$50,000			$200,000	$100,000	
3			$20,000				$20,000			
Bal.	$100,000		$20,000	$150,000	$50,000		$20,000	$200,000	$100,000	
	Totals:		$320,000					$320,000		

An important principle governs the accounting for both the exercise equipment and the building and land. The cost principle requires that we record an asset at the cost to acquire it and continue to show this amount on all balance sheets until we dispose of the asset. With a few exceptions, an asset is not carried at its market value but at its original cost. Why not show the land on future balance sheets at its market value? While this might seem more appropriate in certain instances, the *subjectivity* inherent in determining market values is a major reason for the practice of carrying assets at their historical cost. The cost of an asset is subject to verification by an independent observer and is much more *objective* than market value.

(**4**) *Sale of monthly memberships on account.* The owners open their doors for business. During the first month, they sold 300 monthly club memberships for $50 each, or a total of $15,000. The members have until the 10th of the following month to pay. Glengarry does not have cash from the new members but instead has a promise from each member to pay cash in the future. The promise from a customer to pay an amount owed is another form of asset called an *account receivable.* The other side of this transaction is an increase in the owners' equity (specifically retained earnings) in the business. In other words, the assets have increased by $15,000 without any increase in a liability or a decrease in another asset. The increase in owners' equity indicates that the owners' residual interest in the assets of the business has increased by this amount. More specifically, an inflow of assets resulting from the sale of goods and services by a business is called *revenue*. The change in the accounting equation follows:

| | Assets | | | | | = | Liabilities | + | Owners' Equity | |
NUMBER	CASH	ACCOUNTS RECEIVABLE	EQUIPMENT	BUILDING	LAND		ACCOUNTS PAYABLE	NOTES PAYABLE	CAPITAL STOCK	RETAINED EARNINGS
Bal.	$100,000		$20,000	$150,000	$50,000		$20,000	$200,000	$100,000	
4		$15,000								$15,000
Bal.	$100,000	$15,000	$20,000	$150,000	$50,000		$20,000	$200,000	$100,000	$15,000
Totals:			$335,000					$335,000		

(5) *Sale of court time for cash.* In addition to memberships, Glengarry sells court time. Court fees are paid at the time of use and amount to $5,000 for the first month:

| | Assets | | | | | = | Liabilities | + | Owners' Equity | |
NUMBER	CASH	ACCOUNTS RECEIVABLE	EQUIPMENT	BUILDING	LAND		ACCOUNTS PAYABLE	NOTES PAYABLE	CAPITAL STOCK	RETAINED EARNINGS
Bal.	$100,000	$15,000	$20,000	$150,000	$50,000		$20,000	$200,000	$100,000	$15,000
5	$ 5,000									$ 5,000
Bal.	$105,000	$15,000	$20,000	$150,000	$50,000		$20,000	$200,000	$100,000	$20,000
Totals:			$340,000					$340,000		

The only difference between this transaction and (4) is that cash is received rather than a promise to pay at a later date. Both transactions result in an increase in an asset and an increase in the owners' claim to the assets. In both cases, there is an inflow of assets, in the form of either accounts receivable or cash. Thus, in both cases, the company has earned revenue.

(6) *Payment of wages and salaries.* The wages and salaries for the first month amount to $10,000. The payment of this amount results in a decrease in cash and a decrease in the owners' claim on the assets, that is, a decrease in retained earnings. More specifically, an outflow of assets resulting from the sale of goods or services is called an *expense*. The effect of this transaction is to decrease both sides of the accounting equation:

| | Assets | | | | | = | Liabilities | + | Owners' Equity | |
NUMBER	CASH	ACCOUNTS RECEIVABLE	EQUIPMENT	BUILDING	LAND		ACCOUNTS PAYABLE	NOTES PAYABLE	CAPITAL STOCK	RETAINED EARNINGS
Bal.	$105,000	$15,000	$20,000	$150,000	$50,000		$20,000	$200,000	$100,000	$20,000
6	−10,000									−10,000
Bal.	$ 95,000	$15,000	$20,000	$150,000	$50,000		$20,000	$200,000	$100,000	$10,000
Totals:			$330,000					$330,000		

(7) *Payment of utilities.* The cost of utilities for the first month is $3,000. Glengarry pays this amount in cash. Both the utilities and the salaries and wages are expenses, and they have the same effect on the accounting equation. Cash is decreased with a corresponding decrease in the owners' claim on the assets of the business:

	Assets					=	Liabilities	+	Owners' Equity	
NUMBER	CASH	ACCOUNTS RECEIVABLE	EQUIPMENT	BUILDING	LAND	ACCOUNTS PAYABLE	NOTES PAYABLE	CAPITAL STOCK	RETAINED EARNINGS
Bal.	$95,000	$15,000	$20,000	$150,000	$50,000	$20,000	$200,000	$100,000	$10,000
7	−3,000								−3,000
Bal.	$ 92,000	$15,000	$20,000	$150,000	$50,000	$20,000	$200,000	$100,000	$ 7,000
Totals:			$327,000					$327,000	

(8) *Collection of accounts receivable.* Even though the January monthly memberships are not due until the 10th of the following month, some of the members pay their bill by the end of January. The amount received from members in payment of their accounts is $4,000. The effect of the collection of an open account is to increase cash and decrease accounts receivable:

	Assets					=	Liabilities	+	Owners' Equity	
NUMBER	CASH	ACCOUNTS RECEIVABLE	EQUIPMENT	BUILDING	LAND	ACCOUNTS PAYABLE	NOTES PAYABLE	CAPITAL STOCK	RETAINED EARNINGS
Bal.	$92,000	$15,000	$20,000	$150,000	$50,000	$20,000	$200,000	$100,000	$7,000
8	4,000	−4,000							
Bal.	$ 96,000	$11,000	$20,000	$150,000	$50,000	$20,000	$200,000	$100,000	$7,000
Totals:			$327,000					$327,000	

This is the first transaction we have seen that affects only one side of the accounting equation. In fact, the company simply traded assets: accounts receivable for cash. Thus, note that the totals for the accounting equation remain at $327,000.

(9) *Payment of dividends.* At the end of the month, Mary-Jo and Irene, acting on behalf of Glengarry Health Club, decide to pay a dividend of $1,000 on the shares of stock owned by each of them, or $2,000 in total. The effect of this dividend is to decrease cash and retained earnings. That is, the company is returning cash to the owners, based on the profitable operations of the business for the first month. The transaction not only reduces cash but also decreases the owners' claims on the assets of the company. The effect on the accounting equation follows:

	Assets					=	Liabilities	+	Owners' Equity	
NUMBER	CASH	ACCOUNTS RECEIVABLE	EQUIPMENT	BUILDING	LAND	ACCOUNTS PAYABLE	NOTES PAYABLE	CAPITAL STOCK	RETAINED EARNINGS
Bal.	$96,000	$11,000	$20,000	$150,000	$50,000	$20,000	$200,000	$100,000	$7,000
9	−2,000								−2,000
Bal.	$94,000	$11,000	$20,000	$150,000	$50,000	$20,000	$200,000	$100,000	$5,000
Totals:			$325,000					$325,000	

Nearly all accountants now enter information from source documents into computerized accounting systems rather than make manual entries onto ledger and journal pages. Computerized systems make retrieving and analyzing information for decision making, as this accountant is doing, faster and more accurate.

Balance Sheet and Income Statement for the Health Club

To summarize, Exhibit 3-1 indicates the effect of each transaction on the accounting equation, specifically the individual items increased or decreased by each transaction. Note the *dual* effect of each transaction. At least two items were involved in each transaction. For example, the initial investment by the owners resulted in an increase in an asset and an increase in capital stock. The payment of the utility bill caused a decrease in an asset and a decrease in retained earnings.

You can now see the central idea behind the accounting equation: even though individual transactions may change the amount and composition of the assets and liabilities, the *equation* must always balance *for* each transaction and the *balance sheet* must balance *after* each transaction.

A balance sheet for Glengarry Health Club appears in Exhibit 3-2. All of the information needed to prepare this statement is available in Exhibit 3-1. The balances at the bottom of this exhibit are entered on the balance sheet, with assets on the left side and liabilities and owners' equity on the right side.

An income statement for Glengarry is shown in Exhibit 3-3. An income statement summarizes the revenues and expenses of a company for a period of time. In our example, the statement is for the month of January, as indicated on the third line of the heading of the statement. Glengarry earned revenues from two sources: memberships and court fees. Two types of expenses were incurred: (1) salaries and wages and (2) utilities. The difference between the total revenues of $20,000 and the total expenses of $13,000 is the net income for the month of $7,000. Finally, remember that dividends appear on a statement of retained earnings, rather than an income statement. They are a *distribution* of net income of the period, not a *determinant* of net income as are expenses.

EXHIBIT 3-1   Glengarry Health Club Transactions for the Month of January

	Assets					=	Liabilities	+	Owners' Equity	
NO.	CASH	ACCOUNTS RECEIVABLE	EQUIPMENT	BUILDING	LAND		ACCOUNTS PAYABLE	NOTES PAYABLE	CAPITAL STOCK	RETAINED EARNINGS
1	$100,000								$100,000	
2				$150,000	$50,000			$200,000		
Bal.	$100,000			$150,000	$50,000			$200,000	$100,000	
3			$20,000				$20,000			
Bal.	$100,000		$20,000	$150,000	$50,000		$20,000	$200,000	$100,000	
4		$15,000								$ 15,000
Bal.	$100,000	$15,000	$20,000	$150,000	$50,000		$20,000	$200,000	$100,000	$ 15,000
5	5,000									5,000
Bal.	$105,000	$15,000	$20,000	$150,000	$50,000		$20,000	$200,000	$100,000	$ 20,000
6	− 10,000									− 10,000
Bal.	$ 95,000	$15,000	$20,000	$150,000	$50,000		$20,000	$200,000	$100,000	$ 10,000
7	− 3,000									− 3,000
Bal.	$ 92,000	$15,000	$20,000	$150,000	$50,000		$20,000	$200,000	$100,000	$ 7,000
8	4,000	− 4,000								
Bal.	$ 96,000	$11,000	$20,000	$150,000	$50,000		$20,000	$200,000	$100,000	$ 7,000
9	− 2,000									− 2,000
Bal.	$ 94,000	$11,000	$20,000	$150,000	$50,000		$20,000	$200,000	$100,000	$ 5,000

Total assets: $325,000   Total liabilities and owners' equity: $325,000

We have seen how transactions are analyzed and how they affect the accounting equation and ultimately the financial statements. While the approach we took to analyzing the nine transactions of the Glengarry Health Club was manageable, can you imagine using this type of analysis for a company with *thousands* of transactions in any one month? We now turn our attention to various *tools* used by the accountant to process a large volume of transactions in an effective and efficient way.

The Account:
Basic Unit for Recording Transactions

An **account** is the record used to accumulate monetary amounts for each asset, liability, and component of owners' equity, such as capital stock, retained earnings, and dividends. It is the basic recording unit for each element in the financial statements. Each revenue and expense has its own account. In the Glengarry Health Club example, nine accounts were used: Cash, Accounts Receivable, Equipment, Building, Land, Accounts Payable, Notes Payable, Capital Stock, and Retained Earnings. (Recall that revenues and expenses were recorded directly in the Retained Earnings account.) In the real world, a company might have hundreds, or even thousands, of individual accounts.

EXHIBIT 3-2   Balance Sheet for Glengarry Health Club

GLENGARRY HEALTH CLUB
BALANCE SHEET
JANUARY 31, 1995

ASSETS		LIABILITIES AND OWNERS' EQUITY	
Cash	$ 94,000	Accounts payable	$ 20,000
Accounts receivable	11,000	Notes payable	200,000
Equipment	20,000	Capital stock	100,000
Building	150,000	Retained earnings	5,000
Land	50,000		
		Total liabilities	
Total assets	$325,000	and owners' equity	$325,000

No two entities have exactly the same set of accounts. To a certain extent, the accounts used by a company depend on its business. For example, a manufacturer normally has three inventory accounts: Raw Materials, Work in Process, and Finished Goods. A retailer uses just one account for inventory, a Merchandise Inventory account. A service business has no need for an inventory account.

Chart of Accounts

Companies need a way to organize the large number of accounts they use to record transactions. A **chart of accounts** is a numerical list of all of the accounts an entity uses. The numbering system is a convenient way to identify accounts. For example, all asset accounts might be numbered from 100 to 199, liability accounts from 200 to 299, equity accounts from 300 to 399, revenues from 400 to 499, and expenses from 500 to 599. A chart of accounts for a hypothetical company, Widescreen Theaters Corporation, is shown in Exhibit 3-4. Note the division of account numbers

FROM CONCEPT TO PRACTICE

READING BEN & JERRY'S BALANCE SHEET AND FOOTNOTES

How many inventory accounts does the company report on its balance sheet? How is the inventory broken down in a footnote?

EXHIBIT 3-3   Income Statement for Glengarry Health Club

GLENGARRY HEALTH CLUB
INCOME STATEMENT
FOR THE MONTH ENDED JANUARY 31, 1995

Revenues:		
Memberships	$15,000	
Court fees	5,000	$20,000
Expenses:		
Salaries and wages	10,000	
Utilities	3,000	13,000
Net income		$ 7,000

EXHIBIT 3-4   Chart of Accounts for a Theater

100–199:	ASSETS
100–109:	Cash
101:	Cash, Checking, Second National Bank
102:	Cash, Savings, Third State Bank
103:	Cash, Change, or Petty Cash Fund (coin and currency)
110–119:	Receivables
111:	Accounts Receivable
112:	Due from Employees
113:	Notes Receivable
120–129:	Prepaid Assets
121:	Cleaning Supplies
122:	Prepaid Insurance
130–139:	Property, Plant, and Equipment
131:	Land
132:	Theater Buildings
133:	Projection Equipment
134:	Furniture and Fixtures
200–299:	LIABILITIES
200–209:	Short-Term Liabilities
201:	Accounts Payable
202:	Wages and Salaries Payable
203:	Taxes Payable
203.1:	Income Taxes Payable
203.2:	Sales Taxes Payable
203.3:	Unemployment Taxes Payable
204:	Short-Term Notes Payable
204.1:	Six-month Note Payable to First State Bank
210–219:	Long-Term Liabilities
211:	Bonds Payable, due in 2010

within each of the financial statement categories. For example, within the asset category, the various cash accounts are numbered from 100 to 109, receivables from 110 to 119, and so forth. Not all of the numbers are currently assigned. For example, only 3 of the available 9 numbers are currently utilized for cash accounts. This allows the company to add accounts as the need arises.

■ ACCOUNTING FOR YOUR DECISIONS   **You Are the Stockholder**

You own 100 shares of stock in General Motors.

1. How many different accounts would you expect GM to have in its chart of accounts?
2. Based on your answer to part 1, how many of these accounts would you want to see on a set of financial statements for GM? Explain your answer.

EXHIBIT 3-4 *(continued)*

300–399:	STOCKHOLDERS' EQUITY	
301:	Preferred Stock	
302:	Common Stock	
303:	Retained Earnings	
400–499:	REVENUES	
401:	Tickets	
402:	Video Rentals	
403:	Concessions	
404:	Interest	
500–599:	EXPENSES	
500–509:	Rentals	
501:	Films	
502:	Videos	
510–519:	Concessions	
511:	Candy	
512:	Soda	
513:	Popcorn	
520–529:	Wages and Salaries	
521:	Hourly Employees	
522:	Salaries	
530–539:	Utilities	
531:	Heat	
532:	Electric	
533:	Water	
540–549:	Advertising	
541:	Newspaper	
542:	Radio	
550–559:	Taxes	
551:	Income Taxes	
552:	Unemployment Taxes	

The General Ledger

Companies store their accounts in different ways, depending on their accounting system. In a manual system, a separate card or sheet is used to record the activity in each account. A **general ledger** is simply the file or book that contains the accounts.[4] For example, the general ledger for Widescreen Theaters Corporation might consist of a file of cards in a cabinet, with a card for each of the accounts listed in the chart of accounts.

In today's business world, most companies have an automated accounting system. The computer is ideally suited for the job of processing vast amounts of data rapidly. *All of the tools discussed in this chapter are as applicable to computerized systems as they are to manual systems. It is merely the appearance of the tools that differs between manual and computerized systems.* For example, the ledger in an automated system might be

LO 4

Define the concept of a general ledger and use the T account as a method for analyzing transactions.

---

[4] In addition to a general ledger, many companies maintain subsidiary ledgers. For example, an accounts receivable subsidiary ledger contains a separate account for each customer. The use of a subsidiary ledger for Accounts Receivable is discussed further in Chapter 7.

contained on a diskette rather than being stored in a file cabinet. Throughout the book, we will use a manual system to explain the various tools, such as ledger accounts. The reason is that it is easier to illustrate and visualize the tools in a manual system. However, all of the ideas apply just as well to a computerized system of accounting.

The Double Entry System

The origin of the double entry system of accounting can be traced to Venice, Italy, in 1494. In that year, Fra Luca Pacioli, a Franciscan monk, wrote a mathematical treatise. Included in his book was the concept of debits and credits that is still used almost universally today.

The T Account

The form for a general ledger account will be illustrated later in the chapter. However, the form of account often used to analyze transactions and thus used in accounting courses is called the *T account,* so named because it resembles the capital letter T. The name of the account appears across the horizontal line. One side is used to record increases and the other side decreases, but as you will see, the same side is not used for increases for every account. As a matter of convention, the *left* side of an *asset* account is used to record *increases* and the right side to record *decreases.* To illustrate a T account, we will look at the Cash account for Glengarry Health Club. The transactions recorded in the account can be traced to Exhibit 3-1.

CASH			
Investment by owners	100,000	Wages and salaries	10,000
Court fees collected	5,000	Utilities	3,000
Accounts collected	4,000	Dividends	2,000
	109,000		15,000
Bal.	94,000		

The amounts $109,000 and $15,000 are called *footings.* They represent the totals of the amounts on each side of the account. Neither these amounts nor the balance of $94,000 represents transactions. They are simply shown to indicate the totals and the balance in the account.

Debits and Credits

LO 5
Explain the rules of debits and credits.

Rather than refer to the left or right side of an account, accountants use specific labels for each side. The *left* side of any account is the **debit** side and the *right* side of any account is the **credit** side. We will also use the terms *debit* and *credit* as verbs. If we *debit* the Cash account, we enter an amount on the left side. Similarly, if we want to enter an amount on the right side of an account, we *credit* the account. To *charge* an account has the same meaning as to *debit* it. No such synonym exists for the act of crediting an account.

Note that *debit* and *credit* are *locational* terms. They simply refer to the left or right side of a T account. They do *not* represent increases or decreases. As we will see, when one type of account is increased (for example, the Cash account), the increase is on the left or *debit* side. When certain other types of accounts are increased, however, the entry will be on the right or *credit* side.

As you would expect from your understanding of the accounting equation, the conventions for using T accounts for assets and liabilities are opposite. Assets are future economic benefits and liabilities are obligations to transfer economic benefits in the future. If an asset is *increased* with a *debit,* how do you think a liability would be increased? *Because assets and liabilities are opposites, if an asset is increased with a debit, a liability is increased with a credit.* Thus, the right side, or credit side, of a liability account is used to record an increase. As is the case with liabilities, owners' equity accounts are on the opposite side of the accounting equation as are assets. *Thus, like a liability, an owners' equity account is increased with a credit.* We can summarize the logic of debits and credits, increases and decreases, and the accounting equation in the following way:

ASSETS		=	LIABILITIES		+	OWNERS' EQUITY	
Debits	Credits		Debits	Credits		Debits	Credits
Increases	Decreases		Decreases	Increases		Decreases	Increases
+	−		−	+		−	+

Note again that debits and credits are location oriented. Debits are always on the left side of an account and credits on the right side.

Debits and Credits for Revenues, Expenses, and Dividends

In our Glengarry Health Club example, revenues were an increase in Retained Earnings. The sale of memberships was not only an increase in the asset Cash but also an increase in the owners' equity account, Retained Earnings. The transaction resulted in an increase in the owners' claim on the assets of the business. It is not practical, however, to record revenues directly in the Retained Earnings account. Instead, separate accounts are maintained for each revenue item. The following logic is used to arrive at the rules for increasing and decreasing revenues:[5]

(1) Retained Earnings is increased with a credit.
(2) Revenue is an increase in Retained Earnings.
(3) Revenue is increased with a credit.
(4) Because revenue is increased with a credit, it is decreased with a debit.

The same logic is applied to the rules for increasing and decreasing expense accounts:

(1) Retained Earnings is decreased with a debit.
(2) Expense is a decrease in Retained Earnings.
(3) Expense is increased with a debit.
(4) Because expense is increased with a debit, it is decreased with a credit.

Recall that dividends reduce cash. But they also reduce the owners' claim on the assets of the business. Earlier we recognized this decrease in the owners' claim as a reduction of Retained Earnings. As we do for revenue and expense accounts, we will use a separate Dividends account:

(1) Retained Earnings is decreased with a debit.
(2) Dividends are a decrease in Retained Earnings.

---

[5] We normally think of both revenues and expenses as being only increased, not decreased. Because we will need to decrease them as part of the closing procedure, it is important to know how to reduce these accounts as well as increase them.

(3) Dividends are increased with a debit.

(4) Because dividends are increased with a debit, they are decreased with a credit.

Summary of the Rules for Debiting and Crediting Accounts

The rules for increasing and decreasing the various types of accounts are summarized as follows:

DEBITS:	CREDITS:
Increases in assets	Decreases in assets
Increases in expenses	Decreases in expenses
Decreases in liabilities	Increases in liabilities
Decreases in owners' equity	Increases in owners' equity
Decreases in revenues	Increases in revenues
Increases in dividends	Decreases in dividends

Normal Account Balances

Each account has a "normal" balance. For example, *assets* normally have *debit* balances. Would it be possible for an asset such as Cash to have a credit balance? Assume that a company has a checking account with a bank. A credit balance in the account would indicate that the decreases in the account, from checks written and other bank charges, were more than the deposits into the account. If this were the case, however, the company would no longer have an asset, Cash, but instead would have a liability to the bank. The normal balances for the accounts we have looked at are as follows:

Accounts Normally with a Debit Balance	Accounts Normally with a Credit Balance
Assets	Liabilities
Expenses	Owners' Equity
Dividends	Revenues

Debits Aren't Bad and Credits Aren't Good

Students often approach their first encounter with debits and credits with preconceived notions. The use of the terms *debit* and *credit* in everyday language leads to many of these notions. "Joe is a real *credit* to his team." "Nancy should be *credited* with saving Mary's career." These both appear to be very positive statements. You must resist the temptation to associate the term *credit* with something good or positive and the term *debit* with something bad or negative. *In accounting, debit means one thing: an entry made on the left side of an account. A credit means an entry made on the right side of an account.*[6]

Debits and Credits Applied to Transactions

Recall the first transaction recorded by Glengarry Health Club: the owners invested $100,000 cash in the business. The transaction resulted in an increase in the Cash

---

[6] Another source of confusion stems from examining your bank statement. Why does the bank debit your account when you write a check? The amount you have on deposit in your account is a liability to the bank. Thus, when you write a check, the bank's liability is reduced. The bank reduces its liability with a debit.

account and an increase in the Capital Stock account. Applying the rules of debits and credits, we would *debit* the Cash account for $100,000 and *credit* the Capital Stock account for the same amount:[7]

CASH		CAPITAL STOCK	
(1) 100,000			100,000 (1)

You now can see why we refer to the **double entry system** of accounting. That is, every transaction is recorded in such a way that the equality of debits and credits is maintained and in the process, the accounting equation is kept in balance. *Every transaction is entered in at least two accounts on opposite sides of T accounts. Our first transaction resulted in an increase in an asset account and an increase in an owners' equity account. For every transaction, the debit side must equal the credit side. The debit of $100,000 to the Cash account equaled the credit of $100,000 to the Capital Stock account.* It naturally follows that if the debit side must equal the credit side for every transaction, it is also true that at any point in time the total of all debits recorded must equal the total of all credits recorded. Thus, the fundamental accounting equation remains in balance.

Transactions for Glengarry Health Club

Three distinct steps are involved in recording a transaction in the accounts. First, we *analyze* the transaction. That is, we must decide what accounts are increased or decreased and by how much. Second, we must *recall* the rules of debits and credits as they apply to the transaction we are analyzing. Finally, we *record* the transaction using the rules of debits and credits.

We return to the transactions of the health club. We have already explained the logic for the debit to the Cash account and the credit to the Capital Stock account for the initial investment by the owners. We will now analyze the remaining eight transactions for the month. Refer to Exhibit 3-1 for a summary of the transactions.

(**2**) A building and land are exchanged for a promissory note.

(**a**) *Analyze:* Two asset accounts are increased: Building and Land. The liability account, Notes Payable, is also increased.

(**b**) *Recall the rules of debits and credits:* An *asset* is *increased* with a *debit* and a *liability* is *increased* with a *credit*.

(**c**) *Record the transaction:*

BUILDING		NOTES PAYABLE	
(2) 150,000			200,000 (2)

LAND	
(2) 50,000	

(**3**) Exercise equipment is purchased from a supplier on open account. The purchase price is $20,000.

(**a**) *Analyze:* An asset account, Equipment, is increased. A liability account, Accounts Payable, is also increased. Thus, the transaction is identical to the last transaction in that an asset or assets are increased and a liability is increased.

---

[7] We will use the numbers of each transaction, as they were labeled earlier in the chapter, to identify the transactions. In practice, a formal ledger account is used and transactions are entered according to their date.

(b) *Recall the rules of debits and credits:* An *asset* is *increased* with a *debit* and a *liability* is *increased* with a *credit.*

(c) *Record the transaction:*

EQUIPMENT		ACCOUNTS PAYABLE	
(3) 20,000			20,000 (3)

(4) Three hundred club memberships are sold for $50 each. The members have until the 10th of the following month to pay.

(a) *Analyze:* The asset account, Accounts Receivable, is increased by $15,000. This amount is an asset because the company has the right to collect it in the future. The owners' claim to the assets is increased by the same amount. Recall, however, that we do not record these claims—revenues—directly in an owners' equity account but instead use a separate revenue account. We will call the account Membership Revenue.

(b) *Recall the rules of debits and credits:* An *asset* is *increased* with a *debit.* *Owners' equity* is *increased* with a *credit.* Because *revenue* is an *increase* in *owners' equity,* it is *increased* with a *credit.*

(c) *Record the transaction:*

ACCOUNTS RECEIVABLE		MEMBERSHIP REVENUE	
(4) 15,000			15,000 (4)

(5) Court fees are paid at the time of use and amount to $5,000 for the first month.

(a) *Analyze:* The asset account, Cash, is increased by $5,000. The owners' claim to the assets is increased by the same amount. The account used to record the increase in the owners' claim is Court Fee Revenue.

(b) *Recall the rules of debits and credits:* An *asset* is *increased* with a *debit.* *Owners' equity* is *increased* with a *credit.* Because *revenue* is an *increase* in *owners' equity,* it is *increased* with a *credit.*

(c) *Record the transaction:*

CASH		COURT FEE REVENUE	
(1) 100,000			5,000 (5)
(5) 5,000			

(6) Wages and salaries amount to $10,000, and they are paid in cash.

(a) *Analyze:* The asset account, Cash, is decreased by $10,000. At the same time, the owners' claim to the assets is decreased by this amount. However, rather than record a decrease directly to Retained Earnings, we set up an expense account, Wage and Salary Expense.

(b) *Recall the rules of debits and credits:* An *asset* is *decreased* with a *credit.* Owners' *equity* is *decreased* with a *debit.* Because *expense* is a *decrease* in *owners' equity,* it is *increased* with a *debit.*

(c) *Record the transaction:*

CASH		WAGE AND SALARY EXPENSE	
(1) 100,000	10,000 (6)	(6) 10,000	
(5) 5,000			

(7) The utility bill of $3,000 for the first month is paid in cash.

(a) *Analyze:* The asset account, Cash, is decreased by $3,000. At the same time, the owners' claim to the assets is decreased by this amount. However, rather than record a decrease directly to Retained Earnings, we set up an expense account, Utility Expense.

(b) *Recall the rules of debits and credits:* An *asset* is *decreased* with a *credit.* Owners' *equity* is *decreased* with a debit. Because *expense* is a *decrease* in *owners' equity,* it is *increased* with a *debit.*

(c) *Record the transaction:*

CASH		UTILITY EXPENSE
(1) 100,000	10,000 (6)	**(7) 3,000**
(5) 5,000	**3,000 (7)**	

(8) Cash of $4,000 is collected from members for their January dues.

(a) *Analyze:* Cash is increased by the amount collected from the members. Another asset, Accounts Receivable, is decreased by the same amount. Glengarry has simply traded one asset for another.

(b) *Recall the rules of debits and credits:* An *asset* is *increased* with a *debit* and *decreased* with a *credit.* Thus, one asset is debited and another is credited.

(c) *Record the transaction:*

CASH		ACCOUNTS RECEIVABLE	
(1) 100,000	10,000 (6)	(4)15,000	**4,000 (8)**
(5) 5,000	3,000 (7)		
(8) 4,000			

(9) Dividends of $2,000 are distributed to the owners.

(a) *Analyze:* The asset account, Cash, is decreased by $2,000. At the same time, the owners' claim to the assets is decreased by this amount. Earlier in the chapter, we decreased Retained Earnings for dividends paid to the owners. Now we will use a separate account, Dividends, to record these distributions.

(b) *Recall the rules of debits and credits:* An *asset* is *decreased* with a *credit. Retained earnings* is *decreased* with a *debit.* Because *dividends* are a decrease in *retained earnings,* they are *increased* with a *debit.*

(c) *Record the transaction:*

CASH		DIVIDENDS
(1) 100,000	10,000 (6)	**(9) 2,000**
(5) 5,000	3,000 (7)	
(8) 4,000	**2,000 (9)**	

The Journal: The Firm's Chronological Record of Transactions

Each of the nine transactions was entered directly in the ledger accounts. By looking at the Cash account, we see that it increased by $5,000 in transaction 5. But what was the other side of this transaction? That is, what account was credited? To have a record of *each entry,* transactions are recorded first in a journal. A **journal** is a chronological record of transactions entered into by a business. Because a journal lists transactions in the order in which they took place, it is called the *book of original* *entry.* Transactions are recorded first in a journal and then are posted to the ledger accounts. **Posting** is the process of transferring a journal entry to the ledger accounts:

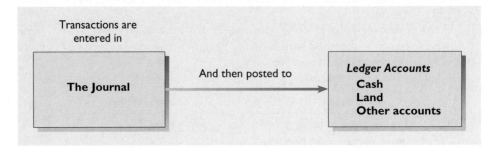

It is important to note that posting does not result in any change in the amounts recorded. It is simply a process of sorting the transactions to go from a chronological order to a topical arrangement.

The Format for a Journal Entry

LO 6
Record journal entries.

A journal entry is recorded for each transaction. **Journalizing** is the process of recording entries in a journal. A standard format is normally used for recording journal entries. To illustrate, consider the original investment by the owners of Glengarry Health Club. The format of the journal entry is as follows:

		Dr.	Cr.
Jan. xx	Cash	100,000	
	Capital Stock		100,000
	To record the issuance of 10,000 shares of stock for cash.		

The following points are important to note:

(**1**) The first line in the entry indicates the date of the transaction. Because we originally used numbers to record each of the transactions, we will use "January xx" in lieu of an actual date. Entries are recorded in a journal in chronological order. The date helps us to trace a transaction to a particular point in time.

(**2**) The account debited is shown on the first line, along with the amount in the column abbreviated *Dr.* This is the abbreviation for the Latin *debere,* meaning "to debit."

(**3**) The account credited is shown on the next line, along with the amount in the column abbreviated *Cr.* This is the abbreviation for the Latin *credere,* meaning "to credit." The credit account is *indented* to clearly distinguish it from the account debited.

(**4**) Our entry involves a single debit account and only one credit account. A **compound journal entry** has more than one account either debited or credited, or both. The second transaction of Glengarry Health Club requires a compound journal entry. A building and land are purchased by signing a promissory note. All accounts debited are shown first, with all accounts credited following and indented.

(**5**) An explanation of the transaction appears on the last line of the entry. If we need to return to the transaction in the future, the explanation makes it easier to recall what took place. It should provide additional information beyond that implied by the accounts listed and amounts shown. For example, our explanation for the entry shown above indicates how many shares of stock were issued.

The General Journal

In lieu of a specialized journal, transactions are recorded in a **general journal.** Specialized journals are used to record repetitive transactions in which either the debit or the credit is always to the same account. For example, a cash receipts journal is used to record all transactions in which cash is received, that is, debited. In this chapter, we will use a general journal to record all transactions.

A general journal for Glengarry Health Club appears in Exhibit 3-5. The format for the entries in the journal is the same as we discussed in the last section. One column needs further explanation. *Post. Ref.* is an abbreviation for *posting reference.* As part of the posting process explained below, the debit and credit amounts are posted to the appropriate accounts, and this column is filled in with the number assigned to the account.

Posting to the Ledger Accounts

Journal entries and ledger accounts are both *tools* used by the accountant. The end result, a set of financial statements, is the most important part of the process. Journalizing provides us with a chronological record of each transaction. So why not just prepare financial statements directly from the journal entries? Isn't it just extra work to *post* the entries to the ledger accounts? In our simple example of Glengarry Health Club, it would be possible to prepare the statements directly from the journal entries. In real-world situations, however, the number of transactions in any given period is so large that it would be virtually impossible, if not terribly inefficient, to bypass the accounts. Accounts provide us with a convenient summary of the activity, as well as the balance, for a specific financial statement item.

The posting process for Glengarry Health Club is illustrated in Exhibit 3-6. Rather than a T-account format for the general ledger accounts, the *running balance form* is illustrated. A separate column indicates the balance in the ledger account after each transaction. The use of the explanation column in a ledger account is optional. Because an explanation of the entry in the account can be found by referring to the journal, this column is often left blank.

The posting process is illustrated for the health club's fifth transaction in which cash is collected for court fees. The steps in the process consist of the following:

(1) Place the date, as it appears in the journal, in the date column of the account that is debited. Remember that we have substituted "xx" for an actual date.

(2) Record the amount that appears in the Debit column in the general journal in the Debit column of the appropriate account in the ledger.

(3) Calculate the balance in the account and place it in the Balance column of the account. As discussed earlier, accounts have a *normal* balance and it is not necessary to indicate whether the balance is a debit or credit amount.

(4) Place the journal page number in the Post. Ref. column of the account debited. For example, the GJ1 in the Post. Ref. column of the Cash account indicates that the $5,000 posted to the account came from page 1 of the general journal (GJ).

(5) Place the account number in the Post. Ref. column of the journal. For example, the 1 in the Post. Ref. column of the general journal on the line for the debit to Cash indicates that the amount has been posted to Account No. 1. The cross-referencing of the journal page number and the account number helps to ensure the accuracy of the posting process, as well as to make it easier to trace amounts at a later time.

(6) Repeat steps (1) through (5) for any other accounts debited and for the account(s) credited in the transaction.

LO 7
Explain how journal entries are transferred to the general ledger.

EXHIBIT 3-5   General Journal for Glengarry Health Club

Date			Account Titles and Explanation	Post. Ref.	Debit	Credit
1995 Jan.	XX		Cash	1	1 0 0 0 0 0	
			Capital Stock	30		1 0 0 0 0 0
			Issued 10,000 shares of stock for cash.			
	XX		Building	10	1 5 0 0 0 0	
			Land	15	5 0 0 0 0	
			Notes Payable	25		2 0 0 0 0 0
			Purchased building and land by issuing promissory note.			
	XX		Equipment	18	2 0 0 0 0	
			Accounts Payable	20		2 0 0 0 0
			Purchased equipment on open account.			
	XX		Accounts Receivable	5	1 5 0 0 0	
			Membership Revenue	40		1 5 0 0 0
			Sold 300 memberships at $50 each.			
	XX		Cash	1	5 0 0 0	
			Court Fee Revenue	44		5 0 0 0
			Collected court fees.			
	XX		Wage and Salary Expense	50	1 0 0 0 0	
			Cash	1		1 0 0 0 0
			Paid wages and salaries.			
	XX		Utility Expense	52	3 0 0 0	
			Cash	1		3 0 0 0
			Paid utility bill.			
	XX		Cash	1	4 0 0 0	
			Accounts Receivable	5		4 0 0 0
			Collected membership fees on account.			
	XX		Dividends	60	2 0 0 0	
			Cash	1		2 0 0 0
			Paid cash dividends to owners.			

The frequency of posting differs among companies, partly based on the degree to which their accounting system is automated. For example, in some computerized systems, amounts are posted to the ledger accounts at the time an entry is recorded in the journal. In a manual system, posting is normally done periodically, for example, daily, weekly, or monthly. Regardless of when performed, the posting process changes nothing. It simply reorganizes the transactions by account.

EXHIBIT 3-6   The Posting Process

General Journal   Page No. 1

Date	Account Titles and Explanation		Post. Ref.	Debit	Credit
1995 Jan.	XX	Accounts Receivable	5	1 5 0 0 0	
		Membership Revenue	40		1 5 0 0 0
		Sold 300 memberships at $50 each.			
	XX	Cash	1	5 0 0 0	
		Court Fee Revenue	44		5 0 0 0
		Collected court fees.			

General Ledger
Cash   Account No. 1

Date	Explanation	Post. Ref.	Debit	Credit	Balance
1995 Jan.	XX		GJ1	1 0 0 0 0 0		1 0 0 0 0 0
	XX		GJ1	5 0 0 0		1 0 5 0 0 0

Court Fee Revenue   Account No. 44

Date	Explanation	Post. Ref.	Debit	Credit	Balance
1995 Jan.	XX		GJ1		5 0 0 0	5 0 0 0

■ ACCOUNTING FOR YOUR DECISIONS   You Are the Manager

You are the community relations manager for a company. You need to determine
whether the company is spending its money wisely in promoting its image in the local
community.

1. What types of accounts would you examine? Give examples of the possible names
   for some of these accounts.
2. Would a general journal or a general ledger be more useful to you in making your
   determination? Explain your answer.

T Accounts for Glengarry Health Club

As mentioned earlier, while the running balance format for ledger accounts is used in practice, T accounts are used for convenience in textbooks and in practice. Now that you have seen the actual posting process from a journal to a formal running balance ledger account, we will return to the use of T accounts. The T accounts for Glengarry Health Club after the transactions for the month of January have been posted are shown in Exhibit 3-7. The entries are identified in the accounts by the original transaction numbers.

The Trial Balance

LO   8

Explain the purpose of a trial balance.

One other tool is used to facilitate the preparation of a set of financial statements. A **trial balance** is a list of each account and its balance at a specific point in time. The trial balance is *not* itself a financial statement but merely a convenient device to prove the equality of the debit and credit balances in the accounts. It can be as informal as an adding machine tape with the account titles penciled in next to the debit and credit amounts. A trial balance for Glengarry Health Club as of January 31, 1995, is shown in Exhibit 3-8.

EXHIBIT 3-7   T Accounts for Glengarry Health Club

	CASH				ACCOUNTS RECEIVABLE		
(1)	100,000	10,000	(6)	(4)	15,000	4,000	(8)
(5)	5,000	3,000	(7)	Bal.	11,000		
(8)	4,000	2,000	(9)				
	109,000	15,000					
Bal.	94,000						

	BUILDING				LAND		
(2)	150,000			(2)	50,000		

	EQUIPMENT				ACCOUNTS PAYABLE		
(3)	20,000					20,000	(3)

	NOTES PAYABLE				CAPITAL STOCK		
		200,000	(2)			100,000	(1)

	MEMBERSHIP REVENUE				COURT FEE REVENUE		
		15,000	(4)			5,000	(5)

	WAGE AND SALARY EXPENSE				UTILITY EXPENSE		
(6)	10,000			(7)	3,000		

	DIVIDENDS		
(9)	2,000		

EXHIBIT 3-8   Trial Balance for Glengarry Health Club

GLENGARRY HEALTH CLUB
TRIAL BALANCE
AT JANUARY 31, 1995

ACCOUNT TITLE	DEBITS	CREDITS
Cash	$ 94,000	
Accounts Receivable	11,000	
Building	150,000	
Land	50,000	
Equipment	20,000	
Accounts Payable		$ 20,000
Notes Payable		200,000
Capital Stock		100,000
Membership Revenue		15,000
Court Fee Revenue		5,000
Wage and Salary Expense	10,000	
Utility Expense	3,000	
Dividends	2,000	
Totals	$340,000	$340,000

Use of the Trial Balance

Certain types of errors are detectable from a trial balance. For example, if the balance of an account is incorrectly computed, the total of the debits and credits in the trial balance will not equal. If a debit is posted to an account as a credit, or vice versa, the trial balance will be out of balance. The omission of part of a journal entry in the posting process will also be detected by the preparation of a trial balance.

Do not attribute more significance to a trial balance, however, than is warranted. It *does* assure us that the balances of all the debit accounts equal the balances of all the credit accounts. But an equality of debits and credits does not necessarily mean that the *correct* accounts were debited and credited in an entry. For example, the entry to record the purchase of land by signing a promissory note *should* result in a debit to Land and a credit to Notes Payable. If the accountant incorrectly debited Cash instead of Land, the trial balance would still show an equality of debits and credits. A trial balance can be prepared at any time. A trial balance is usually prepared as a preliminary step to the release of a set of financial statements.

Finding Errors in the Trial Balance

How do we actually *find* the problem when a trial balance doesn't balance? Although there is no single foolproof method for locating the error, the following procedures are helpful:

(1) Verify the accuracy of the Debit and Credit column totals in the trial balance. It is possible that one of the two columns was simply added incorrectly.

TRANSACTIONS FROM AN AUDITOR'S POINT OF VIEW

Name: Krista Kaland
Profession: CPA
College Major: Accounting

Most people who use financial statements don't really think about the company's internal books and records. Instead, they rely on the company's integrity and/or the auditor's opinion that the company's books are in order—and that the statements that pop out at the end of the year fairly present the company's financial position.

Who exactly are these auditors? They're the nation's CPAs or certified public accountants. Best known for their tax work in the popular press, CPAs audit the books of companies. If the company is public, the government requires such an audit to protect the company's shareholders. If the company is private, the bank may require an audit as a condition of making a loan.

Most companies have a huge quantity of transactions and it would be impossible to examine every one of them. Fortunately, an auditor doesn't have to do that. "Auditing is based on sampling and testing," says Krista Kaland, a partner with Clifton Gunderson, CPAs, a mid-size accounting firm based in Illinois. "You determine on a test basis what documents you need to look at in order to be satisfied that the financial statements are fairly stated," she says.

Kaland has assumed a national role in the profession's auditing and accounting standards, sitting on the Accounting Standards Executive Committee of the American Institute of Certified Public Accountants. As Director of Audit and Accounting for her firm, she advises her colleagues and clients on technical matters. Kaland graduated from the University of Illinois with a degree in accounting and has spent her entire career—nearly 20 years—with Clifton Gunderson.

"I've audited everything from school districts to governments, manufacturing clients, companies with 10 subsidiaries to small retail operations," she says. What would be some typical records she would examine? "We look at their general ledger, which summarizes all of the transactions for the year. "Then we'll look at the subsidiary journals and ledgers and other documentation that supports the entries that went into the general ledger." One such account would be Accounts Receivable. An auditor would send a confirmation to the customer to "confirm" that the

money is really owed. Another test is whether the accounts receivable item is really collectible. "Does the customer really owe it and intend on paying it?"

She and her firm spend a lot of time converting clients from their manual accounting system—the one with real "books"—to a computerized system. "There are so many excellent inexpensive systems that virtually every company should be computerized now."

(2) Find the difference between the Debit and Credit column totals. The difference between the two is often a clue to the error:

(a) The difference may indicate that one side of a transaction was not recorded. Search the trial balance for an account whose balance is the amount of the difference. For example, assume that the debits in our trial balance total to $342,000 and the credits total to $340,000. The $2,000 difference may indicate that Cash was not credited when the dividends of $2,000 were recorded as a debit to the Dividends account. This would be true if the total in the Cash account is $96,000 instead of $94,000.

(b) If the difference is evenly divisible by 9, the error is probably either a transposition or a slide. For example, assume that the debits total to $340,000 in our trial balance but the credits amount to $376,000. The difference between the two is $36,000, which is evenly divisible by 9. The most likely cause of the error is a *transposition*. For example, what if the $15,000 of membership revenue was incorrectly shown on the trial balance as $51,000? The reversing of the 1 and the 5 is called a *transposition*. The difference between the correct number of $15,000 and the incorrect number of $51,000 is $36,000. The key to transposition errors is that they are always evenly divisible by 9. The same is true for *slide errors.* These occur when a decimal point or comma is incorrectly placed. Copying the Building account as $15,000 instead of $150,000 is a slide error.

(c) If the difference is evenly divisible by 2, a debit may have been incorrectly copied as a credit or vice versa. For example, what if the total of the debits is $337,000 and the credits total to $343,000? The difference of $6,000 divided by 2 is $3,000. Search the trial balance for this amount. The error could be caused by copying the Utility Expense of $3,000 as a credit instead of a debit.

(3) Trace each of the amounts in the trial balance back to the ledger accounts. It is possible that a number was simply copied wrong in the trial balance.

(4) If (3) does not yield the error, it may be necessary to trace each of the amounts from the ledger back to the journal. Use the Post. Ref. column in the ledger account to find the page in the journal where the amount was originally recorded.

What Happened to the Retained Earnings Account?

Neither our trial balance nor the set of T accounts used to prepare the trial balance contains the Retained Earnings account. Rather than record revenues, expenses, and dividends *directly* in the Retained Earnings account, separate accounts are used for each of these items. In Chapter 4, we will learn how the balances in these accounts are *closed* to Retained Earnings at the end of each period. The Retained Earnings account *will* have a balance in later periods to reflect accumulated net income, less dividends. There is no balance in the account in our example, however, because this is the *first* month of business.

REVIEW PROBLEM

The following transactions are entered into by Sparkle Car Wash during its first month of operations:

a. Articles of incorporation are filed with the state and 20,000 shares of capital stock are issued. Cash of $40,000 is received from the new owners for the shares.

b. A five-year promissory note is signed at the local bank. The cash received from the loan is $120,000.

c. An existing car wash is purchased for $150,000 in cash. The values assigned to the land, building, and equipment are $25,000, $75,000, and $50,000, respectively.

d. Cleaning supplies are purchased on account for $2,500 from a distributor. All of the supplies are used in the first month.

e. During the first month, $1,500 is paid to the distributor for the cleaning supplies. The remaining $1,000 will be paid next month.

f. Gross receipts from car washes during the first month of operations amount to $7,000.

g. Wages and salaries paid in the first month amount to $2,000.

h. The utility bill of $800 for the month is paid.

i. A total of $1,000 in dividends is paid to the owners.

■ REQUIRED

1. Prepare journal entries for each of the transactions. It is not necessary to use ruled journal paper. In lieu of dates, identify each entry by its respective letter, (a) through (i).

2. Post each of the entries to T accounts. Identify the amount posted to each account by letter.

3. Prepare a trial balance.

■ SOLUTION TO REVIEW PROBLEM

1. Journal entries:

		DR.	CR.
a.	Cash	40,000	
	Capital Stock		40,000
	20,000 shares of capital stock issued for cash.		
b.	Cash	120,000	
	Notes Payable		120,000
	Five-year promissory note signed at the bank.		
c.	Land	25,000	
	Building	75,000	
	Equipment	50,000	
	Cash		150,000
	Existing car wash purchased.		
d.	Supplies Expense	2,500	
	Accounts Payable		2,500
	Cleaning supplies purchased and used.		
e.	Accounts Payable	1,500	
	Cash		1,500
	Payment of account.		
f.	Cash	7,000	
	Car Wash Revenue		7,000
	Cash received from car washes.		
g.	Wage and Salary Expense	2,000	
	Cash		2,000
	Paid wages and salaries.		
h.	Utility Expense	800	
	Cash		800
	Paid utility bill.		
i.	Dividends	1,000	
	Cash		1,000
	Paid cash dividends.		

2. T accounts:

CASH					LAND	
(a)	40,000	150,000	(c)	(c)	25,000	
(b)	120,000	1,500	(e)			
(f)	7,000	2,000	(g)			
		800	(h)			
		1,000	(i)			
	167,000	155,300				
Bal.	11,700					

	BUILDING				EQUIPMENT	
(c)	75,000			(c)	50,000	

	ACCOUNTS PAYABLE				NOTES PAYABLE	
		2,500	(d)			120,000	(b)
(e)	1,500						
		1,000	Bal.				

	CAPITAL STOCK				SUPPLIES EXPENSE	
		40,000	(a)	(d)	2,500	

	CAR WASH REVENUE				WAGE AND SALARY EXPENSE	
		7,000	(f)	(g)	2,000	

	UTILITY EXPENSE				DIVIDENDS	
(h)	800			(i)	1,000	

3.

SPARKLE CAR WASH
TRIAL BALANCE
END OF FIRST MONTH

ACCOUNT TITLE	DEBITS	CREDITS
Cash	$11,700	
Land	25,000	
Building	75,000	
Equipment	50,000	
Accounts Payable		$ 1,000
Notes Payable		120,000
Capital Stock		40,000
Car Wash Revenue		7,000
Supplies Expense	2,500	
Wage and Salary Expense	2,000	
Utility Expense	800	
Dividends	1,000	
Totals	$168,000	$168,000

GUIDANCE ANSWERS TO
ACCOUNTING FOR YOUR DECISIONS

YOU ARE THE STOCKHOLDER

1. A large company such as GM might have hundreds or even thousands of accounts in its chart of accounts. A separate chart of accounts might exist for each of the various divisions, branches, and subsidiaries owned by the company.

2. The point of this question is that you would be overwhelmed if GM presented every single account and its balance in its financial statements. As a reader of the statements, you would quickly suffer from "information overload"! All large companies must combine similar accounts and try to summarize the information for the reader. For example, GM's 1992 consolidated balance sheet contains a single account for inventories and a footnote provides additional detail on this important asset. The consolidated income statement is condensed to the extent that it contains only eight expense accounts, excluding income taxes and a special type of loss.

YOU ARE THE MANAGER

1. Among the possible accounts that you want to examine are Entertainment, Travel, Promotions, Advertising, and Miscellaneous, in addition to any accounts that might contain expenditures related to community relations.

2. You want to examine the general ledger for each of the accounts listed in part 1. The ledger contains a record for each of the accounts and the activity in them during the period.

CHAPTER HIGHLIGHTS

1. **(LO 1)** Both internal and external events affect an entity. External events, such as the purchase of materials, involve the entity and its environment. Internal events, such as the placement of the materials into production, do not involve an outside entity. For any event to be recorded, it must be measurable.

2. **(LO 2)** Source documents are used as the basis for recording events as transactions. Certain transactions are repetitive and a standard source document is used, such as a time card to document the payroll for the week. For other nonrepetitive transactions, a source document has to be generated for the specific event.

3. **(LO 3)** Economic events are the basis for recording transactions. These transactions result in changes in the company's financial position. Transactions change the amount of individual items on the balance sheet, but the statement must balance after each transaction is recorded.

4. **(LO 4)** A separate account is used for each identifiable asset, liability, revenue, expense, and component of owners' equity. No standard set of accounts exists and the types of accounts used depend to a certain extent on the nature of a company's business. A chart of accounts is a numerical list of all the accounts used by an entity. The general ledger in a manual system might consist of a set of cards, one for each account, in a file cabinet. In a computerized system, a magnetic tape or diskette might be used to store the accounts.

5. **(LO 4)** T accounts are used throughout accounting courses as the basic form of analysis of transactions. The left side of an account is used for debits and the right side is for credits. Transactions are recorded in the ledger in more formal accounts than the typical T account.

6. **(LO 5)** By convention, the left side of an asset account is used to record increases. Thus, an asset account is

increased with a debit. Because liabilities are on the opposite side of the accounting equation, they are increased with a credit. Similarly, owners' equity accounts are increased with a credit. Because revenue is an increase in owners' equity, it is increased with a credit. Thus, an expense, as well as a dividend, is increased with a debit.

7. **(LO 5)** According to our double entry system, there are two sides to every transaction. For each transaction, the debit or debits must equal the credit or credits. Do *not* think of credits as "good" and debits as "bad." Debits are simply entries on the left side of an account and credits are entries on the right side of an account.

8. **(LO 6)** Transactions are not recorded directly in the accounts but are recorded initially in a journal. A separate entry is recorded in the journal for each transaction. The account(s) debited appears first in the entry with the account(s) credited indented to distinguish them. Separate columns for debits and credits

are used to indicate the amounts for each. A general journal is used in lieu of any specialized journals.

9. **(LO 7)** Amounts appearing in journal entries are posted to the ledger accounts. Posting can be done either at the time the entry is recorded or periodically. The Post. Ref. column in a journal indicates the account number to which the amount is posted and a similar column in the account acts as a convenient reference back to the particular page number in the journal.

10. **(LO 8)** A trial balance proves the equality of the debits and credits in the accounts. If only one side of a transaction is posted to the accounts, the trial balance will not balance. Other types of errors are detectable from the process of preparing a trial balance. It cannot, however, detect all errors. A trial balance could be in balance even though the wrong asset account is debited in an entry.

KEY TERMS QUIZ

Select from the following list of key terms used in the chapter and fill in the appropriate blank to the left of each description. The solution appears at the end of the chapter.

Event	External event
Internal event	Transaction
Source document	Account
Chart of accounts	General ledger
Debit	Credit
Double entry system	Journal
Posting	Journalizing
Compound journal entry	General journal
Trial balance	

_____ 1. A numerical list of all the accounts used by a company.

_____ 2. A journal entry in which there are multiple debits or credits, or both.

_____ 3. A work sheet showing the balances in each account; used to prove the equality of debits and credits.

_____ 4. A happening of consequence to an entity.

_____ 5. An entry on the right side of an account.

_____ 6. An event occurring entirely within an entity.

_____ 7. A piece of paper, such as a sales invoice, that is used as the evidence to record a transaction.

_____ **8.** The act of recording journal entries.

_____ **9.** An entry on the left side of an account.

_____ **10.** The process of transferring amounts from a journal to the appropriate ledger accounts.

_____ **11.** An event involving interaction between an entity and its environment.

_____ **12.** The record used to accumulate monetary amounts for each individual asset, liability, revenue, expense, and component of owners' equity.

_____ **13.** A book, file, diskette, magnetic tape, or other device containing all of a company's accounts.

_____ **14.** A chronological record of transactions, also known as the *book of original entry*.

_____ **15.** Any event, external or internal, that is recognized in a set of financial statements.

_____ **16.** The journal used in lieu of a specialized journal.

_____ **17.** A system of accounting in which every transaction is recorded with equal debits and credits and the accounting equation is kept in balance.

ALTERNATE TERMS

CREDIT SIDE OF AN ACCOUNT Right side of an account.

DEBIT AN ACCOUNT Charge an account.

DEBIT SIDE OF AN ACCOUNT Left side of an account.

GENERAL LEDGER Set of accounts.

JOURNAL Book of original entry.

JOURNALIZE AN ENTRY Record an entry.

POSTING AN ACCOUNT Transferring an amount from the journal to the ledger.

QUESTIONS

1. What are the two types of events that affect an entity? Describe each.

2. What is the significance of source documents to the recording process? Give two examples of source documents.

3. What are four different forms of cash?

4. How does an account receivable differ from a note receivable?

5. What is meant by the statement "One company's account receivable is another company's account payable"?

6. What do accountants mean when they refer to the "double entry system" of accounting?

7. Owners' equity represents the claim of the owners on the assets of the business. What is the distinction relative to the owners' claim between the Capital Stock account and the Retained Earnings account?

8. If an asset account is increased with a debit, what is the logic for increasing a liability account with a credit?

9. A friend comes to you with the following plight: "I'm confused. An asset is something positive and it is increased with a debit. However, an expense is something negative and it is also increased with a debit. I don't get it." How can you straighten your friend out?

10. The payment of dividends reduces cash. If the Cash account is reduced with a credit, why is the Dividends account debited when dividends are paid?

11. If Cash is increased with a debit, why does the bank credit your account when you make a deposit?

12. Your friend presents the following criticism of the accounting system: "Accounting involves so much duplication of effort. First, entries are recorded in a journal and then the same information is recorded in a ledger. No wonder accountants work such long hours!" Do you agree with this criticism?

13. How does the T account differ from the running balance form for an account? How are they similar?

14. What is a compound journal entry? Give an example of one.

15. What is the benefit of using a cross-referencing system between a ledger and a journal?

16. How often should a company post entries from the journal to the ledger?

17. What is the purpose of a trial balance?

18. What is a transposition error? How can a trial balance be used to detect a transposition error?

19. What is a slide error? How can a trial balance be used to detect a slide error?

20. Why would the trial balance for a new business not contain a Retained Earnings account at the end of the first month of operations?

EXERCISES

(LO 1) EXERCISE 3-1 TYPES OF EVENTS

For each of the following events, identify whether it is an external event that would be recorded as a transaction (E), an internal event that would be recorded as a transaction (I), or not recorded (NR):

_____ **1.** A supplier of a company's raw material is paid an amount owed on account.

_____ **2.** A customer pays its open account.

_____ **3.** A new chief executive officer is hired.

_____ **4.** The biweekly payroll is paid.

_____ **5.** Raw materials are entered into production.

_____ **6.** A new advertising agency is hired to develop a series of newspaper ads for the company.

_____ **7.** The advertising bill for the first month is paid.

_____ **8.** The accountant determines the federal income taxes owed based on the income earned during the period.

(LO 2) EXERCISE 3-2 SOURCE DOCUMENTS MATCHED WITH TRANSACTIONS

Following are a list of source documents and a list of transactions. Indicate by letter next to each transaction the source document that would serve as evidence for the recording of the transaction.

SOURCE DOCUMENTS

a. Purchase invoice

b. Sales invoice

c. Cash register tape

d. Time cards

e. Promissory note

f. Stock certificates

g. Monthly statement from utility company

h. No standard source document would normally be available

TRANSACTIONS

_____ **1.** Utilities expense for the month is recorded.

_____ **2.** A cash settlement is received from a pending lawsuit.

_____ **3.** Owners contribute cash to start a new corporation.

_____ **4.** The biweekly payroll is paid.

_____ **5.** Cash sales for the day are recorded.

_____ **6.** Equipment is acquired on a 30-day open account.

_____ **7.** A sale is made on open account.

_____ **8.** A building is acquired by signing an agreement to repay a stated amount plus interest in six months.

(LO 3) EXERCISE 3-3 THE EFFECT OF TRANSACTIONS ON THE ACCOUNTING EQUATION

For each of the following transactions, indicate whether it increases (I), decreases (D), or has no effect (NE) on the total dollar amount of each of the elements of the accounting equation.

TRANSACTIONS	Assets	= Liabilities	+ Owners' Equity
Example: Common stock is issued in exchange for cash.	I	NE	I

1. Equipment is purchased for cash.

2. Sales are made on account.

3. Cash sales are made.

4. An account payable is paid off.

5. Cash is collected on an account receivable.

6. Buildings are purchased in exchange for a three-year note payable.

7. Advertising bill for the month is paid.

8. Dividends are paid to stockholders.

9. Land is acquired by issuing shares of stock to the owner of the land.

(LO 3) EXERCISE 3-4 TYPES OF TRANSACTIONS

As you found out in reading the chapter, there are three elements to the accounting equation: assets, liabilities, and owners' equity. You also learned that every transaction affects at least two of these elements. This leads to nine possible transactions:

TYPE OF TRANSACTION	Assets	=	Liabilities	+	Owners' Equity
1.	Increase		Increase		
2.	Increase				Increase
3.	Decrease		Decrease		
4.	Decrease				Decrease
5.			Increase		Decrease
6.			Decrease		Increase
7.	Increase Decrease				
8.			Increase Decrease		
9.					Increase Decrease

Transaction types 5, 6, 8, and 9 are more complex and examples of these will be explored in subsequent chapters. However, examples of transaction types 1 through 4 and 7 were introduced in the chapter. For *each* of these five types, write out descriptions of at least *two* transactions that illustrate these types of transactions.

(LO 4) EXERCISE 3-5 BALANCE SHEET ACCOUNTS AND THEIR USE

Choose from the following list of account titles the one that most accurately fits the description of that account or is an example of that account. An account title may be used more than once or not at all.

Cash   **Accounts Receivable**   **Notes Receivable**
Prepaid Asset   **Land**   **Buildings**
Investments   **Accounts Payable**   **Notes Payable**
Taxes Payable   **Retained Earnings**   **Common Stock**
Preferred Stock

_____   **1.** A written obligation to repay a fixed amount, with interest, at some time in the future.

_____   **2.** Twenty acres of land held for speculation.

_____   **3.** An amount owed by a customer.

_____   **4.** Corporate income taxes owed to the federal government.

_____   **5.** Ownership in a company that allows the owner to receive dividends before common shareholders receive any distributions.

_____   **6.** Five acres of land used as the site for a factory.

_____   **7.** Amounts owed to a supplier of raw materials, interest and principal due in 90 days.

_____   **8.** A checking account at the bank.

_____   9. A warehouse used to store merchandise.

_____   10. Claims by the owners on the undistributed net income of a business.

_____   11. Rent paid on an office building in advance of use of the facility.

(LO 5) EXERCISE 3-6 NORMAL ACCOUNT BALANCES

Each account has a normal balance. For the following list of accounts, indicate whether the normal balance of each is a debit or a credit.

ACCOUNT	NORMAL BALANCE
1. Cash	_____
2. Prepaid Insurance	_____
3. Retained Earnings	_____
4. Bonds Payable	_____
5. Investments	_____
6. Capital Stock	_____
7. Advertising Fees Earned	_____
8. Wages and Salaries Expense	_____
9. Wages and Salaries Payable	_____
10. Office Supplies	_____
11. Dividends	_____

(LO 5) EXERCISE 3-7 DEBITS AND CREDITS

The new bookkeeper for Ace Corporation is getting ready to mail the daily cash receipts to the bank for deposit. Because his previous job was at a bank, he is aware that the bank "credits your account" for all deposits and "debits" your account for all checks written. Therefore, he makes the following entry prior to sending the daily receipts to the bank:

June 5	Accounts Receivable	10,000	
	Sales Revenue	2,450	
	Cash		12,450
	To record cash received on June 5: $10,000 on account and $2,450 in cash sales.		

Explain why this entry is wrong and prepare the correct journal entry. Why does the bank refer to cash received from a customer as a *credit* to that customer's account?

(LO 8) EXERCISE 3-8 TRIAL BALANCE

The following list of accounts was taken from the general ledger of Shaw Corporation on December 31, 1995. The bookkeeper thought it would be helpful if the accounts were arranged in alphabetical order! Each account contains the balance normal for that type of account (for example, Cash normally has a debit balance). Prepare a trial balance as of this date, with the accounts arranged in the following order: (1) assets, (2) liabilities, (3) owners' equity, (4) revenues, (5) expenses, and (6) dividends.

ACCOUNT	BALANCE
Accounts Payable	$ 7,650
Accounts Receivable	5,325
Automobiles	9,200
Buildings	150,000
Capital Stock	100,000
Cash	10,500
Commissions Expense	2,600
Commissions Revenue	12,750
Dividends	2,000
Equipment	85,000
Heat, Light, and Water Expense	1,400
Income Tax Expense	1,700
Income Taxes Payable	2,500
Interest Revenue	1,300
Land	50,000
Notes Payable	90,000
Office Salaries Expense	6,000
Office Supplies	500
Retained Earnings	110,025

(LO 8) EXERCISE 3-9 ERRORS IN A TRIAL BALANCE

A customer's account receivable in the amount of $500 is collected. For each of the following independent situations, indicate whether the error involved would, or would not, be disclosed by the preparation of a trial balance.

1. Cash is debited for $500 and Sales is credited for the same amount.

2. Cash is debited for $500 and Accounts Receivable is debited for the same amount.

3. Cash is debited for $500 and Accounts Receivable is credited for $400.

4. Cash is debited for $600 and Accounts Receivable is credited for $600.

MULTI-CONCEPT EXERCISES

(LO 3, 5, 6) EXERCISE 3-10 JOURNAL ENTRIES

Prepare the journal entry to record each of the following independent transactions (use the number of the transaction in lieu of a date for identification purposes):

1. Sales on account of $1,530.

2. Purchases of supplies on account for $1,365.

3. Cash sales of $750.

4. Purchase of equipment for cash of $4,240.

5. Issuance of a promissory note for $2,500.

6. Collections on account for $890.

7. Sale of capital stock in exchange for a parcel of land. The land is appraised at $50,000.

8. Payment of $4,000 in salaries and wages.

9. Payment of open account in the amount of $500.

(LO 3, 5, 6) EXERCISE 3-11 JOURNAL ENTRIES

Following is a list of transactions entered into during the first month of operations of Oak Corporation, a new landscape service. Prepare in journal form the entry to record each transaction.

April 1:   Articles of incorporation are filed with the state and 100,000 shares of common stock are issued for $100,000 in cash.

April 4:   A six-month promissory note is signed at the bank. Interest at 9% per annum will be repaid in six months along with the principal amount of the loan of $50,000.

April 8:   Land and a storage shed are acquired for a lump sum of $80,000. On the basis of an appraisal, 25% of the value is assigned to the land and the remainder to the building.

April 10:   Mowing equipment is purchased from a supplier at a total cost of $25,000. A down payment of $10,000 is made with the remainder due by the end of the month.

April 18:   Customers are billed for services provided during the first half of the month. The total amount billed of $5,500 is due within 10 days.

April 27:   The remaining balance due on the mowing equipment is paid to the supplier.

April 28:   The total amount of $5,500 due from customers is received.

April 30:   Customers are billed for services provided during the second half of the month. The total amount billed is $9,850.

April 30:   Salaries and wages of $4,650 for the month of April are paid.

(LO 6, 7) EXERCISE 3-12 THE PROCESS OF POSTING JOURNAL ENTRIES TO GENERAL LEDGER ACCOUNTS

On June 1, Cubs Corporation purchased 10 acres of land in exchange for a promissory note in the amount of $50,000. Using the formats shown in Exhibit 3-6, prepare the journal entry to record this transaction in a general journal and post it to the appropriate general ledger accounts. The entry will be recorded on page 7 of the general journal. Use whatever account numbers you would like in the general ledger. Assume that none of the accounts to be debited or credited currently contain a balance.

   If at a later date you wanted to review this transaction, would you examine the general ledger or the general journal? Explain your answer.

PROBLEMS

(LO 1) PROBLEM 3-1 EVENTS TO BE RECORDED IN ACCOUNTS

The following events take place at a Fast and Friendly Food Fillup:

1. Food is ordered from vendors to be delivered within the week.

2. Vendors deliver food on account, payment due in 30 days.

3. Employees take frozen food from the freezers and prepare it for customers.

4. Food is served to customers. Sales are rung up on the cash register, to be totaled at the end of the day.

5. Trash is taken to dumpsters and floors are cleaned.

6. Cash registers are cleared at the end of the day.

7. Cash is deposited in the bank night depository.

8. Employees are paid weekly paychecks.

9. Vendors noted in item 2 are paid for the food delivered.

Identify each event as internal (I) or external (E) and indicate whether each event would be recorded in the *accounts* of the company. For each event that is to be recorded, identify the names of at least two accounts that would be affected.

■ REQUIRED

(LO 3) PROBLEM 3-2 TRANSACTION ANALYSIS AND FINANCIAL STATEMENT PREPARATION

Expert Consulting Services, Inc., was organized on March 1, 1995, by two former college roommates. The corporation will provide computer consulting services to small businesses. The following transactions occurred during the first month of operations:

March 2: Received contributions of $20,000 from each of the two principal owners of the new business in exchange for shares of stock.

March 7: Signed a two-year promissory note at the bank and received cash of $15,000. Interest, along with the $15,000, will be repaid at the end of the two years.

March 12: Purchased $700 in miscellaneous supplies on an open account. The company has 30 days to pay for the supplies.

March 19: Billed a client $4,000 for services rendered by Expert in helping to install a new computer system. The client is to pay 25% of the bill upon its receipt and the remaining balance within 30 days.

March 20: Paid $1,300 bill from the local newspaper for advertising for the month of March.

March 22: Received 25% of the amount billed client on March 19.

March 26: Received cash of $2,800 for services provided in assisting a client in selecting software for its computer.

March 29: Purchased a computer system for $8,000 in cash.

March 30: Paid $3,300 of salaries and wages for March.

March 31: Received and paid $1,400 in gas, electric, and water bills.

1. Prepare a table to summarize the preceding transactions as they affect the accounting equation. Use the format in Exhibit 3-1. Identify each transaction with the date.

■ REQUIRED

2. Prepare an income statement for the month of March.

3. Prepare a balance sheet at March 31, 1995.

4. From reading the balance sheet you prepared in part 3, what events would you expect to take place in April? Explain your answer.

(LO 3) PROBLEM 3-3 TRANSACTIONS RECONSTRUCTED FROM FINANCIAL STATEMENTS

The following financial statements are available for Elm Corporation for its first month of operations:

ELM CORPORATION
INCOME STATEMENT
FOR THE MONTH ENDED JUNE 30, 1995

Service revenue		$93,600
Expenses:		
Rent	$ 9,000	
Salaries and wages	27,900	
Utilities	13,800	50,700
Net income		$42,900

ELM CORPORATION
BALANCE SHEET
JUNE 30, 1995

ASSETS		LIABILITIES AND OWNERS' EQUITY	
Cash	$ 22,800	Accounts payable	$ 18,000
Accounts receivable	21,600	Notes payable	90,000
Equipment	18,000		
Building	90,000	Capital stock	30,000
Land	24,000	Retained earnings	38,400
Totals	$176,400	Totals	$176,400

■ **REQUIRED** Using the format illustrated in Exhibit 3-1, prepare a table to summarize the transactions entered into by Elm Corporation during its first month of business. State any assumptions you believe are necessary in reconstructing the transactions.

MULTI-CONCEPT PROBLEMS

(LO 1, 2) PROBLEM 3-4 IDENTIFICATION OF EVENTS WITH SOURCE DOCUMENTS

Many events are linked to a source document. The following is a list of events that occurred in an entity:

a. Paid a one-year insurance policy.

b. Paid employee payroll.

c. Sold merchandise to a customer on account.

d. Identified supplies in the storeroom destroyed by fire.

e. Received payment of bills from customers.

f. Purchased land for future expansion.

g. Calculated taxes due.

h. Entered into a car lease agreement and paid the tax, title, and license.

■ **REQUIRED** For each item *a* through *h:*

1. Indicate whether the event should or should not be recorded in the entity's accounts.

2. For each item that should be recorded in the entity's books

   a. Identify one or more source documents that are generated from the event.

   b. Identify which source document would be used to record an event when it produces more than one source document.

   c. Identify the information from each document that is most useful in recording the event in the accounts.

(LO 3, 5) PROBLEM 3-5 ACCOUNTS USED TO RECORD TRANSACTIONS

A list of accounts, with an identifying number for each, is shown below. Following the list of accounts is a series of transactions entered into by a company during its first year of operations.

1. Cash	**9. Notes Payable**
2. Accounts Receivable	**10. Capital Stock**
3. Office Supplies	**11. Retained Earnings**
4. Buildings	**12. Service Revenue**
5. Automobiles	**13. Wage and Salary Expense**
6. Land	**14. Selling Expense**
7. Accounts Payable	**15. Utilities Expense**
8. Income Tax Payable	**16. Income Tax Expense**

TRANSACTIONS	ACCOUNTS DEBITED	CREDITED
Example: Purchased land and building in exchange for a three-year promissory note.	4, 6	9
a. Issued capital stock for cash.	———	———
b. Purchased 10 automobiles; paid part in cash and signed a 60-day note for the balance.	———	———
c. Purchased land in exchange for note due in six months.	———	———
d. Purchased office supplies; agreed to pay total bill by the 10th of the following month.	———	———
e. Billed clients for services performed during the month and gave them until the 15th of the following month to pay.	———	———
f. Received cash on account from clients for services rendered to them in past months.	———	———
g. Paid employees salaries and wages earned during the month.	———	———
h. Paid newspaper for company ads appearing during the month.	———	———
i. Received monthly gas and electric bill from the utility company; payment is due anytime within first 10 days of the following month.	———	———
j. Computed amount of taxes due based on the income of the period; amount will be paid in following month.	———	———

For each transaction, indicate the account or accounts that should be debited and credited. ■ REQUIRED

(LO 3, 5, 6) PROBLEM 3-6 JOURNAL ENTRIES

Robb Advertising Agency began business on January 2, 1995. Listed below are the transactions entered into by Robb during its first month of operations.

TRANSACTIONS

a. Acquired its articles of incorporation from the state and issued 100,000 shares of capital stock in exchange for $200,000 in cash.

b. Purchased an office building for $150,000 in cash. The building is valued at $110,000 and the remainder of the value is assigned to the land.

c. Signed a three-year promissory note at the bank for $125,000.

d. Purchased office equipment at a cost of $50,000, paying $10,000 down and agreeing to repay the remainder in 10 days.

e. Paid wages and salaries of $13,000 for the first half of the month. Office employees are paid twice a month.

f. Paid the balance due on the office equipment.

g. Sold $24,000 of advertising during the first month. Customers have until the 15th of the following month to pay their bills.

h. Paid wages and salaries of $15,000 for the second half of the month.

i. Recorded $3,500 in commissions earned by the salespeople during the month. They will be paid on the fifth of the following month.

■ REQUIRED   Prepare in journal form the entry to record each transaction.

(LO 3, 4, 5) PROBLEM 3-7 JOURNAL ENTRIES RECORDED DIRECTLY IN T ACCOUNTS
Refer to the transactions for Robb Advertising Agency in Problem 3-6.

■ REQUIRED   Record each transaction directly in T accounts, using the letters preceding each transaction to identify them in the accounts. Each account involved in the problem needs a separate T account.

(LO 3, 5, 8) PROBLEM 3-8 THE DETECTION OF ERRORS IN A TRIAL BALANCE AND PREPARATION OF A CORRECTED TRIAL BALANCE
Chicago Corp. was incorporated on January 1, 1995, with the issuance of capital stock in return for $90,000 of cash contributed by the owners. The only other transaction entered into prior to beginning operations was the issuance of a $75,300 note payable in exchange for building and equipment. The following trial balance was prepared at the end of the first month by the bookkeeper for Chicago Corp.:

CHICAGO CORP.
TRIAL BALANCE
JANUARY 31, 1995

ACCOUNT TITLES	DEBITS	CREDITS
Cash	$ 9,980	
Accounts Receivable	8,640	
Land	80,000	
Building	50,000	
Equipment	23,500	
Notes Payable		$ 75,300
Capital Stock		90,000
Service Revenue		50,340
Wage and Salary Expense	23,700	
Advertising Expense	4,600	
Utilities Expense	8,420	
Dividends		5,000
Totals	$208,840	$220,640

1. Identify the *two* errors present in the trial balance. Explain the nature of the error in both cases and how each of these errors may have occurred (more than one explanation may be possible for each error).

2. Prepare a corrected trial balance.

3. Give examples of at least two other types of errors that would *not* be detected from a trial balance.

■REQUIRED

(LO 3, 5, 6, 8) PROBLEM 3-9 JOURNAL ENTRIES, TRIAL BALANCE, AND FINANCIAL STATEMENTS

Overnight Delivery, Inc., is incorporated on January 2, 1995, and enters into the following transactions during its first month of operations:

January 2:   Filed articles of incorporation with the state and issued 100,000 shares of capital stock. Cash of $100,000 is received from the new owners for the shares.

January 3:   Purchased a warehouse and land for $80,000 in cash. An appraiser values the land at $20,000 and the warehouse at $60,000.

January 4:   Signed a three-year promissory note at the Third State Bank in the amount of $50,000.

January 6:   Purchased five new delivery trucks for a total of $45,000 in cash.

January 31:   Performed services on account during the month that amounted to $15,900. Cash amounting to $7,490 was received from customers on account during the month.

January 31:   Established an open account at a local service station at the beginning of the month. Purchases of gas and oil during January amounted to $3,230. Overnight has until the 10th of the following month to pay its bill.

1. Prepare journal entries on the books of Overnight to record the transactions entered into during the month.

2. Prepare a trial balance at January 31, 1995.

3. Prepare an income statement for the month of January.

4. Prepare a balance sheet at January 31, 1995.

5. Assume that you are considering buying stock in this company. Beginning with the transaction to record the purchase of the property on January 3, list any additional information you would like to have about each of the transactions during the remainder of the month.

■REQUIRED

(LO 3, 5, 6, 8) PROBLEM 3-10 JOURNAL ENTRIES, TRIAL BALANCE, AND FINANCIAL STATEMENTS

Neveranerror, Inc., was organized on June 2, 1995 by a group of accountants to provide accounting and tax services to small businesses. The following transactions occurred during the first month of business:

June 2:   Received contributions of $10,000 from each of the three owners of the business in exchange for shares of stock.

June 5:   Purchased a computer system for $12,000. The agreement with the vendor requires a down payment of $2,500 with the balance due in 60 days.

June 8:   Signed a two-year promissory note at the bank and received cash of $20,000.

June 15:   Billed $12,350 to clients for the first half of June. Clients are billed twice a month for services performed during the month, and the bills are payable within 10 days.

June 17:   Paid a $900 bill from the local newspaper for advertising for the month of June.

June 23:   Received the amounts billed to clients for services performed during the first half of the month.

June 28:   Received and paid gas, electric, and water bills. The total amount is $2,700.

June 29:   Received the landlord's bill for $2,200 for rent on the office space Neveranerror leases. The bill is payable by the 10th of the following month.

June 30:   Paid salaries and wages for June. The total amount is $5,670.

June 30:   Billed $18,400 to clients for the second half of June.

June 30:   Declared and paid dividends in the amount of $6,000.

■ REQUIRED

1. Prepare journal entries on the books of Neveranerror, Inc., to record the transactions for the month of June.

2. Prepare a trial balance at June 30, 1995.

3. Prepare the following financial statements:

   a. Income statement for the month ended June 30, 1995.

   b. Statement of retained earnings for the month ended June 30, 1995.

   c. Balance sheet at June 30, 1995.

4. Assume that you have just graduated from college and have been approached to join this company as an accountant. From your reading of the financial statements for the first month, would you consider joining the company? Explain your answer. Limit your answer to financial considerations only.

ALTERNATE PROBLEMS

(LO 1) PROBLEM 3-1A EVENTS TO BE RECORDED IN ACCOUNTS

The following events take place at Ace Accountants, Inc.:

1. Supplies are ordered from vendors to be delivered within the week.

2. Vendors deliver supplies on account, payment due in 30 days.

3. New computer system is ordered.

4. Old computer system is sold for cash.

5. Services are rendered to customers on account. The invoices are mailed and due in 30 days.

6. Cash received from customer payments is deposited in the bank night depository.

7. Employees are paid weekly paychecks.

8. Vendors noted in item 2 are paid for the supplies delivered.

■ REQUIRED

Identify each event as internal (I) or external (E) and indicate whether each event would be recorded in the *accounts* of the company. For each event that is to be recorded, identify the names of at least two accounts that would be affected.

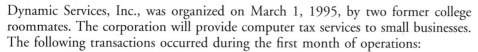

(LO 3) PROBLEM 3-2A TRANSACTION ANALYSIS AND FINANCIAL STATEMENT PREPARATION

Dynamic Services, Inc., was organized on March 1, 1995, by two former college roommates. The corporation will provide computer tax services to small businesses. The following transactions occurred during the first month of operations:

March 2: Received contributions of $10,000 from each of the two principal owners in exchange for shares of stock.

March 7: Signed a two-year promissory note at the bank and received cash of $7,500. Interest, along with the $7,500, will be repaid at the end of the two years.

March 12: Purchased miscellaneous supplies on an open account for $350, payment due in 30 days.

March 19: Billed a client $2,000 for tax preparation services. According to an agreement between the two companies, the client is to pay 25% of the bill upon its receipt and the remaining balance within 30 days.

March 20: Paid a $650 bill from the local newspaper for advertising for the month of March.

March 22: Received 25% of the amount billed client on March 19.

March 26: Received cash of $1,400 for services provided in assisting a client in preparing its tax return.

March 29: Purchased a computer system for $4,000 in cash.

March 30: Paid $1,650 in salaries and wages for March.

March 31: Received and paid $700 of gas, electric, and water bills.

1. Prepare a table to summarize the preceding transactions as they affect the accounting equation. Use the format in Exhibit 3-1. Identify each transaction with the date.

2. Prepare an income statement for the month of March.

3. Prepare a balance sheet at March 31, 1995.

4. From reading the balance sheet you prepared in part 3, what events would you expect to take place in April? Explain your answer.

■ REQUIRED

(LO 3) PROBLEM 3-3A TRANSACTIONS RECONSTRUCTED FROM FINANCIAL STATEMENTS

The following financial statements are available for Oak Corporation for its first month of operations:

OAK CORPORATION
INCOME STATEMENT
FOR THE MONTH ENDED JULY 31, 1995

Service revenue		$75,400
Expenses:		
Rent	$ 6,000	
Salaries and wages	24,600	
Utilities	12,700	43,300
Net income		$32,100

OAK CORPORATION
BALANCE SHEET
JULY 31, 1995

ASSETS		LIABILITIES AND OWNERS' EQUITY	
Cash	$ 13,700	Wages payable	$ 6,000
Accounts receivable	25,700	Notes payable	50,000
Equipment	32,000	Unearned service revenue	4,500
Furniture	14,700	Capital stock	30,000
Land	24,000	Retained earnings	19,600
Totals	$110,100	Totals	$110,100

■ REQUIRED   Describe as many transactions as you can that were entered into by Oak Corporation during the first month of business.

ALTERNATE MULTI-CONCEPT PROBLEMS

(LO 1, 2) PROBLEM 3-4A IDENTIFICATION OF EVENTS WITH SOURCE DOCUMENTS

Many events are linked to a source document. The following is a list of events that occurred in an entity:

a. Paid a security deposit and six months' rent on a building.

b. Hired three employees and agreed to pay them $400 per week.

c. Sold merchandise to a customer for cash.

d. Reported a fire that destroyed a billboard that is on the entity's property and is owned and maintained by another entity.

e. Received payment of bills from customers.

f. Purchased stock in another entity to gain some control over it.

g. Signed a note at the bank and received cash.

h. Contracted with a cleaning service to maintain the interior of the building in good repair. No money is paid at this time.

■ REQUIRED   For each item *a* through *h*:

1. Indicate whether the event should or should not be recorded in the entity's accounts.

2. For each item that should be recorded in the entity's books:

   a. Identify one or more source documents that are generated from the event.

   b. Identify which source document would be used to record an event when it produces more than one source document.

   c. Identify the information from each document that is most useful in recording the event in the accounts.

(LO 3, 5) PROBLEM 3-5A ACCOUNTS USED TO RECORD TRANSACTIONS

A list of accounts, with an identifying number for each, is shown below. Following the list of accounts is a series of transactions entered into by a company during its first year of operations.

1. Cash
2. Accounts Receivable
3. Prepaid Insurance
4. Office Supplies
5. Automobiles
6. Land
7. Accounts Payable
8. Income Tax Payable
9. Notes Payable
10. Capital Stock
11. Retained Earnings
12. Service Revenue
13. Wage and Salary Expense
14. Utilities Expense
15. Income Tax Expense

TRANSACTIONS	ACCOUNTS DEBITED	CREDITED
Example: Purchased office supplies for cash	4	1
a. Issued capital stock for cash.		
b. Purchased an automobile and signed a 60-day note for the total amount.		
c. Acquired land in exchange for capital stock.		
d. Received cash from clients for services performed during the month.		
e. Paid employees salaries and wages earned during the month.		
f. Purchased flyers and signs from a printer, payment due in 10 days.		
g. Paid for the flyers and signs purchased in part f.		
h. Received monthly telephone bill; payment is due within 10 days of receipt.		
i. Paid for a six-month liability insurance policy.		
j. Paid monthly telephone bill.		
k. Computed amount of taxes due based on the income of the period and paid the amount.		

For each transaction, indicate the account or accounts that should be debited and credited.   ■ **REQUIRED**

(LO 3, 5, 6) PROBLEM 3-6A JOURNAL ENTRIES

Bucher Computer Consulting Agency began business in February 1995. Listed below are the transactions entered into by Bucher during its first month of operations.

TRANSACTIONS

a. Acquired articles of incorporation from the state and issued 10,000 shares of capital stock in exchange for $150,000 in cash.
b. Paid monthly rent of $400.
c. Signed a five-year promissory note for $100,000 at the bank.
d. Received $5,000 cash from a customer for services to be performed over the next two months.
e. Purchased software to be used on future jobs. The software costs $950 and is expected to be used on five to eight jobs over the next two years.
f. Billed customers $12,500 for work performed during the month.

g. Paid office personnel $3,000 for the month of February.

h. Received a utility bill of $100. The total amount is due in 30 days.

■ REQUIRED   Prepare in journal form the entry to record each transaction.

(LO 3, 4, 5) PROBLEM 3-7A JOURNAL ENTRIES RECORDED DIRECTLY IN T ACCOUNTS

Refer to the transactions for Bucher Computer Consulting in Problem 3-6A.

■ REQUIRED   Record each transaction directly in T accounts, using the letters preceding each transaction to identify them in the accounts. Each account involved in the problem needs a separate T account.

(LO 3, 4, 5, 8) PROBLEM 3-8A ENTRIES PREPARED FROM A TRIAL BALANCE AND PROOF OF THE CASH BALANCE

Dallas Company was incorporated on January 1, 1995, with the issuance of capital stock in return for $120,000 of cash contributed by the owners. The only other transaction entered into prior to beginning operations was the issuance of a $50,000 note payable in exchange for equipment and fixtures. The following trial balance was prepared at the end of the first month by the Dallas Company bookkeeper:

DALLAS COMPANY
TRIAL BALANCE
JANUARY 31, 1995

ACCOUNT TITLES	DEBITS	CREDITS
Cash	$? ? ?	
Accounts Receivable	30,500	
Equipment and Fixtures	50,000	
Wages Payable		$ 10,000
Notes Payable		50,000
Capital Stock		120,000
Service Revenue		60,500
Wage and Salary Expense	24,600	
Advertising Expense	12,500	
Rent Expense	5,200	
Totals	$240,500	$240,500

■ REQUIRED

1. Determine the balance in the Cash account.

2. Identify all of the transactions that occurred during the month that affected the Cash account. Use a T account to prove what the balance in Cash would be after all transactions are recorded.

(LO 3, 5, 6) PROBLEM 3-9A JOURNAL ENTRIES

Overnight Delivery, Inc., is incorporated on January 2, 1995, and enters into the following transactions during its second month of operations:

February 2: Paid $400 for wages earned by employees for the week ending January 31.

February 3: Paid $3,230 for gas and oil billed on an open account in January.

February 4: Declared and paid $2,000 cash dividends to stockholders.

February 15: Received $8,000 cash from customer accounts.

February 26: Provided $16,800 of services on account during the month.

February 27: Received a $3,400 bill from the local service station for gas and oil used during February.

1. Prepare journal entries on the books of Overnight to record the transactions entered into during February.

2. For the transactions on February 2, 3, 4, and 27, indicate whether the amount is an expense of operating in the month of January or February or is not an expense in either month.

(LO 3, 5, 6) PROBLEM 3-10A JOURNAL ENTRIES AND A BALANCE SHEET

Krittersbegone, Inc., was organized on July 1, 1995 by a group of technicians to provide termite inspections and treatment to homeowners and small businesses. The following transactions occurred during the first month of business:

July 2:   Received contributions of $3,000 from each of the six owners in exchange for shares of stock.

July 3:   Paid $1,000 rent for the month of July.

July 5:   Purchased flashlights, tools, spray equipment, and ladders for $18,000, with a down payment of $5,000 and the balance due in 30 days.

July 17:   Paid a $200 bill for the distribution of door-to-door advertising.

July 28:   Paid August rent and July utilities to the landlord in the amounts of $1,000 and $450, respectively.

July 30:   Received $8,000 in cash from homeowners for services performed during the month. In addition, billed $7,500 to other customers for services performed during the month. Billings are due in 30 days.

July 30:   Paid commissions of $9,500 to the technicians for July.

July 31:   Received $600 from a business client to perform services over the next two months.

1. Prepare journal entries on the books of Krittersbegone for the month of July.

2. Prepare a balance sheet dated July 31, 1995. From the balance sheet, what cash inflow and what cash outflow can you predict in the month of August? Who would be interested in the cash flow information and why?

CASES

READING AND INTERPRETING FINANCIAL STATEMENTS

(LO 3, 5, 6) CASE 3-1 READING AND INTERPRETING BEN & JERRY'S STATEMENT OF CASH FLOWS

Refer to Ben & Jerry's statement of cash flows.

1. What amount did the company spend on additions to property, plant, and equipment during 1992? Prepare the journal entry to record these additions, assuming cash was paid.

2. What amount did the company receive from issuing common stock during 1992? Prepare the journal entry to record the issuance of stock. Do not be concerned at this point with the distinction between par value and additional paid-in capital on the balance sheet. This distinction will be explored in Chapter 11.

3. How did Ben & Jerry's pay for the large amount of "net cash used for investing activities" during 1992? The net amount was $36,378,580.

(LO 1, 3, 5, 6) CASE 3-2 READING AND INTERPRETING UNITED AIRLINE'S BALANCE SHEET

The following item appears in the current liabilities section of UAL Corporation's (the parent company for United Airlines) balance sheet on December 31, 1992:

Advance ticket sales $1,067.6 million

■ **REQUIRED**

1. What economic event caused United to incur this liability? Was it an external or an internal event?

2. Describe the effect on the accounting equation from the transaction to record advance ticket sales.

3. Assume one customer purchases a $500 ticket in advance. Prepare the journal entry on United's books to record this transaction.

4. What economic event will cause United to reduce its liability for advance ticket sales? Is this an external or an internal event?

MAKING FINANCIAL DECISIONS

(LO 2, 3) CASE 3-3 CASH FLOW VERSUS NET INCOME

Kathy Horton started a real estate business in December of last year. After approval by the state for a charter to incorporate, she issued 1,000 shares of stock to herself and deposited $20,000 in a bank account under the name Horton Properties. Because business was "booming," she spent all of her time during the first month selling properties rather than keeping financial records.

At the end of January, Kathy comes to you with the following plight:

I put $20,000 in to start this business last month. My January 31 bank statement shows a balance of $17,000. After all of my efforts, it appears as if I'm "in the hole" already! On the other hand, that seems impossible—we sold five properties for clients during the month. The total sales value of these properties was $600,000, and I receive a commission of 5% on each sale. Granted, one of the five sellers still owes me an $8,000 commission on the sale, but the other four have been collected in full. Three of the sales, totaling $400,000, were actually made by my assistants. I pay them 4% of the sales value of a property. Sure, I have a few office expenses for my car, utilities, and a secretary, but that's about it. How can I have possibly lost $3,000 this month?

You agree to help Kathy figure out how she really did this month. The bank statement is helpful. The total deposits during the month amount to $22,000. Kathy explains that this amount represents the commissions on the four sales collected so far. The canceled checks reveal the following expenditures:

CHECK NO.	PAYEE—MEMO AT BOTTOM OF CHECK	AMOUNT
101	Stevens Office Supply	$2,000
102	Why Walk, Let's Talk Motor Co.—new car	3,000
103	City of Westbrook—heat and lights	500
104	Alice Hill—secretary	2,200
105	Ace Property Management—office rent for month	1,200
106	Jerry Hayes (sales assistant)	10,000
107	Joan Harper (sales assistant)	6,000
108	Don's Fillitup—gas and oil for car	100

According to Kathy, the $2,000 check to Stevens Office Supply represents the down payment on a word processor and a copier for the office. The remaining balance is $3,000 and it must be paid to Stevens by February 15. Similarly, the $3,000 check is the down payment on a car for the business. A $12,000 note was given to the car dealer and is due along with interest in one year.

■REQUIRED

1. Prepare an income statement for the month of January for Horton Properties.

2. Prepare a statement of cash flows for the month of January for Horton Properties.

3. Draft a memorandum to Kathy Horton explaining as simply and as clearly as possible why she *did* in fact have a profitable first month in business but experienced a decrease in her cash account. Support your explanation with any necessary figures.

4. The down payments on the car and the office equipment are reflected on the statement of cash flows. They are assets that will benefit the business for a number of years. Do you think that *any* of the cost associated with the acquisition of these assets should be recognized in some way on the income statement? Explain your answer.

(LO 3, 6, 8) CASE 3-4 LOAN REQUEST

Janet Wilson started a landscaping and lawn care business in April 1995 by investing $20,000 cash in the business in exchange for capital stock. Because her business is in the Midwest the season begins in April and concludes in September. She prepared the following trial balance (with accounts in alphabetical order) at the end of her first season in business.

WILSON LANDSCAPING
TRIAL BALANCE
SEPTEMBER 30, 1995

	DEBITS	CREDITS
Accounts Payable		$ 13,000
Accounts Receivable	$ 23,000	
Capital Stock		20,000
Cash	1,200	
Gas and Oil Expense	15,700	
Insurance Expense	2,500	
Landscaping Revenue		33,400
Lawn Care Revenue		24,000
Mowing Equipment	5,000	
Rent Expense	6,000	
Salaries Expense	22,000	
Truck	15,000	
Totals	$ 90,400	$ 90,400

Janet is pleased with her first year in business. "I paid myself a salary during the year of $22,000, and still have $1,200 in the bank. Sure, I have a few bills outstanding, but my accounts receivable will more than cover those." In fact, Janet is so happy with the first year, that she has come to you in your role as a lending officer at the local bank to ask for a $20,000 loan to allow her to add another truck and mowing equipment for the second season.

■REQUIRED

1. From your reading of the trial balance, what does it appear to you that Janet did with the $20,000 in cash she originally contributed to the business? Reconstruct the journal entry to record the transaction you think took place.

2. Prepare an income statement for the six months ended September 30, 1995.

3. The mowing equipment and truck are assets that will benefit the business for a number of years. Do you think that any of the costs associated with the purchase of these assets should have been recognized as expenses in the first year? How would this have affected the income statement?

4. Prepare a balance sheet as of September 30, 1995. As a banker, what two items on the balance sheet concern you the most? Explain your answer.

5. As a banker, would you loan Janet $20,000 to expand her business during the second year? Draft a memo to respond to Janet's request for the loan, indicating whether you will make the loan.

ACCOUNTING AND ETHICS: WHAT WOULD YOU DO?

(LO 3, 5, 6, 7) CASE 3-5 DELAY IN THE POSTING OF A JOURNAL ENTRY

As assistant controller for a small consulting firm, you are responsible for recording and posting the daily cash receipts and disbursements to the ledger accounts. After you have posted the entries, your boss, the controller, prepares a trial balance and the financial statements. You make the following entries on June 30, 1995:

June 30, 1995	Cash	1,430	
	Accounts Receivable	1,950	
	Service Revenue		3,380
	To record daily cash receipts.		
June 30, 1995	Advertising Expense	12,500	
	Utilities Expense	22,600	
	Rent Expense	24,000	
	Salary and Wage Expense	17,400	
	Cash		76,500
	To record daily cash disbursements.		

The daily cash disbursements are much larger on June 30 than any other day because many of the company's major bills are paid on the last day of the month. After you have recorded these two transactions and *before* you have posted them to the ledger accounts, your boss comes to you with the following request:

> As you are aware, the first half of the year has been a tough one for the consulting industry and for our business in particular. With first-half bonuses based on net income, I am concerned whether you or I will get any bonus this time around. However, I have a suggestion that should allow us to receive something for our hard work and at the same time will not hurt anyone. Go ahead and post the June 30 cash receipts to the ledger but don't bother to post that day's cash disbursements. Even though the treasurer writes the checks on the last day of the month and you normally journalize the transaction on the same day, it is pretty silly to bother posting the entry to the ledger since it takes at least a week for the checks to clear the bank.

■ **REQUIRED**

1. Explain *why* the controller's request will result in an increase in net income.

2. Do you agree with the controller that the omission of the entry on June 30 "will not hurt anyone"? If not, be explicit as to why you don't agree. Whom could it hurt?

3. What would you do? Whom should you talk to about this issue?

(LO 5, 6) CASE 3-6 DEBITS AND CREDITS

You are controller for an architectural firm whose accounting year ends on December 31. As part of the management team, your year-end bonus is directly related to the firm's earnings for the year. One of your duties is to review the journal entries recorded by the bookkeepers. A new bookkeeper prepared the following journal entry:

Dec. 3	Accounts receivable	10,000	
	Service revenue		10,000
	To record deposit from client.		

You notice that the explanation for the journal entry refers to the amount as a deposit and the bookkeeper explains to you that the firm plans to provide the services to the client in March of the following year.

1. Did the bookkeeper prepare the correct journal entry to account for the client's deposit? Explain your answer.

2. What would you do as controller for the firm? Do you have a responsibility to do anything to correct the books?

■ **REQUIRED**

ANALYTICAL SOFTWARE CASE

To the Student: Your instructor may assign one or more parts of the analytical software case that is designed to accompany this chapter. This multi-part case gives you a chance to work with real financial statement data using software that stimulates, guides, and hones your analytical and problem-solving skills. It was created especially to support and strengthen your understanding of the chapter's Learning Objectives.

SOLUTION TO KEY TERMS QUIZ

1. Chart of accounts (p. 121)
2. Compound journal entry (p. 130)
3. Trial balance (p. 134)
4. Event (p. 114)
5. Credit (p. 124)
6. Internal event (p. 114)
7. Source document (p. 114)
8. Journalizing (p. 130)
9. Debit (p. 124)
10. Posting (p. 130)
11. External event (p. 114)
12. Account (p. 120)
13. General ledger (p. 123)
14. Journal (p. 129)
15. Transaction (p. 114)
16. General journal (p. 131)
17. Double entry system (p. 127)

Focus on Financial Results

International Business Machines was once among the strongest companies in the world. Today, it is struggling to reinvent itself. It is moving from a company that focused on big mainframe computers to one that focuses on new technologies: personal computers, local area networks, printers, workstations, software, and mail-order. In 1992, the company's revenues totaled $65 billion. But, its losses on those revenues before taxes were $9 billion.

However, two adjustments to this $9 billion loss nearly cut it in half. The company received a tax credit of more than $2 billion.

Consolidated Statement of Earnings

International Business Machines Corporation and Subsidiary Companies

(Dollars in millions except per share amounts) For the year ended December 31:	1992	1991*†	1990*
Revenue:			
Sales	$ 33,755	$ 37,093	$ 43,959
Software	11,103	10,498	9,865
Maintenance	7,635	7,414	7,198
Services	7,352	5,582	4,124
Rentals and financing	4,678	4,179	3,785
	64,523	64,766	68,931
Cost:			
Sales	19,698	18,571	19,401
Software	3,924	3,865	3,118
Maintenance	3,430	3,379	3,302
Services	6,051	4,531	3,315
Rentals and financing	1,966	1,727	1,579
	35,069	32,073	30,715
Gross Profit	29,454	32,693	38,216
Operating Expenses:			
Selling, general and administrative	19,526	21,375	20,709
Research, development and engineering	6,522	6,644	6,554
Restructuring charges	11,645	3,735	—
	37,693	31,754	27,263
Operating Income	(8,239)	939	10,953
Other Income, principally interest	573	602	495
Interest Expense	1,360	1,423	1,324
Earnings before Income Taxes	(9,026)	118	10,124
Provision for Income Taxes	(2,161)	716	4,157
Net Earnings before Changes in Accounting Principles	(6,865)	(598)	5,967
Effect of Changes in Accounting Principles‡	1,900	(2,263)	—
Net Earnings	$ (4,965)	$ (2,861)	$ 5,967

Another $1.9 billion comes from the Financial Accounting Standards Board. In the late 1980s, the FASB issued *Statement 96*, a treatment of accounting for income tax expense that was controversial because it was complex and lowered earnings. Many corporations delayed implementing the statement, but IBM adopted it early, when the company was profitable. FASB later softened its stance and issued *Statement 109*, which superceded *96*. Since *109* is a more liberal treatment of income tax expense, IBM was able to make a favorable adjustment in 1992: a cumulative effect of an accounting change of $1.9 billion. Although such adjustments are helpful, investors are primarily interested in seeing income from operations.

Chapter 4

Income Measurement and Accrual Accounting

LEARNING OBJECTIVES

After studying this chapter, you should be able to

1. Explain the significance of recognition and measurement in the preparation and use of financial statements.

2. Explain the differences between the cash and accrual bases of accounting.

3. Describe the revenue recognition principle and explain its application in various situations.

4. Describe the matching principle and the various methods for recognizing expenses.

5. Identify the four major types of adjusting entries and prepare them for a variety of situations.

6. Explain the steps in the accounting cycle and the significance of each step.

7. Explain why and how closing entries are made at the end of an accounting period.

8. Understand how to use a work sheet as a basis for preparing financial statements (Appendix 4A).

9. Explain why and how reversing entries are used by some businesses (Appendix 4A).

Linkages

A LOOK AT PREVIOUS CHAPTERS

We focused our attention in Chapter 3 on how accounting information is processed. Debits and credits, journal entries, accounts, and trial balances were introduced as convenient tools to aid in the preparation of periodic financial statements.

A LOOK AT THIS CHAPTER

We begin this chapter by considering the roles of recognition and measurement in the process of preparing financial statements. We explore in detail the accrual basis of accounting and its effect on the measurement of income. The recognition of revenues and expenses in an accrual system is examined, and we look at the role of adjusting entries in this process. In the appendix to this chapter, we see how the accountant uses work sheets and other tools to prepare financial statements.

A LOOK AT UPCOMING CHAPTERS

Chapter 4 completes our overview of the accounting model. In the next section, we will examine accounting for the various types of assets. We begin by looking at accounting by merchandise companies in Chapter 5.

Recognition and Measurement in Financial Statements

LO **I**

Explain the significance of recognition and measurement in the preparation and use of financial statements.

Accounting is a communication process. To successfully communicate information to the users of financial statements, accountants and managers must answer two questions: (1) What economic events should be communicated, or *recognized,* in the statements? and (2) How should the effects of these events be *measured* in the statements? The dual concepts of recognition and measurement are crucial to the success of accounting as a form of communication.

Recognition

"**Recognition** is the process of formally recording or incorporating an item into the financial statements of an entity as an asset, liability, revenue, expense, or the like. Recognition includes depiction of an item in both words and numbers, with the amount included in the totals of the financial statements."[1] We see in this definition the central idea behind general-purpose financial statements. They are a form of communication between the entity and external users. Stockholders, bankers, and other creditors have limited access to relevant information about a company. They depend on the periodic financial statements issued by management to provide the necessary information to make their decisions. Acting on behalf of management, accountants have a moral and ethical responsibility to provide users with financial information that will be useful in making their decisions. The process by which the accountant depicts, or describes, the effects of economic events on the entity is called *recognition.*

The items, such as assets, liabilities, revenues, and expenses, depicted in financial statements are *representations.* Simply stated, the accountant cannot show a stockholder or other user the company's assets, such as cash and buildings. What the user sees in a set of financial statements is a depiction of the real thing. That is, the accountant describes, with words and numbers, the various items in a set of financial statements. The system is imperfect at best and, for that reason, is always in the process of change. As society and the business environment have become more complex, the accounting profession has striven for ways to improve financial statements as a means of communicating with their users.

Measurement

Accountants depict a financial statement item in both words and *numbers.* The accountant must *quantify* the effects of economic events on the entity. In other words, it is not enough to decide that an event is important and thus warrants recognition in the financial statements. To be able to recognize it, the statement preparer must measure the financial effects of the event on the company.

Measurement of an item in financial statements requires that two choices be made. First, the accountant must decide on the *attribute* to be measured. Second, a scale of measurement, or *unit of measure,* must be chosen.

The Attribute to Be Measured
Assume that a company holds a parcel of real estate as an investment. What attribute, or characteristic, of the property should be

---

[1] *Statement of Financial Accounting Concepts No. 5,* "Recognition and Measurement in Financial Statements of Business Enterprises" (Stamford, Conn.: Financial Accounting Standards Board, December 1984), par. 6.

used to measure and thus recognize it as an asset on the balance sheet? The cost of the asset at the time it is acquired is the most logical choice. *Cost* is the amount of cash, or its equivalent, paid to acquire the asset. But how do we report the property on a balance sheet a year from now?

The simplest approach is to show the property on the balance sheet at its original cost, thus the designation **historical cost.** Not only is the use of historical cost simple, but it is also *verifiable.* Assume that two accountants are asked to independently measure the cost of the asset. After examining the sales contract for the land, they should arrive at the same amount.

An alternative to historical cost as the attribute to be measured is **current value.** Current value is the amount of cash, or its equivalent, that could be received currently from the sale of the asset. For the company's piece of property, current value is the *estimated* selling price of the land, reduced by any commissions or other fees involved in making the sale. But the amount is only an estimate, not an actual amount. If the company has not yet sold the property, how can we know for certain its selling price? We have to compare it to similar properties that *have* sold recently.

The choice between current value and historical cost as the attribute to be measured is a good example of the trade-off between *relevance* and *reliability.* As indicated earlier, historical cost is verifiable and is thus to a large extent a reliable measure. But is it as relevant to the needs of the decision makers as current value? Put yourself in the position of a banker trying to decide whether to loan money to the company. In evaluating the company's assets as collateral for the loan, is it more relevant to your decision to know what the firm paid for a piece of land 20 years ago or what it could be sold for today? But what *could* it sell the property for today? Two accountants might not necessarily arrive at the same current value for the land. Whereas value or selling price may be more relevant to your decision on the loan, the reliability of this amount is often questionable.

What events have economic consequences to a business? The destructive effects on businesses throughout the Midwest of the 1993 Mississippi flood will certainly be reflected in flood losses of buildings and other assets—and thus in companies' financial statements. But the long-term consequences of the flood involved loss of future sales due to an eroded customer base, as some people were completely wiped out by the flood. However, only **future income statements will recognize** *these consequences in the form of lower revenues.*

Because of its objective nature, historical cost is the attribute used to measure many of the assets recognized on the balance sheet. However, certain other attributes, such as current value, have increased in popularity in recent years. In various chapters of the book, we will have the opportunity to discuss some of the alternatives to historical cost.

The Unit of Measure   Regardless of the attribute of an item to be measured, it is still necessary to choose a yardstick or unit of measure. The yardstick we currently use is units of money. *Money* is something accepted as a medium of exchange or as a means of payment. The unit of money in the United States is the dollar. In Japan the yen is the medium of exchange, and in Great Britain it is the pound.

The use of the dollar as a unit of measure for financial transactions is widely accepted. The *stability* of the dollar as a yardstick is subject to considerable debate, however. Consider an example. You are thinking about buying a certain parcel of land. As part of your decision process, you measure the dimensions of the property and determine that the lot is 80 feet wide and 120 feet deep. Thus, the unit of measure used to determine the lot's size is the foot. The company that owns the land offers to sell it for $10,000. Although the offer sounds attractive, you decide against the purchase today.

You return in one year to take a second look at the lot. You measure the lot again and, not surprisingly, find the width to still be 80 feet and the depth 120 feet. The owner is still willing to sell the lot for $10,000. This may appear to be the same price as last year. But it is very possible that the *purchasing power* of the unit of measure, the dollar, has changed since last year. Even though the foot is a stable measuring unit, the dollar often is not. A *decline* in the purchasing power of the dollar is evidenced by a continuing *rise* in the general level of prices in an economy. For example, rather than paying $10,000 last year to buy the lot, you could have spent the $10,000 on other goods or services. However, a year later, the same $10,000 may very well not buy the same amount of goods and services.

Inflation, or a rise in the general level of prices in the economy, results in a decrease in purchasing power. In the past, the accounting profession has experimented with financial statements adjusted for the changing value of the dollar. As inflation has declined in recent years, the debate over the use of the dollar as a stable measuring unit has somewhat subsided. It is still important to recognize the inherent weakness in the use of a measuring unit that is subject to change, however.

Summary of Recognition and Measurement in Financial Statements

The purpose of financial statements is to communicate various types of economic information about the company. The job of the accountant is to decide which information should be recognized in the financial statements and how the effects of that information on the entity should be measured. Exhibit 4-1 summarizes the role of recognition and measurement in the preparation of financial statements.

The Accrual Basis of Accounting

The accrual basis of accounting is the foundation for the measurement of income in our modern system of accounting. The best way to understand the accrual basis is to compare it with the simpler cash approach.

EXHIBIT 4-1   Recognition and Measurement in Financial Statements

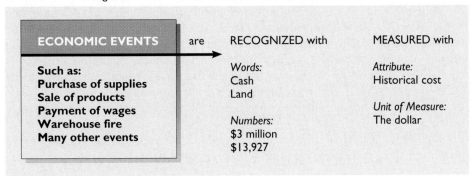

Comparing the Cash and Accrual Bases of Accounting

The cash and accrual bases of accounting differ with respect to the *timing* of the recognition of revenues and expenses. For example, assume that on July 24, Barbara White, a salesperson for Spiffy House Painters, contracts with a homeowner to repaint a house for $1,000. A large crew comes in and paints the house the next day, July 25. The customer has 30 days from the day of completion of the job to pay and does, in fact, pay Spiffy on August 25. *When* should Spiffy recognize the $1,000 as revenue? As soon as the contract is signed on July 24? Or on July 25 when the work is done? Or on August 25 when the customer pays the bill?

In an income statement prepared on the **cash basis,** revenues are recognized when cash is *received.* Thus, on a cash basis, the $1,000 would not be recognized as revenue until the cash is collected on August 25. On an **accrual basis,** revenue is recognized when it is *earned.* On this basis, the $1,000 would be recognized as revenue on July 25 when the house is painted. This is the point at which the revenue is earned.

Recall from Chapter 3 the journal entry to recognize revenue before cash is received. Although cash has not yet been received, another account, Accounts Receivable, is recognized as an asset. This asset represents the right to receive cash in the future. The entry upon completion of the job is as follows:

July 25   Accounts Receivable   1,000
        Service Revenue   1,000
        To recognize revenue from house painting.

Recall from Chapter 3 that the accounting equation must balance after each transaction is recorded. Throughout the remainder of the book, each time we record a journal entry we illustrate the effect of the entry on the equation. The effect of the preceding entry on the equation is as follows:

    Assets   =   Liabilities   +   Owners' Equity
    + 1,000   + 1,000

At the time cash is collected, Accounts Receivable is reduced and Cash is increased:

Aug. 25   Cash   1,000
        Accounts Receivable   1,000
        To record cash received from house painting.

    Assets   =   Liabilities   +   Owners' Equity
    + 1,000
    − 1,000

LO   2

Explain the differences between the cash and accrual bases of accounting.

Assume that Barbara White is paid a 10% commission for all contracts and is paid on the 15th of the month following the month a house is painted. Thus, for this job, she will receive a $100 commission check on August 15. When should Spiffy recognize her commission of $100 as an expense? On July 24 when White gets the homeowner to sign a contract? When the work is completed on July 25? Or on August 15 when she receives the commission check? Again, on a cash basis, commission expense would be recognized on August 15 when cash is *paid* to the salesperson. But on an accrual basis, expenses are recognized when they are *incurred*. In our example, the commission expense is incurred when the house is painted on July 25.

Exhibit 4-2 summarizes the essential differences between the recognition of revenues and expenses on a cash basis and on an accrual basis.

What the Income Statement and the Statement of Cash Flows Reveal

Most business entities, other than the very smallest, use the accrual basis of accounting. Thus, the income statement reflects the accrual basis. Revenues are recognized when they are earned and expenses when they are incurred. At the same time, however, stockholders and creditors are also interested in information concerning the cash flows of an entity. The purpose of a statement of cash flows is to provide this information. Keep in mind that even though we present a statement of cash flows in a complete set of financial statements, the accrual basis is used for recording transactions and for preparing a balance sheet and an income statement.

Recall the example of Glengarry Health Club in Chapter 3. The club earned revenue from two sources, memberships and court fees. Both of these forms of revenue were recognized on the income statement presented in that chapter and are reproduced in the top portion of Exhibit 4-3. Recall, however, that members have 30 days to pay, and at the end of the first month of operation, only $4,000 of the membership fees of $15,000 had been collected.

Now consider the statement of cash flows for the first month of operation as it is partially reproduced in the bottom portion of Exhibit 4-3. Because we want to compare the income statement to the statement of cash flows, only the operating activities section of the statement is shown. (The investing and financing activities sections have been omitted from the statement.) Why is net income for the month a *positive* $7,000, but cash from operating activities a *negative* $4,000? The answer is that of the membership revenue of $15,000 reflected on the income statement, only $4,000 was collected in cash. Glengarry has an accounts receivable for the other

EXHIBIT 4-2 Comparing the Cash and Accrual Bases of Accounting

	Cash Basis	Accrual Basis
Revenue is recognized	**When Received**	**When Earned**
Expense is recognized	**When Paid**	**When Incurred**

EXHIBIT 4-3   Comparing the Income Statement and the Statement of Cash Flows

The income statement for Glengarry Health Club shows the following:

Revenues:

Memberships	$15,000	
Court fees	5,000	$20,000

Expenses:

Salaries and wages	$10,000	
Utilities	3,000	(13,000)
Net income		$ 7,000

A partial statement of cash flows for Glengarry Health Club shows the following:

Net income	$ 7,000
Adjustment to reconcile net income to net cash provided by operating activities:	
Increase in accounts receivable	(11,000)
Cash used by operating activities	$ (4,000)

Another way to look at the cash generated from operations:

Cash received from membership fees	$ 4,000	
Cash received from court fees	5,000	$ 9,000
Cash paid for:		
Salaries and wages	$10,000	
Utilities	3,000	(13,000)
Cash used by operating activities		$ (4,000)

$11,000. Thus, cash from operating activities, as reflected on a statement of cash flows, is $11,000 *less* than net income of $7,000, or a negative $4,000. This is the reason that net income is adjusted downward by $11,000—to account for the fact that net income reflects $15,000 of sales, but only $4,000 of cash was collected—thus requiring an adjustment of $11,000.

The bottom portion of the exhibit provides a proof that cash from operating activities is a negative $4,000. Cash inflows and cash outflows are simply listed, with the result being an excess of cash outflows over inflows in the amount of $4,000. Note that the amount of cash listed as an inflow from membership fees is only $4,000, the amount collected.

Each of these two statements serves a useful purpose. The income statement reflects the revenues actually earned by the business, regardless of whether cash has been collected. The statement of cash flows tells the reader about the actual cash inflows during a period of time. The need for the information provided by both statements is summarized by the Financial Accounting Standards Board as follows:

Statements of cash flows commonly show a great deal about an entity's current cash receipts and payments, but a cash flow statement provides an incomplete basis for assessing prospects for future cash flows because it cannot show interperiod relationships. Many current cash receipts, especially from operations, stem from activities of earlier periods, and many current cash payments are intended or expected to result in future, not current, cash receipts. Statements of earnings and comprehensive income, especially if used in conjunction with statements of financial position, usually provide a better basis for assessing future cash flow prospects of an entity than do cash flow statements alone.[2]

Accrual Accounting and Time Periods

The *time period* assumption was introduced in Chapter 1. We assume that it is possible to prepare an income statement that accurately reflects the earnings of a business for a specific period of time, such as a month or a year. It is somewhat artificial to divide the operations of a business into periods of time as indicated on a calendar. The conflict arises because earning income is a *process* that takes place *over a period of time* rather than *at any one point in time.*

Consider an alternative to our present system of reporting on the operations of a business on a periodic basis. A new business begins operations with an investment of $50,000. The business operates for 10 years during which time no records are kept other than a checkbook for the cash on deposit at the bank. At the end of the 10 years, the owners decide to go their separate ways and convert all of their assets to cash. They split among them the balance of $80,000 in the bank account. What is the profit of the business for the 10-year period? The answer is $30,000, the difference between the original cash of $50,000 contributed and the cash of $80,000 available at liquidation.

The point of this simple example is that we could be very precise and accurate in our measurement of the income of a business if it were not necessary to artificially divide operations according to a calendar. Stockholders, bankers, and other interested parties cannot wait until a business liquidates to make decisions, however. They need information on a periodic basis. Thus, the justification for the accrual basis of accounting lies in the needs of financial statement users for periodic information on the financial position as well as the profitability of the entity.

The Revenue Recognition Principle

LO 3
Describe the revenue recognition principle and explain its application in various situations.

"**Revenues** are inflows or other enhancements of assets of an entity or settlements of its liabilities (or a combination of both) from delivering or producing goods, rendering services, or other activities that constitute the entity's ongoing major or central operations."[3] Two points should be noted about this formal definition of revenues. First, an asset is not always involved when revenue is recognized. It is possible for the recognition of revenue to result from the settlement of a liability rather than the acquisition of an asset. Second, entities generate revenue in different ways: some companies produce goods, others distribute or deliver the goods to users, and still others provide some type of service.

On the accrual basis, revenues are recognized when earned. However, the **revenue recognition principle** actually involves two factors. Revenues are recognized in the income statement when they are *realized* or *realizable* and *earned.* Revenues are *realized* when goods or services are exchanged for cash or claims to cash. *Realizable* has a slightly different meaning that will be explained later when we look at commodities.

[2] *SFAC No. 5,* par. 24c.
[3] *Statement of Financial Accounting Concepts No. 6,* "Elements of Financial Statements" (Stamford, Conn.: Financial Accounting Standards Board, December 1985), par. 78.

When evaluating whether or not to invest in a franchisor, you might look at the popularity of the franchises themselves. But would you think to ask about the franchisor's policies for recognizing revenues from new franchises? These policies can affect how much net income is reported.

Other Applications of the Revenue Recognition Principle

At what point are revenues realized, or realizable, and earned by an entity? As a practical rule, revenue is usually recognized at the time of sale. This is normally interpreted to mean at the time of delivery of the product or service to the customer. However, consider the following examples in which it is necessary either to modify or to interpret the meaning of the revenue recognition principle.

Long-Term Contracts   Assume that a construction company starts two projects during the year. One is a $5 million contract for a bridge. The other is a $4 million contract for a dam. Based on actual costs incurred to date and estimates of costs yet to be incurred, the contractor estimates that at the end of the year the bridge is 20% complete and the dam is 50% complete. Which would be more informative to you as a stockholder of the construction company: (1) a report at the end of the year that indicates no revenue because no contracts are finished yet or (2) a report at the end of the year that indicates revenue of $1 million on the bridge (20% of $5 million) and $2 million on the dam (50% of $4 million), both based on the extent of completion?

The **percentage-of-completion method** allows a contractor to recognize revenue over the life of a project rather than at its completion. For long-term contracts in which the sales price is fixed by contract and the realization of revenue depends only on production, such as constructing the bridge or the dam, the method is a reasonable alternative to deferring the recognition of revenue until the project is completed. The following excerpt from the 1992 annual report of Morrison Knudsen Corporation is an example of how revenue is recognized by many companies in the construction industry:

Recognition of Revenue: The Corporation recognizes revenue on construction contracts . . . on the percentage-of-completion method, based on the proportion of costs incurred on the contract to total estimated contract costs. Construction-management and engineering contract revenue is recognized on the accrual method. Revenue is recognized on long-term rail systems contracts on the delivery of products.

Franchises Over the last 30 years, franchising has achieved enormous popularity as a way to conduct business. It has been especially prevalent in retail sales, including the fast-food (McDonald's), motel (Holiday Inn), and car rental (Hertz) businesses. Typically, the franchisor (such as McDonald's) grants the exclusive right to sell a product or service in a specific geographic area to the franchisee. The franchisor generates revenues from one or both of two sources: (1) from the sale of the franchise and related services, such as help in selecting a site and hiring employees and (2) from continuing fees based on performance, for example, a fixed percentage of sales by the franchisee. The following excerpt from the 1992 annual report of McDonald's Corp. indicates the typical arrangement it has with its franchisees:

> Under the conventional franchise arrangement, franchisees supply capital—initially, by purchasing equipment, signs, seating, and decor, and over the long term, by reinvesting in their businesses. The Company shares the investment by owning or leasing the land and building; franchisees then contribute to McDonald's revenues through payment of rent and service fees based upon a percent of sales, with minimum payments. The conventional franchise arrangement generally lasts for 20 years and, in the U.S., requires an initial investment ranging from approximately $430,000 to $560,000, 60% of which may be financed.

At what point should the revenue from the sale of a franchise be recognized? An FASB standard allows a franchisor to recognize initial franchise fees as revenue only when it has made "substantial performance" of its obligations and collection of the fee is reasonably assured.[4] An excerpt from the 1992 annual report of Ben & Jerry's Homemade, Inc., indicates how one company recognizes the initial franchise fee as revenue:

Revenue Recognition—Franchising Operations
The Company recognizes initial franchise fees for individual stores as income when services required by the franchise agreement have been performed and the franchisee opens for business. Initial franchise fees relating to area franchise agreements are

---

FROM CONCEPT TO PRACTICE

READING BEN & JERRY'S FOOTNOTES AND INCOME STATEMENT

Refer to the income statement in Ben & Jerry's annual report and the footnote at the bottom of this page. Where does the company include franchise fees on its income statement? How significant are these fees?

■ ACCOUNTING FOR YOUR DECISIONS   You Are the Investor

You are considering buying stock in a new franchisor that sells fast-food franchises in large cities. The company charges a large upfront fee to the franchisees in return for assisting them in finding a suitable location and establishing their business. The company follows the policy of recording revenue from these fees at the time a contract is signed. It normally takes six months to one year after the contract is signed before the franchisee opens it doors. The company you are considering investing in has been in business for two years.

1. Is it appropriate for the franchisor to recognize all of the revenue from a franchisee at the time the contract is signed? Explain your answer.
2. What dangers, if any, do you see in investing in this company?

---

[4] *Statement of Financial Accounting Standards No. 45,* "Accounting for Franchise Fee Revenue" (Stamford, Conn.: Financial Accounting Standards Board, December 1981), par. 5.

recognized in proportion to the stores for which the required mandatory services have been substantially performed. Franchise fees recognized as income were $91,250, $95,500 and $117,416 in 1992, 1991 and 1990, respectively. These amounts have been included in net sales of the respective periods.

Commodities   Corn, wheat, gold, silver, and other agricultural and mining products trade on the open market at established prices. Readily convertible assets such as these are interchangeable and can be sold at a quoted price in an active market that can absorb the quantity being sold without significantly affecting the price.[5] Earlier we mentioned that to be recognized, revenues must be either realized or realizable. Revenues are *realizable* when assets received or held are readily convertible to known amounts of cash or claims to cash.

Assume that a company mines gold. Revenues are realizable by the company at the time the product is mined because each ounce of gold is interchangeable with another ounce of gold and the commodities market can absorb all of the gold the company sells without having an effect on the price. This is one of the few instances in which it is considered acceptable to recognize revenue *prior* to the point of sale. The exception is justified because the important event in the revenue generation process is the *production* of the gold, not the sale of it. The **production method** of recognizing revenue is used for precious metals, as well as certain agricultural products and marketable securities.

Installment Sales   Various consumer items, such as automobiles, appliances, and even vacation properties, are sold on an installment basis. A down payment is followed by a series of monthly payments over a period of years. Default on the payments and repossession of the item by the seller are more common in these types of sales than with most other arrangements. For this reason, it is considered acceptable, in limited circumstances, to defer the recognition of revenue on an installment sale until cash is actually collected. The **installment method,** which is essentially a cash basis of accounting, is acceptable only when the seller has no reasonable basis for estimating the degree of collectibility. Note that the production and installment methods are at opposite ends of the spectrum. Under the production method, revenue is recognized *before* a sale takes place; with the installment method, revenue is recognized *after* the sale.

Rent and Interest   In some cases, revenue is earned *continuously* over time. Rent and interest are two examples in which a product or service is not delivered at a specific point in time but instead the earnings process takes place with the passage of time. Interest is the cost associated with the use of someone else's money. When should a bank recognize the interest earned from granting a 90-day loan? Even though the interest may not be received until the loan itself is repaid, interest is earned every day the loan is outstanding. We will look at the process for recognizing interest earned but not yet received later in the chapter. The same procedure is used to recognize revenue from rent that is earned but uncollected.

Long-term contracts, franchises, commodities, installment sales, rent, and interest are not the only situations in which the revenue recognition principle must be interpreted. The intent in examining these particular examples was to make you think about the variety of ways in which businesses generate revenue and the need to apply judgment in deciding when to recognize revenue. These examples should help you to realize the subjective nature of the work of an accountant and to understand that the discipline is not as precise as it may sometimes seem.

[5] *SFAC No. 5,* par. 83a.

LO 4

Describe the matching principle and the various methods for recognizing expenses.

Expense Recognition and the Matching Principle

Companies incur a variety of costs. A new office building is constructed. Inventory is purchased. The payroll is met. The utility bill for the month is received. In each of these situations, the company incurs a cost, regardless of when it pays cash. Conceptually, *any time a cost is incurred, an asset is acquired.* However, recall from the definition of an asset in Chapter 1 that it represents a future economic benefit. An asset ceases being an asset and becomes an expense when the economic benefits from having incurred the cost have expired. Assets are unexpired costs and expenses are expired costs.

At what point do costs expire and become an expense? The expense recognition principle requires that we recognize expenses in different ways, depending on the nature of the cost. The ideal approach to recognizing expenses is to match them with revenues. Under the **matching principle,** the accountant attempts to associate revenues of a period with the costs necessary to generate that revenue. For certain types of expenses, a direct form of matching is possible; for others, it is necessary to associate costs with a particular period. The classic example of direct matching is cost of goods sold expense with sales revenue. Cost of goods sold is the cost of the inventory associated with a particular sale. A cost is incurred and an asset is recorded when the inventory is purchased. The asset, inventory, becomes an expense when it is sold. Another example of a cost that can be matched directly with revenue is commissions. The commission paid to a salesperson can be matched directly with the sale.

An indirect form of matching is used to recognize the benefits associated with certain types of costs, most noticeably long-term assets, such as buildings and equipment. These costs benefit many periods, but usually it is not possible to match them directly with a specific sale of a product. Instead, they are matched with the periods during which they will provide benefits. For example, an office building may be useful to a company for 30 years. *Depreciation* is the process of allocating the cost of a tangible long-term asset to its useful life. Depreciation Expense is the account used to recognize this type of expense.

The benefits associated with the incurrence of certain other costs are treated in accounting as expiring simultaneously with their acquisition. The justification for this treatment is that no future benefits from the incurrence of the cost are discernible. This is true of most selling and administrative costs. For example, the cost of heat and light in a building benefit only the current period and therefore are recognized as an expense as soon as the cost is incurred. Likewise, income taxes incurred during the period do not benefit any period other than the current period and are thus written off as an expense in the period incurred.

The relationships among costs, assets, and expenses are depicted in Exhibit 4-4 using three examples. First, costs incurred for purchases of merchandise result in an asset, Merchandise Inventory, and are eventually matched with revenue at the time the product is sold. Second, costs incurred for office space result in an asset, Office Building, which is recognized as Depreciation Expense over the useful life of the building. Third, the cost of heating and lighting benefits only the current period and is thus recognized immediately as Utilities Expense.

According to the FASB, **expenses** are "outflows or other using up of assets or incurrences of liabilities (or a combination of both) from delivering or producing goods, rendering services, or carrying out other activities that constitute the entity's ongoing major or central operations." [6] The key point to note about expenses is that

[6] *SFAC No. 6,* par. 80.

EXHIBIT 4-4   Relationships Among Costs, Assets, and Expenses

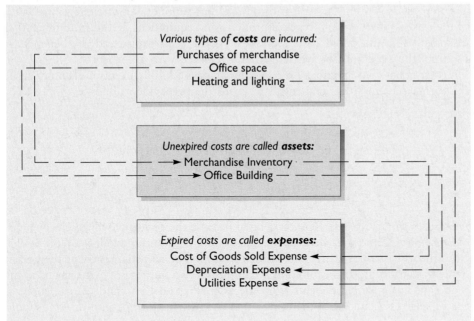

they come about in two different ways: from the use of an asset or the incurrence of a liability. For example, when a retailer sells a product, the asset sacrificed is inventory. Cost of Goods Sold is the expense account that is debited when the Inventory account is credited. As we will see in the next section, the incurrence of an expense may result in a liability.

Accrual Accounting and Adjusting Entries

The accrual basis of accounting necessitates a number of adjustments at the end of a period. **Adjusting entries** are the journal entries made at the end of a period for a company on the accrual basis of accounting. *Adjusting entries are not needed if a cash basis is used. It is the very nature of the accrual basis that results in the need for adjusting entries.* The frequency of the adjustment process depends on how often financial statements are prepared. Adjustments are normally made at the end of each month for most businesses.

Types of Adjusting Entries

Why are there four basic types, or categories, of adjusting entries? The answer lies in the distinction between the cash and accrual bases of accounting. On an accrual basis, *revenue* can be earned either *before* or *after* cash is received. *Expenses* can be incurred *before* or *after* cash is paid. Each of these four distinct situations requires a different type of adjusting entry at the end of the period. We will consider each of the four categories and look at some examples of each.

LO   5

Identify the four major types of adjusting entries and prepare them for a variety of situations.

(1) Cash Paid before Expense Is Incurred (Deferred Expense)   Assets are often acquired prior to their actual use in the business. Insurance policies typically are prepaid, as is often the case with rent. Office supplies are purchased in advance of their use, as is true for all types of property and equipment. Recall from our earlier discussion that unexpired costs are assets. As the costs expire and the benefits are used up, the asset must be written off and replaced with an expense.

Assume that on September 1 a company prepays $2,400 in rent on its office space for the next 12 months. The entry to record the prepayment follows:

Sept. 1	Prepaid Rent	2,400	
	Cash		2,400
	To prepay the rent on office space for 12 months.		

Assets	=	Liabilities	+	Owners' Equity
+ 2,400				
− 2,400				

An asset account, Prepaid Rent, is debited because the company will receive benefits over the next 12 months. Because the rent is for a 12-month period, $200 of benefits from the asset expires at the end of each month. The adjusting entry at the end of September to record this expiration accomplishes two purposes: (1) it recognizes the reduction in unexpired benefits from the asset, Prepaid Rent, and (2) it recognizes the expense associated with the using up of the benefits for one month. You should recall from the last chapter that an asset is decreased with a credit and that an expense is increased with a debit as follows:

Sept. 30	Rent Expense	200	
	Prepaid Rent		200
	To recognize $200 of rent expense for month.		

Assets	=	Liabilities	+	Owners' Equity
− 200				− 200

T accounts are an invaluable aid in understanding adjusting entries. They allow us to focus on the transactions and balances that will be included in the more formal general ledger accounts. The T accounts for Prepaid Rent and Rent Expense appear as follows after posting the original entry on September 1 and the adjusting entry on September 30:

PREPAID RENT					RENT EXPENSE		
9/1	2,400				9/30	200	
		200	9/30				
Bal.	2,200						

FROM CONCEPT TO PRACTICE

**READING BEN & JERRY'S
BALANCE SHEET**

Refer to the balance sheet in Ben & Jerry's annual report. How does Ben & Jerry's classify prepaid expenses? What types of prepaid expenses would you expect the company to have?

The balance in the Prepaid Rent account represents the unexpired benefits from the prepayment of rent for the remaining 11 months: $200 $\times$ 11 = $2,200. The Rent Expense account reflects the expiration of benefits during the month of September.

As discussed earlier in the chapter, depreciation is the process of allocating the cost of a long-term tangible asset over its estimated useful life. The accountant does not attempt to measure the decline in *value* of the asset but simply tries to allocate its cost over its useful life. Thus, the adjusting entry for depreciation is similar to the one we made for rent expense. Assume that on January 1 a company buys a delivery truck, for which it pays $21,000. The entry to record the purchase is as follows:

Jan. 1 Delivery Truck   21,000
    Cash   21,000
   To record purchase of delivery truck for cash.

      Assets = Liabilities + Owners' Equity
      +21,000
      −21,000

Two estimates must be made in depreciating the delivery truck: (1) the useful life of the asset and (2) the salvage value of the truck at the end of its useful life. Estimated salvage value is the amount a company expects to be able to receive when it sells an asset at the end of its estimated useful life. Assume a five-year estimated life for the truck and an estimated salvage value of $3,000 at the end of that time. Thus, the *depreciable cost* of the truck is $21,000 − $3,000, or $18,000. In a later chapter, we will consider alternative methods for allocating the depreciable cost over the useful life of an asset. For now, we use the simplest approach, called the **straight-line method,** to assign an equal amount of depreciation to each period. The monthly depreciation is found by dividing the depreciable cost of $18,000 over the estimated useful life of 60 months, which equals $300 per month.

The debit in the adjusting entry to record depreciation is, of course, to an expense account. Conceptually, the credit is to the asset account, as was the case when writing off prepaid rent. However, for long-term assets, we usually credit a contra account, rather than the asset directly. A **contra account** has a balance that is the opposite of the balance in its related account. For example, Accumulated Depreciation is used to record the decrease in a long-term asset account from depreciation and thus it carries a credit balance. An *increase* in Accumulated Depreciation is recorded with a *credit* because the related asset account is *increased* with a *debit.* The entry to record depreciation at the end of January follows:

Jan. 31 Depreciation Expense   300
     Accumulated Depreciation   300
   To record depreciation on delivery truck.

      Assets = Liabilities + Owners' Equity
      −300   −300

Why do companies credit a contra account for depreciation rather than crediting the long-term asset directly? If depreciation were credited to the asset, its original cost would not be readily determinable from the accounting records. Businesses need to know the original cost of each asset for various reasons. One of the most important of these reasons is the need to know historical cost for computation of depreciation for tax purposes.

The T accounts for the Delivery Truck, Accumulated Depreciation, and Depreciation Expense show the following balances at the end of the first month:

DELIVERY TRUCK		DEPRECIATION EXPENSE	
1/1 21,000		1/31 300	

ACCUMULATED DEPRECIATION	
	300 1/31

On a balance sheet prepared on January 31, the contra account is shown as a reduction in the carrying value of the truck:

Delivery Truck	$21,000	
Less: Accumulated Depreciation	300	$20,700

(2) Cash Received before Revenue Is Earned (Deferred Revenue) You can benefit greatly in your study of accounting by recognizing its *symmetry*. By this we mean that one company's asset is another company's liability. For example, in the earlier example involving the rental of office space, a second company, the landlord, received the cash paid by the first company, the tenant. At the time cash is received, the landlord has a liability because it has taken cash from the tenant but has not yet performed the service to earn the revenue. The revenue will be earned with the passage of time. This is the entry on the books of the landlord on September 1:

Sept. 1	Cash	2,400	
	Rent Collected in Advance		2,400
	To record receipt of rent on office space for 12 months.		

Assets	=	Liabilities	+	Owners' Equity
+2,400		+2,400		

The account Rent Collected in Advance is a liability. Another commonly used name for this account is Unearned Rent Revenue. The landlord is obligated to provide the tenant uninterrupted use of the office facilities for the next 12 months. With the passage of time, the liability is satisfied as the tenant is provided the use of the space. The adjusting entry at the end of each month accomplishes two purposes: it recognizes (1) the reduction in the liability and (2) the revenue earned each month as the tenant occupies the space. Recall that we decrease a liability with a debit and increase revenue with a credit:

Sept. 30	Rent Collected in Advance	200	
	Rent Revenue		200
	To recognize rent earned for month.		

Assets	=	Liabilities	+	Owners' Equity
		−200		+200

The balance in Rent Collected in Advance reflects the remaining liability, and the balance in the Rent Revenue account indicates the amount earned for the month:

RENT COLLECTED IN ADVANCE				RENT REVENUE	
		2,400	9/1	200	9/30
9/30	200				
		2,200	Bal.		

Subscriptions collected in advance

Many magazine subscriptions require the customer to pay in advance. For example, you pay $12 for a one-year subscription to your favorite magazine and the publisher in turn sends you 12 monthly issues. At the time you send money to the publisher, it incurs a liability. That is, it has taken your money but has not yet done anything to earn it. In other words, the publisher has an obligation either to provide you with the magazine over the next 12 months or to refund your $12.

At what point should the publisher recognize revenue from magazine sales? The publisher receives cash at the time the subscription is sold. The revenue has not been *earned* until the company publishes the magazine and mails it to you, however. Thus, a publisher usually recognizes revenue at the time of delivery. An excerpt from page 52 of the 1992 annual report of Marvel Entertainment Group, Inc. (the comic book company) reflects this policy:

> Subscription revenues are generally collected in advance for a one-year subscription. These revenues are deferred and recognized as income on a pro-rata basis over an annual period.

Assume that on March 1 Marvel sells 500 one-year subscriptions to a monthly magazine at a price of $12 each. The entry to record the receipt of cash from the 500 subscribers is as follows:

Mar. 1   Cash   6,000
               Subscriptions Collected in Advance   6,000
               To record receipt of cash from sale of 500 one-year
               subscriptions at $12 each.

Assets	=	Liabilities	+	Owners' Equity
+6,000		+6,000		

Assuming that each of the subscriptions starts with the March issue of the magazine, Marvel would make the following entry at the end of the month:

Mar. 31   Subscriptions Collected in Advance   500
               Subscription Revenue   500
               To recognize subscriptions earned for month.

Assets	=	Liabilities	+	Owners' Equity
		−500		+500

The Subscriptions Collected in Advance and Subscription Revenue accounts appear as follows after posting the two entries:

SUBSCR. COLLECTED IN ADVANCE				SUBSCRIPTION REVENUE	
		6,000	3/1	500	3/31
3/31	500				
		5,500	Bal.		

---

(3) Expense Incurred before Cash Is Paid (Accrued Liability)   This situation is just the opposite of (1). That is, cash is paid *after* an expense is actually incurred rather than *before* its incurrence, as was the case in (1). Consider income taxes, which are incurred as income is earned during the year, but there is a delay in the actual payment of the taxes. Many of the normal operating costs, such as payroll and utilities, also fit this situation. The utility bill is received at the end of the month, but the company has 10 days to pay it. Or consider the biweekly payroll for the Jones Corporation. The company pays a total of $28,000 in wages on every other Friday. Assume that the last payday was Friday, May 31. The next two paydays will be Friday, June 14, and Friday, June 28. The journal entry will be the same on each of these paydays:

June 14	Wages Expense	28,000	
(and	Cash		28,000
June 28)	To pay the biweekly payroll.		

Assets	=	Liabilities	+	Owners' Equity
− 28,000				− 28,000

On a balance sheet prepared as of June 30, a liability must be recognized. Even though the next payment is not until July 12, Jones *owes* employees wages for the last two days of June and must recognize an expense for the wages earned by employees for these two days. We will assume that the company operates seven days a week and that the daily cost is 1/14th of the biweekly amount of $28,000, or $2,000. The double entry system ensures that an entry always has two sides. In addition to crediting a liability, Jones debits an expense account to recognize the cost associated with wages for the last two days of the month:

June 30	Wages Expense	4,000	
	Wages Payable		4,000
	To record wages for last two days of month.		

Assets	=	Liabilities	+	Owners' Equity
		+ 4,000		− 4,000

What entry will be made on the next payday, July 12? Jones will make a *compound entry* (an entry with more than one debit or more than one credit, or both):

July 12	Wages Payable	4,000	
	Wages Expense	24,000	
	Cash		28,000
	To pay the biweekly payroll.		

Assets	=	Liabilities	+	Owners' Equity
− 28,000		− 4,000		− 24,000

The debit to Wages Payable eliminates the liability for the last two days of wages recorded on June 30 because it has now been paid. The debit of $24,000 to Wages Expense recognizes the $2,000 cost per day for each of the 12 days in July. Finally, the credit to Cash represents the amount paid every 14 days, $28,000.

The following time line illustrates the amount of expense incurred in each of the two months, June and July, for the biweekly payroll:

2 days' expense in June: $4,000	12 days' expense in July: $24,000	
×————————————	×————————————————————	×
Friday, June 28: Last payday	Friday, June 30: End of accounting period	Friday, July 12: Next payday

Another typical expense incurred before the payment of cash is interest. In many cases, the interest on a short-term loan is repaid with the amount of the loan, called the *principal,* on the maturity date. Consider an example. Granger Company takes out a 9%, 90-day, $20,000 loan with its bank on March 1. The principal and interest will be repaid on May 30. The entry on Granger's books on March 1 follows:

March 1   Cash   20,000

          Notes Payable   20,000

          To record issuance of 9%, 90-day, $20,000 note.

Assets	=	Liabilities	+	Owners' Equity
+20,000		+20,000		

The basic formula for computing interest follows:

$$I = P \times R \times T,$$

where I = The dollar amount of interest
P = The principal amount of the loan
R = The annual rate of interest as a percentage
T = Time in years (often stated as a fraction of a year).

The total interest on Granger's loan is

$$\$20,000 \times .09 \times 3/12 = \$\underline{450}.$$

Therefore, the amount of interest that must be recognized as expense at the end of March is one-third of $450 because one month of a total of three has passed. Alternatively, the formula for finding the total interest on the loan can be modified to compute the interest for one month:[7]

$$\$20,000 \times .09 \times 1/12 = \$\underline{150}.$$

The adjusting entry for the month of March is

March 31   Interest Expense   150

          Interest Payable   150

          To record interest for one month on 9%,
          $20,000 loan.

Assets	=	Liabilities	+	Owners' Equity
		+150		−150

The same adjusting entry is also made at the end of April:

April 30   Interest Expense   150

          Interest Payable   150

          To record interest for one month on 9%,
          $20,000 loan.

Assets	=	Liabilities	+	Owners' Equity
		+150		−150

[7] In practice, interest is calculated on the basis of days rather than months. For example, the interest for March would be $20,000 × .09 × 30/365, or $147.94, to reflect 30 days in the month of a total of 365 days in the year. The reason the number of days in March is 30 rather than 31 is because it is normal business practice to count the day a note matures in computing interest, but not the day it is signed. Although it is slightly inaccurate, we will use months to simplify the calculations.

The entry on Granger's books on May 30 when it repays the principal and interest is

May 30	Interest Payable	300	
	Interest Expense	150	
	Notes Payable	20,000	
	Cash		20,450
	To record payment of 9%, 90-day, $20,000 loan with interest.		

| Assets | = | Liabilities | + | Owners' Equity |
| −20,450 | | −20,300 | | −150 |

The debit to Interest Payable eliminates the liability recorded at the end of March and April. The debit of $150 to Interest Expense recognizes the cost associated with the month of May.[8] The credit to Cash represents the $20,000 of principal and the total interest of $450 for three months.

(4) Revenue Earned before Cash Is Received (Accrued Asset)   Revenue is sometimes earned before the receipt of cash. Rent and interest are both earned with the passage of time and require an adjusting entry if cash has not yet been received. For example, assume that Grand Management Company rents warehouse space to a number of tenants. Most of its contracts call for prepayment of rent for six months at a time. Its agreement with one tenant allows, however, for it to pay Grand $2,500 in monthly rent anytime within the first 10 days of the following month. The adjusting entry on Grand's books at the end of April, the first month of the agreement, is

Apr. 30	Rent Receivable	2,500	
	Rent Revenue		2,500
	To record rent earned for the month of April.		

| Assets | = | Liabilities | + | Owners' Equity |
| +2,500 | | | | +2,500 |

When the tenant pays its rent on May 7, the entry on Grand's books is

May 7	Cash	2,500	
	Rent Receivable		2,500
	To record rent collected for the month of April.		

Assets	=	Liabilities	+	Owners' Equity
+2,500				
−2,500				

Although we used the example of rent to illustrate this category, this type of situation was presented in Chapter 3 for Glengarry Health Club. Anytime a company records revenue before cash is received, some type of receivable is debited and revenue is credited. In that chapter, the health club earned membership revenue even though members had until the following month to pay their dues.

Accruals and Deferrals

One of the challenges in learning accounting concepts is to gain an understanding of the terminology. Part of the difficulty stems from the alternative terms used by

---

[8] This assumes that Granger did not make a separate entry prior to this to recognize interest for the month of May. If a separate entry had been made, a debit of $450 would be made to Interest Payable.

different accountants to mean the same thing. For example, the asset created when insurance is paid for in advance is termed a *prepaid asset* by some and a *prepaid expense* by others. Someone else might refer to it as a *deferred expense.*

We will use the term **deferral** to refer to a situation in which cash has been either paid or received, but the expense or revenue is deferred to a later point in time. A **deferred expense** indicates that cash has been paid but the recognition of expense is deferred to a later time. An alternative name for deferred expense is *prepaid expense.* Prepaid insurance and office supplies are deferred expenses. An adjusting entry is made periodically to record the portion of the deferred expense that has expired. A **deferred revenue** means that cash has been received, but the recognition of any revenue is deferred until a later time. An alternative name for deferred revenue is *unearned revenue.* Rent collected in advance is deferred revenue. The periodic adjusting entry recognizes the portion of the deferred revenue that is earned in that period.

In this chapter, we have discussed in detail the accrual basis of accounting, which involves recognizing changes in resources and obligations as they occur, not simply when cash changes hands. More specifically, we will use the term **accrual** to refer to a situation in which no cash has been paid or received yet, but it is necessary to recognize, or accrue, an expense or a revenue. An **accrued liability** is recognized at the end of the period in cases in which an expense has been incurred but cash has not yet been paid. Wages payable and interest payable are examples of accrued liabilities. An **accrued asset** is recorded when revenue has been earned but cash has not yet been collected. Rent receivable is an accrued asset.

Summary of Adjusting Entries

The four types of adjusting entries are summarized in Exhibit 4-5. Common examples of each are shown along with the structure of the entries associated with the four categories. Finally, the following generalizations should help you in gaining a better understanding of adjusting entries and how they are used:

(**1**) An adjusting entry is an internal transaction. It does not involve another entity.

(**2**) Because it is an internal transaction, an adjusting entry *never* involves a debit or credit to *Cash.*

EXHIBIT 4-5   Accruals and Deferrals

TYPE	SITUATION	EXAMPLES	ENTRY DURING PERIOD	ENTRY AT END OF PERIOD
Deferred expense	Cash paid before expense incurred	Insurance policy Supplies Rent Buildings, equipment	Asset Cash	Expense Asset
Deferred revenue	Cash received before revenue earned	Deposits, rent Subscriptions Gift certificates	Cash Liability	Liability Revenue
Accrued liability	Expense incurred before cash paid	Salaries, wages Interest Taxes Rent	No Entry	Expense Liability
Accrued asset	Revenue earned before cash received	Interest Rent	No Entry	Asset Revenue

(3) At least one balance sheet account and one income statement account are involved in an adjusting entry. It is the nature of the adjustment process that an asset or liability account is adjusted with a corresponding change in either a revenue or an expense account.

Comprehensive Example of Adjusting Entries

We will now consider a comprehensive example involving the transactions for the first month of operations and the end-of-period adjusting entries for a hypothetical business, Duffy Transit Company. We will also use trial balances to check on the equality of debits and credits at various stages during the journalization process. The transactions entered into by the company during its first month of operations are shown below in the form of journal entries. The transactions are identified by number rather than by date. Assume that the first five transactions were all recorded on the first day of the month.

Journal Entries for the Month of January

1.	Cash	400,000	
	Capital Stock		400,000
	To record issuance of 40,000 shares of stock for cash.		
2.	Cash	150,000	
	Notes Payable		150,000
	To record issuance of 18-month, 12% promissory note.		
3.	Land	20,000	
	Buildings—Garage	160,000	
	Cash		180,000
	To record acquisition of land and garage for cash.		
4.	Equipment—Buses	300,000	
	Cash		300,000
	To record acquisition of 10 buses for cash of $30,000 each.		
5.	Prepaid Insurance	48,000	
	Cash		48,000
	To record purchase of two-year insurance policy.		
6.	Cash	25,000	
	Discount Tickets Sold in Advance		25,000
	To record sale of 25,000 $1 discount tickets.		
7.	Cash	30,000	
	Daily Ticket Revenue		30,000
	To record sale of 20,000 $1.50 daily tickets.		
8.	Gas, Oil, and Maintenance Expense	12,000	
	Cash		12,000
	To record payment of operating expenses for the month.		
9.	Wage and Salary Expense	10,000	
	Cash		10,000
	To record payment of wages and salaries for the month.		
10.	Dividends	5,000	
	Cash		5,000
	To record declaration and payment of cash dividends.		

As discussed in Chapter 3, a trial balance can be prepared at any point in time. We will bypass posting these 10 journal entries to T accounts and prepare a trial balance directly from the journal entries as shown in Exhibit 4-6. Because the trial balance is prepared *before* taking into account adjusting entries, it is called an *unadjusted* trial balance. This is the first month of operations for Duffy. Thus, the Retained Earnings account does not yet appear on the trial balance. After the first month, this account will have a balance and will appear on subsequent trial balances.

Duffy wants to prepare a balance sheet at the end of January and an income statement for its first month of operations. Use of the accrual basis necessitates a number of adjusting entries to update certain asset and liability accounts and to recognize the correct amounts for the various revenues and expenses.

Using a Trial Balance to Prepare Adjusting Entries

A trial balance is an important tool to use in preparing adjusting entries. The deferred expenses on Duffy's trial balance, such as Prepaid Insurance, must be reduced with a corresponding increase in expense. Similarly, any deferred revenues, such as Discount Tickets Sold in Advance, must be adjusted and a corresponding amount of revenue recognized. In addition, any accrued assets, such as Rent Receivable, and accrued liabilities, such as Interest Payable, that do not currently appear on the trial balance must be recognized.

Adjusting Entries at the End of January

In transaction 2, Duffy issued an 18-month, 12%, $150,000 promissory note for cash. Although interest will not be repaid until the loan's maturity date, Duffy must

---

EXHIBIT 4-6   Unadjusted Trial Balance

DUFFY TRANSIT COMPANY
UNADJUSTED TRIAL BALANCE
JANUARY 31

	DR.	CR.
Cash	$ 50,000	
Prepaid Insurance	48,000	
Land	20,000	
Buildings—Garage	160,000	
Equipment—Buses	300,000	
Discount Tickets Sold in Advance		$ 25,000
Notes Payable		150,000
Capital Stock		400,000
Daily Ticket Revenue		30,000
Gas, Oil, and Maintenance Expense	12,000	
Wage and Salary Expense	10,000	
Dividends	5,000	
Totals	$605,000	$605,000

accrue interest for the first month. The calculation of interest for one month is $150,000 × .12 x 1/12. The adjusting entry is

(a) Interest Expense   1,500
         Interest Payable   1,500
      To record interest for one month on 12%, $150,000
      promissory note.

Assets = Liabilities + Owners' Equity
       + 1,500   − 1,500

The wages and salaries recorded in transaction 9 were paid in cash. At the end of the month, Duffy owes employees an additional $2,800 in salaries and wages:

(b) Wage and Salary Expense   2,800
         Wages and Salaries Payable   2,800
      To record wages and salaries owed.

Assets = Liabilities + Owners' Equity
       + 2,800   − 2,800

In transaction 3, Duffy acquired a garage to house the buses at a cost of $160,000. Land is not subject to depreciation. The cost of the land acquired in connection with the purchase of the building will remain on the books until the property is sold. The garage has an estimated useful life of 20 years and an estimated salvage value of $16,000 at the end of its life. The monthly depreciation is found by dividing the depreciable cost of $144,000 by the useful life of 240 months:

$$\frac{\$160,000 - \$16,000}{20 \text{ years} \times 12 \text{ months}} = \frac{\$144,000}{240 \text{ months}} = \underline{\$600} \text{ per month.}$$

The entry to record the depreciation on the garage for January for a full month is

(c) Depreciation Expense—Garage   600
         Accumulated Depreciation—Garage   600
      To record depreciation for the month.

Assets = Liabilities + Owners' Equity
       − 600   − 600

Duffy purchased 10 buses for $30,000 each in transaction 4. The buses have an estimated useful life of five years at which time the company plans to sell them for $6,000 each. The monthly depreciation on the 10 buses is

$$10 \times \frac{\$30,000 - \$6,000}{5 \text{ years} \times 12 \text{ months}} = 10 \times \frac{\$24,000}{60 \text{ months}} = \underline{\$4,000} \text{ per month.}$$

The entry to recognize the depreciation on the buses for the first month is

(d) Depreciation Expense—Buses   4,000
         Accumulated Depreciation—Buses   4,000
      To record depreciation for the month.

Assets = Liabilities + Owners' Equity
       − 4,000   − 4,000

The insurance policy purchased for $48,000 in transaction 5 provides property and liability protection for a 24-month period. The adjusting entry to allocate the cost to expense for the first month is

(e) Insurance Expense   2,000
        Prepaid Insurance   2,000
     To record expiration of insurance benefits.

Assets	=	Liabilities	+	Owners' Equity
− 2,000				− 2,000

In addition to selling tickets on the bus, Duffy sells discount tickets at the terminal. The tickets are good for a ride anytime within 12 months of purchase. Thus, as these tickets are sold, Duffy debits Cash and credits a liability account, Discount Tickets Sold in Advance. The sale of $25,000 worth of these tickets was recorded in transaction 6. At the end of the first month, Duffy counts the number of tickets that have been redeemed. Because $20,400 worth of tickets has been turned in, this is the amount by which the company reduces its liability and recognizes revenue for the month:

(f) Discount Tickets Sold in Advance   20,400
        Discount Ticket Revenue   20,400
     To record redemption of discount tickets.

Assets	=	Liabilities	+	Owners' Equity
		− 20,400		+ 20,400

Duffy does not need all of the space in its garage and rents a section of it to another company for $2,500 per month. The tenant has until the 10th day of the following month to pay its rent. The adjusting entry on Duffy's books on the last day of the month is

(g) Rent Receivable   2,500
        Rent Revenue   2,500
     To record rent earned but not yet received.

Assets	=	Liabilities	+	Owners' Equity
+ 2,500				+ 2,500

Corporations pay estimated taxes on a quarterly basis. Because Duffy is preparing an income statement for the month of January, it must estimate its taxes for the month. We will assume a corporate tax rate of 34% on income before tax. The computation of Income Tax Expense is as follows (the amounts shown for the revenues and expenses reflect the effect of the adjusting entries):

Revenues:		
Daily Ticket Revenue	$30,000	
Discount Ticket Revenue	20,400	
Rent Revenue	2,500	$52,900
Expenses:		
Gas, Oil, and Maintenance Expense	$12,000	
Wage and Salary Expense	12,800	
Depreciation Expense	4,600	
Insurance Expense	2,000	
Interest Expense	1,500	32,900
Net Income before Tax		$20,000
Times the Corporate Tax Rate		× .34
Income Tax Expense		$ 6,800

Based on this estimate of taxes, the final adjusting entry recorded on Duffy's books for the month is

(h)	Income Tax Expense	6,800	
	Income Tax Payable		6,800

To record estimated income taxes for month.

Assets = Liabilities + Owners' Equity
+6,800   −6,800

A trial balance, shown in Exhibit 4-7, indicates the equality of debits and credits after the adjusting entries have been recorded. Note the addition of a number of new accounts on the *adjusted* trial balance that did not appear on the unadjusted trial balance in Exhibit 4-6. The new trial balance includes the accounts that were added when adjusting entries were recorded.

EXHIBIT 4-7   Adjusted Trial Balance

DUFFY TRANSIT COMPANY
ADJUSTED TRIAL BALANCE
JANUARY 31

	DR.	CR.
Cash	$ 50,000	
Prepaid Insurance	46,000	
Land	20,000	
Buildings—Garage	160,000	
Accumulated Depreciation—Garage		$ 600
Equipment—Buses	300,000	
Accumulated Depreciation—Buses		4,000
Gas, Oil, and Maintenance Expense	12,000	
Wage and Salary Expense	12,800	
Dividends	5,000	
Discount Tickets Sold in Advance		4,600
Notes Payable		150,000
Capital Stock		400,000
Daily Ticket Revenue		30,000
Rent Receivable	2,500	
Interest Expense	1,500	
Income Tax Expense	6,800	
Depreciation Expense—Garage	600	
Depreciation Expense—Buses	4,000	
Insurance Expense	2,000	
Interest Payable		1,500
Wages and Salaries Payable		2,800
Income Tax Payable		6,800
Discount Ticket Revenue		20,400
Rent Revenue		2,500
Totals	$623,200	$623,200

Ethical Considerations for a Company on the Accrual Basis

As you have seen, the accrual basis requires the recognition of revenues when earned and expenses when incurred, regardless of when cash is received or paid. It was also noted earlier that adjusting entries are *internal* transactions in that they do not involve an exchange with an outside entity. Because adjustments do not involve another company, accountants may at times feel pressure from others within the organization to either speed or delay the recognition of certain adjustments.

Consider the following two examples for a construction company that is concerned about its "bottom line," that is, its net income. A number of jobs are in progress, but because of inclement weather, none of them are very far along. Management asks the accountant to recognize 50% of the revenue from a job in progress even though by the most liberal estimates it is only 25% complete. Further, the accountant has been asked to delay the recognition of various short-term accrued liabilities (and, of course, the accompanying expenses) until the beginning of the new year.

The "correct" response of the accountant to each of these requests may seem obvious: only 25% of the revenue on the one job should be recognized and all accrued liabilities should be expensed at year-end. The pressures of the daily work environment make these difficult decisions for the accountant, however. It is essential that the accountant always remember that his or her primary responsibility in preparing financial statements is to accurately portray the affairs of the company to the various outside users. Bankers, stockholders, and others rely on the accountant to serve their best interests.

The Accounting Cycle

We have focused our attention in this chapter on accrual accounting and the adjusting entries it necessitates. Adjusting entries are one key component in the **accounting cycle.** The accountant for a business follows a series of steps each period. The objective is always the same: *collect the necessary information to prepare a set of financial statements.* Together, these steps make up the accounting cycle. The name comes from the fact that the steps are repeated each period. It is possible that a company performs all of the steps in the accounting cycle once a *month,* although in practice, certain steps in the cycle may be carried out only once a *year.*

The steps in the accounting cycle are shown in Exhibit 4-8. The point in time at which each step is performed appears on the right side of the exhibit. Note that step 1 involves not only *collecting* information but also *analyzing* it. Transaction analysis is probably the most challenging of all the steps in the accounting cycle. It requires the ability to think logically about an event and its effect on the financial position of the entity. Once the transaction is analyzed, it is recorded in the journal, as indicated by the second step in the exhibit. The first two steps in the cycle take place continuously.

Journal entries are posted to the accounts on a periodic basis. The frequency of posting to the accounts depends on two factors: the type of accounting system employed by a company and the volume of transactions. In a manual system, entries might be posted daily, weekly, or even monthly, depending on the amount of activity. The larger the number of transactions a company records, the more often it posts. In an automated accounting system, posting is likely done automatically by the computer each time a journal entry is recorded.

LO 6

Explain the steps in the accounting cycle and the significance of each step.

EXHIBIT 4-8 Steps in the Accounting Cycle

STEPS	PERFORMED
1. Collect and analyze information from source documents	Continuously
2. Journalize transactions	Continuously
3. Post entries to accounts in the ledger	Periodically: daily or weekly
4. Prepare work sheet	
5. Prepare financial statements	
6. Journalize and post adjusting entries	End of the period
7. Journalize and post closing entries	
8. Prepare post-closing trial balance	
9. Optional: Journalize and post reversing entries	Beginning of following period

The Use of a Work Sheet

Step 4 in Exhibit 4-8 calls for the preparation of a work sheet. The end of an accounting period is a busy time. In addition to recording daily recurring transactions, adjusting entries must be recorded as the basis for preparing financial statements. The time available to prepare the statements is usually very limited. The use of a **work sheet** allows the accountant to gather and organize the information required to adjust the accounts without actually recording and posting the adjusting entries to the accounts. Actually recording adjusting entries and posting them to the accounts can be done after the financial statements are prepared. *A work sheet itself is not a financial statement.* Instead, it is a useful device to *organize* the information needed to prepare the financial statements at the end of the period.

It is not essential that a work sheet be used before preparing financial statements. If it is not used, step 6, journalizing and posting adjusting entries, comes before step 5, preparing the statements. Appendix 4A illustrates how a work sheet is used to facilitate the preparation of financial statements.

The Closing Process

LO 7

Explain why and how closing entries are made at the end of an accounting period.

Two types of accounts appear on an adjusted trial balance. Balance sheet accounts are called **real accounts** because they are permanent in nature. For this reason, they are never closed. The balance in each of these accounts is carried over from one period to the next. In contrast, revenue, expense, and dividend accounts are temporary or **nominal accounts.** The balances in the income statement accounts and the Dividends account are *not* carried forward from one accounting period. For this reason, these accounts are closed at the end of the period.

Closing entries have two important purposes: (1) the balances in all temporary or nominal accounts are returned to zero to start the next accounting period and (2) the net income (or net loss) and the dividends of the period are transferred to the Retained Earnings account.

An account with a debit balance is closed by crediting the account for the amount of the balance. An account with a credit balance is closed by debiting the account for the amount of the balance. Thus, revenue accounts are debited in the closing process. Expense accounts are credited to close them. In this way, the balance of each income statement account is restored to zero to start the next accounting period.

Various approaches are used in practice to accomplish the same two purposes: restore the temporary accounts to zero and update the Retained Earnings account. We will use a holding account called Income Summary to facilitate the closing process. A single entry is made to close all of the revenue accounts. The total amount debited to the revenue accounts is credited to Income Summary. Similarly, a single entry is made to close all of the expense accounts and the offsetting debit is made to Income Summary. This account acts as a temporary storage account. After closing the revenue and expense accounts, Income Summary has a *credit* balance *if revenues exceed expenses*. Finally, the credit balance in Income Summary is itself closed by debiting the account and crediting Retained Earnings for the same amount. The net result of the process is that all of the revenues less expenses, that is, net income, have been transferred to Retained Earnings.

The Dividends account is closed directly to Retained Earnings. Because dividends are *not* an expense, the Dividends account is not closed first to the Income Summary account as is the case for expense accounts. A credit is made to close the Dividends account with an offsetting debit to Retained Earnings.

The closing process for Duffy Transit Company is illustrated with the use of T accounts in Exhibit 4-9. Rather than show each individual revenue and expense account, a single revenue account and a single expense account are used in the exhibit to illustrate the flow in the closing process.

The first closing entry results in a zero balance in each of the three revenue accounts, and the total of the three amounts, $52,900, which represents all of the revenue of the period, is transferred to the Income Summary account. The second entry closes each of the seven expense accounts and transfers the total expenses of $39,700 as a debit to the Income Summary account. At this point, the Income Summary account has a credit balance of $13,200, which represents the net income of the period. The third entry closes this temporary holding account and transfers the net income to the Retained Earnings account. Finally, the fourth entry closes the Dividends account and transfers the $5,000 to the debit side of the Retained Earnings account. The Retained Earnings account is now updated to its correct ending balance of $8,200.

EXHIBIT 4-9   The Closing Process

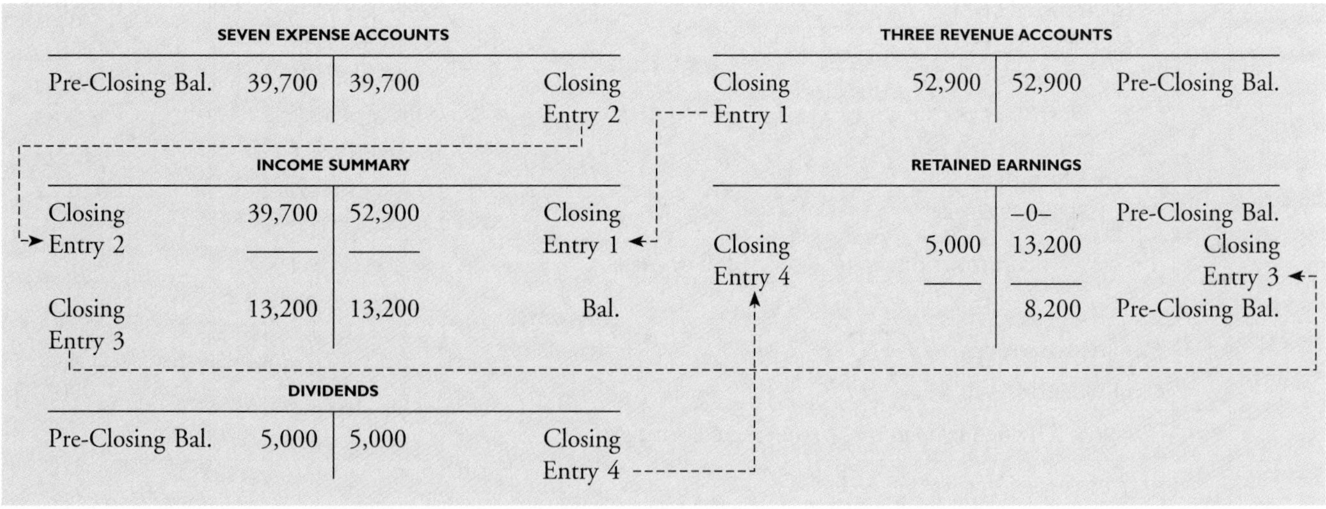

The four closing entries in journal form are shown in Exhibit 4-10. Note that each individual revenue and expense account is closed. The Post. Ref. column has been filled in with the account numbers to indicate that the entries have been posted to the ledger accounts in Exhibit 4-11.

The Ledger Accounts after Posting Adjusting and Closing Entries

The accounts of Duffy Transit Company are shown in Exhibit 4-11 *after* both the adjusting and closing entries are posted. Each account is assigned a number to illustrate the posting process. The notation UB next to an amount indicates the *unadjusted balance* in the account as shown on the unadjusted trial balance in

EXHIBIT 4-10   Closing Entries Recorded in the Journal

Date	Account Titles and Explanation	Post. Ref.	Debit	Credit
Jan. 31	Daily Ticket Revenue	51	30 0 0 0	
	Discount Ticket Revenue	52	20 4 0 0	
	Rent Revenue	53	2 5 0 0	
	Income Summary	99		52 9 0 0
	To close revenue accounts to Income Summary.			
31	Income Summary	99	39 7 0 0	
	Gas, Oil, and Maintenance Expense	61		12 0 0 0
	Wage and Salary Expense	62		12 8 0 0
	Interest Expense	63		1 5 0 0
	Depreciation Expense—Garage	64		6 0 0
	Depreciation Expense—Buses	65		4 0 0 0
	Insurance Expense	66		2 0 0 0
	Income Tax Expense	67		6 8 0 0
	To close expense accounts to Income Summary.			
31	Income Summary	99	13 2 0 0	
	Retained Earnings	33		13 2 0 0
	To close Income Summary to Retained Earnings.			
31	Retained Earnings	33	5 0 0 0	
	Dividends	36		5 0 0 0
	To close Dividends account to Retained Earnings.			

EXHIBIT 4-11   Ledger Accounts after Posting Adjusting and Closing Entries

CASH 1			PREPAID INSURANCE 2		
UB	50,000		UB	48,000	2,000	(e)
			AB	46,000		

LAND 11			BUILDINGS—GARAGE 12	
UB	20,000		UB	160,000	

ACCUMULATED DEPRECIATION—GARAGE 13			EQUIPMENT—BUSES 15	
	600	(c)	UB	300,000
	600	AB		

ACCUMULATED DEPRECIATION—BUSES 16			DISCOUNT TICKETS SOLD IN ADVANCE 21		
	4,000	(d)			25,000	UB
	4,000	AB	(f)	20,400		
					4,600	AB

NOTES PAYABLE 22			CAPITAL STOCK 31	
	150,000	UB		400,000	UB

RETAINED EARNINGS 33			DAILY TICKET REVENUE 51		
	–0–	UB	C1	30,000	30,000	UB
C4	5,000	13,200	C3		–0–	
		8,200	AB			

GAS, OIL, AND MAINTENANCE EXPENSE 61			WAGE AND SALARY EXPENSE 62		
UB	12,000	12,000	C2	UB	10,000	
	–0–			(b)	2,800	
				AB	12,800	12,800	C2
					–0–	

DIVIDENDS 36			INTEREST EXPENSE 63		
UB	5,000	5,000	C4	(a)	1,500	1,500	C2
	–0–				–0–	

DEPRECIATION EXPENSE—GARAGE 64			DEPRECIATION EXPENSE—BUSES 65		
(c)	600	600	C2	(d)	4,000	4,000	C2
	–0–				–0–	

INSURANCE EXPENSE 66			DISCOUNT TICKET REVENUE 52		
(e)	2,000	2,000	C2	C1	20,400	20,400	(f)
	–0–				–0–	

EXHIBIT 4-11 *(continued)*

	RENT RECEIVABLE 3				RENT REVENUE 53		
(g)	2,500			C1	2,500	2,500	(g)
						–0–	

	INTEREST PAYABLE 23				WAGES AND SALARIES PAYABLE 24		
		1,500	(a)			2,800	(b)

	INCOME TAX EXPENSE 67				INCOME TAX PAYABLE 25		
(h)	6,800	6,800	C2			6,800	(h)
	–0–						

	INCOME SUMMARY 99		
C2	39,700	52,900	C1
C3	13,200		
		–0–	

Note: UB indicates an unadjusted balance and AB an adjusted balance. Adjusting entries are lettered (a) through (h) and closing entries are C1 through C4.

Exhibit 4-6. The lettering system used earlier for the adjusting entries is used here as well. Each of the four *closing* entries is identified by the notation C1, C2, C3, or C4. Finally, the notation AB indicates the *adjusted balance* for those accounts that were adjusted during the period but not closed. Keep in mind that in practice neither of the lettering systems used here for adjusting and closing entries is used. Instead, each entry in a formal ledger account is identified by the date of the transaction.

The Post-Closing Trial Balance

After the adjusting and closing entries are posted to the accounts, one final trial balance is prepared. The use of a post-closing trial balance assures us of the equality of debits and credits *after* the closing entries are posted to the accounts. Note that in the post-closing trial balance in Exhibit 4-12, only the *balance sheet* accounts appear. The income statement accounts have been closed.

Reversing Entries

Step 9 in Exhibit 4-8 indicates the preparation of reversing entries as an *optional* procedure. **Reversing entries** are strictly optional and are used by some businesses to *facilitate* the bookkeeping required in the following period. Because they are optional, they are mentioned here and discussed in more detail in Appendix 4A. In the remainder of the text, we will assume that reversing entries have not been made.

EXHIBIT 4-12   Post-Closing Trial Balance

DUFFY TRANSIT COMPANY
POST-CLOSING TRIAL BALANCE
AS OF JANUARY 31

	DR.	CR.
Cash	$ 50,000	
Prepaid Insurance	46,000	
Rent Receivable	2,500	
Land	20,000	
Buildings—Garage	160,000	
Accumulated Depreciation—Garage		$ 600
Equipment—Buses	300,000	
Accumulated Depreciation—Buses		4,000
Discount Tickets Sold in Advance		4,600
Notes Payable		150,000
Interest Payable		1,500
Wages and Salaries Payable		2,800
Income Tax Payable		6,800
Capital Stock		400,000
Retained Earnings		8,200
Totals	$578,500	$578,500

Interim Financial Statements

We mentioned earlier in this chapter that certain steps in the accounting cycle are sometimes carried out only once a year rather than each month as in our example. For ease of illustration, we assumed a monthly accounting cycle. Many companies adjust and close the accounts only once a year, however. They use a work sheet more frequently than this as the basis for preparing interim statements. Statements prepared monthly, quarterly, or at other intervals less than a year in duration are called **interim statements.** Many companies prepare monthly financial statements for their own internal use. Similarly, corporations whose shares are publicly traded on one of the stock exchanges are required to file quarterly financial statements with the Securities and Exchange Commission.

Suppose that a company prepares monthly financial statements for internal use and completes the accounting cycle in its entirety only once a year. In this case, a work sheet is prepared each month as the basis for interim financial statements. Formal adjusting and closing entries are prepared only at the end of each year. The adjusting entries that appear on the monthly work sheet are not posted to the accounts. They are entered on the work sheet as a basis for preparing the monthly financial statements.

USING FINANCIAL STATEMENTS TO MAKE LENDING DECISIONS

Name: Steven Ritzman
Profession: Bank Vice President

One of the first things that Steve Ritzman learned when he got into banking was how to convert accrual basis accounting to the cash basis. "If you've got a company that's showing net income but is consuming cash, then you've got a problem," he says, especially if you're a loan officer and your loan isn't being repaid.

Investors in the stock market often debate whether it's better to use net income or cash flow to evaluate an investment. But bankers are virtually unanimous: cash is king.

At the First National Bank of Omaha, Ritzman's employer for 15 years, the formula is to start with net income and make a series of adjustments for depreciation and other non-cash charges, for changes in receivables, payables, inventory, and other current items. "If their receivable collection is declining or their inventory is building up, then that's cash that's not available to pay their debts. We want to see how much true cash is available to service debt." When does he get worried? When cash flow falls below 1.4 or 1.3 times the debt payment.

"We rate companies from 1 to 6," says Ritzman, "1 being extremely good and 6 being questionable whether we'll ever get our money back." Of course, the bank wouldn't intentionally get involved with a 6. "The key is getting out of a credit before it goes down that roller coaster."

That's where the judgment comes in. "The financials are important, but only part of the decision process when we make a loan," says Ritzman. "Management is very important. I'd rather have a company with financial flaws but superior management because they can turn things around."

Ritzman graduated from the University of Wisconsin with a degree in finance in 1976. He is responsible for a $25 million portfolio of loans. "I spend 30 to 40% of my time with current or prospective customers, another 30% in administration," and the rest of the time in continuing education and training. "It has been my experience that it is very advantageous to hire

people with a strong accounting background as credit analysts because they understand how changes in certain assets affect the balance sheet or the income statement. And when you're dealing with small to medium-size businesses, understanding accounting is extremely important because the owners often don't have accounting backgrounds."

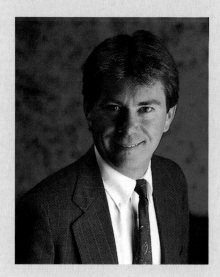

REVIEW PROBLEM

The trial balance of Northern Airlines at January 31 is shown below. It was prepared after posting the recurring transactions for the month of January, but it does not reflect any month-end adjustments.

NORTHERN AIRLINES
UNADJUSTED TRIAL BALANCE
JANUARY 31

Cash	$ 75,000	
Parts Inventory	45,000	
Land	80,000	
Buildings—Hangars	250,000	
Accumulated Depreciation—Hangars		$ 24,000
Aircraft	650,000	
Accumulated Depreciation—Aircraft		120,000
Tickets Sold in Advance		85,000
Capital Stock		500,000
Retained Earnings		368,000
Ticket Revenue		52,000
Maintenance Expense	19,000	
Wage and Salary Expense	30,000	
Totals	$1,149,000	$1,149,000

The following additional information is available:
a. Airplane parts needed for repairs and maintenance are purchased regularly, and the amounts paid are debited to the asset account, Parts Inventory. At the end of each month, the inventory is counted. At the end of January, the amount of parts on hand is $36,100. *Hint:* What entry is needed to reduce the asset account to its proper carrying value? Any expense involved should be included in Maintenance Expense.
b. The estimated useful life of the hangar is 20 years with an estimated salvage value of $10,000 at the end of its life. The original cost of the hangar was $250,000.
c. The estimated useful life of the aircraft is 10 years with an estimated salvage value of $50,000. The original cost of the aircraft was $650,000.
d. As tickets are sold in advance, the amounts are debited to Cash and credited to the liability account, Tickets Sold in Advance. A count of the redeemed tickets reveals that a total of $47,000 were used during January.
e. Wages and salaries owed to employees, but unpaid, at the end of January total $7,600.
f. Northern rents excess hangar space to other companies. The amount owed to Northern, but unpaid at the end of January, is $2,500.
g. Assume a corporate income tax rate of 34%.

1. Set up T accounts for each of the accounts listed on the trial balance. Set up any other T accounts that will be needed to prepare adjusting entries.
2. Post the month-end adjusting entries directly to the T accounts; do not take the time to put the entries in journal format first. Use the letters (a) through (g) from the additional information to identify each entry.

■ REQUIRED

3. Prepare a trial balance to prove the equality of debits and credits after posting the adjusting entries.

■ SOLUTION TO REVIEW PROBLEM

1 and 2:

CASH

Bal.	75,000		

PARTS INVENTORY

Bal.	45,000		
		8,900	(a)
Bal.	36,100		

LAND

Bal.	80,000		

TICKETS SOLD IN ADVANCE

		85,000	Bal.
(d)	47,000		
		38,000	Bal.

BUILDINGS—HANGARS

Bal.	250,000		

EQUIPMENT—AIRCRAFT

Bal.	650,000		

ACCUMULATED DEPRECIATION—HANGARS

		24,000	Bal.
		1,000	(b)
		25,000	Bal.

ACCUMULATED DEPRECIATION—AIRCRAFT

		120,000	Bal.
		5,000	(c)
		125,000	Bal.

CAPITAL STOCK

		500,000	Bal.

RETAINED EARNINGS

		368,000	Bal.

MAINTENANCE EXPENSE

Bal.	19,000		
(a)	8,900		
Bal.	27,900		

TICKET REVENUE

		52,000	Bal.
		47,000	(d)
		99,000	Bal.

WAGE AND SALARY EXPENSE

Bal.	30,000		
(e)	7,600		
Bal.	37,600		

SALARIES AND WAGES PAYABLE

		7,600	(e)

RENT RECEIVABLE

(f)	2,500		

RENT REVENUE

		2,500	(f)

INCOME TAX EXPENSE

(g)	10,200		

INCOME TAXES PAYABLE

		10,200	(g)

DEPRECIATION EXPENSE—HANGARS

(b)	1,000		

DEPRECIATION EXPENSE—AIRCRAFT

(c)	5,000		

3.

NORTHERN AIRLINES
ADJUSTED TRIAL BALANCE
JANUARY 31

Cash	$ 75,000	
Parts Inventory	36,100	
Land	80,000	
Buildings—Hangars	250,000	
Accumulated Depreciation—Hangars		$ 25,000
Aircraft	650,000	
Accumulated Depreciation—Aircraft		125,000
Tickets Sold in Advance		38,000
Capital Stock		500,000
Retained Earnings		368,000
Ticket Revenue		99,000
Maintenance Expense	27,900	
Wage and Salary Expense	37,600	
Depreciation Expense—Hangars	1,000	
Depreciation Expense—Aircraft	5,000	
Rent Receivable	2,500	
Rent Revenue		2,500
Salaries and Wages Payable		7,600
Income Tax Expense	10,200	
Income Taxes Payable		10,200
Totals	$1,175,300	$1,175,300

GUIDANCE ANSWERS TO ACCOUNTING FOR YOUR DECISIONS

YOU ARE THE INVESTOR

1. It is not appropriate for the franchisor to recognize all of the revenue from a new franchisee at the time the contract is signed. According to accounting standards, any initial fee should be recognized only when the franchisor has made "substantial performance" of its obligations. Because the franchisor must assist the franchisee in establishing its business, including finding a suitable location, the fee should not be recognized up front.
2. The danger to the investor if the franchisor recognizes the franchise fee up front is that the franchisor may look much better than it really is in terms of profitability. The franchisor will incur costs in assisting in site location and other start-up activities, and any revenue should be recognized during this time period, not at the time the contract is signed. For a new company such as this, there may be a material overstatement of its revenues at this point.

YOU ARE THE BANKER

1. The publisher should not recognize revenue from the initial sale of subscriptions to the new magazines but rather over the time that the magazines are delivered to the subscribers. Only upon delivery of the product to the customers, in this case the mailing of magazines to them, has revenue been earned.

2. The danger in loaning money to this company is that it has yet to prove that it can be profitable. The sale of the initial subscriptions can give a false sense of security. Will it be able to control costs as it begins publishing and delivering the magazines to subscribers? The company is premature in recognizing revenue at the time it sells the subscriptions.

A P P E N D I X   4 A

ACCOUNTING TOOLS: WORK SHEETS
AND REVERSING ENTRIES

Work sheets and reversing entries were introduced in the chapter as useful tools to aid the accountant. In this appendix we present a detailed discussion of each of these.

Work Sheets

A work sheet is used to organize the information needed to prepare financial statements without recording and posting formal adjusting entries. There is no one single format for a work sheet. We will illustrate a 10-column work sheet by using the information in the chapter for the Duffy Transit Company example. The format for a 10-column work sheet appears in Exhibit 4-13. We will concentrate on the *steps* to complete the work sheet, which has already been completed.

LO   8
Understand how to use a work sheet as a basis for preparing financial statements.

The Unadjusted Trial Balance

Step 1: The Unadjusted Trial Balance Columns   The starting point for the work sheet is the first two columns, which must be filled in with the appropriate amounts from the unadjusted trial balance of Duffy Transit Company as shown on page 187. The trial balance is labeled *unadjusted* because it does not reflect the adjusting entries at the end of the period.

At this point, only the accounts used during the period are entered on the work sheet. Any accounts that are used for the first time during the period because of the adjusting entries will be added in the next step. All but the first two columns of the work sheet should be ignored at this time. Three accounts are included on the work sheet even though they do not have a balance: Accumulated Depreciation—Garage, Accumulated Depreciation—Buses, and Retained Earnings. After this first month of operations, these accounts will always have a balance and will appear on an unadjusted trial balance.

The Adjusting Entries

Step 2: The Adjusting Entries Columns   The third and fourth columns of the work sheet have been completed in Exhibit 4-13. Rather than take the time now to prepare adjusting entries and post them to their respective accounts, the entries are entered in these two columns of the work sheet. Formal entries can be made after the financial statements have been prepared. The addition of these two columns to the work sheet requires that we add the accounts used for the first time in the period because of the adjustment process. Letters are typically used on a work sheet to identify the adjusting entries and are therefore used here. In practice, the work sheet can be many pages long, and the use of identifying letters makes it easier to locate and match the debit and credit sides of each adjusting entry.

The two columns are totaled to ensure the equality of debits and credits for the adjusting entries. Keep in mind that the entries made in these two columns of the work sheet are *not* the actual adjusting entries; those will be recorded in the journal at a later time after the financial statements have been prepared.

EXHIBIT 4-13 The Work Sheet

DUFFY TRANSIT COMPANY
WORK SHEET
FOR THE MONTH ENDED JANUARY 31

ACCOUNT TITLES	UNADJUSTED TRIAL BALANCE DEBIT	UNADJUSTED TRIAL BALANCE CREDIT	ADJUSTING ENTRIES DEBIT	ADJUSTING ENTRIES CREDIT	ADJUSTED TRIAL BALANCE DEBIT	ADJUSTED TRIAL BALANCE CREDIT	INCOME STATEMENT DEBIT	INCOME STATEMENT CREDIT	BALANCE SHEET DEBIT	BALANCE SHEET CREDIT
Cash	50,000				50,000				50,000	
Prepaid Insurance	48,000			(e) 2,000	46,000				46,000	
Land	20,000				20,000				20,000	
Buildings—Garage	160,000				160,000				160,000	
Accumulated Depreciation—Garage		–0–		(c) 600		600				600
Equipment—Buses	300,000				300,000				300,000	
Accumulated Depreciation—Buses		–0–		(d) 4,000		4,000				4,000
Discount Tickets Sold in Advance		25,000	(f) 20,400			4,600				4,600
Notes Payable		150,000				150,000				150,000
Capital Stock		400,000				400,000				400,000
Retained Earnings		–0–				–0–				–0–
Daily Ticket Revenue		30,000				30,000		30,000		
Gas, Oil, and Maintenance Expense	12,000		(b) 2,800		12,000		12,000			
Wage and Salary Expense	10,000		(b) 2,800		12,800		12,800			
Dividends	5,000				5,000				5,000	
	605,000	605,000								
Interest Expense			(a) 1,500		1,500		1,500			
Depreciation Expense—Garage			(c) 600		600		600			
Depreciation Expense—Buses			(d) 4,000		4,000		4,000			
Insurance Expense			(e) 2,000		2,000		2,000			
Discount Ticket Revenue				(f) 20,400		20,400		20,400		
Rent Receivable			(g) 2,500		2,500				2,500	
Rent Revenue				(g) 2,500		2,500		2,500		
Interest Payable				(a) 1,500		1,500				1,500
Wages and Salaries Payable				(b) 2,800		2,800				2,800
Income Tax Expense			(h) 6,800		6,800		6,800			
Income Tax Payable				(h) 6,800		6,800				6,800
			40,600	40,600	623,200	623,200	39,700	52,900	583,500	570,300
Net Income							13,200			13,200
							52,900	52,900	583,500	583,500

The Adjusted Trial Balance

Step 3: The Adjusted Trial Balance Columns   Columns 5 and 6 of the work sheet represent an adjusted trial balance. The amounts entered in these two columns are found by adding or subtracting any debits or credits in the Adjusting Entries columns from the unadjusted trial balance. For example, Cash is not adjusted and, thus, the $50,000 unadjusted amount is carried over to the Debit column of the adjusted trial balance. The $2,000 credit adjustment to Prepaid Insurance is subtracted from the unadjusted debit balance of $48,000, resulting in a debit balance of $46,000 on the adjusted trial balance. Finally, note the equality of the debits and credits on the new trial balance, $623,200.

The Income Statement

Step 4: The Income Statement Columns   An adjusted trial balance is the basis for preparing the financial statements. The purpose of the last four columns of the worksheet is to separate the accounts into those that will appear on the income statement and those that will appear on the balance sheet. The income statement columns will be completed next.

The three revenue accounts appear in the Credit column and the seven expense accounts appear in the Debit column. These amounts are simply carried over, or extended, from the adjusted trial balance. Because Duffy's revenues exceed its expenses, the total of the Credit column, $52,900, exceeds the total of the Debit column, $39,700. The difference between the two columns, the net income of the period of $13,200, is entered in the Debit column. One purpose for showing the net income in this column is to balance the two columns. In addition, the entry in the Debit column will be matched with an entry in the Balance Sheet Credit column to represent the transfer of net income to retained earnings. If revenues were *less* than expenses, the *net loss* would be entered in the Income Statement *Credit* column.

The Balance Sheet

Step 5: The Balance Sheet Columns   Why do the Income Statement columns appear *before* the Balance Sheet columns on the work sheet? The income statement is in fact a *subset* of the balance sheet and information on the work sheet from the Income Statement columns flows into the Balance Sheet columns. Recall that net income causes an increase in the owners' claim to the assets, that is, an increase in owners' equity. The amount of income for the period increases the owners' equity, through the Retained Earnings account and, thus, is entered in the Balance Sheet Credit column of the work sheet. In Exhibit 4-13, the amount of *net income*, $13,200, is carried over from the *Debit* column of the *income statement* to the *Credit* column of the *balance sheet*. If a company experiences a *net loss* for the period, the amount of the loss is entered in the *Credit* column of the *income statement* and in the *Debit* column of the *balance sheet*.

You will note that the Retained Earnings account has a zero balance in the last column of the work sheet because this is the first month of operations for Duffy Transit Company. On future work sheets, the account will reflect the balance from the *end* of the *previous* month. Dividends appear in the Debit column and net income appears in the Credit column. Thus, the ending balance of Retained Earnings can be found be taking its beginning balance, adding the net income of the period, and deducting the dividends. The completed work sheet provides all the necessary information to prepare an income statement, a statement of retained earnings, and a balance sheet.

Reversing Entries

LO 9

Explain why and how reversing entries are used by some businesses.

Reversing entries are *optional* journal entries made on the first day of a new accounting period. Their purpose is to *facilitate* the recording of certain cash receipt and cash disbursement entries in the new period. The mechanics of a reversing entry are easy. An adjusting entry recorded on the last day of a period is reversed on the first day of the following period by debiting the account credited in the adjusting entry and crediting the account debited. It is important to understand two points about reversing entries: (1) they are strictly *optional* and (2) only *certain* adjusting entries are reversed.

Consider the following example. Ellison Company works a five-day workweek and pays its employees every Friday. The following entry is recorded on *Friday, December 27* of Year 1:

19X1			
Dec. 27	Wages Expense	50,000	
	Cash		50,000
	To record payment of wages.		

Assets	=	Liabilities	+	Owners' Equity
− 50,000				− 50,000

An adjusting entry is needed at the end of the accounting period on *Tuesday, December 31.* The purpose of the entry is to record the accrued wages of $10,000 per day for each of the two days worked by employees since the last payday:

19X1			
Dec. 31	Wages Expense	20,000	
	Wages Payable		20,000
	To accrue wages.		

Assets	=	Liabilities	+	Owners' Equity
		+ 20,000		− 20,000

What entry will Ellison record on the next payday, *Friday, January 3* of Year 2? Not all of the $50,000 paid in cash on this date is an expense. The expense is limited to $30,000 for the three days worked in Year 2, January 1, 2, and 3. The other debit of $20,000 removes the liability recorded as part of the adjusting entry on December 31 of Year 1:

19X2			
Jan. 3	Wages Expense	30,000	
	Wages Payable	20,000	
	Cash		50,000
	To record payment of wages.		

Assets	=	Liabilities	+	Owners' Equity
− 50,000		− 20,000		− 30,000

Now assume *instead* that Ellison prepares a reversing entry on January 1 of Year 2. The reversing entry is made by simply reversing the debits and credits from the December 31 adjusting entry:

19X2			
Jan. 1	Wages Payable	20,000	
	Wages Expense		20,000
	To reverse accrual.		

Assets	=	Liabilities	+	Owners' Equity
		− 20,000		+ 20,000

Recall that income statement accounts are closed at the end of a period but that balance sheet accounts remain open. Thus, immediately before the reversing entry is made, Wages Expense is $0 and Wages Payable is $20,000. The reversing entry reduces the Wages Payable account to zero and creates a temporary *negative* balance of $20,000 in the Wages Expense account. How does the use of a reversing entry *facilitate* the entry on January 3 of Year 2? First, it is unnecessary to debit the Wages Payable of $20,000; this was done on January 1. Second, the entire $50,000 debit can be made to Wages Expense; the negative $20,000 that we started the year with is netted against the debit of $50,000, and the *correct* amount of $30,000 is charged to Year 2. The entry on January 3 is

19X2
Jan. 3   Wages Expense   50,000
                 Cash   50,000
            To record payment of wages.

        Assets   =   Liabilities   +   Owners' Equity
        − 50,000   − 50,000

Exhibit 4-14 summarizes the series of entries made with and without the use of a reversing entry. Note that the balance in the T account for Wages Expense is the *same* whether or not a reversing entry is made.

EXHIBIT 4-14   The Use of Reversing Entries

DATE	NO REVERSING ENTRY RECORDED			REVERSING ENTRY RECORDED		
19X1						
Dec. 31	Wages Expense	20,000		Wages Expense	20,000	
	Wages Payable		20,000	Wages Payable		20,000
	To accrue wages.			To accrue wages.		
Dec. 31	Income Summary	20,000		Income Summary	20,000	
	Wages Expense		20,000	Wages Expense		20,000
	To close the expense account.			To close the expense account.		
19X2						
Jan. 1	No Entry			Wages Payable	20,000	
				Wages Expense		20,000
				To reverse accrual.		
Jan. 3	Wages Expense	30,000		Wages Expense	50,000	
	Wages Payable	20,000				
	Cash		50,000	Cash		50,000
	To record payment of wages.			To record payment of wages.		

T ACCOUNTS

	WAGES EXPENSE				**WAGES EXPENSE**	
12/31/X1	20,000	20,000 12/31/X1		12/31/X1	20,000	20,000 12/31/X1
Bal.	−0−			Bal.	−0−	
1/3/X2	30,000			1/3/X2	50,000	20,000 1/1/X2
				Bal.	30,000	

	WAGES PAYABLE				**WAGES PAYABLE**	
1/3/X2	20,000	20,000 12/31/X1		1/1/2	20,000	20,000 12/31/X1
		−0− Bal.				−0− Bal.

Not all adjusting entries are reversed. Only those adjusting entries that *create* an asset or *liability* account are reversed. For example, our adjusting entry for wages on December 31 of Year 1 created a liability account, Wages Payable. Reversing entries are *not* appropriate for adjusting entries in which an asset or liability account is reduced. For example, a reversing entry is not made for the adjusting entry to reduce the Prepaid Insurance account for the cost of insurance expired during the period.

REVIEW PROBLEM

Note to the Student: The following problem is based on the information for the Northern Airlines review problem at the end of this chapter. Try to prepare the work sheet without referring to the adjusting entries you prepared in solving that problem.

■ REQUIRED

Refer to the unadjusted trial balance and the additional information for Northern Airlines as presented on page 199. Prepare a 10-column work sheet for the month of January.

NORTHERN AIRLINES
WORK SHEET
FOR THE MONTH ENDED JANUARY 31

ACCOUNT TITLES	UNADJUSTED TRIAL BALANCE DEBIT	CREDIT	ADJUSTING ENTRIES DEBIT	CREDIT	ADJUSTED TRIAL BALANCE DEBIT	CREDIT	INCOME STATEMENT DEBIT	CREDIT	BALANCE SHEET DEBIT	CREDIT
Cash	75,000				75,000				75,000	
Parts Inventory	45,000			(a) 8,900	36,100				36,100	
Land	80,000				80,000				80,000	
Buildings—Hangars	250,000				250,000				250,000	
Accumulated Depreciation—Hangars		24,000		(b) 1,000		25,000				25,000
Aircraft	650,000				650,000				650,000	
Accumulated Depreciation—Aircraft		120,000		(c) 5,000		125,000				125,000
Tickets Sold in Advance		85,000	(d) 47,000			38,000				38,000
Capital Stock		500,000				500,000				500,000
Retained Earnings		368,000				368,000				368,000
Ticket Revenue		52,000		(d) 47,000		99,000		99,000		
Maintenance Expense	19,000		(a) 8,900		27,900		27,900			
Wage and Salary Expense	30,000		(e) 7,600		37,600		37,600			
	1,149,000	1,149,000								
Depreciation Expense—Hangars			(b) 1,000		1,000		1,000			
Depreciation Expense—Aircraft			(c) 5,000		5,000		5,000			
Rent Receivable			(f) 2,500		2,500				2,500	
Income Tax Expense			(g) 10,200		10,200		10,200			
Wages and Salaries Payable				(e) 7,600		7,600				7,600
Rent Revenue				(f) 2,500		2,500		2,500		
Income Taxes Payable				(g) 10,200		10,200				10,200
			82,200	82,200	1,175,300	1,175,300	81,700	101,500	1,093,600	1,073,800
Net Income							19,800			19,800
							101,500	101,500	1,093,600	1,093,600

CHAPTER HIGHLIGHTS

1. **(LO 1)** The success of accounting as a form of communication depends on two concepts: recognition and measurement. The items depicted in financial statements are representations. The accountant cannot show the reader an asset but instead depicts it with words and numbers.

2. **(LO 1)** Measurement in accounting requires choosing an attribute and a unit of measure. Historical cost is the attribute used for many of the assets included in financial statements. One alternative to historical cost is current value. The dollar as a unit of measure is subject to instability, depending on the level of inflation.

3. **(LO 2)** Under the accrual basis of accounting, revenues are recognized when earned and expenses when incurred. The income statement is prepared on an accrual basis, and the statement of cash flows complements it by providing valuable information about the operating, financing, and investing cash flows of a business.

4. **(LO 3)** According to the revenue recognition principle, revenues are recognized when they are realized or realizable and earned. On a practical basis, revenue is normally recognized at the time a product or service is delivered to the customer. Certain types of sales arrangements, such as long-term contracts and franchises, present special problems in applying the principle.

5. **(LO 4)** The matching principle attempts to associate with the revenue of the period all costs necessary to generate that revenue. A direct form of matching is possible for certain types of costs, such as cost of goods sold and commissions. Other types of costs are recognized as expenses on an indirect basis. Depreciation is the allocation of the cost of a tangible, long-term asset over its useful life. The benefits from most selling and administrative expenses expire immediately and are recognized as expenses in the period the costs are incurred.

6. **(LO 5)** The accrual basis necessitates the use of adjusting entries at the end of a period. The four types of adjusting entries result from differences between the recognition of revenues and expenses on an accrual basis and the receipt or payment of cash.

7. **(LO 5)** Cash paid before expense is incurred results in a deferred expense that is recognized as an asset on the balance sheet. The adjusting entry reduces the asset and recognizes a corresponding amount of expense. Cash received before revenue is earned requires the recognition of a liability, deferred revenue. The adjusting entry reduces the liability and recognizes a corresponding amount of revenue.

8. **(LO 5)** If cash is paid after an expense is incurred, an adjusting entry is needed to recognize the accrued liability and the related expense. Similarly, if cash is received after the revenue is earned, the adjusting entry recognizes the accrued asset and the corresponding revenue. The liability or asset is eliminated in a later period when cash is either paid or received.

9. **(LO 5)** Adjusting entries are prepared by reference to a trial balance and certain additional information. A trial balance prepared after posting the adjustments to the accounts ensures the equality of debits and credits in the ledger.

10. **(LO 6)** Steps in the accounting cycle are carried out each period as a basis for the preparation of financial statements. The entire process may be repeated each month, although in practice, some of the steps, such as closing the accounts, are often performed only at the end of the year.

11. **(LO 7)** After adjusting entries are recorded and posted to the accounts, closing entries are made. They have two important purposes: (1) the balances in all revenue, expense, and dividend accounts are returned to zero to start the following accounting period and (2) the net income (or net loss) and the dividends of the period are transferred to the Retained Earnings account.

12. **(LO 7)** A revenue account is closed by debiting it for the credit balance in the account and crediting Income Summary. An expense account is closed by crediting it and debiting Income Summary. If revenues exceed expenses, Income Summary will have a credit balance at this point, representing the net income of the period. Income Summary is closed by debiting it and crediting Retained Earnings. Finally, the Dividends account is closed with a credit and a corresponding debit to Retained Earnings.

13. **(LO 8)** A work sheet is not itself a financial statement. It is a useful device for organizing the necessary information to prepare financial statements without going through the formal process of recording and posting adjusting entries. The format for a 10-column work sheet includes two columns each (Debits and Credits) for the unadjusted trial balance, the adjustments, the adjusted trial balance, the income statement, and the balance sheet. (Appendix 4A)

14. **(LO 9)** Reversing entries are optional entries made on the first day of a new accounting period to facilitate the recording of certain cash receipt and cash disbursement entries in the new period. Adjusting entries are reversed by simply debiting the account credited and crediting the account debited in the adjusting entry. Not all adjusting entries are reversed; only those that create an asset or liability account are reversed. (Appendix 4A)

KEY TERMS QUIZ

Select from the following list of key terms used in the chapter and fill in the appropriate blank to the left of each description. The solution appears at the end of the chapter.

Recognition	Historical cost
Current value	Cash basis
Accrual basis	Revenues
Revenue recognition principle	Percentage-of-completion method
Production method	Installment method
Matching principle	Expenses
Adjusting entries	Straight-line method
Contra account	Deferral
Deferred expense	Deferred revenue
Accrual	Accrued liability
Accrued asset	Accounting cycle
Work sheet	Real accounts
Nominal accounts	Closing entries
Reversing entries	Interim statements

_____ 1. A device used at the end of the period to gather the information needed to prepare financial statements without actually recording and posting adjusting entries.

_____ 2. Inflows or other enhancements of assets or settlements of liabilities from delivering or producing goods, rendering services, or other activities.

_____ 3. The method in which revenue is recognized at the time a commodity is produced rather than when it is sold.

_____ 4. Journal entries made at the end of a period by a company using the accrual basis of accounting.

_____ 5. Journal entries made at the end of the period to return the balance in all nominal accounts to zero and transfer the net income or loss and the dividends of the period to Retained Earnings.

_____ 6. The method used by contractors to recognize revenue prior to the completion of a long-term contract.

_____ 7. A liability resulting from the receipt of cash prior to the recognition of revenue.

8. The method in which revenue is recognized at the time cash is collected; it is used for various types of consumer items, such as automobiles and appliances.

9. The name given to balance sheet accounts because they are permanent and are not closed at the end of the period.

10. Optional journal entries used by some businesses to facilitate the bookkeeping process. They are made on the first day of a new accounting period.

11. An asset resulting from the recognition of a revenue prior to the receipt of cash.

12. The amount of cash, or its equivalent, that could be received by selling an asset currently.

13. The assignment of an equal amount of depreciation to each period.

14. Cash has either been paid or received, but expense or revenue has not yet been recognized.

15. A system of accounting in which revenues are recognized when earned and expenses when incurred.

16. Cash has not yet been paid or received, but expense has been incurred or revenue earned.

17. Financial statements prepared monthly, quarterly, or at other intervals less than a year in duration.

18. Revenues are recognized in the income statement when they are realized, or realizable, and earned.

19. The process of recording an item in the financial statements as an asset, liability, revenue, expense, or the like.

20. An asset resulting from the payment of cash prior to the incurrence of expense.

21. The name given to revenue, expense, and dividend accounts because they are temporary and are closed at the end of the period.

22. A system of accounting in which revenues are recognized when cash is received and expenses when cash is paid.

23. A liability resulting from the recognition of an expense prior to the payment of cash.

24. The association of revenue of a period with all of the costs necessary to generate that revenue.

25. An account with a balance that is opposite that of a related account.

26. The amount paid for an asset that is used as a basis for recognizing it on the balance sheet and carrying it on later balance sheets.

27. Outflows or other using up of assets or incurrences of liabilities from delivering goods, rendering services, or carrying out other activities.

28. A series of steps performed each period that culminates with the preparation of a set of financial statements.

ALTERNATE TERMS

HISTORICAL COST Original cost.

ASSET Unexpired cost.

DEFERRED EXPENSE Prepaid expense, prepaid asset.

DEFERRED REVENUE Unearned revenue.

EXPENSE Expired cost.

NOMINAL ACCOUNT Temporary account.

REAL ACCOUNT Permanent account.

RENT COLLECTED IN ADVANCE Unearned rent revenue.

QUESTIONS

1. What is meant by the following statement? "The items depicted in financial statements are merely *representations* of the real thing."
2. What is the meaning of the following statement? "The choice between historical cost and current value is a good example of the trade-off in accounting between relevance and reliability."
3. A realtor earns a 10% commission on the sale of a $150,000 home. The realtor listed the home on June 5, the sale takes place on June 12, and the seller pays the realtor the $15,000 commission on July 8. When should the realtor recognize revenue from the sale, assuming (a) the cash basis of accounting and (b) the accrual basis of accounting?
4. What does the following statement mean? "If I want to assess the cash flow prospects for a company down the road, I look at the company's most recent statement of cash flows. An income statement prepared under the accrual basis of accounting is useless for this purpose."
5. What is the relationship between the time period assumption and accrual accounting?
6. Is it necessary for an asset to be acquired when revenue is recognized? Explain your answer.
7. What is the justification for recognizing revenue on a long-term contract by the percentage-of-completion method?
8. Illinois Fried Chicken sells franchises granting the franchisee in a specific geographic area the exclusive right to use the company name and sell chicken using its secret recipe. An initial franchise fee of $50,000 is charged by Illinois, along with a continuing fee of 3% of sales. The initial fee is for Illinois' assistance in selecting a site and training personnel. When should Illinois recognize the $50,000 as revenue?
9. When should a publisher of magazines recognize revenue?
10. What is the justification for recognizing revenue in certain industries at the time the product is *produced* rather than when it is *sold?*
11. A friend says to you, "I just don't get it. Assets cost money. Expenses reduce income. There must be some relationship among *assets, costs,* and *expenses*—I'm just not sure what it is!" What is the relationship? Can you give an example of it?
12. What is the meaning of *depreciation* to the accountant?
13. What are the four basic types of adjusting entries? Give an example of each.
14. What are the rules of debit and credit as they apply to the contra asset account, Accumulated Depreciation?
15. Which of the following steps in the accounting cycle requires the most thought and judgment by the accountant: (a) preparing a trial balance, (b) posting adjusting and closing entries, or (c) analyzing and recording transactions? Explain your answer.

16. What is the difference between a real account and a nominal account?

17. What two purposes are served in making closing entries?

18. Why is the Dividends account closed directly to Retained Earnings rather than to the Income Summary account?

19. What is the purpose of a *post-closing* trial balance? Why do only balance sheet accounts appear on a post-closing trial balance?

20. Assuming the use of a work sheet, are the formal adjusting entries recorded and posted to the accounts before or after the financial statements are prepared? Explain your answer. Would your answer change if a work sheet is not prepared? (Appendix 4A)

21. Some companies use an eight-column work sheet rather than the 10-column format illustrated in the chapter. Which two columns would you think are not used in the eight-column format? Why could these two columns be eliminated? (Appendix 4A)

22. Why do the Income Statement columns appear before the Balance Sheet columns on a work sheet? (Appendix 4A)

23. Does the Retained Earnings account that appears in the Balance Sheet Credit column of a work sheet reflect the beginning or the ending balance in the account? Explain your answer. (Appendix 4A)

24. One asset account will always be carried over from the Unadjusted Trial Balance columns of a work sheet to the Balance Sheet columns of the work sheet without any adjustment. What account is this? (Appendix 4A)

25. Which types of adjusting entries are reversed if a company uses reversing entries? (Appendix 4A)

EXERCISES

(LO 3) EXERCISE 4-1 REVENUE RECOGNITION

The highway department contracted with a private company to collect tolls and maintain facilities on a turnpike. Users of the turnpike can pay cash as they approach the toll booth, or they can purchase a pass. The pass is equipped with an electronic sensor that subtracts the toll fee from the pass balance as the motorist slowly approaches a special toll booth. The passes are issued in $10 increments. Refunds are available to motorists who do not use the pass balance but are issued very infrequently. Last year $3,000,000 was collected at the traditional toll booths, $2,000,000 of passes were issued, and $1,700,000 of passes were used at the special toll booth. How much should the company recognize as revenue for the year? Explain how the revenue recognition rule should be applied in this case.

(LO 4) EXERCISE 4-2 THE MATCHING PRINCIPLE

Three methods of matching costs with revenue were described in the chapter: (a) directly match a specific form of revenue with a cost incurred in generating that revenue, (b) indirectly match a cost with the periods during which it will provide benefits or revenue, and (c) immediately recognize a cost incurred as an expense because no future benefits are expected. For each of the following costs, indicate how it is normally recognized as expense by indicating either *a, b,* or *c.* If you think there is more than one possible answer for any of the situations, explain why.

1. New office copier.
2. Monthly bill from the utility company for electricity.
3. Office supplies.
4. Biweekly payroll for office employees.
5. Commissions earned by salespersons.
6. Interest incurred on a six-month loan from the bank.
7. Cost of inventory sold during the current period.
8. Taxes owed on income earned during current period.
9. Cost of three-year insurance policy.

(LO 5) EXERCISE 4-3 ACCRUALS AND DEFERRALS

For each of the following situations, indicate whether each involves a deferred expense (DE), a deferred revenue (DR), an accrued liability (AL), or an accrued asset (AA):

Example: <u>DE</u>   Office supplies purchased in advance of their use.

_____ 1. Wages earned by employees but not yet paid.

_____ 2. Cash collected from subscriptions in advance of publishing the magazine.

_____ 3. Interest earned on a loan made to a customer but principal and interest not yet collected.

_____ 4. One year's premium on life insurance policy paid in advance.

_____ 5. Office building purchased for cash.

_____ 6. Rent collected in advance from tenant.

_____ 7. State income taxes owed at the end of the year.

_____ 8. Rent owed by a tenant but not yet collected.

(LO 5) EXERCISE 4-4 OFFICE SUPPLIES

Weber Corp. purchases office supplies once a month and prepares monthly financial statements. The asset account, Office Supplies on Hand, has a balance of $1,450 on May 1. Purchases of supplies during May amount to $1,100. Supplies on hand at May 31 amount to $920. Prepare the necessary adjusting entry on Weber's books on May 31. What would be the effect on net income for May if this entry is _not_ recorded?

(LO 5) EXERCISE 4-5 SUBSCRIPTIONS

Great Outdoors publishes a monthly magazine for which a 12-month subscription costs $30. All subscriptions require payment of the full $30 in advance. On August 1, 1995, the balance in the Subscriptions Received in Advance account was $40,500. During the month of August, the company sold 900 yearly subscriptions. After the adjusting entry at the end of August, the balance in the Subscriptions Received in Advance account is $60,000.

1. Prepare the journal entry to record the sale of the 900 yearly subscriptions during the month of August.

2. Prepare the adjusting journal entry on August 31.

3. Assume that the accountant made the correct entry during August to record the sale of the 900 subscriptions but forgot to make the adjusting entry on August 31. Would net income for August be overstated or understated? Explain your answer.

■ REQUIRED

(LO 5) EXERCISE 4-6 WAGES PAYABLE

Elroy Corporation employs 50 workers in its plant. Each employee is paid $10 per hour and works seven hours per day, Monday through Friday. Employees are paid every Friday. The last payday was Friday, October 20.

■ REQUIRED

1. Compute the dollar amount of the weekly payroll.

2. Prepare the journal entry on Friday, October 27, for the payment of the weekly payroll.

3. Elroy prepares monthly financial statements. Prepare the adjusting journal entry on Tuesday, October 31, the last day of the month.

4. Prepare the journal entry on Friday, November 3, for the payment of the weekly payroll.

5. Would net income for the month of October be understated or overstated if Elroy doesn't bother with an adjusting entry on October 31? Explain your answer.

(LO 5) EXERCISE 4-7 PREPAID INSURANCE

On April 1, 1995, Briggs Corp. purchases a 24-month property insurance policy for $72,000. The policy is effective immediately. Briggs prepares a monthly work sheet as the basis for monthly financial statements. Adjusting entries are recorded in the general journal only at the end of the year, however.

■ REQUIRED

1. Compute the monthly cost of the insurance policy.

2. Prepare the journal entry to record the purchase of the policy on April 1, 1995.

3. Prepare the adjusting entry on December 31, 1995.

4. Assume that the accountant forgets to record an adjusting entry on December 31, 1995. Will net income for the year be understated or overstated? Explain your answer.

(LO 5) EXERCISE 4-8 THE EFFECT OF IGNORING ADJUSTING ENTRIES ON NET INCOME

For each of the following independent situations, determine whether the effect of ignoring the required adjusting entry will result in an understatement (U), an overstatement (O), or have no effect (NE) on net income for the period.

EFFECT ON
NET INCOME

SITUATION

O

Example: Taxes owed but not yet paid are ignored.

1. A company fails to record depreciation on equipment.

2. Sales made during the last week of the period are not recorded.

3. A company neglects to record the expired portion of a prepaid insurance policy (its cost was originally debited to an asset account).

4. Interest due but not yet paid on a long-term note payable is ignored.

5. Commissions earned by salespersons but not payable until the 10th of the following month are ignored.

6. A landlord receives cash on the date a lease is signed for the rent for the first six months and credits Unearned Rent Revenue. The landlord fails to make any adjustment at the end of the first month.

(LO 5) EXERCISE 4-9 THE EFFECT OF ADJUSTING ENTRIES ON THE ACCOUNTING EQUATION

Determine whether the effect of recording each of the following adjusting entries is to increase (I), decrease (D), or have no effect (NE) on each of the three elements of the accounting equation.

$$\text{Assets} = \text{Liabilities} + \text{Owners'}$$
$$\text{Equity}$$

Example: Wages earned during the period but not yet paid are accrued.	NE	I	D

1. Prepaid insurance is reduced for the portion of the policy that has expired during the period.

2. Interest incurred during the period but not yet paid is accrued.

3. Depreciation for the period is recorded.

4. Revenue is recorded for the earned portion of a liability for amounts collected in advance from customers.

5. Rent revenue is recorded for amounts owed by a tenant but not yet paid.

6. Income taxes owed but not yet paid are accrued.

(LO 6) EXERCISE 4-10 THE ACCOUNTING CYCLE

The steps in the accounting cycle are listed below in random order. Fill in the blank next to each step to indicate its *order* in the cycle. The first step in the cycle is filled in as an example.

ORDER	PROCEDURE
_____	Prepare a work sheet.
_____	Journalize and post closing entries.
___1___	Collect and analyze information from source documents.
_____	Prepare financial statements.
_____	Post journal entries to accounts in the ledger.
_____	Journalize and post adjusting entries.
_____	Prepare a post-closing trial balance.
_____	Journalize and post reversing entries (optional).
_____	Journalize daily transactions.

(LO 7) EXERCISE 4-11 CLOSING ENTRIES

At the end of the year, the adjusted trial balance for Knox Corporation contains the following amounts for the Income Statement accounts (the balance in each account is the normal balance for that type of account).

ACCOUNT	BALANCE
Advertising Fees Earned	$58,500
Interest Revenue	2,700
Wage and Salary Expense	14,300
Utilities Expense	12,500
Insurance Expense	7,300
Depreciation Expense	16,250
Interest Expense	2,600
Income Tax Expense	3,300
Dividends	2,000

REQUIRED

1. Prepare all necessary journal entries to close Knox Corporation's accounts at the end of the year.
2. Assume that the accountant for Knox forgets to record the closing entries. What will be the effect on net income for the following year? Explain your answer.

(LO 6) EXERCISE 4-12 TRIAL BALANCE

The following account titles, arranged in alphabetical order, are from the records of Winston Realty Corporation. The balance in each account is the normal balance for that account. The balances are as of December 31, after adjusting entries have been made. Prepare an adjusted trial balance, listing the accounts in the following order: (1) assets (2) liabilities (3) owners' equity accounts, including dividends, (4) revenues, and (5) expenses.

Accounts Payable	$12,300
Accounts Receivable	21,230
Accumulated Depreciation—Automobiles	12,000
Accumulated Depreciation—Buildings	15,000
Automobiles	48,000
Buildings	60,000
Capital Stock	25,000
Cash	2,460
Commissions Earned	17,420
Commissions Expense	2,300
Dividends Declared and Paid	1,500
Insurance Expense	300
Interest Expense	200
Interest Payable	200
Land	40,000
Notes Payable	20,000
Office Supplies	1,680
Office Supplies Expense	5,320
Prepaid Insurance	1,200
Rent Expense	2,400
Retained Earnings	85,445
Wages and Salaries Expense	1,245
Wages and Salaries Payable	470

(LO 7) EXERCISE 4-13 PREPARATION OF A STATEMENT OF RETAINED EARNINGS FROM CLOSING ENTRIES

Baxter Corporation reported a Retained Earnings balance of $125,780 on January 1, 1995. Baxter Corporation made the following three closing entries on December

31, 1995 (the entry to transfer net income to Retained Earnings has been intentionally left out). Prepare a statement of retained earnings for Baxter for the year.

Dec.31	Service Revenue		65,400	
	Interest Revenue		20,270	
		Income Summary		85,670
Dec.31	Income Summary		62,345	
		Salary and Wage Expense		23,450
		Rent Expense		20,120
		Interest Expense		4,500
		Utilities Expense		10,900
		Insurance Expense		3,375
Dec.31	Retained Earnings		6,400	
		Dividends		6,400

(LO 7) EXERCISE 4-14 CLOSING ENTRIES FOR BEN & JERRY'S

The following accounts appear on Ben & Jerry's 1992 income statement. The accounts are listed in alphabetical order, and the balance in each account is the normal balance for that account. Prepare closing entries for Ben & Jerry's for 1992.

Cost of Sales	$ 94,389,391
Income Taxes	4,638,797
Interest Expense	181,577
Interest Income	394,817
Net Sales	131,968,814
Other Expenses	235,765
Selling, General, and Administrative Expenses	26,242,761

(LO 7) EXERCISE 4-15 CLOSING ENTRIES

Help U Buy Realty reported the following accounts on its income statement:

Commissions Earned	$54,000
Real Estate Board Fees Paid	5,000
Computer Line Charge	864
Depreciation on Computer	450
Car Expenses	2,200
Travel and Entertainment	4,500
Insurance Expired	780
Advertising Expense	1,460
Office Supplies Used	940

1. Prepare the necessary entries to close the temporary accounts.   ■ REQUIRED

2. Explain why the closing entries are necessary and when they should be recorded.

(LO 9) EXERCISE 4-16 REVERSING ENTRIES (Appendix 4A)

Stevenson Company provides the following information to prepare adjusting entries on December 31, 1993:

a. Accrued wages are $525.

b. Annual depreciation is $11,460.

c. Supplies on hand total only $120. The Supplies account shows a balance of $680.

d. A 30-day, 10%, $7,500 note was signed on December 15, 1993.

■ REQUIRED

1. Prepare the necessary adjusting entries on December 31, 1993.

2. Assuming that Stevenson wants to make reversing entries, prepare the appropriate ones on January 1, 1994.

3. On January 10, 1994, Stevenson issues payroll checks. The total payroll amount is $2,525. Prepare the entry to record payroll on January 10. What is the amount of Wages Expense immediately before and after the January 10 entry?

(LO 8) EXERCISE 4-17 THE DIFFERENCE BETWEEN A FINANCIAL STATEMENT AND A WORK SHEET (Appendix 4A)

The Balance Sheet columns of the work sheet for Jones Corporation shows total debits and total credits of $255,000 each. Dividends for the period are $3,000. Accumulated depreciation is $14,000 at the end of the period. Compute the amount that should appear on the balance sheet (i.e., the formal financial statement) for *total assets.* How do you explain the difference between this amount and the amount that appears as the total debits and total credits on the work sheet?

(LO 8) EXERCISE 4-18 TEN-COLUMN WORK SHEET (Appendix 4A)

Indicate whether each of the following accounts should be spread from the Adjusted Trial Balance columns of the Work Sheet to the Income Statement (IS) columns or to the Balance Sheet (BS) columns. Also indicate whether the account normally has a debit (D) balance or a credit (C) balance.

	ACCOUNT TITLE
BS-D	**Example:** Cash
_____	**1.** Accumulated Depreciation—Trucks
_____	**2.** Subscriptions Sold in Advance
_____	**3.** Accounts Receivable
_____	**4.** Dividends
_____	**5.** Capital Stock
_____	**6.** Prepaid Insurance
_____	**7.** Depreciation Expense—Trucks
_____	**8.** Office Supplies
_____	**9.** Office Supplies Expense
_____	**10.** Subscription Revenue
_____	**11.** Interest Receivable
_____	**12.** Interest Revenue
_____	**13.** Interest Expense
_____	**14.** Interest Payable
_____	**15.** Retained Earnings

MULTI-CONCEPT EXERCISES

(LO 1, 2, 3) EXERCISE 4-19 REVENUE RECOGNITION, CASH AND ACCRUAL BASIS

Beautinbeast Health Club sold three-year memberships at a reduced rate during its opening promotion. One thousand three-year, nonrefundable memberships were sold for $366 each. The club expects to sell 100 additional three-year memberships for $900 each over each of the next two years. Membership fees are paid when clients sign up. The club's bookkeeper has prepared the following income statement for the first year of business and projected income statements for Years 2 and 3.

Cash basis income statements:

	YEAR 1	YEAR 2	YEAR 3
Sales	$366,000	$90,000	$90,000
Equipment*	100,000	–0–	–0–
Salaries and Wages	50,000	50,000	50,000
Advertising	5,000	5,000	5,000
Rent and Utilities	36,000	36,000	36,000
Income (Loss)	$175,000	$(1,000)	$(1,000)

*Equipment was purchased at the beginning of Year 1 for $100,000 and is expected to last for three years and then to be worth $1,000.

1. Convert the income statements for each of the three years to the accrual basis.   ■ REQUIRED

2. Describe how the revenue recognition principle applies. Do you believe that the cash basis or accrual basis income statements are more useful to management? to investors? Why?

(LO 1, 2, 3) EXERCISE 4-20 THE EFFECT OF THE PERCENTAGE-OF-COMPLETION METHOD ON FINANCIAL STATEMENTS

Upnover, Inc., is building a bridge. During the first year of the three-year project, Upnover incurred construction costs of $1.2 million. The company expects to spend an additional $600,000 in each of the next two years of the project. The state has agreed to pay Upnover $4 million for the bridge, $2 million in the first year and $2 million upon completion. The company would like to use the percentage-of-completion method to report revenue and income.

1. Complete the following table, comparing the percentage-of-completion method   ■ REQUIRED
with the cash basis. Use the percentage of costs incurred to date to estimate total costs to determine the percentage of completion.

		INCOME RECOGNIZED UNDER	
YEAR	PERCENTAGE OF COMPLETION		CASH BASIS
1			
2			
3			
Total			

2. Explain how the revenue recognition principle applies to the percentage-of-completion method.

(LO 4, 5) EXERCISE 4-21 DEPRECIATION EXPENSE

During 1995, Carter Company acquired three assets, with the following costs, estimated useful lives, and estimated salvage values:

DATE	ASSET	COST	ESTIMATED USEFUL LIFE	ESTIMATED SALVAGE VALUE
March 28	Truck	$ 18,000	5 years	$ 3,000
June 22	Computer	55,000	10 years	5,000
October 3	Building	250,000	30 years	10,000

The company uses the straight-line method to depreciate all assets and computes depreciation to the nearest month. For example, the computer system will be depreciated for six months in 1995.

■ REQUIRED

1. Compute the depreciation expense that Carter will record on each of the three assets for 1995.

2. Comment on the following statement: "Accountants could save time and money by simply expensing the cost of long-term assets when they are purchased. In addition, this would be more accurate, because depreciation requires estimates of useful life and salvage value."

(LO 4, 5) EXERCISE 4-22 ACCRUAL OF INTEREST ON A LOAN

On July 1, 1995, Paxson Corporation takes out a 12%, two-month, $50,000 loan at Friendly National Bank. Principal and interest are to be repaid on August 31.

■ REQUIRED

1. Prepare the journal entries to be recorded on July 1 to record the borrowing, on July 31 to record the accrual of interest, and on August 31 to record repayment of the principal and interest.

2. Evaluate the following statement: "It would be much easier not to bother with an adjusting entry on July 31 and simply record interest expense on August 31 when the loan is repaid."

(LO 5, 8) EXERCISE 4-23 RE-CREATION OF ADJUSTING ENTRIES FROM UNADJUSTED AND ADJUSTED TRIAL BALANCES AND COMPLETION OF A WORK SHEET (APPENDIX 4A)

Following are the unadjusted and adjusted trial balances for Power Corp. on May 31, 1995:

	UNADJUSTED TRIAL BALANCE DEBITS	CREDITS	ADJUSTED TRIAL BALANCE DEBITS	CREDITS
Cash	$ 3,160		$ 3,160	
Accounts Receivable	7,300		9,650	
Supplies on Hand	400		160	
Prepaid Rent	2,400		2,200	
Equipment	9,000		9,000	
Accumulated Depreciation		$ 2,800		$ 3,200
Accounts Payable		2,600		2,600
Capital Stock		5,000		5,000
Retained Earnings		8,990		8,990
Service Revenue		6,170		8,520
Promotions Expense	2,050		2,050	
Wage Expense	1,250		2,350	
Wages Payable				1,100
Supplies Expense			240	
Depreciation Expense			400	
Rent Expense			200	
Totals	$25,560	$25,560	$29,410	$29,410

■ REQUIRED

1. Enter the unadjusted and adjusted trial balances in the appropriate columns of a 10-column work sheet.

2. Enter the appropriate amounts in the Adjusting Entries columns of the work sheet.

3. Complete the work sheet by filling in the appropriate amounts in the Income Statement and Balance Sheet columns of the work sheet.

(LO 5, 9) EXERCISE 4-24 ADJUSTING AND REVERSING ENTRIES (APPENDIX 4A)

The following two accounts appear among other accounts on the unadjusted trial balance of Wickstrom Corp. on December 31, 1995:

	DEBITS	CREDITS
Prepaid Rent	$9,000	
Notes Payable		$60,000

The Prepaid Rent account represents the one year's rent paid in advance to Wickstrom's landlord on December 1, 1995. The Notes Payable account represents a promissory note signed on December 1, 1995, with the principal amount of $60,000 and interest, at an annual rate of 12%, both payable on January 15, 1996.

1. Prepare the two necessary adjusting entries on December 31, 1995.

2. Assuming that Wickstrom uses reversing entries whenever appropriate, prepare any necessary reversing entries on January 1, 1996.

3. Prepare the necessary entry on January 15, 1996, to record repayment of the note and interest.

4. What are the advantages of preparing reversing entries?

■REQUIRED

PROBLEMS

(LO 3) PROBLEM 4-1 THE REVENUE RECOGNITION PRINCIPLE

Each of the following paragraphs describes a situation involving revenue recognition.

a. ABC Realty receives a 6% commission for every house it sells. It lists a house for a client on April 3 at a selling price of $150,000. ABC receives an offer from a buyer on April 28 to purchase the house at the asking price. The realtor's client accepts the offer on May 1. ABC will receive its 6% commission at a closing scheduled for May 16.

b. Chicken King is a fast-food franchisor on the West Coast. It charges all franchisees $10,000 to open an outlet in a designated city. In return for this fee, the franchisee receives the exclusive right to operate in the area, as well as assistance from Chicken King in selecting a site. On January 5, Chicken King signs an agreement with a franchisee and receives a down payment of $4,000, with the balance of $6,000 due in three months. On March 13, Chicken King meets with the new franchisee and the two parties agree on a suitable site for the business. On April 5, the franchisee pays Chicken King the remaining $6,000.

c. Refer to part b. In addition to the initial fee, Chicken King charges a continuing fee equal to 2% of the franchisee's sales each month. Each month's fee is payable by the 10th of the following month. The franchisee opens for business on June 1. On July 3, Chicken King receives a report from the franchisee indicating its sales for the month of June amount to $60,000. Chicken King receives its 2% fee for June sales on July 8.

d. Goldstar Mining Corporation mines and sells gold and other precious commodities on the open market. During August, the company mines 50 ounces of gold. The market price throughout August is $300 per ounce. The 50 ounces are eventually sold on the open market on September 5 for $310 per ounce.

e. Whatadeal, Inc., sells used cars. Because of the uncertainties involved in collecting from customers, Whatadeal uses the installment basis of accounting. On December 2, Whatadeal sells a car for $10,000 with a 25% down payment and the balance due in 60 days. The company's accounting year ends on December 31. Whatadeal receives the balance of $7,500 on February 1.

■ **REQUIRED**   For each situation, indicate when revenue should be recognized as well as the dollar amount. Give a brief explanation for each answer.

(LO 5) PROBLEM 4-2 ADJUSTING ENTRIES

Water Corporation prepares monthly financial statements and therefore adjusts its accounts at the end of every month. The following information is available for March 1996:

a. Water Corporation takes out a 90-day, 8%, $15,000 note on March 1, 1996, with interest and principal to be paid at maturity.

b. The asset account, Office Supplies on Hand, has a balance of $1,280 on March 1, 1996. During March, Water adds $750 to the account for the purchases of the period. A count of the supplies on hand at the end of March indicates a balance of $1,370.

c. The company purchased office equipment on September 1, 1994, at a cost of $62,600. The equipment has an estimated useful life of six years and an estimated salvage value of $5,000.

d. The company's plant operates seven days per week with a daily payroll of $7,950. Wage earners are paid every Friday. The last day of the month is Sunday, March 31.

e. The company rented an idle warehouse to a neighboring business on February 1, 1996, at a rate of $2,500 per month. On this date, Water Corporation credited Rent Collected in Advance for six months' rent received in advance.

f. On March 1, 1996, Water Corporation credited a liability account, Customer Deposits, for $4,800. This amount represents an amount a customer paid in advance that will be earned evenly by Water over a four-month period.

g. Based on its income for the month, Water Corporation estimates that federal income taxes for March amount to $3,900.

■ **REQUIRED**   **1.** For each of the preceding situations, prepare in general journal form the appropriate adjusting entry to be recorded on March 31, 1996.

2. Assume that Water reports income of $23,000 before taxes and before any of the adjusting entries. What net income will Water report for March?

(LO 5) PROBLEM 4-3 RECURRING AND ADJUSTING ENTRIES

The following are the accounts of Boston Realty Corporation, identified by number. The company has been in the real estate business for 10 years and prepares financial statements monthly. Following the list of accounts is a series of transactions entered into by Boston.

ACCOUNTS

1. Cash

2. Accounts Receivable

3. Prepaid Rent

4. Office Supplies

5. Automobiles

6. Accumulated Depreciation

7. Land

8. Accounts Payable

9. Salaries and Wages Payable

10. Income Tax Payable

11. Notes Payable

12. Capital Stock, $10 par

13. Paid-in Capital in Excess of Par

14. Commissions Revenue

15. Office Supply Expense

16. Rent Expense

17. Salaries and Wages Expense

18. Depreciation Expense

19. Interest Expense

20. Income Tax Expense

	DEBIT	CREDIT	
a. Example: Issued additional shares of stock to owners at amount in excess of par.	1	12,13	■ REQUIRED
b. Purchased automobiles for cash.			
c. Purchased land; made cash down payment and signed a promissory note for the balance.			
d. Paid cash to landlord for rent for next 12 months.			
e. Purchased office supplies on account.			
f. Collected cash for commissions from the properties sold for clients during the month.			
g. Collected cash for commissions from clients for properties sold for them in prior month.			
h. Sold properties for clients during the month for which cash for commissions will be collected next month.			
i. Paid for office supplies purchased on account in an earlier month.			
j. Recorded an adjusting entry to recognize wages and salaries incurred but not yet paid.			
k. Recorded an adjusting entry for office supplies used during the month.			
l. Recorded an adjusting entry for the portion of prepaid rent that expired during the month.			
m. Made required month-end payment on note taken out in (c); payment is part principal and part interest.			
n. Recorded adjusting entry for monthly depreciation on the autos.			
o. Recorded adjusting entry for income taxes.			

For each transaction, enter the number of the account(s) to be debited and credited.

(LO 5) PROBLEM 4-4 USE OF ACCOUNT BALANCES AS A BASIS FOR ADJUSTING ENTRIES

The following account balances are taken from the records of Chauncey Company at December 31, 1995. The Prepaid Insurance account represents the cost of a three-year policy purchased on August 1, 1995. The Rent Collected in Advance account represents the cash received from a tenant on June 1, 1995, for 12 months' rent, beginning on that date. The Note Receivable represents a nine-month promissory note received from a customer on September 1, 1995. Principal and interest at an annual rate of 9% will be received on June 1, 1996.

ACCOUNTS

Prepaid Insurance	$ 7,200 debit	
Rent Collected in Advance		$ 6,000 credit
Notes Receivable	50,000 debit	

■ REQUIRED

I. Prepare the three necessary adjusting entries on the books of Chauncey on December 31, 1995. Assume that Chauncey prepares adjusting entries only once a year, on December 31.

2. Assume that adjusting entries are made at the end of each month rather than only at the end of the year. What would be the balance in Prepaid Insurance *before* the December adjusting entry is made? Explain your answer.

(LO 5) PROBLEM 4-5 USE OF A TRIAL BALANCE AS A BASIS FOR ADJUSTING ENTRIES

Bill Smith operates a real estate business. A trial balance on April 30, 1995, *prior* to recording any adjusting entries, is as follows:

SMITH REALTY COMPANY
UNADJUSTED TRIAL BALANCE
APRIL 30, 1995

	DEBIT	CREDIT
Cash	$15,700	
Prepaid Insurance	450	
Office Supplies	250	
Office Equipment	50,000	
Accumulated Depreciation—Office Equipment		$ 5,000
Automobile	12,000	
Accumulated Depreciation—Automobile		1,400
Accounts Payable		6,500
Unearned Commissions		9,500
Notes Payable		2,000
Capital Stock		10,000
Retained Earnings		40,000
Dividends	2,500	
Commissions Earned		17,650
Utility Expense	2,300	
Salaries Expense	7,400	
Advertising Expense	1,450	
	$92,050	$92,050

OTHER DATA

a. The monthly insurance cost is $50.

b. Office supplies on hand on April 30 amount to $180.

c. The office equipment was purchased on April 1, 1994. On that date, it had an estimated useful life of 10 years.

d. On September 1, 1994, the automobile was purchased; it had an estimated useful life of five years.

e. A deposit is received in advance of providing any services for first-time customers. Amounts received in advance are recorded initially in the account Unearned Commissions. Based on services provided to these first-time customers, the balance in this account at the end of April should be $5,000.

f. Repeat customers are allowed to pay for services one month after the date of the sale of their property. Services rendered during the month but not yet collected or billed to these customers amount to $1,500.

g. Interest owed on the note payable but not yet paid amounts to $20.

h. Salaries owed to employees but unpaid at the end of the month amount to $2,500.

1. Prepare in general journal form the necessary adjusting entries at April 30, 1995. Label the entries *a* through *h* to correspond to the other data. ■ REQUIRED

2. Compute the net increase or decrease in net income for the month from the recognition of the adjusting entries you prepared in part 1.

(LO 5) PROBLEM 4-6 RECONSTRUCTION OF ADJUSTING ENTRIES FROM ACCOUNT BALANCES

Gazebo Corp. records adjusting entries each month before preparing monthly financial statements. The following selected account balances are taken from its trial balances on May 31 and June 30, 1995 (both trial balances reflect month-end adjusting entries):

ACCOUNT TITLE	MAY 31, 1995		JUNE 30, 1995	
	DEBIT	CREDIT	DEBIT	CREDIT
Prepaid Insurance	$3,600		$3,450	
Equipment	9,600		9,600	
Accumulated Depreciation		$1,280		$1,360
Notes Payable		9,600		9,600
Interest Payable		2,304		2,448

1. The company purchased a 36-month insurance policy on June 1, 1994. Reconstruct the adjusting journal entry for insurance on June 30, 1995. ■ REQUIRED

2. What was the original cost of the insurance policy? Explain your answer.

3. The equipment was purchased on February 1, 1994, for $9,600. Gazebo uses straight-line depreciation and estimates that the equipment will have no salvage value. Reconstruct the adjusting journal entry for depreciation on June 30, 1995.

4. What is the equipment's estimated useful life in months? Explain your answer.

5. Gazebo signed a two-year note payable on February 1, 1994, for the purchase of the equipment. Interest on the note accrues on a monthly basis and will be paid at maturity along with the principal amount of $9,600. Reconstruct the adjusting journal entry for interest on June 30, 1995.

6. What is the *monthly* interest rate on the loan? Explain your answer.

(LO 5) PROBLEM 4-7 USE OF A TRIAL BALANCE TO RECORD ADJUSTING ENTRIES IN T ACCOUNTS

Four Star Video has been in the video rental business for five years. An unadjusted trial balance at May 31, 1995, follows.

FOUR STAR VIDEO
UNADJUSTED TRIAL BALANCE
MAY 31, 1995

	DEBIT	CREDIT
Cash	$ 4,000	
Prepaid Rent	6,600	
Video Inventory	25,600	
Display Stands	8,900	
Accumulated Depreciation		$ 5,180
Accounts Payable		3,260
Customer Subscriptions		4,450
Capital Stock		5,000
Retained Earnings		22,170
Rental Revenue		9,200
Wage and Salary Expense	2,320	
Utility Expense	1,240	
Advertising Expense	600	
Totals	$49,260	$49,260

The following additional information is available:

a. Four Star rents a store in a shopping mall and prepays the annual rent of $7,200 on April 1 of each year.

b. The asset account Video Inventory represents the cost of videos purchased from suppliers. When a new title is purchased from a supplier, its cost is debited to this account. When a title has served its useful life and can no longer be rented (even at a reduced price), it is removed from the inventory in the store. Based on the monthly count, the cost of titles on hand at the end of May is $23,140.

c. The display stands have an estimated useful life of five years and an estimated salvage value of $500.

d. Wages and salaries owed to employees but unpaid at the end of May amount to $1,450.

e. In addition to individual rentals, Four Star operates a popular discount subscription program. Customers pay an annual fee of $120 for an unlimited number of rentals. Based on the $10 per month earned on each of these subscriptions, the amount earned for the month of May is $2,440.

f. Four Star accrues income taxes using an estimated tax rate equal to 30% of the income for the month.

■ REQUIRED

1. Set up T accounts for each of the accounts listed on the trial balance. Based on the additional information given, set up any other T accounts that will be needed to prepare adjusting entries.

2. Post the month-end adjusting entries directly to the T accounts but do not bother to put the entries in journal format first. Use the letters *a* through *f* from the additional information to identify the entries.

3. Prepare a trial balance to prove the equality of debits and credits after posting the adjusting entries.

4. On the basis of the information you have, does Four Star appear to be a profitable business? Explain your answer.

MULTI-CONCEPT PROBLEMS

(LO 2, 3) PROBLEM 4-8 CASH AND ACCRUAL INCOME STATEMENTS FOR A MANUFACTURER

Hellar Company was established to manufacture components for the auto industry. The components are shipped the same day they are produced. The following events took place during the first year of operations.

a. Issued common stock for a $50,000 cash investment.

b. Purchased delivery truck at the beginning of the year at a cost of $10,000 cash. The truck is expected to last five years and will be worthless at the end of that time.

c. Manufactured and sold 500,000 components the first year. The costs incurred to manufacture the components are (1) $1,000 monthly rent on a facility that included utilities and insurance; (2) $400,000 of raw materials purchased on account; $100,000 is still unpaid as of year-end but all materials were used in manufacturing; and (3) $190,000 paid in salaries and wages to employees and supervisors.

d. Paid $100,000 to sales and office staff for salaries and wages.

e. Sold all components on account for $2 each. As of year-end, $150,000 is due from customers.

■ REQUIRED

1. How much revenue will Hellar recognize under the cash basis and under the accrual basis?

2. Describe how Hellar should apply the matching principle to recognize expenses.

3. Prepare an income statement under the accrual basis. Ignore income taxes.

(LO 3, 4) PROBLEM 4-9 REVENUE RECOGNITION ON INSTALLMENT SALES AND COMMODITIES

John Deare, an Illinois corn farmer, retired to the ocean in South Carolina. While retired, he volunteered his time at the small business administration office. One day, Frances Hirise, a condominium builder, came in with a question about the amount of sales she should recognize on her income statement. She had constructed a complex of 200 units. Half of the units sell for $50,000 each and the other half sell for $60,000. The developer agreed to finance the sale of all units and at year-end, 40 units at $50,000 and 30 units at $60,000 had been sold. Each buyer made a down payment of 10% cash and agreed to pay the remainder in equal payments plus 5% interest on the unpaid balance over the next nine years. No payments have been received other than the down payments. John advised Frances that she should recognize sales of $11 million (100 × $50,000) + (100 × $60,000).

■ REQUIRED

Do you agree with John? Why did he suggest this amount? What amount would you suggest that Frances recognize in the current and subsequent years as a result of these sales? When should the costs to build the condos (lumber, labor, etc.) be recognized as expenses?

(LO 3, 4, 7) PROBLEM 4-10 REVENUE AND EXPENSE RECOGNITION AND CLOSING ENTRIES

Two years ago, Lu Wong opened a hair salon. Lu reports the following accounts on her income statement:

Sales	$69,000
Advertising expense	3,500
Salaries expense	39,000
Rent expense	10,000

These amounts represent two years of revenue and expenses. Lu has asked you how she can tell how much of the income is from the first year of business and how much is from the second year. She provides the following additional data:

Sales in the second year were double those of the first year.

Advertising expense is for a $500 opening promotion and weekly ads in the newspaper.

Salaries represent one employee for the first nine months and then two employees for the remainder of the time. Each is paid the same salary. No raises have been granted.

Rent has not changed since the salon opened.

■ REQUIRED

1. Prepare income statements for Years 1 and 2.

2. Prepare the closing entries for each year. Close income to Retained Earnings. Prepare a short explanation for Lu about the purpose of closing temporary accounts.

(LO 5, 8) PROBLEM 4-11 TEN-COLUMN WORK SHEET (APPENDIX 4A)

The following unadjusted trial balance is available for Ace Consulting, Inc., on June 30, 1995.

ACE CONSULTING, INC.
UNADJUSTED TRIAL BALANCE
JUNE 30, 1995

Cash	$ 6,320	
Accounts Receivable	14,600	
Supplies on Hand	800	
Prepaid Rent	4,800	
Furniture and Fixtures	18,000	
Accumulated Depreciation		$ 5,625
Accounts Payable		5,200
Capital Stock		10,000
Retained Earnings		17,955
Consulting Revenue		12,340
Utility Expense	4,100	
Wage and Salary Expense	2,500	
Totals	$51,120	$51,120

■ REQUIRED

1. Enter the unadjusted trial balance in the first two columns of a 10-column work sheet.

2. Enter the necessary adjustments in the appropriate columns of the work sheet for each of the following:

a. Wages and salaries earned by employees at the end of June but not yet paid amount to $2,380.

b. Supplies on hand at the end of June amount to $550.

c. Depreciation on furniture and fixtures for June is $375.

d. Ace prepays the rent on its office space on June 1 of each year. The rent amounts to $400 per month.

e. Consulting services rendered and billed but cash not yet received amount to $4,600.

3. Complete the remaining columns of the work sheet.

(LO 5, 8) PROBLEM 4-12 MONTHLY TRANSACTIONS, 10-COLUMN WORK SHEET, AND FINANCIAL STATEMENTS (APPENDIX 4A)

Moonlight Bay Inn is incorporated on January 2, 1995, by its three owners, each of whom contributes $20,000 in cash in exchange for shares of stock in the business. In addition to the sale of stock, the following transactions are entered into during the month of January:

January 2: A Victorian inn is purchased for $50,000 in cash. An appraisal performed on this date indicates that the land is worth $15,000 and the remaining balance of the purchase price is attributable to the house. The owners estimate that the house will have an estimated useful life of 25 years and an estimated salvage value of $5,000.

January 3: A two-year, 12%, $30,000 promissory note was signed at the Second State Bank. Interest and principal will be repaid on the maturity date of January 3, 1997.

January 4: New furniture for the inn is purchased at a cost of $15,000 in cash. The furniture has an estimated useful life of 10 years and no salvage value.

January 5: A 24-month property insurance policy is purchased for $6,000 in cash.

January 6: An advertisement for the inn is placed in the local newspaper. Moonlight Bay pays $450 cash for the ad, which will run in the paper throughout January.

January 7: Cleaning supplies are purchased on account for $950. The bill is payable within 30 days.

January 15: Wages of $4,230 for the first half of the month are paid in cash.

January 16: A guest mails the business $980 in cash as a deposit for a room to be rented for two weeks. The guest plans to stay at the inn during the last week of January and the first week of February.

January 31: Cash receipts from rentals of rooms for the month amount to $8,300.

January 31: Cash receipts from operation of the restaurant for the month amount to $6,600.

January 31: Each stockholder is paid $200 in cash dividends.

1. Prepare journal entries to record each of the preceding transactions.

2. Post each of the journal entries to T accounts.

3. Place the balance in each of the T accounts in the Unadjusted Trial Balance columns of a 10-column work sheet.

4. Enter the appropriate adjustments in the next two columns of the work sheet for each of the following:

a. Depreciation of the house.

b. Depreciation of the furniture.

■ **REQUIRED**

    c. Interest on the promissory note.

    d. Recognition of the expired portion of the insurance.

    e. Recognition of the earned portion of the guest's deposit.

    f. Wages earned during the second half of January amount to $5,120 and will be paid on February 3.

    g. Cleaning supplies on hand on January 31 amount to $230.

    h. A gas and electric bill that is received from the city amounts to $740 and is payable by February 5.

    i. Income taxes are to be accrued at a rate of 30% of income before taxes.

5. Complete the remaining columns of the work sheet.

6. Using the work sheet, prepare in good form the following financial statements:

    a. Income statement for the month of January.

    b. Statement of retained earnings for the month of January.

    c. Balance sheet at January 31, 1995.

7. Assume that you are the loan officer at Second State Bank (refer to the transaction on January 3). What are your reactions to Moonlight's first month of operations? Are you comfortable with the loan you made?

ALTERNATE PROBLEMS

(LO 3) PROBLEM 4-1A THE REVENUE RECOGNITION PRINCIPLE

Each of the following paragraphs describes a situation involving revenue recognition.

a. Zee Zitter, Inc., paints and decorates office buildings. On September 30, 1995, it received $5,750 for work to be completed over the next six months.

b. Tan Us is a tanning salon franchisor in the Midwest. It charges all franchisees a fee of $2,500 to open a salon and an ongoing fee equal to 5% of all revenue during the first five years. The $2,500 is for training and accounting systems to be used in each salon. During January 1995, Tan Us signed an agreement with five individuals to open salons over the next three months.

c. On June 1, 1995, Dan Diver Bridge Building, Inc., entered into a contract with the county to renovate an old covered bridge. The county gives Dan an advance of $500,000 and agrees to pay Dan $75,000 each month for 20 months, at which time the project should be completed.

d. Joe Cropper, a wheat grower, harvested the current year's crop and delivered it to the elevator for storage on October 1, 1995, until it is sold to one of several foreign countries. The expected sales value of the wheat is $450,000.

e. Shop n Here, a convenience store chain, constructed a strip shopping center next to one of its stores. The spaces are being sold to individuals who will open auto parts and repair facilities. One individual is planning to open a brake repair shop, another a transmission repair shop, a third will do 10-minute oil changes, and so on. The store space sells for $25,000 each. There are six spaces, four of which are sold in May of 1995.

■ REQUIRED For each of the preceding situations, indicate when revenue should be recognized as well as the dollar amount. Give a brief explanation for each answer.

(LO 5) PROBLEM 4-2A ADJUSTING ENTRIES

Flood Relief, Inc., prepares monthly financial statements and therefore adjusts its accounts at the end of every month. The following information is available for June 1996:

a. Flood received a $10,000, 4%, two-year note receivable from a customer for services rendered. The principal and interest are due on June 1, 1998. Flood expects to be able to collect the note and interest in full at that time.

b. Office supplies totaling $5,600 were purchased during the month. The asset account Supplies is debited whenever a purchase is made. A count in the storeroom on June 30, 1996, indicated that supplies on hand amount to $507. The supplies on hand at the beginning of the month total $475.

c. The company purchased machines last year for $170,000. The machines are expected to be used for four years and have an estimated salvage value of $2,000.

d. On June 1, the company paid $4,650 for rent for June, July, and August. The asset Prepaid Rent was debited; it did not have a balance on June 1.

e. The company operates seven days per week with a weekly payroll of $49,000. Wage earners are paid every Friday. The last day of the month is Sunday, June 30.

f. Based on its income for the month, Flood estimates that federal income taxes for June amount to $2,900.

REQUIRED

1. For each of the preceding situations, prepare in general journal form the appropriate adjusting entry to be recorded on June 30, 1996.

2. Assume that Flood reports income of $35,000 before taxes and before any of the adjusting entries. What net income will Flood report for June?

(LO 5) PROBLEM 4-3A RECURRING AND ADJUSTING ENTRIES

The following are the accounts of Homes for You, Inc., an interior decorator. The company has been in the construction business for 10 years and prepares quarterly financial statements. Following the list of accounts is a series of transactions entered into by Homes for You.

ACCOUNTS

1. Cash
2. Accounts Receivable
3. Prepaid Rent
4. Office Supplies
5. Office Equipment
6. Accumulated Depreciation
7. Accounts Payable
8. Salaries and Wages Payable
9. Income Tax Payable
10. Interim Financing Notes Payable

11. Capital Stock, $1 par
12. Paid-in Capital in Excess of Par
13. Consulting Revenue
14. Office Supply Expense
15. Rent Expense
16. Salaries and Wages Expense
17. Depreciation Expense
18. Interest Expense
19. Income Tax Expense

REQUIRED

		DEBIT	CREDIT
a.	**Example:** Issued additional shares of stock to owners; shares issued at greater than par.	1	11,12
b.	Purchased office equipment for cash.		
c.	Collected open accounts receivable from customer.		
d.	Purchased office supplies on account.		
e.	Paid office rent for the next six months.		
f.	Paid interest on an interim financing note.		
g.	Paid salaries and wages.		
h.	Purchased office equipment; made a down payment in cash and signed an interim financing note.		
i.	Provided services on account.		
j.	Recorded depreciation on equipment.		
k.	Recorded income taxes due next month.		
l.	Recorded the used office supplies.		
m.	Recorded the used portion of prepaid rent.		

For each transaction, enter the number of the account(s) to be debited and credited.

(LO 5) PROBLEM 4-4A USE OF ACCOUNT BALANCES AS A BASIS FOR ADJUSTING ENTRIES

The following account balances are taken from the records of Laugherty, Inc., at December 31, 1995. The Supplies account represents the cost of supplies on hand at the beginning of the year plus all purchases. A physical count on December 31, 1995, shows only $1,520 of supplies on hand. The Unearned Revenue account represents the cash received from a customer on May 1, 1995, for 12 months of service, beginning on that date. The Note Payable represents a six-month promissory note signed with a supplier on September 1, 1995. Principal and interest at an annual rate of 10% will be paid on March 1, 1996.

ACCOUNTS		
Supplies	$ 5,790 debit	
Unearned Revenue		$ 1,800 credit
Notes Payable		60,000 credit

REQUIRED

1. Prepare the three necessary adjusting entries on the books of Laugherty on December 31, 1995. Assume that Laugherty prepares adjusting entries only once a year, on December 31.

2. Assume that adjusting entries are made at the end of each month rather than only at the end of the year. What would be the balance in Unearned Revenue *before* the December adjusting entry is made? Explain your answer.

(LO 5) PROBLEM 4-5A USE OF A TRIAL BALANCE AS A BASIS FOR ADJUSTING ENTRIES

Tom Stevens operates a graphic arts business. A trial balance on June 30, 1995, *prior* to recording any adjusting entries, is as follows:

TOM STEVENS GRAPHIC ARTS STUDIO
UNADJUSTED TRIAL BALANCE
JUNE 30, 1995

	DEBIT	CREDIT
Cash	$ 7,000	
Prepaid Rent	18,000	
Supplies	15,210	
Office Equipment	46,120	
Accumulated Depreciation—Equipment		$ 4,000
Accounts Payable		1,800
Notes Payable		2,000
Capital Stock		50,000
Retained Earnings		7,550
Dividends		8,400
Revenue		46,850
Utility Expense	2,850	
Salaries Expense	19,420	
Advertising Expense	12,000	
Totals	$120,600	$120,600

OTHER DATA

a. The monthly rent cost is $600.

b. Supplies on hand on June 30, 1995, amount to $1,290.

c. The office equipment was purchased on June 1, 1994. On that date, it had an estimated useful life of 10 years and a salvage value of $6,120.

d. Interest owed on the note payable but not yet paid amounts to $50.

e. Salaries of $620 are owed to employees but unpaid at the end of the month.

1. Prepare in general journal form the necessary adjusting entries at June 30, 1995. Label the entries *a* through *e* to correspond to the other data.

2. Will the recognition of the adjusting entries you prepared in part 1 increase or decrease net income for the month? Support your answer with any necessary calculations.

■ REQUIRED

(LO 5) PROBLEM 4-6A RECONSTRUCTION OF ADJUSTING ENTRIES FROM ACCOUNT BALANCES

Tarp Corporation records adjusting entries each month before preparing monthly financial statements. The following selected account balances are taken from its trial balances on May 31 and June 30, 1995 (both trial balances reflect month-end adjusting entries):

ACCOUNT TITLE	MAY 31, 1995		JUNE 30, 1995	
	DEBIT	CREDIT	DEBIT	CREDIT
Prepaid Rent	$4,000		$3,000	
Equipment	9,600		9,600	
Accumulated Depreciation		$ 800		$ 900
Notes Payable		9,600		9,600
Interest Payable		768		864

■ REQUIRED

1. The company paid for a six-month lease on April 1, 1995. Reconstruct the adjusting journal entry for rent on June 30, 1995.

2. What amount was prepaid on April 1, 1995? Explain your answer.

3. The equipment was purchased on September 30, 1994, for $9,600. Tarp uses straight-line depreciation and estimates that the equipment will have no salvage value. Reconstruct the adjusting journal entry for depreciation on June 30, 1995.

4. What is the equipment's estimated useful life in months? Explain your answer.

5. Tarp signed a two-year note on September 30, 1994, for the purchase of the equipment. Interest on the note accrues on a monthly basis and will be paid at maturity along with the principal amount of $9,600. Reconstruct the adjusting journal entry for interest expense on June 30, 1995.

6. What is the *monthly* interest rate on the loan? Explain your answer.

(LO 5) PROBLEM 4-7A USE OF A TRIAL BALANCE TO RECORD ADJUSTING ENTRIES IN T ACCOUNTS

Lewis and Associates has been in the termite inspection and treatment business for five years. An unadjusted trial balance at June 30, 1995, follows:

LEWIS AND ASSOCIATES
UNADJUSTED TRIAL BALANCE
JUNE 30, 1995

	DEBIT	CREDIT
Cash	$ 6,200	
Accounts Receivable	10,400	
Prepaid Rent	4,400	
Chemical Inventory	9,400	
Equipment	18,200	
Accumulated Depreciation		$ 1,050
Accounts Payable		1,180
Capital Stock		5,000
Retained Earnings		25,370
Treatment Revenue		40,600
Wages and Salary Expense	22,500	
Utility Expense	1,240	
Advertising Expense	860	
Totals	$73,200	$73,200

The following additional information is available:

a. Lewis rents a warehouse with office space and prepays the annual rent of $4,800 on May 1 of each year.

b. The asset account Equipment represents the cost of treatment equipment, which has an estimated useful life of 10 years and an estimated salvage value of $200.

c. Chemical inventory on hand equals $1,300.

d. Wages and salaries owed to employees but unpaid at the end of the month amount to $1,080.

e. Lewis accrues income taxes using an estimated tax rate equal to 30% of the income for the month.

1. Set up T accounts for each of the accounts listed on the trial balance. Based on the additional information given, set up any other T accounts that will be needed to prepare adjusting entries.

■ REQUIRED

2. Post the month-end adjusting entries directly to the T accounts but do not bother to put the entries in journal format first. Use the letters *a* through *e* from the additional information to identify the entries.

3. Prepare a trial balance to prove the equality of debits and credits after posting the adjusting entries.

4. On the basis of the information you have, does Lewis appear to be a profitable business? Explain your answer.

ALTERNATE MULTI-CONCEPT PROBLEMS

(LO 2, 3) PROBLEM 4-8A CASH AND ACCRUAL INCOME STATEMENTS FOR A MANUFACTURER

Alice's Catering Service makes sandwiches for vending machines. The sandwiches are delivered to the vendor on the same day that they are made. The following events have taken place during the first year of operations.

a. On the first day of the year, issued common stock for a $20,000 cash investment and $10,000 investment of equipment. The equipment is expected to last 10 years and will be worthless at the end of that time.

b. Purchased a delivery truck at the beginning of the year at a cost of $14,000 cash. The truck is expected to last five years and will be worthless at the end of that time.

c. Made and sold 50,000 sandwiches during the first year of operations. The costs incurred to make the sandwiches are (1) $800 monthly rent on a facility that included utilities and insurance; (2) $25,000 of meat, cheese, bread, and condiments; all food was purchased on account, and $4,000 is still unpaid at year-end even though all of the food has been used; and (3) $35,000 paid in salaries and wages to employees and supervisors.

d. Paid $12,000 for part-time office staff salaries.

e. Sold all sandwiches on account for $2 each. As of year-end, $25,000 is still due from the vendors.

1. How much revenue will Alice's recognize under the cash basis and under the accrual basis?

■ REQUIRED

2. Explain how accountants apply the revenue recognition principle to Alice's small business. What conditions would allow Alice to use the cash method to recognize revenue?

3. Prepare an income statement according to the accrual method. Ignore income taxes.

(LO 3, 4) PROBLEM 4-9A REVENUE RECOGNITION ON THE PERCENTAGE-OF-COMPLETION AND COMMODITIES METHODS

Judy Darling owns a diamond mine in South Africa. While vacationing on an island in the Caribbean, she discussed with Marty Jones a recent dig that yielded $1.5 million of raw diamonds. The product is stored with an agent until a buyer is located. The agent expects it to take about two and a half years to sell all of the diamonds. Judy's company spent $1 million to extract the diamonds in 1995. Marty's company constructs airplane runways and hangars. He is in the process of building a runway for the island and expects to incur the following costs over the next two and one-half years:

1995	$400,000
1996	500,000
1997	100,000

Local residents and the government have already paid Marty $1 million in 1995 and will pay another $500,000 when the project is completed in 1997.

■ REQUIRED   Explain the difference between revenue and cash flow for Judy and Marty. State the revenue recognition principle and then identify the specific characteristics that allow Judy and Marty to deviate slightly from the revenue recognition principle. How much revenue will each recognize in 1995, 1996, and 1997?

(LO 3, 4, 7) PROBLEM 4-10A REVENUE AND EXPENSE RECOGNITION AND CLOSING ENTRIES

Two years ago, Sue Stern opened an audio book rental shop. Sue reports the following accounts on her income statement:

Sales	$84,000
Advertising expense	10,500
Salaries expense	12,000
Depreciation on tapes	5,000
Rent expense	18,000

These amounts represent two years of revenue and expenses. Sue has asked you how she can tell how much of the income is from the first year and how much is from the second year of business. She provides the following additional data:

Sales in the second year are triple those of the first year.

Advertising expense is for a $1,500 opening promotion and weekly ads in the newspaper.

Salaries represent one employee who was hired eight months ago. No raises have been granted.

Rent has not changed since the shop opened.

■ REQUIRED   1. Prepare income statements for Years 1 and 2.

2. Prepare the closing entries for each year. Prepare a short explanation for Sue about the purpose of closing temporary accounts.

**(LO 5, 7, 8) PROBLEM 4-11A TEN-COLUMN WORK SHEET AND CLOSING ENTRIES
(APPENDIX 4A)**

The unadjusted trial balance for Forever Green Landscaping on August 31, 1995,
follows:

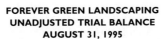

FOREVER GREEN LANDSCAPING
UNADJUSTED TRIAL BALANCE
AUGUST 31, 1995

Cash	$ 6,460	
Accounts Receivable	23,400	
Supplies on Hand	1,260	
Prepaid Insurance	3,675	
Equipment	28,800	
Accumulated Depreciation—Equipment		$ 9,200
Buildings	72,000	
Accumulated Depreciation—Buildings		16,800
Accounts Payable		10,500
Notes Payable		10,000
Capital Stock		40,000
Retained Earnings		42,100
Service Revenue		14,200
Advertising Expense	1,200	
Gasoline and Oil Expense	1,775	
Wage and Salary Expense	4,230	
Totals	$142,800	$142,800

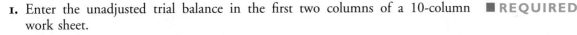

REQUIRED

1. Enter the unadjusted trial balance in the first two columns of a 10-column
   work sheet.

2. Enter the necessary adjustments in the appropriate columns of the work sheet
   for each of the following:

   a. A count of the supplies on hand at the end of August reveals a balance of $730.

   b. The company paid $4,200 in cash on May 1, 1995, for a two-year insur-
      ance policy.

   c. The equipment has a four-year estimated useful life and no salvage value.

   d. The buildings have an estimated useful life of 30 years and no salvage value.

   e. The company leases space in its building to another company. The agreement
      requires the tenant to pay Forever Green $700 on the 10th of each month
      for the previous month's rent.

   f. Wages and salaries earned by employees at the end of August but not yet
      paid amount to $3,320.

   g. The company signed a six-month promissory note on August 1, 1995. Interest
      at an annual rate of 12% and the principal amount of $10,000 are due on
      February 1, 1996.

3. Complete the remaining columns of the work sheet.

4. Assume that Forever Green closes its books at the end of each month before
   preparing financial statements. Prepare the necessary closing entries at August
   31, 1995.

(LO 5, 8) PROBLEM 4-12A TEN-COLUMN WORK SHEET AND FINANCIAL STATEMENTS (APPENDIX 4A)

The following unadjusted trial balance is available for Tenfour Trucking Company on January 31, 1995:

TENFOUR TRUCKING COMPANY
UNADJUSTED TRIAL BALANCE
JANUARY 31, 1995

Cash	$ 27,340	
Accounts Receivable	41,500	
Prepaid Insurance	18,000	
Warehouse	40,000	
Accumulated Depreciation—Warehouse		$ 21,600
Truck Fleet	240,000	
Accumulated Depreciation—Truck Fleet		112,500
Land	20,000	
Accounts Payable		32,880
Notes Payable		50,000
Interest Payable		4,500
Customer Deposits		6,000
Capital Stock		100,000
Retained Earnings		40,470
Freight Revenue		165,670
Gas and Oil Expense	57,330	
Maintenance Expense	26,400	
Wage and Salary Expense	43,050	
Dividends	20,000	
Totals	$533,620	$533,620

■ REQUIRED

1. Enter the unadjusted trial balance in the first two columns of a 10-column work sheet.

2. Enter the necessary adjustments in the appropriate columns of the work sheet for each of the following:

   a. Prepaid insurance represents the cost of a 24-month policy purchased on January 1, 1995.

   b. The warehouse has an estimated useful life of 20 years and an estimated salvage value of $4,000.

   c. The truck fleet has an estimated useful life of six years and an estimated salvage value of $15,000.

   d. The promissory note was signed on January 1, 1994. Interest at an annual rate of 9% and the principal of $50,000 are due on December 31, 1995.

   e. The customer deposits represent amounts paid in advance by new customers. A total of $4,500 of the balance in Customer Deposits was earned during January 1995.

   f. Wages and salaries earned by employees at the end of January but not yet paid amount to $8,200.

   g. Income taxes are accrued at a rate of 30% at the end of each month.

3. Complete the remaining columns of the work sheet.

4. Prepare the following financial statements:

   a. Income statement for the month of January.

   b. Statement of retained earnings for the month ended January 31.

   c. Balance sheet at January 31.

5. Compute Tenfour's current ratio. What does this ratio tell you about the company's liquidity?

6. Explain why it is not possible to compute a gross profit ratio for Tenfour. Describe a ratio that you believe would be a meaningful measure of profitability for a trucking company. Feel free to "invent" a ratio if you think it would be a meaningful measure of profitability.

CASES

READING AND INTERPRETING FINANCIAL STATEMENTS

(LO 3) CASE 4-1 READING AND INTERPRETING BEN & JERRY'S FOOTNOTES—REVENUE RECOGNITION

Refer to the footnote on pages 174–175 in the chapter where Ben & Jerry's explains how it recognizes initial franchise fees as revenue.

1. Is the way in which Ben & Jerry's recognizes franchise fees for individual stores as revenue in accordance with the revenue recognition principle? Explain your answer and include in your explanation any necessary reference to the professional accounting standards.

2. Explain the logic behind the method Ben & Jerry's uses to recognize as revenue franchise fees relating to area franchise agreements.

3. Refer to Ben & Jerry's financial statements. How important are franchise fees as a form of revenue for the company? Support your answer with any necessary computations.

■ REQUIRED

(LO 3, 4) CASE 4-2 WARRANTY FOOTNOTE

The following excerpt is taken from the 1993 annual report for Circuit City Stores, Inc.:

> The Company sells extended warranty contracts beyond the normal manufacturer's warranty period, usually with terms of coverage (including the manufacturer's warranty period) between 12 and 60 months.
>
> All revenue from the sale of extended warranty contracts is deferred and amortized on a straight-line basis over the life of the contracts. Incremental direct contract costs related to the sale of contracts are deferred and charged to expense in proportion to the revenue recognized. All other costs are charged to expense as incurred.

1. Why does Circuit City, Inc., recognize the revenue over the life of the warranty even though it receives the cash at the time of the sale?

2. If a product is sold in Year 1 for $2,500, including a $180 extended warranty plan that will cover three years, how much revenue is recognized in Years 1, 2, and 3? What corresponding account can you look for in the financial statements to determine the amount of warranty revenue that will be recognized in the future?

■ REQUIRED

MAKING FINANCIAL DECISIONS

(LO 2, 3, 4) CASE 4-3 THE USE OF NET INCOME AND CASH FLOW TO EVALUATE A COMPANY

After you have gained five years of experience with a large CPA firm, one of your clients, Software Solutions, asks you to take over as chief financial officer for the business. Software Solutions advises its clients on the purchase of software products and assists them in installing the programs on their computer systems. Because the business is relatively new (it began servicing clients in January 1995), its accounting records are somewhat limited. In fact, the only statement available is an income statement for the first year:

SOFTWARE SOLUTIONS, INC.
STATEMENT OF INCOME
FOR THE YEAR ENDED DECEMBER 31, 1995

Revenues		$1,250,000
Expenses:		
Salaries and wages	$480,000	
Supplies	65,000	
Utilities	30,000	
Rent	120,000	
Depreciation	345,000	
Interest	138,000	
Total expenses		1,178,000
Net income		$ 72,000

Based on its relatively modest profit margin of 5.76% (net income of $72,000 divided by revenues of $1,250,000), you are concerned about joining the new business. To alleviate your concerns, the president of the company is able to give you the following additional information:

a. Clients are given 90 days to pay their bills for consulting services provided by Software Solutions. On December 31, 1995, $230,000 of the revenues is yet to be collected in cash.

b. Employees are paid on a monthly basis. Salaries and wages of $480,000 include the December payroll of $40,000, which will be paid on January 5, 1996.

c. The company purchased $100,000 of operating supplies when it began operations in January. The balance of supplies on hand at December 31 amounts to $35,000.

d. Office space is rented in a downtown high-rise building at a monthly rental of $10,000. When the company moved into the office in January, it prepaid its rent for the next 18 months, beginning January 1, 1995.

e. On January 1, 1995, Software Solutions purchased its own computer system and related accessories at a cost of $1,725,000. The estimated useful life of the system is five years.

f. The computer system was purchased by signing a three-year, 8% note payable for $1,725,000 on the date of purchase. The principal amount of the note and interest for the three years are due on January 1, 1998.

■ **REQUIRED**
1. Based on the income statement and the additional information given, prepare a statement of cash flows for Software Solutions for 1995 (*Hint:* Simply list all of the cash inflows and outflows during the month that relate to operations).

2. On the basis of the income statement given and the statement of cash flows prepared in part 1, do you think it would be a wise decision on your part to join the company as its chief financial officer? Include in your response any additional questions that you believe are appropriate to ask before joining the company.

(LO 4) CASE 4-4 DEPRECIATION

Forestwind, Inc., a graphic arts studio, is considering the purchase of computer equipment and software for a total cost of $18,000. Forestwind can pay for the equipment and software over three years at the rate of $6,000 per year. The equipment is expected to last 10 to 20 years, but because of changing technology, Forestwind believes it may need to replace the system as soon as three to five years. A three-year lease of similar equipment and software is available for $6,000 per year. Forestwind's accountant has asked you if the company should purchase or lease the equipment and software and to make a recommendation as to the length of period over which to depreciate the software and equipment if the company makes the purchase.

Ignoring the effect of taxes, would you recommend the purchase or the lease? Why? Referring to the definition of *depreciation,* what is the appropriate useful life to use for the equipment and software?

■ REQUIRED

ACCOUNTING AND ETHICS: WHAT WOULD YOU DO?

(LO 2, 3, 4, 5) CASE 4-5 REVENUE RECOGNITION AND THE MATCHING PRINCIPLE

Listum & Sellum, Inc., is a medium-size Midwestern real estate company. It was founded five years ago by its two principal stockholders, Willie Listum and Dewey Sellum. Willie is president of the company and Dewey is vice-president of sales. Listum & Sellum has enjoyed tremendous growth since its inception by aggressively seeking out listings for residential real estate and paying a very generous commission to the selling agent.

The company receives a 6% commission for selling a client's property and gives two-thirds of this, or 4% of the selling price, to the selling agent. For example, if a house sells for $100,000, Listum & Sellum receives $6,000 and pays $4,000 of this to the selling agent. At the time of the sale, the company records a debit of $6,000 to Accounts Receivable and a credit of $6,000 to Sales Revenue. The accounts receivable is normally collected within 30 days. Also at the time of sale, the company debits $4,000 to Commissions Expense and credits Commissions Payable for the same amount. Sales agents are paid by the 15th of the month following the month of the sale. In addition to the commissions expense, Listum & Sellum's other two major expenses are advertising of listings in local newspapers and depreciation of the company fleet of Cadillacs (Dewey has always believed that all of the sales agents should drive Cadillacs). The newspaper ads are taken for one month and the company has until the 10th of the following month to pay that month's bill. The automobiles are depreciated over four years (Dewey doesn't believe that any salesperson should drive a car that is more than four years old).

Due to a downturn in the economy in the Midwest, sales have been sluggish for the first 11 months of the current year, which ends on June 30. Willie is very disturbed by the slow sales this particular year because a large note payable to the local bank is due in July, and the company plans to ask the bank to renew it for another three years. Dewey seems less concerned by the unfortunate timing of the recession and has some suggestions as to how they can "paint the rosiest possible picture for the banker" when they go for the loan extension in July. In fact, he has some very specific recommendations for you as to how to account for transactions during June, the last month in the fiscal year.

You are the controller for Listum & Sellum and have been treated very well by Willie and Dewey since joining the company two years ago. In fact, Dewey insists that you personally drive the top-of-the-line Cadillac. Following are his suggestions:

First, for any sales made in June, we can record the 6% commission revenue immediately but delay recording the 4% commission expense until July when the sales agent is paid. We record the sales at the same time we always have, the sales agents get paid when they always have, the bank sees how profitable we have been, we get our loan, and everybody is happy!

Second, since we won't be paying our advertising bills for the month of June until July 10, we can just wait until then to record the expense. The timing seems perfect, given that we are to meet with the bank for the loan extension on July 8.

Third, since we will be depreciating the fleet of Caddys for the year ending June 30, how about just changing the estimated useful life on them to eight years instead of four years? We won't say anything to the sales agents; no need to rile them up about having to drive their cars for eight years. Anyhow, the change to eight years would just be for accounting purposes. In fact, we could even switch back to four years for accounting purposes next year. Likewise, the changes in recognizing commission expense and advertising expense don't need to be permanent either; these are just slight bookkeeping changes to help us get over the hump!

■ REQUIRED

1. Explain why each of the three proposed changes in accounting will result in an increase in net income for the year ending June 30.

2. Identify any concerns you have with each of the three proposed changes in accounting from the perspective of generally accepted accounting principles.

3. Identify any concerns you have with each of the three proposed changes in accounting from an ethical perspective.

4. What would you do? Draft your response to Willie and Dewey in the form of a business memo.

(LO 4) CASE 4-6 ADVICE TO A POTENTIAL INVESTOR

Century Company was organized 15 months ago as a management consulting firm. At that time, the owners invested a total of $50,000 cash in exchange for stock. Century purchased equipment for $35,000 cash and supplies to be used in the business. The equipment is expected to last seven years with no salvage value. Supplies are purchased on account and paid for in the month after the purchase. Century normally has about $1,000 of supplies on hand. Its client base has increased dramatically so the president and chief financial officer have approached an investor to provide additional cash for expansion. The balance sheet and income statement for the first year of business are presented below:

CENTURY COMPANY
BALANCE SHEET
DECEMBER 31, 1995

ASSETS		LIABILITIES AND OWNERS' EQUITY	
Cash	$10,100	Accounts payable	$ 2,300
Accounts receivable	1,200	Common stock	50,000
Supplies	16,500	Retained earnings	10,500
Equipment	35,000		
Total	$62,800	Total	$62,800

CENTURY COMPANY
INCOME STATEMENT
FOR THE YEAR ENDED DECEMBER 31, 1995

Revenues		$82,500
Wages and salaries	$60,000	
Utilities	12,000	72,000
Net income		$10,500

The investor has asked you to look at these financial statements and give an opinion about Century's future profitability. Are the statements prepared in accordance with generally accepted accounting principles? If not, explain why. Based on only these two statements, what would you advise? What additional information would you need in order to give an educated opinion?

■ REQUIRED

ANALYTICAL SOFTWARE CASE

To the Student: Your instructor may assign one or more parts of the analytical software case that is designed to accompany this chapter. This multi-part case gives you a chance to work with real financial statement data using software that stimulates, guides, and hones your analytical and problem-solving skills. It was created especially to support and strengthen your understanding of the chapter's Learning Objectives.

SOLUTION TO KEY TERMS QUIZ

1. Work sheet (p. 192)
2. Revenues (p. 172)
3. Production method (p. 175)
4. Adjusting entries (p. 177)
5. Closing entries (p. 192)
6. Percentage-of-completion method (p. 173)
7. Deferred revenue (p. 185)
8. Installment method (p. 175)
9. Real accounts (p. 192)
10. Reversing entries (p. 196)
11. Accrued asset (p. 185)
12. Current value (p. 167)
13. Straight-line method (p. 179)
14. Deferral (p. 185)
15. Accrual basis (p. 169)
16. Accrual (p. 185)
17. Interim statements (p. 197)
18. Revenue recognition principle (p. 172)
19. Recognition (p. 166)
20. Deferred expense (p. 185)
21. Nominal accounts (p. 192)
22. Cash basis (p. 169)
23. Accrued liability (p. 185)
24. Matching principle (p. 176)
25. Contra account (p. 179)
26. Historical cost (p. 167)
27. Expenses (p. 176)
28. Accounting cycle (p. 191)

INTEGRATIVE PROBLEM

FOR PART I

COMPLETING FINANCIAL STATEMENTS, COMPUTING RATIOS, COMPARING ACCRUAL VS. CASH INCOME, AND EVALUATING THE COMPANY'S CASH NEEDS

Mountain Home Health, Inc. was formed in 1985 to provide home nursing services in the Smokey Mountains of Tennessee. When contacted by a client or referred by a physician, nurses visit with the patient and discuss needed services with the physician.

Mountain Home Health earns revenue from patient services. Most of the revenue comes from billing either insurance companies, the State of Tennessee, or the Medicare program. Amounts billed are recorded in the Billings Receivable account. Insurance companies, states, and the federal government do not fully fund all procedures. For example, the State of Tennessee pays an average 78% of billed amounts. Mountain Home Health has already removed the uncollectible amounts from the Billings Receivable account and reports it and Medical Services Revenue at the net amount. Services extended on Saturday, December 30, and Sunday, December 31, 1995, totaled $16,000, net of allowances for uncollectible amounts. The firm earns a minor portion of its total revenue directly from patients in the form of cash.

Employee salaries, medical supplies, depreciation, and gasoline are the major expenses. Employees are paid every Friday for work performed during the Saturday-to-Friday pay period. Salaries amount to $800 per day. In 1995, December 31 falls on a Sunday. Medical supplies (average use of $1,500 per week) are purchased periodically to support health care coverage. The inventory of supplies on hand on December 31 amounted to $8,653.

The firm owns five automobiles (all purchased at the same time) that average 50,000 miles per year and are replaced every 3 years. They typically have no residual value. The building has an expected life of 20 years with no residual value. Straight-line depreciation is used on all firm assets. Gasoline costs, which are a cash expenditure, average $375 per day. The firm purchases a 3-year, extended warranty contract to cover maintenance costs. The contract costs $9,000 (assume equal use each year).

On December 29, 1995, Mountain Home Health declared a dividend of $10,000, payable on January 15, 1996. The firm makes annual payments of principal and interest each June 30 on the mortgage. The interest rate on the mortgage is 6%.

The following unadjusted trial balance is available for Mountain Home Health on December 31, 1995:

MOUNTAIN HOME HEALTH
UNADJUSTED TRIAL BALANCE
DECEMBER 31, 1995

	DEBIT	CREDIT
Cash	$ 75,000	
Billings Receivable (net)	151,000	
Medical Supplies	73,000	
Extended Warranty	3,000	
Automobiles	90,000	
Accumulated Depreciation—Automobiles		$ 60,000
Building	200,000	
Accumulated Depreciation—Building		50,000
Accounts Payable		22,000

Dividend Payable		10,000
Mortgage Payable		100,000
Capital Stock		100,000
Additional Paid-in-Capital		50,000
Retained Earnings		99,900
Medical Services Revenue		550,000
Salary and Wages Expense	290,400	
Gasoline Expense	137,500	
Utilities Expense	12,000	
Dividends	10,000	
	$1,041,900	$1,041,900

1. Enter the unadjusted balance in the first two columns of a 10-column work sheet.   ■ REQUIRED

2. Enter the necessary adjustments in the appropriate columns (Hint: there are seven adjustments).

3. Complete the remaining columns of the work sheet.

4. Prepare a statement of income and a statement of retained earnings for Mountain Home Health for the year ended December 31, 1995.

5. Prepare a balance sheet for Mountain Home Health as of December 31, 1995.

6. Compute the following as of December 31, 1995:

   a. Working capital

   b. Current ratio

7. Which of the adjusting entries might cause a difference between cash and accrual based income?

8. Mary Francis, controller of Mountain Home, became concerned about the company's cash flow after talking to a local bank loan officer. The firm tries to maintain a 7-week supply of cash to meet the demands of payroll, medical supply purchases, and gasoline. Determine the amount of cash Mountain Home needs to meet the 7-week supply.

A WORD TO STUDENTS ABOUT PART II

In Part I you learned new ways of thinking about events as transactions, and transactions as part of a larger accounting model. You immersed yourself in new terminology. And you drilled in the accounting equation.

Part II tells its own story of what happens when assets flow into a business. Chapter 5 introduces the practicalities of buying and selling merchandise and the internal control necessary for managing a business. Chapter 6 expands on inventory issues raised in Chapter 5, because the business needs to be able to track and cost its inventory of goods for sale. Chapter 7 covers the results of buying and selling: cash and receivables. And Chapter 8 recognizes that the business must invest its cash and receivables in operating assets.

Finally, in Part II and beyond, you can anticipate even more **in-text references to the business environment**—and to how investors and other financial statement users evaluate companies based on inventories, cash flows, and accounts receivable, for example.

Part II

Accounting for Assets

Chapter 5
Merchandise Accounting and Internal Control
Appendix 5A:
Accounting Tools: Completing the Accounting Cycle
for a Merchandiser

Everyone planning a career in business should be sensitive to internal control issues, and should learn how buying, holding, and selling inventory affects the financial statements. Along the way, you'll **confront retail purchasing issues as a manager** (p. 265), **see yourself as a CFO and a controller** (p. 271), and **hear how a chief operating officer uses financial information** (p. 279).

Chapter 6
Inventories and Cost of Goods Sold
Appendix 6A:
Accounting Tools: Inventory Costing Methods with
the Use of a Perpetual Inventory System

Chapter 6 extends the discussion from Chapter 5 a step further into how companies determine the *costs* of their inventories—and how costing methods affect the financial statements. See Wrigley's cash flows statement for what it reveals about its inventories. Along the way, you'll **give a simple auditor's opinion** (p. 328), **react as an analyst** to Quaker Oats's change in how it accounts for inventory (p. 330), and **talk with a real analyst** about cash flows and inventory (p. 341).

Chapter 7
Cash and Receivables

When a company sells inventory, what does it get in exchange? **Cash,** and promises of cash called **receivables.** Being able to manage and invest cash is critical to any business or individual. Along the way, you'll **briefly analyze Wrigley's earnings and cash flows** (p. 375), **assess your company's bad debts situation** (p. 393), and go behind the scenes to **see Kaiser Permanente from a bond analyst's viewpoint** (p. 402).

Chapter 8
Operating Assets: Property, Plant, and Equipment,
Natural Resources, and Intangibles

Strong companies make good decisions about investing cash and receivables in **long-term assets**—productive property, plant, and equipment that allow continued and even increased operations. Accounting for these assets takes judgment, and so does assessing their impact on cash flows. Along the way, you'll **offer simple advice on depreciating landscape improvements** (p. 425), **give a broker's opinion** about Quaker Oats's and Alberto-Culver's intangible assets (p. 440), and **meet an appraiser** who looks at a *building's* financial statements (p. 446).

Integrative Problem for Part II

The Planet We Share.

Focus on Financial Results

McDonald's is the largest food service organization in the world. As such, it has special responsibilities. A few years ago, the company banned the plastic burger box because it was not environmentally biodegradable. Its investor relations packet—the package that goes to prospective shareholders—tells you about the company's numbers: nearly $1 billion in profits on $7 billion in revenues in 1992. But you also get a package on nutrition with instructions on how to choose a diet low in fat and choles-

terol. There's also a booklet entitled "The Planet We Share."

A tour through the company's annual report will include a section on social responsibility—telling you about its diverse workforce, its charitable efforts, and its Ronald McDonald Houses—a home away from home for families of seriously ill children receiving treatment at nearby hospitals.

At Hamburger University, the company's training center, aspiring restaurant managers learn about such topics as delivering customer satisfaction and running a successful operation. One topic of major importance: the internal control of cash—how to make sure that busy young employees understand the basics of transacting the fast flow of cash at the cash register.

McDonald's Corporation
CONSOLIDATED STATEMENT OF INCOME

(In millions of dollars, except per common share data)	Years ended December 31, 1992	1991	1990
Revenues			
Sales by Company-operated restaurants	$5,102.5	$4,908.5	$5,018.9
Revenues from franchised restaurants	2,030.8	1,786.5	1,620.7
Total revenues	7,133.3	6,695.0	6,639.6
Operating costs and expenses			
Company-operated restaurants			
Food and packaging	1,688.8	1,627.5	1,683.4
Payroll and other employee benefits	1,281.4	1,259.2	1,291.0
Occupancy and other operating expenses	1,156.3	1,142.4	1,161.2
	4,126.5	4,029.1	4,135.6
Franchised restaurants—occupancy expenses	348.6	306.5	279.2
General, administrative and selling expenses	860.6	794.7	724.2
Other operating (income) expense—net	(64.0)	(113.8)	(95.3)
Total operating costs and expenses	5,271.7	5,016.5	5,043.7
Operating income	1,861.6	1,678.5	1,595.9
Interest expense—net of capitalized interest of $19.5, $26.2, and $36.0	373.6	391.4	381.2
Nonoperating income (expense)—net	(39.9)	12.3	31.6
Income before provision for income taxes	1,448.1	1,299.4	1,246.3
Provision for income taxes	489.5	439.8	444.0
Net income	$ 958.6	$ 859.6	$ 802.3
Net income per common share	$ 2.60	$ 2.35	$ 2.20
Dividends per common share	$ .39	$ .36	$ .33

The accompanying Financial Comments are an integral part of the consolidated financial statements.

Chapter 5

Merchandise Accounting and Internal Control

LEARNING OBJECTIVES

After studying this chapter, you should be able to

1. Understand how wholesalers and retailers account for sales of merchandise, including sales returns and allowances and sales discounts.
2. Explain the differences between periodic and perpetual inventory systems.
3. Understand how wholesalers and retailers account for cost of goods sold under the periodic system, including purchase returns and allowances, purchase discounts, and transportation-in.
4. Explain the importance of internal control to a business.
5. Describe the basic internal control procedures.
6. Describe the various documents used in recording purchases of merchandise and their role in controlling cash disbursements.
7. Use a 10-column work sheet for a merchandiser (Appendix 5A).
8. Understand the role of closing entries for a merchandiser (Appendix 5A).

Linkages

A LOOK AT PREVIOUS CHAPTERS

Chapter 4 completed our introduction to the accounting model. We examined the role of adjusting entries in an accrual accounting system.

A LOOK AT THIS CHAPTER

In this chapter, we move beyond the basic accounting model to consider the accounting for the various elements on financial statements. We begin by looking at how merchandise companies—retailers and wholesalers—account for their inventory and the effects that buying and selling merchandise have on the income statement. The second part of the chapter introduces the concept of internal control and its applicability to merchandise inventory.

A LOOK AT UPCOMING CHAPTERS

Chapter 6 continues the discussion begun in this chapter by focusing on valuation issues for inventory. In each of the remaining chapters in this part, we look at the accounting for other valuable assets of an entity.

The Income Statement for a Merchandiser

FROM CONCEPT TO PRACTICE

READING BEN & JERRY'S ANNUAL REPORT
Is Ben & Jerry's a merchandiser? What items in the annual report can you cite to support your answer?

To this point, we have concentrated on the accounting for businesses that sell *services*. Banks, hotels, airlines, health clubs, real estate offices, law firms, and accounting firms are all examples of service companies. We turn our attention in this chapter to accounting by merchandisers. Both retailers and wholesalers are merchandisers. They purchase inventory in finished form and hold it for resale. This is in contrast to manufacturers' inventory, which takes three different forms: raw materials, work in process, and finished goods. Accounting for the three different forms of inventory for a manufacturer is more complex and is covered in a follow-up course to this one. We focus our attention in this chapter on accounting for merchandise, that is, inventory held by either a wholesaler or a retailer.

A *condensed* multiple-step income statement for Tabor Hardware Stores is presented in Exhibit 5-1. First note the period covered by the statement: for the year ended December 31, 1995. Tabor ends its fiscal year on December 31; however, many merchandisers end their *fiscal year* on a date other than December 31. Retailers often choose a date toward the end of January because the busy holiday shopping season is over and time can be devoted to closing the records and preparing financial statements. For example, JCPenney's fiscal year ends on the last Saturday in January.

We concentrate our attention in this chapter on the first two items on Tabor's statement: net sales and cost of goods sold. The major difference between this income statement and that for a service company is the inclusion of cost of goods sold. Because a service company does not sell a product, it does not report cost of goods sold. On the income statement of a merchandising company, cost of goods sold is deducted from net sales to arrive at gross margin or gross profit.

Gross margin as a percentage of net sales is a common analytical tool for merchandise companies. Analysts compare the gross margin percentages for various periods or for several companies and express concern if a company's gross margin is dropping. Every industry has its average gross margin ratio and its average overhead cost per square foot of retail space. Analysts can use these facts to see how one company is performing in comparison to others in the same industry.

EXHIBIT 5-1   Condensed Income Statement for a Merchandiser

TABOR HARDWARE STORES
INCOME STATEMENT
FOR THE YEAR ENDED DECEMBER 31, 1995

Net sales	$100,000
Cost of goods sold	60,000
Gross margin	$ 40,000
Selling and administrative expenses	29,300
Net income before tax	$ 10,700
Income tax expense	4,280
Net income	$ 6,420

Net Sales of Merchandise

The first section of Tabor's income statement is presented in Exhibit 5-2. Two deductions—for sales returns and allowances and sales discounts—are made from sales revenue to arrive at **net sales.** Sales revenue, or simply sales, as it is often called, is a *representation of the inflow of assets,* either cash or accounts receivable, from the sale of merchandise during the period. In a merchandising business, cash sales are recorded in the journal daily, based on the total amount shown on the cash register tape. For example, suppose that the cash register tape in the paint department of Tabor Hardware Stores shows sales on March 31, 1995, of $350. The transaction is recorded in the journal as follows:

March 31	Cash	350	
	Sales Revenue		350
	To record daily cash receipts in paint department.		

Assets = **Liabilities** + **Owners' Equity**
+350   +350

Sales on credit do not result in the immediate inflow of cash but in an accounts receivable, a promise by the customer to pay cash at a later date. The entry to record a May 4 sale of tools on credit for $125 is recorded as follows:

May 4	Accounts Receivable	125	
	Sales Revenue		125
	To record sale on credit in tools department.		

Assets = **Liabilities** + **Owners' Equity**
+125   +125

Sales Returns and Allowances

The cornerstone of marketing is to satisfy the customer. Most companies have standard policies that allow the customer to *return* merchandise within a stipulated period of time. Nordstrom, the Seattle-based retailer, has a very liberal policy regarding returns. That policy has, in large measure, fueled its growth from a Pacific Northwest retailer to one with stores in California and on the East Coast. A company's policy might be that a customer who is not completely satisfied can return the merchandise anytime within 30 days of purchase for a full refund. Alternatively, the customer

LO I
Understand how wholesalers and retailers account for sales of merchandise, including sales returns and allowances and sales discounts.

EXHIBIT 5-2   Net Sales Section of the Income Statement

TABOR HARDWARE STORES
PARTIAL INCOME STATEMENT
FOR THE YEAR ENDED DECEMBER 31, 1995

Sales revenue	$103,500	
Less: Sales returns and allowances	2,000	
Sales discounts	1,500	
Net sales		$100,000

may be given an *allowance* for spoiled or damaged merchandise, that is, the customer keeps the merchandise but receives a credit for a certain amount in the account balance. Typically, a single account, **Sales Returns and Allowances,** is used to account for both returns and allowances. If the customer has already paid for the merchandise, either a cash refund is given or the credit amount is applied to future purchases.

The accounting for a return or allowance depends on whether the customer is given a cash refund or credit on an account. Assume that Tabor's paint department gives a $25 cash refund on spoiled paint returned by the customer. The entry follows:

April 25	Sales Returns and Allowances	25	
	Cash		25
	To record return of spoiled paint by customer for a cash refund.		

| **Assets** | = | **Liabilities** | + | **Owners' Equity** |
| −25 | | | | −25 |

Sales Returns and Allowances is a *contra revenue* account. A contra account has a balance opposite to its related account and is deducted from that account on the statement. Thus, the effect of the debit to this account is the same as if Sales Revenue had been debited directly.

The purpose of this entry is to reduce the amount of previously recorded sales. So why didn't we simply debit Sales Revenue for $25? The reason is that management needs to be able to *monitor* the amount of returns and allowances. If we debit sales revenue for returns and at some point need to determine the total dollars of returns for the period, we would need to add up all of the individual debits to the Sales Revenue account. A much more efficient method is to split the sales revenue into two accounts, one that includes only the credits for sales and the other that includes the debits for returns. In this way, the total amount of returns is readily available and the decision-making process is more efficient and thus more effective.

The previous entry illustrates the accounting for a return of merchandise. The same account is normally debited when a credit is given and the customer keeps the merchandise. Assume that on May 7 the customer that made the $125 purchase from Tabor on May 4 notifies it that one of the tools it purchased is defective. Tabor agrees to reduce the customer's unpaid account by $10 because of the defect. The entry to record the allowance follows:

May 7	Sales Returns and Allowances	10	
	Accounts Receivable		10
	To record allowance given for defective merchandise.		

| **Assets** | = | **Liabilities** | + | **Owners' Equity** |
| −10 | | | | −10 |

The Sales Returns and Allowances account gives management and stockholders an important piece of data, that merchandise is being returned or is not completely acceptable. It does not answer the following questions, however. Why is the merchandise being returned? Why are customers getting partial refunds? Is the merchandise shoddy? Are salespeople too aggressive? Should the store's liberal policy regarding returns be changed?

Trade Discounts and Quantity Discounts

Various types of discounts to the list price are given to customers. A **trade discount** is a reduction in the selling price offered to a special class of customers. For example,

If you pick through a stack of lumber at a lumber yard for just the right pieces for a bookshelf, the yard will charge you full retail price. If you buy an entire bundle of lumber to build a deck, you may be able to negotiate a quantity discount. *But if you are a contractor, the yard should grant you a* trade discount *on even the smallest quantities.*

Tabor's plumbing department might offer a special price to building contractors. The difference between normal selling price and this special price is called a *trade discount.* A **quantity discount** is sometimes offered to customers who are willing to buy in large quantities.

   Trade discounts and quantity discounts are *not* recorded in the accounts. Although a company might track the amount of these discounts for control purposes, the reason for ignoring the quantity and trade discounts in the accounting records is that the list price is not the actual selling price. The *net* amount is a more accurate reflection of the amount of a sale. For example, assume that Tabor gives a 20% discount from the normal selling price to any single customer who buys between 10 and 25 kitchen sinks and a 30% discount on purchases of more than 25 sinks. The list price for each unit is $200. The selling price and related journal entry for a single purchase of 40 sinks on July 2 are as follows:

List price	$ 200
Less: 30% quantity discount	60
Selling price	140
× Number of sinks sold	× 40
Sales revenue	$5,600

July 2 Accounts Receivable	5,600	
Sales Revenue		5,600

To record sale of 40 kitchen sinks at list price less 30% quantity discount.

Assets	=	Liabilities	+	Owners' Equity
+5,600				+5,600

Credit Terms and Sales Discounts

Most companies have a standard credit policy. Special notation is normally used to indicate a particular firm's policy for granting credit. For example, credit terms of *n/30* mean that the *net* amount of the selling price, that is, the amount determined after deducting any returns or allowances, is due within 30 days of the date of the invoice. *Net, 10 EOM* means that the net amount is due anytime within 10 days after the end of the month in which the sale took place.

Another common element of the credit terms offered customers is sales discounts, a reduction from the selling price given for early payment. For example, assume that Tabor offers a building contractor credit terms of *1/10, n/30*. This means that the customer may deduct 1% from the selling price if the bill is paid within 10 days of the date of the invoice. Normally the discount period begins with the day *after* the invoice date. If the customer does not pay within the first 10 days, the full invoice amount is due within 30 days. Finally, note that the use of *n* for net in this notation is really a misnomer. Although the amount due is net of any returns and allowances, it is the gross amount that is due within 30 days. That is, no discount is given if the customer does not pay early.

How valuable to the customer is a 1% discount for payment within the first 10 days? Assume that a $1,000 sale is made. If the customer pays at the end of 10 days, the cash paid will be $990, rather than $1,000, a net savings of $10. The customer has saved $10 by paying 20 days earlier than required by the 30-day term. If we assume 360 days in a year, there are 360/20 or 18 periods of 20 days each in a year. Thus, a savings of $10 for 20 days is equivalent to a savings of $10 times 18, or $180 for the year. An annual return of $180/$990, or 18.2%, would be difficult to match with any other type of investment. In fact, a company might want to consider borrowing the money to pay off the account early.

Companies use one of two different methods to account for sales discounts: the gross method or the net method. The two methods are illustrated in Exhibit 5-3 for a $1,000 sale with credit terms of 2/10, net 30. Use of the **gross method** assumes that customers will not necessarily take the discount. Thus, sales are recorded at the gross amount of $1,000, that is, before deducting any discount. If the customer takes advantage of the discount, a *contra revenue* account called **Sales Discounts,** reflecting a reduction in revenue, is used to record the discount of $20. If the customer does not pay within the first 10 days, the entry to record collection is simply a debit to Cash and a credit to Accounts Receivable.

The **net method** is more realistic if a company's customers routinely take advantage of the discount terms offered. The sale is recorded at the net amount of $980, that is, after deducting any applicable discount. If the customer does *not* pay within the first 10 days, a new account is needed to record the additional $20 of cash received over and above the $980 recorded as an account receivable at the time of the sale. This account, Sales Discounts Lost, is normally recorded as other revenue on the seller's records. We have assumed the use of the gross method for Tabor Hardware Stores. This is evident from the line item Sales Discounts in Exhibit 5-2.

Two points are worth noting about the two competing methods for recording sales discounts. First, note in Exhibit 5-3 that the effect on net income is the same whether the gross method or the net method is used. For example, if the discount is taken, the addition to net income reported under both methods is $980: Sales Revenue of $1,000 less Sales Discounts of $20 under the gross method and Sales Revenue of $980 under the net method. If the discount is not taken, either method will add $1,000 to net income: Sales Revenue of $1,000 under the gross method and Sales Revenue of $980 plus Sales Discounts Lost of $20 under the net method.

EXHIBIT 5-3   Comparing the Gross and Net Methods for Recording Sales Discounts

DATE	GROSS METHOD	DR.	CR.	NET METHOD	DR.	CR.

A sale of $1,000 is made with discount terms of 2/10, net 30:

| June 10 | Accounts Receivable | 1,000 | | Accounts Receivable | 980 | |
| | Sales Revenue | | 1,000 | Sales Revenue | | 980 |

$$A = L + O/E$$
$$+1{,}000 \qquad +1{,}000$$

$$A = L + O/E$$
$$+980 \qquad +980$$

Assuming the discount is taken:

June 20	Cash	980		Cash	980	
	Sales Discounts	20				
	Accounts Receivable		1,000	Accounts Receivable		980

$$A = L + O/E$$
$$+\ 980 \qquad -20$$
$$-1{,}000$$

$$A = L + O/E$$
$$+980$$
$$-980$$

Assuming the discount is **not** taken:

July 10	Cash	1,000		Cash	1,000	
				Sales Discounts Lost		20
	Accounts Receivable		1,000	Accounts Receivable		980

$$A = L + O/E$$
$$+1{,}000$$
$$-1{,}000$$

$$A = L + O/E$$
$$+1{,}000 \qquad +20$$
$$-\ 980$$

The second point deals with the concept of materiality. Because sales discounts are rarely material, the method used by a company is normally not disclosed on the financial statements.

The Cost of Goods Sold

The cost of goods sold section of the income statement for Tabor is shown in Exhibit 5-4. We will soon turn our attention to each line item in this section. First let us take a look at the basic model for cost of goods sold.

The Cost of Goods Sold Model

The recognition of cost of goods sold as an expense is an excellent example of the *matching principle*. Sales revenue represents the *inflow* of assets, in the form of cash and accounts receivable, from the sale of products during the period. Likewise, cost of goods sold represents the *outflow* of an asset, inventory, from the sale of those same products. The company needs to *match* the revenue of the period with one of the most important costs necessary to generate the revenue, the *cost* of the merchandise sold.

It may be helpful in understanding cost of goods sold to realize what it is *not*. *Cost of goods sold is not equal to the cost of purchases of merchandise during the period.*

EXHIBIT 5-4   Cost of Goods Sold Section of the Income Statement

TABOR HARDWARE STORES
PARTIAL INCOME STATEMENT
FOR THE YEAR ENDED DECEMBER 31, 1995

Cost of goods sold:			
Inventory, January 1, 1995		$15,000	
Purchases	$65,000		
Less: Purchase returns and allowances	1,800		
Purchase discounts	3,700		
Net purchases	$59,500		
Add: Transportation-in	3,500		
Cost of goods purchased		63,000	
Costs of goods available for sale		$78,000	
Less: Inventory, December 31, 1995		18,000	
Cost of goods sold			$60,000

Except in the case of a new business, a merchandiser starts the year with a certain stock of inventory on hand, called *beginning inventory.* For Tabor, beginning inventory is the dollar amount of merchandise on hand on January 1, 1995. During the year, Tabor *purchases* merchandise. When the cost of goods purchased is added to beginning inventory, the result is **cost of goods available for sale.** Just as the merchandiser starts the period with an inventory of merchandise on hand, a certain amount of *ending inventory* is usually on hand at the end of the year. For Tabor, this is its inventory on December 31, 1995.

Think of cost of goods available for sale as a "pool" of costs to be distributed between what we sold and did not sell. If we subtract from the pool the cost of what we did *not* sell, the *ending inventory,* we will have the amount we *did* sell, the **cost of goods sold.** Cost of goods sold is simply the difference between the cost of goods available for sale and the ending inventory:

Beginning inventory	What is on hand to start the period
+ Purchases	What was acquired for resale during the period
= Cost of goods available for sale	The "pool" of costs to be distributed
− Ending inventory	What was not sold during the period and what is on hand to start the next period
= Cost of goods sold	What was sold during the period

The cost of goods sold model for a merchandiser is illustrated in Exhibit 5-5. The amounts used for the illustration are taken from the cost of goods sold section of Tabor's income statement as shown in Exhibit 5-4. Notice that ending inventory exceeds beginning inventory by $3,000. That means that purchases exceeded cost of goods sold by that same amount. Indeed, a key point for investors is whether inventory is building up. A buildup may indicate that the company's products are becoming less desirable or that prices are becoming uncompetitive.

Inventory Systems: Perpetual and Periodic

Before we look at the journal entries to account for cost of goods sold, it is necessary to understand the difference between the periodic and perpetual inventory systems. All businesses use one of these two distinct approaches to account for inventory. With the **perpetual system,** the Inventory account is updated *perpetually,* or after each sale or purchase of merchandise. Conversely, with the **periodic system,** the Inventory account is updated only at the end of the *period.*

In a perpetual system, every time goods are purchased, the Inventory account is debited and either Cash or Accounts Payable is credited. When goods are sold, two entries are made, one to record a debit to either Cash or Accounts Receivable and a credit to Sales Revenue. A second entry is made to record the *cost of the sale:*

LO   **2**

Explain the differences between periodic and perpetual inventory systems.

Cost of Goods Sold	xxx	
Inventory		xxx

To record the sale of inventory under perpetual system.

Assets = Liabilities + Owners' Equity
 −xxx   −xxx

Thus, at any point during the period, the inventory account is up to date. It has been debited for the cost of the purchases during the period and credited for the cost of the sales.

Why don't all companies use the procedure we just described, the perpetual system? Depending on the volume of inventory transactions, that is, purchases and sales of merchandise, a perpetual system can be extremely costly to maintain. Historically, businesses that have a relatively *small volume* of sales at a *high unit price* have used perpetual systems. For example, dealers in automobiles, furniture, appliances, and jewelry normally use a perpetual system. Each purchase of a unit of merchandise, such as an automobile, can be easily identified and debited to the Inventory account.

EXHIBIT 5-5 The Cost of Goods Sold Model

DESCRIPTION	ITEM	AMOUNT
Merchandise on hand to start the period	Beginning inventory	$15,000
	+	
Acquisitions of merchandise during the period	Cost of goods purchased	63,000
	=	
The pool of merchandise available for sale during the period	Cost of goods available for sale	$78,000
	−	
Merchandise on hand at end of period	Ending inventory	18,000
The expense recognized on the income statement	Cost of goods sold	$60,000

When the auto is sold, the dealer can easily determine the cost of the particular car sold by looking at a perpetual inventory record.

Can you imagine, however, a similar system for a supermarket or a hardware store? Consider a checkout stand in a grocery store. Through the use of a cash register tape, the *sales revenue* for that particular stand is recorded at the end of the day. Because of the tremendous volume of sales of various items of inventory, from cans of vegetables to boxes of soap, it may not be feasible to record the *cost of goods sold* every time a sale takes place. This illustrates a key point in financial information: the cost of the information should never exceed its benefit. If a store manager had to stop and update the records each time a can of Campbell's soup was sold, the retailer's business would obviously be disrupted.

To a certain extent, the ability of mass merchandisers to maintain perpetual inventory records has improved with the advent of point-of-sale terminals. When a cashier runs a can of corn over the sensing glass at the check-out stand and the bar code is read, a message is sent to the company's computer that a can of corn has been sold. In some companies, however, updating the inventory record is in *units* only and is used as a means to determine when a product needs to be reordered. The company still relies on a periodic system to maintain the *dollar* amount of inventory. In the remainder of this chapter, we limit our discussion to the periodic system. We discuss the perpetual system in detail in Chapter 6.

Beginning and Ending Inventories in a Periodic System

In a periodic system, the Inventory account is *not* updated each time a sale or purchase is made. Throughout the year, the Inventory account contains the amount of merchandise on hand at the beginning of the year. The account is adjusted only at the end of the year. A company using the periodic system must physically *count* the units of inventory on hand at the end of the period. The number of units of each product is then multiplied by the cost per unit to determine the dollar amount of ending inventory. Refer to Exhibit 5-4 for Tabor Hardware Stores. The procedure just described was used to determine its ending inventory of $18,000. Because one period's ending inventory is the next period's beginning inventory, the beginning inventory of $15,000 was based on the count at the end of the prior year.

In summary, the ending inventory in a periodic system is determined by a count of the merchandise, not by looking at the Inventory account at the end of the period. The periodic system results in a trade-off. Use of the periodic system reduces record keeping but at the expense of a certain degree of control. Losses of merchandise due to theft, breakage, spoilage, or other reasons may go undetected in a periodic system because management may assume that all merchandise not on hand at the end of the year was sold. In a retail store, some of the merchandise may have been shoplifted rather than sold. In contrast, with a perpetual inventory system, a count of inventory at the end of the period serves as a *control device*. For example, if the Inventory account shows a balance of $45,000 at the end of the year but only $42,000 of merchandise is counted, management is able to investigate the discrepancy. No such control feature exists in a periodic system.

In addition to the loss of control, the use of a periodic system presents a dilemma when a company wants to prepare *interim* financial statements. Because most companies that use a periodic system find it cost-prohibitive to count the entire inventory more than once a year, they use estimation techniques to determine inventory for monthly or quarterly statements. These techniques are discussed in Chapter 6.

The Cost of Goods Purchased

The cost of goods purchased section of Tabor's income statement is shown in Exhibit 5-6. The company purchased $65,000 of merchandise during the period. Two amounts are deducted from purchases to arrive at net purchases: purchase returns and allowances of $1,800 and purchase discounts of $3,700. These same items were discussed earlier from the viewpoint of the seller when we examined the accounting for sales returns and allowances and sales discounts. Now we are looking at them from the viewpoint of the purchaser. The cost of $3,500 incurred by Tabor to ship the goods to its place of business is called **transportation-in** and is added to net purchases of $59,500 to arrive at the cost of goods purchased of $63,000. Another name for *transportation-in* is *freight-in.*

LO 3

Understand how wholesalers and retailers account for cost of goods sold under the periodic system, including purchase returns and allowances, purchase discounts, and transportation-in.

Purchases   Purchases of merchandise are debited to an account titled **Purchases.** Assume that Tabor buys merchandise on account from one of its wholesalers at a cost of $4,000. The journal entry to record the purchase follows:

Feb. 8	Purchases	4,000	
	Accounts Payable		4,000
	To record the purchase of merchandise on account.		

Assets	=	Liabilities	+	Owners' Equity
		+4,000		−4,000

The Purchases account is a temporary account; it is *not* an asset account. It is included in the income statement as an integral part of the calculation of cost of goods sold. Because Purchases is a temporary account, it is closed at the end of the period. The logic for a debit to Purchases can be summarized as follows:

- Purchases are added in the calculation of cost of goods sold for the period.
- Cost of goods sold is an expense.
- An expense account is increased with a debit.
- Therefore, an increase in Purchases is recorded with a debit.

Purchase Returns and Allowances   We discussed returns and allowances earlier in the chapter from the seller's point of view. From the standpoint of the buyer, purchase returns and allowances are reductions in the cost to purchase merchandise.

EXHIBIT 5-6   Cost of Goods Purchased

TABOR HARDWARE STORES
PARTIAL INCOME STATEMENT
FOR THE YEAR ENDED DECEMBER 31, 1995

Purchases	$65,000	
Less: Purchase returns and allowances	1,800	
Purchase discounts	3,700	
Net purchases	$59,500	
Add: Transportation-in	3,500	
Cost of goods purchased		$63,000

Rather than record these reductions as a credit to the Purchases account, a separate account is used. The account, **Purchase Returns and Allowances,** is a *contra account* to Purchases. Because Purchases has a normal debit balance, the normal balance in Purchase Returns and Allowances is a credit balance. The use of a contra account allows management to monitor the amount of returns and allowances. For example, a large number of returns during the period relative to the amount purchased may signal that the purchasing department is not buying from reputable sources.

Suppose that Tabor returns $850 of merchandise to a wholesaler for credit on its account. The journal entry follows:

Sept. 6	Accounts Payable	850	
	Purchase Returns and Allowances		850
	To record the return of merchandise for credit to account.		

Assets	=	Liabilities	+	Owners' Equity
		−850		+850

If Tabor receives a cash refund for merchandise returned to its supplier, the debit is to Cash rather than to Accounts Payable. The entry to record an allowance for merchandise retained rather than returned is the same as the entry for a return.

Purchase Discounts Discounts were discussed earlier in the chapter from the seller's viewpoint. Merchandising companies often purchase inventory on terms that allow for a cash discount for early payment, such as 2/10, net 30. To the buyer, a cash discount is called a purchase discount and results in a reduction of the cost to purchase merchandise. *The same two methods that are used to account for sales discounts are used to account for purchase discounts.* The two methods are compared in Exhibit 5-7. The example assumes a purchase of merchandise for an invoice amount of $500, with credit terms of 1/10, net 30.

Under the gross method, purchases are recorded at the gross amount, that is, before deducting any discount for prompt payment. Any discounts taken are recorded in the **Purchase Discounts** account and deducted from purchases on the income statement. As mentioned earlier in the discussion of sales, the amount the buyer saves by paying early is usually a good investment. Thus, when the net method is used, any discounts missed by not taking advantage of the reduction for early payment are highlighted. The account Purchase Discounts Lost is properly classified as an element of interest expense on the income statement. On the other hand, when the gross method is used, management is aware only of the discounts taken; the discounts lost go undetected. Typically, managers would rather be alerted to bad news than be told the good news. By using the gross method, the company is alerted that it is taking purchase discounts but is not alerted that it is losing purchase discounts, as it would under the net method.

How can you tell, by reference to Exhibit 5-6, which of the two methods Tabor uses? Because the partial income statement shows a separate Purchase Discounts account, you know that Tabor Hardware Stores uses the gross method to record purchase discounts. This account is not used with the net method. Instead, purchases are recorded at the net amount, after considering the discount. Had the net method been used, a Purchase Discounts Lost account may have been displayed.

Shipping Terms and Transportation Costs The *cost principle* governs the recording of all assets. All costs necessary to prepare an asset for its intended use should be included in its cost. The cost of an item to a merchandising company is not necessarily limited to its invoice price. For example, any sales tax paid should

EXHIBIT 5-7   Comparing the Gross and Net Methods for Recording Purchase Discounts

DATE	GROSS METHOD			NET METHOD		

A purchase of $500 is made with discount terms of 1/10, net 30:

| March 13 | Purchases | 500 | | Purchases | 495 | |
| | Accounts Payable | | 500 | Accounts Payable | | 495 |

| | A | = | L | + | O/E | | | A | = | L | + | O/E |
| | | | +500 | | −500 | | | | | +495 | | −495 |

Assuming the discount is taken:

March 23	Accounts Payable	500		Accounts Payable	495	
	Cash		495	Cash		495
	Purchase Discounts		5			

| | A | = | L | + | O/E | | | A | = | L | + | O/E |
| | −495 | | −500 | | +5 | | | −495 | | −495 | | |

Assuming the discount is *not* taken:

April 13	Accounts Payable	500		Accounts Payable	495	
	Cash		500	Purchase Discounts Lost	5	
				Cash		500

| | A | = | L | + | O/E | | | A | = | L | + | O/E |
| | −500 | | −500 | | | | | −500 | | −495 | | −5 |

be included in computing total cost. Any transportation costs incurred by the buyer should likewise be included in the cost of the merchandise.

The buyer does not always pay to ship the merchandise. This depends on the terms of shipment. Goods are normally shipped either **FOB destination point** or **FOB shipping point;** *FOB* stands for *free on board.* When merchandise is shipped FOB destination point, it is the responsibility of the seller to deliver the products to the buyer. Thus, the seller either delivers the product to the customer or pays a trucking firm, railroad, or another carrier to transport it. Alternatively, the agreement between the buyer and seller may provide for the goods to be shipped FOB shipping point. In this case, the merchandise is the responsibility of the buyer as soon as it leaves the seller's premises. When the terms of shipment are FOB shipping point, the buyer incurs transportation costs.

Refer to Exhibit 5-6. Transportation-in represents the freight costs Tabor paid for inbound merchandise. These costs are added to net purchases as shown in the exhibit and increase the cost of goods purchased. Assume that on delivery of a shipment of goods, Tabor pays an invoice for $300 from the Chicago and Southwestern Railroad. The terms of shipment are FOB shipping point. The entry on the books of Tabor follows:

May 10	Transportation-in	300	
	Cash		300
	To record the payment of freight costs.		

| | Assets | = | Liabilities | + | Owners' Equity |
| | −300 | | | | −300 |

The Transportation-in account is an *adjunct* account because it is *added* to the net purchases of the period. The total of net purchases and transportation-in is called *the cost of goods purchased.* Transportation-in will be closed at the end of the period. In summary, cost of goods purchased consists of the following:

> Purchases
> Less: Purchase returns and allowances
>   Purchase discounts
> Equals: Net purchases
> Add: Transportation-in
> Equals: Cost of goods purchased

How should the *seller* account for the freight costs it pays when the goods are shipped FOB destination point? This cost, sometimes called *transportation-out,* is not an addition to the cost of *purchases* of the seller but is instead one of the costs necessary to *sell* the merchandise. Transportation-out is classified as a *selling expense* on the income statement.

Shipping Terms and Transfer of Title to Inventory   Terms of shipment take on additional significance at the end of an accounting period. It is essential that a company establish a proper cutoff at year-end. For example, what if Tabor purchases merchandise that is in transit at the end of the year? To whom does the inventory belong, Tabor or the seller? The answer depends on the terms of shipment. If goods are shipped FOB destination point, they remain the legal property of the seller until they reach their destination. Alternatively, legal title to goods shipped FOB shipping point passes to the buyer as soon as the seller turns them over to the carrier.

The example in Exhibit 5-8 is intended to summarize our discussion about shipping terms and ownership of merchandise. The example involves a shipment of merchandise in transit at the end of the year. Horton, the seller of the goods, pays the transportation charges if the terms are FOB destination point. Horton records a sale for goods in transit at year-end, however, only if the terms of shipment are FOB shipping point. If Horton does not record a sale, because the goods are shipped FOB destination point, the inventory appears on its December 31 balance sheet. Tabor, the buyer,

---

EXHIBIT 5-8   Shipping Terms and Transfer of Title to Inventory

Facts   On December 28, 1995, Horton Wholesale ships merchandise to Tabor Hardware Stores. The trucking company delivers the merchandise to Tabor on January 2, 1996. Tabor's fiscal year-end is December 31.

COMPANY		IF MERCHANDISE IS SHIPPED FOB DESTINATION POINT	IF MERCHANDISE IS SHIPPED FOB SHIPPING POINT
Horton	Pay freight costs?	Yes	No
(seller)	Record sale in 1995?	No	Yes
	Include inventory on balance sheet at December 31, 1995?	Yes	No
Tabor	Pay freight costs?	No	Yes
(buyer)	Record purchase in 1995?	No	Yes
	Include inventory on balance sheet at December 31, 1995?	No	Yes

pays freight costs if the goods are shipped FOB shipping point. Only in this situation does Tabor record a purchase of the merchandise and include it as an asset on its December 31 balance sheet.

■ ACCOUNTING FOR YOUR DECISIONS   **You Are the Retailer**

Assume that you are the general manager of Tabor Hardware Stores. Tabor purchases merchandise from Horton Wholesale with terms of FOB shipping point. The merchandise is in transit at year-end. Should the merchandise be included in the year-end inventory even though it is not on hand to count? If so, how can you ensure that it will be included? Assume a periodic inventory system.

The Accounting Cycle for a Merchandiser

In Chapter 4, we looked at the procedures followed at the end of the period for a service business. These same procedures are applicable to a merchandising company. In addition, assuming a periodic system, the merchandiser must count the ending inventory. The following steps are necessary at the end of the period:

- Count the ending inventory (assuming a periodic system).
- Prepare an unadjusted trial balance.
- Prepare a work sheet.
- Prepare financial statements.
- Journalize and post adjusting entries.
- Journalize and post closing entries.
- Prepare a post-closing trial balance.

The use of a work sheet for a merchandiser is very similar to its use for a service business. The mechanics of preparing a work sheet for a merchandiser as well as the closing entries for this type of business are covered in detail in Appendix 5A.

An Introduction to Internal Control

An employee of a large auto parts warehouse routinely takes spare parts home for personal use. A payroll clerk writes and signs two checks for an employee and then splits the amount of the second check with the worker. Through human error, an invoice is paid for merchandise never received from the supplier. Each of these cases sounds quite different, but they share one important characteristic. They all point to a deficiency in the company's internal control system. An **internal control system** consists of the policies and procedures necessary to ensure the safeguarding of an entity's assets, the reliability of its accounting records, and the accomplishment of its overall objectives.

Three assets are especially critical to the operation of a merchandising company: cash, accounts receivable, and inventory. Activities related to these three assets compose the operating cycle of a business. Cash is used to buy inventory, the inventory is eventually sold, and, assuming a sale on credit, the account receivable from the customer is collected. We turn now to the ways in which a company attempts to *control* the assets at its disposal. This section serves as an introduction to the important

LO **4**

Explain the importance of internal control to a business.

topic of internal control, which is explored further at appropriate points in the book. For example, controls to safeguard cash are discussed in Chapter 7.

The Report of Management: Showing Responsibility for Control

Modern business is characterized by absentee ownership. In most large corporations, it is impossible for the owners—the stockholders—to be actively involved in the daily affairs of the business. Professional managers have the primary responsibility for the business's smooth operation. They are also responsible for the content of the financial statements.

Most annual reports now include a **report of management** to the stockholders. A typical management report, in this case for the Quaker Oats Company, is shown in Exhibit 5-9. The first paragraph of the report clearly spells out management's responsibility for the preparation and integrity of the financial statements. The second paragraph refers to the system of internal controls within the company. One of the features of Quaker's internal control system is the use of an **internal audit staff.**

EXHIBIT 5-9 Report of Management—The Quaker Oats Company

Management is responsible for the preparation and integrity of the Company's financial statements. The financial statements have been prepared in accordance with generally accepted accounting principles and necessarily include some amounts that are based on management's estimates and judgment.

To fulfill its responsibility, management maintains a strong system of internal accounting controls, supported by formal policies and procedures that are communicated throughout the Company. Management also maintains a staff of internal auditors who evaluate the adequacy of and investigate the adherence to these controls, policies and procedures.

Our independent public accountants, Arthur Andersen & Co., have audited the financial statements and have rendered an opinion as to the statements' fairness in all material respects. During the audit, they obtain an understanding of the Company's internal control systems, and perform tests and other procedures to the extent required by generally accepted auditing standards.

The Board of Directors pursues its oversight role with respect to the Company's financial statements through the Audit Committee, which is composed solely of non-management directors. The Committee meets periodically with the independent public accountants, internal auditors and management to assure that all are properly discharging their responsibilities. The Committee approves the scope of the annual audit, and reviews the recommendations the independent public accountants have for improving internal accounting controls. The Board of Directors, on recommendation of the Audit Committee, engages the independent public accountants, subject to shareholder approval.

Both Arthur Andersen & Co. and the internal auditors have unrestricted access to the Audit Committee.

Most large corporations today have a full-time staff of internal auditors who have the responsibility for evaluating the entity's internal control system.

As the third paragraph of Quaker's report of management discusses, the primary concern of the independent public accountants, or external auditors, is whether the financial statements have been presented fairly. Internal auditors focus more on the efficiency with which the organization is run. They are responsible for periodically reviewing both accounting and administrative controls, which we discuss later in this chapter. The internal audit staff also helps to ensure that the company's policies and procedures are followed.

The third paragraph of the report states that the company's independent public accountants have rendered an opinion as to the fairness of presentation in the statements. The management of most corporations would consider it cost prohibitive for the auditors to verify the millions of transactions recorded in a single year. Instead, the auditors rely to a certain degree on the system of internal control as assurance that transactions are properly recorded and reported. The degree of reliance that they are able to place on the company's internal controls is a significant factor in determining the extent of their testing. The stronger the system of internal control, the less testing is necessary. A weak system of internal control requires that the auditors extend their tests of the records.

The **board of directors** of a corporation usually consists of key officers of the corporation as well as a number of directors whom it does not directly employ. For example, Quaker's board of 14 directors consists of 3 officers of the company and 11 outsiders. The outsiders often include presidents and key executive officers of other corporations and sometimes business school faculty. The board of directors is elected by the stockholders.

The **audit committee** of the board of directors provides direct contact between the stockholders and the independent accounting firm. Note that Quaker's audit committee is composed solely of outside directors. Audit committees have assumed a much more active role since the passage of the **Foreign Corrupt Practices Act** in 1977. This legislation was passed in response to a growing concern over various types of improprieties by top management, such as kickbacks to politicians and bribes of foreign officials.

The act includes a number of provisions intended to increase the accountability of management and the board of directors to stockholders. According to the act, management is responsible for keeping accurate records, and various provisions deal with the system of internal controls necessary to ensure the safeguarding of assets and the reliability of the financial statements. Audit committees have become much more involved in the oversight of the financial reporting system since the enactment of the act.

The Internal Control Structure of a Company

According to the American Institute of Certified Public Accountants, an entity's **internal control structure** consists of "the policies and procedures established to provide reasonable assurance that specific entity objectives will be achieved."[1] This is obviously a broad definition. The internal control structure consists of three basic elements: the control environment, the accounting system, and control procedures.

The Control Environment   The success of an internal control system begins with the competence of the people in charge of it. Management's operating style

---

[1] American Institute of Certified Public Accountants, *Professional Standards,* vol. A (New York: AICPA, 1988), sec. AU 319.06.

will have a determinable impact on the effectiveness of various policies. An autocratic style in which a few key officers tightly control operations will result in a different environment than a decentralized organization in which departments have more freedom to make decisions. Personnel policies and practices are another factor in the internal control of a business. An appropriate system for hiring competent employees and firing incompetent ones is crucial to an efficient operation. After all, no internal control system will work very well if employees who are dishonest or poorly trained are on the payroll. On the other hand, too few people doing too many tasks defeats the purpose of an internal control system. Finally, the effectiveness of internal control in a business is influenced by the board of directors, particularly its audit committee.

The Accounting System An **accounting system** consists of all the methods and records used to accurately report an entity's transactions and to maintain accountability for its assets and liabilities. Regardless of the degree of computer automation, the use of a journal to record transactions in debit and credit form is an integral part of all accounting systems. Refinements are sometimes made to the basic components of the system, depending on the company's needs. For example, most companies use specialized journals to record recurring transactions, such as sales of merchandise on credit.

An accounting system can be completely manual, fully computerized, or, as is often the case, a mixture of the two. Internal controls are important to all businesses, regardless of the degree of automation of the accounting system. The system must be capable of handling both the volume and the complexity of transactions entered into by a business. Most businesses use computers because of the sheer volume of transactions. The computer is ideally suited to the task of processing large numbers of repetitive transactions efficiently and quickly.

The cost of computing has dropped so substantially that virtually every business can now afford a system. Today some computer software programs that are designed for home-based businesses cost under $100 and are meant to run on machines that cost less than $1,000. Inexpensive software programs that categorize expenses and print checks, produce financial statements, and analyze financial ratios are available. Still, some people are uncomfortable with computers and are too busy working to spend the considerable amount of time it often takes to learn an automated system.

Internal Control Procedures

LO 5

Describe the basic internal control procedures.

Management establishes policies and procedures on a number of different levels to ensure that corporate objectives will be met. Some procedures are formalized in writing. Others may not be written but are just as important. Certain **administrative controls** within a company are more concerned with the efficient operation of the business and adherence to managerial policies than with the accurate reporting of financial information. For example, a company policy that requires all prospective employees to be interviewed by the personnel department is an administrative control. Other **accounting controls** primarily concern safeguarding assets and ensuring the reliability of the financial statements. We now turn to a discussion of some of the most important internal control procedures:

Proper authorizations.

Segregation of duties.

Independent verification.

Safeguarding of assets and records.

Independent review and appraisal of the system.

The design and use of business documents.

Proper Authorizations   Management grants specific departments the authority to perform various activities. Along with the *authority* goes *responsibility.* Most large organizations give the authority to hire new employees to the personnel department. Management authorizes the purchasing department to order goods and services for the company and the credit department to establish specific policies for granting credit to customers. By specifically authorizing certain individuals to carry out specific tasks for the business, management is able to hold these same people responsible for the outcome of their actions.

The authorizations for some transactions are general in nature; others are specific. For example, a cashier authorizes the sale of a book in a bookstore by ringing up the transaction (a general authorization). It is likely, however, that the bookstore manager's approval is required before a book can be returned (a specific authorization).

Segregation of Duties   What might happen if one employee is given the authority both to prepare checks and to sign them? What could happen if a single employee is allowed to order inventory and receive it from the shipper? Or what if the cashier at a check-out stand also records the daily receipts in the journal? If the employee in each of these situations is both honest and never makes mistakes, nothing bad will happen. However, if the employees in these situations are dishonest or make human errors, the company can experience losses. These situations all point to the need for *segregation of duties,* which is one of the most fundamental of all internal control procedures. Without segregation of duties, an employee is able not only to perpetrate a fraud but also to conceal it. A good system of internal control requires that the *physical custody* of assets be separated from the *accounting* for those same assets.

Independent Verification   Related to the principle of segregation of duties is the idea of independent verification. The work of one department should act as a check on the work of another. For example, the physical count of the inventory in a perpetual inventory system provides such a check. The accounting department maintains the general ledger card for inventory and updates it as sales and purchases are made. The physical count of the inventory by an independent department acts as a check on the work of the accounting department. As another example, consider a bank reconciliation as a control device. The reconciliation of a company's bank account with the bank statement by someone not responsible for either the physical custody of cash or the cash records acts as an independent check on the work of these parties. We will take a closer look at the use of a bank reconciliation as a control device in Chapter 7.

Safeguarding Assets and Records   Adequate safeguards must be in place to protect assets and the accounting records from losses of various kinds. Cash registers, safes, and lockboxes are important safeguards for cash. Secured storage areas with limited access are essential for the safekeeping of inventory. Protection of the accounting records against misuse is equally important. For example, access to a computerized accounting record should be limited to those employees authorized to prepare journal entries. This can be done with the use of a personal identification number and a password to access the system.

Independent Review and Appraisal   A well-designed system of internal control provides for periodic review and appraisal of the accounting system as well as the

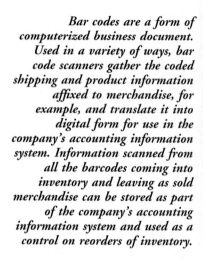

Bar codes are a form of computerized business document. Used in a variety of ways, bar code scanners gather the coded shipping and product information affixed to merchandise, for example, and translate it into digital form for use in the company's accounting information system. Information scanned from all the barcodes coming into inventory and leaving as sold merchandise can be stored as part of the company's accounting information system and used as a control on reorders of inventory.

people operating it. The two groups primarily responsible for review and appraisal of the system are the internal audit staff and the independent accounting firm. Each provides management with periodic reports as to the effectiveness of the control system and the efficiency of operations.

The Design and Use of Business Documents   *Business documents* are the crucial link between economic transactions entered into by an entity and the accounting record of these events. These are often called *source documents*. Some source documents are manual; others are computer generated. The source document for the recognition of the expense of an employee's wages is the *time card*. The source documents for a sale include the sales order, the sales invoice, and the related shipping document. Business documents must be designed so they capture all relevant information about an economic event. They are also designed to ensure that related transactions are properly classified.

Business documents must themselves be properly controlled. For example, a key feature for documents is a *serial numbering system* just like you have for your personal checks. This system results in a complete accounting for all documents in the series and negates the opportunity for an employee to misdirect one. Another key feature of well-designed business documents is the use of *multiple copies.* The various departments involved in a particular activity, such as sales or purchasing, are kept informed of the status of outstanding orders through the use of copies of documents. After we consider some of the limitations on internal control, we will turn to an example that involves the use of multiple copies.

Limitations on Internal Control

Internal control is a relative term. No system of internal control is totally foolproof. An entity's size affects the degree of control that it can obtain. In general, large organizations are able to devote a substantial amount of resources to safeguarding assets and records because these companies have the assets to justify the cost. Because the installation and maintenance of controls can be costly, an internal audit staff is a luxury that many small businesses cannot afford. The mere segregation of duties can result in added costs if two employees must be involved in a task previously performed by only one.

Segregation of duties can be effective in preventing collusion, but no system of internal control can ensure that it will not happen. It does no good to have one employee count the cash at the end of the day and another to record it if the two act in concert to steal from the company. Rotation of duties can help to lessen the likelihood for problems of this sort. An employee is less likely to work with someone to steal if the assignment is a temporary one. Another control feature, a system of authorizations, is meaningless if management continually overrides it. Management must believe in a system of internal control enough to support it.

Intentional acts to misappropriate company assets are not the only problem. All sorts of human errors can weaken a system of internal control. Misunderstanding instructions, carelessness, fatigue, and distraction can all lead to errors. A well-designed system of internal control should result in the best possible people being hired to perform the various tasks, but no human being is perfect.

■ ACCOUNTING FOR YOUR DECISIONS   You Are the Controller

The president of Mt. St. Helens Soap Company has informed you that you are going to be promoted to chief financial officer as soon as you can find a replacement for yourself as the controller. Where would you look for a new controller? What qualifications should this person have?

Internal Control for a Merchandising Company

Specific internal controls are necessary to control cash receipts and cash disbursements in a merchandising company. In addition to the separation of the custodianship of cash from the recording of it in the accounts, two other fundamental principles apply to its control. First, all cash receipts should be deposited *intact* in the bank on a *daily* basis. *Intact* means that no disbursements should be made from the cash received from customers. The second basic principle is related to the first: all cash disbursements should be made by check. The use of serially numbered checks results in a clear record of all disbursements. The only exception to this rule is the use of a petty cash fund to make cash disbursements for minor expenditures such as postage stamps and repairs. The use of such a fund is explained in Chapter 7.

Control over Cash Receipts

Most merchandisers receive checks and currency from customers in two distinct ways: (1) cash received over the counter, that is, from cash sales and (2) cash received in the mail, that is, cash collections from credit sales. Each of these types of cash receipts poses its own particular control problems.

Cash Received over the Counter   Several control mechanisms are used to handle these cash payments. First, cash registers allow the customer to see the display, which deters the salesclerk from ringing up a sale for less than the amount received from the customer and pocketing the difference. A locked-in cash register tape is another control feature. At various times during the day, an employee other than the clerk unlocks the register, removes the tape, and forwards it to the accounting department. At the end of the shift, the sales clerk remits the coin and currency from the register to a central cashier. Any difference between the amount of cash remitted to the cashier and the amount on the tape submitted to the accounting department is investigated.

Finally, prenumbered customer receipts, prepared in duplicate, are a useful control mechanism. The customer is given a copy and the salesclerk retains another. The salesclerk is accountable for all numbers in a specific series of receipts and must be able to explain any differences between the amount of cash remitted to the cashier and the amount collected per the receipts.

Cash Received in the Mail   Most customers send checks rather than currency through the mail. Any form of cash received in the mail from customers should be applied to their account balances. The customer wants assurance that the account is appropriately reduced for the amount of the payment. The company must be assured that all cash received is deposited in the bank and that the account receivable is reduced accordingly.

To achieve a reasonable degree of control, two employees should be present when the mail is opened. The first employee opens the mail in the presence of the second employee, counts the money received, and prepares a control list of the amount received on that particular day. The list is often called a *prelist* and is prepared in triplicate. The second employee takes the original to the cashier along with the total cash received on that day. The cashier is the person who makes the bank deposit. One copy of the prelist is forwarded to the accounting department to be used as the basis for recording the debit to Cash and the credit to Accounts Receivable. The other copy is retained by one of the persons opening the mail. A comparison of the prelist to the bank deposit slip is a timely way to detect receipts that do not make it to the bank. Because the two employees acting in concert could circumvent the control process, rotation of duties is important.

Monthly customer statements act as an additional control device for customer payments received in the mail. Assume that the two employees responsible for opening the mail and remitting it to the cashier decide to pocket a check received from a customer. Checks made payable to a company *can* be stolen and cashed. The customer provides the control element. Because the check is not remitted to the cashier, the accounting department will not be notified to reduce the customer's account for the payment. The monthly statement, however, should alert the customer to the problem. The amount the customer thought was owed will be smaller than the balance due on the statement. At this point, the customer should ask the company to investigate the discrepancy. As evidence of its payment on account, the customer will be able to point to a canceled check—which was cashed by the unscrupulous employees.

Finally, keep in mind that the use of customer statements as a control device will be effective only if the employees responsible for the custody of cash received through the mail, for record keeping, and for authorization of adjustments to customers' accounts are not allowed to prepare and mail statements to customers. Employees allowed to do so are in a position to alter customers' statements.

Cash Over and Short   Discrepancies occur occasionally due to theft by dishonest employees and to human error. For example, if a salesclerk either intentionally or unintentionally gives the wrong amount of change, the amount remitted to the cashier will not agree with the cash register tape. Assume that a cash register tape shows total sales for March 13 of $500 but the amount in the drawer to be remitted to the cashier is only $490. Which amount should be recorded as sales revenue? Actual sales for the day are $500 and the journal entry should be as follows:

March 13	Cash	490	
	Cash Over and Short	10	
	Sales Revenue		500
	To record daily sales.		

Assets	=	Liabilities	+	Owners' Equity
+490				− 10
				+500

Any material amount in the Cash Over and Short account should be investigated. Of particular significance are *recurring* differences between the amount remitted by any one cashier and the amount on the cash register tape. A debit balance in the Cash Over and Short account at the end of the period indicates a shortage of cash. At the end of the period, the account is closed by crediting it and debiting a miscellaneous expense account. If the amount of cash on hand exceeds the amount recorded as sales revenue, the Cash Over and Short account will contain a credit balance. The account is then closed by debiting it and crediting a miscellaneous revenue account.

The Role of Computerized Business Documents in Controlling Cash Disbursements

A company makes cash payments for a variety of purposes: to purchase merchandise, supplies, plant, and equipment; to pay operating expenditures; and to cover payroll expenses, to name a few. We will concentrate on the disbursement of cash to purchase goods for resale, focusing particularly on the role of business documents in the process. Merchandising companies rely on a smooth and orderly inflow of quality goods for resale to customers. It is imperative that suppliers be paid on time so that they will continue to make goods available.

Business documents play a vital role in the purchasing function. The example that follows begins with a requisition for merchandise by the tool department of Tabor Hardware Stores. The example continues through the receipt of the goods and the eventual payment to the supplier. The entire process is summarized in Exhibit 5-10. You will want to refer back to this exhibit throughout the remainder of the chapter.

Purchase Requisition The tool department at Tabor Hardware Stores reviews its stock weekly to determine whether any items need replenishing. On the basis of its needs, the supervisor of the tool department fills out the **purchase requisition form** shown in Exhibit 5-11. The form indicates the preferred supplier or vendor, A-1 Tool.

The purchasing department has the responsibility to make the final decision on a vendor. Giving the purchasing department this responsibility means that it is held accountable for acquiring the goods at the lowest price, given certain standards for merchandise quality. Tabor assigns a separate item number to each of the thousands of individual items of merchandise it stocks. Note that the requisition also indicates the vendor's number for each item. The unit of measure for each item is indicated in the quantity column. For example, "24 ST" means 24 sets and "12 CD" means 12 cards. The original and a copy of the purchase requisition are sent to the purchasing department. The tool department keeps one copy for its records.

LO   6
Describe the various documents used in recording purchases of merchandise and their role in controlling cash disbursements.

EXHIBIT 5-10 Document Flow for the Purchasing Function

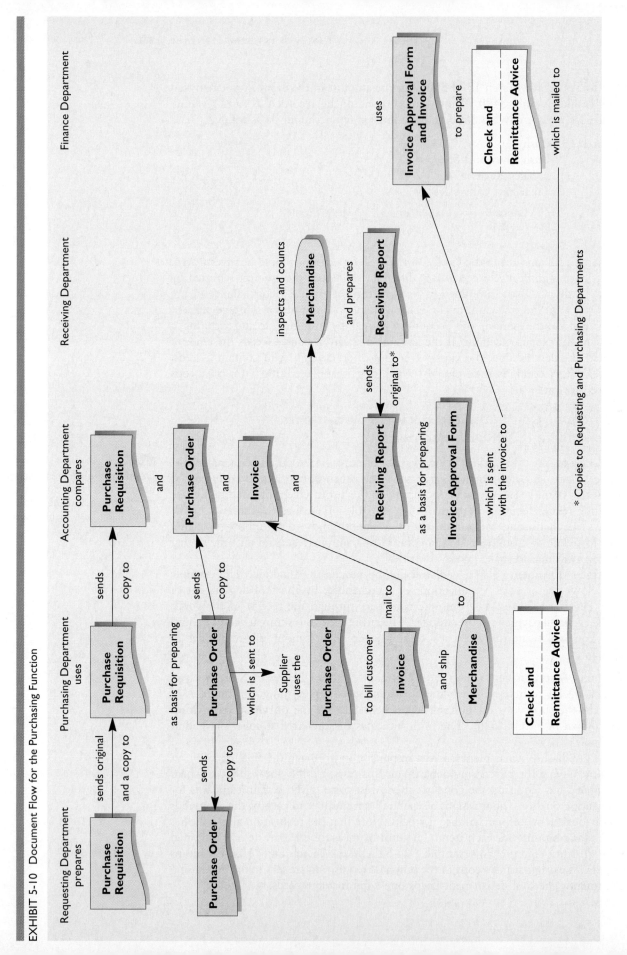

EXHIBIT 5-11   Purchase Requisition

Tabor Hardware Stores
676 Glenwood St.
Chicago, IL

PURCHASE REQUISITION

Date   5/28/95   **PR 75638**

Preferred vendor   A-1 Tool Co.

Date needed by   6/5/95

The following items are requested for   weekly dept. order

Item No.	Quantity	Description/Vendor No.
314627	24 ST	Hobby tool set/5265
323515	12 CD	Hobby blades 5 pk/7512
323682	6 ST	Screwdriver set 5/PC/1589

Requested by   *Joe Smith*   **Department**   Tool department

Purchase Order   Like many businesses, Tabor uses a computerized purchasing system. Most computer manufacturers either have developed software themselves or have arrangements with outsiders to develop the software, which performs such functions as purchasing, sales, and payroll. The software is capable not only of increasing the speed and accuracy of the process but also of generating the necessary documents.

A computer-generated **purchase order** is shown in Exhibit 5-12. Purchase orders are usually prenumbered; a company should investigate periodically any missing numbers. The purchasing department uses its copy of the purchase requisition as a basis for preparing the purchase order. An employee in the purchasing department keys in the relevant information from the purchase requisition and adds the unit cost for each item gathered from the vendor's price guide. The software program generates the purchase order as shown in Exhibit 5-12. You should trace all of the information for at least one of the three items ordered from the purchase requisition to the purchase order. The purchase order indicates the instructions for shipping, FOB destination point, and the terms for payment, 2/10, net 30.

The system generates the original purchase order and three copies. As indicated in Exhibit 5-10, the original is sent to the supplier after a supervisor in the purchasing department approves it. One copy is sent to the accounting department where it will be matched with the original requisition. A second copy is sent to the tool department as confirmation that its request for the items has been attended to by the purchasing department. The purchasing department keeps the third copy for its records.

A purchase order is not the basis for recording a purchase and a liability. Legally, the order is merely an offer by the company to purchase goods from the supplier. Technically, the receipt of goods from the supplier is the basis for the purchaser's

EXHIBIT 5-12 Computer-Generated Purchase Order

```
                          Tabor Hardware Stores
                           676 Glenwood St.
                             Chicago, IL

                            PURCHASE ORDER

  TO:                                                      PO 54296
  A-1 Tool Co.
  590 West St.
  Milwaukee, WI
  Date 5/30/95          Ship by  Best Express    Instructions  FOB destination point
  Terms 2/10, net 30                             Date required 6/5/95


  Item No.    Quantity    Description/Vendor No.    Unit price     Amount
  314627      24 ST       Hobby tool set/5265       $28.59         $686.16
  323515      12 CD       Hobby blades 5 pk/7512      .69             8.28
  323682       6 ST       Screwdriver set 5/PC/1589  4.49            26.94
                                                                  _____
                                                                  $721.38
                                                                  =======

                       Mary Jones
  Approved by _____
```

recognition of a liability. As a matter of practice, however, most companies record the payable upon receipt of the invoice.

Invoice   When A-1 Tool ships the merchandise, it also mails an invoice to Tabor, requesting payment according to the agreed-upon terms, in this case 2/10, net 30. The **invoice** may be mailed separately or included with the shipment of merchandise. A-1 Tool, the seller, calls this document a *sales invoice;* it is the basis for recording a sale and an account receivable. Tabor, the buyer, calls the same document a *purchase invoice,* which is the basis for recording a purchase and an account payable. The invoice that A-1 sent to Tabor's accounting department is shown in Exhibit 5-13.

Receiving Report   The accounting department receives the invoice for the three items ordered. Within a few days before or after the receipt of the invoice, the merchandise arrives at Tabor's warehouse. As soon as the items are unpacked, the receiving department inspects and counts them. The same software program that generated the purchase order also generates a receiving report, as shown in Exhibit 5-14.

Tabor uses a **blind receiving report.** The column for the quantity received is left blank and is filled in by the receiving department. Rather than being able simply to indicate that the number ordered were received, an employee must count the items to determine that the number ordered is actually received. You should trace all of the relevant information for one of the three items ordered from the purchase order to the receiving report. The accounting system generates an original receiving report and three copies. The receiving department keeps one copy for its records and sends the original to the accounting department. One copy is sent to the purchasing department to be matched with the purchase order, and the other copy is sent

EXHIBIT 5-13 Invoice

NO. 427953

A-1 Tool Co.
590 West St.
Milwaukee, WI

INVOICE

Sold to Tabor Hardware Stores   **Date** 6/2/95

676 Glenwood St.   **Order No.** 54296

Chicago, IL   **Shipped via** Best Express

Ship to Same   **Date shipped** 6/2/95

Terms 2/10, net 30   **Ship terms** FOB destination

Quantity	Description/No.	Price	Amount
24 ST	Hobby tool set/5265	$28.59	$686.16
12 CD	Hobby blades 5 pk/7512	.69	8.28
6 ST	Screwdriver set 5 PC/1589	4.49	26.94
			$721.38

EXHIBIT 5-14 Computer-Generated Receiving Report

Tabor Hardware Stores
676 Glenwood St.
Chicago, IL

Receiving Report

RR 23637

Purchase Order No. 54296   Date ordered 5/30/95
Vendor A-1 Tool Co.   Date required 6/5/95
Ship via Best Express   Instructions FOB Destination
Terms 2/10, net 30

Quantity received	Our Item No.	Description/Item No.	Remarks
24 ST	314627	Hobby tool set/5265	Box damaged but merchandise ok
12 CD	323515	Hobby blades 5 pk/7512	
6 ST	323682	Screwdriver set 5/PC/1589	

Received by *Bob Reed*   Date   6/4/95

to the tool department as verification that the items it originally requested have been received.

Invoice Approval Form   At this point, Tabor's accounting department has copies of the purchase requisition from the tool department, the purchase order from the purchasing department, the invoice from the supplier, and the receiving report from the warehouse. The accounting department uses an **invoice approval form** to document the accuracy of the information on each of these other forms. The invoice approval form for Tabor Hardware is shown in Exhibit 5-15.

The invoice is compared to the purchase requisition to ensure that the company is billed for goods that it in fact requested. A comparison of the invoice with the purchase order ensures that the goods were in fact ordered. Finally, the receiving report is compared with the invoice to verify that all goods it is being billed for were received. An accounting department employee must also verify the extensions on the invoice and the footings, that is, the calculation of the total amount owed. The date the invoice must be paid to take advantage of the discount is noted so that the finance department will be sure to send the check by this date. At this point, the accounting department prepares the journal entry to debit Purchases and credit Accounts Payable. The invoice approval form and the invoice are then sent to the finance department. Some businesses call the invoice approval form a *voucher;* it is used for all expenditures, not just those for the purchase of merchandise. Finally, it

EXHIBIT 5-15 Invoice Approval Form

Tabor Hardware Stores
676 Glenwood St.
Chicago, IL

Invoice Approval Form

	No.	**Check**
Purchase Requisition	PR 75638	✔
Purchase Order	PO 54296	✔
Receiving Report	RR 23637	✔

Invoice:

No.   427953

Date   6/2/95

Price   ✔

Extensions   ✔

Footings   ✔

Last Day to Pay for Discount   6/12/95

Approved for Payment by   *Alice Johnson*

USING FINANCIAL INFORMATION FOR INTERNAL CONTROL AND FOR INVESTMENT

Name: Steven P. Eldredge
Profession: Chief Operating Officer
College Major: Finance

One of the nation's fastest growing industries is mutual funds. There are now more mutual funds than there are companies to invest in. Fueling the growth is the public's appetite for higher returns and a need for professional management in the increasingly complex investment markets. Even with its bumpy ride, the stock market as a whole has outperformed most other investments, including real estate, bonds, and gold. Since the 1920s, stocks have handsomely outrun inflation, too.

The fast growth of the mutual fund industry has led to fast-track careers for its executives. Mr. Steven Eldredge is in his mid-30s, yet he is already the chief operating officer of ABT Funds, a mutual fund company in Florida. He is also responsible for the company's municipal bond portfolios including ABT Florida Tax-Free Fund, ABT Florida High Income Municipal Bond Fund and ABT Florida Limited Term Tax-Free Fund.

That means he uses financial information two ways. First, as a portfolio manager, Mr. Eldredge monitors the bonds in his portfolios, making sure that the entities can generate sufficient cash flow to pay the bond interest and principal. Most municipalities provide about the same financial information as regular corporations. "They give you the three basic financial statements, including footnotes," he says.

Secondly, Mr. Eldredge uses financial information to run his company. For that, the key report is the income statement. "I'm interested in what our budget says we're going to make this month and what our actual income and expenses look like. Our CFO provides variance reports once a month. Maybe we have overspent in marketing because we ran a campaign that we weren't anticipating when we were completing our budget." Of course, the company's income depends a great deal upon how the market does. Since most mutual funds are paid a fraction of the money they manage, a down market hurts income.

By the way, knowing about FIFO and LIFO is handy if you're going to be a mutual fund investor. Buying shares of a mutual fund is like acquiring inventory layers in merchandising.

FOCUS ON USERS

On April 15th, you need to know which mutual fund "layers" you sold in order to compute your taxes. LIFO, FIFO, and average cost accounting are among the available options.

*Variance reports are internal reports to management showing how actual performance—such as sales, costs, and so on—compares to budgeted performance.

is worth noting that some businesses do not use a separate invoice approval form but simply note approval directly on the invoice itself.

Check with Remittance Advice   Tabor's finance department has the responsibility for issuing checks. This results from the need to segregate custody of cash (the signed check) from record keeping (the updating of the ledger). Upon receipt of the invoice approval form from the accounting department, a clerk in the finance department types a check with a remittance advice attached as shown in Exhibit 5-16.

Before the check is signed, the documents referred to on the invoice approval form are reviewed and canceled to prevent reuse. The clerk then forwards the check to one of the officers of the company authorized to sign checks. According to one

EXHIBIT 5-16 Check with Remittance Advice

3690

Tabor Hardware Stores
676 Glenwood St.
Chicago, IL

June 12 19 95

PAY TO THE
ORDER OF ___ A-1 Tool Co. _____ $706.95

Seven hundred six and 95/100 _____ DOLLARS

Second National Bank
Chicago, IL
3690 035932 9321

John B. Martin

Purchase Order No.	Invoice No.	Invoice Date	Description	Amount
PO 54296	427953	6/2/95	24 ST Hobby tool set	$686.16
			12 CD Hobby blades 5pk	8.28
			6 ST Screwdriver set 5PC	26.94
			Total	721.38
			Less: 2% discount	14.43
			Net remitted	706.95

of Tabor's internal control policies, only the treasurer and the assistant treasurer are authorized to sign checks. Both officers must sign check amounts above a specified dollar limit. To maintain separation of duties, the finance department should mail the check. The remittance advice informs the supplier as to the nature of the payment and is torn off by the supplier before cashing the check.

REVIEW PROBLEM

Mickey's Marts, which operates a chain of department stores, uses the periodic inventory system. The cost of inventory on hand at January 1 amounts to $12,000, and on January 31, it is $9,500. The following transactions are entered into by Mickey's during January:

a. Purchased merchandise on account from various vendors for $25,000. All merchandise is bought with terms of 1/10, net 30. The gross method is used to record purchase discounts.

b. Reduced the total amount owed to vendors by $20,000. This is *not* the amount paid but the amount before taking the 1% discount. All accounts are paid within 10 days of the date of the invoice.

c. Recognized purchase returns and allowances of $1,900 during the month.

d. Recognized total sales of $42,000 for the month, of which $28,000 is cash sales and the remainder is on account.

e. Made collections on account of $17,000 for the month.

f. Applied $3,200 of sales returns and allowances for the month to customers' account balances.

g. Paid the freight cost of $2,700 on *incoming* purchases of merchandise.

1. Prepare the necessary journal entries to record each of the transactions (a) through (g).   ■ **REQUIRED**

2. Prepare a *partial* income statement for the month of January. The last line on the partial statement should be gross margin.

■ SOLUTION TO REVIEW PROBLEM

1. Journal entries:

a. Purchases   25,000
    Accounts Payable   25,000
    To record purchases on account.

Assets	**=**	**Liabilities**	**+**	**Owners' Equity**
+25,000				−25,000

b. Accounts Payable   20,000
    Purchase Discounts   200
    Cash   19,800
    To record payment of amounts owed on account, less 1% discount for early payment.

Assets	**=**	**Liabilities**	**+**	**Owners' Equity**
−19,800		−20,000		+200

c. Accounts Payable   1,900
    Purchase Returns and Allowances   1,900
    To record purchase returns and allowances for the month.

Assets	**=**	**Liabilities**	**+**	**Owners' Equity**
		−1,900		+1,900

d. Cash   28,000
  Accounts Receivable   14,000
    Sales Revenue   42,000
    To record sales for the month.

Assets	**=**	**Liabilities**	**+**	**Owners' Equity**
+28,000				+42,000
+14,000				

e. Cash   17,000
    Accounts Receivable   17,000
    To record collections on account for the month.

Assets	**=**	**Liabilities**	**+**	**Owners' Equity**
+17,000				
−17,000				

f. Sales Returns and Allowances 3,200
    Accounts Receivable 3,200
    To record sales returns and allowances for the month.

Assets	=	Liabilities	+	Owners' Equity
−3,200				−3,200

g. Transportation-in 2,700
    Cash 2,700
    To record payment of freight bill on incoming merchandise.

Assets	=	Liabilities	+	Owners' Equity
−2,700				−2,700

2. Partial income statement:

MICKEY'S MARTS
PARTIAL INCOME STATEMENT
FOR THE MONTH OF JANUARY

Sales revenue			$42,000
Less: Sales returns and allowances			3,200
Net sales			$38,800
Cost of goods sold:			
Inventory, January 1		$12,000	
Purchases	$25,000		
Less: Purchase discounts	200		
Purchase returns and allowances	1,900		
Net purchases	$22,900		
Add: Transportation-in	2,700		
Cost of goods purchased		25,600	
Cost of goods available for sale		$37,600	
Less: Inventory, January 31		9,500	
Cost of goods sold			28,100
Gross margin			$10,700

GUIDANCE ANSWERS TO ACCOUNTING FOR YOUR DECISIONS

YOU ARE THE RETAILER

Merchandise is in transit at year-end that was shipped FOB shipping point should be included in ending inventory. With a periodic inventory system, a count of ending inventory is needed to determine cost of goods sold. The controller will need to examine the outstanding purchase invoices to determine the amount of inventory in transit at year-end that should be included in ending inventory.

YOU ARE THE CONTROLLER

One of the most important attributes of an internal control system is to have qualified people with integrity working for you. You would look for someone who had been a controller at another industrial company or someone who has been on the audit staff of a well-respected accounting firm. Both types of candidates would possess the accounting skills necessary to produce the financial statements and tax returns—as well as the experience in setting up and working with internal accounting systems. Equally important: does this person possess the degree of integrity necessary to work for your company in such an important capacity?

┌───┐
│   │
│   **A P P E N D I X   5 A**   │
│   │
└───┘

ACCOUNTING TOOLS: COMPLETING THE ACCOUNTING CYCLE FOR A MERCHANDISER

The discussion that follows focuses on the preparation of the *work sheet* and the *closing entries* for a merchandising company. The year-end process for a merchandiser using a periodic system begins with a count of the inventory on hand. The mechanics of the other steps in the accounting cycle are identical to those for a service company, as illustrated in Chapter 4.

Work Sheet for a Merchandising Company

LO **7**

Use a 10-column work sheet for a merchandiser.

The unadjusted trial balance for Tabor Hardware Stores appears in the first two columns of the 10-column work sheet in Exhibit 5-17. The first thing you should notice from the list of account titles is the inclusion of the various merchandising accounts introduced in this chapter. For ease of reference, they are highlighted. Four adjusting entries were made in the third and fourth columns of the work sheet. Although adjusting entries are not a primary concern in this chapter, you should review them briefly. Do not be concerned with how the amounts were calculated. The following are the four adjustments:

  a. Recognize as an expense the expired portion of prepaid insurance.

  b. Record depreciation expense on the buildings and equipment.

  c. Accrue salaries and wages unpaid at the end of the period; note that $1,100 of the accrual is classified as a selling expense and that $600 is an administrative expense.

  d. Accrue income taxes unpaid at the end of the period.

After the Adjusted Trial Balance columns of the work sheet are completed, each of the account balances is entered in one of the two Income Statement columns or one of the two Balance Sheet columns. Pay particularly close attention to the highlighted merchandising accounts. *Beginning inventory* is entered in the *Income Statement Debit* column because it is *added* in the cost of goods sold *expense* section of the income statement. Because we are assuming that Tabor uses a periodic inventory system, *ending inventory* is determined by a count of the merchandise on hand. It is entered in the *Income Statement Credit* column because it is *subtracted* in the cost of goods sold *expense* section of the income statement. Finally, note that *ending inventory* is also entered in the *Balance Sheet Debit* column because it is an *asset* at the end of the period. Each of the other merchandising accounts with debit balances, such as Sales Returns and Allowances, is entered in the Income Statement Debit column. Each of the accounts with credit balances, such as Sales, is entered in the Credit column.

The difference between the Income Statement Credit column total of $127,000 and the Income Statement Debit column total of $120,580 is the net income of $6,420. This amount is entered in the Income Statement Debit column as a balancing figure and in the Balance Sheet Credit column because net income results in an increase in retained earnings. Note that cost of goods sold does not specifically appear on the work sheet because it is not an *account* in the periodic system but a calculated *amount*. Instead, each of the accounts necessary to prepare the cost of goods sold

EXHIBIT 5-17 Work Sheet for a Merchandiser

TABOR HARDWARE STORES
WORK SHEET
FOR THE YEAR ENDED DECEMBER 31, 1995

ACCOUNT TITLES	UNADJUSTED TRIAL BALANCE DEBIT	UNADJUSTED TRIAL BALANCE CREDIT	ADJUSTING ENTRIES DEBIT	ADJUSTING ENTRIES CREDIT	ADJUSTED TRIAL BALANCE DEBIT	ADJUSTED TRIAL BALANCE CREDIT	INCOME STATEMENT DEBIT	INCOME STATEMENT CREDIT	BALANCE SHEET DEBIT	BALANCE SHEET CREDIT
Cash	8,590				8,590				8,590	
Accounts receivable	27,400				27,400				27,400	
Prepaid insurance	10,000			(a) 6,000	4,000				4,000	
Merchandise inventory	15,000				15,000		15,000	18,000	18,000	
Land	125,000				125,000				125,000	
Buildings and equipment	250,000				250,000				250,000	
Accumulated depreciation		40,000		(b) 10,000		50,000				50,000
Accounts payable		18,740				18,740				18,740
Capital stock		200,000				200,000				200,000
Retained earnings		154,350				154,350				154,350
Dividends	2,500				2,500				2,500	
Sales revenue		103,500				103,500		103,500		
Sales returns and allowances	2,000				2,000		2,000			
Sales discounts	1,500				1,500		1,500			
Purchases	65,000				65,000		65,000			
Purchase returns and allowances		1,800				1,800		1,800		
Purchase discounts		3,700				3,700		3,700		
Transportation-in	3,500				3,500		3,500			
Salaries and wages expense—selling	4,000		(c) 1,100		5,100		5,100			
Salaries and wages expense—admin.	3,300		(c) 600		3,900		3,900			
Advertising expense	3,400				3,400		3,400			
Utilities expense	900				900		900			
	522,090	522,090								
Insurance expense			(a) 6,000		6,000		6,000			
Depreciation expense			(b) 10,000		10,000		10,000			
Salaries and wages payable				(c) 1,700		1,700				1,700
Income tax expense			(d) 4,280		4,280		4,280			
Income tax payable				(d) 4,280		4,280				4,280
			21,980	21,980	538,070	538,070	120,580	127,000	435,490	429,070
Net income							6,420			6,420
							127,000	127,000	435,490	435,490

section of the income statement is included in the income statement columns of the work sheet. Thus, cost of goods sold as an expense is represented on the work sheet. An alternative procedure in which cost of goods sold is entered on the work sheet with the use of an adjusting entry is illustrated later in this appendix.

The Income Statement and Balance Sheet for a Merchandising Company

The income statement for Tabor Hardware Stores is shown in Exhibit 5-18. The condensed income statement presented earlier in Exhibit 5-1 has been expanded to show each of the accounts on the work sheet. The statement in Exhibit 5-18 consists of five major sections: (1) net sales, (2) cost of goods sold, (3) selling expenses, (4) administrative expenses, and (5) income tax expense.

EXHIBIT 5-18   Detailed Income Statement for a Merchandiser

TABOR HARDWARE STORES
INCOME STATEMENT
FOR THE YEAR ENDED DECEMBER 31, 1995

Sales revenue		$103,500	
Less: Sales returns and allowances		2,000	
Sales discounts		1,500	
Net sales			$100,000
Cost of goods sold:			
Inventory, January 1, 1995		$ 15,000	
Purchases	$65,000		
Less: Purchase returns and allowances	1,800		
Purchase discounts	3,700		
Net purchases	$59,500		
Add: Transportation-in	3,500		
Cost of goods purchased		63,000	
Cost of goods available for sale		$ 78,000	
Less: Inventory, December 31, 1995		18,000	
Cost of goods sold			60,000
Gross margin			$ 40,000
Selling expenses:			
Salaries and wages		$ 5,100	
Advertising		3,400	8,500
Administrative expenses:			
Salaries and wages		$ 3,900	
Insurance		6,000	
Utilities		900	
Depreciation		10,000	20,800
Income before tax			$ 10,700
Income tax expense			4,280
Net income			$ 6,420

EXHIBIT 5-19   Balance Sheet for a Merchandising Company

TABOR HARDWARE STORES
BALANCE STATEMENT
AT DECEMBER 31, 1995

Current assets			**Current liabilities**	
Cash		$ 8,590	Accounts payable	$ 18,740
Accounts receivable		27,400	Salaries and wages payable	1,700
Merchandise inventory		18,000	Income taxes payable	4,280
Prepaid insurance		4,000	**Total current liabilities**	$ 24,720
Total current assets		$ 57,990	Capital stock	200,000
Land		125,000	Retained earnings	158,270
Buildings and equipment	250,000		**Total liabilities and**	
Less: Accumulated depreciation	(50,000)	200,000	**stockholders' equity**	$382,990
Total assets		$382,990		

Tabor's balance sheet is presented in Exhibit 5-19. The ending inventory of $18,000 is classified as merchandise inventory under current assets because by its nature it will be sold within the next operating cycle of the business.

Although a statement of retained earnings is not shown, it is possible to verify the ending balance of retained earnings by looking at the work sheet. The ending balance of $158,270 consists of the beginning balance of $154,350, plus net income of $6,420, minus dividends of $2,500.

The Closing Entries
for a Merchandising Company

Closing entries serve two purposes. First, all income statement accounts are returned to a zero balance to start the next accounting period. Second, net income and dividends of the period are transferred to the Retained Earnings account. Many different procedural approaches are used in practice to close the accounts of a merchandising company. The approach illustrated here involves making two entries to close the income statement accounts. One entry closes all accounts with credit balances and the second closes all accounts with debit balances. Using the work sheet in Exhibit 5-17 as a guide, the first closing entry is as follows:

LO 8

Understand the role of closing entries for a merchandiser.

Dec. 31	Merchandise Inventory, December 31	18,000	
	Sales Revenue	103,500	
	Purchase Returns and Allowances	1,800	
	Purchase Discounts	3,700	
	Income Summary		127,000

To record ending inventory per physical count and close accounts with credit balances.

Assets	=	**Liabilities**	+	**Owners' Equity**
+18,000				−103,500
				− 1,800
				− 3,700
				+127,000

The credit to Income Summary is simply the total of the debits to the various accounts. However, this amount can be verified by comparing it to the total amount in the Income Statement Credit column of the work sheet. The debit to Merchandise Inventory serves an additional purpose: It adds the ending balance of $18,000 to this account on the balance sheet.

The second entry closes all of the income statement accounts with debit balances and in addition removes the beginning inventory balance of $15,000 from this account:

Dec. 31	Income Summary	120,580	
	Merchandise Inventory, January 1		15,000
	Sales Returns and Allowances		2,000
	Sales Discounts		1,500
	Purchases		65,000
	Transportation-in		3,500
	Salaries and Wages Expense—Selling		5,100
	Salaries and Wages Expense—Administrative		3,900
	Advertising Expense		3,400
	Utilities Expense		900
	Insurance Expense		6,000
	Depreciation Expense		10,000
	Income Tax Expense		4,280

To close accounts with debit balances to Income Summary.

Assets	=	Liabilities	+	Owners' Equity
− 15,000				− 120,580
				+ 2,000
				+ 1,500
				+ 65,000
				+ 3,500
				+ 33,580

Note that the debit to Income Summary is the same as the column total on the work sheet. The effect of the credit of $15,000 to Merchandise Inventory is to remove the beginning inventory from the records. The effect of the two entries on the Inventory account is shown in T-account form as follows:

MERCHANDISE INVENTORY

Bal. on Jan. 1	15,000			
Closing entry 1	18,000			
		15,000	Closing entry 2	
Bal. on Dec. 31	18,000			

At this point, the Income Summary account has a credit balance of $6,420. A third entry is made to close it and transfer net income to Retained Earnings:

Dec. 31	Income Summary	6,420	
	Retained Earnings		6,420

To close the Income Summary account to Retained Earnings.

Assets	=	Liabilities	+	Owners' Equity
				− 6,420
				+ 6,420

The fourth and final entry closes the Dividends account and reduces Retained Earnings accordingly:

Dec. 31   Retained Earnings   2,500
               Dividends   2,500
           To close Dividends to Retained Earnings.

Assets   =   Liabilities   +   Owners' Equity
                                          − 2,500
                                          + 2,500

Alternative Procedure
for Closing the Merchandising Accounts

The procedure illustrated above for preparing a work sheet and closing entries for a merchandiser is only one of a number of acceptable techniques. Cost of goods sold did not appear as an expense either on the work sheet or in the closing entries. Instead, each of the merchandising accounts was carried forward to one of the two Income Statement columns on the work sheet. By closing the merchandising accounts, the *amount* of cost of goods sold of $60,000 was closed to the Income Summary account without the use of a Cost of Goods Sold account. An alternative procedure is sometimes used in which the Cost of Goods Sold account appears on the work sheet and is then included in a closing entry.

A work sheet using the alternative technique is presented in Exhibit 5-20. Entries (a) through (d) in the Adjusting Entries columns record the expired portion of prepaid insurance, record depreciation, accrue salaries and wages, and accrue income taxes. Entry (e) closes the merchandising accounts and transfers the balance to cost of goods sold. Along with the other four adjusting entries, this entry will eventually be entered in the general journal. Entry (e) in journal form follows:

Dec. 31   Merchandise Inventory, December 31   18,000
           Cost of Goods Sold   60,000
           Purchase Returns and Allowances   1,800
           Purchase Discounts   3,700
               Merchandise Inventory, January 1   15,000
               Purchases   65,000
               Transportation-in   3,500
           To close merchandising accounts and transfer balance to Cost
           of Goods Sold.

Assets   =   Liabilities   +   Owners' Equity
+ 18,000   − 60,000
− 15,000   − 1,800
                                            − 3,700
                                            + 65,000
                                            + 3,500

Note the two entries to Merchandise Inventory. The debit establishes $18,000 as the ending inventory on the balance sheet, and the credit of $15,000 removes the beginning inventory from the records. On the work sheet, cost of goods sold of $60,000 is carried forward to the Adjusted Trial Balance and also to the Income Statement Debit column. To recap, the first two figures in this entry represent the

EXHIBIT 5-20 Alternative Work Sheet Procedure

TABOR HARDWARE STORES
WORK SHEET
FOR THE YEAR ENDED DECEMBER 31, 1995

ACCOUNT TITLES	UNADJUSTED TRIAL BALANCE DEBIT	UNADJUSTED TRIAL BALANCE CREDIT	ADJUSTING ENTRIES DEBIT	ADJUSTING ENTRIES CREDIT	ADJUSTED TRIAL BALANCE DEBIT	ADJUSTED TRIAL BALANCE CREDIT	INCOME STATEMENT DEBIT	INCOME STATEMENT CREDIT	BALANCE SHEET DEBIT	BALANCE SHEET CREDIT
Cash	8,590				8,590				8,590	
Accounts receivable	27,400				27,400				27,400	
Prepaid insurance	10,000			(a) 6,000	4,000				4,000	
Merchandise inventory	15,000		(e) 18,000	(e) 15,000	18,000				18,000	
Land	125,000				125,000				125,000	
Buildings and equipment	250,000				250,000				250,000	
Accumulated depreciation		40,000		(b) 10,000		50,000				50,000
Accounts payable		18,740				18,740				18,740
Capital stock		200,000				200,000				200,000
Retained earnings		154,350				154,350				154,350
Dividends	2,500				2,500				2,500	
Sales revenue		103,500				103,500		103,500		
Sales returns and allowances	2,000				2,000		2,000			
Sales discounts	1,500				1,500		1,500			
Purchases	65,000			(e) 65,000						
Purchase returns and allowances		1,800	(e) 1,800							
Purchase discounts		3,700	(e) 3,700							
Transportation-in	3,500			(e) 3,500						
Salaries and wages expense—selling	4,000		(c) 1,100		5,100		5,100			
Salaries and wages expense—admin.	3,300		(c) 600		3,900		3,900			
Advertising expense	3,400				3,400		3,400			
Utilities expense	900				900		900			
	522,090	522,090								
Insurance expense			(a) 6,000		6,000		6,000			
Depreciation expense			(b) 10,000		10,000		10,000			
Salaries and wages payable				(c) 1,700		1,700				1,700
Income tax expense			(d) 4,280		4,280		4,280			
Income tax payable				(d) 4,280		4,280				4,280
Cost of goods sold			(e) 60,000		60,000		60,000			
			105,480	105,480	532,570	532,570	97,080	103,500	435,490	429,070
Net income							6,420			6,420
							103,500	103,500	435,490	435,490

distribution of costs between ending inventory and cost of goods sold. The other figures make up the pool of costs or simply the cost of goods available for sale.

Because the merchandising accounts have been closed in an adjusting entry, they will not be involved in the closing entries. The first closing entry follows:

Dec. 31   Sales Revenue   103,500
            Income Summary   103,500
            To close Sales Revenue to Income Summary.

> **Assets = Liabilities + Owners' Equity**
>   −103,500
>   +103,500

The second closing entry removes the balance from all the income statement accounts with debit balances, including the Cost of Goods Sold account that was created in the adjusting entry:

Dec. 31   Income Summary   97,080

Sales Returns and Allowances	2,000	
Sales Discounts	1,500	
Salaries and Wages Expense—Selling	5,100	⎫
Salaries and Wages Expense—Administrative	3,900	⎪
Advertising Expense	3,400	⎪
Utilities Expense	900	⎬ 93,580
Insurance Expense	6,000	⎪
Depreciation Expense	10,000	⎪
Income Tax Expense	4,280	⎪
Cost of Goods Sold	60,000	⎭

            To close accounts with debit balances to Income Summary.

> **Assets = Liabilities + Owners' Equity**
>   −97,080
>   + 2,000
>   + 1,500
>   +93,580

Note that the debit to Income Summary is the same as the Income Statement Debit column subtotal on the work sheet. The balance of $6,420 in Income Summary is now transferred to Retained Earnings in the third closing entry:

Dec. 31   Income Summary   6,420
            Retained Earnings   6,420
            To close the Income Summary account to Retained Earnings.

> **Assets = Liabilities + Owners' Equity**
>   −6,420
>   +6,420

The fourth and final entry closes the Dividends account and reduces Retained Earnings accordingly:

Dec. 31   Retained Earnings   2,500
            Dividends   2,500
            To close Dividends to Retained Earnings.

> **Assets = Liabilities + Owners' Equity**
>   −2,500
>   +2,500

CHAPTER HIGHLIGHTS

1. **(LO 1)** Merchandise is inventory purchased in finished form and held for resale. Both wholesalers and retailers sell merchandise. Sales revenue is a representation of the inflow of assets from the sale of merchandise during the period.

2. **(LO 1)** Two deductions are made from sales revenue on the income statement. Sales returns and allowances and sales discounts are both subtracted from sales revenue to arrive at net sales. Sales discounts appears on the income statement only if a company uses the gross method. If the net method is used, all sales are recorded net of the discount. Under this method, Sales Discounts Lost is credited if a customer pays the full amount after the end of the discount period.

3. **(LO 2)** A perpetual inventory system requires the updating of the Inventory account at the time of each purchase and each sale of merchandise. With the periodic system, the Inventory account is updated only at the end of the year. Separate accounts are used during the period to record purchases, purchase returns and allowances, purchase discounts, and transportation-in. The periodic system relies on a count of the inventory on the last day of the period to determine ending inventory.

4. **(LO 3)** Cost of goods sold is recognized as an expense under the matching principle. It represents the cost associated with the merchandise sold during the period and is matched with the revenue of the period.

5. **(LO 3)** The purchases of the period are reduced by purchase returns and allowances and by purchase discounts. Any freight costs paid to acquire the merchandise, called *transportation-in,* are added. The result, cost of goods purchased, is added to the beginning inventory to determine cost of goods available for sale. Cost of goods sold is found by deducting ending inventory from cost of goods available for sale.

6. **(LO 3)** Either the gross method or the net method is used to record purchase discounts. The account Purchase Discounts is used only with the gross method to record discounts taken. The account Purchase Discounts Lost is used with the net method to record the payment of an account after the discount period.

7. **(LO 3)** *FOB destination point* means that the seller is responsible for the cost of delivering the merchandise to the buyer. Title to the goods does not transfer to the buyer until the buyer receives the merchandise from the carrier. *FOB shipping point* means that the buyer pays shipping costs. Title to the goods transfers to the buyer as soon as the seller turns them over to the carrier.

8. **(LO 4)** The purpose of an internal control system is to provide assurance that overall company objectives are met. Specifically, accounting controls are designed to safeguard the entity's assets and provide the company with reliable accounting records. Management has the primary responsibility for the reliability of the financial statements. Many companies employ a full-time internal audit staff to monitor and evaluate the internal control system.

9. **(LO 5)** Segregation of duties is the most fundamental of all internal control procedures. Possession of assets must be kept separate from the record-keeping function. Other important control procedures include a system of independent verifications, proper authorizations, adequate safeguards for assets and their records, independent review and appraisal of the accounting system, and the design and use of business documents.

10. **(LO 5)** Control over cash requires that all receipts be deposited intact on a daily basis and that all disbursements be made by check. Control procedures are important for cash received over the counter as well as for cash received in the mail. Any material amount in the Cash Over and Short account at the end of the period should be investigated.

11. **(LO 6)** Business documents play a vital role in various activities of the business such as the purchase of merchandise. The requesting department fills out a purchase requisition form and sends it to the purchasing department. The purchasing department uses the requisition to complete a purchase order, which it sends to the supplier. The supplier mails an invoice to the buyer's accounting department. The accounting department also gets a receiving report from the warehouse to indicate the quantity and condition of the goods delivered. The accounting department fills out an invoice approval form, which it sends with the invoice to the finance department, which uses them as the basis for preparing and sending a check to the supplier.

12. **(LO 7, 8)** Merchandisers use the same accounting procedures at the end of the period that service businesses employ. These procedures include the use of a work sheet and closing entries. In addition, if the merchandiser uses the periodic system, inventory must be counted. (Appendix 5A)

KEY TERMS QUIZ

Because of the large number of terms introduced in this chapter, there are two key terms quizzes. Select from the following list of key terms used in the chapter and fill in the appropriate blank to the left of each description. The solution appears at the end of the chapter.

Quiz 1: Merchandise Accounting

Net sales

Sales Returns and Allowances

Quantity discount

Gross method

Cost of goods sold

Perpetual system

Transportation-in

Purchases

Purchase Discounts

Trade discount

Sales Discounts

Net method

Cost of goods available for sale

Periodic system

Purchase Returns and Allowances

FOB destination point

FOB shipping point

_____   1. A reduction in selling price for buying a large number of units of a product.

_____   2. The contra revenue account used to record both refunds to customers and reductions of their accounts.

_____   3. The recording of either a purchase or a sale at the full amount less the applicable discount for early payment.

_____   4. The adjunct account used to record freight costs paid by the buyer.

_____   5. A reduction in selling price offered to a special class of customers.

_____   6. The system in which the Inventory account is increased at the time of each purchase of merchandise and decreased at the time of each sale.

_____   7. The contra purchases account used in a periodic inventory system when a refund is received from a supplier or a reduction given in the balance owed to the supplier.

_____   8. The contra revenue account used to record discounts given customers for early payment of their accounts.

_____   9. Terms that require the seller to pay for the cost of shipping the merchandise to the buyer.

_____   10. Terms that require the buyer to pay the shipping costs.

_____   11. The recording of either a purchase or sale at the full amount, before deducting any discount for early payment.

_____   12. The system in which the Inventory account is updated only at the end of the period.

_____   13. Beginning inventory plus cost of goods purchased.

_____   14. The contra purchases account used to record reductions in purchase price for early payment to the supplier.

_____ 15. The account used in a periodic inventory system to record acquisitions of merchandise.

_____ 16. Sales revenue less sales returns and allowances and sales discounts.

_____ 17. Cost of goods available for sale minus ending inventory.

Quiz 2: Internal Control

Internal control system   Internal audit staff
Report of management   Audit committee
Board of directors   Internal control structure
Foreign Corrupt Practices Act   Accounting controls
Administrative controls   Purchase requisition form
Accounting system   Invoice
Purchase order   Invoice approval form
Blind receiving report

_____ 1. The form sent by the seller to the buyer as evidence of a sale.

_____ 2. The group composed of key officers of a corporation and outside members responsible for the general oversight of the affairs of the entity.

_____ 3. The methods and records used to accurately report an entity's transactions and to maintain accountability for its assets and liabilities.

_____ 4. A subset of the board of directors that acts as a direct contact between the stockholders and the independent accounting firm.

_____ 5. Procedures concerned with safeguarding the assets or the reliability of the financial statements.

_____ 6. The form a department uses to initiate a request to order merchandise.

_____ 7. A form the accounting department uses before making payment to document the accuracy of all the information about a purchase.

_____ 8. A written statement in the annual report indicating the responsibility of management for the financial statements.

_____ 9. The policies and procedures established to provide assurance that entity objectives are achieved.

_____ 10. A form used by the receiving department to account for the quantity and condition of merchandise received from a supplier.

_____ 11. Legislation intended to increase the accountability of management for accurate records and reliable financial statements.

_____ 12. Procedures concerned with efficient operation of the business and adherence to managerial policies.

_____ 13. The form sent by the purchasing department to the supplier.

_____ 14. The department responsible for monitoring and evaluating the internal control system.

_____ 15. Policies and procedures necessary to ensure the safeguarding of an entity's assets, the reliability of its accounting records, and the accomplishment of overall company objectives.

ALTERNATE TERMS

GROSS MARGIN Gross profit.

INVOICE Purchase invoice, sales invoice.

INVOICE APPROVAL FORM Voucher.

MERCHANDISER Wholesaler, retailer.

REPORT OF MANAGEMENT Management's report.

SALES REVENUE Sales.

TRANSPORTATION-IN Freight-in.

QUESTIONS

1. When a company gives a cash refund on returned merchandise, why doesn't it just debit Sales Revenue instead of using a contra revenue account?
2. Why are trade discounts and quantity discounts not accorded accounting recognition (the sale is simply recorded net of either of these types of discounts)?
3. What do credit terms of *3/20, n/60* mean? How valuable to the customer is the discount offered in these terms?
4. What is the difference between a periodic inventory system and a perpetual inventory system?
5. How have point-of-sale terminals improved the ability of mass merchandisers to use a perpetual inventory system?
6. In a periodic inventory system, what kind of account is Purchases? Is it an asset or an expense or neither?
7. Which method of recording discounts is being used if Purchase Discounts Lost appears on a trial balance? What is the advantage of this method?
8. Why are shipping terms, such as FOB shipping point or FOB destination point, important in deciding ownership of inventory at the end of the year?
9. How and why are transportation-in and transportation-out recorded differently?
10. Is ending inventory entered in the Income Statement Debit or Credit column when a work sheet is prepared and the periodic inventory system is used? Where else does it appear on the work sheet? (Appendix 5A)
11. How do the duties of an internal audit staff differ from those of the external auditors?
12. What is the typical composition of a board of directors of a publicly held corporation?
13. What basic internal control procedure could have prevented the following misuse of company assets? An order clerk fills out a purchase requisition for an expensive item of inventory and the receiving report when the merchandise arrives. The clerk takes the inventory home and then sends the invoice to the accounting department so that the supplier will be paid.
14. What are some of the limitations on a company's effective system of internal control?
15. What two basic procedures are essential to an effective system of internal control over cash?

16. How would you evaluate the following statement? "The only reason a company positions its cash register so that the customers can see the display is so that they feel comfortable they are being charged the correct amount for a purchase."

17. Assuming that the amount involved is not material, what is the proper disposition of the Cash Over and Short account at the end of the period?

18. Which document, a purchase order or an invoice, is the basis for recording a purchase and a corresponding liability? Explain your answer.

19. What is a blind receiving report and how does it act as a control device?

20. What is the purpose in comparing a purchase invoice with a purchase order? in comparing a receiving report with a purchase invoice?

EXERCISES

(LO 1) EXERCISE 5-1 JOURNAL ENTRIES TO RECORD SALES

Prepare the journal entries to record the following transactions on the books of Ace Corporation for March 3, 1995:

a. Sold merchandise on credit for $500 with terms of 2/10, net 30. Ace uses the net method of recording sales discounts.

b. Recorded cash sales for the day of $1,250 from the cash register tape.

c. Granted a cash refund of $135 to a customer for spoiled merchandise returned.

d. Granted a customer a credit of $190 on its outstanding bill and allowed the customer to keep a defective product.

e. Applied cash of $2,300 received through the mail to customers' accounts. All amounts received qualify for the discount for early payment.

(LO 1) EXERCISE 5-2 JOURNAL ENTRIES FOR SALES DISCOUNTS

Prepare the journal entries on the books of Rambler Corporation for the following transactions, using (a) the gross method for recording sales discounts and (b) the net method for recording sales discounts (all sales on credit are made with terms of 2/10, net 30).

June 2: Sold merchandise on credit to Huskie Corp. for $1,200.

June 4: Sold merchandise on credit to Hawkeye Company for $2,000.

June 13: Collected cash from Hawkeye Company.

June 30: Collected cash from Huskie Corp.

(LO 3) EXERCISE 5-3 MISSING AMOUNTS IN COST OF GOODS SOLD MODEL

For each of the following independent cases, fill in the missing amounts:

	CASE 1	CASE 2	CASE 3
Beginning inventory	$ (a)	$2,350	$1,890
Purchases (gross)	6,230	5,720	(e)
Purchase returns and allowances	470	800	550
Purchase discounts	200	(c)	310
Transportation-in	150	500	420
Cost of goods available for sale	7,110	(d)	8,790
Ending inventory	(b)	1,750	1,200
Cost of goods sold	5,220	5,570	(f)

(LO 3) EXERCISE 5-4 JOURNAL ENTRIES FOR PURCHASE DISCOUNTS

Prepare the journal entries on the books of Buffalo Corporation for the following transactions, using (a) the gross method for recording purchase discounts and (b) the net method for recording purchase discounts (all purchases on credit are made with terms of 1/10, net 30, and Buffalo uses the periodic system of inventory):

July   3: Purchased merchandise on credit from Wildcat Corp. for $3,500.

July   6: Purchased merchandise on credit from Cyclone Company for $7,000.

July   12: Paid amount owed to Wildcat Corp.

August 5: Paid amount owed to Cyclone Company.

(LO 3) EXERCISE 5-5 JOURNAL ENTRIES FOR PURCHASES—PERIODIC SYSTEM

Prepare journal entries for the following transactions entered into by Wolverine Corporation (the net method is used to record purchase discounts):

March 3: Purchased merchandise from Spartan Corp. for $2,500 with terms of 2/10, net/30. Shipping costs of $250 were paid to Neverlate Transit Company.

March 7: Purchased merchandise from Boilermaker Company for $1,400 with terms of net/30.

March 12: Paid amount owed to Spartan Corp.

March 15: Received a credit of $500 on defective merchandise purchased from Boilermaker Company. The merchandise was kept.

March 18: Purchased merchandise from Gopher Corp. for $1,600 with terms of 2/10, net 30.

March 22: Received a credit of $400 from Gopher Corp. for spoiled merchandise returned to them. This is the amount of credit exclusive of any discount.

April   6: Paid amount owed to Boilermaker Company.

April 18: Paid amount owed to Gopher Corp.

(LO 3) EXERCISE 5-6 SHIPPING TERMS AND TRANSFER OF TITLE

On December 23, 1995, Butler Wholesalers ships merchandise to Beaman Retailers with terms of FOB destination point. The merchandise arrives at Beaman's warehouse on January 3, 1996.

■ REQUIRED

1. Identify who pays to ship the merchandise.

2. Determine whether the inventory should be included as an asset on Beaman's December 31, 1995, balance sheet. Should the sale be included on Butler's 1995 income statement?

3. Explain how your answers to part 2 would have been different if the terms of shipment had been FOB shipping point.

(LO 5) EXERCISE 5-7 INTERNAL CONTROL

The university drama club is planning a raffle. The president overheard you talking about internal control to another accounting student, so she has asked you to set up some guidelines to "be sure" that all money collected for the raffle is accounted for by the club.

■ REQUIRED

1. Describe guidelines that the club should follow to achieve an acceptable level of internal control.

2. Comment on the president's request that she "be sure" all money is collected and recorded.

(LO 5) EXERCISE 5-8 SEGREGATION OF DUTIES

The following tasks are performed by three employees, each of whom is capable of performing all of them. Do not concern yourself with the time required to perform the tasks but with the need to provide for segregation of duties. Assign the duties by using a check mark to indicate which employee should perform each task. Remember that you may assign any one of the tasks to any of the employees.

		EMPLOYEE	
TASK	MARY	SUE	JOHN
Prepare invoices			
Mail invoices			
Pick up mail from post office			
Open mail, separate checks			
List checks on deposit slip in triplicate			
Post payment to customer's account			
Deposit checks			
Prepare monthly schedule of accounts receivable			
Reconcile bank statements			

(LO 8) EXERCISE 5-9 CLOSING ENTRIES FROM A TRIAL BALANCE (APPENDIX 5A)

Using the adjusted trial balance shown below for Windsor Corporation, prepare the appropriate journal entries to close the books at the end of the period (a count of the ending inventory indicates a balance of $12,600):

	DEBITS	CREDITS
Cash	$ 6,230	$
Accounts receivable	12,300	
Prepaid rent	2,400	
Merchandise inventory	15,230	
Land	20,000	
Buildings and equipment	40,000	
Accumulated depreciation		15,000
Accounts payable		11,140
Capital stock		50,000
Retained earnings		8,860
Dividends	5,000	
Sales revenue		90,400
Sales returns and allowances	3,200	
Sales discounts	800	
Purchases	55,200	
Purchase returns and allowances		2,550
Transportation-in	5,400	
Salaries and wages expense	4,890	
Depreciation expense	2,500	
Rent expense	570	
Income tax expense	4,230	
Totals	$177,950	$177,950

MULTI-CONCEPT EXERCISES

(LO 1, 3) EXERCISE 5-10 INCOME STATEMENT FOR A MERCHANDISER

Fill in the missing amounts in the following income statement for Marshfields Department Store, Inc.:

Sales revenue		$125,600	
Less: Sales returns and allowances		(a) ?	
Net sales			$122,040
Cost of goods sold:			
Beginning inventory		23,400	
Purchases	(b) ?		
Less: Purchase discounts	1,300		
Net purchases	74,600		
Add: Transportation-in	6,550		
Cost of goods purchased		81,150	
Cost of goods available for sale		104,550	
Less: Ending inventory		(d) ?	
Cost of goods sold			(c) ?
Gross margin			38,600
Operating expenses			(e) ?
Income before tax			26,300
Income tax expense			10,300
Net income			$ 16,000

(LO 1, 3, 8) EXERCISE 5-11 CLOSING ENTRIES FOR A MERCHANDISER (APPENDIX 5A)

The following data are available from two similar companies, both in their first month of business. One uses the net method for recording sales and purchases, the other uses the gross method.

	ALPHA CO.	BETA CO.
Sales	$10,000	$9,800
Sales discounts	180	
Sales returns and allowances	500	500
Sales discounts lost		20
Purchases	8,500	8,500
Purchases returns and allowances	50	50
Transportation-in	450	450
Ending inventory	4,000	4,000

REQUIRED

1. Which company uses the net method and which uses the gross method for recording sales discounts? Explain your answer.

2. Prepare each company's first month income statement.

3. Prepare the closing entries for each company.

PROBLEMS

(LO 1) PROBLEM 5-1 TRADE DISCOUNTS

Keisling, Inc., offers the following discounts to customers who purchase large quantities:

10% discount: 10–25 units

20% discount: >25 units

Mr. Keisling, the president, would like to record all sales at the list price and record the discount as an expense.

■ **REQUIRED**
1. Explain to Mr. Keisling why trade discounts do not enter into the accounting records.

2. Even though trade discounts do not enter into the accounting records, is it still important to have some record of these? Explain your answer.

(LO 5) PROBLEM 5-2 INTERNAL CONTROL PROCEDURES

You are opening a summer business, a chain of three drive-thru snow cone stands. You have hired other college students to work and have purchased a cash register with locked-in tapes. You retain one key and the other is available to the lead person on each shift.

■ **REQUIRED**
1. Write a list of the procedures for all employees to follow when ringing up sales and giving change.

2. Write a list of the procedures for the lead person to follow in closing out at the end of the day. Be as specific as you can so employees will have few if any questions.

3. What is your main concern in the design of internal control for the snow cone stands? How did you address that concern? Be specific.

(LO 6) PROBLEM 5-3 THE DESIGN OF INTERNAL CONTROL DOCUMENTS

Motel $24.99 has purchased a large warehouse to store all supplies used by housekeeping departments in the company's expanding chain of motels. In the past, each motel bought supplies from local distributors and paid for the supplies from cash receipts.

■ **REQUIRED**
1. Name some potential problems with the old system.

2. Design a purchase requisition form and a receiving report to be used by the housekeeping departments and the warehouse. Indicate how many copies of each form should be used and who should receive each copy.

(LO 7) PROBLEM 5-4 COMPLETION OF A WORK SHEET FOR A MERCHANDISER (APPENDIX 5A)

Marshall Merchandise, Inc., provides the following unadjusted trial balance and additional information:

MARSHALL MERCHANDISE, INC.
WORK SHEET
FOR THE YEAR ENDED DECEMBER 31, 1995

ACCOUNT TITLES	DEBITS	CREDITS
Cash	$ 6,300	
Accounts receivable	2,000	
Office supplies	540	
Merchandise inventory	15,000	
Land	40,500	
Buildings and fixtures	78,000	
Accumulated depreciation		$ 23,850
Accounts payable		1,800
Capital stock		100,000
Retained earnings		14,520
Sales revenue		60,508
Sales discounts	1,008	
Purchases	29,780	
Purchase discounts		908
Transportation-in	2,458	
Salaries expense	19,000	
Advertising expense	5,800	
Utilities expense	1,200	
	201,586	201,586

Additional Data

Ending inventory, $14,700.

Depreciation expense, $2,300.

Accrued salaries, $1,200.

Supplies on hand, $75.

Ignore taxes.

REQUIRED

1. Enter the information above in the first two columns of a 10-column work sheet.

2. Enter the adjustments in the appropriate columns of the work sheet.

3. Complete the remaining columns of the work sheet, using the approach illustrated in Exhibit 5-17 to report beginning and ending inventory on the work sheet.

4. Compare the amounts of beginning and ending inventory. From this comparison, determine the amount by which cost of goods sold exceeded purchases of the period or by how much purchases exceeded cost of goods sold.

MULTI-CONCEPT PROBLEMS

(LO 1, 2, 3) PROBLEM 5-5 JOURNAL ENTRIES FOR A MERCHANDISER

The following transactions were entered into by West Coast Tires, Inc., during the month of June:

June 2:   Purchased 1,000 tires at a cost of $60 per tire. Terms of payment are 1/10, net 45.

June 4: Paid trucking firm $1,200 to ship the tires purchased on June 2.

June 5: Purchased 600 tires at a cost of $60 per tire. Terms of payment are 2/10, net 30.

June 6: Paid trucking firm $800 to ship the tires purchased on June 5.

June 7: Returned 150 of the tires purchased on June 2 because they were defective. Received a credit on open account from the seller.

June 11: Paid for tires purchased on June 2.

June 13: Sold 700 tires from those purchased on June 2. The selling price was $90 per tire. Terms are 1/10, net 30.

June 22: Received cash from sale of tires on June 13.

June 30: Paid for tires purchased on June 5.

■ REQUIRED

1. Prepare the journal entries to record these transactions on the books of West Coast Tires, Inc. The company uses the net method of recording purchase discounts and the gross method of recording sales discounts. West Coast employs a periodic inventory system.

2. Given the nature of its product, do you think it would be feasible for West Coast to use a perpetual inventory system? Why? If so, what advantages would accrue to the company by using a perpetual system?

(LO 1, 3) PROBLEM 5-6 JOURNAL ENTRIES AND PARTIAL INCOME STATEMENT FOR A MERCHANDISER

Weekend Wonders, Inc., operates a chain of discount hardware stores. The company uses a periodic inventory system. Inventory on hand on June 1, 1995, amounts to $25,670 and on June 30, 1995, it is $30,200. The company uses the net method to record purchase discounts and the gross method to record sales discounts. The following transactions take place during the month of June:

a. Purchased merchandise from suppliers at a cost of $80,000 with credit terms of 2/10, net 30.

b. Paid freight costs of $4,250 to the common carrier for merchandise purchased.

c. Returned defective merchandise to suppliers and received credits of $2,300, the amount of credit before taking into account any purchase discounts.

d. Realized $92,000 in sales for the month, of which $68,000 is on credit and the remainder are cash sales. The credit sales are made with terms of 2/10, net 45.

e. Gave sales returns and allowances on credit sales of $4,000 during the month.

f. Made cash payments of $62,000 to suppliers for earlier purchases on account. All amounts paid during the month are made within the discount period.

g. Received $56,000 in cash collections on account from customers. All amounts received during the month are within the discount period.

■ REQUIRED

1. Prepare the journal entries on the books of Weekend Wonders, Inc., to record each of the transactions.

2. Prepare a partial income statement for the month of June. The last line on the statement should be gross margin.

3. Assume that Weekend Wonders decides as a matter of policy to forgo the discount for early payment on purchases (credit terms are 2/10, net 30). What return would Weekend Wonders need to earn on the money it invests by not paying early to justify this decision? Provide any necessary calculations to support your answer.

(LO 1, 2, 3) PROBLEM 5-7 PURCHASES AND SALES OF MERCHANDISE, CASH FLOWS

On-A-Roll, a bike shop, opened for business on April 1. It uses a periodic inventory system and records purchases at gross. The following transactions occurred during the first month of business:

April 1: Purchased five units from Duhan, Co. for $500 with terms 3/10, net 30, FOB destination.

April 10: Paid for the April 1 purchase.

April 15: Sold one unit for $200 cash.

April 18: Purchased 10 more units from Clinton, Inc., for $900, with terms 3/10, net/30, FOB destination.

April 25: Sold three units for $200 each, cash.

April 28: Paid for April 18 purchase.

1. Prepare the journal entries to record the April transactions.

2. Determine the income for the month of April. On-A-Roll paid $100 for rent and $50 for miscellaneous expenses during April. Ending inventory is $967.

3. Assuming that the only transactions during April are given (including rent and miscellaneous expenses), compute net cash flow from operating activities.

4. Explain why cash outflow is so much larger than expenses on the income statement.

■ REQUIRED

(LO 4, 5) PROBLEM 5-8 INTERNAL CONTROL

At Morris Mart, Inc., all sales are on account. Mary Morris-Manning is responsible for mailing invoices to customers, recording the amount billed, opening mail, and recording the payment. Mary is very devoted to the family business and never takes off more than one or two days for a long weekend. The customers know Mary and sometimes send personal notes with their payments. Another clerk handles all aspects of accounts payable. Mary's brother, who is president of Morris Mart, has hired an accountant to help with expansion.

1. List some problems with the current accounts receivable system.

2. What suggestions would you make to improve internal control?

3. How would you explain to Mary that she personally is not the problem?

■ REQUIRED

(LO 1, 3, 7, 8) PROBLEM 5-9 CLOSING ENTRIES FROM WORK SHEET, FINANCIAL STATEMENTS (APPENDIX 5A)

Following are the last four columns of a 10-column work sheet for Stone, Inc., for the year ended 12/31/95.

ACCOUNT TITLES	INCOME STATEMENT		BALANCE SHEET	
	DEBITS	CREDITS	DEBITS	CREDITS
Cash			$ 590	
Accounts receivable			2,359	
Inventory	$ 6,400	$ 7,500	7,500	
Interest receivable			100	
Buildings and equipment, net			55,550	
Land			20,000	
Capital stock				$ 50,000
Retained earnings				32,550
Dividends			6,000	
Sales		84,364		
Sales returns	780			
Purchases	40,200			
Purchase discounts		800		
Transportation-in	375			
Salaries expense	25,600			
Advertising expense	4,510			
Utilities expense	3,600			
Depreciation expense	2,300			
Salaries payable				650
Income tax expense	3,200			
Income tax payable				3,200

■ REQUIRED

1. Determine cost of goods sold for 1995.

2. Determine net income for 1995.

3. Prepare the closing entries for Stone, Inc. using the first approach illustrated in Appendix 5A rather than the alternative procedure to close inventory.

4. Prepare a balance sheet dated December 31, 1995.

5. Determine the balance in retained earnings on *January 1,* 1995.

ALTERNATE PROBLEMS

(LO 1) PROBLEM 5-1A DISCOUNTS

Austin, Inc., a recording distributor, would like to offer discounts to customers who purchase large quantities. Austin is unsure about the terms to use and how to account for discounts extended to customers. The company also wants to consider a cash discount for early payment by customers. Austin expects sales of about $3 million this year. All sales are on account to about 100 different outlets located within 500 miles of the warehouse. Deliveries are made by Austin's own trucks and cost about $25 per 100 miles driven. A full truck will hold 1,000 units.

■ REQUIRED

1. Explain the difference between a quantity discount and a discount for early payment. How is each accounted for in the accounting records? What are the reasons to extend the different discounts to customers?

2. Set up a quantity discount plan and a sales discount plan for Austin to extend to customers. Be able to explain why you chose your bases for the discounts and the amount of discounts.

(LO 5) PROBLEM 5-2A INTERNAL CONTROL PROCEDURES

The loan department in a bank is subject to regulation. Internal auditors work for the bank to ensure that the loan department complies with requirements. The internal auditors must verify that each car loan file has a note signed by the maker, verification of insurance, and a title issued by the state that names the bank as co-owner.

1. Explain why the bank and the regulatory agency are concerned with these documents.   ■ REQUIRED

2. Describe the internal control procedures that should be in place to ensure that these documents are obtained and safeguarded.

(LO 6) PROBLEM 5-3A THE DESIGN OF INTERNAL CONTROL DOCUMENTS

Tiger's Group is a newly formed company that produces and sells children's movies about an imaginary character. The movies are in such great demand that they are shipped to retail outlets as soon as they are produced. The company must pay a royalty to several actors for each movie that is sold to retail outlets.

1. Describe some internal control features that should be in place to ensure that all   ■ REQUIRED royalties are paid to the actors.

2. Design the shipping form that Tiger's Group should use for the movies. Be sure to include authorizations and indicate the number of copies and routing of the copies.

(LO 7) PROBLEM 5-4A COMPLETION OF THE WORK SHEET OF A MERCHANDISER (APPENDIX 5A)

Gallagher Art Supply, Inc., provides the following unadjusted trial balance and additional information.

GALLAGHER ART SUPPLY, INC.
WORK SHEET
FOR THE YEAR ENDED DECEMBER 31, 1995

ACCOUNT TITLES	DEBITS	CREDITS
Cash	7,200	
Accounts receivable	34,890	
Office supplies	865	
Merchandise inventory	45,430	
Unearned revenue		17,900
Accounts payable		23,900
Capital stock		60,000
Retained earnings		14,520
Sales revenue		60,508
Purchases	55,650	
Purchase discounts		1,113
Transportation-in	2,458	
Salaries expense	24,448	
Advertising expense	5,800	
Utilities expense	1,200	
	177,941	177,941

Additional Data

Ending inventory, $42,621.

Supplies on hand, $65.

Revenue unearned to date is $11,900.

Ignore taxes.

■ REQUIRED

1. Enter the unadjusted trial balance in the first two columns of a 10-column work sheet.

2. Enter the adjusting entries in the next two columns of the work sheet.

3. Complete the remaining columns of the work sheet, using the approach illustrated in Exhibit 5-17 to report beginning and ending inventory on the work sheet.

4. Compare the amounts of beginning and ending inventory. From this comparison, determine the amount by which cost of good sold exceeded purchases of the period or by which purchases exceeded cost of goods sold.

ALTERNATE MULTI-CONCEPT PROBLEMS

(LO 1, 3) PROBLEM 5-5A JOURNAL ENTRIES FOR A MERCHANDISER

The following transactions were entered into by Southern Sausage, Inc., during the month of July:

July 2: Purchased 1,000 pounds of sausage at a cost of $3 per pound. Terms of payment are 2/10, net 30.

July 4: Paid trucking firm $500 to ship the sausage purchased on July 2.

July 5: Purchased 600 pounds of sausage at a cost of $3 per pound. Terms of payment are 2/10, net 45.

July 6: Paid trucking firm $300 to ship the sausage purchased on July 5.

July 7: Returned 100 pounds of the sausage purchased on July 2 due to expired dates on some packages. Received a credit on open account from the seller.

July 11: Paid for sausage purchased on July 2.

July 13: Sold 1,200 pounds of sausage from those purchased on July 2 and July 5. The selling price was $7 per pound, cash.

July 30: Paid for sausage purchased on July 5.

■ REQUIRED

1. Prepare the journal entries to record these transactions on the books of Southern Sausage, Inc. The company uses the net method of recording purchase discounts. Southern employs a periodic inventory system.

2. Southern assumes a $3 per pound cost of inventory when planning profit and setting prices. Is this accurate? Explain.

(LO 1, 3) PROBLEM 5-6A JOURNAL ENTRIES AND PARTIAL INCOME STATEMENT FOR A MERCHANDISER

Toppsie Turn, Inc., operates a chain of T-shirt stores. The company uses a periodic inventory system. Inventories on hand on June 1 and June 30, 1995, amount to $12,840. The company uses the net method to record purchase discounts. The following transactions take place during the month of June:

a. Purchased merchandise from suppliers at a cost of $62,000 with credit terms of 2/10, net 30.

b. Paid freight cost of $3,400 to the common carrier for merchandise purchased.

c. Realized $124,000 of sales for the month, all of which are cash sales.

d. Paid for merchandise purchased during the month within the discount period.

e. Accepted $500 in returned merchandise during the month.

1. Prepare the journal entries on the books of Toppsie Turn, Inc., to record each of the transactions. ■ REQUIRED

2. Determine the gross margin that Toppsie Turn would report on the income statement for the month of June.

3. Toppsie is thinking about extending credit to some of its major customers to encourage credit customers to pay quickly. Toppsie expects existing sales will increase by 10% and at the new sales level, 60% of sales will be credit sales. Should Toppsie extend credit terms of 2/10, net 30? Explain your answer.

(LO 1, 2, 3) PROBLEM 5-7A PURCHASES AND SALES OF MERCHANDISE

Appleton Corp., a ski shop, opened for business on October 1. It uses a periodic inventory system and records purchases at net. The following transactions occurred during the first month of business:

October 1: Purchased three units from Oshkosh, Inc., for $249, terms 2/10, net 30, FOB destination.

October 10: Paid for the October 1 purchase.

October 15: Sold one unit for $200 cash.

October 18: Purchased 10 more units from Wausau Company for $800, with terms 2/10, net/30, FOB destination.

October 25: Sold three units for $200 each, cash.

October 30: Paid for October 18 purchase.

1. Prepare the journal entries to record the October transactions. ■ REQUIRED

2. Determine the number of units on hand on October 31.

3. If Appleton started the month with $2,000, determine its balance in cash at the end of the month, assuming that these are the only transactions that occurred during October. Why has the cash balance decreased when the company reported a profit?

(LO 4, 5) PROBLEM 5-8A INTERNAL CONTROL

Abbott, Inc., is expanding and needs to hire more personnel in the accounting office. Barbara Barker, the chief accounting clerk, knew that her cousin Cheryl was looking for a job. Barbara and Cheryl are also roommates. Barbara offered Cheryl a job as her assistant. Barbara will be responsible for Cheryl's performance reviews and training.

1. List some problems with the proposed personnel situations in the accounting department. ■ REQUIRED

2. Explain why accountants are concerned with hiring of personnel. What suggestions would you make to improve internal control at Abbott?

3. How would you explain to Barbara and Cheryl that they personally are not the problem?

(LO 7, 8) PROBLEM 5-9A CLOSING ENTRIES FROM WORK SHEET (APPENDIX 5A)

Following are the last four columns of a 10-column work sheet for Smith, Inc., for the year ended December 31, 1995.

ACCOUNT TITLES	INCOME STATEMENT		BALANCE SHEET	
	DEBITS	CREDITS	DEBITS	CREDITS
Cash			$22,340	
Accounts receivable			56,359	
Inventory	$ 6,400	$ 5,900	5,900	
Wages payable				$ 120
Capital stock				50,000
Retained earnings				????
Dividends			6,000	
Sales		112,768		
Sales returns	1,008			
Purchases	62,845			
Purchase discounts		1,237		
Transportation-in	375			
Wages and salaries expense	23,000			
Advertising expense	12,900			
Utilities expense	1,800			
Salaries payable				650
Income tax expense	1,450			
Income tax payable				1,450

Net income for 1995 is $10,127.

■ REQUIRED

1. Determine the balance in Retained Earnings at the beginning of the year and at the end of the year. Explain how you arrived at each of these balances.

2. Prepare the closing entries for Smith, Inc., using the first approach illustrated in Appendix 5A rather than the alternative procedure to close inventory.

CASES

READING AND INTERPRETING FINANCIAL STATEMENTS

(LO 3) CASE 5-1 READING AND INTERPRETING BEN & JERRY'S FINANCIAL STATEMENTS

Refer to the 1992 financial statements included in Ben & Jerry's annual report.

■ REQUIRED

1. Determine the amount of cost of sales for 1992.

2. Read the note below the consolidated statement of income about cost of sales. Is Ben & Jerry's a merchandiser, manufacturer, or service provider? What items that are included in Ben & Jerry's statement would not be included in the cost of sales of a merchandiser?

3. Look at the statement of cash flows. Under the operating activities, you will find an adjustment for depreciation, yet there is no mention of depreciation on the income statement. Depreciation on equipment and buildings used in the manufac-

turing process is included in cost of sales. Make a list of other expenses that you would expect to be included in Ben & Jerry's cost of sales rather than listed separately on the income statement.

(LO 4) CASE 5-2 READING AND INTERPRETING WAL-MART'S MANAGEMENT REPORT

The financial report for Wal-Mart Stores, Inc., dated January 31, 1993, includes a section on page 19 called "Responsibility for Financial Statements." Included in the section is the following:

> Management has developed and maintains a system of accounting and controls, including an extensive internal audit program, designed to provide reasonable assurance that the Company's assets are protected from improper use and that accounting records provide a reliable basis for the preparation of financial statements. This system is continually reviewed, improved, and modified in response to changing business conditions and operations and to recommendations made by the independent auditors and the internal auditors. Management believes that the accounting and control systems provide reasonable assurance that assets are safeguarded and financial information is reliable.

■REQUIRED

1. Why did management include this section and this statement in the financial report?

2. What does management mean by "assets are protected from improper use"?

3. Based on what you know about retail stores, and Wal-Mart stores in particular, list the kinds of accounting and system controls the company may have in place to safeguard assets.

MAKING FINANCIAL DECISIONS

(LO 1, 3) CASE 5-3 GROSS MARGIN FOR A MERCHANDISER

Emblems For You sells specialty sweat shirts. The purchase price is $10 per unit, plus 10% tax and shipping cost of 50¢ per unit. When the units arrive, they must be labeled at an additional cost of 75¢ per unit. Emblems purchased, received, and labeled amounted to 1,500 units, of which 750 units were sold during the month for $20 each. The controller has prepared the following income statement:

Sales	$15,000
Cost of sales ($11 × 750)	8,250
Gross margin	$ 6,750
Shipping expense	750
Labeling expense	1,125
Net income	$ 4,875

Emblem is aware that a gross margin of 40% is standard for the industry. The marketing manager believes that Emblem should lower the price because the gross margin is higher than the industry average.

■REQUIRED

1. Calculate Emblem's gross margin ratio.

2. Explain why you believe that Emblem should or should not lower its selling price.

(LO 2) CASE 5-4 USE OF A PERPETUAL INVENTORY SYSTEM

Darrell Keith is starting a new business. He would like to keep a tight control over it. Therefore, he wants to know *exactly* how much gross profit he earns on each unit he sells. Darrell has set up an elaborate numbering system to identify each item as it is purchased and then to match the item with a sales price. Each unit is assigned a number as follows:

0000-000-00-000.

a. The first four numbers represent the month and day an item was received.

b. The second three numbers are the last three numbers of the purchase order that authorized the purchase of the item.

c. The third set of two numbers is the department code assigned to different types of products.

d. The last three numbers are a chronological code assigned to units as they are received during a given day.

■ REQUIRED

1. Write a short memo to Darrell explaining the benefits and costs involved in a perpetual inventory system in conjunction with his quest to know *exactly* how much he will earn on each unit.

2. Comment on Darrell's inventory system, assuming that he is selling (a) automobiles or (b) trees, shrubs, and plants.

ACCOUNTING AND ETHICS: WHAT WOULD YOU DO?

(LO 1) CASE 5-5 SALES RETURNS AND ALLOWANCES

You are the controller for a large chain of discount merchandise stores. You receive a memorandum from the sales manager for the Midwestern region in which he raises an issue regarding the proper treatment of sales returns. The manager urges you to discontinue the "silly practice" of debiting Sales Returns and Allowances each time a customer returns a product. In the manager's mind, this is a waste of time and unduly complicates the financial statements. The manager recommends that "things could be kept a lot simpler by just debiting Sales Revenue when a product is returned."

■ REQUIRED

1. What do you think the sales manager's *motivation* might be for writing you the memo? Is it because he believes that the present practice is a waste of time and unduly complicates the financial statements?

2. Do you agree with the sales manager's recommendation? Explain why you agree or disagree.

3. Write a brief memo to the sales manager outlining your position on this matter.

(LO 4, 5) CASE 5-6 CASH RECEIPTS IN A BOOKSTORE

You were recently hired by a large retail bookstore chain. Your training involved spending a week at the largest and most profitable store in the district. The store manager assigned the head cashier to train you on the cash register and closing procedures required by the company's home office. In the process, the head cashier instructed you to keep an envelope for cash over and short that would include cash or IOUs equal to the net amount of overages or shortages in the cash drawer. "It is impossible to balance exactly, so just put extra cash in this envelope and use the cash when you are short." You studied accounting for one semester in college and remembered your professor saying that "all deposits should be made intact, daily."

■ REQUIRED

Draft a memorandum to the store manager detailing any problems you see with the current system.

To the Student: Your instructor may assign one or more parts of the analytical software case that is designed to accompany this chapter. This multi-part case gives you a chance to work with real financial statement data using software that stimulates, guides, and hones your analytical and problem-solving skills. It was created especially to support and strengthen your understanding of the chapter's Learning Objectives.

SOLUTION TO KEY TERMS QUIZZES

Quiz 1

1. Quantity discount (p. 255)
2. Sales Returns and Allowances (p. 254)
3. Net method (p. 256)
4. Transportation-in (p. 261)
5. Trade discount (p. 254)
6. Perpetual system (p. 259)
7. Purchase Returns and Allowances (p. 262)
8. Sales Discounts (p. 256)
9. FOB destination point (p. 263)
10. FOB shipping point (p. 263)
11. Gross method (p. 256)
12. Periodic system (p. 259)
13. Cost of goods available for sale (p. 258)
14. Purchase Discounts (p. 262)
15. Purchases (p. 261)
16. Net sales (p. 253)
17. Cost of goods sold (p. 258)

Quiz 2

1. Invoice (p. 276)
2. Board of directors (p. 267)
3. Accounting system (p. 268)
4. Audit committee (p. 267)
5. Accounting controls (p. 268)
6. Purchase requisition form (p. 273)
7. Invoice approval form (p. 278)
8. Report of management (p. 266)
9. Internal control structure (p. 267)
10. Blind receiving report (p. 276)
11. Foreign Corrupt Practices Act (p. 267)
12. Administrative control (p. 268)
13. Purchase order (p. 275)
14. Internal audit staff (p. 266)
15. Internal control system (p. 265)

Focus on Financial Results

Procter & Gamble markets a broad range of laundry, cleaning, paper, beauty care, health care, food, and beverage products in more than 140 countries around the world, with such brand names as Tide, Crest, Max Factor, and Pampers. Founded more than 150 years ago, P&G generated revenues of $30 billion in fiscal 1993, up almost 4% from the prior year.

Like many consumers products companies, Procter & Gamble found itself cutting

prices to compete with "private label" brands on grocery shelves.

When P&G marks down its prices to compete with generics, there is only one way to make it up: more volume. Take a look at the company's income statement: cost of goods sold stays the same; marketing and administrative expenses stay the same—the only way to keep operating income constant with declining prices is to sell more units. This has held true for P&G until 1993 when the company decided that it would have to take a big write-off to reflect the closure of 30 manufacturing plants worldwide—a sure sign that the company is trying to become more efficient because of the newfound pressure on the price of its products.

Consolidated Statement Of Earnings

Years Ended June 30 (Millions of Dollars Except Per Share Amounts)	1993	1992	1991
Net Sales	$30,433	$29,362	$27,026
Cost of products sold	17,683	17,324	16,081
Marketing, administrative, and other expenses	9,589	9,171	8,243
Provision for restructuring (see Note #2)	2,705	—	—
Operating Income	456	2,867	2,702
Interest and other income	445	528	380
Interest expense	552	510	395
Earnings Before Income Taxes & Prior Years' Effect of Accounting Changes	349	2,885	2,687
Income taxes	80	1,013	914
Net Earnings Before Prior Years' Effect of Accounting Changes	269	1,872	1,773
Prior years' effect of accounting changes, net of tax	(925)	—	—
Net Earnings/(Loss)	$ (656)	$ 1,872	$ 1,773
Per Common Share:			
Net Earnings Before Prior Years' Effect of Accounting Changes	$ 0.25	$ 2.62	$ 2.46
Prior years' effect of accounting changes, net of tax	$(1.36)	—	—
Net Earnings/(Loss)	$(1.11)	$ 2.62	$ 2.46
Net Earnings/(Loss) Assuming Full Dilution	$(0.96)	$ 2.45	$ 2.31
Dividends	$ 1.10	$1.025	$ .975
Average Shares Outstanding (in millions)	680.4	677.4	689.5

Consolidated Statement Of Retained Earnings

Years Ended June 30 (Millions of Dollars)	1993	1992	1991
Balance at Beginning of Year	$7,810	$6,775	$6,581
Net earnings/(loss)	(656)	1,872	1,773
Dividends to shareholders			
Common	(748)	(694)	(675)
Preferred, net of applicable tax relief	(102)	(94)	(78)
Excess of cost over the stated value of common shares purchased for treasury	(56)	(49)	(826)
Balance at End of Year	$6,248	$7,810	$6,775

See accompanying Notes To Consolidated Financial Statements.

Chapter 6

Inventories and Cost of Goods Sold

LEARNING OBJECTIVES

After studying this chapter, you should be able to

1. Identify the forms of inventory held by different types of businesses and the types of costs incurred.
2. Explain the relationship between the valuation of inventory and the measurement of income.
3. Analyze the effects of an inventory error on various financial statement items.
4. Apply the inventory costing methods of specific identification, weighted average, FIFO, and LIFO using a periodic system.
5. Analyze the effects of the different costing methods on inventory, net income, income taxes, and cash flow.
6. Apply the lower of cost or market rule to the valuation of inventory.
7. Use the gross profit method to estimate inventory.
8. Use the retail inventory method to estimate inventory.
9. Explain the effects of inventory transactions on the statement of cash flows.
10. Explain the differences between a periodic and a perpetual inventory system (Appendix 6A).
11. Apply the inventory costing methods using a perpetual system (Appendix 6A).

Linkages

◯◯ A LOOK AT PREVIOUS CHAPTERS

In Chapter 5, we introduced inventory for merchandisers and examined how they account for purchases and sales of their products. We saw that companies track their inventory using one of two systems, periodic or perpetual.

◯◯ A LOOK AT THIS CHAPTER

In this chapter, we continue our examination of inventory by considering inventory costing methods. Specific identification, FIFO, LIFO, and weighted average are choices available to a company in assigning a value to inventory on the balance sheet and in determining cost of goods sold on the income statement. Other inventory topics discussed in the chapter include the lower of cost or market rule, the gross profit method, and the retail inventory method.

◯◯ A LOOK AT UPCOMING CHAPTERS

Chapter 7 concludes our look at accounting for current assets. When a company makes a sale of inventory on credit, it records an account receivable. The collection of the receivable adds to the company's cash balance. Chapter 7 looks at accounting issues for cash and receivables.

The Nature of Inventory

LO   I

Identify the forms of inventory held by different types of businesses and the types of costs incurred.

Inventory is an asset held for *resale* in the normal course of business. The distinction between inventory and an operating asset is the *intent* of the owner. For example, some of the computers that IBM owns are operating assets because they are used in various activities of the business such as the payroll and accounting functions. Many of the computers owned by IBM are inventory, however, because the company intends to sell them. This chapter is concerned with the proper valuation of inventory and the related effect on cost of goods sold.

It is important to distinguish between the *types* of inventory costs incurred and the *form* the inventory takes. Wholesalers and retailers incur a single type of cost, the *purchase price,* of the inventory they sell. They use a single account for inventory on the balance sheet titled **Merchandise Inventory.** Wholesalers and retailers buy merchandise in finished form and offer it for resale without transforming the product in any way. Because they do not use factory buildings, assembly lines, or production equipment, merchandise companies have a relatively small dollar amount in operating assets and a large amount in inventory. For example, on its January 27, 1993, balance sheet, Kmart Corporation reported merchandise inventories of more than $8.7 billion and total assets of approximately $19 billion. It is not unusual for inventories to account for nearly one-half of the total assets of a merchandise company.

The cost of inventory to a merchandiser is limited to the price paid to purchase the product, which may include such costs as taxes and transportation-in. Conversely, three distinct *types* of *costs* are incurred by a *manufacturer:* direct materials, direct labor, and manufacturing overhead. Direct materials, also called **raw materials,** are the ingredients used in making a product. The costs of direct materials used in manufacturing an automobile include the costs of steel, glass, and rubber. Direct labor consists of the amounts paid to workers to manufacture the product. The $20 per hour paid to an assembly line worker is a primary ingredient in the cost to manufacture the automobile. Manufacturing overhead includes all other costs that are related to the manufacturing process but cannot be directly matched to specific units of output. Depreciation of a factory building and the salary of a supervisor are two examples of overhead costs. Accountants have developed various allocation techniques to assign these manufacturing overhead costs to specific products.

In addition to the three types of costs incurred in a production process, the inventory of a manufacturer takes three distinct *forms.* The three forms or stages in the development of inventory are raw materials, work in process, and finished goods. Direct materials or raw materials enter a production process in which they are transformed into a finished product by the addition of direct labor and manufacturing overhead. At any point in time, including the end of an accounting period, some of the materials have entered the process and some labor costs have been incurred, but the product is not finished. The cost of unfinished products is appropriately called **work in process.** Inventory that has completed the production process and is available for sale is called **finished goods.** Manufacturers disclose the dollar amounts of each of the three forms of inventory in their annual report. For example, IBM disclosed in its 1992 annual report the following amounts, stated in millions of dollars:

Current inventories:	
Finished goods	$2,100
Work in process	6,115
Raw materials	170
Total current inventories	$8,385

Exhibit 6-1 summarizes the relationships between the types of costs incurred and the forms of inventory for different types of businesses.

Inventory Valuation and the Measurement of Income

Valuation is the major problem in accounting for inventories. Because of the additional complexities involved in valuing the inventory of a manufacturer, we will concentrate in this chapter on the valuation of *merchandise inventory*. Accounting for the inventory costs incurred by a manufacturing firm is covered in detail in management accounting textbooks.

One of the most fundamental concepts in accounting is the relationship between *asset valuation* and the *measurement of income*. Recall a point made in Chapter 4: Assets are unexpired costs, and expenses are expired costs. Thus, the value assigned to an asset on the balance sheet determines the amount eventually recognized as an expense on the income statement. For example, the amount recorded as the cost of an item of plant and equipment will dictate the amount of depreciation expense recognized on the income statement over the life of the asset. Similarly, the amount recorded as the cost of inventory determines the amount recognized as cost of goods

LO 2

Explain the relationship between the valuation of inventory and the measurement of income.

EXHIBIT 6-1   Relationships between Types of Businesses and Inventory Costs and Forms

TYPE OF BUSINESS	TYPE OF COSTS INCURRED	INVENTORY FORM
Wholesalers and retailers	Purchase costs	Merchandise inventory
Manufacturers	**Direct materials** Such as steel, glass, and rubber	**Raw materials** Materials on hand for use in production
	are combined with	
	Direct labor Wages and salaries	
	and	
	Manufacturing overhead Wages and salaries, supplies, depreciation, and other related production costs	*to create:*
		Work in process Goods partially complete as to materials, labor, and overhead
		and
		Finished goods Goods complete and ready for sale

sold on the income statement when the asset is sold. An error in assigning the proper amount to inventory on the balance sheet will affect the amount recognized as cost of goods sold on the income statement. The relationship between inventory as an asset and cost of goods sold is evident by recalling the cost of goods sold section of the income statement. Assume the following example:

Beginning inventory	$ 500
Add: Purchases	1,200
Cost of goods available for sale	$1,700
Less: Ending inventory	600
Cost of goods sold	$1,100

The amount assigned to ending inventory is deducted from cost of goods available for sale to determine cost of goods sold. If this amount is incorrect, cost of goods sold will be wrong, and, thus, the net income of the period will be in error as well.

Inventory Errors

LO 3

Analyze the effects of an inventory error on various financial statement items.

The importance of inventory valuation to the measurement of income can be illustrated by considering inventory errors. Many different types of inventory errors exist. Some errors are mathematical; for example, a bookkeeper may add a column total incorrectly. Other errors relate specifically to the physical count of inventory at year-end. For example, the count might inadvertently omit one section of a warehouse. Other errors arise from cut-off problems at year-end.

For example, assume that merchandise in transit at the end of the year is shipped FOB (free on board) shipping point. Under these shipment terms, the inventory belongs to the buyer at the time it is shipped. Because the shipment has not arrived at the end of the year, however, it cannot be included in the physical count. Unless some type of control is in place, the amount in transit may be erroneously omitted from the valuation of inventory at year-end.

Inventory errors sometimes occur when goods are held on consignment. A **consignment** is a legal arrangement in which inventory owned by one company, the consignor, is turned over to another company, the consignee, to sell. Most art galleries operate on a consignment basis. The artist agrees to split the profits with the gallery owner in exchange for having the art on display. Typically, a consignment arrangement relieves the gallery owner of taking a risk that the artwork will not be sold. During the consignment period, title to the goods remains with the consignor. The consignee acts as a selling agent for the consignor. Even though the consignor does not have physical possession of the goods at the end of the period, it must still include them in inventory on the balance sheet. Conversely, the consignee must be sure *not* to include any consigned goods in the physical count of its own merchandise at year-end.

To demonstrate the effect of an inventory error on the income statement, consider the following example. Through a scheduling error, two different inventory teams were assigned to count the inventory in the same warehouse on December 31, 1993. The correct amount of ending inventory is $250,000, but because two different teams counted the same inventory in one warehouse, the amount recorded is $300,000. The effect of this error on net income is analyzed in the left half of Exhibit 6-2.

The *overstatement* of *ending inventory* in 1993 leads to an *understatement* of the 1993 cost of goods sold *expense*. Because cost of goods sold is understated, *gross margin* for the year is *overstated*. Operating expenses are unaffected by an inventory error. Thus, *net income* is *overstated* by the same amount of overstatement of gross

EXHIBIT 6-2   Effects of Inventory Error on the Income Statement

	1993 REPORTED	1993 CORRECTED	EFFECTS OF ERROR	1994 REPORTED	1994 CORRECTED	EFFECTS OF ERROR
Sales	$1,000*	$1,000		$1,500	$1,500	
Cost of goods sold:						
Beginning inventory	200	200		**300**	**250**	$50 OS
Add: Purchases	700	700		1,100	1,100	
Cost of goods available for sale	$ 900	$ 900		**$1,400**	**$1,350**	50 OS
Less: Ending inventory	**300**	**250**	$50 OS†	350	350	
Cost of goods sold	$ **600**	$ **650**	50 US‡	**$1,050**	**$1,000**	50 OS
Gross margin	$ **400**	$ **350**	50 OS	$ **450**	$ **500**	50 US
Operating expenses	100	100		120	120	
Net income	$ **300**	$ **250**	50 OS	$ **330**	$ **380**	50 US

Note: Figures that differ as a result of the error are bold.
*All amounts are in thousands of dollars.
† OS = Overstatement
‡ US = Understatement

margin.[1] The most important conclusion from the exhibit is that an overstatement of ending inventory leads to a corresponding overstatement of net income.

Unfortunately, the effect of a misstatement of the year-end inventory is not limited to the net income for that year. As indicated in the right portion of Exhibit 6-2, the error also affects the income statement for the following year. This happens simply because *the ending inventory of one period is the beginning inventory of the following period.* The *overstatement* of the 1994 *beginning inventory* leads to an *overstatement* of *cost of goods available for sale.* Because cost of goods available for sale is overstated, *cost of goods sold* is also *overstated.* The *overstatement* of cost of goods sold *expense* results in an *understatement* of *gross margin* and thus an *understatement* of *net income.*

Exhibit 6-2 illustrates the nature of a *counterbalancing error.* The effect of the overstatement of net income in the first year, 1993, is offset or counterbalanced by the understatement of net income by the same dollar amount in the following year. If the net incomes of two successive years are misstated in the opposite direction by the same amount, what is the effect on retained earnings? Assume that retained earnings at the beginning of 1993 is correctly stated at $300,000. The counterbalancing nature of the error is seen by analyzing retained earnings. For 1993 the analysis would indicate the following (OS = overstated and US = understated):

	1993 REPORTED	1993 CORRECTED	EFFECT OF ERROR
Beginning retained earnings	$300,000	$300,000	Correct
Add: Net income	300,000	250,000	$50,000 OS
Ending retained earnings	$600,000	$550,000	$50,000 OS

[1] An overstatement of gross margin also results in an overstatement of income tax expense. Thus, because tax expense is overstated, the overstatement of net income is not so large as the overstatement of gross margin. For now we will ignore the effect of taxes, however.

An analysis for 1994 would show this:

	1994 REPORTED	1994 CORRECTED	EFFECT OF ERROR
Beginning retained earnings	$600,000	$550,000	$50,000 OS
Add: Net income	330,000	380,000	$50,000 US
Ending retained earnings	$930,000	$930,000	Correct

Thus, even though retained earnings is overstated at the end of the first year, it is correctly stated at the end of the second year. This is the nature of a counterbalancing error.

The effect of the error on the balance sheet is shown in Exhibit 6-3. The only accounts affected by the error are Inventory and Retained Earnings. The overstatement of the 1993 ending inventory results in an overstatement of total assets at the end of the first year. Similarly, as our earlier analysis indicates, the overstatement of 1993 net income leads to an overstatement of retained earnings by the same amount. Because the error is counterbalancing, the 1994 year-end balance sheet is correct; that is, ending inventory is not affected by the error, and, thus, the amount for total assets at the end of 1994 is also correct. The effect of the error on retained earnings is limited to the first year because of the counterbalancing nature of the error.

The effects of inventory errors on various financial statement items are summarized in Exhibit 6-4. Our analysis focused on the effects of an overstatement of inventory. The effects of an understatement are just the opposite and are summarized in the bottom portion of the exhibit.

Not all errors are counterbalancing. For example, if a section of a warehouse *continues* to be omitted from the physical count every year, both the beginning and ending inventory will be incorrect each year and the error will not counterbalance.

Part of the auditor's job is to perform the necessary tests to obtain reasonable assurance that inventory has not been overstated or understated. If there is an error and inventory is wrong, however, the balance sheet and the income statement will both be distorted. For example, if ending inventory is overstated, inflating total assets,

EXHIBIT 6-3 Effects of Inventory Error on the Balance Sheet

	1993 REPORTED	1993 CORRECTED	1994 REPORTED	1994 CORRECTED
Inventory	$ **300***	$ **250**	$ 350	$ 350
All other assets	1,700	1,700	2,080	2,080
Total assets	**$2,000**	**$1,950**	$2,430	$2,430
Total liabilities	$ 400	$ 400	$ 500	$ 500
Capital stock	1,000	1,000	1,000	1,000
Retained earnings	**600**	**550**	930	930
Total liabilities and stockholders' equity	**$2,000**	**$1,950**	$2,430	$2,430

Note: Figures that differ as a result of the error are bold.
*All amounts are in thousands of dollars.

EXHIBIT 6-4 Summary of the Effects of Inventory Errors

	EFFECT OF OVERSTATEMENT OF ENDING INVENTORY ON	
	---	---
	CURRENT YEAR	FOLLOWING YEAR
Cost of goods sold	Understated	Overstated
Gross margin	Overstated	Understated
Net income	Overstated	Understated
Retained earnings, end of year	Overstated	Correctly stated
Total assets, end of year	Overstated	Correctly stated
	EFFECT OF UNDERSTATEMENT OF ENDING INVENTORY ON	
	CURRENT YEAR	FOLLOWING YEAR
Cost of goods sold	Overstated	Understated
Gross margin	Understated	Overstated
Net income	Understated	Overstated
Retained earnings, end of year	Understated	Correctly stated
Total assets, end of year	Understated	Correctly stated

then cost of goods sold will be understated, boosting profits. Thus, such an error overstates the financial health of the organization in two ways. A lender or an investor must make a decision based on the current year's statement and cannot wait until the next accounting cycle when this error is reversed. This is one reason that investors and creditors insist on audited financial statements.

Inventory Costs—What Should Be Included?

All assets, including inventory, are recorded initially at cost. Cost is defined as

the price paid or consideration given to acquire an asset. As applied to inventories, cost means in principle the sum of the applicable expenditures and charges directly or indirectly incurred in bringing an article to its existing condition and location.[2]

Note the reference to the existing *condition* and *location.* For example, any freight costs incurred by the buyer in shipping inventory to its place of business should be included in the cost of the inventory. The cost of insurance taken out during the time inventory is in transit should be added to the cost of the inventory. The cost of storing inventory prior to the time it is ready to be sold should be included in cost. Various types of taxes paid, such as excise and sales taxes, are other examples of costs necessary to put the inventory into a position to be able to sell it.

It is often very difficult, however, to allocate many of these incidental costs among the various items of inventory purchased. For example, consider a $500 freight bill that a supermarket paid on a shipment of merchandise that includes 100 different items of inventory. To address the practical difficulty in assigning this type of cost to the different products, many companies have a policy by which transportation costs are charged to expense of the period if they are immaterial in amount. Thus, shipments of merchandise are simply recorded at the net invoice price, that is, after

---

[2] *Accounting Research Bulletin No. 43,* "Inventory Pricing" (New York: American Institute of Certified Public Accountants, June 1953), ch. 4, statement 3.

taking any cash discounts for early payment. It is a practical solution to a difficult allocation problem. Once again, the company must apply the cost/benefit test to accounting information.

Inventory Costing Methods with a Periodic System

LO 4

Apply the inventory costing methods of specific identification, weighted average, FIFO, and LIFO using a periodic system.

To this point, we have assumed that the cost to purchase an item of inventory is constant. For most merchandisers, however, the unit cost of inventory changes frequently. Consider a simple example. Everett Company purchases merchandise twice during the first year of business. The dates, the number of units purchased, and the costs are as follows:

> February 4   200 units purchased at $1.00 per unit   = $200
>
> October 13   200 units purchased at $1.50 per unit   = $300

Everett sells 200 units during the first year. Individual sales of the units take place relatively evenly throughout the year. The question is: *Which* 200 units did the company sell, the $1.00 units or the $1.50 units or some combination of each? Recall the earlier discussion of the relationship between asset valuation and income measurement. The question is important because the answer determines not only the value assigned to the 200 units of ending inventory *but also* the amount allocated to cost of goods sold for the 200 units sold.

One possible method of assigning amounts to ending inventory and cost of goods sold is to *specifically identify* which 200 units were sold and which 200 units are on hand. This method is feasible for a few types of businesses in which units can be identified by serial numbers but is totally impractical in most situations. As an alternative to specific identification, we could make an *assumption* as to which units were sold and which are on hand. Three different answers are possible:

(1) 200 units sold at $1.00 each   = $200 cost of goods sold
     and 200 units on hand at $1.50 each = $300 ending inventory
     or
(2) 200 units sold at $1.50 each   = $300 cost of goods sold
     and 200 units on hand at $1.00 each = $200 ending inventory
     or
(3) 200 units sold at $1.25 each   = $250 cost of goods sold
     and 200 units on hand at $1.25 each = $250 ending inventory

The third alternative assumes an *average cost* for the 200 units on hand and the 200 units sold. The average cost is the cost of the two purchases of $200 and $300, or $500, divided by the 400 units available to sell, which is $1.25 per unit.

None of the three methods illustrated is necessarily correct if we are concerned with the actual *physical flow* of the units of inventory. The only approach that will yield a "correct" answer in terms of the actual flow of *units* of inventory is the specific identification method. In the absence of a specific identification approach, it is impossible to say which particular units were *actually* sold. In fact, there may have been sales from each of the two purchases, that is, some of the $1.00 units may have been sold and some of the $1.50 units may have been sold. To solve the problem of assigning a cost to identical units, accountants have developed inventory costing assumptions or methods. Each of these methods makes a specific *assumption* about the *flow of costs* rather than the physical flow of units. The only approach that uses the actual flow of the units in assigning costs is the specific identification method.

To take a closer look at specific identification as well as three alternative approaches to valuing inventory, we will use the following example:

	UNITS	UNIT COST	TOTAL COST
Beginning inventory			
January 1	500	$10	$ 5,000*
Purchases			
January 20	300	11	3,300
April 8	400	12	4,800
September 5	200	13	2,600
December 12	100	14	1,400
Total purchases	1,000 units		$12,100
Available for sale	1,500 units		$17,100
Units sold	900 units		?
Units in ending inventory	600 units		?

*Beginning inventory of $5,000 is carried over as the ending inventory from the prior period. It is highly unlikely that each of the four methods we will illustrate would result in the same dollar amount of inventory at any point in time. It is helpful when first learning the methods, however, to assume the same amount of beginning inventory.

The question marks indicate the dilemma. What portion of the cost of goods available for sale of $17,100 should be assigned to the 900 units sold? What portion should be assigned to the 600 units remaining in ending inventory? The purpose of an inventory costing method is to provide a reasonable answer to these two questions.

Specific Identification Method

It is not always necessary to make an assumption about the flow of costs. In certain situations, it may be possible to specifically identify which units are sold and which units are on hand. A serial number on an automobile allows a dealer to identify a car on hand and thus its unit cost. An appliance dealer with 15 refrigerators on hand at the end of the year can identify the unit cost of each by matching a tag number with the purchase records. To illustrate the use of the **specific identification method** for our example, assume that the merchandiser is able to identify the specific units in the inventory at the end of the year, and, thus, their costs as follows:

DATE	UNITS	COST	TOTAL
January 20	100	$11	$1,100
April 8	300	12	3,600
September 5	200	13	2,600
Ending inventory	600		$7,300

One of two techniques can be used to find cost of goods sold. We can deduct ending inventory from the cost of goods available for sale:

Cost of goods available for sale	$17,100
Less: Ending inventory	7,300
Equals: Cost of goods sold	$ 9,800

Or we can calculate cost of goods sold independently by matching the units sold with their respective unit costs. By eliminating the units in ending inventory from the original acquisition schedule, the units sold and their costs are as follows:

DATE	UNITS	COST	TOTAL
January 1	500	$10	$5,000
January 20	200	11	2,200
April 8	100	12	1,200
December 12	100	14	1,400
Cost of goods sold	900		$9,800

The practical difficulty in keeping track of individual items of inventory sold is not the only problem with the use of this method. The method also allows management to *manipulate income.* For example, assume that a company is not having a particularly good year. Management may be tempted to do whatever it can to boost net income. One way it can do this is by selectively selling units with the lowest possible unit cost. By doing so, the company can keep cost of goods sold down and net income up. Because of the potential for manipulation with the specific identification method, coupled with the practical difficulty of applying it in most situations, it is not widely used.

Weighted Average Cost Method

The **weighted average cost method** is a relatively easy approach to costing inventory. It assigns the same unit cost to all units available for sale during the period. The weighted average cost is calculated as follows for our example:

Widespread use of bar codes and readers like this one have made it possible for even very small companies to track each item's current cost, current selling price, availability, and order information. As discussed on p. 331, this technology has popularized the use of what is called the perpetual inventory system, the focus of Appendix 6A.

$$\frac{\text{Cost of Goods Available for Sale}}{\text{Units Available for Sale}} = \text{Weighted Average Cost}$$

$$\frac{\$17,100}{1,500} = \$11.40$$

Ending inventory is found by multiplying the weighted average unit cost by the number of units on hand:

Weighted Average Cost	$\times$	Number of Units In Ending Inventory	$=$	Ending Inventory
$11.40	$\times$	600	$=$	$6,840

Cost of goods sold can be calculated in one of two ways:

	Cost of goods available for sale	$17,100
Less:	Ending inventory	6,840
Equals:	Cost of goods sold	$10,260

or

Weighted Average Cost	$\times$	Number of Units Sold	$=$	Cost of Goods Sold
$11.40	$\times$	900	$=$	$10,260

Note that the computation of the weighted average cost is based on the cost of *all* units available for sale during the period, not just the beginning inventory or purchases. Also note that the method is called the *weighted* average cost method. As the name indicates, each of the individual unit costs is multiplied by the number of units acquired at each price. The simple arithmetic average of the unit costs for the beginning inventory and the four purchases is ($10 + $11 + $12 + $13 + $14)/ 5 = $12. The weighted average cost is slightly less than $12 ($11.40), however, because more units were acquired at the lower prices than at the higher prices.

First-in, First-out Method (FIFO)

The **FIFO method** assumes that the first units in, or purchased, are the first units out, or sold. The first units sold during the period are assumed to come from the beginning inventory. After the beginning inventory is sold, the next units sold are assumed to come from the first purchase during the period and so forth. Thus, ending inventory consists of the most recent purchases of the period. In many businesses, this cost-flow assumption is a fairly accurate reflection of the *physical* flow of products. For example, to maintain a fresh stock of products, the physical flow in a grocery store is first-in, first-out.

To calculate *ending inventory*, we start with the *most recent* inventory acquired and work *backward*:

DATE	UNITS	COST	TOTAL
December 12	100	$14	$1,400
September 5	200	13	2,600
April 8	300	12	3,600
Ending inventory	600		$7,600

Cost of goods sold can be found using either approach:

Cost of goods available for sale $17,100
Less: Ending inventory   7,600
Equals: Cost of goods sold $ 9,500

Or because the FIFO method assumes the first units in are the first ones sold, cost of goods sold can be calculated by starting with the *beginning inventory* and working *forward:*

DATE	UNITS	COST	TOTAL
January 1	500	$10	$5,000
January 20	300	11	3,300
April 8	100	12	1,200
Units sold	900	Cost of goods sold	$9,500

Last-in, First-out Method (LIFO)

The **LIFO method** assumes that the last units in, or purchased, are the first units out, or sold. The first units sold during the period are assumed to come from the latest purchase made during the period and so forth. Can you think of any businesses where the *physical* flow of products is last-in, first-out? Although this situation is not nearly so common as a first-in, first-out physical flow, a stockpiling operation, such as in a rock quarry, operates on this basis.

To calculate *ending inventory* using LIFO, we start with the *beginning inventory* and work *forward:*

DATE	UNITS	COST	TOTAL
Beginning inventory	500	$10	$5,000
January 20	100	11	1,100
Ending inventory	600		$6,100

Once again, one of two methods is used to find cost of goods sold:

Cost of goods available for sale $17,100
Less: Ending inventory   6,100
Equals: Cost of goods sold $11,000

Or because the LIFO method assumes that the last units in are the first ones sold, *cost of goods sold* can be calculated by starting with the most *recent* inventory acquired and working *backward:*

DATE	UNITS	COST	TOTAL
December 12	100	$14	$ 1,400
September 5	200	13	2,600
April 8	400	12	4,800
January 20	200	11	2,200
Units sold	900	Cost of goods sold	$11,000

Selecting an Inventory Costing Method

The mechanics of each of the inventory costing methods are straightforward. But how does a company decide on the best method to use to value its inventory? According to the accounting profession, *the primary determinant in selecting an inventory costing method should be the ability of the method to accurately reflect the net income of the period.* But how and why does a particular costing method accurately reflect the net income of the period? Because there is no easy answer to this question, a number of arguments have been raised by accountants to justify the use of one method over the others. We turn now to some of these arguments.

LO 5

Analyze the effects of the different costing methods on inventory, net income, income taxes, and cash flow.

Costing Methods and Cash Flow

Comparative income statements for our example are presented in Exhibit 6-5. Note that with the use of the weighted average method, net income is between the amount for FIFO and LIFO. Because the weighted average method normally yields results between the other two methods, we concentrate on the two extremes, LIFO and FIFO. The major advantage from use of the weighted average method is its simplicity.

The original data for our example involved a situation in which prices were *rising* throughout the period: beginning inventory cost $10 per unit, and the last purchase during the year was at $14. With LIFO, the most recent costs are assigned to cost of goods sold; with FIFO, the older costs are assigned to expense. Thus, in a period of rising prices, the assignment of the *higher* prices to cost of goods sold under LIFO results in *lower gross margin* as compared to FIFO ($7,000 for LIFO and $8,500 for FIFO). Because operating expenses are not affected by the choice of inventory method, lower gross margin under LIFO results in lower income before tax, which in turn leads to lower taxes. If we assume a 40% tax rate, income tax expense with LIFO is only $2,000 as compared to $2,600 with FIFO, a savings of $600 in taxes.

EXHIBIT 6-5 Income Statements for the Inventory Costing Methods

	WEIGHTED AVERAGE	FIFO	LIFO
Sales revenue—$20 each	$18,000	$18,000	$18,000
Beginning inventory	5,000	5,000	5,000
Purchases	12,100	12,100	12,100
Cost of goods available for sale	$17,100	$17,100	$17,100
Ending inventory	**6,840**	**7,600**	**6,100**
Cost of goods sold	**$10,260**	**$ 9,500**	**$11,000**
Gross margin	**$ 7,740**	**$ 8,500**	**$ 7,000**
Operating expenses	2,000	2,000	2,000
Net income before tax	**$ 5,740**	**$ 6,500**	**$ 5,000**
Income tax expense (40%)	**2,296**	**2,600**	**2,000**
Net income	**$ 3,444**	**$ 3,900**	**$ 3,000**

Note: Figures that differ among the three methods are bold.

Another way to look at the taxes saved by using LIFO is to focus on the difference in the expense under each method:

	LIFO cost of goods sold	$11,000
−	FIFO cost of goods sold	9,500
	Additional expense from use of LIFO	$ 1,500
×	Tax rate	.40
	Tax savings from the use of LIFO	$ 600

To summarize, *during a period of rising prices,* the two methods result in the following:

ITEM	LIFO	RELATIVE TO	FIFO
Cost of goods sold	Higher		Lower
Gross margin	Lower		Higher
Income before taxes	Lower		Higher
Taxes	Lower		Higher

In conclusion, lower taxes with the use of LIFO results in cash savings.

The tax savings available during a period of rising prices from the use of LIFO are largely responsible for its popularity. Keep in mind, however, that the cash saved from a lower tax bill with LIFO is only a temporary savings, or what is normally called a *tax deferral.* At some point in the life of the business, the inventory that is carried at the older, lower-priced amounts will be sold. This will result in a relatively higher tax bill, as compared to FIFO. Even a tax deferral is beneficial; given the opportunity, it is better to pay less tax today and more in the future because today's tax savings can be invested.

The tax deferral from the use of LIFO may not be beneficial, however, if tax rates go up. If inventory carried at older lower-priced amounts is sold after tax rates increase, a higher amount of tax will be paid than was originally expected to be paid. In 1993, tax rates on corporations rose from 34% to 35%. This increase in rates has made the tax deferral aspects of previous LIFO deductions less advantageous.

LIFO Liquidation

Recall the assumption made about which costs remain in inventory when LIFO is used. The cost of the oldest units remain in inventory and if prices are rising, these units will have a relatively low unit cost, compared to more recent purchases. Now assume that the company *sells more units during the period than it buys.* When a company using LIFO experiences a liquidation, some of the units assumed to be sold will come from the older layers with a relatively low unit cost. This situation, called a **LIFO liquidation,** presents a dilemma for the company.

A partial or complete liquidation of the older, lower-priced units will result in a low cost of goods sold figure and a correspondingly high gross margin for the period. In turn, the company faces a large tax bill because of the relatively high gross margin. In fact, a liquidation causes the tax advantages of using LIFO to reverse on the company, and it is faced with paying off some of the taxes that were deferred in earlier periods. Should a company facing this situation buy inventory at the end of the year to avoid the consequences of a liquidation? This is a difficult question to answer and depends on many factors, including the company's cash position. At the least, the accountant must be aware of the potential for a large tax bill if a liquidation occurs.

Of course, a LIFO liquidation also benefits—and may even distort—reported earnings if the liquidation is large enough. For this reason and the tax problem, many companies are reluctant to liquidate their LIFO inventory. The problem often festers and companies find themselves with inventory costed at decade-old price levels.

The LIFO Conformity Rule

Would it be possible for a company to have the best of both worlds? That is, could it use FIFO to report its income to stockholders, thus maximizing the amount of net income reported to this group, and use LIFO to report to the IRS, minimizing its taxable income and the amount paid to the government? Unfortunately, the IRS says that if a company chooses LIFO for reporting cost of goods sold on its tax return, then it must also use LIFO on its books, that is, in preparing its income statement. This is called the **LIFO conformity rule.** Note that the rule applies only to the use of LIFO on the tax return. A company is free to use different methods in preparing its tax return and its income statement, as long as the method used for the tax return is *not* LIFO.

The LIFO Reserve: Estimating the Effect on Income and on Taxes Paid from Using LIFO

If a company decides to use LIFO, an investor can still determine how much more profitable the company would be had it used FIFO. In addition, he or she can approximate the tax savings to the company from the use of LIFO. Consider the following footnote from the 1992 annual report for Albertson's, Inc., the retail grocery chain:

> Approximately 96% of the Company's inventories are valued using the last-in, first-out (LIFO) method. If the first-in, first-out (FIFO) method had been used, inventories would have been $185,150,000, $172,470,000 and $160,877,000 higher at the end of 1992, 1991, and 1990, respectively.

The following steps explain the logic for using the information in the inventory footnote to estimate the effect on income and on taxes from using LIFO:

1. The excess of the value of a company's inventory stated at FIFO as compared to LIFO is called the **LIFO reserve.** The *cumulative* excess of the value of Albertsons' inventory on a FIFO basis as compared to a LIFO basis is $185,150,000 at the end of 1992.

2. Because Albertsons reports less inventory on its balance sheet using LIFO, it will report a higher cost of goods sold amount on the income statement. Thus, the LIFO reserve not only represents the excess of the inventory balance on a FIFO basis, compared to LIFO, but *it also represents the cumulative amount by which cost of goods sold on a LIFO basis exceeds cost of goods sold on a FIFO basis.*

3. The increase in Albertsons LIFO reserve in 1992 was $12,680,000 ($185,150,000 − $172,470,000). This means that the increase in cost of goods sold for 1992 from using LIFO as compared to FIFO was also this

amount. Thus, income before tax for 1992 was $12,680,000 lower because the company used LIFO.

4. If we assume a corporate tax rate of 35%, the tax savings to Albertsons from using LIFO amounted to $12,680,000 × .35, or $4,438,000.

Because of low inflation, the LIFO reserve is insignificant for some companies and may in fact go down from one period to the next. As an example, consider the following disclosure in Quaker Oats' 1992 annual report:

> If the LIFO method of valuing certain inventories were not used, total inventories would have been $13.9 million, $18.9 million and $27.9 million higher than reported at June 30, 1992, 1991 and 1990, respectively.

What does this note tell you? First, it notes that inventory on a FIFO basis as compared to a LIFO basis was $13.9 million higher at the end of 1992. The excess of FIFO over LIFO was $18.9 million at the end of the prior year, however. Thus, the net decrease in the LIFO reserve of $18.9 − $13.9, or $5 million, is the amount by which *FIFO cost of goods sold exceeded LIFO cost of goods sold* in 1992. Assuming a tax rate of 35%, Quaker paid $5 million × .35, or $1,750,000, more by using LIFO in 1992. This is another way to show that LIFO provides tax benefits to a company only when inflation is present.

■ ACCOUNTING FOR YOUR DECISIONS   **You Are the Auditor**

Your client, Yale Company, is a manufacturer of components for personal computers. It uses the FIFO method of inventory accounting. The chief financial officer asks you whether the company should switch to LIFO in order to save taxes. How would you respond?

Costing Methods and Inventory Profits

FIFO, LIFO, and weighted average are all cost-based methods to value inventory. They vary in terms of which costs are assigned to inventory and which to cost of goods sold, but nevertheless all three assign *historical costs* to inventory. In our previous example, the unit cost for inventory purchases gradually increased during the year from $10 for the beginning inventory to a high of $14 on the date of the last purchase.

An alternative to assigning any of the historical costs incurred during the year to ending inventory and cost of goods sold would be to base each of these on **replacement cost.** Assume that the cost to replace a unit of inventory at the end of the year is $15. Use of a replacement cost system results in the following:

Ending inventory	600 units × $15 per unit	=	$ 9,000
Cost of goods sold	900 units × $15 per unit	=	$13,500

A replacement cost approach is not acceptable under the profession's current standards, but many believe that it provides more relevant information to users. Inventory must be replaced if a company is to remain in business. Many accountants argue that the use of historical cost in valuing inventory leads to what is called **inventory profit,** particularly if *FIFO* is used in a period of rising prices. For example, cost of goods sold in our illustration was only $9,500 on a FIFO basis, as compared to $13,500 if replacement cost of $15 per unit is used. The difference between the two cost of goods sold figures of $4,000 is a profit from holding the inventory during a period of rising prices and is called *inventory profit*. To look at this another way, assume that the units are sold for $20 each. The following analysis reconciles the difference between gross margin on a FIFO basis and on a replacement cost basis:

Sales revenue 900 units × $20 =		$18,000
Cost of goods sold—FIFO basis		9,500
Gross margin—FIFO basis		$ 8,500
Cost of goods sold—replacement cost basis	$13,500	
Cost of goods sold—FIFO basis	9,500	
Profit from holding inventory during a period of inflation		4,000
Gross margin on a replacement cost basis		$ 4,500

Those who argue in favor of a replacement cost approach would report only $4,500 of gross margin. They believe that the additional $4,000 of profit reported on a FIFO basis is simply due to holding the inventory during a period of rising prices. According to this viewpoint, if the 900 units sold during the period are to be replaced, a necessity if the company is to continue operating, the use of replacement cost in calculating cost of goods sold results in a better measure of gross margin than if it is calculated using FIFO.

Given that our current standards require the use of historical costs rather than replacement costs, does any one of the costing methods result in a better approximation of replacement cost of goods sold than the others? Because *LIFO* assigns the cost of the most recent purchases to cost of goods sold, it most nearly approximates the results with a replacement cost system. The other side of the argument, however, is that while *LIFO* results in the best approximation of *replacement cost of goods sold* on the *income statement, FIFO* most nearly approximates the amount assigned to *inventory* on the *balance sheet*. A comparison of the amounts from our example verifies this:

	ENDING INVENTORY	COST OF GOODS SOLD
Weighted average	$6,840	$10,260
FIFO	7,600	9,500
LIFO	6,100	11,000
Replacement cost	9,000	13,500

Changing Inventory Methods

The purpose of each of the inventory costing methods is to match costs with revenues. If a company believes that a different method would result in a better matching than the one currently being used, it should change methods. A company must be able to justify a change in methods, however. A change to take advantage of the tax breaks offered by LIFO is not a valid justification for a change in methods.

It is very important for a company to *disclose* any change in accounting principle, including a change in the method of costing inventory. For example, in its 1989 annual report, The Quaker Oats Company disclosed the following:

Effective July 1, 1988, the Company adopted the LIFO cost flow assumption for valuing the majority of remaining U.S. Grocery Products inventories. The Company believes that the use of the LIFO method better matches current costs with current revenues. The cumulative effect of this change on retained earnings at the beginning of the year is not determinable, nor are the pro forma effects of retroactive application of LIFO to prior years. The effect of this change on fiscal 1989 was to decrease net income by $16.0 million, or $.20 per share.

■ ACCOUNTING FOR YOUR DECISIONS   **You Are the Investment Analyst**

Does changing accounting methods for inventory have any impact on your opinion of Quaker Oats as a stock?

Popularity of the Costing Methods

An annual survey conducted by the AICPA indicates the relative popularity of the inventory costing methods. The inventory methods used by the 600 corporations in the survey are reported in Exhibit 6-6. Note in the top half of the exhibit that the number of companies each year totals more than 600. This happens because many companies use more than one method to determine the total cost of inventory. That is, weighted average may be used to value certain types of inventory, while LIFO is used for certain others. The survey indicates the relatively equal popularity of LIFO and FIFO in practice. The second part of the exhibit indicates the relative proportion of inventory that is costed by the LIFO method.

The exhibit indicates that the use of LIFO is diminishing somewhat, probably because LIFO depends on inflation to be advantageous. As of this writing, inflation continues to be low, as it has been since the early 1980s. Without significant inflation, a company has to be concerned about LIFO liquidation, LIFO reserves, and the complications that arise in the computation and disclosure of LIFO inventory.

Your introduction to LIFO, FIFO, and average cost may actually come not as an accountant but as an investor in mutual funds. If you buy shares in a mutual fund,

FROM CONCEPT TO PRACTICE

READING BEN & JERRY'S ANNUAL REPORT

Which inventory method does Ben & Jerry's use? Where did you find this information? Do you think the company is justified in using the method it does?

EXHIBIT 6-6 Inventory Cost Determination—AICPA Survey

	NUMBER OF COMPANIES			
	1992	1991	1990	1989
METHODS				
First-in, first-out (fifo)	415	421	411	401
Last-in, first-out (lifo)	358	361	366	366
Average cost	193	200	195	200
Other	45	50	44	48
USE OF LIFO				
All inventories	23	23	20	26
50% or more of inventories	189	186	186	191
Less than 50% of inventories	91	95	92	99
Not determinable	55	57	68	50
Companies using LIFO	358	361	366	366

SOURCE: *Accounting Trends & Techniques*, 47th ed. (New York: American Institute of Certified Public Accountants, 1993).

you will find yourself keeping track of a different form of inventory—not widgets but shares of a fund. When you go to sell shares in the fund, you'll need to compute your costs. You can use a form of specific identification to determine which shares you sold, but that will get complicated if your fund automatically reinvests dividends in new shares. So you'll have a choice of FIFO, LIFO, or average cost to determine how to "cost" your inventory layers of mutual fund shares. Most mutual fund investors have no idea that calculating their profits can be so complicated. After all, the reason that they bought mutual funds in the first place was simplicity. Many mutual fund companies have decided to do the computations for the investor as a free service.

Two Inventory Systems: Periodic and Perpetual

In the examples so far in this chapter, we have assumed a periodic system to concentrate our attention on the various cost-flow assumptions. Recall from Chapter 5 that with this system, a count of the inventory is necessary at the end of the period to determine the number of units sold and the number on hand. The reason is that the Inventory account is not updated each time a purchase is made and each time a sale is made.

For many years, the simplicity of the periodic system resulted in its widespread use. Because of the need in a perpetual system to record the *cost* of every individual sale when it occurs, its use was limited to businesses that sold products with a relatively high unit cost and low turnover, such as those of an automobile dealer. The ability to *computerize* the inventory system has resulted, however, in an increase in the use of the perpetual system in all types of businesses. A company can use any one of the costing methods we have discussed with either a periodic or a perpetual inventory system. The application of the methods when a company maintains a perpetual inventory system is illustrated in Appendix 6A.

Valuing Inventory at Lower of Cost or Market

LO 6

Apply the lower of cost or market rule to the valuation of inventory.

One of the components sold by an electronics firm has become economically obsolete. A particular style of suit sold by a retailer is outdated and can no longer be sold at regular price. In each of these instances, it is likely that the retailer will have to sell the merchandise for less than the normal selling price. In these situations, a *departure* from the cost basis of accounting is necessary because the *market value* of the inventory is less than its *cost* to the company. The departure is called the **lower of cost or market (LCM) rule.**

At the end of each accounting period, the original cost, as determined using one of the costing methods such as FIFO, is compared with the market price of the inventory. If market is less than cost, the inventory is written down to the lower amount with an adjusting entry of the following form:

Dec. 31   Loss on Decline in Value of Inventory   xxx
                    Inventory   xxx
            To record decline in value of inventory.

Assets	=	Liabilities	+	Owners' Equity
− xxx				− xxx

Note that the entry reduces both assets, in the form of inventory, and owners' equity. The reduction in owners' equity is the result of reporting the debit to Loss on Decline in Value of Inventory on the income statement as an item of other expense.

Why Replacement Cost Is Used as a Measure of Market

A better name for the lower of cost or market rule would be the lower of cost or replacement cost rule because accountants define *market* as *replacement cost.*[3] To understand why replacement cost is used as a basis to compare with original cost, consider the following example. A clothier pays $150 for a man's double-breasted suit and normally sells it for $200. Thus, the normal markup on selling price is $50/$200, or 25%, as indicated in the column Before Price Change in Exhibit 6-7. Now assume that double-breasted suits fall out of favor with the fashion world. The retailer checks with the distributor and finds that because of the style change, the cost to the retailer to replace a double-breasted suit is now only $120. The retailer realizes that if double-breasted suits are to be sold at all, they will have to be offered at a reduced price. The selling price is dropped from $200 to $160. If the retailer now buys a suit for $120 and sells it for $160, the gross margin will be $40 and the gross margin percentage will be maintained at 25%, as indicated in the right-hand column of Exhibit 6-7.

To compare the results with and without the use of the LCM rule, assume the same facts as before and that the retailer has 10 double-breasted suits in inventory on December 31, 1995. In addition, assume that all 10 suits are sold at a clearance sale in January 1996 at the reduced price of $160 each. If the lower of cost or market rule is not used, the results for the two years will be as follows:

LCM RULE NOT USED	1995	1996	TOTAL
Sales revenue ($160 per unit)	$–0–	$1,600	$1,600
Cost of goods sold			
(original cost of $150 per unit)	–0–	(1,500)	(1,500)
Gross margin	$–0–	$ 100	$ 100

If the LCM rule is not applied, the gross margin is distorted: Instead of the normal 25%, a gross margin percentage of $100/$1,600 or 6.25% is reported in 1996 when the 10 suits are sold. If the LCM rule is applied, however, the results in each of the two years are as follows:

LCM RULE USED	1995	1996	TOTAL
Sales revenue ($160 per unit)	$ –0–	$1,600	$1,600
Cost of goods sold			
(replacement cost of $120 per unit)	–0–	(1,200)	(1,200)
Loss on decline in value of inventory: 10 units × ($150 − $120)	(300)	–0–	(300)
Gross margin	$(300)	$ 400	$ 100

The use of the LCM rule serves two important functions: (1) to report the loss in value of the inventory, $30 per suit or $300 in total, in the year the loss occurs and (2) to report in the year the suits are actually sold the normal gross margin of $400/$1,600, or 25%, which is not affected by a change in the selling price.

[3] Technically, the use of replacement cost as a measure of market value is subject to two constraints. First, market cannot be more than the net realizable value of the inventory. Second, inventory should not be recorded at less than net realizable value less a normal profit margin. The rationale for these two constraints is covered in intermediate accounting texts. For our purposes, we assume that replacement cost falls between the two constraints.

EXHIBIT 6-7   Gross Margin Percentage before and after Price Change

	BEFORE PRICE CHANGE	AFTER PRICE CHANGE
Selling price	$200	$160
Cost	150	120
Gross margin	$ 50	$ 40
Gross margin percentage	25%	25%

Conservatism Is the Basis for the Lower of Cost or Market Rule

The departure from the cost basis is normally justified on the basis of *conservatism*. According to the accounting profession, conservatism is "a prudent reaction to uncertainties to try to insure that uncertainties and risks inherent in business situations are adequately considered."[4] In our example, the future selling price of a suit is uncertain because of the style changes. The use of the LCM rule serves two purposes. First, the inventory of suits is written down from $150 to $120 each. Second, the decline in value of the inventory is recognized at the time it is first observed rather than waiting until the suits are sold. An investor in a company with deteriorating inventory has good reason to be alarmed. Merchandisers who do not make the proper adjustments to their product lines go out of business as they compete with the lower-priced warehouse clubs and the lower overhead of mail-order catalogs and even home shopping networks.

You should realize that the write-down of the suits violates the historical cost principle, which says that assets should be carried on the balance sheet at their original cost. But the LCM rule is considered a valid exception to the principle because it is a prudent reaction to the uncertainty involved and, thus, an application of conservatism in accounting.

Application of the LCM Rule

We have yet to consider how the LCM rule is applied to the entire inventory of a company. Three different interpretations of the rule are possible: (1) the lower of the total cost or the total market value for the entire inventory could be reported, (2) the lower of cost or market value for each individual product or item could be reported, or (3) a group approach could be used. A company is free to choose any one of these approaches in applying the lower of cost or market rule. Three different answers are possible, depending on the approach selected. The three approaches are illustrated in Exhibit 6-8.

The total approach results in a loss of $150. This happens because the total cost of the inventory is $19,500, but its total market value is determined to be $19,350. The item-by-item approach requires the selection of the cost or the market value for *each* individual product and produces a carrying amount for the total inventory of $18,600, and thus a loss of $900. Note that the loss of $450 with use of the group approach falls between the two extremes.

[4] *Statement of Financial Accounting Concepts No. 2,* "Qualitative Characteristics of Accounting Information" (Stamford, Conn.: Financial Accounting Standards Board, May 1980), par. 95.

EXHIBIT 6-8   Application of the Lower of Cost or Market Rule

GROUP	PRODUCT	QUANTITY	FIFO COST PER UNIT	TOTAL COST	COST TO REPLACE PER UNIT	TOTAL COST TO REPLACE	ITEM BY ITEM	GROUP BY GROUP
Suits	3 piece	25	$200	$ 5,000	$210	$ 5,250	$ 5,000	
	2 piece	30	150	4,500	150	4,500	4,500	
	Dbl-breasted	10	150	1,500	120	1,200	1,200	
	Group total			$11,000		$10,950		$10,950
Jackets	Regular	40	$ 80	$ 3,200	$ 85	$ 3,400	3,200	
	Dbl-breasted	15	100	1,500	60	900	900	
	Group total			$ 4,700		$ 4,300		4,300
Slacks	Straight	100	$ 20	$ 2,000	$ 20	$ 2,000	2,000	
	With cuffs	60	30	1,800	35	2,100	1,800	
	Group total			$ 3,800		$ 4,100		3,800
Total cost				$19,500				
Total replacement cost						$19,350		
Total market: Item by item							$18,600	
Total market: Group by group								$19,050

If LCM is applied using the	The loss will be			
Total approach	$19,500–19,350 =		$ 150	
Item by item approach	$19,500–18,600 =			$ 900
Group by group approach	$19,500–19,050 =			$ 450

Why does the item-by-item approach result in a carrying value for the inventory that is *more conservative* and a larger loss than that obtained with the total approach? The reason is that with the total approach, increases in market value above cost are allowed to offset decreases in value. For example, consider three-piece suits. Total market is *higher* than total cost ($5,250 versus $5,000), and the former amount is included in the total market to be compared with total cost. Under the item-by-item approach, only the lower of the two is considered; the higher market value is ignored.

The item-by-item approach is the most popular of the three approaches in practice for two reasons. First, as we have seen, it produces the most conservative result. Second, it is the method required for tax purposes, although unlike LIFO, it is not required for book purposes merely because it is used for tax computations.

Consistency is important in deciding which of these approaches to use in applying the LCM rule. As is the case with the selection of one of the inventory costing methods discussed earlier in the chapter, the approach chosen to apply the rule should be used consistently from one period to the next.

Methods for Estimating Inventory Value

Situations arise in which it may not be practicable or even possible to measure inventory at cost. At times it may be necessary to *estimate* the amount of inventory.

EXHIBIT 6-9   The Gross Profit Method for Estimating Inventory

INCOME STATEMENT MODEL	GROSS PROFIT METHOD MODEL
Beginning Inventory	Beginning Inventory
+	+
Purchases	Purchases
=	=
Cost of Goods Available for Sale	Cost of Goods Available for Sale
−	−
Ending Inventory (per count)	Estimated Cost of Goods Sold
=	=
Cost of Goods Sold	Estimated Inventory

Two similar methods are used for very different purposes to estimate the amount of inventory. They are the gross profit method and the retail inventory method.

Gross Profit Method

A company that uses a periodic inventory system may experience a problem if inventory is stolen or destroyed by fire, flooding, or some other type of damage. Without a perpetual inventory record, what is the cost of the inventory stolen or destroyed? The **gross profit method** is a useful technique to estimate the cost of inventory lost in these situations. The method relies *entirely* on the ability to reliably estimate the *ratio of gross profit to sales,* thus the name the gross profit method.[5]

Exhibit 6-9 illustrates how the normal income statement model that we use to find cost of goods sold can be rearranged to estimate inventory. The model on the left shows the components of cost of goods sold as they appear on the income statement. Assuming a periodic system, the inventory on hand at the end of the period is counted and is subtracted from cost of goods available for sale to determine cost of goods sold. The model is rearranged on the right as a basis for estimating inventory under the gross profit method. The only difference in the two models is in the reversal of the last two components: ending inventory and cost of goods sold. Rather than attempting to estimate *ending* inventory, we are trying to estimate the amount of inventory that should be on hand at a specific date, such as the date of a fire or flood. The estimate of cost of goods sold is found by estimating gross profit and deducting this estimate from sales revenue.

To illustrate the method, assume that on March 12, 1995, a portion of Hardluck Company's inventory is destroyed in a fire. The company determines by a physical count that the cost of the merchandise not destroyed is $200. Hardluck needs to estimate the cost of the inventory lost for purposes of insurance reimbursement. If the insurance company pays Hardluck an amount equivalent to the cost of the inventory destroyed, no loss will be recognized. A loss will be recorded for any amount by which the cost of the inventory destroyed exceeds the amount reimbursed by the insurance company.

LO **7**
Use the gross profit method to estimate inventory.

[5] The terms *gross profit* and *gross margin* are synonymous in this context. Although we have used *gross margin* in referring to the excess of sales over cost of goods sold, the method is typically called the *gross profit method.*

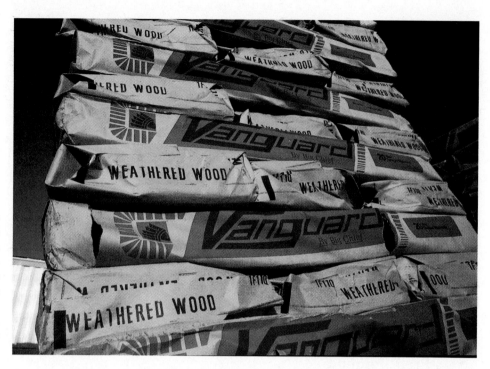

If its supply of wood shingles caught on fire, could the roofing company accurately estimate the loss to its inventory? If it uses the gross profit method and accounts for its inventory on a periodic basis, one way would be to calculate the amount of loss from information in the records as shown below.

Assume that the insurance company agrees to pay Hardluck $250 as full settlement for the inventory lost in the fire. From its records, Hardluck is able to determine the following amounts for the period from January 1 to the date of the fire, March 12:

Net sales from January 1 to March 12	$6,000
Beginning inventory—January 1	1,200
Purchases from January 1 to March 12	3,500

Assume that based on recent years' experience, Hardluck estimates its gross profit ratio as 30% of net sales. The steps it will take to estimate the inventory lost follow:

(**1**) Determine gross profit:

Net Sales $\times$ Gross Profit Ratio = Gross Profit
$6,000 $\times$ 30%   = $1,800

(**2**) Determine cost of goods sold:

Net Sales $-$ Gross Profit   = Cost of Goods Sold
$6,000 $-$ $1,800   = $4,200

(**3**) Determine cost of goods available for sale at time of fire:

Beginning Inventory $+$ Purchases = Cost of Goods
                                     Available for Sale
$1,200 $+$ $3,500   = $4,700

(**4**) Determine inventory at time of the fire:

Cost of Goods $-$ Cost of Goods Sold   = Inventory
  Available for Sale
$4,700 $-$ $4,200   = $500

(**5**) Determine amount of inventory destroyed:

Inventory at Time $-$ Inventory not   = Inventory Destroyed
  of Fire   Destroyed
$500 $-$ $200   = $300

Hardluck would record the following journal entry to recognize a loss for the excess of the cost of the inventory lost over the amount of reimbursement from the insurance company:

Mar 12   Loss on Insurance Settlement   50
             Cash (from insurance company)   250
                 Inventory   300
             To record the insurance settlement from fire.

Assets	=	Liabilities	+	Owners' Equity
+250				−50
−300				

Another situation in which the gross profit method is used is for *interim financial statements.* Most companies prepare financial statements at least once every three months. In fact, the Securities and Exchange Commission requires a quarterly report from corporations whose stock is publicly traded. Companies using the periodic inventory system, however, find it cost prohibitive to count the inventory every three months. The gross profit method is used to estimate the cost of the inventory at these interim dates. A company is allowed to use the method only in interim reports. Inventory reported in the annual report must be based on actual, not estimated, cost.

Retail Inventory Method

The counting of inventory in most retail businesses is an enormous undertaking. Imagine the time involved to count all of the various items stocked in a hardware store. Because of the time and cost involved in counting inventory, most retail businesses take a physical inventory only once a year. The **retail inventory method** is a technique used to estimate inventory for interim statements, typically prepared monthly.

LO 8

Use the retail inventory method to estimate inventory.

Use of the Retail Method for Interim Statements   The steps a retailer uses to estimate the cost of inventory at the end of the month are illustrated in Exhibit 6-10. The first step is to find the goods available for sale at both cost and retail. The retail value of the beginning inventory is simply the retail value of the ending inventory from the prior period. Likewise, the cost of the inventory at the beginning of the period is the same as last month's ending inventory. The method does require that the retailer keep records of purchases both on a cost and a retail basis. Net

EXHIBIT 6-10   Use of the Retail Method for Interim Statements

	COST	RETAIL
Inventory, January 1	$ 7,500	$ 9,750
Add: Net purchases in January	40,500	50,250
Goods available for sale	$48,000	$60,000
Ratio of cost to retail: $48,000/$60,000 = 80%		
Less: Net sales in January		43,000
Inventory, January 31, at retail		$17,000
Times: Cost to retail ratio		× .80
Inventory, January 31, at cost	$13,600	

purchases are added to beginning inventory to find the goods available for sale at both cost and retail. Next, the ratio of cost to retail of 80% is found by dividing the *cost* of goods available for sale by the *retail* value of goods available for sale. The next step is to deduct net sales for the month from the retail value of merchandise available for sale to determine the estimated ending inventory at retail value, in this case $17,000. Finally, the ending inventory at retail of $17,000 is multiplied by the cost-to-retail ratio of 80% to find the estimated inventory on a cost basis of $13,600.

Use of the Retail Method at Year-End   As mentioned earlier, all businesses count the inventory at least once a year. In a periodic system, it is a necessity to determine the amount on hand. In a perpetual system, the count acts as a check on the amount that appears in the records. Consider the year-end inventory count in a large supermarket. One employee counts the number of tubes of toothpaste on the shelf and relays the relevant information to either another employee or to a tape recording device: "16 tubes of 8 ounce ABC brand toothpaste at $1.69." The key is that the price recorded is the *selling price* or *retail* price of the product, not its cost. It is much quicker to count the inventory at retail than it would be to trace the cost of each item to purchase invoices. The retail method can then be used to convert the inventory from retail to cost. The methodology is very similar to that used for interim purposes and is illustrated for a different retailer in Exhibit 6-11.

The first two steps are the same as those used in Exhibit 6-10. First, net purchases during the period, in this case for a year rather than a month, are added to beginning inventory, on both a cost basis and a retail basis. Second, the ratio of cost to retail of 70% is found by dividing the goods available for sale at cost of $350,000 by the amount at retail of $500,000. Ending inventory at cost of $126,000 is then approximated by multiplying the ending inventory at retail of $180,000, as determined by count, by the cost to retail ratio of 70%.

Finally, we should note that the merchandise of retailers is often subject to numerous markups and markdowns from the original selling price. Popular items are marked up by a retailer because they are moving particularly well. Conversely, the end of a selling season may necessitate that certain products be marked down to sell them. The modifications necessary to take markups and markdowns into account in applying the retail method are covered in detail in intermediate accounting textbooks.

EXHIBIT 6-11   Use of the Retail Method at Year-End

	COST	RETAIL
Inventory, January 1	$100,000	$145,000
Add: Net purchases during the year	250,000	355,000
Goods available for sale	$350,000	$500,000
Ratio of cost to retail: $350,000/$500,000 = 70%		
Inventory, December 31, at retail value, per a physical count		$180,000
Times: Cost to retail ratio		× .70
Inventory, December 31, at cost	$126,000	

Analyzing the Management of Inventory Turnover

Managers must strike a balance between maintaining enough inventory to meet customers' needs and incurring the high cost of carrying inventory. The cost of storage and the lost income from the money tied up to own inventory make it very expensive to keep on hand. Investors are also concerned with a company's inventory management. They pay particular attention to a company's *inventory turnover:*

$$\text{Inventory Turnover} = \frac{\text{Cost of Goods Sold}}{\text{Average Inventory}}$$

Typically, the faster the inventory turnover, the better. For example, a company with cost of goods sold of $1,000,000 and average inventory of $100,000 turns over its inventory 10 times per year. If we assume 360 days in a year, that is once every 36 days. Now assume the same cost of goods sold for a company with an average inventory balance of $200,000. The result in this case is a turnover of only five times per year, or once every 72 days.

FROM CONCEPT TO PRACTICE

READING BEN & JERRY'S FINANCIAL STATEMENTS
Compute Ben & Jerry's inventory turnover for 1992. What is the average length of time it takes to sell its inventory? Does this seem reasonable for the type of business the company is in?

How Inventories Affect Cash Flows Statement

The effects on the income statement and the statement of cash flows from inventory-related transactions differ significantly. We have focused our attention in the last two chapters on how the purchase and sale of inventory are reported on the income statement. We found that the cost of the inventory sold during the period is deducted on the income statement as cost of goods sold.

The appropriate reporting on a statement of cash flows for inventory transactions depends on whether the direct or indirect method is used. If the direct method is used to prepare the operating activities section of the statement, the amount of cash paid to suppliers of inventory is shown as a deduction in this section of the statement.

If the indirect method is used, it is necessary to make adjustments to net income for the changes in two accounts: inventories and accounts payable. An increase in inventory is deducted because it indicates that the company is building up its stock of inventory and thus expending cash. A decrease in inventory is added to net income. An increase in accounts payable is added because it indicates that during the period, the company has increased the amount it owes suppliers and has therefore conserved its cash. A decrease in accounts payable is deducted because the company actually reduced the amount owed suppliers during the period.

LO 9

Explain the effects of inventory transactions on the statement of cash flows.

Reading a Statement of Cash Flows

To test your understanding of these concepts, refer to Wrigley's statement of cash flows as shown below and answer the following questions:

1. Does Wrigley use the direct or the indirect method to prepare the operating activities section of the statement?

2. Did inventories increase or decrease during 1992? Why was the change in the account added to net income in the operating activities section of the statement?

3. Did accounts payable increase or decrease during 1992? Why was the change in the account added to net income in the operating activities section of the statement?

STATEMENT OF
CONSOLIDATED CASH FLOWS

WM. WRIGLEY JR. COMPANY AND WHOLLY OWNED ASSOCIATED COMPANIES

YEAR ENDED DECEMBER 31	1992	1991	1990
	In thousands of dollars		
CASH FLOWS—OPERATING ACTIVITIES			
Net earnings	**$141,295**	128,652	117,362
Adjustments to reconcile net earnings to net cash flows from operating activities:			
Depreciation	**29,806**	28,695	26,860
Gain on sales of property, plant and equipment	**(3,985)**	(365)	(254)
(Increase) decrease in:			
Accounts receivable	**(10,652)**	(6,812)	(5,518)
Inventories	**205**	(7,924)	(22,371)
Other current assets	**(115)**	(1,198)	(5,328)
Other assets and deferred charges	**(6,216)**	(1,452)	(637)
Increase (decrease) in:			
Accounts payable	**7,937**	(5,444)	(4,079)
Accrued expenses	**9,724**	3,938	(293)
Income and other taxes payable	**8,944**	1,963	329
Deferred income taxes	**(11,551)**	(1,161)	787
Other noncurrent liabilities	**23,876**	573	2,438
Net cash flows—operating activities	**189,268**	139,465	109,296
CASH FLOWS—INVESTING ACTIVITIES			
Additions to property, plant and equipment	**(66,682)**	(45,235)	(45,463)
Proceeds from property retirements	**7,983**	4,671	4,606
Net (increase) decrease in short-term investments	**(26,132)**	4,355	9,491
Net cash flows—investing activities	**(84,831)**	(36,209)	(31,366)
CASH FLOWS—FINANCING ACTIVITIES			
Dividends paid	**(72,511)**	(64,609)	(58,060)
Common stock purchased	**(17,579)**	(3,318)	(8,200)
Net cash flows—financing activities	**(90,090)**	(67,927)	(66,260)
Effect of exchange rate changes on cash and cash equivalents	**(3,538)**	(385)	2,836
Net increase in cash and cash equivalents	**10,809**	34,944	14,506
Cash and cash equivalents at beginning of year	**73,335**	38,391	23,885
Cash and cash equivalents at end of year	**$ 84,144**	73,335	38,391
SUPPLEMENTAL CASH FLOW INFORMATION			
Income taxes paid	**$ 78,938**	79,935	69,734
Interest paid	**$ 1,177**	1,369	1,173
Interest and dividends received	**$ 10,893**	10,845	13,938

See accompanying accounting policies and notes.

The answers to these questions are as follows:

1. Wrigley uses the indirect method because the operating activities section starts with the net income or "net earnings" for the period.

2. The change in inventories was added to net earnings and according to the description, this indicates that inventories decreased during the year. When they do decrease, the company is not replacing its inventory as quickly as it is selling it, which in effect saves the company cash.

3. The change in accounts payable was added to net earnings and according to the description, the amounts owed suppliers increased during the year. Wrigley slowed down the payment of cash to suppliers during the year, which resulted in a savings of cash.

A WALL STREET ANALYST LOOKS AT WHAT INVENTORIES REVEAL ABOUT A COMPANY'S PROSPECTS

Name: Mike LaTronica
Profession: Research Director
College Major: Economics

Among the most voracious consumers of financial statements are Wall Street analysts. Their job is to dissect them on behalf of their clients, the nation's investment community.

Michael LaTronica has been a stockbroker, a credit analyst, and a stock market analyst following technology, aerospace, and defense electronics stocks. He is currently director of research at Gruntal & Co., a major Wall Street brokerage firm. His job is to make sure that his research analysts are emphasizing the right investment sectors—the ones that are going to do well in the future. In addition, he is responsible for developing upcoming analysts, defining market strategy, and sculpting Gruntal's research niche in the investment community.

One area on the balance sheet where an analyst can make a judgment about a company is its inventory. "Inventory accounting became an important topic in the late 1970s when inflation was very high," says LaTronica, whose firm is the 10th largest in the United States. "There was a shift from FIFO to LIFO at that time." But today, LIFO is less

popular because inflation has waned. "FIFO is the traditional inventory valuation method for companies that I follow. Goods that are shipped first are the ones that are assumed to be produced first," he says. The result: inventory on the balance sheet is valued at the most current price level. Unlike the 1970s, inventory doesn't sit around very long, anyway. "Just-in-time" inventory techniques have helped companies manage inventories more effectively at leaner levels.

"If you see an inventory buildup starting to occur, that can mean that the product is not shipping," he says. Or it can mean that a new product is

ramping up and awaiting delivery—just like an airplane backs up on a runway. "The balance sheet presentation will look identical." The analysts' job is to get to know the company well enough to be able to decide which is happening.

To be a successful investment analyst, a knowledge of accounting is important. But it takes more than that. "You have to have a sense of market timing, a sense of what drives stocks," says LaTronica. And a good gut instinct.

REVIEW PROBLEM

Stewart Distributing Company sells a single product for $2 per unit and uses a periodic inventory system. The following data are available for the year:

DATE	TRANSACTION	NUMBER OF UNITS	UNIT COST	TOTAL
1/1	Beginning inventory	500	$1.00	$500.00
2/5	Purchase	350	1.10	385.00
4/12	Sale	(550)		
7/17	Sale	(200)		
9/23	Purchase	400	1.30	520.00
11/5	Sale	(300)		

■ REQUIRED

1. Compute cost of goods sold, assuming the use of the weighted average costing method.

2. Compute the dollar amount of ending inventory, assuming the FIFO costing method.

3. Compute gross margin, assuming the LIFO costing method.

4. Assume a 40% tax rate. Compute the amount of taxes saved if Stewart uses the LIFO method rather than the FIFO method.

■ SOLUTION TO REVIEW PROBLEM

1. Cost of goods sold, weighted average cost method:
Cost of goods available for sale
   $500 + $385 + $520 = $1,405
Divided by:
Units available for sale:
   500 + 350 + 400 =   1,250   units
Weighted average cost $1.124   per unit
× Number of units sold:
   550 + 200 + 300 =   1,050   units
Cost of goods sold $1,180.20

2. Ending inventory, FIFO cost method:
Units available for sale   1,250
 − Units sold   1,050
 = Units in ending inventory   200
 × Most recent purchase price of $ 1.30
 = Ending inventory $ 260

3. Gross margin, LIFO cost method:
Sales revenue 1,050 units × $2 each $2,100
Cost of goods sold
   400 units × $1.30 = $520
   350 units × $1.10 =   385
   300 units × $1.00 =   300   1,205
Gross margin $ 895

4. Taxes saved from using LIFO instead of FIFO:

LIFO Cost of goods sold		$1,205
− FIFO Cost of goods sold:		
Cost of goods available for sale	$1,405	
Ending inventory from part 2	260	
Cost of goods sold expense		1,145
Additional expense from use of LIFO		$ 60
× Tax rate		.40
Tax savings from the use of LIFO		$ 24

GUIDANCE ANSWERS TO ACCOUNTING FOR YOUR DECISIONS

YOU ARE THE AUDITOR

When inflation was significant, LIFO typically produced lower income taxes. The reason: the "last out" inventory usually cost more money, lowering profits and, thus, taxes. In a low inflationary environment—which may actually be deflationary in some industries, such as computers—using LIFO doesn't provide material tax savings. Therefore, it probably isn't worthwhile to switch, even if it could be justified.

YOU ARE THE INVESTMENT ANALYST

It should not. For one thing, the effect of the accounting change, 20 cents per share, is probably a small proportion of the company's earnings. Moreover, the company's fundamental outlook as a business has nothing to do with whether it uses LIFO or FIFO. The effect of the change to LIFO was negative. In spite of the fact, analysts should react positively because the company is probably achieving a real savings in terms of cash flow by cutting its tax bill.

APPENDIX 6A

ACCOUNTING TOOLS: INVENTORY COSTING METHODS WITH THE USE OF A PERPETUAL INVENTORY SYSTEM

LO 10

Explain the differences between a periodic and a perpetual inventory system.

The illustrations of the inventory costing methods in the chapter assumed the use of a periodic inventory system. In this appendix, we will see how the methods are applied when a company maintains a perpetual inventory system. Prior to doing so, however, it is useful to look closer at the differences between the two systems.

Journal Entries for the Two Systems

To highlight the differences between the two systems, consider the following three transactions:

1. Purchased on account 500 units at $8 each.
2. Returned for credit 100 units damaged in transit.
3. Sold on account 200 units at $10 each.

Exhibit 6-12 shows the journal entries for the three transactions under each of the two inventory systems. Because the inventory account is updated only *periodically* with the periodic system, the purchase of 500 units of merchandise is accumulated in the temporary account Purchases. The cost of the 100 units returned in the second transaction is credited to the *contra purchases* account Purchase Returns and Allowances. The only entry made at the time of a sale records the revenue earned. Because the inventory account has not been updated for purchases and sales during the period, a *physical count* of the merchandise is required at year-end. This establishes the amount to be shown on the balance sheet as the cost of the inventory and helps determine the amount to appear on the income statement for cost of goods sold. Cost of goods sold is in fact a calculated figure determined in the following way:

Beginning inventory	The inventory at the end of the prior period
+ Net purchases	The balance in the Purchases account, plus any freight-in, less any purchase returns and allowances and any purchase discounts
= Cost of goods available for sale	
− Ending inventory	Based on a physical count
= Cost of goods sold	

As you see in the right side of Exhibit 6-12, in a perpetual system, purchases of merchandise are debited directly to the Inventory account and any returns of merchandise are credited to it. Unlike the periodic system, *two* entries are made at the time of each sale. The first entry is the same under both systems: to record the sales revenue. Because the inventory account is kept *perpetually* up to date, however, a

EXHIBIT 6-12   Comparison of the Periodic and Perpetual Inventory Systems

PERIODIC SYSTEM	DR.	CR.	PERPETUAL SYSTEM	DR.	CR.
1. Purchases	4,000		Inventory	4,000	
Accounts Payable		4,000	Accounts Payable		4,000
To record purchase of 500 units.			To record purchase of 500 units.		

$$A = L + OE$$
$$+4,000 \quad -4,000$$

$$A = L + OE$$
$$+4,000 \quad +4,000$$

2. Accounts Payable	800		Accounts Payable	800	
Purchase Returns and Allowances		800	Inventory		800
To record return of 100 damaged units.			To record return of 100 damaged units.		

$$A = L + OE$$
$$-800 \quad +800$$

$$A = L + OE$$
$$-800 \quad -800$$

3. Accounts Receivable	2,000		Accounts Receivable	2,000	
Sales Revenue		2,000	Sales Revenue		2,000
To record sale of 200 units at $10 each.			To record sale of 200 units at $10 each.		

$$A = L + OE$$
$$+2,000 \quad +2,000$$

$$A = L + OE$$
$$+2,000 \quad +2,000$$

			Cost of Goods Sold	1,600	
			Inventory		1,600
			To record 200 units sold at a cost of $8 each.		

$$A = L + OE$$
$$-1,600 \quad -1,600$$

second entry is made to reduce this account with a corresponding debit to expense for the cost of the merchandise sold. Finally, because the Inventory account has been updated for each purchase and sale of merchandise, a physical count is not the basis for valuing the inventory at the end of the period in a perpetual system. For control purposes, however, most businesses that use a perpetual system count the inventory once a year. Any differences between the amount on hand per the count and the amount appearing in the Inventory account require an adjusting entry in the records and should be investigated.

Inventory Costing Methods with a Perpetual System

It is important to understand the difference between inventory *costing systems* and inventory *methods*. The two inventory systems differ in terms of how often the inventory account is updated, either periodically or perpetually. However, when a company sells identical units of product and the cost to purchase each unit is subject

LO II

Apply the inventory costing methods using a perpetual system.

to change, it also must choose an inventory costing method, such as FIFO, LIFO, or weighted average.

Earlier in the chapter, we illustrated the various costing methods with a periodic system. We now use the same data to illustrate how the methods differ when a perpetual system is used. Keep in mind that if a company uses specific identification, the results will be the same regardless of whether it uses the periodic or the perpetual system. To compare the periodic and perpetual systems for the other methods, one important piece of information, the date of each of the sales, must be added. The original data as well as number of units sold on the various dates are summarized below:

DATE	PURCHASES	SALES	BALANCE
Beginning inventory			500 units @ $10
January 20	300 units @ $11		800 units
February 18		450 units	350 units
April 8	400 units @ $12		750 units
June 19		300 units	450 units
August 5	200 units @ $13		650 units
October 20		150 units	500 units
December 12	100 units @ $14		600 units

FIFO Costing with a Perpetual System

Exhibit 6-13 illustrates the FIFO method on a perpetual basis. The basic premise of FIFO applies whether a periodic or a perpetual system is used: The first units purchased are assumed to be the first units sold. With a perpetual system, however, this concept is applied *at the time of each sale.* For example, note in the exhibit which 450 units are assumed to be sold on February 18. The 450 units sold are taken from the beginning inventory of 500 units with a unit cost of $10. Thus, the inventory or balance after this sale as shown in the last three columns is 50 units at $10 and 300 units at $11, for a total of $3,800. The purchase on April 8 of 400 units at $12 is added to the running balance. On a FIFO basis, the sale of 300 units on June 19 comes from the remainder of the beginning inventory of 50 units and another 250 units from the first purchase at $11 on January 20. The balance after this sale is 50 units at $11 and 400 units at $12. You should follow through the last three transactions in the exhibit to make sure that you understand the application of FIFO or a perpetual basis. An important point to note about the ending inventory of $7,600 is that it is the same amount that we calculated for FIFO periodic earlier in the chapter:

FIFO periodic (Exhibit 6-5) $7,600

FIFO perpetual (Exhibit 6-13) $7,600

Whether the method is applied each time a sale is made or only at the end of the period, the earliest units in are the first units out, and the two systems will yield the same ending inventory.

EXHIBIT 6-13 Perpetual System—FIFO Cost-Flow Assumption

	PURCHASES			SALES			BALANCE		
DATE	UNITS	UNIT COST	TOTAL COST	UNITS	UNIT COST	TOTAL COST	UNITS	UNIT COST	BALANCE
1/1							500	$10	$5,000
1/20	300	$11	$3,300				500	10	
							300	11	8,300
2/18				450	$10	$4,500	50	10	
							300	11	3,800
4/8	400	12	4,800				50	10	
							300	11	
							400	12	8,600
6/19				50	10	500	50	11	
				250	11	2,750	400	12	5,350
8/5	200	13	2,600				50	11	
							400	12	
							200	13	7,950
10/20				50	11	550	300	12	
				100	12	1,200	200	13	6,200
12/12	100	14	1,400				300	12	
							200	13	
							100	14	7,600

LIFO Costing with a Perpetual System

A LIFO cost flow with the use of a perpetual system is illustrated in Exhibit 6-14. First, note which 450 units are assumed to be sold on February 18. The sale consists of the most recent units acquired, 300 units at $11, and then 150 units from the beginning inventory at $10. Thus, the balance after this sale is simply the remaining 350 units from the beginning inventory priced at $10. The purchase on April 8 results in a balance of 350 units at $10 and 400 units at $12.

Note what happens with LIFO when it is applied on a perpetual basis. In essence, a gap is created. Units acquired at the earliest price of $10 and units acquired at the most recent price of $12 are on hand, but none of those at the middle price of $11 remain. This situation arises because LIFO is applied every time a sale is made rather than only at the end of the year. Because of this difference, the amount of ending inventory differs, depending on which system is used:

LIFO periodic (Exhibit 6-5) $6,100
LIFO perpetual (Exhibit 6-14) $6,750

EXHIBIT 6-14   Perpetual System—LIFO Cost-Flow Assumption

	PURCHASES			SALES			BALANCE		
DATE	UNITS	UNIT COST	TOTAL COST	UNITS	UNIT COST	TOTAL COST	UNITS	UNIT COST	BALANCE
1/1							500	$10	$5,000
1/20	300	$11	$3,300				500	10	
							300	11	8,300
2/18				300	$11	$3,300			
				150	10	1,500	350	10	3,500
4/8	400	12	4,800				350	10	
							400	12	8,300
6/19				300	12	3,600	350	10	
							100	12	4,700
8/5	200	13	2,600				350	10	
							100	12	
							200	13	7,300
10/20				150	13	1,950	350	10	
							100	12	
							50	13	5,350
12/12	100	14	1,400				350	10	
							100	12	
							50	13	
							100	14	6,750

EXHIBIT 6-15   Perpetual System—Moving Average Cost-Flow Assumption

	PURCHASES			SALES			BALANCE		
DATE	UNITS	UNIT COST	TOTAL COST	UNITS	UNIT COST	TOTAL COST	UNITS	UNIT COST	BALANCE
1/1							500	$10	$5,000
1/20	300	$11	$3,300				800	10.38*	8,304
2/18				450	$10.38	$4,671	350	10.38	3,633
4/8	400	12	4,800				750	11.24†	8,430
6/19				300	11.24	3,372	450	11.24	5,058
8/5	200	13	2,600				650	11.78‡	7,657
10/20				150	11.78	1,767	500	11.78	5,890
12/12	100	14	1,400				600	12.15§	7,290

The moving average prices per unit are calculated as follows:
*($5,000 + $3,300) / 800 units = $10.38 (rounded to nearest cent)
†($3,633 + $4,800) / 750 units = $11.24
‡($5,058 + $2,600) / 650 units = $11.78
§($5,890 + $1,400) / 600 units = $12.15

Moving Average with a Perpetual System

When a weighted average cost assumption is applied with a perpetual system, it is sometimes called a **moving average.** As indicated in Exhibit 6-15, each time a purchase is made, a new weighted average cost must be computed, thus the name *moving average.* For example, the goods available for sale after the January 20 purchase consist of 500 units at $10 and 300 units at $11, which results in an average cost of $10.38. This is the unit cost applied to the 450 units sold on February 18. The 400 units purchased on April 8 require the computation of a new unit cost, as indicated in the second footnote to the exhibit. As you might have suspected, the ending inventory with an average cost flow does differ, depending on whether a periodic or a perpetual system is used:

Weighted average periodic (Exhibit 6-5) $6,840
Moving average perpetual (Exhibit 6-15) $7,290

CHAPTER HIGHLIGHTS

1. **(LO 1)** A manufacturer's inventory consists of raw materials, work in process, and finished goods. The inventory of a retailer or wholesaler is in a single form called *merchandise inventory.*

2. **(LO 2, 3)** The amount of cost of goods sold reported on the income statement is inherently tied to the value assigned to ending inventory on the balance sheet. Errors in valuing inventory affect cost of goods sold and thus affect the amount of income reported for the period. An understatement of ending inventory will result in an understatement of net income; an overstatement of ending inventory will result in an overstatement of net income.

3. **(LO 3)** All costs necessary to put inventory into a condition and location for sale should be included in its cost. Freight costs, storage costs, excise and sales taxes, and insurance during the time the merchandise is in transit are all candidates for inclusion in the cost of the asset. As a practical manner, however, some of these costs are very difficult to allocate to individual products and are therefore accounted for as expenses of the period.

4. **(LO 4)** The purchase of identical units of a product at varying prices necessitates the use of a costing method to assign a dollar amount to ending inventory and cost of goods sold. As alternatives to the use of a specific identification method, which is impractical in many instances as well as subject to manipulation, accountants have devised cost-flow assumptions.

5. **(LO 4)** The weighted average method assigns the same average unit cost to all units available for sale during the period. It is widely used because of its simplicity.

6. **(LO 4)** The FIFO method assigns the most recent costs incurred to ending inventory. The older costs are assigned to cost of goods sold. A first-in, first-out approach does tend to parallel the physical flow of products in many businesses, although the actual flow is not our primary concern in choosing a costing method.

7. **(LO 4)** LIFO assigns the most recent costs to cost of goods sold, and the older costs remain in inventory. In a period of rising prices, this method results in a relatively higher amount assigned to cost of goods sold

and, thus, a lower amount of net income is reported. Lower net income results in a lower amount of taxes due, and the tax advantages have resulted in the widespread use of the LIFO method.

A company that chooses to take advantage of the tax break from using LIFO on its tax return must also use the method in preparing the income statement. A concern with the use of LIFO is the possibility of a liquidation. If more units are sold than are bought in any one period, some of the units sold will come from the older, lower-priced units, resulting in a low cost of goods sold and a high gross margin. The high gross margin will necessitate a larger tax amount due.

8. **(LO 5)** Many accountants favor LIFO because it results in the nearest approximation to the current cost of goods sold. On the other hand, LIFO results in an inventory amount on the balance sheet which in many cases is very outdated. FIFO gives a much closer approximation to current cost on the balance sheet. It leads, however, to what accountants describe as inventory profit: that portion of the gross margin that is due simply to holding the inventory during an inflationary period.

9. **(LO 6)** As used in the lower of cost or market rule, *market* means *replacement cost.* The purpose of valuing inventory at original cost or replacement cost, whichever is lower, is to anticipate declines in the selling price of goods subject to obsolescence, spoilage, and other types of loss. By being conservative and reducing the carrying value of the inventory at the end of the year, a company is more likely to report its normal gross margin when the units are sold at a reduced price in the next period. The rule can be applied on an item-by-item basis, group basis, or to the entire inventory.

10. **(LO 7)** The gross profit method is used to estimate the cost of inventory lost by theft, fire, flooding, and other types of damage. The method is also useful to estimate the amount of inventory on hand for interim reports, such as quarterly financial statements. It relies on a trustworthy estimate of the gross profit ratio.

11. **(LO 8)** Retailers use the retail inventory method to estimate the cost of inventory for interim financial statements and as a device to convert the year-end inventory, per a physical count, from retail to cost.

12. (LO 9) The payment of cash to suppliers of inventory represents a cash outflow from operating activities on the statement of cash flows. If a company uses the indirect method, however, adjustments are made to net income for the increase or decrease in the Inventory and Accounts Payable accounts.

13. (LO 10) The periodic system relies on a count of inventory on hand at the end of the year to allocate costs between ending inventory and cost of goods sold. No entry is made in a periodic system to record the cost of inventory sold at the time of sale. Acquisitions of inventory during the period are recorded in the temporary account Purchases. (Appendix 6A)

14. (LO 10) The Inventory account is updated at the time of each sale and purchase of merchandise in a perpetual system. The computer has made the perpetual system much more feasible for many businesses. (Appendix 6A)

15. (LO 11) Ending inventory costed at FIFO will be the same, whether the periodic system or the perpetual system is used. This is not the case when the LIFO method is used. The results under a periodic and a perpetual system differ. Likewise, ending inventory differs when a weighted average approach is applied in a periodic system as opposed to a perpetual system. The average method with a perpetual system is really a moving average approach. (Appendix 6A)

KEY TERMS QUIZ

Select one of the following key terms used in the chapter and fill in the appropriate blank to the left of each description. The solution appears at the end of the chapter.

Merchandise Inventory
Work in process
Consignment
Weighted average cost method
LIFO method
LIFO conformity rule
Replacement cost
Lower of cost or market rule
Retail inventory method

Raw materials
Finished goods
Specific identification method
FIFO method
LIFO liquidation
LIFO reserve
Inventory profit
Gross profit method
Moving average (Appendix 6A)

_____   **1.** The name given to an average cost method when it is used with a perpetual inventory system.

_____   **2.** The cost of unfinished products in a manufacturing company.

_____   **3.** An inventory costing method that assigns the same unit cost to all units available for sale during the period.

_____   **4.** The account wholesalers and retailers use to report inventory held for sale.

_____   **5.** A conservative approach to valuing inventory, which is an attempt to anticipate declines in the value of inventory prior to its actual sale.

_____   **6.** An inventory costing method that assigns the most recent costs to ending inventory.

_____   **7.** The inventory of a manufacturer before the addition of any direct labor or manufacturing overhead.

_____   **8.** The current cost of a unit of inventory.

_____   **9.** An inventory costing method that assigns the most recent costs to cost of goods sold.

_____ 10. A technique used to establish an estimate of the cost of inventory stolen, destroyed, or otherwise damaged, or the amount of inventory on hand at an interim date.

_____ 11. The inventory of a manufacturer that is complete and ready for sale.

_____ 12. A technique used by retailers to convert the retail value of inventory to a cost basis.

_____ 13. The IRS requires that if LIFO is used on the tax return, it must also be used in reporting income to stockholders.

_____ 14. An inventory costing method that relies on matching unit costs with the actual units sold.

_____ 15. A legal arrangement in which inventory owned by one company is turned over to another one for sale.

_____ 16. That portion of the gross profit due to holding inventory during a period of rising prices.

_____ 17. The result of selling more units than are purchased during the period, which can have negative tax consequences if a company is using LIFO.

_____ 18. The excess of the value of a company's inventory stated at FIFO as compared to that stated at LIFO.

ALTERNATE TERMS

GROSS MARGIN Gross profit.

INTERIM STATEMENTS Quarterly or monthly statements.

MARKET (value for inventory) Replacement cost.

RAW MATERIALS Direct materials.

RETAIL PRICE Selling price.

QUESTIONS

1. What are three distinct types of costs that manufacturers incur? Describe each of them.
2. What is the relationship between the valuation of inventory as an asset on the balance sheet and the measurement of income?
3. Who owns consigned goods and what is the significance of the ownership for accounting purposes?
4. Delevan Corp. uses a periodic inventory system and is counting its year-end inventory. Due to a lack of communication, two different teams count the same section of the warehouse. What effect will this error have on net income?
5. What is the justification for including freight costs incurred in acquiring incoming goods in the cost of the inventory rather than simply treating the cost as an expense of the period? What is the significance of this decision for accounting purposes?
6. What are the characteristics of a company's inventory that would allow it to use the specific identification method? Give at least two examples of inventory for which the method is appropriate.
7. How can the specific identification method allow management to manipulate income?

8. What is the significance of the adjective *weighted* in the weighted average cost method? Use an example to illustrate your answer.

9. Which inventory method, FIFO or LIFO, more nearly approximates the physical flow of products in most businesses? Explain your answer.

10. York, Inc., manufactures notebook computers and has experienced noticeable declines in the purchase price of many of the components it uses, including computer chips. Which inventory costing method should York use if it wants to maximize net income? Explain your answer.

11. Which inventory costing method should a company use if it wants to minimize taxes? Does your response depend on whether prices are rising or falling? Explain your answers.

12. The president of Ace Retail is commenting on the company's new controller: "The woman is brilliant! She has shown us how we can maximize our income and at the same time minimize the amount of taxes we have to pay the government. Because the cost to purchase our inventory constantly goes up, we will use FIFO to calculate cost of goods sold on the income statement to minimize the amount charged to cost of goods sold and thus maximize net income. For tax purposes, however, we will use LIFO because this will minimize taxable income and thus minimize the amount we have to pay in taxes." Should the president be enthralled with the new controller? Explain your answer.

13. What does the term *LIFO liquidation* mean? How can it lead to poor buying habits?

14. Historical-based costing methods are sometimes criticized for leading to inventory profits. In a period of rising prices, which inventory costing method will lead to the most "inventory profit"? Explain your answer.

15. Is it acceptable for a company to disclose in its annual report that it is switching from some other inventory costing method to LIFO *to save on taxes?*

16. What is the rationale for valuing inventory at the lower of cost or market?

17. Why is it likely that application of the lower of cost or market rule using a total approach, that is, by comparing total cost to total market value, will produce a different result than if the rule is applied on an item-by-item basis?

18. Patterson's controller makes the following suggestion: "I have a brilliant way to save us money. Because we are already using the gross profit method for our quarterly statements, we start using it to estimate the year-end inventory for the annual report and save the money normally spent to have the inventory counted on December 31." What do you think of his suggestion?

19. Why does a company save time and money by using the retail inventory method at the end of the year?

20. (Appendix 6A) In simple terms, how do the inventory costing methods, such as FIFO and LIFO, and inventory systems, such as periodic and perpetual, differ?

21. (Appendix 6A) Why is the weighted average cost method called a *moving average* when a company uses a perpetual inventory system?

EXERCISES

(LO 1) EXERCISE 6-1 CLASSIFICATION OF INVENTORY COSTS

Put an X in the appropriate column next to the inventory item to indicate its most likely classification on the books of a company that manufactures furniture and then sells it in retail company stores.

	CLASSIFICATION			
INVENTORY ITEM	RAW MATERIAL	WORK IN PROCESS	FINISHED GOODS	MERCHANDISE INVENTORY
Fabric				
Lumber				
Unvarnished tables				
Chairs on the showroom floor				
Cushions				
Decorative knobs				
Drawers				
Sofa frames				
Chairs in the plant warehouse				
Chairs in the retail storeroom				

(LO 1) EXERCISE 6-2 INVENTORIABLE COSTS

During the first month of operations, ABC Company incurred the following costs in ordering and receiving merchandise for resale. No inventory has been sold.

List price $100, 200 units purchased.

Volume discount, 10% off list price.

Paid freight costs, $56.

Insurance cost while goods were in transit, $32.

Long-distance phone charge to place orders, $4.35.

Purchasing department salary, $1,000.

Supplies used to label goods at retail price, $9.75.

Interest paid to supplier, $46.

REQUIRED What amount do you recommend the company record as merchandise inventory on its balance sheet? Explain your answer. For any items not to be included in inventory, indicate their appropriate treatment in the financial statements.

(LO 2) EXERCISE 6-3 INVENTORY AND INCOME MANIPULATION

The president of SOS, Inc., is concerned that the net income at year-end will not reach the expected figure. When the sales manager receives a large order on the last day of the fiscal year, the president tells the accountant to record the sale but to ignore any inventory adjustment because the physical inventory has already been taken. How will this affect the current year's net income? Next year's income? What would you do if you were the accountant? Assume SOS uses a periodic inventory system.

(LO 3) EXERCISE 6-4 INVENTORY ERRORS

For each of the following independent situations, fill in the blanks to indicate the effect of the error on each of the various financial statement items. Indicate an understatement (U), an overstatement (O), or no effect (NE). Assume that each of the companies uses a periodic inventory system.

	BALANCE SHEET		INCOME STATEMENT	
ERROR	INVENTORY	RETAINED EARNINGS	COST OF GOODS SOLD	NET INCOME
1. A consignor doesn't include goods out on consignment in its ending inventory.	_____	_____	_____	_____
2. One section of a warehouse is counted twice during the year-end count of inventory.	_____	_____	_____	_____
3. A consignee includes goods held on consignment in its count of inventory at year-end.	_____	_____	_____	_____
4. During the count at year-end, the inventory sheets for one of the stores of a discount retailer is lost.	_____	_____	_____	_____

(LO 5) EXERCISE 6-5 EVALUATION OF INVENTORY COSTING METHODS

Write the letter of the method that is most applicable to each statement.

a. Specific identification.

b. Average cost.

c. First-in, first-out (FIFO).

d. Last-in, first-out (LIFO).

_____ **1.** Most realistic ending inventory.

_____ **2.** Results in cost of goods sold being closest to current product costs.

_____ **3.** Results in highest income during periods of inflation.

_____ **4.** Results in highest ending inventory during periods of inflation.

_____ **5.** Smooths out costs during periods of inflation.

_____ **6.** Not practical for most businesses.

_____ **7.** Puts more weight on the cost of the larger number of units purchased.

_____ **8.** An assumption that most closely reflects the physical flow of goods for most businesses.

(LO 7) EXERCISE 6-6 GROSS PROFIT METHOD

On February 12, a hurricane destroys the entire inventory of Suncoast Corporation. An estimate of the amount of inventory lost is needed for insurance purposes. The following information is available:

Inventory on January 1	$ 15,400
Net sales from January 1 to February 12	105,300
Purchases from January 1 to February 12	84,230

Suncoast estimates its gross profit ratio as 25% of net sales. The insurance company has agreed to pay Suncoast $10,000 as a settlement for the inventory destroyed. Prepare the journal entry on Suncoast's books to recognize the inventory lost and the insurance reimbursement.

■ REQUIRED

(LO 8) EXERCISE 6-7 RETAIL METHOD USED FOR INTERIM REPORTING

Z-Mart, a large retail chain, would like to prepare quarterly financial statements. The following information is available:

	COST	RETAIL
Sales		$8,580,000
Beginning inventory	$ 327,500	$ 584,000
Purchases	$4,635,000	$8,265,000

■ REQUIRED

1. Calculate the estimated cost of the ending inventory.

2. Calculate the gross margin Z-Mart should report on its quarterly income statement.

(LO 8) EXERCISE 6-8 INVENTORY TURNOVER FOR SEARS

The following amounts are available from the 1992 annual report of Sears, Roebuck & Co. for its Merchandising Group (all amounts are in millions of dollars):

Cost of sales, buying and occupancy expenses	$20,717.5
Inventories, December 31, 1992	4,047.9
Inventories, December 31, 1991	4,459.4

■ REQUIRED

1. Compute Sears Merchandise Group's inventory turnover ratio for 1992.

2. What is the average length of time it takes to sell an item of inventory? Explain your answer.

3. Do you think the average length of time it took Sears to sell inventory in 1992 is reasonable? What other information do you need to fully answer this question?

(LO 10) EXERCISE 6-9 PERIODIC AND PERPETUAL JOURNAL ENTRIES (APPENDIX 6A)

Record the journal entries to reflect the following transactions, assuming (a) a periodic system and (b) a perpetual system. Arrange your entries in parallel columns for comparison purposes.

October 1:   Purchased 100 units on account for $7 each.
October 3:   Returned 5 defective units for full credit.
October 8:   Paid $16 freight charges on the October 1 shipment.
October 20: Sold 75 units on account for $10 each.

MULTI-CONCEPT EXERCISES

(LO 4, 5) EXERCISE 6-10 INVENTORY COSTING METHODS—PERIODIC SYSTEM

The following information is available concerning the inventory of Carter, Inc.:

	UNITS	UNIT COST
Beginning inventory	200	$10
Purchases during year:		
March 5	300	11
June 12	400	12
August 23	250	13
October 2	150	15

During the year, Carter sold 1,000 units. It employs a periodic inventory system.

1. Calculate ending inventory and cost of goods sold for each of the following three methods: ■ **REQUIRED**

   a. Weighted average.

   b. FIFO.

   c. LIFO.

2. Assume an estimated tax rate of 30%. How much more or less (indicate which) will Carter pay in taxes by using FIFO instead of LIFO? Explain your answer.

(LO 2, 6) EXERCISE 6-11 LOWER OF COST OR MARKET RULE

Awards Etc. carries an inventory of trophies and ribbons for local sports teams and school clubs. The cost of trophies has dropped in the past year, which pleases the company except for the fact that it has considerable inventory on hand that was purchased at the higher prices. The president is not pleased with the lower profit margin the company is earning. "The lower profit margin will continue until we sell all of this old inventory," he grumbled to the new staff accountant. "Not really," replied the accountant. "Let's write down the inventory to the replacement cost this year, and then next year our profit margin will be in line with the competition."

Explain why the inventory can be carried at an amount less than its cost. Which accounts will be affected by the write-down? What will be the effect on the income of the current year and future years? ■ **REQUIRED**

(LO 5, 11) EXERCISE 6-12 INVENTORY COSTING METHODS—PERPETUAL SYSTEM (APPENDIX 6A)

The following information is available concerning Oshkosh, Inc.:

	UNITS	UNIT COST
Beginning inventory	200	$10
Purchases		
March 5	300	11
June 12	400	12
August 23	250	13
October 2	150	15

Oshkosh, which employs a perpetual system, sold 1,000 units for $22 each during the year. Sales occurred on the following dates:

	UNITS
February 12	150
April 30	200
July 7	200
September 6	300
December 3	150

1. Calculate ending inventory and cost of goods sold for each of the following three methods: ■ **REQUIRED**

   a. Weighted average.

   b. FIFO.

   c. LIFO.

2. For each of the three methods, compare the results with those for Carter in Exercise 6-10. Which of the methods gives a different answer, depending on whether a company uses a periodic or a perpetual inventory system?

3. Assume the use of the perpetual system and an estimated tax rate of 30%. How much more or less (indicate which) will Oshkosh pay in taxes by using LIFO instead of FIFO? Explain your answer.

PROBLEMS

(LO 1) PROBLEM 6-1 INVENTORY COSTS IN VARIOUS BUSINESSES

Businesses incur various costs in selling goods and services. Each business must decide which costs are expenses of the period and which should be included in the cost of the inventory. Various types of businesses are listed below along with certain types of costs they incur:

		ACCOUNTING TREATMENT		
		EXPENSE OF THE PERIOD	INVENTORY COST	OTHER TREATMENT
BUSINESS	TYPES OF COSTS			
Retail shoe store	Shoes for sale			
	Shoe boxes			
	Advertising signs			
Grocery store	Canned goods on the shelves			
	Produce			
	Cleaning supplies			
	Cash registers			
Frame shop	Wooden frame supplies			
	Nails			
	Glass			
Walk-in print shop	Paper			
	Copy machines			
	Toner cartridges			
Restaurant	Frozen food			
	China and silverware			
	Prepared food			
	Spices			

■ REQUIRED Fill in the table to indicate the correct accounting for each of these types of costs by placing an X in the appropriate column. For any costs that receive other treatment, explain what the appropriate treatment is for accounting purposes.

(LO 3) PROBLEM 6-2 INVENTORY ERROR

The following highly condensed income statements and balance sheets are available for Budget Stores for a two-year period (all amounts are stated in thousands of dollars):

INCOME STATEMENTS	1996	1995
Revenues	$20,000	$15,000
Cost of goods sold	13,000	10,000
Gross profit	$ 7,000	$ 5,000
Operating expenses	3,000	2,000
Net income	$ 4,000	$ 3,000

BALANCE SHEETS	DECEMBER 31, 1996	DECEMBER 31, 1995
Cash	$ 1,700	$ 1,500
Inventory	4,200	3,500
Other current assets	2,500	2,000
Long-term assets	15,000	14,000
Total assets	$23,400	$21,000
Liabilities	$ 8,500	$ 7,000
Capital stock	5,000	5,000
Retained earnings	9,900	9,000
Total liabilities and owners' equity	$23,400	$21,000

Before releasing the 1996 annual report, Budget's controller learns that the inventory of one of the stores (amounting to $600,000) was inadvertently omitted from the count on December 31, 1995. The inventory of the store was correctly included in the December 31, 1996, count.

REQUIRED

1. Prepare revised income statements and balance sheets for Budget Stores for each of the two years. Ignore the effect of income taxes.

2. If Budget did not prepare revised statements before releasing the 1996 annual report, what would be the net amount of overstatement or understatement of net income for the two-year period? What would be the overstatement or understatement of retained earnings at December 31, 1996, if revised statements were not prepared?

3. Given your answers in part 2, does it matter if Budget bothers to restate the financial statements of the two years to rectify the error?

(LO 5) PROBLEM 6-3 EVALUATION OF INVENTORY COSTING METHODS

Users of financial statements rely on the information available to them to decide whether to invest in a company or lend it money. As an investor, you are comparing three companies in the same industry. The cost to purchase inventory is rising in the industry. Assume that all expenses incurred by the three companies are the same except for cost of goods sold. The companies use the following methods to value ending inventory:

Company A—weighted average cost.

Company B—first-in, first-out (FIFO).

Company C—last-in, first-out (LIFO).

REQUIRED

1. Which of the three companies will report the highest net income? Explain your answer.

2. Which of the three companies will pay the least in income taxes? Explain your answer.

3. Which method of inventory costing do you believe is superior to the others in providing information to potential investors? Explain.

(LO 6) PROBLEM 6-4 LOWER OF COST OR MARKET RULE

Trendy, a clothing retailer, sells three product lines. Due to a decline in popularity of the Purple line, its replacement price has decreased, and Trendy anticipates a decline in its selling price. Trendy's year-end inventory count provides the following data:

PRODUCT LINE	ORIGINAL COST	COST TO REPLACE	UNITS ON HAND
Black	$4.50	$6.00	2,000
Purple	6.00	2.88	1,000
Red	7.50	9.00	500

■ REQUIRED

1. Compute the ending inventory, applying the lower of cost or market rule

  a. On a total basis.

  b. On an item-by-item basis.

2. Trendy's accountant believes that the company should report the most conservative results. What does conservative mean? What amount should Trendy report on its balance sheet as the value of ending inventory?

(LO 7) PROBLEM 6-5 GROSS PROFIT METHOD OF ESTIMATING INVENTORY LOSSES

On August 1, an office supply store was destroyed by an explosion in its basement. A small amount of inventory valued at $4,500 was saved. An estimate of the amount of inventory lost is needed for insurance purposes. The following information is available:

Inventory, January 1	$ 3,200
Purchases, January–July	164,000
Sales, January–July	113,500

The normal gross profit ratio is 40%. The insurance company will pay the store $65,000.

■ REQUIRED

1. Using the gross profit method, estimate the amount of inventory lost in the explosion.

2. Prepare the journal entry to record the inventory loss and the insurance reimbursement.

(LO 8) PROBLEM 6-6 RETAIL METHOD OF ESTIMATING AND REPORTING INVENTORY

Honeycomb, a retailer, hired a temporary service to count year-end inventory at the retail price marked on the goods. The following information is available:

	COST	RETAIL
Sales		$12,780,000
Beginning inventory	$ 80,000	160,000
Purchases	6,400,000	12,800,000
Ending inventory (per count)		150,000

■ REQUIRED

1. Ignoring the inventory count at retail value, estimate the amount of ending inventory you would expect Honeycomb to report on its year-end balance sheet.

2. Convert the year-end count of inventory at retail value to cost.

3. Compare your answers in parts 1 and 2. Why would the company experience a difference between the amount of expected inventory and the amount actually reported in the physical count?

MULTI-CONCEPT PROBLEMS

(LO 2, 4, 5) PROBLEM 6-7 COMPARISON OF INVENTORY COSTING METHODS—PERIODIC SYSTEM

Bitten Company's inventory records show 600 units on hand on October 1 with a unit cost of $5 each. The following transactions occurred during the month of October:

BALANCE ON HAND	UNIT PURCHASES	UNIT SALES
October 4		500 @ $10.00
8	800 @ $5.40	
9		700 @ $10.00
18	700 @ $5.76	
20		800 @ $11.00
29	800 @ $5.90	

All expenses other than cost of goods sold amount to $3,000 for the month. The company uses an estimated tax rate of 30% to accrue monthly income taxes.

1. Prepare a chart comparing cost of goods sold and ending inventory using the periodic system and the following costing methods: ■ **REQUIRED**

	COST OF GOODS SOLD	ENDING INVENTORY	TOTAL
Weighted average			
FIFO			
LIFO			

2. What does the Total column represent?

3. Prepare income statements for each of the three methods.

4. Will the company pay more or less tax if it uses FIFO as compared to LIFO? How much more or less?

(LO 2, 5, 11) PROBLEM 6-8 COMPARISON OF INVENTORY COSTING METHODS—PERPETUAL SYSTEM (APPENDIX 6A)

Repeat Problem 6-7 using the perpetual system.

(LO 2, 4, 5) PROBLEM 6-9 INVENTORY COSTING METHODS—PERIODIC SYSTEM

Following is an inventory acquisition schedule for Weber Corp. for 1995:

	UNITS	UNIT COST
Beginning inventory	5,000	$10
Purchases:		
February 4	3,000	9
April 12	4,000	8
September 10	2,000	7
December 5	1,000	6

During the year, Weber sold 12,500 units at $12 each. All expenses except cost of goods sold amounted to $20,000. The tax rate is 30%.

■ REQUIRED

1. Compute cost of goods sold and ending inventory under each of the following three methods (assume a periodic inventory system):

   a. Weighted average.

   b. FIFO.

   c. LIFO.

2. Prepare income statements under each of the three methods.

3. Which method do you recommend so that Weber pays the least amount of taxes during 1995? Explain your answer.

4. Weber anticipates that unit costs for inventory will increase throughout 1996. Will it be able to switch from the method you recommended it use in 1995 to another method to take advantage of the increase in prices for tax purposes? Explain your answer.

(LO 4, 8) PROBLEM 6-10 INTERPRETING WAL-MART'S FINANCIAL STATEMENTS

The 1993 annual report for Wal-Mart Stores, Inc., includes the following:

> Note 1. Inventories. Inventories are stated principally at cost (last-in, first-out), which is not in excess of market, using the retail method for inventories in stores.

A friend knows that you are studying accounting and asks you what this note means.

■ REQUIRED

1. Wal-Mart uses the last-in, first-out method. Does this mean that it sells its newest merchandise first?

2. Does Wal-Mart report inventories on its balance sheet at their retail value?

ALTERNATE PROBLEMS

(LO 1) PROBLEM 6-1A INVENTORY COSTS IN VARIOUS BUSINESSES

Sound Traxs, Inc., sells and rents videos to retail customers. The accountant is aware that at the end of the year she must account for inventory but is unsure what videos are considered inventory and how to value them. Videos purchased by the company are placed on the shelf for rental. Every three weeks the company performs a detailed analysis of the rental income from each video and decides whether to keep it as a rental or to offer it for sale in the resale section of the store. Resale videos sell for $10 each regardless of the price Sound Traxs paid for the tape.

■ REQUIRED

1. How should Sound Traxs account for each of the two types of tapes—rentals and resales—on its balance sheet?

2. How would you suggest Sound Traxs account for the videos as they are transferred from one department to another?

(LO 3) PROBLEM 6-2A INVENTORY ERROR

The following condensed income statements and balance sheets are available for Planter Stores, for a two-year period (all amounts are stated in thousands of dollars):

INCOME STATEMENTS	1996	1995
Revenues	$35,982	$26,890
Cost of goods sold	12,594	9,912
Gross profit	$23,388	$16,978
Operating expenses	13,488	10,578
Net income	$ 9,900	$ 6,400

BALANCE SHEETS	DECEMBER 31, 1996	DECEMBER 31, 1995
Cash	$ 9,400	$ 4,100
Inventory	4,500	5,400
Other current assets	1,600	1,250
Long-term assets, net	24,500	24,600
Total assets	$40,000	$35,350
Current liabilities	$ 9,380	$10,600
Capital stock	18,000	18,000
Retained earnings	12,620	6,750
Total liabilities and owners' equity	$40,000	$35,350

Before releasing the 1996 annual report, Planter's controller learns that the inventory of one of the stores (amounting to $500,000) was counted twice in the December 31, 1995, inventory. The inventory was correctly counted in the December 31, 1996, inventory count.

REQUIRED

1. Prepare revised income statements and balance sheets for Planter Stores for each of the two years. Ignore the effect of income taxes.

2. Compute the current ratio at December 31, 1995 before the statements are revised and then compute the current ratio at the same date after the statements are revised. If Planter applied for a loan in early 1996 and the lender required a current ratio of at least 1 to 1, would the error have affected the loan?

3. If Planter did not prepare revised statements before releasing the 1996 annual report, what would be the net amount of overstatement or understatement of net income for the two-year period? What would be the overstatement or understatement of retained earnings at December 31, 1996, if revised statements were not prepared?

4. Given your answers in parts 2 and 3, does it matter if Planter bothers to restate the financial statements of the two years for the error?

(LO 5) PROBLEM 6-3A EVALUATION OF INVENTORY COSTING METHODS

Three large mass merchandisers use the following methods to value ending inventory:

Company X—weighted average cost.
Company Y—first-in, first-out (FIFO).
Company Z—last-in, first-out (LIFO).

The cost of inventory has steadily increased over the past 10 years of the product life. Recently, however, prices have started to decline slightly due to foreign competition.

REQUIRED

1. Will all three companies be equally pleased with the decline in cost of the goods sold? Explain your answer.

2. Company Z would like to change its inventory costing method from LIFO to FIFO. Write an acceptable footnote for its annual report to justify the change.

(LO 6) PROBLEM 6-4A LOWER OF COST OR MARKET INVENTORY RULE

Walden, an outdoor equipment retailer, sells four product lines. Due to a decline in popularity of the Rough line, its replacement price has decreased, and Walden anticipates a decline in the selling price of the Rough line. Walden's year-end inventory count provides the following data:

PRODUCT LINE	ORIGINAL COST	COST TO REPLACE	UNITS ON HAND
Ready	$2.50	$3.00	1,000
Rough	6.00	2.88	2,000
Rugged	7.50	9.00	500
Pansy	9.00	9.50	5,000

REQUIRED

1. Compute the ending inventory, applying the lower of cost or market rule

   a. On a total basis.

   b. On an item-by-item basis.

2. Walden's chief operating officer does not want to alarm investors and views the decline in price as a positive factor in future operations. Explain how a decline in the cost of merchandise may affect an investor's evaluation of the company. How does the lower of cost or market rule affect the company's income statement?

(LO 7) PROBLEM 6-5A GROSS PROFIT METHOD OF ESTIMATING INVENTORY LOSSES

On July 1, an explosion destroyed a fireworks supply company. A small amount of inventory valued at $4,500 was saved. An estimate of the amount of inventory lost is needed for insurance purposes. The following information is available:

Inventory, January 1	$14,200
Purchases, January–June	77,000
Sales, January–June	93,500

The normal gross profit ratio is 70%. The insurance company will pay the supply company $50,000.

REQUIRED

1. Using the gross profit method, estimate the amount of inventory lost in the explosion.

2. Prepare the journal entry to record the inventory loss and the insurance reimbursement.

3. The owner has worked for the past six months making fireworks. She would like the insurance company to pay her for the retail value of the fireworks rather than for part of the cost of supplies. She also believes that she should be able to write off a loss at an amount to reflect her potential loss of sales. Respond to her comments.

(LO 8) PROBLEM 6-6A RETAIL METHOD OF ESTIMATING AND REPORTING INVENTORY

Seifert Company, a retailer, hired a temporary service to count inventory at the end of its first year of business. The inventory was counted at the retail price marked on the goods. The following information is available:

	COST	RETAIL
Sales		$6,575,000
Purchases	$3,580,000	8,950,000
Ending inventory (per count)		2,200,000

■ REQUIRED

1. Ignoring the inventory count at retail value, estimate the amount of ending inventory you would expect Seifert to report on its year-end balance sheet.
2. Convert the year-end count of inventory at retail value to cost.
3. Compare your answers in parts 1 and 2. Why would the company experience a difference between the amount of expected inventory and the amount actually reported in the physical count?

ALTERNATE MULTI-CONCEPT PROBLEMS

(LO 2, 4, 5) PROBLEM 6-7A COMPARISON OF INVENTORY COSTING METHODS

Stellar Inc.'s inventory records show 300 units on hand on November 1 with a unit cost of $4 each. The following transactions occurred during the month of November:

	UNIT PURCHASES	UNIT SALES
November 4		200 @ $9.00
8	500 @ $4.50	
9		500 @ $9.00
18	700 @ $4.75	
20		400 @ $9.50
29	600 @ $5.00	

All expenses other than cost of goods sold amount to $2,000 for the month. The company uses an estimated tax rate of 25% to accrue monthly income taxes.

■ REQUIRED

1. Prepare a chart comparing cost of goods sold and ending inventory using the periodic system and the following costing methods:

	COST OF GOODS SOLD	ENDING INVENTORY	TOTAL
Weighted average			
FIFO			
LIFO			

2. What does the Total column represent?
3. Prepare income statements for each of the three methods.
4. Will the company pay more or less tax if it uses FIFO as compared to LIFO? How much more or less?

(LO 2, 5, 11) PROBLEM 6-8A COMPARISON OF INVENTORY COSTING METHODS— PERPETUAL SYSTEM (APPENDIX 6A)

Repeat Problem 6-7A, using the perpetual system.

(LO 2, 4, 5) PROBLEM 6-9A INVENTORY COSTING METHODS—PERIODIC SYSTEM

Following is an inventory acquisition schedule for Keese Corp. for 1995:

	UNITS	UNIT COST
Beginning inventory	4,000	$20
Purchases:		
February 4	2,000	18
April 12	3,000	16
September 10	1,000	14
December 5	2,500	12

During the year, Keese sold 11,000 units at $30 each. All expenses except cost of goods sold amounted to $60,000. The tax rate is 30%.

■ REQUIRED

1. Compute cost of goods sold and ending inventory under each of the following three methods (assume a periodic inventory system):

   a. Weighted average.

   b. FIFO.

   c. LIFO.

2. Prepare income statements under each of the three methods.

3. Which method do you recommend so that Keese pays the least amount of taxes during 1995? Explain your answer.

4. Keese anticipates that unit costs for inventory will increase throughout 1996. Will it be able to switch from the method you recommended it use in 1995 to another method to take advantage of the increase in prices for tax purposes? Explain your answer.

(LO 1, 5) PROBLEM 6-10A INTERPRETING WASHINGTON POST'S FINANCIAL STATEMENTS

The 1993 annual report of The Washington Post Company includes the following note:

   Inventories. Inventories are valued at the lower of cost or market. Cost of newsprint is determined by the first-in, first-out method and cost of magazine paper is determined by the specific-cost method.

■ REQUIRED

1. What *types* of inventory cost does The Washington Post Company carry? What about newspapers? Aren't these considered inventory?

2. Why would the company choose two different methods to value its inventory?

CASES

READING AND INTERPRETING FINANCIAL STATEMENTS

(LO 1, 4) CASE 6-1 READING AND INTERPRETING BEN & JERRY'S ANNUAL REPORT

Refer to the financial statements for Ben & Jerry's included in its annual report.

1. Before you look at Ben & Jerry's annual report, what types of inventory accounts do you expect? What types of inventory accounts does Ben & Jerry's actually report (refer to the footnote on inventories)?

2. What inventory costing method does Ben & Jerry's use? Look in the footnotes to the financial statements.

3. What portion of total assets is represented by inventory at the end of 1991? at the end of 1992? Do these portions seem reasonable for a company in this business? Explain your answer.

(LO 9) CASE 6-2 READING BEN & JERRY'S STATEMENT OF CASH FLOWS

Refer to the statement of cash flows in Ben & Jerry's 1992 annual report and answer the following questions:

1. Did inventories increase or decrease during 1992? Why was the change in the account deducted from net income in the operating activities section of the statement?

2. Comment on the size of change in inventories during 1992. Is there any explanation in the annual report for the large change in inventories during the year?

3. Did accounts payable increase or decrease during 1992? Why was the change in the account added to net income in the operating activities section of the statement?

(LO 5) CASE 6-3 READING AND INTERPRETING HERMAN MILLER'S INVENTORY FOOTNOTE—THE LIFO RESERVE

The following disclosure is from the footnotes to the 1992 annual report for Herman Miller, Inc., a manufacturer of office furniture:

> The inventories of Herman Miller, Inc., are valued using the last-in, first-out (LIFO) method. The inventories of the company's subsidiaries are valued using the first-in, first-out (FIFO) method. Inventories valued using the LIFO method amounted to $38.4 and $43.6 million at May 30, 1992, and June 1, 1991, respectively.
>
> If all inventories had been valued using the first-in, first-out method, inventories would have been $17.0 and $19.0 million higher than reported at May 30, 1992, and June 1, 1991, respectively. The LIFO method increased net income by $1.3 million ($.05 per share) in 1992, decreased net income by $1.1 million ($.04 per share) in 1991, and had no material effect on net income in 1990.

1. Provide a possible justification for Herman Miller's use of LIFO for certain units of the business and FIFO for others (its subsidiaries).

2. What is the amount of the LIFO reserve on May 30, 1992? on June 1, 1991?

3. Explain the meaning of the increase or decrease in the LIFO reserve during the year ended May 30,1992. What does this tell you about inventory costs for the company? Are they rising or falling? Explain your answer.

4. The LIFO reserve decreased during the year ended May 30, 1992 from $19 million to $17 million, or $2 million. The footnote indicates, however, that the LIFO method increased net income by only $1.3 million. What accounts for this difference?

MAKING FINANCIAL DECISIONS

(LO 4, 5) CASE 6-4 INVENTORY COSTING METHODS

You are the controller for Georgetown Company. At the end of its first year of operations, the company is experiencing cash flow problems. The following information has been accumulated during the year:

PURCHASES

January	1,000 units @ $8
March	1,200 units @ 8
October	1,500 units @ 9

During the year, Georgetown sold 3,000 units at $15 each. The expected tax rate is 35%. The president doesn't understand how to report inventory in the financial statements because no record of the cost of the units sold was kept as each sale was made.

■ REQUIRED
1. What inventory *system* must Georgetown use?

2. Determine the number of units on hand at the end of the year.

3. Explain cost-flow assumptions to the president and the method you recommend. Prepare income statements to justify your position, comparing your recommended method with at least one other method.

(LO 3) CASE 6-5 INVENTORY ERRORS

You are the controller of a rapidly growing mass merchandiser. The company uses a periodic inventory system. As the company has grown and accounting systems have developed, errors have occurred in both the physical count of inventory and the valuation of inventory on the balance sheet. You have been able to identify the following errors as of December 1994:

■ In 1992 one section of the warehouse was not counted. The error resulted in inventory understated on December 31, 1992, by approximately $45,600.

■ In 1993 the replacement cost of some inventory was less than the FIFO value used on the balance sheet. The inventory would have been $6,000 less on the balance sheet dated December 31, 1993.

■ In 1994 the company used the gross profit method to estimate inventory for its quarterly financial statements. At the end of the second quarter, the controller made a math error and overstated the inventory by $20,000 on the quarterly report. The error was not discovered until the end of the year.

■ REQUIRED   What, if anything, should you do to correct each of these errors? Explain your answers.

ACCOUNTING AND ETHICS: WHAT WOULD YOU DO?

(LO 6) CASE 6-6 WRITE-DOWN OF OBSOLETE INVENTORY

As a newly hired staff accountant, you are assigned the responsibility of physically counting inventory at the end of the year. The inventory count proceeds in a timely fashion. The inventory is outdated, however. You suggest that the inventory could not be sold for the cost at which it is carried and that the inventory should be written down to a much lower level. The controller replies that experience has taught her how the market changes and she knows that the units in the warehouse will be more marketable again. The company plans to keep the goods until they are back in style.

■ REQUIRED
1. What effect will writing off the inventory have on the current year's income?

2. What effect does not writing off the inventory have on the year-end balance sheet?

3. What factors should you consider in deciding whether to persist in your argument that the inventory should be written down?

(LO 5) CASE 6-7 SELECTION OF AN INVENTORY METHOD

As controller of a widely held public company, you are concerned with making the best decisions for the stockholders. At the end of its first year of operations, you are faced with the choice of method to value inventory. Specific identification is out of the question because the company sells a large quantity of diversified products. You are trying to decide between FIFO and LIFO. Inventory costs have increased 33% over the year. The chief executive officer has instructed you to do whatever it takes in all areas to report the highest income possible.

1. Which method will satisfy the CEO?

2. Which method do you believe is in the best interest of the stockholders? Explain your answer.

3. Write a brief memo to the CEO to convince him that reporting the highest income is not always the best approach for the shareholders.

■ REQUIRED

ANALYTICAL SOFTWARE CASE

To the Student: Your instructor may assign one or more parts of the analytical software case that is designed to accompany this chapter. This multi-part case gives you a chance to work with real financial statement data using software that stimulates, guides, and hones your analytical and problem-solving skills. It was created especially to support and strengthen your understanding of the chapter's Learning Objectives.

SOLUTION TO KEY TERMS QUIZ

1. Moving average (p. 349)
2. Work in process (p. 314)
3. Weighted average cost method (p. 322)
4. Merchandise Inventory (p. 314)
5. Lower of cost or market rule (p. 331)
6. FIFO method (p. 323)
7. Raw materials (p. 314)
8. Replacement cost (p. 328)
9. LIFO method (p. 324)
10. Gross profit method (p. 335)
11. Finished goods (p. 314)
12. Retail inventory method (p. 337)
13. LIFO conformity rule (p. 327)
14. Specific identification method (p. 321)
15. Consignment (p. 316)
16. Inventory profit (p. 328)
17. LIFO liquidation (p. 327)
18. LIFO reserve (p. 327)

Focus on Financial Results

Xerox Corporation has one of the best-known brand names in the world. In recent years, however, Xerox has faced stiff competition from Japanese photocopy companies such as Canon and Minolta—but has recently regained market share. In addition, Xerox has diversified into printers, fax machines, scanners, workstations, networks, computer software, and supplies. In 1992, the company generated $600 million in income ($5.36 per share) on worldwide revenue of $15 billion from these products. Revenues from "document processing" grew from $13.8 billion in 1991 to $14.7 billion in 1992.

In recent years, however, the company had been held back by its financial services division. Xerox's 1992 balance sheet was divided into (1) Document Processing and (2) Insurance and Other Financial Services ("IOFS"), because these two core businesses were so different. In the current assets section, Document Processing contained almost no cash and no marketable securities but had a healthy $5 billion in receivables. IOFS had Investments Held for Sale of $11.7 billion but much more modest receivables. The businesses clearly *are* different. In late 1992, Xerox decided to sell its financial services division to concentrate on document processing.

Consolidated Balance Sheets

December 31 (in millions)	1992	1991
Assets		
Document Processing		
Cash	$ 2	$ 10
Accounts Receivable, net	1,751	1,781
Finance Receivables, net	3,162	2,550
Inventories	2,257	2,091
Deferred Taxes and Other Current Assets	864	680
Total Current Assets	8,036	7,112
Finance Receivables Due after One Year, net	5,337	4,621
Land, Building and Equipment, net	2,150	1,950
Investments in Affiliates, at Equity	957	856
Other Assets	660	639
Total Document Processing Assets	17,140	15,178
Insurance and Other Financial Services		
Cash	85	70
Investments Held for Sale	11,740	11,171
Reinsurance Receivables	445	560
Premiums and Other Receivables	1,086	1,011
Goodwill	427	930
Deferred Taxes and Other Assets	1,957	1,514
Total Insurance and Other Financial Services Assets	15,740	15,256
Investment in Discontinued Operations, net	1,171	1,896
Total Assets	$34,051	$32,330
Liabilities and Equity		
Document Processing		
Short-Term Debt and Current Portion of Long-Term Debt	$ 2,533	$ 2,038
Accounts Payable	544	543
Accrued Compensation and Benefit Costs	722	780
Unearned Income	363	317
Other Current Liabilities	1,296	1,152
Total Current Liabilities	5,458	4,830
Allocated Long-Term Debt	4,950	4,422
Liability for Postretirement Medical Benefits	927	–
Deferred Taxes and Other Liabilities	1,625	1,653
Total Document Processing Liabilities	12,960	10,905
Insurance and Other Financial Services		
Unpaid Losses and Loss Expenses	6,892	6,400
Policyholders' Funds on Deposit	3,682	3,341
Unearned Income	850	832
Other Liabilities	1,361	1,133
Total Insurance and Other Financial Services Operating Liabilities	12,785	11,706
Insurance and Other Financial Services Allocated Debt	2,532	2,388
Discontinued Operations Allocated Debt	623	1,015
Deferred ESOP Benefits	(681)	(720)
Minorities' Interests in Equity of Subsidiaries	885	818
Preferred Stock	1,072	1,078
Common Shareholders' Equity	3,875	5,140
Total Liabilities and Equity	$34,051	$32,330

Shares of common stock issued and outstanding at December 31, 1992 and 1991 (in thousands) were 95,066 and 92,846, respectively.

The accompanying notes are an integral part of the consolidated financial statements.

Chapter 7

Cash and Receivables

LEARNING OBJECTIVES

After studying this chapter, you should be able to

1. Identify and describe the various forms of cash reported on a balance sheet.
2. Understand the accounting for investments of idle cash in financial instruments such as certificates of deposit.
3. Explain the use of a bank reconciliation as a control device for cash.
4. Explain the use of a petty cash fund as a control device for cash.
5. Understand how to account for accounts receivable, including bad debts.
6. Understand how to account for interest-bearing notes receivable.
7. Understand how to account for non-interest-bearing notes receivable.
8. Explain various techniques that companies use to accelerate the inflow of cash from sales.
9. Explain the effects of transactions involving liquid assets on the statement of cash flows.

Linkages

A LOOK AT PREVIOUS CHAPTERS

In the two preceding chapters, we discussed the accounting for inventories, a major asset for many companies. The emphasis in Chapter 5 was on merchandise inventory and the accounting for purchases and sales of it. In Chapter 6, we considered how inventory is valued in the accounts, using a costing method such as weighted average, FIFO, or LIFO.

A LOOK AT THIS CHAPTER

We now turn our attention to assets, namely cash and receivables, that come into existence because a company sells its inventory. We examine the composition of cash and the controls necessary to protect it. The second part of the chapter covers various valuation issues relative to both accounts receivable and notes receivable.

A LOOK AT UPCOMING CHAPTERS

Chapter 8 focuses attention on the long-term operational assets necessary to run a business, such as property, plant, and equipment and intangibles. In Chapters 9 and 10 we explore the use of liabilities to finance the purchase of assets.

Wm. Wrigley Jr. Company, like all businesses, relies on *liquid assets* to function smoothly. *Liquidity* is a relative term. It deals with a company's ability to pay its debts as they fall due. Most obligations must be paid in cash, and therefore cash is considered the most liquid of all assets. Accounts and notes receivable are not as liquid as cash. Their collection does result in an inflow of cash, however. Because cash in its purest form does not earn a return, most businesses invest in various types of securities as a way to use idle cash over the short term. The current asset section of Wrigley's balance sheet, as shown in Exhibit 7-1, indicates three highly liquid assets: cash and cash equivalents, short-term investments, and accounts receivable. Inventories are not considered as liquid as these three assets because they depend on a sale to be realized.

We begin the chapter by considering the various forms cash can take. We consider the use of various types of financial instruments, such as bank certificates of deposit, as a way to invest idle cash over the short term. We discuss two important cash control features, bank reconciliations and petty cash systems. The chapter concludes with a discussion of the accounting for both accounts receivable and notes receivable.

What Constitutes Cash?

LO   1

Identify and describe the various forms of cash reported on a balance sheet.

Cash takes many different forms. Coin and currency on hand and cash on deposit in the form of checking, savings, and money market accounts are the most obvious forms of cash. Also included in cash are various forms of checks, including undeposited checks from customers, cashier's checks, and certified checks. The proliferation of different types of financial instruments on the market today makes it very difficult to decide on the appropriate classification of these various items. The key to the classification of an amount as cash is that it be *readily available to pay debts*. Technically, a bank has the legal right to demand that the customer notify it before making withdrawals from savings accounts, or time deposits, as they are often called. Because this right is rarely exercised, however, savings accounts are normally classified as cash. In contrast, a certificate of deposit has a specific maturity date and carries a penalty for early withdrawal and is therefore not included in cash.

Cash Equivalents and the Statement of Cash Flows

Note that the first item on Wrigley's balance sheet is titled Cash and Cash Equivalents. Examples of items normally classified as cash equivalents are commercial paper issued by corporations, treasury bills issued by the federal government, and money market funds offered by financial institutions. According to current accounting standards, classification as a **cash equivalent** is limited to those investments that are readily convertible to known amounts of cash and that have an original maturity to the investor of three months or less. Note that according to this definition, a *six-month* bank certificate of deposit would *not* be classified as a cash equivalent.

The statement of cash flows that accompanies Wrigley's balance sheet is shown in Exhibit 7-2. Note the direct tie between this statement and the balance sheet (refer to the current asset section of Wrigley's balance sheet as shown in Exhibit 7-1). The cash and cash equivalents of $84,144,000 at the end of 1992, as shown at the bottom of the statement of cash flows, is the same amount that appears as the first line on the balance sheet. The reason for this is that the statement of cash flows traces the flow of cash from the beginning balance of cash for the year—

EXHIBIT 7-1 Wrigley's Partial Balance Sheet

CONSOLIDATED BALANCE SHEET

WM. WRIGLEY JR. COMPANY AND WHOLLY OWNED ASSOCIATED COMPANIES

AS OF DECEMBER 31	1992	1991
	In thousands of dollars	
ASSETS		
Current assets:		
Cash and cash equivalents	$ 84,144	73,335
Short-term investments, at cost which approximates market	98,314	71,575
Accounts receivable		
(less allowance for doubtful accounts: **1992—$2,357;** 1991—$2,454)	95,939	92,527
Inventories—		
Finished goods	38,352	37,736
Raw materials and supplies	117,403	117,770
	155,755	155,506
Other current assets	10,270	10,415
Deferred income taxes - current	4,217	—
Total current assets	448,639	403,358

$73,335,000—to the year's ending balance, $84,144,000. Cash inflow from operating activities, $189,268,000, minus cash outflow from investing activities, $84,831,000 minus cash outflow from financing activities, $90,090,000, minus the effects of currency fluctuations, $3,538,000, equals a net increase in cash of $10,809,000. Add $10,809,000 to the beginning cash balance to arrive at $84,144,000.

Note the third item listed under Cash Flows—Investing Activities on the statement of cash flows. The net (increase) decrease in short-term investments represents the net purchases or sales of short-term investments during the year. Therefore, any purchases or sales of items classified as short-term investments are considered significant and worthy of reporting on the statement of cash flows. Any purchases or sales of items classified as cash equivalents, however, are not considered significant activities. Instead, they are included with cash on the balance sheet and considered to be its "equivalent."

Investing Idle Cash

The seasonal nature of most businesses leads to the potential for a shortage of cash during certain times of the year and an excess of cash during other times. Companies typically deal with *cash shortages* by borrowing on a short-term basis, either from a bank in the form of notes or from other entities in the form of commercial paper.

LO **2**

Understand the accounting for investments of idle cash in financial instruments such as certificates of deposit.

EXHIBIT 7-2   Wrigley's Statement of Cash Flows

STATEMENT OF
CONSOLIDATED CASH FLOWS

WM. WRIGLEY JR. COMPANY AND WHOLLY OWNED ASSOCIATED COMPANIES

YEAR ENDED DECEMBER 31	1992	1991	1990
	In thousands of dollars		
CASH FLOWS—OPERATING ACTIVITIES			
Net earnings	**$141,295**	128,652	117,362
Adjustments to reconcile net earnings to net cash flows from operating activities:			
Depreciation	**29,806**	28,695	26,860
Gain on sales of property, plant and equipment	**(3,985)**	(365)	(254)
(Increase) decrease in:			
Accounts receivable	**(10,652)**	(6,812)	(5,518)
Inventories	**205**	(7,924)	(22,371)
Other current assets	**(115)**	(1,198)	(5,328)
Other assets and deferred charges	**(6,216)**	(1,452)	(637)
Increase (decrease) in:			
Accounts payable	**7,937**	(5,444)	(4,079)
Accrued expenses	**9,724**	3,938	(293)
Income and other taxes payable	**8,944**	1,963	329
Deferred income taxes	**(11,551)**	(1,161)	787
Other noncurrent liabilities	**23,876**	573	2,438
Net cash flows—operating activities	**189,268**	139,465	109,296
CASH FLOWS—INVESTING ACTIVITIES			
Additions to property, plant and equipment	**(66,682)**	(45,235)	(45,463)
Proceeds from property retirements	**7,983**	4,671	4,606
Net (increase) decrease in short-term investments	**(26,132)**	4,355	9,491
Net cash flows—investing activities	**(84,831)**	(36,209)	(31,366)
CASH FLOWS—FINANCING ACTIVITIES			
Dividends paid	**(72,511)**	(64,609)	(58,060)
Common stock purchased	**(17,579)**	(3,318)	(8,200)
Net cash flows—financing activities	**(90,090)**	(67,927)	(66,260)
Effect of exchange rate changes on cash and cash equivalents	**(3,538)**	(385)	2,836
Net increase in cash and cash equivalents	**10,809**	34,944	14,506
Cash and cash equivalents at beginning of year	**73,335**	38,391	23,885
Cash and cash equivalents at end of year	**$ 84,144**	73,335	38,391
SUPPLEMENTAL CASH FLOW INFORMATION			
Income taxes paid	**$ 78,938**	79,935	69,734
Interest paid	**$ 1,177**	1,369	1,173
Interest and dividends received	**$ 10,893**	10,845	13,938

See accompanying accounting policies and notes.

■ **ACCOUNTING FOR YOUR DECISIONS**   **You Are the Investment Analyst**

According to Exhibit 7-2, Wrigley earned $141.3 million in 1992, but the company's cash balance only increased by $10.8 million. How do you account for most of the difference? What is the more impressive trend: the company's three-year earnings record or its three-year record in generating cash flow from operating activities?

The maturities of the bank notes or the commercial paper generally range anywhere from 30 days to six months.

To highlight the need to deal with *excess cash* during certain times of the year, consider as an example the seasonal nature of the ice cream business. Ben & Jerry's 1992 annual report admits the obvious by stating, "The Company typically experiences more demand for its products during the summer than during the winter months." A footnote from the same report highlights the seasonality of the business:

	FIRST QUARTER	SECOND QUARTER	THIRD QUARTER	FOURTH QUARTER
Net sales	$27,336,410	$35,820,845	$40,823,659	$27,987,900

Because the third quarter of the year (the months of July, August, and September) generated sales that were almost 150% of the sales of the first quarter of the year, it is natural that Ben & Jerry's had excess cash to invest at the end of the summer selling season. According to the annual report:

Cash equivalents represent highly liquid investments with maturities of three months or less at date of purchase. Investments representing bank certificates of deposit and tax-exempt debt instruments with a maturity of between three months and one year, are stated at aggregate amortized cost, which approximates market.

Thus, we see that Ben & Jerry's uses various financial instruments, including certificates of deposits, as a way to invest excess cash during the slower winter months, prior to the use of those funds to build up inventory during the busier summer months.

Accounting for an Investment in a Certificate of Deposit (CD)

Assume that on October 2, 1995, Ben & Jerry's invests $100,000 of excess cash in a 120-day certificate of deposit. The CD matures on January 30, 1996, at which time Ben & Jerry's receives the $100,000 invested and interest at an annual rate of 6%. The entry to record the purchase of the CD is

```
1995
Oct. 2   Short-Term Investments—CD              100,000
             Cash                                           100,000
         To record purchase of 6%, 120-day CD.
```

Assets	**=**	**Liabilities**	**+**	**Owners' Equity**
+ 100,000				
− 100,000				

Assuming December 31 is the end of Ben & Jerry's fiscal year, an entry is needed on this date to record interest earned during 1995, even though no cash will be received until the CD matures in 1996:

```
1995
Dec. 31  Interest Receivable                              1,500
             Interest Revenue                                     1,500
         To record interest earned: $100,000 × .06 × 90/360
```

Assets	=	Liabilities	+	Owners' Equity
+1,500				+1,500

The basic formula to compute interest is as follows:

$$\text{Interest (I)} = \text{Principal (P)} \times \text{Interest Rate (R)} \times \text{Time (T)}$$

Because interest rates are normally stated on an annual basis, time is interpreted to mean the fraction of a year that the investment is outstanding. The amount of interest is based on the principal or amount invested ($100,000), times the rate of interest (6%), times the fraction of a year the CD was outstanding in 1995 (29 days in October + 30 days in November + 31 days in December = 90 days). To simplify calculations, it is easiest to assume 360 days in a year in computing interest. With the availability of computers to do the work, however, most businesses now use 365 days in a year to calculate interest. Throughout this book, we assume 360 days in a year to allow us to focus on concepts rather than detailed calculations. Thus, in our example, the fraction of a year that the CD is outstanding during 1995 is 90/360.

The entry on January 30 to record the receipt of the principal amount of the CD of $100,000 and interest for 120 days is

```
1996
Jan. 30  Cash                                            102,000
             Short-Term Investments—CD                          100,000
             Interest Receivable                                  1,500
             Interest Revenue                                       500
         To record the maturity of $100,000 CD.
```

Assets	=	Liabilities	+	Owners' Equity
+102,000				+500
−100,000				
−1,500				

This combination journal entry results in the removal of both the CD and interest receivable from the records and the recognition of $500 in interest earned during the first 30 days of 1996: $100,000 × .06 × 30/360 = $500.

Classification of Short-Term Investments

Recall our earlier discussion in this chapter about cash equivalents. Accountants classify an item as a cash equivalent if it is convertible to a known amount of cash and has an original maturity to the investor of three months or less. For example, Ben & Jerry's would classify any of its certificates of deposit with a maturity of three months or less as cash equivalents. Because all others mature in more than 90 days, they are classified as short-term investments. The same distinction holds true for all other liquid financial instruments, such as Treasury bills of the federal government and commercial paper issued by large corporations: if the original maturity is three months or less, the investments are classified as cash equivalents; otherwise, they are classified as short-term investments.

In addition to investments in highly liquid financial instruments, some companies invest in the stocks and bonds of other corporations, as well as bonds issued by various government agencies. Securities issued by corporations as a form of ownership in the business, such as common stock and preferred stock, are called **equity securities.** Because these securities are a form of ownership, they do not have a maturity date. Alternatively, bonds issued by corporations and governmental bodies as a form of borrowing are called **debt securities.** The term of a bond can be relatively short, such as 5 years, or much longer, such as 20 or 30 years.

Assume that Jacobsen Corporation buys 100 shares of General Motors common stock as an investment. Should the shares be classified as a short-term investment and thus included in the current asset section of the balance sheet or should they be shown among the long-term assets? The answer depends on Jacobsen's *intent* and the *marketability* of the stock. Certainly shares of GM stock are marketable, that is, Jacobsen could sell them if it so desires. Thus, if the company intends to sell the 100 shares of GM stock within one year of the date of the balance sheet or within the operating cycle of the business, whichever is longer, the shares are classified as a short-term investment. Otherwise, they must be classified as long term.

A company is not guaranteed a specific amount upon selling an investment just because it is "marketable." An investor reviewing his or her portfolio during the fourth quarter of 1987 could attest to that. The October 19, 1987, stock market crash cut the value of the Dow Jones Industrial Averages by 508 points. The securities were marketable but at very depressed prices.

Current accounting standards recognize two distinct types of equity securities: trading securities and available-for-sale securities. *Trading securities* are purchased and held principally to sell in the near future and are therefore always classified as current assets. *Available-for-sale securities* are marketable, but the company's intent dictates whether they are classified as current or noncurrent. The valuation of investments in equity securities as well as investments in debt securities is discussed in Chapter 13.

One popular form of short-term investment is the certificate of deposit at banks that we discussed earlier. The federal government insures CDs up to $100,000 per account. Their chief drawback, however, is their lack of liquidity. That is, if the company needs the money right away, it may have to pay a penalty or forfeit interest to get cash. U.S. Treasury bonds, commercial paper (short-term notes issued by large industrial companies), and government and corporate bonds and stocks are more liquid but involve some degree of risk. Treasury bonds are backed by the "full faith and credit of the U.S. government," but they can trade at a discount if interest rates have risen. Commercial paper and corporate bonds also involve risk, and it's conceivable that the company issuing the debt could go out of business.

Control over Cash

In Chapter 5, we discussed the concept of internal control and the critical role it plays for an asset such as cash. Because cash is universally accepted as a medium of exchange, control over it is critical to the smooth functioning of any business, no matter how large or small.

Cash Management

In addition to the need to guard against theft and other abuses related to the physical custody of cash, management of this asset is also important. Cash management is necessary to ensure that at any point in time a company has neither too little nor too much cash on hand. The necessity to have enough cash on hand is obvious: suppliers, employees, taxing agencies, banks, and all other creditors must be paid on time if an entity is to remain in business. It is equally important that a company not maintain cash on hand and on deposit in checking accounts beyond a minimal amount that is necessary to support ongoing operations. This is so because cash is essentially a nonearning asset. Granted, some checking accounts pay a very meager rate of interest. The superior return that could be earned by investing idle cash in various forms of marketable securities dictates, however, that companies carefully monitor the amount of cash on hand at all times.

A company that has too much cash on its balance sheet could find itself a takeover target. For one thing, the idle cash could be used to finance the transaction. For another, a company's board of directors could be persuaded by a potential buyer that the company is not investing its assets optimally. The board of directors should be aware, however, that investing idle cash in marketable securities carries a certain degree of risk. Stocks and bonds are not guaranteed investments. Even U.S. Treasury securities, which are guaranteed at maturity, can drop in value when interest rates rise.

An important tool in the management of cash, the cash flows statement, is discussed in detail in Chapter 15. Cash budgets, which are also critical to the management of cash, are discussed in management accounting and business finance texts. Cash management is one important aspect of control over cash. Beyond cash management, companies often use two other cash control features: bank reconciliations and petty cash funds. Before we turn to these control devices, we need to review the basic features of a bank statement.

Reading a Bank Statement

Two fundamental principles of internal control discussed in Chapter 5 are worth repeating: All cash receipts should be deposited daily intact and all cash payments should be made by check. Checking accounts at banks are critical in this regard. These accounts allow the company to carefully monitor and control cash receipts and cash payments. Control is aided further by the monthly **bank statement.** Most banks mail their customers a monthly bank statement for each account. The statement provides a detailed list of all activity for a particular account during the month. An example of a typical bank statement is shown in Exhibit 7-3. Note that the bank statement indicates the activity in one of the cash accounts maintained by Weber Products, Inc., at the Mt. Etna State Bank.

Before we look at the various items that appear on a bank statement, it is important to understand the route a check takes after it is written. Assume that Weber writes a check on its account at the Mt. Etna State Bank. Weber mails the check to one of its suppliers, Keese Corp., which deposits the check in its account at the Second City Bank. At this point, Second City presents the check to Mt. Etna for payment and Mt. Etna reduces the balance in Weber's account accordingly. The canceled check has now "cleared" the banking system. Either the canceled check itself, or a copy of it, is returned with Weber's next bank statement.

The following types of items appear on Weber's bank statement:

Canceled checks—The checks written by Weber that cleared the bank during the month of June are listed with the corresponding check number and the date paid.

EXHIBIT 7-3 Bank Statement

MT. ETNA STATE BANK
CHICAGO, ILLINOIS

STATEMENT OF ACCOUNT

Weber Products, Inc.
502 Dodge St.
Chicago, IL 66606

FOR THE MONTH ENDING   June 30, 1995
ACCOUNT   0371-22-514

DATE	DESCRIPTION	DEBITS	CREDITS	BALANCE
6-01	Previous balance			3,236.41
6-01	Check 497	723.40		2,513.01
6-02	Check 495	125.60		2,387.41
6-06	Check 491	500.00		1,887.41
6-07	Deposit		1,423.16	3,310.57
6-10	Check 494	185.16		3,125.41
6-13	NSF check	245.72		2,879.69
6-15	Deposit		755.50	3,635.19
6-18	Check 499	623.17		3,012.02
6-20	Check 492	125.00		2,887.02
6-22	Deposit		1,875.62	4,762.64
6-23	Service charge	20.00		4,742.64
6-24	Check 493	875.75		3,866.89
6-24	Check 503	402.10		3,464.79
6-26	Customer note, interest		550.00	4,014.79
6-26	Service fee on note	16.50		3,998.29
6-27	Check 500	1,235.40		2,762.89
6-28	Deposit		947.50	3,710.39
6-30	Check 498	417.25		3,293.14
6-30	Interest earned		15.45	3,308.59
6-30	Statement Totals	5,495.05	5,567.23	

Keep in mind that some of these checks may have been written by Weber in a previous month, but they were not presented for payment to the bank until June. You also should realize that Weber may have written some checks during June that do not yet appear on the bank statement because they have not yet been presented for payment. A check written by a company but not yet presented to the bank for payment is called an **outstanding check.**

Deposits—In keeping with the internal control principle calling for the deposit of all cash receipts intact, most companies deposit all checks, coin, and currency on a

*For control purposes, cash receipts should be deposited daily at the bank. Since banks can make mistakes in entering and processing deposits and withdrawals, businesses should perform a **bank reconciliation** after receiving every statement. For better service, many banks maintain commercial windows or drive-up lanes for their business customers.*

daily basis. For the sake of brevity, we have limited to four the number of deposits that Weber made during the month. Keep in mind that Weber also may have made a deposit on the last day or two of the month and that this deposit may not yet be reflected on the bank statement. This type of deposit is called a **deposit in transit.**

NSF check—NSF is an abbreviation for *not sufficient funds.* The NSF check listed on the bank statement on June 13 is a customer's check that Weber recorded on its books, deposited, and thus included in its bank account. When Mt. Etna State Bank learned that the check was not good because the customer did not have sufficient funds on hand in its bank account to cover the check, the bank deducted the amount from Weber's account. Weber needs to contact its customer to collect the amount due; ideally, the customer will issue a new check once it has sufficient funds in its account.

Service charge—Banks charge for various services they provide to customers. Three of the most common bank service charges are fees charged for new checks, for the rental of a lock box at the bank in which to store valuable company documents, and for the collection of customer notes by the bank.

Customer note and interest—It is often convenient to have customers pay amounts owed to a company directly to that company's bank. The bank simply acts as a collection agency for the company.

Interest earned—Most checking accounts pay interest on the average daily balance in the account. Rates paid on checking accounts are usually significantly less than could be earned on most other forms of investment.

The Bank Reconciliation

LO 3

Explain the use of a bank reconciliation as a control device for cash.

A **bank reconciliation** should be prepared for each individual bank account as soon as the bank statement is received. Ideally, the reconciliation should be performed, or at a minimum, thoroughly reviewed, by someone independent of custody, record-keeping, and authorization responsibilities relating to cash. As the name implies, the purpose of a bank reconciliation is to *reconcile* the balance that the bank shows for an account with the balance that appears on the company's books. Differences between the two amounts are investigated and, if necessary, journal entries are prepared. The following are the steps in preparing a bank reconciliation:

1. Trace deposits listed on the bank statement to the books. Any deposits recorded on the books but not yet shown on the bank statement are deposits in transit. Prepare a list of the deposits in transit.

2. Arrange the canceled checks in numerical order and trace each of them to the books. Any checks recorded on the books but not yet listed on the bank statement are outstanding. List the outstanding checks.

3. List all items shown as additions or credits on the bank statement, other than deposits, such as interest paid by the bank for the month and amounts collected by the bank from one of the company's customers. When the bank pays interest or collects an amount owed to a company by one of the company's customers, the bank increases or *credits* its liability to the company on its own books. For this reason, these items are called **credit memoranda.**

4. List all amounts shown as deductions or debits on the bank statement, other than canceled checks, such as any NSF checks and the various service charges mentioned earlier. When a company deposits money in a bank, a liability is created on the books of the bank. Therefore, when the bank reduces the amount of its liability for these various items, it *debits* the liability on its own books. For this reason, these items are called **debit memoranda.**

5. Identify any errors made by the bank or by the company in recording the various cash transactions.

6. Use the information collected in steps 1 through 5 to prepare a bank reconciliation.

Companies use a number of different *formats* in preparing bank reconciliations. For example, some companies take the balance shown on the bank statement and reconcile this amount to the balance shown on the books. Another approach, which we will illustrate for Weber Products, involves reconciling the bank balance and the book balance to an adjusted balance, rather than one to the other. As we will see, the advantage of this approach is that it yields the correct balance and makes it easy for the company to make any necessary adjustments to its books. A bank reconciliation for Weber Products is shown in Exhibit 7-4. The following are explanations for the various items on the reconciliation:

1. The balance per bank statement of $3,308.59 is taken from the June statement as shown in Exhibit 7-3.

2. Weber's records showed a deposit for $642.30 made on June 30 that is not reflected on the bank statement. The deposit in transit is listed as an addition to the balance per the bank statement.

3. The accounting records indicate three checks written that have not yet been reflected on the bank statement. The three outstanding checks are as follows:

496	$ 79.89
501	$213.20
502	$424.75

EXHIBIT 7-4   Bank Reconciliation

WEBER PRODUCTS
BANK RECONCILIATION
JUNE 30, 1995

Balance per bank statement, June 30			$3,308.59
Add:	Deposit in transit		642.30
Deduct:	Outstanding checks:		
	No. 496	$ 79.89	
	No. 501	213.20	
	No. 502	424.75	(717.84)
Adjusted balance, June 30			$3,233.05
Balance per books, June 30			$2,895.82
Add:	Customer note collected	$500.00	
	Interest on customer note	50.00	
	Interest earned during June	15.45	
	Error in recording check 498	54.00	619.45
Deduct:	NSF check	$245.72	
	Collection fee on note	16.50	
	Service charge for lock box	20.00	(282.22)
Adjusted balance, June 30			$3,233.05

Outstanding checks are just the opposite of deposits in transit and therefore are deducted from the balance per the bank statement.

4. The adjusted balance of $3,233.05 is found by adding the deposit in transit and deducting the outstanding checks from the balance per the bank statement.

5. The $2,895.82 balance per the books on June 30 is taken from the company's records as of that particular date.

6. According to the bank statement, $550 was credited to the account on June 26 for the collection of a note with interest. We assume that the repayment of the note itself accounted for $500 of this amount and that the other $50 was for interest. The bank statement notifies Weber that the note with interest has been collected. Therefore, Weber must add $550 to the balance currently shown on its books.

7. An entry on June 30 on the bank statement shows a credit of $15.45 for interest earned on the bank account during June. This amount is added to the balance per the books.

8. A review of the canceled checks returned with the bank statement detected an error made by Weber. The company records indicated that check 498 was recorded incorrectly as $471.25, but the check was actually written for $417.25 and reflected as such on the bank statement. This error, referred to as a *transposition error,* resulted from transposing the 7 and the 1 in recording the check in the books. The error is the difference between the amount of $471.25 recorded and the amount of $417.25 that should have been recorded,

or $54.00. Because Weber recorded the cash payment at too large an amount, $54.00 must be added back to the balance per books.

9. In addition to canceled checks, three other deductions appear on the bank statement. Each of these must be deducted from the balance shown on the books:

   a. A customer's NSF check for $245.72 (see June 13 entry on bank statement).

   b. A $16.50 fee charged by the bank to collect the customer's note discussed in item 6 (see June 26 entry on bank statement).

   c. A service fee of $20.00 charged by the bank for rental of a lock box (see June 23 entry on bank statement).

10. The additions of $619.45 and deductions of $282.22 resulted in an adjusted cash balance of $3,233.05. Note that this adjusted balance agrees with the adjusted balance per the bank statement on the bank reconciliation (see item 4). As such, all differences between the two balances have been explained.

The Bank Reconciliation and the Need for Adjustments to the Records

After it completes the bank reconciliation, Weber must prepare a number of journal entries. In fact, all of the information for these journal entries will be from one section of the bank reconciliation. Do you think that the adjustments made to the bank balance or the adjustments made to the book balance are the basis for the journal entries? It is logical that the adjustments to the Cash account *on the books* should be the basis for the journal entries because these are items that Weber was unaware of prior to receiving the bank statement. Conversely, the adjustments to the bank's balance, that is, the deposits in transit and the outstanding checks, are items that Weber has already recorded on its books.

The first journal entry recognizes the bank's collection of the customer's note, with interest:

June 30	Cash	550.00	
	Notes Receivable		500.00
	Interest Revenue		50.00
	To record the collection of note and interest.		

Assets	=	Liabilities	+	Owners' Equity
+550				+50
−500				

The next entry is needed to record interest earned and paid by the bank on the average daily balance maintained in the checking account during June:

June 30	Cash	15.45	
	Interest Revenue		15.45
	To record interest earned on checking account.		

Assets	=	Liabilities	+	Owners' Equity
+15.45				+15.45

Recall the error in recording check 498: it was actually written for $417.25, the amount paid by the bank. Weber recorded the cash disbursement on its books as $471.25, however. If we assume that the purpose of the cash payment was to buy supplies, the Cash account is understated and the Supplies account is overstated by the amount of the error. The entry needed to correct both accounts is

| June 30 | Cash | 54.00 | |
| | Supplies | | 54.00 |

To correct for error in recording purchase of supplies.

Assets = Liabilities + Owners' Equity
+54
−54

The customer's NSF check is handled by reducing the Cash account and reinstating the Account Receivable:

| June 30 | Accounts Receivable | 245.72 | |
| | Cash | | 245.72 |

To record customer's NSF check.

Assets = Liabilities + Owners' Equity
+245.72
−245.72

Finally, two entries are needed to recognize the expenses incurred in connection with the fees charged by the bank to collect the customer's note and for rental of the lock box:

| June 30 | Collection Fee Expense | 16.50 | |
| | Cash | | 16.50 |

To record collection fee on note.

Assets = Liabilities + Owners' Equity
−16.50 −16.50

| June 30 | Rent Expense—Lock Box | 20.00 | |
| | Cash | | 20.00 |

To record rental charge on lock box.

Assets = Liabilities + Owners' Equity
−20 −20

Note that we made a separate entry to record each of the increases and decreases in the Cash account. Some companies combine all of the increases in Cash in a single journal entry and all of the decreases in a second entry. Finally, we should note that supervisory review and approval should take place before any of these entries are posted.

Petty Cash Fund

LO 4
Explain the use of a petty cash fund as a control device for cash.

Recall one of the fundamental rules in controlling cash: all disbursements should be made by check. Most businesses make an exception to this rule in the case of minor expenditures for which they use a **petty cash fund.** The necessary steps in setting up and maintaining a petty cash fund follow:

1. A check is written for a lump sum amount, such as $100 or $500. The check is cashed and the coin and currency are entrusted to a petty cash custodian.

2. A journal entry is made to record the establishment of the fund.

3. Upon presentation of the necessary documentation, minor disbursements are made from the fund. In essence, cash is traded from the fund in exchange for a receipt.

4. Periodically, the fund is replenished by writing and cashing a check in the amount necessary to bring the fund back to its original balance.

5. At the time the fund is replenished, a journal entry is made both to record its replenishment and to recognize the various expenses incurred.

The use of this fund is normally warranted on the basis of cost versus benefits. That is, the benefits in time saved in making minor disbursements from cash are thought to outweigh the cost associated with the risk of loss from decreased control over cash disbursements.

An Example of a Petty Cash Fund

Assume that on March 1, the treasurer of Keese Corporation cashes a check for $200 and remits the cash to the newly appointed petty cash custodian. On this date, the following journal entry is made:

March 1	Petty Cash Fund	200.00	
	Cash		200.00
	To record establishment of petty cash fund.		

Assets	=	Liabilities	+	Owners' Equity
+200				
−200				

During March the custodian disburses coin and currency to various individuals who present receipts to the custodian for the following:

U.S. Post Office	$ 55.00
Overnight Delivery Service	69.50
Office Supply Express	45.30
Total expenditures	$169.80

At the end of March, the custodian counts the coin and currency on hand and determines the balance to be $26.50. Next, the treasurer writes and cashes a check in the amount of $173.50, which is the amount needed to return the balance in the account to $200.00. The treasurer remits the cash to the custodian. The following entry is made:

March 31	Postage Expense	55.00	
	Delivery Expense	69.50	
	Office Expense	45.30	
	Cash Over and Short	3.70	
	Cash		173.50
	To record replenishment of petty cash fund.		

Assets	=	Liabilities	+	Owners' Equity
−173.50				−55.00
				−69.50
				−45.30
				−3.70

The Cash Over and Short account is necessary because the total expenditures for the month were only $169.80, but a check in the amount of $173.50 was necessary to restore the fund balance to $200.00. The discrepancy of $3.70 could be due to any number of factors, such as an error in making change. Any large discrepancies would be investigated, particularly if they recur. Assuming that the discrepancy is immaterial, a debit balance in the Cash Over and Short account is normally closed to Miscellaneous Expense. A credit balance in the account is closed to Other Income.

Accounts Receivable

LO   5

Understand how to account for accounts receivable, including bad debts.

To appreciate the significance of credit sales for many businesses, consider the case of the Merchandising Group of Sears, Roebuck & Co. This unit of Sears operates retail outlets throughout the United States and around the world. The balance sheet of the Sears Merchandise Group reported total assets of $27 billion at the end of 1992. Of this total amount, retail customer receivables accounted for $13.9 billion, or over 50%, of total assets. Sears or any other company would rather not sell on credit but to make all sales for cash. Selling on credit causes two problems: it slows down the inflow of cash to the company and it raises the possibility that the customer may not pay its bill on time or possibly ever. To remain competitive, however, Sears and most other businesses must sell their products and services on credit. Large retailers such as Sears often extend credit through the use of their own credit cards.

To be sure, retailers usually are able to charge very high rates of interest on their charge cards, generally several points above the prime rate, to compensate them for the few people who don't pay their bills. As we discuss later in the chapter, some retailers offer credit via VISA, MasterCard, Discover, American Express, or some other card to be reimbursed quickly. The trade-off is that the retailer doesn't earn any interest and actually pays a fee of 3 to 5% to these credit card companies.

The two most common types of short-term receivables are accounts receivable and notes receivable. The distinction is whether the customer signs a written promise to pay. The asset resulting from a sale on credit with an oral promise from the customer to pay within a specified period of time is called an *account receivable.* This type of account is non-interest bearing and often gives the customer a discount for early payment. For example, the terms of sale might be 2/10, net 30, which means the customer can deduct 2% from the amount due if the bill is paid within 10 days of the date of sale; otherwise, payment in full is required within 30 days. In some instances, businesses require a written promise from a customer at the time of sale in the form of a promissory note. The asset resulting from a sale on credit with a written promise from the customer to pay within a specified period of time is called a *note receivable.* This type of account usually bears interest.

The Use of a Subsidiary Ledger

Ben & Jerry's sells its ice cream through distributors and directly to retail outlets. Assume that it sells $25,000 of ice cream to ABC Distributors on an open account. The journal entry to record the sale would be

Accounts Receivable	25,000	
Sales Revenue		25,000
To record sale on open account.		

Assets	=	Liabilities	+	Owners' Equity
+25,000				+25,000

It is important for control purposes that Ben & Jerry's keeps a record of *whom* the sale was to and include this amount on a periodic statement or *bill* sent to the customer. What if a company has a hundred or a thousand different customers? Some mechanism is needed to track the balance each of these customers owes. The mechanism companies use is called a **subsidiary ledger.**

A subsidiary ledger contains the necessary detail on each of a number of items that collectively make up a single general ledger account, called the **control account.** In theory, any one of the accounts in the general ledger could be supported by a subsidiary ledger. In addition to Accounts Receivable, two other common accounts supported by subsidiary ledgers are Plant and Equipment and Accounts Payable. An accounts payable subsidiary ledger contains a separate account for each of the suppliers or vendors from which a company purchases inventory. A plant and equipment subsidiary ledger consists of individual accounts, along with their balances, for each of the various long-term tangible assets the company owns.

It is important to understand that a subsidiary ledger does *not* take the place of the control account in the general ledger. Instead, at any point in time, the balances of the accounts that make up the subsidiary ledger should total to the single balance in the related control account. In the remainder of this chapter we will only illustrate the use of the control account. Whenever a specific customer's account is debited or credited we will, however, note the name of the customer next to the control account in the journal entry.

The Valuation of Accounts Receivable

The following presentation of accounts receivable is taken from Ben & Jerry's 1992 annual report:

	DEC. 26, 1992	DEC. 28, 1991
Accounts receivable, less allowance for doubtful accounts: $350,000 in 1992 and 1991	$8,849,326	$6,939,975

Ben & Jerry's does not sell its ice cream to distributors under the assumption that any particular customer will *not* pay its bill. In fact, the credit department of a business is responsible for performing a reference check on all potential customers before they are granted credit. Management of Ben & Jerry's is not naive enough, however, to believe that all customers will be able to pay their accounts when due. This would be the case only if (1) all customers are completely trustworthy and (2) customers never experience unforeseen financial difficulties that make it impossible to pay on time.

The reduction in Ben & Jerry's accounts receivable for an allowance for doubtful accounts is the way in which most companies deal with bad debts in their accounting records. Bad debts are unpaid customer accounts that a company gives up trying to collect. Some companies refer to allowance for doubtful accounts as allowance for uncollectible accounts. Using the end of 1992 as an example, Ben & Jerry's believes that the *net recoverable amount* of its accounts receivable is $8,849,326, even though the *gross* amount of accounts receivable is $350,000 higher than this amount. The company has reduced the gross accounts receivable for an amount that it believes is necessary to reflect the asset on the books at the *net recoverable amount* or *net realizable value.* We now take a closer look at how a company accounts for bad debts.

Two Methods to Account for Bad Debts

Assume that Roberts Corp. makes a $500 sale to Dexter, Inc., on November 10, 1995, with credit terms of 2/10, net 60. Roberts makes the following entry on its books on this date:

```
1995
Nov. 10   Accounts Receivable—Dexter                      500
               Sales Revenue                                      500
          To record sale on credit; terms of 2/10, net 60.
```

Assets	=	Liabilities	+	Owners' Equity
+500				+500

Assume further that Dexter not only misses taking advantage of the discount for early payment but is also unable to pay within 60 days. After pursuing the account for four months into 1996, the credit department of Roberts informs the accounting department that it has given up on collecting the $500 from Dexter and advises that the account should be written off. To do so, the accounting department makes the following entry:

```
1996
May 1     Bad Debts Expense                               500
               Accounts Receivable—Dexter                       500
          To write off Dexter account.
```

Assets	=	Liabilities	+	Owners' Equity
−500				−500

This approach to accounting for bad debts is called the **direct write-off method.** Do you see any problems with its use? What about Roberts' balance sheet at the end of 1995? By ignoring the possibility that not all of its outstanding accounts receivable will be collected, Roberts is overstating the value of this asset at December 31, 1995. Also, what about the income statement for 1995? By ignoring the possibility of bad debts on sales made during 1995, Roberts has violated the *matching principle.* This principle requires that all costs associated with making sales in a period should be matched with the sales of that period. Roberts has overstated net income for 1995 by ignoring bad debts as an expense. The problem is one of *timing:* Even though any one particular account may not prove to be uncollectible until a later period (e.g., the Dexter account), the cost associated with making sales on credit (bad debts) should be recognized in the period of sale.

Accountants use the **allowance method** to overcome the deficiencies of the direct write-off method. They *estimate* the amount of bad debts before they actually occur. For example, assume that Roberts' total sales during 1995 amount to $600,000 and that at the end of the year the outstanding accounts receivable total $250,000. Also assume that Roberts estimates that on the basis of past experience, 1% of the sales of the period, or $6,000, eventually will prove to be uncollectible. Under the allowance method, Roberts makes the following adjusting entry at the end of 1995:

```
1995
Dec. 31   Bad Debts Expense                             6,000
               Allowance for Doubtful Accounts                 6,000
          To record estimated bad debts for the year.
```

Assets	=	Liabilities	+	Owners' Equity
−6,000				−6,000

The debit recognizes the cost associated with the reduction in value of the asset, Accounts Receivable. The cost is charged to the income statement, in the form of Bad Debts Expense. A contra asset account is used to reduce the asset to its net realizable value. This is accomplished by crediting a valuation allowance account, Allowance for Doubtful Accounts. Roberts presents accounts receivable as follows on its December 31, 1995, balance sheet:

Accounts receivable	$250,000
Less: Allowance for doubtful accounts	(6,000)
Net accounts receivable	$244,000

An alternative would be for Roberts to follow the form used by Ben & Jerry's described earlier in the chapter:

Accounts receivable, less allowance for doubtful accounts of $6,000:	$244,000

Write-Offs of Uncollectible Accounts with the Allowance Method

As with the direct write-off method, the write-off of a specific customer's account under the allowance method reduces accounts receivable. If the account receivable no longer exists, there is no need for the related allowance account and thus this account is reduced as well. For example, assume as we did earlier that Dexter's $500 account is written off on May 1, 1996. Under the allowance method, the following entry is recorded:

1996			
May 1	Allowance for Doubtful Accounts	500	
	Accounts Receivable—Dexter		500
	To record the write-off of Dexter account.		

Assets	=	Liabilities	+	Owners' Equity
+500				
−500				

To summarize, whether the direct write-off method or the allowance method is used, the entry to write off a specific customer's account reduces Accounts Receivable. It is the debit that differs between the two methods, however: Under the direct write-off method, the *expense* account is debited and under the allowance method, the *allowance* account is debited or reduced.

Two Approaches to the Allowance Method of Accounting for Bad Debts

Because it results in a better *matching,* accounting standards require the use of the allowance method rather than the direct write-off method, unless bad debts are immaterial in amount. Accountants use one of two different variations of the allowance method to estimate bad debts. One approach emphasizes matching bad debts expense with revenue on the income statement and bases bad debts on a percentage of the sales of the period. This was the method we illustrated earlier for Roberts Company. The other approach emphasizes the net realizable amount (value) of accounts receivable on the balance sheet and bases bad debts on a percentage of the accounts receivable balance at the end of the period.

Percentage of Net Credit Sales Approach If a company has been in business for enough years, it may be able to use the past relationship between bad debts and *net* credit sales to predict bad debt amounts. *Net* means that credit sales have been adjusted for sales discounts and returns and allowances. Assume that the accounting records for Bosco Corp. reveal the following:

YEAR	NET CREDIT SALES	BAD DEBTS
1990	$1,250,000	$ 26,400
1991	1,340,000	29,350
1992	1,200,000	23,100
1993	1,650,000	32,150
1994	2,120,000	42,700
	$7,560,000	$153,700

Although the exact percentage varied slightly over the five-year period, the average percentage of bad debts to net credit sales is very close to 2% ($153,700/$7,560,000 = .02033). Bosco needs to determine whether this estimate is realistic for the current period. For example, are current economic conditions considerably different than in the prior years? Has the company made sales to any new customers with significantly different credit terms? If the answers to these types of questions are yes, Bosco should consider adjusting the 2% experience rate to estimate future bad debts. Otherwise, it should proceed with this estimate. Assuming that it uses the 2% rate and its net credit sales during 1995 are $2,340,000, Bosco makes the following entry:

```
1995
Dec. 31   Bad Debts Expense                              46,800
              Allowance for Doubtful Accounts                      46,800
          To record estimated bad debts: .02 × $2,340,000.
```

Assets	=	Liabilities	+	Owners' Equity
− 46,800				− 46,800

Thus, Bosco matches bad debt expense of $46,800 with sales revenue of $2,340,000.

Percentage of Accounts Receivable Approach Some companies believe they can more accurately estimate bad debts by relating them to the balance in the Accounts Receivable account at the end of the period rather than to the sales of the period. The objective with both approaches is the same, however, namely to use past experience with bad debts to predict future amounts. Assume that the records for Cougar Corp. reveal the following:

YEAR	BALANCE IN ACCOUNTS RECEIVABLE DECEMBER 31	BAD DEBTS
1990	$ 650,000	$ 5,250
1991	785,000	6,230
1992	854,000	6,950
1993	824,000	6,450
1994	925,000	7,450
	$4,038,000	$32,330

The ratio of bad debts to the ending balance in Accounts Receivable over the past five years is $32,330/$4,038,000, or approximately .008 (.8%). Assuming balances in Accounts Receivable and the Allowance for Doubtful Accounts on December 31, 1995, of $865,000 (debit) and $2,100 (credit), respectively, Cougar records the following entry:

```
1995
Dec. 31  Bad Debts Expense                        4,820
              Allowance for Doubtful Accounts            4,820
         To record estimated bad debts:
         Credit balance required in allowance
           account after adjustment
           ($865,000 × 0.8%)                        $6,920
         Less: Credit balance in allowance
           account before adjustment                 2,100
         Amount for bad debt expense entry          $4,820
```

Assets	=	Liabilities	+	Owners' Equity
− 4,820				− 4,820

Note the one major difference between this approach and the percentage of sales approach: *Under the percentage of net sales approach, the balance in the allowance account is ignored; bad debts expense is simply a percentage of the sales of the period. Under the percentage of accounts receivable approach, however, the balance in the allowance account must be considered.* A T account for Allowance for Doubtful Accounts with the balance before and after adjustment appears as follows:

ALLOWANCE FOR DOUBTFUL ACCOUNTS

	2,100	Bal. before adjustment
	4,820	Adjusting entry
	6,920	Bal. after adjustment

In other words, making an adjustment for $4,820 results in a balance in the account of $6,920, which is .8% of the Accounts Receivable balance of $865,000. The net realizable value of accounts receivable is determined as follows:

Accounts receivable	$865,000
Less: Allowance for doubtful accounts	6,920
Net realizable value	$858,080

Aging of Accounts Receivable Some companies use a variation of the percentage of accounts receivable approach to estimate bad debts. This variation is actually a refinement of the approach because it considers the length of time that the receivables have been outstanding. In other words, it stands to reason that the older an account receivable is, the less likely that it will be collected. An **aging schedule** categorizes the various accounts by length of time outstanding. An example of an aging schedule is shown in Exhibit 7-5. We assume that the company's policy is to allow 30 days for payment of an outstanding account. After that time, the account is past due. An alphabetical list of customers appears in the first column with the balance in each account shown in the appropriate column to the right. The dotted lines after A. Matt's account indicate that many more accounts appear in the records, but we have included just a few to show the format of the schedule. The totals on the aging schedule are used as the basis for estimating bad debts as shown in Exhibit 7-6.

EXHIBIT 7-5   Aging Schedule

CUSTOMER	CURRENT	NUMBER OF DAYS PAST DUE 1–30	31–60	61–90	OVER 90
L. Ash	$ 4,400				
B. Budd	3,200				
C. Cox		$ 6,500			
E. Fudd					$6,300
G. Hoff			$ 900		
A. Matt	5,500				
......					
......					
......					
T. West				$ 3,100	
M. Young				4,200	
Totals*	$85,600	$31,200	$24,500	$18,000	$9,200

*Only a few of the customer accounts are illustrated; thus the column totals are higher than the amounts for the accounts illustrated.

Note that the estimated percentage of uncollectibles increases as the period of time the accounts have been outstanding lengthens. If we assume that the Allowance for Doubtful Accounts has a credit balance of $1,230 before adjustment, the adjusting entry is as follows:

1995			
Dec. 31	Bad Debts Expense	13,324	
	Allowance for Doubtful Accounts		13,324
	To record estimated bad debts:		
	Credit balance required in allowance		
	account after adjustment		$14,554
	Less: Credit balance in allowance		
	account before adjustment		1,230
	Amount for bad debt expense entry		$13,324

$$\text{Assets} = \text{Liabilities} + \text{Owners' Equity}$$
$$-13,324 \qquad\qquad\qquad -13,324$$

EXHIBIT 7-6   Use of an Aging Schedule to Estimate Bad Debts

CATEGORY	AMOUNT	ESTIMATED PERCENT UNCOLLECTIBLE	ESTIMATED AMOUNT UNCOLLECTIBLE
Current	$ 85,600	1%	$ 856
Past due:			
1–30 days	31,200	4%	1,248
31–60 days	24,500	10%	2,450
61–90 days	18,000	30%	5,400
Over 90 days	9,200	50%	4,600
Totals	$168,500		$14,554

■ **ACCOUNTING FOR YOUR DECISIONS**   **You Are the CFO**

After viewing your company's accounts receivable aging schedule and resulting estimate of bad debts in Exhibits 7-5 and 7-6, you are uncomfortable. What factors should be considered to determine if the bad debt percentage is too high? What actions could be taken to reduce bad debts?

The net realizable value of accounts receivable would be determined as follows:

Accounts receivable	$168,500
Less: Allowance for doubtful accounts	14,554
Net realizable value	$153,946

Recoveries of Accounts Previously Written Off

Occasionally, a company collects an account previously written off. Assume that E. Fudd's account listed on the aging schedule in Exhibit 7-5 in the amount of $6,300 is written off on June 30, 1996. The entry to record the write-off follows:

1996
June 30   Allowance for Doubtful Accounts   6,300
                   Accounts Receivable—E. Fudd   6,300
           To record write-off of E. Fudd account.

Assets   =   Liabilities   +   Owners' Equity
+6,300
−6,300

Now assume that on September 2, 1996, Fudd mailed a check for $6,300 to pay the account in full. Two entries are made on this date. The first entry *restores* the balance in the customer's account:

1996
Sept. 2   Accounts Receivable—E. Fudd   6,300
                   Allowance for Doubtful Accounts   6,300
           To record E. Fudd account previously written off.

Assets   =   Liabilities   +   Owners' Equity
+6,300
−6,300

Note that this entry is an exact reversal of the entry on June 30 to write off the account. A second entry is necessary to record the collection of cash:

1996
Sept. 2   Cash   6,300
                   Accounts Receivable (E. Fudd)   6,300
           To record collection of account receivable.

Assets   =   Liabilities   +   Owners' Equity
+6,300
−6,300

Could the company save time and simply *combine* these last two entries and eliminate the debit to Accounts Receivable in the first entry and a credit to the same account and for the same amount in the second entry? Certainly, it could from the perspective of the general ledger. Recording the two entries results in a more complete history of E. Fudd's account in the subsidiary ledger, however.

Analyzing the Accounts Receivable Rate of Collection

Managers, investors, and creditors are keenly interested in how well a company manages its accounts receivable. One simple measure is to compare a company's sales to its accounts receivable. The result is the accounts receivable turnover ratio:

$$\text{Accounts Receivable Turnover} = \frac{\text{Net Credit Sales}}{\text{Average Accounts Receivable}}$$

Typically, the faster the turnover, the better. For example, if a company has sales of $10 million and an average accounts receivable of $1 million, it turns over its accounts receivable 10 times per year. If we assume 360 days in a year, that is once every 36 days. An observer would compare that figure with historical figures to see if the company is experiencing slower or faster collections. A comparison could also be made to other companies in the same industry. If receivables are turning over too slowly, that could mean that the company's credit department is not operating effectively and the company therefore is missing opportunities with the cash that isn't available. On the other hand, a turnover rate that is too fast might mean that the company's credit policies are too stringent and that sales are being lost as a result.

Notes Receivable

A **promissory note** is a written promise to repay a definite sum of money on demand or at a fixed or determinable date in the future. Promissory notes normally require the payment of interest for the use of someone else's money. The party that agrees to repay money is the **maker** of the note and the party that receives money in the future is the **payee.** A company that holds a promissory note received from another company has an asset, called a **note receivable;** the company that makes or gives a promissory note to another company has a liability in the form of a **note payable.** Over the life of the note, the maker incurs interest expense on its note payable and the payee earns interest revenue on its note receivable. The following summarizes this:

PARTY	RECOGNIZES ON BALANCE SHEET	RECOGNIZES ON INCOME STATEMENT
Maker	Note payable	Interest expense
Payee	Note receivable	Interest revenue

Promissory notes are used for a variety of purposes. Banks normally require a company to sign a promissory note to borrow money. They are often used in the sale of consumer durables with relatively high purchase prices, such as appliances and automobiles. At times a promissory note is issued to replace an existing overdue account receivable.

Important Terms Connected with Promissory Notes

It is important to understand the following terms when dealing with promissory notes:

Principal The amount of cash received, or the fair value of the products or services received, by the maker when a promissory note is issued.

Maturity date The date that the promissory note is due.

Term The length of time a note is outstanding. That is, the period of time between the date it is issued and the date it matures.

Maturity value The amount of cash the maker is to pay the payee on the maturity date of the note.

Interest The difference between the principal amount of the note and its maturity value.

In some cases, the interest rate on a promissory note is stated explicitly on the face of the note. Even though the note's term may be less than a year, the interest rate is stated on an annual basis. In other cases, an interest rate does not appear on the face of the note. As we will see, however, there is *implicit* interest, because more is to be repaid at maturity than is owed at the time the note is signed. Notes in which an interest rate is explicitly stated are called **interest-bearing notes.** Notes in which interest is implicit in the agreement are called **non-interest-bearing notes.** We now look at the accounting for each of these types of notes.

Interest-Bearing Notes

Assume that on December 13, 1995, HighTec sells a computer to Baker Corp. at an invoice price of $15,000. Because Baker is short of cash, it gives HighTec a 90-day, 12% promissory note. The total amount of interest due on the maturity date is:

LO 6

Understand how to account for interest-bearing notes receivable.

$$\$15,000 \times .12 \times 90/360 = \underline{\$450}$$

The entry to record receipt of the note by HighTec is

```
1995
Dec. 13   Notes Receivable                              15,000
              Sales Revenue                                      15,000
          To record sale of computer in exchange for promissory
          note.
```

	Assets	=	Liabilities	+	Owners' Equity
	+ 15,000				+ 15,000

If we assume that December 31 is the end of HighTec's accounting year, an entry is needed to recognize interest earned but not yet received. It is required when a company uses the accrual basis of accounting. The question is: How many days of interest have been earned during December? *It is normal practice to count the day a note matures in computing interest but not the day it is signed.* Thus, in our example, interest would be earned for 18 days (December 14 to December 31) during 1995 and for 72 days in 1996:

MONTH	NUMBER OF DAYS OUTSTANDING
December 1995	18 days
January 1996	31 days
February 1996	28 days
March 1996	13 days (matures on March 13, 1996)
Total days	90 days

An adjusting entry is made on December 31 to record interest earned during 1995:

1995
Dec. 31   Interest Receivable   90
                   Interest Revenue   90
          To record interest earned: $15,000 × .12 × 18/360.

Assets	=	Liabilities	+	Owners' Equity
+90				+90

On March 13, 1996, HighTec collects the principal amount of the note and interest from Baker and records this entry:

1996
March 13   Cash   15,450
                   Notes Receivable   15,000
                   Interest Revenue   360
                   Interest Receivable   90
          To record collection of promissory note.

Assets	=	Liabilities	+	Owners' Equity
+15,450				+360
−15,000				
−90				

This entry accomplishes a number of purposes. First, it removes the amount of $15,000 originally recorded in the Notes Receivable account by crediting that account. Second, it credits interest earned during the 72 days in 1996 that the note is outstanding to Interest Revenue. The calculation of interest earned during 1996 is

$$\$15,000 \times .12 \times 72/360 = \underline{\$360}$$

Third, the entry credits Interest Receivable for $90 to remove this account from the records now that the note has been collected. Finally, it debits Cash for $15,450, which represents the principal amount of the note, $15,000, plus interest of $450 for 90 days.

Non-Interest-Bearing Notes

LO 7
Understand how to account for non-interest-bearing notes receivable.

Assume that you walk in to an automobile dealership on November 1, 1995, and find the car of your dreams. After extensive negotiation, the dealer agrees to sell you the car outright for $10,000. Because you are short of cash, you give the dealer $1,000 as a down payment and sign a promissory note to pay $9,900 in six months. Even though interest is never mentioned, it is *implicitly* built into the transaction. You owe the car dealer $10,000 − $1,000, or $9,000, today, and you have agreed to pay $9,900 in six months. The $900 excess of the amount to be paid in six months over the amount owed today is *interest*. The note is called a non-interest-bearing note because no interest is *explicitly* stated. Anytime it is necessary to pay more in the future than is owed today interest is involved. The *effective interest rate* can be found as follows:

1. The amount of interest implicit in the note: $9,900 − $9,000, or $900.
2. The length of the note: 6 months.
3. The number of 6-month periods in a year: 12/6 = 2.
4. The amount of interest that would apply to a full year: $900 × 2, or $1,800.
5. The effective annual interest rate is $1,800/$9,000, or 20%.

In essence, the car dealer has you sign a promissory note in the amount of $9,900 but gave you credit equivalent to only $9,000 in cash, that is, the difference between the value of the car today, $10,000, and the amount of your down payment, $1,000. The dealer deducted interest of $900 in advance and gave you the equivalent of a $9,000 loan. Another name for this non-interest-bearing note is a **discounted note.** On the date the note is signed, the car dealer makes this entry:

```
1995
Nov. 1   Cash                                      1,000
         Notes Receivable                          9,900
             Discount on Notes Receivable                      900
             Sales Revenue                                  10,000
         To record sale in exchange for note.
```

Assets	=	Liabilities	+	Owners' Equity
+1,000				+10,000
+9,900				
−900				

The debit to Cash represents the down payment. The debit to Notes Receivable is for $9,900, the maturity amount of the promissory note. The credit to Sales Revenue represents the amount the car could be sold for today. Discount on Notes Receivable is a contra account to the Notes Receivable account and represents the interest that the dealer will earn over the next six months. As interest is earned, this account will be reduced and Interest Revenue will be credited. For example, at the end of the year, the dealer will make an entry to recognize that two months' interest of the total of six months' interest has been earned:

```
1995
Dec. 31   Discount on Notes Receivable              300
              Interest Revenue                                300
          To record interest earned for two months: $900 × 2/6.
```

Assets	=	Liabilities	+	Owners' Equity
+300				+300

The current assets section of the dealer's balance sheet at December 31, 1995, includes the following:

```
Notes receivable                          $9,900
Less: Discount on notes receivable           600      $9,300
```

The entry on April 30 to record collection of the maturity amount of the note and to recognize the remaining interest earned is

```
1996
April 30   Cash                                     9,900
           Discount on Notes Receivable              600
               Notes Receivable                               9,900
               Interest Revenue                                 600
           To record collection of note.
```

Assets	=	Liabilities	+	Owners' Equity
+9,900				+600
+600				
−9,900				

Accelerating the Inflow of Cash from Sales

LO   8

Explain various techniques that companies use to accelerate the inflow of cash from sales.

Earlier in the chapter we pointed out why cash sales are preferable to credit sales: Credit sales slow down the inflow of cash to the company and create the potential for bad debts. To remain competitive, most businesses find it necessary to grant credit to customers. That is, if one company won't grant credit to a customer, the customer may find another company willing to do so. Companies have found it possible, however, to circumvent the problems inherent in credit sales in various ways. We discussed the use of sales discounts to motivate timely repayment of accounts receivable in Chapter 5. We now consider other approaches that companies use to speed up the flow of cash from sales.

Credit Card Sales

Most retail establishments, as well as many service businesses, accept one or more major credit cards. Among the most common cards are MasterCard, VISA, American Express, Carte Blanche, Discover Card, and Diners Club. Most merchants believe that they must honor at least one or more of these credit cards to remain competitive. In return for a fee, the merchant passes the responsibility for collection on to the credit card company. Thus, the credit card issuer assumes the risk of nonpayment. The basic relationships among the three parties, the customer, the merchant, and the credit card company, are illustrated in Exhibit 7-7. Assume that Joe Smith entertains clients at Club Cafe and charges $100 in meals to his Diners Club credit card. When Joe is presented with his bill at the end of the evening he is asked to sign a multiple-copy **credit card draft** or invoice. Joe keeps one copy of the draft and leaves the other two copies at the Club Cafe. The restaurant keeps one copy as the basis for recording its sales for the day and sends the other copy to Diners Club for payment. Diners Club uses the copy of the draft it gets for two purposes: to reimburse Club Cafe $95 (keeping $5 or 5% of the original sale as a collection fee) and to include Joe Smith's $100 purchase on the monthly bill it mails him.

Assume that total credit card sales on June 5 amount to $800. The entry on Club Cafe's books on that day is

June 5	Accounts Receivable—Diners Club	800	
	Sales Revenue		800
	To record daily credit card sales.		

Assets	=	Liabilities	+	Owners' Equity
+800				+800

Assume that Club Cafe remits the credit card drafts to Diners Club once a week and that the total sales for the week ending June 11 amount to $5,000. Further assume that on June 13 Diners Club pays the amount due to Club Cafe, after deducting a 5% collection fee. The entry on Club Cafe's books is

June 13	Cash	4,750	
	Collection Fee Expense	250	
	Accounts Receivable—Diners Club		5,000
	To record weekly receipts from credit card company.		

Assets	=	Liabilities	+	Owners' Equity
+4,750				−250
−5,000				

EXHIBIT 7-7 Basic Relationships among Parties with Credit Card Sales

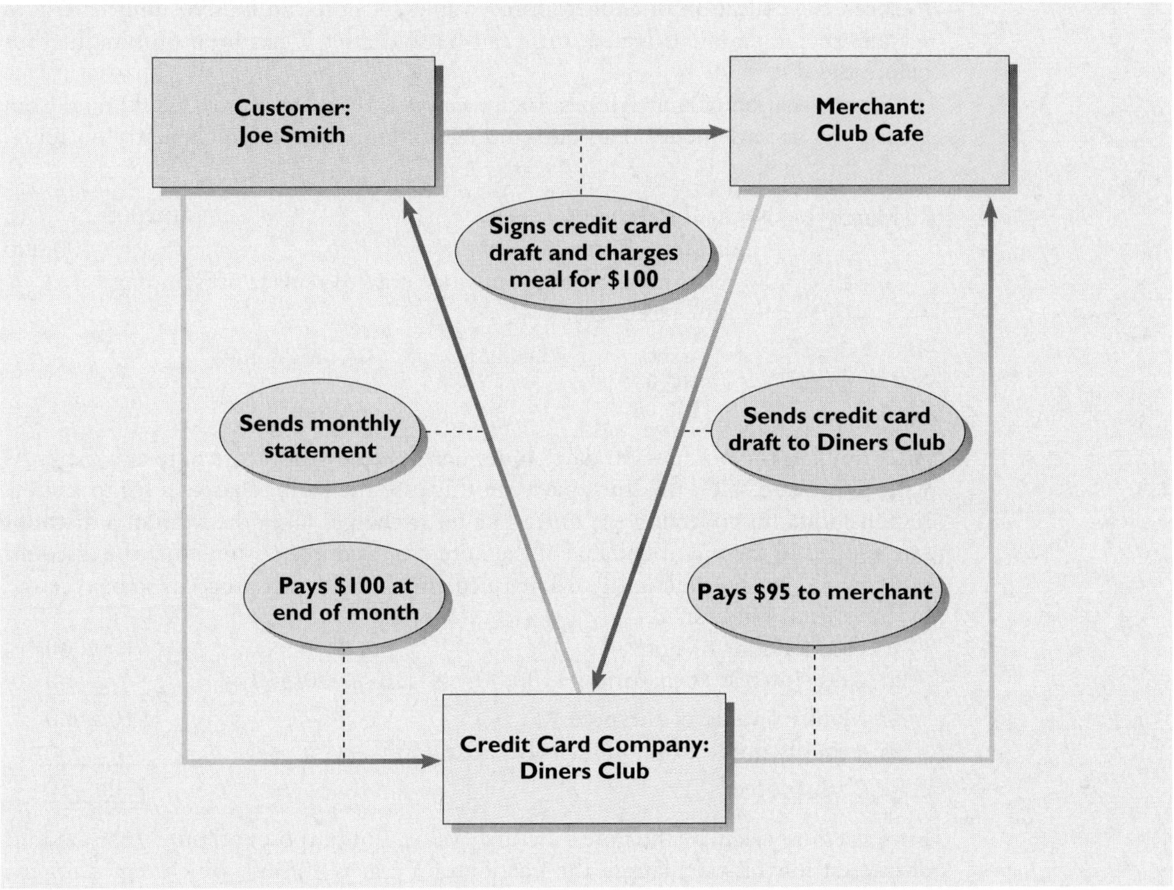

Some credit cards, such as MasterCard and VISA, allow a merchant to present a credit card draft directly for deposit in a bank account, in much the same way the merchant deposits checks, coins, and currency. Obviously, this type of arrangement is even more advantageous for the merchant because the funds are available as soon as the drafts are credited to the bank account. Assume that on July 9 Club Cafe presents VISA credit card drafts to its bank for payment in the amount of $2,000 and that the collection charge is 4%. The entry on its books on the date of deposit is

July 9	Cash	1,920	
	Collection Fee Expense	80	
	Sales Revenue		2,000
	To record credit card sales.		

$$\begin{array}{ccccc} \textbf{Assets} & = & \textbf{Liabilities} & + & \textbf{Owners' Equity} \\ +1,920 & & & & -80 \\ & & & & +2,000 \end{array}$$

Discounting Notes Receivable

Promissory notes are negotiable, which means that they can be endorsed and given to someone else for collection. In other words, a company can sign the back of a note, just as it would a check, sell it to a bank, and receive cash before the note's maturity date. This process is called **discounting** and is another way for companies to speed the collection of cash from receivables. A note can be sold immediately to a bank on the date it is issued, or it can be sold after it has been outstanding but before the due date.

Assume that on March 1 Jones, Inc., receives a 10%, 90-day $100,000 note from a customer as settlement on an outstanding account receivable. The entry on Jones' books on this date is

March 1	Notes Receivable	100,000	
	Accounts Receivable		100,000
	To record receipt of promissory note to replace outstanding account receivable.		

$$\text{Assets} \quad = \quad \text{Liabilities} \quad + \quad \text{Owners' Equity}$$
$$+100,000$$
$$-100,000$$

After holding the note for 30 days, Jones decides to discount the note at a bank. As with credit card sales, the third party, in this case the bank, charges a fee to assume responsibility for collecting the note. The fee it charges takes the form of a discount rate applied to the maturity value of the note. For example, assume that the discount rate charged by the bank is 12%. The calculation of the cash proceeds to be received by Jones is as follows:

1. Face amount of note: $100,000
2. Add: Interest at maturity: $100,000 \times .10 \times 90/360 =$ 2,500
3. Maturity value of the note: $102,500
4. Less discount: $102,500 \times .12 \times 60/360 =$ (2,050)
5. Cash proceeds $100,450

First, we must calculate the note's maturity value. For purposes of finding the amount of interest for this calculation, the fraction of a year is 90/360, which represents the part of a year the note will be outstanding. The second step is to calculate the amount of discount the bank charged. Note that the rate is the bank's discount rate, not the original rate on the note. Also note that 60/360 is used to represent the remaining part of the year that the note will be outstanding. The discount is deducted from the maturity value to find the amount of cash the bank paid Jones. Finally, the difference between the face amount of the note and the cash proceeds is recorded as interest revenue if the cash proceeds exceed the face amount or as interest expense if the cash proceeds are less than the face amount.

The entry on Jones's books to record discounting of the note at the bank is

March 31	Cash	100,450	
	Notes Receivable		100,000
	Interest Revenue		450
	To record discounting of note at the bank.		

$$\text{Assets} \quad = \quad \text{Liabilities} \quad + \quad \text{Owners' Equity}$$
$$+100,450 \qquad\qquad\qquad\qquad\qquad +450$$
$$-100,000$$

To understand the nature of a discounted note, it is helpful to calculate the interest Jones *would have earned for the month of March had it held the note to maturity.* Interest for one month would be

$$\$100,000 \times .10 \times 30/360 = \underline{\$833}$$

Why did Jones record only $450 of interest revenue even though interest for the month amounted to $833? The difference between what it would have earned had it held the note to maturity, $833 for the month of March, and the amount it did earn, $450, is the cost associated with discounting the note with the bank.

Discounting Notes and Contingent Liabilities   When a note is discounted at a bank, it is normally done *with recourse.* This means that if the original customer fails to pay the bank the total amount due on the maturity date of the note, the company that sold the note to the bank is liable for the full amount. Because there is *uncertainty* as to whether the company will have to make good on any particular note that it discounts at the bank, a *contingent liability* exists from the time the note is discounted until its maturity date. We explore the topic of contingent liabilities in more detail in Chapter 9. As we will see, the accounting profession has adopted guidelines to decide whether a particular uncertainty requires that the company record a contingent liability on its balance sheet. Under these guidelines, the contingency created by the discounting of a note with recourse is not recorded as a liability. However, a *footnote* to the financial statements is used to inform the reader of the existing uncertainty. For example, if we assume that Jones discounted the note with recourse and that it prepared financial statements at the end of April, it includes the following footnote:

> The Company is contingently liable for a $100,000 note receivable discounted at the bank on March 31. The due date of the promissory note is May 30.

Accounting for Dishonored Notes   Assume that on May 30 Jones receives notice from the bank that the customer had not paid the amount due. Because the note was sold with recourse, it is now Jones's responsibility to attempt to collect the amount of the note from the customer. Because Jones will have to pay the maturity value of the note to the bank, it makes the following entry on its books:

May 30	Accounts Receivable—		
	Dishonored Notes	102,500	
	Cash		102,500
	To record payment of cash to bank for promissory note dishon-ored by customer.		

Assets	=	Liabilities	+	Owners' Equity
+102,500				
−102,500				

The debit is made to a special type of account receivable for dishonored notes to separate it from the normal type of account receivable. It is then up to the credit department to attempt to collect the maturity value of the note from the customer.

How Liquid Assets Affect the Cash Flows Statement

LO 9

Explain the effects of transactions involving liquid assets on the statement of cash flows.

As we discussed earlier in the chapter, cash equivalents are combined with cash on the balance sheet. These items are very near maturity and do not present any significant risk of collectibility. Because of this, any purchases or redemptions of cash equivalents are not considered significant activities to be reported on a statement of cash flows.

The purchase and sale of short-term investments are considered significant activities and are therefore reported on the statement of cash flows. Under current accounting standards, however, the purchases and sales of certain types of these investments are classified as investing activities while others are categorized as operating activities.

We will return to a full discussion of the various types of investments and their presentation on the statement of cash flows in Chapter 13.

The collection of accounts receivable generates cash for a business and appears in the operating activities section of the statement of cash flows. How the collection of receivables appears, however, depends on whether the company uses the direct or the indirect method of presenting cash flow from operating activities. If a company uses the direct method, it lists the amount of cash collected on account from customers simply as a cash inflow. Most companies, however, use the indirect method and begin the statement of cash flows with the net income of the period. Net income includes the sales revenue of the period. Therefore, a decrease in accounts receivable during the period indicates that the company collected more cash than it recorded in sales revenue. Thus, when it uses the indirect method, *a decrease in accounts receivable must be added back to net income because more cash was collected than is reflected in the sales revenue number.* Alternatively, an increase in accounts receivable indicates that the company recorded more sales revenue than cash collected during

---

INVESTING IN MUNICIPAL BONDS

Name: Audrey Quaye
Profession: Municipal Bond Analyst
Education: MBA (Accounting and Finance), University of Southern California

Corporations and individuals with idle cash to invest often invest in municipal bonds. A big draw: they're usually tax-free. When compared to other investments that are taxable, municipal bonds can stack up very well. In states such as California, a profitable corporation can pay nearly half of its income taxes to the federal and state governments. So, a municipal bond paying 5% is equivalent to another taxable investment paying approximately 10%. Given the relative safety of municipal bonds, many corporate and individual investors find them very attractive.

Making sure that these bonds are safe is one of the duties of Audrey Quaye, a municipal credit analyst for The Benham Group, a large mutual fund company based in Mountain View, California. "What I do is advise the portfolio managers on the credit

quality of fixed income securities that are being considered for purchase," she says. "In addition, I monitor the bond issuers' ongoing performance to determine if the credit rating, assigned by the rating agencies, is likely to remain unchanged or change in a positive or negative direction."

Ms. Quaye, a CPA by training, says that the focus of her analysis is to make sure than an entity can pay its debt as it becomes due. "Can it generate sufficient cash flow from its operating activities? What are its future borrowing needs given its forecasted capital expenditures?" The way she does this is by reviewing the municipalities' financial statements and operating statistics. Some red flags? Declining profitability and cash flow, a low ratio of cash flow to capital expenditures and debt service payments, and a high debt to capitalization rate.

For example, Kaiser Permanente, a nonprofit health maintenance organization, issues tax-exempt bonds through a state government agency. In addition to all of the normal financial ratios and operating statistics, Ms. Quaye would analyze Kaiser for subjective factors

such as how well it is likely to do in the changing health-care environment. The answer is that it should do well because it is already providing health care in a form—managed care—that is likely to be the future of the health care industry.

What advice would she give to college students? "Having an accounting degree gives you a superior understanding of financial statements. It's definitely an advantage in this field."

the period. Therefore, an increase in accounts receivable requires a deduction from the net income of the period to arrive at cash flow from operating activities.

Reading Wrigley's Statement of Cash Flows

To test your understanding of these concepts, refer to Wrigley's statement of cash flows as shown in Exhibit 7-1 and answer the following questions:

1. Does Wrigley use the direct or the indirect method to prepare the operating activities section of the statement?

2. What was the dollar amount and direction of change in Wrigley's accounts receivable during 1992? Why was the change deducted in the operating activities section of the statement?

3. Did Wrigley buy or sell short-term investments during 1992? How much?

The answers follow:

1. Wrigley uses the indirect method because the operating activities section starts with the net income or net earnings for the period.

2. Wrigley's accounts receivable increased during 1992 by $10,652,000. This indicates that Wrigley recorded more in sales revenue than it collected in cash. Because sales revenue is included in the net earnings figure, the excess of sales over cash collections, that is, the increase in accounts receivable, is deducted.

3. According to the investing activities section of the statement, short-term investments increased by $26,132,000. This indicates that Wrigley purchased short-term investments for this amount.

REVIEW PROBLEM

The following items pertain to the current asset section of the balance sheet for Jackson Corp. at the end of its accounting year, December 31, 1995. Each item must be considered and any necessary accounting entry must be recorded. Additionally, the accountant for Jackson wishes to develop the current asset section of the balance sheet as of the end of 1995.

a. Cash in a savings account at the Second State Bank amounts to $13,200.

b. Cash on hand in the petty cash fund amounts to $400.

c. A 9%, 120-day certificate of deposit was purchased on December 1, 1995, for $10,000.

d. The balance on the books for a checking account at the Second State Bank is $4,230. The bank statement indicates that one of Jackson's customers paid a $1,500 promissory note, along with $120 in interest, directly to the bank. The bank deducted a $25 collection fee from the amount it credited to Jackson's account. The statement also indicated that the bank had charged Jackson's account $50 to print new checks.

e. Gross accounts receivable at December 31, 1995, amount to $44,000. Before adjustment, the balance in the Allowance for Doubtful Accounts is $340. Based on past experience, the accountant estimates that 3% of the gross accounts receivable outstanding at December 31, 1995, will prove to be uncollectible.

f. A customer's 12%, 90-day promissory note in the amount of $6,000 is held at the end of the year. (*Note:* This is a different note than the one in item d.) The note has been held for 45 days during 1995.

■ REQUIRED

1. Record the accounting entries required in parts a–f.

2. Prepare the current asset section of Jackson's balance sheet as of December 31, 1995. In addition to items a–f, the balances in Inventory and Prepaid Insurance on this date are $65,000 and $4,800, respectively.

■ SOLUTION TO REVIEW PROBLEM

1. The following entries are recorded at December 31, 1995:

a. & b. No entries required.

c. Jackson needs an adjusting entry to record interest earned on the certificate of deposit at the Second State Bank. The CD has been outstanding for 30 days during 1995, and therefore the amount of interest earned is

$$\$10,000 \times .09 \times 30/360 = \underline{\$75}$$

The adjusting entry is

1995			
Dec. 31	Interest Receivable	75	
	Interest Revenue		75
	To record interest earned during 1995.		

Assets	**=**	**Liabilities**	**+**	**Owners' Equity**
+75				+75

d. Entries are needed to record the bank's collection of the promissory note and interest, the collection charge on the note, and the charge for the new checks:

1995			
Dec. 31	Cash	1,620	
	Notes Receivable		1,500
	Interest Revenue		120
	To record collection of note and interest.		

Assets	**=**	**Liabilities**	**+**	**Owners' Equity**
+1,620				+120
−1,500				

1995			
Dec. 31	Collection Fee Expense	25	
	Cash		25
	To record deduction from account for collection fee on note.		

Assets	**=**	**Liabilities**	**+**	**Owners' Equity**
−25				−25

1995			
Dec. 31	Miscellaneous Expense	50	
	Cash		50
	To record deduction from account for new checks.		

Assets	**=**	**Liabilities**	**+**	**Owners' Equity**
−50				−50

e. Based on gross accounts receivable of $44,000 at year-end and an estimate that 3% of this amount will be uncollectible, the balance in the Allowance for Doubtful Accounts is $1,320 ($44,000 × 3%). Given a current balance of $340, an adjusting entry for $980 ($1,320 − $340) is needed to bring the balance to the desired amount of $1,320:

1995
Dec. 31   Bad Debts Expense   980
                Allowance for Doubtful Accounts   980
                To record estimated bad debts for the year.

Assets	**=**	**Liabilities**	**+**	**Owners' Equity**
− 980				− 980

f. An adjusting entry is needed to accrue interest on the promissory note ($6,000 × .12 × 45/360 = $90):

1995
Dec. 31   Interest Receivable   90
                Interest Revenue   90
                To record interest earned on promissory note.

Assets	**=**	**Liabilities**	**+**	**Owners' Equity**
+ 90				+ 90

2. The current assets section of Jackson's balance sheet appears as follows:

JACKSON CORP.
PARTIAL BALANCE SHEET
DECEMBER 31, 1995

CURRENT ASSETS

Cash		$ 19,375*
Certificate of deposit		10,000
Accounts receivable	$44,000	
Less: Allowance for doubtful accounts	1,320	42,680
Notes receivable		6,000
Interest receivable		165‡
Inventory		65,000
Prepaid insurance		4,800
Total current assets		$148,020

*Savings account	$13,200
Petty cash fund	400
Checking account ($4,230 + $1,620 − $25 − $50)	5,775
Total	$19,375

‡$75 from CD and $90 from promissory note.

GUIDANCE ANSWERS TO ACCOUNTING FOR YOUR DECISIONS

YOU ARE THE INVESTMENT ANALYST

Most of the cash went to buy property, plant, and equipment, invest in short-term investments, pay dividends, and purchase the company's own stock. Between 1990 and 1991, Wrigley's earnings rose about 10%. But its net cash flows from operations rose 28% during the same period. Between 1991 and 1992, the company's earnings rose another 10% but its net cash flows from operations rose 36%. Its cash flow trend is more impressive.

YOU ARE THE CFO

Out of a total accounts receivable of $168,500, the estimated bad debt expense is $14,554 or 9%. This is probably twice as high as it should be. A bad debt is very damaging to the bottom line. After all, you have incurred all of the expenses of a sale—without getting the sales proceeds. You must qualify your customers more carefully before you sell to them. If they are a new account, check their credit references and their credit report by TRW or other credit rating agencies. True, you may lose some sales. But you won't incur the cost of those sales, either.

CHAPTER HIGHLIGHTS

1. **(LO 1)** The amount of cash reported on the balance sheet includes all items that are readily available to satisfy obligations. Items normally included in cash are coin and currency, petty cash funds, customers' undeposited checks, cashier's checks, certified checks, savings accounts, and checking accounts.

2. **(LO 1)** Cash equivalents include such items as commercial paper, money market funds, and treasury bills. They are included with cash on the balance sheet and are limited to those investments that are readily convertible to known amounts of cash and have original maturities of three months or less.

3. **(LO 2)** Companies classify an investment as short term when it is readily marketable and the intent is to sell it within the next year or the operating cycle, whichever is longer. Included are stocks, bonds, and other types of financial instruments, such as certificates of deposit. Companies often use these financial instruments to invest idle cash during various times of the year.

4. **(LO 3)** A bank reconciliation is normally prepared monthly for all checking accounts to reconcile the amount of cash recorded on the books with the amount reported on the bank statement. One popular form for the reconciliation, and the one illustrated in the chapter, reconciles the balance on the bank statement and the balance on the books to the correct balance. Journal entries are made for all adjustments made in the balance per books section of the reconciliation.

5. **(LO 4)** Many companies use a petty cash fund to disburse small amounts of cash that would otherwise require the use of a check and a more lengthy approval process. The fund is established by writing and cashing a check and placing the coin and currency in a secure place controlled by a custodian. At this point, a journal entry is made to record the establishment of the fund. On presentation of a supporting receipt to the custodian, disbursements are made from the fund. The fund periodically is replenished and a journal entry is made to record the replenishment and to recognize the various expenses incurred.

6. **(LO 5)** The allowance method of accounting for bad debts matches the cost associated with uncollectible accounts with the revenue of the period in which the sale took place. One of two variations is used to estimate bad debts under the allowance method. Some companies base bad debts on a percentage of net credit sales. Others use an aging schedule as a basis for relating the amount of bad debts to the balance in Accounts Receivable at the end of the period.

7. **(LO 6)** A promissory note is a written promise to repay a definite sum of money on demand or at a fixed or determinable date in the future. Situations in which a promissory note is used include the purchase of consumer durables, the lending of money to another party, or in satisfaction of an existing account receivable. Interest earned but not yet collected should be accrued at the end of an accounting period.

8. **(LO 7)** The interest on certain promissory notes is implicitly included in the agreement instead of stated explicitly as a percentage of the principal amount of the note. Any difference between the cash purchase price of an item or, in the case of a loan, the amount borrowed and the amount to be repaid at maturity is interest. As is the case for interest-bearing notes, any interest earned but not yet collected is recognized as income at the end of an accounting period.

9. **(LO 8)** Many businesses accept credit cards in lieu of cash. In return for a fee, the credit card company assumes responsibility for collecting the customer charges. A credit card draft or invoice is the basis for

recording a credit card sale and an account receivable. When the drafts are presented to the credit card company for payment, the excess of accounts receivable for these sales over the amount of cash received represents the expense associated with accepting credit cards. In some instances, companies do not have to wait to collect from the credit card company but can instead present the drafts for deposit to their bank account.

10. (LO 8) Because a promissory note is negotiable, it can be sold to another party, such as a bank. The sale of a note is called *discounting* and is a way for a company to accelerate the inflow of cash. If the note is sold or discounted with recourse, the company sell-ing it is contingently liable until the maturity date of the loan. A footnote is used to report this contingency to financial statement readers.

11. (LO 9) Cash equivalents are included with cash on the balance sheet and therefore changes in them do not appear as significant activities on a statement of cash flows. Purchases and sales of short-term investments do appear in the statement of cash flows. The collection of accounts receivable results in an inflow of cash from operating activities under the direct method of determining cash from operating activities. Under the indirect method, an increase in accounts receivable is deducted from net income; a decrease is added back to net income.

KEY TERMS QUIZ

Because of the large number of terms introduced in this chapter, it has two key terms quizzes. Select from the list of key terms used in the chapter and fill in the appropriate blank to the left of each description. The solution appears at the end of the chapter.

Quiz 1:

Cash equivalent   Equity securities
Debt securities   Bank statement
Outstanding check   Deposit in transit
Bank reconciliation   Credit memoranda
Debit memoranda   Petty cash fund

_____ 1. Additions on a bank statement for such items as interest paid on the account and notes collected by the bank for the customer.

_____ 2. An investment that is readily convertible to a known amount of cash and has an original maturity to the investor of three months or less.

_____ 3. Deductions on a bank statement for such items as NSF checks and various service charges.

_____ 4. A deposit recorded on the books but not yet reflected on the bank statement.

_____ 5. Securities issued by corporations as a form of ownership in the business.

_____ 6. A check written by a company but not yet presented to the bank for payment.

_____ 7. Bonds issued by corporations and governmental bodies as a form of borrowing.

_____ 8. A detailed list provided by the bank of all the activity for a particular account during the month.

_____ 9. A form used by the accountant to reconcile the balance shown on the bank statement for a particular account with the balance shown in the accounting records.

_____ 10. Money kept on hand for making minor disbursements of coin and currency rather than by writing checks.

Quiz 2:

Subsidiary ledger	Control account
Direct write-off method	Allowance method
Aging schedule	Promissory note
Maker	Payee
Note receivable	Note payable
Principal	Maturity date
Term	Maturity value
Interest	Interest-bearing note
Non-interest-bearing note	Discounted note
Credit card draft	Discounting

_____ **1.** A method of estimating bad debts on the basis of either the net credit sales of the period or the amount of accounts receivable at the end of the period.

_____ **2.** The party to a promissory note that will receive the money at some future date.

_____ **3.** A written promise to repay a definite sum of money on demand or at a fixed or determinable date in the future.

_____ **4.** A liability resulting from the signing of a promissory note.

_____ **5.** The date that a promissory note is due.

_____ **6.** A multiple-copy document used by a company that accepts a credit card for a sale.

_____ **7.** An asset resulting from the acceptance of a promissory note from another company.

_____ **8.** The length of time a promissory note is outstanding.

_____ **9.** The process of selling a promissory note.

_____ **10.** The party to a promissory note that agrees to repay the money at some future date.

_____ **11.** A promissory note in which the interest rate is explicitly stated.

_____ **12.** The amount of cash received, or the fair value of the products or services received, by the maker when a promissory note is issued.

_____ **13.** A form used to categorize the various individual accounts receivable according to the length of time each has been outstanding.

_____ **14.** The difference between the principal amount of a promissory note and its maturity value.

_____ **15.** An alternative name for a non-interest-bearing promissory note.

_____ **16.** The detail for a number of individual items that collectively make up a single general ledger account.

_____ **17.** The amount of cash to be paid by the maker to the payee on the maturity date of a promissory note.

_____ **18.** A promissory note in which interest is not explicitly stated but is implicit in the agreement.

_____ **19.** The recognition of bad debts expense at the point an account is written off as uncollectible.

_____ **20.** The general ledger account that is supported by a subsidiary ledger.

ALTERNATE TERMS

ALLOWANCE FOR DOUBTFUL ACCOUNTS Allowance for Uncollectible Accounts.

CREDIT CARD DRAFT Invoice.

DEBT SECURITIES Bonds.

EQUITY SECURITIES Stocks.

NET REALIZABLE VALUE Net recoverable amount.

NON-INTEREST-BEARING NOTE Discounted note.

SHORT-TERM INVESTMENTS Marketable securities.

QUESTIONS

1. What is a cash equivalent? Why is it included with cash on the balance sheet?
2. Why does the purchase of an item classified as a cash equivalent *not* appear on the statement of cash flows as an investing activity?
3. A friend says to you: "I understand why it is important to deposit all receipts intact and not keep coin and currency sitting around the business. Beyond this control feature, however, I believe that a company should strive to keep the maximum amount possible in checking accounts to always be able to pay bills on time." How would you evaluate your friend's statement?
4. A friends says to you: "I'm confused. I have a memo included with my bank statement indicating a $20 service charge for printing new checks. If the bank is deducting this amount from my account, why do they call it a 'debit memorandum'? I thought a decrease in a cash account would be a credit, not a debit." How can you explain this?
5. Different formats for bank reconciliations are possible. What is the format for a bank reconciliation in which a service charge for a lock box is *added* to the balance per the bank statement? Explain your answer.
6. Why is a journal entry not made when a disbursement is made from a petty cash fund?
7. What conditions are necessary to classify an investment as short term?
8. On December 31 Stockton, Inc., invests idle cash in two different certificates of deposit. The first is an 8%, 90-day CD and the second has an interest rate of 9% and matures in 120 days. How is each of these CDs classified on the December 31 balance sheet?
9. What is the theoretical justification for the allowance method of accounting for bad debts?
10. In estimating bad debts, why is the balance in Allowance for Doubtful Accounts considered when the percentage of accounts receivable approach is used but not when the percentage of net credit sales approach is used?
11. When estimating bad debts on the basis of a percentage of accounts receivable, what is the advantage to using an aging schedule?
12. What is wrong with recording this *one* entry to recognize the recovery of an account receivable previously written off?

Cash	xxx	
Allowance for Doubtful Accounts		xxx

13. What is the distinction between an account receivable and a note receivable?
14. How would you evaluate the following statement? "Given the choice, it would always be better to require an interest-bearing note from a customer as opposed to a non-interest-bearing note. This is so because interest on a note receivable is a form of revenue and it is only in the case of an interest-bearing note that interest will be earned."
15. Why does the discounting of a note receivable with recourse result in a contingent liability? Should the liability be reported on the balance sheet?

EXERCISES

(LO 3) EXERCISE 7-1 ITEMS ON A BANK RECONCILIATION

Assume that a company is preparing a bank reconciliation for the month of June. It reconciles the bank balance and the book balance to the correct balance. For each of the following items, indicate whether the item is an addition to the bank balance (A-Bank), an addition to the book balance (A-Book), a deduction from the bank balance (D-Bank), a deduction from the book balance (D-Book), or would not appear on the June reconciliation (NA).

1. Check written in June but not yet returned to the bank for payment.
2. Customer's NSF check.
3. Customer's check written in the amount of $54 recorded on the books in the amount of $45.*
4. Service charge for new checks.
5. Principal and interest on a customer's note collected for the company by the bank.
6. Customer's check deposited on June 30 but not reflected on the bank statement.
7. Check written on the company's account paid by the bank and returned with the bank statement.
8. Check for $123 written on the company's account but recorded on the books as $132.*
9. Interest on the checking account for the month of June.

* Answer in terms of the adjustment needed to correct for the error.

(LO 4) EXERCISE 7-2 PETTY CASH FUND

On January 2, 1995, Cleaver Video Stores decided to set up a petty cash fund. The treasurer established the fund by writing and cashing a $300 check and placing the coin and currency in a locked petty cash drawer. Edward Haskell was designated as the custodian for the fund. During January, the following receipts were given to Haskell in exchange for cash from the fund:

U. S. Post Office (stamps)	$76.00
Speedy Delivery Service	45.30
Cake N Cookies (party for retiring employee)	65.40
Office Supply Superstore (paper, pencils)	36.00

A count of the cash in the drawer on January 31 revealed a balance of $74.10. The treasurer wrote and cashed a check on the same day to restore the fund to its original balance of $300. Prepare the necessary journal entries, with explanations, for January. Assume that all stamps and office supplies were used during the month.

(LO 2) EXERCISE 7-3 CERTIFICATE OF DEPOSIT

On May 31, 1995, Elmer Corp. purchased a 120-day, 9% certificate of deposit for $50,000. The CD was redeemed on September 28, 1995. Prepare the journal entries on Elmer's books to account for the CD, including any entry on June 30, the end of the company's fiscal year. Assume 360 days in a year.

(LO 5) EXERCISE 7-4 COMPARISON OF THE DIRECT WRITE-OFF AND ALLOWANCE METHODS OF ACCOUNTING FOR BAD DEBTS

In its first year of business, Mulch Landscapers has net income of $145,000, exclusive of any adjustment for bad debt expense. The president of the company has asked you to calculate net income under each of two alternatives of accounting for bad debts: the direct write-off method and the allowance method. The president would like to use the method that will result in the higher net income. So far, no entries have been made to write off uncollectible accounts or to estimate bad debts. The relevant data are as follows:

Write-offs during the year of uncollectible accounts	$ 10,500
Net credit sales	$650,000
Estimated percentage of net credit sales that will be uncollectible	2%

Compute net income under each of the two alternatives. Does Mulch have a choice as to which method to use? Should it base its choice on which method will result in the higher net income? (Ignore income taxes.)

■ REQUIRED

(LO 5) EXERCISE 7-5 ALLOWANCE METHOD OF ACCOUNTING FOR BAD DEBTS— COMPARISON OF THE TWO APPROACHES

The following data are available for the Griffith Corp.:

Accounts receivable, 12/31/95	$255,000 (dr.)
Allowance for doubtful accounts	$ 1,200 (cr.)
Net credit sales during 1995	$720,000 (cr.)

Prepare the journal entry in each case to recognize bad debts under the following assumptions: (1) bad debts expense should be 1% of net credit sales for the year and (2) 3% of the year-end balance in Accounts Receivable will prove to be uncollectible.

■ REQUIRED

(LO 6) EXERCISE 7-6 INTEREST-BEARING NOTES RECEIVABLE

On December 1, 1995, Boxer Corp. accepted a six-month, 8%, $50,000 note from a customer to settle an outstanding open account. The customer paid the note and interest to Boxer on May 31, 1996. Boxer's fiscal year ends on December 31 each year. Prepare all necessary journal entries on Boxer's books in connection with the note.

(LO 8) EXERCISE 7-7 CREDIT CARD SALES

Darlene's Diner accepts American Express from its customers. Darlene's is closed on Sundays and on that day records the weekly sales and remits the credit card drafts to American Express. For the week ending on Sunday, June 12, cash sales totaled $2,430 and credit card sales amounted to $3,500. On June 15, Darlene's received $3,360 from American Express as payment for the credit card drafts. Prepare the necessary journal entries on Darlene's books on June 12 and June 15. As a percentage, what collection fee is American Express charging Darlene?

(LO 5) EXERCISE 7-8 ACCOUNTS RECEIVABLE TURNOVER FOR QUAKER OATS

The 1993 annual report of The Quaker Oats Company reported the following amounts (in millions of dollars). The company's fiscal year ends on June 30. The accounts receivable balances are net of allowances for doubtful accounts.

Net sales	$5,730.6
Trade accounts receivable, June 30, 1993	478.9
Trade accounts receivable, June 30, 1992	575.3

■ REQUIRED

1. Compute Quaker's accounts receivable turnover ratio for 1993. (Assume all sales are on credit.)

2. What is the average collection period, in days, for an account receivable? Explain your answer.

3. Give some examples of the types of customers you would expect Quaker Oats to have. Do you think the average collection period for sales to these customers is reasonable? What other information do you need to fully answer this question?

MULTI-CONCEPT EXERCISES

(LO 1, 2) EXERCISE 7-9 COMPOSITION OF CASH

Indicate a Y for yes or an N for no whether each of the following items should be included in cash and cash equivalents on the balance sheet. If an item should not be included in cash and cash equivalents, indicate where it should appear on the balance sheet.

_____ 1. Checking account at Third County Bank.

_____ 2. Petty cash fund.

_____ 3. Coin and currency.

_____ 4. Postage stamps.

_____ 5. An IOU from an employee.

_____ 6. Savings account at the Ft. Worth Savings & Loan.

_____ 7. A six-month CD.

_____ 8. Undeposited customer checks.

_____ 9. A customer's check returned by the bank and marked NSF.

_____ 10. Sixty-day U.S. treasury bills.

_____ 11. A cashier's check.

(LO 1, 2) EXERCISE 7-10 CLASSIFICATION OF CASH EQUIVALENTS AND INVESTMENTS ON A BALANCE SHEET

Classify each of the following items as either a cash equivalent (CE), a short-term investment (STI), or a long-term investment (LTI).

_____ 1. A 120-day certificate of deposit.

_____ 2. Three hundred shares of GM common stock. The company plans on selling the stock in six months.

_____ 3. A six-month U.S. Treasury bill.

_____ 4. A 60-day certificate of deposit.

_____ 5. Ford Motor Co. bonds maturing in 15 years. The company intends to hold the bonds until maturity.

_____ 6. Commercial paper issued by ABC Corp., maturing in four months.

_____ 7. Five hundred shares of Chrysler common stock. The company plans to sell the stock in 60 days to help pay for a note due at that time at the bank.

_____ 8. Two hundred shares of GE preferred stock. The company intends to hold the stock for 10 years and at that point sell it to help finance construction of a new factory.

_____ **9.** Ten-year U.S. Treasury bonds. The company plans to sell the bonds on the open market in six months.

_____ **10.** A 90-day U.S. Treasury bill.

PROBLEMS

(LO 3) PROBLEM 7-1 BANK RECONCILIATION AND JOURNAL ENTRIES

The following information is available to assist you in preparing a bank reconciliation for Sunshine Florists on May 31, 1995:

a. The balance on the May 31, 1995, bank statement is $8,432.11.

b. Not included on the bank statement is a $1,250.00 deposit made by Sunshine late on May 31.

c. A comparison of the canceled checks returned with the bank statement with the company records indicated that the following checks are outstanding at May 31:

No. 123	$ 23.40
No. 127	145.00
No. 128	210.80
No. 130	67.32

d. The Cash account on the company's books shows a balance of $9,965.34.

e. The bank acts as a collection agency for interest earned on some municipal bonds held by Sunshine. The May bank statement indicates interest of $465.00 earned during the month.

f. Interest earned on the checking account and credited to Sunshine's account during May was $54.60. Miscellaneous bank service charges amounted to $50.00.

g. A customer's NSF check in the amount of $166.00 was returned with the May bank statement.

h. A comparison of the deposits listed on the bank statement with the company's books revealed that a customer's check in the amount of $123.45 was recorded on the books during May but never credited to the company's account. The bank erroneously credited the check to the account of Sunshine Bakery, which also has an account at the same bank.

i. The comparison of deposits per the bank statement with those per the books revealed that another customer's check in the amount of $101.10 was correctly credited to the company's account. In recording the check on the company's books, however, the accountant erroneously debited the Cash account for $1,011.00.

1. Prepare a bank reconciliation in good form.

2. Prepare the necessary journal entries on the books of Sunshine Florists.

3. A friend says to you: "I don't know why companies bother to prepare bank reconciliations—it seems a waste of time. Why don't they just do like I do and adjust the cash account for any difference between what the bank shows as a balance and what shows up in the books?" Explain to your friend _why_ a bank reconciliation should be prepared as soon as a bank statement is received.

■ **REQUIRED**

(LO 5) PROBLEM 7-2 AGING SCHEDULE TO ACCOUNT FOR BAD DEBTS

Sparkle Jewels distributes fine stones. It sells on credit to retail jewelry stores and extends terms of 2/10, net 60. For accounts that are not overdue, Sparkle has found that there is a 95% probability of collection. For accounts up to one month past due, the likelihood of collection decreases to 80%. If accounts are between one and two months past due, the probability of collection is 60%, and if an account is more than two months past due, Jewel estimates that there is only a 40% chance of collecting the receivable.

On December 31, 1995, the credit balance in Allowance for Doubtful Accounts is $12,300. The amounts of gross receivables, by age, on this date are as follows:

CATEGORY	AMOUNT
Current	$200,000
Past due:	
Less than one month	45,000
One to two months	25,000
More than two months	10,000

■ REQUIRED
1. Prepare a schedule to estimate the amount of uncollectible accounts at December 31, 1995.

2. On the basis of the schedule in part 1, prepare the journal entry on December 31, 1995, to estimate bad debts.

3. Show how accounts receivable would be presented on the December 31, 1995, balance sheet.

(LO 7) PROBLEM 7-3 NON-INTEREST-BEARING NOTES RECEIVABLE

Western Nursery sells a large stock of trees and shrubs to a landscaping business on May 31, 1995. The landscaper makes a down payment of $5,000 and signs a promissory note agreeing to pay $20,000 on August 29, 1995, the end of its busy season. The cash selling price of the nursery stock on May 31 was $24,000.

■ REQUIRED
1. Prepare the appropriate journal entry on Western's books on each of the following dates:

a. May 31, 1995, to record the receipt of the down payment and the promissory note.

b. June 30, 1995, the end of Western's fiscal year.

c. August 29, 1995, to record collection of the note.

2. Compute the effective rate of interest earned by Western on the note. Explain your answer.

(LO 8) PROBLEM 7-4 DISCOUNT OF A NOTE RECEIVABLE

Cougar Company sold merchandise on credit to a customer on May 31, 1995. The customer gave Cougar a down payment of $20,000 and an 8%, 120-day promissory note in the amount of $60,000. Cougar's year-end is June 30. On July 30, Cougar sold the note, with recourse, to Granite State Bank at a discount rate of 10%. On September 28, Granite notified Cougar that the original customer had paid the amount due on the note in full.

■ REQUIRED
1. Prepare the necessary journal entries on Cougar's books on the following dates (if an entry is not needed, explain why):

a. May 31, 1995.

b. June 30, 1995.

c. July 30, 1995.

d. September 28, 1995.

2. Should Cougar record a contingent liability on its books on July 30, 1995? Would it make a difference if the note had been discounted at the bank without recourse?

3. Assume that instead of paying the amount due the bank on September 28, the customer defaulted on the loan (assume for this part that the note was sold to the bank with recourse). Prepare any necessary journal entry on Cougar's books on this date.

(LO 4) PROBLEM 7-5 THE EFFECT OF PETTY CASH ON CASH AND INCOME

ABC Company established a petty cash fund in the amount of $500. One month later, it replenished the fund based on the following receipts:

a. $40 postage due on computer supplies used in the administrative offices.

b. $5.80 postage stamps used by the president when she is on the road and without access to the postage meter.

c. $180 advertising fliers, to be used by the marketing department, sent COD to the company.

d. $95 office supplies, purchased at a local store for use in administrative offices.

1. Prepare the journal entry to establish the petty cash fund. Cash on hand at the end of the first month is $174. Do you believe that the $500 amount was an appropriate amount for ABC's petty cash fund? Explain.

2. Prepare the journal entry to replenish the petty cash fund at the end of the month. What is the effect of this entry on the total assets of the company? on income?

3. Explain why a petty cash fund is allowed since proper accounting control over cash requires all payments to be made by check.

■ REQUIRED

(LO 8) PROBLEM 7-6 CREDIT CARD SALES

Gas stations sell gasoline at a lower price to customers who pay cash than to customers who use a charge card. A local gas station owner pays 2% of the sales price to the credit card company when customers pay with a credit card. He pays $ .75 per gallon of gasoline and must earn at least $ .25 per gallon of gross margin to stay competitive.

1. Determine the price the owner must charge credit card customers and the price he must charge cash customers.

2. Why has the policy of offering a lower price to cash customers not carried over to retail department stores?

■ REQUIRED

MULTI-CONCEPT PROBLEMS

(LO 1, 2) PROBLEM 7-7 CASH AND LIQUID ASSETS ON THE BALANCE SHEET

The following accounts are listed in a company's general ledger. The accountant is aware that the items should be placed in order of liquidity on the balance sheet.

Accounts Receivable
Certificates of Deposit (six months)
Marketable Securities
Prepaid Rent
Money Market Fund
Cash in Drawers

Rank the accounts in terms of liquidity. Identify items to be included in the total of cash, and explain why the items not included in cash on the balance sheet are not as liquid as cash. Explain how these items should be classified.

■ REQUIRED

(LO 5, 6) PROBLEM 7-8 ACCOUNTS AND NOTES RECEIVABLE

Linus Corp. sold merchandise for $5,000 to C. Brown on May 15, 1995, with credit terms of net 30. Subsequent to this, Brown experienced cash flow problems and was unable to pay its debt. On August 10, 1995, Linus stopped trying to collect the outstanding receivable from Brown and wrote the account off as uncollectible. On December 1, 1995, Brown sent Linus a check for $1,000 and offered to sign a two-month, 9% $4,000 promissory note to satisfy the remaining obligation. Brown paid the entire amount due Linus, with interest, on January 31, 1996. Linus ends its accounting year on December 31 each year and it uses the allowance method to account for bad debts.

■ REQUIRED

1. Prepare all of the necessary journal entries on the books of Linus Corp. from May 15, 1995, to January 31, 1996.

2. Why would Brown bother to send Linus a check for $1,000 on December 1 and agree to sign a note for the balance, given that such a long period of time had passed since the original purchase?

ALTERNATE PROBLEMS

(LO 3) PROBLEM 7-1A BANK RECONCILIATION

The following information is available to assist you in preparing a bank reconciliation for Maude's Marvelous Cheesecakes on March 31, 1995:

a. The balance on the March 31, 1995, bank statement is $6,506.10.

b. Not included on the bank statement is a deposit made by Maude's late on March 31 in the amount of $423.00.

c. A comparison of the canceled checks listed on the bank statement with the company records indicated that the following checks are outstanding at March 31:

No. 112	$ 42.92
No. 117	$307.00
No. 120	$ 10.58
No. 122	$ 75.67

d. The bank acts as a collection agency for checks returned for insufficient funds. The March bank statement indicates that one such check in the amount of $45.00 was collected and deposited and a collection fee of $4.50 was charged.

e. Interest earned on the checking account and credited to Maude's account during March was $4.30. Miscellaneous bank service charges amounted to $22.00.

f. A comparison of the deposits listed on the bank statement with the company's books revealed that a customer's check in the amount of $1,250.00 was recorded on the bank deposit in March but never credited to the customer's account.

g. The comparison of checks cleared per the bank statement with those per the books revealed that the wrong amount was charged to the company's account for a check. The amount of the check was $990.00. The proof machine encoded the check in the amount of $909.00, the amount charged against the company's account.

■ REQUIRED

1. Determine the balance on the books before any adjustments as well as the corrected balance to be reported on the balance sheet.

2. What would you recommend Maude do as a result of the bank error in **g.** above? Why?

(LO 5) PROBLEM 7-2A AGING SCHEDULE TO ACCOUNT FOR BAD DEBTS

Rough Stuff is a distributor of large rocks. It sells on credit to commercial landscaping companies and extends terms of 2/10, net 60. For accounts that are not overdue, Rough has found that there is a 90% probability of collection. For accounts up to one month past due, the likelihood of collection decreases to 75%. If accounts are between one and two months past due, the probability of collection is 65%, and if an account is more than two months past due, Rough estimates that there is only a 25% chance of collecting the receivable.

On December 31, 1995, the credit balance in Allowance for Doubtful Accounts is $34,590. The amounts of gross receivables, by age, on this date are as follows:

CATEGORY	AMOUNT
Current	$135,000
Past due:	
Less than one month	60,300
One to two months	35,000
More than two months	45,000

1. Prepare a schedule to estimate the amount of uncollectible accounts at December 31, 1995.

2. Rough knows that $40,000 of the $45,000 amount that is more than two months overdue is due from one customer that is in severe financial trouble. It is rumored that the customer will be filing for bankruptcy in the near future. As controller for Rough Stuff, how would you handle this situation?

3. Show how accounts receivable would be presented on the December 31, 1995, balance sheet.

■ REQUIRED

(LO 7) PROBLEM 7-3A NON-INTEREST-BEARING NOTE RECEIVABLE

Southern Poultry sells a large stock of birds to a processor on May 31, 1995. The processor makes a $12,000 down payment and signs a $36,900 promissory note agreeing to pay the remainder on August 29, 1995, the end of its busy season. The cash selling price of the birds on May 31 was $48,000.

1. Compute the effective rate of interest earned by Southern on the note. Explain your answer.

2. Write the footnote in Southern's annual report describing the terms of the note and expected collection. Southern's accounting year ends on June 30.

■ REQUIRED

(LO 8) PROBLEM 7-4A DISCOUNT OF A NOTE RECEIVABLE

Ram Company sold merchandise on credit to a customer on July 31, 1995. The customer gave Ram a down payment of $1,000 and a 10%, 45-day promissory note in the amount of $4,000. Ram's year-end is September 30. On August 15, Ram sold the note, with recourse, to Slate Savings and Loan at a discount rate of 12%. On September 14, Slate notified Ram that the original customer had paid the amount due on the note in full.

1. What amount of cash would Ram have accepted instead of the note?

2. What is the result of the sale of merchandise and discounting of the note on Ram's asset's and liabilities as of September 30, 1995, and income for the year ended September 30, 1995? Should an investor be notified if the company's sales are usually handled with a note that is discounted at a financial institution? Write a footnote to explain this sales payment method.

■ REQUIRED

(LO 4) PROBLEM 7-5A THE EFFECT OF PETTY CASH ON CASH AND INCOME

Arlington, Inc., established a petty cash fund in the amount of $50. One month later, it replenished the fund based on the following receipts:

a. $4 postage due on computer supplies purchased for the administrative offices.

b. $5.80 in postage stamps used by the receptionist so he does not need to leave his desk to use the postage meter.

c. $18 for a cake for the secretary's birthday.

d. $20 of materials purchased at a local store for use by the sales staff.

■ **REQUIRED**

1. Prepare the journal entry to establish the petty cash fund. Cash on hand at the end of the month is $1.15. Do you believe that the $50 amount was an appropriate amount for Arlington's petty cash fund? Explain.

2. Prepare the journal entry to replenish the petty cash fund at the end of the month. What is the effect of this entry on the total assets of the company? on income?

3. Who should oversee the petty cash fund? Write a short description of how the process should be handled in the company.

(LO 8) PROBLEM 7-6A CREDIT CARD SALES

A local fast-food store is considering the use of major credit cards in its outlets. Current annual sales are $800,000 per outlet. The company can purchase the equipment needed to handle credit cards and have an additional phone line installed in each outlet for approximately $800 per outlet. The equipment will be an expense in the year it is installed. The employee training time is minimal. The credit card company will charge a fee equal to 1.5% of sales for the use of credit cards. The company is unable to determine how much, if any, sales will increase and whether cash customers will use a credit card rather than cash. No other fast-food stores in the local area accept credit cards for sales payment.

■ **REQUIRED**

1. Assuming only 5% of existing cash customers will use a credit card, what increase in sales is necessary to pay for the credit card equipment in the first year?

2. What other factors might the company consider in addition to an increase in sales dollars?

ALTERNATE MULTI-CONCEPT PROBLEMS

(LO 1, 2) PROBLEM 7-7A CASH AND LIQUID ASSETS ON THE BALANCE SHEET

The following accounts are listed in a company's general ledger:

	DECEMBER 31, 1995	DECEMBER 31, 1994
Accounts receivable	$12,300	$10,000
Certificates of deposit (three months)	10,000	10,000
Marketable securities	4,500	4,000
Prepaid rent	1,200	1,500
Money market fund	25,800	28,000
Cash in checking account	6,000	6,000

■ **REQUIRED**

1. Which items are cash equivalents?

2. Explain where items that are not cash equivalents should be classified on the balance sheet.

3. What are the amount and direction of change in cash and cash equivalents for 1995? Is the company as liquid at the end of 1995 as it was at the end of 1994? Explain your answer.

(LO 5, 6) PROBLEM 7-8A ACCOUNTS AND NOTES RECEIVABLE

Tweedy, Inc., sold merchandise for $6,000 to P.D. Cat on July 31, 1995, with credit terms of net 30. Subsequent to this, Cat experienced cash flow problems and was unable to pay its debt. On December 24, 1995, Tweedy stopped trying to collect the outstanding receivable from Cat and wrote the account off as uncollectible. On January 15, 1996, Cat sent Tweedy a check for $1,500 and offered to sign a two-month, 8% $4,500 promissory note to satisfy the remaining obligation. Cat paid the entire amount due Tweedy, with interest, on March 15, 1996. Tweedy ends its accounting year on December 31 each year.

REQUIRED

1. Prepare all of the necessary journal entries on the books of Tweedy, Inc., from July 31, 1995, to March 15, 1996.

2. Why would Cat bother to send Tweedy a check for $1,500 on January 15 and agree to sign a note for the balance, given that such a long period of time had passed since the original purchase?

CASES

READING AND INTERPRETING FINANCIAL STATEMENTS

(LO 5) CASE 7-1 READING AND INTERPRETING BEN & JERRY'S FINANCIAL STATEMENTS

Refer to the financial statements for 1992 included in Ben & Jerry's annual report.

REQUIRED

1. What is the balance in the Allowance for Doubtful Accounts at the end of each of the two years presented?

2. Calculate the ratio of the Allowance for Doubtful Accounts to Gross Accounts Receivable at the end of each of the two years.

3. Why would the balance in the Allowance for Doubtful Accounts be unchanged at the end of each of the two years, even though Gross Accounts Receivable actually increased from the end of 1991 to the end of 1992? Does this mean that there was no activity in the allowance account during 1992? Explain your answer.

(LO 9) CASE 7-2 READING BEN & JERRY'S STATEMENT OF CASH FLOWS

Refer to the financial statements for 1992 included in Ben & Jerry's annual report.

REQUIRED

1. Did the company buy or sell any investments during 1992? If so, what was the dollar amount?

2. Relate the change in investments on the statement of cash flows to a number on the balance sheet. How is this number categorized on the balance sheet?

3. What was the dollar amount of increase or decrease in accounts receivable for 1992? Why is this number deducted on the statement of cash flows?

MAKING FINANCIAL DECISIONS

(LO 1, 2) CASE 7-3 LIQUIDITY

T Rex and R Rex both distribute films to movie theatres. The following are the current assets for each at the end of the year (all amounts are in millions of dollars):

	T REX	R REX
Cash	$10	$ 5
Six-month certificates of deposit	9	0
Short-term investments in stock	0	6
Accounts receivable	15	23
Allowance for doubtful accounts	(1)	(1)
Total current assets	$33	$33

■ REQUIRED   As a loan officer for the First National Bank of Jurassic Park, assume that both companies have come to you asking for a $10 million, six-month loan. If you could lend money to only one of the two, which one would it be? Justify your answer by writing a brief memo to the president of the bank.

(LO 6, 7) CASE 7-4 NOTES RECEIVABLE

Larson Land Development is considering two offers for a lot. Builder A has offered to pay $12,000 down and sign a 10%, $80,000 promissory note, with interest and principal due in one year. Builder B would make a down payment of $20,000 and sign a non-interest bearing, one-year note for $80,000. The president believes the deal with Builder A is better because it involves interest and the loan to Builder B does not. The vice-president of marketing thinks the offer from Builder B is better because it involves more money "up front." The sales manager is indifferent, reasoning that both builders would eventually pay $100,000 in total and because the lot was recently appraised at $75,000, both would be paying more than fair market value.

■ REQUIRED   1. Regardless of which offer it accepts, how much revenue should Larson recognize from the sale of the lot? Explain your answer.

2. Which offer do you think Larson should accept? Or is the sales manager correct that it doesn't matter which one is accepted? Explain your answer.

ACCOUNTING AND ETHICS: WHAT WOULD YOU DO?

(LO 5) CASE 7-5 TREATMENT OF CUSTOMER'S ACCOUNT

Ledermen Furniture Company has always experienced a problem collecting accounts. As of the end of 1995, Accounts Receivable was reported as follows:

Accounts receivable	$125,600
Allowance for bad debts	32,800
Accounts receivable, net	$ 92,800

During 1995 Ledermen wrote off $10,800 of accounts deemed to be uncollectible. Early in 1996, a former customer repaid $4,500, which had been written off in 1995. The chief financial officer recorded the receipt of the cash as a sale. He and the marketing vice president have an ongoing conflict regarding the credibility of customers. The financial officer believes that the marketing department is too generous in granting credit and that marketing has even overridden the finance's credit rejections. The marketing vice president believes that the credit department does not understand the business and without marketing's efforts, the company would not exist.

■ REQUIRED   1. Do you believe that the receipt of the $4,500 in cash was handled correctly?

2. What remedy could you recommend to resolve this conflict between the chief financial officer and the marketing vice president?

(LO 7) CASE 7-6 NOTES RECEIVABLE

Patterson Company is a large diversified company with a unit of the business that sells commercial real estate. As a company, Patterson has been profitable in recent years with the exception of the real estate business, where economic conditions have resulted in weak sales. The vice-president of the real estate division is aware of the poor performance of his group and needs to find ways to "show a profit."

During the current year the division was successful in selling a 100-acre tract of land for a new shopping center. The original cost of the property to Patterson was $4 million. The buyer has agreed to sign a $10 million note with payments of $2 million due at the end of each of the next 5 years. The property was appraised late last year at a market value of $7.5 million. The vice-president has come to you in your role as controller and asked that you record the sale as

Notes Receivable	10,000,000	
Sales Revenue		10,000,000
To record sale of 100-acre tract.		

■ REQUIRED

1. Does the entry suggested by the vice-president to record the sale violate any accounting principle? If so, explain what principle it violates.

2. What would you do? Write a brief memo to the vice-president explaining the proper accounting for the sale.

ANALYTICAL SOFTWARE CASE

To the Student: Your instructor may assign one or more parts of the analytical software case that is designed to accompany this chapter. This multi-part case gives you a chance to work with real financial statement data using software that stimulates, guides, and hones your analytical and problem-solving skills. It was created especially to support and strengthen your understanding of the chapter's Learning Objectives.

SOLUTIONS TO KEY TERMS QUIZ

Quiz 1:
1. Credit memoranda (p. 381)
2. Cash equivalent (p. 372)
3. Debit memoranda (p. 381)
4. Deposit in transit (p. 380)
5. Equity securities (p. 377)
6. Outstanding check (p. 379)
7. Debt securities (p. 377)
8. Bank statement (p. 378)
9. Bank reconciliation (p. 380)
10. Petty cash fund (p. 384)

Quiz 2:
1. Allowance method (p. 388)
2. Payee (p. 394)
3. Promissory note (p. 394)
4. Note payable (p. 394)

5. Maturity date (p. 395)
6. Credit card draft (p. 398)
7. Note receivable (p. 394)
8. Term (p. 395)
9. Discounting (p. 400)
10. Maker (p. 394)
11. Interest-bearing note (p. 395)
12. Principal (p. 394)
13. Aging schedule (p. 391)
14. Interest (p. 395)
15. Discounted note (p. 397)
16. Subsidiary ledger (p. 387)
17. Maturity value (p. 395)
18. Non-interest-bearing note (p. 395)
19. Direct write-off method (p. 388)
20. Control account (p. 387)

Focus on Financial Results

One of the most difficult issues for accountants is how to put a value on intangible assets. If a company is working on a cure for cancer and has a patent for a promising treatment, what should go on the balance sheet? The legal fees and administrative expenses associated with filing a patent would be included—but not the potential benefits to society if the treatment were to be widely effective. Regardless of the number placed on the balance sheet, biotechnology

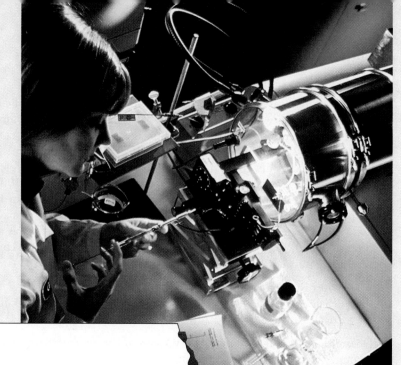

companies are valued by investors based on their potential for curing illness.

Genentech, Inc. is one of the most successful biotechnology companies, having developed several pharmaceutical products. Despite its success, the company does not display patents separately on the balance sheet—indeed, patents are buried in "other assets" of $64 million. The real expense of discovery is in research & development (R&D), which was $300 million in 1993—*about half the company's expenses*. However, the Financial Accounting Standards Board (FASB) requires that R&D must be written off immediately and is not disclosed as an asset on the balance sheet. Therefore, the balance sheet will never really tell the whole story for Genentech investors.

GENENTECH, INC.
CONSOLIDATED STATEMENTS OF INCOME
(in thousands, except per share amounts)

YEAR ENDED DECEMBER 31	1993	1992	1991
Revenues			
Product sales	$457,360	$390,975	$383,260
Royalties (including amounts from related parties:1993–$5,488; 1992–$5,378; 1991–$2,367)	112,872	91,682	63,384
Contract and other (including amounts from related parties: 1993–$8,869; 1992–$7,234; 1991–$1,601)	37,957	16,727	20,501
Interest	41,560	44,881	48,779
Total revenues	649,749	544,265	515,924
Costs and expenses			
Cost of sales	70,514	66,824	68,437
Research and development (including contract related: 1993–$4,235; 1992–$8,468; 1991–$8,340)	299,396	278,615	221,270
Marketing, general and administrative	214,410	172,486	175,277
Interest	6,527	4,406	4,771
Total costs and expenses	590,847	522,331	469,755
Income before taxes	58,902	21,934	46,169
Income tax provision	—	1,097	1,847
Net income	$ 58,902	$ 20,837	$ 44,322

Chapter 8

Operating Assets: Property, Plant, and Equipment, Natural Resources, and Intangibles

LEARNING OBJECTIVES

After studying this chapter, you should be able to

1. Understand balance sheet disclosures for operating assets.
2. Determine the acquisition cost of an operating asset.
3. Explain how to calculate the acquisition cost of assets purchased for a lump sum.
4. Describe the impact of capitalizing interest as part of the acquisition cost of an asset.
5. Compare depreciation calculated by alternative methods.
6. Understand the impact of a change in the estimate of the asset life or residual value.
7. Determine which expenditures should be capitalized as asset costs and which should be treated as expenses.
8. Analyze the effect of the disposal of an asset at a gain or loss.
9. Understand the balance sheet presentation of intangible assets.
10. Describe the proper amortization of intangible assets.
11. Explain the impact of long-term assets on the statement of cash flows.

Linkages

A LOOK AT PREVIOUS CHAPTERS

Chapter 2 introduced the topic of long-term assets as an important aspect of a classified balance sheet. The short-term assets of inventory, cash, and receivables were presented in previous chapters.

A LOOK AT THIS CHAPTER

This chapter presents the accounting for long-term operating assets. The first section of the chapter discusses assets that are generally classified as tangible assets or as property, plant, and equipment. We examine asset acquisition issues concerned with use and depreciation, and the sale or disposition of these assets. The second section of the chapter discusses assets generally classified as intangible assets. The accounting issues involved with the acquisition, use, and disposition of intangible assets are examined. The unique features of certain intangible assets are discussed separately.

A LOOK AT UPCOMING CHAPTERS

Subsequent chapters discuss the financing of long-term assets. Chapter 10 presents long-term liabilities as a source of financing. Chapter 11 describes the use of stock as a source of funds for financing long-term assets.

Operating Assets: Property, Plant, and Equipment

Balance Sheet Presentation

LO   1
Understand balance sheet disclosures for operating assets.

Operating assets constitute the major productive assets of many companies. Current assets are important to a company's short-term liquidity; operating assets are absolutely essential to its long-term future. These assets must be used to produce the goods or services the company sells to customers. The dollar amount invested in operating assets may be very large, as is the case with most manufacturing companies. On the other hand, operating assets on the balance sheet may be insignificant to a company's value, as is the case with a computer software firm. Companies use the value of physical assets as collateral when attempting to obtain financing; reliance on something less tangible—though no less valuable—such as intellectual assets, may make obtaining a loan difficult.

The terms used to describe the operating assets and the balance sheet presentation of those assets vary somewhat by company. Some firms refer to this category of assets as *fixed* or *plant* assets. Other firms prefer to present operating assets in two categories: *Tangible Assets* and *Intangible Assets.* The balance sheet of Ben & Jerry's uses another way to classify operating assets. Ben & Jerry's presents two classes of operating assets: *Property, Plant, and Equipment* and *Other Assets.* Because the latter term can encompass a variety of items, we will use the more descriptive term *intangible assets* for the second category. We begin by examining the accounting issues concerned with the first category of property, plant, and equipment.

Ben & Jerry's 1992 balance sheet presents the property, plant, and equipment category as follows:

Property, plant, and equipment	$39,312,513
Less accumulated depreciation	(12,575,088)
	$26,737,425

The amount of property, plant, and equipment less accumulated depreciation is sometimes referred to as *net property, plant, and equipment.* Ben & Jerry's footnote that accompanies the balance sheet indicates that the property, plant, and equipment classification consists of the following types of assets:

Land and improvements.

Land under capital lease.

Buildings.

Equipment and furniture.

Equipment under capital lease.

Leasehold improvements.

Transportation equipment.

Construction in progress.

The term *land improvements* refers to items such as landscaping, paving, or other improvements of the land. Construction in progress refers to the cost of assets that are being built over a long period of time. Note that Ben & Jerry's also has assets acquired by capital lease arrangements. Capital leases are discussed in Chapter 10 and will not be addressed in this chapter. The acquisition of operating assets by other means and the use of those assets are the focus of this chapter.

■ ACCOUNTING FOR YOUR DECISIONS   **You Are the Appraiser**

Dr. Jones, a dentist, has hired you to appraise his office property in support of a loan to make certain landscaping improvements. A landscape architect has estimated that the improvements will cost the dentist $100,000, which the dentist can probably depreciate over 10 years. Can you think of a scenario in which the tax benefits of this new depreciation could be offset by other taxes?

Acquisition of Property, Plant, and Equipment

Assets classified as property, plant, and equipment are initially recorded in 1992 at acquisition cost (also referred to as *historical cost*). As indicated on Ben & Jerry's balance sheet, these assets are normally presented on the balance sheet at original acquisition cost minus accumulated depreciation. It is important, however, to define the term *acquisition cost* (also known as original cost) in a more exact manner. What items should be included as part of the original acquisition? **Acquisition cost** should include all of the costs necessary to acquire the asset and prepare it for its intended use. Items included in acquisition cost would generally include the following:

LO   2
Determine the acquisition cost of an operating asset.

Purchase price.

Taxes paid at time of purchase (for example, sales tax).

Transportation charges.

Installation costs.

Repair costs, if necessary to prepare the asset for use.

Acquisition cost should not include expenditures unrelated to the acquisition or costs incurred subsequent to the time the asset was installed and use begun. An accountant must exercise careful judgment to determine which costs are "normal" and "necessary" and should be included in the calculation of the acquisition cost of operating assets.

Group Purchase   Quite often a firm purchases several assets as a group and pays a lump-sum amount. This is most common when a company purchases land and a building situated on it and pays a lump-sum amount for them. It is important to measure separately the acquisition cost of the land and of the building. Land is not a depreciable asset, but the amount allocated to the building is subject to depreciation. In cases such as this, the purchase price should be allocated between land and building on the basis of the proportion of the *fair market values* of each.

LO   3
Explain how to calculate the acquisition cost of assets purchased for a lump sum.

For example, assume that on January 1, Tammy Company purchased a building and the land that it is situated on for $100,000. The accountant was able to establish that the fair market values of the two assets on January 1 were as follows:

Land	$30,000
Building	90,000
Total	$120,000

On the basis of the estimated market values, the purchase price should be allocated as follows:

To land $100,000 × $30,000/$120,000 = $25,000
To building $100,000 × $90,000/$120,000 = $75,000

The journal entry to record the purchase would be as follows:

Jan. 1	Land	25,000	
	Building	75,000	
	Cash		100,000

To record the purchase of land and building for a lump-sum amount.

Assets	=	Liabilities	+	Owners' Equity
+25,000				
+75,000				
−100,000				

Market value is best established by an independent appraisal of the property. If such appraisal is not possible, the accountant must rely on the market value of other similar assets, on the value of the assets in tax records, or on other available evidence.

These efforts to allocate dollars between land and buildings will permit the appropriate allocation for depreciation. But when an investor or lender views the balance sheet, one of the first things that he or she does is adjust these accounts to current market value. The best things that can be said about historical cost are that it is a verifiable number and that it is conservative. But it is still up to the lender or the investor to determine the appropriate value for these assets.

LO 4

Describe the impact of capitalizing interest as part of acquisition cost.

Capitalization of Interest We have seen that acquisition cost may include several items. But should the acquisition cost of an asset include the interest cost necessary to finance the asset? That is, should interest be treated as an asset, or should it be treated as an expense of the period?

Generally, interest should be treated as an expense of the period. If a company buys an asset and borrows money to finance the purchase, the interest on borrowed money is not considered part of the asset's cost. Its acquisition is treated as a business decision that is separate from the decision concerning the financing of the asset. Therefore, interest is treated as a period cost and should appear on the income statement as interest expense in the period incurred.

There is one exception to this general guideline, however. If a company *constructs* an asset over a period of time and borrows money to finance the construction, the amount of interest during the construction period is not treated as interest expense. Instead, the interest must be included as part of the acquisition cost of the asset. This is referred to as **capitalization of interest.** The amount of interest that is capitalized (treated as an asset) is based on the *average accumulated expenditures* and is limited to an amount that is not more than the amount of actual interest incurred. The logic of using the average accumulated expenditure is that this number represents an average amount of money tied up in the project over a year. If it takes $200,000 to construct a building, the interest should not be figured on the full $200,000 because there were times during the year when no money was being used. We will illustrate the concept with the example that follows.

Assume that on January 1, 1995, Sanchez Company began to construct a large piece of factory equipment. Construction occurred evenly throughout 1995 and

A restaurant under construction, along with the equipment purchased and under capital lease and such items as paving and landscaping, represent operating assets for the company that owns or will acquire it.

resulted in average expenditures of $100,000. To finance the construction, Sanchez borrowed $250,000 from a local bank on January 1, 1995. According to the terms of the loan, annual interest of 10% is to be paid at year-end. Sanchez had no other loans or obligations during 1995. Therefore, it would calculate the following amounts for 1995:

Average Accumulated Expenditures = $100,000

$$\text{Interest Incurred on Loan} = \$250,000 \times 10\%$$
$$= \$25,000$$

Interest to Be Capitalized = Average Accumulated Expenditures times interest rate

$$= \$100,000 \times 10\%$$
$$= \$10,000$$

Because the amount of interest to be capitalized is not larger than the amount of interest incurred, Sanchez should include $10,000 of interest as part of the acquisition cost of the asset. The journal entries to record the construction of the asset, the loan, and the interest are as follows:

```
1995
Jan. 1   Cash                                      250,000
            Note Payable                                      250,000
         To record loan for construction of an asset.
```

Assets	=	Liabilities	+	Owners' Equity
+ 250,000		+ 250,000		

```
1995
Dec. 31   Factory Equipment                          200,000
             Cash                                              200,000
          To record the cost of constructing factory equipment for
          the year.
```

Assets	=	Liabilities	+	Owners' Equity
+ 200,000				
− 200,000				

```
1995
Dec. 31   Interest Expense                            15,000
          Factory Equipment                           10,000
             Cash                                              25,000
          To record the payment of interest and the capitalization of
          interest to factory equipment.
```

Assets	=	Liabilities	+	Owners' Equity
+ 10,000				− 15,000
− 25,000				

In this example, the acquisition cost of the factory equipment should be considered to be $210,000. Depreciation of the factory equipment should be based on that amount, less any residual value.

Land Improvements   It is important to distinguish between land and other costs associated with it. The acquisition cost of land should be kept in a separate account because land has an unlimited life and is not subject to depreciation. Other costs associated with land should be recorded in an account such as Land Improvements. For example, the costs of paving a parking lot or landscaping costs are properly treated as **land improvements,** which have a limited life. Therefore, the acquisition costs of land improvements should be depreciated over their useful lives.

Use and Depreciation of Property, Plant, and Equipment

LO 5

Compare depreciation calculated by alternative methods.

All property, plant, and equipment, except land, have a limited life and decline in usefulness over time. The accrual accounting process requires a proper *matching* of expenses and revenue to accurately measure income. Therefore, the accountant must estimate the decline in usefulness of operating assets and allocate the acquisition cost over their useful lives in a manner consistent with the decline in usefulness. This allocation is the process generally referred to as **depreciation.**

Unfortunately, estimating and determining the decline in usefulness of operating assets is not easy because of the many factors involved. An asset's decline in usefulness is related to *physical deterioration* factors such as wear and tear. In some cases, the physical deterioration results from heavy use of the asset in the production process, but it may also result from the passage of time or exposure to the elements.

The decline in an asset's usefulness is also related to *obsolescence* factors. Some operating assets, such as computers, decline in usefulness simply because they have been surpassed by a newer model or newer technology. Finally, the decline in an asset's usefulness is related to a company's *repair and maintenance* policy. A company with an aggressive and extensive repair and maintenance program will not experience a decline in usefulness of operating assets as rapidly as one without such a policy.

Because the decline in an asset's usefulness is related to a variety of factors, several depreciation methods have been developed. In theory, a company should use a depreciation method that best measures the decline in an asset's usefulness and allows the company to accurately match that expense to the revenue generated by the asset. We will present four methods of depreciation: *straight line, units of production, sum of years' digits,* and *double declining balance.*

All depreciation methods are based on the asset's original acquisition cost. In addition, all methods require an estimate of two additional factors: the asset's *life* and *residual value.* The residual value (also referred to as *salvage value*) should represent the amount that could be obtained from selling or disposing of it at the end of its useful life. Often this may be a small amount or even zero.

Straight-Line Method   **Straight-line depreciation** assumes that the decline in an asset's usefulness occurs evenly over time. This method calculates the annual depreciation as follows:

$$\text{Depreciation} = (\text{Acquisition Cost} - \text{Residual Value})/\text{Life}$$

For example, assume that on January 1, 1995, Farley Company purchased an operating asset for $20,000. The company estimated that the asset life would be five years and its residual value at the end of 1999 would be $2,000. The annual depreciation should be calculated as follows:

$$\begin{aligned} \text{Depreciation} &= (\text{Acquisition Cost} - \text{Residual Value})/\text{Life} \\ \text{Depreciation} &= (\$20,000 - \$2,000)/5 \\ &= \$3,600 \end{aligned}$$

An asset's **book value** is defined as its acquisition cost minus its total amount of accumulated depreciation. Thus, the book value of the asset in this example is $16,400 at the end of 1995:

$$\begin{aligned} \text{Book Value} &= \text{Acquisition Cost} - \text{Accumulated Depreciation} \\ \text{Book Value} &= \$20,000 - \$3,600 \\ &= \$16,400 \end{aligned}$$

The book value at the end of 1996 is $12,800:

$$\begin{aligned} \text{Book Value} &= \text{Acquisition Cost} - \text{Accumulated Depreciation} \\ \text{Book Value} &= \$20,000 - (2 \times \$3,600) \\ &= \$12,800 \end{aligned}$$

The most attractive features of the straight-line method are its ease and simplicity. It is the most popular method for presenting depreciation in the annual report to stockholders.

Units-of-Production Method   In some cases, the decline in an asset's usefulness is directly related to wear and tear as a result of the number of units it produces. In those cases, depreciation should be calculated by the **units-of-production method.** With this method, the asset's life is expressed in terms of the number of units that the asset can produce. The depreciation *per unit* can be calculated as

$$\begin{aligned} \text{Depreciation per Unit} = (\text{Acquisition Cost} - \text{Residual Value})/ \\ \text{Total Number of Units in Asset's Life} \end{aligned}$$

The annual depreciation for a given year can be calculated based on the number of units produced during that year as

$$\text{Annual Depreciation} = \text{Depreciation per Unit} \times \text{Units Produced in Current Year}$$

For example, assume that Farley Company in the previous example wished to use the units-of-production method for 1995. Also assume that Farley has been able to estimate that the total number of units that will be produced during the asset's five-year life is 18,000. During 1995 Farley produced 4,000 units. The depreciation per unit for Farley's asset can be calculated as

$$\text{Depreciation per Unit} = (\text{Acquisition Cost} - \text{Residual Value})/\text{Life in Units}$$

$$\text{Depreciation per Unit} = (\$20,000 - \$2,000)/18,000$$
$$= \$1 \text{ per Unit}$$

The amount of depreciation that should be recorded as an expense for 1995 is

$$\text{Annual Depreciation} = \text{Depreciation per Unit} \times \text{Units Produced in 1995}$$
$$\text{Annual Depreciation} = \$1 \text{ per Unit} \times 4,000 \text{ Units}$$
$$= \$4,000$$

Depreciation will be recorded until the asset produces 18,000 units. The asset cannot be depreciated below its residual value of $2,000.

The units-of-production method is most appropriate when the accountant is able to estimate the total number of units that will be produced over the asset's life. For example, if a factory machine is used to produce a particular item, the life of the asset may be expressed in terms of the number of units produced. Further, the units produced must be related to particular time periods so that depreciation expense can be matched accurately with the related revenue.

Accelerated Depreciation Methods   The decline in usefulness of some assets occurs more in early years than in later ones. For those assets, an accelerated method of depreciation is appropriate. The term **accelerated depreciation** refers to several methods of depreciation by which a higher amount of depreciation is recorded in the early years than in later ones. One common method of accelerated depreciation is the **sum-of-the-years' digits method,** which takes its name from the fact that the depreciation for each period is determined by comparing the number of years of life remaining to the sum of the years' digits making up the asset's life.

The asset purchased by Farley Company will again be used as an example. The first step is to total the digits of asset life. If the asset life is five years, the sum is 15:

$$1 + 2 + 3 + 4 + 5 = 15$$

Instead of summing the digits, a formula is available to calculate the sum-of-the-digits' life:

$$\text{Sum of Digits} = n \times (n + 1)/2$$

where

$$n = \text{Life of the Asset}$$

For our example, the formula is calculated as

$$\text{Sum of Digits} = 5 \times (5 + 1)/2 = 15$$

The amount of depreciation to be recorded for 1995 is based on the fraction 5/15, for 1996 on 4/15, for 1997 on 3/15, and so on. Therefore, Farley should record depreciation for 1995 calculated as follows:

$$\text{Depreciation} = (\text{Acquisition Cost} - \text{Residual Value}) \times \text{Rate}$$
$$\text{Depreciation} = (\$20,000 - \$2,000) \times 5/15$$
$$= \$6,000$$

The amount of depreciation for 1996 is calculated as

$$\text{Depreciation} = (\text{Acquisition Cost} - \text{Residual Value}) \times \text{Rate}$$
$$\text{Depreciation} = (\$20,000 - \$2,000) \times 4/15$$
$$= \$4,800$$

Note that the residual value is deducted from the acquisition cost to determine the depreciable amount.

The sum-of-the-years'-digit method does result in an accelerated depreciation in that a higher amount of depreciation is recorded in the early years of the asset life than in later ones. This method is most appropriate when the decline in the usefulness of the asset follows that pattern.

Another form of accelerated depreciation is the **double declining-balance method.** Using this method, depreciation is calculated at double the straight-line rate but on a declining amount. The first step is to calculate the straight-line rate as a percentage. The straight-line rate for the Farley asset with a five-year life is

$$100\%/5 \text{ Years} = 20\%$$

The second step is to double the straight-line rate:

$$2 \times 20\% = 40\%$$

This rate will be applied in all years to the asset's beginning book value. As depreciation is recorded, the book value declines. Thus, a constant rate is applied to a declining amount. This constant rate is applied to the full cost or initial book value, not to cost minus residual value as in the other methods. However, the asset cannot be depreciated below its residual value.

The amount of depreciation for 1995 would be calculated as

$$\text{Depreciation} = \text{Beginning Book Value} \times \text{Rate}$$
$$\text{Depreciation} = \$20,000 \times 40\%$$
$$= \$8,000$$

The amount of depreciation for 1996 would be calculated as

$$\text{Depreciation} = \text{Beginning Book Value} \times \text{Rate}$$
$$\text{Depreciation} = (\$20,000 - \$8,000) \times 40\%$$
$$= \$4,800$$

The complete depreciation schedule for Farley Company for all five years of asset life would be as follows:

YEAR	RATE	BOOK VALUE AT BEGINNING OF YEAR	DEPRECIATION	BOOK VALUE AT END OF YEAR
1995	40%	$20,000	$ 8,000	$12,000
1996	40	12,000	4,800	7,200
1997	40	7,200	2,880	4,320
1998	40	4,320	1,728	2,592
1999	40	2,592	592	2,000
Total			$18,000	

In the Farley Company example, the depreciation for 1999 cannot be calculated as $2,592 \times 40\%$ because this would result in an accumulated depreciation amount more than $18,000. The total amount of depreciation recorded in Years 1 through

4 is $17,408. The accountant should record only $592 depreciation ($18,000 − $17,408) in 1999 so that the remaining value of the asset is $2,000 at the end of 1999.

The double declining-balance method of depreciation results in an accelerated depreciation pattern. It is most appropriate for assets subject to a rapid decline in usefulness as a result of technical or obsolescence factors. Like the sum-of-the-years'-digits method, double declining depreciation is not widely used for financial statement purposes but may be appropriate for certain assets. As discussed earlier, most companies use straight-line depreciation for financial statement purposes because it generally produces the highest net income, especially in growing companies that have a stable or expanding base of assets.

Comparison of Depreciation Methods   In this section, you have learned about several methods of depreciating operating assets. Exhibit 8-1 presents a comparison of the depreciation and book values of the Farley Company asset for 1995–1999 using the straight-line, sum-of-the-years'-digit, and double declining-balance methods (we have excluded the units-of-production method). Note that all methods result in a depreciation total of $18,000 over the five-year time period. The amount of depreciation per year depends, however, on the method of depreciation chosen.

Nonaccountants often misunderstand the accountant's concept of depreciation. Accountants do not consider depreciation to be a process of *valuing* the asset. That is, depreciation does not describe the increase or decrease in the market value of the asset. Accountants consider depreciation to be a process of *cost allocation*. The purpose is to allocate the original acquisition cost to the periods benefited by the asset. The depreciation method chosen should be based on the decline in the asset's usefulness. A company can choose a different depreciation method for each individual fixed asset or for each class or category of fixed assets.

The choice of depreciation method can have a significant impact on the bottom line. If two companies are essentially identical in every other respect, a different depreciation method for fixed assets can make one company look more profitable than another. Or a company that uses accelerated depreciation for one year can find that its otherwise declining earnings are no longer declining if it switches to straight-line depreciation. Investors should pay some attention to depreciation methods when comparing companies. Statement users must be aware of the different depreciation methods to understand the calculation of income and to compare companies that may not use the same methods.

Some investors ignore depreciation altogether when evaluating a company, not because they do not know that assets depreciate but because they wish to focus

FROM CONCEPT TO PRACTICE

READING BEN & JERRY'S ANNUAL REPORT

What amount did Ben & Jerry's report as depreciation in 1992? Where is it disclosed? What depreciation method was used?

EXHIBIT 8-1   Comparison of Depreciation and Book Values of Straight-Line and Accelerated Methods

YEAR	STRAIGHT LINE		SUM-OF-THE-YEARS' DIGITS		DOUBLE DECLINING BAL.	
	DEPREC.	BOOK VALUE	DEPREC.	BOOK VALUE	DEPREC.	BOOK VALUE
1995	$ 3,600	$16,400	$ 6,000	$14,000	$ 8,000	$12,000
1996	3,600	12,800	4,800	9,200	4,800	7,200
1997	3,600	9,200	3,600	5,600	2,880	4,320
1998	3,600	5,600	2,400	3,200	1,782	2,592
1999	3,600	2,000	1,200	2,000	592	2,000
Total	$18,000		$18,000		$18,000	

on cash flow instead of earnings. Depreciation is a "noncash" charge that reduces net income.

Depreciation and Income Taxes   Financial accounting involves the presentation of financial statements to external users of accounting information such as investors and creditors. When depreciating an asset for financial accounting purposes, the accountant's goal should be to choose a depreciation method that is consistent with the asset's decline in usefulness and properly allocates its cost to the periods that benefit from its use.

Depreciation is also deducted for income tax purposes. Sometimes depreciation is referred to as a *tax shield* because it reduces (as do other expenses) the amount of income tax that would otherwise have to be paid. When depreciating an asset for tax purposes, a company should generally choose a depreciation method that reduces the present value of its tax burden to the lowest possible amount over the life of the asset. Normally, this is best accomplished with an accelerated depreciation method because it allows a company to save more income tax in the early years of the asset. This happens because the higher depreciation charges reduce taxable income more than the straight-line method does. The method allowed for tax purposes is referred to as *MACRS,* which stands for Modified Accelerated Cost Recovery System. It is a form of accelerated depreciation and is similar to the methods we have examined in that it results in a larger amount of depreciation in the early years of asset life and a smaller amount in later years.

Therefore, it is not unusual for a company to use *two* depreciation methods for the same asset, one for financial reporting purposes and another for tax purposes. This may seem somewhat confusing, but it is the direct result of the differing goals of financial and tax accounting. See Chapter 10 for more about this issue.

Change in Depreciation Estimate

An asset's acquisition cost is known at the time it is purchased, but its life and its residual value must be estimated. These estimates are then used as the basis for depreciating it. Occasionally, an estimate of the asset's life or residual value must be altered after the depreciation process has begun. This is an example of an accounting change that is referred to as a **change in estimate.**

Assume the same facts as in the Farley Company example (see page 429). The company purchased an asset on January 1, 1995, for $20,000. Farley estimated that the asset's life would be five years and its residual value at the end of five years would be $2,000. Assume that Farley has depreciated the asset using the straight-line method for two years. At the beginning of 1997, Farley believes that the total asset life will be seven years, or another five years beyond the two years the asset has been used. Thus, depreciation must be adjusted to reflect the new estimate of the asset's life.

A change in estimate should be recorded *prospectively,* meaning that the depreciation recorded in prior years is not corrected or restated. Instead, the new estimate should affect the current year and future years. The Farley Company should depreciate the remaining depreciable amount during 1997 through 2001. The amount to be depreciated over that time period should be calculated as

Acquisition Cost, Jan. 1, 1995	$20,000
Less: Accumulated Depreciation	
(2 years at $3,600 per year)	7,200
Book Value, Jan. 1, 1997	$12,800
Less: Residual Value	2,000
Remaining Depreciable Amount	$10,800

LO **6**
Understand the impact of a change in the estimate of the asset life or residual value.

The remaining depreciable amount should be recorded as depreciation over the remaining life of the asset. In the Farley Company case, the depreciation amount for 1997 and the following four years would be $2,160:

$$\text{Depreciation} = \text{Remaining Depreciable Amount/Remaining Life}$$
$$\text{Depreciation} = \$10,800 \: / \: 5 \text{ Years}$$
$$= \$2,160$$

The journal entry to record depreciation for the year 1997 is as follows:

1997			
Dec. 31	Depreciation Expense	2,160	
	Accumulated Depreciation		2,160
	To record depreciation for 1997 based on remaining life of five years.		

Assets	=	Liabilities	+	Owners' Equity
−2,160				−2,160

If the change in estimate is a material amount, the company should disclose in the footnotes to the 1997 financial statements that depreciation has changed as a result of a change in estimate. The company's auditors have to be very careful that management's decision to change its estimate of the depreciable life of the asset is not simply an attempt to manipulate earnings. Particularly in capital-intensive manufacturing concerns, lengthening the useful life of equipment can have a material impact on earnings.

A change in estimate of an asset's residual value is treated in a manner similar to a change in an asset's life. There should be no attempt to correct or restate the income statements of past periods that were based on the original estimate. Instead, the accountant should use the new estimate of residual value to calculate depreciation for the current and future years.

A change in estimate is not treated the same way as a *change in principle*. If a company changes its *method* of depreciation, for example from accelerated depreciation to the straight-line method, this constitutes a change in accounting principle that must be disclosed separately on the income statement. A complete discussion of items treated as a change in accounting principle can be found in Chapter 12.

Capital versus Revenue Expenditures

Accountants must often decide whether certain expenditures related to operating assets should be treated as an addition to the cost of the asset or as an expense. One of the most common examples involving this decision concerns repairs to an asset. Should the repairs constitute capital expenditures or revenue expenditures? A **capital expenditure** is a cost that is added to the acquisition cost of the asset. A **revenue expenditure** is not treated as part of the cost of the asset, but as an expense on the income statement. Thus, the company must decide whether to treat an item as an asset (balance sheet) and depreciate its cost over its life or to treat it as an expense (income statement) of a single period.

The distinction between capital and revenue expenditures is a matter of judgment. Generally, the guideline that should be followed is that if an expenditure increases the life of the asset or its productivity, it should be treated as a capital expenditure and added to the asset account. If an expenditure simply maintains an asset in its normal operating condition, however, it should be treated as an expense. The *materiality* of the expenditure must also be considered. Most companies establish a policy of treating an expenditure smaller than a specified amount as a revenue expenditure (an expense on the income statement).

It is very important that a company not improperly capitalize a material expenditure that should have been written off right away. The capitalization policies of companies become grist for Wall Street analysts trying to assess the true value of these companies. When a company is accused of capitalizing rather than expensing certain items to artificially boost earnings, that revelation can be very damaging to the stock price.

Expenditures related to operating assets may be classified in several categories. For each type of expenditure, its treatment as capital or revenue should be as follows:

CATEGORY	EXAMPLE	ASSET OR EXPENSE
Normal maintenance	Repainting	Expense
Minor repair	Replace spark plugs	Expense
Major repair	Replace a vehicle's engine	Asset, if life or productivity is enhanced
Addition	Add a wing to a building	Asset

An item treated as a capital expenditure affects the amount of depreciation that should be recorded over the asset's remaining life. We return to the Farley Company example to illustrate. Assume again that Farley purchased an operating asset on January 1, 1995, for $20,000. Farley estimated that the residual value of the asset at the end of five years would be $2,000 and has depreciated the asset using the straight-line method for 1995 and 1996. At the beginning of 1997, Farley made a $3,000 overhaul to the asset, extending its life by three years. Because the expenditure qualifies as a capital expenditure, the journal entry to record the overhaul is as follows:

```
1997
Jan. 1    Asset                                       3,000
              Cash                                            3,000
          To record the overhaul of an operating asset.
```

Assets	=	Liabilities	+	Owners' Equity
+3,000				
−3,000				

For the years 1995 and 1996, Farley recorded depreciation of $3,600 per year:

$$\text{Depreciation} = (\text{Acquisition Cost} - \text{Residual Value})/\text{Life}$$
$$\text{Depreciation} = (\$20,000 - \$2,000)/5$$
$$= \$3,600$$

Beginning in 1997, Farley should record depreciation of $2,300 per year, computed as follows:

Original Cost, Jan. 1, 1995	$20,000
Less: Accumulated Depreciation (2 years × $3,600)	7,200
Book Value, Jan. 1, 1997	$12,800
Plus: Major Overhaul	3,000
Less: Residual Value	(2,000)
Remaining Depreciable Amount	$13,800

$$\text{Depreciation} = \text{Remaining Depreciable Amount/Remaining Life}$$
$$\text{Depreciation per Year} = \$13,800/6 \text{ Years}$$
$$= \$2,300$$

The entry to record depreciation for the year 1997 follows:

1997			
Dec. 31	Depreciation Expense	2,300	
	Accumulated Depreciation-Asset		2,300
	To record annual depreciation on operating asset.		

Assets	=	Liabilities	+	Owners' Equity
− 2,300				− 2,300

Environmental Aspects of Operating Assets

As the number of the government's environmental regulations has increased, businesses have been required to expend more money complying with them. A common example involves costs to comply with federal requirements to clean up contaminated soil surrounding plant facilities. Should such costs be considered an expense and recorded entirely in one accounting period or should they be treated as a capital expenditure and added to the cost of the asset? At the present time, there is little accounting guidance on such issues and management must exercise careful judgment on a case-by-case basis. It is important, however, for companies at least to conduct a thorough investigation to determine the potential environmental considerations that may affect the value of operating assets and to ponder carefully the accounting implications of new environmental regulations.

Should the costs of cleaning up a contaminated factory be considered an expense of one period or a capital expenditure added to the cost of the plant asset? To make the best decision, management should gather all the facts about the extent of the proposed cleanup and its environmental impact.

Disposal of Operating Assets

An asset may be disposed of in any of several different ways. One common method is to sell the asset for cash. Sale of an asset involves two important considerations. First, depreciation must be recorded up to the date of sale. If the sale does not occur at the fiscal year-end, usually December 31, depreciation must be recorded for a partial period from the beginning of the year to the date of sale. Second, the company selling the asset must calculate and record the gain or loss on its sale.

Refer again to the Farley Company example. Assume that Farley purchased a machine on January 1, 1995, for $20,000, estimated its life to be five years and the residual value to be $2,000. Farley used the straight-line method of depreciation. Assume that Farley sold the machine on July 1, 1997, for $12,400. Depreciation for the six-month time period from January 1 to July 1, 1997, is $1,800 ($3,600 per year times one-half of a year) and should be recorded as follows:

```
1997
July 1    Depreciation Expense                              1,800
              Accumulated Depreciation—Machine                        1,800
          To record depreciation for a six-month time period.
```

Assets	=	Liabilities	+	Owners' Equity
− 1,800				− 1,800

After recording the July 1 entry, the balance of the Accumulated Depreciation—Machine account is $9,000, which reflects depreciation for the 2½ yearsfrom the date of purchase to the date of sale. The entry to record the sale follows:

```
1997
July 1    Accumulated Depreciation—Machine                  9,000
          Cash                                             12,400
              Machine                                               20,000
              Gain on Sale of Asset                                  1,400
          To record the sale of the machine.
```

Assets	=	Liabilities	+	Owners' Equity
+ 9,000				+ 1,400
+ 12,400				
− 20,000				

When an asset is sold, all accounts related to it must be removed. In the preceding entry the Machine account is credited to eliminate the account, and the Accumulated Depreciation—Machine account is debited to eliminate it. The **Gain on Sale of Asset** indicates the amount by which the sale price of the asset *exceeds* the book value. Thus, the gain can be calculated as

Asset Cost	$20,000
Less: Accumulated Depreciation	9,000
Book Value	$11,000
Sale Price	12,400
Gain on Sale of Asset	$ 1,400

The account Gain on Sale of Asset is an income statement account and should appear in the Other Income/Expense category of the statement. The Gain on Sale of Asset account is not treated as revenue because it does not constitute the company's ongoing or central activity. Instead, it appears as income but in a separate category to denote its incidental nature.

The calculation of a loss on the sale of an asset is similar to that of a gain. Assume in the above example that Farley had sold the machine on July 1, 1997, for $10,000

LO 8

Analyze the effect of the disposal of an asset at a gain or loss.

cash. The entry to record six months of depreciation has already been presented. However, the following is the entry to record the sale of the asset:

1997			
July 1	Accumulated Depreciation—Machine	9,000	
	Cash	10,000	
	Loss on Sale of Asset	1,000	
	Machine		20,000
	To record the sale of a machine.		

Assets	=	Liabilities	+	Owners' Equity
+9,000				−1,000
+10,000				
−20,000				

The **Loss on Sale of Asset** indicates the amount by which the asset's sales price *is less than* its book value. Thus, the loss could be calculated as

Asset Cost	$20,000
Less: Accumulated Depreciation	9,000
Book Value	$11,000
Sale Price	10,000
Loss on Sale of Asset	$ 1,000

The Loss on Sale of Asset account is an income statement account with a debit balance and should appear in the Other Income/Expense category of the income statement.

Operating Assets: Natural Resources

An important operating asset for some companies consists of a natural resource such as coal fields, oil wells, other mineral deposits, and timberlands. Natural resources share one common characteristic: the resource is consumed as it is used. For example, the coal a utility company uses to make electricity is consumed in the process. Most natural resources cannot be replenished in the foreseeable future. Coal and oil, for example, can be replenished only by nature over millions of years. Timberlands may be replenished in a shorter time period, but even trees must grow for many years to be usable for lumber.

Natural resources should be carried in the Property, Plant, and Equipment category of the balance sheet as an operating asset. As with other assets in the category, natural resources should be initially recorded at *acquisition cost*. Acquisition cost should include the cost of acquiring the natural resource and the costs necessary to prepare the asset for use. The preparation costs for natural resources may often be very large; for example, a utility may spend large sums to remove layers of dirt before the coal can be mined. These preparation costs should be added to the cost of the asset.

Depletion of Natural Resources

When a natural resource is used or consumed, it should be treated as an expense. The process of recording the expense is similar to the depreciation or amortization process but is usually referred to as *depletion*. The amount of depletion expense recorded each period should reflect the portion of the natural resource that was used up during the current year.

Assume, for example, that Black Coal Company purchased a coal field on January 1, 1995, for $1 million. The company employed a team of engineering experts who estimated the total coal in the field to be 200,000 tons and determined that the field's residual value after removal of the coal would be zero. Black Coal should calculate the depletion per ton as follows:

$$\text{Depletion per Ton} = (\text{Acquisition Cost} - \text{Residual Value})/$$
$$\text{Total Number of Tons in Asset's Life}$$
$$(\$1,000,000 - 0)/200,000 \text{ tons}$$
$$= \$5 \text{ per ton}$$

Depletion expense for each year should be calculated as

$$\text{Depletion Expense} = \text{Depletion per Ton} \times \text{Tons Mined during Year}$$

Assume that Black Coal Company mined 10,000 tons of coal during 1995. The depletion expense for 1995 for Black Coal is

$$\$5 \times 10,000 \text{ tons} = \$50,000$$

Black Coal should record the depletion as in the following journal entry:

```
1995
Dec. 31   Depletion Expense                        50,000
              Accumulated Depletion—Coal Field            50,000
          To record depletion for 1995.
```

Assets	=	**Liabilities**	+	**Owners' Equity**
−50,000				−50,000

Rather than using an accumulated depletion account, some companies may credit the asset account directly.

There is an interesting parallel between depletion of natural resources and depreciation of plant and equipment. That is, depletion is very similar to depreciating an asset using the units-of-production method. Both require an estimate of the useful life of the asset in terms of the total amount that can be produced (for units-of-production method) or consumed (for depletion) over the asset's life.

Natural resources may be important assets for some companies. For example, Exhibit 8-2 highlights the asset portion of the 1992 balance sheet and the accompanying footnote of Georgia-Pacific Corporation. Georgia-Pacific had timber and

---

EXHIBIT 8-2 Georgia-Pacific Corporation and Subsidiaries 1992 Assets Section and Natural Resources Footnote

GEORGIA-PACIFIC CORPORATION AND SUBSIDIARIES BALANCE SHEETS

(MILLIONS, EXCEPT SHARES AND PER SHARE AMOUNTS)	DECEMBER 31 1992	DECEMBER 31 1991
Timber and timberlands, net	1,402	1,377
Property, plant and equipment, net	5,831	5,567
Goodwill	1,891	1,949
Other assets	159	167

> **Timber and Timberlands** The Corporation depletes its investment in timber based on the total fiber that will be available during the estimated growth cycle. Timber carrying costs are expensed as incurred.

timberlands, net of depletion, of $1,402 million as of December 31, 1992. The footnote indicates that the company records depletion based on the total fiber available during the estimated growth cycle of the timber.

Operating Assets: Intangible Assets

Intangible assets are long-term assets with no physical properties. Because one cannot see or touch most intangible assets, it is easy to overlook their importance. Intangibles are recorded as assets, however, because they provide future economic benefits to the company. In fact, an intangible asset may be the most important asset a company owns or controls. For example, a pharmaceutical company may own some property, plant, and equipment, but its most important asset may be its patent for a particular drug or process. Likewise, the company that publishes this textbook may consider the copyrights to textbooks to be among its most important revenue-producing assets.

Patents, copyrights, brand names, intellectual property—all of these intangibles produce future economic benefit to the organization. The hard part for the investment community is trying to put a value on such intangibles, but they should not rely solely on balance sheet amounts; once again, balance sheets reflect the cost, not the value.

Balance Sheet Presentation

LO 9

Understand the balance sheet presentation of intangible assets.

Intangible assets are long-term assets and should be shown separately from property, plant, and equipment. Some companies develop a separate category, Intangible Assets, for the various types of intangibles. For example, Exhibit 8-3 presents the asset section and the accompanying footnote of the 1992 balance sheet of Quaker Oats Company. Quaker presents only one line for intangible assets, but the footnote indicates that intangibles consist primarily of goodwill (see below), which is amortized on a straight-line basis. The presentation of intangible assets varies widely, however.

Exhibit 8-4 presents the asset section and the accompanying footnote of the 1992 balance sheet of Alberto-Culver Company. Alberto-Culver presents the intangible assets of goodwill and trade names immediately after the property, plant, and equipment category. Both accounts are presented net of the accumulated amortization. The footnote indicates that amortization was computed on the straight-line basis. Exhibit 8-5 contains a list of the most common intangible assets.

■ ACCOUNTING FOR YOUR DECISIONS   **You Are the Stockbroker**

Your colleagues at the investment house where you work insist that the intangible assets on the Quaker Oats and Alberto-Culver balance sheets are worthless and should be removed before any analysis can be completed on the two companies. Would you agree or disagree with their position?

The nature of most intangible assets is fairly evident, but two of them are not so easily understood. **Organization costs** represent the costs incurred at the time a new corporation is formed. These costs include legal fees, registration fees, and other costs involved in starting the company. These costs are not treated as an expense when incurred because the benefit of incorporating occurs over a long time period.

EXHIBIT 8-3   The Quaker Oats Company and Subsidiaries 1992 Assets Section and Intangibles Footnote

THE QUAKER OATS COMPANY AND SUBSIDIARIES CONSOLIDATED BALANCE SHEET

ASSETS JUNE 30	1992
Current assets:	
Cash and cash equivalents	$ 95.2
Trade accounts receivable—net of allowances	575.3
Inventories:	
Finished goods	302.8
Grain and raw materials	93.7
Packaging materials and supplies	38.8
Total inventories	435.3
Other current assets	150.4
Net current assets of discontinued operations	—
Total current assets	1,256.2
Other receivables and investments	83.0
Property, plant and equipment	2,066.1
Less accumulated depreciation	792.8
Properties—Net	1,273.3
Intangible assets, net of amortization	427.4
Net non-current assets of discontinued operations	—
Total assets	**$3,039.9**

> **Intangibles** Intangible assets consist principally of excess purchase price over net tangible assets of businesses acquired (goodwill). Goodwill is amortized on a straight-line basis over periods not exceeding 40 years. Accumulated goodwill amortization as of June 30, 1992, 1991 and 1990 was $103.2 million, $86.5 million and $71.2 million, respectively.

Instead, the costs are treated as an asset, Organization Costs, and amortized over a future time period.

Goodwill represents the amount of the purchase price paid in excess of the market value of the individual net assets when a business is purchased. (See Chapter 13 for more details.) Goodwill is recorded only when a business is purchased. It is not recorded when a company engages in other activities that do not involve the purchase of another business entity. For example, customer loyalty or a good management team may represent "goodwill" but neither meets the accountants' criteria to be recorded as an asset on a firm's financial statements.

Some investors believe that goodwill is not an asset and eliminate it when analyzing a company. According to their view, goodwill is nothing more than a bad business decision to pay an excessive amount over the fair market value of assets. These investors simply reduce the amount shown on the balance sheet by the amount of

EXHIBIT 8-4   Alberto-Culver Company and Subsidiaries 1992 Assets Section and Intangibles Footnote

ALBERTO-CULVER COMPANY AND SUBSIDIARIES
CONSOLIDATED BALANCE SHEETS

(DOLLARS IN THOUSANDS, EXCEPT SHARE DATA)	SEPTEMBER 30	
ASSETS	1992	1991
Current assets:		
Cash and cash equivalents	$ 75,758	80,103
Short-term investments	4,400	4,492
Receivables, less allowance for doubtful accounts (1992-$4,839; 1991-$4,105)	127,767	127,073
Inventories:		
Raw materials	28,758	29,212
Work-in-process	4,703	4,523
Finished goods	164,543	151,512
Total inventories	198,004	185,247
Prepaid expenses	6,420	7,026
Total current assets	412,349	403,941
Property, plant and equipment		
Land	5,997	5,191
Buildings	70,599	63,234
Machinery and equipment	134,776	120,807
Total property, plant and equipment	211,372	189,232
Accumulated depreciation	89,669	74,322
Property, plant and equipment, net	121,703	114,910
Goodwill, net	44,472	27,803
Trade names, net and other intangible assets, net	15,611	17,412
Other assets	16,265	10,347
	$610,400	574,413

> **Goodwill and Trade Names** The cost of goodwill and trade names is amortized on a straight-line basis over periods ranging from ten to forty years.

goodwill, deducting it from total assets and reducing stockholders' equity by the same amount. That is similar to the accounting for goodwill that occurs in many foreign countries. International accounting standards allow firms *either* to present goodwill separately as an asset or to deduct it from stockholders' equity at the time of purchase. The result is that the presentation of goodwill on the financial statements of non–U.S. companies can look much different from that for U.S. companies.

EXHIBIT 8-5   Most Common Intangible Assets

INTANGIBLE ASSET	DESCRIPTION
Patent	Right to use, manufacture, or sell a product; granted by the U.S. Patent Office. Patents have a legal life of 17 years.
Copyright	Right to reproduce or sell a published work. Copyrights are granted for 50 years plus the life of the creator.
Trademark	A symbol or name that allows a product or service to be identified. Provides legal protection for 20 years plus an indefinite number of renewal periods.
Organization costs	Costs incurred at the time a new corporation is created. Costs include legal and registration fees.
Goodwill	The excess of the purchase price to acquire a business over the value of the individual net assets acquired.

Acquisition Cost of Intangible Assets

As was the case with property, plant, and equipment, the acquisition cost of an intangible asset includes all of the costs to acquire the asset and prepare it for its intended use. This should include all necessary costs such as legal costs incurred at the time of acquisition. Acquisition cost also should include costs after acquisition that are necessary to the existence of the asset. For example, if a firm must pay legal fees to protect a patent from infringement, the costs should be considered part of the acquisition cost and should be included in the patent account.

You should also be aware of one item that is similar to intangible assets but is *not* on the balance sheet. **Research and development costs** are expenditures incurred in the discovery of new knowledge and the translation of research into a design or plan for a new product or service or in a significant improvement to an existing product or service. Firms that engage in research and development do so because they believe such activities provide future benefit to the company. In fact, many firms have become leaders in an industry by engaging in research and development and the discovery of new products or technology. It is often very difficult, however, to identify the amount of future benefits of research and development and to associate those benefits with specific time periods. Because of the difficulty in predicting future benefits, the FASB has ruled that firms are not allowed to treat research and development costs as an asset; all such expenditures must be treated as expenses in the period incurred. Many firms, especially high technology ones, argue that this accounting rule results in seriously understated balance sheets. In their view, an important "asset" is not portrayed on their balance sheet. They also argue that they are at a competitive disadvantage when compared to foreign companies that are allowed to treat at least a portion of research and development as an asset. Users of financial statements somehow need to be aware of those "hidden assets" when analyzing the balance sheets of companies that must expense research and development costs.

It is important to distinguish between patent costs and research and development costs. Patent costs include legal and filing fees necessary to acquire a patent. Such costs are capitalized as an intangible asset, Patent. However, the Patent account should not include the costs of research and development of a new product. Those costs are not capitalized but are treated as an expense, Research and Development.

LO   **10**

Describe the proper amortization of intangible assets.

Amortization of Intangibles

Intangibles should be reported on the balance sheet at acquisition cost less accumulated amortization. *Amortization* is very similar to depreciation of property, plant, and equipment. Amortization involves allocating the acquisition cost of the intangible asset to the period benefited by the use of the asset; the period may not exceed 40 years. In most cases, companies use the straight-line method of amortization. You may see instances of an accelerated form of amortization, however, if the decline in usefulness of the intangible asset does not occur evenly over time.

Assume that KJ Company developed a patent for a new product on January 1, 1995. The costs involved with patent approval were $10,000, and the company wishes to record amortization on the straight-line basis over a five-year life with no residual value. The accounting entry to record the amortization for 1995 is as follows:

1995		
Dec. 31	Patent Amortization Expense	2,000	
	Accumulated Amortization—Patent		2,000
	To record amortization of patent for one year.		

Assets	=	Liabilities	+	Owners' Equity
−2,000				−2,000

Rather than use an accumulated amortization account, some companies credit the intangible asset account directly. In that case, the preceding transaction is recorded as follows:

1995		
Dec. 31	Patent Amortization Expense	2,000	
	Patent		2,000
	To record amortization of patent for one year.		

Assets	=	Liabilities	+	Owners' Equity
−2,000				−2,000

No matter which of the two preceding entries is used, the asset should be reported on the balance sheet at acquisition cost ($10,000) less accumulated amortization ($2,000), or $8,000, as of December 31, 1995.

Some question exists about the time period over which to amortize intangible assets. The general guideline is that an intangible should be amortized *over its legal life or useful life, whichever is shorter.* For example, a patent has a legal life of 17 years, but many are not useful that long because new products and technology may surpass them. The patent should be amortized over the number of years in which the firm receives benefits, which is a period shorter than its legal life.

Certain intangibles have no legal life and their useful life is very difficult to determine. Goodwill is the primary example. Some accountants argue that goodwill has an unlimited life and should not be amortized. Others argue that the benefits of goodwill are too difficult to determine and this intangible asset should be written off as an expense in its entirety in the year of acquisition. The current accounting guideline takes a compromise approach. Goodwill must be amortized over a time period that cannot exceed 40 years. Thus, goodwill must be amortized in a manner similar to the amortization of other intangible assets over its estimated useful life. But if it is not possible to determine the useful life, the maximum amortization period is 40 years.

Finally, it is important to monitor the usefulness of intangible assets as time passes. An intangible asset that will not produce future benefit should be written off as an expense. Assume in the KJ example that KJ learns on January 1, 1996, when accumulated amortization is $2,000 (or the book value of the patent is $8,000), that a competing company has developed a new product that renders KJ's patent worthless. KJ should record an entry to write off the asset as follows:

1996			
Jan. 1	Loss on Patent	8,000	
	Accumulated Amortization—Patent	2,000	
	Patent		10,000
	To record the write-off of patent.		

Assets	=	Liabilities	+	Owners' Equity
+2,000				−8,000
−10,000				

This entry is consistent with the treatment of all assets. Assets existing on the balance sheet date represent future benefits or revenue. If an item does not have future usefulness, it must be removed from the balance sheet and treated as a loss or expense.

Analyzing Long-Term Assets for Average Life and Asset Turnover

Because long-term assets constitute the major productive assets of most companies, it is important to analyze the age and composition of these assets. This can be accomplished fairly easily for those companies that use the straight-line method of depreciation. A rough measure of the *average life* of the assets can be calculated as follows:

Average Life = Property, Plant, and Equipment/Depreciation Expense

The *average age* of the assets can be calculated as

Average Age = Accumulated Depreciation/Depreciation Expense.

For example, a reference earlier in this chapter (see page 424) indicated that at the end of 1992, Ben & Jerry's had property, plant, and equipment of $39,312,513 and accumulated depreciation of $12,575,088. A careful reading of the annual report also indicates depreciation expense of $3,455,720 for 1992. Therefore, the average life of Ben & Jerry's assets is calculated as follows:

Average Life = Property, Plant, and Equipment/Depreciation Expense
Average Life = $39,312,513/$3,455,720
            = 11.4 Years

This is a rough estimate because it assumes that the company has purchased assets fairly evenly over time. Because it is an average, it indicates that some assets have a life longer than 11.4 years and others shorter lives.

The average age of Ben & Jerry's assets is calculated as follows:

Average Age = Accumulated Depreciation/Depreciation Expense
Average Age = $12,575,088/$3,455,720
            = 3.6 Years

This indicates that Ben & Jerry's assets are, on average, fairly new and should be productive for several more years.

The asset category of the balance sheet is also important in analyzing the company's *profitability*. The asset turnover ratio is a measure of the productivity of the assets and is measured as

APPRAISING REAL ESTATE

Name: Ed Miesen
Occupation: Real estate appraiser
Major: Urban planning

Accountants value real estate conservatively. If it goes down in value, they mark it down. If it goes up in value, they ignore the good fortune. So if the accounting profession won't put a value on appreciated real estate, then who does?

That's where Ed Miesen, Seattle real estate appraiser, comes in. Miesen has seen his share of appreciated real estate—both residential and commercial—in his booming city. Often, banks hire him to make sure that their loan has sufficient collateral. "The appraiser's job is to estimate the value of the property so that the bank knows that if they have to foreclose, they'll have something to take back that's of value," he says.

Appraisers are also hired by investors or sellers to get an independent opinion of the value of a piece of property. Nobody wants to pay too much or sell for too little. Attorneys might hire them when there is a partnership dispute or a divorce to make sure each party is getting an equal distribution.

Miesen uses three different valuation approaches: (1) the cost, (2) the income and (3) the sales comparison methods. The cost approach looks at the land value and adds the cost of the building plus improvements less depreciation. The income approach tries to project the cash flows from the build-ing's tenants over the next several years. The sales comparison approach focuses on sales of similar property. Does Miesen take an average of the three? "No," says Miesen, "we look at where our best data is coming from and use that method."

The building's financial statements are most relevant to the income approach. "We would ask for three years' income and expense data," he says. Among the important expense categories are property taxes, insurance, maintenance, utilities, and management fees. "Sometimes the owners put expenses in that appraisers don't include in their analysis. If the owner pays himself a big salary, then we wouldn't include that because it's not typical of the operation of the building."

Does depreciation count? "Depreciation is, in theory, an expense that occurs as the building needs to be replaced. But in actuality, buildings are still standing that have been fully depreciated," says Miesen. "With repairs, they can stand for 100 years."

$$\text{Asset Turnover} = \text{Net Sales/Average Total Assets}$$

This ratio is a measure of how many dollars of asset are necessary for every dollar of sales. If a company is using its assets efficiently, each dollar of asset will create a high amount of sales. Technically, the ratio is based on average *total assets,* but long-term assets often constitute the largest portion of a company's total assets. For more discussion of ratio analysis, see Chapter 15.

How Long-Term Assets Affect the Statement of Cash Flows

Determining the impact that acquisition, depreciation, and sale of long-term assets have on the statement of cash flows is important. Each of these business activities has an impact on the statement of cash flows.

The acquisition of a long-term asset is an investing activity and should be reflected in the Investing Activities category of the statement of cash flows. The acquisition should appear as a deduction or negative item in that section because it requires the use of cash to purchase the asset. This applies whether the long-term asset is property, plant, and equipment or an intangible asset; the acquisition of the asset should appear in the Investing Activities category of the statement of cash flows.

The depreciation or amortization of a long-term asset is *not* a cash item. It was referred to earlier as a noncash charge to earnings. Nevertheless, it must be presented on the statement of cash flows (if the indirect method is used for the statement). The reason is that it was deducted from earnings in calculating the net income figure. Therefore, it must be eliminated or "added back" if the net income amount is used to indicate the amount of cash generated from operations. Thus, depreciation and amortization should be presented in the Operating Activities category of the statement of cash flows as an addition to net income. For example, the first few lines of the 1992 statement of cash flows for Ben & Jerry's indicate the following:

Cash flows from operating activities:	
Net income	$6,675,340
Adjustments to reconcile net income to net cash	
provided by operating activities:	
Depreciation and amortization	3,455,720

The sale or disposition of long-term assets is an investing activity. When an asset is sold, the amount of cash received should be reflected as an addition or plus amount in the Investing Activities category of the statement of cash flows. If the asset was sold at a gain or loss, however, one additional aspect should be reflected. Because the gain or loss was reflected on the income statement, it should be eliminated from the net income amount presented in the Operating Activities category (if the indirect method is used). A sale of an asset is not an activity related to normal, ongoing operations, and all amounts involved with the sale should be removed from the Operating Activities category. For more detail on this issue, see Chapter 14.

LO [11]

Explain the impact of long-term assets on the statement of cash flows.

FROM CONCEPT TO PRACTICE

READING BEN & JERRY'S STATEMENT OF CASH FLOWS
Refer to Ben & Jerry's 1992 annual report. What amount of assets was bought and sold during the year? Was there a gain or loss? Where is it presented?

REVIEW PROBLEM

The accountant for Beavis Company wishes to develop a balance sheet as of December 31, 1995. A review of the asset records has revealed the following information.

a. Asset A was purchased on July 1, 1993, for $40,000 and has been depreciated on the straight-line basis using an estimated life of six years and a residual value of $4,000.

b. Asset B was purchased on January 1, 1994, for $66,000. The straight-line method has been used for depreciation purposes. Originally, the estimated life of the asset was projected to be six years with a residual value of $6,000; however, at the beginning of 1995, the accountant learned that the remaining life of the asset was only three years with a residual value of $2,000.

c. Asset C was purchased on January 1, 1994, for $50,000. The sum-of-the-years'-digits basis has been used for depreciation purposes with an estimated five-year life and a residual value estimate of $5,000.

d. Asset D was purchased on January 1, 1994, for $50,000. The double declining-balance method has been used for depreciation purposes with a four-year life and a residual value estimate of $5,000.

■ REQUIRED

1. Assume that the assets above represent pieces of equipment. Calculate the acquisition cost, accumulated depreciation, and book value of each asset as of December 31, 1995.

2. How would the assets appear on the balance sheet on December 31, 1995?

3. Assume that Beavis Company sold Asset B on January 2, 1996, for $25,000. Calculate the amount of the resulting gain or loss and prepare the proper journal entry to record the sale. Where would the gain or loss appear on the income statement?

■ SOLUTION TO REVIEW PROBLEM

I.

ASSET A

1993	Depreciation	($40,000 − $4,000)/6 × 1/2 Year	=	$ 3,000
1994		($40,000 − $4,000)/6	=	6,000
1995		($40,000 − $4,000)/6	=	6,000
	Accumulated Depreciation			$15,000

ASSET B

1994	Depreciation	($66,000 − $6,000)/6	=	$10,000
1995		($66,000 − $10,000 − $2,000)/3	=	18,000
	Accumulated Depreciation			$28,000

Note the impact of the change in estimate on 1995 depreciation.

ASSET C

1994	Depreciation	$50,000 − $5,000 = $45,000 × 5/15	=	$15,000
1995		$45,000 × 4/15	=	12,000
	Accumulated Depreciation			$27,000

ASSET D

1994	Depreciation	$50,000 × (25% × 2)	=	$25,000
1995		($50,000 − $25,000) × (25% × 2)	=	12,500
	Accumulated Depreciation			$37,500

BEAVIS COMPANY
SUMMARY OF ASSET COST AND ACCUMULATED DEPRECIATION
AS OF DECEMBER 31, 1995

ASSET	ACQUISITION COST	ACCUMULATED DEPRECIATION	BOOK VALUE
A	$ 40,000	$ 15,000	$25,000
B	66,000	28,000	38,000
C	50,000	27,000	23,000
D	50,000	37,500	12,500
Totals	$206,000	$107,500	$98,500

2. The assets would appear in the long-term asset category of the balance sheet as follows:

Assets	$206,000	
Less: Accumulated Depreciation	107,500	
Assets (net)		$98,500

3.

Asset B Book Value	$38,000
Selling Price	25,000
Loss on Sale of Asset	$13,000

The journal entry to record the sale is as follows:

1996			
Jan. 2	Cash	25,000	
	Accumulated Depreciation	28,000	
	Loss on Sale of Asset	13,000	
	Asset B		66,000
	To record the sale of asset B.		

Assets	=	Liabilities	+	Owners' Equity
+25,000				−13,000
+28,000				
−66,000				

The Loss on Sale of Asset account should appear in the Other Income/Other Expense Category of the income statement. It is similar to an expense but is not the company's major activity.

GUIDANCE ANSWERS TO ACCOUNTING FOR YOUR DECISIONS

YOU ARE THE APPRAISER

It is very possible that making these land improvements would increase the assessed market value of the property by $100,000 or even more. In some states, property taxes are very high in relation to the assessed value—as much as 3%. Therefore, the dentist may achieve a $10,000 tax deduction for the new depreciation, which could be worth $3,100 if he is in the 31% federal tax bracket. On the other hand, the additional $100,000 in land improvements may cost an additional $3,000 in property taxes. Therefore, the dentist should make the improvements if he thinks it is going to benefit his business—not solely because there might be tax savings.

YOU ARE THE STOCKBROKER

An asset can be "intangible" and still be valuable. If the intangible asset is goodwill, then the question to ask is whether the business that was acquired is creating profits in excess of that obtained by Quaker or Alberto-Culver. If the answer is yes, then the goodwill has a future economic benefit and should be counted as an asset in an investment analysis. If the intangible asset is a trademark, then the question to ask is whether the product has a uniqueness in the marketplace that could not have emerged without the trademark—thus conferring a future economic benefit on Alberto-Culver. The problem is that the answers to these questions are not necessarily presented in the financial statements—and the reader is relying on the auditor's judgment that these assets are real. Moreover, the auditor is making a judgment from an accounting viewpoint and not an investment viewpoint. This is a tough issue to resolve, but it is important because intangible assets often comprise a large proportion of shareholders' equity.

CHAPTER HIGHLIGHTS

1. **(LO 1)** Operating assets are normally presented on the balance sheet in one category for property, plant, and equipment and a second category for intangibles.

2. **(LO 1)** Operating assets should be presented at original acquisition cost less accumulated depreciation or amortization.

3. **(LO 2)** Acquisition cost should include all costs necessary to acquire the asset and prepare it for its intended use.

4. **(LO 3)** When assets are purchased for a lump sum, acquisition cost should be determined as the proportion of the market values of the assets purchased.

5. **(LO 4)** Interest on assets constructed over time should be capitalized. The amount of interest capitalized should be the average accumulated expenditures times an interest rate but cannot be more than the amount of actual interest incurred.

6. **(LO 5)** Several alternative depreciation methods are available to describe the decline in usefulness of operating assets. The straight-line method is the most commonly used and assigns the same amount of depreciation to each time period over the asset life.

7. **(LO 5)** Accelerated depreciation allocates a greater expense to the earlier years of an asset's life and less to later years. Two methods of accelerated depreciation are the sum-of-the-years'-digits method and the double declining-balance method.

8. **(LO 6)** Depreciation is based on an estimate of the life of the asset and the residual value. When it is necessary to change the estimate, the amount of depreciation expense is adjusted for the current year and future years. Past depreciation amounts are not restated.

9. **(LO 7)** Capital expenditures are costs that increase an asset's life or its productivity. Capital expenditures should be added to the cost of the asset. Revenue expenditures should be treated as an expense in the period incurred because they benefit only the current period.

10. **(LO 8)** The gain or loss on disposal of an asset is the difference between the asset's book value and its selling price.

11. **(LO 9)** Intangible assets should be presented on the balance sheet at acquisition cost less accumulated amortization. Acquisition cost should include all costs necessary to acquire the asset.

12. **(LO 9)** Research and development costs are not treated as an intangible asset. Instead, they are treated as an expense in the year incurred.

13. **(LO 10)** Intangibles should be amortized over the shorter of their legal or useful life. All intangibles, including goodwill, should be amortized over a period that cannot exceed 40 years.

14. **(LO 11)** Acquisition of long-term assets should be reflected in the investing activities category of the statement of cash flows.

KEY TERMS QUIZ

Select from the following list of key terms used in the chapter and fill in the appropriate blank to the left of each description. The solution appears at the end of the chapter.

Acquisition cost
Capitalization of interest
Land improvements
Depreciation
Straight-line depreciation
Book value
Units-of-production method
Accelerated depreciation
Sum-of-the-years'-digits method
Double declining-balance method

Change in estimate
Capital expenditure
Revenue expenditure
Gain on Sale of Asset
Loss on Sale of Asset
Intangible assets
Organization costs
Goodwill
Research and development costs

_____ **1.** This amount includes all of the costs normally necessary to acquire an asset and prepare it for its intended use.

_____ **2.** Additions made to a piece of property such as paving or landscaping a parking lot. The costs are treated separately from land for purposes of recording depreciation.

_____ **3.** A method by which the same dollar amount of depreciation is recorded in each year of asset use.

_____ **4.** A method by which depreciation is determined as a function of the number of units the asset produces.

_____ **5.** A method by which depreciation is recorded as a function of the total of the digits of the asset's life.

_____ **6.** The process of treating the cost of interest on constructed assets as a part of the asset cost rather than as an expense.

_____ **7.** A change in the life of an asset or in its expected residual value.

_____ **8.** The allocation of the original acquisition cost of an asset to the periods benefited by its use.

_____ **9.** A cost that improves an operating asset and is added to the asset account.

_____ **10.** The original acquisition cost of an asset minus the amount of accumulated depreciation.

_____ **11.** A cost that keeps an operating asset in its normal operating condition and is treated as an expense of the period.

_____ **12.** An account whose amount indicates that the selling price received on an asset's disposal exceeds its book value.

_____ **13.** An account whose amount indicates that the book value of an asset exceeds the selling price received on its disposal.

_____ **14.** A term that refers to several methods by which a higher amount of depreciation is recorded in the early years of an asset's life and a lower amount is recorded in the later years.

_____ **15.** A long-term asset that has no physical properties, for example patents, copyrights, and goodwill.

16. Costs that are incurred at the initial formation of a corporation and are treated as an intangible asset.

17. A method by which depreciation is recorded at twice the straight-line rate but the depreciable balance is reduced in each period.

18. The amount indicating that the purchase price of a business exceeded the total fair market values of the identifiable net assets at the time the business was acquired.

19. Expenditures incurred in the discovery of new knowledge and the translation of research into a design or plan for a new product.

ALTERNATE TERMS

ACCUMULATED DEPRECIATION Allowance for depreciation.

ACQUISITION COST Historical cost.

CAPITALIZE Treat as asset.

CONSTRUCTION IN PROGRESS Construction in process.

GOODWILL Purchase price in excess of the market value of assets.

HIDDEN ASSETS Unrecorded or off-balance sheet assets.

PROPERTY, PLANT, AND EQUIPMENT Fixed assets.

PROSPECTIVE Current and future years.

RESIDUAL VALUE Salvage value.

REVENUE EXPENDITURE An expense of the period.

QUESTIONS

1. What are several examples of operating assets? Why are operating assets essential to a company's long-term future?

2. What is the meaning of the term *acquisition cost* of operating assets? Give some examples of costs that should be included in the acquisition cost.

3. When assets are purchased as a group, how should the acquisition cost of the individual assets be determined?

4. Why is it important to account separately for the cost of land and building, even when the two assets are purchased together?

5. Under what circumstances should interest be capitalized as part of the cost of an asset? How much interest should be capitalized?

6. What factors may contribute to the decline in usefulness of operating assets? Should the choice of depreciation method be related to these factors?

7. Why do you think that most companies use the straight-line method of depreciation?

8. How should the residual value of an operating asset be treated when using the straight-line method? How should it be treated when using the double declining-balance method?

9. Why do many companies use one method to calculate depreciation for the financial statement developed for stockholders and another method for income tax purposes?

10. What should a company do if it finds that the original estimate of the life of the asset or the residual value of the asset must be changed?

11. What are the meanings of the terms *capital expenditures* and *revenue expenditures?* What determines whether an item is a capital or revenue expenditure?

12. How is the gain or loss on the sale of an operating asset calculated? Where would the Gain on Sale of Asset account appear on the financial statements?

13. What are several examples of items that constitute intangible assets? In what category of the balance sheet should intangible assets appear?

14. What is the meaning of the term *goodwill?* Give an example of a transaction that would result in goodwill being recorded on the balance sheet.

15. Do you agree with the FASB's ruling that all research and development costs should be treated as an expense on the income statement? Why or why not?

16. Do you agree with some accountants who argue that intangible assets have an unlimited life and should therefore not be subject to amortization?

17. When an intangible asset is amortized, should the asset's amortization occur over its legal life or over its useful life? Give an example where the legal life exceeds the useful life.

18. Suppose that an intangible asset is being amortized over a 10-year time period, but a competitor has just introduced a new product that will have a serious negative impact on the asset's value. Should the company continue to amortize the intangible asset over the 10-year life?

EXERCISES

(LO 2) EXERCISE 8-1 ACQUISITION COST

Allen Company purchased a piece of equipment with a list price of $40,000 on January 1, 1995. The following amounts were related to the equipment purchase:

Terms of the purchase were 2/10, net 30. Allen paid for the purchase on January 8.

Freight costs of $1,000 were incurred.

A state agency required that a pollution control device be installed on the equipment at a cost of $2,500.

During installation, the equipment was damaged and repair costs of $4,000 were incurred.

Architect's fees of $6,000 were paid to redesign the work space to accommodate the new equipment.

Allen purchased liability insurance to cover possible damage to the asset. The three-year policy cost $8,000.

Allen financed the purchase with a bank loan. Interest of $3,000 was paid on the loan during 1995.

Determine the amount that should be considered in the acquisition cost of the equipment.   ■ REQUIRED

(LO 3) EXERCISE 8-2 LUMP-SUM PURCHASE

Davison Company purchased several assets on January 1, 1995, for $30,000 cash and a note payable to the seller for $90,000. An appraiser was hired to assess the value of the assets and determined that the market value of the items was land, $40,000, land improvements, $50,000, and building, $70,000.

■ REQUIRED

1. Determine the acquisition cost of the assets and record the journal entry for January 1, 1995.

2. Assume that Davison wishes to record depreciation on the straight-line basis using a life of 20 years for operating assets. Determine the amount of depreciation expense for 1995 on the acquired assets.

3. How would the assets appear on the balance sheet of December 31, 1995?

(LO 5) EXERCISE 8-3 STRAIGHT-LINE AND UNITS-OF-PRODUCTION METHODS

Assume that Schumer Company purchased factory equipment on January 1, 1995, for $50,000. The asset has an estimated life of five years and an estimated residual value of $5,000. Schumer's accountant is considering whether to use the straight-line or the units-of-production method to depreciate the asset. Because the company is beginning a new production process, the equipment will be used to produce 10,000 units in 1995, but production subsequent to 1995 will increase by 10,000 units each year.

■ REQUIRED

Calculate the depreciation expense, accumulated depreciation, and the book value of the asset under both methods for each of the five years of asset life. Do you think that the units-of-production method yields reasonable results in this situation?

(LO 5) EXERCISE 8-4 ACCELERATED DEPRECIATION METHODS

Assume the same facts as in Exercise 8-3. Compare the depreciation expense, accumulated depreciation, and book value of the asset using the sum-of-the-years'-digits method and the double declining-balance method for each of the five years of asset life.

(LO 6) EXERCISE 8-5 CHANGE IN ESTIMATE

Assume that Bloomer Company purchased an asset on January 1, 1995, for $80,000. The asset was estimated to have a useful life of nine years and a residual value of $8,000. Bloomer has chosen to use the straight-line method of depreciation. On January 1, 1997, Bloomer discovered that the asset would not be useful beyond December 31, 2000, and estimated its value at that time to be $2,000.

■ REQUIRED

1. Calculate the depreciation expense, accumulated depreciation, and book value of the asset for each year 1995 to 2000.

2. Was the depreciation recorded in 1995 and 1996 wrong? If so, why was it not corrected?

(LO 8) EXERCISE 8-6 ASSET DISPOSAL

Assume that Wendell Company purchased an asset on January 1, 1993, for $60,000. The asset had an estimated life of six years and an estimated residual value of $6,000. The company used the straight-line method to depreciate the asset. On July 1, 1995, the asset was sold for $40,000 cash.

■ REQUIRED

1. Make the journal entry to record depreciation for 1995. Also record all transactions necessary for the sale of the asset.

2. How should the gain or loss on the sale of the asset be presented on the income statement?

(LO 8) EXERCISE 8-7 ASSET DISPOSAL

Refer to Exercise 8-6. Assume that Wendell Company sold the asset on July 1, 1995, and received $15,000 cash and a note signed by the seller for an additional $15,000.

1. Make the journal entry to record depreciation for 1995. Also record all transactions ■ REQUIRED necessary for the sale of the asset.

2. How should the gain or loss on the sale of the asset be presented on the income statement?

(LO 10) EXERCISE 8-8 AMORTIZATION OF INTANGIBLES

For each of the following intangible assets, indicate the amount of amortization expense that should be recorded for the year 1995 and the amount of accumulated amortization as of December 31, 1995.

	GOODWILL	PATENT	ORGANIZATION COSTS	TRADEMARK
Cost	$40,000	$50,000	$60,000	$80,000
Date of purchase	1/1/88	1/1/90	1/1/92	1/1/93
Useful life	50 yrs.	10 yrs.	10 yrs.	20 yrs.
Legal life	undefined	17 yrs.	undefined	20 yrs.
Method	SL*	SL	SL	SL

*Represents the straight-line method.

MULTI-CONCEPT EXERCISES

(LO 1, 7) EXERCISE 8-9 CAPITAL VERSUS REVENUE EXPENDITURES

On January 1, 1993, Jose Company purchased a building for $100,000 and a delivery truck for $20,000. The following expenditures have been incurred during 1995 related to the building and the truck:

The building was painted at a cost of $5,000.

To prevent leaking, new windows were installed at a cost of $10,000.

To allow an improved flow of production, a new conveyor system was installed at a cost of $40,000.

The delivery truck was repainted with a new company logo at a cost of $1,000.

To allow better handling of large loads, a hydraulic lift system was installed on the truck at a cost of $5,000.

The truck's engine was overhauled at a cost of $4,000.

1. Determine which of these costs should be capitalized and then make the appro- ■ REQUIRED priate journal entry for them. Assume that all costs were incurred on January 1, 1995.

2. Record depreciation for the year 1995. The company uses the straight-line method and depreciates the building over 25 years and the truck over 6 years. Assume zero residual value for all assets.

3. How would the assets appear on the balance sheet of December 31, 1995?

(LO 9, 10) EXERCISE 8-10 RESEARCH AND DEVELOPMENT AND PATENTS

Butch Company incurred the following costs during 1995.

a. Research and development costs of $20,000 were incurred. The research was conducted to discover a new product to sell to customers in future years. A product was successfully developed and a patent for the new product was granted during 1995. Butch is unsure of the period benefited by the research but believes the product will result in increased sales over the next five years.

b. Legal costs and application fees of $10,000 for the patent were incurred on January 1, 1995. The patent was granted for a life of 17 years.

c. A patent infringement suit was successfully defended at a cost of $8,000. Assume that all costs were incurred on January 1, 1996.

■ REQUIRED Determine how the costs in **a** and **b** above should be presented on Butch's financial statements as of December 31, 1995. Also determine the amount of amortization of intangible assets that Butch should record in 1995 and 1996.

PROBLEMS

(LO 4) PROBLEM 8-1 CAPITALIZATION OF INTEREST

In 1995 McHale Company constructed a building to use as a warehouse. The company began construction on January 1, 1995, and completed the building on December 31 of the same year with average expenditures of $100,000. You may assume that construction occurred evenly throughout the year.

To finance the construction project, McHale borrowed $80,000 from a local bank and used $120,000 of cash that had been previously set aside for the project. The bank loan requires annual interest of 10% to be paid and recorded each December 31. McHale has no other loans outstanding.

■ REQUIRED
1. Determine the amount of interest cost incurred in 1995 and record a journal entry for the payment of interest and the capitalization of interest to the building account.

2. Assume that the company wishes to depreciate the building on a straight-line basis over 20 years with a $5,000 residual value. Determine the amount of depreciation expense for 1995 and 1996 and make a journal entry to record depreciation each year.

3. Assume that McHale Company had borrowed $200,000 from the bank to finance the construction project. How would the larger loan affect the capitalization of interest?

(LO 3) PROBLEM 8-2 LUMP-SUM PURCHASE OF ASSETS AND SUBSEQUENT EVENTS

Cameo Development Company purchased, for cash, a large tract of land that was immediately platted and deeded into smaller sections:

Section 1, retail development with highway frontage.

Section 2, multifamily apartment development.

Section 3, single-family homes in the largest section.

Based on recent sales of similar property, the fair market values of each of the three sections are

Section 1, $525,000.

Section 2, $315,000.

Section 3, $210,000.

1. What value is assigned to each section of land if the tract was purchased for (a) $1,050,000, (b) $1,250,000, or (c) $500,000? ■ REQUIRED

2. How does the purchase of the tract affect the balance sheet?

3. Why would Cameo be concerned with the value assigned to each individual section? Would Cameo be more concerned with the values assigned if instead of purchasing three sections of land, it purchased land with buildings? Why or why not?

(LO 5) PROBLEM 8-3 DEPRECIATION AS A TAX SHIELD

The term *tax shield* refers to the amount of income tax saved by deducting depreciation for income tax purposes. Assume that Sorry Company is considering the purchase of an asset as of January 1, 1995. The cost of an asset with a five-year life and zero residual value is $100,000. The company will use the straight-line method of depreciation.

Sorry's income for tax purposes before recording depreciation on the asset will be $50,000 per year for the next five years. The corporation is currently in the 35% tax bracket.

Calculate the amount of income tax that Sorry must pay each year if the asset is not purchased. Calculate the amount of income tax that Sorry must pay each year if the asset is purchased. What is the amount of the depreciation tax shield? ■ REQUIRED

(LO 5) PROBLEM 8-4 BOOK VERSUS TAX DEPRECIATION

Jiffy Company purchased an asset on January 1, 1995, for $90,000. The asset has a five-year life and zero residual value. Assume that you have proposed to your boss that Jiffy use two methods of depreciation: the straight-line method for the annual report to be sent to stockholders and an accelerated method for income tax purposes. The accelerated method will result in $30,000 of depreciation in 1995 and will decline by $6,000 each year thereafter. You believe that the use of an accelerated depreciation method offers tax advantages. Your boss, however, disagrees with your suggestion. He points out that either method of depreciation will result in a total of $90,000 of depreciation over the five-year time frame.

Calculate depreciation expense for each year under the two methods of depreciation. Draft a memo to your boss to support your position in favor of accelerated depreciation for tax purposes. ■ REQUIRED

(LO 5) PROBLEM 8-5 DEPRECIATION AND CASH FLOW

Simplified Company's only asset as of January 1, 1995, was a limousine. During 1995 only three transactions occurred:

Provided services of $100,000 on account.

Collected all accounts receivable.

Depreciation on the limousine was $15,000.

1. Develop an income statement for Simplified for 1995. ■ REQUIRED

2. Determine the amount of the net cash inflow for Simplified for 1995.

3. Explain in one or more sentences why the amount of the net income on Simplified's income statement does not equal the amount of the net cash inflow.

4. If Simplified developed a cash flow statement for 1995 using the indirect method, what amount would appear in the category titled Cash Flow from Operating Activities?

MULTI-CONCEPT PROBLEMS

(LO 7, 10) PROBLEM 8-6 COST OF ASSETS AND SUBSEQUENT BOOK VALUE

The following events took place at Head, Inc., a small machine repair company:

a. On January 1, purchased a truck for $15,000, added a cab and tool chest at a cost of $3,200. The truck is expected to last five years and be sold for $200 at the end of that time. Head uses straight-line depreciation for its trucks.

b. On January 1, purchased for $2,250 several tools and equipment from a competitor who was retiring:

A saw, fair market value $1,400.

A router, fair market value $900.

Ladders, fair market value $1,200.

The saw and router are expected to last three years, but the ladders are expected to last only this year. The company uses the straight-line method to depreciate its tools and equipment.

c. On April 1, sold an old truck for $500. The truck was purchased exactly five years earlier for $10,000, had an expected salvage value of $1,000, and was depreciated over a 10-year life using the straight-line method.

d. On July 1, purchased a $12,000 patent for a unique process to produce a new good. The patent is valid for 15 more years; however, the company expects to produce and market the good for only four years. The patent's value at the end of the four years is undeterminable.

■ REQUIRED For each situation, explain the value assigned to the asset when it is purchased and the book value of each asset at the end of the year (or for part c., when sold). Be able to explain why the values are appropriate.

(LO 2, 5) PROBLEM 8-7 COST OF ASSETS AND THE EFFECT ON DEPRECIATION

Early in its first year of business, Cameo Company, a fitness and training center, purchased new workout equipment. The acquisition included the following costs:

Purchase Price	$150,000
Tax	15,000
Transportation	4,000
Setup*	25,000
Painting*	3,000

*The equipment was adjusted to Cameo's specific needs and painted to match the other equipment in the gym.

The bookkeeper recorded an asset, Equipment, $165,000 (purchase price and tax). The remaining costs were expensed for the year. Cameo used straight-line depreciation. The equipment was expected to last 10 years with zero salvage value.

■ REQUIRED

1. How much depreciation did Cameo report on its income statement related to this equipment in Year 1? What do you believe is the correct amount of depreciation to report in Year 1 related to this equipment?

2. Income is $100,000, before costs related to the equipment are reported. How much income will Cameo report in Year 1? What amount of income should it report? You may ignore income tax.

3. Using the equipment as an example, explain the difference between a cost and an expense.

(LO 7, 8) PROBLEM 8-8 CAPITAL EXPENDITURES, DEPRECIATION, AND DISPOSAL

Marley Company purchased a factory building at a cost of $260,000 on January 1, 1994. Marley estimated that the building's life would be 25 years and the residual value at the end of 25 years would be $10,000.

On January 1, 1995, the company made several expenditures related to the building. The entire building was painted and floors were refinished at a cost of $15,000. A federal agency required Marley to install additional pollution control devices in the building at a cost of $30,000. With the new devices, Marley believed it was possible to extend the life of the building by an additional six years.

In 1996 Marley altered its corporate strategy dramatically. The company sold the factory building on April 1, 1996, for $280,000 in cash and located all factory operations in another state.

■ REQUIRED

1. Determine the amount of depreciation that should be recorded for 1994 and 1995.

2. Explain why the cost of the pollution control equipment was not expensed in 1995. What conditions would have allowed Marley to expense the equipment? If Marley has a choice, would it prefer to expense or capitalize the equipment?

3. What amount of gain or loss did Marley record when it sold the building? What amount of gain or loss would have been reported if the pollution control equipment had been expensed in 1995?

(LO 6, 10) PROBLEM 8-9 AMORTIZATION OF INTANGIBLE, REVISION OF RATE

Harry Company purchased Wrong Company on January 1, 1995, for $600,000. To determine the value of the assets and liabilities purchased, Harry requested an appraisal of Wrong. The appraiser determined that the fair market values of the items purchased as of January 1, 1995, were as follows:

ASSETS	FAIR MARKET VALUE
Cash	$ 80,000
Receivables	200,000
Building	370,000
LIABILITIES	
Accounts Payable	$100,000

Harry Company decided to amortize any goodwill recorded in the transaction on a straight-line basis over the maximum possible time period.

On January 1, 1996, Harry Company's accountant met with a group of lenders who had serious doubts about the amortization period chosen for goodwill. Accordingly, Harry Company agreed to amortize all remaining goodwill for a period of 10 more years.

■ REQUIRED   **1.** Determine the amount of goodwill that should be recorded in the January 1, 1995, purchase of Wrong Company.

2. Determine the amount of goodwill that should be amortized in 1995 and make the appropriate journal entry.

3. Determine the amount of goodwill that should be amortized in 1996 and make the appropriate journal entry.

ALTERNATE PROBLEMS

(LO 4) PROBLEM 8-1A CAPITALIZATION OF INTEREST

In 1995 Shelbey Company constructed a building to use as an office. The company began construction on January 1, 1995, and it completed the building on December 31 of the same year with average expenditures of $75,000. You may assume that construction occurred evenly throughout the year.

To finance the construction project, Shelbey borrowed $100,000 from a local bank and issued $50,000 in stock. The company previously reported earnings per share equal to about 10% of the stock price. The bank loan carries an interest rate of 10% payable each December 31. Shelbey has no other loans outstanding.

■ REQUIRED   **1.** What amount of interest is the company required to capitalize?

2. Write a short memo to the president explaining the terms *capitalize* and *expense.* Then give at least one example of how the company will benefit from capitalizing the interest and one example of how the company will benefit from expensing it.

(LO 3) PROBLEM 8-2A LUMP-SUM PURCHASE OF ASSETS AND SUBSEQUENT EVENTS

Brown Manufacturing purchased, for cash, three large pieces of equipment. Based on recent sales of similar equipment, the fair market values of each of the three are as follows:

Piece 1 $125,000.

Piece 2 $125,000.

Piece 3 $275,000.

■ REQUIRED   **1.** What value is assigned to each piece of equipment if the equipment were purchased for (a) $600,000, (b) $550,000, or (c) $500,000?

2. How does the purchase of the equipment affect total assets?

(LO 5) PROBLEM 8-3A DEPRECIATION AS A TAX SHIELD

The term *tax shield* refers to the amount of income tax saved by deducting depreciation for income tax purposes. Assume that Rummy Company is considering the purchase of an asset as of January 1, 1995. The cost of an asset with a five-year life and zero residual value is $50,000. The company will use the double declining-balance method of depreciation.

Rummy's income for tax purposes before recording depreciation on the asset will be $45,000 per year for the next five years. The corporation is currently in the 28% tax bracket.

■ REQUIRED

Calculate the amount of income tax that Rummy must pay each year if the asset is not purchased and then the amount of income tax that Rummy must pay each year if the asset is purchased. What is the amount of tax shield over the life of the asset? What is the amount of tax shield for Rummy if it uses the straight-line method over the life of the asset? Why would Rummy choose to use the accelerated method?

(LO 5) PROBLEM 8-4A BOOK VERSUS TAX DEPRECIATION

Speedy Company purchased an asset on January 1, 1995, for $8,000. The asset has a four-year life and zero residual value. Assume that you have proposed to your boss that Speedy use two methods of depreciation, the straight-line method for the annual report to be sent to stockholders and an accelerated method for income tax purposes. The accelerated method will result in $3,200 depreciation in 1995 and will decline by $800 per year. You believe that an accelerated depreciation method offers tax advantages. Your boss, however, disagrees with your suggestion. She points out that either method of depreciation will result in a total of $8,000 of depreciation over the four-year time frame. Speedy is currently in the 25% tax bracket, but it is possible that the tax bracket may change to 15% next year and continue at that rate.

■ REQUIRED

Calculate depreciation expense for each year under the two methods of depreciation. Calculate the amount of tax shield under each method at 25% for 1995 and 15% for years thereafter. Draft a memo to your boss to support your position in favor of accelerated depreciation for tax purposes, especially in light of the decreased tax rate.

(LO 5) PROBLEM 8-5A AMORTIZATION AND CASH FLOW

Simplified Company's only asset as of January 1, 1995, was a copyright. During 1995, only three transactions occurred:

Royalties earned from copyright use, $400,000 in cash.

Cash paid for advertising and clerical services, $50,000.

Amortization of copyright, $40,000.

■ REQUIRED

1. What amount of income will Simplified report in 1995?

2. What is the amount of cash on hand at December 31, 1995?

3. Explain how the cash balance increased from zero at the beginning of the year to its end-of-year balance. Why does the increase in cash not equal the income?

ALTERNATE MULTI-CONCEPT PROBLEMS

(LO 5, 10) PROBLEM 8-6A COST OF ASSETS AND SUBSEQUENT BOOK VALUE

The following events took place at Tasty-Toppins, Inc., a pizza shop that specializes in home delivery:

a. January 1, purchased a truck for $12,000 and added a cab and oven at a cost of $8,200. The truck is expected to last five years and be sold for $200 at the end of that time. The company uses straight-line depreciation for its trucks.

b. January 1, purchased equipment for $2,250 from a competitor who was retiring. The equipment is expected to last three years with zero salvage value. The company uses the double declining-balance method to depreciate its equipment.

c. April 1, sold an old truck for $1,500. The truck had been purchased for $8,000 exactly five years earlier, had an expected salvage value of $1,000, and was depreciated over a 10-year life using the straight-line method.

d. July 1, purchased a $12,000 patent for a unique baking process to produce a new product. The patent is valid for 15 more years; however, the company expects to produce and market the product for only four years. The patent's value at the end of the four years is indeterminable.

■ REQUIRED   For each situation, explain the amount of depreciation or amortization recorded for each asset in the current year and the book value of each asset at the end of the year. Be able to justify your answer when alternatives are available.

(LO 2, 5) PROBLEM 8-7A COST OF ASSETS AND THE EFFECT ON DEPRECIATION

Early in its first year of business, Lock-it, Inc., a locksmith and security consultant, purchased new equipment. The acquisition included the following costs:

Purchase Price	$150,000
Tax	15,000
Transportation	4,000
Setup*	1,000
Operating cost for first year	24,000

*The equipment was adjusted to Lock-it's specific needs.

The bookkeeper recorded the asset, Equipment, at $194,000. Lock-it used straight-line depreciation. The equipment was expected to last 10 years with zero residual value.

■ REQUIRED   1. How much depreciation did Lock-it report on its income statement related to this equipment in Year 1? How much should have been reported?

2. If Lock-it's income before the costs associated with the equipment is $50,000, what amount of income did Lock-it report? What amount should it have reported? You may ignore income tax.

3. Explain how Lock-it should determine the amount to capitalize when recording an asset. What is the effect of Lock-it's error?

(LO 7, 8) PROBLEM 8-8A CAPITAL EXPENDITURES, DEPRECIATION, AND DISPOSAL

Webster Company purchased a retail shopping center at a cost of $510,000 on January 1, 1994. Webster estimated that the life of the building would be 25 years and the residual value at the end of 25 years would be $10,000.

On January 1, 1995, the company made several expenditures related to the building. The entire building was painted and floors were refinished at a cost of $96,000. A local zoning agency required Webster to install additional fire protection equipment, including sprinklers and built-in alarms, at a cost of $73,000. With the new protection, Webster believed it was possible to increase the residual value of the building to $25,000.

In 1996 Webster altered its corporate strategy dramatically. The company sold the retail shopping center on January 1, 1996, for $300,000 of cash.

■ REQUIRED   1. Determine the amount of depreciation that should be recorded for 1994 and 1995.

2. Explain why the cost of the fire protection equipment was not expensed in 1995. What conditions would have allowed Webster to expense it? If Webster has a choice, would it prefer to expense or capitalize the improvement?

3. What amount of gain or loss did Webster record when it sold the building? What amount of gain or loss would have been reported if the fire protection equipment had been expensed in 1995?

(LO 6, 10) PROBLEM 8-9A AMORTIZATION OF INTANGIBLE, REVISION OF RATE

Dick, Inc., purchased Under Company on January 1, 1995, for $400,000. To determine the value of the assets and liabilities purchased, Dick requested an appraisal of Under's assets and liabilities. The appraiser determined that the fair market values of the items purchased as of January 1, 1995, were as follows:

ASSETS	FAIR MARKET VALUE
Cash	$ 60,000
Receivables	100,000
Building	230,000
LIABILITIES	
Accounts Payable	$100,000

Dick decided to amortize any goodwill recorded in the transaction on a straight-line basis over the maximum possible time period.

On January 1, 1996, Dick's accountant met with one of Under's largest customers. The customer owed Under $70,000 at the time of purchase, but the appraiser did not expect to collect any of the money because the customer was in bankruptcy. The customer has resolved his financial problems and has paid Dick $70,000.

1. Determine the amount of goodwill that should be recorded in the January 1, 1995, purchase of Under Company and the amount to be amortized in 1995.

2. How would you recommend that Dick handle the receipt of $70,000 from Under's customer? What amount of goodwill should be amortized in 1996?

■ REQUIRED

CASES

READING AND INTERPRETING FINANCIAL STATEMENTS

(LO 1, 9) CASE 8-1 BEN & JERRY'S

Refer to the financial statements included in the 1992 annual report of Ben & Jerry's.

1. What items does Ben & Jerry's list in the Property, Plant, and Equipment category?

2. What method is used to depreciate the operating assets?

3. What is the estimated useful life of the operating assets?

4. What are the accumulated depreciation and book values of property, plant, and equipment for the most recent fiscal year?

5. Were any assets purchased or sold during the most recent fiscal year?

6. In what category of the balance sheet are intangible assets included?

7. Ben & Jerry's financial statement does not disclose the useful life for the account Land under Capital Lease. Why?

■ REQUIRED

(LO 1, 9, 10) CASE 8-2 JCPENNEY

The 1992 & 1991 consolidated balance sheets and notes for JCPenney Company, Inc., included the following account balances and disclosures:

BALANCE SHEET ACCOUNT BALANCES

ASSETS	1992	1991
Property, net	$3,725,000	$3,602,000

Note:

PROPERTIES	1992	1991
Land	$ 210,000,000	$ 203,000,000
Buildings owned	1,992,000,000	1,814,000,000
Capital leases	237,000,000	244,000,000
Fixtures & equipment	2,686,000,000	2,633,000,000
Leasehold improvements	545,000,000	570,000,000
Accumulated depreciation	(1,945,000,000)	(1,862,000,000)
Properties, net	$3,725,000,000	$3,602,000,000

CAPITAL EXPENDITURES	1992
Land	$ 8,000,000
Buildings	189,000,000
Fixtures & equipment	269,000,000
Leasehold improvements	27,000,000
Total capital expenditures	$493,000,000

■ REQUIRED

1. What events could have affected the Properties account during 1992?

2. What events could have affected the Accumulated Depreciation account during 1992?

3. The statement of cash flows indicates that a net amount of $453,000,000 was used for capital expenditures. Why is this figure different from the $493,000,000 reported in the note?

4. Using the information given in the comparative balance sheets and the note, determine the amount of land that was sold in 1992.

(LO 11) CASE 8-3 BEN & JERRY'S STATEMENT OF CASH FLOWS

Refer to the statement of cash flows in Ben & Jerry's 1992 annual report and answer the following questions:

1. What amount of cash was used to purchase property, plant, and equipment during 1992?

2. Did Ben & Jerry's sell any property, plant, and equipment during 1992? What amount of cash was received? Were the assets sold for a gain or loss?

3. What amount was recorded for depreciation and amortization during 1992? Does the fact that depreciation and amortization are listed as a cash flow from operating activities mean that Ben & Jerry's created cash by recording depreciation?

MAKING FINANCIAL DECISIONS

(LO 1, 5) CASE 8-4 COMPARING COMPANIES

Assume that you are a financial analyst attempting to compare the financial results of two companies. The 1995 income statement of Straight Company is as follows:

Sales		$600,000
Cost of goods sold		300,000
Gross profit		300,000
Administrative costs	$ 80,000	
Depreciation expense	100,000	180,000
Income before tax		120,000
Tax expense (40%)		48,000
Net income		$ 72,000

Straight Company depreciates all operating assets using the straight-line method for tax purposes and for the annual report provided to stockholders. All operating assets were purchased on the same date, and all assets had an estimated life of five years when purchased. Straight Company's balance sheet reveals that on December 31, 1995, the balance of the Accumulated Depreciation account was $200,000.

   You wish to compare the annual report of Straight Company to that of Accelerated Company. Both companies are in the same industry, and both have exactly the same assets, sales, and expenses except that Accelerated uses the double declining-balance method for depreciation for income tax purposes and for the annual report provided to stockholders.

Develop Accelerated Company's 1995 income statement. As a financial analyst interested in investing in one of the companies, which company do you find more attractive? Because depreciation is a "noncash" expense, should you be indifferent between the two companies? Explain your answer.

■ **REQUIRED**

(LO 5) CASE 8-5 DEPRECIATION ALTERNATIVES

Medical Associates, Inc., produces supplies used in hospitals and nursing homes. Its sales, production, and costs to produce are expected to remain constant over the next five years. The corporate income tax rate is expected to increase over the next three years. The current rate, 15%, is expected to increase to 20% next year and then to 25% and continue at that rate indefinitely.

   Medical Associates is considering the purchase of new equipment that is expected to last for five years and to cost $150,000 with zero salvage value. As the controller, you are aware that the company can use one method of depreciation for accounting purposes and another method for tax purposes. You are trying to decide between the straight-line and the sum-of-the-years'-digits methods.

■ REQUIRED   Recommend which method to use for accounting purposes and which to use for tax purposes. Be able to justify your answer on both a numerical and a theoretical basis. How does a noncash adjustment to income, such as depreciation, affect cash flow?

ACCOUNTING AND ETHICS: WHAT WOULD YOU DO?

(LO 3) CASE 8-6 VALUING ASSETS

Rockies Company recently hired Joe Cora as an accountant. He was given responsibility for all accounting functions related to fixed asset accounting. Donna Baylor, Joe's boss, asked him to review all transactions involving the current year's acquisition of fixed assets and to take necessary action to ensure that acquired assets were recorded at proper values. Joe is satisfied that all transactions are proper except for an April 15 purchase of an office building and the land on which it is situated. The purchase price of the acquisition was $200,000. Rockies has not separately recorded the land and building, however.

Joe hired an appraiser to determine the market values of the land and the building. The appraiser reported that his best estimates of the values were $150,000 for the building and $70,000 for the land. When Joe proposed that these values be used to determine the acquisition cost of the assets, Ms. Baylor disagreed. She told Joe to request another appraisal of the property and asked him to stress to the appraiser that the land component of the acquisition could not be depreciated for tax purposes. The second appraiser estimated that the values were $180,000 for the building and $40,000 for the land. Joe and Ms. Baylor agreed that the second appraisal should be used to determine the acquisition cost of the assets.

■ REQUIRED   Did Joe and Ms. Baylor act ethically in this situation? Explain your answer.

(LO 9, 10) CASE 8-7 AMORTIZATION POLICY

In 1993 Dreaming, Inc., purchased for $50,000 the copyright of a song written by an up-and-coming country rap star. Dreaming believed that the country rap market was untapped and that the company had made an investment that would yield sales for at least the next 10 years. Dreaming amortized the copyright accordingly. In 1995 its accountant evaluated the amortization policy and determined that the copyright was of little value. Dreaming's owners disagreed with the accountant, citing her lack of knowledge of trends in the music industry and her conservative nature.

Dreaming's management ordered the accountant to continue the amortization policy.

■ REQUIRED   If you were the accountant, what would you do?

ANALYTICAL SOFTWARE CASE

To the Student: Your instructor may assign one or more parts of the analytical software case that is designed to accompany this chapter. This multi-part case gives you a chance to work with real financial statement data using software that stimulates, guides, and hones your analytical and problem-solving skills. It was created especially to support and strengthen your understanding of the chapter's Learning Objectives.

SOLUTION TO KEY TERMS QUIZ

1. Acquisition cost (p. 425)
2. Land improvements (p. 428)
3. Straight-line depreciation (p. 429)
4. Units-of-production method (p. 429)
5. Sum-of-the-years'-digits method (p. 430)
6. Capitalization of interest (p. 426)
7. Change in estimate (p. 433)
8. Depreciation (p. 428)
9. Capital expenditure (p. 434)
10. Book value (p. 429)
11. Revenue expenditure (p. 434)
12. Gain on Sale of Asset (p. 437)
13. Loss on Sale of Asset (p. 438)
14. Accelerated depreciation (p. 430)
15. Intangible asset (p. 440)
16. Organization costs (p. 440)
17. Double declining-balance method (p. 431)
18. Goodwill (p. 441)
19. Research and development costs (p. 443)

INTEGRATIVE PROBLEM

FOR PART II

CORRECT AN INCOME STATEMENT AND STATEMENT OF CASH FLOWS AND ASSESS THE IMPACT OF A CHANGE IN INVENTORY METHOD; COMPUTE THE EFFECT OF A BAD DEBT RECOGNITION.

The following income statement, statement of cash flows, and additional information are available for PEK Company:

PEK COMPANY
INCOME STATEMENT
FOR THE YEAR ENDED DECEMBER 31, 1995

Sales revenue		$1,250,000
Cost of goods sold		636,500
Gross profit		$ 613,500
Depreciation on plant equipment	$58,400	
Depreciation on buildings	12,000	
Interest expense	33,800	
Other expenses	83,800	188,000
Income before taxes		$ 425,500
Income tax expense (30% rate)		127,650
Net income		$ 297,850

PEK COMPANY
STATEMENT OF CASH FLOWS
FOR THE YEAR ENDED DECEMBER 31, 1995

Cash flows from operating activities:	
Net income	$ 297,850
Adjustments to reconcile net income to net cash provided by operating activities (includes depreciation expense)	83,200
Net cash provided by operating activities	$ 381,050
Cash flows from financing activities:	
Dividends	(35,000)
Net increase in cash	$ 346,050

Additional information:

1. Beginning inventory and purchases for the one product the company sells follows:

	UNITS	UNIT COST
Beginning inventory	50,000	$2.00
Purchases:		
February 5	25,000	2.10
March 10	30,000	2.20
April 15	40,000	2.50
June 16	75,000	3.00
September 5	60,000	3.10
October 3	40,000	3.25

2. During the year the company sold 250,000 units at $5 each.

3. PEK uses the periodic FIFO method to value its inventory and the straight-line method to depreciate all of its long-term assets.

4. During the year-end audit it was discovered that a January 3, 1995 transaction for the lump-sum purchase of a mixing machine and a boiler was not recorded. The fair market values of the mixing machine and the boiler were $200,000 and $100,000 respectively. Each asset has an estimated useful life of ten years with no residual value expected. The purchase of the assets was financed by issuing a $270,000 five-year promissory note directly to the seller. Interest of 8% is paid annually on December 31.

1. Prepare a revised income statement and a revised statement of cash flows to take into account the omission of the entry to record the purchase of the two assets. (Hint: you will need to take into account any change in income taxes as a result of changes in any income statement items. Assume that income taxes are paid on December 31 of each year.)

■ REQUIRED

2. Assume the same facts as above, except that the company is considering the use of the sum-of-the-years' digits method rather than the straight-line method for the assets purchased on January 3, 1995. All other assets would continue to be depreciated on a straight-line basis. Prepare a revised income statement and a revised statement of cash flows, assuming the company decides to use the sum-of-the-years' digits method for these two assets rather than the straight-line method.

Treat the answers in requirements 3 and 4 as independent of the other parts.

3. Assume PEK decides to use the LIFO method rather than the FIFO method to value its inventory and recognize cost of goods sold for 1995. Compute the effect (amount of increase or decrease) this would have on:

a. Cost of goods sold

b. Income tax expense

c. Net income

4. Assume PEK failed to record an estimate of bad debts for 1995 (bad debt expense is normally included in "other expenses"). Before any adjustment, the balance in Allowance for Doubtful Accounts is $8,200. The credit manager estimates that 3% of the $800,000 of sales on account will prove to be uncollectible. Based on this information, compute the effect (amount of increase or decrease) of recognition of the bad debt estimate on:

a. Other expenses

b. Income tax expense

c. Net income

Annual Report

A WORD TO STUDENTS ABOUT PART III

By now it's obvious that this book, like most other financial accounting books, is following a rough balance sheet order—Part II covered assets; Part III will cover liabilities and equity. **Read the linkages, and you can begin to think of Part III as continuing the story of the flow of assets through the company:** unless the firm pays cash, it purchases assets with promises of repayment called liabilities. As we'll see, taking on liabilities to pay for assets is a way to provide financing for the future of the company.

Part III

Accounting for Liabilities and Owners' Equity

Chapter 9
Current Liabilities, Contingent Liabilities, and the
Time Value of Money
Appendix 9A:
Accounting Tools: Payroll Accounting

Current liabilities are a way to finance operations. You'll learn their impact on McDonald's statement of cash flows. And you'll be impressed by how much insight is needed to reflect some possible liabilities in the balance sheet. Along the way, you'll **evaluate a biotech firm** (p. 486), **see how Dow Corning's contingent liabilities could affect its credit rating** (p. 495), and briefly **assess your own "time value of money" situation** (p. 496).

Chapter 10
Long-Term Liabilities

Businesses often finance their operations using long-term liabilities such as bonds. (The time value of money, which you studied as part of Chapter 9, is essential to understanding this chapter.) Along the way, you'll **assess factors you'd use to rate bonds** (p. 545), **chair the pension committee** (p. 558), and **talk to an investment banker** about debt issues (p. 559).

Chapter 11
Stockholders' Equity
Appendix 11A:
Accounting Tools: Unincorporated Businesses

By the end of this chapter you should be able to classify the components of stockholders' equity and develop a basis for evaluating a company. Along the way, you'll **make an investment decision about which stock to purchase** (p. 589), **give rudimentary advice about an Intel Corp. stock split** (p. 600), and **meet a mergers and acquisitions specialist who looks at a bank's stockholders' equity** (p. 603).

Chapter 12
Additional Corporate Accounting Issues

This chapter deals with accounting for a variety of events on a multiple-step income statement, reading a retained earnings statement, and analyzing profitability and cash flows. Along the way, you'll **make an investment decision about Motorola's earnings** (p. 641), **decide how to handle your audit client's objections** (p. 647), and **meet an investor relations specialist** (p. 649).

Integrative Problem for Part III

Focus on Financial Results

Mattel, Inc., is one of the most successful toy companies in the world. Its Barbie doll is the leading product in the toy industry, racking up worldwide sales in 1992 approaching $1 billion, more than one half of Mattel's total sales. Other products include dolls licensed from Disney and toys tied to Nickelodeon. Net income rose from $95.5 million in 1990 to $143.9 million in 1992.

Mattel spends more than 15% of its revenues on advertising and promotion expenses. Such heavy spending on marketing is typical for toy companies and other consumer-oriented businesses such as McDonald's and Nike.

A less glamorous—but an equally effective—promotional method is the use of redeemable coupons in cereal boxes and other food containers. Since the coupons permit the holder to buy Mattel toys at a discount, it is appropriate for Mattel to accrue a liability on its balance sheet. But even with the coupon program, Mattel's balance sheet is strong. Current assets are more than double current liabilities—and long-term liabilities are just half of shareholders' equity.

Mattel, Inc. and Subsidiaries

Consolidated Balance Sheets

ASSETS (In thousands)	December 31, 1992	December 31, 1991
Current Assets		
Cash	$ 281,072	$ 198,410
Marketable securities	14,114	8,723
Accounts receivable, less allowances of $12,188 at December 31, 1992 and $8,897 at December 31, 1991	377,565	342,212
Inventories	156,665	146,433
Prepaid expenses and other current assets	43,083	30,510
Total current assets	872,499	726,288
Property, Plant and Equipment		
Land	7,484	7,950
Buildings	74,195	70,072
Machinery and equipment	115,503	101,769
Capitalized leases	38,209	38,209
Leasehold improvements	40,384	33,686
	275,775	251,666
Less: Accumulated depreciation	101,560	84,545
	174,215	167,121
Tools, dies and molds, net	48,987	42,367
Property, plant and equipment, net	225,202	209,488
Other Noncurrent Assets		
Intangible assets, net	132,192	129,319
Sundry assets	32,400	34,137
	$1,260,293	$1,099,232

The accompanying notes are an integral part of these statements.

Chapter 9

Current Liabilities, Contingent Liabilities, and the Time Value of Money

LEARNING OBJECTIVES

After studying this chapter, you should be able to

1. Identify the components of the current liability category of the balance sheet.
2. Explain how to record transactions that involve the accrual of current liabilities.
3. Understand how changes in current liabilities affect the statement of cash flows.
4. Determine when contingent liabilities should be recorded or disclosed in footnotes and how to calculate their amounts.
5. Explain the difference between simple and compound interest.
6. Calculate amounts using the future value and present value concepts.
7. Apply the compound interest concepts to some common accounting situations.
8. Understand the deductions and expenses for payroll accounting. (Appendix 9A)
9. Determine when compensated absences must be accrued as a liability. (Appendix 9A)

Linkages

A LOOK AT PREVIOUS CHAPTERS

Chapter 2 introduced the concept of classified balance sheets, which emphasize the distinction between current and noncurrent assets and liabilities. Current liabilities generally represent items to be paid within one year.

A LOOK AT THIS CHAPTER

The first part of this chapter examines more closely the items that appear in the current liability category of the balance sheet. The second part examines whether contingent liabilities should be recorded, disclosed in the footnotes, or ignored altogether. The third part of the chapter presents the time value of money concept.

A LOOK AT UPCOMING CHAPTERS

Chapter 10 presents the accounting for long-term liabilities. The time value of money concept developed in Chapter 9 will be applied to several long-term liability issues in Chapter 10.

Current Liabilities

LO | 1

Identify the components of the current liability category of the balance sheet.

A classified balance sheet presents financial statement items by category in order to provide more information to financial statement users. The balance sheet generally presents two categories of liabilities, current and long term.

Current liabilities finance the working capital of the company. At any given time during the year, current liabilities may fluctuate substantially. What's important is that the company generate sufficient cash flow to retire these debts as they come due. As long as the company's ratio of current assets to current liabilities stays fairly constant from quarter to quarter or year to year, financial statement users are not going to be too concerned.

The current liability portion of McDonald's Corporation 1992 balance sheet is shown in Exhibit 9-1. Note the practice of listing the accounts in the current liability category in the order of payment due date. That is, the account that requires payment first should be listed first, the account requiring payment next should be listed second, and so forth. This allows users of the statement to assess the cash flow implications of each account.

Current liabilities were first introduced to you in Chapter 2 of this text. In general, a **current liability** is an obligation that will be satisfied within one year. Although current liabilities are not due immediately, they are still recorded at face value, that is, the time until payment is not taken into account. If it were, current liabilities would be recorded at a slight discount to reflect interest that would be earned between now and the due date. The face value amount is generally used for all current liabilities because the time period involved until payment is short enough that it is not necessary to record or calculate an interest factor. In addition, low interest rates further diminish the need to worry about interest that could be earned in this short period of time. We will find in Chapter 10 that many long-term liabilities must be stated at their present value on the balance sheet.

The current liability classification is important because it is closely tied to the concept of *liquidity.* Management of the firm must be prepared to pay current liabilities within a very short time period. Therefore, management must have access to liquid assets, cash, or other assets that can be converted to cash in amounts sufficient to pay the current liabilities. Firms that do not have sufficient resources to pay their current liabilities are often said to have a liquidity problem.

A handy ratio to help creditors or potential creditors determine a company's liquidity is the current ratio. A current ratio of current assets to current liabilities of 2:1 is usually a very comfortable margin. If the firm has a large amount of inventory, it is sometimes useful to delete inventory when computing the ratio. That gives you the "quick" ratio. Usually, one would expect a quick ratio of at least 1.5:1 to feel secure that the company could pay its bills on time.

The accounting for current liabilities is an area in which U.S. accounting standards are very similar to those of most other countries. Nearly all countries encourage firms to provide a breakdown of liabilities into current and long term in order to allow users to evaluate liquidity.

Accounts Payable

Accounts payable represent amounts owed for the purchase of inventory, goods, or services acquired in the normal course of business. Generally, Accounts Payable is the first account listed in the current liability category because it requires the payment

EXHIBIT 9-1 McDonald's Corporation 1992 Consolidated Balance Sheet

McDonald's Corporation
CONSOLIDATED BALANCE SHEET

(In millions of dollars)	December 31, 1992	1991
Assets		
Current assets		
Cash and equivalents	$ 436.5	$ 220.2
Accounts receivable	245.9	238.4
Notes receivable	33.7	36.0
Inventories, at cost, not in excess of market	43.5	42.6
Prepaid expenses and other current assets	105.1	108.8
Total current assets	864.7	646.0
Other assets and deferred charges		
Notes receivable due after one year	99.0	123.1
Investments in and advances to affiliates	399.7	374.2
Miscellaneous	330.7	278.2
Total other assets and deferred charges	829.4	775.5
Property and equipment		
Property and equipment, at cost	12,658.0	12,368.0
Accumulated depreciation and amortization	(3,060.6)	(2,809.5)
Net property and equipment	9,597.4	9,558.5
Intangible assets—net	389.7	369.1
Total assets	$11,681.2	$11,349.1
Liabilities and shareholders' equity		
Current liabilities		
Notes payable	$ 411.0	$ 278.3
Accounts payable	343.3	313.9
Income taxes	109.7	157.2
Other taxes	74.8	82.3
Accrued interest	133.3	185.7
Other accrued liabilities	203.1	201.4
Current maturities of long-term debt	269.4	69.1
Total current liabilities	1,544.6	1,287.9
Long-term debt	3,176.4	4,267.4
Security deposits by franchisees and other long-term liabilities	225.2	224.5
Deferred income taxes	748.6	734.2
Common equity put options	94.0	
Shareholders' equity		
Preferred stock, no par value; authorized—165.0 million shares; issued—5.8 and 9.9 million	680.2	298.2
Common stock, no par value; authorized—1.25 billion shares; issued—415.2 million	46.2	46.2
Additional paid-in capital	260.2	201.9
Guarantee of ESOP Notes	(271.3)	(286.7)
Retained earnings	6,727.3	5,925.2
Foreign currency translation adjustment	(127.4)	32.3
	7,315.2	6,217.1
Common stock in treasury, at cost; 51.6 and 56.5 million shares	(1,422.8)	(1,382.0)
Total shareholders' equity	5,892.4	4,835.1
Total liabilities and shareholders' equity	$11,681.2	$11,349.1

The accompanying Financial Comments are an integral part of the consolidated financial statements.

of cash before other current liabilities. McDonald's is somewhat unique because it lists Notes Payable before Accounts Payable.

If we assume a perpetual inventory system, a typical entry to record inventory purchases on June 1 may be the following:

June 1	Inventory	800	
	Accounts Payable		800
	To record a purchase of inventory priced at $800.		

Assets	=	Liabilities	+	Owners' Equity
+800		+800		

Normally, a firm has an established relationship with several suppliers, and formal contractual arrangements with those suppliers are unnecessary. Accounts payable usually do not require the payment of interest, but terms may be given to encourage early payment. For example, terms may be stated as 2/10, n30, which means that a 2% discount is available if payment occurs within the first 10 days, and if not paid within 10 days, the full amount must be paid within 30 days. The accounting entry to record the payment of an account payable on June 4, assuming that no discount is available, is

June 4	Accounts Payable	800	
	Cash		800
	To record the payment of an $800 account payable.		

Assets	=	Liabilities	+	Owners' Equity
−800		−800		

Timely payment of accounts payable is an important aspect of the management of cash flow. Generally, it is to the company's benefit to take advantage of discounts when they are available. After all, if your supplier is going to give you a 2% discount for paying on Day 10 instead of Day 30, that means you are earning 2% on your money over 20/360 of a year. If you were to take a 2% discount throughout the year, you would be getting a 36% annual return on your money, since there are 18 periods of 20 days each in a year. It is essential therefore that the accounts payable system be established in a manner that alerts management to take advantage of offered discounts.

Notes Payable

The first current liability on McDonald's balance sheet is notes payable of $411 million. How is a note payable different from an account payable? The most important difference is that an account payable is not a formal contractual arrangement, but a **note payable** is represented by a formal agreement or note signed by the parties to the transaction. Notes payable may arise from dealing with a supplier or when acquiring a cash loan from a bank or creditor. Those notes that are expected to be paid within one year of the balance sheet date should be classified as current liabilities.

The accounting for notes payable depends on whether the interest is paid on the note's due date or is deducted in advance before the borrower receives the loan proceeds. With the first type of note, the terms stipulate that the borrower receives a short-term loan and agrees to repay the principal and interest at the note's due date. For example, assume that Glengarry Health Club receives a one-year loan from First National Bank on January 1, 1995. The face amount of the note of $1,000 must be repaid on December 31 along with interest at the rate of 12%. Glengarry would make the following entries to record the loan and its repayment:

Jan. 1   Cash   1,000
    Notes Payable   1,000
   To record loan of $1000.

       Assets = Liabilities + Owners' Equity
       +1,000   +1,000

Dec. 31   Notes Payable   1,000
    Interest Expense   120
     Cash   1,120
   To record the repayment of loan with interest.

       Assets = Liabilities + Owners' Equity
       −1,120   −1,000   −120

   Banks also use another form of note for which the interest is deducted in advance. Suppose that on January 1, 1995, First National Bank granted to Glengarry a $1,000 loan, due on December 31, 1995, but deducted the interest in advance and gave Glengarry the remaining amount of $880 ($1,000 face amount of the note less interest of $120). This is sometimes referred to as *discounting a note;* the reason will become obvious in the entries that are recorded. On January 1, Glengarry must record the following entry:

Jan. 1
    Cash   880
    Discount on Notes Payable   120
     Notes Payable   1,000
   To record loan of $1,000 less interest deducted in
   advance.

       Assets = Liabilities + Owners' Equity
       +880   −120
           +1,000

The account titled **Discount on Notes Payable** has a debit balance and thus should be treated as a reduction of Notes Payable. If a balance sheet were developed immediately after the January 1 entry, the note would appear in the current liability category as follows:

Notes payable	$1,000
Less: Discount on notes payable	120
Net liability	$ 880

The original balance in the Discount on Notes Payable account represents interest and must be transferred to interest expense over the life of the note. If Glengarry wishes to present annual financial statements, then it must make an adjusting entry as of December 31 as follows:

Dec. 31   Interest Expense   120
    Discount on Notes Payable   120
   To record interest on note payable.

       Assets = Liabilities + Owners' Equity
        +120   −120

When the note is repaid on December 31, 1995, Glengarry must repay the full amount of the note as follows:

Dec. 31	Notes Payable	1,000	
	Cash		1,000
	To record payment of the note on its due date.		

Assets	=	Liabilities	+	Owners' Equity
− 1,000		− 1,000		

It is important to compare the two types of notes payable. In the previous two examples, the stated interest rate on each note was 12%. The dollar amount of interest incurred in each case was $120. However, the interest *rate* on a discounted note, the second example, is always higher than it appears. Glengarry received the use of only $880, yet it was required to repay $1,000. Therefore, the interest rate incurred on the note was actually 120/880, or approximately 13.6%.

Current Maturities of Long-Term Debt

Another account that appears in the current liability category of McDonald's balance sheet is **Current Maturities of Long-Term Debt.** On other companies' balance sheets, this item may appear as Long-Term Debt, Current Portion. This account should appear when a firm has a liability and must make periodic payments. For example, assume that on January 1, 1995, your firm obtained a $10,000 loan from the bank. The terms of the loan require you to make payments to reduce the principal in the amount of $1,000 per year for 10 years, payable each January 1, beginning January 1, 1996. On December 31, 1995, an entry should be made to classify a portion of the balance as a current liability as follows:

Dec. 31	Long-Term Liability	1,000	
	Current Portion of Liability		1,000
	To record the current portion of bank loan.		

Assets	=	Liabilities	+	Owners' Equity
		− 1,000		
		+ 1,000		

When an investor or creditor reads a balance sheet, he or she wants to distinguish between debt that is permanent and debt that is short term. Therefore, it is important to segregate that portion of the debt that becomes due within one year. Typically, investors calculate a ratio known as *debt-to-total equity* to determine the degree to which the company has fixed obligations to creditors. The ratio usually excludes current debt because it is deemed to be temporary.

The December 31, 1995, balance sheet should indicate that the liability for the note payable is classified into two portions: a $1,000 current liability that must be repaid within one year and a $9,000 long-term liability.

On January 1, 1996, the company must pay $1,000, and the entry should be recorded as follows:

Jan. 1	Current Portion of Liability	1,000	
	Cash		1,000
	To record payment of $1,000 on bank loan.		

Assets	=	Liabilities	+	Owners' Equity
− 1,000		− 1,000		

On December 31, 1996, the company should again record the current portion of the liability. Therefore, the 1996 year-end balance sheet should indicate that the liability is classified into two portions: $1,000 current liability and $8,000 long-term liability. The process should be repeated each year until the bank loan has been fully paid.

The balance sheet category labeled Current Maturities of Long-Term Debt should include only the amount of principal to be paid. The amount of interest that has been incurred but is unpaid should be listed separately in an account such as Interest Payable.

Taxes Payable

Corporations pay a variety of taxes, including federal and state income taxes, property taxes, and other taxes. Usually, the largest dollar amount is incurred for state and federal income taxes. Taxes are an expense of the business and should be accrued in the same manner as any other business expense. A company that ends its accounting year on December 31 is not required to pay its tax amounts to the government until the following March 15 or April 15, depending on the type of business. Therefore, the business must make an accounting entry, usually as one of the year-end adjusting entries, to record the amount of tax that has been incurred but is unpaid. Normally, the entry would be recorded as

LO **2**

Explain how to record transactions that involve the accrual of current liabilities.

Dec. 31	Tax Expense	xxx	
	Tax Payable		xxx
	To accrue income tax for the year.		

Assets = Liabilities + Owners' Equity
+ xxx   − xxx

The calculation of the amount of tax a business owes is very complex. Appendix 2 to your text goes into much more detail concerning this topic and you should refer to that appendix if you are interested. For now, the important point is that taxes are an expense when incurred (not when they are paid) and must be recorded as a liability as incurred.

Some analysts prefer to measure a company's profits before it pays taxes. For one thing, tax rates change from year to year. President Clinton's budget package in 1993 raised the corporate tax rate from 34% to 35%. It is possible that the only reason that a business did worse in 1993 than in 1992 is because its tax rate went up, not because its operations did not hold the line on expenses. In some industries, such as the grocery industry where margins are razor thin, a one-point swing in the tax rate can make a big difference to the bottom line. Investors would want to note the tax change as a one-time event, not as a recurring element of the business.

Other Accrued Liabilities

McDonald's 1992 balance sheet listed an amount of $203.1 million as current liability under the category of Other Accrued Liabilities. What items might be included in this category?

In previous chapters, especially Chapter 4, we covered many examples of accrued liabilities. **Accrued liabilities** include any amount that has been incurred due to the passage of time but has not been paid as of the balance sheet date. A common example is salary or wages payable. Suppose that your firm has a payroll of $1,000 per day, Monday through Friday, and that employees are paid at the close of work each Friday. Also suppose that December 31 is the end of your accounting year and falls on a Tuesday. Your firm will then have to record the following entry as of December 31:

Dec. 31	Salary Expense	2,000	
	Salary Payable		2,000
	To record two days' salary as expense.		

| **Assets** | **=** | **Liabilities** | **+** | **Owners' Equity** |
| | | + 2,000 | | − 2,000 |

The amount of the salary payable would be classified as a current liability and could appear in a category such as Other Accrued Liabilities.

Interest is another item that often must be accrued at year-end. Assume that you received a one-year loan of $10,000 on December 1. The loan carries an interest rate of 12%. On December 31, an accounting entry must be made to record interest, even though the money may not actually be due:

Dec. 31	Interest Expense	100	
	Interest Payable		100
	To record one month's interest as expense.		

| **Assets** | **=** | **Liabilities** | **+** | **Owners' Equity** |
| | | + 100 | | − 100 |

The Interest Payable account should be classified as a current liability, assuming that it is to be paid within one year of the December 31 date.

We have illustrated two examples of liabilities that must be accrued. Had these accruals not been made, a financial statement user would be unpleasantly surprised when the entire obligation suddenly became due.

Reading Statement of Cash Flows for Changes in Current Liabilities

LO 3
Understand how changes in current liabilities affect the statement of cash flows.

Most current liabilities are directly related to a firm's ongoing operations. Therefore, the change in the balance of each current liability account should be reflected in the operating activities category of the statement of cash flows. A decrease in a current liability account indicates that cash has been used to pay the liability.

The cash flow statement of McDonald's Corporation is presented in Exhibit 9-2. Note that one of the items in the operating activities category is listed as Taxes and Other Liabilities of ($68.2) million. This means that the balance of those current liabilities decreased by $68.2 million, resulting in a decrease of cash.

Almost all current liabilities appear in the operating activities category of the statement of cash flows, but there are exceptions. If a current liability is not directly related to operating activities, it should not appear in that category. For example, McDonald's uses some notes payable as a means of financing, distinct from operating activities. Therefore, cash generated from the use of notes is reflected in the financing activities category rather than as operating activities.

FROM CONCEPT TO PRACTICE

READING BEN & JERRY'S STATEMENT OF CASH FLOWS

Refer to Ben & Jerry's statement of cash flows for 1992. What was the change in Accounts Payable and where was it reported? What conclusion might you draw?

LO 4
Determine when contingent liabilities should be recorded or disclosed in footnotes and how to calculate their amounts.

Contingent Liabilities

We have seen that accountants must exercise a great deal of expertise and judgment in deciding what to record and in determining the amount to record. This is certainly

EXHIBIT 9-2 McDonald's Corporation 1992 Consolidated Statement of Cash Flows

McDonald's Corporation
CONSOLIDATED STATEMENT OF CASH FLOWS

(In millions of dollars)	Years ended December 31, 1992	1991	1990
Operating activities			
Net income	$ 958.6	$ 859.6	$ 802.3
Adjustments to reconcile to cash provided by operations			
Depreciation and amortization	554.9	514.2	493.3
Deferred income taxes	22.4	64.7	70.8
Changes in operating working capital items			
Accounts receivable increase	(29.1)	(40.9)	(26.6)
Inventories, prepaid expenses and other current assets (increase) decrease	2.2	.4	(32.1)
Accounts payable increase (decrease)	.8	(22.7)	(14.5)
Accrued interest increase (decrease)	(27.4)	27.5	(1.7)
Taxes and other liabilities increase (decrease)	(68.2)	85.2	80.5
Other—net	11.7	(64.8)	(71.0)
Cash provided by operations	1,425.9	1,423.2	1,301.0
Investing activities			
Property and equipment expenditures	(1,086.9)	(1,128.8)	(1,570.7)
Sales of restaurant businesses	124.5	159.8	130.8
Purchases of restaurant businesses	(64.1)	(30.1)	(81.9)
Notes receivable additions	(31.8)	(38.8)	(46.2)
Property sales	52.2	58.6	39.5
Notes receivable reductions	78.5	53.1	61.2
Other	(71.1)	(13.5)	(55.2)
Cash used for investing activities	(998.7)	(939.7)	(1,522.5)
Financing activities			
Notes payable and commercial paper net borrowings supported by line of credit agreements	17.0	(676.7)	987.9
Other long-term debt borrowings	509.5	1,004.1	1,070.7
Other long-term debt repayments	(1,041.5)	(606.9)	(1,561.0)
Treasury stock purchases	(79.7)	(109.2)	(160.3)
Preferred stock issuances	484.9	100.0	
Common and preferred stock dividends	(160.5)	(148.3)	(133.3)
Other	59.4	30.9	23.4
Cash provided by (used for) financing activities	(210.9)	(406.1)	227.4
Cash and equivalents increase	216.3	77.4	5.9
Cash and equivalents at beginning of year	220.2	142.8	136.9
Cash and equivalents at end of year	$ 436.5	$ 220.2	$ 142.8
Supplemental cash flow disclosures			
Interest paid	$ 395.7	$ 368.1	$ 370.5
Income taxes paid	$ 531.6	$ 313.5	$ 326.5

The accompanying Financial Comments are an integral part of the consolidated financial statements.

true regarding contingent liabilities. A **contingent liability** is an obligation that involves an existing condition for which the outcome is not known with certainty and depends on some event that will occur in the future. The actual amount of the liability must be estimated because we cannot clearly predict the future. The important accounting issues are whether contingent liabilities should be recorded and, if so, in what amounts.

This is a judgment call that usually is resolved through discussions among the company's management and its outside auditors. Management usually would rather not disclose contingent liabilities until they become actual liabilities. The reason is that management is judged by investors and creditors based on the company's earnings, and the recording of a contingent liability must be accompanied by a charge to earnings. Auditors, on the other hand, want the management to disclose as much as possible because the auditors are essentially representing the interests of investors and creditors who want to have as much information as possible.

Contingent Liabilities That Are Recorded

A contingent liability should be accrued and recorded if it is probable and if the amount can be reasonably estimated. But when is an event *probable* and what does *reasonably estimated* mean? The terms must be defined based on the facts of each situation. A financial statement user would want the company to err on the side of full disclosure. On the other hand, the company should not be required to disclose every remote possibility.

A common contingent liability that must be recorded by firms involves product warranties or guarantees. Many firms sell products for which they provide the customer a warranty against defects that may develop in the products. If a product becomes defective within the warranty period, the selling firm ensures that it will repair or replace the item. This is an example of a contingent liability because the expense of fixing a product depends on some of the products becoming defective—an uncertain, although likely, event.

At the end of each period, the selling firm must estimate how many of the current year's sales will become defective in the future and the cost of repair or replacement. This type of contingent liability is often referred to as an **estimated liability** to emphasize that the costs are not known at year-end and must be estimated.

As an example, assume that Quickkey Computer sells a computer product for $5,000. When the customer buys the product, Quickkey provides a one-year warranty in case it must be repaired. Assume that in 1995 Quickkey sold 100 computers for a total sales revenue of $500,000. At the end of 1995, Quickkey must record an estimate of the warranty costs that will occur on 1995 sales. Based on analysis of past warranty records, Quickkey estimates that repairs will average 2% of total sales. Therefore, Quickkey should record the following transaction at the end of 1995:

Dec. 31	Warranty Expense	10,000	
	Estimated Liability		10,000
	To record estimated liability at 2% of sales.		

Assets	=	Liabilities	+	Owners' Equity
		+10,000		−10,000

The amount of warranty expense a company records is of interest to investors and potential creditors. If the expense as a percentage of sales begins to rise, one might conclude that the product is becoming less reliable.

Warranties are an excellent example of the matching principle. In our Quickkey example, the warranty costs related to 1995 sales were estimated and recorded in

Product warranties are a contingent liability that must be recorded. This is because some amount of returns for warranty work is probable and can be estimated based on information about past returns. Many retailers offer their own warranties in addition to those of the manufacturer. As the level of warranty expense rises, often so does the skepticism of investors toward these retailers.

1995. This was done to match the 1995 sales with the expenses related to those sales. If actual repair of the computers occurred in 1996, it does not result in an expense. The repair costs incurred in 1996 should be treated as a reduction in the liability that had previously been estimated.

Because items such as warranties involve estimation, you may wonder what happens if the amount estimated is not accurate. The company must analyze past warranty records carefully and incorporate any changes in customer buying habits, usage, technological changes, and other changes. Still, even with careful analysis, the actual amount of the expense is not likely to equal the estimated amount. Generally, firms do not change the amount of the expense recorded in past periods for such differences. They may compensate in future periods, however.

Warranties provide an example of a contingent liability that must be estimated and recorded. Other examples are premium or coupon offers that accompany many products. Cereal boxes are an everyday example of premium offers. The boxes often allow customers to purchase a toy or game at a reduced price if the purchase is accompanied by cereal box tops or proof of purchase. The offer given to cereal customers represents a contingent liability. At the end of each year, the cereal company must estimate the number of premium offers that will be redeemed and the cost involved and must record a contingent liability for that amount.

Contingent Liabilities That Are Disclosed

Any contingent liability that both is probable and can be reasonably estimated must be recorded as a liability. We have used warranty liabilities in the preceding section as an example. We now must consider contingent liabilities that do not meet the probable criterion or cannot be reasonably estimated. In either case a contingent liability must be disclosed in the footnotes but not recorded on the balance sheet if the contingent liability is at least reasonably possible.

Although information in the footnotes to the financial statements contains very important data on which investors make decisions, some accountants believe that footnote disclosure does not have the same impact as balance sheet disclosure. For one thing, footnote disclosure does not impact the important financial ratios that investors use to make decisions.

A lawsuit that has been filed against a firm is an example of a contingent liability that is disclosed. In today's business environment, lawsuits are a fact of life. They represent a contingent liability because an event has occurred but the outcome of that event, the resolution of the lawsuit, is not known. The defendant in the lawsuit must make a judgment about the outcome of the lawsuit in order to decide whether the item should be recorded, disclosed, or neither. As you might imagine, firms are usually not anxious to record contingent lawsuits as liabilities because it is often difficult to estimate an amount of loss. Also, some may view the accountant's decision as an admission of guilt if a lawsuit is recorded as a liability before the courts have made a decision. Even if the lawsuit is not recorded, however, it must be disclosed if it is reasonably possible that a loss will occur. What constitutes *reasonably possible* is also a matter of judgment. Accountants must often consult with lawyers or other legal experts to determine the probability of loss of a lawsuit. In cases involving contingencies, it is especially important that the accountant make an independent judgment based on the facts and not be swayed by the desires of other parties.

Exhibit 9-3 provides the footnote disclosure that accompanied the 1992 financial statements of Quaker Oats Company concerning litigation over the words *thirst-aid*

FROM CONCEPT TO PRACTICE

READING BEN & JERRY'S ANNUAL REPORT
Does Ben & Jerry's have any lawsuits? Have these been recorded or are they presented in the footnotes?

EXHIBIT 9-3   Quaker Oats' 1992 Footnote Disclosure on Pending Litigation

Note 19

Litigation

On December 18, 1990, Judge Prentice H. Marshall of the United States District Court for the Northern District of Illinois issued a memorandum opinion stating that the Court would enter judgment against the Company in favor of Sands, Taylor & Wood Co. The Court found that the use of the words "thirst aid" in advertising *Gatorade* thirst quencher infringed the Plaintiff's rights in the trademark THIRST-AID. On July 9, 1991, Judge Marshall entered a judgment of $42.6 million, composed of $31.4 million in principal, plus prejudgment interest of $10.6 million and fees, expenses and costs of $0.6 million. The order enjoined use of the phrase "THIRST-AID" in connection with the advertising or sale of *Gatorade* thirst quencher in the United States. The Company and its subsidiary, Stokely-Van Camp, Inc., ceased use of the words "thirst aid" in December 1990. The Company subsequently appealed the judgment. On September 2, 1992, the Court of Appeals for the Seventh Circuit vacated the District Court's judgment. The appellate court affirmed the finding of infringement, but found that the monetary award was an inequitable "windfall" to the Plaintiff. The case was remanded to the District Court for further proceedings. The Company filed a request for rehearing that was denied. The Company also filed a Petition for Certiorari with the U.S. Supreme Court that was denied. On June 7, 1993, Judge Marshall issued a judgment on remand of $26.5 million, composed of $20.7 million in principal, prejudgment interest of $5.4 million and fees, expenses and costs of $0.4 million. The Company has filed a Notice of Appeal with respect to this judgment. Management, with advice from outside legal counsel, has determined that the amount of liability that might ultimately exist in this case will not be material.

The Company is not a party to any pending legal proceedings that it believes will have a material adverse effect on its financial position or results of operations.

used to advertise the product Gatorade. Quaker Oats did not record a liability for the lawsuit on the financial statements but provided the footnote disclosure so that statement users could be aware of the existence of the lawsuit.

Lawsuits may be the most common type of contingent liabilities that are disclosed in financial statement footnotes, but there are several other types. A contingent liability can arise if a company guarantees the debt of another company or individual. Also, contingent liabilities may arise from tax disputes with the Internal Revenue Service. Exhibit 9-4 provides the 1990 footnote of Noland Company that discloses a contingency involving its tax returns.

Contingent liabilities are another example of the difference between accrual and cash accounting. The amount and timing of the cash outlays associated with contingent liabilities are especially difficult to determine. Lawsuits, for example, may extend several years into the future, and the dollar amount of possible loss may be subject to great uncertainty.

Contingent Liabilities versus Contingent Assets

Contingent liabilities that are probable and can be reasonably estimated must be recorded before the outcome of the future events is known. This accounting rule applies only to contingent losses or liabilities. It does not apply to contingencies by which the firm may gain. Generally, contingent gains or **contingent assets** are not recorded until the gain actually occurs. That is, contingent liabilities may be accrued but contingent assets are not accrued. This may seem inconsistent—it is. Remember, however, that accounting is a discipline based on a conservative set of principles. It is prudent and conservative to delay the recording of a gain until an asset is actually received but to record contingent liabilities in advance.

Of course, just because the contingent assets are not recorded does not mean that they do not exist. Wall Street analysts make their living trying to place a value on contingent assets that they believe exist. By buying stock of a company that has

---

EXHIBIT 9-4   Noland Company's 1990 Footnote Disclosure on
Contingent Liability for Tax Assessments

10. Contingencies

The Federal income tax returns of the
Company for the years ended December
31, 1986 and 1985 are currently under
examination by the Internal Revenue
Service. In the opinion of management, any
assessments which may result will not have
a material effect on the financial condition
or the results of operations of the
Company.

unrecorded assets, or advising their clients to do so, the investment analysts hope to make money when those assets become a reality.

■ **ACCOUNTING FOR YOUR DECISIONS**   **You Are the Investor**

You are an investor in a biotechnology company that is applying to the Food & Drug Administration to market a new drug that has shown promise in the treatment of lymphoma, a form of cancer. The company has no revenues nor earnings, yet the stock is selling at $25 per share. The balance sheet is bare, also—the stock's book value is $1. Do you think it would make a difference to the stock price if the company were permitted to record a contingent asset on its balance sheet reflecting the possibility that the FDA approves the drug?

Time Value of Money Concepts

Imagine that you have won the state lottery worth $10 million. You have been given the choice of receiving the money as one lump sum immediately or receiving $1 million per year for 10 years. Assume that tax considerations do not affect your decision. Which option are you likely to choose? Most people are likely to take the lump-sum amount because of the time value of money.

The **time value of money** concept means that people prefer a payment at the present time rather than a future payment because of the interest factor. If an amount is received at the present time, it can be invested and the resulting accumulation will be larger than if the same amount were received in the future. To understand the interest rate calculations, we must understand the way compound interest works and the concepts of future values and present values.

We will find that compound interest is a powerful concept that applies to many accounting situations. The valuation of Bonds Payable, Notes Receivable, Leases, and other accounts are all based on compound interest calculations. The accounting applications of compound interest concepts will become evident as these topics are introduced in future chapters. The time value of money concept is used in virtually every advanced business course. For example, a course on investments will spend a great deal of time comparing cash flows from one investment to cash flow from another. To make the cash flows comparable, it is necessary to convert them from "future" dollars to "current" dollars using time value of money concepts.

In the working world, the time value of money is a factor considered by many different decision makers. Accountants use it to value liabilities on the balance sheet. Bankers consider it when making lending decisions. Investment managers use the time value of money to consider rates of return on various investment opportunities.

Simple Interest

LO 5

Explain the difference between simple and compound interest.

Simple interest is interest earned on the principal amount. If the amount of principal is unchanged from year to year, the interest per year will remain the same. Interest can be calculated by the following formula:

$$I = P \times R \times T$$

where:

$$I = \text{Dollar amount of interest per year}$$
$$P = \text{Principal}$$
$$R = \text{Interest rate as a percentage}$$
$$T = \text{Time in years}$$

For example, assume that our firm has signed a two-year note payable for $3,000. Interest and principal are to be paid at the due date with simple interest at the rate of 10% per year. The amount of interest on the note would be $600 calculated as $3,000 $\times$ .10 $\times$ 2. We would be required to pay $3,600 on the due date: $3,000 principal and $600 interest.

Compound Interest

Compound interest means that interest is calculated on the principal plus previous amounts of accumulated interest. Thus, interest is compounded, or we can say that there is interest on interest. For example, assume a $3,000 note payable for which interest and principal are due in two years with interest compounded annually at 10% per year. Interest would be calculated as follows:

YEAR	PRINCIPAL AMOUNT AT BEGINNING OF YEAR	INTEREST AT 10%	ACCUMULATED AT YEAR-END
1	$3,000	$300	$3,300
2	3,300	330	3,630

We would be required to pay $3,630 at the end of two years, $3,000 principal and $630 interest. A comparison of the note payable with 10% simple interest in the first example with the note payable with 10% compound interest in the second example clearly indicates that the amount accumulated with compound interest is always a higher amount because of the interest on interest feature.

Interest Compounding

For most accounting problems, we will assume that compound interest is compounded annually. In actual business practice, compounding usually occurs over much shorter intervals. This can be confusing because the interest rate is often stated as an annual rate even though it is compounded over a shorter period. If compounding is not done annually, you must adjust the interest rate by dividing the annual rate by the number of compounding periods per year.

LO 6

Calculate amounts using the future value and present value concepts.

For example, assume that the note payable from the previous example carried a 10% interest rate, compounded semiannually, for two years. The 10% annual rate should be converted to 5% per period for four semiannual periods. The amount of interest would be compounded, as in the previous example, but for four periods instead of two. The compounding process is as follows:

PERIOD	PRINCIPAL AMOUNT AT BEGINNING OF YEAR	INTEREST AT 5% PER PERIOD	ACCUMULATED AT END OF PERIOD
1	$3,000	$150	$3,150
2	3,150	158	3,308
3	3,308	165	3,473
4	3,473	174	3,647

Assume you won the lottery and this check were yours. Which payment option would you take— a lump sum or an amount every year for 10 years? Only by understanding time value of money concepts would you make an intelligent decision.

The example illustrates that compounding more frequently results in a larger amount accumulated. In fact, many banks and financial institutions now compound interest on savings accounts on a daily basis.

In the remainder of this section, we will assume that compound interest is applicable. Four compound interest calculations must be understood:

1. Future value of a single amount
2. Present value of a single amount
3. Future value of an annuity
4. Present value of an annuity

Future Value of a Single Amount

We are often interested in the amount of interest plus principal that will be accumulated at a future time. This is called a *future amount* or *future value*. The future amount is always larger than the principal amount (payment) because of the interest that accumulates. The formula to calculate the **future value of a single amount** is

$$FV = p(1 + i)^n$$

where:

FV = Future value to be calculated
p = Payment or principal amount
i = Interest rate
n = Number of periods of compounding

Example: Grandpa Phil passed away and left your three-year-old son, Robert, $50,000 in cash and securities. If the funds were left in the bank and in the stock market and received an annual return of 10%, how much would be there in 15 years when Robert starts college?

Solution:
$$FV = \$50,000(1 + .10)^{15}$$
$$= \$50,000(4.177)$$
$$= \$208,850$$

In some cases, we will use time diagrams to illustrate the relationships. A time diagram to illustrate a future value would be of the following form:

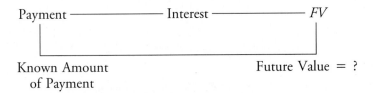

Payment —————— Interest —————— *FV*

Known Amount   Future Value = ?
of Payment

For example, consider a $2,000 note payable that carries interest at the rate of 10% compounded annually. The note is due in two years, and the principal and interest must be paid at that time. The amount that must be paid in two years is the future value. The future value can be calculated in the manner we have used in the previous examples as

YEAR	PRINCIPAL AMOUNT AT BEGINNING OF YEAR	INTEREST AT 10%	ACCUMULATED AT YEAR-END
1	$2,000	$200	$2,200
2	2,200	220	2,420

The future value can also be calculated by using the following formula:
$$FV = \$2,000(1 + .10)^2$$
$$= \$2,000(1.21)$$
$$= \$2,420$$

Many calculators are capable of performing compound interest calculations. The future value formula is programmed into the calculator so that you do not see the calculations once you have entered the proper values.

Tables can also be constructed to assist in the calculations. Table 9-1 on page 499 indicates the future value of $1 at various interest rates and for various time periods. To find the future value of a two-year note at 10% compounded annually, you read across the line for two periods and down the 10% column and see an interest rate factor of 1.210. Because the table has been constructed for future values of $1, we would determine the future value of $2,000 as

$$FV = \$2,000 \times 1.210$$
$$= \$2,420$$

We mentioned that compounding does not always occur annually. How does this affect the calculation of future value amounts? Suppose we wish to find the future value of a $2,000 note payable due in two years. The note payable requires interest to be compounded quarterly at the rate of 12% per year. To calculate the future value, we must adjust the interest rate to a quarterly basis by dividing the 12% rate by the number of compounding periods per year, which in the case of quarterly compounding is four:

$$12\%/4 \text{ Quarters} = 3\% \text{ per Quarter}$$

Also, the number of compounding periods is eight, four per year times two years.

The future value of the note can be found in two ways. First, we can insert the proper values into the future value formula:

$$FV = \$2,000(1 + .03)^8$$
$$= \$2,000(1.267)$$
$$= \$2,534$$

We can arrive at the same future value amount with the use of Table 9-1. Refer to the interest factor in the table indicated for 8 periods and 3%. The future value would be calculated as

$$FV = \$2,000(\text{interest factor})$$
$$= \$2,000(1.267)$$
$$= \$2,534$$

Present Value of a Single Amount

In many situations, we do not wish to calculate how much will be accumulated at a future time. Rather, we wish to determine the amount at the present time that is equivalent to an amount at a future time. This is the present value concept. The **present value of a single amount** represents the value today of a single amount to be received or paid at a future time. This can be portrayed in a time diagram as follows:

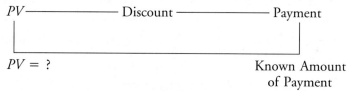

The time diagram portrays discount, rather than interest, because we often speak of "discounting" the future payment back to the present time.

Suppose that you know that you will receive $2,000 in two years. You also know that if you had the money now, it could be invested at 10% compounded annually. What is the present value of the $2,000? Another way to ask the same question is: What amount must be invested today at 10% compounded annually in order to have $2,000 accumulated in two years?

The formula used to calculate present value is

$$PV = \text{Payment} \times (1 + i)^{-n}$$

where:

$$PV = \text{Present value amount in dollars}$$
$$\text{Payment} = \text{Amount to be received in the future}$$
$$i = \text{Interest rate or discount rate}$$
$$n = \text{Number of periods}$$

We can use the present value formula to solve for the present value of the $2,000 note as follows:

$$PV = \$2,000 \times (1 + .10)^{-2}$$
$$= \$2,000 \times (.826)$$
$$= \$1,652$$

Example: A recent magazine article projects that it will cost $100,000 to attend a four-year college 10 years from now. If that is true, how much money would you have to put into an account today to fund that education, assuming a 5% rate of return?

Solution:
$$PV = \$100,000(1 + .05)^{-10}$$
$$= \$100,000(.614)$$
$$= \$61,400$$

Tables have also been developed to determine the present value of $1 at various interest rates and number of periods. Table 9-2 on page 500 presents the present value or discount factors for an amount of $1 to be received at a future time. To use the table for our two-year note example, you must read across the line for two periods and down the 10% column to the discount factor of .826. The present value of $2,000 would be calculated as

$$PV = \$2,000(\text{discount factor})$$
$$= \$2,000(.826)$$
$$= \$1,652$$

Two other points are important. First, the example illustrates that the present value amount is always less than the future payment. This happens because of the discount factor. In other words, if we had a smaller amount at the present (the present value), we could invest it and earn interest that would accumulate to an amount equal to the larger amount (the future payment). Second, study of the present value and future value formulas indicates that they are reciprocals of each other. When we wish to calculate a present value amount, we normally use Table 9-2 and multiply a discount factor times the payment. However, we could also use Table 9-1 and divide by the interest factor. Thus, the present value of the $2,000 to be received in the future could also be calculated as

$$PV = \$2,000/1.210$$
$$= \$1,652$$

Future Value of an Annuity

The present value and future value amounts presented to this point have been useful when a single amount is involved. Many accounting situations involve an annuity, however. **Annuity** means a series of payments of equal amounts. We will now consider the calculation of the future value when a series of payments is involved.

Suppose that you were to receive $3,000 per year at the end of each of the next four years. Also assume that each payment received could be invested at an interest rate of 10% compounded annually. How much would be accumulated in principal and interest by the end of the fourth year? This is an example of an annuity of payments of equal amounts. A time diagram would portray the payments as follows:

$$\$3,000 \qquad \$3,000 \qquad \$3,000 \qquad \$3,000$$

| Interest | Interest | Interest |

$$FV = \ ?$$

Because we are interested in calculating the future value, we could use the future value of $1 concept and calculate the future value of each $3,000 payment using Table 9-1 as follows:

$3,000 × 1.331 Interest for 3 Periods	$3,993
3,000 × 1.210 Interest for 2 Periods	$3,630
3,000 × 1.100 Interest for 1 Period	3,300
3,000 × 1.000 Interest for 0 Periods	3,000
Total Future Value	$13,923

It should be noted that four payments would be received but only three of them would draw interest because the payments are received at the end of each period.

Fortunately, there is an easier method to calculate the **future value of an annuity.** Table 9-3 on page 501 has been constructed to indicate the future value of a series of payments of $1 per period at various interest rates and number of periods. The table can be used for the previous example by reading across the four-period line and down the 10% column to a table factor of 4.641. The future value of an annuity of $3,000 per year can be calculated as follows:

$$FV = \$3,000(\text{table factor})$$
$$= \$3,000(4.641)$$
$$= \$13,923$$

Example: You just had a baby girl two weeks ago and are already thinking about college. When she is 15, how much money would be in her college account if you deposit $2,000 into it on each of her first 15 birthdays? The interest rate is 10%.

Solution: $FV = \$2,000(\text{table factor})$
$$= \$2,000(31.772)$$
$$= \$63,544$$

When compounding occurs more frequently than annually, adjustments must be made to the interest rate and number of periods similar to those discussed previously for single amounts. For example, how would the future value be calculated if the previous example were modified so that we were to receive $1,000 semiannually, and the interest rate was 10% compounded semiannually (or 5% per period) for 15 years? Table 9-3 could be used by reading across the line for 30 periods and down the column for 5% to obtain a table factor of 66.439. The future value would be calculated as

$$FV = \$1,000(\text{table factor})$$
$$= \$1,000(66.439)$$
$$= \$66,439$$

Comparing the two examples illustrates once again that more frequent compounding results in larger accumulated amounts.

Present Value of an Annuity

Many accounting applications of the time value of money concept concern situations for which we wish to know the present value of a series of payments that will occur in the future. This involves calculating the present value of an annuity.

An annuity is a series of payments of equal amounts. Suppose that you will receive an annuity of $4,000 per year for four years, with the first received one year from today. The amounts that are received can be invested at a rate of 10% compounded annually. What amount would we need at the present time to have an amount equivalent to the series of payments and interest in the future? To answer this question, we must calculate the **present value of an annuity.** A time diagram of the series of payments would appear as follows:

$4,000	$4,000	$4,000	$4,000
Discount	Discount	Discount	Discount

PV = ?

Because we are interested in calculating the present value, we could refer to the present value of $1 concept and discount each of the $4,000 payments individually using table factors from Table 9-2 as follows:

$4,000 × 0.683 Factor for Four Periods	$ 2,732
4,000 × 0.751 Factor for Three Periods	3,004
4,000 × 0.826 Factor for Two Periods	3,304
4,000 × 0.909 Factor for One Period	3,636
Total Present Value	$12,676

For a problem of any size, it is very cumbersome to calculate the present value of each payment individually. Therefore, tables have been constructed to ease the computational burden. Table 9-4 on page 502 provides table factors to calculate the present value of an annuity of $1 per year at various interest rates and number of periods. The previous example can be solved by reading across the four-year line and down the 10% column to obtain a table factor of 3.170. The present value would then be calculated as follows:

$$PV = \$4,000(\text{table factor})$$
$$= \$4,000(3.170)$$
$$= \$12,680$$

You should note that there is a $4 difference in the present value calculated by the first and second methods. This difference is caused by a small amount of rounding in the table factors that were used.

Example: You just won the lottery. You can take your $1 million in a lump sum today, or you can receive $100,000 per year over the next 12 years. Assuming a 5% interest rate, which would you prefer, ignoring tax considerations?

Solution:

$$PV = \$100,000(\text{table factor})$$
$$= \$100,000(8.863)$$
$$= \$886,300$$

Because the present value of the payments over 12 years is less than the $1 million immediate payment, you should prefer the immediate payment.

Solving for Unknowns

In some cases, the present value or future value amounts will be known but the interest rate, or the number of payments, must be calculated. The formulas that have been presented thus far can be used for such calculations, but you must be careful to analyze each problem to be sure that you have chosen the correct relationship. We will use two examples to illustrate the power of the time value of money concepts.

Assume that you have just purchased a new automobile for $14,420 and must decide how to pay for it. Your local bank has graciously granted you a five-year loan. Because you are a good credit risk, the bank will allow you to make annual payments on the loan at the end of each year. The amount of the loan payments, which include principal and interest, is $4,000 per year. You are concerned that your total payments will be $20,000 ($4,000 per year for five years) and wish to calculate the interest rate that is being charged on the loan.

Because the market or present value of the car, as well as the loan, is $14,420, a time diagram of our example would appear as follows:

$4,000	$4,000	$4,000	$4,000	$4,000
Discount	Discount	Discount	Discount	Discount

$PV = 14,420$

The interest rate that we must solve for represents the discount rate that was applied to the $4,000 payments to result in a present value of $14,420. Therefore, the applicable formula is the following:

$$PV = \$4,000(\text{table factor})$$

In this case, PV is known, so the formula can be rearranged as

$$\text{Table Factor} = PV/\$4,000$$
$$= \$14,420/\$4,000$$
$$= 3.605$$

The value of 3.605 represents a table factor in Table 9-4. We must read across the five-year line until we find a table factor of 3.605. In this case, that table factor is found in the 12% column. Therefore, the rate of interest being paid on the auto loan is 12%.

The second example involves solving for the number of interest periods. Assume that you wish to accumulate $12,000 as a down payment on a home. You believe that you can save $1,000 per semiannual period, and your bank will pay interest of 8% per year, or 4% per semiannual period. How long will it take you to accumulate the desired amount?

The accumulated amount of $12,000 represents the future value of an annuity of $1,000 per semiannual period. Therefore, we can use the interest factors of Table 9-3 to assist in the solution. The applicable formula in this case is

$$FV = \$1,000(\text{table factor})$$

A CREDIT ANALYST EXAMINES LIABILITIES ON AND OFF THE BALANCE SHEET

Name: Doris S. Nakamura
Profession: Credit Analyst
College Degree: MBA

The nation's credit-rating agencies in large measure determine whether a company can issue debt to the public. Depending on the rating by these companies, a firm may have to pay more than the market rate of interest to borrow money. If the rating is poor enough, it may not be able to offer a bond issue.

One of the major credit-rating agencies is Duff & Phelps Credit Rating Co. Based in Chicago, Duff & Phelps has a scale of 19 ratings for industrial companies, the highest being AAA. The firm's analysts comb through a company's financial statements, looking for strengths and weaknesses in its business and financial affairs.

Doris Nakamura is a senior analyst at the firm responsible for industrial companies primarily in the consumer, paper, and forest products; cable television; and media sectors. She's been with the firm since 1982. She earned an MBA from the University of Chicago at night while working during the day.

Although a rating agency focuses on debt, it analyzes the big picture, too. "We look at a company's business and financial risk factors," she says. "Business risk factors include the degree to which a company is sensitive to the business cycle, labor issues, competition, and exposure to government regulation." For example, an auto company might have high business risk in all four areas. As the economy gets worse, so do its fortunes. As it competes with car companies throughout the world it is affected by labor unions and government regulation regarding such factors as safety and emissions.

Financial risk includes the amount of debt a company already has on the books. A credit analyst would examine long-term debt, of course, but also working capital accounts such as accounts receivable and inventory and would be concerned if those accounts showed excessive growth given business conditions. The analyst would also look at current liabilities. "If you saw cash growing and you saw accounts payable growing, then you'd know that one of the reasons for the growth in cash is that it's financed by a growth in payables," says Nakamura. In other words, bills are piling up.

Not everything can be found on the balance sheet, however. Certain companies are downgraded because they have contingent liabilities such as pending litigation. "For example, we have Dow Corning on our 'Rating Watch' list due to the litigation over silicone breast implants. We can't quantify the ultimate liability, but we know it impacts credit quality," she says. Where does she find out about contingent liabilities? "A detailed reading of the financial footnotes and in-depth meetings with management."

The future value is known to be $12,000 and we must solve for the interest factor or table factor. Therefore, we can rearrange the formula as follows:

$$\text{Table factor} = FV/\$1,000$$
$$= \$12,000/\$1,000$$
$$= 12.00$$

Using Table 9-3, we must scan down the 4% column until we find a table value that is near 12.00. The closest table value we find is 12.006. That table value corresponds to 10 periods. Therefore, if we deposit $1,000 per semiannual period and invest the money at 8% per semiannual period, it will take 10 semiannual periods (five years) to accumulate $12,000.

■ ACCOUNTING FOR YOUR DECISIONS   You Handle the Money in the Family

How many different personal financial situations can you think of in which the time value of money is relevant? Where it's irrelevant?

REVIEW PROBLEM

Part A

The accountant for Albright Express wishes to develop a balance sheet as of December 31, 1995. The following items pertain to the liability category and must be considered in order to determine the items that should be recorded in the current liability section of the balance sheet. You may assume that Albright began business on January 1, 1995, and therefore the beginning balance of all accounts was zero.

1. During 1995 Albright purchased $100,000 of inventory on account from suppliers. By year-end $40,000 of the balance has been eliminated as a result of payments. All items were purchased on terms of 2/10, n/30. Albright uses the gross method of recording payables.

2. On April 1, 1995, Albright borrowed $10,000 on a one-year note payable from Foss Bank. Terms of the loan indicate that Albright must repay the principal and 12% interest at the due date of the note.

3. On October 1, 1995, Albright also borrowed $8,000 from Dove Bank on a one-year note payable. Dove Bank deducted 10% interest in advance and gave to Albright the net amount. At the due date, Albright must repay the principal of $8,000.

4. On January 1, 1995, Albright borrowed $20,000 from Owens Bank by signing a 10-year note payable. Terms of the note indicate that Albright must make annual payments of principal each January 1 beginning in 1996 and also must pay interest each January 1 in the amount of 8% of the outstanding balance of the loan.

5. The accountant for Albright has completed an income statement for 1995 that indicates that income before taxes was $10,000. Albright must pay tax at the rate of 40% and must remit the tax to the Internal Revenue Service by April 15, 1996.

6. As of December 31, 1995, Albright owes to employees salaries of $3,000 for work performed in 1995. The employees will be paid on the first payday of 1996.

7. During 1995 two lawsuits were filed against Albright. In the first lawsuit, a customer sued for damages because of an injury that occurred on Albright's premises. Albright's legal counsel advised that it is probable that the lawsuit will be settled in 1996 at an amount of $7,000. The second lawsuit involves a patent infringement suit of $14,000 filed against Albright by a competitor. The legal counsel has advised that there is some possibility that Albright may be at fault but loss does not appear probable at this time.

Part B

1. What amount will be accumulated by January 1, 1999, if $5,000 is invested on January 1, 1995, at 10% interest compounded semiannually?

2. Assume that we are to receive $5,000 on January 1, 1999. What amount at January 1, 1995, is equivalent to the $5,000 that is to be received in 1999? Assume that interest is compounded annually at 10%.

3. What amount will be accumulated by January 1, 1999, if $5,000 is invested each semiannual period for eight periods beginning with June 30, 1995, and ending December 31, 1998? Interest will accumulate at 10% compounded semiannually.

4. Assume that we are to receive $5,000 each semiannual period for eight periods beginning on June 30, 1995. What amount at January 1, 1995, is equivalent to the future series of payments? Assume that interest will accrue at 10% compounded semiannually.

5. Assume that a new bank has begun a promotional campaign to attract savings accounts. The bank advertisement indicates that customers who invest $1,000 will double their money in 10 years' time. Assuming annual compounding of interest, what rate of interest is the bank offering?

1. Consider all items in part A. Develop the current liability section of Albright's balance sheet as of December 31, 1995. To make investment decisions about this company, what additional data would you need? You do not need to consider the footnotes that accompany the balance sheet.

2. Answer the five questions in part B.

■ **REQUIRED**

■ SOLUTION TO PART A

The accountant's decisions for questions 1 to 7 of part A should be as follows:

1. The balance of the Accounts Payable account should be $60,000. The payables should be recorded at the gross amount and discounts would not be recorded until the time of payment.

2. The note payable to Foss Bank of $10,000 should be included as a current liability. Also, interest payable of $900 ($10,000 $\times$ 12% $\times$ 9/12) should be considered a current liability.

3. The note payable to Dove Bank should be considered a current liability and listed at $8,000 minus the contra account Discount on Note Payable of $600 ($8,000 $\times$ 10% $\times$ 9/12 remaining).

4. The debt to Owens Bank should be split between current liability and long-term liability with the current portion shown as $2,000. Also, interest payable of $1,600 ($20,000 $\times$ 8% x 1 year) should be considered a current liability.

5. Income taxes payable of $4,000 ($10,000 $\times$ 40%) is a current liability.

6. Salaries payable of $3,000 is a current liability.

7. The lawsuit involving the customer must be recorded as a current liability of $7,000 because the possibility of loss is probable. The second lawsuit should not be recorded but should be disclosed as a footnote to the balance sheet.

ALBRIGHT EXPRESS
PARTIAL BALANCE SHEET
AS OF DECEMBER 31, 1995

Current Liabilities:

Accounts payable		$60,000
Interest payable ($900 + $1,600)		2,500
Salaries payable		3,000
Taxes payable		4,000
Note payable to Foss Bank		10,000
Note payable to Dove Bank	$8,000	
Less: Discount on note payable	(600)	7,400
Current maturity of long-term debt		2,000
Contingent liability for pending lawsuit		7,000
Total Current Liabilities		$95,900

Other data necessary to make an investment decision might include current assets, total assets, and current liabilities as of December 31, 1994 and 1995. If current assets were significantly larger than current liabilities, you can be comfortable that the company was capable of paying its short-term debt. The dollar amount of current assets and liabilities must be evaluated with regard to the size of the company. The larger the company, the less significant $95,900 in current liabilities would be. Knowing last year's current liabilities would give you an idea about the trend in current liabilities. If they are rising, you would want to know why.

■ SOLUTION TO PART B

1.
$$FV = \$5,000(\text{table factor}) \quad \text{using Table 9-1}$$
$$= \$5,000(1.477) \quad \text{where } i = 5\%, n = 8$$
$$= \$7,385$$

2.
$$PV = \$5,000(\text{table factor}) \quad \text{using Table 9-2}$$
$$= \$5,000(.683) \quad \text{where } i = 10\%, n = 4$$
$$= \$3,415$$

3.
$$FV \text{ annuity} = \$5,000(\text{table factor}) \quad \text{using Table 9-3}$$
$$= \$5,000(9.549) \quad \text{where } i = 5\%, n = 8$$
$$= \$47,745$$

4.
$$PV \text{ annuity} = \$5,000(\text{table factor}) \quad \text{using Table 9-4}$$
$$= \$5,000(6.463) \quad \text{where } i = 5\%, n = 8$$
$$= \$32,315$$

5.
$$FV = \$1,000(\text{table factor}) \quad \text{using Table 9-1}$$

Because the future value is known to be $2,000, the formula can be written as
$$\$2,000 = \$1,000(\text{table factor})$$
and rearranged as
$$\text{Table Factor} = \$2,000/\$1,000 = 2.0.$$
In Table 9-1, the table factor of 2.0 and 10 years corresponds with an interest rate of between 7% and 8%.

GUIDANCE ANSWERS TO ACCOUNTING FOR YOUR DECISIONS

YOU ARE THE INVESTOR

The FASB does not permit the recording of a contingent asset such as this. However, stockholders may still know about the contingency, from other sources, and are betting that the FDA gives the company the green light. Therefore, recording of the item as an asset probably would not affect the stock price. Here's one example of many that illustrate that a company's financial statements rarely tell the whole story about the company's stock price.

YOU HANDLE THE MONEY IN THE FAMILY

Relevant: Deciding whether to refinance your mortgage. Deciding how much money to put away every month for the kids' college fund. Deciding whether to lease or buy a car. Deciding whether you should go back to school to get retraining for a new career. Deciding whether to make a loan to your sister so that she can start a business. Irrelevant: Deciding whether to take a family vacation. Deciding whether to replace a broken refrigerator with a $1,500 model or a $3,000 model. Deciding whether to give $1,000 or $2,000 to charity this year.

TABLE 9-1   Future Value of $1

| (n) PERIODS | RATE OF INTEREST IN % | | | | | | | | | | | |
	2	3	4	5	6	7	8	9	10	11	12	15
1	1.020	1.030	1.040	1.050	1.060	1.070	1.080	1.090	1.100	1.110	1.120	1.150
2	1.040	1.061	1.082	1.103	1.124	1.145	1.166	1.188	1.210	1.232	1.254	1.323
3	1.061	1.093	1.125	1.158	1.191	1.225	1.260	1.295	1.331	1.368	1.405	1.521
4	1.082	1.126	1.170	1.216	1.262	1.311	1.360	1.412	1.464	1.518	1.574	1.749
5	1.104	1.159	1.217	1.276	1.338	1.403	1.469	1.539	1.611	1.685	1.762	2.011
6	1.126	1.194	1.265	1.340	1.419	1.501	1.587	1.677	1.772	1.870	1.974	2.313
7	1.149	1.230	1.316	1.407	1.504	1.606	1.714	1.828	1.949	2.076	2.211	2.660
8	1.172	1.267	1.369	1.477	1.594	1.718	1.851	1.993	2.144	2.305	2.476	3.059
9	1.195	1.305	1.423	1.551	1.689	1.838	1.999	2.172	2.358	2.558	2.773	3.518
10	1.219	1.344	1.480	1.629	1.791	1.967	2.159	2.367	2.594	2.839	3.106	4.046
11	1.243	1.384	1.539	1.710	1.898	2.105	2.332	2.580	2.853	3.152	3.479	5.652
12	1.268	1.426	1.601	1.796	2.012	2.252	2.518	2.813	3.138	3.498	3.896	5.350
13	1.294	1.469	1.665	1.886	2.133	2.410	2.720	3.066	3.452	3.883	4.363	6.153
14	1.319	1.513	1.732	1.980	2.261	2.579	2.937	3.342	3.797	4.310	4.887	7.076
15	1.346	1.558	1.801	2.079	2.397	2.759	3.172	3.642	4.177	4.785	5.474	8.137
16	1.373	1.605	1.873	2.183	2.540	2.952	3.426	3.970	4.595	5.311	6.130	9.358
17	1.400	1.653	1.948	2.292	2.693	3.159	3.700	4.328	5.054	5.895	6.866	10.761
18	1.428	1.702	2.026	2.407	2.854	3.380	3.996	4.717	5.560	6.544	7.690	12.375
19	1.457	1.754	2.107	2.527	3.026	3.617	4.316	5.142	6.116	7.263	8.613	14.232
20	1.486	1.806	2.191	2.653	3.207	3.870	4.661	5.604	6.727	8.062	9.646	16.367
21	1.516	1.860	2.279	2.786	3.400	4.141	5.034	6.109	7.400	8.949	10.804	18.822
22	1.546	1.916	2.370	2.925	3.604	4.430	5.437	6.659	8.140	9.934	12.100	21.645
23	1.577	1.974	2.465	3.072	3.820	4.741	5.871	7.258	8.954	11.026	13.552	24.891
24	1.608	2.033	2.563	3.225	4.049	5.072	6.341	7.911	9.850	12.239	15.179	28.625
25	1.641	2.094	2.666	3.386	4.292	5.427	6.848	8.623	10.835	13.585	17.000	32.919
26	1.673	2.157	2.772	3.556	4.549	5.807	7.396	9.399	11.918	15.080	19.040	37.857
27	1.707	2.221	2.883	3.733	4.822	6.214	7.988	10.245	13.110	16.739	21.325	43.535
28	1.741	2.288	2.999	3.920	5.112	6.649	8.627	11.167	14.421	18.580	23.884	50.066
29	1.776	2.357	3.119	4.116	5.418	7.114	9.317	12.172	15.863	20.624	26.750	57.575
30	1.811	2.427	3.243	4.322	5.743	7.612	10.063	13.268	17.449	22.892	29.960	66.212

TABLE 9-2   Present Value of $1

(n) PERIODS	2	3	4	5	6	7	8	9	10	11	12	15
1	0.980	0.971	0.962	0.952	0.943	0.935	0.926	0.917	0.909	0.901	0.893	0.870
2	0.961	0.943	0.925	0.907	0.890	0.873	0.857	0.842	0.826	0.812	0.797	0.756
3	0.942	0.915	0.889	0.864	0.840	0.816	0.794	0.772	0.751	0.731	0.712	0.658
4	0.924	0.888	0.855	0.823	0.792	0.763	0.735	0.708	0.683	0.659	0.636	0.572
5	0.906	0.863	0.822	0.784	0.747	0.713	0.681	0.650	0.621	0.593	0.567	0.497
6	0.888	0.837	0.790	0.746	0.705	0.666	0.630	0.596	0.564	0.535	0.507	0.432
7	0.871	0.813	0.760	0.711	0.665	0.623	0.583	0.547	0.513	0.482	0.452	0.376
8	0.853	0.789	0.731	0.677	0.627	0.582	0.540	0.502	0.467	0.434	0.404	0.327
9	0.837	0.766	0.703	0.645	0.592	0.544	0.500	0.460	0.424	0.391	0.361	0.284
10	0.820	0.744	0.676	0.614	0.558	0.508	0.463	0.422	0.386	0.352	0.322	0.247
11	0.804	0.722	0.650	0.585	0.527	0.475	0.429	0.388	0.350	0.317	0.287	0.215
12	0.788	0.701	0.625	0.557	0.497	0.444	0.397	0.356	0.319	0.286	0.257	0.187
13	0.733	0.681	0.601	0.530	0.469	0.415	0.368	0.326	0.290	0.258	0.229	0.163
14	0.758	0.661	0.577	0.505	0.442	0.388	0.340	0.299	0.263	0.232	0.205	0.141
15	0.743	0.642	0.555	0.481	0.417	0.362	0.315	0.275	0.239	0.209	0.183	0.123
16	0.728	0.623	0.534	0.458	0.394	0.339	0.292	0.252	0.218	0.188	0.163	0.107
17	0.714	0.605	0.513	0.436	0.371	0.317	0.270	0.231	0.198	0.170	0.146	0.093
18	0.700	0.587	0.494	0.416	0.350	0.296	0.250	0.212	0.180	0.153	0.130	0.081
19	0.686	0.570	0.475	0.396	0.331	0.277	0.232	0.194	0.164	0.138	0.116	0.070
20	0.673	0.554	0.456	0.377	0.312	0.258	0.215	0.178	0.149	0.124	0.104	0.061
21	0.660	0.538	0.439	0.359	0.294	0.242	0.199	0.164	0.135	0.112	0.093	0.053
22	0.647	0.522	0.422	0.342	0.278	0.226	0.184	0.150	0.123	0.101	0.083	0.046
23	0.634	0.507	0.406	0.326	0.262	0.211	0.170	0.138	0.112	0.091	0.074	0.040
24	0.622	0.492	0.390	0.310	0.247	0.197	0.158	0.126	0.102	0.082	0.066	0.035
25	0.610	0.478	0.375	0.295	0.233	0.184	0.146	0.116	0.092	0.074	0.059	0.030
26	0.598	0.464	0.361	0.281	0.220	0.172	0.135	0.106	0.084	0.066	0.053	0.026
27	0.586	0.450	0.347	0.268	0.207	0.161	0.125	0.098	0.076	0.060	0.047	0.023
28	0.574	0.437	0.333	0.255	0.196	0.150	0.116	0.090	0.069	0.054	0.042	0.020
29	0.563	0.424	0.321	0.243	0.185	0.141	0.107	0.082	0.063	0.048	0.037	0.017
30	0.552	0.412	0.308	0.231	0.174	0.131	0.099	0.075	0.057	0.044	0.033	0.015

RATE OF INTEREST IN %

TABLE 9-3   Future Value of Annuity of $1

(n) PERIODS	RATE OF INTEREST IN %											
	2	3	4	5	6	7	8	9	10	11	12	15
1	1.000	1.000	1.000	1.000	1.000	1.000	1.000	1.000	1.000	1.000	1.000	1.000
2	2.020	2.030	2.040	2.050	2.060	2.070	2.080	2.090	2.100	2.110	2.120	2.150
3	3.060	3.091	3.122	3.153	3.184	3.215	3.246	3.278	3.310	3.342	3.374	3.473
4	4.122	4.184	4.246	4.310	4.375	4.440	4.506	4.573	4.641	4.710	4.779	4.993
5	5.204	5.309	5.416	5.526	5.637	5.751	5.867	5.985	6.105	6.228	6.353	6.742
6	6.308	6.468	6.633	6.802	6.975	7.153	7.336	7.523	7.716	7.913	8.115	8.754
7	7.434	7.662	7.898	8.142	8.394	8.654	8.923	9.200	9.487	9.783	10.089	11.067
8	8.583	8.892	9.214	9.549	9.897	10.260	10.637	11.028	11.436	11.859	12.300	13.727
9	9.755	10.159	10.583	11.027	11.491	11.978	12.488	13.021	13.579	14.164	14.776	16.786
10	10.950	11.464	12.006	12.578	13.181	13.816	14.487	15.193	15.937	16.722	17.549	20.304
11	12.169	12.808	13.486	14.207	14.972	15.784	16.645	17.560	18.531	19.561	20.655	24.349
12	13.412	14.192	15.026	15.917	16.870	17.888	18.977	20.141	21.384	22.713	24.133	29.002
13	14.680	15.618	16.627	17.713	18.882	20.141	21.495	22.953	24.523	26.212	28.029	34.352
14	15.974	17.086	18.292	19.599	21.015	22.550	24.215	26.019	27.975	30.095	32.393	40.505
15	17.293	18.599	20.024	21.579	23.276	25.129	27.152	29.361	31.772	34.405	37.280	47.580
16	18.639	20.157	21.825	23.657	25.673	27.888	30.324	33.003	35.950	39.190	42.753	55.717
17	20.012	21.762	23.698	25.840	28.213	30.840	33.750	36.974	40.545	44.501	48.884	65.075
18	21.412	23.414	25.645	28.132	30.906	33.999	37.450	41.301	45.599	50.396	55.750	75.836
19	22.841	25.117	27.671	30.539	33.760	37.379	41.446	46.018	51.159	56.939	63.440	88.212
20	24.297	26.870	29.778	33.066	36.786	40.995	45.762	51.160	57.275	64.203	72.052	102.444
21	25.783	28.676	31.969	35.719	39.993	44.865	50.423	56.765	64.002	72.265	81.699	118.810
22	27.299	30.537	34.248	38.505	43.392	49.006	55.457	62.873	71.403	81.214	92.503	137.632
23	28.845	32.453	36.618	41.430	46.996	53.436	60.893	69.532	79.543	91.148	104.603	159.276
24	30.422	34.426	39.083	44.502	50.816	58.177	66.765	76.790	88.497	102.174	118.155	184.168
25	32.030	36.459	41.646	47.727	54.865	63.249	73.106	84.701	98.347	114.413	133.334	212.793
26	33.671	38.553	44.312	51.113	59.156	68.676	79.954	93.324	109.182	127.999	150.334	245.712
27	35.344	40.710	47.084	54.669	63.706	74.484	87.351	102.723	121.100	143.079	169.374	283.569
28	37.051	42.931	49.968	58.403	68.528	80.698	95.339	112.968	134.210	159.817	190.699	327.104
29	38.792	45.219	52.966	62.323	73.640	87.347	103.966	124.135	148.631	178.397	214.583	377.170
30	40.568	47.575	56.085	66.439	79.058	94.461	113.283	136.308	164.494	199.021	241.333	434.745

TABLE 9-4   Present Value of Annuity of $1

(n) PERIODS	RATE OF INTEREST IN %											
	2	3	4	5	6	7	8	9	10	11	12	15
1	0.980	0.971	0.962	0.952	0.943	0.935	0.926	0.917	0.909	0.901	0.893	0.870
2	1.942	1.913	1.886	1.859	1.833	1.808	1.783	1.759	1.736	1.713	1.690	1.626
3	2.884	2.829	2.775	2.723	2.673	2.624	2.577	2.531	2.487	2.444	2.402	2.283
4	3.808	3.717	3.630	3.546	3.465	3.387	3.312	3.240	3.170	3.102	3.037	2.855
5	4.713	4.580	4.452	4.329	4.212	4.100	3.993	3.890	3.791	3.696	3.605	3.352
6	5.601	5.417	5.242	5.076	4.917	4.767	4.623	4.486	4.355	4.231	4.111	3.784
7	6.472	6.230	6.002	5.786	5.582	5.389	5.206	5.033	5.868	4.712	4.564	4.160
8	7.325	7.020	6.733	6.463	6.210	5.971	5.747	5.535	5.335	5.146	4.968	4.487
9	8.162	7.786	7.435	7.108	6.802	6.515	6.247	5.995	5.759	5.537	5.328	4.772
10	8.983	8.530	8.111	7.722	7.360	7.024	6.710	6.418	6.145	5.889	5.650	5.019
11	9.787	9.253	8.760	8.306	7.887	7.499	7.139	6.805	6.495	6.207	5.938	5.234
12	10.575	9.954	9.385	8.863	8.384	7.943	7.536	7.161	6.814	6.492	6.194	5.421
13	11.348	10.635	9.986	9.394	8.853	8.358	7.904	7.487	7.103	6.750	6.424	5.583
14	12.106	11.296	10.563	9.899	9.295	8.745	8.244	7.786	7.367	6.982	6.628	5.724
15	12.849	11.938	11.118	10.380	9.712	9.108	8.559	8.061	7.606	7.191	6.811	5.847
16	13.578	12.561	11.652	10.838	10.106	9.447	8.851	8.313	7.824	7.379	6.974	5.954
17	14.292	13.166	12.166	11.274	10.477	9.763	9.122	8.544	8.022	7.549	7.120	6.047
18	14.992	13.754	12.659	11.690	10.828	10.059	9.372	8.756	8.201	7.702	7.250	6.128
19	15.678	14.324	13.134	12.085	11.158	10.336	9.604	8.950	8.365	7.839	7.366	6.198
20	16.351	14.877	13.590	12.462	11.470	10.594	9.818	9.129	8.514	7.963	7.469	6.259
21	17.011	15.415	14.029	12.821	11.764	10.836	10.017	9.292	8.649	8.075	7.562	6.312
22	17.658	15.937	14.451	13.163	12.042	11.061	10.201	9.442	8.772	8.176	7.645	6.359
23	18.292	16.444	14.857	13.489	12.303	11.272	10.371	9.580	8.883	8.266	7.718	6.399
24	18.914	16.936	15.247	13.799	12.550	11.469	10.529	9.707	8.985	8.348	7.784	6.434
25	19.523	17.413	15.622	14.094	12.783	11.654	10.675	9.823	9.077	8.422	7.843	6.464
26	20.121	17.877	15.983	14.375	13.003	11.826	10.810	9.929	9.161	8.488	7.896	6.491
27	20.707	18.327	16.330	14.643	13.211	11.987	10.935	10.027	9.237	8.548	7.943	6.514
28	21.281	18.764	16.663	14.898	13.406	12.137	11.051	10.116	9.307	8.602	7.984	6.534
29	21.844	19.188	16.984	15.141	13.591	12.278	11.158	10.198	9.370	8.650	8.022	6.551
30	22.396	19.600	17.292	15.372	13.765	12.409	11.258	10.274	9.427	8.694	8.055	6.566

```
A P P E N D I X   9   A
```

ACCOUNTING TOOLS: PAYROLL ACCOUNTING

LO   8

Understand the deductions and expenses for payroll accounting.

Salaries payable was one of the current liabilities discussed in Chapter 2. At the end of each accounting period, the accountant must accrue salaries that have been earned by the employees but have not yet been paid. To this point, we have not considered the accounting that must be done for payroll deductions and other payroll expenses.

Payroll deductions and expenses occur not only at year-end but every time, throughout the year, that employees are paid. The amount of cash paid for salaries and wages is the largest cash outflow for many firms. It is imperative that sufficient cash be available not only to meet the weekly or monthly payroll but also to remit the payroll taxes to the appropriate government agency when required. The purpose of this appendix is to introduce the calculations and the accounting entries that are necessary when payroll is recorded.

The issue of payroll expenses is of great concern to businesses, particularly small entrepreneurial ones. One of the large issues facing companies is how to meet the increasing cost of hiring people. Salary is just one component. How are they going to pay salaries plus benefits such as health insurance, life insurance, disability, unemployment benefits, workers' compensation, and so on? More and more companies are trying to keep their payrolls as small as possible. Unfortunately, this has been a contributing factor in the widespread layoffs throughout U.S. business.

Calculation of Gross Wages

We will cover the payroll process by indicating the basic steps that must be performed. The first step is normally to calculate the **gross wages** of all employees. The gross wage represents the wage amount before deductions. Companies often have two general classes of employees, hourly and salaried. The gross wage of each hourly employee is calculated by multiplying the number of hours worked times his or her hourly wage rate. Salaried employees are not paid on a per hour basis but at a flat rate per week, month, or year. For both hourly and salaried employees, the payroll accountant must also consider any overtime, bonus, or other salary supplement that may affect gross wages.

Calculation of Net Pay

The second step in the payroll process is to calculate the deductions from each employee's paycheck to calculate **net pay.** Deductions from the employees' checks represent a current liability to the employer because the employer must remit the amounts at a future time to the proper agency or government office, for example to the Internal Revenue Service. The deductions that are made depend on the type of company and the employee. The most important deductions are indicated in the following sections.

Income Tax

The employer must withhold federal income tax from most employees' paychecks. The amount withheld depends on the employees' earnings and the number of *exemptions* claimed by that employee. An exemption reflects the number of dependents a taxpayer can claim. The more exemptions, the lower the withholding amount required by the government. Withholding tables are available from the Internal Revenue Service to calculate the proper amount that should be withheld. This amount must be remitted to the Internal Revenue Service periodically; the frequency depends on the company's size and its payroll. Income tax withheld represents a liability to the employer and is normally classified as a current liability.

Many states also have an income tax, and the employer must often withhold additional amounts for the state tax.

FICA—Employees' Share

FICA stands for Federal Insurance Contributions Act and it is commonly called the *social securities tax.* The FICA tax is assessed on both the employee and the employer. The employees' portion must be withheld from paychecks at the applicable rate. Currently, the tax is assessed at the rate of 7.65% on the first $60,600 paid to the employee each year. Other rates and special rules apply to certain types of workers and to self-employed individuals. The amounts withheld from the employees' checks must be remitted to the federal government periodically.

FICA taxes withheld from employees' checks represent a liability to the employer until remitted. It is important to remember that the employees' portion of the FICA tax does not represent an expense to the employer.

Voluntary Deductions

If you have ever received a paycheck, you are probably aware that a variety of items was deducted from the amount you earned. Many of these are voluntary deductions chosen by the employee. They may include health insurance, pension or retirement contributions, savings plans, contributions to charities, union dues, and others. Each of these items is deducted from the employees' paychecks, held by the employer, and remitted at a future time. Therefore, each represents a current liability to the employer until remitted.

Employer Payroll Taxes

The payroll items discussed thus far do not represent expenses to the employer because they are assessed on the employees and deducted from their paychecks. However, there are taxes that the employer must pay. The two most important are FICA and unemployment taxes.

FICA—Employer's Share

The FICA tax is assessed on both the employee and the employer. The employee amount is withheld from the employees' paychecks and represents a liability but is not an expense to the employer. Normally, an equal amount is assessed on the employer. Therefore, the employer must pay an additional 7.65% of employee wages to the federal government. The employer's portion represents an expense to the employer and should be recorded in a Payroll Tax Expense account or similar type of account. This portion is a liability to the employer until it is remitted.

Unemployment Tax

Most employers must also pay unemployment taxes. This tax is designed to collect amounts from employers to fund payments to workers who lose their jobs through a program sponsored jointly by the state and federal governments. The maximum rate of unemployment taxes is 3.4%, of which 2.7% is the state portion and .7% the federal, on an employee's first $7,000 of wages earned each year. The rate is adjusted according to a company's employment history, however. If a company has been fairly stable and few of its employees have filed for employment benefits, the rate is adjusted downward.

Unemployment taxes are levied against the employer, not the employee. Therefore, the tax represents an expense to the employer and should be recorded in a Payroll Tax Expense account or similar type of account. The tax also represents a liability to the employer until it is remitted.

An Example

Assume that Felver Company has calculated the gross wages of all employees for the month of July to be $100,000. Also assume that the following amounts have been withheld from the employees' paychecks:

Income Tax	$20,000
FICA	7,000
United Way Contributions	5,000
Union Dues	3,000

In addition, assume that Felver's unemployment tax rate is 3%, that no employees have reached the $7,000 limit, and that Felver's portion of FICA matches the employees' share. Felver must make the following entries to record the payroll, to pay the employees, and to record the employer's payroll expenses.

July 31	Salary Expense	100,000	
	Salary Payable		65,000
	Income Tax Payable		20,000
	FICA Payable		7,000
	United Way Payable		5,000
	Union Dues Payable		3,000
	To record July salary and deductions.		

Assets	=	Liabilities	+	Owners' Equity
		+65,000		−100,000
		+20,000		
		+7,000		
		+5,000		
		+3,000		

July 31	Salary Payable	65,000	
	Cash		65,000
	To record payment of employee salaries.		

Assets	=	Liabilities	+	Owners' Equity
−65,000		−65,000		

July 31   Payroll Tax Expense   10,000
         FICA Payable   7,000
         Unemployment Tax Payable   3,000
      To record employer's payroll taxes.

Assets	=	Liabilities	+	Owners' Equity
		+7,000		−10,000
		+3,000		

Periodically, Felver must remit amounts to the appropriate government body or agency. The accounting entry to record remittance, assuming remittance at the end of July, is as follows.

July 31   Income Tax Payable   20,000
         FICA Payable   14,000
         United Way Payable   5,000
         Union Dues Payable   3,000
         Unemployment Tax Payable   3,000
         Cash   45,000
      To record remittance of withheld amounts.

Assets	=	Liabilities	+	Owners' Equity
−45,000		−20,000		
		−14,000		
		−5,000		
		−3,000		
		−3,000		

Compensated Absences

LO   9

Determine when compensated absences must be accrued as a liability.

Most employers allow employees to accumulate a certain number of sick days and to take a certain number of paid vacation days each year. This causes an accounting question when recording payroll amounts. When should the sick days and vacation days be treated as an expense, in the period they are earned or in the period they are taken by the employee?

The FASB has coined the term **compensated absences.** These are absences from employment, such as vacation, illness, and holidays, for which it is expected that employees will be paid. The FASB has ruled that an expense should be accrued if certain conditions are met: the services have been rendered, the rights (days) accumulate, and payment is probable and can be reasonably estimated. The result of the FASB ruling is that most employers are required to record a liability and expense for vacation days when earned, but sick days are not recorded until employees are actually absent.

Compensated absence is another example of the matching principle at work and so it is consistent with good accounting theory. Unfortunately, it has also resulted in some complex calculations and additional work for payroll accountants. Part of the complexity is due to unresolved legal issues about compensated absences. For example, in 1993 the Oregon Supreme Court ruled that an employee of Portland General Electric was entitled to use his accumulated sick time to care for a sick child. The company had maintained that the employee was legally entitled to unpaid parental leave only.

U.S. accounting standards on this issue are much more detailed and extensive than those of many foreign countries. The International Accounting Standards Committee has not issued a rule that parallels the FASB rule. As a result, U.S. companies may believe that they are subject to higher record-keeping costs than their foreign competitors.

CHAPTER HIGHLIGHTS

1. **(LO 1)** Balance sheets generally have two categories of liability, current liabilities and long-term liabilities. Current liabilities are obligations that will be satisfied within one year or within the next operating cycle.

2. **(LO 2)** Current liabilities should be valued at the face amount or the amount necessary to settle the obligation. They are not recorded at the present value because of the short time span until payment.

3. **(LO 2)** Accounts payable represent amounts owed for the purchase of inventory, goods, or services. Accounts payable usually do not require the payment of interest, but a discount may be available to encourage prompt payment.

4. **(LO 2)** The accounting for notes payable depends on the terms of the note. Some notes payable require the payment of interest at the due date. If so, accounting entries must be made to accrue interest expense to the proper periods. Interest is an expense when incurred, not when paid. Alternatively, the terms of the note may require interest to be deducted in advance. The interest deducted should initially be recorded in a Discount on Notes Payable account and transferred to interest expense over the life of the note.

5. **(LO 2)** Accrued liabilities include any amount that is owed but not actually due as of the balance sheet date. These liabilities may be grouped together in an account such as Other Accrued Liabilities.

6. **(LO 3)** The changes in current liabilities affect the cash flow statement and, for most items, are reflected in the operating activities category. Decreases in current liabilities indicate a reduction of cash; increases in current liabilities indicate an increase in cash.

7. **(LO 4)** Contingent liabilities involve an existing condition whose outcome depends on some future event. If a contingent liability is probable and the amount of loss can reasonably be estimated, it should be recorded on the balance sheet. If a contingent liability is reasonably possible, it must be disclosed but not recorded.

8. **(LO 5)** Simple interest is interest earned on the principal amount. It is often calculated by the well-known formula of principal times rate times time. Compound interest is calculated on the principal plus previous amounts of interest accumulated.

9. **(LO 6)** The future value of a single amount represents the amount of interest plus principal that will be accumulated at a future time. The future value of a single amount can be calculated by formula or by the use of Table 9-1.

10. **(LO 6)** The present value of a single amount represents the amount at a present time that is equivalent to an amount at a future time. The present value of a single amount can be calculated by formula or by the use of Table 9-2.

11. **(LO 6)** An annuity is a series of payments of equal amount. The future value of an annuity represents the amount that will be accumulated in principal and interest if a series of payments is invested for a specified time and for a specified rate. The future value of an annuity can be calculated by formula or by the use of Table 9-3.

12. **(LO 6)** The present value of an annuity represents the amount at a present time that is equivalent to a series of payments in the future that will occur for a specified time and at a specified interest or discount rate. The present value of an annuity can be calculated by formula or by the use of Table 9-4.

13. **(LO 7)** The compound interest concepts are also useful when solving for unknowns such as the number of interest periods or the interest rate on a series of payments using compound interest techniques.

14. **(LO 8)** There are two types of payroll deductions and expenses. Deductions from the employee's check are made to determine net pay and represent a current liability to the employer. Employer's payroll taxes are also assessed directly on the employer and represent an expense. (Appendix 9A)

15. **(LO 9)** Compensated absences such as sick pay and vacation pay are expenses and must be accrued by the employer if certain conditions are met. (Appendix 9A)

KEY TERMS QUIZ

Select one of the following key terms used in the chapter and fill in the appropriate blank to the left of each description. The solution appears at the end of the chapter.

Current liability
Notes payable
Current Maturities of Long-Term
  Debt
Contingent liability
Contingent asset
Time value of money
Compound interest
Present value of a single amount
Future value of an annuity
Gross wages (Appendix 9A)

Accounts payable
Discount on Notes Payable
Accrued liability
Estimated liability
Simple interest
Future value of a single amount
Annuity
Present value of an annuity
Net pay (Appendix 9A)
Compensated absences
  (Appendix 9A)

_____   1. Accounts that will be satisfied within one year or the next operating cycle.

_____   2. The amount needed at the present time to be equivalent to a series of payments and interest in the future.

_____   3. Amounts owed for the purchase of inventory, goods, or services acquired in the normal course of business.

_____   4. A contra liability account that represents interest on a loan or note deducted in advance.

_____   5. A series of payments of equal amount.

_____   6. The portion of a long-term liability that will be paid within one year of the balance sheet date.

_____   7. A liability that has been incurred but has not been paid as of the balance sheet date.

_____   8. Amounts owed that are represented by a formal contractual agreement. These amounts usually require the payment of interest.

_____   9. A liability that involves an existing condition for which the outcome is not known with certainty and depends on some future event.

_____   10. Interest that is earned or paid on the principal amount only.

_____   11. A contingent liability that is accrued and recorded on the balance sheet. Common examples are warranties, guarantees, and premium offers.

_____   12. An amount that involves an existing condition dependent on some future event by which the company stands to gain. These amounts are not normally recorded.

_____   13. Interest calculated on the principal plus previous amounts of interest accumulated.

_____   14. The concept that indicates that people should prefer to receive an immediate amount at the present time over an equal amount in the future.

_____   15. The amount that will be accumulated in the future when one amount is invested at the present time and accrues interest until the future time.

_____   16. The amount that will be accumulated in the future when a series of payments is invested and accrues interest until the future time.

————————————————— **17.** The amount at the present time that is equivalent to one amount at a future time.

————————————————— **18.** The amount of an employee's wages before deductions.

————————————————— **19.** Absences from employment such as sick days and vacation days for which it is expected that employees will be paid.

————————————————— **20.** The amount of an employee's paycheck after deductions.

ALTERNATE TERMS

ACCRUED INTEREST Interest payable.

COMPENSATED ABSENCES Accrued vacation or sick pay.

COMPOUND INTEREST Interest on interest.

CONTINGENT ASSET Contingent gain.

CURRENT LIABILITY Short-term liability.

CURRENT MATURITIES OF LONG-TERM DEBT Long-term debt, current portion.

DISCOUNTING A NOTE Interest in advance.

FICA Social Security.

FUTURE VALUE OF AN ANNUITY Amount of an annuity.

GROSS WAGES Gross pay.

INCOME TAX LIABILITY Income tax payable.

WARRANTIES Guarantees.

QUESTIONS

1. What is the definition of *current liabilities?* Why is it important to distinguish between current and long-term liabilities?
2. Most firms attempt to pay their accounts payable within the discount period to take advantage of the discount. Why is that normally a sound financial move?
3. Assume that your local bank gives you a $1,000 loan at 10% per year but deducts the interest in advance. Is 10% the "real" rate of interest that you will pay? How could the true interest rate be calculated?
4. Is the account Discount on Notes Payable an income statement or balance sheet account? Does it have a debit or credit balance?
5. A firm's year ends on December 31. Its tax is computed and submitted to the IRS on March 15 of the following year. When should the taxes be recorded as a liability?
6. What is a contingent liability? Why are contingent liabilities accounted for differently than contingent assets?
7. Many firms believe that it is very difficult to estimate the amount of a possible future contingency. Should a contingent liability be recorded even if the dollar amount of the loss is not known? Should it be disclosed in the footnotes?
8. Assume that a lawsuit has been filed against your firm. Your legal counsel has assured you that the likelihood of loss is not probable. How should the lawsuit be disclosed on the financial statements?

9. What is the difference between simple and compound interest? Would the amount of interest be higher or lower if the interest is simple rather than compound?

10. What is the effect if interest is compounded quarterly versus annually?

11. What is the meaning of the terms *present value* and *future value?* How can you determine whether to calculate the present value of an amount versus the future value?

12. What is the meaning of the word *annuity?* Could the present value of an annuity be calculated as a series of single amounts? If so, how?

13. Assume that you know the total dollar amount of a loan and the amount of the monthly payments on the loan. How could you determine the interest rate as a percentage of the loan?

14. The present value and future value concepts are applied to measure the amount of several accounts commonly encountered in accounting. What are some accounts that are valued in this manner?

15. Your employer withholds federal income tax from your paycheck and remits it to the IRS. How is the federal tax treated on the employer's financial statements? (Appendix 9A)

16. Unemployment tax is a tax on the employer rather than on the employee. How should unemployment taxes be treated on the employer's financial statements? (Appendix 9A)

17. What is the meaning of the term *compensated absences?* Give some examples. (Appendix 9A)

18. Do you agree or disagree with the following statement? "Vacation pay should be recorded as an expense when the employee takes the vacation." (Appendix 9A)

EXERCISES

(LO 1) EXERCISE 9-1 CURRENT LIABILITIES

The items listed below are accounts on Smith's balance sheet of December 31, 1995.

> Taxes Payable
>
> Accounts Receivable
>
> Notes Payable, 9%, due in 90 days
>
> Investment in Bonds
>
> Capital Stock
>
> Accounts Payable
>
> Estimated Warranty Payable in 1996
>
> Retained Earnings
>
> Trademark
>
> Mortgage Payable ($10,000 due every year until 2012)

Identify which of the above accounts should be classified as a current liability on Smith's balance sheet. For each item that is not a current liability, indicate the category of the balance sheet in which it would be classified.

(LO 1) EXERCISE 9-2 CURRENT LIABILITIES

The following items all represent liabilities on a firm's balance sheet.

a. An amount of money owed to a supplier based on the terms 2/20, net 40, for which *no* note was executed.

b. An amount of money owed to a creditor on a note due April 30, 1996.

c. An amount of money owed to a creditor on a note due August 15, 1997.

d. An amount of money owed to employees for work performed during the last week in December.

e. An amount of money owed to a bank for the use of borrowed funds due on March 1, 1996.

f. An amount of money owed to a creditor as an annual installment payment on a 10-year note.

g. An amount of money owed to the federal government, based on the company's annual income.

1. For each lettered item, state whether it should be classified as a current liability on the December 31, 1995, balance sheet. Assume that the operating cycle is shorter than one year. If the item should not be classified as a current liability, indicate where on the balance sheet it should be presented.

2. For each item identified as a current liability in part 1, state the account title that is normally used to report the item on the balance sheet.

3. Why would an investor or creditor be interested in whether an item is a current or long-term liability?

■ **REQUIRED**

(LO 1) EXERCISE 9-3 CURRENT LIABILITIES SECTION

Jensen Company had the following accounts and balances on December 31, 1995:

Income Taxes Payable	$61,250
Allowance for Doubtful Accounts	17,800
Accounts Payable	24,400
Interest Receivable	5,000
Unearned Revenue	4,320
Wages Payable	6,000
Notes Payable, 10%, due June 2, 1996	1,000
Accounts Receivable	67,500
Discount on Notes Payable	150
Current Maturities of Long-Term Debt	6,900
Interest Payable	3,010

Prepare the current liabilities section of Jensen Company's balance sheet as of December 31, 1995.

(LO 2) EXERCISE 9-4 TRANSACTION ANALYSIS

The following transactions were entered into by Ray's Sporting Goods Store during the current calendar year:

a. The firm purchased inventory on account for $40,000 from a new supplier. Assume that Ray's uses a periodic inventory system.

b. On April 1, office equipment was purchased for $5,000. A 30% down payment was made and a one-year, 10% note was signed for the balance.

c. Ray's returned $6,000 worth of inventory purchased in item a to the supplier. Ray's account was credited.

d. Ray's paid the balance owed on account for inventory purchases.

e. On July 1, Ray received $94,000 from Big Bank for which he signed a one-year note for $100,000.

f. Sales of products for the year amounted to $200,000, of which 70% was for cash and the remainder on account. In addition, state sales tax of 4% applied to all sales. The sales tax was charged to customers and must be remitted to the state next year.

g. Ray's sold 100 gift certificates that cost $20 each for cash. Sales of certificates are credited to the Sales Revenue account. At year-end, only 40% of the gift certificates had been redeemed.

■ REQUIRED

1. Record general journal entries to record items a through g.

2. Assume that Ray's accounting year ends December 31. Record all adjusting entries necessary to properly reflect the preceding items on the annual financial statements.

(LO 2) EXERCISE 9-5 CURRENT LIABILITIES AND RATIOS

Listed below are several accounts that appeared on Heartroy's 1995 balance sheet.

Accounts Payable	$ 55,000
Marketable Securities	40,000
Accounts Receivable	180,000
Notes Payable, 12%, due in 60 days	20,000
Capital Stock	1,150,000
Salaries Payable	10,000
Cash	15,000
Equipment	950,000
Taxes Payable	15,000
Retained Earnings	250,000
Inventory	85,000
Allowance for Doubtful Accounts	20,000
Land	600,000

■ REQUIRED

1. Prepare the current liabilities section of Heartroy's 1995 balance sheet.

2. Compute Heartroy's working capital.

3. Compute Heartroy's current ratio. What does this ratio indicate about Heartroy's condition?

(LO 2) EXERCISE 9-6 DISCOUNTS

Each of the following situations involves the use of discounts.

1. Calculate the dollar amount of discount available in each transaction.

    a. A company buys printing supplies costing $100 subject to terms of 2/10, net 30.

    b. A company buys equipment costing $1,500 subject to terms of 3/15, net 30.

2. Calculate the discount *rate* for each transaction.

   a. A company bought printing supplies costing $800 on credit and paid the account within the discount period for $776.

   b. A company bought equipment costing $1,000 on credit and paid for it within the discount period for $955.

3. Refer to parts 1A and 1B. On an annualized basis, what returns does the company receive by taking the discounts?

(LO 2) EXERCISE 9-7 NOTES PAYABLE AND INTEREST

On July 1, 1995, Jo's Flower Shop borrowed $25,000 from the bank. Jo signed a 10-month, 9% promissory note for the entire amount. Jo's uses a calendar year-end.

1. Prepare the journal entry on July 1 to record the promissory note.   ■ REQUIRED

2. Prepare any adjusting entries needed at year-end.

3. Prepare the journal entry on May 1 to record the payment of principal and interest.

(LO 4) EXERCISE 9-8 WARRANTIES

Jet Corporation manufactures and sells dishwashers. Jet provides all customers with a two-year warranty guaranteeing to repair, free of charge, any defects reported during this time period. During the year, it sold 100,000 dishwashers, for $300 each. Analysis of past warranty records indicates that 15% of all sales will be returned for repair within the warranty period. Jet expects to incur expenditures of $10 to repair each dishwasher. The account Estimated Liability for Warranties had a credit balance of $110,000 on January 1. Jet incurred $140,000 in actual expenditures during the year.

   Prepare all journal entries necessary to record the events related to the warranty ■ REQUIRED
transactions during the year. Determine the adjusted ending balance in the Estimated Liability for Warranties account.

(LO 5) EXERCISE 9-9 SIMPLE VERSUS COMPOUND INTEREST

Part 1. For each of the following notes, calculate the simple interest due at the end of the term.

NOTE	FACE VALUE (PRINCIPAL)	RATE	TERM
1.	$10,000	4%	6 years
2.	10,000	6%	4 years
3.	10,000	8%	3 years

Part 2. Now assume that the interest on the notes are compounded annually. Calculate the amount of interest due at the end of the term for each note. What conclusion can you draw from a comparison of your results in part 1 and part 2?

(LO 6) EXERCISE 9-10 PRESENT VALUE, FUTURE VALUE

Nolan, Inc., estimates it will need $150,000 in 10 years to expand its manufacturing facilities. A bank has agreed to pay Nolan 5% interest, compounded annually, if it deposits the entire amount now needed to accumulate $150,000 in 10 years. How much money does Nolan need to deposit now?

(LO 6) EXERCISE 9-11 EFFECT OF COMPOUNDING PERIOD

Roon Company deposited $1,000 in the bank on January 1, 1995, earning 8% interest. Roon Company withdraws the deposit plus accumulated interest on January 1, 1997. Compute the amount of money Roon withdraws from the bank, assuming interest is compounded (a) annually, (b) semiannually, and (c) quarterly.

(LO 6) EXERCISE 9-12 PRESENT VALUE, FUTURE VALUE

The following situations involve time value of money calculations.

1. A deposit of $7,000 is made on January 1, 1995. The deposit will earn interest at a rate of 8%. How much will be accumulated on January 1, 2000, assuming interest is compounded (a) annually, (b) semiannually, and (c) quarterly?

2. A deposit is made on January 1, 1995, to earn interest at an annual rate of 8%. The deposit will accumulate to $15,000 by January 1, 2000. How much money was originally deposited, assuming interest is compounded (a) annually, (b) semi-annually, and (c) quarterly?

(LO 6) EXERCISE 9-13 PRESENT VALUE, FUTURE VALUE

The following are situations requiring the application of the time value of money.

1. On January 1, 1995, $16,000 is deposited. Assuming a 8% interest rate, calculate the amount accumulated on January 1, 2000, if interest is compounded (a) annually, (b) semiannually, and (c) quarterly.

2. Assume that a deposit made on January 1, 1995, earns 8% interest. The deposit plus interest accumulated to $20,000 on January 1, 2000. How much was invested on January 1, 1995, if interest was compounded (a) annually, (b) semiannually, and (c) quarterly?

(LO 7) EXERCISE 9-14 ANNUITY

Rick Spaulding has decided to start saving for his son's college education by depositing $1,000 at the end of every year for 15 years. A bank has agreed to pay interest at the rate of 4% compounded annually. How much will Rick have in the bank immediately after his 15th deposit?

(LO 7) EXERCISE 9-15 CALCULATION OF YEARS

Julie Smith has decided to start saving for her daughter's college education. She wants to accumulate $30,000. The bank will pay interest at the rate of 4% compounded annually. If Julie plans to make payments of $2,000 at the end of each year, how long will it take her to accumulate $30,000?

(LO 7) EXERCISE 9-16 VALUE OF PAYMENTS

Pat Coop signs an agreement to buy a car that requires Pat to pay $2,000 at the end of each year for eight years. The car dealer used a 12% rate, compounded annually, to determine the amount of the payments. What should Pat consider to be the value of the car?

(LO 8) EXERCISE 9-17 PAYROLL ENTRIES (Appendix 9A)

The following items relate to Costner Corporation's payroll for the month of January:

Gross Salaries and Wages	$500,000
Federal Income Tax Rate	28%
State Income Tax Rate	5%
FICA Tax Rate	7.65%
Federal Unemployment Rate	.7%
State Unemployment Rate	2.7%

All tax rates should be computed as a percentage of gross salaries and wages. Additional deductions amounted to $10,000 for health insurance and $1,200 for union dues. No employee has earned more than $6,000 for the current year.

■ REQUIRED

1. Prepare the journal entry to record salaries and wages for Costner Corporation's January payroll.
2. Prepare the entry to record the employer's portion of payroll taxes for the January payroll.

(LO 8) EXERCISE 9-18 PAYROLL, EMPLOYER'S PORTION (Appendix 9A)

Stein's Bakery Shop has six employees on its payroll. Payroll records include the following information on employee earnings:

NAME	EARNINGS FROM 1/1 TO 6/30/1995	EARNINGS FOR 3RD QUARTER, 1995
Dell	$ 23,490	$11,710
Fin	4,240	2,660
Hook	34,100	15,660
Patty	51,000	26,200
Tuss	30,050	19,350
Woo	6,300	3,900
Totals	$149,180	$79,480

FICA taxes are levied at 7.65% on the first $60,600 of the current year's earnings. The unemployment tax rates are .7% for federal and 2.7% for state unemployment. Assume that unemployment taxes are levied on the first $7,000 of current year's earnings.

■ REQUIRED

1. Calculate the employer's portion of payroll taxes incurred by Stein's Bakery for each employee for the third quarter of 1995. Round your answers to the nearest dollar.
2. Prepare the journal entry that Stein's should make to record the employer's portion of payroll taxes.

(LO 9) EXERCISE 9-19 COMPENSATED ABSENCES (Appendix 9A)

Feather, Inc., has a monthly payroll of $72,000 for its 24 employees. In addition to their salary, employees earn one day of vacation and one sick day for each month that they work. There are 20 workdays in a month. Prepare the end-of-the-month journal entry, if necessary, to record (a) vacation benefits and (b) sick days. From the owner's perspective, should the company offer the employees vacation and sick pay that accumulates year to year?

MULTI-CONCEPT EXERCISES

(LO 6, 7) EXERCISE 9-20 COMPARE ALTERNATIVES

Allison Bower has won the lottery and has four options for receiving her winnings:

1. Receive $100,000 at the beginning of the current year.
2. Receive $108,000 at the end of the year.

3. Receive $20,000 at the end of each year for 8 years.

4. Receive $10,000 at the end of each year for 30 years.

Allison can invest her winnings at an interest rate of 9% compounded annually at a major bank. Which of the payment options should Allison choose?

(LO 6, 7) EXERCISE 9-21 TWO SITUATIONS

The following situations involve the application of the time value of money concept.

1. Solomon Company just purchased a piece of equipment with a value of $53,300. Solomon financed this purchase with a loan from the bank and must make annual loan payments of $13,000 at the end of each year for the next five years. Interest is compounded annually on the loan. What is the interest rate on the bank loan?

2. Sandstrom Company needs to accumulate $200,000 to repay bonds due in six years. Sandstrom estimates it can save $13,300 at the end of each semiannual period at a local bank offering an annual interest rate of 8% compounded semiannually. Will Sandstrom have enough money saved at the end of six years to repay the bonds?

PROBLEMS

(LO 2) PROBLEM 9-1 NOTES AND INTEREST

During 1995 Puckett Corporation entered into the following transactions involving notes payable. Puckett makes all adjusting entries at fiscal year-end, which is September 30.

a. January 1: Signed a one-year, 12% loan for $50,000. Interest on the note is paid semiannually. The loan principal is to be repaid on the due date.

b. January 15: Signed an agreement that established a $450,000 line of credit. The agreement stipulates that a 10% interest rate will be charged on all borrowed funds.

c. April 1: Borrowed $200,000 using the established line of credit.

d. April 15: Signed a 90-day non-interest-bearing note for $10,000. Interest at the rate of 8% per year is deducted in advance by the bank.

e. July 1: Repaid $100,000 of the line of credit, plus accrued interest.

f. July 1: Paid accrued interest on the term loan.

g. July 14: Repaid the non-interest-bearing note in item d on the due date.

h. August 1: Borrowed an additional $300,000 using the established line of credit.

i. September 30: Made all necessary adjusting entries.

j. December 31: Repaid the one-year term loan principal plus interest.

■ REQUIRED   Record all the journal entries necessary to reflect the preceding transactions. For purposes of interest calculations, assume a 360-day year.

(LO 4) PROBLEM 9-2 WARRANTIES

Juraska Company manufactures and sells high-quality television sets. The most popular line sells for $1,000 each and is accompanied by a three-year warranty to repair, free of charge, any defective unit. Average costs to repair each defective unit will be

$90 for replacement parts and $60 for labor. Juraska estimates that warranty costs of $12,600 will be incurred during 1995. The company actually sold 600 television sets and incurred replacement part costs of $3,600 and labor costs of $5,400 during the year. The adjusted 1995 ending balance in the Estimated Liability for Warranties account is $10,200.

1. How many defective units from this year's sales does Juraska Company estimate will be returned for repair?

2. What percentage of sales does Juraska Company estimate will be returned for repair?

■ **REQUIRED**

(LO 4) PROBLEM 9-3 WARRANTIES

Bombeck Company sells a product for $1,500. When the customer buys it, Bombeck provides a one-year warranty. Bombeck sold 120 products during 1995. Based on analysis of past warranty records, Bombeck estimates that repairs will average 3% of total sales.

1. Prepare the journal entry to record the estimated liability.

■ **REQUIRED**

2. Assume that products under warranty must be repaired during 1995 using repair parts from inventory costing $4,950. Prepare the journal entry to record the repair of products.

(LO 5) PROBLEM 9-4 COMPARISON OF SIMPLE AND COMPOUND INTEREST

On June 30, 1995, Reaves, Inc., borrowed $25,000 from its bank, signing a 7%, two-year note.

1. Assuming that the bank charges simple interest on the note, prepare the journal entry Reaves will record on each of the following dates:

■ **REQUIRED**

December 31, 1995

December 31, 1996

June 30, 1997

2. Assume instead the bank charges 7% on the note, which is compounded semiannually. Prepare the necessary journal entries on the dates in part 1.

3. What amount of additional interest expense is recognized in part 2 over part 1?

(LO 6) PROBLEM 9-5 INVESTMENT WITH VARYING INTEREST RATE

Shari Thompson invested $1,000 in a financial institution on January 1, 1995. She leaves her investment in the institution until December 31, 1999. How much money does Shari accumulate if she earned interest, compounded annually, at the following rates?

1995	4%
1996	5
1997	6
1998	7
1999	8

(LO 6) PROBLEM 9-6 COMPARISON OF ALTERNATIVES

Compare the following options using the time value of money concept. (Hint: Calculate the present values as of January 1, 1995.) Assume that interest can be earned at an annual rate of 7%.

1. Receive $150,000 on January 1, 1995.

2. Receive $170,000 on January 1, 1997.

3. Receive $170,000 on December 31, 1996.

4. Receive four annual payments of $40,000 beginning on December 31, 1995.

5. Receive three annual payments of $62,000 beginning on December 31, 1996.

(LO 8) PROBLEM 9-7 PAYROLL ENTRIES (Appendix 9A)

Waters Company has calculated the gross wages of all employees for the month of August to be $170,000. The following amounts have been withheld from the employee's paychecks:

Income Tax	$34,000
FICA	12,000
Heart Fund Contributions	5,000
Union Dues	3,500

Waters' unemployment tax rate is 3%, and its portion of FICA matches the employees' share.

■ REQUIRED

1. Prepare the journal entry to record the payroll as an amount payable to employees.

2. Prepare the journal entry that would be recorded to pay the employees.

3. Prepare the journal entry to record the employer's payroll costs.

4. Prepare the journal entry to remit the withholdings.

(LO 9) PROBLEM 9-8 COMPENSATED ABSENCES (Appendix 9A)

TPL, Inc., pays its employees every Friday. For every four weeks that employees work, they earn one vacation day. For every six weeks that they work without calling in sick, they earn one sick day. If employees quit or retire, they can receive a lump-sum payment for their unused vacation days and unused sick days.

■ REQUIRED

Write a short memo to the bookkeeper explaining how and when he should record vacation and sick days. Explain how the matching principle applies and why you believe that the timing you recommend is appropriate.

MULTI-CONCEPT PROBLEMS

(LO 2, 5) PROBLEM 9-9 INTEREST IN ADVANCE VERSUS INTEREST PAID WHEN LOAN IS DUE

On July 1, 1995, Lewis Company needs exactly $103,200 in cash to pay an existing obligation. Lewis has decided to borrow from State Bank, which charges 14% interest on loans. The loan will be due in one year. Lewis is unsure, however, whether to ask the bank for (a) an interest-bearing loan with interest and principal payable at the end of the year or (b) a loan due in one year but with interest deducted in advance.

■ REQUIRED

1. What will be the face value of the note assuming that

   a. interest is paid when the loan is due?

   b. interest is deducted in advance?

2. Calculate the effective interest rate on the note assuming that

   a. interest is paid when the loan is due.

   b. interest is deducted in advance.

3. Assume that Lewis negotiates and signs the one-year note with the bank on July 1, 1995. Also assume that Lewis's accounting year ends December 31. Prepare all the journal entries necessary to record the issuance of the note and the interest on the note, assuming that

   a. interest is paid when the loan is due.

   b. interest is deducted in advance.

4. Prepare the appropriate balance sheet presentation for July 1, 1995, immediately after the note has been issued, assuming that

   a. interest is paid when the loan is due.

   b. interest is deducted in advance.

(LO 1, 4) PROBLEM 9-10 CONTINGENT LIABILITIES

Listed below are several items for which the outcome of events is unknown at year-end.

a. A company is being sued in connection with a safety hazard that exists in one of its manufactured products. The company's legal counsel believes that an unfavorable verdict is reasonably possible and has provided an estimate of the amount of the possible loss.

b. A company sells ovens and extends a one-year warranty to all customers. Management estimates that 5% of all sales will require repair within the warranty period.

c. A company is being sued for patent infringement. The company's legal counsel believes that an unfavorable verdict is unlikely but if the company loses the lawsuit, it will have to pay a large dollar amount.

d. A cereal manufacturer has included a premium offer available to purchasers. The manufacturer estimates that 50% of the offers will be redeemed at a cost of $1 each.

e. A company is involved in a tax dispute with the IRS. The company's tax experts and legal counsel believe that a $200,000 refund will probably be awarded to the company.

1. Identify which of the items a through e should be recorded at year-end.

2. Identify which of the items a through e should not be recorded but should be disclosed on the year-end financial statements.

■ REQUIRED

(LO 6, 7) PROBLEM 9-11 FOUR SITUATIONS

The following situations involve the application of the time value of money concept.

a. Janelle Carter deposited $9,750 in the bank on January 1, 1978, at an interest rate of 11% compounded annually. How much has accumulated in the account by January 1, 1995?

b. Mike Smith deposited $21,600 in the bank on January 1, 1985. On January 2, 1995, this deposit has accumulated to $42,487. Interest is compounded annually on the account. What is the rate of interest that Mike earned on the deposit?

c. Lee Spony made a deposit in the bank on January 1, 1988. The bank pays interest at the rate of 8% compounded annually. On January 1, 1995, the deposit has accumulated to $15,000. How much money did Lee originally deposit on January 1, 1988?

d. Nancy Holmes deposited $5,800 in the bank on January 1 a few years ago. The bank pays an interest rate of 10% compounded annually, and the deposit is now worth $15,026. How many years has the deposit been invested?

(LO 6, 7) PROBLEM 9-12 COMPARISON OF ALTERNATIVES

Jeanne's uncle has decided to give her money as a college graduation gift. He has given Jeanne three options on how she may receive the gift.

a. Receive $900 immediately. Assume that interest is compounded semiannually.

b. Receive $400 at the end of each year for three years. Assume that interest is compounded annually.

c. Receive $197 at the end of each six-month period for three years. Assume that interest is compounded semiannually.

■ REQUIRED Using future value calculations, decide which option allows Jeanne to receive the maximum gift. Assume that an annual interest rate of 10% can be earned on the money received.

ALTERNATE PROBLEMS

(LO 2) PROBLEM 9-1A NOTES AND INTEREST

During 1995 Packett Corporation entered into the following transactions involving notes payable. Packett makes all adjusting entries at fiscal year-end, which is September 30.

a. January 1: Signed a one-year, 12% loan for $100,000. Interest on the note is paid semiannually. The loan principal is to be repaid on the due date.

b. January 15: Signed an agreement that established a $900,000 line of credit. The agreement stipulates that a 10% interest rate will be charged on all borrowed funds.

c. April 1: Borrowed $400,000 using the established line of credit.

d. April 15: Signed a 90-day non-interest-bearing note for $20,000. Interest at the rate of 8% per year is deducted in advance by the bank.

e. July 1: Repaid $200,000 of the line of credit, plus accrued interest.

f. July 1: Paid accrued interest on the term loan.

g. July 14: Repaid the non-interest-bearing note in item d on the due date.

h. August 1: Borrowed an additional $600,000 using the established line of credit.

i. September 30: Made all necessary adjusting entries.

j. December 31: Repaid the one-year term loan principal plus interest.

■ REQUIRED Record all the journal entries necessary to reflect the preceding transactions. For purposes of interest calculations, assume a 360-day year.

(LO 4) PROBLEM 9-2A WARRANTIES

Rusk Company manufactures and sells high-quality stereo sets. The most popular line sells for $2,000 each and is accompanied by a three-year warranty to repair, free of charge, any defective unit. Average costs to repair each defective unit will be $180 for replacement parts and $120 for labor. Rusk estimates that warranty costs of $25,200 will be incurred during 1995. The company actually sold 600 sets and incurred replacement part costs of $7,200 and labor costs of $10,800 during the year. The adjusted 1995 ending balance in the Estimated Liability for Warranties account is $20,400.

■ REQUIRED

1. How many defective units from this year's sales does Rusk Company estimate will be returned for repair?

2. What percent of sales does Rusk Company estimate will be returned for repair?

(LO 4) PROBLEM 9-3A WARRANTIES

Beck Company sells a product for $3,000. When the customer buys it, Beck provides a one-year warranty. Beck sold 120 products during 1995. Based on analysis of past warranty records, Beck estimates that repairs will average 3% of total sales.

■ REQUIRED

1. Prepare the journal entry to record the estimated liability.

2. Assume during 1995 that products under warranty must be repaired using repair parts from inventory costing $9,800. Prepare the journal entry to record the repair of products.

3. Assume that the balance of the Estimated Liabilities for Warranties account as of the beginning of 1995 was an $800 credit. Calculate the balance of the account as of the end of 1995.

(LO 5) PROBLEM 9-4A COMPARISON OF SIMPLE AND COMPOUND INTEREST

On June 30, 1995, Rolls, Inc., borrowed $25,000 from its bank, signing a 6% note. Principal and interest are due at the end of two years.

■ REQUIRED

1. Assuming the note earns simple interest for the bank, calculate the amount of interest accrued on each of the following dates:
      December 31, 1995
      December 31, 1996
      June 30, 1997

2. Assume instead that the note earns 6% for the bank, but is compounded semiannually. Calculate the amount of interest accrued on the same dates as part 1.

3. What amount of additional interest expense is recognized in part 2 over part 1?

(LO 6) PROBLEM 9-5A INVESTMENT WITH VARYING INTEREST RATE

Trena Thompson invested $2,000 in a financial institution on January 1, 1995. She leaves her investment in the institution until December 31, 1999. How much money did Trena accumulate if she earned interest, compounded annually, at the following rates?

1995	4%
1996	5
1997	6
1998	7
1999	8

(LO 6) PROBLEM 9-6A COMPARISON OF ALTERNATIVES

Compare the following options using the time value of money concept. (Hint: Calculate the present values as of January 1, 1995.) Assume that interest can be earned at an annual rate of 7%.

1. Receive $300,000 on January 1, 1995.

2. Receive $340,000 on January 1, 1997.

3. Receive $340,000 on December 31, 1996.

4. Receive four annual payments of $80,000 beginning on December 31, 1995.

5. Receive three annual payments of $124,000 beginning on December 31, 1996.

(LO 8) PROBLEM 9-7A PAYROLL ENTRIES (Appendix 9A)

Watts Company has calculated the gross wages of all employees for the month of August to be $340,000. The following amounts have been withheld from the employee's paychecks:

Income Tax	$68,000
FICA	24,000
Heart Fund Contributions	10,000
Union Dues	7,000

Watts' unemployment tax rate is 3% and its portion of FICA matches the employees' share.

■ REQUIRED

1. Prepare the journal entry to record the payroll as an amount payable to employees.

2. Prepare the journal entry that would be recorded to pay the employees.

3. Prepare the journal entry to record the employer's payroll costs.

4. Prepare the journal entry to remit the withholdings, including FICA, and the unemployment tax.

(LO 9) PROBLEM 9-8A COMPENSATED ABSENCES (Appendix 9A)

Assume that you are the accountant for a large company with several divisions. The divisional manager of Division B has contacted you with a concern. During 1995, several employees retired from Division B. The company's policy is that employees can be paid for days of sick leave accrued at the time they retire. Payment occurs in the year following retirement. The divisional manager has been told by corporate headquarters that she cannot replace the employees in 1996 because the payment of the accrued sick pay will be deducted from Division B's budget in that year.

■ REQUIRED

Write a memo to the manager of Division B that explains the proper accounting for accrued sick pay. Do you think that the policies of corporate headquarters should be revised?

ALTERNATE MULTI-CONCEPT PROBLEMS

(LO 2, 5) PROBLEM 9-9A INTEREST IN ADVANCE VERSUS INTEREST PAID WHEN LOAN IS DUE

On July 1, 1995, Lever Company needs exactly $206,400 in cash to pay an existing obligation. Lever has decided to borrow from State Bank, which charges 14% interest on loans. The loan will be due in one year. Lever is unsure, however, whether to ask the bank for (a) an interest-bearing loan with interest and principal payable at the end of the year or (b) a non-interest-bearing loan due in one year but with interest deducted in advance.

■ REQUIRED

1. What will be the face value of the note, assuming that
   a. interest is paid when the loan is due?
   b. interest is deducted in advance?

2. Calculate the effective interest rate on the note, assuming that
   a. interest is paid when the loan is due.
   b. interest is deducted in advance.

3. Assume that Lever negotiates and signs the one-year note with the bank on July 1, 1995. Also assume that Lever's accounting year ends December 31. Prepare all the journal entries necessary to record the issuance of the note and the interest on it, assuming that

a. interest is paid when the loan is due.

b. interest is deducted in advance.

4. Prepare the appropriate balance sheet presentation for July 1, 1995, immediately after the note has been issued, assuming that

a. interest is paid when the loan is due.

b. interest is deducted in advance.

(LO 1, 4) PROBLEM 9-10A CONTINGENT LIABILITIES

Listed below are several events for which the outcome is unknown at year-end.

a. A company sells ovens and extends a one-year warranty to all customers. Management estimates that 5% of all sales will require repair within the warranty period.

b. A company is being sued for patent infringement. Its legal counsel believes that an unfavorable verdict is unlikely, but if the company loses, it will have to pay a large dollar amount.

c. A candy manufacturer has included a premium offer available to consumers who purchase it. The manufacturer estimates that 50% of the offers will be redeemed at a cost of $1 each.

d. A company is involved in a tax dispute with the IRS. The company's tax experts and legal counsel believe that a $400,000 refund will probably be awarded to the company.

e. A company is being sued in connection with a safety hazard that exists in one of its manufactured products. The company's legal counsel believes that it is reasonably possible that an unfavorable verdict will be rendered and has provided an estimate of the amount of the possible loss.

1. Identify which of the items a through e should be recorded at year-end.

2. Identify which of the items a through e should not be recorded but should be disclosed on the year-end financial statements.

■ REQUIRED

(LO 6, 7) PROBLEM 9-11A FOUR SITUATIONS

The following situations involve the application of the time value of money concept.

a. Jan Cain deposited $19,500 in the bank on January 1, 1978, at an interest rate of 11% compounded annually. How much has been accumulated in the account by January 1, 1995?

b. Mark Schultz deposited $43,200 in the bank on January 1, 1985. On January 2, 1995, this deposit has accumulated to $84,974. Interest is compounded annually on the account. What is the rate of interest that Mark earned on the deposit?

c. Les Hinckle made a deposit in the bank on January 1, 1988. The bank pays interest at the rate of 8% compounded annually. On January 1, 1995, the deposit has accumulated to $30,000. How much money did Les originally deposit on January 1, 1988?

d. Val Hooper deposited $11,600 in the bank on January 1 a few years ago. The bank pays an interest rate of 10% compounded annually, and the deposit is now worth $30,052. For how many years has the deposit been invested?

(LO 6, 7) PROBLEM 9-12A COMPARISON OF ALTERNATIVES

Jack's uncle has decided to give him money as a college graduation gift. He has given Jack three options on how he may receive the gift.

a. Receive $2,000 immediately. Assume that interest is compounded semiannually.

b. Receive $1,200 at the end of each year for three years. Assume that interest is compounded annually.

c. Receive $394 at the end of each six-month period for three years. Assume that interest is compounded semiannually.

■ **REQUIRED**

Using future value calculations, decide which option allows Jack to receive the maximum gift. Assume that an annual interest rate of 10% can be earned on the money received.

CASES

READING AND INTERPRETING FINANCIAL STATEMENTS

(LO 1, 2, 4) CASE 9-1 ANALYSIS OF CURRENT LIABILITIES

Refer to the Ben & Jerry's annual report and write a response to the following questions based on Ben & Jerry's balance sheet.

1. Ben & Jerry's total current liabilities increased from $12.7 million in 1991 to $17.5 million in 1992. What were the major factors that caused the increase in current liabilities during that time period?

2. Does the increase in Ben & Jerry's current liabilities indicate that the firm was experiencing liquidity problems? What numbers or ratios could be used to determine its liquidity?

3. Refer to footnote number 4. What amounts are included in the category Accounts Payable and Accrued Expenses?

4. The amount listed as Current Portion of Long-Term Debt and Obligations under Capital Lease increased from $514,905 in 1991 to $628,098 in 1992. What do those amounts represent? Does the increase from 1991 to 1992 mean that Ben & Jerry's has been unable to pay its loan commitments as they come due?

(LO 3) CASE 9-2 BEN & JERRY'S CASH FLOW STATEMENT

1. Ben & Jerry's balance sheet indicates that accounts payable and accrued expenses increased by $4,907,611. Where is this amount shown on the statement of cash flows? Does it represent an increase or decrease in cash?

2. In 1991, Ben & Jerry's borrowed $8,900,000 of short-term debt and also repaid that amount. Which category of the statement of cash flows presents those amounts? For the purposes of the statement of cash flows, does it matter whether the borrowings were short-term or long-term?

3. Ben & Jerry's December 28, 1991, balance sheet indicated an amount as income tax payable. When this amount is paid, should it be disclosed in the operating category of the statement of cash flows?

(LO 4) CASE 9-3 FORD MOTOR COMPANY'S CONTINGENT LIABILITIES

The following is an excerpt from Ford's 1992 annual report (italics have been added for emphasis):

> Various legal actions, governmental investigations and proceedings and claims are pending or may be instituted or asserted in the future against the company and its subsidiaries, including those arising out of alleged defects in the company's products, governmental regulations relating to safety, emissions and fuel economy, financial services, intellectual property rights, product warranties and environmental matters. . . .
>
> Litigation is subject to many uncertainties, the outcome of individual litigated matters is not predictable with assurance, and it is *reasonably possible* that some of the foregoing matters could be decided unfavorably to the company or the subsidiary involved. Although the amount of liability at December 31, 1992 with respect to these matters cannot be ascertained, the company believes that any resulting liability should not *materially* affect the consolidated financial position of the company. . . .

■ REQUIRED

After reading this footnote to the financial statements, what accounts would you look for in the balance sheet? income statement? Explain the significance of the words in italics in the excerpt. How did these words affect the way in which Ford reported its contingent liabilities?

MAKING FINANCIAL DECISIONS

(LO 1, 2) CASE 9-4 CURRENT RATIO LOAN PROVISION

Assume that you are the controller of a small, growing sporting goods company. The prospects for your firm in the future are quite good, but, like most firms, it has been experiencing some cash flow difficulties because all available funds have been used to purchase inventory and finance start-up costs associated with a new business. At the beginning of the current year, your local bank advanced a loan to your company. Included in the loan is the following provision.

> The company is obligated to pay interest payments each month for the next five years. Principal is due and must be paid at the end of Year 5. The company is further obligated to maintain a current assets to current liabilities ratio of 2 to 1 as indicated on quarterly statements to be submitted to the bank. If the company fails to meet any loan provisions, all amounts of interest and principal are due immediately upon notification by the bank.

You, as controller, have just gathered the following information as of the end of the first month of the current quarter.

Current Liabilities:	
Accounts Payable	$400,000
Taxes Payable	100,000
Accrued Expenses	50,000
Total Current Liabilities	$550,000

You are concerned about the loan provision that requires a 2-to-1 ratio of current assets to current liabilities.

■ REQUIRED

1. Indicate what actions could be taken during the next two months to meet the loan provision. Which of the available actions should be recommended?

2. What is the meaning of the term *window-dressing* financial statements? What are the long-run implications of actions taken to window-dress financial statements?

(LO 5) CASE 9-5 ALTERNATIVE PAYMENT OPTIONS

Kathy Adams owns a small company that makes ice machines for restaurants and food-service facilities. Kathy knows a lot about producing ice machines but is less familiar with the best terms to extend to her customers. One customer is opening a new business and has asked Kathy to consider any of the following options to pay for his new $20,000 ice machine.

a. Term 1: 10% down, the remainder paid at the end of the year plus 8% simple interest.

b. Term 2: 10% down, the remainder paid at the end of the year plus 8% interest, compounded quarterly.

c. Term 3: $0 down but $21,600 at the end of the year.

■ REQUIRED   Make a recommendation to Kathy. She believes that 8% is a fair return on her money at this time. Should she accept option a, b, or c, or take the $20,000 cash at the time of the sale? Justify your recommendation with calculations. What factors, other than the actual amount of cash received from the sale, should be considered?

ACCOUNTING AND ETHICS: WHAT WOULD YOU DO?

(LO 4) CASE 9-6 WARRANTY COST ESTIMATE

John Walsh is an accountant for ABC Auto Dealers, a large auto dealership in a metropolitan area. ABC sells both new and used cars. New cars are sold with a five-year warranty, the cost of which is carried by the manufacturer. For several years, however, ABC has offered a two-year warranty on used cars. The cost of the warranty is an expense to ABC, and John has been asked by his boss, Mr. Seaver, to review warranty costs and recommend the amount to accrue on the year-end financial statements.

For the past several years, ABC has recorded as warranty expense 5% of used car sales. John has analyzed past repair records and found that repairs, although fluctuating somewhat from year to year, have averaged near the 5% level. John is convinced, however, that 5% is inadequate for the coming year. He bases his judgment on industry reports of increased repair costs and on the fact that ABC has recently sold several cars on warranty that have experienced very high repair costs. John believes that the current year's repair accrual must be at least 10%. He discussed the higher expense amount with Mr. Seaver, who is controller of ABC.

Mr. Seaver was not happy with John's decision concerning warranty expense. He reminded John of the need to control expenses during the recent sales downturn. He also reminded John that ABC is seeking a large loan from the bank and the bank loan officers would not be happy with recent operating results, especially if ABC begins to accrue larger amounts for future estimated amounts such as warranties. Finally, Mr. Seaver reminded John that most of the employees of ABC, including Mr. Seaver, were members of the company's profit-sharing plan and would not be happy with the reduced share of profits. Mr. Seaver thanked John for his judgment concerning warranty cost but told him that the accrual for the current year would remain at 5%.

John left the meeting with Mr. Seaver somewhat frustrated. He was convinced that his judgment concerning the warranty costs was correct. He knew that the owner of ABC would be visiting the office next week and wondered whether he should discuss the matter with him personally at that time. John also had met one of the loan officers from the bank several times and considered calling her to discuss his concern about the warranty expense amount on the year-end statements.

Discuss the courses of action available to John. What should John do concerning his judgment of warranty costs?

■ REQUIRED

(LO 4) CASE 9-7 RETAINER FEES AS SALES

Bunch'o Ballons markets ballon arrangements to companies who wish to thank clients and employees. They have a unique style that has put them in high demand. Consequently, Bunch'o Ballons has asked clients to establish an account with them. Clients are asked to pay a retainer fee equal to about three months of client purchases. The fee will be used to cover the cost of arrangements delivered and will be reevaluated at the end of each month. At the end of the current month Bunch'o Ballons has $43,900 of retainer fees in its possession. The controller is anxious to show this amount as sales because "it represents certain sales for the company."

Do you agree with the controller? When should the sales be recorded? Why would the controller be anxious to record the cash receipts as sales?

■ REQUIRED

ANALYTICAL SOFTWARE CASE

To the Student: Your instructor may assign one or more parts of the analytical software case that is designed to accompany this chapter. This multi-part case gives you a chance to work with real financial statement data using software that stimulates, guides, and hones your analytical and problem-solving skills. It was created especially to support and strengthen your understanding of the chapter's Learning Objectives.

SOLUTION TO KEY TERMS QUIZ

1. Current liability (p. 474)
2. Present value of an annuity (p. 493)
3. Accounts payable (p. 474)
4. Discount on Notes Payable (p. 477)
5. Annuity (p. 491)
6. Current Maturities of Long-Term Debt (p. 478)
7. Accrued liability (p. 479)
8. Notes payable (p. 476)
9. Contingent liability (p. 482)
10. Simple interest (p. 486)
11. Estimated liability (p. 482)
12. Contingent asset (p. 485)
13. Compound interest (p. 487)
14. Time value of money (p. 486)
15. Future value of a single amount (p. 488)
16. Future value of an annuity (p. 492)
17. Present value of a single amount (p. 490)
18. Gross wages (p. 503)
19. Compensated absences (p. 506)
20. Net pay (p. 503)

Focus on Financial Results

When you think of debt, you think of banks. Banks make billions of dollars' worth of long-term loans to companies, to individuals, to governments. And banks get into trouble for making bad loans. **Wells Fargo,** the largest bank on the West Coast with assets exceeding $50 billion, had major problems when the California real estate market went soft in the early 1990s. Businesses and individuals would borrow long-term debt and secure their loan with

Consolidated Balance Sheet

WELLS FARGO & COMPANY AND SUBSIDIARIES

LIABILITIES AND STOCKHOLDERS' EQUITY	1992	1991
Deposits:		
Noninterest-bearing—domestic	$ 9,190	$ 8,216
Interest-bearing—domestic	33,048	35,253
Interest-bearing—foreign	6	250
Total deposits	42,244	43,719
Federal funds purchased and securities sold under repurchase agreements	1,311	951
Commercial paper and other short-term borrowings	202	266
Acceptances outstanding	97	180
Accrued interest payable	88	146
Other liabilities	746	794
Senior debt	2,159	2,537
Subordinated debt	1,881	1,683
Total liabilities	48,728	50,276

The accompanying notes are an integral part of these statements.

their real estate assets. But when that real estate falls in value—as it did all over California—the loan becomes less secure. Wells Fargo had to write off the loans, and the bank's stockholders suffered.

Banks also *borrow* money —from depositors, other banks, the Federal Reserve, and the public through the invesment banking system. Take a look at Wells Fargo's balance sheet and you'll see deposits, federal funds, commercial paper, senior and subordinated debt. Most of this debt is purchased by big institutional investors such as pension funds, university endowments, and insurance companies. When Wells Fargo's fortunes improved in the mid-1990s, the investment managers of these big institutions could sleep a little easier at night.

Chapter 10

Long-Term Liabilities

Linkages

⚭ A LOOK AT PREVIOUS CHAPTERS

The topic of long-term liabilities was introduced in Chapter 2 as an important aspect of a classified balance sheet, which segregates short-term and long-term assets and liabilities. Chapter 9 introduced compound interest and present value calculations as a method used to value long-term liabilities.

⚭ A LOOK AT THIS CHAPTER

This chapter examines those items that typically appear in the long-term liability category of the balance sheet. The first section of the chapter will cover bonds, an important source of financing for many companies. The second section covers several other important long-term liabilities: leases, pensions, and deferred taxes. Although these liabilities are based on very complex financial arrangements, our primary purpose is to introduce these topics so that you are aware of their existence when reading a financial statement.

⚭ A LOOK AT UPCOMING CHAPTERS

Chapter 11 will examine the presentation of stockholders' equity, the other major category on the right-hand side of the balance sheet. Chapter 12 introduces other accounting issues related to liabilities and stockholders' equity.

LEARNING OBJECTIVES

After studying this chapter, you should be able to

1. Identify the components of the long-term liability category of the balance sheet.
2. Define the important characteristics of bonds payable.
3. Determine the issue price of a bond using compound interest techniques.
4. Understand the effect of issuance of bonds.
5. Find the amortization of premium or discount using two methods of amortization.
6. Find the gain or loss on retirement of bonds.
7. Determine whether a lease agreement must be recorded as a liability on the balance sheet.
8. Explain deferred taxes and calculate the deferred tax liability.
9. Understand the meaning of a pension obligation and record accounting entries to recognize pensions as a long-term liability.
10. Explain the effects of transactions involving long-term liabilities on the statement of cash flows.

Balance Sheet Presentation

LO 1

Identify the components of the long-term liability category of the balance sheet.

In general, **long-term liabilities** are obligations that will not be satisfied within one year. Essentially, all liabilities that are not classified as current liabilities are classified as long term. We will concentrate on the long-term liabilities of bonds or notes, pension obligations, leases, and deferred taxes. On the balance sheet, the items are listed after current liabilities. For example, the noncurrent liabilities section of Kmart's balance sheet appears in Exhibit 10-1.

Bonds Payable

Characteristics of Bonds

LO 2

Define the important characteristics of bonds payable.

A bond is a security or financial instrument that allows firms to borrow money and repay the loan over a long period of time. The bonds are sold, or *issued,* to investors who have amounts to invest and wish a return on their investment. The *borrower* (issuing firm) promises to pay interest on specified dates, usually annually or semiannually. The borrower also promises to repay the principal on a specified date, the *due date* or maturity date.

A bond certificate, illustrated in Exhibit 10-2, is issued at the time of purchase and indicates the *terms* of the bond. Generally, bonds are issued in denominations of $1,000. The denomination of the bond is usually referred to as the **face value**

EXHIBIT 10-1 Kmart Corporation Liability Section of the Balance Sheet

Consolidated Balance Sheets

($ Millions)	January 27, 1993	January 29, 1992
Current Liabilities:		
Long-term debt due within one year	$ 117	$ 39
Notes payable	590	—
Accounts payable—trade	2,959	2,722
Accrued payrolls and other liabilities	1,215	1,014
Taxes other than income taxes	368	322
Income taxes	246	211
Total current liabilities	5,495	4,308
Capital Lease Obligations	1,698	1,638
Long-Term Debt	3,237	2,287
Other Long-Term Liabilities (includes restructuring obligations)	697	641
Deferred Income Taxes	268	234

EXHIBIT 10-2   Bond Certificate

or par value. This is the amount that the firm must pay on the maturity date of the bond.

Firms issue bonds in very large amounts, often in millions in a single issue. After bonds are issued, they may be traded on the New York Bond Exchange in the same way that stock is sold on the stock exchanges. Therefore, many bonds are not held until maturity by the initial investor but may change hands several times before their eventual due date. Because bond maturities are as long as 30 years, the "secondary" market in bonds—the market for bonds already issued—is a critical factor in a company's ability to raise money. Investors in bonds may wish to sell them if interest rates paid by competing investments become more attractive or if the issuer becomes less creditworthy. Buyers of these bonds may be betting that interest rates will reverse course or that the company gets back on its feet. Trading in the secondary market does not affect the financial statements of the issuing company; thus, no journal entries are required.

We have described the general nature of bonds, but it should not be assumed that all bonds have the same terms and features. Following are some important features that often appear in the bond certificate.

Collateral   The bond certificate should indicate the *collateral* of the loan. Collateral represents the assets that back the bonds in case the issuer cannot make the interest and principal payments and must default on the loan. **Debenture bonds** are not backed by specific collateral of the issuing company. Rather, the investor must examine the general creditworthiness of the issuer. If a bond is a *secured bond,* the certificate indicates specific assets that serve as collateral in case of default.

Due Date   The bond certificate specifies the date that the bond principal must be repaid. Normally, bonds are *term bonds,* meaning that the entire principal amount

Debenture bonds, like this one from Southwestern Bell Telephone, are backed by the general creditworthiness of the issuing company, not by its assets as collateral. Buyers of such bonds should check the issuer's credit rating, know how to read the firm's financial statements—and learn as much as possible about its operations.

is due on a single date. Alternatively, bonds may be issued as **serial bonds** for which the principal does not all come due on the same date. For example, a firm may issue serial bonds that have a portion of the principal due each year for the next 10 years. Issuing firms often prefer serial bonds because it is not necessary to accumulate the entire principal amount for repayment at one point in time.

Other Features   Some bonds are issued as convertible or callable bonds. *Convertible bonds* can be converted into common stock at a future time. This feature allows the investor to buy a security that pays a fixed interest rate but can be converted at a future date into an equity security (stock) if the issuing firm is growing and profitable. The conversion feature is also advantageous to the issuing firm because convertible bonds normally carry a lower rate of interest.

Callable bonds may be retired before their specified due date. Callable generally refers to the issuer's right to retire the bonds. If the buyer or investor has the right to retire the bonds, they are referred to as redeemable bonds. Usually, callable bonds stipulate the price to be paid at redemption; this price is referred to as the *redemption price* or the *reacquisition price*. The callable feature is like an insurance policy for the company. Say a bond pays 10% but interest rates plummet to 6%. Rather than continuing to pay 10%, the company is willing to offer a slight premium over face

This bond trader buys and sells bonds to investors on the secondary market—that is, after they have been issued. On the board behind her, she tallies bond availability information including company names ("Great Atl. & Pac."), bond rates ("9.125" for 9.125%), maturity dates ("1/15/ 98" for January 15, 1998) and the issue price ("99.50," or 99.5% of face value).

value for the right to retire those 10% bonds so that it can borrow at 6%. Of course, the investor is invariably disappointed when the company invokes its call privilege.

As you can see, a variety of terms and features is associated with bonds. Each firm seeks to structure the bond agreement in the manner that best meets its financial needs and will attract investors at the most favorable rates.

Bonds are a popular source of financing because of the tax advantages when compared to the issuance of stock. Interest paid on bonds is deductible for tax purposes but dividends paid on stock are not. This may explain why the amount of debt on many firms' balance sheets has increased in recent years. Debt became popular in the 1980s to finance mergers and again in the early 1990s when interest rates reached 20-year lows. Still, investors and creditors tend to downgrade a company to the extent that it has debt on the balance sheet.

Issuance of Bonds

When bonds are issued, the issuing firm must recognize the incurrence of a liability in exchange for cash. If bonds are issued at their face amount, the accounting entry is straightforward. For example, assume that on April 1 a firm issues bonds with a face amount of $10,000 and receives $10,000. In this case, the accounting entry is

Apr. 1	Cash	10,000	
	Bonds Payable		10,000
	To record the issuance of bonds at face value.		

Assets	=	**Liabilities**	+	**Owners' Equity**
+10,000		+10,000		

Factors Affecting Bond Price

When dealing with bonds payable, two interest rates are always involved. The **face rate of interest** (also called the *stated rate, nominal rate, contract rate,* or *coupon rate*) is the rate specified on the bond certificate. It is the amount of interest that will be paid each interest period. For example, if $10,000 worth of bonds is issued with an 8% annual face rate of interest, then interest of $800 ($10,000 × 8% × 1 year) would be paid at the end of each annual period. Alternatively, bonds often require the payment of interest semiannually. If the bonds in our example required the 8% annual face rate to be paid semiannually (at 4%), then interest of $400 ($10,000 × 8% × 1/2 year) would be paid each semiannual period.

The second important interest rate is the market rate of interest (also called the *effective rate* or *bond yield*). The **market rate of interest** refers to the rate that bondholders could obtain by investing in other bonds that are similar to the issuing firm's bonds. The issuing firm does not set the market rate of interest. That rate is determined by the bond market on the basis of many transactions for similar bonds. The market rate incorporates all of the "market's" knowledge about economic conditions and expectations about future conditions. Normally, issuing firms try to set a face rate for their bonds that is equal to the market rate. However, because the market rate changes daily, there are almost always small differences between the face rate and the market rate at the time bonds are issued.

In addition to the number of interest payments and the maturity length of the bond, the face rate and the market rate of interest must both be known in order to calculate the issue price of a bond. The **bond issue price** equals the *present value* of the cash flows that the bond will produce. Bonds produce two types of cash flows

LO **3**

Determine the issue price of a bond using compound interest techniques.

for the investor, interest receipts and repayment of principal (face value). The interest receipts constitute an annuity of payments each interest period over the life of the bonds. The repayment of principal (face value) is a one-time receipt that occurs at the end of term of the bonds. We must calculate the present value of the interest receipts (using Table 9-4) and the present value of the principal amount (using Table 9-2). The total of the two present value calculations represents the issue price of the bond.

An Example   Suppose that on January 1, 1995, Discount Firm wishes to issue bonds with a face value of $10,000. The face or coupon rate of interest has been set at 8%. The bonds will pay interest annually, and the principal amount is due in four years. Also suppose that the market rate of interest for other similar bonds is currently 10%. Because the market rate of interest exceeds the coupon rate, investors will not be willing to pay $10,000 but something less. We wish to calculate the amount that will be obtained from the issuance of Discount Firm's bonds.

Discount's bond will produce two sets of cash flows for the investor, an annual interest payment of $800 ($10,000 × 8%) per year for four years and repayment of the principal of $10,000 at the end of the fourth year. To calculate the issue price, we must calculate the present value of the two sets of cash flows. A time diagram portrays the cash flows as follows:

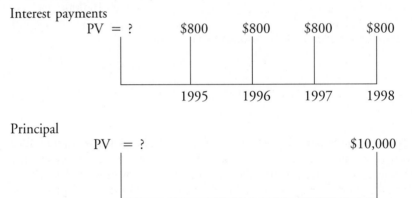

Interest payments

Principal

We can calculate the issue price by using the compound interest tables found in Chapter 9, as follows:

$800 × 3.170 (factor from Table 9-4 for 4 periods, 10%)	$2,536
$10,000 × .683 (factor from Table 9-2 for 4 periods, 10%)	6,830
Issue Price	$9,366

The table factors used represent four periods and 10% interest. This is a very key point. The issue price of a bond is always calculated using the market rate of interest. The face rate of interest determines the amount of the interest payments, but the market rate determines the present value of the payments and the present value of the principal (and therefore the issue price).

Our example of Discount Firm reveals that the bonds with $10,000 face value amount would be issued for $9,366. The bond markets and the financial press often state the issue price as a percentage of the face amount. The percentage for Discount's bonds can be calculated as ($9,366/$10,000) × 100, or 93.66%. Therefore, when you read that bonds were issued "at 93.66," this means that the bonds were issued at 93.66% of face value.

Premium or Discount on Bonds

We will continue with the Discount Firm example to illustrate the concepts of premium and discount on bonds. **Premium** or **discount** represents the difference between the face value and the issue price of a bond. We may state the relationship as follows:

LO **4**
Understand the effect of issuance of bonds.

$$\text{Premium} = \text{Issue Price} - \text{Face Value}$$
$$\text{Discount} = \text{Face Value} - \text{Issue Price}$$

In other words, when issue price exceeds face value, the bonds have sold at a premium, and when the face value exceeds the issue price, the bonds have sold at a discount.

Discount Firm's bonds sold at a discount calculated as

$$\text{Discount} = \$10,000 - \$9,366$$
$$\text{Discount} = \$634.$$

Discount Firm would record the discount at the time that the issuance of the bonds was recorded in the following journal entry:

Jan. 1	Cash	9,366	
	Discount on Bonds Payable	634	
	Bonds Payable		10,000
	To record the issuance of bonds payable.		

Assets	=	Liabilities	+	Owners' Equity
+9,366		− 634		
		+10,000		

The Discount on Bonds Payable account is shown as a contra liability on the balance sheet in conjunction with the Bonds Payable account and is a deduction from that account. If Discount Firm were to prepare a balance sheet immediately after the bond issuance, the following would appear in the long-term liability category of the balance sheet:

Long-Term Liabilities:	
Bonds Payable	$10,000
Less: Discount on Bonds Payable	634
	$ 9,366

The Discount Firm example has illustrated a situation in which the market rate of a bond issue is higher than the face rate. Now we will examine the opposite situation when the face rate exceeds the market rate. Again, we are interested in calculating the issue price of the bonds.

Issuing at a Premium   Suppose that on January 1, 1995, Premium Firm wishes to issue the same bonds as in the previous example: $10,000 face value bonds, with an 8% face rate of interest, and with interest paid annually each year for four years. Assume, however, that the market rate of interest is 6% for similar bonds. The issue price is calculated as the present value of the annuity of interest payments and the present value of the principal at the market rate of interest. The calculations are as follows:

$800 × 3.465 (factor from Table 9-4 for 4 periods, 6%)	$ 2,772
$10,000 × .792 (factor from Table 9-2 for 4 periods, 6%)	7,920
Issue Price	$10,692

We have calculated that the bonds would be issued for $10,692. Because the bonds would be issued at an amount that is higher than the face value amount, they would be issued at a premium. The amount of the premium is calculated as

$$\text{Premium} = \$10,692 - \$10,000$$
$$\text{Premium} = \$692.$$

The premium is recorded at the time of bond issuance in the following entry:

Jan. 1	Cash	10,692	
	Bonds Payable		10,000
	Premium on Bonds Payable		692
	To record the issuance of bonds payable.		

Assets	=	Liabilities	+	Owners' Equity
+10,692		+10,000		
		+692		

The account Premium on Bonds Payable is an addition to the Bonds Payable account. If Premium Firm presented a balance sheet immediately after the bond issuance, the long-term liability category of the balance sheet would appear as follows:

Long-Term Liabilities:	
Bonds Payable	$10,000
Plus: Premium on Bonds Payable	692
	$10,692

You should learn two important points from the Discount Firm and Premium Firm examples. First, you should be able to determine whether a bond will sell at a premium or discount by the relationship that exists between the face rate and market rate of interest. *Premium* and *discount* do not mean "good" and "bad." Premium or discount arises solely because of the difference that exists between the face rate and market rate of interest for a bond issue. The same relationship always exists so that the following statements hold true:

If Market Rate = Face Rate THEN bonds are issued at face value amount

If Market Rate > Face Rate THEN bonds are issued at a discount

If Face Rate > Market Rate THEN bonds are issued at a premium

The examples also illustrate a second important point. The relationship between interest rates and bond prices is always inverse. To understand the term *inverse relationship,* refer to the Discount Firm and Premium Firm examples. The bonds of the two firms are identical in all respects except for the market rate of interest. When the market rate was 10%, the bond issue price was $9,366 (the Discount Firm example). When the market rate was 6%, the bond issue price increased to $10,692 (the Premium Firm example). The examples illustrate that as interest rates decrease, prices on the bond markets increase and as interest rates increase, they decrease.

Many investors in the *stock market* perceive that they are taking a great deal of risk with their capital. In truth, *bond investors* are taking substantial risk, too. The most obvious risk is that the company will fail and not be able to pay its debts. But another risk is that interest rates on comparable investments will rise. Interest rate risk can have a devastating impact on the current market value of bonds. One way to minimize interest rate risk is to hold the bond to maturity, at which point the company must pay the face amount.

Bond Amortization

Straight-Line Method   The amount of interest that should be reflected on a firm's income statement for bonds payable is the true, or effective, interest. The effective interest should reflect the face rate of interest as well as interest that results from issuing the bond at a premium or discount. To reflect that interest component, the amount initially recorded in the Premium on Bonds Payable account or the Discount on Bonds Payable must be amortized or spread over the life of the bond.

Amortization refers to the process of transferring an amount from the discount or premium to interest expense each time period to adjust interest expense. Two commonly used methods of amortization are straight line and effective interest. We will illustrate both methods, first to amortize a discount amount and then to amortize a premium amount.

To illustrate amortization of a discount, we need to return to our Discount Firm example introduced earlier (see page 534). We have seen that the issue price of the bond could be calculated as $9,366, resulting in a debit balance of $634 in the Discount on Bonds Payable account (see the entry on page 535). But what does the initial balance of the Discount account really represent? The discount should be thought of as additional interest that Discount Firm must pay over and above the 8% face rate. Remember that Discount received only $9,366 but must repay the full principal of $10,000 at the bond due date. For that reason, the $634 of discount is an additional interest cost that must be reflected as interest expense. It is reflected as interest expense by the process of amortization. In other words, interest expense is made up of two components: cash interest and amortization. We will now consider the methods available to amortize premium or discount.

The easiest method to amortize the discount is the straight-line method. The **straight-line method of amortization** reduces the discount balance by the same amount each period over the life of the bonds. If we use straight-line amortization for the Discount Firm bonds, the discount balance must be reduced by $158.50 ($634/4) each period for four periods. Therefore, the interest entries for the first annual period could be recorded as two entries. The first entry is simply to record the payment of interest at the face rate of 8%:

LO 5
Find the amortization of premium or discount using two methods of amortization.

Dec. 31	Interest Expense	800	
	Cash		800
	To record annual interest payment on bonds payable.		

Assets	=	Liabilities	+	Owners' Equity
− 800				− 800

The second entry is to record amortization of the annual portion of discount:

Dec. 31	Interest Expense	158.50	
	Discount on Bonds Payable		158.50
	To amortize annual portion of discount on bonds payable.		

Assets	=	Liabilities	+	Owners' Equity
		+ 158.50		− 158.50

The T accounts related to the bonds would appear as follows as of December 31, 1995:

BONDS PAYABLE		DISCOUNT ON BONDS PAYABLE			
	10,000 1/1/95	1/1/95	634.00		
				158.50	12/31/95
		Bal.	475.50		

INTEREST EXPENSE	
12/31/95 800.00	
12/31/95 158.50	
Bal. 958.50	

On the balance sheet presented as of December 31, 1995, the *unamortized* portion of discount appears as the balance of the Discount on Bonds Payable as follows:

Long-Term Liabilities:

Bonds Payable	$10,000.00
Less: Discount on Bonds Payable	475.50
	$ 9,524.50

The same process of amortization would occur each year for four years until the balance of the Discount on Bonds Payable account is reduced to zero. As of December 31, 1998, the account appears as follows:

DISCOUNT ON BONDS PAYABLE			
1/1/95 634.00			
		158.50	12/31/95
		158.50	12/31/96
		158.50	12/31/97
		158.50	12/31/98
Bal. –0–			

Essentially, all of the balance of the Discount on Bonds Payable account has been transferred to the Interest Expense account over the four-year period. Amortization of the discount has occurred to properly reflect the true interest (sometimes called the *effective interest*) incurred as a result of issuing bonds at less than face value.

Effective Interest Method—Impact on Expense   The straight-line method of amortization is the easiest amortization method, but it is not conceptually sound. The straight-line method produces the same dollar amount of amortization each period. This results in the same dollar amount of interest expense each period, but the *rate* of interest appears to vary from period to period.

To illustrate this point, we introduce two new terms. The **carrying value** of bonds is represented by the following:

$$\text{Carrying Value} = \text{Face Value} - \text{Unamortized Discount}$$

For example, the carrying value of the bonds for our Discount Firm example, as of the date of issuance of January 1, 1995, could be calculated as

$$\$10,000 - \$634 = \$9,366$$

In those situations in which there is a premium instead of a discount, carrying value is represented by the following:

$$\text{Carrying Value} = \text{Face Value} + \text{Unamortized Premium}$$

For example, the carrying value of the bonds for our Premium Firm example, as of the date of issuance of January 1, 1995, could be calculated as

$$\$10,000 + \$692 = \$10,692$$

The second term has been suggested earlier. The *effective rate of interest* is

$$\text{Effective Rate} = \text{Annual Interest Expense/Carrying Value}$$

For example, when using straight-line amortization in the Discount Firm example, the effective rate of interest for 1995 is calculated as $958.50/$9,366, or 10.23%. In 1996, however, the dollar amount of interest expense remains as $958.50, but the carrying value increases to $9,524.50 ($10,000 less unamortized discount of $475.50). Therefore, the effective interest rate for 1996 is 10.06%. Conceptually, this is not correct. The true effective rate on the bonds does not vary from year to year, but straight-line amortization provides a result that appears to vary from year to year. The effective interest method of amortization is intended to overcome this conceptual difficulty.

The **effective interest method of amortization** amortizes discount or premium in a manner that produces a constant effective interest rate from period to period. The objective of amortization is still the same. The amount of discount on bonds must be reflected as an adjustment of interest expense over the life of the bonds. By the bond's due date, the balance of the Discount on Bonds Payable account must be reduced to zero. Unlike the straight-line method, however, the amount of amortization is not the same each period.

Effective Interest Method—An Example   The amortization table in Exhibit 10-3 illustrates effective interest amortization of the bond discount for our Discount Firm example of the previous section.

As illustrated in Exhibit 10-3, the effective interest method of amortization is based on several important concepts. The relationships can be stated in equation form as follows:

$$\text{Cash Interest (in Column 1)} = \text{Bond Face Value} \times \text{Face Rate}$$

$$\text{Interest Expense (in Column 2)} = \text{Carrying Value} \times \text{Market Rate}$$

$$\text{Discount Amortized (in Column 3)} = \text{Interest Expense} - \text{Cash Interest}$$

The first column of the exhibit indicates that the cash interest to be paid is $800 ($10,000 × 8%). The second column indicates the annual interest expense at the market rate or effective rate of interest. This is a constant rate of interest (10% in our example) and is calculated by multiplying the carrying value as *of the beginning of the period* times the market rate of interest. In 1995 the interest expense is $937 ($9,366 × 10%). Note that the amount of interest expense changes each year because the carrying value changes as discount is amortized. The amount of discount amortized each year in Column 3 is the difference between the cash interest in Column 1 and the interest expense in Column 2. Again, note that the amount of discount amortized changes in each of the four years. Finally, the carrying value in Column 4 is the

EXHIBIT 10-3   Discount Amortization
Effective Interest Method of Amortization

DATE	COLUMN 1 CASH INTEREST	COLUMN 2 INTEREST EXPENSE	COLUMN 3 DISCOUNT AMORTIZED	COLUMN 4 CARRYING VALUE
	8%	10%	COL. 2 – COL. 1	
1/1/95				$9,366
12/31/95	$800	$937	$137	9,503
12/31/96	800	950	150	9,653
12/31/97	800	965	165	9,818
12/31/98	800	982	182	10,000

previous year's carrying value plus the discount amortized in Column 3. When bonds are issued at a discount, the carrying value starts at an amount less than face value and increases each period until it reaches the face value amount.

The amortization table in Exhibit 10-3 is the basis for the accounting entries that must be recorded. Discount Firm may record two entries for each period. The first entry at the end of 1995 is recorded to reflect the cash interest payment:

Dec. 31   Interest Expense   800
          Cash   800
          To record annual payment on bonds payable.

           Assets = **Liabilities** + **Owners' Equity**
           −800   −800

The second entry is recorded to amortize a portion of the discount and to reflect that amount as an adjustment of interest expense:

Dec. 31   Interest Expense   137
          Discount on Bonds Payable   137
          To amortize annual portion of discount on bonds
          payable.

           Assets = **Liabilities** + **Owners' Equity**
                    +137   −137

Instead of making two entries as above, it is quite common for firms to make one entry that combines the two. Thus, the entry for 1995 could also be recorded in the following manner:

Dec. 31   Interest Expense   937
          Cash   800
          Discount on Bonds Payable   137
          To record annual interest payment and amortize
          annual portion of discount on bonds payable.

           Assets = **Liabilities** + **Owners' Equity**
           −800   +137   −937

The T accounts of the issuing firm as of December 31, 1995, would appear as follows:

BONDS PAYABLE			DISCOUNT ON BONDS PAYABLE		
	10,000	1/1/95	1/1/95	634	
					137 12/31/95
			Bal.	497	

INTEREST EXPENSE	
12/31/95 800	
12/31/95 137	
Bal. 937	

The amortization of a premium has an impact opposite from the amortization of a discount. We will use our Premium Firm example to illustrate. Recall that on January 1, 1995, Premium Firm issued $10,000 face value bonds with a face rate of interest of 8%. At the time the bonds were issued, the market rate was 6%, resulting in an issue price of $10,692 and a credit balance in the Premium on Bonds Payable account of $692 (see page 536).

The amortization table in Exhibit 10-4 illustrates effective interest amortization of the bond premium for Premium Firm. As the exhibit illustrates, effective interest amortization of a premium is based on the same concepts as amortization of a discount. The following relationships still hold true:

Cash Interest (in Column 1) =
Bond Face Value × Face Rate

Interest Expense (in Column 2) =
Carrying Value × Market Rate

The first column of the exhibit indicates that the cash interest to be paid is $800 ($10,000 × 8%). The second column indicates the annual interest expense at the market rate. In 1995 the interest expense is $642 ($10,692 × 6%). Note, however, two differences between Exhibit 10-3 and Exhibit 10-4. When amortizing a premium,

EXHIBIT 10-4   Premium Amortization Effective Interest Method of Amortization

DATE	COLUMN 1 CASH INTEREST	COLUMN 2 INTEREST EXPENSE	COLUMN 3 PREMIUM AMORTIZED	COLUMN 4 CARRYING VALUE
	8%	6%	COL. 1 − COL. 2	
1/1/95				$10,692
12/31/95	$800	$642	$158	10,534
12/31/96	800	632	168	10,366
12/31/97	800	622	178	10,188
12/31/98	800	612	188	10,000

the cash interest in Column 1 exceeds the interest expense in Column 2. Therefore, the premium amortized is defined as follows:

Premium Amortized (in Column 3) =
Cash Interest − Interest Expense

Also note that the carrying value in Column 4 starts at an amount higher than the face value of $10,000 ($10,692) and is amortized downward until it reaches face value. Therefore, the carrying value at the end of each year is the carrying value at the beginning of the period minus the premium amortized for that year. For example, the carrying value in Exhibit 10-4 at the end of 1995 ($10,534) was calculated by subtracting the premium amortized for 1995 ($158 in Column 3) from the carrying value at the beginning of 1995 ($10,692).

The amortization table in Exhibit 10-4 again serves as the basis for the accounting entries that must be recorded. Premium Firm may record two entries for each period. The first entry at the end of 1995 is recorded to reflect the cash interest payment.

Dec. 31   Interest Expense   800
       Cash   800
       To record annual payment on bonds payable.

Assets	=	Liabilities	+	Owners' Equity
− 800				− 800

The second entry is recorded to amortize a portion of the premium and to reflect that amount as an adjustment of interest expense.

Dec. 31   Premium on Bonds Payable   158
       Interest Expense   158
       To amortize annual portion of premium on bonds payable.

Assets	=	Liabilities	+	Owners' Equity
		− 158		+ 158

Of course, Premium Firm could combine the preceding two entries into one entry as follows:

Dec. 31   Interest Expense   642
       Premium on Bonds Payable   158
       Cash   800
       To record annual interest payment and amortize annual portion of premium on bonds payable.

Assets	=	Liabilities	+	Owners' Equity
− 800		− 158		− 642

The T accounts of Premium Firm as of December 31, 1995, appear as follows:

BONDS PAYABLE			PREMIUM ON BONDS PAYABLE		
	10,000	1/1/95		692	1/1/95
			12/31/95 158		
				534	Bal.

INTEREST EXPENSE	
12/31/95 800	
	158 12/31/95
Bal. 642	

Redemption of Bonds

Redemption at Maturity   The term *redemption* refers to retirement of bonds by repayment of the principal. If bonds are retired on their due date, the accounting entry is not difficult. Refer again to the Discount Firm example from the previous sections of this chapter. If Discount Firm retires its bonds on the due date of December 31, 1998, it must repay the principal of $10,000 and records the following entry:

Dec. 31   Bonds Payable   10,000
         Cash   10,000
         To record the retirement of bonds payable.

Assets	=	Liabilities	+	Owners' Equity
− 10,000		− 10,000		

This assumes that the interest payment that was paid on December 31, 1998, and the discount amortization on that date have already been recorded.

Retired Early at a Gain   A firm may wish to retire bonds before their due date for several reasons. A firm may simply have excess cash and may determine that the best use of those funds is to repay outstanding bond obligations. Bonds may also be retired early because of changing interest rate conditions. If interest rates in the economy decline, firms may find it advantageous to retire bonds that have been issued at higher rates. Of course, what is advantageous to the issuer is not necessarily so for the investor. Unfortunately, early retirement of bonds is a fact of life when interest rates drop sharply, as they did in the early 1990s. Large institutional investors expect such a development and merely reinvest the money elsewhere. Many individual investors are more seriously inconvenienced when a bond issue is called.

LO 6
Find the gain or loss on retirement of bonds.

Bond terms generally specify that if bonds are retired before their due date, they are not retired at the face value amount but at a call price or redemption price indicated on the bond certificate. Also the amount of unamortized premium or discount on the bonds must be considered when bonds are retired early. The retirement results in a **gain or loss on redemption** that must be calculated as follows:

$$\text{Gain} = \text{Carrying Value} - \text{Redemption Price}$$
$$\text{Loss} = \text{Redemption Price} - \text{Carrying Value}$$

In other words, the issuing firm must calculate the carrying value of the bonds at the time of redemption and compare it to the total redemption price. If the carrying value is higher than the redemption price, the issuing firm must record a gain. If the carrying value is lower than the redemption price, the issuing firm must record a loss.

We will use the Premium Firm example from the previous section to illustrate the calculation of gain or loss. Assume that on December 31, 1995, Premium Firm wishes to retire its bonds due in 1998. Assume, as in the previous section, that the bonds were issued at a premium of $692 at the beginning of 1995. Premium Firm has used the effective interest method of amortization and has recorded the interest and amortization entries for the year (see page 542). This has resulted in a balance of $534 in the Premium on Bonds Payable account as of December 31, 1995. Assume also that Premium Firm's bond certificates indicate that the bonds may be retired early at a call price of 102 (meaning 102% of face value). Thus, the redemption price is 102% of $10,000, or $10,200.

Premium Firm's retirement of bonds would result in a gain. The gain can be calculated using two steps. First, we must calculate the carrying value of the bonds as of the date they are retired. The carrying value of Premium Firm's bonds at that date is as follows:

$$\begin{aligned} \text{Carrying Value} &= \text{Face Value} + \text{Unamortized Premium} \\ &= \$10,000 + \$534 \\ &= \$10,534 \end{aligned}$$

Note that the carrying value we have calculated is the same amount indicated for December 31, 1995, in Column 4 of the effective interest amortization table of Exhibit 10-4.

The second step is to calculate the gain:

$$\begin{aligned} \text{Gain} &= \text{Carrying Value} - \text{Redemption Price} \\ &= \$10,534 - (\$10,000 \times 1.02) \\ &= \$10,534 - \$10,200 \\ &= \$334 \end{aligned}$$

It is important to remember that when bonds are retired, the balance of the Bonds Payable account and the remaining balance of the Premium on Bonds Payable account must be eliminated from the balance sheet.

Retired Early at a Loss   To illustrate retirement of bonds at a loss, assume that Premium Firm retires bonds at December 31, 1995, as in the previous section. However, assume that the call price for the bonds is 107 (or 107% of face value).

We can again perform the calculations in two steps. The first step is to calculate the carrying value:

$$\begin{aligned} \text{Carrying Value} &= \text{Face Value} + \text{Unamortized Premium} \\ &= \$10,000 + \$534 \\ &= \$10,534 \end{aligned}$$

The second step is to compare the carrying value with the redemption price to calculate the amount of the loss.

$$\begin{aligned} \text{Loss} &= \text{Redemption Price} - \text{Carrying Value} \\ &= (\$10,000 \times 1.07) - \$10,534 \\ &= \$10,700 - \$10,534 \\ &= \$166 \end{aligned}$$

In this case, a loss of $166 has resulted from the retirement of Premium Firm bonds. A loss means that the company paid more to retire the bonds than the amount at which the bonds were recorded on the balance sheet.

Financial Statement Presentation of Gain or Loss   The accounts Gain on Bond Redemption and Loss on Bond Redemption are income statement accounts. A gain on bond redemption increases Premium Firm's income; a loss decreases its income. In that respect, the accounts are similar to gains or losses that occur on the sale of equipment or other assets. There is an important difference, however. The FASB has ruled that gains and losses that occur on bond redemption merit separate recognition on the income statement. Such gains and losses are considered *extraordinary items* and must be shown in a separate section of the income statement.[1] This allows income statement readers to understand that bond redemption is not a part of the firm's "normal operating" activities. That is not to say that investors are not

---

[1] *Statement of Financial Accounting Standards No. 4,* "Reporting Gains and Losses from Extinguishment of Debt" (Stamford, Conn.: FASB, 1975).

interested in such one-time gains or losses. Although redemptions on bonds are not part of normal operations, a large gain suggests that the company's financial managers are astute enough to take advantage of opportunities in the financial markets. (For a more complete discussion of the treatment of extraordinary items on the income statement, see Chapter 12).

Analyzing Debt to Assess a Firm's Solvency

Bonds are a component of the "capital structure" of the company and are included in the calculation of the debt-to-equity ratio:

$$\text{Debt-to-Equity Ratio} = \frac{\text{Total Liabilities}}{\text{Total Stockholders' Equity}}$$

For example, the debt-to-equity ratio of Kmart Corporation is approximately 1.5, which means that Kmart has 1.5 times as much debt as equity, a situation not unusual for companies in the retail industry. Most investors would prefer to see equity rather than debt on the balance sheet. Debt, with its fixed interest charges, is a fixed obligation that must be repaid in a finite period of time. In contrast, equity never has to be repaid, and the dividends that are declared on it are optional. Stock investors view debt as a claim against the company that must be satisfied before they get a return on their money.

Other ratios used to measure the degree of debt obligation include the times interest earned ratio

$$\text{Times Interest Earned} = \frac{\text{Income before Interest and Tax}}{\text{Interest Expense}}$$

and the debt service coverage ratio

$$\text{Debt service coverage ratio} = \frac{\text{Cash Flow from Operations before Interest and Tax}}{\text{Interest and Principal Payments}}.$$

Lenders want to be sure that borrowers can pay the interest and repay the principal on a loan. Both of the preceding ratios reflect the degree to which a company can make its debt payments out of current cash flow.

■ ACCOUNTING FOR YOUR DECISIONS   You Rate the Bonds

One of the factors that determine the rate of interest on a bond is the rating by a rating agency such as Standard & Poors or Moody's Investor Service. What factors would you use to rate the bonds issued by a company such as Turner Broadcasting Company, owner of CNN?

Other Long-Term Liabilities

Long-term bonds and notes payable are important sources of financing for many large corporations and are quite prominent in the long-term liability category of the balance sheet for many firms. But other important elements of that category of the balance sheet also represent long-term obligations. We will introduce you to three items: leases, pensions, and deferred taxes. In some cases, they are required to be reported on the financial statements and are important components of the long-term liability section of the balance sheet. In other cases, the items are not required to be recorded on the financial statement and can be discerned only by a careful reading of the footnotes to the financial statements.

Leases

A *lease* is a contractual arrangement between two parties that allows one party, the *lessee,* the right to use the asset in exchange for making payments to its owner, the *lessor.* A common example of a lease arrangement involves the rental of an apartment. The tenant in that case is the lessee and the landlord is the lessor.

Lease agreements are a form of financing. In some cases, it is more advantageous to lease an asset than to borrow money to purchase it. The lessee can conserve cash because a lease does not require a large initial cash outlay. A wide variety of lease arrangements exists, ranging from simple agreements to complex ones that span a long time period. Lease arrangements are popular because of their flexibility. The terms of a lease can be structured in many ways to meet the needs of the lessee and lessor. This results in difficult accounting questions:

1. Should the right to use property be recorded as an asset by the lessee?
2. Should the obligation to make payments be recorded as a liability by the lessee?
3. Should all leases be accounted for in the same manner regardless of the terms of the lease agreement?

The answers are that some leases should be recorded as an asset and liability by the lessee and some should not. The accountant must examine the terms of the lease agreement and compare those terms with a set of criteria that has been established.

The contractor on this construction site has leased some of its equipment—such as tools, trucks, the crane. How the contractor accounts for any liability arising from these leases has a direct effect on its balance sheet, and thus on investors' evaluation of the company.

Lease Criteria   From the viewpoint of the lessee, there are two types of lease agreements, operating and capital leases. In an **operating lease,** the lessee acquires the right to use an asset for a limited period of time. The lessee is *not* required to record the right to use the property as an asset or to record the obligation for payments as a liability. Therefore, the lessee is able to attain a form of *off-balance-sheet financing.* That is, the lessee has attained the right to use property but has not recorded that right, or the accompanying obligation, on the balance sheet. By escaping the balance sheet, the lease does not add to debt or impair the debt-to-equity ratio that investors usually calculate. Management has a responsibility to make sure that such off-balance-sheet financing is not in fact a long-term obligation. The company's auditors are supposed to analyze the terms of the lease carefully to make sure that management has exercised its responsibility.

The second type of lease agreement is a **capital lease.** In this type of lease, the lessee has acquired sufficient rights of ownership and control of the property to be considered its owner. The lease is called a *capital lease* because it is capitalized (recorded) on the balance sheet by the lessee.

The FASB has ruled that a lease should be considered a capital lease by the lessee if *one or more* of the following criteria are met:[2]

1. The lease transfers ownership of the property to the lessee at the end of the lease term.

2. The lease contains a bargain purchase option to purchase the asset at an amount lower than its fair market value.

3. The lease term is 75% or more of the property's economic life.

4. The present value of the minimum lease payments is 90% or more of the fair market value of the property at the inception of the lease.

If none of the criteria are met, the lease agreement is accounted for as an operating lease. This is an area in which it is important for the accountant to exercise professional judgment. In some cases, firms may take elaborate measures to evade or manipulate the criteria that would require lease capitalization. The accountant should determine what is full and fair disclosure based on an unbiased evaluation of the substance of the transaction.

Operating Leases   You have already accounted for operating leases in previous chapters when recording rent expense and prepaid rent. A rental agreement for a limited time period is also a lease agreement.

Suppose, for example, that Lessee Firm wishes to lease a car for a new salesperson. A lease agreement is signed with Lessor Dealer on January 1, 1995, to lease a car for the year for $4,000, payable on December 31, 1995. Typically, a car lease does not transfer title at the end of the term, does not include a bargain purchase price, and does not last for more than 75% of the car's life. In addition, the present value of the lease payments is not 90% of the car's value. Because the lease does not meet any of the specified criteria, it should be recorded as an operating lease. Lessee Firm records the following entry at the time of the lease payment:

Dec. 31	Lease Expense	4,000	
	Cash		4,000
	To record the annual lease payment.		

Assets	=	Liabilities	+	Owners' Equity
−4,000				−4,000

[2] *Statement of Financial Accounting Standards No. 13,* "Accounting for Leases" (Stamford, Conn.: FASB, 1976).

Although operating leases are not recorded on the balance sheet by the lessee, they are mentioned in financial statement footnotes. The FASB requires footnote disclosure of the amount of future lease obligations for leases that are considered operating leases. Exhibit 10-5 provides a portion of the footnote from Hartmarx Corporation's 1992 annual report. The footnote reveals that Hartmarx has used operating leases as an important source of financing and has significant off-balance-sheet commitments in future periods as a result. An investor might want to add this off-balance-sheet item to the debt on the balance sheet to get a conservative view of the company's real obligations.

Capital Leases Capital leases are recorded as assets and liabilities by the lessee because they meet one or more of the criteria specified by the FASB. Suppose that Lessee Firm in the previous example wished to lease a car for a longer period of time. Assume that on January 1, 1995, Lessee signs a lease agreement with Lessor Dealer to lease a car. The terms of the agreement specify that Lessee will make annual lease payments of $4,000 per year for five years, payable each December 31. Assume also that the lease specifies that at the end of the lease agreement, the title to the car is transferred to Lessee Firm. Lessee must decide how to account for the lease agreement.

The contractual arrangement between Lessee Firm and Lessor Dealer is called a lease agreement, but clearly the agreement is much different than a year-to-year lease arrangement. Essentially, Lessee Firm has acquired the right to use the asset for its entire life and does not need to return it to Lessor Dealer. You may call this agreement a lease, but it actually represents a purchase of the asset by Lessee with payments made over time.

The lease should be treated as a capital lease by Lessee because it meets at least one of the four criteria specified by the FASB (it meets the first criteria concerning transfer of title). A capital lease must be recorded by Lessee as an asset and as an obligation. As of January 1, 1995, we must calculate the present value of the annual payments. If we assume an interest rate of 8%, the present value of the payments is $15,972 ($4,000 × an annuity factor of 3.993 from Table 9-4). The first entry is made on the basis of the present value as follows:

Jan. 1	Leased Asset	15,972	
	Lease Obligation		15,972
	To record a capital lease agreement.		

Assets	=	Liabilities	+	Owners' Equity
+ 15,972		+ 15,972		

The Leased Asset account is a long-term asset similar to plant and equipment and represents the fact that Lessee has acquired the right to use and retain the asset. Because the leased asset represents depreciable property, depreciation must be recorded for each of the five years of asset use. On December 31, 1995, Lessee records depreciation of $3,194 ($15,972/5 years) as follows, assuming that the straight-line method is adopted:

Dec. 31	Depreciation Expense	3,194	
	Accumulated Depreciation—Leased Assets		3,194
	To record depreciation of leased assets.		

Assets	=	Liabilities	+	Owners' Equity
− 3,194				− 3,194

Depreciation of leased assets is referred to as *amortization* by some firms.

EXHIBIT 10-5 Hartmarx Corporation Footnote Disclosure of Leases

Leases

The Company and its subsidiaries lease office, manufacturing, warehouse/distribution, showroom and retail space, automobiles, computers and other equipment under various noncancellable operating leases. A number of the leases contain renewal options ranging up to 10 years. Some retail leases provide for contingent rental payments, generally based on the sales volume of the retail unit.

At November 30, 1992, total minimum rentals are as follows (000's omitted):

Years	Amount
1993	$20,781
1994	19,137
1995	16,204
1996	11,158
1997	7,085
Thereafter	10,468
Total minimum rentals due	$84,833

Rental expense, including rentals under short term leases, comprised the following (000's omitted):

	1992	1991	1990
Minimum rentals	**$58,742**	$64,630	$65,056
Contingent rentals	**2,418**	4,916	4,923
Sublease income	**(896)**	(1,070)	(564)
Total rental expense	**$60,264**	$68,476	$69,415

Most leases provide for additional payments of real estate taxes, insurance, and other operating expenses applicable to the property, generally over a base period level. Total rental expense

On December 31, Lessee Firm also must make a payment of $4,000 to Lessor Dealer. A portion of each payment represents interest on the obligation (loan), and the remainder represents a reduction of the principal amount. Each payment must be separated into its principal and interest components. Generally, the effective interest method is used for that purpose. An effective interest table can be established using the same concepts as when using the effective interest method to amortize premium or discount on bonds payable.

Exhibit 10-6 illustrates the effective interest method applied to the Lessee Firm example. Note that the table begins with an obligation amount equal to the present value of the payments of $15,972. Each payment is separated into principal and interest amounts in a manner so that the amount of the loan obligation at the end of the lease agreement equals zero. The amortization table is the basis for the accounting entries that are recorded. Exhibit 10-6 indicates that the $4,000 payment in 1995 should be considered as interest of $1,278 (8% of $15,972) and reduction of principal of $2,722. On December 31, 1995, Lessee Firm records the following entry for the annual payment:

Dec. 31	Interest Expense	1,278	
	Lease Obligation	2,722	
	Cash		4,000
	To record annual lease payment.		

Assets	=	Liabilities	+	Owners' Equity
−4,000		−2,722		−1,278

Therefore, for a capital lease, Lessee Firm must record both an asset and a liability. The asset is reduced by the process of depreciation. The liability is reduced by reductions of principal using the effective interest method. On the balance sheet as of December 31, 1995, Lessee Firm reports the following balances related to the lease obligation:

Assets:		
Leased Assets	$15,972	
Less: Accumulated Depreciation	3,194	
		$12,778
Current Liabilities:		
Lease Obligation		$ 2,940
Long-Term Liabilities:		
Lease Obligation		$10,310

Notice that the depreciated asset does not equal the present value of the lease obligation. That is not really unusual. For example, an automobile often may be completely depreciated but still have payments due on it.

According to Exhibit 10-6, the total lease obligation as of December 31 is $13,250. This amount must be separated into current and long-term categories. The portion of the liability that will be paid within one year of the balance sheet should be considered as a current liability. Reference to Exhibit 10-6 indicates that the liability will be reduced by $2,940 in 1996 and that amount should be considered a current liability. The remaining amount of the liability, $10,310, should be considered long term.

The criteria established by the FASB to determine whether a lease is an operating or capital lease have provided a standard accounting treatment for all leases. The accounting for leases in foreign countries generally follows guidelines similar to those

EXHIBIT 10-6   Lease Amortization
Effective Interest Method of Amortization

DATE	COLUMN 1 LEASE PAYMENT	COLUMN 2 INTEREST EXPENSE	COLUMN 3 REDUCTION OF OBLIGATION	COLUMN 4 LEASE OBLIGATION
		8%	COL. 1 – COL. 2	
1/1/95				$15,972
12/31/95	$4,000	$1,278	$2,722	13,250
12/31/96	4,000	1,060	2,940	10,310
12/31/97	4,000	825	3,175	7,135
12/31/98	4,000	571	3,429	3,706
12/31/99	4,000	294	3,706	–0–

used in the United States. The criteria used in foreign countries to determine whether a lease is a capital lease are usually less detailed and less specific, however. As a result, capitalization of leases occurs less frequently in foreign countries than in the United States because of the increased use of judgment necessary in applying the accounting rules.

Deferred Tax

The financial statements of most major firms include an item titled Deferred Income Tax or Deferred Tax (see Kmart's deferred taxes in Exhibit 10-1). In most cases, the account appears in the long-term liability section of the balance sheet, and the dollar amount may be large enough to catch the user's attention. For example, Exhibit 10-7 illustrates the presentation of deferred tax in the 1991 and 1992 comparative balance sheets of American Maize-Products Company, a producer of corn products and cigars and smokeless tobacco products. The Deferred Income Taxes account is listed immediately after Long-Term Debt and should be considered a long-term liability. At the end of 1992, the firm had more than $37 million of deferred tax. The size of that account relative to the other liabilities should raise questions concerning its exact meaning. In fact, deferred income taxes represent one of the most misunderstood aspects of financial statements. In this section, we will attempt to address some of the questions concerning deferred taxes.

Deferred tax is an amount that reconciles the differences between the accounting done for purposes of financial reporting to stockholders ("book" purposes) and the accounting done for tax purposes. It may surprise you that U.S. firms are allowed to use different accounting methods for financial reporting than are used for tax calculations. The reason is that the Internal Revenue Service defines income and expense differently than does the Financial Accounting Standards Board. As a result, companies tend to use accounting methods that minimize income for tax purposes but maximize income in the annual report to stockholders. This is not true in some foreign countries where financial accounting and tax accounting are more closely aligned. Firms in those countries do not report deferred tax because the differences between methods is not significant.

When differences between financial and tax reporting do occur, we can classify the differences into two types: permanent and temporary. **Permanent differences** occur when an item is included in the tax calculation and is never included for book

LO **8**

Explain deferred taxes and calculate the deferred tax liability.

EXHIBIT 10-7   American Maize-Products Company and Its Subsidiaries Consolidated Balance Sheets

SUMMARY CONSOLIDATED BALANCE SHEETS
DOLLARS IN THOUSANDS

AT DECEMBER 31,	1992	1991
ASSETS		
Cash and cash equivalents	$ 72,085	$ 49,050
Receivables	45,802	47,585
Inventories	80,577	82,129
Prepaid expenses and other	9,261	9,871
Total current assets	207,725	188,635
Property, plant, and equipment, net	234,821	232,266
Goodwill	14,381	14,385
Other assets	27,076	24,353
Total	$484,003	$459,639
LIABILITIES AND STOCKHOLDERS' EQUITY		
Short-term debt	$ 9,200	$ 10,000
Current portion of long-term debt	4,580	892
Accounts payable	10,283	11,413
Accrued expenses	27,356	25,727
Total current liabilities	51,419	48,032
Long-term debt	136,227	127,542
Deferred income taxes	37,931	44,840
Other liabilities	4,782	4,846
Minority interest	85,404	75,714
Stockholders' equity	168,240	158,665
Total	$484,003	$459,639

purposes—or vice versa, when an item is included for book purposes but not for tax purposes.

For example, the tax laws allow taxpayers to exclude interest from certain investments, usually state and municipal bonds, from their income. These are generally called *tax-exempt bonds.* If a corporation buys tax-exempt bonds, it does not have to declare the interest as income for tax purposes. When the corporation develops its income statement for stockholders (book purposes), however, the interest is included and appears in the Interest Income account. Therefore, tax-exempt interest represents a permanent difference between tax and book calculations.

Temporary differences occur when an item affects both the book and tax calculation but not in the same time period. A difference caused by depreciation methods is the most common type of temporary difference. You have learned in previous chapters that depreciation may be calculated using a straight-line method or one of several accelerated (sum-of-the-years'-digits or declining-balance) methods. Most firms do not use the same depreciation method for book and tax purposes, however. Generally, straight-line depreciation is used for book purposes and an accelerated method is used for tax purposes because accelerated depreciation lowers taxable income—at least in early years—and therefore reduces the tax due. The IRS refers to this method as the *Modified Accelerated Cost Recovery System* (*MACRS*). It is similar to other accelerated depreciation methods in that it allows the firm to take larger depreciation deductions for tax purposes in the early years of the asset and smaller deductions in the later years. Over the life of the depreciable asset, the total depreciation using straight-line is equal to that using MACRS. Therefore, this difference is an example of a temporary difference between book and tax reporting.

The Deferred Tax account is used to reconcile the differences between the accounting for book purposes and for tax purposes. It is important to distinguish between permanent and temporary differences because the FASB has ruled that not all differences should affect the Deferred Tax account. The Deferred Tax account should reflect temporary differences but not items that are permanent differences between book accounting and tax reporting.[3]

Example of Deferred Tax Assume that Startup Firm begins business on January 1, 1995. During 1995 the firm has sales of $6,000 and has no expenses other than depreciation and income tax at the rate of 40%. Startup has depreciation on only one asset. That asset was purchased on January 1, 1995, for $10,000 and has a four-year life. Startup has decided to use the straight-line depreciation method for financial reporting purposes. Startup's accountants have chosen to use MACRS for tax purposes, however, resulting in $4,000 depreciation in 1995 and a decline of $1,000 per year thereafter.

The depreciation amounts for each of the four years for Startup's asset are as follows:

YEAR	TAX DEPRECIATION	BOOK DEPRECIATION	DIFFERENCE
1995	$ 4,000	$ 2,500	$1,500
1996	3,000	2,500	500
1997	2,000	2,500	(500)
1998	1,000	2,500	($1,500)
Total	$10,000	$10,000	$ –0–

---

[3] *Statement of Financial Accounting Standards No. 109,* "Accounting for Income Taxes" (Stamford, Conn.: FASB, 1992).

Startup's tax calculation for 1995 is based on the accelerated depreciation of $4,000, as follows:

Sales	$6,000
Depreciation Expense	4,000
Taxable Income	$2,000
x Tax Rate	40%
Tax payable to IRS	$ 800

For the year 1995, Startup owes $800 of tax to the Internal Revenue Service. This amount is ordinarily recorded as tax payable until the time it is remitted.

Startup wishes also to develop an income statement to send to the stockholders. What amount should be shown as tax expense on the income statement? You may guess that the Tax Expense account on the income statement should reflect $800 because that is the amount to be paid to the IRS. That is not true in this case, however. Remember that the tax payable amount was calculated using the depreciation method Startup chose to use for tax purposes. The income statement must be calculated using the straight-line method that Startup uses for book purposes. Therefore, Startup's income statement for 1995 appears as follows:

Sales	$6,000
Depreciation Expense	2,500
Income before Tax	$3,500
Tax Expense (40%)	1,400
Net Income	$2,100

Startup must make the following accounting entry to record the amount of tax expense and tax payable for 1995:

Dec. 31	Tax Expense	1,400	
	Tax Payable		800
	Deferred Tax		600
	To record income tax for the year 1995.		

Assets	=	Liabilities	+	Owners' Equity
		+800		−1,400
		+600		

The Deferred Tax account is a balance sheet account. A credit balance in it reflects the fact that Startup has received a tax benefit by recording accelerated depreciation, in effect delaying the ultimate obligation to the IRS. To be sure, the amount of deferred tax still represents a liability of Startup. The Deferred Tax account balance of $600 represents the amount of the 1995 temporary difference of $1,500 times the tax rate of 40% ($1,500 × 40% = $600).

What can we learn from the Startup example? First, when you see a firm's income statement, the amount listed as tax expense does not represent the amount of cash paid to the government for taxes. Accrual accounting procedures require that the tax expense amount be calculated using the accounting methods chosen for book purposes.

Second, when you see a firm's balance sheet, the amount in the Deferred Tax account reflects all of the temporary differences between the accounting methods chosen for tax and book purposes. The accounting and financial communities are severely divided on whether the Deferred Tax account represents a "true" liability. For one thing, many investment analysts do not view it as a real liability because they have noticed that it continues to grow year after year. Others look at it as a bookkeeping item that is simply there to balance the books. The FASB has taken the stance that deferred tax is an amount that results in a future obligation and meets the definition of a liability. The controversy concerning deferred taxes is likely to continue for many years.

Pensions

Many large firms establish pension plans to provide income to employees after their retirement. These pension plans often cover a large number of employees and involve millions of dollars. The funds in pension funds have become a major force in our economy, representing billions of dollars in stocks and bonds. In fact, pension funds are among the major "institutional investors" that have an enormous economic impact on our stock and bond exchanges.

Pensions are complex financial arrangements that involve difficult estimates and projections developed by specialists and actuaries. Pension plans also involve very difficult accounting issues requiring a wide range of estimates and assumptions about future cash flows.

We will concern ourselves with two accounting questions related to pensions. First, the employer must record the cost of the pension plan as an expense over some time period. How should that expense be recorded? Second, the employer's financial statement should reflect a measure of the liability associated with a pension plan. What is the liability for future pension amounts and how should it be recorded or disclosed? Our discussion will begin with the recording of pension expense.

Pensions on the Income Statement Most pension plans are of the following form:

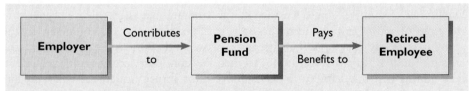

Normally, the employer must make payments to the pension fund at least annually, perhaps more frequently. This is often referred to as *funding the pension* or as *the* **funding payment.** *Funding* simply means that the employer has contributed cash to the pension fund. The pension fund is usually administered by a trustee, often a bank or other financial institution. The trustee must invest the employer's funds so that they earn interest and dividends sufficient to pay amounts owed to retired employees.

Our first accounting question concerns the amount that should be shown by the employer as pension expense. This is another example of the difference between cash basis accounting and accrual accounting. The cash paid as the funding payment is not the same as the expense. When using the accrual basis of accounting, we must consider the amount of pension cost incurred, not the amount paid. Pension expense should be accrued in the period that the employee earns the benefits, regardless of the amount paid to the pension trustee. The amount expensed and the amount paid involve two separate decisions.

The FASB has specified the methods to use to calculate the amount of annual pension expense to record on the employer's income statement.[4] The accountant must determine the cost of the separate components of pension cost and total them

---

[4] *Statement of Financial Accounting Standards No. 87,* "Employers' Accounting for Pension Plans" (Stamford, Conn.: FASB, 1985).

Understand the meaning of a pension obligation and record accounting entries to recognize pensions as a long-term liability.

to determine the amount of pension expense. The components consider the employee's service during the current year, the interest cost, the earnings on pension investments, and other factors. The details of those calculations are beyond our discussion.

To illustrate, suppose that Employer Firm has calculated its annual pension expense to be $80,000 for 1995. Also suppose that Employer has determined that it will make a funding payment of $60,000 to the pension fund. On the basis of those decisions, Employer should make the following accounting entry for the year:

Dec. 31	Pension Expense	80,000	
	Cash		60,000
	Accrued Pension Cost		20,000
	To record annual pension expense and funding payment.		

Assets	=	**Liabilities**	+	**Owners' Equity**
− 60,000		+ 20,000		− 80,000

The Pension Expense account is an income statement account and is reflected on Employer's 1995 income statement.

Pensions on the Balance Sheet

The **Accrued Pension Cost** in the preceding entry is a balance sheet account. The account could have a credit or debit balance, depending on whether the amount expensed is more or less than the amount of the funding payment. If the account has a debit balance, it is reported by Employer Firm as an asset and labeled as Prepaid Pension Cost. Normally, the account has a credit balance as in the entry here. In that case, the Accrued Pension Cost is reported by Employer Firm as a long-term liability.

But what is the meaning of the Accrued Pension Cost account? Is it really a liability? It certainly is not a measure of the amount that is owed to employees at the time of retirement. In fact, the only true meaning that can be given to the account is to say that it is the difference between the amount expensed and the amount funded.[5] In that regard, the Accrued Pension Cost account is inadequate in determining a firm's liability to its employees for future retirement benefits. The FASB requires a great deal of footnote information for pension plans. This footnote section can be used to develop a clearer picture of the status of a firm's pension obligation.

Pension Footnote Information

Readers of financial statements are often interested in the *funding status* of pension plans. This indicates whether sufficient assets are available in the pension fund to cover the amounts to be paid to employees as retirement benefits. We will use the footnote disclosures of an actual firm to illustrate the use of pension information.

Exhibit 10-8 presents portions of the 1992 pension footnote for Household International, a large financial institution. We need to define several items in Household's footnote. First, Household has disclosed the amount of *plan assets* at fair value. This is a measure of the total dollar amount of assets that have been accumulated in the pension fund. The footnote indicates that as of year-end 1992, Household had assets of $586.6 million. Second, there are two measures of the amount of pension benefits owed to employees at the time of retirement. One measure is referred to as the **accumulated benefit obligation** (ABO). This is a measure of the amount

---

[5] Some pension plans that are underfunded may be required to report an additional amount as a liability. This is referred to as the *minimum liability provision*. Refer to *SFAS No. 87* for more detail.

EXHIBIT 10-8 Household International's Pension Footnote for 1992

The funded status of defined benefit pension plans at December 31 was as follows (in millions):

	1992	1991
Actuarial present value of:		
Vested benefits obligation	$305.7	$309.3
Nonvested benefits obligation	32.6	29.4
Accumulated benefit obligation	338.3	338.7
Effects of anticipated future compensation levels	27.3	24.6
Projected benefit obligation	365.6	363.3
Plan assets at fair value	586.6	595.4
Plan assets in excess of projected benefit obligation	$221.0	$232.1

of pension benefits payable to employees if they were to retire at their existing salary levels. The footnote indicates that as of year-end 1992, Household had an accumulated benefit obligation of $338.3 million.

Another measure provides a higher estimate of that obligation. The **projected benefit obligation** (PBO) is a measure of the amount of pension benefits payable to employees if an assumption is made concerning the future salary increases that will be earned by the employees. This is probably a more realistic view of the amount of the obligation to employees, but it is a less objective number because of the difficulty in estimating future salary increases for employees. The footnote indicates that as of year-end 1992, Household had a projected benefit obligation of $365.6 million.

To determine the funding status of the pension plan, we must compare the amount of plan assets with the ABO and PBO. At the end of 1992, Household had pension plan assets of $586.6 million, which was $221.0 million higher than the PBO and $248.3 million higher than the ABO. When the amount of assets exceeds the amount of the obligation, the plan is referred to as *overfunded,* indicating that the pension plan is healthy and well managed. Overfunding is also an example of an "off-balance-sheet" asset that investors use to assess the desirability of a company's stock.

Household International pension plans certainly appear to be quite healthy, but not all firms are as fortunate. There have been many press reports of firms whose pension plans are seriously *underfunded* and for which it is quite questionable whether sufficient assets are available to pay impending employee retirement benefits. Such underfunded plans must be considered an off-balance-sheet liability by investors or creditors in assessing the company's health.

Users of the financial statements of U.S. firms are somewhat fortunate because the disclosure of pensions on the balance sheet and in the footnotes is quite extensive. The accounting for pensions by firms outside the United States varies considerably. Many countries do not require firms to accrue pension costs, and the expense is recorded only when paid to retirees. Furthermore, within the statements and footnotes, there is much less disclosure, making an assessment of the funding status of pensions much more difficult.

Postretirement Benefits

Pensions represent a benefit paid to employees after their retirement. In addition to pensions, other benefits may be paid to employees after their retirement. For example, many firms promise to pay a portion of retirees' health care costs. The accounting question is whether postretirement benefits should be considered an expense when paid or during the period that the employee worked for the firm.

Until recently, most firms treated postretirement benefits as an expense when they were paid to the retiree. It was widely believed that costs such as those for health care after retirement are too uncertain to be accrued as an expense and that such costs do not meet the definition of a liability and thus do not merit recording. The result of this expense-as-you-pay accounting was that firms had an obligation to future retirees that was not recorded as a liability. As health care costs began to escalate, this unrecorded—and often undisclosed—cost became a concern for many firms as well as stockholders, analysts, and employees.

The FASB has modified the accounting for other postemployment benefits to be consistent with pension costs. Under the matching principle, postretirement costs must now be accrued as an expense during the period that the employee helps the firm generate revenues and *earns* the benefits. The accountant must determine the cost of the separate components of postretirement benefits and total them to calculate the amount of the expense. Normally, the form of the adjusting entry made to record the expense is as follows:

Dec. 31   Postretirement Expense   xxxx
           Accrued Postretirement Cost   xxxx
      To accrue postretirement costs.

Assets	=	Liabilities	+	Owners' Equity
		+ xxxx		− xxxx

Accrued Postretirement Cost represents a liability that must be reflected on the balance sheet. There is still much controversy concerning the accounting for postretirement costs. Many firms object to the accounting requirements because of uncertainty involved in measuring an obligation that extends far into the future. They also object because the requirements result in reduced profits on the income statement and huge liabilities on the balance sheet. Interestingly, this new accounting rule had little impact on the stock market because the investment community already knew the magnitude of the postretirement obligations.

■ ACCOUNTING FOR YOUR DECISIONS   **You Chair the Pension Committee**

Now that postretirement benefits are accrued on the income statement, should you offer fewer benefits to employees?

How Long-Term Liabilities Affect the Statement of Cash Flows

Most long-term liabilities are related to a firm's financing activities. Therefore, the change in the balance of each long-term liability account should be reflected in the financing activities category of the statement of cash flows. The decrease in a long-

HELPING FIRMS
RAISE DEBT CAPITAL

Name: Kenneth A. Mabbs
Profession: Investment Banker
College Major: Chemistry

Debt played a big role in the mega-deals of the 1980s. It financed the merger of Time and Warner Communications. It drove the "leveraged buyout" of RJR Nabisco by management and outside investors. Indeed, it was the "leverage" that made these deals go. Today, the world of high finance is less driven by debt than it was in the 1980s. One reason is that many companies that borrowed big money to do deals went bankrupt, leaving investors in those bonds holding the bag.

Although his transactions didn't always make *The Wall Street Journal*, Ken Mabbs was a player in the 1980s, the heyday of investment banking. After spending nearly a decade with Bear Stearns in New York and Boston, Mabbs joined First Albany Corporation to set up its corporate finance department. Corporate finance specialists help companies raise money through stock or bond offerings. The firm's brokers sell the securities to their clients: insurance companies, pension funds, wealthy individuals, and so on.

Investment bankers read financial statements to see if the company is strong enough to sell its securities. Because they are paid a percentage of the deal, they have an incentive to make deals that are acceptable to the market. Mabbs says raising debt usually fetches 2%. Raising equity can earn the investment banker a hefty 7% fee, although the deals tend to be smaller.

"If you're dealing with technology companies, the balance sheet isn't as important as the people," says Mabbs, who has an MBA from Wharton and a Ph.D. in physics from Harvard University. He says that you don't usually find much long-term debt on technology clients' balance sheets. The reasons: no collateral as well as the dynamic markets in which they sell their products. "If you're dealing with mature companies that require lots of capital—such as an oil company—they have a 'leveragable' balance sheet with hard assets and they do business in a more established market."

If a company does have a lot of debt, then Mabbs looks at consistency in cash flow and earnings. "You want a steady business, a relatively more stable business." In the 1980s, "people were willing to accept less coverage of debt," he says. "They were willing to emphasize business plans as opposed to historical performance."

But even though the go-go 1980s are gone, the market for high-yield debt—the engine that powered that decade—has quietly made a comeback. Indeed, the debt of lower-quality companies is one of the few ways that investors can get double-digit current yields anymore.

term liability account indicates that cash has been used to pay the liability. Therefore, in the cash flow statement, a decrease in a long-term liability account should appear as a subtraction or reduction. The increase in a long-term liability account indicates that the firm has obtained additional cash via a long-term obligation. Therefore, an increase in a long-term liability account should appear in the cash flow statement as an addition.

The cash flow statement of McDonald's Corporation is presented in Exhibit 10-9. Note that the Financing Activities category contains two large items related to long-term liabilities. In 1992 long-term debt borrowings increased by $509.5 million and are an addition to cash. This indicates that McDonald's increased its cash position by borrowings. Second, the other long-term debt repayment is listed as a deduction

EXHIBIT 10-9 McDonald's Corporation Consolidated Statement of Cash Flows

McDonald's Corporation

CONSOLIDATED STATEMENT OF CASH FLOWS

(In millions of dollars)	Years ended December 31, 1992	1991	1990
Operating activities			
Net income	$ 958.6	$ 859.6	$ 802.3
Adjustments to reconcile to cash provided by operations			
Depreciation and amortization	554.9	514.2	493.3
Deferred income taxes	22.4	64.7	70.8
Changes in operating working capital items			
Accounts receivable increase	(29.1)	(40.9)	(26.6)
Inventories, prepaid expenses and other current assets (increase) decrease	2.2	.4	(32.1)
Accounts payable increase (decrease)	.8	(22.7)	(14.5)
Accrued interest increase (decrease)	(27.4)	27.5	(1.7)
Taxes and other liabilities increase (decrease)	(68.2)	85.2	80.5
Other—net	11.7	(64.8)	(71.0)
Cash provided by operations	1,425.9	1,423.2	1,301.0
Investing activities			
Property and equipment expenditures	(1,086.9)	(1,128.8)	(1,570.7)
Sales of restaurant businesses	124.5	159.8	130.8
Purchases of restaurant businesses	(64.1)	(30.1)	(81.9)
Notes receivable additions	(31.8)	(38.8)	(46.2)
Property sales	52.2	58.6	39.5
Notes receivable reductions	78.5	53.1	61.2
Other	(71.1)	(13.5)	(55.2)
Cash used for investing activities	(998.7)	(939.7)	(1,522.5)
Financing activities			
Notes payable and commercial paper net borrowings supported by line of credit agreements	17.0	(676.7)	987.9
Other long-term debt borrowings	509.5	1,004.1	1,070.7
Other long-term debt repayments	(1,041.5)	(606.9)	(1,561.0)
Treasury stock purchases	(79.7)	(109.2)	(160.3)
Preferred stock issuances	484.9	100.0	
Common and preferred stock dividends	(160.5)	(148.3)	(133.3)
Other	59.4	30.9	23.4
Cash provided by (used for) financing activities	(210.9)	(406.1)	227.4
Cash and equivalents increase	216.3	77.4	5.9
Cash and equivalents at beginning of year	220.2	142.8	136.9
Cash and equivalents at end of year	$ 436.5	$ 220.2	$ 142.8
Supplemental cash flow disclosures			
Interest paid	$ 395.7	$ 368.1	$ 370.5
Income taxes paid	$ 531.6	$ 313.5	$ 326.5

The accompanying Financial Comments are an integral part of the consolidated financial statements.

of $1,041.5. This indicates that McDonald's paid long-term liabilities resulting in a reduction of cash.

Although most long-term liabilities are reflected in the financing category of the statement of cash flows, there are exceptions. The most notable exception involves the Deferred Tax account. The change in this account is reflected in the operating category of the statement of cash flows. This presentation is necessary because the Deferred Tax account is related to an operating item, income tax expense. For example, in Exhibit 10-9, McDonald's listed $22.4 million in the operating category of the 1992 statement of cash flows. This indicates that $22.4 million that was recorded as expense was not paid out in cash but was *deferred* to a future period. Therefore, the amount is a positive amount in or an addition to the operating category.

FROM CONCEPT TO PRACTICE

READING BEN & JERRY'S STATEMENT OF CASH FLOWS

Refer to Ben & Jerry's statement of cash flows for 1992. What were the changes in long-term liabilities? Where are they reported?

REVIEW PROBLEM

The following items pertain to the liabilities of Brandon Foods. You may assume that Brandon Foods began business on January 1, 1995, and therefore the beginning balance of all accounts was zero.

a. On January 1, 1995, Brandon Foods issued bonds with a face value of $50,000. The bonds are due in five years and have a face interest rate of 10%. The market rate on January 1 for similar bonds was 12%. The bonds pay interest annually each December 31. Brandon has chosen to use the effective interest method of amortization for any premium or discount on the bonds.

b. On December 31, Brandon Foods signed a lease agreement with Simak Leasing. The agreement requires Brandon to make annual lease payments of $3,000 per year for four years, with the first payment due on December 31, 1996. The agreement stipulates ownership of the property is transferred to Brandon at the end of the four-year lease. Assume that an 8% interest rate is used for the leasing transaction.

c. Brandon has calculated the amount of expense on its employee pension plan to be $40,000. The company wishes to make a funding payment of $30,000 to the pension fund on December 31, 1995.

d. Brandon must calculate and record the correct amount of deferred tax for 1995. The only difference between the accounting methods chosen for tax purposes and the accounting methods used for financial reporting purposes concerns depreciation on an asset purchased January 1, 1995, for $120,000. For tax purposes, Brandon is allowed to depreciate the asset on a straight-line basis over five years. For financial reporting purposes, Brandon wishes to use straight-line depreciation over eight years. You may assume that Brandon pays income tax at the rate of 40%.

e. On January 1, 1996, Brandon redeems its bonds payable at the specified redemption price of 101. Because this item occurs in 1996, it does not affect the balance sheet prepared for year-end 1995.

1. Record the accounting entries necessary on December 31, 1995 to reflect the information in items a, b, and c of the review problem.

2. For item d, calculate the amount of the Deferred Tax account on the year-end balance sheet. You do not need to develop an accounting entry.

■ **REQUIRED**

3. Develop the long-term liability section of Brandon Foods' balance sheet as of December 31, 1995, based on items a through d. You do not need to consider the footnotes that accompany the balance sheet.

4. Please consider the following questions. Would the company prefer to treat the lease in item b as an operating lease? Why? Also, in item d why would the company prefer a shorter depreciation period for tax purposes than for financial reporting (book) purposes?

5. Calculate the gain or loss on the bond redemption for item e and indicate how it should be reported on the 1996 income statement.

■ SOLUTION TO REVIEW PROBLEM

1. The issue price of the bonds on January 1 must be calculated as the present value of the interest payments and the present value of the principal as follows:

$5,000 × 3.605	$18,025
50,000 × .567	28,350
Issue price	$46,375

The amount of the discount is

$$\$50,000 - \$46,375 = \$3,625$$

The following is the entry on December 31, 1995, to record interest and amortize discount:

Dec. 31	Interest Expense	5,565	
	Cash		5,000
	Discount on Bonds Payable		565
	To record interest and amortize discount.		

Assets	=	Liabilities	+	Owners' Equity
−5,000		+565		−5,565

The interest expense is calculated using the effective interest method by multiplying the carrying value of the bonds times the market rate of interest ($46,375 × 12%).

Brandon must show two accounts in the long-term liability category of the balance sheet: Bonds Payable of $50,000 and Discount on Bonds Payable of $3,060 ($3,625 less $565 amortized).

The lease meets the criteria to be a capital lease. Brandon must record the lease as an asset and record the obligation for lease payments as a liability. The entry should be recorded at the present value of the lease payments of $9,936 (computed by multiplying $3,000 times the annuity factor of 3.312). The accounting entry should be as follows:

Dec. 31	Leased Asset	9,936	
	Lease Obligation		9,936
	To record lease as a capital lease.		

Assets	=	Liabilities	+	Owners' Equity
+9,936		+9,936		

Because the lease agreement was signed on December 31, 1995, it is not necessary to amortize the Lease Obligation account. The account should be stated in the long-term liability section of Brandon's balance sheet at $9,936.

The difference between the amount of pension expense and the amount of pension funding should be considered as accrued pension cost. The following is Brandon's accounting entry to record pension amounts:

Dec. 31	Pension Expense	40,000	
	Cash		30,000
	Accrued Pension Cost		10,000
	To record the annual pension expense and payment.		

Assets	=	Liabilities	+	Owners' Equity
−30,000		+10,000		−40,000

The Accrued Pension Cost account should be stated in the long-term liability category of Brandon's balance sheet.

2. The amount of deferred tax for 1995 is the result of the difference between the amount of depreciation calculated for tax purposes ($120,000/5 years = $24,000) and the amount calculated for financial reporting purposes ($120,000/8 years = $15,000) times the tax rate of 40%. The Deferred Tax account balance therefore is

$$(\$24,000 - \$15,000) \times 40\% = \$3,600$$

The Deferred Tax account should be stated in the long-term liability section of the balance sheet.

3. The long-term liability category of Brandon's balance sheet for December 31, 1995, on the basis of items a to d is as follows:

BRANDON FOODS
PARTIAL BALANCE SHEET
AS OF DECEMBER 31, 1995

Long-Term Liabilities:		
Bonds payable	$50,000	
Less: Unamortized discount on bonds payable	3,060	$46,940
Lease obligation		9,936
Deferred tax		3,600
Accrued pension cost		10,000
Total Long-Term Liabilities		$70,476

4. The company would prefer that the lease be an operating lease because it would not have to record the asset or liability on the balance sheet. This off-balance-sheet financing may give a more favorable impression of the company.

The company would prefer a shorter life for tax purposes because it allows taxes to be reduced. At the same time, a longer life for book purposes allows the firm to report a higher income to the stockholders and investors.

5. Brandon must calculate the loss on the bond redemption as the difference between the carrying value of the bonds ($46,940) and the redemption price ($50,000 × 1.01). The amount of the loss is

$$\$50,500 - \$46,940 = \$3,560 \text{ loss on redemption}$$

The loss should be reported as an extraordinary item on the 1996 income statement.

GUIDANCE ANSWERS TO ACCOUNTING FOR YOUR DECISIONS

YOU RATE THE BONDS

A bond receives a higher rating to the extent that there is assurance that the company will not default on its obligation. Turner Broadcasting Company was a heavy issuer of "junk" bonds in the 1980s because its balance sheet was heavily laden with high-interest debt. Since that time, however, the company has improved its balance sheet and become profitable. In addition, prospects for the cable television industry have improved. The bonds of Turner Broadcasting should get a higher rating to the extent that 1) the other debt on Turner's balance sheet is shrinking, 2) the ratings of CNN are rising, 3) business and regulatory prospects in the cable-TV industry are improving.

YOU CHAIR THE PENSION COMMITTEE

On the one hand, offering fewer benefits might impact the financial statements in a positive way. In particular, the cost of postretirement health insurance is very high. On the other hand, such benefits are a great attraction to employees who are concerned about not having health insurance once they are no longer employed. To some extent, you are going to finance health care benefits by keeping salaries lower than they otherwise might be—thus, creating an offsetting factor on the financial statements. Another attraction to employee benefits: they are not taxed as income to the employee. The task is to make sure the company communicates the attractions of these benefits to employees so that they appreciate them rather than complaining about small salary and wage increases.

CHAPTER HIGHLIGHTS

1. **(LO 1)** Balance sheets generally have two categories of liabilities, current liabilities and long-term liabilities. Long-term liabilities are obligations that will not be satisfied within one year.

2. **(LO 2)** The terms of a bond payable are given in the bond certificate. The denomination of a bond is its face value. The interest rate stated in the bond certificate is referred to as the *face rate* or *stated rate of interest.* Term bonds all have the same due date. Serial bonds are not all due on the same date. Convertible bonds can be converted into common stock by the bondholders. Callable bonds may be redeemed or retired before their due date.

3. **(LO 3)** The issue price of a bond is the present value of the cash flows that the bond will provide to the investor. You must calculate the present value of the annuity of interest payments and of the principal amount to determine the price. The present values must be calculated at the market rate of interest.

4. **(LO 3)** A bond sells at a discount or premium, depending on the relationship of the face rate to the market rate of interest. If the face rate exceeds the market rate, a bond is issued at a premium. If the face rate is less than the market rate, it will be issued at a discount.

5. **(LO 5)** Premium or discount must be amortized by transferring a portion of premium or discount each period to interest expense. Straight-line amortization reduces the balance of the premium or discount account by the same amount each period. The effective interest method of amortization reduces the balance in a manner so that the effective interest rate on the bond is constant over its life.

6. **(LO 4)** The carrying value of the bond equals the face value plus unamortized premium or minus unamortized discount.

7. **(LO 6)** When bonds are redeemed before their due date, a gain or loss on redemption results. The gain or loss is the difference between the bond carrying value at the date of redemption and the redemption price. The gain or loss is treated as an extraordinary item on the income statement.

8. **(LO 7)** A lease is a contractual arrangement between two parties that allows the lessee the right to use the property in exchange for making payments to the lessor.

9. **(LO 7)** There are two major categories of lease agreements, operating and capital. The lessee does not record an operating lease as an asset and does not record the obligation to make payments as a liability. Capital leases are recorded as assets and liabilities by the lessee. Leases are recorded as capital leases if they meet one or more of the four criteria specified by the FASB.

10. **(LO 7)** Capital lease assets must be depreciated by the lessee over the life of the lease agreement. Capital lease payments must be separated into interest expense and reduction of principal using the effective interest method.

11. **(LO 8)** There are many differences between the accounting for tax purposes and for financial reporting purposes. Permanent differences occur when an item affects one calculation but never affects the other.

Temporary differences affect both book and tax calculations but not in the same time period.

12. **(LO 8)** The amount of tax payable is calculated using the accounting method chosen for tax purposes. The amount of tax expense is calculated using the accounting method chosen for financial reporting purposes. The Deferred Tax account reconciles the differences between tax expense and tax payable. It reflects all of the temporary differences times the tax rate. Deferred taxes is a controversial item on the balance sheet, raising questions as to whether it is a true liability.

13. **(LO 9)** Pensions represent an obligation to compensate retired employees for service performed while employed.

14. **(LO 9)** Pension expense is recorded on the income statement and is calculated on the basis of several complex components that have been specified by the FASB.

15. **(LO 9)** Pension expense does not represent the amount of cash paid by the employer to the pension fund. The cash payment is referred to as the *funding payment*. An Accrued Pension account is recorded as the difference between the amount of pension expense and the amount of the funding.

16. **(LO 9)** The required footnote information on pensions can be used to evaluate the funding status of a firm's pension plan. If the amount of assets in the pension fund exceeds the pension obligation, the fund is considered to be overfunded, generally indicating that it is healthy and well managed. An overfunded plan is an example of an "off-balance-sheet" asset that an investor can count toward the value of the company's stock.

17. **(LO 10)** Long-term liabilities represent methods of financing. Therefore, changes in the balances of long-term liability accounts should be reflected in the financing activities category of the statement of cash flows.

KEY TERMS QUIZ

Select one of the following key terms used in the chapter and fill in the appropriate blank to the left of each description. The solution appears at the end of the chapter.

Long-term liability
Face value
Debenture bonds
Serial bonds
Callable bonds
Face rate of interest
Market rate of interest
Bond issue price
Premium on bonds
Discount on bonds
Straight-line method of amortization
Effective interest method of amortization

Carrying value
Gain or loss on redemption
Operating lease
Capital lease
Deferred tax
Permanent difference
Temporary difference
Pension
Funding payment
Accrued pension cost
Accumulated benefit obligation
Projected benefit obligation

1. The principal amount of the bond as stated on the bond certificate.

2. Bonds that do not all have the same due date. A portion of the bonds come due each time period.

3. The interest rate stated on the bond certificate. It is also called the *nominal* or *coupon rate.*

4. The total of the present value of the cash flows produced by a bond. It is calculated as the present value of the annuity of interest payments plus the present value of the principal.

5. An obligation that will not be satisfied within one year.

6. The excess of the issue price over the face value of bonds. It occurs when the face rate on the bonds exceeds the market rate.

7. Bonds that are backed by the general creditworthiness of the issuer and are not backed by specific collateral.

8. The excess of the face value of bonds over the issue price. It occurs when the market rate on the bonds exceeds the face rate.

9. Bonds that may be redeemed or retired before their specified due date.

10. The process of transferring a portion of premium or discount to interest expense. This method transfers the same dollar amount each period.

11. The process of transferring a portion of premium or discount to interest expense. This method transfers an amount resulting in a constant effective interest rate.

12. The face value of a bond plus the amount of unamortized premium or minus the amount of unamortized discount.

13. The interest rate that bondholders could obtain by investing in other bonds that are similar to the issuing firm's bonds.

_____ 14. The difference between the carrying value and the redemption price at the time bonds are redeemed. This amount is recorded as an income statement account.

_____ 15. A measure of the amount owed to employees for pensions that incorporates an estimate of the future salary increases that employees will receive.

_____ 16. A lease that does not meet any of the four FASB criteria and is not recorded by the lessee.

_____ 17. A payment made by the employer to the pension fund or its trustee.

_____ 18. A lease that meets one or more of the four FASB criteria and is recorded as an asset by the lessee.

_____ 19. A difference between the accounting for tax purposes and the accounting for financial reporting purposes. This type of difference affects both book and tax calculations but not in the same time period.

_____ 20. The account used to reconcile the difference between the amount recorded as income tax expense and the amount that is payable as income tax.

_____ 21. A difference between the accounting for tax purposes and the accounting for financial reporting purposes. This type of difference occurs when an item affects one set of calculations but never affects the other set.

_____ 22. An obligation to pay retired employees as compensation for service performed while employed.

_____ 23. An account that represents the difference between the amount of pension recorded as an expense and the amount of the funding payment made to the pension fund.

_____ 24. A measure of the amount owed to employees for pensions if the employees retired at their existing salary levels.

ALTERNATE TERMS

ACCUMULATED BENEFIT OBLIGATION ABO.

BOND FACE VALUE Bond par value.

BONDS PAYABLE Notes payable.

BOND RETIREMENT Extinguishment of bonds.

CARRYING VALUE OF BOND Book value of bond.

EFFECTIVE INTEREST AMORTIZATION Interest method of amortization.

FACE RATE OF INTEREST Stated rate or nominal rate or coupon rate of interest.

LONG-TERM LIABILITIES Noncurrent liabilities.

MARKET RATE OF INTEREST Yield or effective rate of interest.

POSTRETIREMENT COSTS Other postemployment benefits.

PROJECTED BENEFIT OBLIGATION PBO.

REDEMPTION PRICE Reacquisition price.

TEMPORARY DIFFERENCE Timing difference.

QUESTIONS

1. Which interest rate, the face rate or the market rate, should be used when calculating the issue price of a bond? Why?

2. What is the tax advantage that companies experience when bonds are issued instead of stock?

3. Does the issue of bonds at a premium indicate that the face rate is higher or lower than the market rate of interest?

4. Why is the effective interest method of amortization theoretically superior to the straight-line method?

5. What is the meaning of the following sentence: "Amortization affects the amount of interest expense"? How does amortization of premium affect the amount of interest expense? How does amortization of discount affect the amount of interest expense?

6. Does amortization of premium increase or decrease the bond carrying value? Does amortization of discount increase or decrease the bond carrying value?

7. Is there always a gain or loss when bonds are redeemed? How is the gain or loss calculated?

8. Why is it important to show gains or losses on bond redemption separately on the income statement as an extraordinary item?

9. What are the reasons that not all leases are accounted for in the same manner? Do you think it would be possible to develop a new accounting rule that would treat all leases in the same manner?

10. What is the meaning of the term off-balance-sheet financing? Why do some firms want to engage in off-balance-sheet transactions?

11. What are the effects on the financial statements if a lease is considered an operating rather than a capital lease?

12. Should depreciation be recorded on leased assets? If so, over what period of time should depreciation occur?

13. What is the reason that firms have a Deferred Tax account? Where should that account be shown on the financial statements?

14. How can you determine whether an item should reflect a permanent or temporary difference when calculating the deferred tax amount?

15. Does the amount of income tax expense recorded on the income statement represent the amount of tax actually paid? Why or why not?

16. When an employer has a pension plan for employees, what information is shown on the financial statements concerning the pension plan?

17. How can you determine whether a pension plan is overfunded or underfunded?

18. What is the difference between the two measures of a pension plan's obligation, the projected benefit obligation and the accumulated benefit obligation?

19. Do you agree with the statement "All liabilities could be legally enforced in a court of law"?

EXERCISES

(LO 2) EXERCISE 10-1 RELATIONSHIPS

The following components are computed annually when a bond is issued for other than its face value:

- Cash interest payment
- Interest expense
- Amortization of discount/premium
- Carrying value of bond

State whether each component will increase (I), decrease (D), or remain constant (C) as the bond approaches maturity given the following situations. ■ **REQUIRED**

1. Issued at a discount; straight-line amortization.
2. Issued at a discount; effective interest amortization.
3. Issued at a premium; straight-line amortization.
4. Issued at a premium; effective interest amortization.

(LO 3) EXERCISE 10-2 ISSUE PRICE

Preston Company plans to issue $500,000 par value bonds with a stated interest rate of 10%; they mature in 10 years. Interest is paid semiannually. At the date of issuance, assume that the market rate is (a) 10%, (b) 12%, and (c) 8%.

Calculate the price at which the bonds would be issued under each of the three ■ **REQUIRED** market interest rates.

(LO 3) EXERCISE 10-3 ISSUE PRICE

The following terms relate to independent bond issues:

a. 500 bonds; $1,000 par value; 8% stated rate; 5 years; annual interest payments.

b. 500 bonds; $1,000 par value; 8% stated rate; 5 years; semiannual interest payments.

c. 700 bonds; $1,000 par value; 6% stated rate; 10 years; semiannual interest payments.

d. 2,000 bonds; $500 par value; 12% stated rate; 15 years; semiannual interest payments.

Assuming the market rate of interest is 10%, calculate the selling price for each ■ **REQUIRED** bond issue.

(LO 4) EXERCISE 10-4 IMPACT OF TWO BOND ALTERNATIVES

Carlson Company wishes to issue 100 bonds, $1,000 par value, in January. The bonds will have a 10-year life and pay interest annually. The market rate of interest on January 1 will be 9%. Carlson is considering two alternative bond issues: (a) bonds with a face rate of 8% and (b) bonds with a face rate of 10%.

1. Could the company save money by issuing bonds with an 8% face rate? If it ■ **REQUIRED** chooses alternative (a), what would be the interest cost as a percentage?
2. Could the company benefit by issuing bonds with a 10% face rate? If it chooses alternative (b), what would be the interest cost as a percentage?

(LO 6) EXERCISE 10-5 REDEMPTION OF BONDS

Spelling Corporation issued $75,000 par value bonds at a discount of $2,500. The bonds contain a call price of 103. Spelling decides to redeem the bonds early when the unamortized discount is $1,750.

■ REQUIRED

1. Calculate Spelling Corporation's gain or loss on the early redemption of the bonds.

2. Describe where the gain or loss should be presented on the financial statements.

(LO 7) EXERCISE 10-6 LEASED ASSET

Hopper Corporation signed a 10-year capital lease on January 1, 1995. The lease requires annual payments of $6,000 every December 31.

■ REQUIRED

1. Assuming an interest rate of 9 percent, calculate the present value of the minimum lease payments.

2. Explain why the value of the leased asset and accompanying lease obligation is not recorded at $60,000.

(LO 7) EXERCISE 10-7 FINANCIAL STATEMENT IMPACT OF A LEASE

Benjamin's Warehouse signed a six-year capital lease on January 1, 1995, with payments due every December 31. Interest is calculated annually at 10 percent, and the present value of the minimum lease payments is $13,065.

■ REQUIRED

1. Calculate the amount of the annual payment that Benjamin must make every December 31.

2. Calculate the amount of the lease obligation that would be presented on the December 31, 1996, balance sheet (after two lease payments have been made).

(LO 8) EXERCISE 10-8 TEMPORARY AND PERMANENT DIFFERENCES

Madden Corporation wishes to determine the amount of deferred tax that should be recorded on its 1995 financial statements. It has compiled a list of differences between the accounting conducted for tax purposes and the accounting for financial reporting (book) purposes. For each of the following items, indicate whether the difference should be classified as a permanent or temporary difference.

1. During 1995, Madden received interest on state bonds purchased as an investment. The interest can be treated as tax-exempt interest for tax purposes.

2. During 1995, Madden paid for a life insurance premium on two key executives. Madden's accountant has indicated that the amount of the premium cannot be deducted for income tax purposes.

3. During December 1995, Madden received money for renting a building to a tenant. Madden must report the rent as income on its 1995 tax form. For book purposes, however, the rent will be considered income on the 1996 financial statement.

4. Madden owns several pieces of equipment that it depreciates using the straight-line method for book purposes. An accelerated method of depreciation is used for tax purposes, however.

5. Madden offers a warranty on the products it sells. The corporation records the expense of the warranty repair costs in the year the product is sold (the accrual method) for book purposes. For tax purposes, however, Madden is not allowed to deduct the expense until the period when the product is repaired.

6. During 1995, Madden was assessed a large fine by the federal government for polluting the environment. Madden's accountant has indicated that the fine cannot be deducted as an expense for income tax purposes.

(LO 8) EXERCISE 10-9 DEFERRED TAX

On January 1, 1995, Marshall Corporation purchased an asset for $12,000. Assume this is the only asset owned by the corporation. Marshall has decided to use the straight-line method to depreciate it. For tax purposes, it will be depreciated over three years. It will be depreciated over five years, however, for the financial statements provided to stockholders. Assume that Marshall Corporation is subject to a 40% tax rate.

Calculate the balance that should be reflected in the deferred tax account for Marshall Corporation for each year 1995 through 1999.   ■ REQUIRED

(LO 9) EXERCISE 10-10 PENSION ANALYSIS

The following information was extracted from a footnote found in the annual report of a Fortune 500 company.

Plan Assets	$2.6 billion
Accumulated Benefit Obligation	$1.7 billion
Projected Benefit Obligation	$2.1 billion

1. Determine whether the pension plan is overfunded or underfunded.   ■ REQUIRED

2. Explain what your response to part 1 implies about the ability of the plan to provide benefits to future retirees.

MULTI-CONCEPT EXERCISES

(LO 4, 5) EXERCISE 10-11 IMPACT OF A DISCOUNT

Berol Corporation sold 20-year bonds on January 1, 1995. The face value of the bonds was $100,000, and they carry a 9% stated rate of interest, which is paid on December 31 of every year. Berol received $96,400 in return for the issuance of the bonds. Any premium or discount is amortized using the straight-line method.

1. Prepare the journal entry to record the sale of the bonds on January 1, 1995,   ■ REQUIRED
and the proper balance sheet presentation on this date.

2. Prepare the journal entry to record interest expense on December 31, 1995, and the proper balance sheet presentation on this date.

3. Explain why it was necessary for Berol to issue the bonds for only $96,400 rather than $100,000.

(LO 4, 5) EXERCISE 10-12 IMPACT OF A PREMIUM

Assume the same set of facts for Berol Corporation as in Exercise 10-11 except that it received $105,480 in return for the issuance of the bonds.

1. Prepare the journal entry to record the sale of the bonds on January 1, 1995,   ■ REQUIRED
and the proper balance sheet presentation on this date.

2. Prepare the journal entry to record interest expense on December 31, 1995, and the proper balance sheet presentation on this date.

3. Explain why the company was able to issue the bonds for $105,400 rather than for the face amount.

PROBLEMS

(LO 3) PROBLEM 10-1 FACTORS THAT AFFECT THE BOND ISSUE PRICE

Hunter Company is considering the issue of $100,000 face value, five-year term bonds. The bonds will pay 6% interest each December 31. The current market rate is 6%; therefore the bonds will be issued at face value.

■ REQUIRED

1. For each of the following independent situations, indicate whether you believe that the company will receive a premium on the bonds or will issue them at a discount or at par. Without using numbers, explain your position.

   a. Interest is paid semiannually instead of annually.

   b. Assume instead that the market rate of interest is 7%; the nominal rate is still 6%.

2. For each situation in part 1, prove your statement by determining the issue price of the bonds given the changes in parts a and b.

(LO 5) PROBLEM 10-2 AMORTIZATION OF DISCOUNT

Printer Company issued five-year, 10% bonds with par value of $10,000 on January 1, 1995. Interest is paid annually on December 31. The market rate of interest on this date is 12%, and Printer Company receives proceeds of $9,275 on the bond issuance.

■ REQUIRED

1. Prepare a five-year table (similar to Exhibit 10-3) to amortize the discount using the effective interest method.

2. What is the total interest expense over the life of the bonds? cash interest payment? discount amortization?

3. Prepare the journal entry to record interest expense on December 31, 1997 (the third year), and the balance sheet presentation of the bonds on that date.

(LO 5) PROBLEM 10-3 AMORTIZATION OF PREMIUM

Assume the same set of facts for Printer Company as in Problem 10-2 except that the market rate of interest of January 1, 1995, is 8% and the proceeds from the bond issuance equal $10,803.

■ REQUIRED

1. Prepare a five-year table (similar to Exhibit 10-4) to amortize the premium using the effective interest method.

2. What is the total interest expense over the life of the bonds? cash interest payment? premium amortization?

3. Prepare the journal entry to record interest expense on December 31, 1997 (the third year), and the balance sheet presentation of the bonds on that date.

(LO 6) PROBLEM 10-4 REDEMPTION OF BONDS

Kay Company issued $200,000 par value bonds at a premium of $4,500. The bonds contain a call provision of 101. Kay decides to redeem the bonds due to a significant decline in interest rates. On that date, Kay had amortized only $1,500 of the premium.

■ REQUIRED

1. Calculate the gain or loss on the early redemption of the bonds.

2. Calculate the gain or loss on the redemption, assuming that the call provision is 103 instead of 101.

3. Indicate where the gain or loss should be presented on the financial statements.

(LO 7) PROBLEM 10-5 FINANCIAL STATEMENT IMPACT OF A LEASE

Pender Company signed a four-year capital lease on January 1, 1995, requiring annual payments of $2,500 every December 31. Interest expense is calculated at 7%. The present value of the minimum lease payments is $8,467. Pender uses straight-line depreciation for all long-term assets.

■ REQUIRED

1. Prepare the journal entry to record the lease transaction on January 1, 1995.

2. Prepare a table (similar to Exhibit 10-6) to show the four-year amortization of the lease obligation.

3. Prepare the journal entries necessary on December 31, 1996 (the second year of the lease).

4. Develop the balance sheet presentation on December 31, 1996, for the leased asset and lease obligation.

(LO 8) PROBLEM 10-6 DEFERRED TAX

Norwood Corporation has compiled its 1995 financial statements. Included in the long-term liability category of the balance sheet are the following amounts:

	1995	1994
Deferred Tax	$180	$100

Included in the income statement are the following amounts related to income taxes:

	1995	1994
Income before Tax	$500	$400
Tax Expense	200	160
Net Income	$300	$240

In the footnotes that accompany the 1995 statement are the following amounts:

	1995
Current Provision for Tax	$120
Deferred Portion	80

■ REQUIRED

1. Prepare the journal entry recorded in 1995 for income tax expense, deferred tax, and income tax paid.

2. Assume that a stockholder has inquired about the meaning of the numbers recorded and disclosed about deferred tax. Explain why the Deferred Tax liability account exists. Also, what do the terms *current provision* and *deferred portion* mean? Why is the deferred amount in the footnote $80 when the deferred amount on the 1995 balance sheet is $180?

(LO 8) PROBLEM 10-7 DEFERRED TAX CALCULATIONS

Abramovich, Inc., has reported income for book purposes as follows for the past three years:

(IN THOUSANDS)	YEAR 1	YEAR 2	YEAR 3
Income before Taxes	100	120	130

Abramovich has identified two items that are treated differently in the financial records than for taxes. The first one is interest income of $10,000 each year, which is recorded for financial accounting but is tax exempt and does not show up on the company's tax return. The other item is an auto that is depreciated using the straight-line method at the rate of $15,000 each year for financial accounting, but for tax purposes, the auto is being depreciated at the rate of $30,000 in Year 1, $10,000 in Year 2, and $5,000 in Year 3.

■ REQUIRED

1. Determine the amount of cash paid for income taxes each year by Abramovich. Assume a 50% tax rate for all three years.

2. Prepare the T account for Deferred Taxes for Years 1 through 3. What is the balance in the account at the end of Year 3? Why?

(LO 9) PROBLEM 10-8 FINANCIAL STATEMENT IMPACT OF A PENSION

Smith Financial Corporation prepared the following schedule relating to its pension expense and pension funding payment for the years 1993 through 1995.

YEAR	EXPENSE	PAYMENT
1993	$100,000	$90,000
1994	85,000	105,000
1995	112,000	100,000

At the beginning of 1993, the Prepaid/Accrued Pension Cost account had a credit balance of $8,000.

■ REQUIRED

1. Prepare the journal entries to record Smith Financial Corporation's pension expense for 1993, 1994, and 1995.

2. Calculate the balance in the Prepaid/Accrued Pension Cost account at the end of 1995.

3. Explain the effects that pension expense, the funding payment, and the balance in the Prepaid/Accrued Pension Cost account have on the 1995 financial statements.

MULTI-CONCEPT PROBLEMS

(LO 4, 6) PROBLEM 10-9 ENTRIES FOR BONDS

Lamberts Company issued $1,000,000 par value, eight-year, 12% bonds on April 1, 1995, when the market rate of interest was 12%. Interest payments are due every October 1 and April 1. Lamberts uses a calendar year-end.

■ REQUIRED

1. Prepare the journal entry to record the issuance of the bonds on April 1, 1995.

2. Prepare the journal entry to record the interest payment on October 1, 1995.

3. Explain why additional interest must be recorded on December 31, 1995. What impact does this have on the amounts paid on April 1, 1996?

4. Determine the total cash inflows and outflows that occurred on the bonds over the eight-year life.

ALTERNATE PROBLEMS

(LO 3) PROBLEM 10-1A FACTORS THAT AFFECT THE BOND ISSUE PRICE

Gathering, Inc., is considering the issue of $500,000 face value, 10-year term bonds. The bonds will pay 5% interest each December 31. The current market rate is 5%; therefore the bonds will be issued at face value.

1. For each of the following independent situations, indicate whether you believe that the company will receive a premium on the bonds or will issue them at a discount or at par. Without using numbers, explain your position.

    a. Interest is paid semiannually instead of annually.

    b. Assume instead that the market rate of interest is 4%; the nominal rate is still 5%.

2. For each situation in part 1, prove your statement by determining the issue price of the bonds given the changes in parts a and b.

■ REQUIRED

(LO 5) PROBLEM 10-2A AMORTIZATION OF DISCOUNT

Painter Company issued five-year, 5% bonds with par value of $50,000 on January 1, 1995. Interest is paid annually on December 31. The market rate of interest on this date is 8%, and Painter Company receives proceeds of $44,011 on the bond issuance.

1. Prepare a five-year table (similar to Exhibit 10-3) to amortize the discount using the effective interest method.

2. What is the total interest expense over the life of the bonds? cash interest payment? discount amortization?

3. Prepare the journal entry to record interest expense on December 31, 1997 (the third year), and the balance sheet presentation of the bonds on that date.

■ REQUIRED

(LO 5) PROBLEM 10-3A AMORTIZATION OF PREMIUM

Assume the same set of facts for Painter Company as in Problem 10-2A except that the market rate of interest of January 1, 1995, is 4% and the proceeds from the bond issuance equal $52,230.

1. Prepare a five-year table (similar to Exhibit 10-4) to amortize the premium using the effective interest method.

2. What is the total interest expense over the life of the bonds? cash interest payment? premium amortization?

3. Prepare the journal entry to record interest expense on December 31, 1997 (the third year), and the balance sheet presentation of the bonds on that date.

■ REQUIRED

(LO 6) PROBLEM 10-4A REDEMPTION OF BONDS

Elliot Company issued $100,000 par value bonds at a premium of $5,500. The bonds contain a call provision of 101. Elliot decides to redeem the bonds due to a significant decline in interest rates. On that date, Elliot has amortized only $3,500 of the premium.

■ REQUIRED

1. Calculate the gain or loss on the early redemption of the bonds.

2. Calculate the gain or loss on the redemption, assuming that the call provision is 103 instead of 101.

3. Why do you suppose that the call price of the bonds is normally an amount higher than 100?

(LO 7) PROBLEM 10-5A FINANCIAL STATEMENT IMPACT OF A LEASE

Piper Company signed a three-year capital lease on January 1, 1995, requiring annual payments of $4,200 every December 31. Interest expense is calculated at 6%. The present value of the minimum lease payments is $11,227. Piper uses straight-line depreciation for all long-term assets.

■ REQUIRED

1. Prepare the journal entry to record the lease transaction on January 1, 1995.

2. Prepare a table (similar to Exhibit 10-6) to show the three-year amortization of the lease obligation.

3. Prepare the journal entries necessary on December 31, 1996 (the second year of the lease).

4. What accounts would have been recorded if this transaction had been a purchase of the asset and the company had signed a note to pay for the purchase?

(LO 8) PROBLEM 10-6A DEFERRED TAX

Tanner Corporation has compiled its 1995 financial statements. Included in the long-term liability category of the balance sheet are the following amounts:

	1995	1994
Deferred Tax	$180	$200

Included in the income statement are the following amounts related to income taxes:

	1995	1994
Income before Tax	$500	$400
Tax Expense	100	150
Net Income	$400	$250

■ REQUIRED

1. Prepare the journal entry recorded in 1995 for income tax expense, deferred tax, and income tax paid.

2. Assume that a stockholder has inquired about the meaning of the numbers recorded. Explain why the Deferred Tax liability account exists.

(LO 8) PROBLEM 10-7A DEFERRED TAX CALCULATIONS

Clemente, Inc., has reported income for book purposes as follows for the past three years:

(IN THOUSANDS)	YEAR 1	YEAR 2	YEAR 3
Income before Taxes	$120	$120	$120

Clemente has identified two items that are treated differently in the financial records than for taxes. The first one is Interest Income on municipal bonds, which is recognized on the financial reports to the extent of $5,000 each year but does not show up as a revenue item on the company's tax return. The other item is equipment that is depreciated using the straight-line method, at the rate of $20,000 each year for financial accounting, but for tax purposes, the equipment is being depreciated at the rate of $30,000 in Year 1, $20,000 in Year 2, and $10,000 in Year 3.

1. Determine the amount of cash paid for income taxes each year by Clemente. Assume that a 50% tax rate applies to all three years.

2. Prepare the T account for Deferred/Prepaid Taxes for Years 1 through 3. What is the balance in the account at the end of Year 3? Why?

■ REQUIRED

(LO 9) PROBLEM 10-8A FINANCIAL STATEMENT IMPACT OF A PENSION

Jones Consulting Corporation prepared the following schedule relating to its pension expense and pension funding payment for the years 1993 through 1995:

YEAR	EXPENSE	PAYMENT
1993	$100,000	$110,000
1994	85,000	80,000
1995	112,000	100,000

At the beginning of 1993, the Prepaid/Accrued Pension Cost account had a debit balance of $5,000.

1. Prepare the journal entries to record Jones Consulting Corporation's pension expense for 1993, 1994, and 1995.

2. Calculate the balance in the Prepaid/Accrued Pension Cost account at the end of 1995.

3. Explain the effects that pension expense, the funding payment, and the balance in the Prepaid/Accrued Pension Cost account have on the 1995 financial statements.

■ REQUIRED

ALTERNATE MULTI-CONCEPT PROBLEMS

(LO 4, 6) PROBLEM 10-9A FINANCIAL STATEMENT IMPACT OF A BOND

Stevenson Company issued $1,000,000 par value, six-year, 10% bonds on July 1, 1995, when the market rate of interest was 12%. Interest payments are due every July 1 and January 1. Stevenson uses a calendar year-end.

1. Prepare the journal entry to record the issuance of the bonds on July 1, 1995.

2. Prepare the adjusting journal entry on December 31, 1995, to accrue interest expense. Use the straight-line amortization method.

3. Prepare the journal entry to record the interest payment on January 1, 1996.

4. Prepare the journal entry to record the retirement of the bonds on the maturity date.

5. Why is the journal entry necessary on December 31? How would the income statement and balance sheet be affected if the adjusting entry is not prepared?

■ REQUIRED

CASES

READING AND INTERPRETING FINANCIAL STATEMENTS

(LO 1, 7) CASE 10-1 READING AND INTERPRETING BEN & JERRY'S BALANCE SHEET

Refer to the financial statements included in Ben & Jerry's annual report.

■ REQUIRED

1. What is the total amount of long-term liabilities for Ben & Jerry's as of December 29, 1992?

2. Discuss whether deferred income taxes should be included when calculating the total amount of Ben & Jerry's liabilities.

3. Ben & Jerry's has an account titled Long-Term Debt and Obligation under Capital Leases. If that account is a long-term item, why is a portion shown in the current liability category?

4. Footnote 6 indicates that $5.83 million of debentures was redeemed in August 1991. How were these bonds paid off? Should debentures that are convertible into stock be classified as a liability or as stock on the balance sheet?

5. Assume that you are an analyst who must review Ben & Jerry's financial condition. Assume that Ben & Jerry's has indicated that it plans to issue debt of nearly $10 million. Your boss is concerned that the amount of long-term debt may be excessive and has asked you to review the financial statements. Prepare a memo to your boss with a response to her concerns. Include in the memo a discussion of the factors that you considered to determine whether the amount of long-term debt is too high.

(LO 10) CASE 10-2 READING BEN & JERRY'S STATEMENT OF CASH FLOWS

Refer to the statement of cash flows in Ben & Jerry's 1992 annual report and answer the following questions:

■ REQUIRED

1. Ben & Jerry's has leased assets using capital lease arrangements. When payments are made to reduce capital lease obligations, in which category of the cash flow statement are the payments disclosed?

2. In 1991, Ben & Jerry's redeemed $5.83 million of debentures. Why is that not evident on the statement of cash flows?

3. Ben & Jerry's has a Deferred Tax account listed in the asset category of its balance sheet. Would an increase in that account result in an addition or subtraction on the statement of cash flows? In which category?

MAKING FINANCIAL DECISIONS

(LO 1, 7) CASE 10-3 MAKING A LOAN DECISION

Assume that you are a loan officer at a major bank in charge of reviewing loan applications from potential new clients. You are considering an application from

Molitor Corporation, which is a fairly new company with a limited credit history. It has provided a balance sheet for its most recent fiscal year as follows:

MOLITOR CORPORATION
BALANCE SHEET
DECEMBER 31, 199X

ASSETS		LIABILITIES	
Cash	$ 10,000	Accounts payable	$100,000
Receivables	50,000	Notes payable	200,000
Inventory	100,000		
Equipment	500,000	STOCKHOLDERS' EQUITY	
		Common stock	80,000
		Retained earnings	280,000
Total assets	$660,000	Total liabilities and stockholders' equity	$660,000

Your bank has established certain guidelines that must be met before making a favorable loan recommendation. These include minimum levels for several financial ratios. You are particularly concerned about the bank's policy that loan applicants must have a total assets-to-debt ratio of at least 2 to 1 to be acceptable. Your initial analysis of Molitor's balance sheet has indicated that the firm has met the minimum assets-to-debt ratio requirement. On reading the footnotes that accompany the financial statements, however, you discover the following statement:

Molitor has engaged in a variety of innovative financial techniques resulting in the acquisition of $200,000 of assets at very favorable rates. The company is obligated to make a series of payments over the next five years to fulfill its commitments in conjunction with these financial instruments. Current generally accepted accounting principles do not require the assets acquired nor the related obligations be reflected on the financial statements.

■ REQUIRED

1. How should this footnote affect your evaluation of Molitor's loan application? Calculate a revised total assets-to-debt ratio for Molitor.

2. Do you believe that the bank's policy concerning a minimum of total assets-to-debt ratio can be modified to consider financing techniques that are not reflected on the financial statements? Write a statement that expresses your position on this issue.

(LO 6) CASE 10-4 BOND REDEMPTION DECISION

Arlington Areo Ace, a flight training school, issued $100,000 of 20-year bonds at face value when the market rate was 10%. The bonds have been outstanding for ten years. The company pays annual interest on January 1. The current rate for similar bonds is 4%. On January 1, the controller would like to purchase the bonds on the open market to be retired, then issue $100,000 of ten-year bonds to pay 4% annual interest.

■ REQUIRED

Draft a memo to the controller advising him to retire the outstanding bonds and issue new debt. Ignore taxes. (Hint: find the selling price of bonds that pay 10% when the market rate is 4%.)

ACCOUNTING AND ETHICS: WHAT WOULD YOU DO?

(LO 7) CASE 10-5 DETERMINATION OF ASSET LIFE

Jan Kelly is an accountant for Buff's Manufacturing Company. Buff has entered into an agreement to lease a piece of equipment from EZ Leasing. Jan must decide how to record the lease agreement on Buff's financial statements.

Jan has reviewed the lease contract carefully. She has also reviewed the four lease criteria specified in the accounting rules. She has been able to determine that the lease does not meet three of the criteria. However, she is concerned about the criterion that indicates that if the term of the lease is 75% or more of the life of the property, the lease should be classified as a capital lease. Jan is fully aware that Buff does not want to record the lease agreement as a capital lease but prefers to show it as a type of off-balance-sheet financing.

Jan's reading of the lease contract indicates the asset has been leased for seven years. She is unsure of the life of such assets, however, and has consulted two sources to determine it. One of them indicates that similar equipment owned by Buff is depreciated over nine years. The other, a trade publication of the equipment industry, indicates that equipment of this type will usually last for 12 years.

■ REQUIRED

1. How should Jan record the lease agreement?

2. If Jan decides to record the lease as an off-balance-sheet arrangement, has she acted ethically?

(LO 9) CASE 10-6 OVERFUNDED PENSION PLAN

Willis Company has sponsored a pension plan for employees for several years. Each year Willis has paid cash to the pension fund and the pension trustee has used that cash to invest in stocks and bonds. Because the trustee has invested wisely, the amount of the pension assets exceeds the accumulated benefit obligation as of December 31, 1995.

The president of Willis Company wishes to pay a dividend to the stockholders at the end of 1995. The president believes that it is important to maintain a stable dividend pattern. Unfortunately, the company, while profitable, does not have enough cash on hand to pay a dividend and must find a way to raise the necessary cash if the dividend is declared. Several executives of the company have recommended that assets be withdrawn from the pension fund. They point out that the fund is currently "overfunded." Further, they have stated withdrawal of assets will not have an impact on the financial statements because the overfunding is an "off-balance-sheet item."

■ REQUIRED

Comment on the proposal to withdraw assets from the pension fund to pay a dividend to stockholders. Do you believe it is unethical?

ANALYTICAL SOFTWARE CASE

To the Student: Your instructor may assign one or more parts of the analytical software case that is designed to accompany this chapter. This multi-part case gives you a chance to work with real financial statement data using software that stimulates, guides, and hones your analytical and problem-solving skills. It was created especially to support and strengthen your understanding of the chapter's Learning Objectives.

SOLUTION TO KEY TERMS QUIZ

1. Face value (p. 530)
2. Serial bonds (p. 532)
3. Face rate of interest (p. 533)
4. Bond issue price (p. 533)
5. Long-term liability (p. 530)
6. Premium on bonds (p. 535)
7. Debenture bonds (p. 532)
8. Discount on bonds (p. 535)
9. Callable bonds (p. 532)
10. Straight-line method of amortization (p. 537)
11. Effective interest method of amortization (p. 539)
12. Carrying value (p. 538)
13. Market rate of interest (p. 533)
14. Gain or loss on redemption (p. 543)
15. Projected benefit obligation (p. 557)
16. Operating lease (p. 547)
17. Funding payment (p. 555)
18. Capital lease (p. 547)
19. Temporary difference (p. 553)
20. Deferred tax (p. 551)
21. Permanent difference (p. 551)
22. Pension (p. 555)
23. Accrued pension cost (p. 556)
24. Accumulated benefit obligation (p. 556)

Focus on Financial Results

Since early 1993, Sears Roebuck has accomplished what many big corporations have failed to do: make big changes and become more efficient. But the transition was painful. Thousands of loyal employees were laid off and the Sears Catalog, nearly a century old, was eliminated.

For 1992, Sears reported a loss from continuing operations of nearly $2.6 billion, or $7.02 per share. But just one year later, the results couldn't be more different. For1993, the company reported earnings of

$1.7 billion or $4.36 a share.

How did Sears turn around so quickly? For one thing, the company sold its non-retailing subsidiaries—primarily brokerage, insurance, and real estate—to return to its roots as a merchant. For another, the company entered the 1990s world of marketing by sponsoring rock concerts and producing television informercials.

But even at the company's worst moment, the company had fundamental balance sheet strength. With a total shareholders' equity at the end of 1992 of $10.8 billion, or book value of roughly $29 per share, Sears stock was able to operate from a position of strength and make the necessary changes. The strategy certainly paid off for Sears stockholders. By the summer of 1993, the stock reached $60 per share.

Sears, Roebuck and Co.

Consolidated Statements of Financial Position

millions		December 31
	1992	1991
Shareholders' equity (note 14)		
Preferred shares ($1 par value, 50 shares authorized)		
8.88% Preferred Shares, First Series (3.25 shares issued and outstanding)	325.0	325.0
Series A Mandatorily Exchangeable Preferred Shares (7.1875 shares issued and outstanding)	1,236.3	—
Common shares ($.75 par value, 1,000 shares authorized, 345.8 and 344.1 shares outstanding)	290.6	289.5
Capital in excess of par value	2,194.6	2,153.4
Retained income	8,772.2	13,514.3
Treasury stock (at cost)	(1,734.3)	(1,746.4)
Deferred ESOP expense (note 6)	(699.8)	(739.4)
Unrealized net capital gains on marketable equity securities	428.0	365.5
Cumulative translation adjustments	(39.4)	26.3
Total shareholders' equity	**10,773.2**	**14,188.2**
Total liabilities and shareholders' equity	**$83,533.2**	**$77,951.7**

See accompanying notes and the summarized Group financial statements.

Chapter 11

Stockholders' Equity

LEARNING OBJECTIVES

After studying this chapter, you should be able to

1. Identify the components of the stockholders' equity category of the balance sheet and the accounts found in each component.

2. Understand the characteristics of common and preferred stock and the differences between the classes of stock.

3. Determine the impact when stock is issued for cash, for other consideration, or on a subscription basis.

4. Describe the impact of stock treated as treasury stock.

5. Compute the amount of cash dividends when a firm has issued both preferred and common stock.

6. Understand the difference between cash and stock dividends and account for the effect of stock dividends.

7. Determine the difference between stock dividends and stock splits.

8. Understand how investors use ratios to evaluate owners' equity.

9. Determine the impact of transactions involving stockholders' equity on the statement of cash flows.

10. Describe the important differences between the sole proprietorship and partnership forms of organization versus the corporate form (Appendix 11A).

Linkages

A LOOK AT PREVIOUS CHAPTERS

Chapters 9 and 10 covered the current and long-term liability portions of the balance sheet. Liabilities are one source of financing of business activities.

A LOOK AT THIS CHAPTER

This chapter examines the other major source of financing available to companies, stock and stock transactions. The chapter begins with an overview of the stockholders' equity category of Ben & Jerry's balance sheet. The impact of stock issuance and repurchase is examined along with the declaration and payment of cash and stock dividends.

The discussion in this chapter centers on the corporate form of organization and the stockholders' equity of corporations. The accounts contained in the equity category of a sole proprietorship or partnership are presented in the appendix to this chapter.

A LOOK AT UPCOMING CHAPTERS

Chapter 12 examines other events in a company's activities that affect stockholders' equity. It introduces the statement of stockholders' equity as a summary of all events affecting that section of the balance sheet.

An Overview of Stockholders' Equity

The basic accounting equation is often stated as

$$\text{Assets} = \text{Liabilities} + \text{Owners' Equity}$$

Owners' equity is viewed as a residual amount. That is, the owners of a corporation have a claim to all assets after the claims represented by liabilities to creditors have been satisfied.

In this chapter, we concentrate on the corporate form of organization and refer to the owners' equity as *stockholders' equity.* Therefore, the basic accounting equation for a corporation can be stated as

$$\text{Assets} = \text{Liabilities} + \text{Stockholders' Equity}$$

The stockholders are the owners of a corporation. They have a residual interest in its assets after the claims of all creditors have been satisfied.

The stockholders' equity category of all corporations has two major components or subcategories:

$$\text{Total Stockholders' Equity} = \text{Contributed Capital} \\ + \\ \text{Retained Earnings}$$

Contributed capital represents the amount the corporation has received from the sale of stock to stockholders. Retained earnings is the amount of net income that the corporation has earned but not paid as dividends. Instead, the corporation retains and reinvests the income.

Although all corporations maintain the two primary categories of contributed capital and retained earnings, within these categories they use a variety of accounts, which have several alternative titles. The next section illustrates the stockholders' equity category with the use of an actual firm's balance sheet.

Identifying the Components of the Stockholders' Equity Section of the Balance Sheet

LO 1

Identify the components of the stockholders' equity category of the balance sheet and the accounts found in each component.

The complete financial statements of Ben & Jerry's are provided in its annual report. We will focus on the stockholders' equity category of the balance sheet, which is included as Exhibit 11-1. All corporations, including Ben & Jerry's, begin the stockholders' equity category with a list of the firm's contributed capital. Generally, there are two categories of stock: common stock and preferred stock (the latter is discussed later in this chapter). Common stock normally carries voting rights, and the common stockholders elect the officers of the corporation and establish its by-laws and governing rules. It is not unusual for corporations to have more than one type of common stock, each with different rights or terms. Ben & Jerry's has two classes of common stock referred to in its balance sheet as *Class A common stock* and *Class B common stock.* The annual report indicates that both classes of stock have voting rights, but Class B common stock has 10 votes per share on all matters, is generally nontransferable, and is convertible into Class A common stock.

Number of Shares   It is important to determine the number of shares of stock for each stock account. Corporate balance sheets report the number of shares in three categories: **authorized, issued,** and **outstanding shares.**

EXHIBIT 11-1   Ben & Jerry's Stockholders' Equity (Partial Balance Sheet)

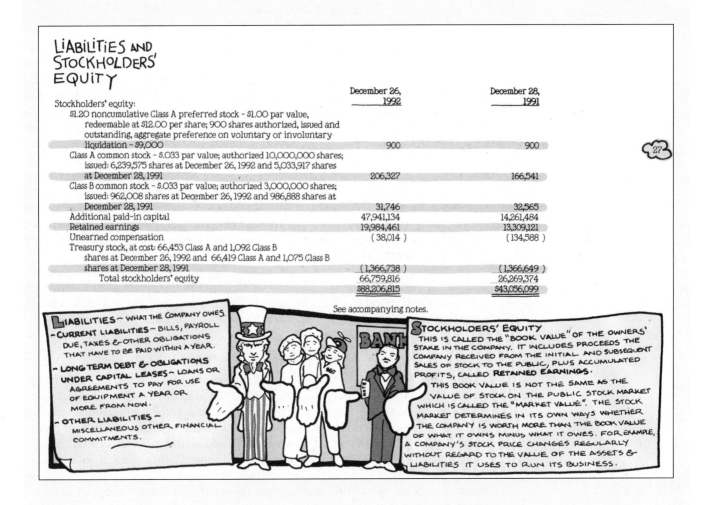

LIABILITIES AND STOCKHOLDERS' EQUITY

Stockholders' equity:	December 26, 1992	December 28, 1991
$1.20 noncumulative Class A preferred stock - $1.00 par value, redeemable at $12.00 per share; 900 shares authorized, issued and outstanding, aggregate preference on voluntary or involuntary liquidation - $9,000	900	900
Class A common stock - $.033 par value; authorized 10,000,000 shares; issued: 6,239,575 shares at December 26, 1992 and 5,033,917 shares at December 28, 1991	206,327	166,541
Class B common stock - $.033 par value; authorized 3,000,000 shares; issued: 962,008 shares at December 26, 1992 and 986,888 shares at December 28, 1991	31,746	32,565
Additional paid-in capital	47,941,134	14,261,484
Retained earnings	19,984,461	13,309,121
Unearned compensation	(38,014)	(134,588)
Treasury stock, at cost: 66,453 Class A and 1,092 Class B shares at December 26, 1992 and 66,419 Class A and 1,075 Class B shares at December 28, 1991	(1,366,738)	(1,366,649)
Total stockholders' equity	66,759,816	26,269,374
	$88,206,815	$43,056,099

See accompanying notes.

LIABILITIES – WHAT THE COMPANY OWES.
– CURRENT LIABILITIES – BILLS, PAYROLL DUE, TAXES & OTHER OBLIGATIONS THAT HAVE TO BE PAID WITHIN A YEAR.
– LONG TERM DEBT & OBLIGATIONS UNDER CAPITAL LEASES – LOANS OR AGREEMENTS TO PAY FOR USE OF EQUIPMENT A YEAR OR MORE FROM NOW.
– OTHER LIABILITIES – MISCELLANEOUS OTHER FINANCIAL COMMITMENTS.

STOCKHOLDERS' EQUITY
THIS IS CALLED THE "BOOK VALUE" OF THE OWNERS' STAKE IN THE COMPANY. IT INCLUDES PROCEEDS THE COMPANY RECEIVED FROM THE INITIAL AND SUBSEQUENT SALES OF STOCK TO THE PUBLIC, PLUS ACCUMULATED PROFITS, CALLED RETAINED EARNINGS.
THIS BOOK VALUE IS NOT THE SAME AS THE VALUE OF STOCK ON THE PUBLIC STOCK MARKET WHICH IS CALLED THE "MARKET VALUE". THE STOCK MARKET DETERMINES IN ITS OWN WAYS WHETHER THE COMPANY IS WORTH MORE THAN THE BOOK VALUE OF WHAT IT OWNS MINUS WHAT IT OWES. FOR EXAMPLE, A COMPANY'S STOCK PRICE CHANGES REGULARLY WITHOUT REGARD TO THE VALUE OF THE ASSETS & LIABILITIES IT USES TO RUN ITS BUSINESS.

To become incorporated, a business must develop articles of incorporation and apply to the proper state authorities for a corporate charter. The corporation must specify the maximum number of shares that it will be allowed to issue. This maximum number of shares is called the *authorized stock*. A corporation applies for authorization to issue many more shares than it will issue immediately to allow for future growth and other events that may occur over its long life. For example, Ben & Jerry's indicates that it has 10,000,000 shares of Class A common stock authorized but that only 6,239,575 shares had been issued as of December 26, 1992.

The number of shares *issued* indicates the number of shares that have been sold or transferred to stockholders. The number of shares issued does not necessarily mean, however, that those shares are currently *outstanding*. The term *outstanding* indicates shares actually in the hands of the stockholders. Shares that have been issued by the corporation and then repurchased are counted as shares issued but not as shares outstanding. Quite often corporations repurchase their own stock as treasury stock (explained in more detail later in this chapter). Treasury stock reduces the number of shares outstanding. The number of Ben & Jerry's shares of Class A common stock outstanding at December 26, 1992, could be calculated as follows:

Number of shares issued	6,239,575
Less: Treasury stock	66,453
Number of shares outstanding	6,173,122

Par Value: The Firm's "Legal Capital"   The stockholders' equity category of many balance sheets refers to an amount as the *par value* of the stock. For example, Ben & Jerry's Class A common stock has a par value of $.033 per share. **Par value** is an arbitrary amount stated on the face of the stock certificate and represents the legal capital of the corporation. Most corporations set the par value of the stock at very low amounts because there are legal difficulties if stock is sold at less than par. Therefore, par value does not indicate the stock's value or the amount that is obtained when it is sold on the stock exchange; it is simply an arbitrary amount that exists to fulfill legal requirements. A company's legal requirement depends on its state of incorporation. Some states do not require corporations to indicate a par value; others require them to designate the *stated value* of the stock. A stated value is accounted for in the same manner as a par value and appears in the stockholders' equity category in the same manner as a par value.

The amount of the par value is the amount that is recorded in the stock account. That is, the dollar amount in a firm's stock account can be calculated as its par value per share times number of shares issued. For Ben & Jerry's, the dollar amount appearing in the Class A common stock account can be calculated as follows:

$.033 Par Value Per Share × 6,239,575 Shares Issued = $205,906 Balance in the Class A Common Stock Account

Additional Paid-in Capital   The dollar amounts of the stock accounts in the stockholders' equity category do not indicate the amount that was received when the stock was sold to stockholders. The Common Stock and Preferred Stock accounts indicate only the par value of the stock. When stock is issued for an amount higher than the par value, the excess is recorded as **additional paid-in capital.** Several alternative titles are used for this account, including Paid-in Capital in Excess of Par, Capital Surplus (an old term that should no longer be used), and Premium on Stock. Regardless of the title, the account represents the amount received in excess of par when stock was issued.

Ben & Jerry's balance sheet indicates Additional Paid-in Capital of $47,941,135 at December 26, 1992. Ben & Jerry's, as well as many other corporations, presents only one amount for additional paid-in capital for all stock transactions. Therefore, we are unable to determine whether the amount resulted from the issuance of Class A common stock, Class B common stock, preferred stock, or other stock transactions. As a result, it is often impossible to determine the issue price of each category of stock even with a careful analysis of the balance sheet and the accompanying footnotes.

Retained Earnings: The Amount Not Paid as Dividends   **Retained earnings** represents net income that the firm has earned but has *not* paid as dividends. Remember that retained earnings is an amount that is accumulated over the entire life of the corporation and does not represent the income or dividends for a specific year. For example, the balance of the Retained Earnings account on Ben & Jerry's balance sheet at December 26, 1992, is $19,984,461. That does not mean that Ben and Jerry's had a net income of that amount in 1992 but that over the life of the corporation, it has had $19,984,461 more net income than it paid as dividends to stockholders.

It is also important to remember that the balance of the Retained Earnings account does not mean that liquid assets of that amount are available to the stockholders. Corporations decide to retain income because they have needs other than paying dividends to stockholders. The needs may include purchase of assets, retirement of debt, or other financial needs. Money spent for those needs usually benefits the stockholders in the long run, but liquid assets equal to the balance of the Retained Earnings account are not necessarily available to stockholders. In fact, shareholders may believe that income should be retained because the company can reinvest the money and get a better return within the business than the shareholders can get on their own, particularly when interest rates are low. Additionally, the federal income tax code encourages companies to reinvest profits. The reason for this is that money paid out is taxed twice, once when the company earns it and again when the shareholder reports it as income. In summary, Retained Earnings is a stockholders' equity account. Although the company's assets have increased, retained earnings does not represent a pool of liquid assets.

A prospective stockholder may purchase shares and receive certificates, as here, either directly from the company or through a stockbroker. Usually, however, a broker purchases shares in its own name for the investor's account—and the investor never sees a certificate.

What Is Preferred Stock?

Many companies have a class of stock called *preferred stock.* One of the advantages of preferred stock is the flexibility it provides because its terms and provisions can

LO   **2**

Understand the characteristics of common and preferred stock and the differences between the classes of stock.

be tailored to meet the firm's needs. These terms and provisions are detailed in the stock certificate. Generally, preferred stock offers holders a preference to dividends declared by the corporation. That is, if a dividend is declared, the preferred stockholders must receive it before the holders of common stock can receive a dividend.

The dividend rate on preferred stock may be stated in two ways. First, it may be stated as a percentage of the stock's par value. For example, if a stock is presented in the balance sheet as $100 par, 7% preferred stock, its dividend rate is $7 per share ($100 times 7%). Second, the dividend may be stated as a per-share amount. For example, a stock may appear in the balance sheet as $100 par, $7 preferred stock, meaning that the dividend rate is $7 per share. Investors in common stock should note the dividend requirements of the preferred shareholder. The greater the obligation to the preferred shareholder, the less desirable the common stock becomes.

Several important provisions of preferred stock relate to the payment of dividends. Some preferred stock issues have a **cumulative feature,** which means that if a dividend is not declared to the preferred stockholders in one year, dividends are considered to be *in arrears.* Before a dividend can be declared to common stockholders in a subsequent period, the preferred stockholders must be paid all dividends in arrears as well as the current year's dividend. The cumulative feature ensures that the preferred stockholders will receive a dividend before one is paid to common stockholders. It does not guarantee a dividend to preferred stockholders, however. There is no legal requirement to mandate that a corporation declare a dividend, and preferred stockholders have a legal right only to receive a dividend once it has been declared.

Some preferred stocks have a **participating feature.** Its purpose is to allow the preferred stockholders to receive a dividend in excess of the regular rate when a firm has been particularly profitable and declares an abnormally large dividend. When the participating feature is present and a firm declares a dividend, the preferred stockholders first have a right to the current year's dividend and then the common stockholders must receive an equal portion (usually based on the par or stated value of the stocks) of the dividend. The participating feature then applies to any dividend declared in excess of the amounts in the first two steps. The preferred stockholders are allowed to share in the excess, normally on the basis of the total par value of the preferred and common stock. The participating feature is explained in more detail in the section of this chapter concerning dividends.

Preferred stock may also be **convertible** or **callable.** The convertible feature allows the preferred stockholders to convert their stock holdings to common stock. Convertible preferred stock offers stockholders the advantages of the low risk generally associated with preferred stock and the possibility of higher return that is associated with common stock. The callable feature allows the issuing firm to retire the stock after it has been issued. Normally, the call price is specified as a fixed dollar amount. Firms may exercise the call option to eliminate a certain class of preferred stock so that control of the corporation is maintained in the hands of fewer stockholders. The call option also may be exercised when the dividend rate on the preferred stock is too high and other more cost-effective financing alternatives are available.

Preferred stock is attractive to many investors because it offers a return in the form of a dividend at a level of risk that is lower than that of most common stocks. Usually, the dividend available on preferred stock is more stable from year to year and, as a result, the market price of the stock is also more stable. In fact, if preferred stock carries certain provisions, it is very similar to bonds or notes payable. Management must evaluate whether such securities really represent debt and should be presented in the liability category of the balance sheet or whether they represent equity and should be presented in the equity category. Such a decision involves the concept of *substance over form.* That is, a company must look not only at the legal form but also at the economic substance of the security to decide whether it is debt or equity.

■ ACCOUNTING FOR YOUR DECISIONS

You have a choice between buying the 6% preferred stock of an industrial company or the common stock of the same company that pays a 2% dividend. However, counting stock appreciation, both securities are providing a total return of 8%. You have just been informed that the chairman of the Federal Reserve Board has decided to raise short-term interest rates by a quarter of a point. All other things being equal, which security would seem to be more attractive?

Issuance of Stock

Stock Issued for Cash

Stock may be issued in several different ways. It may be issued for cash or in a transaction in which noncash assets are received in return or on a subscription basis. When stock is issued for cash, the amount of its par value should be recorded in the stock account and the amount in excess of par should be recorded in an additional paid-in capital account. For example, assume that on July 1 a firm issued 1,000 shares of $10 par common stock for $15 per share. The transaction is recorded as follows:

July 1	Cash	15,000	
	Additional Paid-in Capital—		
	Common		5,000
	Common Stock		10,000
	To record the issuance of 1,000 shares of common stock at $15 per share.		

Assets	=	Liabilities	+	Owners' Equity
+15,000				+ 5,000
				+10,000

LO 3
Determine the impact when stock is issued for cash, for other consideration, or on a subscription basis.

As noted earlier, the Common Stock account and the Additional Paid-in Capital account are both presented in the stockholders' equity category of the balance sheet and represent the contributed capital component of the corporation.

If no-par stock is issued, the corporation does not distinguish between common stock and additional paid-in capital. If the firm in the previous example had issued no-par stock on July 1 for $15 per share, the transaction would be recorded as follows:

July 1	Cash	15,000	
	Common Stock		15,000
	To record the issuance of 1,000 shares of common stock at $15 per share.		

Assets	=	Liabilities	+	Owners' Equity
+15,000				+15,000

Stock Issued for Noncash Consideration

Occasionally, stock is issued in return for something other than cash. For example, a corporation may issue stock to obtain land, buildings, or other consideration. When such a transaction occurs, the company faces the difficult task of deciding what value to place on the transaction. This is especially difficult when the market values of the elements of the transaction are not known with complete certainty. The general guideline that should be followed is that the transaction should be recorded at fair market value. Market value may be indicated by the value of the consideration given (stock) or the value of the consideration received (property), whichever can be most readily determined.

Assume that on July 1 a firm issued 500 shares of $10 par preferred stock to acquire a building. The stock is not widely traded and the current market value of the stock is not evident. The building has recently been appraised by an independent firm as having a market value of $12,000. In this case, the issuance of the stock is recorded as follows:

July 1	Building	12,000	
	Additional Paid-in Capital—		
	Preferred		7,000
	Preferred Stock		5,000
	To record the issuance of preferred stock for building.		

Assets	=	Liabilities	+	Owners' Equity
+ 12,000				+ 7,000
				+ 5,000

In other situations, the market value of the stock may be more readily determined and should be used as the best measure of the value of the transaction. Market value may be represented by the current stock market quotation or from a recent cash sale of the stock. The company should attempt to develop the best estimate of the market value of the noncash transaction and should neither intentionally overstate nor understate the assets received by the issuance of stock.

Stock Issued on a Subscription Basis

Some corporations issue stock on a subscription basis. An investor who signs a **subscription agreement** agrees to purchase a specified number of shares at a specified price but to pay for the stock at a future date. The stock certificates are not actually issued to the investors until the specified amount has been received in cash. The issuing corporation receives an asset, a receivable, however, when the subscription agreement is signed and must record a transaction at that time. For example, assume that on January 1 an investor signs a subscription agreement to purchase 1,000 shares of Sosa Company common stock for $25 per share. The stock carries a par value of $10 per share. Sosa records the following transaction at the time of the signing of the subscription agreement, with the par value per share recorded in the Common Stock Subscribed account:

Jan. 1	Subscription Receivable	25,000	
	Additional Paid-in Capital—		
	Common		15,000
	Common Stock Subscribed		10,000
	To record the subscription agreement at $25 per share.		

Assets	=	Liabilities	+	Owners' Equity
+ 25,000				+ 15,000
				+ 10,000

The Subscriptions Receivable account is considered an asset account; the Common Stock Subscribed account is considered a stockholders' equity account and indicates that an investor has agreed to purchase stock but has not yet paid for it. When the investor pays and the stock certificates are issued, the balance of the Common Stock Subscribed account is transferred to the Common Stock account.

Assume that the investor pays Sosa $25,000 on April 1 and the stock certificates are issued. Sosa should record two accounting entries. First, it must record the receipt of cash and eliminate the balance of the Subscriptions Receivable account as follows:

April 1	Cash	25,000
	Subscriptions Receivable	25,000
	To record receipt of cash for stock subscriptions.	

Assets	=	**Liabilities**	+	**Owners' Equity**
+25,000				
−25,000				

Second, Sosa should record the issuance of the stock to the investor as follows:

April 1	Common Stock Subscribed	10,000
	Common Stock	10,000
	To record issuance of stock to an investor.	

Assets	=	**Liabilities**	+	**Owners' Equity**
				−10,000
				+10,000

What Is Treasury Stock?

The stockholders' equity category of Ben & Jerry's annual report includes **treasury stock** in the amount of $1,366,738. The Treasury Stock account is created when a corporation buys its own stock sometime after issuing it. For an amount to be treated as treasury stock, (1) it must be the corporation's own stock, (2) it must have been issued to the stockholders at some point, (3) it must have been repurchased from the stockholders, and (4) it must not have been retired but must be held for some purpose. Treasury stock is not considered outstanding stock and does not have voting rights.

A corporation may repurchase stock as treasury stock for several reasons. The most common is to have stock available to distribute to employees for bonuses or as part of an employee benefit plan. Firms also may buy treasury stock to maintain a favorable market price for the stock or to improve the appearance of the firm's financial ratios. More recently, firms have purchased their stock to maintain control of the ownership and to prevent unwanted takeover or buyout attempts. Of course, the lower the stock price, the more likely a company is to buy back its own stock and wait for the shares to rise in value before reissuing it.

The two methods to account for treasury stock transactions are the cost method and the par value method. We will present the more commonly used cost method. Assume that the stockholders' equity section of Rezin Company's balance sheet on December 31, 1994, appears as follows:

Common stock, $10 par value	$10,000
1,000 shares issued and outstanding	
Additional paid-in capital—common	12,000
Retained earnings	15,000
Total stockholders' equity	$37,000

LO **4**

Describe the impact of stock treated as treasury stock.

Assume that on February 1, 1995, Rezin buys 100 of its shares as treasury stock at $25 per share. Rezin records the following transaction at that time:

Feb. 1	Treasury Stock	2,500	
	Cash		2,500
	To record the purchase of 100 shares of treasury stock.		

Assets	=	Liabilities	+	Owners' Equity
− 2,500				− 2,500

The purchase of treasury stock does not directly affect the Common Stock account itself. The Treasury Stock account is considered to be a contra account and is subtracted from the total of contributed capital and retained earnings in the stockholders' equity section. Treasury Stock is *not* an asset account. When a company buys its own stock, it is contracting its size and reducing the equity of the stockholders. Therefore, the normal balance of the account is a debit balance and is increased by debiting and decreased by crediting the account.

The stockholders' equity section of Rezin's balance sheet on February 1, 1995, after the purchase of the treasury stock, appears as follows:

Common stock, $10 par value	$10,000
1,000 shares issued, 900 outstanding	
Additional paid-in capital—common	12,000
Retained earnings	15,000
Total contributed capital and retained earnings	$37,000
Less: Treasury stock, 100 shares at cost	2,500
Total stockholders' equity	$34,500

Corporations may choose to reissue stock to investors after it has been held as treasury stock. When treasury stock is resold for more than it cost, the difference between the sales price and cost appears in the Additional Paid-in Capital—Treasury Stock account. For example, if Rezin resold 100 shares of treasury stock on May 1, 1995, for $30 per share, the transaction is recorded as follows:

May 1	Cash	3,000	
	Treasury Stock		2,500
	Additional Paid-in Capital—Treasury Stock		500
	To record the reissuance of treasury stock.		

Assets	=	Liabilities	+	Owners' Equity
+ 3,000				+ 2,500
				+ 500

When treasury stock is resold for an amount less than its cost, the difference between the sales prices and cost is deducted from the Additional Paid-in Capital—Treasury Stock account. If that account does not exist, the difference should be deducted from the Retained Earnings account. For example, assume that Rezin Company had resold 100 shares of treasury stock on May 1, 1995, for $20 per share, instead of $30 in the previous example. In this example, Rezin has had no other treasury stock transactions and, therefore, no balance existed in the Additional Paid-in Capital—Treasury Stock account. The entry is recorded as follows:

May 1	Cash	2,000	
	Retained Earnings	500	
	Treaury Stock		2,500
	To record the reissuance of treasury stock.		

Assets	=	Liabilities	+	Owners' Equity
+2,000				− 500
				+2,500

Thus, the Additional Paid-in Capital—Treasury Stock account may have a credit or zero balance, but entries that result in a negative or debit balance in the account should not be made.

Note that *income statement accounts are never involved* in treasury stock transactions. Regardless of whether treasury stock is reissued for more or less than its cost, the effect is reflected in the stockholders' equity accounts. It is simply not possible for a firm to engage in transactions involving its own stock and have the result affect the performance of the firm as reflected on the income statement.

Retirement of Stock

Retirement of stock occurs when a corporation buys back its stock after it has been issued to investors and does not intend to reissue it. Retirement often occurs because the corporation wishes to eliminate a particular class of stock or a particular group of stockholders. When stock is repurchased and retired, the balances of the stock account and paid-in capital account that were created when the stock was issued must be eliminated. When the original issue price is higher than the repurchase price of the stock, the difference should be reflected in the Paid-in Capital from Stock Retirement account. For example, assume that Pippen and Company issued 1,000 shares of $10 par common stock on January 1 at $50 per share, resulting in the following transaction:

Jan. 1	Cash	50,000	
	Additional Paid-in Capital—		
	Common		40,000
	Common Stock		10,000
	To record the issuance of stock.		

Assets	=	Liabilities	+	Owners' Equity
+50,000				+40,000
				+10,000

Assume that on August 1 Pippen repurchased the stock for retirement at $45 per share. The entry to repurchase and retire the stock is recorded as follows:

Aug. 1	Additional Paid-in Capital—		
	Common	40,000	
	Common Stock	10,000	
	Paid-In Capital from Stock Retirement		5,000
	Cash		45,000
	To record the repurchase and retirement of common stock.		

Assets	=	Liabilities	+	Owners' Equity
−45,000				−10,000
				−40,000
				+ 5,000

When the repurchase price of the stock is more than the original issue price, the difference reduces the Retained Earnings account. For example, assume that on August 1 Pippen repurchased the stock for retirement at a price of $55 per share instead of $45 per share. The entry to repurchase and retire the stock is recorded as follows:

Aug. 1	Additional Paid-in Capital—		
	Common	40,000	
	Common Stock	10,000	
	Retained Earnings	5,000	
	Cash		55,000
	To record the repurchase and retirement of common stock.		

Assets	=	Liabilities	+	Owners' Equity
− 55,000				− 40,000
				− 10,000
				− 5,000

The general principle for retirement of stock is the same as for treasury stock transactions. No income statement accounts are affected by the retirement. The effect is reflected in the Cash account and the stockholders' equity accounts.

Dividends: Distribution of Income to Shareholders

Cash Dividends

Corporations may declare and issue several different types of dividends, the most common of which is a cash dividend to stockholders. Cash dividends may be declared quarterly, annually, or at other intervals. Normally, cash dividends are declared on one date, referred to as the *date of declaration,* and paid out on a later date, referred to as the *payment date.*

Generally, two requirements must be met before the board of directors can declare a cash dividend. First, sufficient cash must be available by the payment date to pay to the stockholders. Second, the Retained Earnings account must have a sufficient credit balance. Dividends reduce the balance of the account, and therefore Retained Earnings must have a balance prior to the dividend declaration. Most firms have an established policy concerning the portion of income that will be declared as dividends. The **dividend payout ratio** is calculated as the annual dividend amount divided by the annual net income. The dividend payout ratio for many firms is 50% or 60% and seldom exceeds 70%. Typically, utilities pay a high proportion of their earnings. In contrast, fast-growing companies in technology often pay nothing to shareholders. Some investors want and need the current income of a high-dividend payout, but others would rather not receive dividend income and prefer to gamble that the stock price will appreciate.

Cash dividends become a liability on the date they are declared. An accounting entry should be recorded on that date to acknowledge the liability and reduce the balance of the Retained Earnings account. For example, assume that on July 1 the board of directors of Grant Company declared a cash dividend of $7,000 to be paid on September 1. Grant records the declaration as follows:

July 1	Retained Earnings	7,000	
	Cash Dividend Payable		7,000
	To record the declaration of a cash dividend.		

Assets	=	Liabilities	+	Owners' Equity
		+7,000		−7,000

The Cash Dividend Payable account is a liability and is normally shown in the current liability category of the balance sheet.

Grant records the following accounting transaction on September 1 when the cash dividend is paid:

Sept. 1	Cash Dividend Payable	7,000	
	Cash		7,000
	To record the payment of cash dividend.		

Assets	=	Liabilities	+	Owners' Equity
−7,000		−7,000		

The important point to remember is that dividends reduce the amount of retained earnings *when declared.* When dividends are paid, the company reduces the liability to stockholders reflected in the Cash Dividend Payable account.

Cash Dividends for Preferred and Common Stock

When cash dividends involving more than one class of stock are declared, the corporation must determine the proper amount to allocate to each class of stock. As indicated earlier, the amount of dividends that preferred stockholders have rights to depends on the terms and provisions of the preferred stock. We will illustrate the proper allocation of cash dividends with an example of a firm that has two classes of stock, preferred and common.

Assume that on December 31, 1995, Boomer Company has outstanding 10,000 shares of $10 par, 8% preferred stock and 40,000 shares of $5 par common stock. Boomer was unable to declare a dividend in 1993 or 1994 but wishes to declare a $70,000 dividend for 1995. The dividend is to be allocated to preferred and common stockholders in accordance with the terms of the stock agreements.

Noncumulative Preferred Stock   If the terms of the stock agreement indicate that the preferred stock is not cumulative, the preferred stockholders do not have a right to dividends in arrears. The dividends that were not declared in 1993 and 1994 are simply lost and do not affect the distribution of the dividend in 1995. Therefore, the cash dividend declared in 1995 is allocated between preferred and common stockholders as follows:

LO   5

Compute the amount of cash dividends when a firm has issued both preferred and common stock.

	TO PREFERRED	TO COMMON
Step 1: Distribute current year dividend to preferred (10,000 shares × $10 par × 8% × 1 year)	$8,000	
Step 2: Remaining dividend to common ($70,000 − $8,000)		$62,000
Total allocated	$8,000	$62,000
Dividend per share		
Preferred: $8,000/10,000 shares	$.80	
Common: $62,000/40,000 shares		$1.55

Cumulative Preferred Stock   If the terms of the stock agreement indicate that the preferred stock is cumulative, the preferred stockholders have a right to dividends in arrears before the current year's dividend is distributed. Therefore, Boomer performs the following steps:

	TO PREFERRED	TO COMMON
Step 1: Distribute dividend in arrears to preferred (10,000 shares × $10 par × 8% × 2 years)	$16,000	
Step 2: Distribute current year dividend to preferred (10,000 shares × $10 par × 8% × 1 year)	8,000	
Step 3: Distribute remainder to common ($70,000 − $24,000)		$46,000
Total allocated	$24,000	$46,000
Dividend per share		
Preferred: $24,000/10,000 shares	$2.40	
Common: $46,000/40,000 shares		$1.15

Cumulative and Participating Preferred Stock   If the terms of the stock agreement indicate that the preferred stock is both cumulative and participating, the preferred stockholders have a right to dividends in arrears (the cumulative feature) and to share in the portion of the current year's dividend that exceeds a specified amount (the participating feature). Assume that Boomer Company preferred stockholders participate in any dividend in excess of 8% of total par value and that the participation is on the basis of the proportion of the total par value of the preferred and common stock. The 1995 dividend is distributed as follows:

	TO PREFERRED	TO COMMON
Step 1: Distribute dividend in arrears to preferred (10,000 shares × $10 par × 8% × 2 years)	$16,000	
Step 2: Distribute current year dividend to preferred (10,000 shares × $10 par × 8% × 1 year)	8,000	
Step 3: Distribute equal percentage to common (40,000 shares × $5 par × 8%)		$16,000
Step 4: Remainder to preferred and common on basis of total par value		
Preferred: ($70,000 − $40,000) × $100,000[a]/$300,000 =	10,000	
Common: ($70,000 − $40,000) × $200,000[b]/$300,000 =		20,000
Total allocated	$34,000	$36,000
Dividend per share		
Preferred: $34,000/10,000 shares	$3.40	
Common: $36,000/40,000 shares		$.90

[a] 10,000 shares × $10 par   [b] 40,000 shares × $5 par

The Boomer Company example illustrates the flexibility available with preferred stock. The provisions and terms of the preferred stock can be established to make the stock attractive to investors and to provide an effective form of financing for the corporation. The cumulative and participating features make the preferred stock more attractive. However, these features may make the *common stock* less attractive because more dividends to the preferred stockholders may mean less dividends are left for the common stockholders.

Stock Dividends

Cash dividends are the most popular and widely used form of dividend, but corporations may at times use stock dividends instead of, or in addition to, cash dividends. A **stock dividend** occurs when a corporation declares and issues additional shares of its own stock to its existing stockholders. Firms use stock dividends for several reasons. First, a corporation may simply not have sufficient cash available to declare a cash dividend. Stock dividends do not require the use of the corporation's resources and allow cash to be retained for other purposes. Second, stock dividends result in additional shares of stock outstanding and may decrease the market price per share of stock if the dividend is large (small stock dividends tend to have little effect on market price). The lower price may make the stock more attractive to a wider range of investors and allow enhanced financing opportunities. Finally, stock dividends normally do not represent taxable income to the recipients and may be attractive to some wealthy stockholders.

LO 6
Understand the difference between cash and stock dividends and account for the effect of stock dividends.

   Similar to cash dividends, stock dividends are normally declared by the board of directors on a specific date and the stock is distributed to the stockholders at a later date. The corporation records the stock dividend on the date of declaration. Assume that Shah Company's stockholders' equity category of the balance sheet appears as follows as of January 1, 1995:

Common stock, $10 par, 5,000 shares issued and outstanding	$ 50,000
Additional paid-in capital—common	30,000
Retained earnings	70,000
Total stockholders' equity	$150,000

Assume that on January 2, 1995, Shah declares a 10% stock dividend to common stockholders to be distributed on April 1, 1995. Small stock dividends (usually those of 20 to 25% or less) normally are recorded at the *market value* of the stock as of the date of declaration. Assume that Shah's common stock is selling at $40 per share on that date. Therefore, the total market value of the stock dividend is $20,000 (10% of 5,000 shares outstanding, or 500 shares times $40 per share). Shah records the transaction on the date of declaration as follows, with the par value per share recorded in the Common Stock Dividend Distributable account:

Jan. 2	Retained Earnings	20,000	
	Additional Paid-in Capital—Common		15,000
	Common Stock Dividend Distributable		5,000
	To record the declaration of a stock dividend.		

Assets	=	Liabilities	+	Owners' Equity
				− 20,000
				+ 15,000
				+ 5,000

The Common Stock Dividend Distributable account represents shares of stock to be issued; it is not a liability account because no cash or assets are to be distributed to the stockholders. Thus, it should be treated as an account in the stockholders'

Stockbrokers like this one evaluate whether a company declares and pays dividends, in what form—cash or stock—and the size of the distribution as a basic part of her job of matching prospective companies' stocks to a client's investment profile.

equity section of the balance sheet and is a part of the contributed capital component of equity.

Note that the declaration of a stock dividend does not affect the total stockholders' equity of the corporation although the retained earnings are reduced. That is, the stockholders' equity section of Shah's balance sheet on January 2, 1995, is as follows after recording the declaration of the dividend:

Common stock, $10 par, 5,000 shares issued and outstanding	$ 50,000
Common stock dividend distributable, 500 shares	5,000
Additional paid-in capital—common	45,000
Retained earnings	50,000
Total stockholders' equity	$150,000

The account balances are different but total stockholders' equity is $150,000 both before and after the declaration of the stock dividend. In effect, retained earnings has been capitalized (transferred permanently to the contributed capital accounts). When a corporation actually issues a stock dividend, an entry is necessary to transfer an amount from the Stock Dividend Distributable account to the appropriate stock account.

Our stock dividend example has illustrated the general rule that stock dividends should be recorded at fair market value. That is, in the transaction to record the stock dividend, retained earnings is debited in the amount of the fair market value per share of the stock times the number of shares to be distributed. When a large stock dividend is declared, however, accountants do not follow the general rule we have illustrated. A large stock dividend has been established to be a stock dividend of more than 20% to 25% of the number of shares of stock outstanding. In that case, the stock dividend is recorded at *par value* rather than at fair market value.

That is, Retained Earnings is debited in the amount of the par value per share times the number of shares to be distributed.

Refer again to the Shah Company example. Assume that, instead of a 10% dividend, on January 2, 1995, Shah declares a 100% stock dividend to be distributed on April 1, 1995. The stock dividend results in 5,000 additional shares being issued and certainly meets the definition of a large stock dividend. Shah records the following transaction at the time of dividend declaration:

Jan. 2	Retained Earnings	50,000	
	Common Stock Dividend Distributable		50,000
	To record the declaration of a large stock dividend.		

Assets	=	Liabilities	+	Owners' Equity
				− 50,000
				+ 50,000

The accounting transaction to be recorded when the stock is actually distributed is as follows:

April 1	Common Stock Dividend Distributable	50,000	
	Common Stock		50,000
	To record the distribution of a stock dividend.		

Assets	=	Liabilities	+	Owners' Equity
				− 50,000
				+ 50,000

The stockholders' equity category of Shah's balance sheet as of April 1 after the stock dividend is as follows:

Common stock, $10 par, 10,000 shares issued	
and outstanding	$100,000
Additional paid-in capital—common	30,000
Retained earnings	20,000
Total stockholders' equity	$150,000

Again, you should note that the stock dividend has not affected total stockholders' equity. Shah has $150,000 of stockholders' equity both before and after the stock dividend. The difference between large and small stock dividends is the amount transferred from retained earnings to the contributed capital portion of equity.

Stock Splits

A **stock split** is similar to a stock dividend in that it results in additional shares of stock outstanding and is nontaxable. In fact, firms may use a stock split for nearly the same reasons as a stock dividend: to increase the number of shares, reduce the market price per share, and make the stock more accessible to a wider range of investors. There is an important legal difference, however. Stock dividends do not affect the par value per share of the stock whereas stock splits reduce the par value per share. There also is an important accounting difference. An accounting transaction is *not recorded* when a corporation declares and executes a stock split. None of the stockholders' equity accounts are affected by the split. Rather, the footnote information accompanying the balance sheet must disclose the additional shares and the reduction of the par value per share.

Return to the Shah Company example. Assume that on January 2, 1995, Shah chose to declare a 2-for-1 stock split instead of a stock dividend. The split results

LO 7

Determine the difference between stock dividends and stock splits.

in an additional 5,000 shares of stock outstanding but should not be recorded in a formal accounting transaction. Therefore, the stockholders' equity of Shah Company on January 2, 1995, is as follows:

Common stock, $5 par, 10,000 shares issued and outstanding	$ 50,000
Additional paid-in capital—common	30,000
Retained earnings	70,000
Total stockholders' equity	$150,000

You should note that the par value per share has been reduced from $10 to $5 per share of stock as a result of the split. Like a stock dividend, the split does not affect total stockholders' equity because no assets have been transferred. Therefore, the split simply results in more shares of stock with claims to the same net assets of the firm.

The footnotes to Ben & Jerry's annual report indicate that the company executed a 2-for-1 stock split in June 1992 on its Class A common stock. This doubled the number of shares of stock, an increase of 2,498,667 shares. Thus, after the stock split, each stockholder had twice as many shares of stock but still had the same proportional ownership of the company. Although a stock split does not increase the wealth of the shareholder, it is usually a good sign. Companies with rising stock prices declare a stock split to make the stock more marketable to the small investor who would be more likely to buy a stock at $50 per share than at $100.

■ ACCOUNTING FOR YOUR DECISIONS   **You Are the Stockbroker**

Your firm recently recommended the shares of Intel Corp., a large semiconductor manufacturer based in northern California. The stock had been trading at about $100 per share when the company announced a 2:1 stock split. You have been receiving calls from your clients asking you why the company split its stock, even though there is no change in anyone's ownership interest as a result of the split. How would you answer your clients?

What Analyzing Owners' Equity Reveals about a Firm's Value

Book Value per Share

LO   8
Understand how investors use ratios to evaluate owners' equity.

Users of financial statements are often interested in computing the *value* of a corporation's stock. This is a difficult task because value is not a well-defined term and means different things to different users. One measure of value is the book value of the stock. **Book value per share** of common stock represents the rights that each share of common stock has to the net assets of the corporation. The term *net assets* refers to the total assets of the firm minus total liabilities. In other words, net assets equal the total stockholders' equity of the corporation. Therefore, when only common stock is present, book value per share is measured as follows:

Book Value per Share =
   Total Stockholders' Equity/Number of Shares of Stock Outstanding

The stockholders' equity of Motorola, Inc., as of 1992 appears in Exhibit 11-2. As of December 31, 1992, the total stockholders' equity of Motorola is $5,144 million and the number of outstanding shares of common stock is 269.7 million. Therefore, the book value per share for Motorola is $19.07, calculated as follows:

$$\$5,144/269.7 = \$19.07$$

This means that the company's common stockholders have the right to $19.07 per share of net assets in the corporation.

The book value per share indicates the recorded minimum value per share of the stock. In a sense, it indicates the rights of the common stockholders in the event that the company is liquidated. It does not indicate the market value of the common stock. That is, book value per share does not indicate the price that should be paid by those who wish to buy or sell stock on the stock exchange. Book value also represents an incomplete measure of value because the corporation's net assets are normally measured on the balance sheet at the original historical cost, not at the current value of the assets. Thus, book value per share does not provide a very accurate measure of the price that a stockholder would be willing to pay for a share of stock. The book value of a stock is often thought to be the "floor" of a stock price. An investor's decision to pay less than book value for a share of stock suggests that he or she thinks that the company is going to continue to lose money, thus shrinking book value.

Calculating Book Value When Preferred Stock Is Present

The focus of the computation of book value per share is always on the value per share of the *common* stockholders. Therefore, the computation must be adjusted for corporations that have both preferred and common stock. The numerator of the fraction, total stockholders' equity, should be reduced by the rights that preferred stockholders have to the corporation's net assets. Normally, this can be accomplished by deducting the redemption value or liquidation value of the preferred stock along with any dividends in arrears on cumulative preferred stock. The denominator of

---

EXHIBIT 11-2   Motorola, Inc., Stockholder's Equity

MOTOROLA, INC., AND CONSOLIDATED SUBSIDIARIES
STOCKHOLDERS' EQUITY
DECEMBER 31, 1992

IN MILLIONS	1992	1991
Stockholders' equity		
Common stock, $3 par value		
Authorized shares: 1992, 300.0; 1991, 300.0		
Outstanding: 1992, 269.7; 1991, 264.3	$ 809	$ 398
Preferred stock, $100 par issuable in series		
Authorized shares: 0.5 (none issued)	—	—
Additional paid-in capital	701	945
Retained earnings	3,634	3,287
Total stockholders' equity	**$5,144**	**$4,630**

FROM CONCEPT TO PRACTICE

READING BEN & JERRY'S ANNUAL REPORT
Refer to Ben & Jerry's 1992 report. What was the book value per share of the common stock? How did that relate to the market value of the stock?

should not include the number of shares of preferred stock.

To illustrate the computation of book value per share when both common and preferred stock are present, we will refer to the stockholders' equity of Household International, Inc., a large financial institution. Household provided an analysis of the number of shares of stock in its 1992 annual report, which is presented in Exhibit 11-3. When calculating book value per share, we wish to consider only the *common* stockholders' equity. Fortunately, Household has provided that amount in the statement of stockholders' equity (not shown here) as $1,608.4 million. The number of shares of common stock outstanding can be calculated from Exhibit 11-3 as follows:

55.55 million shares issued
− 14.11 million treasury shares
41.44 million shares outstanding

Therefore, the computation of book value per share is as follows:

$1,608.4/41.44 = $38.81 Book Value Per Share

This indicates that if the company were liquidated and the assets sold at their recorded values, the stockholders would receive $38.81 per share. Of course, if the company went bankrupt and had to liquidate assets at distressed values, stockholders would not receive book value but something less.

Market Value per Share

The market value of the stock is a more meaningful measure of the value of the stock to those financial statement users interested in buying or selling shares of stock. The **market value per share** is the price at which stock is currently selling. When stock is sold on a stock exchange, the price can be determined by its most recent selling price. For example, the listing for General Motors stock on the financial pages of a newspaper may indicate the following:

52-WEEK		DAILY			
HIGH	LOW	HIGH	LOW	LAST	CHANGE
44 3/8	26 3/4	31 3/8	30 7/8	31 1/8	+ 5/8

EXHIBIT 11-3 Household International's Number of Shares of Stock

HOUSEHOLD INTERNATIONAL, INC., AND SUBSIDIARIES **NUMBER OF SHARES OF STOCK** **DECEMBER 31**				
SHARES IN MILLIONS	NONCONVERTIBLE PREFERRED	COMMON STOCK	TREASURY STOCK	
Balance, Dec. 31, 1991	2,500	54,556	(14,779)	
Exercise of stock options		149		
Conversion of preferred		843		
Reissuance of stock			669	
Issuance of preferred	50			
Balance, Dec. 31, 1992	2,550	55,548	(14,110)	

last 52-week period. General Motors sold as high as $44 3/8 and as low as $26 3/4 during that time period. The right-hand portion indicates the high and low for the previous day's trading and the closing price. General Motors sold as high as $31 3/8 per share and as low as $30 7/8 per share and closed at $31 1/8. For the day, the stock increased by 5/8 or $0.625 per share.

The market value of the stock depends on many factors. Stockholders must evaluate

a corporation's earnings and liquidity as indicated in the financial statements. They must also consider a variety of economic factors and project all of the factors into the future to determine the proper market value per share of the stock. Many investors use sophisticated investment techniques, including large databases, to identify factors that affect a company's stock price.

How Changes in Stockholders' Equity Affect the Statement of Cash Flows

It is important to determine the impact that the issuance of stock, the repurchase of stock, and the payment of dividends have on the statement of cash flows. Each of these business activities has an impact on cash that must be reflected on the statement.

The issuance of stock is a method to finance the business. Therefore, the cash *inflow* from sale of stock to stockholders should be reflected as an inflow in the financing activities section of the statement of cash flows. Generally, companies do not disclose separately the amount received for the par value of the stock and the amount received in excess of par. Rather, one amount is listed to indicate the total inflow of cash.

The repurchase or retirement of stock also represents a financing activity. Therefore, the cash *outflow* should be reflected as a reduction of cash in the financing activities section of the statement of cash flows. Again, companies do not distinguish between the amount paid for the par of the stock and amounts paid in excess of par. One amount is generally listed to indicate the total cash outflow to retire stock.

Dividends paid to stockholders represent a cost of financing the business with stock. Therefore, dividends paid should be reflected as a cash *outflow* in the financing section of the statement of cash flows. It is important to distinguish between the declaration of dividends and the payment of dividends. The cash outflow occurs at the time the dividend is paid and should be reflected on the statement of cash flows in that period.

REVIEW PROBLEM

Andrew Company was incorporated on January 1, 1995, under a corporate charter that authorized the issuance of 50,000 shares of $5 par common stock and 20,000 shares of $100 par, 8% preferred stock. The following events occurred during 1995. Andrew wishes to record the events and develop financial statements on December 31, 1995.

a. Issued for cash 10,000 shares of common stock at $25 per share and 1,000 shares of preferred stock at $110 per share on January 15, 1995.

b. Acquired a patent on April 1 in exchange for 2,000 shares of common stock. At the time of the exchange, the common stock was selling on the local stock exchange for $30 per share.

c. Repurchased 500 shares of common stock on May 1 at $20 per share. The corporation is holding the stock to be used for an employee bonus plan.

d. Decided that some of the reacquired stock was not needed and on June 1 resold 200 shares of treasury stock at $25 per share.

e. Declared a cash dividend of $1 per share to common stockholders and an 8% dividend to preferred stockholders on July 1. The preferred stock is noncumulative, nonparticipating. The dividend will be distributed on August 1.

f. Distributed the cash dividend on August 1.

g. Declared and distributed to preferred stockholders a 10% stock dividend on September 1. At the time of the dividend declaration, preferred stock was valued at $130 per share.

h. Calculated the annual net income on December 31 as $200,000. Andrew wishes to transfer the net income from the Income Summary account to the Retained Earnings account.

1. Record the accounting entries required in items a through h.

■REQUIRED

2. Develop the stockholders' equity section of Andrew Company's balance sheet at December 31, 1995. You do not need to consider the footnotes that accompany the balance sheet.

3. Determine the book value per share of the common stock. Assume that the preferred stock can be redeemed at par.

■SOLUTION TO REVIEW PROBLEM

1. The following entries should be recorded:

a. The entry to record the issuance of stock:

Jan. 15	Cash	360,000	
	Common Stock		50,000
	Additional Paid-in Capital—Common		200,000
	Preferred Stock		100,000
	Additional Paid-in Capital—Preferred		10,000
	To record the issuance of stock for cash.		

Assets	=	Liabilities	+	Owners' Equity
+360,000				+ 50,000
				+200,000
				+100,000
				+ 10,000

b. The patent received for stock should be recorded at the fair market value:

April 1	Patent	60,000	
	Common Stock		10,000
	Additional Paid-in Capital—Common		50,000
	To record the issuance of stock for patent.		

Assets	=	Liabilities	+	Owners' Equity
+60,000				+10,000
				+50,000

c. Stock reacquired constitutes treasury stock and should be recorded as follows:

May 1	Treasury Stock	10,000	
	Cash		10,000
	To record the purchase of treasury stock.		

Assets	=	Liabilities	+	Owners' Equity
−10,000				−10,000

d. Reissued stock does not result in a gain on the income statement. The transaction is recorded as follows:

June 1   Cash   5,000
             Treasury Stock   4,000
             Additional Paid-in Capital—Treasury
                Stock   1,000
          To record the reissuance of treasury stock.

Assets	=	Liabilities	+	Owners' Equity
+5,000				+4,000
				+1,000

e. A cash dividend should be declared on the number of shares of stock outstanding as of July 1. The dividend is recorded as follows:

July 1   Retained Earnings   19,700
             Dividends Payable—Common   11,700
             Dividends Payable—Preferred   8,000
          To record the declaration of a cash dividend.

Assets	=	Liabilities	+	Owners' Equity
		+11,700		−19,700
		+ 8,000		

The number of shares of common stock outstanding should be calculated as the number of shares issued (12,000) less the number of shares of treasury stock (300). The preferred stock dividend should be calculated as 1,000 shares times $100 par times 8%.

f. The entry to record the distribution of a cash dividend is recorded as follows:

Aug. 1   Dividends Payable—Common   11,700
            Dividends Payable—Preferred   8,000
            Cash   19,700
          To record the payment of cash dividend.

Assets	=	Liabilities	+	Owners' Equity
−19,700		−11,700		
		− 8,000		

g. A stock dividend on the number of shares of stock outstanding should be declared and recorded at the market value of the stock as follows:

Sept. 1   Retained Earnings   13,000
              Preferred Stock   10,000
              Additional Paid-in Capital—Preferred   3,000
          To record the declaration of a stock dividend.

Assets	=	Liabilities	+	Owners' Equity
				−13,000
				+10,000
				+ 3,000

The amount of the debit to Retained Earnings should be calculated as the number of shares outstanding (1,000) times 10% times $130 per share.

h. The entry to close the Income Summary to stockholders' equity should be recorded as follows:

Dec. 31	Income Summary	200,000	
	Retained Earnings		200,000
	To record the annual net income.		

Assets	**=**	**Liabilities**	**+**	**Owners' Equity**
				− 200,000
				+ 200,000

2. The stockholders' equity for Andrew Company after completing these transactions appears as follows:

Preferred stock, $100 par, 8%,	
20,000 authorized, 1,100 issued	$110,000
Common stock, $5 par, 50,000 authorized,	
12,000 issued	60,000
Additional paid-in capital—preferred	13,000
Additional paid-in capital—common	250,000
Additional paid-in capital—treasury stock	1,000
Retained earnings	167,300*
Total contributed capital and retained	
earnings	$601,300
Less: Treasury stock, 300 shares, common	(6,000)
Total stockholders' equity	$595,300

*$200,000 − $19,700 − $13,000

3. The book value per share of the common stock is

$$(\$595,300 - \$110,000)/11,700 \text{ shares} = \$41.48.$$

GUIDANCE ANSWERS TO ACCOUNTING FOR YOUR DECISIONS

YOU ARE THE INVESTOR

The preferred stock provides mostly dividend income while the common stock provides mostly capital appreciation. In an environment of rising interest rates, the security that focuses on a fixed income (dividends) generally does poorer that the security that focuses on capital appreciation. However, rising interest rates are not generally good for any kind of stock.

YOU ARE THE STOCKBROKER

Although a stock split does not provide immediate income to current shareholders, it is an indication of the company's optimism about the future. In order to maintain interest from individual shareholders, many companies like to keep the price of their stock under $100. A stock split keeps the shares at an affordable price and allows a broader range of potential investors. From an investors' perspective, a stock split is usually a positive sign.

APPENDIX 11A

ACCOUNTING TOOLS: UNINCORPORATED BUSINESSES

The focus of Chapter 11 has been on the corporate form of organization. Most of the large, influential companies in the United States are organized as corporations. They have a legal and economic existence that is separate from that of the owners of the business, the stockholders. Many other companies in the economy are organized as sole proprietorships or partnerships. The purpose of the appendix is to show briefly how the characteristics of such organizations affect the accounting, particularly the accounting for the owners' equity category of the balance sheet.

Sole Proprietorships

LO ▌10▐

Describe the important differences between sole proprietorship and partnership forms of organization versus the corporate form.

A **sole proprietorship** is a business owned by one person. Most sole proprietorships are small in size with the owner as the operator or manager of the company. The primary advantage of the sole proprietorship form of organization is its simplicity. The owners' equity category of the balance sheet consists of one account, the owner's capital account. The owner answers to no one but himself or herself. A disadvantage of the sole proprietorship is that all the responsibility for the success or failure of the venture attaches to the owner, who often has limited resources.

There are three important points to remember about this form of organization. First, a sole proprietorship is not a separate entity for legal purposes. This means that the law does not distinguish between the assets of the business and those of its owner. If an owner loses a lawsuit, for example, the law does not limit an owner's liability to the amount of assets of the business but extends them to the owner's personal assets. Thus, the owner is said to have *unlimited liability*.

Second, accountants adhere to the *entity principle* and maintain a distinction between the owner's personal assets and the assets of the sole proprietorship. The balance sheet of a sole proprietorship should reflect only the "business" assets and liabilities with the difference reflected as owner's capital.

Third, a sole proprietorship is not treated as a separate entity for federal income tax purposes. That is, the sole proprietorship does not pay tax on its income. Rather, the business income must be declared as income on the owner's personal tax return and income tax is assessed at the personal tax rate rather than the rate that applies to companies organized as corporations. This may or may not be advantageous, depending on the amount of income involved and the owner's tax situation. Between 1986 and 1992, the top corporate tax rate of 34% was higher than the top individual rate. Therefore, the sole proprietorship form usually saved the taxpayer money. Beginning in 1993, the top individual rate reached as high as 39.6% on income above $250,000 per year. The top corporate rate was 35%. Therefore, it might be advantageous for the very successful proprietor to incorporate.

Typical Transactions   When the owners of a corporation, the stockholders, invest in the corporation, they normally do so by purchasing stock. When investing in a sole proprietorship, the owner simply contributes more cash, or other assets, into the business. For example, assume that on January 1, 1995, Peter Tom began a new business by investing $10,000 cash. Peter Tom Company records the transaction as follows:

Jan. 1   Cash   10,000
         Peter Tom, Capital   10,000
      To record the investment of cash to the business.

        Assets   =   Liabilities   +   Owners' Equity
        + 10,000   **+ 10,000**

The capital account is an owner's equity account and reflects the rights of the owner to the business assets.

An owner's withdrawal of assets from the business is recorded as a reduction of owner's equity. Assume that on July 1, 1995, Peter Tom took an auto valued at $6,000 from the business to use as his personal auto. The transaction is recorded as follows:

July 1   Peter Tom, Drawing   6,000
         Equipment   6,000
      To record the withdrawal of auto from the business.

        Assets   =   Liabilities   +   Owners' Equity
        − 6,000   **− 6,000**

The Peter Tom, Drawing account is a contra equity account. Sometimes a drawing account is referred to as a *withdrawals account* as in Peter Tom, Withdrawal. The normal balance of the account is debit, and it is increased by debit and reduced by credit entries. At the end of the fiscal year, the drawing account should be closed to the capital account as follows:

Dec. 31   Peter Tom, Capital   6,000
         Peter Tom, Drawing   6,000
      To close the drawing account to capital.

        Assets   =   Liabilities   +   Owners' Equity
                                                 − 6,000
                                                 + 6,000

The amount of the net income of the business should also be reflected in the capital account. Assume that all revenue and expense accounts of Peter Tom Company have been closed to the Income Summary account, resulting in a credit balance of $4,000, the net income for the year. The Income Summary account is closed to capital as follows:

Dec. 31   Income Summary   4,000
         Peter Tom, Capital   4,000
      To close income summary to the capital account.

        Assets   =   Liabilities   +   Owners' Equity
                                                 − 4,000
                                                 + 4,000

The owners' equity section of the balance sheet for Peter Tom Company consists of one account, the capital account, calculated as follows:

Beginning balance, Jan. 1, 1995	$ −0−
Plus: Investments	10,000
Net income	4,000
Less: Withdrawals	6,000
Ending balance, Dec. 31, 1995	$ 8,000

Partnerships

A **partnership** is a company owned by two or more persons. Like sole proprietorships, most partnerships are fairly small businesses formed when individuals combine their capital and managerial talents for a common business purpose. Other partnerships are large, national organizations. For example, the major public accounting firms are very large, national companies but are organized in most states as partnerships.

Partnerships have characteristics similar to those of sole proprietorships rather than corporations. The following are the most important characteristics of partnerships:

1. *Unlimited liability.* Legally, the assets of the business are not separate from the partners' personal assets. Each partner is personally liable for the debts of the partnership. Creditors have a legal claim, first to the assets of the partnership, and then to the assets of the individual partners.

2. *Limited life.* Corporations have a separate legal existence and an unlimited life but partnerships do not. The life of a partnership is limited; it exists as long as the contract between the partners is valid. The partnership ends when a partner withdraws or a new partner is added. A new partnership must be created for the business to continue.

3. *Not taxed as a separate entity.* Partnerships are subject to the same tax features as sole proprietorships. The partnership itself does not pay federal income tax. Rather, the income of the partnership is treated as personal income on each of the partner's individual tax returns and is taxed as personal income. All partnership income is subject to federal income tax on the individual partners' returns even if it is not distributed to the partners. A variety of other factors affects the tax consequences of partnerships versus the corporate form of organization. These aspects are quite complex and beyond the scope of this text.

A partnership is based on a **partnership agreement.** It is very important that the partners agree in writing about all aspects of the partnership. The agreement should detail items such as how much capital each partner is to invest, the time each is expected to devote to the business, the salary of each, and how income of the partnership is to be divided. If a partnership agreement is not present, the courts may be forced to settle disputes among partners. Therefore, the partners should develop a partnership agreement when the firm is first established and should review the agreement periodically to determine whether changes are necessary.

Investments and Withdrawals In a partnership it is important to account separately for the capital of each of the partners. A capital account should be established in the owners' equity section of the balance sheet for each partner of the company. Investments into the company should be credited to the partner making the investment. For example, assume that on January 1, 1995, Page Waters and Amy Rebec begin a partnership named AP Company. Page contributes $10,000 cash, and Amy contributes equipment valued at $5,000. The accounting transaction that should be recorded by AP Company follows:

Jan. 1	Cash	10,000	
	Equipment	5,000	
	Page Waters, Capital		10,000
	Amy Rebec, Capital		5,000
	To record the contribution of assets to the business.		

Assets	=	Liabilities	+	Owners' Equity
+10,000				+10,000
+ 5,000				+ 5,000

A drawing account also should be established for each owner of the company to account for withdrawals of assets that occur. Assume that on April 1, 1995, each owner withdraws $2,000 of cash from AP Company. The accounting entry is recorded:

April 1	Page Waters, Drawing	2,000	
	Amy Rebec, Drawing	2,000	
	Cash		4,000
	To record the withdrawal of assets from the business.		

Assets	=	Liabilities	+	Owners' Equity
− 4,000				− 2,000
				− 2,000

Distribution of Income The partnership agreement governs the manner in which income should be allocated to partners. The distribution may recognize the partners' relative investment in the business, their time and effort, their expertise and talents, or other factors. We will illustrate three methods of income allocation, but you should be aware that partnerships use many other possible allocation methods. Although these allocation methods are straightforward, partnerships dissolve often because one or more of the partners believes that the allocation is unfair. It is very difficult to devise a method that will make all partners happy.

One way to allocate income is to divide it evenly between or among the partners. In fact, when a partnership agreement is not present, the courts specify that an equal allocation must be applied, regardless of the relative contribution or effort of the partners. For example, assume that AP Company has $30,000 net income for the period and has established an agreement that income should be allocated evenly between the two partners, Page and Amy. The accounting entry that AP Company records during the closing entry process is as follows:

Dec. 31	Income Summary	30,000	
	Page Waters, Capital		15,000
	Amy Rebec, Capital		15,000
	To record the allocation of income between partners.		

Assets	=	Liabilities	+	Owners' Equity
				− 30,000
				+ 15,000
				+ 15,000

An equal distribution of income to all partners is easy to apply but is not fair to those partners who have contributed more in money or time to the partnership.

Another way to allocate income is to specify in the partnership agreement that income be allocated according to a *stated ratio*. For example, Page and Amy may specify that all income of AP Company should be allocated on a 2-to-1 ratio, with Page receiving the larger portion. If that allocation method is applied to the preceding example, AP Company records the following transaction at year-end:

Dec. 31	Income Summary	30,000	
	Page Waters, Capital		20,000
	Amy Rebec, Capital		10,000
	To record the allocation of income between partners.		

Assets	=	Liabilities	+	Owners' Equity
				− 30,000
				+ 20,000
				+ 10,000

Finally, we illustrate an allocation method that more accurately reflects the partners' input. It is based on salaries, interest on invested capital, and a stated ratio. Assume that the partnership agreement of AP Company specifies that Page and Amy be allowed a salary of $6,000 and $4,000, respectively, that each partner receive 10% on her capital balance, and that any remaining income be allocated equally. Assume that AP Company has been in operation for several years and the capital balances of the owners at the end of 1995, prior to the income distribution, are as follows:

Page Waters, Capital	$40,000
Amy Rebec, Capital	50,000

If AP Company calculated that its 1995 net income (before partner salaries) was $30,000, income would be allocated between the partners as follows:

	PAGE	AMY
Distributed for salaries:	$ 6,000	$ 4,000
Distributed for interest:		
Page: ($40,000 × 10%)	4,000	
Amy: ($50,000 × 10%)		5,000
Remainder = $30,000 − $10,000 − $9,000 = $11,000		
Remainder distributed equally:		
Page: ($11,000/2)	5,500	
Amy: ($11,000/2)		5,500
Total distributed	$15,500	$14,500

The accounting transaction to transfer the income to the capital accounts is as follows:

Dec. 31	Income Summary	30,000	
	Page Waters, Capital		15,500
	Amy Rebec, Capital		14,500
	To record the allocation of income to partners.		

Assets	=	Liabilities	+	Owners' Equity
				−30,000
				+15,500
				+14,500

Finally, it should be emphasized that for tax purposes, the income of the partnership is treated as personal income on the partners' individual tax returns regardless of whether or not the income is actually paid in cash to the partners. This aspect often encourages partners to withdraw income from the business and makes it difficult to retain sufficient capital for the business to operate profitably.

CHAPTER HIGHLIGHTS

1. (LO 1) The stockholders' equity category is composed of two parts. Contributed capital is the amount derived from stockholders and other external parties. Retained earnings is the amount of net income not paid as dividends.

2. (LO 1) The stockholders' equity category reveals the number of shares authorized, issued, and outstanding. Treasury stock is stock that the firm has issued and repurchased but not retired.

3. (LO 2) *Preferred stock* refers to a stock which has preference to dividends declared. If a dividend is declared, the preferred stockholders must receive a dividend before the common stockholders.

4. (LO 3) When stock is issued for cash, the par value of the stock should be recorded in the stock account and the amount in excess of par should be recorded in an Additional Paid-in Capital account.

5. (LO 3) When stock is issued for a noncash asset, the transaction should reflect the value of the stock given or the value of the property received, whichever is more evident.

6. (LO 4) Treasury stock is accounted for as a reduction of stockholders' equity. When treasury stock is reissued and the cost is less than reissue price, the difference is credited to Additional Paid-in Capital. When cost exceeds reissue price, Additional Paid-in Capital or Retained Earnings is reduced for the difference.

7. (LO 5) The amount of cash dividends to be paid to common and preferred stockholders depends on the terms of the preferred stock. If the stock is cumulative, preferred stockholders have the right to dividends in arrears before current year dividends are paid. Participating preferred stock indicates that preferred stockholders can share in the amount of the dividend that exceeds a specified amount.

8. (LO 6) Stock dividends involve the issuance of additional shares of stock. The dividend should normally be recorded at the fair market value of the additional shares.

9. (LO 7) Stock splits are similar to stock dividends except that splits reduce the par value per share of the stock. No accounting entry is necessary for stock splits.

10. (LO 8) Book value per share is calculated as net assets divided by the number of shares of common stock. It indicates the rights that stockholders have, based on recorded values, to the net assets in the event of liquidation and is therefore not a measure of the market value of the stock.

11. (LO 8) When a corporation has both common and preferred stock, the net assets attributed to the rights of the preferred stockholders must be deducted from the amount of net assets to determine the book value per share of the common stockholders.

12. (LO 9) Transactions involving stockholders' equity accounts should be reflected in the financing activities category of the statement of cash flows.

13. (LO 10) A sole proprietorship is a business owned by one person. It is not a separate entity for legal purposes and does not pay taxes on its income. However, a balance sheet should present the assets and liabilities of the business, separate from those of the owner. (Appendix 11A)

14. (LO 10) A partnership is a company owned by two or more persons. Like sole proprietorships, partnerships are not a separate legal or tax entity. The balance sheet of the partnership should present the assets and liabilities of the business, separate from those of the owners. (Appendix 11A)

KEY TERMS QUIZ

Select from the following list of key terms used in the chapter and fill in the appropriate blank to the left of each description. The solution appears at the end of the chapter.

Authorized shares   Subscription agreement
Issued shares   Treasury stock
Outstanding shares   Retirement of stock
Par value   Dividend payout ratio
Additional paid-in capital   Stock dividend
Retained earnings   Stock split
Cumulative feature   Market value per share
Participating feature   Convertible stock
Callable stock   Book value per share
Sole Proprietorship (Appendix 11A)   Partnership agreement (Appendix
Partnership (Appendix 11A)   11A)

1. The number of shares sold or distributed to stockholders.

2. An arbitrary amount stated on the face of the stock certificate that represents the legal capital of the firm.

3. Net income that has been made by the corporation but not paid out as dividends.

4. The holders of this stock have a right to dividends in arrears before the current year dividend is distributed.

5. Allows preferred stock to be returned to the corporation in exchange for common stock.

6. An agreement by an investor to purchase stock and pay for it at a later date.

7. Stock issued by the firm and then repurchased but not retired.

8. The annual dividend amount divided by the annual net income.

9. A business with a single owner.

10. Creation of additional shares of stock and reduction of the par value of the stock.

11. Total stockholders' equity divided by the number of shares of common stock outstanding.

12. A business owned by two or more individuals and with the characteristic of unlimited liability.

13. The selling price of the stock as indicated by the most recent stock transactions on, for example, the stock exchange.

14. The maximum number of shares a corporation may issue as indicated in the corporate charter.

15. The number of shares issued less the number of shares held as treasury stock.

16. A document that specifies how much each owner should invest, the salary of each owner, and how profits are to be shared.

17. The amount received for the issuance of stock in excess of the par value of the stock.

_____ **18.** Stock that has a provision allowing the stockholders to share in the distribution of an abnormally large dividend on a percentage basis.

_____ **19.** Allows the issuing firm to eliminate a class of stock by paying the stockholders a fixed amount.

_____ **20.** When the stock of a corporation is repurchased with no intention to reissue at a later date.

_____ **21.** Declaration and issuance of additional shares of its own stock by a corporation to existing stockholders.

ALTERNATE TERMS

ADDITIONAL PAID-IN CAPITAL Paid-in capital in excess of par value.

ADDITIONAL PAID-IN CAPITAL—TREASURY STOCK Paid-in capital from treasury stock transactions.

CALLABLE Redeemable.

CAPITAL ACCOUNT Owners' equity account.

CONTRIBUTED CAPITAL Paid-in capital.

RETAINED EARNINGS Retained income.

SMALL STOCK DIVIDEND Stock dividend less than 20%.

STOCKHOLDERS' EQUITY Owners' equity.

WITHDRAWAL ACCOUNT Drawing account.

QUESTIONS

1. What are the two major components of stockholders' equity? Which accounts generally appear in each component?
2. Corporations disclose the number of shares authorized, issued, and outstanding. What is the meaning of these terms? What causes a difference between the number of shares issued and outstanding?
3. Why do firms designate an amount as the par value of stock? Does par value indicate the selling price or market value of the stock?
4. If a firm has a net income for the year, will the balance in the Retained Earnings account equal the net income? What is the meaning of the balance of the account?
5. What is the meaning of the statement that preferred stock has a preference to dividends declared by the corporation? Do preferred stockholders have the right to dividends in arrears on preferred stock?
6. Why might some stockholders be inclined to buy preferred stock rather than common stock? What are the advantages of investing in preferred stock?
7. Why are common shareholders sometimes called _residual owners_ when a company has both common and preferred stock outstanding?
8. When stock is issued in exchange for an asset, at what amount should the asset be recorded? How could the fair market value be determined?

9. What is treasury stock? Why do firms use it? Where does it appear on a corporation's financial statements?

10. When treasury stock is bought and sold, the transactions do not result in gains or losses recorded on the income statement. What account or accounts are used instead? Why are no income statement amounts recorded?

11. Many firms operate at a dividend payout ratio of less than 50%. Why do firms not pay a larger percentage of income as dividends?

12. What is a *stock dividend*? How should it be recorded?

13. Would you rather receive a cash dividend or stock dividend from a company? Explain.

14. What is the difference between stock dividends and stock splits? How should stock splits be recorded?

15. How is the ratio book value per share calculated? Does the amount calculated as book value per share mean that stockholders will receive a dividend equal to the book value?

16. Can the market value per share of stock be determined by the information on the income statement?

17. What is an advantage of organizing a company as a corporation rather than a partnership? Why don't all companies incorporate? (Appendix 11A)

18. What are some ways that partnerships could share income among the partners? (Appendix 11A)

EXERCISES

(LO 1) EXERCISE 11-1 STOCKHOLDERS' EQUITY ACCOUNTS

MJ Company has identified the following items. Indicate whether each item is included in an account in the stockholders' equity category of the balance sheet. Also indicate whether the normal balance of the account should be debit or credit.

1. Preferred stock issued by MJ.

2. Amount received by MJ in excess of par value when preferred stock was issued.

3. Dividends in arrears on MJ preferred stock.

4. Cash dividend declared but unpaid on MJ stock.

5. Stock dividend declared but unissued by MJ.

6. Treasury stock.

7. Amount received in excess of cost when treasury stock is reissued by MJ.

8. Retained earnings.

9. MJ stockholders signed subscription agreements but have not paid the amounts specified by the agreement.

(LO1) EXERCISE 11-2 SOLVE FOR UNKNOWNS

The stockholders' equity category of Paxson Company's balance sheet appears below. Determine the missing values, which are indicated by question marks.

Common Stock, $10 par, ?? issued,	
?? outstanding	$ 50,000
Additional paid-in capital	200,000
Total contributed capital	??
Retained earnings	100,000
Treasury stock, 500 shares at cost	10,000
Total stockholders' equity	??

(LO 3) EXERCISE 11-3 STOCK ISSUANCE

Horace Company had the following transactions during 1995, its first year of business.

a. Issued 5,000 shares of $5 par common stock for cash at $15 per share.

b. Received from investors subscription agreements to purchase 10,000 shares of common stock at $20 per share on March 1. They paid $5 per share on March 1 and agreed to pay the remaining portion by April 1.

c. Received the balance of the subscriptions on April 1 and issued the stock certificates.

d. Issued 7,000 shares of common stock on May 1 to acquire a factory building from Barkley Company. Barkley had acquired the building in 1991 at a price of $150,000. Horace estimated that the building was worth $175,000 on May 1, 1995.

e. Issued 2,000 shares of stock on June 1 to acquire a patent. The accountant has been unable to estimate the value of the patent but has determined that Horace's common stock was selling at $25 per share on June 1.

1. Determine the impact of each of the events on the accounting equation.

2. Determine the amounts to present on the balance sheet for common stock and additional paid-in capital.

■ REQUIRED

(LO 4) EXERCISE 11-4 TREASURY STOCK

The stockholders' equity category of Rodney Company's balance sheet on January 1, 1995, appeared as follows:

Common stock, $10 par, 10,000 shares issued	
and outstanding	$100,000
Additional paid-in capital	50,000
Retained earnings	80,000
Total stockholders' equity	$230,000

The following transactions occurred during 1995.

a. Reacquired 2,000 shares of common stock at $20 per share on July 1.

b. Resold 500 shares of treasury stock at $20 per share on August 1.

c. Resold 400 shares of treasury stock at $30 per share on September 1.

d. Resold the remaining shares of treasury stock at $18 per share on October 1.

1. Record the entries in journal form.

2. Did the company benefit from the treasury stock transactions? If so, where is the amount of the "gain" presented on the balance sheet?

■ REQUIRED

(LO 4) EXERCISE 11-5 TREASURY STOCK TRANSACTIONS

The stockholders' equity category of Big Bertha's balance sheet on January 1, 1995, appeared as follows:

Common stock, $10 par, 20,000 shares issued	
and outstanding	$200,000
Additional paid-in capital	90,000
Retained earnings	100,000
Total stockholders' equity	$390,000

The following transactions occurred during 1995.

a. Reacquired 4,000 shares of common stock at $20 per share on January 1.

b. Resold 1,000 shares of treasury stock at $20 per share on February 1.

c. Resold 800 shares of treasury stock at $18 per share on March 1.

d. Resold the remaining shares of treasury stock at $30 per share on April 1.

■ REQUIRED

1. Determine the impact of the events on the accounting equation.

2. Did the company benefit from the treasury stock transactions? Where is the "gain" or "loss" presented on the financial statements?

(LO 5) EXERCISE 11-6 CASH DIVIDENDS

The stockholders' equity category of Jackson Company's balance sheet as of January 1, 1995, appeared as follows:

Preferred stock, $100 par, 8%,	
2,000 issued and outstanding	$200,000
Common stock, $10 par, 5,000 issued	
and outstanding	50,000
Additional paid-in capital	300,000
Total contributed capital	$550,000
Retained earnings	400,000
Total stockholders' equity	$950,000

The footnotes that accompany the financial statements indicate that Jackson has not paid dividends for the two years prior to 1995. On July 1, 1995, Jackson wishes to declare a dividend of $100,000 to preferred and common stockholders to be paid on August 1.

■ REQUIRED

1. Determine the amount of the dividend to be allocated to preferred and common stockholders, assuming that the preferred stock is noncumulative, nonparticipating stock.

2. Record the appropriate journal transactions on July 1 and August 1, 1995.

3. Determine the amount of the dividend to be allocated to preferred and common stockholders, assuming instead that the preferred stock is cumulative, nonparticipating stock.

(LO 5) EXERCISE 11-7 CASH DIVIDENDS—PARTICIPATING FEATURE

Refer to Jackson Company's stockholders' equity category in Exercise 11-6. Assume that the footnotes that accompany the financial statements indicate that Jackson has not paid dividends for the two years prior to 1995. On July 1, 1995, Jackson wishes to declare a dividend of $100,000 to preferred and common stockholders to be paid on August 1.

1. Determine the amount of the dividend to be allocated to preferred and common stock, assuming that the preferred stock is cumulative and participates in dividends in proportion to the total par value of preferred and common stock.

2. Record the appropriate journal transactions on July 1 and August 1, 1995.

■ REQUIRED

(LO 6) EXERCISE 11-8 CASH DIVIDENDS AND STOCK DIVIDENDS

The stockholders' equity category of Worthy Company's balance sheet as of January 1, 1995, appeared as follows:

Common stock, $10 par, 40,000 shares issued	
and outstanding	$400,000
Additional paid-in capital	100,000
Retained earnings	400,000
Total stockholders' equity	$900,000

The following transactions occurred during 1995:

a. Declared a 10% stock dividend to common stockholders on January 15. At the time of the dividend, the common stock was selling for $30 per share. The stock dividend was to be issued to stockholders on January 30, 1995.

b. Distributed the stock dividend to the stockholders on January 30, 1995.

1. Record the 1995 transactions in journal entry form.

2. Develop the stockholders' equity category of Worthy Company's balance sheet as of January 31, 1995, after the stock dividend was issued.

■ REQUIRED

(LO 7) EXERCISE 11-9 STOCK DIVIDENDS VERSUS STOCK SPLITS

Scott Company wishes to increase the number of shares of its common stock outstanding and is considering a stock dividend versus a stock split. The stockholders' equity of the firm on its most recent balance sheet appeared as follows:

Common stock, $10 par, 50,000 shares issued	
and outstanding	$ 500,000
Additional paid-in capital	750,000
Retained earnings	880,000
Total stockholders' equity	$2,130,000

If a stock dividend is chosen, the firm wishes to declare a 100% stock dividend. Because the stock dividend qualifies as a "large stock dividend," it must be recorded at par value. If a stock split is chosen, Scott will declare a 2-for-1 split.

1. Compare the effect of the two alternatives on the accounting equation.

2. Develop the stockholders' equity category of Scott's balance sheet that will result from the stock dividend and from the stock split.

■ REQUIRED

(LO 8) EXERCISE 11-10 PAYOUT RATIO AND BOOK VALUE PER SHARE

Divac Company has developed a statement of stockholders' equity for the year 1995 as follows:

	PREFERRED STOCK	PAID-IN CAPITAL— PREFERRED	COMMON STOCK	PAID-IN CAPITAL— COMMON	RETAINED EARNINGS
Balance Jan. 1	$100,000	$50,000	$400,000	$40,000	$200,000
Stock issued			100,000	10,000	
Net income					80,000
Cash dividend					− 45,000
Stock dividend	10,000	5,000			− 15,000
Balance Dec. 31	$110,000	$55,000	$500,000	$50,000	$220,000

Divac's preferred stock is $100 par, 8% stock. If the stock is liquidated or redeemed, stockholders are entitled to $120 per share. There are no dividends in arrears on the stock. The common stock has a par value of $5 per share.

■ REQUIRED
1. Determine the dividend payout ratio for the common stock.
2. Determine the book value per share of Divac's common stock.

(LO 10) EXERCISE 11-11 SOLE PROPRIETORSHIP (APPENDIX 11A)

Pain Stewart opened Par Golf as a sole proprietor by investing $50,000 cash on January 1, 1995. Because the business was new, it operated at a net loss of $10,000 for 1995. During the year, Pain withdrew $20,000 from the business for living expenses. Pain also had $4,000 of interest income from sources unrelated to the business.

■ REQUIRED
1. Record all the necessary entries for 1995 on the books of Par Golf.
2. Present the owners' equity category of Par Golf's balance sheet as of December 31, 1995.

PROBLEMS

(LO 1) PROBLEM 11-1 STOCKHOLDERS' EQUITY CATEGORY

Peeler Company was incorporated as a new business on January 1, 1995. The corporate charter approved on that date authorized the issuance of 1,000 shares of $100 par, 7% cumulative, nonparticipating preferred stock and 10,000 shares of $5 par common stock. On January 10, Peeler issued for cash 500 shares of preferred stock at $120 per share and 4,000 shares of common at $80 per share. On January 20, it issued 1,000 shares of common stock to acquire a building site at a time when the stock was selling for $70 per share.

During 1995 Peeler established an employee benefit plan and acquired 500 shares of common stock at $60 per share as treasury stock for that purpose. Later in 1995, it resold 100 shares of the stock at $65 per share.

On December 31, 1995, Peeler determined its net income for the year to be $40,000. The firm declared the annual cash dividend to preferred stockholders and a cash dividend of $5 per share to the common stockholders. The dividend will be paid in 1996.

■ REQUIRED
Develop the stockholders' equity category of Peeler's balance sheet as of December 31, 1995. Indicate on the statement the number of shares authorized, issued, and outstanding for both preferred and common stock.

(LO 2) PROBLEM 11-2 INVESTING IN PREFERRED STOCK

Ruth Larkin received a windfall from one of her investments. She would like to invest $100,000 of the money in Kennedale, Inc., which is offering common stock, preferred stock, and bonds on the open market. The common stock has paid $5 per share in dividends for the past three years and the company expects to be able to perform as well in the current year. The current market price of the common stock is $100 per share. The preferred stock has a 5% dividend rate, cumulative and nonparticipating. The bonds are selling at par with a 5% stated rate.

1. Explain one benefit that each type of investment has over the others.   ■ REQUIRED

2. Recommend one type of investment over the others to Ruth, and justify your reason.

(LO 7) PROBLEM 11-3 DIVIDENDS AND SPLITS

The stockholders' equity category of Perkins Company as of January 1, 1995, appeared as follows:

Preferred stock, $100 par, 8%,	
2,000 shares issued and outstanding	$200,000
Common stock, $10 par, 5,000 shares issued	
and outstanding	50,000
Additional paid-in capital	300,000
Total contributed capital	$550,000
Retained earnings	400,000
Total stockholders' equity	$950,000

The following transactions occurred during 1995.

a. Declared on February 1 a 10% stock dividend on common stock, when the stock was selling at $50 per share. The stock dividend was to be distributed on March 1, 1995.

b. Distributed the stock dividend on March 1.

c. Approved a 2-for-1 stock split of the preferred stock on July 1, when it was selling for $140 per share.

1. Record the transactions in journal entry form and develop the stockholders' equity   ■ REQUIRED
category of Perkins's balance sheet as of December 31, 1995.

2. Write a paragraph that explains the difference between a stock dividend and a stock split.

(LO 5) PROBLEM 11-4 DIVIDENDS FOR PREFERRED AND COMMON STOCK

The stockholders' equity category of Griswold Company's balance sheet as of December 1, 1995, appeared as follows:

Preferred stock, $100 par, 8%,	
1,000 shares issued and outstanding	$100,000
Common stock, $10 par, 20,000 shares issued	
and outstanding	200,000
Additional paid-in capital	250,000
Total contributed capital	$ 550,000
Retained earnings	450,000
Total stockholders' equity	$1,000,000

The footnotes to the financial statements indicate that dividends were not declared or paid for 1993 or 1994. Griswold wishes to declare a dividend of $59,000 for 1995.

Determine the total and the per-share amounts that should be declared to the preferred   ■ REQUIRED
and common stockholders under the following assumptions.

1. The preferred stock is noncumulative, nonparticipating.

2. The preferred stock is cumulative, nonparticipating.

3. The preferred stock is cumulative and participating on the basis of the proportion of the total par values of the preferred and common stock.

(LO 6) PROBLEM 11-5 EFFECT OF STOCK DIVIDEND

Favre Company has a history of paying cash dividends on its common stock. The firm did not have a particularly profitable year, however, in 1995. At the end of the year, Favre found itself without the necessary cash for a dividend and therefore declared a stock dividend to its common stockholders. A 50% stock dividend was declared to stockholders on December 31, 1995. The board of directors is unclear about the effect of a stock dividend on Favre's balance sheet and has requested your assistance.

■ REQUIRED

1. Write a statement to indicate the effect that the stock dividend has on the financial statements of Favre Company.

2. A group of common stockholders has contacted the firm to express its concern about the effect of the stock dividend and to question the effect the stock dividend may have on the market price of the stock. Write a statement to address the stockholders' concerns.

(LO 10) PROBLEM 11-6 INCOME DISTRIBUTION OF A PARTNERSHIP (APPENDIX 11A)

Louise Abbott and Buddie Costello are partners in a comedy club business. The partnership agreement specifies the manner in which income of the business is to be distributed. Louise is to receive a salary of $20,000 for managing the club, and Buddie is to receive interest at the rate of 10% on her capital balance of $300,000. Remaining income is to be distributed on a 2-to-1 ratio.

■ REQUIRED

Determine the amount that should be distributed to each partner, assuming that the business net income is

1. $15,000.

2. $50,000.

3. $80,000.

MULTI-CONCEPT PROBLEMS

(LO 1, 4) PROBLEM 11-7 ANALYSIS OF STOCKHOLDERS' EQUITY

The stockholders' equity section of the December 31, 1995, balance sheet of Eldon Company appeared as follows:

Preferred stock, $30 par value, 5,000 shares authorized, ? shares issued	$120,000
Common stock, no par, 10,000 shares authorized, 7,000 shares issued	630,000
Additional paid-in capital—preferred	6,000
Additional paid-in capital—treasury stock	1,000
Total contributed capital	$757,000
Retained earnings	40,000
Less: Treasury stock, preferred, 100 shares	3,200
Total stockholders' equity	$793,800

■ REQUIRED

Determine the following items based on Eldon's balance sheet.

1. The number of shares of preferred stock issued.

2. The number of shares of preferred stock outstanding.

3. The average per-share sales price of the preferred stock when issued.

4. The cost of the treasury stock per share.

5. The average per-share sales price of the common stock when issued.

6. The per-share book value of the common stock, assuming that there are no dividends in arrears and that the preferred stock can be redeemed at its par value.

(LO 3, 4, 6, 7) PROBLEM 11-8 STOCKHOLDERS' EQUITY TRANSACTIONS

The following transactions occurred at Horton, Inc., during its first year of operation:

a. Issued 100,000 shares of common stock at $5 each; 1,000,000 shares are authorized at $1 par value.

b. Issued 10,000 shares of common stock for a building and land. The building was appraised for $20,000, but the value of the land is undeterminable. The stock is selling for $10 on the open market.

c. Purchased 1,000 shares of its own common stock on the open market for $16 per share.

d. Declared a dividend of $.10 per share on outstanding common stock. The dividend is to be paid after the end of the first year of operations. Market value of the stock is $26.

e. Declared a 2-for-1 stock split. The market value of the stock was $37 before the stock split.

f. Reported $180,000 of income for the year.

1. Indicate the effect of each transaction on the assets, liabilities, and owners' equity of Horton, Inc.   ■ REQUIRED

2. Prepare the owners' equity section of the balance sheet.

3. Write a paragraph that explains the number of shares of stock issued and outstanding at the end of the year.

(LO 2, 4) PROBLEM 11-9 OWNERS' EQUITY SECTION OF THE BALANCE SHEET

The newly hired accountant at Ives, Inc., prepared the following balance sheet.

ASSETS	
Cash	$ 3,500
Account receivable	2,000
Common stock subscriptions receivable	3,000
Treasury stock	500
Plant, property, and equipment	108,000
Retained earnings	1,000
Total assets	$118,000

LIABILITIES	
Accounts payable	$ 2,500
Dividends payable	1,500
Common stock subscribed	3,000

OWNERS' EQUITY	
Common stock, $1 par, 100,000 issued	100,000
Additional paid-in capital	11,000
Total liabilities and owners' equity	$118,000

1. Prepare a corrected balance sheet. Write a short explanation for each correction.   ■ REQUIRED

2. Why does the Retained Earnings account have a debit balance?

ALTERNATE PROBLEMS

(LO 1) PROBLEM 11-1A STOCKHOLDERS' EQUITY CATEGORY

Kebler Company was incorporated as a new business on January 1, 1995. The corporate charter approved on that date authorized the issuance of 2,000 shares of $100 par 7% cumulative, nonparticipating preferred stock and 20,000 shares of $5 par common stock. On January 10, Kebler issued for cash 1,000 shares of preferred stock at $120 per share and 8,000 shares of common at $80 per share. On January 20, it issued 2,000 shares of common stock to acquire a building site at a time when the stock was selling for $70 per share.

During 1995 Kebler established an employee benefit plan and acquired 1,000 shares of common stock at $60 per share as treasury stock for that purpose. Later in 1995, it resold 100 shares of the stock at $65 per share.

On December 31, 1995, Kebler determined its net income for the year to be $80,000. The firm declared the annual cash dividend to preferred stockholders and a cash dividend of $5 per share to the common stockholders. The dividend will be paid in 1996.

■ REQUIRED   Develop the stockholders' equity category of Kebler's balance sheet as of December 31, 1995. Indicate on the statement the number of shares authorized, issued, and outstanding for both preferred and common stock.

(LO 2) PROBLEM 11-2A INVESTING IN PREFERRED STOCK

Rob Louder would like to invest $100,000 in Overman, Inc., which is offering common stock, preferred stock, and bonds on the open market. The common stock has paid $1 per share in dividends for the past three years and the company expects to be able to double the dividend in the current year. The current market price of the common stock is $10 per share. The preferred stock has an 8% dividend rate. The bonds are selling at par with a 5% stated rate.

■ REQUIRED   **1.** Explain Overman's obligation to pay dividends or interest on each instrument.

2. Recommend one type of investment over the others to Rob and justify your reason.

(LO 7) PROBLEM 11-3A DIVIDENDS AND SPLITS

The stockholders' equity category of Patrick Company as of January 1, 1995, appeared as follows:

Preferred stock, $100 par, 8%,	
4,000 shares issued and outstanding	$400,000
Common stock, $10 par, 10,000 shares issued	
and outstanding	100,000
Additional paid-in capital	600,000
Total contributed capital	$1,100,000
Retained earnings	800,000
Total stockholders' equity	$1,900,000

The following transactions occurred during 1995.

a. Declared a 10% stock dividend on common stock on February 1 when the stock was selling at $50 per share. The stock dividend was to be distributed on March 1, 1995.

b. Distributed the stock dividend on March 1.

c. Approved a 2-for-1 stock split of the preferred stock on July 1 when the preferred stock was selling for $140 per share.

1. Determine the impact of the transactions on the accounting equation.

2. Develop the stockholders' equity category of Patrick's balance sheet as of December 31, 1995.

(LO 5) PROBLEM 11-4A DIVIDENDS FOR PREFERRED AND COMMON STOCK

The stockholders' equity category of Gumby Company's balance sheet as of December 31, 1995, appeared as follows:

Preferred stock, $100 par, 8%,	
2,000 shares issued and outstanding	$200,000
Common stock, $10 par, 40,000 shares issued	
and outstanding	400,000
Additional paid-in capital	500,000
Total contributed capital	$1,100,000
Retained earnings	900,000
Total stockholders' equity	$2,000,000

The footnotes to the financial statements indicate that dividends were not declared or paid for 1993 or 1994. Gumby wishes to declare a dividend of $118,000 for 1995.

Determine the total and the per-share amounts that should be declared to the preferred and common stockholders under the following assumptions.

1. The preferred stock is noncumulative, nonparticipating.

2. The preferred stock is cumulative, nonparticipating.

3. The preferred stock is cumulative and participating on the basis of the proportion of the total par values of the preferred and common stock.

(LO 6) PROBLEM 11-5A EFFECT OF STOCK DIVIDEND

Flavor Company has a history of paying cash dividends on its common stock. The firm did not have a particularly profitable year, however, in 1995. At the end of the year, Flavor found itself without the necessary cash for a dividend and therefore declared a stock dividend to its common stockholders. A 50% stock dividend was declared to stockholders on December 31, 1995. The board of directors is unclear about the effect of a stock dividend on Flavor's balance sheet and has requested your assistance.

1. Write a statement to indicate the effect that the stock dividend has on the financial statements of Flavor Company.

2. A group of common stockholders has contacted the firm to express its concern about the effect of the stock dividend and to question the effect that the stock dividend may have on the market price of the stock. Write a statement to address the stockholders' concerns.

(LO 10) PROBLEM 11-6A INCOME DISTRIBUTION OF A PARTNERSHIP (APPENDIX 11A)

Kay Katz and Doris Kan are partners in a dry cleaning business. The partnership agreement specifies the manner in which income of the business is to be distributed. Kay is to receive a salary of $40,000 for managing the business. Doris is to receive interest at the rate of 10% on her capital balance of $600,000. Remaining income is to be distributed on a 2-to-1 ratio.

Determine the amount that should be distributed to each partner assuming that the business net income is

1. $30,000.

2. $100,000.

3. $160,000.

ALTERNATE MULTI-CONCEPT PROBLEMS

(LO 1, 4) PROBLEM 11-7A ANALYSIS OF STOCKHOLDERS' EQUITY

The stockholders' equity section of the December 31, 1995, balance sheet of Everett Company appeared as follows:

Preferred stock, $30 par value, 10,000 shares authorized, ? shares issued	$ 240,000
Common stock, no par, 20,000 shares authorized, 14,000 shares issued	1,260,000
Additional paid-in capital—preferred	12,000
Additional paid-in capital—treasury stock	2,000
Total contributed capital	$1,514,000
Retained earnings	80,000
Less: Treasury stock, preferred, 100 shares	6,400
Total stockholders' equity	$1,587,600

Determine the following items based on Everett's balance sheet.

1. The number of shares of preferred stock issued.
2. The number of shares of preferred stock outstanding.
3. The average per-share sales price of the preferred stock when issued.
4. The cost of the treasury stock per share.
5. The average per-share sales price of the common stock when issued.
6. The per-share book value of the common stock, assuming that there are no dividends in arrears and that the preferred stock can be redeemed at its par value.

(LO 3, 4, 6, 7) PROBLEM 11-8A STOCKHOLDERS' EQUITY TRANSACTIONS

The following transactions occurred at Hilton, Inc., during its first year of operation:

a. Issued 10,000 shares of common stock at $10 each; 100,000 shares are authorized at $1 par value.

b. Issued 10,000 shares of common stock for a patent, which is expected to be effective for the next 15 years. The value of the patent is undeterminable. The stock is selling for $10 on the open market.

c. Purchased 1,000 shares of its own common stock on the open market for $10 per share.

d. Declared a dividend of $.50 per share of outstanding common stock. The dividend is to be paid after the end of the first year of operations. Market value of the stock is $10.

e. Sold 500 shares of the stock purchased in (c) for $12 each.

f. Income for the year is reported as $340,000.

■ REQUIRED

1. Indicate the effect of each transaction on the assets, liabilities, and owners' equity of Hilton, Inc.

2. Hilton's president has asked you to explain the difference between contributed capital and retained earnings. Discuss these terms as they relate to Hilton.

3. Determine the book value per share of the stock at the end of the year.

(LO 2, 4) PROBLEM 11-9A EQUITY SECTION OF THE BALANCE SHEET

The newly hired accountant at Grainfield, Inc., is considering the following list of accounts as he prepares the balance sheet. All of the accounts have their normal balances. The company is authorized to issue 1,000,000 shares of common stock and 10,000 shares of preferred stock. The treasury stock was purchased at $5 per share.

Treasury Stock (common)	$ 15,000
Retained Earnings	54,900
Dividends Payable	1,500
Common Stock Subscribed	30,000
Common Stock, $1 par	100,000
Additional Paid-in Capital	68,400
Preferred Stock, $10 par, 5%	50,000

1. Prepare the owners' equity section of the balance sheet for Grainfield.

2. Explain why some of the listed accounts are not shown in the owners' equity section.

■ REQUIRED

CASES

READING AND INTERPRETING FINANCIAL STATEMENTS

(LO 1, 2) CASE 11-1 BEN & JERRY'S STOCKHOLDERS' EQUITY CATEGORY

Refer to the Ben & Jerry's 1992 annual report and answer the following questions.

1. What is the number of shares of preferred stock authorized, issued, and outstanding as of the balance sheet date?

2. The preferred stock indicates an "aggregate preference on voluntary or involuntary liquidation." What does that provision of the preferred stock mean?

3. Calculate the book value per share of the common stock.

4. The balance of the Retained Earnings account increased during the year. What are the possible factors that affect its balance?

5. The total stockholders' equity as of December 31, 1992, is $66,759,816. Does that mean that stockholders would receive that amount if the company were liquidated?

■ REQUIRED

(LO 4) CASE 11-2 STOCK PURCHASE PLANS

Many companies offer stock purchase plans to their employees. The 1993 annual report of Circuit City Stores, Inc., included the following notes:

> The Company had an Employee Stock Purchase Plan for all employees meeting certain eligibility criteria. Under the Plan, eligible employees may purchase shares of the company's stock . . . at 85 percent of its fair market value. At February 28, 1993, a total of 483,334 shares remained eligible for issuance under the Plan. . . . The purchase price discount is charged to operations and totaled $1,135,930 . . . in fiscal 1993.

How should the company account for the shares it has purchased to issue to employees? What accounts are affected when the stock is issued to employees? Why does the company charge the purchase price discount to operations?

■ REQUIRED

(LO 9) CASE 11-3 READING BEN & JERRY'S STATEMENT OF CASH FLOWS

Refer to the 1992 statement of cash flows in Ben & Jerry's annual report and answer the following questions.

1. During 1992 Ben & Jerry's issued common stock. What amount of cash was received? What category of the statement of cash flows reflects this amount?

■ REQUIRED

2. If Ben & Jerry's had paid a dividend in 1992, where would it appear on the statement of cash flows?

3. Why do you think investors are willing to purchase stock in Ben & Jerry's when the company does not pay a dividend on the stock?

MAKING FINANCIAL DECISIONS

(LO 1, 2) CASE 11-4 DEBT VERSUS EQUITY

Assume that you are an analyst attempting to compare the financial structure of two companies. In particular, you must analyze the debt and equity categories of the two firms and calculate a debt-to-equity ratio for each firm. The liability and equity categories of First Company at year-end appeared as follows:

LIABILITIES	
Accounts Payable	$ 500,000
Loan Payable	800,000
STOCKHOLDERS' EQUITY	
Common Stock	300,000
Retained Earnings	600,000
Total Debt and Equity	$2,200,000

First Company's loan payable bears interest at 8%, which is paid annually. The principal is due in five years.

The liability and equity categories of Second Company at year-end appeared as follows:

LIABILITIES	
Accounts Payable	$ 500,000
STOCKHOLDERS' EQUITY	
Common Stock	300,000
Preferred Stock	800,000
Retained Earnings	600,000
Total Debt and Equity	$2,200,000

Second Company's preferred stock is 8%, cumulative stock. A provision of the stock agreement specifies that the stock must be redeemed at face value in five years.

■ REQUIRED

1. It appears that the loan payable of First Company and the preferred stock of Second Company are very similar. What are the differences between the two securities?

2. When calculating the debt-to-equity ratio, do you believe that the Second Company preferred stock should be treated as debt or stockholders' equity? Write a statement expressing your position on this issue.

(LO 2) CASE 11-5 PREFERRED VERSUS COMMON STOCK

Rohnan, Inc., needs to raise $500,000. It is considering two options.

a. Issue preferred stock, $100 par, 8%, cumulative, nonparticipating, callable at $110. The stock could be issued at par.

b. Issue common stock, $1 par, market $10. Currently, the company has 400,000 shares outstanding equally in the hands of five owners. The company has never paid a dividend.

Rohnan has asked you to consider both options and make a recommendation. It is equally concerned with cash flow and company control. Write your recommendations.   ■ REQUIRED

ACCOUNTING AND ETHICS: WHAT WOULD YOU DO?

(LO 8) CASE 11-6 INSIDE INFORMATION

Jim Brock was an accountant with Hubbard, Inc., a large corporation with stock that was publicly traded on the New York Stock Exchange. One of Jim's duties was to manage the corporate reporting department, which was responsible for developing and issuing Hubbard's annual report. At the end of 1995, Hubbard closed its accounting records, and initial calculations indicated a very profitable year. In fact, the income exceeded the net income that had been projected during the year by the financial analysts that followed Hubbard's stock.

Jim was very pleased with the company's financial performance. In January 1996, he suggested that his father buy Hubbard's stock because he was sure the stock price would increase when the company announced its 1995 results. Jim's father followed the advice and bought a block of stock at $25 per share.

On February 15, 1996, Hubbard announced its 1995 results and issued the annual report. The company received favorable press coverage about its performance and the stock price on the stock exchange increased to $32 per share.

What was Jim's professional responsibilities to Hubbard, Inc., concerning the issuance of the 1995 annual report? Did Jim act ethically in this situation?

(LO 5) CASE 11-7 DIVIDEND POLICY

Hancock, Inc., is owned by nearly 100 shareholders. Judith Stitch owns 48% of the stock. She needs cash to fulfill her commitment to donate the funds to construct a new art gallery. Some of her friends have agreed to vote for Hancock to pay a larger than normal dividend to shareholders. Judith has asked you to vote for the large dividend because she knows that you also support the arts. When informed that the dividend may create a working capital hardship on Hancock, Judith responded, "There is plenty of money in Retained Earnings. The dividend will not affect the cash of the company." Respond to her comment. What ethical questions do you and Judith face? How would you vote?

ANALYTICAL SOFTWARE CASE

To the Student: Your instructor may assign one or more parts of the analytical software case that is designed to accompany this chapter.

SOLUTION TO KEY TERMS QUIZ

1. Issued shares (p. 584)
2. Par value (p. 586)
3. Retained earnings (p. 586)
4. Cumulative feature (p. 588)
5. Convertible stock (p. 588)
6. Subscription agreement (p. 590)
7. Treasury stock (p. 591)
8. Dividend payout ratio (p. 594)
9. Sole Proprietorship (p. 608)
10. Stock split (p. 599)
11. Book value per share (p. 600)
12. Partnership (p. 610)
13. Market value per share (p.602)
14. Authorized shares (p. 584)
15. Outstanding shares (p. 584)
16. Partnership agreement (p. 610)
17. Additional paid-in capital (p. 586)
18. Participating feature (p. 588)
19. Callable stock (p. 588)
20. Retirement of stock (p. 593)
21. Stock dividend (p. 597)

Focus on Financial Results

Corporate America usually gets criticized by the national media. Yet many companies such as **General Electric** sponsor events and projects that help them be better corporate neighbors. And many big companies offer their employees relatively generous pensions and postretirement health and life insurance benefits. Because of the vast obligations that companies have made over the years, the Financial Accounting Standards Board (FASB) changed an accounting rule a few years ago to require companies to record these liabilities on their

Statement of Earnings

	General Electric Company and consolidated affiliates		
For the years ended December 31 (In millions)	**1993**	1992	1991
Earnings from continuing operations before income taxes and accounting changes	**6,575**	6,273	5,726
Provision for income taxes (note 9)	**(2,151)**	(1,968)	(1,742)
Earnings from continuing operations before accounting changes	**4,424**	4,305	3,984
Earnings from discontinued operations, net of income taxes of $44, $248 and $259, respectively (note 2)	75	420	451
Gain on transfer of discontinued operations, net of income taxes of $752	678	—	—
Earnings from discontinued operations	753	420	451
Earnings before accounting changes	**5,177**	4,725	4,435
Cumulative effects of accounting changes (notes 6 and 22)	**(862)**	—	(1,799)
Net earnings	**$ 4,315**	$ 4,725	$ 2,636

books. As a result, most of these firms had to record the cumulative effect of this accounting change on their balance sheet and income statement.

Accordingly, in 1991, GE recorded a $1.8 billion charge to earnings for such benefits. Following the FASB requirement, the effect of the change was listed separately so that analysts could focus on earnings from continuing operations. Many companies had to make the same type of adjustment. The question for investors is how to interpret such a large adjustment. It is a one-time charge that catches up all the promises made to employees over the past several years. There is no immediate cash flow impact. Still, it does indicate the company has a very large obligation to its employees at a future time.

Chapter 12

Additional Corporate Accounting Issues

LEARNING OBJECTIVES

After studying this chapter, you should be able to

1. Understand a multi-step corporate income statement and its categories.
2. Describe the appropriate presentation and disclosure of discontinued operations.
3. Determine when items should be considered extraordinary and develop the income statement presentation when such items are present.
4. Analyze accounting changes and determine the effect on the income statement.
5. Use the earnings per share ratio as a measure of a company's profitability.
6. Identify the proper retained earnings statement presentation of corrections of errors.
7. Understand the effect of appropriations and other restrictions on retained earnings.
8. Prepare a statement of stockholders' equity.
9. Understand the meaning and importance of comprehensive income.
10. Determine the impact of income statement transactions on the statement of cash flows.

Linkages

A LOOK AT PREVIOUS CHAPTERS

In previous chapters, you studied the basic concepts of income statement presentation. Chapter 2 introduced the multi-step income statement for corporations.

A LOOK AT THIS CHAPTER

This chapter develops the corporate income statement in more detail. The first section presents the proper classification and income statement presentation for a multi-step income statement.

The second section of the chapter examines the retained earnings statement. The section also reviews the elements of stockholders' equity and presents a statement of stockholders' equity that many large corporations use.

The final sections of the chapter develop ratio analysis of profitability with the earnings per share ratio and the impact of various transactions on the statement of cash flows.

A LOOK AT UPCOMING CHAPTERS

Chapter 13 will examine gains and losses on investment securities in more detail, Chapter 14 takes a closer look at the statement of cash flows, and Chapter 15 will present a more complete discussion of ratio analysis of profitability.

Reading a Corporate Income Statement

Categories on the Multi-Step Income Statement

LO   I

Understand a multi-step corporate income statement and its categories.

The purpose of the income statement is to report the amount of net income for the corporation for a given time period. It is an expression of the basic accounting equation:

$$\text{Revenue} - \text{Expenses} = \text{Net Income}$$

Most corporations do not report all revenue in one category and all expense in another. Rather, they have found that it is more meaningful to provide categories of revenues and expenses. This is referred to as a **multi-step income statement.**

Ben & Jerry's income statement is an example of a multi-step statement; the 1992 statement is included as Exhibit 12-1. Ben and Jerry's income statement has four main categories of income. The purpose of the first category is to determine the amount of the gross profit or gross margin. **Gross profit** is expressed as

$$\text{Net Sales} - \text{Cost of Sales} = \text{Gross Profit}$$

EXHIBIT 12-1   Ben & Jerry's Multiple-Step Income Statement

		Years Ended	
	December 26, 1992	December 28, 1991	December 29, 1990
CONSOLIDATED STATEMENT OF INCOME			
Net sales	$ 131,968,814	$ 96,997,339	$ 77,024,037
Cost of sales	94,389,391	68,500,402	54,202,387
Gross profit	37,579,423	28,496,937	22,821,650
Selling, general and administrative expenses	26,242,761	21,264,214	17,639,357
Operating income	11,336,662	7,232,723	5,182,293
Other income (expenses):			
Interest income	394,817	147,058	296,329
Interest expense	(181,577)	(736,248)	(868,736)
Other	(235,765)	(139,627)	(136,578)
	(22,525)	(728,817)	(708,985)
Income before income taxes	11,314,137	6,503,906	4,473,308
Income taxes	4,638,797	2,764,523	1,864,063
Net income	$ 6,675,340	$ 3,739,383	$ 2,609,245
Net income per common share	$ 1.07	$ 0.67	$ 0.50
Weighted average number of common shares outstanding	6,253,825	5,572,368	5,224,667

See accompanying notes.

STATEMENT OF INCOME
- NET SALES- THIS IS THE TOTAL SALES OF THE COMPANY MINUS THE VALUE OF PRODUCT DISCOUNTED OR RETURNED.
- COST OF SALES - WHAT IT COST TO MAKE & STORE THE PRODUCTS UNTIL THEY ARE SOLD. INCLUDES INGREDIENTS, PACKAGING, LABOR COSTS, & THE COST TO RUN PRODUCTION & STORAGE MACHINERY.
- GROSS PROFIT- NET SALES MINUS COST OF SALES.
- SELLING & ADMINISTRATIVE EXPENSES - THESE ARE THE COSTS OF MARKETING & SELLING THE PRODUCT AFTER IT HAS BEEN MADE, PLUS ALL OF THE ADMINISTRATIVE COSTS TO RUN THE COMPANY.

- OPERATING INCOME- GROSS PROFIT MINUS SELLING, GENERAL & ADMINISTRATIVE EXPENSES. THIS MEASURES HOW MUCH A COMPANY EARNS (BEFORE TAXES) FROM THE CORE BUSINESS IT IS IN.
- INCOME BEFORE TAXES, INCOME TAXES & NET INCOME. INCOME TAXES ARE THE AMOUNT OF FEDERAL & STATE TAXES PAID OR DUE BASED ON THE COMPANY'S BOOK INCOME. SUBTRACTING THOSE TAXES FROM INCOME BEFORE TAXES RESULTS IN NET INCOME OR THE "BOTTOM LINE." (REMEMBER, BEN & JERRY'S HAS TWO "BOTTOM LINES." CONTINUED →

For the year 1992, Ben & Jerry's had net sales of $131,968,814 and cost of sales (often referred to as *cost of goods sold*) of $94,389,391, resulting in gross profit of $37,579,423. A gross profit, as opposed to a gross loss, means that Ben & Jerry's is selling its products for more than it costs to buy or produce them. This is a favorable indication of the company's profitability, but the amount of the gross profit should be compared to that of similar firms to determine whether it is adequate. For such comparison, a **gross profit percentage** is often computed:

Gross Profit / Net Sales = Gross Profit Percentage

This determination allows companies of different sizes to be compared on the basis of the percentage, rather than the dollar amount, of gross profit. Ben & Jerry's gross profit percentage for 1992 was approximately 28.8% ($37,579,423/$131,968,814) and appears to be adequate when compared to that of other companies in the same line of business. Sufficient gross profit must be available to cover all of the firm's expenses for it to be profitable. An analysis of the gross profit percentage over time also indicates the company's ability to pass higher costs to customers or to survive price-cutting competitors. Remember, however, that gross profit is only an initial measure of profitability and considers only one revenue, sales revenue, and one expense, cost of goods sold.

The second category of income on Ben & Jerry's income statement is the operating income. **Operating income** is expressed as

Gross Profit − Operating Expenses = Operating Income

Some firms disclose several categories of operating expenses. For example, many firms disclose the amount of selling, general, and administrative expenses in separate categories. Ben & Jerry's has only one operating expense category: selling, general, and administrative expenses. For the year 1992, the firm had $26,242,761 of operating expenses. When that amount is deducted from the amount of the gross profit, an operating income of $11,336,662 resulted for 1992:

$37,579,423 − $26,242,761 = $11,336,662

Operating income is a measure of the amount of income derived from the firm's primary or central activities. Ben & Jerry's is in the business of selling food products to distributors and retailers, and its main source of income must be from such activities if it is to be profitable.

The third category of income on Ben & Jerry's income statement includes those items that enter into the computation of **income before income taxes.** This amount for Ben & Jerry's can be expressed as

Operating Income + Interest Income − Interest Expense − Other Expense =
Income before Income Taxes

The items listed in this category of the income statement involve income and expense items that are *not* the firm's primary or central activities. Interest expense and interest revenue reflect the decisions the firm has made concerning how to finance its operations and invest its excess funds. The financing decision is extremely important, but it is separate from the operating decisions of the firm and is therefore listed with other expenses and losses on the income statement. The category labeled as "other" encompasses a variety of transactions and may be referred to as *miscellaneous income* or *expense* by some firms. Ben & Jerry's had operating income of $11,336,662 for 1992, but after considering interest income, interest expense, and other expenses, the income before income taxes was $11,314,137:

$11,336,662 + $394,817 − $181,577 − $235,765 = $11,314,137

The fourth category of income involves the computation of *net income.* Because income tax is a very important item, most firms separate that expense from the other expenses. Therefore, a line titled *income before tax* is presented and income tax expense is deducted to arrive at net income. The relationship can be expressed as follows:

$$\text{Income before Income Tax} - \text{Income Tax} = \text{Net Income}$$

For 1992 Ben & Jerry's had income before income taxes of \$11,314,137, but after deducting the income tax expense, the net income was \$6,675,340:

$$\$11,314,137 - \$4,638,797 = \$6,675,340$$

Note that the term *net income* is reserved for the bottom line of the income statement. It is a measure of profit after all revenues and all expenses, including income tax expense, have been considered.

Analysts may disagree about which income figure is most important. Ask a banker and he or she might tell you that cash flow is the most critical factor in determining whether a loan is repaid. A Wall Street analyst might tell you that operating income is the most important figure, because it excludes nonrecurring items. An industry analyst might focus on gross profit, because statistics regarding materials and labor are plentiful across companies and thus are comparable. The public, however, puts more faith in the bottom line than any other number. That's the figure that the press quotes when a company releases its earnings.

Three other items also must be displayed on the income statement. These items occur infrequently and are not included in normal business operations. They usually are material when they do occur, however, and should be reported after income from continuing or normal operations. These items are income (loss) from discontinued operations, extraordinary gains or losses, and the cumulative effect of changes in accounting principles. They are discussed in the following sections.

Discontinued Operations

Users of financial statements desire income statements that might help them predict the income and cash flow that will occur for a firm in the future. Normally, the current year income statement provides a good indication of those activities that will continue in future periods. Viewed over several years, there is usually a trend in revenues, cost of goods sold, and administrative expenses. Problems arise, however, if a company sells major segments or divisions during a year. In that case, it is necessary to separate the results of activities that will continue in the future from the results of activities that were conducted by the portion of the business that has been sold or discontinued.

The **discontinued operations** section should be presented when a company sells a major division or segment. For a transaction to qualify as a discontinued operation, it must be a separate, identifiable portion of the business. Further, the sale must change the nature of the company's operations in a way that affects the financial statement user's ability to predict future activities. For example, assume that a large auto firm has two divisions, one that manufactures and sells autos and another that finances and leases them. If the company decides to sell the financing and leasing division, the transaction should be reported as a discontinued operation on the income statement.

When a transaction meets the criteria to be classified as a discontinued operation, it should appear in a separate category of the income statement. For example, assume

LO   2

Describe the appropriate presentation and disclosure of discontinued operations.

that Wirtz Company decided on December 31, 1995, to sell one of its major divisions and on that date received as the selling price an amount that was $1,000 less than the book value of the assets. During 1995 the division that was sold had sales to customers of $12,000 and operating expenses (not including income tax) of $15,000. Wirtz pays income tax at the rate of 30%. The transaction should be portrayed on the income statement as follows:

Income from continuing operations	$XXXXX
Discontinued operations:	
Loss from operations	
($3,000 less tax effect of $900)	(2,100)
Loss from disposal of assets	
($1,000 less tax effect of $300)	(700)
Net income	$XXXXX

The first item indicates the loss from *operating* the division during 1995. The second item indicates the loss from *selling* the division. Note that both items should be shown *net* of the tax effect involved. The tax effect may be confusing and should be analyzed carefully. Essentially, a loss results in a tax savings. For example, the company had a $3,000 loss from operating the division in 1995, reducing the firm's income by $3,000. As a result, the firm paid $900 less tax than it would have paid if the loss had not occurred. Therefore, the $900 is a tax savings or tax benefit and reduces the amount of the loss net of taxes to $2,100.

The consolidated income statement of Ryder System, Inc., for the year 1991 is presented in Exhibit 12-2. Ryder is perhaps best known for its rental trucks and vehicles but has several other related business activities. The 1991 income statement indicates that Ryder had an income of $65,720,000 from continuing operations but had a loss of $51,703,000 from discontinued operations, resulting in net earnings of $14,017,000:

$$\$65,720,000 - \$51,703,000 = \$14,017,000$$

The footnotes to the annual report indicate that the company discontinued its aircraft leasing business and sold aircraft and other related assets. This caused a loss and is the reason that the company recorded $51,703,000 in the category labeled as *discontinued operations.*

Ryder's *net income* figure is a good indication of the firm's overall performance or activity for the year. Because the aircraft leasing business was discontinued, however, it is probably not a good indication of future income. Users of the statement should place primary importance on the amount of *income from continuing operations* to indicate Ryder's future activities. Of course, it would be easier to predict future income if Ryder's "earnings from continuing operations before income taxes" were going in one direction. In 1989, the total is $90.3 million; it rises to $138.6 million in 1990 but then falls to $114.9 million in 1991. That makes it difficult to forecast 1992 results.

Extraordinary Items

When developing an income statement, management makes a variety of judgments concerning the proper presentation and communication of results. An example of the application of judgment concerns the determination of extraordinary items. The accountant classifies extraordinary items separately so that the statement user can easily determine the nature of the item and consider whether such items should be expected in future periods. This requires careful judgment on the part of the company's accountant and management.

EXHIBIT 12-2 Ryder System, Inc. 1991 Consolidated Income Statement

CONSOLIDATED STATEMENTS OF EARNINGS

Ryder System, Inc. and Consolidated Subsidiaries

| | Years ended December 31 | | |
	1991	1990	1989
(Thousands of dollars, except per share amounts)			
Revenue	$3,860,557	3,956,827	3,900,128
Net sales	1,200,539	1,205,506	1,130,054
Total Revenue and Net Sales	5,061,096	5,162,333	5,030,182
Operating expense	3,193,354	3,240,775	3,141,467
Cost of sales	943,570	940,338	881,273
Depreciation, net of gains	603,415	616,082	601,955
Interest expense	206,481	234,923	257,765
Unusual charges	–	–	90,000
Miscellaneous income	(599)	(8,336)	(32,593)
	4,946,221	5,023,782	4,939,867
Earnings from continuing operations before income taxes	114,875	138,551	90,315
Provision for income taxes	49,155	56,335	37,877
Earnings from continuing operations	65,720	82,216	52,438
Loss from discontinued operations	(51,703)	(39,536)	(249)
Earnings before extraordinary item	14,017	42,680	52,189
Extraordinary loss	–	–	(6,203)
Net Earnings	14,017	42,680	45,986
Preferred dividend requirements	10,500	10,594	7,647
Earnings Available to Common Shares	$ 3,517	32,086	38,339
Earnings (loss) per common share:			
Continuing operations	$ 0.75	0.96	0.58
Discontinued operations	(0.70)	(0.53)	–
Extraordinary loss	–	–	(0.08)
Earnings Per Common Share	$ 0.05	0.43	0.50

See accompanying notes to consolidated financial statements.

LO 3

Determine when items should be considered extraordinary and develop income statement presentation when such items are present.

An item should be treated as an **extraordinary item** if it is both *unusual and infrequent.* The accountant must judge what constitutes unusual and infrequent with regard to the environment of each individual firm. Thus, an occurrence may be unusual and infrequent to one firm but not to another. For example, if a tornado destroys a firm's assets, the loss probably should be considered extraordinary. If the firm is located in a geographic area known for tornadoes or if it has experienced tornado losses several times in past years, however, the loss is not considered extraordinary.

Typically, management prefers that a major *loss* be categorized as extraordinary because the investment community tends to ignore extraordinary events when predicting future income levels. A loss that is part of continuing operations will probably hurt the company's stock price. On the other hand, management would rather not categorize an unusual *gain* as extraordinary, because it would want investors to believe that such a gain was part of continuing operations. Accountants must develop a careful, professional judgment based on all the facts available concerning the transaction and the environment of the firm to determine whether an item is extraordinary.

An item or transaction that is deemed to be extraordinary should be presented in a separate category of the income statement. For example, assume that Lily Company had a large fire loss of $6,000 and pays income tax at the rate of 30%. The fire loss should be presented as follows:

Income before extraordinary item	$XXXXX
Extraordinary loss	
($6,000 less tax effect of $1,800)	(4,200)
Net income	$XXXXX

As was the case with discontinued items, extraordinary items should always be presented net of tax. Thus, the $6,000 loss in the preceding example is reduced by $1,800, the amount of the *taxes saved* as a result of the loss. The amount of $4,200 is reported on the income statement. If the extraordinary item results in a gain, the amount should be reduced by the amount of *additional taxes* that result from the gain to obtain the net-of-tax amount.

Chapter 10 referred to gains and losses on the redemption of bonds payable as extraordinary items. Gains and losses on bond redemption are a special type of extraordinary item. The accountant is not required to determine whether the items are "unusual and infrequent." The FASB has ruled that all gains and losses on the redemption of bonds should be classified as extraordinary items by the firm that issued the bonds. This is one of the most frequent types of extraordinary items, and you will see these gains or losses reflected on the financial statements of many companies.

Refer again to the income statement of Ryder System, Inc., in Exhibit 12-2. Ryder's 1991 income statement indicated that an extraordinary loss of $6,203,000 occurred in 1989. The footnotes to the financial statement indicate that "in 1989 the company exercised its option to redeem all of its outstanding collateral trust bonds and senior secured notes creating an extraordinary loss of $6.2 million, net

An extraordinary gain or loss must be both unusual and infrequent, and determining this is a matter of judgment. On January 17, 1994, a major earthquake hit the Northridge area near Los Angeles and affected homes and businesses in a wide area of Southern California, including Anaheim Stadium (shown here). Can such damage be considered an extraordinary loss for any company in the Los Angeles area, which is prone to quakes? Can such damage be extraordinary if the firm lies on a previously unknown fault line? On an active fault?

of tax benefits of $3 million." This means that the loss before taxes was $9.2 million ($6.2 + $3.0). Ryder's income statement reports income before extraordinary items of $52,189,000 and an extraordinary loss of $6,203,000, resulting in net earnings of $45,986,000:

$$\$52,189,000 - \$6,203,000 = \$45,986,000$$

Ryder was required to treat the item as an extraordinary loss, regardless of whether it was unusual and infrequent. Still, the bond redemption should be considered a one-time occurrence that is unlikely to occur again for Ryder. Therefore, although the net income of Ryder may be a good measure of the overall performance of the firm, it is probably not a good indication of the activities that will continue in the future. Users should consider the company's earnings *before* the extraordinary item as a more accurate reflection of future activities.

Change in Accounting Principle

One of the important concepts of accounting information is consistency. The consistency principle states that firms should normally use the same accounting methods from year to year to allow users of the financial statements to accurately evaluate the firm's performance. It is necessary on some occasions, however, for a firm to change its accounting methods. The accountant must then evaluate the effect of the change and determine the proper way to present it on the financial statements.

LO **4**

Analyze accounting changes and determine the effect on the income statement.

A **change in accounting principle** occurs when a firm changes from one generally accepted accounting method to another method that is also generally accepted. A common example of a change in principle occurs when a firm changes to the straight-line method of depreciation from an accelerated method. Another example involves changes in inventory methods, for example, from the first-in, first-out method to the weighted average method. When a change in accounting principle occurs, the company must present the **cumulative effect** of the change in a separate category of the income statement in the year of change. The cumulative effect is the total difference in income as a result of applying the previous accounting method versus the adopted method for all years prior to the current year.

Assume that Zielinski Company was formed in 1993 and adopted an accelerated method to depreciate all assets. In 1995 Zielinski finds it appropriate to change to the straight-line method. Also assume that the company pays income tax at the rate of 30%. To calculate the cumulative effect of the change in depreciation, the company must first determine the amount of depreciation for each method for the previous years, 1993 and 1994. Assume that the following depreciation schedules have been developed.

YEAR	STRAIGHT-LINE	ACCELERATED	DIFFERENCE
1993	$50,000	$100,000	$50,000
1994	50,000	80,000	30,000
Total			$80,000

In this example, the cumulative effect of the change in accounting principle is $80,000 before tax. It should be presented on the 1995 income statement, net of tax, as follows:

Income before cumulative effect	$XXXXX
Plus: Cumulative effect of a change in principle	
($80,000 less tax effect of $24,000)	56,000
Net income	$XXXXX

Campbell's.

CONSOLIDATED STATEMENTS OF EARNINGS

(millions, except per share amounts)	**1993 (52 weeks)**	1992 (53 weeks)	1991 (52 weeks)
Net sales	**$6,586.2**	$6,263.2	$6,204.1
Cost and expenses			
Cost of products sold	**4,027.8**	3,963.1	4,095.5
Marketing and selling expenses	**1,208.3**	1,050.0	956.2
Administrative expenses	**306.7**	282.3	306.7
Research and development expenses	**68.8**	59.7	56.3
Interest expense (Note 4)	**82.8**	101.9	116.2
Interest income	**(9.0)**	(15.3)	(26.0)
Other expense (Note 5)	**28.0**	22.2	31.8
Divestiture and restructuring charges (Note 6)	**353.0**	—	—
Total costs and expenses	**6,066.4**	5,463.9	5,536.7
Earnings before taxes	**519.8**	799.3	667.4
Taxes on earnings (Note 9)	**262.6**	308.8	265.9
Earnings before cumulative effect of accounting changes	**257.2**	490.5	401.5
Cumulative effect of accounting changes (Note 2)	**249.0**	—	—
Net earnings	**$ 8.2**	$ 490.5	$ 401.5
Per share (Note 20)			
Earnings before cumulative effect of accounting changes	**$ 1.02**	$ 1.95	$ 1.58
Cumulative effect of accounting changes	**.99**	—	—
Net earnings	**$ .03**	$ 1.95	$ 1.58
Weighted average shares outstanding	**251.9**	251.7	254.0

The accompanying Summary of Significant Accounting Policies and Notes on pages 29 to 36 are an integral part of the financial statements.

Note 2

In the fourth quarter of 1993, the Company adopted Statements of Financial Accounting Standards No. 106, "Employers' Accounting for Postretirement Benefits Other Than Pensions," No. 109, "Accounting for Income Taxes," and No. 112, "Employers' Accounting for Postemployment Benefits." FAS No. 106 requires accrual of the estimated cost of retiree health and life benefits during the years that employees render service. The Company previously expensed these costs as claims were made. The Company elected to recognize the effect of the transition liability for past service costs by recording a one-time, non-cash charge against earnings of $229.7 or .91 per share. Adoption of FAS No. 106 also decreased 1993 earnings per share by $.07 as a result of a $28.0 pre-tax incremental annual charge. FAS No. 112 requires the Company to account for postemployment benefits on the accrual basis. The cumultaive effect of this change in accounting decreased 1993 net earnings by $22.3 or $.09 per share. FAS No. 109 requires the Company to recognize the benefit of certain deferred tax assets not permitted under FAS No. 96. The cumulative effect of this change in accounting increased 1993 net earnings by $3.0 or $.01 per share.

As you will see on the following pages, due to a ruling by the Financial Accounting Standards Board, a number of companies were forced to change their method of accounting for postretirement benefits. In doing so they had to take huge one-time noncash charges against earnings. Many did so in 1992; Campbell's Soup chose 1993. This excerpt from Campbell's income statement for that year shows how making this change (along with two other changes due to FASB rulings) dropped its net earnings by $249 million. Note 2 summarizes the rulings and explains the changes.

If the straight-line method had been used in 1993 and 1994, less depreciation would have been taken, and income would have been higher. Therefore, the cumulative effect must be added to income. Other accounting changes may require an amount to be *deducted* in the income statement. For example, if Zielinski Company had changed from straight-line depreciation to an accelerated method, it would have been necessary to deduct the cumulative effect of the change in principle.

The 1992 income statement of Motorola appears in Exhibit 12-3. Motorola is one of the world's largest producers of communications and electronic equipment. In 1992 the company changed its method of accounting for postretirement benefits. Previously, the firm had recorded the costs as an expense when paid, but the FASB issued a new accounting rule that required firms to accrue the retirement costs as an expense over the period that the employee worked for the company. Because of the new accounting rule, Motorola changed its accounting method for retirement

EXHIBIT 12-3   Motorola, Inc. 1992 Income Statement

STATEMENTS OF CONSOLIDATED EARNINGS

(In millions, except per share amounts)			Motorola, Inc. and Consolidated Subsidiaries
Years ended December 31	**1992**	1991	1990
Net sales	**$13,303**	$11,341	$10,885
Costs and expenses			
Manufacturing and other costs of sales	**8,508**	7,245	6,882
Selling, general and administrative expenses	**2,838**	2,468	2,414
Depreciation expense	**1,000**	886	790
Interest expense, net	**157**	129	133
Total costs and expenses	**12,503**	10,728	10,219
Earnings before income taxes and cumulative effect of change in accounting principle	**800**	613	666
Income taxes provided on earnings	**224**	159	167
Net earnings before cumulative effect of change in accounting principle	**$ 576**	$ 454	$ 499
Cumulative effect of change in accounting principle, net of tax	**123**	–	–
Net earnings	**$ 453**	$ 454	$ 499
Net earnings per share before cumulative effect of change in accounting principle	**$ 2.16**	$ 1.72	$ 1.90
Cumulative effect of change in accounting principle per share	**0.46**	–	–
Net earnings per share	**$ 1.70**	$ 1.72	$ 1.90
Average shares outstanding	**267.0**	263.9	262.5

See accompanying notes to consolidated financial statements.

■ **ACCOUNTING FOR YOUR DECISIONS**   **You Are the Analyst**

Which per-share figure would you emphasize in your investment decision regarding Motorola—earnings before income taxes and cumulative effect of change in accounting principle, net earnings before cumulative effect of change in accounting principle, or net earnings?

costs in 1992. Its income statement presents an amount as earnings before the cumulative effect of a change in accounting principle of $576 million. The cumulative effect of the change in the accounting for postretirement costs is $123 million. Because this amount represents additional expense, it is deducted to arrive at the net income amount of $453 million for the year:

$$\$576 - \$123 = \$453 \text{ million}$$

The cumulative effect amount on Motorola's income statement represents a one-time charge and is unlikely to occur in the future.

As it turns out, in 1992 many companies had a similar item on their income statement as a result of the FASB's new rule requiring companies to record postretirement health and other benefits as liabilities today even though the amounts will not be paid for many years. Previously, companies merely charged earnings for these costs as they went along. Because the FASB mandated the rule change, companies really had little choice but to display this "cumulative effect of an accounting change."

What can be troubling is when companies change accounting principles because their results will look better under the new method, not because the new principle better reflects business reality. Companies that change accounting methods must justify the change and should not be attempting merely to increase their income as a result. When a change in accounting principle does occur, the income statement line referred to as income *before* the cumulative effect of a change in accounting principle is perhaps a better measure of the activities that will continue in the future.

Analyzing Profitability
Using Earnings Per Share

Ratios are often helpful to evaluate the profitability of a firm and to compare the performance of one firm with that of another. The most common ratio to evaluate a firm's profitability is **earnings per share.** All public companies are required to disclose this important ratio on their income statement. Earnings per share is calculated as

LO   5

Use the earnings per share ratio as a measure of a company's profitability.

Net Income − Preferred Dividends /
Weighted Average Number of Shares of Common Stock

The purpose of the earnings per share calculation is to determine the amount of earnings that have been earned by the *common* stockholder. When a firm has both preferred and common stock, the preferred stockholders have a claim to earnings in the amount of the preferred stock dividend. Therefore, preferred stock dividends must be deducted in the numerator; the remaining amount represents the earnings of the common stockholder.

The denominator represents the number of shares of *common* stock outstanding for the firm. The income number, the numerator of the fraction, measures income of a specific time period, in this case a year. Therefore, it is necessary that the denominator of the fraction, the number of shares, also be measured over a time period. For that reason, a **weighted average of shares** is used as the denominator of the earnings per share calculation. The weighted average is calculated by weighting the number of shares by the time period those shares were outstanding during the period.

The following example illustrates the calculation of a weighted average. Assume that a firm had 1,000 shares of common stock issued as of the beginning of 1995. On September 1, 1995, the firm issued an additional 600 shares of common stock. The September 1 transaction was the only transaction during the year affecting the number of shares. On December 31, 1995, the firm had 1,600 shares of common stock outstanding, but this is not the number that is used as the denominator when calculating earnings per share. The weighted average number of shares is calculated as follows:

$$\text{Beginning Shares} + (\text{Increase in Shares} \times \text{Time Factor}) =$$
$$\text{Weighted Average Shares}$$
$$1,000 + 600 \ (4/12) = 1,200$$

The shares must be weighted by the time period the shares were outstanding, so the 600 shares are weighted by 4/12 (4 months divided by 12 months).

Companies must compute earnings per share based on the bottom line net income figure and for other categories of income on the income statement. For example, if a firm's income statement has an extraordinary item, earnings per share for income before extraordinary items is calculated as

$$\text{Income before Extraordinary Items} - \text{Preferred Dividends} \ /$$
$$\text{Weighted Average Number of Shares of Common Stock}$$

Thus, the income statement of most corporations reveals several earnings per share numbers corresponding to the income categories disclosed on the income statement.

The income statement of Motorola in Exhibit 12-3 is an excellent example of the presentation of earnings per share. Note that toward the bottom of the statement, the company has indicated that the "average shares outstanding" for 1992 were 267 million. This represents the weighted average number of shares of common stock and was used as the denominator for calculating earnings per share. Because Motorola had a change in accounting principle during 1992, the income statement presents earnings per share both before and after the change in principle. The earnings per share based on earnings before the cumulative effect of a change in principle was $2.16, the earnings per share for the cumulative effect itself was a negative $.46, and the earnings per share based on the bottom line net income amount was $1.70.

The earnings per share ratio is a very important measure of a firm's profitability. Investors commonly use it to determine the proper market price of a firm's stock. A company's management is expected to meet the earnings per share predicted for the company by analysts and investors. If a company does not meet such goals, the stock price often falls in response.

The earnings per share ratio represents the *earnings* per share of the firm, however, not the *dividend* that the stockholders will receive. A firm's disclosure of earnings per share of $2 does not mean that stockholders will receive a dividend of $2 per

FROM CONCEPT TO PRACTICE

READING BEN & JERRY'S INCOME STATEMENT

Refer to Ben & Jerry's income statement. What amount was reported as earnings per share? How was the amount calculated?

share. Most firms pay only a portion of their earnings to stockholders as dividends. Others, such as Ben & Jerry's, do not regularly pay any dividends. The amounts not paid as dividends are retained by the firm to finance its future growth.

Transactions Affecting Stockholders' Equity

Chapter 11 discussed a variety of transactions that affect the stockholders' equity category of the balance sheet. This section of Chapter 12 introduces several additional transactions. The items discussed here are all examples of transactions that affect the stockholders' equity category but are not part of the income statement. Each of the items is recorded directly to an account in the stockholders' equity category.

Prior Period Adjustments

A **prior period adjustment** is an adjustment to the income of previous years. Because the income of each period affects the Retained Earnings account, a prior period adjustment is an item that is recorded directly in the Retained Earnings account rather than on the income statement. The most common example of a prior period adjustment is a correction of an error in a previous period. For example, assume that Heidi Company purchased a $10,000 asset on January 1, 1993. The asset has a 10-year life, and Heidi had planned to use straight-line depreciation. In 1995, however, the accountant for Heidi discovered that the company has neglected to record depreciation on the asset since the time of purchase.

LO   **6**

Identify the proper retained earnings statement presentation of corrections of errors.

This situation is an example of the need for a correction of an error that should be treated as a prior period adjustment. The accountant for Heidi should first determine the amount of the error for the prior periods as follows:

$$\$10,000/10 \text{ Years} = \$1,000 \text{ Depreciation per Year} \times 2 \text{ Years}$$
$$\text{Error before Tax} = \underline{\$2,000}$$

Note that the error in Retained Earnings is the amount of error for *prior* periods, 1993 and 1994 in this example. It does not include the amount for the current year, 1995, because that amount can be corrected by taking $1,000 for depreciation expense on the 1995 income statement. Depreciation was understated each year for two years. Depreciation expense for 1993 and 1994 cannot be corrected, however, by changing the Depreciation Expense account. Depreciation Expense is a temporary account that was closed each year. The result was that net income was overstated each year. Net income is closed to the Retained Earnings account at year-end; therefore, Retained Earnings is overstated. To correct for the error, the beginning balance of Retained Earnings as of January 1, 1995, must be decreased.

Prior period adjustments must be presented *net* of the tax effect of the item. Assume that the tax rate for Heidi Company is 40%. The error, net of taxes, would be computed as follows:

Error before tax	$2,000
Tax effect at 40%	(800)
Error net of tax	$1,200

The prior period adjustment would appear on the 1995 statement of retained earnings as follows:

Retained earnings, January 1, 1995	$XXXXX
Less: Correction of error (net of $800 tax effect)	($1,200)
Corrected balance, January 1, 1995	$XXXXX

When an error occurs and a prior period adjustment item is presented, it should be presented as the first item after the beginning balance on the retained earnings statement. The beginning balance of the Retained Earnings account should be shown as previously reported. The correction of error should then be presented to arrive at a corrected beginning balance. After the corrected beginning balance, the other items on the retained earnings statement, such as net income and dividends, should be handled as we have indicated in previous chapters.

Although prior adjustments due to errors occur with some frequency on the unaudited financial statements of privately held companies, it is most unusual to see such an adjustment on the audited financial statements of a publicly held company.

Appropriations of Retained Earnings

LO 7

Understand the effect of appropriations and other restrictions on retained earnings.

Another example of an item that does not affect the income of the company but does affect retained earnings is appropriations of retained earnings. An **appropriation of retained earnings** occurs when a company designates a portion of the balance of retained earnings for a specific purpose, thereby making the amount appropriated unavailable for dividends. The amount can be recorded in a separate account or reported in a footnote. Appropriations of retained earnings are used less frequently than in past years and are usually reported in a footnote.

Assume, for example, that the board of directors of Dran Company has voted to engage in a plant expansion program. As part of the program, the directors voted on January 1, 1995, to appropriate $10,000 of retained earnings for plant expansion. If the appropriation is recorded in a separate account, the following journal entry records the transaction:

Jan. 1	Retained Earnings	10,000	
	Retained Earnings Appropriated for Plant Expansion		10,000
	To record the appropriation of retained earnings.		

Assets	=	Liabilities	+	Owners' Equity
				− 10,000
				+ 10,000

The account Retained Earnings Appropriated for Plant Expansion is an account in the stockholders' equity category of the balance sheet. The normal balance of the account is a credit, and the account is increased by crediting or decreased by debiting. Dran Company now has two accounts within the retained earnings category. The first account, Retained Earnings, represents the amount that is available for dividend purposes. The second account, Retained Earnings Appropriated for Plant Expansion, represents the amount designated for a specific purpose. It is important to remember, however, that appropriated retained earnings does not represent assets and does not ensure sufficient assets are available for plant expansion. It merely represents the balance of an account in the stockholders' equity category of the balance sheet. The assets of the company may be committed to receivables, inventory, property, plant, and equipment, not to cash or investments that can be used for plant expansion.

What then is the purpose of appropriating retained earnings? It may serve at least two purposes. First, appropriating retained earnings reduces the company's ability to pay dividends to stockholders. Dividends are declared from the Retained Earnings account, which was reduced when the entry to appropriate was recorded. Second, appropriating retained earnings serves a signaling effect. It is a visible sign to stockholders and other statement users that the firm has future plans and needs to retain funds for those plans. Many firms may disclose such intentions in a footnote or a parenthetical disclosure attached to the Retained Earnings account in lieu of a Retained Earnings Appropriated account.

At times, the board of directors may vote to cancel an appropriation of retained earnings. Assume that in the preceding example, the plant expansion was completed and the board of directors voted on December 31, 1995, to cancel the appropriation. If the footnote method had been used, no footnote would be needed on the year-end balance sheet. If a separate account had been used, the entry to return the appropriated retained earnings to the Retained Earnings account is as follows:

Dec. 31   Retained Earnings Appropriated
               for Plant Expansion   10,000
                    Retained Earnings   10,000
           To record the return of retained earnings appropriated.

Assets	**=**	**Liabilities**	**+**	**Owners' Equity**
				−10,000
				+10,000

Other Transactions

Thus far in this section, we have presented two examples of items that are not recorded on the income statement but are recorded directly in the Retained Earnings account. Additional items are not recorded on the income statement but are recorded directly to other accounts in the stockholders' equity category. We mention these briefly because you may see these items on the financial statements of many large corporations. First, the stockholders' equity category of some firms reveals the account **Unrealized Gain/Loss—Available-for-Sale Securities,** which occurs when a firm adjusts its investments in securities for changes in the market value of the securities. For example, if a company buys stock in another company and the value of that stock changes, it may be necessary to write up or down the stock to market value. (See Chapter 13 for more detail.) The adjustment of available-for-sale investments is not considered a gain or loss on the income statement. Instead, the adjustment on these items is recorded directly to the stockholders' equity category, and an account for such items is reflected on the balance sheet after retained earnings. The Unrealized Gain/Loss—Available-for-Sale Securities account is a stockholders' equity account. Debits to the account represent declines in value of securities and credits represent increases in value.

Although it is true that unrealized gains and losses on some investments are not presented on the income statement precisely because they are unrealized, such information is still of interest to investors. For example, one would question the money management ability of a company that showed significant unrealized losses during a period when the stock market had been rising for several years, as it did in the early 1990s. Today, managing money is a big part of managing a company's resources.

A second item that may appear in the stockholders' equity category is the account Foreign Currency Translation Adjustments. Most large corporations operate in several countries, and their assets may be held in the currency of several denominations, such as U.S. dollars and Japanese yen. Generally, when these international companies present their financial statements, they are required to present all of their assets in one currency. For example, U.S. companies must state their financial statements in U.S. dollars, requiring restatement of all their assets to U.S. dollars. When assets of another currency are restated to U.S. dollars, a gain or loss on restatement occurs. The gain or loss is not the result of selling the assets but results from differences in the values of the two currencies involved.

This gain or loss is not presented on the income statement. Instead, it is presented as an account in the stockholders' equity category of the balance sheet. The account Foreign Currency Translation Adjustments may have either a debit or credit balance. If a loss has resulted from the translation, the balance of the account is a debit; if a gain has resulted, its balance is a credit.

You should note that there is considerable controversy about the importance of translation adjustment amounts on companies' annual reports. Companies consider the translation adjustments to be "paper" gains or losses because they are unrealized and do not directly result in any cash inflows or outflows. The gains or losses are realized only if foreign assets are transferred to U.S. dollars. Most international firms do not actually intend such transactions and calculate the translation adjustments only for the purpose of presenting financial statements. We return to a detailed explanation of these adjustments in Chapter 13.

Statement of Stockholders' Equity

LO 8

Prepare a statement of stockholders' equity.

In addition to a balance sheet, income statement, and cash flow statement, many annual reports contain a **statement of stockholders' equity.** The purpose of this statement is to explain all of the reasons for the difference between the beginning and ending balance of each of the accounts in the stockholders' equity category of the balance sheet. Of course, if the only changes are the result of dividends, a statement of retained earnings is sufficient. When other changes have occurred in stockholders' equity accounts, this more complete statement is necessary.

The statement of stockholders' equity of Household International, a large financial institution, is presented in Exhibit 12-4 for the year 1992. The statement starts with the beginning balances of each of the accounts as of December 31, 1991. Household's

EXHIBIT 12-4 Household International 1992 Statement of Stockholders' Equity

STATEMENTS OF CHANGES IN PREFERRED STOCK AND COMMON SHAREHOLDERS' EQUITY						
	Nonconvertible Preferred Stock	Common Stock	Additional Paid-in Capital	Retained Earnings	Other	Total Common Shareholders' Equity
Balance at December 31, 1991	250.0	54.6	252.9	2,015.4	(798.0)	1,524.9
Net income				190.9		190.9
Cash dividends–preferred, at stated rates				(30.4)		(30.4)
Cash dividends–common, $2.29 per share				(94.2)		(94.2)
Foreign currency translation adjustments[2]					(37.5)	(37.5)
Conversion of preferred stock		.9	17.3			18.2
Exercise of stock options		.1	5.9			6.0
Unrealized loss on investments, net					(0.9)	(0.9)
Issuance of common stock			1.1		31.9	33.0
Issuance of nonconvertible preferred stock	50.0		(1.6)			(1.6)
Balance at December 31, 1992	**$300.0**	**$55.6**	**$275.6**	**$2,081.7**	**$(804.5)**	**$1,608.4**

■ **ACCOUNTING FOR YOUR DECISIONS** **You Are the Auditor**

Your client is being very tough with you on your fees, trying to cut corners wherever possible. He suggests that the company forego the preparation of the statement of changes in preferred stock and common shareholder's equity, which you stated would cost the company another $5,000 for you to audit on top of the $100,000 audit fee. What should you do?

---

stockholders' equity is presented in five categories (the columns on the statement) as of December 31, 1991, as follows:

Nonconvertible preferred stock	$250.0 million
Common stock	54.6
Additional paid-in capital	252.9
Retained earnings	2,015.4
Other	(798.0)

A footnote indicates that the other category includes items such as foreign currency translation adjustments, unrealized losses on marketable equity securities, and treasury stock.

During 1992 nine items or transactions affected stockholders' equity as follows:

ITEM	EFFECT
Net income	Increased retained earnings by $190.9
Cash dividends—preferred	Decreased retained earnings by $30.4
Cash dividends—common	Decreased retained earnings by $94.2
Foreign currency translation adjustments	Reduced other category by $37.5
Preferred stock converted to common stock	Increased common stock by $0.9 and additional paid-in capital by $17.3
Stock options exercised	Issued stock resulting in increase in common stock capital of $0.1 and additional paid-in capital of $5.9
Loss on investments	Decrease in other category of $0.9
Issued common stock held as treasury stock	Increased additional paid-in capital by $1.1 and increased other by $31.9
Issued nonconvertible preferred stock	Increased preferred stock by $50.0 and decreased additional paid-in capital by $1.6

Amounts in millions.

These nine events or transactions explain the ending balances indicated for December 31, 1992. The statement indicates that total *common* shareholders' equity as of December 31, 1992, was $1,608.4 million. To arrive at total shareholders' equity, including preferred stock, we must add the balance of nonconvertible preferred stock of $300.0 million to arrive at a total of $1,908.4 million.

Based on Household International's statement of changes in stockholders' equity, the reader can see that the company paid out more than half its income in dividends, reduced its equity through foreign currency translation adjustments (which may be temporary), and boosted its equity by issuing new shares of common and preferred stock.

What Is Comprehensive Income?

LO 9

Understand the meaning and importance of comprehensive income.

There has always been some question about which items or transactions should be shown on the income statement and be included in the calculation of net income. Generally, the accounting rule-making bodies have held that the income statement should reflect an *all-inclusive* approach. That is, all events and transactions that affect income should be shown on the income statement. This approach prevents items from being recorded directly to Retained Earnings and the other stockholders' equity accounts. It also prevents the manipulation of the income figure by those who would like to show "good news" on the income statement and "bad news" directly on the retained earnings statement or the statement of stockholders' equity. The result of the all-inclusive approach is that the income statement includes items that are not necessarily under management's control, such as losses from natural disasters, and may not be a true reflection of a company's future potential.

Recently, the FASB has accepted certain exceptions to the all-inclusive approach and has allowed items to be recorded directly to the stockholders' equity category. This chapter has presented several examples of such items: prior period adjustments, foreign currency translation adjustments, and unrealized losses on some investment securities. Items such as these have been excluded from the income statement for various reasons. Quite often, the justification is a concern for the volatility of the net income number. The items we have cited are often large dollar amounts and, if included in the income statement, would cause income to fluctuate widely from period to period. Therefore, the income statement is deemed to be more useful if the items are excluded.

A new term has been coined to incorporate the "income-type" items that escape the income statement. **Comprehensive income** is the increase in the amount of net assets resulting from all transactions during a time period (except for effects of investments by owners and distributions to owners). The comprehensive income measure is truly all-inclusive because it includes transactions such as unrealized gains and prior period adjustments. Firms are not currently required to disclose comprehensive income, but its inclusion provides a more complete measure of the performance of modern corporations.

How Income Statement Transactions Affect the Statement of Cash Flows

LO 10

Determine the impact of income statement transactions on the statement of cash flows.

In this chapter, we have reviewed several accounting issues and have studied the impact of those issues on the income statement. In this section, we concentrate on transactions involving extraordinary items and changes in accounting principle to determine their cash flow impact and the proper way to disclose such items on the statement of cash flows.

Some extraordinary items do not have a cash flow impact. For example, assume that a company's plant, with a book value of $600,000, is destroyed by a fire. If the company did not have fire insurance, the result would be an extraordinary loss of $600,000 on the income statement (assuming no tax effect). Because no cash was received, the event has no cash flow impact. If the indirect method is used for the

INVESTOR RELATIONS

Name: Randall Oliver
Profession: Senior Financial Analyst
College Major: Public Relations

An emerging profession that draws upon accounting and communication skills is the field of investor relations. "IR" people tell their company's story to Wall Street—why earnings are up or down, why debt is dropping, and more complicated messages such as how a change in a FASB rule could affect the stock.

Among other duties at Houston Industries, Randall Oliver (center) is the company's IR contact for Wall Street investors as well as individual shareholders. Houston Industries, a holding company with electric utility and cable television subsidiaries, has more than its share of individual investors. Utilities often do, since the stocks pay healthy dividends, which retirees like to collect to supplement their Social Security. That means Mr. Oliver has to answer questions that range from the extremely complex—those posed by the electric utility securities analysts—to the extremely simple. "Sometimes the questions relate to our operations, such as how particular plants are performing, the impact of adverse weather—or it could be a regulatory change from the Public Utility Commission." Or the question could be financial. Investors might want to know more about earnings, cash flow, return on equity, refinancings, or sales growth.

Oliver, who also holds an MBA in finance from UCLA, produces the company's annual report, writes speeches for executives and puts out a monthly newsletter that goes to securities analysts. Of course, he never discloses information that is not already public, because that would be illegal. Indeed, a major focus of the investor relations profession is how to disclose new information in such a way that no one gets an unfair advantage. That means issuing press releases in the widest possible media, and being careful that questions are never answered in a manner that would reveal inside information.

Investor relations specialists throughout the country have spent a great deal of time explaining a relatively new FASB rule—106, for example, which refers to postretirement employee benefits. Many companies had one-time charges in 1992 or 1993 to reflect this change in accounting, which essentially created a liability for workers' health and life insurance benefits promised after retirement. Another one, in 1994, is a one-time accounting change reflecting a liability for people on long-term disability. (We discuss these issues in Chapter 10.)

Another one-time change that Oliver had to explain is peculiar to the utility industry. "In the past, we recorded electric revenues as they've been billed," he says. "Now, we are recording revenues at the time that the electricity is consumed." Why is that important? Because the change threw off the year-to-year comparisons. Without knowing, an analyst would falsely assume that the company's results were worse in 1993 compared to 1992, when they actually were better.

statement of cash flows, the loss should be disclosed by *adding back* the amount to the net income in the operating category of the statement. Adding back the item *does not* mean that it was a source of cash. Because the loss was deducted in calculating net income, however, it must be added back to indicate that it did not involve cash, in the same way that depreciation and other noncash items are added back in the operating category.

Extraordinary gains must also be disclosed on the statement of cash flows. A gain increases net income, so the item must be *deducted* on the statement of cash flows to remove the effect from the operating category of the statement.

When a company makes a change in accounting principle, the cumulative effect of the change should appear on the income statement in the year of the change. The company does not pay cash or receive cash, however, as a result of making a change in its accounting methods. It is a bookkeeping change that affects net income but does not involve cash. Changes in accounting principles should be reflected on the statement of cash flows in a manner similar to that described for extraordinary items. If a change in principle resulted in a cumulative effect that was deducted on the income statement (a debit), the change should be *added back* on the statement of cash flows. The item should appear in the operating category to show that changes in accounting principle are not a part of normal operating activities.

If a change in principle resulted in a cumulative effect that was added on the income statement (a credit), the change should be *deducted* on the statement of cash flows. Again, the item should be deducted from the operating category to indicate that changes in principle do not result in cash and are not part of normal operating activities.

FROM CONCEPT TO PRACTICE

READING MOTOROLA'S INCOME STATEMENT
Refer to Exhibit 12-3. Where would the accounting change for Motorola appear on the statement of cash flows? Would the item be added or subtracted?

REVIEW PROBLEM

The accountant for Jalen Company wishes to develop an income statement for 1995. The following preliminary amounts have been calculated at year-end:

Gross profit	$500,000
Selling and administrative expense	100,000
Interest expense	20,000
Other income and expense	–0–
Income tax rate	40%

These amounts were calculated before several items and transactions were considered. The following items must be considered before Jalen can develop an income statement.

a. Jalen determined that it was holding some obsolete inventory. The goods in inventory had been purchased in 1994 for $8,000 and were now considered to be worthless.

b. On December 31, 1995, Jalen decided to drastically change the nature of its business. The board of directors voted to sell a major division of the company in 1996. It was estimated that the loss on the division would amount to $10,000 when sold in 1996. (*Hint:* This item should be reported on the 1995 income statement.)

c. During 1995 a fire caused $40,000 of damage to one of Jalen's plants. Jalen had a long history of safe operating conditions and had never experienced a fire loss to its property prior to 1995. The fire loss is uninsured.

d. On January 1, 1995, Jalen changed its method of recording inventory from the first-in, first-out method to a weighted average method. Jalen has calculated that if the new inventory method had been used in past periods, income would have been higher by $20,000 before considering the tax effect of the change.

e. During 1995 Jalen discovered that the company had neglected to record an expense of $9,000 in 1993. It must make the proper corrections on the 1995 financial statements.

f. During 1995 Jalen's board of directors voted to appropriate $20,000 of retained earnings for possible inventory losses. The amount of the inventory loss for the year was $8,000, as indicated in item a.

g. Jalen must present the necessary earnings per share figures to accompany the income statement. Its capital structure consists of one class of stock. On January 1, 1995, 5,000 shares of stock were outstanding; an additional 2,000 shares were issued on July 1, 1995; no other stock transactions occurred during the year.

1. Indicate the category of the income statement where each of the items a through f should be presented and the dollar amount for that category. Develop a revised 1995 income statement for Jalen Company beginning with gross profit, as given.

■ REQUIRED

2. At the bottom of the income statement, present the necessary earnings per share figures for Jalen's income statement.

3. Which line of the income statement would be the most useful for predicting Jalen's future income?

■ SOLUTION TO REVIEW PROBLEM

1. The items in the review problem should be treated in the following manner.

a. A loss on obsolete inventory is *not* considered to be an extraordinary item. The loss of $8,000 should be presented in the other expense category of the income statement. Because the item in this case is a loss, it should be deducted in arriving at Jalen's income.

b. A company's sale of a major division should be presented as a discontinued operation. The amount of $10,000 is before the tax effect. The amount net of the tax effect is $6,000, or $10,000 × 60% (100% − 40%). Note that this estimated loss is presented on the 1995 income statement even though the division will not be sold until 1996.

c. The fire loss appears to meet the criteria to be classified as an extraordinary item. The loss of $40,000 does not consider the tax benefit of the loss. The amount net of the tax effect is $24,000, or $40,000 × 60% (100% − 40%).

d. The change in inventory methods represents a change in accounting principle and should be presented in a separate category of the income statement. The cumulative effect of the change was an increase in income of $20,000 before tax. The amount net of the tax effect is $12,000, or $20,000 × 60% (100% − 40%).

e. The failure to record an expense in 1993, discovered in 1995, is an error that must be corrected. The correction is *not* presented on the income statement. Rather, the error correction is presented on the retained earnings statement, net of its tax effect, as an adjustment of the beginning balance of retained earnings.

f. An appropriation of retained earnings is *not* presented on the income statement. It represents a reduction of the Retained Earnings account and the creation of the separate retained earnings account Appropriated Retained Earnings. Note that the income statement impact is the amount of the actual loss that occurred, as reflected in item a. The appropriation of retained earnings does not have an impact on the income statement.

After considering items a through f, the revised income statement appears as follows:

JALEN COMPANY
PARTIAL INCOME STATEMENT
FOR THE YEAR ENDED DECEMBER 31, 1995

Gross profit		$500,000
Selling and administrative expenses		(100,000)
Income from operations		400,000
Other income and expense:		
Interest expense	($20,000)	
Loss on obsolete inventory	(8,000)	(28,000)
Income from continuing operations before tax		372,000
Income tax expense		(148,800)
Income from continuing operations		223,200
Discontinued operations:		
Expected loss on disposal of division,		
$10,000, less tax effect of $4,000		(6,000)
Income before extraordinary item		217,200
Extraordinary loss—loss from fire,		
$40,000, less tax effect of $16,000		(24,000)
Income before cumulative effect		193,200
Cumulative effect of change in inventory		
method, $20,000, less tax effect of		
$8,000		12,000
Net income		$205,200

2. For purposes of calculating earnings per share, the weighted average number of shares are computed as 6,000 shares:

$$5,000 + 2,000 \ (6/12) = 6,000 \text{ shares}$$

Earnings per share should be presented as follows:

Income from continuing operations	$223,200/6,000 = $37.20
Discontinued operations:	
Expected loss on disposal of division	(6,000)/6,000 = (1.00)
Income before extraordinary item	217,200/6,000 = $36.20
Extraordinary loss—loss from fire	(24,000)/6,000 = (4.00)
Income before cumulative effect	193,200/6,000 = $32.20
Cumulative effect of change in inventory	12,000/6,000 = 2.00
Net Income	$205,200/6,000 = $34.20

3. The income statement line labeled Income from Continuing Operations is the best indication of Jalen's future income potential.

GUIDANCE ANSWERS TO ACCOUNTING FOR YOUR DECISIONS

YOU ARE THE ANALYST

A good first choice would be the middle one—earnings before the cumulative effect of the accounting change. Since taxes are an ongoing expense for the corporation, there would be no reason to look at earnings before taxes. However, a cumulative effect of an accounting change is a one-time charge that is unrelated to the company's ongoing results. Unfortunately, users often pick up the Net Earnings Per Share figure of $1.70, since it's the "bottom line."

YOU ARE THE AUDITOR

Some companies who file with the SEC are required to provide a statement of stockholders' equity and the auditor must audit the statement. For other companies the statement is not required. Smart investors can get all of the information on this statement from other parts of the annual report. However, you should encourage your client to provide the report. The increase in fees is a small amount for the additional information.

CHAPTER HIGHLIGHTS

1. **(LO 1)** Most corporations present the revenues and expenses of the period on the income statement in a multi-step, rather than single-step, format to provide more relevant information to users of the statement.

2. **(LO 1)** The amount of operating income is a measure of the amount derived from the firm's primary or central activities. It does not include other income and expenses such as interest.

3. **(LO 2)** A discontinued operations category indicates that a company has taken action to sell a major segment of the company. The amount of the gain or loss on disposal should be presented separately on the income statement net of the income tax effect of the transaction.

4. **(LO 3)** An item should be considered extraordinary if it is both unusual and infrequent. Management must consider the criteria with regard to the company's environment. If an item is considered extraordinary, the amount of the gain or loss should be presented separately on the income statement net of the income tax effect of the transaction.

5. **(LO 3)** Gains or losses on the redemption of bonds payable should always be considered extraordinary and are not required to be judged as unusual and infrequent.

6. **(LO 4)** An accounting change occurs when a company changes its method of accounting for an item from one year to the next. The cumulative effect of the change in accounting principle should be presented on the income statement in the year of the change net of the income tax effect of the transaction.

7. **(LO 4)** The cumulative effect of a change in accounting principle is the total difference in income between the previous accounting method and the adopted method for all years prior to the current year.

8. **(LO 5)** Earnings per share is a measure of the rights of the common stockholder to the income of the company. It is generally calculated by subtracting preferred stock dividends from the net income and dividing by the weighted average number of shares of common stock outstanding.

9. **(LO 6)** Corrections of errors of prior periods are not recorded on the income statement. They are presented as an adjustment to the beginning balance of the Retained Earnings account.

10. **(LO 7)** An appropriation of retained earnings occurs when a company designates a portion of the balance of retained earnings and creates a separate Retained Earnings account for that purpose. The Appropriated

Retained Earnings account is an account within the stockholders' equity category of the balance sheet.

11. (LO 8) A statement of stockholders' equity explains the changes in the balances of all stockholders' equity accounts. It is similar to a statement of retained earnings except that it explains the changes in all stockholders' equity accounts.

12. (LO 8) Several items that are recorded as part of stockholders' equity do not affect net income. The items include the adjustment for changes in the market value of available-for-sale securities and foreign currency translation adjustments.

13. (LO 9) Comprehensive income is the increase in the amount of net assets resulting from all transactions during a time period except for effects of investments by owners and distributions to owners. It is the broadest measure of income available and provides a more complete measure of a company's performance.

14. (LO 10) When the indirect method is used to prepare the statement of cash flows, adjustments are necessary in the operating activities section for extraordinary items and cumulative effects. Those items that were deductions on the income statement must be added back and those that were additions on the income statement must be deducted.

KEY TERMS QUIZ

Select one of the following key terms used in the chapter and fill in the appropriate blank to the left of each description. The solution appears at the end of the chapter.

Multi-step income statement	Gross profit
Gross profit percentage	Operating income
Income before income taxes	Discontinued operations
Extraordinary item	Change in accounting principle
Cumulative effect	Earnings per share
Weighted average of shares	Prior period adjustment
Appropriation of retained earnings	Unrealized Gain/Loss—Available-
Statement of stockholders' equity	for-Sale Securities
Comprehensive income	

_____ **1.** A ratio calculated as the gross profit divided by the net sales.

_____ **2.** A subtotal on the income statement calculated as operating income plus other income items, such as interest, and minus other expense items.

_____ **3.** The amount of net sales minus the amount of cost of sales.

_____ **4.** A category on the income statement indicating that a major segment or division of the company has been or will be sold.

_____ **5.** A subtotal on the income statement calculated as gross profit minus operating expenses.

_____ **6.** An income statement item that occurs when a company changes from one accounting method to another.

_____ **7.** A correction that is not recorded on the income statement but is presented as an adjustment to the balance of the Retained Earnings account.

_____ **8.** An item that is considered both unusual and infrequent and is presented in a separate category of the income statement.

_____ **9.** An income statement that presents revenues and expenses by category.

_____   **10.** A statement that indicates the differences between beginning and ending balances for all accounts in the stockholders' equity category.

_____   **11.** The total effect of a change in accounting principle for all years prior to the current year.

_____   **12.** An account in the stockholders' equity category that reflects that the investment in certain securities was adjusted to market value.

_____   **13.** The number of shares of stock weighted by the time period that the stock was outstanding.

_____   **14.** The amount that reflects the total change in net assets from all sources except investment or withdrawals by the owners of the company.

_____   **15.** An account that indicates that a company has designated a portion of the balance of Retained Earnings for a specific purpose.

_____   **16.** A number that represents the rights of the common stockholders to the income of the company; calculated as net income minus preferred dividends divided by the number of shares of common stock outstanding.

ALTERNATE TERMS

CHANGE IN PRINCIPLE Change in accounting method.

DISCONTINUED OPERATIONS Disposal of a segment.

EARNINGS PER SHARE Net income per share.

EXTRAORDINARY ITEMS Unusual and infrequent items.

GROSS PROFIT Gross margin.

OPERATING INCOME Income from operations.

OPERATING EXPENSES Selling, general, and administrative expenses.

PRIOR PERIOD ADJUSTMENT Correction of error.

STOCKHOLDERS' EQUITY Shareholders' equity.

QUESTIONS

1. Why do most firms consider a multi-step income statement to be better than a single-step statement?
2. How is gross profit calculated? What does the gross profit amount tell financial statement users about a company?
3. How is the gross profit percentage calculated? How would you determine whether a company's gross profit percentage was at an acceptable level?
4. Where does the term *net income* appear on the income statement? Is net income calculated before or after income tax is deducted on the income statement?
5. If you see an income statement that has a discontinued operations category, what does it indicate about the company's operations? Is the amount in the discontinued operations before or after the tax effect of the transaction?
6. If a company has a gain on a transaction, will the tax effect increase or reduce the gain? If a company has a loss on a transaction, will the income tax effect increase or reduce the loss?
7. What are the two criteria that must be met for an item to be considered an extraordinary item?

8. How are extraordinary items presented on the income statement? How should the tax effect of the transaction be presented?

9. How are gains and losses on the redemption of bonds payable presented on the income statement?

10. When a company changes from one accounting method to another, how should the effect of the change be presented on the income statement? Give an example of a change in accounting principle.

11. What does the cumulative effect of a change in accounting principle mean? How is the amount calculated?

12. When calculating earnings per share, why are preferred stock dividends deducted? Does the amount of earnings per share indicate the amount of dividend that will be paid?

13. How is the weighted average number of shares of stock calculated when calculating earnings per share?

14. When a company discovers that an error has occurred, how should it present the correction on the financial statements? Give an example of a prior period adjustment.

15. What is an appropriation of retained earnings and why would it be used?

16. What is an example of an item that is not recorded on the income statement but is recorded directly to the stockholders' equity category? What are possible reasons that such items are not recorded on the income statement?

17. What is the difference between a statement of stockholders' equity and a retained earnings statement?

18. What is meant by the term *comprehensive income?* How does comprehensive income differ from the net income figure presented on the traditional income statement?

EXERCISES

(LO 1) EXERCISE 12-1 MULTI-STEP INCOME STATEMENT

Dara Company has compiled the following single-step income statement for 1995.

Revenues:		
Sales revenue	$100,000	
Interest revenue	15,000	
Total revenue		$115,000
Expenses:		
Cost of goods sold	$ 60,000	
Selling and administrative expense	20,000	
Interest expense	10,000	
Income taxes	15,000	
Total expenses		$105,000
Net income		$ 10,000

■ REQUIRED

1. Develop a multi-step income statement for Dara Company for 1995.

2. Calculate the gross profit percentage. Explain what this ratio means for Dara Company.

(LO 3) EXERCISE 12-2 EXTRAORDINARY ITEMS

Battie Company has developed the following preliminary income statement for the year 1995.

Revenues	$100,000	
Cost of goods sold	60,000	
Gross profit		$40,000
Selling and administrative expenses		20,000
Income before tax		$20,000
Income tax		8,000
Net income		$12,000

The preliminary income statement does not include the impact of one additional event. During 1995 a fire destroyed a building that had a book value of $30,000; the loss was not covered by insurance. Assume that the tax rate applicable to the loss was the same as the rate on other transactions for Battie.

1. Develop a revised 1995 income statement for Battie Company to reflect the fire loss. You do not need to include the earnings per share calculations.

2. How would Battie's income statement differ if the fire were not treated as an extraordinary item?

■ REQUIRED

(LO 3) EXERCISE 12-3 EXTRAORDINARY ITEMS

Assume that Battie Company has developed the same preliminary income statement as in Exercise 12-2. One additional event has not been reflected on the 1995 income statement. During 1995 Battie retired bonds payable at a gain of $30,000. Assume that the gain is taxed at the same rate as the gain on other transactions.

1. Develop a revised income statement for 1995 for Battie Company to reflect the bond retirement. You do not need to include the earnings per share calculations.

2. Compare the tax effect on the extraordinary items in Exercises 12-2 and 12-3. Why is the tax effect positive in one case and negative in the other?

■ REQUIRED

(LO 3) EXERCISE 12-4 EXTRAORDINARY ITEMS

Consider the following items independently.

a. Loss on inventory as a result of obsolescence.

b. Write-off of receivables because a customer was unsatisfied with the product purchased.

c. Client notification of bankruptcy and the inability to pay its accounts receivable. The client is a major customer that has constituted at least 50% of the firm's sales each year for several years.

d. A gain or loss on the sale of equipment.

e. A loss recorded on equipment as a result of a flood.

f. A loss experienced by a company located in California due to structural damage to a building resulting from an earthquake.

g. A loss on the redemption of bonds payable, which were retired prior to the due date because of changing interest rate conditions.

h. A gain on the redemption of bonds payable, which were retired prior to the due date because of changing interest rate conditions.

i. Discovery that a piece of the company's equipment purchased three years ago has no recorded depreciation.

j. The decision by the company during the current year to change its method of inventory from the FIFO method to the weighted average method. Because of the composition of the inventory, the change had a very large impact on the current year income.

■ REQUIRED Indicate whether each of the above items should be treated as extraordinary on the income statement. If the situation does not qualify as an extraordinary item, indicate the section or category of the statement in which it should be reported.

(LO 4) EXERCISE 12-5 CHANGE IN ACCOUNTING PRINCIPLE

Assume that on January 1, 1992, Tarpley Company purchased a $150,000 asset. Tarpley chose to depreciate the asset over five years using the sum-of-years'-digit basis. For depreciation purposes, Tarpley assumed a zero salvage value. On January 1, 1995, Tarpley changed to the straight-line method of depreciation. The company continued to assume a zero salvage value and did not revise its estimate of the life of the asset.

■ REQUIRED **1.** Calculate the amount that should be reflected on Tarpley's 1995 income statement as the cumulative effect of the change in accounting principle. Assume that a 40% tax rate applies to the transaction.

2. Calculate the amount that should be recorded as depreciation expense by Tarpley on the 1995 income statement. Compare the 1994 depreciation to that recorded in 1995.

(LO 5) EXERCISE 12-6 EARNINGS PER SHARE

Chaney Company calculated its net income for the year ended December 31, 1995, as $50,000. The stockholders' equity category of Chaney's December 31, 1995, balance sheet contains the following:

Preferred stock, $10 par, 8%, cumulative, 5,000 shares issued and outstanding	$50,000
Common stock, $1 par, 10,000 shares issued and outstanding	10,000

Two stock transactions occurred during 1995. On March 1, 2,000 shares of common stock were issued for cash. On July 1, an additional 2,000 shares were issued for cash.

■ REQUIRED Calculate the earnings per share amount that should be disclosed on Chaney's 1995 income statement.

(LO 6) EXERCISE 12-7 ERROR CORRECTION

Benson Company has begun to prepare its 1995 financial statements. The following two situations involve errors that occurred in recording Benson Company transactions in years prior to 1995.

a. In 1994 Benson Company overstated ending inventory by $40,000; the error was discovered during 1995. The ending inventory for 1995 was calculated and recorded correctly.

b. In 1992 Benson purchased a new computer for $8,000 and recorded the purchase correctly. During 1995, however, Benson discovered that the company failed to record depreciation on the computer in all past periods. Assume that the asset has a five-year life, no salvage value, and that the company wishes to record depreciation using the straight-line method.

■ REQUIRED **1.** For each situation, record a transaction in journal form to correct the error. You may assume that tax does not apply to these transactions.

2. Describe how the two items should be presented on Benson's financial statements.

(LO 7) EXERCISE 12-8 APPROPRIATIONS OF RETAINED EARNINGS

On January 1, 1995, Nadler Company had a credit balance in the Retained Earnings account of $400,000. The following transactions occurred in 1995.

a. On March 1, Nadler's board of directors voted to appropriate $100,000 of retained earnings for possible future fire losses.

b. On June 1, a fire completely destroyed one of Nadler's buildings. The building originally cost $100,000; the accumulated depreciation on June 1 was $60,000. There was no insurance to cover the loss.

c. On December 15, 1995, Nadler's board of directors voted to eliminate the appropriation of retained earnings and to return the amount to the Retained Earnings account.

d. On December 31, 1995, Nadler recorded closing entries and calculated the net income for the year as $80,000.

1. Record these transactions in journal form.

2. Determine the amount that is available for dividend purposes after each transaction.

■ REQUIRED

(LO 9) EXERCISE 12-9 COMPREHENSIVE INCOME

Assume that you are the accountant for Hunter Corporation, which has issued its 1995 annual report. You have received an inquiry from a stockholder who has questions about several items in the annual report, including why Hunter has not shown certain transactions on the income statement. In particular, Hunter's 1995 balance sheet revealed two accounts—Unrealized Gain/Loss—Available-for-Sale Securities and Loss on Foreign Currency Translation Adjustments—in stockholders' equity for which the dollar amounts involved had not been recorded on the income statement.

Draft a written response to the stockholder's inquiry that explains the nature of the two accounts and the reason that the amounts involved were not recorded on the 1995 income statement. Do you think the concept of comprehensive income would be useful to explain the impact of all events for Hunter Corporation?

■ REQUIRED

MULTI-CONCEPT EXERCISES

(LO 1, 2) EXERCISE 12-10 DISCONTINUED OPERATIONS

Kidd Company has developed the following preliminary income statement for the year 1995.

Revenues	$100,000	
Cost of goods sold	60,000	
Gross profit		$40,000
Selling and administrative expenses		20,000
Income before tax		$20,000
Income tax		8,000
Net income		$12,000

Kidd Company is composed of two major divisions, A and B. On December 31, 1995, Kidd agreed to sell or eliminate Division A. Assume that all of Division A's assets will be sold at book value, resulting in zero gain or loss. The preliminary income statement must be altered, however, to reflect the discontinued operations of Division A. All of the division's revenues and expenses must appear on a separate line, income or loss from discontinued operations. Assume that when the income statement is altered, the income from continuing operations line is $8,400. During 1995 the results of Division A were as follows:

Revenue	$30,000
Expenses (except tax)	24,000
Tax	40%

■ REQUIRED   Develop a revised income statement for Kidd Company for 1995, beginning with income from continuing operations. You do not need to include the earnings per share calculations on the income statement.

PROBLEMS

(LO 1) PROBLEM 12-1 MULTI-STEP INCOME STATEMENT

Thomas Company has the following income statement accounts for 1995.

Sales revenue	$100,000
Interest revenue	20,000
Gain on sale of equipment	10,000
Cost of goods sold	60,000
Selling and administrative expenses	25,000
Interest expense	15,000
Loss on discontinued operations	5,000

■ REQUIRED   Develop a multi-step income statement for Thomas Company for 1995. Assume that a 40% tax rate applies to all transactions. Include the appropriate earnings per share calculations to accompany the 1995 income statement. Thomas had 20,000 shares of common stock and 10,000 shares of preferred stock outstanding throughout 1995. The preferred stockholders received a dividend of $1 per share.

(LO 2) PROBLEM 12-2 SALE OF SEGMENTS

Los Cruces Company, a New Mexico dairy producer, owns more than 3,000 head of cattle as well as land, buildings, and equipment. Included in the assets are a fleet of trucks and a chain of convenience stores. During 1995 Los Cruces sold 500 head of cattle and purchased 700 more. The company sold all of its trucks at a $10,000 gain and entered into a long-term agreement with a trucking firm to transport milk. The convenience stores reported losses for the past three years, so Los Cruces decided on December 31, 1995, to sell them. The amount of loss from convenience store operations during 1995 was $40,000, and the company estimated that future losses related to the segment would be $30,000. The company sold an investment in stock resulting in a $1,200 loss. Los Cruces's tax rate is 28%.

■ REQUIRED   **1.** Explain which, if any, of these transactions should be reported as a separate item on the income statement after income from continuing operations.

2. Assume that the income from continuing operations in 1995 has been calculated correctly as $624,500. Present the items that would appear on the income statement after the income from continuing operations line. You may ignore earnings per share calculations.

(LO 5) PROBLEM 12-3 EARNINGS PER SHARE

Laube Company had 10,000 shares of common stock outstanding on January 1, 1995. During 1995 the following common stock transactions occurred:

March 1, issued 2,000 shares of stock for cash.

April 1, purchased 1,000 shares as treasury stock.

July 1, reissued 1,000 shares of stock held as treasury stock.

October 1, issued 3,000 shares of stock for cash.

Laube also had 100 shares of $100 par, 8% cumulative preferred stock outstanding as of January 1, 1995. No preferred stock transactions occurred during 1995.

■ REQUIRED

1. Assume that the net income of Laube Company for 1995 was $60,000. Compute the earnings per share amount that should accompany the 1995 income statement.

2. Does the amount calculated as earnings per share indicate the dividend the stockholders can expect to receive? Explain.

(LO 7) PROBLEM 12-4 APPROPRIATIONS OF RETAINED EARNINGS

Genske Company's stockholders' equity section includes the following items on December 31, 1993:

Common stock, $1 par, 100,000 issued	$ 100,000
Additional paid-in capital	500,000
Retained earnings, unappropriated	462,300
Retained earnings, appropriated for land	200,000
Treasury stock, at cost, 5,000 shares	(75,000)
Total stockholders' equity	$1,187,300

At the annual meeting, the chief financial officer is asked to explain the nature of the items in the stockholders' equity section. A group of stockholders is pushing for a $4 per share dividend.

■ REQUIRED

1. Write a brief summary to be used by the CFO to explain the meaning of each of the items in the stockholders' equity section to a group of shareholders that are not trained in accounting.

2. Answer the following questions by stockholders:

"Why is treasury stock subtracted from the total? Doesn't the company actually own the stock?"

"In which bank is the $200,000 for the land and is it earning interest?"

"Why can't we have the $4 per share dividend? Why should we leave the money in retained earnings when we could put it in the bank to earn interest?"

(LO 8) PROBLEM 12-5 STATEMENT OF STOCKHOLDERS' EQUITY

Peeler Company was incorporated as a new business on January 1, 1995. The corporate charter approved on that date authorized the issuance of 1,000 shares of $100 par, 7% cumulative, nonparticipating preferred stock and 10,000 shares of $5 par common stock. On January 10, Peeler issued for cash 500 shares of preferred at $120 per share and 4,000 shares of common at $80 per share. On January 20, Peeler issued 1,000 shares of common stock to acquire a building site at a time when the stock was selling for $70 per share.

During 1995 Peeler established an employee benefit plan and acquired 500 shares of common stock at $60 per share as treasury stock for that purpose. One hundred shares of the stock were later resold during 1995 at $65 per share.

On December 31, 1995, Peeler determined that its net income for the year was $40,000. The firm declared the annual cash dividend to preferred stockholders and a cash dividend of $5 per share to the common stockholders. The dividend will be paid in 1996.

■ **REQUIRED** Develop a statement of stockholders' equity for Peeler Company for 1995. The statement should begin with the beginning balance of each stockholders' equity account and explain the changes that occurred in that account to arrive at the 1995 ending balance.

MULTI-CONCEPT PROBLEMS

(LO 3, 4) PROBLEM 12-6 EXTRAORDINARY ITEMS AND CHANGES IN ACCOUNTING PRINCIPLES

Grinde Company has developed the following preliminary income statement for the year 1995.

Revenues	$200,000	
Cost of goods sold	120,000	
Gross profit		$80,000
Selling and administrative expenses		40,000
Income before tax		$40,000
Income tax		16,000
Net income		$24,000

The preliminary income statement does not reflect two additional transactions that occurred in 1995. First, Grinde experienced a tornado loss of $50,000 during the year. You may assume that tornado losses are rare where Grinde is located. Second, on January 1, 1995, Grinde changed depreciation method for its only depreciable asset, which was originally purchased on January 1, 1993, for $150,000. Grinde depreciated the asset using an estimated life of five years and the sum-of-years'-digit method of depreciation for 1993 and 1994. Grinde changed to the straight-line method over a five-year life beginning in 1995. The 1995 depreciation is reflected in the Selling and Administrative Expenses account.

■ **REQUIRED** Prepare a revised 1995 income statement for Grinde Company to reflect the two additional transactions. Also present the earnings per share amounts to accompany the income statement. Grinde had 1,000 shares of common stock outstanding at all times during 1995. Assume a 40% tax rate applies to additional transactions.

(LO 1, 6, 10) PROBLEM 12-7 ERRORS AND RETAINED EARNINGS PRESENTATION

The preliminary income statement of Weaver Company for 1995 is as follows.

Revenues	$200,000	
Cost of goods sold	120,000	
Gross profit		$80,000
Selling and administrative expenses		40,000
Income before tax		$40,000
Income tax		16,000
Net income		$24,000

The preliminary income statement does not reflect one additional event. On January 1, 1993, Weaver appropriately recorded goodwill of $15,000 as a result of the purchase of another company. Weaver has discovered, however, that the goodwill has not been amortized in 1993 or any subsequent period.

1. Record an entry or entries to correct for the failure to amortize goodwill. Weaver wishes to amortize the goodwill over a five-year time period using the straight-line method. You may assume that there is no tax impact of the correction.

2. Prepare a revised income statement for Weaver for 1995. You may omit the required earnings per share calculations.

3. Prepare a statement of retained earnings for Weaver for 1995. The balance of the Retained Earnings account on January 1, 1995, was $50,000. During 1995 Weaver declared dividends to stockholders of $20,000.

4. Explain how the amortization of goodwill should appear on the cash flow statement.

■ REQUIRED

ALTERNATE PROBLEMS

(LO 1) PROBLEM 12-1A MULTI-STEP INCOME STATEMENT

Jones Company has the following income statement accounts for 1995.

Sales revenue	$250,000
Interest revenue	12,000
Loss on sale of land	40,000
Cost of goods sold	45,000
Selling and administrative expenses	13,500
Interest expense	7,500
Loss on discontinued operations	2,000

Develop a multi-step income statement for Jones Company for 1995. Assume that a 35% tax rate applies to all transactions. Jones had 100,000 shares of common stock and 2,000 shares of 8%, $100 par value, preferred stock outstanding throughout 1995. Include the appropriate earnings per share calculations to accompany the 1995 income statement.

■ REQUIRED

(LO 2) PROBLEM 12-2A SALE OF SEGMENTS

Carolina Company, a furniture manufacturer, owns more than 30,000 acres of forests, buildings, and equipment. Included in the assets are a fleet of trucks, a lumber-processing facility, and a chain of office supply stores. During 1994 Carolina sold lumber to its customers at its processing facility and purchased other specialty lumber from outside suppliers. An unusual fire destroyed several acres of timber, resulting in a $5,600 loss. Fires are infrequent in this area. A new furniture warehouse was constructed in 1994. During construction, Carolina rented warehouse space at a cost of $7,800. All the trucks were sold because the company entered into a long-term agreement with a trucking firm to transport finished pieces of furniture across the country. Three office supply stores were sold at a $12,000 loss because they were not as profitable as the average stores. The company purchased additional land in seven cities for expansion of profitable office supply stores. The company sold an investment in stock resulting in a $3,400 loss. Carolina's tax rate is 28%.

1. Explain which, if any, of these transactions should be reported as a separate item on the income statement after income from continuing operations.

2. Assume that 1994 income from continuing operations has been correctly calculated as $590,500. Prepare the sections of the income statement that follow the income from continuing operations line. You may ignore earnings per share calculations.

(LO 5) PROBLEM 12-3A EARNINGS PER SHARE

Brietlow Company had 100,000 shares of common stock outstanding on January 1, 1995. During 1995 the following common stock transactions occurred:

March 1, issued 12,000 shares of stock for cash.
April 1, purchased 8,000 shares as treasury stock.
October 1, issued 16,000 shares of stock for land.

Brietlow Company also had 1,000 shares of $100 par, 8% cumulative preferred stock outstanding as of January 1, 1995. No preferred stock transactions occurred during 1995.

1. Assume that the net income of Brietlow Company for 1995 was $116,000. Compute the earnings per share amount that should accompany the 1995 income statement.

2. Do Brietlow's preferred stockholders have a right to a dividend? If so, what are those rights?

(LO 7) PROBLEM 12-4A APPROPRIATIONS OF RETAINED EARNINGS

Kubiniski Company's stockholders' equity section includes the following items on December 31, 1993:

Common stock, $1 par, 500,000 shares issued	$ 500,000
Additional paid-in capital	890,000
Retained earnings, unappropriated	1,483,900
Retained earnings, appropriated for buildings	300,000
Treasury stock, at cost, 5,000 shares	(75,000)
Total stockholders' equity	$3,098,900

At the annual board meeting, the chief financial officer asked the board to appropriate $1,000,000 for future expansion of the manufacturing facilities that have become inefficient. The CFO also plans to recommend that the board approve the issuance of $1,000,000 of bonds to finance the construction of new facilities. One stockholder asks why the bonds are needed if the company is already using the retained earnings to build new facilities.

1. Write a response to the stockholder's question about the need for bonds.

2. Answer the following questions by other stockholders:

"How is the amount of retained earnings calculated?"
"How does the company report a gain or loss when it sells its treasury stock?"
"Does the company report a gain or loss if it issues stock at an amount greater than the par value? Why? Why not?"

(LO 8) PROBLEM 12-5A STATEMENT OF STOCKHOLDERS' EQUITY

Kebler Company was incorporated as a new business on January 1, 1995. The corporate charter approved on that date authorized the issuance of 2,000 shares of $100 par, 7% cumulative, nonparticipating preferred stock and 20,000 shares of $5 par common stock. On January 10, Kebler issued for cash 1,000 shares of preferred at $120 per share and 8,000 shares of common at $80 per share. On January 20,

Kebler issued 2,000 shares of common stock to acquire a building site at a time when the stock was selling for $70 per share.

During 1995 Kebler established an employee benefit plan and acquired 1,000 shares of common stock at $60 per share as treasury stock for that purpose. Later in 1995 it resold 100 shares of the stock at $65 per share.

On December 31, 1995, Kebler determined that its net income for the year was $80,000. The firm declared the annual cash dividend to preferred stockholders and a cash dividend of $5 per share to the common stockholders. The dividend will be paid in 1996.

Develop the statement of stockholders' equity for Kebler for the year ended December 31, 1995. The statement should begin with the beginning balance of each account and explain the changes in each account that resulted in the ending balances. ■ REQUIRED

ALTERNATE MULTI-CONCEPT PROBLEMS

(LO 3, 4, 10) PROBLEM 12-6A EXTRAORDINARY ITEMS AND CHANGES IN ACCOUNTING PRINCIPLES

Smoother Company has developed the following preliminary income statement for the year 1995.

Revenues	$340,000	
Cost of goods sold	170,000	
Gross profit		$170,000
Selling and administrative expenses		125,000
Income from continuing operations		$ 45,000
Income tax		13,500
Net income		$31,500

The preliminary income statement does not reflect two additional transactions that occurred in 1995. First, Smoother experienced a freeze loss of $12,000 during the year. You may assume that freeze losses are rare where Smoother is located. Second, on January 1, 1995, Smoother changed its method for recognizing exploration costs. Exploration costs of $150,000 had been incurred on January 1, 1993. The company used to capitalize costs, and amortize such costs over five years. After the change, the company will expense all costs. Exploration costs incurred in 1995 were correctly included in Selling and Administrative Expenses.

1. Prepare a revised 1995 income statement for Smoother Company to reflect the freeze loss and exploration costs. Also present the earnings per share amounts to accompany the income statement. Smoother had 10,000 shares of common stock outstanding at all times during 1995. Assume a 30% tax rate applies to the two additional transactions. ■ REQUIRED

2. What is the effect of the two transactions on Smoother's 1995 cash flow? How should the items appear on the statement of cash flows?

(LO 1, 6, 10) PROBLEM 12-7A ERRORS AND RETAINED EARNINGS PRESENTATION

The preliminary income statement of Whightsil Company for 1995 is as follows.

Revenues	$350,000	
Selling and administrative expenses	301,000	
Income before tax		$49,000
Income tax		14,700
Net income		$34,300

The preliminary income statement does not reflect one additional event. On January 1, 1993, Whightsil failed to record depreciation of $6,900. Depreciation was recorded correctly in 1994 and 1995.

1. Record an entry if needed to correct for the failure to depreciate. You may ignore income taxes.
2. Prepare a statement of retained earnings for Whightsil for 1995. The balance of the Retained Earnings account on January 1, 1995, was $35,000. During 1995 Whightsil declared dividends to stockholders of $14,000.
3. Explain how the depreciation should be shown on the statement of cash flows.

CASES

READING AND INTERPRETING FINANCIAL STATEMENTS

(LO 1, 5) CASE 12-1 READING BEN & JERRY'S INCOME STATEMENT
Refer to the financial statements included in Ben & Jerry's annual report.

■ **REQUIRED**
1. Calculate the gross profit percentage for each of the three years of the financial statements. Has the percentage increased or decreased over time? What are the reasons for the trend in the percentage?
2. Analyze the income statement and retained earnings statement to determine what portion of earnings has been declared as dividends to stockholders each period. What are the possible reasons that Ben & Jerry's has not paid a dividend in recent years?
3. From the income statement and balance sheet, determine the number of shares of common stock outstanding as of the balance sheet date for each year and the weighted average number of shares outstanding each year. Why do these numbers differ?
4. What are the items contained in the other income (expense) category of Ben & Jerry's income statement? Why are those items separated from operating income?

(LO 10) CASE 12-2 READING BETHLEHEM STEEL'S CASH FLOW STATEMENT
A portion of Bethlehem Steel's 1992 consolidated statement of cash flows is presented below.

(Dollars in millions)	
Operating activities:	
Net loss	$(449.3)
Adjustments for items not affecting cash from operating activities:	
Depreciation	261.7
Cumulative effect of changes in accounting principles	250.0
Deferred income taxes	(40.0)
Other—net	26.5
Working capital:	
Receivables	5.2
Inventories	156.8
Accounts payable	(59.2)
Employment costs and other	(17.6)
Other—net	1.0
Cash provided from operating activities	$135.1

1. Write a paragraph explaining how the company could incur a net loss of $449.3 million and yet generate cash from operating activities of $135.1 million.

2. Was the cumulative effect of changes in accounting principles a positive or negative amount on the income statement? Did the changes in accounting principle increase or decrease the amount of cash?

■ REQUIRED

MAKING FINANCIAL DECISIONS

(LO 2, 3, 10) CASE 12-3 COMPARING TWO COMPANIES

Assume that you are a financial analyst who must compare two companies. You are particularly concerned about the amount of income tax expense recorded by Companies A and B. The 1995 income statement of Company A is as follows:

Revenues	$200,000	
Cost of goods sold	120,000	
Gross profit		$80,000
Selling and administrative expenses		40,000
Income before tax		$40,000
Income tax		16,000
Net income		$24,000

The 1995 income statement of Company B is as follows:

Revenues	$150,000	
Cost of goods sold	90,000	
Gross profit		$60,000
Selling and administrative expenses		30,000
Income before tax		$30,000
Income tax expense		12,000
Income from continuing operations		$18,000
Loss from discontinued operations (net of 40% tax)		(9,000)
Income before extraordinary item		$ 9,000
Extraordinary gain (net of 40% tax)		15,000
Net income		$24,000

Compare the amount of income tax incurred by Company A and Company B. Does the amount of income tax expense on the income statement represent the amount of income tax paid to the Internal Revenue Service? What other factors need to be considered to determine the amount of cash actually paid for income taxes?

(LO 2) CASE 12-4 SALE OF SEGMENT

A diverse company owns a chain of barbecue restaurants. It is probable that the city in which a majority of the restaurants are located will pass an ordinance to ban smoking in all public places. Sales are expected to drop if the ordinance passes because most of the restaurant's customers are smokers. The company has an opportunity to sell all of its restaurants to an investor who plans to open health food stores. The president does not want to sell the segment, which will result in a loss that will affect the current year income. He proposes to keep the segment and "bury" the annual operating losses evenly over the next few years and then to sell. The sales price of the restaurants at a future date is undeterminable.

■ REQUIRED   How would the sale be disclosed on the income statement? Is it better to keep the restaurants and spread the loss over the next few years?

ACCOUNTING AND ETHICS: WHAT WOULD YOU DO?

(LO 6) CASE 12-5 CHANGE IN ESTIMATE

Regina Lewis is an accountant for Ajax, a large industrial company. In the process of preparing the 1995 financial statements, she has become concerned about the accounting for the company's warranty costs. Ajax sells a product with a one-year warranty. Analysis of information indicates that the cost of warranty repairs has averaged approximately 5% of sales price. Ajax uses the accrual method and records the warranty costs as an expense in the year that the product is sold.

Ms. Lewis has discovered that the accrual of warranty costs for 1994 was estimated at 1% of sales. When she questioned the individuals who made the estimate, she learned that the estimate was below the historical average because Ajax was under pressure to meet certain performance measures. Specifically, Ajax creditors had become concerned about the company's sagging profit and had required it to be more profitable in 1994.

Ms. Lewis reported the matter to her superior, Mr. Russell, who agreed that the warranty accrual in 1994 had been too low. He suggested that this matter was an example of a "change in estimate" and should be recorded on the 1995 income statement. He recommended a 7% accrual to compensate for 1994. Mr. Russell reminded Ms. Lewis that accruals are always estimates and that corrections or adjustments are not unusual.

■ REQUIRED   Based on the information Ms. Lewis has gathered, what action should she take concerning the warranty accrual for 1994 and 1995?

(LO 6) CASE 12-6 CHANGE IN ESTIMATE

Refer to Case 12-5. Would your answer be the same if the 1994 accrual had been overstated (at 8%), rather than understated (at 1%)?

ANALYTICAL SOFTWARE CASE

To the Student: Your instructor may assign one or more parts of the analytical software case that is designed to accompany this chapter. This multi-part case gives you a chance to work with real financial statement data using software that stimulates, guides, and hones your analytical and problem-solving skills. It was created especially to support and strengthen your understanding of the chapter's Learning Objectives.

SOLUTION TO KEY TERMS QUIZ

1. Gross profit percentage (p. 633)
2. Income before income taxes (p. 633)
3. Gross profit (p. 632)
4. Discontinued operations (p. 634)
5. Operating income (p. 633)
6. Change in accounting principle (p. 638)
7. Prior period adjustment (p. 643)
8. Extraordinary item (p. 636)
9. Multi-step income statement (p. 632)

INTEGRATIVE PROBLEM

FOR PART III

EVALUATING FINANCING OPTIONS FROM ASSET ACQUISITION AND THEIR IMPACT ON FINANCIAL STATEMENTS

Following are the financial statements for Worldwide, Inc., for the year 1995:

WORLDWIDE, INC.
BALANCE SHEET
AS OF DECEMBER 31, 1995
(IN MILLIONS)

Assets		Liabilities	
Cash	$1.6	Current portion of lease obligation	$1.0
Other current assets	6.4	Other current liabilities	3.0
Leased assets (net of accumulated depreciation)	7.0	Lease obligation—long term	6.0
Other long-term assets	45.0	Other long-term liabilities	6.0
		Total liabilities	$16.0
		Stockholders' Equity:	
		Preferred stock	$1.0
		Additional paid-in capital on preferred stock	2.0
		Common stock	4.0
		Additional paid-in capital on common stock	16.0
		Retained earnings	21.0
		Total stockholders' equity	44.0
		Total liabilities and	
Total assets	$60.0	stockholders' equity	$60.0

WORLDWIDE, INC.
INCOME STATEMENT
FOR THE YEAR ENDED DECEMBER 31, 1995
(IN MILLIONS)

Revenues		$50.0
Expenses:		
Depreciation of leased asset	$ 1.0	
Depreciation—other assets	3.2	
Interest on leased asset	.5	
Other expenses	27.4	
Income tax (30% rate)	5.4	
Total expenses		37.5
Income before extraordinary loss		$12.5
Extraordinary loss (net of		
$.9 taxes)		(2.1)
Net income		$10.4
EPS before extraordinary loss		$3.10
EPS extraordinary loss		(.53)
EPS—net income		$2.57

Additional information:

Worldwide, Inc. has authorized 500,000 shares of 10%, $10 par value cumulative preferred stock. There were 100,000 shares issued and outstanding at all times during 1995. The firm has also authorized 5 million shares of $1 par common stock, with 4 million shares issued and outstanding.

On January 1, 1995, Worldwide, Inc. acquired an asset, a piece of specialized heavy equipment, for $8 million with a capital lease. The lease contract indicates that the term of the lease is 8 years. Payments of $1.5 million are to be made each December 31. The first lease payment was made December 31, 1995 and consisted of $1 million principal and $.5 million of interest expense. The capital lease is depreciated using the straight-line method over 8 years with zero salvage value.

■ REQUIRED

1. Assuming the acquisition of the equipment using a capital lease, provide the entries for the acquisition, depreciation, and lease payment.

2. The management of Worldwide, Inc. is considering the financial statement impact of other methods of financing, rather than the capital lease, that could have been used to acquire the equipment. For each alternative A, B, and C, provide all necessary entries, the impact on the accounting equation for each entry, revised 1995 financial statements, and calculate, as revised, the following amounts or ratios:

    a. Current ratio
    b. Debt-to-equity ratio
    c. Net income
    d. EPS—net income

Assume that the following alternative actions would have taken place on January 1, 1995.

A. Instead of acquiring the equipment with a capital lease, assume that the company negotiated an operating lease to use the asset. The lease would require annual year-end payments of $1.5 million and would result in "off-balance-sheet" financing. (Hint: the $1.5 million should be treated as rental expense.)

B. Instead of acquiring the equipment with a capital lease, assume that Worldwide, Inc. had issued bonds for $8 million and purchased the equipment with the proceeds of the bond issue. Assume the bond interest of $.5 million would have been accrued and paid on December 31, 1995. A portion of the principal also is paid each year for 8 years. On December 31, 1995, the company would have paid $1 million of principal and would anticipate another $1 million of principal to be paid in 1996. Assume the equipment would have an 8-year life and would be depreciated on a straight-line basis with zero salvage value.

C. Instead of acquiring the equipment with a capital lease, assume that Worldwide, Inc. issued 200,000 additional shares of 10% preferred stock to raise $8 million, and purchased the equipment for $8 million with the proceeds from the stock issue. Dividends on the stock are declared and paid annually. Assume that a dividend payment would have beeen made on December 31, 1995. Assume the equipment would have an 8-year life and would be depreciated on a straight-line basis with zero salvage value.

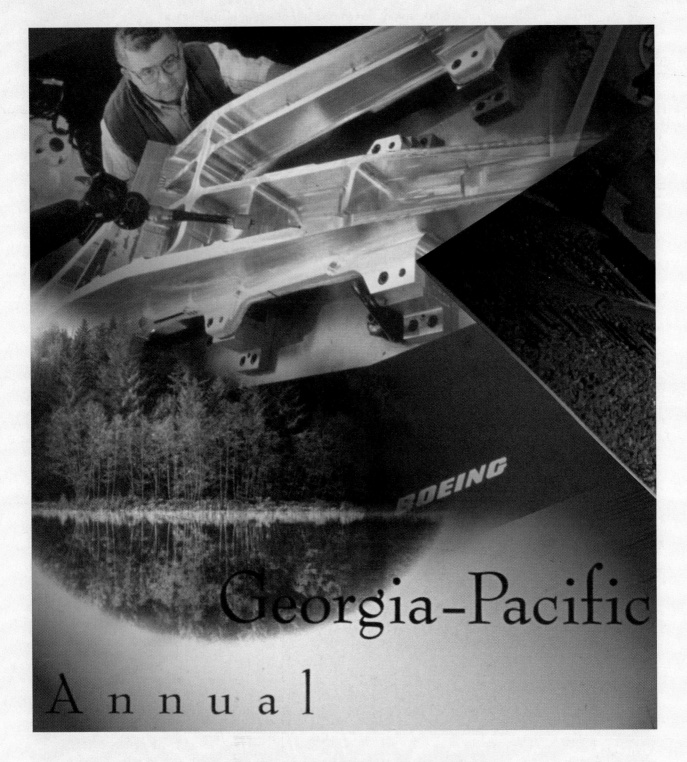

Georgia-Pacific

Annual

A WORD TO STUDENTS ABOUT PART IV

Part IV will be fascinating and even fun—as long as you **keep practicing the concepts and reading the linkages from chapter to chapter.** *How does an international corporation report its earnings?* Chapter 13 uses Whirlpool Inc., a major international company, to show how. *What is the heart of reporting a business's activities?* See Chapter 14 to learn how to evaluate a company from its cash flows. *Can you find the trends in a company's performance?* Practice the analysis concepts and skills available to you in Chapter 15 with any set of financial statements you can find.

Part IV

Additional Topics in Financial Reporting

Chapter 13
Accounting and Reporting Issues for the Global Corporation

For Whirlpool Corporation, our featured company at the beginning of the chapter and at the end, operating globally is second nature; Whirlpool also illustrates how companies invest in other companies. On your "world tour," you'll **take the roles of a bond analyst looking at a bond price drop** (p. 680) and a **money manager looking at foreign currency risk** (p. 700), and you'll **think strategically with a chief financial officer** (p. 711).

Chapter 14
The Statement of Cash Flows

Appendix 14A:
Accounting Tools: A Worksheet Approach to the Statement of Cash Flows

Learn to put together and use cash flows statements, and you grow close to the company's most revealing financial interrelationships. Along the way, you'll **take the roles of an investment analyst reviewing IBM's cash flows** (p. 748) and a **CEO explaining your cash situation to Wall Street** (p. 769). You'll also **meet a stockbroker for whom cash flows are key** (p. 776).

Chapter 15
Financial Statement Analysis

In Chapter 15, you'll add depth and sophistication to the small arsenal of analysis tools you've acquired in past chapters. Along the way, you'll **become an analyst looking broadly at inventory turnover by industry** (p. 830), **give your views to a client about a company's P/E ratio** (p. 840), and **see how a major fund manager and CEO evaluates companies** (p. 841).

Integrative Problem for Part IV

Focus on Financial Results

Whirlpool Corporation embodies what many investors consider to be the success formula for American business: a global strategy. Although the U.S. economy was fairly strong during the early to mid-1990s, other economies around the world were stronger. Emerging markets in Eastern Europe, the Far East, and Latin America are a tremendous business opportunity for American companies that are strong enough to do business there. Whirlpool is one such

• MANAGEMENT'S DISCUSSION AND ANALYSIS •

Revenues by Business Unit were as follows:

(millions of dollars)	1992	1991	1990
North American Appliance Group	$ 4,059	$ 3,843	$ 3,836
Whirlpool Europe	2,476	2,312	2,213
Whirlpool Overseas Corporation	336	141	102
Other, less intercompany transactions	226	254	273
Total Appliance Business	7,097	6,550	6,424
Whirlpool Financial Corporation	235	233	210
Less intercompany transactions	31	26	29
Total Revenues	$ 7,301	$ 6,757	$ 6,605

• WHIRLPOOL CORPORATION •

[*About The Company*]

Whirlpool Corporation is the world's leading manufacturer and marketer of major home appliances. The company manufactures in 12 countries and markets products in more than 120 countries under major brand names such as *Whirlpool, KitchenAid, Roper, Estate, Bauknecht, Ignis, Laden* and *Inglis.* Whirlpool is also the principal supplier to Sears, Roebuck and Co. of many major home appliances marketed under the *Kenmore* brand name.

◆

company, with subsidiaries and operations in all three of these areas. For example, one of its subsidiaries is Brastemp S.A. (shown here), which manufactures and markets a full line of appliances that are sold throughout South and Central America, the Caribbean, and the Middle East.

In Mexico and the rest of Latin America, the passage of NAFTA in late 1993 stimulated trade by eliminating trade barriers that discouraged American companies from doing business there.

See Whirlpool's revenues by business unit, located in the Management Discussion and Analysis portion of the 1992 annual report. Its North American Appliance Group grew slightly, as did its Europe operations. But the revenues of tiny Whirlpool Overseas Corporation, which manages the company's interests in these so-called emerging markets, tripled in size.

Chapter 13

Accounting and Reporting Issues for the Global Corporation

LEARNING OBJECTIVES

After studying this chapter, you should be able to

1. Explain the various reasons that one company might invest in another company.

2. Understand the accounting and reporting requirements for held-to-maturity securities.

3. Understand the accounting and reporting requirements for trading securities.

4. Understand the accounting and reporting requirements for available-for-sale securities.

5. Understand the accounting and reporting requirements for equity investees.

6. Explain the different forms of business combinations and how to account for a merger using the purchase method.

7. Explain when, why, and how consolidated financial statements are prepared.

8. Understand how to account for foreign currency transactions.

9. Understand how to translate foreign financial statements into U.S. dollars.

10. Describe the reporting requirements for segments of a business.

Linkages

A LOOK AT PREVIOUS CHAPTERS

In the previous three chapters, we considered accounting for various types of securities issued by corporations. Specifically, in Chapter 10 we looked at how companies account for the issuance of bonds, notes, and other forms of borrowing on a long-term basis. Chapters 11 and 12 focused on permanent types of financing in the form of capital stock.

A LOOK AT THIS CHAPTER

In this chapter, we look at the "other side of the fence." That is, we explore the accounting by companies that invest in the stocks and bonds of other corporations, using Whirlpool Corporation as an example.

A LOOK AT UPCOMING CHAPTERS

Many of the topics discussed in Chapter 13 have cash flow implications. In Chapter 14 we turn our attention to an expanded consideration of the preparation and use of the statement of cash flows. The analysis of this statement, as well as the other financial statements, is the focus of Chapter 15.

Operating in a Global Environment

Whirlpool Corporation is a typical corporation of the 1990s. Its core business is major home appliances, of which it is the world's leading manufacturer and marketer. In addition, it operates Whirlpool Financial Corporation (WFC), which provides financing services for dealers, distributors, and consumers. This unit makes loans for the purchase of Whirlpool products and in this respect is similar to General Motors Acceptance Corporation (GMAC), the financing arm of General Motors.

In addition to the complexities of operating a manufacturing business and a financing business, Whirlpool must deal with other challenges. It generates a significant portion of its revenues from sales to Sears, Roebuck & Co. Whirlpool is the principal supplier to Sears of many appliances marketed under the Kenmore brand name. Thus, Sears' success in selling its products directly impacts on Whirlpool's success.

Until the late 1980s, Whirlpool sold its washers, dryers, refrigerators, ranges, and other appliances almost exclusively in the United States. The competitive nature of the U.S. business climate led to a corporate decision in 1988 to dramatically increase its presence in foreign markets. By the end of 1992, Whirlpool manufactured in 12 countries and sold products in more than 120 countries.

Exhibit 13-1 illustrates the global nature of Whirlpool's business. The company operates in four major world markets: North America (the United States, Canada, and Mexico), Europe, Latin America (Central and South America and the Caribbean), and Asia. To accomplish its global goals, the business is organized into a number of units. Operations in North America are carried out by the parent, Whirlpool Corporation. A subsidiary, Whirlpool Europe B.V., is responsible for European operations. Another subsidiary, Whirlpool Overseas Corporation, manages the company's businesses in Latin America and Asia.

As we discuss in the chapter, a **subsidiary** is a separate legal entity that is controlled by another entity, the **parent.** Normally, control over another entity results from ownership of a majority of that company's stock. In many cases, the parent owns all of the stock of a subsidiary, thus making it a **wholly owned subsidiary.**

In addition to subsidiaries, Whirlpool has investments in a number of affiliates. Although Whirlpool doesn't control the **affiliate,** it owns enough of the other company to exercise significant influence over it. For example, Whirlpool has direct voting rights, ranging from 28% to 49%, in three Brazilian companies and in a Mexican manufacturer. In May 1992 the company bought a 43.8% stake in Whirlpool Tatramat a.s., a joint venture in Slovakia (a country that was part of the former Czechoslovakia). Domestically, Whirlpool owns a minority share of Matsushita Floor Care Company, a manufacturer of vacuum cleaners.

This introduction to the business of Whirlpool raises a number of questions:

1. What is the appropriate accounting for the acquisition of another business? How should a company account for a significant investment in another business?

2. How should a subsidiary be reported in the financial statements of a parent corporation? Does it matter if the subsidiary is engaged in an entirely different line of business than the parent?

3. How should a corporation report on an affiliate in its financial statements?

4. What if a subsidiary or an affiliate keeps its books in a foreign currency? What needs to be done to *translate* the relevant amounts into dollars?

EXHIBIT 13-1   Organization of Whirlpool Corporation

NAAG   Subsidiaries
North   • **Whirlpool Financial Corporation**
American   • **Inglis Limited (Canada)**
Appliance   Affiliates
Group   • **Matsushita Floor Care Company**
                 • **Vitromatic S.A. de C.V.**

Europe   Subsidiary
          • **Whirlpool Europe B.V. (Netherlands)**
          Affiliate
          • **Whirlpool Tatramat a.s. (Slovakia)**

Latin   Subsidiaries
America   • **Whirlpool Argentina**
             • **Whirlpool Overseas Corporation**
             Affiliates
             • **Brasmotor S.A. (Brazil)**
             • **Brastemp S.A. (Brazil)**
             • **Consul S.A. (Brazil)**
             • **Embraco S.A. (Brazil)**
             • **South American Sales Company
               (Brazil)**

Asia   Subsidiary
          • **Whirlpool Overseas Corporation**
          Affiliate
          • **TVS Whirlpool Limited (India)**

5. If a company operates in more than one industry, what supplementary disclosures would be useful to the financial statement reader? Similarly, what disclosures would be useful regarding a company's various geographic segments?

6. Is it important for financial statement readers to know if a company relies on any one customer or customers for a significant portion of its sales? If so, what specific information should be disclosed and how should it be disclosed?

We first try to provide general answers to each of these questions in the context of current accounting standards. We begin by looking at various types of investments in stocks and bonds, some of which give the investor influence over the company and some of which do not. Then we will return to consider how Whirlpool actually addresses these issues in its annual report.

Intercompany Investments

LO 1

Explain the various reasons that one company might invest in another company.

Corporations frequently invest in the securities of other businesses. These investments take two forms: debt securities and equity securities. A **debt security** results when one company loans money to another company; an **equity security** represents one company's ownership interest in another entity. The most common type of debt security is a bond; equity securities are usually in the form of either common or preferred stock.

Why One Company Invests in Another Company

Corporations have varying motivations for investing in the stock and bonds of other companies. We will refer to the company that invests as the *investor* and the company whose stock or bonds are purchased as the *investee.* At times, companies invest excess funds in stocks and bonds over the short run. The seasonality of certain businesses may result in otherwise idle cash being available during certain times of the year. In other cases, stocks and bonds are purchased as a way to invest cash over the long run. Often these types of investments are made in anticipation of a need for cash at some distant point in the future. For example, a company may invest today in a combination of stocks and bonds because it will need cash 10 years from today to build a new plant. The investor may be primarily interested in periodic income in the form of interest and dividends, in appreciation in the value of the securities, or in some combination of the two.

Sometimes shares of stock in another company are bought with a different purpose in mind. If a company buys a relatively large percentage of the common stock of the investee, it may be able to secure significant influence over the policies of this company. For example, a company may buy 30% of the common stock of a supplier of its raw materials to ensure a steady source of inventory. When an investor is able to secure influence over the investee, the **equity method** of accounting is used. According to current accounting standards, this method is appropriate when an investor owns at least 20% of the common stock of the investee.

Finally, a corporation may buy stock in another company with the purpose of obtaining control over that other entity. Normally, this requires an investment in excess of 50% of the common stock of the investee. When an investor owns more than half of the stock of another company, accountants normally prepare a set of **consolidated financial statements.** This involves combining the financial statements of the individual entities into a single set of statements. As we noted earlier concerning

Whirlpool, an investor with an interest of more than 50% in another company is called the *parent* and the investee in these situations is called the *subsidiary*.

Companies normally disclose the method or methods they use to account for investees as part of the first footnote to the financial statements. For example, in its Summary of Principal Accounting Policies, Whirlpool states:

> Principles of Consolidation: The consolidated financial statements include all majority-owned subsidiaries. Investments in affiliated companies are accounted for by the equity method.[1]

In the next section of this chapter, we consider how companies account for investments in stocks and bonds that do *not* give them any significant influence over the other company. After that, we discuss how to account for investments in which there is significant influence, that is, when the equity method is used. Finally, we turn to the accounting for investments that give the investor control over the other company and require the use of consolidated statements.

Investments without Significant Influence

Companies face a number of major issues in deciding how to account for and report on investments in the stocks and bonds of other companies. These include the following:

1. What should be the basis for the recognition of periodic income from an investment? That is, what event causes income to be recognized?

2. How should an investment be valued and thus reported at the end of an accounting period? At original cost? At fair value?

3. How should an investment be classified on a balance sheet? As a current asset? As a noncurrent asset?

The answer to each of these questions depends on the type of investment. Accountants classify investments in the securities of other companies into one of three categories:[2]

Held-to-maturity securities are investments in the bonds of other companies when the investor has the positive intent and the ability to hold the securities to maturity. *Note that only bonds can qualify as held-to-maturity securities because shares of stock do not have a maturity date.*

Trading securities are stocks and bonds of other companies that are bought and held for the purpose of selling them in the near term. These securities are usually held for only a short period of time with the objective of generating profits on short-term appreciation in the market price of the stocks and bonds.

Available-for-sale securities are stocks and bonds that are not classified as either held-to-maturity or trading securities.

Investments in Held-to-Maturity Securities

By their nature, only bonds, not stock, can qualify as held-to-maturity securities. A bond is categorized as a held-to-maturity security if the investor plans to hold it

LO **2**

Understand the accounting and reporting requirements for held-to-maturity securities.

[1] 1992 Whirlpool Annual Report, p. 31.
[2] *Statement of Financial Accounting Standards No. 115,* "Accounting for Certain Investments in Debt and Equity Securities" (Stamford, Conn.: Financial Accounting Standards Board, May 1993), par. 7–12.

until it matures. In Chapter 10, we looked at the accounting by an *issuer* of bonds. Accounting by an *investor* in bonds parallels this accounting. An investor may buy the bonds either on the original issuance date or later. If the investor buys them on the date they are originally issued, the purchase is from the issuer. It is also possible, however, that an investor buys bonds on the *open market* after they have been outstanding for a period of time.

Typically, the buyer of bonds directly from an issuer is an investor with a great deal of clout. When an investment banker arranges for an issuer to sell bonds, investors line up to purchase big chunks of the issuance. These buyers typically get the best possible price; once the bonds are in the open market, it is unlikely that an investor can buy them at such a favorable price.

To illustrate an open market purchase of bonds, consider the following example. On January 1, 1995, Homer buys $100,000 in face value of Simpson bonds at 103. This means that the bonds are currently selling in the market at 103% of face value. The coupon rate is 10%, with interest payable semiannually on June 30 and December 31. The original term of the bonds was 20 years; they were issued on January 1, 1990. Thus, at the time of Homer's purchase, the bonds have a remaining life of 15 years. The entry on Homer's books to record the purchase of the bonds is

1995			
Jan. 1	Investment in Bonds	103,000	
	Cash		103,000
	To record purchase of Simpson bonds at 103.		

Assets	=	**Liabilities**	+	**Owners' Equity**
+ 103,000				
− 103,000				

Two points are worth noting. First, the premium of $3,000 paid for the bonds is not recorded separately as it is by issuers of bonds. Although it is possible to use a separate premium account, the premium is often simply included in the Investment in Bonds account.[3] Second, recall what the premium paid by Homer indicates: The stated rate or coupon rate of 10% must be higher than the effective or market rate of interest at this time because an investor is willing to pay more than face value for the bonds. In the early 1990s, bonds paying 10% were usually classified as "noninvestment grade." That is, an issuer had to pay investors a higher rate of interest, such as 10%, because its credit quality was suspect. These so-called high-yield bonds were commonly known as *junk bonds* in the 1980s.

On June 30, Homer must record the receipt of semiannual interest and recognize amortization of the premium. As is true for the issuer, accounting standards require Homer to use the effective interest method to recognize interest income and the amortization of the premium, unless the results from use of the straight-line method are not materially different. Recall from Chapter 10 that under the effective interest method, interest expense for a period is computed by multiplying the carrying value of the bonds at the beginning of that period by the effective or market rate of interest. Companies use an amortization schedule to track the carrying value from one period to the next as the basis for computing interest expense. With the straight-line method, interest expense is the same each period.

---

[3] Recall from Chapter 10 that bonds can be issued at either a premium or a discount. As is the case for a premium, most investors do not record a discount separately. Instead, the discount is netted against the investment account.

To keep our calculations simple, we assume that the results are not materially different and that Homer elects to use the straight-line method. The entry on June 30 is

1995
June 30	Cash	5,000	
	Investment in Bonds		100
	Interest Income		4,900
	To record interest income on Simpson bonds.		

Assets	=	**Liabilities**	+	**Owners' Equity**
+5,000				+4,900
−100				

The amount of cash received is equal to the semiannual rate of interest of 5% times the face value of the bonds of $100,000. Straight-line amortization of the premium is computed as follows:

Amount of premium	$3,000
Divided by:	
Number of six-month periods in remaining life of bonds of 15 years	30
Premium amortized for six months	= $ 100

Under the straight-line method, the amount of interest income recognized is the difference between the amount of cash received of $5,000 and the amount of premium amortized of $100. The fact that the actual income earned for the six-month period is less than cash received is logical given the nature of a *premium*. Because Homer paid more for the bonds, $103,000, than it will receive when they mature, $100,000, interest income is less than the cash received in interest each six months.

The approach just illustrated to account for an investment in held-to-maturity bonds is the **amortized cost method.** The investment was recorded initially at cost, including any premium paid or less any discount. The basis for the recognition of income on the bonds was the receipt of interest (if interest was not received at the end of an accounting period, a company should accrue interest earned but not yet received). Because a premium paid reduces the amount of interest earned, it is amortized over the remaining life of the bonds. Similarly, a discount increases the interest earned, and it is amortized in the same way as a premium is amortized. Finally, by its nature, an investment in held-to-maturity bonds is normally classified as a *noncurrent asset.* Any held-to-maturity bonds that are one year or less from maturity, however, are classified in the current asset section of a balance sheet.

Assume that prior to the maturity date, Homer needs cash and decides to sell the bonds. Keep in mind that this is a definite change in Homer's plans since the bonds were initially categorized as held-to-maturity securities. The principles that were applied in Chapter 10 in accounting for the retirement of bonds early by the issuer apply here. Any difference between the proceeds received from the sale of the bonds and their carrying value on the date of the sale is recognized as either a gain or a loss.

Assume that on January 1, 1998, Homer sells all of its Simpson bonds at 99. This means that the amount of cash received is .99 × $100,000, or $99,000. The carrying value of the bonds on this date is

Amount paid for bonds on 1/1/95	$103,000
Less: Three years of amortization at $200 per year ($100 each six months)	600
Carrying value of bonds on 1/1/98	$102,400

The entry on January 1 is as follows:

```
1998
Jan. 1    Cash                                    99,000
          Loss on Sale of Bonds                    3,400
              Investment in Bonds                          102,400
          To record sale of Simpson bonds.
```

Assets	=	Liabilities	+	Owners' Equity
+ 99,000				− 3,400
− 102,400				

The $3,400 loss on the sale is the excess of the carrying value of $102,400 over the cash proceeds of $99,000. The loss is reported in the other income and expenses section on the 1998 income statement. Recall from Chapter 10 that a gain or loss to the *issuer* from early extinguishment of debt is reported as an *extraordinary* item on its income statement.

■ ACCOUNTING FOR YOUR DECISIONS   **You Are the Bond Analyst**

What are some reasons why the Simpson bonds dropped in price?

Investments in Trading Securities

LO ⬛ 3

Understand the accounting and reporting requirements for trading securities.

A company invests in trading securities as a way to profit from increases in the market prices of these securities over the short term. Because the intent is to hold them for the short term, trading securities are classified as current assets. All trading securities are recorded initially at cost, including any brokerage fees, commissions, or other fees paid to acquire the shares. Assume that Dexter Corp. invests in the following securities on November 30, 1995:

SECURITY	COST
Stuart common stock	$50,000
Menlo preferred stock	25,000
Total cost	$75,000

The entry on Dexter's books on the date of purchase is

```
1995
Nov. 30   Investment in Stuart Common Stock       50,000
          Investment in Menlo Preferred Stock     25,000
              Cash                                          75,000
          To record purchase of trading securities for cash.
```

Assets	=	Liabilities	+	Owners' Equity
+ 50,000				
+ 25,000				
− 75,000				

Many companies attempt to pay dividends every year as a signal to investors of their overall financial strength and profitability.[4] Assume that on December 10, 1995, Dexter received dividends of $1,000 from Stuart and $600 from Menlo. The dividends received from trading securities are recognized as income as shown in the following entry on Dexter's books:

1995
Dec. 10   Cash   1,600
                 Dividend Income   1,600
          To record receipt of dividends on trading securities.

Assets	=	Liabilities	+	Owners' Equity
+ 1,600				+ 1,600

Unlike interest on a bond or a note, dividends do not accrue over time. In fact, a company does not have a legal obligation to pay dividends until its board of directors declares them. Up to that point in time, the investor has no guarantee that dividends will ever be paid.

Buying stocks in companies that pay large dividends has a serious tax disadvantage. The drawback relates to the notion of *double taxation*. The company paying the dividend has already paid tax on the income from which the dividend is generated. Then the investing company has to pay tax on the dividend income, currently paying 35% at the federal level and as much as 10% at the state level. (Some portion of the dividends received from investments in domestic companies may be excluded from taxation as discussed in Appendix 2 at the end of the book.) Investing in fast-growing companies that pay no dividends avoids these problems. On the other hand, fast-growing companies that fall off of their growth track usually suffer a severe drop in market price.

As noted earlier, trading securities are purchased with the intention of holding them for a short period of time. Assume that Dexter sells the Stuart stock on December 15, 1995, for $53,000. In this case, Dexter recognizes a gain for the excess of the cash proceeds, $53,000, over the amount recorded on the books, $50,000:

1995
Dec. 15   Cash   53,000
                 Investment in Stuart Common Stock   50,000
                 Gain on Sale of Stock   3,000
          To record sale of Stuart common stock.

Assets	=	Liabilities	+	Owners' Equity
+ 53,000				+ 3,000
− 50,000				

For accounting purposes, the gain is considered realized and is classified on the income statement as other income. Although a company such as Dexter is not in the business of selling stock and bonds, money management has become a very

---

[4] IBM's March 1993 dividend was the computer company's 312th consecutive quarterly dividend, an uninterrupted string of 78 years in which it paid dividends. In the aftermath of a 1992 net loss of almost $5 billion, however, the March 1993 dividend was set at $.54, a cut of more than 50% from the previous quarterly dividend of $1.21 per share. Later in the same year, the dividend was reduced to $.25 per share.

important element of corporate success. Other income is a component of net income and sometimes exceeds operating income. For tax purposes, this gain is referred to as a *capital gain* and is taxed at a rate of 28% as opposed to 35% on regular income and dividends. The tax rate on capital gains has historically been less than ordinary income to provide an incentive to invest in the economy. Appendix 2 to this book provides more detail on the taxation of capital gains and ordinary income.

Assume that on December 22, 1995, Dexter replaces the Stuart stock in its portfolio by purchasing Canby common stock for $40,000. The entry on this date follows:

1995
Dec. 22   Investment in Canby Common Stock   40,000
                Cash   40,000
            To record purchase of trading securities for cash.

                    Assets   =   Liabilities   +   Owners' Equity
                    + 40,000
                    − 40,000

Now assume that Dexter ends its accounting period on December 31. Should it adjust the carrying value of its investments to reflect their fair values on this date? According to the accounting profession, fair values should be used to report investments in trading securities on a balance sheet. The fair values are thought to be relevant information to the various users of financial statements. Assume the following information for Dexter on December 31, 1995:

SECURITY	TOTAL COST	TOTAL FAIR VALUE ON DECEMBER 31, 1995	GAIN (LOSS)
Menlo preferred stock	$25,000	$27,500	$ 2,500
Canby common stock	40,000	39,000	(1,000)
Totals	$65,000	$66,500	$ 1,500

The entry on Dexter's books on this date follows:

1995
Dec. 31   Investment in Menlo Preferred Stock   2,500
                Investment in Canby Common Stock   1,000
                Unrealized Gain—Trading Securities   1,500
                    (Income Statement)
            To adjust trading securities to fair value.

                    Assets   =   Liabilities   +   Owners' Equity
                    + 2,500   + 1,500
                    − 1,000

Note that this entry results in each security being written up or down so that it will appear on the December 31 balance sheet at its market or fair value. This type of fair value accounting for trading securities is often referred to as a *mark to market* approach, because at the end of each period the value of each security is adjusted to its current market value. Also, it is important to realize that for trading securities, the changes in value are recognized on the income statement. The difference of $1,500 between the original cost of the two securities, $65,000, and their fair values, $66,500, is recorded in the account Unrealized Gain—Trading Securities to call attention to the fact that the securities have not been sold. Even though we use the term *unrealized,* however, the gain or loss is recognized on the income statement as a form of other income or loss.

Assume one final entry in our Dexter example: On January 20, 1996, Dexter sells the Menlo stock for $27,000. The entry on Dexter's books on this date follows:

```
1996
Jan. 20   Loss on Sale of Stock (Income Statement)        500
          Cash                                         27,000
              Investment in Menlo Preferred Stock                27,500
          To record sale of Menlo preferred stock.
```

	Assets	=	Liabilities	+	Owners' Equity
	+27,000				−500
	−27,500				

The important point to note about this entry is that the $500 loss represents the difference between the cash proceeds of $27,000 and the *fair value of the stock at the most recent reporting date,* $27,500. Because the Menlo stock was adjusted to a fair value of $27,500 on December 31, the excess of this amount over the cash proceeds of $27,000 results in a loss of $500.

Investments in Available-for-Sale Securities

Stocks and bonds that do not qualify as trading securities and bonds that are not intended to be held to maturity are categorized as available-for-sale securities. Accounting for these securities is similar to the accounting for trading securities with one major exception. *Even though fair value accounting is used to report available-for-sale securities at the end of an accounting period, any gains or losses are not reported on the income statement but instead are accumulated in a stockholders' equity account.* This inconsistency is justified by the accounting profession on the grounds that the inclusion of fluctuations in the value of securities that are available for sale, but not necessarily being actively traded, could lead to volatility in reported earnings. Regardless, reporting gains and losses on the income statement for one class of securities but not for others is a subject of considerable debate.

To illustrate the use of fair value accounting for available-for-sale securities, assume that Lenox Corp. purchases two different stocks late in 1995. The cost and fair values at the end of 1995 are as follows:

LO   4
Understand the accounting and reporting requirements for available-for-sale securities.

SECURITY	TOTAL COST	FAIR VALUE ON DECEMBER 31, 1995	GAIN (LOSS)
Adair preferred stock	$15,000	$16,000	$ 1,000
Casey common stock	35,000	32,500	(2,500)
Totals	$50,000	$48,500	$(1,500)

The entry on Lenox's books on this date appears on the following page:

1995
Dec. 31   Unrealized Gain/Loss—Available-for-
              Sale Securities (Stockholders' Equity)   1,500
          Investment in Adair Preferred Stock   1,000
              Investment in Casey Common Stock   2,500
          To adjust available-for-sale securities to fair value.

Assets	=	Liabilities	+	Owners' Equity
+ 1,000				− 1,500
− 2,500				

Note the similarity between this entry and the one we made at the end of the period in the example for trading securities. In both instances, the individual investments are adjusted to their fair values for purposes of presenting them on the year-end balance sheet. The unrealized loss of $1,500 does not, however, affect income in this case. Instead, the loss is shown as a reduction of stockholders' equity on the balance sheet.

Now assume that Lenox sells its Casey stock for $34,500 on June 30, 1996. The entry on this date is as follows:

1996
June 30   Cash   34,500
          Loss on Sale of Stock (Income Statement)   500
              Investment in Casey Common Stock   32,500
              Unrealized Gain/Loss—Available-for-
              Sale Securities (Stockholders' Equity)   2,500
          To record sale of Casey common stock.

Assets	=	Liabilities	+	Owners' Equity
+ 34,500				− 500
− 32,500				+ 2,500

Lenox records a *realized* loss of $500, which represents the excess of the cost of the stock of $35,000 over the cash proceeds of $34,500. Note, however, that the Investment in Casey Common Stock is removed from the books at $32,500, the fair value at the end of the prior period. Thus, it is also necessary to adjust the unrealized gain/loss account for the difference between the original cost of $35,000 and the fair value at the end of 1995 of $32,500.

Finally, assume that Lenox does not buy any additional securities during the remainder of 1996 and that the fair value of the one investment it holds, the Adair preferred stock, is $19,000 on December 31, 1996. The entry to adjust the Adair stock to fair value on this date is as follows:

1996
Dec. 31   Investment in Adair Preferred Stock   3,000
              Unrealized Gain/Loss—Available-for-
              Sale Securities (Stockholders' Equity)   3,000
          To adjust available-for-sale securities to fair value.

Assets	=	Liabilities	+	Owners' Equity
+ 3,000				+ 3,000

The debit to the Investment in Adair Preferred Stock account results in a balance of $19,000 in this account, the fair value of the stock. The stockholders' equity account now has a *credit* balance of $4,000 as reflected in the following T account:

UNREALIZED GAIN/LOSS—AVAILABLE-FOR-SALE SECURITIES

12/31/95 bal.	1,500		
		2,500	6/30/96 entry
		1,000	6/30/96 bal.
		3,000	12/31/96 entry
		4,000	12/31/96 bal.

The balance of $4,000 in this account represents the excess of the $19,000 fair value of the one security now held over its original cost of $15,000.

Where Investments Appear on the Statement of Cash Flows

Purchases of stocks and bonds in other companies require the use of cash, and the sales of these investments result in the inflow of cash to the business. The classification of these activities on the statement of cash flows depends on the type of investment. Cash flows from purchases, sales, and maturities of held-to-maturity securities and available-for-sale securities are classified as *investing* activities. On the other hand, these same types of cash flows for trading securities are classified as *operating* activities. We present a complete discussion of the statement of cash flows, including the reporting of investments, in Chapter 14.

Summary of Accounting and Reporting Requirements

A summary of the accounting and reporting requirements for each of the three categories of investments is shown in Exhibit 13-2. Periodic income from each of these types of investments is recognized in the form of interest and dividends. Held-to-maturity bonds are reported on the balance sheet at *amortized cost*. Both trading securities and available-for-sale securities are reported on the balance sheet at fair value. Unrealized gains and losses from holding trading securities are recognized on the income statement, however, while these same gains and losses for available-for-sale securities are accumulated in a stockholders' equity account.

The Controversy over Fair Value Accounting

Only recently have accounting standards changed to require that certain investments be reported at fair value. Prior to the change, the lower of cost or market rule was followed when accounting for these investments. The use of fair values is clearly an exception to the cost principle as first introduced in Chapter 1. Whether the exception is justified has been, and will continue to be, a matter of debate.

One concern of financial statement users is the hybrid system now employed to report assets on a balance sheet. Consider the following types of assets and how we report them on the balance sheet:

ASSET	REPORTED ON THE BALANCE SHEET AT
Inventories	Lower of cost or market
Investments	Either amortized cost or fair value
Property, plant, and equipment	Original cost, less accumulated depreciation

EXHIBIT 13-2 Accounting for Investments (without significant influence)

CATEGORIES	TYPES	CLASSIFIED ON BALANCE SHEET AS	RECOGNIZE AS INCOME	REPORT ON BALANCE SHEET AT	REPORT CHANGES IN FAIR VALUE ON
Held to maturity	Bonds	Noncurrent*	Interest	Amortized cost	Not applicable
Trading	Bonds, stock	Current	Interest, dividends	Fair value	Income statement
Available for sale	Bonds, stock	Current or noncurrent	Interest, dividends	Fair value	Balance sheet (in stockholders' equity)

*Reclassified as current if they mature within one year of the balance sheet date.

LO 5

Understand the accounting and reporting requirements for equity investees.

It is difficult to justify so many different valuation methods to report the assets of a single company. Recall that the lower of cost or market approach to valuing inventory is based on conservatism. Why should it be used for inventories and fair value be used for investments? Proponents of fair values believe that the information provided to the reader of the statements is more relevant and argue that the subjectivity inherent in valuing other types of assets is not an issue when dealing with securities that have a ready market. The controversy surrounding the valuation of assets on a balance sheet is likely to continue, particularly given the divergent methods now used to value different types of assets.

Investments in Stock Using the Equity Method

The accounting profession has set 20% as the minimum investment in the common stock of another company to be able to exercise significant influence over the policies of that other company. These policies include key decisions related to the investee's operating, investing, and financing activities. For example, an equity investor normally has a significant voice in such decisions as the amount of dividends to be paid by the investee, whether the investee should expand its plant, and whether to borrow more funds. The 20% rule is somewhat arbitrary and there are exceptions to it; however, it provides a useful reference for determining how a company should account for an investment in common stock.

Assume that on January 2, 1995, Marlin Corp. buys as a form of long-term investment 3,000 of the 10,000 outstanding shares of Cougar, Inc., at a price of $25 per share, plus commissions of $1,000. An investee such as Cougar is usually referred to by the investor, Marlin, as an *affiliate*. Marlin records the investment in its new affiliate:

1995
Jan. 2   Investment in Stock   76,000
        Cash   76,000
     To record purchase of 3,000 shares of Cougar stock
     at $25 per share, plus commissions of $1,000.

Assets	=	Liabilities	+	Owners' Equity
+76,000				
−76,000				

Assume that during 1995 Cougar reports net income of $50,000 and declares and pays dividends of $30,000. *The equity method gets its name from the fact that the investor increases the investment account for its proportionate share of the increase in the investee's stockholders' equity.* For example, what effect did the recognition of net income have on Cougar's stockholders' equity? The net income *increases* Cougar's stockholders' equity by $50,000. Thus, Marlin will increase its investment account by 30% of $50,000, or $15,000. The other side of the entry is an increase in income. That is, *income reported under the equity method is based on the investor's proportionate share of the income reported by the investee.* The entry on Marlin's books to record its share of the investee's income is

1995
Dec. 31   Investment in Stock   15,000
          Equity Income   15,000
          To record 30% share of Cougar's reported income
          of $50,000.

Assets	=	Liabilities	+	Owners' Equity
+15,000				+15,000

Note that the basis for recognition of income under the equity method is different than under the cost method. With the cost method, dividends received are recognized as income. Under the equity method, income is based on the investor's proportionate share of the investee's income, not dividends. Equity income is usually reported as a separate line item on the investor's income statement.

Turning to dividends, what is the effect on Cougar's stockholders' equity from declaring and paying dividends? The 1995 dividends *reduce* Cougar's equity by $30,000. Thus, it is appropriate under the equity method for Marlin to reduce its long-term investment account for the dividends it receives from Cougar with the following entry:

1995
Dec. 31   Cash   9,000
          Investment in Stock   9,000
          To record dividends received from Cougar:
          .30 × $30,000.

Assets	=	Liabilities	+	Owners' Equity
+9,000				
−9,000				

A T account for Marlin's investment account is helpful to understand why these two entries are made:

INVESTMENT IN STOCK

1/1/95 bal.	76,000	9,000	Dividends
Income	15,000		
12/31/95 bal.	82,000		

Thus, we see that the increase in Marlin's investment account during 1995 was $6,000. According to the concept behind the equity method, this should represent 30% of the increase in the investee's stockholders' equity, as shown on page 688:

Investee's reported net income	$50,000
Less: Investee's dividends	30,000
Increase in investee's stockholders' equity	$20,000
× Investor's percentage ownership	.30
Increase in Investment in Stock account	$ 6,000

Two final points can be made about the use of the equity method. First, if an investor sells an investment accounted for under the equity method, a gain or loss normally results. The gain or loss, however, is not the difference between the cash proceeds and the *historical cost*. Because the investment account has been adjusted upward for a share of the investee's income and downward for the dividends received, it is the difference between the cash proceeds and this adjusted balance that results in a gain or loss. The second point concerns the valuation at the end of the period of an investment accounted for by the equity method. Unlike trading securities and available-for-sale securities, equity investments are *not* periodically adjusted to fair value. Although the equity method is not an attempt to reflect the securities at fair value, the investment is adjusted to reflect the investor's share of increases in the investee's equity.

Business Combinations

The popularity of mergers and acquisitions peaked in this country in 1988. In that year alone, the value of announced domestic mergers and acquisitions (M&A) was approximately $350 billion. After 1988, the number of mergers and acquisitions decreased, primarily because the engine of 1980s-style deal making—the highly leveraged transaction in which large amounts of debt were used—went out of favor. The market for "junk" bonds dried up with the demise of Drexel Burnham Lambert, the infamous investment firm that controlled that market. In addition, the companies that went deep into debt to complete these transactions couldn't make their payments because their economic assumptions were often too optimistic.

After a few years, the M&A business gradually came back to life, this time with much less debt and much more strategic rationale. *The Wall Street Journal* reported on October 14, 1993, that the "merger bandwagon is rolling again." The story was in the aftermath of the announcement of a planned acquisition of Tele-Communication Inc., a cable TV company, by Bell Atlantic Corp., a regional phone company. Why would a phone company want to buy a cable operator? We begin our study of business combinations by considering why companies combine.

Why Corporations Combine

Sometimes *competitors* combine. This is called a **horizontal combination** because it involves companies operating on the same level. The combination of Jeep in the late 1980s with Chrysler Corp. was an example of a horizontal combination. United Airlines' purchase of Air Wisconsin in 1992 was also a combination of competitors. In the same year, Marvel Entertainment Group, Inc., the famous comic book company, acquired Fleer, the trading card company. Marvel saw Fleer as a good fit as it continued to compete for the youth entertainment market.

On other occasions, a company may combine with either one of its *suppliers* or one of its *customers*. For example, a combination with a supplier may be viewed as a way to ensure a reliable source of raw material for a product. A company also might combine with one of its customers to be assured of a steady market for its products. Because the company is either reaching down in terms of the product chain to combine with a supplier or up to combine with a customer, this is called a **vertical combination.**

Finally, some business combinations involve companies without any obvious tie to each other. For example, at one time Sears, Roebuck & Co. owned Allstate, an insurance company, Dean Witter, a brokerage firm, and Coldwell Banker, a real estate company. This type of corporation, with widely varying business interests, is termed a **conglomerate.** According to *The Wall Street Journal* article just mentioned, "The conglomerate theory held that companies operating in many different businesses would be less vulnerable to downturns in individual sectors and could benefit from centralized management." The planned acquisition of Tele-Communications Inc. by Bell Atlantic Corp. is an example of this type of combination.

Legal Forms of Business Combinations

Before we consider how to account for a business combination, it is important to understand the different *legal forms* for business combinations. Assume that two competitors, A and B, decide to combine their operations. In a **statutory merger,** A acquires all of the assets of B and assumes all of its liabilities and B ceases to exist. In effect, B is merged into A and goes out of business as a separate legal entity. In a **statutory consolidation,** A and B combine, but instead of B being merged into A, a new corporation, C, is created to continue the business of the two former entities. It is important to understand that in both of these instances, a *single* entity survives, that is, either one of the two combining companies or a new entity.

In contrast, in a **stock acquisition,** two companies combine, but after the combination, both entities maintain their legal identities. Both entities survive in this type of business combination because of the structure of the transaction. Instead of A acquiring B's *assets and liabilities,* as is the case in a merger, A acquires the *stock* of B.

The three legal forms for business combinations are summarized in Exhibit 13-3. Note that both entities survive when the combination is structured as a stock acquisition as opposed to a single entity in either a statutory merger or a statutory consolidation.

Methods of Accounting for Business Combinations

Regardless of the legal form a business combination takes, one of two methods is used to account for it. Unlike depreciation or inventory methods, a company is not free to choose between the two methods. One or the other should be used based on the facts in a particular combination. One is called the **purchase method** and occurs when a significant amount of cash, other assets, or debt is used to effect the combination. The other method is the **pooling of interests method** and is used in limited situations in which shares of stock in the two companies are exchanged. Because the pooling of interests method is used less frequently, we focus our attention on the purchase method. Both methods are covered in detail in advanced accounting textbooks.

LO 6

Explain the different forms of business combinations and how to account for a merger using the purchase method.

EXHIBIT 13-3 Legal Forms for Business Combinations

LEGAL FORM	WHAT HAPPENS	AFTER THE COMBINATION
Statutory merger	A acquires net assets of B.	A is surviving entity. B goes out of existence.
Statutory consolidation	A and B combine net assets.	A and B go out of existence. New entity, C, is created.
Stock acquisition	A acquires the stock of B.	A and B continue to exist.

Marvel Comics used the format it knows best for its own 1992 annual report—producing an instant collectible in the process. Here is management's summary of Marvel's increases in revenue and income—due in part to its purchase of Fleer Corporation in 1992.

Use of the Purchase Method to Record a Merger

As we have seen in previous chapters, any asset acquired by a company should be recorded initially at its cost. Under the purchase method, the same idea holds true. The investor company is simply buying a "basket" of assets. Thus, the individual assets should be recorded on the investor's books at their market value, which represents cost at the time of purchase.

Assume that on January 1, 1995, Garth Corp. purchases the assets and agrees to assume the liabilities of Brooks, Inc., for $40 million in cash. Thus, the legal form is a statutory merger. Condensed balance sheets for each of the two companies prior to the purchase are shown in Exhibit 13-4.

Three amounts are relevant in a business combination accounted for as a purchase:

1. The *cost* or *purchase price.*
2. The *book value* of the net assets (assets minus liabilities) acquired.
3. The *fair value* of the net assets acquired.

In our example, the *purchase price* is $40 million. One of two approaches can be used to find the *book value* of the net assets acquired by Garth. One way is to compute the book value of Brooks' assets minus its liabilities as shown on its balance sheet:

Book value of assets $10 + $10 + $15	$35
Less: Book value of liabilities $3 + $7	10
Book value of net assets acquired	$25

EXHIBIT 13-4   Premerger Balance Sheets for Two Companies

GARTH CORP. AND BROOKS, INC.
BALANCE SHEETS
JANUARY 1, 1995
(IN MILLIONS OF DOLLARS)

	GARTH CORP.	BROOKS, INC.
Current assets	$300	$10
Land	200	10
Buildings, net of depreciation	300	15
Total assets	$800	$35
Current liabilities	$ 50	$ 3
Bonds payable	200	7
Capital stock, $1 par	100	5
Additional paid-in capital	300	10
Retained earnings	150	10
Total equities	$800	$35

According to the accounting equation, assets minus liabilities equal stockholders' equity. Thus, another way to find the book value of a company's net assets, that is, assets minus liabilities, is to add the components of Brooks' stockholders' equity on its balance sheet:

Capital stock, $1 par	$ 5
Additional paid-in capital	10
Retained earnings	10
Book value of stockholders' equity	$25

Why did Garth pay $40 million, or $15 million *more* than book value of $25 million, to acquire the net assets of Brooks? Two explanations are possible. First, the book value of Brooks' assets and liabilities may not be equal to their fair values. Second, not all of Brooks' value as a company may be currently recognized on the balance sheet in the form of assets. Brooks may have some unrecorded assets, such as its reputation, number of years in business, and location, that are valuable assets but are not currently recorded on the books. In addition, the high price could be the result of an old-fashioned bidding war. Accountants refer to the excess of the purchase price for a business over the fair value of its net assets as **goodwill.**

Recall from Chapter 8 that goodwill exists in most businesses, but it is normally not recorded because of the difficulty in valuing it. In fact, goodwill is recorded as an asset only when it is purchased, that is, when one company buys another company. In this instance, the accountant records goodwill for the excess of the purchase price of a business over the fair value of the net assets acquired.

As part of the negotiation process, an acquiring company often hires an appraiser to value the assets of the acquired firm. Assume that on the basis of an appraisal, the accountant prepares the following analysis to compare the cost of the net assets purchased from Brooks with the *fair value* of those net assets:

Cost (purchase price)		$40
Fair value of net assets acquired:		
Current assets	10	
Land	15	
Buildings	18	
Current liabilities	(3)	
Bonds payable	(10)*	30
Excess of cost over fair value of net assets acquired (goodwill)		$10

According to this analysis, the net assets now recognized on Brooks' books are worth $30 million, even though they are currently recorded on the books at only $25 million. Thus, an excess of fair value over book value explains $5 million of the excess purchase price. The other $10 million is attributable to unrecorded assets, that is, goodwill. The following summarizes these points:

Excess of cost over book value of net assets acquired: $40 − $25	$15
Excess of fair values of net assets over book values: $30 − $25	5
Excess of cost over fair values of net assets acquired (goodwill): $40 − $30	$10

At this point, we will record a journal entry on Garth's books to record the purchase of the other company. The entry is similar to one to record the acquisition of any asset, although it involves a number of assets, as well as the recognition of the liabilities:

1995			
Jan. 1	Current Assets	10 ⎫	
	Land	15 ⎪ 53	
	Buildings	18 ⎬	
	Goodwill	10 ⎭	
	Current Liabilities		3 ⎫ 13
	Bonds Payable		10 ⎭
	Cash		40
	To record purchase of Brooks, Inc.		

Assets	=	Liabilities	+	Owners' Equity
+53		+13		
−40				

Note that the assets and liabilities are recorded on Garth's books at their individual fair values. Because the amount of cash paid exceeded the fair value of the net assets acquired, a new intangible asset, labeled Goodwill, is recorded. Goodwill, like other intangible assets, should be amortized over its useful life. According to current accounting standards, the maximum amortization period for goodwill is 40 years.

---

* Bonds have a different market or fair value as compared to their book value because of changes in interest rates. In this case, market rates of interest have gone down since Brooks issued its bonds, making the Brooks' bonds relatively more valuable.

EXHIBIT 13-5 Post-Merger Balance Sheet

GARTH CORP.
BALANCE SHEET
JANUARY 1, 1995
(IN MILLIONS OF DOLLARS)

Current assets	$270
Land	215
Buildings, net of depreciation	318
Goodwill	10
Total assets	$813
Current liabilities	$ 53
Bonds payable	210
Capital stock, $1 par	100
Additional paid-in capital	300
Retained earnings	150
Total equities	$813

Thus, if Garth chooses the maximum write-off period for its goodwill and the method most often used for intangibles, straight-line amortization, it will recognize amortization expense beginning in 1995 equal to $10 million divided by 40 years, or $250,000 per year.

Many analysts and lenders ignore goodwill. They add back the amortization on the income statement to remove its effect. Even though accountants recognize it, these other groups do not, because goodwill does not have value as collateral. That is, if a loan goes bad, a lender cannot repossess goodwill.

A balance sheet prepared immediately after the purchase of Brooks by Garth is presented in Exhibit 13-5. Keep in mind that the only surviving entity is Garth. Brooks has gone out of existence and has effectively been merged with Garth. The balance sheet is prepared by posting each of the amounts in the journal entry directly to Garth's accounts. The calculation of the amount of current assets deserves special attention. The balance of $270 million is found by adding Brooks' current assets of $10 million to Garth's current assets of $300 and deducting the cash of $40 million paid to acquire Brooks. Finally, note the recognition of $10 million of goodwill.

Consolidated Financial Statements

Work sheets are normally used to aid the accountant in consolidating two or more entities. For our purposes, however, it is more important to understand *when* and *why* these types of statements are prepared than to be able to prepare the worksheets.

LO 7

Explain when, why, and how consolidated financial statements are prepared.

When Are Consolidated Financial Statements Prepared?

Consolidated financial statements are prepared when one company *controls* another company. The two companies are legally separate but under common control. Recall our earlier discussion of the three types of business combinations: statutory merger, statutory consolidation, and stock acquisition. Which of these three types of combinations results in the need for consolidated financial statements? The answer is that *only when a business combination is effected as a stock acquisition is there a need for consolidated statements, because it is the only case in which the two combining entities survive.* The two companies continue their separate legal identities, but through ownership of a majority of the stock, one company controls the affairs of the other.

As we described earlier, the company that owns the majority of the stock in another company is called the *parent company*. The company that has a majority of its stock held by another entity is called a *subsidiary*. In today's global environment, many companies have foreign subsidiaries. With national boundaries no longer a constraint, it is not uncommon for a parent to control more than 100 subsidiaries. Although exceptions exist, the normal rule that accountants follow to decide whether a company controls another and should therefore prepare consolidated statements is ownership of more than 50% of the common stock of that other company. Many times the parent owns 100% of the subsidiary's stock, in which case the subsidiary is referred to as a *wholly owned subsidiary*.

Why Are Consolidated Statements Prepared?

Two important accounting concepts justify the preparation of consolidated statements: substance over form and the economic entity concept. Consolidated statements are an example in accounting of *substance over form.* In form, a parent and its subsidiary are separate legal entities. This is the very nature of a stock acquisition. Recall that if a company buys the assets of another company, a merger takes place and only a single entity survives. In a stock acquisition, however, the two companies continue their legal identities. For our purposes, it is equally important to recognize that the two companies continue to keep their own sets of records. That is, for accounting purposes, the companies are kept separate, but in *substance,* the companies are controlled by a single entity, the parent company.

Recall from Chapter 1 the *economic entity concept.* This concept requires that an identifiable, specific entity be the subject of a set of financial statements. In the case of consolidated statements, the parent corporation and its subsidiaries form one identifiable entity under common control.

What Happens in a Stock Acquisition?

To illustrate a stock acquisition, and eventually, consolidated financial statements, we return to the example of Garth Corp. Assume the same facts in the Garth and Brooks example with one exception. *Instead of paying $40 million to buy the assets and assume the liabilities of Brooks, Garth buys all of the shares of Brooks' stock.* As noted in Brooks' balance sheet in Exhibit 13-4, we observe that it has $5 million of $1 par value per share stock outstanding. Thus, Brooks has 5 million shares of stock, and if Garth paid $40 million for all of the shares, the purchase price was $8 per share.

Exhibit 13-6 describes what happens in a stock acquisition. The key to understanding what happens is to understand who buys the shares and what happens to the prior stockholders. Assume that before the acquisition, three stockholders, A, B, and C, own all of Garth's stock. Similarly, three stockholders, D, E, and F, own all of Brooks' stock. Garth management, acting on behalf of the corporation's stockholders, goes directly to D, E, and F and buys their 5 million shares of Brooks' stock for $40 million. *The owners of the Brooks stock sell their ownership interests to Garth, and Brooks now has a single stockholder: Garth.* Stockholders D, E and F have been bought out and are no longer associated with Brooks.

Balance sheets for each of the two entities immediately *after* the stock acquisition are presented in Exhibit 13-7. At this point, compare these balance sheets with those

EXHIBIT 13-6 What Happens in a Stock Aquisition

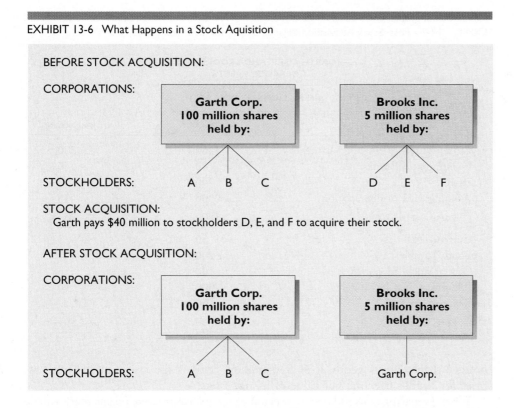

BEFORE STOCK ACQUISITION:

CORPORATIONS:

> **Garth Corp.**
> **100 million shares**
> **held by:**

> **Brooks Inc.**
> **5 million shares**
> **held by:**

STOCKHOLDERS: A B C D E F

STOCK ACQUISITION:
  Garth pays $40 million to stockholders D, E, and F to acquire their stock.

AFTER STOCK ACQUISITION:

CORPORATIONS:

> **Garth Corp.**
> **100 million shares**
> **held by:**

> **Brooks Inc.**
> **5 million shares**
> **held by:**

STOCKHOLDERS: A B C Garth Corp.

in Exhibit 13-4, which reflected the financial positions of the two companies prior to any combination. Garth took $40 million of cash and used it to buy shares of stock in Brooks. Thus, its balance sheet in Exhibit 13-7 shows a reduction in current assets from $300 million to $260 million and a new asset, Investment in Brooks, for $40 million. Note that Brooks' balance sheets are identical in the two exhibits since the stock acquisition does not directly affect Brooks as an entity. The transaction was between Garth and the stockholders of Brooks.

Consolidated Balance Sheet

A consolidated balance sheet for Garth, Inc., is shown in Exhibit 13-8. At this point, compare this balance sheet to the one shown in Exhibit 13-5. Why are these two balance sheets identical? You will recall that the balance sheet in Exhibit 13-5 reported the financial position of Garth immediately after Brooks had been merged into Garth. *Whether one company is legally merged into the other, as in Exhibit 13-5, or one company controls the other through ownership of a majority of its stock, as in Exhibit 13-8, the combined financial position of the two should be the same.*

Consolidation involves two steps: aggregation and elimination. *Aggregation* means that similar accounts on the balance sheets of the two companies are added together. For example, Garth's current assets of $260 million are added to Brooks' current assets of $10 million with a result of $270 million on the consolidated balance sheet. Note, however, that land on the consolidated balance sheet in Exhibit 13-8 amounts to $215 million; the individual amounts were $200 million on Garth's books and $10 million on Brooks' books. The additional $5 million is due to the excess of the fair value of Brooks' land over its book value. The same is true of buildings and bonds payable. The amounts on the consolidated balance sheet for Brooks represent fair values rather than book values. As was the case in the merger, the consolidated

EXHIBIT 13-7   Post–Stock Acquisition Balance Sheets for Two Companies

GARTH CORP. AND BROOKS, INC.
BALANCE SHEETS
JANUARY 1, 1995
(IN MILLIONS OF DOLLARS)

	GARTH CORP.	BROOKS, INC.
Current assets	$260	$10
Investment in Brooks	40	0
Land	200	10
Buildings, net of depreciation	300	15
Total assets	$800	$35
Current liabilities	$ 50	$ 3
Bonds payable	200	7
Capital stock, $1 par	100	5
Additional paid-in capital	300	10
Retained earnings	150	10
Total equities	$800	$35

balance sheet reflects goodwill of $10 million. This is the excess of the purchase price for Brooks over the fair value of its net assets.

When preparing consolidated financial statements, *elimination* means that to avoid *double counting,* any *reciprocal* accounts should be eliminated when preparing the consolidated statements. Reciprocal accounts are opposite but related accounts. In our example, there is one set of reciprocal accounts. The Investment in Brooks account on Garth's books is related to the stockholders' equity accounts on Brooks' books because it represents Garth's interest in the equity of Brooks. Note that neither the investment account from Garth's books nor the stockholders' equity accounts

EXHIBIT 13-8   Consolidated Balance Sheet

GARTH CORP. AND SUBSIDIARY
CONSOLIDATED BALANCE SHEET
JANUARY 1, 1995
(IN MILLIONS OF DOLLARS)

Current assets	$270
Land	215
Buildings, net of depreciation	318
Goodwill	10
Total assets	$813
Current liabilities	$ 53
Bonds payable	210
Capital stock, $1 par	100
Additional paid-in capital	300
Retained earnings	150
Total equities	$813

from Brooks' books have been included on the consolidated balance sheet. The investment account is eliminated and replaced with the individual assets and liabilities of Brooks. The stockholders' equity accounts of Brooks are eliminated. Because the owners of Garth own Brooks, only the stockholders' equity accounts for Garth remain on the consolidated balance sheet.

Consolidated work sheets typically contain a number of other types of eliminations. For example, assume that a parent company that manufactures athletic shoes owns a subsidiary that supplies it with rubber for the soles of the shoes. At any point in time, it is likely that the parent company will owe money to the subsidiary on open account. That is, the parent will report Accounts Payable on its separate balance sheet and the subsidiary will report Accounts Receivable. On a consolidated balance sheet, however, neither of these accounts is reported. The reason is that the debt is "in the family." On the consolidated work papers, the intercompany accounts, Accounts Payable and Accounts Receivable, are eliminated.

Consolidated Income Statement

The rationale for all consolidated statements is the same: to report on legally separate entities as if they were one because they are under common control. Thus, the purpose of a consolidated income statement is to report the results of operations for a period of time for a parent and its subsidiaries. The work paper procedures used by the accountant to prepare a consolidated income statement are beyond the scope of this text and are the subject of advanced accounting courses.

For our purposes, it is important to understand that a consolidated income statement combines the revenues and the expenses of the parent and its subsidiaries. For example, sales revenues for the two or more entities are combined and reported as a single amount on the consolidated income statement. Likewise, purchases are added together as one of the components to arrive at cost of goods sold for the two entities. However, recall our example of the athletic shoe manufacturer. The amount bought from the rubber subsidiary is included in the shoemaker's purchases for any one period. Similarly, the subsidiary reports on its own income statement the sales that it made to the parent. For purposes of preparing a consolidated income statement, the purchases from the records of the parent and the sales from the books of the subsidiary must be eliminated. Any other intercompany revenue and expense items are also subject to elimination in the preparation of a consolidated income statement.

What Is Minority Interest?

In certain situations, a parent company may own less than 100% of the stock of a subsidiary. When this is the case, a **minority interest** exists. Minority interest is that portion of the subsidiary's stockholders' equity that is owned by stockholders other than the parent corporation. For example, assume that a parent company owns 90% of a subsidiary. This means there is a 10% minority interest. Even when a minority interest exists, a consolidated balance sheet reports *all* of the assets under the control of the parent entity. That is, even if only 90% of a subsidiary is owned, 100% of its assets are included on the consolidated balance sheet. It would be artificial to split the assets of the subsidiary as if only part of them are controlled. The point is that all of the assets are under the control of the parent.

Turning to the right side of the balance sheet, recall that in preparing a consolidated balance sheet, the accountant eliminates the stockholders' equity of the subsidiary. However, what about that portion of the stockholders' equity of the subsidiary that is *not* attributable to the parent but represents the claim of the minority shareholders? This portion of stockholders' equity is not eliminated.

How should minority interest be reported on the right side of a consolidated balance sheet? Some accountants argue that minority shareholders are truly outsiders and therefore report minority interest in the liabilities section of the consolidated balance sheet. The difficulty with this argument is that there is no legal obligation or due date for the minority interest. Others argue that it represents equity in a portion of the consolidated entity and report it as an element of stockholders' equity. Interestingly, in published financial statements, the theoretical issue of the proper treatment of minority interest is normally avoided by placing it *between* liabilities and stockholders' equity on the consolidated balance sheet. This approach sidesteps the question as to whether it is debt or equity.

Many family businesses that go public have minority interests—often it is the public that is in the minority. That is, the family owns most of the stock. One famous example is Hugh Hefner, the majority owner of Playboy Enterprises, Inc. Many investors question whether it is a good idea to buy stock in a company that is controlled by a family. Management is more likely to act in the best interests of the family shareholders. Minority shareholders often find it difficult to sell their stock because of the lack of an active market for it.

FROM CONCEPT TO PRACTICE

READING BEN & JERRY'S FOOTNOTES
Locate the footnote in which the company describes its consolidation policies. What percentage of the stock does Ben & Jerry's own in its subsidiaries? Given the nature of its business, what kinds of subsidiaries would you expect Ben & Jerry's to own?

Accounting for the Global Corporation

U.S. corporations are increasingly looking abroad to expand their business opportunities. In 1992 only 41% of IBM's revenues were attributable to its U.S. operations. Almost 50% of McDonald's 1992 revenues were generated outside the United States. At the end of 1992, McDonald's had restaurants in 65 countries, with 1,653 of them in the Pacific, 1,549 in Europe and Africa, and 274 in Latin America. The first McDonald's in Russia opened its doors in that year. The dramatic political changes in Eastern Europe and the former Soviet Union, along with the passage of the North American Free Trade Agreement, have only added to the opportunities abroad for American businesses.

When a company does business internationally, the currency of the local country often becomes an issue. For example, assume that a company purchases inventory from a supplier in Mexico. The agreement is that the U.S. company will pay the Mexican supplier 10,000 pesos for the purchase. How does the U.S. company account for this *foreign currency transaction?* As another example, assume that a U.S. parent owns a subsidiary in France. The French sub keeps its books in the currency of that country, the franc. How does the parent *translate the foreign financial statements* into U.S. dollars prior to consolidating them with the parent's statements? We now turn to a brief consideration of each of these issues.

Foreign Currency Transactions

LO 8
Understand how to account for foreign currency transactions.

To understand how foreign currency transactions are accounted for, you must first understand the meaning of an **exchange rate.** An exchange rate measures the relative worth of two different currencies. To illustrate, consider the following published exchange rates on October 22, 1993:

British (pound)	$1.480500
Canada (dollar)	.767342
France (franc)	.171380
Germany (mark)	.599161
Japan (yen)	.009240
Mexico (peso)	.321337

Each of these quotations represents the relationship of one foreign currency unit to the U.S. dollar. For example, one British pound was worth $1.48 of U.S. currency on this date. One German mark was worth approximately $.60.

A **foreign currency transaction** occurs when a company agrees to either accept payment or make payment in a foreign currency. In other words, if Quaker Oats sells $10,000 of grocery products to a wholesaler in Canada and requires payment in U.S. dollars, there is no foreign currency transaction. Foreign currency transactions arise from a decision to deal in foreign currency. As we will see, this can subject a company to certain risks.

Consider the following example. On October 22, 1993, a U.S. steel manufacturer, Sturdy Steel, makes a sale to a German auto maker. The selling price is 1,000,000 marks and the terms are net 30. Based on the exchange rate quoted above for German marks, the entry on Sturdy Steel's books on the date of the sale is

1993
Oct. 22   Accounts Receivable   599,161
              Sales Revenue   599,161
          To record sale: 1,000,000 marks × .599161.

Assets	**=**	**Liabilities**	**+**	**Owners' Equity**
+599,161				+599,161

Because each mark on this date is worth $.599161, Sturdy records the sale at 1,000,000 marks times $.599161, or a total of $599,161. Now assume that the German auto maker pays Sturdy on November 22, 1993. It will be up to Sturdy to take the 1,000,000 marks to a bank or other financial institution that deals in foreign currencies and exchange them for U.S. dollars. Assume that the exchange rate on November 22 has dropped to $.575242. The drop in the rate means that Sturdy will receive only 1,000,000 × $.575242, or $575,242. Because the original sale was recorded at an amount that reflected the higher exchange rate, Sturdy records a loss at the time it collects from the German customer. The entry on Sturdy's books on this date is

1993
Nov. 22   Cash   575,242
          Foreign Exchange Loss   23,919
              Accounts Receivable   599,161
          To record collection on account.

Assets	**=**	**Liabilities**	**+**	**Owners' Equity**
+575,242				−23,919
−599,161				

The loss represents the decline in value of the asset, Accounts Receivable, from $599,161 on October 22 to $575,242 when it was collected on November 22. Sturdy has incurred a loss because it was willing to accept foreign currency at a later date. This is one of many different *risks* faced by companies dealing across national boundaries. Another way to look at the loss is that it represents the decline in value of the mark over the month:

Value of one mark on 10/22/93	$.599161
Value of one mark on 11/22/93	.575242
Decline in value of the mark	$.023919
Number of marks	1,000,000
Foreign exchange loss	$ 23,919

What if the value of the German mark rose between the time of the sale and the time of collection? In this case, Sturdy records a gain. Foreign exchange gains and losses are normally reported in other revenues and expenses on the income statement.

■ **ACCOUNTING FOR YOUR DECISIONS**   **You Are the Money Manager**

International investing is very popular today, yet foreign currency risk has not diminished. How would you minimize the risk of foreign currency fluctuations on your investments?

Translation of Foreign Financial Statements

LO 9

Understand how to translate foreign financial statements into U.S. dollars.

Two major issues arise in the translation of foreign financial statements. First, it may be necessary to restate various accounts on the statements of a foreign subsidiary or affiliate to conform with U.S. accounting standards. For example, it is common in other English-speaking countries of the world, such as England, Australia, South Africa, and Canada, to report plant and equipment at an amount in excess of historical cost on the balance sheet. If a U.S. company operates a subsidiary in London, it may be necessary to restate its plant and equipment accounts in historical cost terms if they have been adjusted to reflect current values. This is done prior to the consolidation of the subsidiary with the U.S. parent.

The second issue has to do with how to translate the *amounts* on the other statements. The British subsidiary most likely keeps its records in pounds, not U.S. dollars. Thus, it is necessary to *translate* those statements into U.S. dollars prior to consolidating them with the statements of the parent. **Foreign currency translation** is the process of restating the financial statements of a company from one currency to another.

Assume that at the beginning of the year, Mel's Motor City Manufacturing in Detroit opens a wholly owned subsidiary, Windsor Wheels, in Windsor, Canada. Windsor Wheels begins operations with an investment of 250,000 Canadian dollars (CD) from Motor City. All of the capital stock is held by the parent, Motor City, because the sub is wholly owned. After the initial investment, Windsor Wheels buys a new plant for one million CD by signing a five-year, 10% note with a Toronto bank. The plant will be depreciated on a straight-line basis over 20 years. The relevant exchange rates are as follows:

DATE	EXCHANGE RATE PER CANADIAN DOLLAR
Beginning of year	$.80
End of year	$.70
Average for year	$.75

One critical question must be answered before we translate the income statement for the year and the balance sheet at the end of the first year into U.S. dollars: What exchange rate should be used to translate? The answer to this question depends on the **functional currency.** This is the currency of the primary economic environment in which the foreign entity operates. For example, if Windsor sells most of its wheels in the United States and remits most of its cash to its parent, Motor City, the U.S. dollar might be designated as the functional currency. It is more common, however, that the functional currency is the local currency of the foreign country. Because this is the case, we focus on situations in which the local currency is the functional currency. The appropriate treatment for situations in which the reporting currency, that is, the U.S. dollar, is the functional currency and for situations in which the foreign entity operates in a highly inflationary economy are covered in advanced accounting courses.

If we assume that the Canadian dollar is the functional currency, the translation process is very straightforward. All *income statement items* are translated using the *average* exchange rate for the year. The rationale for this treatment is that most revenues are earned and most expenses are incurred evenly over the period. An income statement for Windsor Wheels is shown in Exhibit 13-9, in Canadian dollars and translated into U.S. dollars. Note that each item on the income statement is translated using the average exchange rate for the year, $.75 per Canadian dollar. The amounts in U.S. dollars are found by simply multiplying the amount of Canadian dollars times the exchange rate. For example, sales in U.S. dollars of $750,000 are calculated by multiplying 1,000,000 CD times the average exchange rate of $.75 per CD.

The translation of items on a balance sheet is also easy when the local currency of the subsidiary is the functional currency. All *assets and liabilities* are translated using the current rate, meaning the *rate at the end of the year*. A balance sheet for

This international bank offers to manage the risk to global corporations from foreign exchange exposure—that is, fluctuations in the exchange rate affecting the translation of their foreign subsidiaries' financial statements.

EXHIBIT 13-9   Translation of a Foreign Income Statement

WINDSOR WHEELS
INCOME STATEMENT
FOR THE FIRST YEAR

ITEMS	CANADIAN DOLLARS	EXCHANGE RATE	U.S. DOLLARS
Sales	1,000,000 CD	.75 per CD	$750,000
Cost of sales	(600,000)	.75	(450,000)
Depreciation	(50,000)	.75	(37,500)
Interest expense	(40,000)	.75	(30,000)
Other expenses	(60,000)	.75	(45,000)
Net income	250,000 CD		$187,500

Windsor Wheels, first in Canadian dollars and then translated into U.S. dollars, is presented in Exhibit 13-10. Note that all of the assets and liabilities are translated using the exchange rate at the end of the year. Common stock is translated to U.S. dollars, however, using the rate at the beginning of the year, the point at which the stock was issued. Measurement of the original contributed capital of the foreign entity using the rate when the stock was first issued, that is, the historical exchange rate, provides a base, and this rate is used in the translation of all subsequent balance sheets. Also, note that an exchange rate is not used to translate retained earnings. Because this is a new business and because the sub paid no dividends in the first year, retained earnings at year-end in U.S. dollars is simply the net income for the first year, $187,500.

EXHIBIT 13-10   Translation of a Foreign Balance Sheet

WINDSOR WHEELS
BALANCE SHEET
AT THE END OF THE FIRST YEAR

ITEMS	CANADIAN DOLLARS	EXCHANGE RATE	U.S. DOLLARS
Cash	200,000 CD	$.70 per CD	$ 140,000
Accounts receivable	450,000	.70	315,000
Inventory	200,000	.70	140,000
Plant, net	950,000	.70	665,000
Totals	1,800,000 CD		$1,260,000
Current liabilities	300,000 CD	$.70	$ 210,000
Notes payable	1,000,000	.70	700,000
Common stock	250,000	.80	200,000
Retained earnings	250,000		187,500
Totals	1,800,000 CD		
Translation adjustment			(37,500)
Totals			$1,260,000

How should the reader of the financial statements interpret the **translation adjustment**? Note that it is simply a "plug number." For Windsor Wheels, it is

Assets	$1,260,000
Liabilities, common stock, and retained earnings	$1,297,500
Negative translation adjustment	$ (37,500)

The translation adjustment is the amount needed to balance the two sides of the balance sheet. In this particular case, the adjustment is a negative amount because the value of the Canadian dollar relative to the value of the U.S. dollar decreased during the period from $.80 at the beginning of the year to $.70 at the end of the year. The amount is not considered to be realized in any sense, however. The investment in the subsidiary is not being sold. There are presently no *cash flow* implications from the decrease in the exchange rate during the period. Thus, the negative translation adjustment appears in stockholders' equity as a contra account. Note that a positive translation adjustment would appear at the end of the first year if the exchange rate had gone up during the period instead of down.

Reporting Requirements for Segments of a Business

Earlier in the chapter, we focused attention on the need for consolidated financial statements when two or more entities are under common control. We described the process of preparing consolidated statements as being one of *aggregation.* The problem with aggregation, however, is that it can make judging the performance and financial position of the various segments of the business difficult. Users of financial statements, particularly investors and creditors, find it useful at times to assess the individual *segments* of the business. Current accounting standards require a company to present *supplementary* information in a company's footnotes about its segments. Essentially, the reporting requirements require a reverse process from consolidation, that is, a *disaggregation* of the operations and financial position of a business.

LO   10

Describe the reporting requirements for segments of a business.

Accounting standards require four areas of disclosure. These relate to the following elements of a company:

1. Operations in different industries.
2. Operations in foreign countries.
3. Major customers.
4. Export sales.

The accounting standards in this area are quite detailed. If certain criteria are met that deal with how significant an industry, a foreign segment, a major customer, or export sales are to a business, certain disclosures are required. For example, the following disclosures appear in the footnotes or in a separate schedule for a company that has significant operations in more than one *industry.* For each reportable industry, the following segment disclosures are required:

1. Revenues.
2. Operating profit or loss.
3. Carrying value of the assets.
4. Depreciation, depletion, and amortization.
5. Capital expenditures.

In addition to disclosures about industry segments, *geographic* segmentation may be required. Companies with significant foreign operations are required to disclose the first three items noted above: revenues, operating profit or loss, and carrying value of assets, each by geographic segment. The grouping of foreign operations by countries is left to the accountant's discretion. For example, it is common to report on operations by continents: Europe, Asia, South America, and so forth. In addition, a company with a significant amount of export sales (sales generated in this country but the product shipped outside the United States) is required to disclose the amount of these sales.

Finally, disclosures are required when a company relies on any one or a number of its customers to a significant extent. The accounting standards require a disclosure if 10 percent or more of revenue is derived from sales to any single customer. The amount of revenue from each such customer must also be disclosed. The need for this type of information is obvious; it is important for investors and creditors to be aware of an entity's reliance on any single customer in the event that the customer itself experiences financial difficulties.

The requirements to report segment information began in 1977. Many analysts find this information to be among the most useful in the financial statements. Many companies would rather not disclose details about their various divisions, because they don't want their competition to find out key information about them. Nonetheless, many investors prefer to place values on parts of the enterprise and the fate of the stock price is affected if one of these parts is sold or discontinued.

Reporting by a Global Company: Whirlpool Corporation

At the beginning of this chapter, we introduced Whirlpool Corporation. We asked a number of questions about how it should account for and report on its global operations. We now look at the answers to these questions by reviewing the company's 1992 annual report.

Business Acquisitions

The second footnote in Whirlpool's annual report is entitled Business Acquisitions. This footnote describes all significant acquisitions of other businesses in recent years. One paragraph is devoted to a description of the way Whirlpool acquired its original interest in its operations in Europe:

> The Company acquired the original 53% interest in Whirlpool Europe on January 2, 1989 for Dfl 750 million or approximately $361 million in cash. The acquisition was accounted for as a purchase transaction with the purchase price allocated to the assets acquired and liabilities assumed based on their respective estimated fair values at the date of acquisition. The cost of the acquisition in excess of net tangible assets acquired was Dfl 480 million or approximately $238 million.[5]

The following points can be made by relating this footnote to items discussed in the chapter:

1. Because Whirlpool acquired Whirlpool Europe by a payment of cash, the combination was accounted for as a *purchase,* rather than a pooling of interests.

[5] 1992 Whirlpool Annual Report, p. 32.

2. The purchase involved a *foreign currency transaction*. The purchase price was Dfl 750 million. Whirlpool purchased this interest from a Dutch company, Philips Electronics N.V. The purchase was denominated, or transacted, in the local currency of the Netherlands, the guilder, which carries the designation Dfl (as compared to the $ sign used in the United States). The exchange rate at the time of the transaction can be found by dividing $361 million by the local currency units of 750 million (Dfl), or approximately $.48 per Dfl.

3. The amount paid in excess of the fair values of the net assets acquired was $238 million. As we know from our earlier discussion, this is goodwill. Thus, if the purchase price was $361 million, the fair value of the net assets acquired is determined as follows:

Purchase price (cost)	$361 million
Excess of purchase price over fair value of net assets acquired (goodwill)	238 million
Fair value of net assets acquired	$123 million

This tells us that Whirlpool paid a relatively large amount, $238 million, for assets not even recorded on the other company's books. The reason is that Whirlpool perceived the importance of establishing a European presence and was willing to pay a high price to enter this market. Of course, many other U.S. companies had the same idea in mind. As a result, Whirlpool may have been forced by competitive pressures to pay such a high price. Unfortunately, Europe was in a serious recession in 1992, so it was not clear at the time whether the investment would pay off.

4. Goodwill is included on Whirlpool's consolidated balance sheet in Exhibit 13-11 under the account title Intangibles, net. Included in the footnotes is a description of how the company amortizes its goodwill that arises from paying amounts for other businesses in excess of the value of the net assets acquired:

Intangibles: The cost of business acquisitions in excess of net tangible assets acquired is amortized on a straight-line basis principally over 40 years. Accumulated amortization aggregated $89 million at December 31, 1992 and $65 million at December 31, 1991.[6]

Thus, we see that Whirlpool uses a *straight-line* approach to writing off goodwill and that it uses the maximum write-off period allowed by accounting rules, 40 years.

Consolidations

Whirlpool's first footnote describes its consolidation policies:

Principles of Consolidation: The consolidated financial statements include all majority-owned subsidiaries. Investments in affiliated companies are accounted for by the equity method. Intercompany transactions and amounts between Whirlpool Corporation and Whirlpool Financial Corporation included in the supplemental consolidating data have been eliminated from the consolidated financial statements. The eliminations relate primarily to intercompany financing, interest and leasing transactions.[7]

Prior to 1988, companies had more latitude than they have now in deciding which subsidiaries to report on a consolidated basis. For example, many companies chose not to consolidate subsidiaries that were in a completely different type of business. Whirlpool Financial Corporation is a good example. Its primary business

---

[6] 1992 Whirlpool Annual Report, p. 31.
[7] 1992 Whirlpool Annual Report, p. 31.

EXHIBIT 13-11 Whirlpool's Balance Sheets

• CONSOLIDATED BALANCE SHEETS •

Supplemental Consolidating Data

December 31 (millions of dollars)	Whirlpool Corporation (Consolidated) 1992	1991	Whirlpool with WFC on an Equity Basis 1992	1991	Whirlpool Financial Corporation (WFC) 1992	1991
Assets						
Current Assets						
Cash and equivalents	$ 66	$ 42	$ 52	$ 31	$ 14	$ 11
Trade receivables, less allowances of $35 in 1992 and $47 in 1991	851	846	851	846	–	–
Financing receivables and leases, less allowances	980	1,190	–	–	980	1,190
Inventories	650	698	650	698	–	–
Prepaid expenses and other	119	111	98	85	20	27
Deferred income taxes	74	33	74	33	–	–
Total Current Assets	2,740	2,920	1,725	1,693	1,014	1,228
Other Assets						
Investment in affiliated companies	282	296	282	296	–	–
Investment in WFC	–	–	293	269	–	–
Financing receivables and leases, less allowances	912	893	–	–	912	900
Intangibles, net	795	909	795	909	–	–
Other	64	27	59	23	5	5
	2,053	2,125	1,429	1,497	917	905
Property, Plant and Equipment						
Land	73	78	73	78	–	–
Buildings	588	586	588	586	–	–
Machinery and equipment	2,052	2,026	2,031	1,997	21	18
Accumulated depreciation	(1,388)	(1,290)	(1,377)	(1,279)	(11)	(8)
	1,325	1,400	1,315	1,382	10	10
Total Assets	$6,118	$6,445	$4,469	$4,572	$1,941	$2,143

These receivables relate only to the financing sub.

Investment in the financing sub at equity.

Why did this investment decrease? As reported on the Income Statement in Exhibit 14-12, the affiliates reported losses in 1992.

The financing sub has insignificant P. P+E.

Supplemental Consolidating Data

December 31 (millions of dollars)	Whirlpool Corporation (Consolidated) 1992	1991	Whirlpool with WFC on an Equity Basis 1992	1991	Whirlpool Financial Corporation (WFC) 1992	1991
Liabilities and Stockholders' Equity						
Current Liabilities						
Notes payable	$ 1,425	$ 1,467	$ 322	$ 385	$ 1,050	$ 1,082
Accounts payable	688	742	646	677	41	66
Employee compensation	164	177	157	170	7	7
Accrued expenses	495	478	477	465	18	11
Income taxes	87	38	79	41	8	–
Current maturities of long-term debt	28	29	14	16	67	13
Total Current Liabilities	2,887	2,931	1,695	1,754	1,191	1,179
Other Liabilities						
Deferred income taxes	213	166	109	70	104	96
Accrued pensions and expenses	203	305	203	305	–	–
Long-term debt	1,215	1,528	862	928	378	624
	1,631	1,999	1,174	1,303	482	720
Stockholders' Equity						
Capital stock	76	75	76	75	8	8
Paid-in capital	47	37	47	37	26	26
Retained earnings	1,721	1,593	1,721	1,593	236	209
Unearned restricted stock	(18)	(12)	(18)	(12)	–	–
Cumulative translation adjustments	(49)	(1)	(49)	(1)	(2)	1
Treasury stock - at cost	(177)	(177)	(177)	(177)	–	–
	1,600	1,515	1,600	1,515	268	244
Total Liabilities and Stockholders' Equity	$6,118	$6,445	$4,469	$4,572	$1,941	$2,143

Nearly 3/4 of the consolidated notes are owed by the financing sub.

The value of the foreign currencies have decreased relative to the value of the U.S. dollar.

is loaning money. The main business of the parent, of course, is making and selling appliances. Beginning in 1988, however, the accounting profession ruled that virtually all subsidiaries should be consolidated, regardless of the industry in which they operate.

This change in accounting rules to require consolidation of virtually all subsidiaries has been controversial. A company such as Whirlpool or General Motors with relatively low debt would be forced to add the liabilities of a financial subsidiary, which has huge "liabilities," but in a different sense of the word. Think of a bank's deposits. Those are liabilities under this definition, as are similar obligations of finance companies. As we will see, the change in accounting rules has led Whirlpool and many other companies to add additional disclosures.

Refer back to Whirlpool's two-year comparative balance sheets in Exhibit 13-11. You will see that in addition to the first two columns that show the consolidated financial position of the company at the end of the two years, two additional sets of columns appear. The heading over both of these sets of columns indicates that this information is "supplemental consolidating data." Management's Discussion and Analysis provides an explanation for this additional information:

> The accompanying consolidated financial statements include supplemental consolidating data reflecting the Company's investment in Whirlpool Financial Corporation ("WFC") on an equity basis rather than as a consolidated subsidiary. Management believes this presentation provides more meaningful information about the major home appliance and financial services businesses.[8]

Whirlpool believes that it is more meaningful to look at the financial statements for its home appliance business separately from those for its finance subsidiary. *Thus, it has complied with the accounting rules by including all subsidiaries on a consolidated basis in the first set of columns but has added the other two sets of columns to allow the reader to look at the two types of businesses separately.*

Whirlpool with WFC on an Equity Basis   The purpose of this balance sheet is to show the financial position of the parent and all subsidiaries on a consolidated basis, with the exception of the financial subsidiary. This allows the reader to focus attention on the part of the business that makes and sells appliances. Note that this results in the need to report the Investment in WFC as an asset ($293 million at the end of 1992). This asset appears when WFC is reported on the equity basis (the middle columns) but not when it is consolidated (the first set of columns). In this case, the investment account has been eliminated.

Whirlpool Financial Corporation (WFC)   The purpose of the last two columns is to report the financial position of the financial services subsidiary. It is informative to note the *types* of assets and liabilities that both appear and do not appear, given the nature of this type of business:

Financing Receivables and Leases   When Whirlpool sells an appliance, it often allows the customer to pay for the purchase over time. The amounts due from customers within the next year are classified as current assets, and all other amounts are classified as other assets. Note that financing receivables and leases relate entirely to Whirlpool Financial Corporation. When the financing subsidiary is put on an equity basis in the middle columns, nothing appears on the line for financing receivables and leases because the parent corporation itself does not have any of these assets.

---

[8] 1992 Whirlpool Annual Report, p. 22.

Property, Plant, and Equipment   Note in the last two columns that WFC has no land or buildings and that the amount of machinery and equipment is insignificant ($10 million compared to total assets of $1,941 million).

Notes Payable   In contrast, a majority of the consolidated notes payable shown as the first item under current liabilities is attributable to the financing subsidiary. In fact, at the end of 1992, of the consolidated notes payable of $1,425 million, $1,050 million of this was owed by WFC.

Consolidated Income Statement   As it did for the balance sheets, Whirlpool presents three different income statements for each of the two years, as shown in Exhibit 13-12. The advantages to the reader of this presentation are apparent by focusing on the revenues. Note on the first line of the income statements that *all* of the corporation's net sales are attributable to the parent and subsidiaries other than WFC. Conversely, all of the company's revenues from financial services on the

EXHIBIT 13-12   Whirlpool's Income Statements

• CONSOLIDATED STATEMENTS OF EARNINGS •

Supplemental Consolidating Data

(Years ended December 31 (millions of dollars except share data)	Whirlpool Corporation (Consolidated)			Whirlpool with WFC on an Equity Basis			Whirlpool Financial Corporation (WFC)		
	1992	1991	1990	1992	1991	1990	1992	1991	1990
Revenues									
Net sales	$7,097	$6,550	$6,424	$7,097	$6,550	$6,424	$ –	$ –	$ –
Financial services	204	207	181	–	–	–	235	233	210
	7,301	6,757	6,605	7,097	6,550	6,424	235	233	210
Expenses									
Cost of products sold	5,365	4,967	4,955	5,365	4,967	4,955	–	–	–
Selling and administrative	1,323	1,257	1,180	1,242	1,181	1,133	113	102	76
Financial services interest	82	91	85	–	–	–	95	101	99
Intangible amortization	27	27	14	27	27	14	–	–	–
Restructuring costs	25	22	22	16	22	22	9	–	–
	6,822	6,364	6,256	6,650	6,197	6,124	217	203	175
Operating Profit	479	393	349	447	353	300	18	30	35
Other Income (Expense)									
Interest and sundry	38	49	19	21	33	13	20	18	8
Interest expense	(145)	(138)	(148)	(134)	(130)	(136)	–	–	–
Earnings Before Income Taxes and Other Items	372	304	220	334	256	177	38	48	43
Income taxes	154	130	110	142	113	94	12	17	16
Earnings Before Equity Earnings (Losses) and Other Items	218	174	110	192	143	83	26	31	27
Equity in net earnings of WFC	–	–	–	26	31	27	–	–	–
Equity in net earnings (losses) of affiliated companies and other	(13)	(4)	(38)	(13)	(4)	(38)	–	–	–
Net Earnings	$ 205	$ 170	$ 72	$ 205	$ 170	$ 72	$ 26	$ 31	$ 27
Per share of common stock:									
Primary earnings	$ 2.90	$ 2.45	$ 1.04						
Fully diluted earnings	$ 2.79	$ 2.40	$ 1.04						
Cash dividends	$ 1.10	$ 1.10	$ 1.10						
Average number of common shares outstanding (millions)	70.6	69.5	69.4						

second line were earned by the financial subsidiary. The revenue for WFC of $235 million in 1992 is higher than the consolidated revenue of $204 million because a small portion of WFC's revenue was intercompany. As we saw earlier in the consolidations footnote, intercompany amounts have been eliminated in the consolidated data.

It is also informative to note the treatment given to the operations of the financing subsidiary when it is reported on an equity basis (the middle columns of Exhibit 13-12). As we saw earlier, WFC's specific revenues and expenses are not reported individually when it is reported on an equity basis. This allows the reader to focus attention instead on the revenues and expenses related to making and selling appliances. Instead, the profitability of the subsidiary is summarized on a single line, equity in net earnings of WFC. Finally, note that this same amount, $26 million of equity in net earnings of WFC in 1992, can be traced back to the income statement of the subsidiary in the third set of columns.

Investments in Affiliates

As mentioned in the consolidations footnote, Whirlpool uses the equity method to account for investments in affiliates. These are the domestic and foreign companies in which Whirlpool holds between 20% and 50% of the common stock and thus exerts significant influence. Referring back to the consolidated balance sheets in Exhibit 13-11, you will note that Whirlpool reports an investment in affiliated companies of $282 million at the end of 1992. Why did this investment decrease by $14 million from the end of 1991?

The answer can be found by referring to the income statement in Exhibit 13-12. In the first column, the last line before net earnings is "equity in net earnings (losses) of affiliated companies and other." The negative amount reported on this line for 1992 means that Whirlpool's share of the net losses reported by these affiliates during the year was $13 million. The decrease in the investment account on the balance sheet of $14 million is primarily due to Whirlpool's share of the affiliate's losses.

Translation Adjustments

Many of Whirlpool's subsidiaries and affiliates are located in foreign countries. Whirlpool has to translate the statements for the subsidiaries from the local currency into U.S. dollars prior to consolidation. As we noted earlier in the chapter, translation adjustments result from the translation of the various assets and liabilities at current exchange rates and the stockholders' equity at historical exchange rates. Because these adjustments merely result from the translation process, they are not included on the income statement but instead are reported in the stockholders' equity section of the balance sheet.

Note on the consolidated balance sheets in Exhibit 13-11 that the *negative* translation adjustment increased from $1 million at the end of 1991 to $49 million at the end of 1992. Recall the negative amount for the translation adjustment in our earlier example in the chapter for Windsor Wheels. A negative adjustment indicates that over time the value of the foreign currency units has *decreased* relative to the value of the dollar. Although the translation adjustment is not reflected on the income statement, it is still significant. Recall from our earlier discussion that any cash flow implications from the translation adjustment only arise if the foreign entity is sold.

Segmental Disclosures

Whirlpool reports on its geographic and industry segments in a footnote to the financial statements. The schedules for each of these presentations are shown in Exhibit 13-13. Whirlpool reports on two major geographic markets: North America

EXHIBIT 13-13 Whirlpool's Segment Disclosures

Business Segment Information
• NOTE 14 •

Geographic Segments

(millions of dollars)	North America	Europe	Other and (Eliminations)	Consolidated
Revenues				
1992	$ 4,471	$ 2,645	$ 185	$ 7,301
1991	$ 4,224	$ 2,479	$ 54	$ 6,757
1990	$ 4,157	$ 2,405	$ 43	$ 6,605
Operating profit				
1992	$ 359	$ 101	$ 19	$ 479
1991	$ 314	$ 82	$ (3)	$ 393
1990	$ 269	$ 86	$ (6)	$ 349

North American 1990 operating profit includes Canadian losses of $31 million resulting primarily from certain of the restructuring costs described in Note 10.

[*Notes to Consolidated Financial Statements (continued)*]

	North America	Europe	Other and (Eliminations)	Consolidated
Identifiable assets				
1992	$ 3,511	$ 1,917	$ 690	$ 6,118
1991	$ 3,672	$ 2,284	$ 489	$ 6,445
1990	$ 3,216	$ 1,905	$ 493	$ 5,614
Depreciation expense				
1992	$ 142	$ 132	$ 1	$ 275
1991	$ 129	$ 104	$ –	$ 233
1990	$ 140	$ 107	$ –	$ 247
Net capital expenditures				
1992	$ 174	$ 111	$ 3	$ 288
1991	$ 183	$ 104	$ –	$ 287
1990	$ 158	$ 106	$ 1	$ 265

Industry Segments

(millions of dollars)	Major Home Appliances	Financial Services	Other and (Eliminations)	Consolidated
Revenues				
1992	$ 7,097	$ 235	$ (31)	$ 7,301
1991	$ 6,550	$ 233	$ (26)	$ 6,757
1990	$ 6,424	$ 210	$ (29)	$ 6,605
Operating profit				
1992	$ 447	$ 18	$ 14	$ 479
1991	$ 353	$ 30	$ 10	$ 393
1990	$ 300	$ 35	$ 14	$ 349
Identifiable assets				
1992	$ 3,612	$ 1,941	$ 565	$ 6,118
1991	$ 3,835	$ 2,143	$ 467	$ 6,445
1990	$ 3,513	$ 1,632	$ 469	$ 5,614
Depreciation expense				
1992	$ 271	$ 3	$ 1	$ 275
1991	$ 228	$ 3	$ 2	$ 233
1990	$ 243	$ 3	$ 1	$ 247
Net capital expenditures				
1992	$ 284	$ 4	$ –	$ 288
1991	$ 283	$ 5	$ (1)	$ 287
1990	$ 260	$ 5	$ –	$ 265

TODAY'S ACCOUNTANTS MUST THINK STRATEGICALLY

Name: Keith Ogata
Profession: CFO
College Major: Business Administration

An increasing number of American-based companies are finding that a key to growth in revenues, earnings, and shareholder value can be found outside the United States. By diversifying abroad, a company can take advantage of new markets and achieve economies of scale—spreading their product development costs over a larger base of customers. One example: National Education Corporation, based in Irvine, Cal., is the world's largest training company with operations in Australia, Canada, England, and Germany.

Working for a company with international operations presents special challenges to management. Among many other duties, NEC's chief financial officer, Keith Ogata, must consolidate the financial statements and the tax returns of the company's international operations. Each foreign division keeps a set of books to conform to its country's accounting standards. But the statements must also be converted to U.S. generally accepted accounting principles. Mr. Ogata, who volunteered for the Peace Corps after graduating from the University of Southern California, is also involved in foreign exchange transactions, banking relationships, investing idle cash, as well as the strategic planning of these subsidiaries.

In some organizations, the CFO position is narrowly defined to accounting and financial tasks. At NEC, Mr. Ogata has a broad range of duties, including investor relations, human resources, data processing, and insurance. "We have a large fleet of automobiles, and I'm very active in the company's safety programs," he says. "Through these programs, we try to keep our losses to a minimum, because insurance premiums are a function of losses."

Mr. Ogata began his career with Price Waterhouse in Newport Beach in 1980, becoming a CPA shortly after receiving his MBA at Duke University. After a short stint in public accounting, he came to National Education Corp. as a financial analyst, quickly moving up to controller, treasurer, and CFO. "My advice to college students is to try to get as broad a background as possible," he says. "Today, the job of CFO requires more teamwork, more involvement with operations and strategic direction of the company."

and Europe. Note that the consolidated amounts for revenues, operating profit, and identifiable assets in this schedule are the same amounts that appear on the consolidated balance sheets and income statements in Exhibits 13-11 and 13-12. The geographic information tells the reader that Whirlpool relies on its European operations for a very significant share of its revenues and operating profits.

The company reports on two industry segments: major home appliances and financial services. Again, the amounts in the consolidated columns can be traced to the consolidated income statements and balance sheets. Note what this information tells the reader. The financial services business generated a very insignificant amount of the consolidated revenues and operating profits (slightly over 3% in 1992). The identifiable assets of these businesses are considerably more significant, however, due mainly to the large amounts of receivables on the balance sheet of Whirlpool Financial Corporation. Many investment analysts do not look at the consolidated totals because they believe that the finance subsidiary's receivables and payables are a distortion. That is why the company has chosen to present the finance subsidiary using the equity method in addition to the required method.

Finally, recall the accounting rule that requires a company to disclose information about any customer that it relies on for a significant amount of its sales. The same footnote that provides Whirlpool's information on geographic and industry segments includes the following statement:

Percentages of consolidated net sales to Sears, Roebuck and Co., a North American major home appliance customer, were 19% in 1992, 19% in 1991 and 20% in 1990.[9]

REVIEW PROBLEM

Cubs Corp. is a large, diversified company. On January 1, 1995, Cubs entered into two transactions:

a. Cubs paid $750,000 to acquire all of the assets and assume all of the debts of Cardinals, Inc. After the purchase, Cardinals will cease to exist as an entity. The following condensed balance sheet was available for Cardinals on this date:

Current assets	$150,000	Current liabilities	$ 50,000
Land	100,000	Long-term debt	250,000
Plant and equipment	350,000	Capital stock	100,000
		Retained earnings	200,000
Total	$600,000	Total	$600,000

All of these amounts represent fair values with the exception of the land and the plant and equipment, which were appraised at $200,000 and $500,000, respectively, on January 1, 1995.

b. Cubs paid the market price to acquire 3,000 shares of the common stock of Mets, Inc. On this date Mets had 10,000 shares of stock outstanding, and they were trading on the market at $25 per share. During 1995 Mets reported net income of $90,000 and declared and paid dividends of $40,000.

■ REQUIRED

1. What is the legal form of the business combination with Cardinals, Inc.? Explain your answer.

2. Compute the amount of goodwill arising from the purchase of Cardinals.

3. Prepare the entry on Cubs' books on January 1, 1995, to record the purchase of Cardinals.

4. Prepare the entry on Cubs' books on January 1, 1995, to record the purchase of shares of stock of Mets, Inc.

5. Prepare the entries on Cubs' books at the end of 1995 to account for its investment in Mets.

[9] 1992 Whirlpool Annual Report, p. 41.

■ SOLUTION TO REVIEW PROBLEM

1. The business combination with Cardinals is a statutory merger because Cubs is purchasing the assets and assuming the debts of the other company. Cardinals will cease to exist and thus is being merged into Cubs.

2. Computation of goodwill:

Cost		$750,000
Fair value of net assets acquired:		
Current assets	$150,000	
Land	200,000	
Plant and equipment	500,000	
Current liabilities	(50,000)	
Long-term debt	(250,000	550,000
Excess of cost over fair value of net assets acquired (goodwill)		$200,000

3. Entry on Cubs' books to record merger of Cardinals:

1995
Jan. 1

Current Assets	150,000 ⎫	
Land	200,000 ⎪ 1,050,000	
Plant and Equipment	500,000 ⎬	
Goodwill	200,000 ⎭	
Current Liabilities		50,000 ⎫
Long-term Debt		250,000 ⎬ 300,000
Cash		750,000

To record purchase of Cardinals, Inc.

Assets	=	Liabilities	+	Owners' Equity
+ 1,050,000		+ 300,000		
− 750,000				

4. Entry to record purchase of shares of stock of Mets:

1995
Jan. 1

Long-term Investment	75,000	
Cash		75,000

To record purchase of 3,000 shares of stock at $25 per share.

Assets	=	Liabilities	+	Owners' Equity
+ 75,000				
− 75,000				

5. Entries at the end of the first year:

1995
Dec. 31

Long-term Investment	27,000	
Equity Income		27,000

To record share of income of investee:

$$(3,000/10,000) \times \$90,000 = .3 \times \$90,000$$

Assets	=	Liabilities	+	Owners' Equity
+ 27,000				+ 27,000

1995
Dec. 31   Cash   12,000
      Long-term Investment   12,000
    To record share of dividends paid by investee:
      .3 × $40,000

Assets	=	Liabilities	+	Owners' Equity
+ 12,000				
− 12,000				

GUIDANCE ANSWERS TO ACCOUNTING FOR YOUR DECISIONS

YOU ARE THE BOND ANALYST

One reason could be that long-term interest rates have risen, which reduces the value of all bonds of similar maturity. Another reason could be that the industry that Simpson is part of has come on hard times, requiring the bond rating agencies to reduce the rating on Simpson bonds. Also, the bonds could have received a lower rating because Simpson itself is having trouble servicing its debt.

YOU ARE THE MONEY MANAGER

One way to minimize this risk is to invest in foreign companies whose currency is stable in relation to the U.S. dollar. Another way to minimize the risk is to buy shares of stock in foreign companies denominated in U.S. dollars. One way to do this is to purchase American Depositary Receipts (ADRs), which trade on the New York Stock Exchange. Foreign currency risk can also be hedged using the futures and options markets. Short of all of this, foreign currency risk is a downside to international investing and it cannot be removed entirely as a risk. However, many areas of the world are growing much faster than the United States—such as Latin America and the Far East—and so it is an area of investment that cannot be ignored.

CHAPTER HIGHLIGHTS

1. (LO 1) Corporations invest for various reasons in the debt and equity securities of other companies. Some investments are made without the intention of influencing or controlling the other company. Accountants classify these investments as either held-to-maturity securities, trading securities, or available-for-sale securities. Other investments are made to exert significant influence over the policies of the other companies. The equity method is used in these instances. Finally, companies may buy enough of the common stock of another company to control it. This situation normally results in the presentation of consolidated financial statements.

2. (LO 2) Held-to-maturity securities are bonds that are purchased with the intention of holding them until they mature. The principles that govern the accounting by the issuer of these bonds apply as well to an investor in bonds. The amortized cost method results in the recognition of periodic interest income and the amortization of any premium or discount over the remaining life of the bonds.

3. (LO 3) Trading securities are stocks and bonds held for the short term with the intention of profiting from appreciation in their trading price. Dividends received are recognized as income. Trading securities are adjusted to their fair value at the end of each period, and any increase or decrease in value is reported on the income statement.

4. **(LO 4)** Available-for-sale securities are investments that are not classified as either held-to-maturity or trading securities. The accounting and reporting requirements for this category are similar to the rules for trading securities. The primary difference is that unrealized gains and losses from holding available-for-sale securities (changes in fair value from one period to the next) are not recognized on the income statement. Instead, these amounts are reported as a separate component of stockholders' equity.

5. **(LO 5)** The equity method is used to account for an investment in the common stock of another company that allows the investor to exert significant influence over the investee. The general rule is that the method should be used when the investor owns at least 20% of the common stock of the investee. Under the equity method, the investor recognizes as income its proportionate share of the income of the investee. Dividends received from the investee reduce the investment account.

6. **(LO 6)** Corporations combine for many different reasons. Three different legal forms of combination are possible. In a statutory merger, one company goes out of existence, and in a statutory consolidation, both combining entities cease to exist and are replaced by a new entity. In a stock acquisition, one company buys the stock of the other and both entities survive. Regardless of the legal form, one of two different accounting methods is used to record a business combination. A pooling of interests is used in limited situations in which shares of stock in the two companies are exchanged. The purchase method occurs when one company uses cash, other assets, or debt to acquire the other. In a purchase, all assets and liabilities are recorded at their fair values. Goodwill is recognized for the excess of the purchase price over the fair value of the net assets acquired.

7. **(LO 7)** When two companies combine by means of a stock acquisition, both survive the combination even though one company controls the other. Because of this control, consolidated statements are prepared to report on the two entities as if they were one. Consolidated financial statements are prepared to reflect the combined position and results of operations for a parent and its subsidiaries. Any intercompany transactions are eliminated in the consolidation process.

8. **(LO 8)** A foreign currency transaction is one that is billed in a foreign currency. When a company either agrees to accept or to make payment in a foreign currency at a later date, it will recognize a gain or a loss if the exchange rate changes between the time of the original transaction and the settlement date.

9. **(LO 9)** Prior to consolidation, financial statements for a foreign subsidiary must be restated to conform to accounting standards in the United States if any differences exist. After this, the statements must be translated from the local currency into the reporting currency, the U.S. dollar. Assuming that the local currency is the functional currency, income statement items are translated using the average exchange rate for the period. Assets and liabilities are translated using the exchange rate at the end of the period. A translation adjustment results from this process and is reported in stockholders' equity.

10. **(LO 10)** Many companies are required to disclose supplementary information in their annual report for their operations in different industries and in different geographic markets. The purpose of these disclosures is to allow the user of consolidated financial statements to analyze the various segments of the business on a disaggregated basis. Disclosures about major customers and significant export sales are also required.

KEY TERMS QUIZ

Select one of the following key terms used in the chapter and fill in the appropriate blank to the left of each description. The solution appears at the end of the chapter.

Subsidiary   Parent
Wholly owned subsidiary   Affiliate
Debt securities   Equity securities
Equity method   Consolidated financial statements
Held-to-maturity securities   Trading securities
Available-for-sale securities   Amortized cost method
Horizontal combination   Vertical combination
Conglomerate   Statutory merger
Statutory consolidation   Stock acquisition
Purchase method   Pooling of interests method
Goodwill   Minority interest
Exchange rate   Foreign currency transaction
Foreign currency translation   Functional currency
Translation adjustment

_____ **1.** A combination of a company with either a supplier or a customer.

_____ **2.** An accounting approach for recording a business combination that is used when one company uses cash, other assets, or debt to acquire the other company.

_____ **3.** A business combination in which a new entity is created to carry on the activities of the entities involved in the combination.

_____ **4.** Securities issued by a corporation as a form of borrowing.

_____ **5.** A method of accounting for investments in which income is recognized as a proportionate share of the income of the investee.

_____ **6.** A combination of companies with operations in different industries.

_____ **7.** Securities issued by a corporation that represent a form of ownership in the business.

_____ **8.** A separate legal entity controlled by another entity.

_____ **9.** A company that has enough of its stock held by another company to give the other entity significant influence over it.

_____ **10.** A business combination in which only one of the two entities survives.

_____ **11.** A subsidiary in which the parent owns all of the common stock.

_____ **12.** A business combination in which one company acquires a majority of the common stock of the other company.

_____ **13.** The amount needed to balance the two sides of a balance sheet when financial statements are translated from one currency into another currency.

_____ **14.** The process of restating the financial statements of a company from one currency to another.

_____ **15.** An accounting approach to recording a business combination that is sometimes used when shares of stock in the two companies are exchanged.

_____ **16.** A method of accounting for investments in bonds in which the investment account is adjusted periodically to recognize the amortization of premium or discount.

_____ **17.** The owners' equity of a subsidiary not attributable to the interest of the parent.

_____ **18.** An entity that controls another entity by ownership of a majority of the other company's common stock.

_____ **19.** Stocks and bonds of other companies bought and held for the purpose of selling them in the near term to generate profits on appreciation in their price.

_____ **20.** A measure of the relative worth of two different currencies.

_____ **21.** Stocks and bonds that are not classified as either held-to-maturity or trading securities.

_____ **22.** Statements that report on the parent corporation and any separate legal entities called *subsidiaries*.

_____ **23.** A transaction in which a company agrees to receive or make payment in a foreign currency.

_____ **24.** The currency of the primary economic environment in which an entity operates.

_____ **25.** Investments in bonds of other companies in which the investor has the positive intent and the ability to hold the securities to maturity.

_____ **26.** An intangible asset that represents the excess of the purchase price for a business over the fair value of the net assets acquired.

_____ **27.** A combination of businesses that are in competition with each other.

ALTERNATE TERMS

AFFILIATE Equity investee.

DEBT SECURITIES Bonds.

EQUITY SECURITIES Common stock, preferred stock.

MERGERS AND ACQUISITIONS Business combinations.

QUESTIONS

1. Stanzel Corp. purchased 1,000 shares of IBM common stock. What will determine whether the shares are classified as trading securities or available-for-sale securities?

2. How does a company decide when to use the amortized cost method to account for an investment in bonds? What is the amortized cost method?

3. A company buys $10,000 face value of Ace Corp. bonds at 98. In addition, it incurs $300 of brokerage fees in making the purchase. What amount should the company record as the cost of the investment?

4. Basset, Inc., purchases 5,000 shares of the 20,000 shares of common stock of Beagle Corp. What method of accounting should Basset use? What is the justification for this method?

5. What is the theoretical justification for preparing consolidated financial statements?

6. What is the primary difference in the accounting requirements for trading securities and available-for-sale securities? How is the primary difference justified?

7. Why are changes in the fair value of trading securities recorded in the account Unrealized Gains/Losses—Trading Securities even though the gains and losses are reported on the income statement?

8. Why should dividends received from an investee that is accounted for using the equity method be treated as a reduction in the investment account? Why aren't the dividends recognized as income?

9. Can you give an example of a horizontal combination that would occur by the combination of two real-world companies? A vertical combination?

10. What is the difference between a statutory merger and a statutory consolidation?

11. Which is the only one of the three legal forms of business combination that requires the preparation of periodic consolidated financial statements? Explain your answer.

12. Why do accountants record goodwill only when a business is purchased?

13. Why would one company pay more than the fair market value for the net assets of another company?

14. A parent buys raw materials on account from one of its subsidiaries. Why would any accounts payable on the books of the parent and any accounts receivable on the books of the subsidiary be eliminated when preparing consolidated financial statements?

15. Should minority interest be classified on a consolidated balance sheet as a liability or as a component of stockholders' equity? Explain your answer.

16. Do all sales by U.S. companies to foreign companies result in foreign currency transactions? Explain your answer.

17. A U.S. corporation sells on account to a London firm with payment in British pounds. The exchange rate at the time of the sale was $1.50 per pound and at the time of collection of the account was $1.60. Will the U.S. corporation report a foreign exchange gain or loss when it collects the receivable? Explain your answer.

18. Assuming that the local currency is the functional currency, what exchange rate is used to translate income statement items? What is the rationale for using this rate?

19. Assuming that the local currency is the functional currency, what exchange rate is used to translate balance sheet items? Are all items on the balance sheet translated at the same rate? Explain your answer.

20. What is the purpose of requiring disclosure of a significant amount of sales a company makes to a single customer?

21. What is the inherent weakness in consolidated financial statements that is addressed by supplemental disclosure of segmental information for a company?

EXERCISES

(LO 2) EXERCISE 13-1 INVESTMENT IN BONDS—STRAIGHT-LINE AMORTIZATION

On January 1, 1995, Marquette Corp. purchased $50,000 face value of the bonds of Georgetown, Inc. The bonds are dated January 1, 1995, and have a term of 20 years. They were purchased for $41,506, which reflects an effective rate of interest of 10%. Interest of 8% is paid annually on December 31. Marquette will use the straight-line method to amortize any discount or premium.

1. Prepare the journal entry on Marquette's records on January 1, 1995, to account for the purchase of the bonds.

2. Prepare the journal entry on Marquette's records on December 31, 1995, to account for the receipt of interest and the amortization of any discount or premium.

3. Why was Marquette able to buy the bonds for less than it will receive when they mature?

■ REQUIRED

(LO 2) EXERCISE 13-2 INVESTMENT IN BONDS—EFFECTIVE INTEREST AMORTIZATION

Assume the same facts as in Exercise 13-1, except that Marquette uses the effective interest method to amortize any discount or premium.

1. Prepare the journal entry on Marquette's records on January 1, 1995, to account for the purchase of the bonds.

2. Prepare the journal entry, or entries, on Marquette's records on December 31, 1995, to account for the receipt of interest and the amortization of any discount or premium.

3. Why was Marquette able to buy the bonds for less than it will receive when they mature?

■ REQUIRED

(LO 2) EXERCISE 13-3 INVESTMENT IN BONDS—STRAIGHT-LINE AMORTIZATION

On January 1, 1995, Xavier Corp. purchased $100,000 face value of the bonds of Fordham, Inc. The bonds are dated January 1, 1995, and have a term of 10 years. The bonds were purchased for $113,400, which reflects an effective rate of interest of 8%. Interest of 10% is paid annually on December 31. Xavier uses the straight-line method to amortize any discount or premium.

1. Prepare the journal entry on Xavier's records on January 1, 1995, to account for the purchase of the bonds.

2. Prepare the journal entry on Xavier's records on December 31, 1995, to account for the receipt of interest and the amortization of any discount or premium.

3. Why was Xavier willing to pay more for the bonds than it will receive when they mature?

■ REQUIRED

(LO 2) EXERCISE 13-4 INVESTMENT IN BONDS—EFFECTIVE INTEREST AMORTIZATION

Assume the same facts as in Exercise 13-3, except that Xavier uses the effective interest method to amortize any discount or premium.

1. Prepare the journal entry on Xavier's records on January 1, 1995, to account for the purchase of the bonds.

2. Prepare the journal entry, or entries, on Xavier's records on December 31, 1995, to account for the receipt of interest and the amortization of any discount or premium.

3. Why was Xavier willing to pay more for the bonds than it will receive when they mature?

■ REQUIRED

(LO 3) EXERCISE 13-5 INVESTMENT IN STOCK

On December 1, 1995, Chicago Corp. purchased 1,000 shares of the preferred stock of Denver Corp. for $40 per share. Chicago expected the price of the stock to increase over the next few months and plans to sell it for a profit. On December 20, 1995, Denver declares a dividend of $1 per share to be paid on January 15, 1996. On December 31, 1995, Chicago's accounting year-end, the Denver stock is trading on the market at $42 per share. Chicago sells the stock on February 12, 1996, at a price of $45 per share.

REQUIRED

1. Should Chicago classify its investment as held-to-maturity, trading, or available-for-sale securities? Explain your answer.

2. Prepare all necessary entries on Chicago's books in connection with its investment, beginning with the purchase on December 1, 1995, and ending with the sale on February 12, 1996. Indicate next to each account title in your entries whether the account appears on the balance sheet (BS) or the income statement (IS).

3. How should Chicago classify its investment on its December 31, 1995, balance sheet?

(LO 4) EXERCISE 13-6 INVESTMENT IN STOCK

On August 15, 1995, Cubs Corp. purchases 5,000 shares of common stock in Sox, Inc., at a market price of $15 per share. In addition, Cubs pays brokerage fees of $1,000. Cubs plans to hold the stock indefinitely rather than as a part of its active trading portfolio. The market value of the stock is $13 per share on December 31, 1995, the end of Cub's accounting year. On July 8, 1996, Cubs sells the Sox stock for $10 per share.

REQUIRED

1. Should Cubs classify its investment as held-to-maturity, trading, or available-for-sale securities? Explain your answer.

2. Prepare all necessary entries on Cub's books in connection with its investment, beginning with the purchase on August 15, 1995, and ending with the sale on July 8, 1996. Indicate next to each account title in your entries whether the account appears on the balance sheet (BS) or the income statement (IS).

3. How should Cubs classify its investment on its December 31, 1995, balance sheet?

(LO 5) EXERCISE 13-7 EQUITY METHOD

On January 1, 1995, Beaman buys on the open market 3,000 shares of common stock in Roberts at $15 per share. Beaman incurs $1,000 in various fees to make the purchase. Roberts has 10,000 shares of stock outstanding on this date. Roberts declares a dividend of $1 per share each quarter in 1995 and reports net income for the year of $60,000.

REQUIRED

1. What amount should Beaman report on its December 31, 1995, balance sheet for its investment in Roberts? Explain your answer.

2. Compute the amount of gain or loss Beaman would have if it sold all of its Roberts shares on January 10, 1996, for $20 per share. Explain your answer.

(LO 6) EXERCISE 13-8 BUSINESS COMBINATIONS AND GOODWILL

On January 1, 1995, Keller Corp. purchases all of the assets and assumes all of the liabilities of Newton, Inc. for $400,000 in cash. After this date, Newton ceases to exist as an entity. On this date, Newton's balance sheet reported total assets of $500,000 and total liabilities of $200,000. According to an appraisal performed on this date, all assets are recorded at their fair values except for a parcel of real estate. It is included on the balance sheet at a cost of $100,000, but an appraisal indicates that it is worth $140,000.

REQUIRED

1. What type of business combination is this legally? Explain your answer.

2. Determine the amount at which Keller should record the real estate on its books.

3. Compute the amount of goodwill Keller should recognize in connection with this business combination.

4. Why would Keller pay more than fair market value to acquire the net assets of Newton?

(LO 8) EXERCISE 13-9 FOREIGN EXCHANGE GAINS AND LOSSES

For each of the following situations, determine the dollar amount of foreign exchange gain or loss that the U.S. company would recognize on the settlement date of each of the following foreign currency transactions. Also indicate whether it is a foreign exchange gain (G) or a foreign exchange loss (L).

_____ **1.** On August 8, Boston sells merchandise to a London firm. The buyer agrees to pay Boston 10,000 British pounds on September 30. The exchange rate on August 8 is $1.50 per British pound and then falls to $1.40 on September 30.

_____ **2.** On May 3, San Diego sells inventory to a Tokyo company. The buyer agrees to pay 100,000 Japanese yen on June 15. The exchange rate on May 3 is $.008 per Japanese yen and then rises to $.009 on June 15.

_____ **3.** On March 5, St. Louis buys supplies from a Mexican vendor. The seller agrees to accept 50,000 pesos on March 31. The exchange rate on March 5 is $.30 per Mexican peso and then rises to $.35 per peso on March 31.

_____ **4.** On October 7, Seattle buys inventory from a company in Germany. The German company agrees to accept 20,000 German marks on November 15. The exchange rate on October 7 is $.60 per German mark; it falls to $.50 per mark on November 15.

(LO 9) EXERCISE 13-10 TRANSLATION OF A FOREIGN SUBSIDIARY

Carson Corp. opened a new subsidiary in France at the beginning of the year with an investment of 200,000 French francs. Capital stock in the same amount was issued. At the time, this was equivalent to $36,000 (that is, the exchange rate at this time was $.18 per French franc). The functional currency for the subsidiary is the local currency, the French franc. The exchange rate at the end of the year had risen to $.20. At the end of the year, the subsidiary's balance sheet reported assets of 400,000 francs and liabilities of 80,000 francs. The subsidiary's net income for the year amounted to the equivalent of $10,000.

1. What dollar amount should appear for total assets on a balance sheet for the subsidiary at the end of the year translated from French francs to U.S. dollars?

■ **REQUIRED**

2. What dollar amount should appear on the same balance sheet for the translation adjustment?

3. Interpret the translation adjustment. How does it affect the subsidiary's net income and its cash flow?

MULTI-CONCEPT EXERCISES

(LO 1, 3, 4, 5, 7) EXERCISE 13-11 CLASSIFICATION OF INVESTMENTS

Red Oak makes the following investments in the stock of other companies during 1995. For each investment, indicate how it would be accounted for and reported on using the following designations: trading security (T), available-for-sale security (AS), equity investee (E), or a subsidiary included in consolidated statements (S).

_____ **1.** 500 shares of ABC common stock to be held for short-term share appreciation.

_____ **2.** 20,000 shares of the 50,000 shares of Ace common stock to be held for the long term.

_____ **3.** 100 shares of Creston preferred stock to be held for an indefinite period of time.

_____ **4.** 80,000 of the 100,000 shares of Orient common stock.

_____ **5.** 10,000 of the 40,000 shares of Omaha preferred stock to be held for the long term.

(LO 2, 3, 4) EXERCISE 13-12 CLASSIFICATION OF INVESTMENTS

Fill in the blanks below to indicate whether each of the following investments should be classified as a held-to-maturity security (HM), a trading security (T), or an available-for-sale security (AS):

_____ **1.** Shares of IBM stock to be held indefinitely.

_____ **2.** GM bonds due in 10 years. The intent is to hold them until they mature.

_____ **3.** Shares of Motorola stock. Plans are to hold the stock until the price goes up by 10% and then sell it.

_____ **4.** Ford Motor Company bonds due in 15 years. The bonds are part of a portfolio that turns over on the average of every 60 days.

_____ **5.** Chrysler bonds due in ten years. Plans are to hold them indefinitely.

PROBLEMS

(LO 6) PROBLEM 13-1 BUSINESS COMBINATION

On March 1, 1995, Mantle, Inc., a software developer, paid $2,700,000 to acquire all of the assets and assume all of the liabilities of Maris Corp., a regional competitor. After the acquisition, Maris ceased to exist as a separate entity. The individual balance sheets of the two companies prior to the merger were as follows:

	MANTLE, INC.	MARIS CORP.
Cash	$2,900,000	$ 500,000
Accounts receivable	2,200,000	750,000
Prepayments	210,000	120,000
Furniture and fixtures	1,000,000	250,000
Copyrights	3,500,000	1,200,000
Total assets	$9,810,000	$2,820,000
Accounts payable	$ 200,000	$ 120,000
Long-term notes payable	2,400,000	1,200,000
Common stock, $1 par	1,000,000	500,000
Retained earnings	6,210,000	1,000,000
Total equities	$9,810,000	$2,820,000

Mantle is able to determine that all of Maris' assets and liabilities are on its books at their fair values with the exception of the copyrights. Mantle estimates that they are worth $2,000,000.

■ **REQUIRED**

1. What type of business combination is this from a legal perspective? Explain your answer.

2. Compute the amount of goodwill that Mantle should record in connection with the combination.

3. Prepare the journal entry on Mantle's books to record the combination.

4. How does the estimate of the fair value assigned to the copyrights of Maris affect the amount of goodwill that is recognized? Why is it important for Mantle to have reliable estimates of the values of each of these assets?

(LO 7) PROBLEM 13-2 CONSOLIDATED FINANCIAL STATEMENTS

On June 30, 1995, Waylon, Inc., buys all of the outstanding stock of Willie Corp. for $300 million in cash. Prior to the acquisition, balance sheets for each of the two companies appeared as follows (amounts are in millions of dollars):

	JUNE 30, 1995 WAYLON	WILLIE
Cash	$350	$ 30
Accounts receivable	100	50
Inventory	80	60
Land	200	100
Buildings, net	250	150
Total assets	$980	$390
Accounts payable	$ 80	$ 20
Long-term debt	200	100
Capital stock, $10 par	100	50
Additional paid-in capital	400	150
Retained earnings	200	70
Total equities	$980	$390

All of the recorded values for Willie's assets are equivalent to their fair market values, with the exception of the land. It has an estimated fair value of $120 million.

REQUIRED

1. From a legal perspective, what type of business combination is this? Explain your answer.
2. Prepare the journal entry on Waylon's books to record its purchase of the Willie stock.
3. Compute the amount of goodwill that should be recognized on a consolidated balance sheet prepared immediately after the combination.
4. Prepare a consolidated balance sheet for Waylon and Willie.

(LO 7) PROBLEM 13-3 CONSOLIDATED FINANCIAL STATEMENTS

On January 1, 1995, Tucker, Inc., acquires all of the outstanding common stock of Campton Corp. at a price of $45 per share. The fair values of Campton's current assets and its liabilities are equal to their book values. However, Campton's land, buildings, and intangibles were appraised at $200 million, $350 million, and $150 million, respectively.

Prior to the acquisition, the individual condensed balance sheets for each of the two companies appeared as follows (all amounts are in millions of dollars):

	TUCKER, INC.	CAMPTON, INC.
Current assets	$ 600	$ 50
Land	400	150
Buildings, net of depreciation	800	300
Intangibles	500	100
Total assets	$2,300	$600
Current liabilities	$ 400	$100
Long-term notes payable	700	250
Common stock, $10 par	500	100
Retained earnings	700	$150
Total equities	$2,300	$600

■ REQUIRED

I. What type of business combination is this from a legal perspective? Explain your answer.

2. Prepare the journal entry on Tucker's books to record the acquisition of the Campton stock.

3. Prepare balance sheets for each of the two companies as they would appear immediately after the acquisition.

4. Prepare a consolidated balance sheet as it would appear immediately after the acquisition.

5. For purposes of a consolidated income statement, what is the proper accounting treatment for any goodwill arising from the combination?

(LO 8) PROBLEM 13-4 FOREIGN CURRENCY TRANSACTIONS

During January 1995, Rogers, Inc., entered into the following transactions with foreign companies:

Jan. 5   Purchased inventory from a company in Toronto. Rogers agrees to pay the supplier 20,000 Canadian dollars by the end of the month. The exchange rate on January 5 is $.90 per Canadian dollar.

Jan. 12   Sold inventory to a company in Mexico. The company agrees to pay Rogers 50,000 pesos by the end of the month. The exchange rate on January 12 is $.25 per Mexican peso.

Jan. 15   Sold inventory to a company in London. The firm agrees to pay Rogers $15,000 by January 25. The exchange rate on January 15 is $1.30 per British pound.

Jan. 18   Purchased inventory from a company in France for 15,000 French francs and immediately made payment. The exchange rate on this date was $.20 per French franc.

Jan. 25   Received payment for inventory sold on January 15. The exchange rate on January 25 is $1.40 per British pound.

Jan. 30   Paid for inventory purchased on January 5. The exchange rate on January 30 is $.95 per Canadian dollar.

Jan. 31   Received payment for inventory sold on January 12. The exchange rate on January 31 is $.30 per Mexican peso.

■ REQUIRED

I. Prepare all necessary journal entries on Rogers' books during the month of January to record these transactions. Assume Rogers uses a periodic inventory system.

2. Compute the net amount of foreign exchange gain or loss Rogers would report on an income statement for the month of January.

3. How can a company do business with foreign suppliers and customers but avoid the risks associated with dealing in foreign currency?

(LO 9) PROBLEM 13-5 TRANSLATION OF A FOREIGN SUBSIDIARY

On January 1, 1995, Smith Enterprises, a large New York–based conglomerate, opened a new subsidiary in Germany by issuing common stock for a total of 1,000,000 German marks. The subsidiary, Thomas, Inc., will produce parts for one of Smith's products. Thomas' income statement for 1995 and a balance sheet prepared as of December 31, 1995, are as follows:

THOMAS, INC.
INCOME STATEMENT
FOR THE YEAR ENDED DECEMBER 31, 1995
(ALL AMOUNTS IN GERMAN MARKS)

Sales revenue	6,000,000
Cost of goods sold	3,200,000
Gross profit	2,800,000
Selling and administrative expenses	1,700,000
Interest expense	200,000
Net income	900,000

THOMAS, INC.
BALANCE SHEET
AS OF DECEMBER 31, 1995
(ALL AMOUNTS IN GERMAN MARKS)

Cash	600,000	Accounts payable	500,000
Accounts receivable	900,000	Notes payable	1,600,000
Inventories	800,000	Common stock	1,000,000
Plant, net	1,700,000	Retained earnings	900,000
Totals	4,000,000	Totals	4,000,000

At the beginning of 1995, the exchange rate was $.60 per German mark and at the end of the year, it was $.40. The average exchange rate for the year was $.50. Assume that the German mark is the functional currency.

■ **REQUIRED**

1. Prepare an income statement for Thomas translated from German marks into U.S. dollars.

2. Prepare a balance sheet as of December 31, 1995, for Thomas, translated from German marks into U.S. dollars.

3. Why is it necessary to create the account Translation Adjustment? Is it an addition to or a deduction from stockholders' equity? What are the cash flow implications to the parent, Smith, from this adjustment?

MULTI-CONCEPT PROBLEMS

(LO 2, 3) PROBLEM 13-6 INVESTMENTS IN BONDS AND STOCK

Iowa Corp. enters into the following transactions during 1995:

July 1   Paid $9,450 to acquire on the open market $10,000 face value of Idaho bonds. The bonds have a stated annual interest rate of 6% with interest paid semiannually on June 30 and December 31. The remaining life of the bonds on the date of purchase is 5½ years.

Oct. 23   Purchased 600 shares of Colorado common stock at $20 per share.

Nov. 21   Purchased 200 shares of Montana preferred stock at $30 per share.

Dec. 10   Received dividends of $1.50 per share on the Colorado stock and $2.00 per share on the Montana stock.

Dec. 28   Sold 400 shares of Colorado common stock at $25 per share.

Dec. 31   Received interest from the Idaho bonds.

Dec. 31   Noted market price of $29 per share for the Colorado stock and $26 per share for the Montana stock.

REQUIRED

1. Prepare all necessary journal entries on Iowa's records to account for its investments during 1995. Iowa classifies the bonds as held-to-maturity securities and all stock investments as trading securities. The straight-line method is used to amortize any bond discount or premium.

2. Prepare a partial balance sheet at December 31 to indicate the proper presentation of the investments.

3. Indicate the items, and the amount of each, that will appear on the 1995 income statement relative to the investments.

(LO 3, 4) PROBLEM 13-7 INVESTMENTS IN STOCK

Atlas Superstores occasionally finds itself with excess cash to invest and consequently entered into the following transactions during 1995:

Jan. 15   Purchased 200 shares of Sears common stock at $50 per share, plus $500 in commissions.

May 23   Received dividends of $2 per share on the Sears stock.

June 1   Purchased 100 shares of Ford Motor Co. stock at $74 per share, plus $300 in commissions.

Oct. 20   Sold all of the Sears stock at $42 per share, less commissions of $400.

Dec. 15   Received notification from Ford Motor Co. that a $1.50 per share dividend had been declared. The checks will be mailed to stockholders on January 10, 1996.

Dec. 31   Noted that the Ford Motor Co. stock was quoted on the stock exchange at $85 per share.

REQUIRED

1. Prepare journal entries on the books of Atlas Superstores during 1995 to record these transactions, including any necessary entry on December 15 when the dividend is declared and at the end of the year. Assume that Atlas categorizes all investments as available-for-sale securities.

2. What is the total amount of income that Atlas should recognize from its investments during 1995, including any income effect from the entry on December 31?

3. Assume all of the same facts except that Atlas categorizes all investments as trading securities. How would your answer to part 2 change? Explain why your answer would change.

(LO 5, 9) PROBLEM 13-8 FOREIGN EQUITY INVESTEE

Edgar Enterprises holds 30% of the common stock of Kyoto Corp., an affiliate in Japan. The Investment in Kyoto was reported on Edgar's December 31, 1994, balance sheet at $5 million. Edgar's 30% investment gives it the ability to exert significant influence over Kyoto. The affiliate presents the following income statement for the year ended December 31, 1995 (all amounts are stated in millions of Japanese yen):

KYOTO CORP.
INCOME STATEMENT
FOR THE YEAR ENDED DECEMBER 31, 1995

Revenues	2,500
Operating expenses	(1,500)
Interest expense	(400)
Net income	600

On June 1, 1995, Kyoto declared and paid dividends totaling 200 million yen. On December 31, 1995, it declared and paid another dividend of 150 million yen. The Japanese yen is the functional currency. The following exchange rates are available:

DATE	EXCHANGE RATE PER JAPANESE YEN
January 1	$.0100
June 1	.0095
December 31	.0080
Average for the year	.0090

■REQUIRED

1. Translate Kyoto's income statement from Japanese yen into U.S. dollars. Why is it necessary for Edgar to translate the statement?

2. What amount of income, in dollars, should Edgar recognize from its investment in Kyoto for 1995?

3. At what amount should Edgar report the Investment in Kyoto account on its December 31, 1995, balance sheet? Support your answer with any necessary computations. (*Hint:* Dividends should be translated at the exchange rate in effect when they were paid.)

ALTERNATE PROBLEMS

(LO 6) PROBLEM 13-1A BUSINESS COMBINATION

On March 1, 1995, Mays, Inc., a software developer, paid $5,400,000 to acquire all of the assets and assume all of the liabilities of Aaron Corp., a regional competitor. After the acquisition, Aaron ceased to exist as a separate entity. The individual balance sheets of the two companies prior to the merger were as follows:

	MAYS, INC.	AARON CORP.
Cash	$ 5,800,000	$1,000,000
Accounts receivable	4,400,000	1,500,000
Prepayments	420,000	240,000
Furniture and fixtures	2,000,000	500,000
Copyrights	7,000,000	2,400,000
Total assets	$19,620,000	$5,640,000
Accounts payable	$ 400,000	$ 240,000
Long-term notes payable	4,800,000	2,400,000
Common stock, $1 par	2,000,000	1,000,000
Retained earnings	12,420,000	2,000,000
Total equities	$19,620,000	$5,640,000

Mays is able to determine that all of Aaron's assets and liabilities are on its books at their fair values with the exception of the copyrights. Mays estimates that they are worth $4,000,000.

REQUIRED
1. What type of business combination is this from a legal perspective? Explain your answer.

2. Compute the amount of goodwill that Mays should record in connection with the combination.

3. Prepare the journal entry on Mays' books to record the combination.

4. How does the estimate of the fair value assigned to the copyrights of Aaron affect the amount of goodwill that is recognized? Why is it important for Mays to have reliable estimates of the values of each of these assets?

(LO 7) PROBLEM 13-2A CONSOLIDATED FINANCIAL STATEMENTS

On January 1, 1995, Travis, Inc., buys all of the outstanding stock of Tritt Corp. for $490 million in cash. Prior to the acquisition, balance sheets for each of the two companies appeared as follows (amounts are in millions of dollars):

| | JANUARY 1, 1995 | |
	TRAVIS	TRITT
Cash	$ 550	$ 60
Accounts receivable	120	80
Inventory	200	90
Land	300	150
Buildings, net	450	250
Total assets	$1,620	$630
Accounts payable	$ 90	$ 60
Long-term debt	500	150
Capital stock, $10 par	200	100
Additional paid-in capital	400	200
Retained earnings	430	120
Total equities	$1,620	$630

All of the recorded values for Tritt's assets are equivalent to their fair market values, with the exception of the land. It has an estimated fair value of $180 million.

REQUIRED
1. From a legal perspective, what type of business combination is this? Explain your answer.

2. Prepare the journal entry on Travis' books to record its purchase of the Tritt stock.

3. Compute the amount of goodwill that should be recognized on a consolidated balance sheet prepared immediately after the combination.

4. Prepare a consolidated balance sheet for Travis and Tritt.

(LO 7) PROBLEM 13-3A CONSOLIDATED FINANCIAL STATEMENTS

On January 1, 1995, Huskie, Inc., acquires all of the outstanding common stock of Carrier Corp. at a price of $50 per share. The fair values of Carrier's current assets and its liabilities are equal to their book values. However, Carrier's land, buildings, and intangibles were appraised at $400 million, $700 million, and $300 million, respectively.

Prior to the acquisition, the individual condensed balance sheets for each of the two companies appeared as follows (all amounts are in millions of dollars):

	HUSKIE, INC.	CARRIER CORP.
Current assets	$1,200	$ 100
Land	800	300
Buildings, net of depreciation	1,600	600
Intangibles	1,000	200
Total assets	$4,600	$1,200
Current liabilities	$ 800	$ 200
Long-term notes payable	1,400	500
Common stock, $10 par	1,000	200
Retained earnings	1,400	300
Total equities	$4,600	$1,200

■ REQUIRED

1. What type of business combination is this from a legal perspective? Explain your answer.

2. Prepare the journal entry on Huskie's books to record the acquisition of the Carrier stock.

3. Prepare balance sheets for each of the two companies as they would appear immediately after the acquisition.

4. Prepare a consolidated balance sheet as it would appear immediately after the acquisition.

5. For purposes of a consolidated income statement, what is the proper accounting treatment for any goodwill arising from the combination?

(LO 8) PROBLEM 13-4A FOREIGN CURRENCY TRANSACTIONS

During January 1995, Roscoe, Inc., entered into the following transactions with foreign companies:

Jan. 5   Purchased inventory from a company in Toronto. Roscoe agrees to pay the supplier 10,000 Canadian dollars by the end of the month. The exchange rate on January 5 is $.95 per Canadian dollar.

Jan. 12   Sold inventory to a company in Mexico. The company agrees to pay Roscoe 60,000 pesos by the end of the month. The exchange rate on January 12 is $.30 per Mexican peso.

Jan. 15   Sold inventory to a company in London. The firm agrees to pay Roscoe $25,000 by January 25. The exchange rate on January 15 is $1.30 per British pound.

Jan. 18   Purchased inventory from a company in France for 20,000 French francs and immediately made payment. The exchange rate on this date was $.25 per French franc.

Jan. 25   Received payment for inventory sold on January 15. The exchange rate on January 25 is $1.40 per British pound.

Jan. 30   Paid for inventory purchased on January 5. The exchange rate on January 30 is $.90 per Canadian dollar.

Jan. 31   Received payment for inventory sold on January 12. The exchange rate on January 31 is \$.40 per Mexican peso.

■ REQUIRED

1. Prepare all necessary journal entries on Roscoe's books during the month of January to record these transactions. Assume Roscoe uses a periodic inventory system.

2. Compute the net amount of foreign exchange gain or loss Roscoe would report on an income statement for the month of January.

3. How can a company do business with foreign suppliers and customers but avoid the risks associated with dealing in foreign currency?

(LO 9) PROBLEM 13-5A TRANSLATION OF A FOREIGN SUBSIDIARY

On January 1, 1995, Aikman Enterprises, a large Chicago-based conglomerate, opened a new subsidiary in London by issuing common stock for a total of 500,000 British pounds. The subsidiary, Kelly, Ltd., will produce parts for one of Aikman's products. Kelly's income statement for 1995 and a balance sheet prepared as of December 31, 1995, are as follows:

KELLY, LTD.
INCOME STATEMENT
FOR THE YEAR ENDED DECEMBER 31, 1995
(ALL AMOUNTS IN BRITISH POUNDS)

Sales revenue	3,000,000
Cost of goods sold	1,600,000
Gross profit	1,400,000
Selling and administrative expenses	850,000
Interest expense	100,000
Net income	450,000

KELLY, LTD.
BALANCE SHEET
AS OF DECEMBER 31, 1995
(ALL AMOUNTS IN BRITISH POUNDS)

Cash	300,000	Accounts payable	250,000
Accounts receivable	450,000	Notes payable	800,000
Inventories	400,000	Common stock	500,000
Plant, net	850,000	Retained earnings	450,000
Totals	2,000,000	Totals	2,000,000

At the beginning of 1995, the exchange rate was \$1.40 per British pound and at the end of the year, it was \$1.60. The average exchange rate for the year was \$1.50. Assume that the British pound is the functional currency.

■ REQUIRED

1. Prepare an income statement for Kelly, translated from British pounds into U.S. dollars.

2. Prepare a balance sheet as of December 31, 1995, for Kelly, translated from British pounds into U.S. dollars.

3. Why is it necessary to create the account Translation Adjustment? Is it an addition to or a deduction from stockholders' equity? What are the cash flow implications to the parent, Aikman, from this adjustment?

ALTERNATE MULTI-CONCEPT PROBLEMS

(LO 2, 3) PROBLEM 13-6A INVESTMENTS IN BONDS AND STOCK

Vermont Corp. enters into the following transactions during 1995:

July 1   Paid $10,700 to acquire on the open market $10,000 face value of Maine bonds. The bonds have a stated annual interest rate of 8% with interest paid semiannually on June 30 and December 31. The remaining life of the bonds on the date of purchase is $3^{1}/_{2}$ years.

Oct. 23   Purchased 1,000 shares of Virginia common stock at $15 per share.

Nov. 21   Purchased 600 shares of Carolina preferred stock at $8 per share.

Dec. 10   Received dividends of $.50 per share on the Virginia stock and $1.00 per share on the Carolina stock.

Dec. 28   Sold 700 shares of Virginia common stock at $19 per share.

Dec. 31   Received interest from the Maine bonds.

Dec. 31   The Virginia stock and the Carolina stock have market prices of $20 per share and $11 per share, respectively.

■ REQUIRED

1. Prepare all necessary journal entries on Vermont's records to account for its investments during 1995. Vermont classifies the bonds as held-to-maturity securities and all stock investments as trading securities. The straight-line method is used to amortize any bond discount or premium.

2. Prepare a partial balance sheet at December 31 to indicate the proper presentation of the investments.

3. Indicate the items, and the amount of each, that will appear on the 1995 income statement relative to the investments.

(LO 3, 4) PROBLEM 13-7A INVESTMENTS IN STOCK

Trendy Supercenter occasionally finds itself with excess cash to invest and consequently entered into the following transactions during 1995:

Jan. 15   Purchased 100 shares of IBM common stock at $50 per share, plus $250 in commissions.

May 23   Received dividends of $1 per share on the IBM stock.

June 1   Purchased 200 shares of General Motors stock at $60 per share, plus $300 in commissions.

Oct. 20   Sold all of the IBM stock at $65 per share, less commissions of $400.

Dec. 15   Received notification from General Motors that a $.75 per share dividend had been declared. The checks will be mailed to stockholders on January 10, 1996.

Dec. 31   Noted that the General Motors stock was quoted on the stock exchange at $45 per share.

■ REQUIRED

1. Prepare journal entries on the books of Trendy Supercenter during 1995 to record these transactions, including any necessary entry on December 15 when the dividend was declared and at the end of the year. Assume that Trendy categorizes all investments as available-for-sale securities.

2. What is the total amount of income that Trendy should recognize from its investments during 1995, including any income effect from the entry on December 31?

3. Assume all of the same facts except that Trendy categorizes all investments as trading securities. How would your answer to part 2 change? Explain why your answer would change.

(LO 5, 9) PROBLEM 13-8A FOREIGN EQUITY INVESTEE

Elston Enterprises holds 40% of the common stock of Norris, Ltd., an affiliate in Canada. The Investment in Norris was reported on Elston's December 31, 1994, balance sheet at $210 million. Elston's 40% investment gives it the ability to exert significant influence over Norris. The affiliate presents the following income statement for the year ended December 31, 1995 (all amounts are stated in millions of Canadian dollars):

NORRIS, LTD.
INCOME STATEMENT
FOR THE YEAR ENDED DECEMBER 31, 1995

Revenues	500
Operating expenses	(300)
Interest expense	(50)
Net income	150

On June 1, 1995, Norris declared and paid dividends totaling 50 million Canadian dollars. On December 31, 1995, it declared and paid another dividend of 30 million Canadian dollars. The Canadian dollar is the functional currency. The following exchange rates are available:

DATE	EXCHANGE RATE PER CANADIAN DOLLAR
January 1	$.80
June 1	.75
December 31	.60
Average for the year	.70

■ **REQUIRED**

1. Translate Norris's income statement from Canadian dollars into U.S. dollars. Why is it necessary for Elston to translate the statement?

2. What amount of income, in dollars, should Elston recognize from its investment in Norris for 1995?

3. At what amount should Elston report the Investment in Norris account on its December 31, 1995, balance sheet? Support your answer with any necessary computations. (*Hint:* Dividends should be translated at the exchange rate in effect when they were paid.)

CASES

READING AND INTERPRETING FINANCIAL STATEMENTS

(LO 6) CASE 13-1 MARVEL'S ACQUISITION OF FLEER

In 1992 Marvel Entertainment Group, Inc., the comic book company, acquired Fleer, the company that sells sports trading cards. Marvel acquired all of the issued and outstanding shares of Fleer common stock for $28 per share, or approximately

$286 million. The following footnote is from page 50 of Marvel's 1992 annual report (all amounts in the footnote, including the schedule, are in thousands of dollars):

> The acquisition was accounted for using the purchase method of accounting. The purchase price was allocated to the assets and liabilities of Fleer based on their estimated respective fair values at September 1, 1992, including an obligation of $65,000 to former Fleer stockholders who did not tender their shares, of which $27,716 was outstanding at December 31, 1992. The fair values of the assets and liabilities are summarized below. The purchase price and expenses associated with the acquisition exceeded the fair value of Fleer's net assets by $232,000, which has been assigned to goodwill and is being amortized over forty years on the straight-line basis.

Cash and cash equivalents	$ 19,296
Accounts receivable, net	35,311
Inventories	9,188
Current deferred income tax assets and other	12,830
Noncurrent assets	14,914
Accounts payable	(11,326)
Accrued expenses and other	(32,711)
Noncurrent liabilities	(6,211)
	$41,291

■REQUIRED

1. Why was the acquisition accounted for using the purchase method of accounting rather than the pooling of interests method?

2. According to the schedule, the fair value of Fleer's net assets acquired was approximately $41 million. Why did Marvel pay $286 million to acquire Fleer's stock? Do you think this was a wise business decision by Marvel?

3. Marvel's consolidated balance sheet reported goodwill of approximately $48 million at the beginning of 1992 and $277 million at the end of the year. What caused the large net increase during the year? Aside from the net increase, what caused a reduction in goodwill during the year?

4. From the information you have, what large cash outflow would you expect to find on Marvel's 1992 statement of cash flows, and in which section of the statement would it appear?

(LO 9) CASE 13-2 JOHNSON & JOHNSON FOREIGN OPERATIONS

The 1992 Johnson & Johnson annual report includes the following (emphasis added):

> In consolidating international subsidiaries, balance sheet currency effects are recorded as a separate component of stockholders' equity. This equity account includes the results of translating all balance sheet assets and liabilities at current exchange rates, except for those located in highly inflationary economies, principally Brazil, which are reflected in operation results. The translation adjustments do not exist in terms of *functional cash flows;* such adjustments are not reported as part of operating results since *realization is remote* unless the international businesses were sold or liquidated.

An analysis of the changes during 1992 and 1991 in the separate component of stockholders' equity for cumulative currency translation adjustments follows (all amounts in millions of dollars):

	1992	1991
Beginning of year (credit balance)	$ 134	241
Translation adjustments	(280)	(107)
End of year	$(146)	134

■ REQUIRED

1. What does Johnson & Johnson mean by "functional cash flows" and "realization is remote"?

2. Over the two-year period shown, the translation adjustment has gone from a credit balance of $241 million to a debit balance of $146 million. What does this tell you about the value of the U.S. dollar relative to the functional currencies of those countries in which Johnson & Johnson has operations? Explain your answer.

3. Should Johnson & Johnson be concerned by the large decrease in this component of stockholders' equity? Explain your answer.

MAKING FINANCIAL DECISIONS

(LO 10) CASE 13-3 SEGMENT INFORMATION

Carburetor Corp. started in business 25 years ago as a manufacturer of auto parts that it sells to each of the Big Three auto manufacturers and to auto parts wholesalers. Ten years ago, the company decided that it should diversify and began a business to distribute sporting goods to retail outlets. The following segment information is included in Carburetor's footnotes to its 1995 annual report (amounts in millions of dollars):

	AUTO PARTS	SPORTING GOODS
Sales revenue	$375	$250
Operating profit	20	75
Carrying value of assets	800	450
Depreciation expense	225	50
Capital expenditures	100	10

Sales to Ford, GM, and Chrysler during 1995 amounted to $120 million, $160 million, and $60 million, respectively.

■ REQUIRED

1. Which segment of the business appears to you to be doing better? Justify your response with any computations or ratios you believe are relevant.

2. What percentage of the revenues of the auto parts division is from each of the Big Three? What percentage of the revenues of this segment do the Big Three account for on a combined basis?

3. Assume that the chief financial officer of Carburetor has come to you for a $100 million loan. Carburetor wants to spend $80 million to build a new plant to manufacture auto parts and another $20 million to add another warehouse to its sporting goods distribution operation. Will you make the loan? Explain why or why not.

(LO 1) CASE 13-4 ALTERNATIVE INVESTMENTS

The research and development division of a sports medicine supplier, Troy, Inc., has advised the company that it will be necessary to have funds available to manufacture a new product. Production is expected to begin in three to five years. The capital expenditures needed to make the new product are expected to be between $1 million and $1.25 million. Troy plans to invest $250,000 for each of the next three to five years to fund the capital expenditures. It is considering the following investments:

- 5% municipal bonds.

- Preferred stock of several current and potential customers.

- A widely held portfolio of common stock managed by the assistant to the chief financial officer.

■ REQUIRED

1. Is it possible for Troy to plan without a more specific time frame and required investment? Explain.

2. Write a memo to the chief financial officer recommending one of the investments Troy is considering.

ACCOUNTING AND ETHICS: WHAT WOULD YOU DO?

(LO 3, 4) CASE 13-5 FAIR MARKET VALUES FOR INVESTMENTS

Kennedy Corp. operates a chain of discount stores. The company regularly holds stock of various companies in a trading securities portfolio. One of these investments is 10,000 shares of Clean Air, Inc., stock purchased for $100 per share during December 1995.

Clean Air manufactures highly specialized equipment used to test automobile emissions. Unfortunately, the market price of Clean Air's stock dropped during December 1995 and closed the year trading at $75 per share. Kennedy expects the Clean Air stock to experience a turnaround, however, as states pass legislation to require an emissions test on all automobiles.

As controller for Kennedy, you have followed the fortunes of Clean Air with particular interest. You and the company's treasurer are both concerned with the negative impact that a write-down of the stock to fair value would have on Kennedy's earnings for 1995. You have calculated net income for 1995 to be $400,000, exclusive of the recognition of any loss on the stock.

The treasurer comes to you on January 31, 1996, with the following idea:

> Since you haven't closed the books yet for 1995 and we haven't yet released the 1995 financials, let's think carefully about how Clean Air should be classified. I realize that we normally treat these types of investments as trading securities, but if we categorize the Clean Air stock on the balance sheet as available-for-sale rather than a trading security, we won't need to report the adjustment to fair value on the income statement. I don't see anything wrong with this since we would still report the stock at its fair value on the balance sheet.

■ REQUIRED

1. Compute Kennedy's net income for 1995, under two different assumptions: (a) the stock is classified as a trading security and (b) the stock is classified as an available-for-sale security.

2. Which classification do you believe is appropriate, according to accounting standards? Explain your answer.

3. Would you have any ethical concerns in following the treasurer's advice? Explain your answer.

(LO 5) **CASE 13-6 EQUITY METHOD**

Pizza Express is a nationwide pizza delivery company. A few years ago, the company purchased 20% of the common stock of Top Tomato, a supplier of tomato sauce and other fresh vegetables. Because Pizza Express has significant influence over the operations of Top Tomato, it uses the equity method to account for its investment. Recently, Top Tomato has experienced significant volatility in its earnings, due in large part to the unpredictable weather in locales where its products are grown. In fact, the supplier reported a net loss of $20 million for 1995. Top Tomato paid dividends of $5 million in 1995, the same amount it has paid for many years.

Pizza Express had a good year in 1995. Exclusive of any adjustment for its share of Top Tomato's loss, Pizza Express's net income amounted to $6 million. You are the controller for Pizza Express and are approached by its president in January 1996, before the release of the 1995 financial statements. He is concerned that the recognition of a share of Top Tomato's net loss will put a serious damper on an otherwise successful year for Pizza Express. After all, he reasons, "My bonus, your bonus, and our ability to attract new capital from banks and other lenders hinge on our profitability."

He goes on to offer the following remedy:

I understand that accounting rules require you to use the equity method, given our 20% stake in Top Tomato. I believe we should instruct the treasurer to sell 1% of our holdings in this company. This would relieve you of the responsibility to use this peculiar accounting method that requires us to share in their profits and losses. Instead of picking up a share of their net loss, we can recognize as income the dividends they paid us. This approach to recognizing income on an investment makes much more sense to me anyhow. Besides, divesting ourselves of such a minor percentage of Top Tomato's stock shouldn't jeopardize at all our ability to continue to have a strong voice in their strategic decisions.

■ **REQUIRED**

1. Compute net income for Pizza Express under two different assumptions: (a) the use of the equity method to account for the investment in Top Tomato and (b) the use of the method proposed by the president. Assume that the market value of Top Tomato's stock did not change over the year.

2. Does the president's proposal violate generally accepted accounting principles? Explain your answer.

3. Does the president's proposal present you with an ethical dilemma in your role as controller of the company? Explain your answer.

ANALYTICAL SOFTWARE CASE

To the Student: Your instructor may assign one or more parts of the analytical software case that is designed to accompany this chapter. This multi-part case gives you a chance to work with real financial statement data using software that stimulates, guides, and hones your analytical and problem-solving skills. It was created especially to support and strengthen your understanding of the chapter's Learning Objectives.

SOLUTION TO KEY TERMS QUIZ

1. Vertical combination (p. 688)
2. Purchase method (p. 689)
3. Statutory consolidation (p. 689)
4. Debt securities (p. 676)
5. Equity method (p. 676)
6. Conglomerate (p. 689)
7. Equity securities (p. 676)
8. Subsidiary (p. 674)
9. Affiliate (p. 674)
10. Statutory merger (p. 689)
11. Wholly owned subsidiary (p. 674)
12. Stock acquisition (p. 689)
13. Translation adjustment (p. 703)
14. Foreign currency translation (p. 699)
15. Pooling of interests method (p. 689)
16. Amortized cost method (p. 679)
17. Minority interest (p. 697)
18. Parent (p. 674)
19. Trading securities (p. 677)
20. Exchange rate (p. 698)
21. Available-for-sale securities (p. 677)
22. Consolidated financial statements (p. 676)
23. Foreign currency transaction (p. 701)
24. Functional currency (p. 701)
25. Held-to-maturity securities (p. 677)
26. Goodwill (p. 691)
27. Horizontal combination (p. 688)

Focus on Financial Results

The major airlines are in a predicament. Competitive pressures make it difficult to make a profit when price is the main variable used by the public to make their purchase decision. After all, if you have to travel from Dallas to New York City and there are four equally convenient and reputable airlines going there, you'll probably pick the airline that offers the lowest price. The airlines know that, too. When one lowers a price, they all have to match, even if it

means losing money. The reason: if they don't match the price, it means even larger losses. An empty flight costs almost as much as a full one.

As a result, **AMR,** the parent of American Airlines, lost nearly a billion dollars in 1992, compared to a $240 million loss in 1991 and a $40 million loss in 1990. You could find a brighter picture, though, if you examine its statement of cash flows—which shows that the company's cash balance only dropped by $49 million. Adding back depreciation, an accounting change, and other adjustments, AMR generated $843 million in cash from operations. But the relief is short-lived. The company *spent* more than $3 billion on capital items. And instead of being financed by profits, these expenditures were financed by debt.

AMR CORPORATION

CONSOLIDATED STATEMENT OF CASH FLOWS (in millions)	1992	1991	1990
CASH FLOW FROM OPERATING ACTIVITIES:			
Net loss	$ (935)	$ (240)	$ (40)
Adjustments to reconcile net loss to net cash provided by operating activities:			
Depreciation and amortization	1,041	883	723
Deferred income tax	(101)	(110)	(152)
Provisions for losses	165	77	32
Cumulative effect of accounting changes	460	-	-
Change in assets and liabilities:			
Increase in receivables	(144)	(152)	(76)
Proceeds from transfer of receivables	-	300	-
Increase in inventories	(85)	(55)	(102)
Increase (decrease) in accounts payable and accrued liabilities	(17)	15	63
Increase in air traffic liability	366	40	248
Other, net	93	(14)	(10)
Net cash provided by operating activities	843	744	686
CASH FLOW FROM INVESTING ACTIVITIES:			
Capital expenditures	(3,299)	(3,536)	(2,901)
Acquisitions of routes and other related assets	(36)	(744)	(467)
Net decrease (increase) in short-term investments	342	(319)	(355)
Other, net	39	28	(15)
Net cash used for investing activities	(2,954)	(4,571)	(3,738)
CASH FLOW FROM FINANCING ACTIVITIES:			
Proceeds from:			
Issuance of long-term debt	1,787	2,742	923
Sale-leaseback transactions	610	1,637	1,342
Issuance of common stock	454	300	-
Short-term borrowings with maturities of 90 days or less, net of repayments	18	(246)	689
Other short-term borrowings	104	425	486
Payments on other short-term borrowings	(153)	(978)	(129)
Payments on long-term debt and capital lease obligations	(779)	(118)	(282)
Other, net	21	45	17
Net cash provided by financing activities	2,062	3,807	3,046
Net decrease in cash	(49)	(20)	(6)
Cash at beginning of year	94	114	120
Cash at end of year	$ 45	$ 94	$ 114
CASH PAYMENTS (REFUNDS) FOR:			
Interest (net of amounts capitalized)	$ 458	$ 292	$ 191
Income taxes	(7)	39	140
FINANCING ACTIVITIES NOT AFFECTING CASH:			
Capital lease obligations incurred	$ 418	$ 425	$ 158
Installment promissory notes issued for assets	162	-	-

Year Ended December 31,

The accompanying notes are an integral part of these financial statements.

Chapter 14

The Statement of Cash Flows

LEARNING OBJECTIVES

After studying this chapter, you should be able to

1. Explain the purpose of a statement of cash flows.
2. Explain what cash equivalents are and how they are treated on the statement of cash flows.
3. Describe operating, investing, and financing activities, and give examples of each.
4. Describe the difference between the direct and the indirect methods of computing cash flow from operating activities.
5. Use T accounts to prepare a statement of cash flows, using the direct method to determine cash flow from operating activities.
6. Use T accounts to prepare a statement of cash flows, using the indirect method to determine cash flow from operating activities.
7. Use a work sheet to prepare a statement of cash flows, using the indirect method to determine cash flow from operating activities (Appendix 14A).

Linkages

A LOOK AT PREVIOUS CHAPTERS

Chapter 13 completed our examination of the accounting and reporting issues for a company's various assets and liabilities. Specifically, in that chapter, we considered how companies account for investments in other entities. In addition, we looked at issues related to the consolidation of a group of entities under common control and those related to foreign currency.

We have seen in previous chapters that assets and liabilities involve important cash flows to a business at one time or another. In Chapters 1 and 2, we introduced the statement of cash flows along with the other financial statements.

A LOOK AT THIS CHAPTER

Now that we have a fuller appreciation of how to account for the various assets and liabilities of a business, we turn our attention in this chapter to an in-depth examination of the statement of cash flows.

A LOOK AT THE UPCOMING CHAPTER

Stockholders, creditors, and other groups use financial statements, including the statement of cash flows, to analyze a company. We called attention in earlier chapters to various ratios often used to aid in these analyses. In the final chapter, we discuss the use of ratios and other types of analysis to better understand the financial strength and health of companies.

Cash Flows and Accrual Accounting

The *bottom line* is a phrase used in many different ways in today's society. "I wish politicians would cut out all of the rhetoric and get to the bottom line." "The bottom line is that the manager was fired because the team wasn't winning." "Our company's bottom line is twice what it was last year." This last use of the phrase, in reference to a company's net income, is probably the way in which *bottom line* was first used. In recent years, managers, stockholders, creditors, analysts, and other users of financial statements have become more and more wary of focusing on any one number as an indicator of a company's overall performance. Most experts now agree that there has been a tendency to rely far too heavily on net income and its companion, earnings per share, and in many cases to ignore a company's cash flows. More than anything else, the economic downturn of the last decade probably has been responsible for the renewed interest in cash flows. As you know by now in your study of accounting, you can't pay bills with net income; it takes cash!

To illustrate the difference between a company's bottom line and its cash flow, consider the case of IBM in 1992. The computer giant suffered the largest net loss in its history, nearly $5 billion. During the same 12-month period, however, IBM's cash position actually improved by over 12%, from $3.9 billion at the beginning of the year to $4.4 billion at year-end. How is this possible? First, net income is computed on an accrual basis, not a cash basis. Second, the income statement primarily reflects events related to the operating activities of a business, that is, selling products or providing services.

If you think about it, any one of four combinations is possible. That is, a company's cash position can increase or decrease during a period, and it can report a net profit or a net loss. Exhibit 14-1 illustrates this point by showing the performance of four well-known companies, including IBM, during 1992. Quaker Oats is the only one of the four companies that both improved its cash position in 1992 and reported a net profit. Eastman Kodak reported a net profit, but for reasons that should be evident by looking at its statement of cash flows, it experienced a decrease in cash. Both Sears, Roebuck and IBM reported large net losses in 1992 and both started the year with almost the same amount of cash on hand. By the end of the year, however, IBM had a cash balance of over $4.4 billion, compared to just over $2.6 billion for Sears. To summarize, a company with a profitable year does not necessarily increase its cash position, nor does a company with an unprofitable year always experience a decrease in cash.

EXHIBIT 14-1   Cash Flows and Net Income for Four Companies in 1992
(all amounts in millions of dollars)

COMPANY	BEGINNING BALANCE IN CASH	ENDING BALANCE IN CASH	INCREASE (DECREASE) IN CASH	NET INCOME (LOSS)
Quaker Oats	$ 75	$ 95	$ 20	$ 248
Eastman Kodak	783	374	(409)	1,146
Sears, Roebuck	3,943	2,627	(1,316)	(3,932)
IBM	3,945	4,446	501	(4,965)

EASTMAN KODAK COMPANY AND SUBSIDIARY COMPANIES
- - - - -
CONSOLIDATED STATEMENT OF CASH FLOWS

	1992	1991 (IN MILLIONS)	1990
Cash flows from operating activities:			
Net earnings	$ 1,146	$ 17	$ 703
Adjustments to reconcile net earnings to net cash provided by operating activities:			
Depreciation and amortization	1,539	1,477	1,309
Provision (benefit) for deferred taxes	1	(153)	(192)
Loss on sale and retirement of properties	148	131	154
Decrease (increase) in receivables	216	(15)	(88)
(Increase) decrease in inventories	(150)	114	82
Increase in liabilities excluding borrowings	271	755	414
Cumulative effect of change in accounting	(152)	—	—
Other items, net	347	145	35
Total adjustments	2,220	2,454	1,714
Net cash provided by operating activities	3,366	2,471	2,417
Cash flows from investing activities:			
Additions to properties	(2,092)	(2,135)	(2,037)
Proceeds from sale of investments	189	33	10
Proceeds from sale of properties	85	53	83
Marketable securities—purchases	(159)	(60)	(128)
Marketable securities—sales	114	102	126
Other items	3	16	90
Net cash used in investing activities	(1,860)	(1,991)	(1,856)
Cash flows from financing activities:			
Net (decrease) increase in commercial paper borrowings of 90 days or less	(629)	(111)	114
Proceeds from other borrowings	549	1,535	1,691
Repayment of other borrowings	(1,184)	(1,207)	(2,102)
Dividends to shareowners	(650)	(649)	(649)
Other items	16	2	1
Net cash used in financing activities	(1,898)	(430)	(945)
Effect of exchange rate changes on cash	(17)	(2)	24
Net (decrease) increase in cash and cash equivalents	(409)	48	(360)
Cash and cash equivalents, beginning of year	783	735	1,095
Cash and cash equivalents, end of year	$ 374	$ 783	$ 735

(See notes on pages 40 through 48)

As Exhibit 14-1 makes clear, Eastman Kodak experienced net profit in 1992 of $1.146 billion, but had a decrease in cash of $409 million. How? Look at Kodak's 1992 statement of cash flows, excerpted here. Kodak paid over $2 billion for additions to property, repaid $1.184 billion of borrowings, and distributed $650 million in dividends.

Purpose of the Statement of Cash Flows

The **statement of cash flows** is an important complement to the other major financial statements. It summarizes the operating, investing, and financing activities of a business over a period of time. The balance sheet summarizes the cash on hand and the balances in other assets and the liabilities and owners' equity accounts, providing a snapshot at a specific point in time. The statement of cash flows reports the changes in cash over a period of time and, most important, *explains these changes.*

LO 1

Explain the purpose of a statement of cash flows.

EXHIBIT 14-2   Income Statement for Fox River Realty

FOX RIVER REALTY
INCOME STATEMENT
FOR THE YEAR ENDED DECEMBER 31, 1995

Revenues	$400,000
Depreciation expense	$ 50,000
All other expenses	100,000
Total expenses	$150,000
Net income	$250,000

The income statement summarizes performance on an accrual basis. As you have learned in your study of accrual accounting, income on this basis is considered a better indicator of *future* cash inflows and outflows than a statement limited to current cash flows. The statement of cash flows complements the accrual-based income statement by allowing users to assess a company's performance on a cash basis. As we will see in the following simple example, however, it also goes beyond presenting data related to operating performance and looks at other activities that affect a company's cash position.

An Example

Consider the following discussion between the owner of Fox River Realty and the company accountant. After a successful first year in business in 1994 in which it earned a profit of $100,000, the owner reviews the income statement for the second year, as presented in Exhibit 14-2.

The owner is pleased with the results and asks to see the balance sheet. Comparative balance sheets for the first two years are presented in Exhibit 14-3.

EXHIBIT 14-3   Balance Sheets for Fox River Realty

FOX RIVER REALTY
COMPARATIVE BALANCE SHEETS
DECEMBER 31

	DECEMBER 31	
	1995	**1994**
Cash	$ 50,000	$ 150,000
Plant and equipment	600,000	350,000
Accumulated depreciation	(150,000)	(100,000)
Total assets	$ 500,000	$ 400,000
Notes payable	$ 100,000	$ 150,000
Common stock	250,000	200,000
Retained earnings	150,000	50,000
Total equities	$ 500,000	$ 400,000

Where Did the Cash Go?   At first glance, the owner is surprised to see the significant decline in the Cash account. She immediately presses the accountant for answers. With such a profitable year, where has the cash gone? Specifically, why has cash decreased from $150,000 to $50,000, even though income rose from $100,000 in the first year to $250,000 in the second year?

The accountant begins his explanation to the owner by pointing out that income on a strict cash basis is even *higher* than the reported $250,000. Because depreciation expense is an expense that does not use cash (cash was used when the plant and equipment was purchased, not when it is depreciated), cash provided from operating activities is calculated as follows:

Net income	$250,000
Add back: Depreciation expense	50,000
Cash provided by operating activities	$300,000

Further, the accountant reminds the owner of the additional $50,000 that she invested in the business during the year. Now the owner is even more bewildered: with cash from operations of $300,000 and her own infusion of $50,000, why did cash *decrease* by $100,000? The accountant refreshes the owner's memory on three major outflows of cash during the year. First, even though the business earned $250,000, she withdrew $150,000 in dividends during the year. Second, the comparative balance sheets indicate that notes payable with the bank were reduced from $150,000 to $100,000, requiring the use of $50,000 in cash. Finally, the comparative balance sheets show an increase in plant and equipment for the year from $350,000 to $600,000—a sizable investment of $250,000 in new long-term assets.

Statement of Cash Flows   To summarize what happened to the cash, the accountant prepares a statement of cash flows as shown in Exhibit 14-4. Although the owner is not particularly happy with the decrease in cash for the year, she is at least satisfied with the statement as an explanation of where the cash came from and how it was used. The statement summarizes the important cash activities for the year and fills a void created with the presentation of just an income statement and a balance sheet.

Reporting Requirements
for a Statement of Cash Flows

Accountants have prepared variations of the statement of cash flows for many years. Names for these statements included *statement of sources and uses of funds, funds statement,* and *statement of changes in financial position.* For most companies, the definition of funds was broader than cash and included all working capital (current asset and current liability) accounts. Most often, the top of the statement merely listed all sources of funds; all uses of funds were listed below them. In 1987 the accounting profession decided that more standardization was necessary in the preparation of the statement and mandated two important changes.[1] First, the statement must be prepared on a cash basis. Second, the cash flows must be classified into three categories: operating, investing, and financing activities. We now take a closer look at each of these important requirements in preparing a statement of cash flows.

[1] *Statement of Financial Accounting Standards No. 95,* "Statement of Cash Flows" (Stamford, Conn.: Financial Standards Board, November 1987).

EXHIBIT 14-4   Statement of Cash Flows for Fox River Realty

FOX RIVER REALTY
STATEMENT OF CASH FLOWS
FOR THE YEAR ENDED DECEMBER 31, 1995

Cash provided (used) by operating activities:	
Net income	$ 250,000
Add back: Depreciation expense	50,000
Net cash provided (used) by operating activities	$ 300,000
Cash provided (used) by investing activities:	
Purchase of new plant and equipment	$(250,000)
Cash provided (used) by financing activities:	
Additional investment by owner	$ 50,000
Cash dividends paid to owner	(150,000)
Repayment of notes payable to bank	(50,000)
Net cash provided (used) by financing activities	$(150,000)
Net increase (decrease) in cash	$(100,000)
Cash balance at beginning of year	150,000
Cash balance at end of year	$ 50,000

The Definition of Cash: Cash and Cash Equivalents

LO   2

Explain what cash equivalents are and how they are treated on the statement of cash flows.

The purpose of the statement of cash flows is to provide information about a company's cash inflows and outflows. Thus, it is essential to have a clear understanding of what the definition of cash includes. According to accounting standards, certain items are recognized as being equivalent to cash and are combined with cash on the balance sheet and for purposes of preparing a statement of cash flows. No prudent corporate treasurer would put cash in non-interest-bearing accounts; even cash that's used for everyday purposes should earn some return in a checking account. Money that isn't going to be used immediately to pay bills should be placed in a cash equivalent.

Commercial paper (short-term notes issued by corporations), money market funds, and Treasury bills are examples of cash equivalents. To be classified as a **cash equivalent,** an item must be readily convertible to a known amount of cash and have an original maturity *to the investor* of three months or less. For example, a three-year Treasury note purchased two months before its maturity is classified as a cash equivalent. The same note purchased two years before maturity is not classified as a cash equivalent but as an investment.

To understand why cash equivalents are combined with cash when preparing a statement of cash flows, assume that a company has a cash balance of $10,000 and no assets that qualify as cash equivalents. Further assume that the $10,000 is used to purchase 90-day Treasury bills and is recorded by the following entry:

Investment in Treasury Bills	10,000	
Cash		10,000
To record purchase of 90-day Treasury bills.		

Assets	=	Liabilities	+	Owners' Equity
+ 10,000				
− 10,000				

For record-keeping purposes, it is important to recognize this transaction as a transfer between cash in the bank and an investment in a government security. In the strictest sense, the investment represents an outflow of cash. The purchase of a security with such a short maturity does not, however, involve any significant degree of risk in terms of price changes and thus is not reported on the statement of cash flows as an outflow. Instead, for purposes of classification on the balance sheet and the statement of cash flows, this is merely a transfer *within* the cash and cash equivalents category. The important point is that before the purchase of the Treasury bills, the company had $10,000 in cash and cash equivalents and after the purchase, it still had $10,000 in cash and cash equivalents. Because nothing changed, the transaction is not reported on the statement of cash flows.

Consider a different transaction involving the $10,000 and the following entry:

| Investment in GM Common Stock | 10,000 | |
| Cash | | 10,000 |

To record the purchase of GM common stock.

Assets	=	Liabilities	+	Owners' Equity
+10,000				
−10,000				

This purchase involves a certain amount of risk for the company making the investment. The GM stock is not convertible to a known amount of cash because its market value is subject to change. Thus, for balance sheet purposes, the investment is not considered a cash equivalent and is not therefore combined with cash but is classified as either a trading security or an available-for-sale security, depending on the company's intent in holding the stock (the distinction between these two types was discussed in Chapter 13). When preparing a statement of cash flows, the investment in stock of another company is considered a significant activity and thus is reported on the statement of cash flows.

Classification of Cash Flows

For the statement of cash flows, companies are required to classify activities into three categories: operating, investing, or financing. These categories represent the major functions of an entity, and classifying activities in this way allows users to look at important relationships. For example, one important financing activity for many businesses is borrowing money. Grouping the cash inflows from borrowing money during the period with the cash outflows from repayments of loans during the period makes it easier for analysts and other users of the statements to evaluate the company.

LO 3
Describe operating, investing, and financing activities, and give examples of each.

Each of the three types of activities can result in both cash inflows and cash outflows to the company. Thus, the general format for the statement is as shown in Exhibit 14-5. Note the direct tie between the bottom portion of this statement and the balance sheet. The beginning and ending balances in cash and cash equivalents shown as the last two lines on the statement of cash flows are taken directly from the comparative balance sheets. Some companies end their statement of cash flows with the figure for the net increase or decrease in cash and cash equivalents and do not report the beginning and ending balances in cash and cash equivalents directly on the statement of cash flows. Instead, the reader must turn to the balance sheet for these amounts. We now take a closer look at the types of activities that appear in each of the three categories on the statement of cash flows.

Operating Activities **Operating activities** involve acquiring and selling products and services. The specific activities of a business depend on its type. For example,

EXHIBIT 14-5   Format for the Statement of Cash Flows

THE SMITH CORPORATION
STATEMENT OF CASH FLOWS
FOR THE YEAR ENDED DECEMBER 31, 1995

Cash flows from operating activities:		
Inflows	$ xxx	
Outflows	(xxx)	
Net cash provided (used) by operating activities		$xxx
Cash flows from investing activities:		
Inflows	xxx	
Outflows	(xxx)	
Net cash provided (used) by investing activities		xxx
Cash flows from financing activities:		
Inflows	xxx	
Outflows	(xxx)	
Net cash provided (used) by financing activities		xxx
Net increase (decrease) in cash and cash equivalents		$xxx
Cash and cash equivalents at beginning of year		xxx
Cash and cash equivalents at end of year		$xxx

the purchase of raw materials is an important operating activity for a manufacturer. For a retailer, the purchase of inventory from a distributor constitutes an operating activity. For a realty company, the payment of a commission to a salesperson is an operating activity. All three types of businesses sell either products or services, and their sales are important operating activities.

A statement of cash flows reflects the cash effects, either inflows or outflows, associated with each of these activities. For example, the manufacturer's payment for purchases of raw materials results in a cash outflow. The receipt of cash from collecting an account receivable results in a cash inflow. The income statement reports operating activities on an accrual basis. The statement of cash flows reflects a company's operating activities on a cash basis.

Investing Activities   **Investing activities** involve acquiring and disposing of long-term assets. Replacing worn-out plant and equipment and expanding the existing base of long-term assets are essential to all businesses. In fact, cash paid for these acquisitions, often called *capital expenditures,* is usually the largest single item in the investing activities section of the statement, as evidenced by this section in The Quaker Oats Company's 1992 statement of cash flows (amounts in millions of dollars):

CASH FLOWS FROM INVESTING ACTIVITIES

Additions to property, plant, and equipment	(176.4)
Change in other receivables and investments	(20.0)
Disposals of property, plant, and equipment	39.6)
Net Cash Used in Investing Activities	(156.8)

Sales of long-term assets, such as plant and equipment, are not generally a significant source of cash. They are acquired to be used in producing goods and services, or to support this function, rather than being resold, as is true for inventory. Occasionally, however, plant and equipment may wear out or no longer be needed and are offered for sale. In fact, the excerpt from The Quaker Oats Company report indicates that it generated $39.6 million of cash in 1992 from disposals of property, plant, and equipment.

In Chapter 13 we explained why companies sometimes invest in the stocks and bonds of other companies. The classification of these investments on the statement of cash flows depends on the type of investment. The acquisition of one company by another, whether in the form of a merger or a stock acquisition, is an important *investing* activity to bring to the attention of statement readers. Cash flows from purchases, sales, and maturities of held-to-maturity securities (bonds) and available-for-sale securities (stocks and bonds) are classified as *investing* activities. On the other hand, these same types of cash flows for trading securities are classified as *operating* activities. This apparent inconsistency in the accounting rules is based on the idea that trading securities are held for the express purpose of generating short-term profits and thus are operating in nature.

Financing Activities   All businesses rely on internal financing, external financing, or a combination of the two in meeting their needs for cash. Initially, a new business must have a certain amount of investment by the owners to begin operations. After this, many companies use notes, bonds, and other forms of debt to provide financing.[2] Issuing stock and various forms of debt results in cash inflows that appear in the **financing activities** section of the statement of cash flows. On the other side, the repurchase of a company's own stock and the repayment of borrowings are important cash outflows to be reported in the financing section of the statement. Another important activity listed in the financing section of the statement is the payment of dividends to stockholders. IBM's 1992 and 1991 statements of cash flows list most of the common cash inflows and outflows from financing activities (amounts in millions of dollars):

CASH FLOWS FROM FINANCING ACTIVITIES	1992	1991
Proceeds from new debt	$10,045	$ 5,776
Payments to settle debt	(10,735)	(4,184)
Short-term borrowings less than 90 days—net	4,199	2,676
Proceeds from (payments to) employee stock plans—net	(90)	67
Payments to purchase and retire capital stock	—	(196)
Cash dividends paid	(2,765)	(2,771)
Net cash provided from (used in) financing activities	$ 654	$ 1,368

In 1992 IBM received just over $10 billion from issuing new debt and paid $10.7 billion to retire old debt. In analyzing IBM, your next step would probably be to

---

[2] Wm. Wrigley Jr. Company is unusual is this regard in that it relies almost solely on funds generated from stockholders, in the form of common stock, for financing. The company had no short-term notes payable at December 31, 1992, and total long-term liabilities accounted for less than 9% of the total liabilities and stockholders' equity on the balance sheet on that date.

■ **ACCOUNTING FOR YOUR DECISIONS**   **You Are the Investment Analyst**

Why do you think that IBM would have "Proceeds from new debt" of $10,045 million
and "Payments to settle debt" of $10,735 million?

read the long-term debt footnote to see whether the company essentially refinanced
the old debt with new debt at a lower interest rate and if it did, what the interest
saving is, because it will continue to be a benefit for many years.

Summary of the Three Types of Activities   To summarize the categorization
of the activities of a business as operating, investing, and financing, refer to Exhibit
14-6. The exhibit lists examples of each of the three activities along with the account
that it relates to on the balance sheet and the classification of that account on the
balance sheet.

In the exhibit, operating activities center on the acquisition and sale of products
and services and related costs, such as wages and taxes. Two important observations
can be made about the cash flow effects from the operating activities of a business.
*First, the cash flows from these activities are the cash effects of transactions that enter
into the determination of net income.* For example, the sale of a product enters into
the calculation of net income. The cash effect of this transaction, that is, the collection
of the account receivable, results in a cash inflow from operating activities. *Second,
cash flows from operating activities usually relate to an increase or decrease in either a
current asset or a current liability.* For example, the payment of taxes to the government
results in a decrease in taxes payable, which is a current liability on the balance sheet.

Note that investing activities normally relate to long-term assets on the balance sheet.
For example, the purchase of new plant and equipment increases long-term assets,

EXHIBIT 14-6   Classification of Items on the Statement of Cash Flows

ACTIVITY	EXAMPLES	EFFECT ON CASH	RELATED BALANCE SHEET ACCOUNT	CLASSIFICATION ON BALANCE SHEET
Operating	Collection of customer accounts	Inflow	Accounts receivable	Current asset
	Payment to suppliers for inventory	Outflow	Accounts payable Inventory	Current liability Current asset
	Payment of wages	Outflow	Wages payable	Current liability
	Payment of taxes	Outflow	Taxes payable	Current liability
Investing	Capital expenditures	Outflow	Plant and equipment	Long-term asset
	Purchase of another company	Outflow	Long-term investment	Long-term asset
	Sale of plant and equipment	Inflow	Plant and equipment	Long-term asset
	Sale of another company	Inflow	Long-term investment	Long-term asset
Financing	Sale of capital stock	Inflow	Capital stock	Stockholders' equity
	Sale of bonds	Inflow	Bonds payable	Long-term liability
	Issuance of bank note	Inflow	Notes payable	Long-term liability
	Repurchase of stock	Outflow	Treasury stock	Stockholders' equity
	Retirement of bonds	Outflow	Bonds payable	Long-term liability
	Repayment of notes	Outflow	Notes payable	Long-term liability
	Payment of dividends	Outflow	Retained earnings	Stockholders' equity

and the sale of these same assets reduces long-term assets on the balance sheet. Finally, *note that financing activities usually relate to either long-term liabilities or stockholders' equity accounts.* There are exceptions to each of these observations about the type of balance sheet account involved with each of the three types of activities, but these rules of thumb are useful as we begin to analyze transactions and attempt to determine their classification on the statement of cash flows.

Two Methods of Reporting Cash Flow from Operating Activities

Companies use one of two different methods to report the amount of cash flow from operating activities. The first approach, called the **direct method,** involves reporting major classes of gross cash receipts and cash payments. For example, cash collected from customers is reported separately from any interest and dividends received. Each of the major types of cash payments related to the company's operations follows, such as cash paid for inventory, for salaries and wages, for interest, and for taxes.

An acceptable alternative to this approach is the **indirect method.** Under the indirect method, net cash flow from operating activities is computed by adjusting net income to remove the effect of all deferrals of past operating cash receipts and payments, and all accruals of future operating cash receipts and payments. Although the Financial Accounting Standards Board prefers that companies use the direct method, it is used much less frequently in practice. In fact, an annual survey of 600 companies reported that 585 companies used the indirect method and only 15 companies used the direct method.[3]

To compare and contrast the two methods, assume that Boulder Company begins operations on January 1, 1995, with the owner's investment of $10,000 in cash. An income statement for 1995 and a balance sheet as of December 31, 1995, are presented in Exhibits 14-7 and 14-8, respectively.

Direct Method   To report cash flow from operating activities under the direct method, we look at each of the items on the income statement and determine how much cash each of these activities either generated or used. For example, revenues for the period were $80,000. If the balance sheet at the end of the period shows a balance in Accounts Receivable of $13,000, however, Boulder collected only $80,000 − $13,000, or $67,000, from its sales of the period. Thus, the first line on the statement of cash flows in Exhibit 14-9 reports $67,000 in cash collected from

> **LO 4**
> Describe the difference between the direct and the indirect methods of computing cash flow from operating activities.

[3] *Accounting Trends & Techniques,* 47th ed. (New York: American Institute of Certified Public Accountants, 1993).

EXHIBIT 14-7   Boulder Company Income Statement

BOULDER COMPANY
INCOME STATEMENT
FOR THE YEAR ENDED DECEMBER 31, 1995

Revenues	$80,000
Operating expenses	64,000
Income before tax	$16,000
Income tax expense	4,000
Net income	$12,000

EXHIBIT 14-8   Boulder Company Balance Sheet

BOULDER COMPANY
BALANCE SHEET
AS OF DECEMBER 31, 1995

ASSETS		LIABILITIES AND STOCKHOLDERS' EQUITY	
Cash	$15,000	Accounts payable	$ 6,000
Accounts receivable	13,000	Capital stock	10,000
		Retained earnings	12,000
Total	$28,000	Total	$28,000

customers. Remember that the *net increase* in Accounts Receivable must be deducted from sales to find cash collected. For a new company, this is the same as the ending balance because it starts the year without a balance in Accounts Receivable.

The same logic can be applied to determine the amount of cash expended for operating purposes. Operating expenses on the income statement are reported at $64,000. According to the balance sheet, however, $6,000 of the expense is unpaid at the end of the period as evidenced by the balance in Accounts Payable. Thus, the amount of cash expended for operating purposes as reported on the statement of cash flows in Exhibit 14-9 is $64,000 − $6,000, or $58,000. The other cash payment in the operating activities section of the statement is $4,000 for income taxes. Because no liability for income taxes is reported on the balance sheet, we know that $4,000 represents both the income tax expense of the period and the amount paid to the government. The only other item on the statement of cash flows in Exhibit 14-9 is the cash inflow from financing activities for the amount of cash invested by the owner in return for capital stock.

EXHIBIT 14-9   Statement of Cash Flows Using the Direct Method

BOULDER COMPANY
STATEMENT OF CASH FLOWS
FOR THE YEAR ENDED DECEMBER 31, 1995

CASH FLOWS FROM OPERATING ACTIVITIES	
Cash collected from customers	$ 67,000
Cash payments for operating purposes	(58,000)
Cash payments for taxes	(4,000)
Net cash inflow from operating activities	$ 5,000
CASH FLOWS FROM FINANCING ACTIVITIES	
Issuance of capital stock	$ 10,000
Net increase in cash	$ 15,000
Cash balance, beginning of period	–0–
Cash balance, end of period	$ 15,000

Indirect Method When the indirect method is used, the first line in the operating activities section of the statement of cash flows as shown in Exhibit 14-10 is the net income of the period. Net income is then adjusted to reconcile it to the amount of cash provided by operating activities. As reported on the income statement, this net income figure includes the sales of $80,000 for the period. As we know, however, the amount of cash collected was $13,000 less than this because not all customers paid Boulder the amount due. *The increase in Accounts Receivable for the period is deducted from net income on the statement because it indicates that the company sold more during the period than it collected in cash.*

The logic for the addition of the increase in Accounts Payable is similar although the effect is the opposite. The amount of operating expenses deducted on the income statement was $64,000. We know, however, that the amount of cash paid was $6,000 less than this as the balance in Accounts Payable indicates. *The increase in Accounts Payable for the period is added back to net income on the statement because it indicates that the company paid less during the period than it recognized in expense on the income statement.* One observation can be noted about this example. Because this is the first year of operations for Boulder, we wouldn't be too concerned that accounts receivable is increasing faster than accounts payable. If this becomes a trend, however, we would try to improve the accounts receivable collections process.

Two important observations should be made in comparing the two methods illustrated in Exhibits 14-9 and 14-10. First, the amount of cash provided by operating activities is the same under the two methods; the two methods are simply different computational approaches to arrive at the cash generated from operations. Second, the remainder of the statement of cash flows is the same, regardless of which method is used. The only difference between the two is in the operating activities section of the statement.

Noncash Investing and Financing Activities

Occasionally, companies engage in important investing and financing activities that do not affect cash. For example, assume that at the end of the year Wolk Corp.

FROM CONCEPT TO PRACTICE

READING BEN & JERRY'S STATEMENT OF CASH FLOWS

Does Ben & Jerry's use the direct or the indirect method in the operating activities section of its statement of cash flows? How can you tell which it is?

EXHIBIT 14-10 Statement of Cash Flows Using the Indirect Method

BOULDER COMPANY
STATEMENT OF CASH FLOWS
FOR THE YEAR ENDED DECEMBER 31, 1995

CASH FLOWS FROM OPERATING ACTIVITIES	
Net income	$ 12,000
Adjustments to reconcile net income to net cash from operating activities:	
Increase in accounts receivable	(13,000)
Increase in accounts payable	6,000
Net cash inflow from operating activities	$ 5,000
CASH FLOWS FROM FINANCING ACTIVITIES	
Issuance of capital stock	$ 10,000
Net increase in cash	$ 15,000
Cash balance, beginning of period	–0–
Cash balance, end of period	$ 15,000

issues capital stock to an inventor in return for the exclusive rights to a patent. Although the patent has no ready market value, the stock could have been sold on the open market for $25,000. Thus, the following entry is made on Wolk's books:

Patent	25,000	
Capital Stock		25,000
To record issuance of stock in exchange for patent.		

Assets	=	Liabilities	+	Owners' Equity
+25,000				+25,000

This transaction does not involve cash and is therefore not reported on the statement of cash flows. However, what if we changed the scenario slightly? Assume that Wolk wants the patent, but the inventor is not willing to accept stock in return for it. So instead, Wolk sells stock on the open market for $25,000 and then pays this amount in cash to the inventor for the rights to the patent. Now Wolk records two journal entries; the first is

Cash	25,000	
Capital Stock		25,000
To record issuance of capital stock for cash.		

Assets	=	Liabilities	+	Owners' Equity
+25,000				+25,000

It next records this entry:

Patent	25,000	
Cash		25,000
To record acquisition of patent for cash.		

Assets	=	Liabilities	+	Owners' Equity
+25,000				
−25,000				

How would each of these two transactions be reported on a statement of cash flows? The first entry appears as a cash inflow in the financing activities section of the statement; the second is reported as a cash outflow in the investing activities section. The point is that even though the *form* of this arrangement—with stock sold for cash and then the cash paid to the inventor—differs from the first arrangement—with stock exchanged directly for the patent—the *substance* of the two arrangements is the same. That is, both involve a significant financing activity, the issuance of stock, and an important investing activity, the acquisition of a patent. Because the substance is what matters, accounting standards require that any significant noncash transactions be reported either in a separate schedule or in a footnote to the financial statements. For our transaction in which stock was issued directly to the inventor, presentation in a schedule is as follows:

SUPPLEMENTAL SCHEDULE OF NONCASH INVESTING AND FINANCING ACTIVITIES

Acquisition of patent in exchange for capital stock	$25,000

To this point, we have concentrated on the purpose of a statement of cash flows and the major reporting requirements related to it. We turn our attention next to a methodology to use in actually preparing the statement.

How the Statement of Cash Flows Is Put Together

Two interesting observations can be made about the statement of cash flows. First, the "answer" to a statement of cash flows is known before we start to prepare it. That is, the change in cash for the period is known by comparing two successive balance sheets. Thus, it is not the change in cash itself that is emphasized on the statement of cash flows but the *explanations* for the change in cash. That is, each item on a statement of cash flows helps to explain why cash changed by the amount it did during the period. The second important observation about the statement of cash flows relates even more specifically to how we prepare it. Both an income statement and a balance sheet are prepared simply by taking the balances in each of the various accounts in the general ledger and putting them in the right place on the right statement. This is not true for the statement of cash flows, however. Instead, it is necessary to analyze the transactions during the period and attempt to (1) determine which of these affected cash and (2) classify each of the cash effects into one of the three categories.

In the simple examples presented so far in the chapter, we prepared the statement of cash flows without the use of any special tools. In more complex situations, however, some type of methodology is needed. We first review the basic accounting equation and then illustrate a T-account approach for preparing the statement. Appendix 14A presents a work sheet approach to the preparation of the statement of cash flows.

The Accounting Equation and the Statement of Cash Flows

The basic accounting equation is

$$\text{Assets} = \text{Liabilities} + \text{Owners' Equity}$$

Next, consider this refinement of the equation:

$$\text{Cash} + NCCA + LTA = CL + LTL + CS + RE$$

where

$NCCA$ = noncash current assets
LTA = long-term assets
CL = current liabilities
LTL = long-term liabilities
CS = capital stock
RE = retained earnings

The equation can be rearranged so that cash is on the left side and all other items are on the right side:

$$\text{Cash} = CL + LTL + CS + RE - NCCA - LTA$$

Finally, it stands to reason that any changes in cash must be accompanied by a corresponding change in the right side of the equation. For example, an increase or inflow of cash could result from an *increase* in long-term liabilities in the form of issuing bonds payable, an important financing activity for many companies. Or an increase in cash could come from a *decrease* in long-term assets in the form of a sale of fixed assets. The various possibilities for inflows and outflows of cash can be summarized by activity as follows:

ACTIVITY	LEFT SIDE	RIGHT SIDE	EXAMPLE
Operating	+ Cash	− *NCCA*	Collect accounts receivable
	− Cash	+ *NCCA*	Prepay insurance
	+ Cash	+ *CL*	Collect customer's deposit
	− Cash	− *CL*	Pay suppliers
	+ Cash	+ *RE*	Make a cash sale
Investing	+ Cash	− *LTA*	Sell equipment
	− Cash	+ *LTA*	Buy equipment
Financing	+ Cash	+ *LTL*	Issue bonds
	− Cash	− *LTL*	Retire bonds
	+ Cash	+ *CS*	Issue capital stock
	− Cash	− *CS*	Buy treasury stock
	− Cash	− *RE*	Pay dividends

What becomes clear by considering these examples is that inflows and outflows of cash relate to increases and decreases in the various balance sheet accounts. We now turn our attention to a methodology for analyzing these accounts as a way to assemble a statement of cash flows.

A Master T-Account Approach to Preparing the Statement of Cash Flows: Direct Method

LO 5

Use T accounts to prepare a statement of cash flows, using the direct method to determine cash flow from operating activities.

The following steps can be used to prepare a statement of cash flows:

1. **Set up three master T accounts with the following headings:**

   a. Cash Flows from Operating Activities

   b. Cash Flows from Investing Activities

   c. Cash Flows from Financing Activities

   These master T accounts take the place of the Cash account. As we analyze the transactions that affect each of the noncash balance sheet accounts, any cash effects are entered in the appropriate master account. When completed, the three master accounts contain all of the information needed to prepare a statement of cash flows.

2. **Determine the cash flows from operating activities.** Generally, this requires analyzing each item on the *income statement* and the *current asset and current liability* accounts. Draft journal entries for each transaction, using a lettering system for identification purposes, and post them to the appropriate balance sheet accounts. In many instances, these will be summary entries for the entire period. For example, we make one entry for all credit sales for the period, one entry for all collections on account, and so forth. Enter any debits to cash on the left side of the Cash Flow from Operating Activities master T account and any credits on the right side.

3. **Determine the cash flows from investing activities.** Generally, this requires analyzing the *long-term asset* accounts and any additional information provided. Draft journal entries for each transaction and post them to the appropriate

balance sheet accounts. Enter any debits to cash on the left side of the Cash Flow from Investing Activities master T account and any credits on the right side. Enter any significant noncash activities on a supplemental schedule.

4. **Determine the cash flows from financing activities.** Generally, this requires analyzing the *long-term liability* and *stockholders' equity* accounts and any additional information provided. Draft journal entries for each transaction. Enter any debits to cash on the left side of the Cash Flow from Financing Activities master T account and any credits on the right side of the T account. Enter any significant noncash activities on a supplemental schedule.

Remember that these are general rules that the cash effects of changes in current accounts are reported in the operating activities section, those relating to long-term asset accounts in the investing section, and those relating to long-term liabilities and stockholders' equity in the financing section. The general rules for classification of activities have a few exceptions, but we will not concern ourselves with them.

The Master T-Account Approach: A Comprehensive Example

To illustrate this approach, refer to the income statement in Exhibit 14-11 and the comparative balance sheets in Exhibit 14-12, along with the additional information provided for Julian Corp.

Determine the Cash Flows from Operating Activities To do this, it is necessary to consider each of the items on the income statement and any related current assets or liabilities from the balance sheet.

Sales Revenue and Accounts Receivable Sales as reported on the income statement in Exhibit 14-11 amounted to $670,000. The journal entry is

(a) Accounts Receivable   670,000
      Sales Revenue   670,000
    To record sales on account.

	Assets	=	**Liabilities**	+	**Owners' Equity**
	+670,000				+670,000

Based on the beginning and ending balances from Exhibit 14-12, a T account for Accounts Receivable appears as follows after posting the debit for the sales of the period:

ACCOUNTS RECEIVABLE

Bal. Jan. 1	57,000		
(a) Sales on account	670,000	?	Cash collections (b)
Bal. Dec. 31	63,000		

Accounts Receivable increased by $6,000 for the period. *This indicates that Julian had $6,000 more in sales to its customers than it collected in cash from them* (assuming that all sales are on credit). Thus, cash collections must have been $670,000 − $6,000, or $664,000. Another way to look at this is

Beginning accounts receivable	$ 57,000
+ Sales revenue	670,000
− Cash collections	(X)
= Ending accounts receivable	$ 63,000

EXHIBIT 14-11   Julian Corp. Income Statement

JULIAN CORP.
INCOME STATEMENT
FOR THE YEAR ENDED DECEMBER 31, 1995

Revenues and gains:		
Sales revenue	$670,000	
Interest revenue	15,000	
Gain on sale of machine	5,000	
Total revenues and gains		$690,000
Expenses and losses:		
Cost of goods sold	$390,000	
Salaries and wages	60,000	
Depreciation	40,000	
Insurance	12,000	
Interest	15,000	
Income taxes	50,000	
Loss on retirement of bonds	3,000	
Total expenses and losses		570,000
Net income		$120,000

Solving for X, we can find cash collections:

$$57,000 + 670,000 - X = 63,000$$
$$X = \underline{664,000}$$

The journal entry to record cash collections would be

(b) Cash   664,000
     Accounts Receivable   664,000
   To record cash collected on account.

Assets	=	Liabilities	+	Owners' Equity
+664,000				
-664,000				

At this point, note the debit to Cash for $664,000 as shown in the master T account, Cash Flows from Operating Activities, in Exhibit 14-13.

Interest Revenue   Julian reported interest revenue on the income statement of $15,000. Did the company actually receive this amount of cash or was it merely an accrual of revenue earned but not yet received? The answer can be found by examining the current asset section of the balance sheet. *Because there is no Interest Receivable account, the amount of interest earned was the amount of cash received:*

(c) Cash   15,000
     Interest Revenue   15,000
   To record interest earned and received.

Assets	=	Liabilities	+	Owners' Equity
+15,000				+15,000

EXHIBIT 14-12   Julian Corp. Comparative Balance Sheets

JULIAN CORP.
COMPARATIVE BALANCE SHEETS

	DECEMBER 31	
	1995	1994
Cash	$ 35,000	$ 46,000
Accounts receivable	63,000	57,000
Inventory	84,000	92,000
Prepaid insurance	12,000	18,000
Total current assets	$ 194,000	$ 213,000
Long-term investments	$ 120,000	$ 90,000
Land	150,000	100,000
Property and equipment	320,000	280,000
Accumulated depreciation	(100,000)	(75,000)
Total long-term assets	$ 490,000	$ 395,000
Total assets	$ 684,000	$ 608,000
Accounts payable	$ 38,000	$ 31,000
Salaries and wages payable	7,000	9,000
Income taxes payable	8,000	5,000
Total current liabilities	$ 53,000	$ 45,000
Notes payable	$ 85,000	$ 35,000
Bonds payable	200,000	260,000
Total long-term liabilities	$ 285,000	$ 295,000
Capital stock	$ 100,000	$ 75,000
Retained earnings	246,000	193,000
Total stockholders' equity	$ 346,000	$ 268,000
Total liabilities and stock. equity	$ 684,000	$ 608,000

Additional Information

1. Long-term investments were purchased for $30,000. The securities are classified as available for sale.
2. Land was purchased by issuing a $50,000 note payable.
3. Equipment was purchased for $75,000.
4. A machine with an original cost of $35,000 and a book value of $20,000 was sold for $25,000.
5. Bonds with a face value of $60,000 were retired by paying $63,000 in cash.
6. Capital stock was issued in exchange for $25,000 in cash.
7. Dividends of $67,000 were paid.

The debit should be entered in the master T account, Cash Flows from Operating Activities, as shown in Exhibit 14-13.

Gain on Sale of Machine   A gain on the sale of machine of $5,000 is reported as the next line on the income statement. Any cash received from sale of a long-term asset is reported in the investing activities section of the statement of cash flows. Thus, we ignore the gain when reporting cash flows from operating activities under the direct method.

Cost of Goods Sold, Inventory, and Accounts Payable   Cost of goods sold, as reported on the income statement, amounts to $390,000 and is recorded with this entry:

(d) Cost of Goods Sold   390,000
        Inventory   390,000
     To record cost of goods sold.

Assets	=	Liabilities	+	Owners' Equity
− 390,000				− 390,000

We see that $390,000 is not the amount of cash expended to pay suppliers of inventory. First, cost of goods sold represents the cost of the inventory sold during the period, not the amount purchased. Thus, we must analyze the Inventory account to determine the purchases of the period. Second, the amount of purchases is not the same as the cash paid to suppliers because purchases are normally on account. Thus, we must analyze the Accounts Payable account to determine the cash payments.

Based on the beginning and ending balances from Exhibit 14-12, a T account for Inventory appears as follows after posting the credit for cost of goods sold:

INVENTORY

Bal. Jan. 1	92,000		
(e) Purchases on account	?	390,000	Cost of goods sold (d)
Bal. Dec. 31	84,000		

Note the $8,000 net decrease in Inventory. *This means that the cost of inventory sold was $8,000 more than the purchases of the period.* Thus, purchases must have been $390,000 − $8,000, or $382,000. Another way to look at this is

Beginning inventory	$ 92,000
+ Purchases	X
− Cost of goods sold	(390,000)
= Ending inventory	$ 84,000

EXHIBIT 14-13   Master T Account for Cash Flows from Operating Activities

CASH FLOWS FROM OPERATING ACTIVITIES			
Cash receipts from:		Cash payments for:	
(b) Sales on account	664,000	(f) Inventory	375,000
(c) Interest	15,000	(h) Salaries and wages	62,000
		(k) Insurance	6,000
		(l) Interest	15,000
		(n) Taxes	47,000

Solving for *X,* we can find purchases:

$$92,000 + X - 390,000 = 84,000$$
$$X = \underline{382,000}$$

The journal entry to record purchases is

(e) Inventory	382,000	
Accounts Payable		382,000
To record purchases on account.		

| **Assets** | **=** | **Liabilities** | **+** | **Owners' Equity** |
| +382,000 | | +382,000 | | |

From Exhibit 14-12, a T account for Accounts Payable, after posting the credit for purchases of the period, is as follows:

ACCOUNTS PAYABLE

		31,000	Bal. Jan. 1
(f) Cash payments	?	382,000	Purchases (e)
		38,000	Bal. Dec. 31

Note the $7,000 net increase in Accounts Payable. *This means that Julian's purchases were $7,000 more during the period than its cash payments.* Thus, cash payments must have been $382,000 − $7,000, or $375,000. Another way to look at this is

	Beginning accounts payable	$ 31,000
+	Purchases	382,000
−	Cash payments	(X)
=	Ending accounts payable	$ 38,000

Solving for *X,* we can find cash payments:

$$31,000 + 382,000 - X = 38,000$$
$$X = \underline{375,000}$$

The journal entry to record payments on account is

(f) Accounts Payable	375,000	
Cash		375,000
To record cash payments on account.		

| **Assets** | **=** | **Liabilities** | **+** | **Owners' Equity** |
| −375,000 | | −375,000 | | |

At this point, the credit to cash should be entered in the master T account, Cash Flows from Operating Activities, as shown in Exhibit 14-13.

Salaries and Wages Expense and Salaries and Wages Payable The entry to record salaries and wages expense is

(g) Salaries and Wages Expense	60,000	
Salaries and Wages Payable		60,000
To record salaries and wages.		

| **Assets** | **=** | **Liabilities** | **+** | **Owners' Equity** |
| | | +60,000 | | −60,000 |

When this entry is posted to Salaries and Wages Payable, note the $2,000 net decrease in the account for the period.

SALARIES AND WAGES PAYABLE

		9,000	Bal. Jan. 1
(h) Cash payments	?	60,000	Expense (g)
		7,000	Bal. Dec. 31

This means that the amount of cash paid to employees was $2,000 more than the amount of expense accrued. Another way to look at the cash payments of $60,000 + $2,000, or $62,000, is

Beginning salaries and wages payable	$ 9,000
+ Salaries and wages expense	60,000
− Cash payments to employees	(X)
= Ending accounts payable	$ 7,000

Solving for *X*, we can find cash payments:

$$9,000 + 60,000 - X = 7,000$$
$$X = \underline{\underline{62,000}}$$

The journal entry to record the cash paid is

(h) Salaries and Wages Payable   62,000
       Cash   62,000
       To record cash paid to employees.

Assets	=	Liabilities	+	Owners' Equity
− 62,000		− 62,000		

As you see in Exhibit 14-13, the credit of $62,000 in this entry appears in the T account for Cash Flows from Operating Activities.

Depreciation Expense   The next item on the income statement is depreciation of $40,000. The entry to record depreciation is

(i) Depreciation Expense   40,000
       Accumulated Depreciation   40,000
       To record depreciation.

Assets	=	Liabilities	+	Owners' Equity
− 40,000				− 40,000

Depreciation of tangible long-term assets, amortization of intangible assets, and depletion of natural resources are different from most other expenses in that they have no effect on cash flow. The only related cash flows are from the purchase and sale of these long-term assets, and these are reported in the investing activities section of the statement of cash flows.

Insurance Expense and Prepaid Insurance   According to the income statement in Exhibit 14-11, Julian recorded Insurance Expense of $12,000 during 1995. This amount is not the cash payments for insurance, however, because Julian has a Prepaid

Insurance account on the balance sheet. The entry to record expense involves a reduction in the Prepaid Insurance account as follows:

(j) Insurance Expense   12,000
　　　　Prepaid Insurance   12,000
　　　To record expiration of insurance.

Assets　=　Liabilities　+　Owners' Equity
− 12,000　　　　　　　　　　　　　　− 12,000

When the credit to Prepaid Insurance is posted, note the $6,000 net decrease in the account for the period:

PREPAID INSURANCE

Bal. Jan. 1	18,000		
(k) Cash payments	?	12,000	Expense (j)
Bal. Dec. 31	12,000		

This means that the amount of cash paid for insurance was $6,000 less than the amount of expense recognized. Thus, the cash payments must have been $12,000 − $6,000, or $6,000. Another way to look at the cash payments is

Beginning prepaid insurance	$18,000
+ Cash payments for insurance	X
− Insurance expense	(12,000)
= Ending prepaid insurance	$12,000

Solving for X, we can find the amount of cash paid:

$$18,000 + X - 12,000 = 12,000$$
$$X = \underline{6,000}$$

The journal entry to record the cash paid is

(k) Prepaid Insurance   6,000
　　　　Cash   6,000
　　　To record cash paid to employees.

Assets　=　Liabilities　+　Owners' Equity
+ 6,000
− 6,000

Note that the credit to Cash is entered in Exhibit 14-13 in the T account for Cash Flows from Operating Activities.

Interest Expense　The amount of interest expense reported on the income statement is $15,000. Because the balance sheet does not report an accrual of interest owed but not yet paid (an Interest Payable account), we know that $15,000 is also the amount of cash paid:

(l) Interest Expense   15,000
　　　　Cash   15,000
　　　To record interest expense.

Assets　=　Liabilities　+　Owners' Equity
− 15,000　　　　　　　　　　　　　　− 15,000

The entry is recorded as a cash outflow in Exhibit 14-13. Whether interest paid is properly classified as an operating activity is subject to considerable debate. The

Financial Accounting Standards Board decided in favor of classification of *interest* as an *operating* activity because, unlike dividends, it appears on the income statement. This, it was argued, provides a direct link between the statement of cash flows and the income statement. Many argue, however, that it is inconsistent to classify dividends paid as a financing activity but interest paid as an operating activity. After all, both represent returns paid to providers of capital: interest to creditors and dividends to stockholders.

Income Tax Expense and Income Taxes Payable   The entry to record Income Tax Expense is

(m) Income Taxes Expense	50,000	
Income Taxes Payable		50,000
To record income taxes.		

Assets	=	Liabilities	+	Owners' Equity
		+50,000		−50,000

When the credit to Income Taxes Payable is posted, note the $3,000 net increase in the account for the period:

INCOME TAXES PAYABLE

		5,000	Bal. Jan. 1
(n) Cash payments	?	50,000	Expense (m)
		8,000	Bal. Dec. 31

This means that the amount of cash paid to the government in taxes was $3,000 less than the amount of expense accrued. Another way to look at the cash payments of $50,000 − $3,000, or $47,000, is

Beginning income taxes payable	$ 5,000
+ Income tax expense	50,000
− Cash payments for taxes	(X)
= Ending income taxes payable	$ 8,000

Solving for X, we can find the amount of cash paid:

$$5,000 + 50,000 - X = 8,000$$
$$X = \underline{47,000}$$

The journal entry to record cash paid is

(n) Income Taxes Payable	47,000	
Cash		47,000
To record cash paid in taxes.		

Assets	=	Liabilities	+	Owners' Equity
−47,000		−47,000		

As you see by examining Exhibit 14-13, the cash payments for taxes is the last item in the T account for Cash Flows from Operating Activities.

Loss on Retirement of Bonds   A $3,000 loss on the retirement of bonds is reported as the last item under expenses and losses on the income statement in Exhibit 14-11. Any cash paid to retire a long-term liability is reported in the financing activities section of the statement of cash flows. Thus, we ignore the loss when reporting cash flows from operating activities under the direct method.

Comparing Net Income to Net Cash Flow from Operating Activities

At this point, all of the items on the income statement have been analyzed (with the exception of the gain and the loss), as have all of the current asset and current liability accounts. All of the information needed to prepare the operating activities section of your statement of cash flows has been gathered.

To summarize, the preparation of the operating activities section of the statement of cash flows requires the conversion of each item on the income statement to a cash basis. The current asset and liability accounts are analyzed to discover the cash effects of each item on the income statement. Exhibit 14-14 summarizes this conversion process.

Note in the exhibit the various adjustments made to put each income statement item on a cash basis. For example, the $6,000 increase in accounts receivable for the period is deducted from sales revenue of $670,000 to arrive at cash collected from customers. Similar adjustments are made to each of the other income statement items with the exception of depreciation and the gain and the loss. Depreciation is ignored because it does not have an effect on cash flow. The gain relates to the sale of a long-term asset, and any cash effect is reflected in the investing activities section of the statement of cash flows. Similarly, the loss resulted from the retirement of bonds, and any cash flow effect is reported in the financing activities section. The bottom of the exhibit highlights an important point: Julian reported net income of $120,000 but actually generated $174,000 in cash from operations.

Determine the Cash Flows from Investing Activities At this point, we turn our attention to the long-term asset accounts and any additional information available about these accounts. Julian has three long-term assets on its balance sheet: Long-term Investments, Land, and Property and Equipment.

Long-term Investments Item 1 in the additional information in Exhibit 14-12 indicates that Julian purchased $30,000 of investments during the year. The $30,000 net increase in the Long-term Investments account confirms this (no mention is made of the sale of any investments during 1995):

LONG-TERM INVESTMENTS

Bal. Jan. 1	90,000
(o) Purchases	?
Bal. Dec. 31	120,000

The entry to record the purchase is

(o) Long-term Investments	30,000	
Cash		30,000
To record purchase of investments.		

Assets	=	Liabilities	+	Owners' Equity
+30,000				
−30,000				

The credit in this entry is the first cash outflow in the master T account, Cash Flows from Investing Activities, as shown in Exhibit 14-15.

Land Note the $50,000 net increase in land:

LAND

Bal. Jan. 1	100,000
(p) Acquisitions	?
Bal. Dec. 31	150,000

EXHIBIT 14-14 Conversion of Income Statement Items to Cash Basis

INCOME STATEMENT	AMOUNT	ADJUSTMENTS	CASH FLOWS
Sales revenue	$670,000		$670,000
		+ Decreases in accounts receivable	–0–
		− Increases in accounts receivable	(6,000)
		Cash collected from customers	$664,000
Interest revenue	15,000		$ 15,000
		+ Decreases in interest receivable	–0–
		− Increases in interest receivable	–0–
		Cash collected in interest	$ 15,000
Gain on sale of machine	5,000	*Not an operating activity*	$ –0–
Cost of goods sold	390,000		$390,000
		+ Increases in inventory	–0–
		− Decreases in inventory	(8,000)
		+ Decreases in accounts payable	–0–
		− Increases in accounts payable	(7,000)
		Cash paid to suppliers	$375,000
Salaries and wages	60,000		$ 60,000
		+ Decreases in salaries/wages payable	2,000
		− Increases in salaries/wages payable	–0–
		Cash paid to employees	$ 62,000
Depreciation	40,000	*No cash flow effect*	$ –0–
Insurance	12,000		$ 12,000
		+ Increases in prepaid insurance	–0–
		− Decreases in prepaid insurance	(6,000)
		Cash paid for insurance	$ 6,000
Interest	15,000		$ 15,000
		+ Decreases in interest payable	–0–
		− Increases in interest payable	–0–
		Cash paid for interest	$ 15,000
Income taxes	50,000		$ 50,000
		+ Decreases in income taxes payable	–0–
		− Increases in income taxes payable	(3,000)
		Cash paid for taxes	$ 47,000
Loss on retirement of bonds	3,000	*Not an operating activity*	$ –0–
Net income	$120,000	Net cash flow from operating activities	$174,000

Item 2 in the additional information indicates that Julian purchased land by issuing a $50,000 note payable. The entry to record the purchase is

(p) Land 50,000
    Notes Payable 50,000
To record acquisition of land in exchange for note.

Assets	=	**Liabilities**	+	**Owners' Equity**
+50,000		+50,000		

EXHIBIT 14-15   Master T Account for Cash Flows from Investing Activities

CASH FLOWS FROM INVESTING ACTIVITIES		
Cash inflows from:	Cash outflows for:	
(r) Sale of machine 25,000	(o) Purchase of investments	30,000
	(q) Purchase of plant and	
	equipment	75,000

This entry obviously does not involve cash. The transaction has both an important financing element as well as an investing component, however. The issuance of the note is a financing activity and the acquisition of land is an investing activity. Because no cash was involved, the transaction is reported in a separate schedule instead of directly on the statement of cash flows:

SUPPLEMENTAL SCHEDULE OF NONCASH INVESTING AND FINANCING ACTIVITIES

Acquisition of land in exchange for note payable $50,000

Property and Equipment   Property and equipment increased by $40,000 during 1995. However, Julian both acquired equipment and sold a machine (items 3 and 4 in the additional information). The acquisition of the equipment for $75,000 results in this journal entry:

(q) Property and Equipment   75,000
      Cash   75,000
    Acquisition of equipment for cash.

Assets	**=**	**Liabilities**	**+**	**Owners' Equity**
+75,000				
−75,000				

As we discussed earlier in the chapter, acquisitions of new plant and equipment are important investing activities for most businesses. Thus, the credit to Cash appears in the master T account, Cash Flows from Investing Activities in Exhibit 14-15.

After this entry is posted to the Property and Equipment account, it appears as follows:

PROPERTY AND EQUIPMENT

Bal. Jan. 1	280,000		
(q) Acquisitions	75,000	?	Disposals (r)
Bal. Dec. 31	320,000		

Julian obviously disposed of fixed assets during the period. In fact, item 4 in the additional information reports the sale of a machine with an original cost of $35,000. An analysis of the Property and Equipment account at this point confirms this amount:

Beginning property and equipment	$280,000
+ Acquisitions	75,000
− Disposals	(X)
= Ending property and equipment	$320,000

Solving for *X*, we can find the *cost* of the fixed assets sold during the year:

$$280,000 + 75,000 - X = 320,000$$
$$X = \underline{\$35,000}$$

A T account for Accumulated Depreciation appears as follows after posting Depreciation Expense in entry (i) on page 760:

ACCUMULATED DEPRECIATION

		75,000	Bal. Jan. 1
(r) Disposals	?	40,000	Depreciation expense (i)
		100,000	Bal. Dec. 31

The additional information also indicates that the book value of the machine sold was $20,000. This means that if the original cost was $35,000 and the book value was $20,000, the Accumulated Depreciation on the machine sold must have been $35,000 − $20,000, or $15,000. A similar analysis to the one we just looked at for Property and Equipment confirms this amount:

Beginning accumulated depreciation	$ 75,000
+ Depreciation expense (entry i)	40,000
− Accumulated depreciation on assets sold	(*X*)
= Ending accumulated depreciation	$100,000

Solving for *X*, we can find the accumulated depreciation on the assets disposed of during the year:

$$75,000 + 40,000 - X = 100,000$$
$$X = \underline{\$15,000}$$

Finally, we are told in the additional information that the machine was sold for $25,000. *If the selling price was $25,000 and the book value was $20,000, Julian reports a gain on sale of $5,000, an amount that is confirmed on the income statement in Exhibit 14-11.* The journal entry to record the sale of the machine is

(r) Cash	25,000	
Accumulated Depreciation	15,000	
Property and Equipment		35,000
Gain on Sale of Machine (Retained Earnings)		5,000
To record sale of machine.		

Assets	=	Liabilities	+	Owners' Equity
+25,000				+5,000
+15,000				
−35,000				

To summarize, the machine was sold for $25,000, an amount that exceeded its book value of $20,000, thus generating a gain of $5,000. The debit to Cash is entered in the master T account for Cash Flows from Investing Activities in Exhibit 14-15.

Determine the Cash Flows from Financing Activities These activities generally involve long-term liabilities and stockholders' equity. We first consider Julian's two long-term liabilities, Notes Payable and Bonds Payable, and then the two stockholders' equity accounts: Capital Stock and Retained Earnings.

Notes Payable   Recall that item 2 in the additional information reported that Julian purchased land in exchange for a $50,000 note payable. The T account for Notes Payable confirms this amount:

NOTES PAYABLE		
	35,000	Bal. Jan. 1
	?	Additional issuances (p)
	85,000	Bal. Dec. 31

In our discussion of investing activities, we recorded entry (p) on page 764 to account for this exchange and entered the transaction on a supplemental schedule of noncash activities because it was a significant financing activity, but did not involve cash.

Bonds Payable   A T account for Bonds Payable appears as follows:

BONDS PAYABLE		
	260,000	Bal. Jan. 1
(s) Retirement ?		
	200,000	Bal. Dec. 31

Item 5 in the additional information in Exhibit 14-12 indicates that bonds with a face value of $60,000 were retired by paying $63,000 in cash. The book value of the bonds retired is the same as the face value of $60,000 because there is no unamortized discount or premium on the records. *When a company has to pay more in cash ($63,000) to settle a debt than the book value of the debt ($60,000), it reports a loss.* Recall the $3,000 loss reported on the income statement in Exhibit 14-11. The entry to record the retirement of the bonds is

(s) Loss on Retirement of Bonds (Retained Earnings)	3,000	
Bonds Payable	60,000	
Cash		63,000

To record retirement of bonds.

Assets	=	**Liabilities**	+	**Owners' Equity**
− 63,000		− 60,000		− 3,000

The credit to Cash in this entry is presented in the master T account, Cash Flows from Financing Activities, as shown in Exhibit 14-16.

Capital Stock   The Capital Stock account indicates a $25,000 net increase during 1995:

CAPITAL STOCK		
	75,000	Bal. Jan. 1
	?	Stock issued (t)
	100,000	Bal. Dec. 31

EXHIBIT 14-16   Master T Account for Cash Flows from Financing Activities

CASH FLOWS FROM FINANCING ACTIVITIES			
Cash inflows from:		Cash outflows for:	
(t) Issuance of stock	25,000	(s) Retirement of bonds	63,000
		(u) Cash dividends	67,000

Julian issued capital stock in exchange for $25,000, according to item 6 in the additional information in Exhibit 14-12. Some companies issue additional stock after the initial formation of a corporation to raise needed capital. The entry is

(t) Cash	25,000	
Capital Stock		25,000

To record issuance of stock in exchange for cash.

Assets	= Liabilities	+ Owners' Equity
+ 25,000		+ 25,000

The debit to Cash in this entry is presented as a cash inflow in the master T account, Cash Flows from Financing Activities, as shown in Exhibit 14-16.

Retained Earnings   An analysis of the Retained Earnings account indicates the following:

<table>
<tr><td colspan="4" align="center">RETAINED EARNINGS</td></tr>
<tr><td></td><td></td><td>193,000</td><td>Bal. Jan. 1</td></tr>
<tr><td>(u) Cash dividends</td><td>?</td><td>120,000</td><td>Net income for 1995</td></tr>
<tr><td></td><td></td><td>246,000</td><td>Bal. Dec. 31</td></tr>
</table>

We can determine the amount of cash dividends for 1995 in the following manner:

Beginning retained earnings	$193,000
+ Net income	120,000
− Cash dividends	X
= Ending retained earnings	$246,000

Solving for X, we can find the amount of cash dividends paid during the year:[4]

$$193,000 + 120,000 - X = 246,000$$
$$X = \underline{\$67,000}$$

Item 7 in the additional information confirms that this was in fact the amount of dividends paid during the year. The final entry is

(u) Retained Earnings	67,000	
Cash		67,000

To record cash dividends paid.

Assets	= Liabilities	+ Owners' Equity
− 67,000		− 67,000

The credit to Cash in this entry appears in the master T account, Cash Flows from Financing Activities, as presented in Exhibit 14-16.

Using the Master T Accounts to Prepare a Statement of Cash Flows

All of the information needed to prepare a statement of cash flows is now available in the three master T accounts, along with the supplemental schedule prepared

---

[4] Any decrease in Retained Earnings represents the dividends *declared* during the period rather than the amount paid. If there had been a Dividends Payable account, we would analyze it to find the amount of dividends paid. The lack of a balance in such an account at either the beginning or the end of the period tells us that Julian paid the same amount of dividends that it declared during the period.

earlier. From the information gathered in Exhibits 14-13, 14-15, and 14-16, a completed statement of cash flows appears in Exhibit 14-17.

What does Julian's statement of cash flows tell us? Cash flow from operations totaled $174,000. Cash used to acquire investments and equipment amounted to $80,000, after receiving $25,000 from the sale of a machine. A net amount of $105,000 was used for financing activities. Thus, Julian used more cash than it generated, and that's why the cash balance declined. That's okay for a year or two, but if it continues, the company won't be able to pay its bills.

■ ACCOUNTING FOR YOUR DECISIONS   **You Are the CEO of Julian Corp.**

You are on a tour of Wall Street, setting up meetings with securities analysts who follow your stock. At one luncheon, an analyst asks you why there is such a big disparity between your net income of $120,000 and the net decrease in cash of $11,000. What is your response?

A Master T-Account Approach to Preparing the Statement of Cash Flows: Indirect Method

The purpose of the operating activities section of the statement changes when we use the indirect method. Instead of reporting cash receipts and cash payments, *the objective is to reconcile net income to net cash flow from operating activities.* The other two sections of the completed statement in Exhibit 14-17, the investing and financing sections, are unchanged. The use of the indirect or direct method for presenting cash flow from operating activities does not affect these two sections.

A T-account methodology, similar to that used for the direct method, can be used to prepare the operating activities section of the statement of cash flows under the indirect method.

LO	6

Use T accounts to prepare a statement of cash flows, using the indirect method to determine cash flow from operating activities.

Net Income   Recall that the first line in the operating activities section of the statement under the indirect method is net income. That is, we start with the assumptions that all revenues and gains reported on the income statement increase cash flow and that all expenses and losses decrease cash flow. Julian's net income of $120,000, as reported on its income statement in Exhibit 14-11, is reported as the first item in the operating activities section of the statement of cash flows as shown in Exhibit 14-18.

Increase in Accounts Receivable   The net increase in Accounts Receivable, as shown below in T-account form, indicates that Julian recorded more sales during the period than cash collections:

ACCOUNTS RECEIVABLE	
Bal. Jan. 1 57,000	
Net increase 6,000	
Bal. Dec. 31 63,000	

Because net income includes sales, as opposed to cash collections, the $6,000 *net increase* must be *deducted* to adjust net income to cash from operations. To help you

FROM CONCEPT TO PRACTICE

READING BEN & JERRY'S STATEMENT OF CASH FLOWS
Did Accounts Receivable increase or decrease during 1992? Why is the change in this account deducted on the statement of cash flows?

EXHIBIT 14-17   Completed Statement of Cash Flows for Julian Corp.

JULIAN CORP.
STATEMENT OF CASH FLOWS
FOR THE YEAR ENDED DECEMBER 31, 1995

CASH FLOWS FROM OPERATING ACTIVITIES

Cash receipts from:

Customers	$ 664,000
Interest	15,000
Total cash receipts	$ 679,000

Cash payments for:

Inventory	$(375,000)
Salaries and wages	(62,000)
Insurance	(6,000)
Interest	(15,000)
Income taxes	(47,000)
Total cash payments	$(505,000)
Net cash provided by operating activities	$ 174,000

CASH FLOWS FROM INVESTING ACTIVITIES

Purchase of long-term investments	$ (30,000)
Purchase of equipment	(75,000)
Sale of machine	25,000
Net cash used by investing activities	$ (80,000)

CASH FLOWS FROM FINANCING ACTIVITIES

Retirement of bonds payable	$ (63,000)
Issuance of capital stock	25,000
Payment of cash dividends	(67,000)
Net cash used by financing activities	$(105,000)
Net decrease in cash	$ (11,000)
Cash balance, December 31, 1994	46,000
Cash balance, December 31, 1995	$ 35,000

SUPPLEMENTAL SCHEDULE OF NONCASH INVESTING AND FINANCING ACTIVITIES

Acquisition of land in exchange for note payable	$ 50,000

remember to deduct the net increase in accounts receivable in the operating activities section of the statement, consider the following. The $6,000 net increase appears in the preceding T account as a *debit*. Think of the deduction on the statement of cash flows as the equivalent of a *credit*. That is, the debit is to Accounts Receivable and the credit is recorded as a bracketed amount (i.e., as a deduction on the statement of cash flows).

Gain on Sale of Machine   The gain itself did not generate any cash, but the *sale* of the machine did. And as we found earlier, the cash generated by selling the machine was reported in the investing activities section of the statement. The cash

EXHIBIT 14-18 Indirect Method for Reporting Cash Flows from Operating Activities

JULIAN CORP.
PARTIAL STATEMENT OF CASH FLOWS
FOR THE YEAR ENDED DECEMBER 31, 1995

NET CASH FLOWS FROM OPERATING ACTIVITIES

Net income	$120,000
Adjustments to reconcile net income to net cash provided by operating activities:	
Increase in accounts receivable	(6,000)
Gain on sale of machine	(5,000)
Decrease in inventory	8,000
Increase in accounts payable	7,000
Decrease in salaries and wages payable	(2,000)
Depreciation expense	40,000
Decrease in prepaid insurance	6,000
Increase in income taxes payable	3,000
Loss on retirement of bonds	3,000
Net cash provided by operating activities	$174,000

proceeds included the gain. Because the gain is included in the net income figure, it must be *deducted* to determine cash from operations. Also note that the gain is included twice in cash inflows if it is not deducted from the net income figure in the operating activities section. Note the deduction of $5,000 in Exhibit 14-18.

Decrease in Inventory As the $8,000 net decrease in the Inventory account indicates, Julian liquidated a portion of its stock of inventory during the year:

INVENTORY			
Bal. Jan. 1	92,000		
		8,000	Net decrease
Bal. Dec. 31	84,000		

A net decrease in this account indicates that the company sold more products than it purchased during the year. As shown in Exhibit 14-18, the *net decrease* of $8,000 is *added back* to net income. As discussed for Accounts Receivable, note the debit and credit logic for this adjustment. Because Inventory is credited in the T account for the decrease, the statement of cash flows shows an increase, which is equivalent to a debit to Cash.

Increase in Accounts Payable Julian owed suppliers $31,000 at the start of the year. By the end of the year, this balance had grown to $38,000. A T account for Accounts Payable follows:

ACCOUNTS PAYABLE			
		31,000	Bal. Jan. 1
		7,000	Net increase
		38,000	Bal. Dec. 31

FROM CONCEPT TO PRACTICE

READING BEN & JERRY'S STATEMENT OF CASH FLOWS
Did the disposal of assets during 1992 result in a gain or a loss? What is the amount? Why is it deducted on the statement of cash flows?

Effectively, the company has saved cash by delaying the payment of some of its outstanding accounts payable. The *net increase* of $7,000 in this account is *added back* to net income, as shown in Exhibit 14-18.

Decrease in Salaries and Wages Payable A T account for Salaries and Wages Payable indicates a net decrease of $2,000:

SALARIES AND WAGES PAYABLE

		9,000	Bal. Jan. 1
Net decrease	2,000		
		7,000	Bal. Dec. 31

The rationale for *deducting* the $2,000 *net decrease* in this liability in Exhibit 14-18 follows from what we just said about an increase in Accounts Payable. The payment to employees of $2,000 more than the amount included in expense on the income statement requires an additional deduction under the indirect method.

Depreciation Expense Depreciation is a noncash expense. Because it was deducted to arrive at net income, we must *add back* $40,000, the amount of depreciation, to find cash from operations. The same holds true for amortization of intangible assets and depletion of natural resources.

Decrease in Prepaid Insurance This account decreased by $6,000, according to the T account:

PREPAID INSURANCE

Bal. Jan. 1	18,000		
		6,000	Net decrease
Bal. Dec. 31	12,000		

A decrease in this account indicates that Julian deducted more on the income statement for the insurance expense of the period than it paid in cash for new policies. That is, the cash outlay for insurance protection was not as large as the amount of expense reported on the income statement. Thus, the *net decrease* in the account is *added back* to net income in Exhibit 14-18.

Increase in Income Taxes Payable A T account for Income Taxes Payable indicates a net increase of $3,000:

INCOME TAXES PAYABLE

		5,000	Bal. Jan. 1
		3,000	Net increase
		8,000	Bal. Dec. 31

The *net increase* of $3,000 in this liability is *added back* to net income in Exhibit 14-18 because the payments to the government were $3,000 less than the amount included on the income statement.

Loss on Retirement of Bonds The $3,000 loss from retiring bonds was reported on the income statement as a deduction. There are two parts to the explanation for *adding back* the loss to net income to eliminate its effect in the operating activities section of the statement. First, any cash outflow from retiring bonds is properly classified as a financing activity, not an operating activity. The entire cash outflow should be reported in one classification rather than being allocated between two classifications. Second, the amount of the cash outflow is $63,000, not $3,000. To summarize, to convert net income to a cash basis, the loss is added back in the operating activities section to eliminate its effect. The actual use of cash to retire the bonds is shown in the financing section of the statement.

Summary of Adjustments to Net Income under the Indirect Method

Following is a list of the most common adjustments to net income when the indirect method is used to prepare the operating activities section of the statement of cash flows:

ADDITIONS TO NET INCOME	DEDUCTIONS FROM NET INCOME
Decrease in accounts receivable	Increase in accounts receivable
Decrease in inventory	Increase in inventory
Decrease in prepayments	Increase in prepayments
Increase in accounts payable	Decrease in accounts payable
Increase in accrued liabilities	Decrease in accrued liabilities
Losses on sales of long-term assets	Gains on sales of long-term assets
Losses on retirements of bonds	Gains on retirements of bonds
Depreciation, amortization, and depletion	

Comparison of the Indirect and Direct Methods

The relative merits of the two methods have stirred considerable debate in the accounting profession. The Financial Accounting Standards Board has expressed a strong preference for the direct method but allows companies to use the indirect method.

If a company uses the indirect method, it must separately disclose two important cash payments: income taxes paid and interest paid. Thus, if Julian uses the indirect method, it reports the following either at the bottom of the statement of cash flows or in a footnote:[5]

Income taxes paid	$47,000
Interest paid	$15,000

Advocates of the direct method believe that the information provided with this approach is valuable in evaluating a company's operating efficiency. For example, the use of the direct method allows the analyst to follow any trends in cash receipts from customers and compare them with cash payments to suppliers. The information presented in the operating activities section of the statement under the direct method is certainly user friendly. Someone without a technical background in accounting can easily tell where cash came from and where it went during the period.

Advocates of the indirect method argue two major points. Many companies believe that the use of the direct method reveals too much about their business by telling readers exactly the amount of cash receipts and cash payments from operations. Whether the use of the direct method tells the competition too much about a company is subject to debate. The other argument made for the indirect method is that it focuses attention on the differences between income on an accrual basis and

[5] The same *Accounting Trends & Techniques* survey referred to earlier in the chapter indicated that of those companies using the indirect method, approximately 60% disclose interest and taxes paid in notes to the financial statements and approximately 40% report these amounts at the bottom of the statement of cash flows.

a cash basis. In fact, this reconciliation of net income and cash provided by operating activities is considered to be important enough that *if a company uses the direct method, it must present a separate schedule to reconcile net income to net cash from operating activities.* This schedule, in effect, is the same as the operating activities section for the indirect method.

The Use of Cash Flow Information

The statement of cash flows is a critical disclosure to a company's investors and creditors. Many investors focus on cash flow from operations as their key statistic rather than net income. Companies such as Time Warner and RJR Nabisco that took on a great deal of debt during the 1980s merger mania are evaluated almost exclusively on their cash flows. Similarly, many bankers are as concerned with cash flow from operations as they are with net income because they care about a company's ability to pay its bills. There is the concern that accrual accounting can mask cash flow problems. For example, a company with smooth earnings could be building up accounts receivable and inventory. This may not become evident until the company is in deep trouble.

The statement of cash flows provides investors, analysts, bankers, and other users with a valuable starting point as they attempt to evaluate a company's financial health. From this point, these groups must decide *how* to use the information presented on the statement. They pay particular attention to the *relationships* among various items on the statement, as well as to other financial statement items. In fact, many large banks have their own cash flow models, which typically involve a rearrangement of the items on the statement of cash flows to suit their needs. We now turn our attention to two examples of how various groups use cash flow information.

Managers, investors, and brokers gauge the relative strengths of retailers by observing which stores are the most popular. But they also study the financial statements, particularly the statement of cash flows for such indicators as cash flow adequacy, as the most fundamental way to measure a firm's strength.

Creditors and Cash Flow Adequacy

Bankers and other creditors are especially concerned with a company's ability to meet its principal and interest obligations. *Cash flow adequacy* is a measure intended to help in this regard.[6] It gauges the cash available to meet future debt obligations after paying taxes and interest costs and making capital expenditures. Because capital expenditures on new plant and equipment are a necessity for most companies, analysts are concerned with the cash available to repay debt *after* the company has replaced and updated its existing base of long-term assets.

Cash flow adequacy can be computed as follows:

$$\text{Cash Flow Adequacy} = \frac{\text{Cash Flow from Operating Activities} - \text{Capital Expenditures}}{\text{Average Amount of Debt Maturing over Next 5 Years}}$$

How could you use the information in an annual report to measure a company's cash flow adequacy? First, whether a company uses the direct or indirect method to report cash flow from operating activities, this number represents cash flow *after* paying interest and taxes. Thus, the numerator of the ratio is determined by deducting capital expenditures, as they appear in the investing activities section of the statement, from cash flow from operating activities. A disclosure required by the Securities and Exchange Commission provides the information needed to calculate the denominator of the ratio. This regulatory body requires companies to report the annual amount of long-term debt maturing over each of the next five years.

Quaker Oats' Cash Flow Adequacy   As an example of the calculation of this ratio, consider the following disclosures from Quaker Oats' statement of cash flows for the year ended June 30, 1993 (amounts in millions of dollars):

Net cash provided by operating activities	$558.2
Additions to property, plant, and equipment	172.3

Note 6 in Quaker's 1993 annual report provides the following information:

Aggregate required payments of maturities of long-term debt for the next five fiscal years are as follows (dollars in millions):

	1994	1995	1996	1997	1998
Required payments	$48.9	$45.3	$37.2	$54.0	$67.4

We can now compute Quaker's cash flow adequacy for the year ended June 30, 1993, as follows:

$$\text{Cash Flow Adequacy} = \frac{\$558.2 - \$172.3}{(\$48.9 + \$45.3 + \$37.2 + \$54.0 + \$67.4)/5} = \frac{\$385.9}{\$50.6} = 7.6$$

Would you feel comfortable lending to Quaker if you knew that its ratio of cash flow from operations, after making necessary capital expenditures, to average maturities of debt over the next five years was 7.6 to 1? Before answering this question, you would want to compare the ratio with prior years as well as with the ratio for

[6] An article appearing in the January 10, 1994, edition of *The Wall Street Journal* reported that Fitch Investors Service, Inc., has published a rating system to compare the cash flow adequacy of companies that it rates single-A in its credit ratings. The rating system is intended to help corporate bond investors assess the ability of these companies to meet their maturing debt obligations. Lee Berton. "Investors Have a New Tool for Judging Issuers' Health: 'Cash-Flow Adequacy,' " p. C1.

WITHOUT UNDERSTANDING FINANCIAL STATEMENTS, THIS STOCKBROKER COULD NOT DO THE JOB HER CLIENTS EXPECT

Name: Suzanne McGrath
Profession: Stockbroker
College Major: Mathematics

In a company's annual report, the statement of cash flows usually comes third—after the balance sheet and the income statement. But to Suzanne P. McGrath, stockbroker and managing director of Piper Jaffray Inc., it gets equal billing to the other two statements. "It doesn't take very long for a company with inadequate cash flow to be out of business," she says.

McGrath, who has been in the investment business since 1983, is also a CPA who was in the accounting profession for a decade. "Many people can be very successful investors without knowing how to read a financial statement," she says. "But if you have an accounting background, you probably won't go out and buy a stock just because you like the product or service." That's not to say that she ignores such qualitative factors as busy shopping malls in Atlanta being a sign that retail stocks are back in vogue, or that Starbucks Coffee shops are springing up on every corner in the Pacific Northwest. But unlike some stockbrokers, she won't recommend a stock unless she is satisfied with the financial statements.

Of course, the company's income statement provides earnings per share data. It's also a place to see whether a company's gross margins are rising or falling. That's particularly important for retailers. And the balance sheet is an easy place to find out how much debt the company has. "A highly leveraged balance sheet would not be a suitable investment for some of my clients," she says. But it is the statement of cash flows that offers perhaps the most investment information. The cash flow from operations section could signal that a company's true performance is better than its earnings per share would indicate. That's certainly going to be the case with real estate companies which have a lot of depreciation. Then she might calculate cash flow after capital improvements "to make sure that there is plenty of money left not just to operate but to expand the plant and equipment and to modernize and keep the business up to date." The cash flow from financing activities section can reveal whether the company has refinanced its debt at a lower interest rate, providing savings for years to come.

"Most of my day is spent talking with customers about why certain investments fit their needs or why they don't," says McGrath. Some clients want stocks that will pay large dividends. These securities, such as utilities, appreciate slowly in value but provide substantial income. Others want stocks that will appreciate in value but pay little if any dividends. Starbucks Coffee is an example of such a "growth" stock. "I help clients save for their kids' college educations, plan for retirement and evaluate the investments that they already have."

Any advice for budding stockbrokers? "Find a broker that you know and admire and ask to work as his or her assistant. By apprenticing under a broker with seniority, you are learning the proper way to do business from someone who has been in the market a lot of years instead of just the current cycle."

companies of similar size in similar lines of business to those of Quaker. As a starting point, however, Quaker's ratio of 7.6 indicates that its 1993 cash flow was certainly sufficient to repay its average annual debt over the next five years.

Stockholders and Cash Flow per Share

As we will see in Chapter 15, one measure of the relative worth of an investment in a company is the ratio of the stock's market price per share to the company's earnings per share (that is, the price/earnings ratio). But many stockholders and Wall Street analysts are even more interested in the price of the stock in relation to the company's cash flow per share. Cash flow for purposes of this ratio is normally limited to cash flow from operating activities. This ratio has been used by these groups to evaluate investments even though the accounting profession has expressly forbidden the reporting of cash flow per share information in the financial statements. The belief is that this type of information is not an acceptable alternative to earnings per share as an indicator of company performance. Obviously, differences of opinion exist among various groups as to the usefulness of cash flow per share information.

```
┌─────────────────────────────────────────────────────────────┐
│              R E V I E W   P R O B L E M                      │
└─────────────────────────────────────────────────────────────┘
```

An income statement and comparative balance sheets for Dexter Company are shown below:

DEXTER COMPANY
INCOME STATEMENT
FOR THE YEAR ENDED DECEMBER 31, 1995

Sales revenue	$89,000
Cost of goods sold	57,000
Gross margin	$32,000
Depreciation expense	6,500
Advertising expense	3,200
Salaries expense	12,000
Total operating expenses	$21,700
Operating income	$10,300
Loss on sale of land	2,500
Income before tax	$ 7,800
Income tax expense	2,600
Net income	$ 5,200

DEXTER COMPANY
COMPARATIVE BALANCE SHEETS

	DECEMBER 31	
	1995	1994
Cash	$ 12,000	$ 9,500
Accounts receivable	22,000	18,400
Inventory	25,400	20,500
Prepaid advertising	10,000	8,600
Total current assets	$ 69,400	$ 57,000
Land	120,000	80,000
Equipment	190,000	130,000
Accumulated depreciation	(70,000)	(63,500)
Total long-term assets	$240,000	$146,500
Total assets	$309,400	$203,500
Accounts payable	$ 15,300	$ 12,100
Salaries payable	14,000	16,400
Income taxes payable	1,200	700
Total current liabilities	$ 30,500	$ 29,200
Capital stock	$200,000	$100,000
Retained earnings	78,900	74,300
Total stockholders' equity	$278,900	$174,300
Total liabilities and stockholders' equity	$309,400	$203,500

ADDITIONAL INFORMATION

1. Land was acquired during the year for $70,000.

2. An unimproved parcel of land was sold during the year for $27,500. Its original cost to Dexter was $30,000.

3. A specialized piece of equipment was acquired in exchange for capital stock in the company. The value of the capital stock was $60,000.

4. In addition to the capital stock issued in item 3, stock was sold for $40,000.

5. Dividends of $600 were paid.

■ **REQUIRED** Prepare a statement of cash flows for 1995 using the direct method in the operating activities section of the statement. Include supplemental schedules to report any noncash investing and financing activities and to reconcile net income to net cash provided by operating activities.

■ SOLUTION TO REVIEW PROBLEM

DEXTER COMPANY
STATEMENT OF CASH FLOWS
FOR THE YEAR ENDED DECEMBER 31, 1995

CASH FLOWS FROM OPERATING ACTIVITIES

Cash collections from customers	$ 85,400
Cash payments:	
To suppliers	$(58,700)
For advertising	(4,600)
To employees	(14,400)
For income taxes	(2,100)
Total cash payments	$(79,800)
Net cash provided by operating activities	$ 5,600

CASH FLOWS FROM INVESTING ACTIVITIES

Purchase of land	$(70,000)
Sale of land	27,500
Net cash used by investing activities	$(42,500)

CASH FLOWS FROM FINANCING ACTIVITIES

Issuance of capital stock	$ 40,000
Payment of cash dividends	(600)
Net cash provided by financing activities	$ 39,400
Net increase in cash	$ 2,500
Cash balance, December 31, 1994	9,500
Cash balance, December 31, 1995	$ 12,000

SUPPLEMENTAL SCHEDULE OF NONCASH INVESTING AND FINANCING ACTIVITIES

Acquisition of specialized equipment in exchange for capital stock	$ 60,000

RECONCILIATION OF NET INCOME TO NET CASH PROVIDED BY OPERATING ACTIVITIES

Net income	$ 5,200
Adjustments to reconcile net income to net cash provided by operating activities:	
Increase in accounts receivable	(3,600)
Increase in inventory	(4,900)
Increase in prepaid advertising	(1,400)
Increase in accounts payable	3,200
Decrease in salaries payable	(2,400)
Increase in income taxes payable	500
Depreciation expense	6,500
Loss on sale of land	2,500
Net cash provided by operating activities	$ 5,600

GUIDANCE ANSWERS TO
ACCOUNTING FOR YOUR DECISIONS

YOU ARE THE INVESTMENT ANALYST

In 1992, interest rates were dropping very rapidly. It is likely that IBM was refinancing its debt to get a better interest rate. Go to the financial statement footnotes to learn more.

YOU ARE THE CEO OF JULIAN CORP.

It is true that our cash balance dropped $11,000 while our net income totaled $120,000. But that shouldn't make the investment community think less of Julian Corp. May I point out that net cash flow provided by operating activities—the day-to-day business itself—amounted to $174,000. We took that money and reinvested in equipment, retired long-term bonds, and paid our healthy dividend. So the cash was spent wisely.

A P P E N D I X   1 4 A

ACCOUNTING TOOLS: A WORK SHEET APPROACH TO THE STATEMENT OF CASH FLOWS

In the chapter, we illustrated the use of T accounts to aid in the preparation of a statement of cash flows. We pointed out that T accounts are simply tools to help in analyzing the transactions of the period. As an alternative tool, we now consider the use of a work sheet to organize the information needed to prepare the statement. We will use the information given in the chapter for Julian Corp. (refer to Exhibits 14-11 and 14-12 for the income statements and comparative balance sheets). Although it is possible to use a work sheet to prepare the statement when the operating activities section is prepared under the direct method, we illustrate the use of a work sheet using the more popular *indirect* method.

A work sheet for Julian Corp. is presented in Exhibit 14-19. The following steps were followed in preparing the work sheet:

> LO 7
>
> Use a work sheet to prepare a statement of cash flows, using the indirect method to determine cash flow from operating activities.

EXHIBIT 14-19 Julian Corp.

STATEMENT OF CASH FLOWS WORK SHEET (INDIRECT METHOD)
(all amounts in thousands of dollars)

ACCOUNTS	BALANCES 12/31/95	BALANCES 1/1/95	CHANGES	CASH INFLOWS (OUTFLOWS) OPERATING	CASH INFLOWS (OUTFLOWS) INVESTING	CASH INFLOWS (OUTFLOWS) FINANCING	NONCASH ACTIVITIES
Cash	35	46	$(11)^{16}$				
Accounts receivable	63	57	6^{10}	$(6)^{10}$			
Inventory	84	92	$(8)^{11}$	8^{11}			
Prepaid insurance	12	18	$(6)^{12}$	6^{12}			
Long-term investments	120	90	30^1		$(30)^1$		
Land	150	100	50^2				$(50)^2$
Property and equipment	320	280	75^3		$(75)^3$		
			$(35)^4$		25^4		
Accumulated depreciation	(100)	(75)	15^4				
			$(40)^9$	40^9			
Accounts payable	(38)	(31)	$(7)^{13}$	7^{13}			
Salaries and wages payable	(7)	(9)	2^{14}	$(2)^{14}$			
Income taxes payable	(8)	(5)	$(3)^{15}$	3^{15}			
Notes payable	(85)	(35)	$(50)^2$				50^2
Bonds payable	(200)	(260)	60^5			$(63)^5$	
Capital stock	(100)	(75)	$(25)^6$			25^6	
Retained earnings	(246)	(193)	67^7	$(5)^4$		$(67)^7$	
				3^5			
			$(120)^8$	120^8			
Totals	–0–	–0–	–0–	174	(80)	(105)	–0–
Net decrease in cash				$(11)^{16}$			

Source: The authors are grateful to Jeannie Folk for the development of this worksheet.

Step 1: The balances in each account at the end and at the beginning of the period are entered in the first two columns of the work sheet. For Julian, these balances can be found in its comparative balance sheets in Exhibit 14-12. Note that credit balances are bracketed on the work sheet. Because the work sheet lists all balance sheet accounts, the total of the debit balances must equal the total of the credit balances, and, thus, the totals at the bottom for each of these first two columns equal $0.

Step 2: The additional information listed at the bottom of Exhibit 14-12 is used to record the various investing and financing activities on the work sheet (the item numbers discussed below correspond to the superscript numbers on the worksheet in Exhibit 14-19):

1. Long-term investments were purchased for $30,000. Because this transaction required the use of cash, it is entered as a bracketed amount in the Investing column and as an addition to the Long-term Investments account in the Changes column.

2. Land was acquired by issuing a $50,000 note payable. This transaction is entered on two lines on the work sheet. First, $50,000 is added to the Changes column for Land and a corresponding deduction in the Noncash column (the last column on the work sheet). Likewise, $50,000 is added to the Changes column for Notes Payable and the same amount in the Noncash column.

3. Item 3 in the additional information indicates the acquisition of equipment for $75,000. This amount appears on the work sheet as an addition to Property and Equipment in the Changes column and as a deduction (cash outflow) in the Investing column.

4. A machine with an original cost of $35,000 and a book value of $20,000 was sold for $25,000, resulting in four entries on the work sheet. First, the amount of cash received, $25,000, is entered as an addition in the Investing column on the line for property and equipment. On the same line, the cost of the machine, $35,000, is entered as a deduction in the Changes column. The difference between the cost of the machine, $35,000, and its book value, $20,000, is its accumulated depreciation of $15,000. This amount is shown as a deduction from this account in the Changes column. Because the gain of $5,000 is included in net income, it is deducted from Retained Earnings in the Operating column.

5. Bonds with a face value of $60,000 were retired by paying $63,000 in cash, resulting in the entry of three amounts on the work sheet. The face value of the bonds, $60,000, is entered as a reduction of Bonds Payable in the Changes column. The proceeds from selling the bonds, $63,000, is entered on the same line in the Financing column. The loss of $3,000 is added in the Operating column because it was a deduction to arrive at net income.

6. Capital stock was issued for $25,000. This amount is entered on the Capital Stock line under the Changes column (as an increase in the account) and under the Financing column as an inflow.

7. Dividends of $67,000 were paid. This amount is entered as a reduction in Retained Earnings in the Changes column and as a cash outflow in the Financing Activities column.

Step 3: Because the indirect method is being used, net income of $120,000 for the period is entered as an addition to Retained Earnings in the Operating Activities column of the worksheet (entry 8). The amount is also entered as an increase (bracketed) in the Changes column.

Step 4: Any noncash revenues or expenses are entered on the work sheet on the appropriate lines. For Julian, depreciation expense of $40,000 is added (bracketed) to Accumulated Depreciation in the Changes column and in the Operating column. This entry is identified on the work sheet as entry 9.

Step 5: Each of the changes in the noncash current asset and current liability accounts is entered in the Changes column and in the Operating column. These entries are identified on the work sheet as entries 10 through 15.

Step 6: Totals are determined for the Operating, Investing, and Financing columns and entered at the bottom of the work sheet. The total for the final column, Noncash Activities, of $0, is also entered.

Step 7: The net cash inflow (outflow) for the period is determined by adding the total of the three columns. For Julian, the net cash *outflow* amounts to $11,000, shown as entry 16 at the bottom of the statement. This same amount is then transferred to the line for Cash in the Changes column. Finally, the total of the Changes column at this point should net to $0.

CHAPTER HIGHLIGHTS

1. **(LO 1)** The purpose of a statement of cash flows is to summarize the cash flows of an entity during a period of time. The cash inflows and outflows are categorized into three activities: operating, investing, and financing.

2. **(LO 2)** Cash equivalents are convertible to a known amount of cash and are therefore included with cash on the balance sheet. Because such items as commercial paper, money market funds, and Treasury bills do not involve any significant risk, neither their purchase nor sale is shown as investing activities on the statement of cash flows.

3. **(LO 3)** Operating activities are generally the effects of items that enter into the determination of net income, such as the effects of buying and selling products and services. Other operating activities include payments of compensation to employees, taxes to the government, and interest to creditors. Preparation of the operating activities section of the statement of cash flows requires an analysis of the current assets and current liabilities.

4. **(LO 3)** Investing activities are critical to the success of a business because they involve the replacement of existing productive assets and the addition of new ones. Capital expenditures are normally the single largest cash outflow for most businesses. Occasionally, companies generate cash from the sale of existing plant and equipment. The information needed to prepare the investing activities section of the statement of cash flows is found by analyzing the long-term asset accounts.

5. **(LO 3)** All businesses rely on financing in one form or another. At least initially, all corporations sell stock to raise funds. Many turn to external sources as well, generating cash from the issuance of promissory notes and bonds. The repayment of debt and the reacquisition of capital stock are important uses of cash for some companies. Given the nature of financing activities, long-term liability and stockholders' equity accounts must be examined in preparing this section of the statement of cash flows.

6. **(LO 4)** Two different methods are acceptable to report cash flow from operating activities. Under the direct method, cash receipts and cash payments related to operations are reported. Under the indirect method, net income is reconciled to net cash flow from operating activities. Regardless of which method is used, the amount of cash generated from operations is the same.

7. **(LO 5)** Preparation of the operating activities section under the direct method requires the conversion of income statement items from an accrual basis to a cash basis. Certain items, such as depreciation, do not have a cash effect and are not included on the statement. Gains and losses typically relate to either investing or financing activities and are not included in this section of the statement. When the direct method is used to present cash flow from operating activities, a separate schedule is required to reconcile net income to net cash flow from operating activities. This schedule is the same as the operating activities section under the indirect method. Some type of methodology, such as a T-account approach, can be helpful in preparing the statement for more complex situations.

8. **(LO 6)** When the indirect method is used, the reconciliation of net income to net cash flow from operating activities appears on the face of the statement. Adjustments are made for the changes in each of the operating-related current asset and current liability accounts, as well as adjustments for noncash items, such as depreciation. The effects of gains and losses on net income must also be removed to convert to a cash basis. If the indirect method is used, a company must separately disclose the amount of cash paid for taxes and for interest.

9. **(LO 7)** A work sheet is sometimes used in preparing a statement of cash flows. Similar to T accounts, the work sheet acts as a tool to aid in the preparation of the statement. (Appendix 14A)

KEY TERMS QUIZ

Select one of the following key terms used in the chapter and fill in the appropriate blank to the left of each description. The solution appears at the end of the chapter.

Statement of cash flows   **Cash equivalent**
Operating activities   **Investing activities**
Financing activities   **Direct method**
Indirect method

_____ **1.** Activities concerned with the acquisition and sale of products and services.

_____ **2.** The approach to preparing the operating activities section of the statement of cash flows in which net income is reconciled to net cash flow from operations.

_____ **3.** The financial statement that summarizes an entity's cash receipts and cash payments during the period from operating, investing, and financing activities.

_____ **4.** An item readily convertible to a known amount of cash and with an original maturity to the investor of three months or less.

_____ **5.** Activities concerned with the acquisition and disposal of long-term assets.

_____ **6.** The approach to preparing the operating activities section of the statement of cash flows in which cash receipts and cash payments are reported.

_____ **7.** Activities concerned with the raising and repayment of funds in the form of debt and equity.

ALTERNATE TERMS

BOTTOM LINE Net income.

CASH FLOW FROM OPERATING ACTIVITIES Cash flow from operations.

STATEMENT OF CASH FLOWS Cash flows statement.

QUESTIONS

1. What is the purpose of the statement of cash flows? As a flows statement, explain how it differs from the income statement.

2. What is a cash equivalent? Why is it included with cash for purposes of preparing a statement of cash flows?

3. Preston Corp. acquires a piece of land by signing a $60,000 promissory note and making a down payment of $20,000. How should this transaction be reported on the statement of cash flows?

4. Hansen, Inc., made two purchases in December 1995. One was a $10,000 Treasury bill that matures in 60 days from the date of purchase. The other was a $20,000 investment in Motorola common stock that will be held indefinitely. How should each of these be treated for purposes of preparing a statement of cash flows?

5. Companies are required to classify cash flows as either operating, investing, or financing. Which of these three categories do you think will most likely have a net cash *outflow* over a number of years? Explain your answer.

6. A fellow student says to you: "The statement of cash flows is the easiest of the basic financial statements to prepare because you know the answer before you start. You compare the beginning and ending balances in cash on the balance sheet and compute the net inflow or outflow of cash. What could be easier!" Do you agree? Explain your answer.

7. What is your evaluation of the following statement? "Depreciation is responsible for providing some of the highest amounts of cash for capital-intensive businesses. This is obvious by examining the operating activities section of the statement of cash flows. Other than the net income of the period, depreciation is often the largest amount reported in this section of the statement."

8. Which method for preparing the operating activities section of the statement of cash flows, the direct or the indirect method, do you believe provides the most information to users of the statement? Explain your answer.

9. Assume that a company uses the indirect method to prepare the operating activities section of the statement of cash flows. Why would a decrease in accounts receivable during the period be added back to net income?

10. Why is it necessary to analyze both inventory and accounts payable in trying to determine cash payments to suppliers when the direct method is used?

11. A company has a very profitable year. What explanations might there be for a decrease in cash?

12. A company reports a net loss for the year. Is it possible that cash could increase during the year? Explain your answer.

13. What effect does a decrease in income taxes payable for the period have on cash generated from operating activities? Does it matter whether the direct or indirect method is used?

14. Why do accounting standards require a company to separately disclose income taxes paid and interest paid if it uses the indirect method?

15. Is it logical that interest paid is classified as a cash outflow in the *operating* activities section of the statement of cash flows but dividends paid are included in the *financing* activities section? Explain your answer.

16. Jackson Company prepays the rent on various office facilities. The beginning balance in Prepaid Rent was $9,600 and the ending balance was $7,300. The income statement reports Rent Expense of $45,900. Under the direct method, what amount would appear for cash paid in rent in the operating activities section of the statement of cash flows?

17. Baxter, Inc., buys 2,000 shares of its own common stock at $20 per share and places them in the treasury. How is this transaction reported on the statement of cash flows?

18. Duke Corp. sells a delivery truck for $9,000. Its original cost was $25,000, and the book value at the time of the sale was $11,000. How does the transaction to record the sale appear on a statement of cash flows prepared under the indirect method?

19. Billings Company has a patent on its books with a balance at the beginning of the year of $24,000. The ending balance for the asset was $20,000. The company neither bought nor sold any patents during the year, nor does it use an Accumulated Amortization account. Assuming that the company uses the indirect method in preparing a statement of cash flows, how is the decrease in the Patents account reported on the statement?

20. Ace, Inc., declared and distributed a 10% stock dividend during the year. Explain how, if at all, you think this transaction should be reported on a statement of cash flows.

EXERCISES

(LO 3) EXERCISE 14-1 CLASSIFICATION OF ACTIVITIES

Indicate how each of the following transactions is reported on a statement of cash flows by filling in the blank if it would appear in the operating activities section (O), in the investing activities section (I), or in the financing activities section (F). Put an *S* in the blank if the transaction does not affect cash but is reported in a supplemental schedule of noncash activities.

_____ **1.** A company purchases its own common stock in the open market and immediately retires it.

_____ **2.** A company issues preferred stock in exchange for land.

_____ **3.** A six-month bank loan is obtained.

_____ **4.** Twenty-year bonds are issued.

_____ **5.** A customer's open account is collected.

_____ **6.** Income taxes are paid.

_____ **7.** Cash sales for the day are recorded.

_____ **8.** Cash dividends are declared and paid.

_____ **9.** A creditor is given shares of common stock in the company in return for cancellation of a long-term loan.

_____ **10.** A new piece of machinery is acquired for cash.

_____ **11.** Stock of another company is acquired as an investment.

_____ **12.** Interest is paid on a bank loan.

_____ **13.** Factory workers are paid.

(LO 6) EXERCISE 14-2 ADJUSTMENTS TO NET INCOME WITH THE INDIRECT METHOD

Assume that a company uses the indirect method to prepare the operating activities section of the statement of cash flows. For each of the following items, fill in the blank to indicate whether they would be added to net income (A), deducted from net income (D), or not reported in this section of the statement under the indirect method (NR).

_____ **1.** Depreciation expense.

_____ **2.** Gain on sale of used delivery truck.

_____ **3.** Bad debts expense.

_____ **4.** Increase in accounts payable.

_____ **5.** Purchase of new delivery truck.

_____ **6.** Loss on retirement of bonds.

_____ **7.** Increase in prepaid rent.

_____ **8.** Decrease in inventory.

_____ **9.** Increase in short-term investments (classified as trading securities).

_____ **10.** Amortization of patents.

(LO 5) EXERCISE 14-3 OPERATING ACTIVITIES SECTION—DIRECT METHOD

The following account balances for the noncash current assets and liabilities of Beagle Company are available:

	DECEMBER 31	
	1995	1994
Accounts receivable	$ 4,000	$ 6,000
Inventory	32,000	25,000
Office supplies	7,000	10,000
Accounts payable	7,500	4,500
Salaries and wages payable	1,500	2,500
Interest payable	500	1,000
Income taxes payable	4,500	3,000

In addition, the income statement for 1995 is as follows:

	1995
Sales revenue	$100,000
Cost of goods sold	75,000
Gross profit	$ 25,000
General and administrative expense	$ 8,000
Depreciation expense	3,000
Total operating expenses	$ 11,000
Income before interest and taxes	$ 14,000
Interest expense	3,000
Income before tax	$ 11,000
Income tax expense	5,000
Net income	$ 6,000

■ REQUIRED

1. Prepare the operating activities section of the statement of cash flows using the direct method.

2. In preparing the operating activities section of the statement, what does the use of the direct method reveal about a company that the indirect method does not?

(LO 5) EXERCISE 14-4 DETERMINATION OF MISSING AMOUNTS—CASH FLOW FROM OPERATING ACTIVITIES

The computation of cash provided by operating activities requires analysis of the noncash current asset and current liability accounts. Using T accounts, determine the missing amounts for each of the following independent cases:

CASE I	
Accounts receivable, beginning of year	$150,000
Accounts receivable, end of year	100,000
Credit sales for the year	175,000
Cash sales for the year	60,000
Write-offs of uncollectible accounts	35,000
Total cash collections for the year	?

CASE 2

Inventory, beginning of year	$ 80,000
Inventory, end of year	55,000
Accounts payable, beginning of year	25,000
Accounts payable, end of year	15,000
Cost of goods sold	175,000
Cash payments for inventory (assume all purchases of inventory are on account)	?

CASE 3

Prepaid insurance, beginning of year	$ 17,000
Prepaid insurance, end of year	20,000
Insurance expense	15,000
Cash paid for new insurance policies	?

CASE 4

Income taxes payable, beginning of year	$ 95,000
Income taxes payable, end of year	115,000
Income tax expense	300,000
Cash payments for taxes	?

(LO 5) EXERCISE 14-5 DIVIDENDS ON THE STATEMENT OF CASH FLOWS

The following selected account balances are available from the records of Simpson Company:

	DECEMBER 31	
	1995	**1994**
Dividends payable	$ 30,000	$ 20,000
Retained earnings	375,000	250,000

Other information available for 1995 follows:

a. Simpson reported $285,000 net income for the year.

b. It declared and distributed a small stock dividend of $50,000 during the year.

c. It declared cash dividends at the end of each quarter and paid them within the next 30 days of the following quarter.

1. With the use of T accounts, determine the amount of cash dividends *paid* during the year for presentation in the cash flows from financing activities section of the statement of cash flows.

■ REQUIRED

2. Should the small stock dividend described in part b appear on a statement of cash flows? Explain your answer.

(LO 6) EXERCISE 14-6 OPERATING ACTIVITIES SECTION—INDIRECT METHOD

The following account balances for the noncash current assets and liabilities of Des Moines Company are available:

	DECEMBER 31	
	1995	1994
Accounts receivable	$43,000	$35,000
Inventory	30,000	40,000
Prepaid rent	17,000	15,000
Totals	$90,000	$90,000
Accounts payable	$26,000	$19,000
Income taxes payable	6,000	10,000
Interest payable	15,000	12,000
Totals	$47,000	$41,000

Net income for 1995 is $40,000. Depreciation expense is $20,000. Assume that all sales and all purchases are on account.

■ REQUIRED

1. Prepare the operating activities section of the statement of cash flows using the indirect method.

2. Provide a brief explanation as to why cash flow from operating activities is more or less than the net income of the period.

(LO 6) EXERCISE 14-7 LONG-TERM ASSETS ON THE STATEMENT OF CASH FLOWS— INDIRECT METHOD

The following account balances are taken from the records of Martin Corp. for the past two years (credit balances are in parentheses):

	DECEMBER 31	
	1995	1994
Plant and equipment	$750,000	$500,000
Accumulated depreciation	(160,000)	(200,000)
Patents	92,000	80,000
Retained earnings	(825,000)	(675,000)

Other information available for 1995 follows:

a. Net income for the year was $200,000.

b. Depreciation expense on plant and equipment was $50,000.

c. Plant and equipment with an original cost of $150,000 were sold for $64,000 (you will need to determine the book value of the assets sold).

d. Amortization expense on patents was $8,000.

e. Both new plant and equipment and patents were purchased for cash during the year.

■ REQUIRED Indicate, with amounts, how all items related to these long-term assets would be reported in the 1995 statement of cash flows, including any adjustments in the operating activities section of the statement. Assume that Martin uses the indirect method.

(LO 6) EXERCISE 14-8 RETIREMENT OF BONDS PAYABLE ON THE STATEMENT OF CASH FLOWS—INDIRECT METHOD

Schultz, Inc., has the following debt outstanding on December 31, 1995:

10% bonds payable, due 12/31/99	$500,000	
Discount on bonds payable	(40,000)	$460,000

On this date, Schultz retired the entire bond issue by paying cash of $510,000.

■ REQUIRED

1. Prepare the journal entry to record the bond retirement.
2. Describe how the bond retirement would be reported on the statement of cash flows, assuming that Schultz uses the indirect method.

MULTI-CONCEPT EXERCISES

(LO 2, 3) EXERCISE 14-9 CLASSIFICATION OF ACTIVITIES

For each of the following transactions, indicate how it would be reported on the statement of cash flows using the following legend (assume that the stocks and bonds of other companies are classified as available-for-sale securities):

II = Inflow from investing activities
OI = Outflow from investing activities
IF = Inflow from financing activities
OF = Outflow from financing activities
CE = Classified as a cash equivalent and included with cash for purposes of preparing the statement of cash flows

_____ 1. Purchased a six-month certificate of deposit.

_____ 2. Purchased a 60-day Treasury bill.

_____ 3. Issued 1,000 shares of common stock.

_____ 4. Purchased 1,000 shares of stock in another company.

_____ 5. Purchased 1,000 shares of its own stock to be held in the treasury.

_____ 6. Invested $1,000 in a money market fund.

_____ 7. Sold 500 shares of stock of another company.

_____ 8. Purchased 20-year bonds of another company.

_____ 9. Issued 30-year bonds.

_____ 10. Repaid a six-month bank loan.

(LO 3, 5) EXERCISE 14-10 CLASSIFICATION OF ACTIVITIES

For each of the following transactions, indicate how it would be reported on the statement of cash flows using the following legend (assume that the company uses the direct method in the operating activities section):

IO = Inflow from operating activities
OO = Outflow from operating activities
II = Inflow from investing activities
OI = Outflow from investing activities
IF = Inflow from financing activities
OF = Outflow from financing activities
NR = Not reported in the body of the statement of cash flows, but in a supplemental schedule

_____ 1. Collected $10,000 in cash from customers' open accounts for the period.

_____ 2. Paid one of the company's inventory suppliers $500 in settlement of an open account.

_____ 3. Purchased a new copier for $6,000; signed a 90-day note payable.

_____ 4. Issued bonds at face value of $100,000.

_____ 5. Made $23,200 in cash sales for the week.

_____ 6. Purchased an empty lot adjacent to the factory for $50,000. The seller of the land agrees to accept a five-year promissory note as consideration.

_____ 7. Renewed the property insurance policy for another six months. Cash of $1,000 is paid for the renewal.

_____ 8. Purchased a machine for $10,000.

_____ 9. Paid cash dividends of $2,500.

_____ 10. Reclassified as short-term a long-term note payable of $5,000 that is due within the next year.

_____ 11. Purchased 500 shares of the company's own stock on the open market for $4,000.

_____ 12. Sold 500 shares of Nike stock for book value of $10,000 (they had been classified as available-for-sale securities).

(LO 1, 5) EXERCISE 14-11 INCOME STATEMENT, STATEMENT OF CASH FLOWS (DIRECT METHOD), AND BALANCE SHEET

The following events occurred at Handsome Hounds Grooming Company during its first year of business:

1. To establish the company, the two owners contributed a total of $50,000 in exchange for common stock.

2. Grooming service revenue for the first year amounted to $150,000, of which $40,000 was on account.

3. Customers owe $10,000 at the end of the year from the services provided on account.

4. At the beginning of the year a storage building was rented. The company was required to sign a three-year lease for $12,000 per year and make a $2,000 refundable security deposit. The first year's lease payment and the security deposit were paid at the beginning of the year.

5. At the beginning of the year the company purchased a patent at a cost of $100,000 for a revolutionary system to be used for dog grooming. The patent is expected to be useful for 10 years. The company paid 20% down in cash and signed a four-year note at the bank for the remainder.

6. Operating expenses, including amortization of the patent and rent on the storage building, totaled $80,000 for the first year. No expenses were accrued or unpaid at the end of the year.

7. The company declared and paid a $20,000 cash dividend at the end of the first year.

■ REQUIRED

1. Prepare an income statement for the first year.

2. Prepare a statement of cash flows for the first year, using the direct method in the operating activities section.

3. Did the company generate more or less cash flow from operations than it earned in net income? Explain why there is a difference.

4. Prepare a balance sheet as of the end of the first year.

PROBLEMS

(LO 6) PROBLEM 14-1 STATEMENT OF CASH FLOWS—INDIRECT METHOD

The following balances are available for Tippin Company:

	DECEMBER 31	
	1995	1994
Cash	$ 8,000	$ 10,000
Accounts receivable	20,000	15,000
Inventory	15,000	25,000
Prepaid rent	9,000	6,000
Land	75,000	75,000
Plant and equipment	400,000	300,000
Accumulated depreciation	(65,000)	(30,000)
Totals	$462,000	$401,000
Accounts payable	$ 12,000	$ 10,000
Income taxes payable	3,000	5,000
Short-term notes payable	35,000	25,000
Bonds payable	75,000	100,000
Common stock	200,000	150,000
Retained earnings	137,000	111,000
Totals	$462,000	$401,000

Bonds were retired during 1995 at face value, plant and equipment were acquired for cash, and common stock was issued for cash. Depreciation expense for the year was $35,000. Net income was reported at $26,000.

1. Prepare a statement of cash flows for 1995, using the indirect method in the operating activities section.   ■ REQUIRED

2. Did Tippin generate sufficient cash from operations to pay for its investing activities? How else did it generate cash other than from operations? Explain your answers.

(LO 7) PROBLEM 14-2 STATEMENT OF CASH FLOWS USING A WORK SHEET— INDIRECT METHOD (APPENDIX 14A)

Refer to all of the facts in Problem 14-1.

1. Using the format in Appendix 14A, prepare a statement of cash flows work sheet.   ■ REQUIRED

2. Prepare a statement of cash flows, using the indirect method in the operating activities section.

3. Did Tippin generate sufficient cash from operations to pay for its investing activities? How else did it generate cash other than from operations? Explain your answers.

(LO 5) PROBLEM 14-3 STATEMENT OF CASH FLOWS—DIRECT METHOD

Peoria Corp. has just completed another very successful year as indicated by the following income statement:

	FOR THE YEAR ENDED DECEMBER 31, 1995
Sales revenue	$1,250,000
Cost of goods sold	700,000
Gross profit	$ 550,000
Operating expenses	150,000
Income before interest and taxes	$ 400,000
Interest expense	25,000
Income before taxes	$ 375,000
Income tax expense	150,000
Net income	$ 225,000

Presented below are comparative balance sheets:

	DECEMBER 31	
	1995	1994
Cash	$ 52,000	$ 90,000
Accounts receivable	180,000	130,000
Inventory	230,000	200,000
Prepayments	15,000	25,000
Total current assets	$ 477,000	$ 445,000
Land	$ 750,000	$ 600,000
Plant and equipment	700,000	500,000
Accumulated depreciation	(250,000)	(200,000)
Total long-term assets	$1,200,000	$ 900,000
Total assets	$1,677,000	$1,345,000
Accounts payable	$ 130,000	$ 148,000
Other accrued liabilities	68,000	63,000
Income taxes payable	90,000	110,000
Total current liabilities	$ 288,000	$ 321,000
Long-term bank loan payable	$ 350,000	$ 300,000
Common stock	$ 550,000	$ 400,000
Retained earnings	489,000	324,000
Total stockholders' equity	$1,039,000	$ 724,000
Total liabilities and stockholders' equity	$1,677,000	$1,345,000

Other information follows:

a. Dividends of $60,000 were declared and paid during the year.

b. Operating expenses include $50,000 of depreciation.

c. Land and plant and equipment were acquired for cash and additional stock was issued for cash. Cash was also received from additional bank loans.

The president has asked you some questions about the year's results. She is very impressed with the profit margin of 18% (net income divided by sales revenue). She is bothered, however, by the decline in the cash balance during the year. One of the conditions of the existing bank loan is that the company always maintain a minimum cash balance of $50,000.

1. Prepare a statement of cash flows for 1995, using the direct method in the operating activities section.

2. On the basis of your statement in requirement 1, draft a brief memo to the president to explain why cash decreased during such a profitable year. Include in your explanation any recommendations for improving the company's cash flow in future years.

■ REQUIRED

(LO 6) PROBLEM 14-4 STATEMENT OF CASH FLOWS—INDIRECT METHOD

Refer to all of the facts in Problem 14-3.

1. Prepare a statement of cash flows for 1995, using the indirect method in the operating activities section.

2. On the basis of your statement in requirement 1, draft a brief memo to the president to explain why cash decreased during such a profitable year. Include in your explanation any recommendations for improving the company's cash flow in future years.

■ REQUIRED

(LO 7) PROBLEM 14-5 STATEMENT OF CASH FLOWS USING A WORK SHEET— INDIRECT METHOD (APPENDIX 14A)

Refer to all of the facts in Problem 14-3.

1. Using the format in Appendix 14A, prepare a statement of cash flows work sheet.

2. Prepare a statement of cash flows, using the indirect method in the operating activities section.

3. On the basis of your statement in requirement 2, draft a brief memo to the president to explain why cash decreased during such a profitable year. Include in your explanation any recommendations for improving the company's cash flow in future years.

■ REQUIRED

(LO 5) PROBLEM 14-6 STATEMENT OF CASH FLOWS—DIRECT METHOD

The income statement for Astro, Inc., for 1995 follows:

	FOR THE YEAR ENDED DECEMBER 31, 1995
Sales revenue	$ 500,000
Cost of goods sold	400,000
Gross profit	$ 100,000
Operating expenses	180,000
Loss before interest and taxes	$ (80,000)
Interest expense	20,000
Net loss	$ (100,000)

Presented below are comparative balance sheets:

	DECEMBER 31	
	1995	1994
Cash	$ 95,000	$ 80,000
Accounts receivable	50,000	75,000
Inventory	100,000	150,000
Prepayments	55,000	45,000
Total current assets	$ 300,000	$ 350,000
Land	475,000	400,000
Plant and equipment	870,000	800,000
Accumulated depreciation	(370,000)	(300,000)
Total long-term assets	$ 975,000	$ 900,000
Total assets	$1,275,000	$1,250,000
Accounts payable	$ 125,000	$ 100,000
Other accrued liabilities	35,000	45,000
Interest payable	15,000	10,000
Total current liabilities	$ 175,000	$ 155,000
Long-term bank loan payable	$ 340,000	$ 250,000
Common stock	450,000	400,000
Retained earnings	310,000	445,000
Total stockholders' equity	$ 760,000	$ 845,000
Total liabilities and stockholders' equity	$1,275,000	$1,250,000

Other information follows:

a. Dividends of $35,000 were declared and paid during the year.

b. Operating expenses include $70,000 of depreciation.

c. Land and plant and equipment were acquired for cash and additional stock was issued for cash. Cash was also received from additional bank loans.

The president has asked you some questions about the year's results. He is disturbed with the $100,000 net loss for the year. He notes, however, that the cash position at the end of the year is improved. He is confused about what appear to be conflicting signals: "How could we have possibly added to our bank accounts during such a terrible year of operations?"

■ REQUIRED

1. Prepare a statement of cash flows for 1995, using the direct method in the operating activities section.

2. On the basis of your statement in requirement 1, draft a brief memo to the president to explain why cash increased during such an unprofitable year. Include in your memo your recommendations for improving the company's bottom line.

(LO 6) PROBLEM 14-7 STATEMENT OF CASH FLOWS—INDIRECT METHOD
Refer to all of the facts in Problem 14-6.

■ REQUIRED

1. Prepare a statement of cash flows for 1995, using the indirect method in the operating activities section.

2. On the basis of your statement in requirement 1, draft a brief memo to the president to explain why cash increased during such an unprofitable year. Include in your memo your recommendations for improving the company's bottom line.

(LO 6) PROBLEM 14-8 YEAR-END BALANCE SHEET AND STATEMENT OF CASH FLOWS—INDIRECT METHOD

The balance sheet of Terrier Company at the end of 1994 is presented below along with certain other information for 1995:

	DECEMBER 31, 1994
Cash	$ 140,000
Accounts receivable	155,000
Total current assets	$ 295,000
Land	$ 300,000
Plant and equipment	500,000
Accumulated depreciation	(150,000)
Investments	100,000
Total long-term assets	$ 750,000
Total assets	$1,045,000
Current liabilities	$ 205,000
Bonds payable	$ 300,000
Common stock	400,000
Retained earnings	140,000
Total stockholders' equity	$ 540,000
Total liabilities and stockholders' equity	$1,045,000

Other information follows:

a. Net income for 1995 was $70,000.

b. Included in operating expenses was $20,000 in depreciation.

c. Cash dividends of $25,000 were declared and paid.

d. An additional $150,000 of bonds was issued for cash.

e. Common stock of $50,000 was purchased for cash and retired.

f. Cash purchases of plant and equipment during the year were $200,000.

g. An additional $100,000 of bonds was issued in exchange for land.

h. Sales exceeded cash collections on account during the year by $10,000. All sales are on account.

i. The amount of current liabilities remained unchanged during the year.

1. Prepare a statement of cash flows for 1995, using the indirect method in the operating activities section. Include a supplemental schedule for noncash activities.

2. Prepare a balance sheet at December 31, 1995.

3. Provide a possible explanation as to why Terrier decided to issue additional bonds for cash during 1995.

■ REQUIRED

MULTI-CONCEPT PROBLEMS

(LO 5, 6) **PROBLEM 14-9 STATEMENT OF CASH FLOWS—DIRECT AND INDIRECT METHODS**

Batavia Corp. is in the process of preparing its statement of cash flows for the year ended June 30, 1995. An income statement for the year and comparative balance sheets follow:

	FOR THE YEAR ENDED JUNE 30, 1995
Sales revenue	$550,000
Cost of goods sold	350,000
Gross profit	$200,000
General and administrative expenses	$ 55,000
Depreciation expense	75,000
Loss on sale of plant assets	5,000
Total expenses and losses	$135,000
Income before interest and taxes	$ 65,000
Interest expense	15,000
Income before taxes	$ 50,000
Income tax expense	17,000
Net income	$ 33,000

	JUNE 30	
	1995	1994
Cash	$ 31,000	$ 40,000
Accounts receivable	90,000	75,000
Inventory	80,000	95,000
Prepaid rent	12,000	16,000
Total current assets	$ 213,000	$ 226,000
Land	$ 250,000	$ 170,000
Plant and equipment	750,000	600,000
Accumulated depreciation	(310,000)	(250,000)
Total long-term assets	$ 690,000	$ 520,000
Total assets	$ 903,000	$ 746,000
Accounts payable	$ 155,000	$ 148,000
Other accrued liabilities	32,000	26,000
Income taxes payable	8,000	10,000
Total current liabilities	$ 195,000	$ 184,000
Long-term bank loan payable	$ 100,000	$ 130,000
Common stock	$ 350,000	$ 200,000
Retained earnings	258,000	232,000
Total stockholders' equity	$ 608,000	$ 432,000
Total liabilities and stockholders' equity	$ 903,000	$ 746,000

Dividends of $7,000 were declared and paid during the year. New plant assets were purchased for $195,000 in cash during the year. Also, land was purchased for cash.

Plant assets were sold during 1995 for $25,000 in cash. The original cost of the assets sold was $45,000, and their book value was $30,000. Additional stock was issued for cash and a portion of the bank loan was repaid.

■ REQUIRED

1. Prepare a statement of cash flows, using the direct method in the operating activities section.

2. Prepare a statement of cash flows, using the indirect method in the operating activities section.

3. Evaluate the following statement: "Whether a company uses the direct or the indirect method to report cash flows from operations is irrelevant because the amount of cash flow from operating activities is the same regardless of which method is used."

(LO 2, 5) **PROBLEM 14-10 STATEMENT OF CASH FLOWS—DIRECT METHOD**

Odon Company has not yet prepared a formal statement of cash flows for 1995. Comparative balance sheets as of December 31, 1995 and 1994, and a statement of income and retained earnings for the year ended December 31, 1995, follow:

ODON COMPANY
BALANCE SHEET
DECEMBER 31
(THOUSANDS OMITTED)

ASSETS	1995	1994
Current assets:		
Cash	$ 60	$ 100
U.S. Treasury bills (six month)	–0–	50
Accounts receivable	610	500
Inventory	720	600
Total current assets	$1,390	$1,250
Long-term assets:		
Land	$ 80	$ 70
Buildings and equipment	710	600
Accumulated depreciation	(180)	(120)
Patents (less amortization)	105	130
Total long-term assets	$ 715	$ 680
Total assets	$2,105	$1,930
LIABILITIES AND OWNERS' EQUITY		
Current liabilities:		
Accounts payable	$ 360	$ 300
Taxes payable	25	20
Notes payable	400	400
Total current liabilities	$ 785	$ 720
Term notes payable—due 1999	200	200
Total liabilities	$ 985	$ 920
Owners' equity:		
Common stock outstanding	$ 830	$ 700
Retained earnings	290	310
Total owners' equity	$1,120	$1,010
Total liabilities and owners' equity	$2,105	$1,930

ODON COMPANY
STATEMENT OF INCOME AND RETAINED EARNINGS
FOR THE YEAR ENDED DECEMBER 31, 1995
(THOUSANDS OMITTED)

Sales		$2,408
Less expenses and interest:		
Cost of goods sold	$1,100	
Salaries and benefits	850	
Heat, light, and power	75	
Depreciation	60	
Property taxes	18	
Patent amortization	25	
Miscellaneous expense	10	
Interest	55	2,193
Net income before income taxes		$ 215
Income taxes		105
Net income		$ 110
Retained earnings—January 1, 1995		310
		$ 420
Stock dividend distributed		130
Retained earnings—December 31, 1995		$ 290

■ REQUIRED

1. For purposes of a statement of cash flows, are the U.S. Treasury bills cash equivalents? If not, how should they be classified? Explain your answers.

2. Prepare a statement of cash flows, using the direct method in the operating activities section.

(CMA adapted)

ALTERNATE PROBLEMS

(LO 6) **PROBLEM 14-1A STATEMENT OF CASH FLOWS—INDIRECT METHOD**

The following balances are available for Toppsie Company:

	DECEMBER 31	
	1995	**1994**
Cash	$ 12,000	$ 10,000
Accounts receivable	10,000	12,000
Inventory	8,000	7,000
Prepaid rent	1,200	1,000
Land	75,000	75,000
Plant and equipment	200,000	150,000
Accumulated depreciation	(75,000)	(25,000)
Totals	$231,200	$230,000
Accounts payable	$ 15,000	$ 15,000
Income taxes payable	2,500	2,000
Short-term notes payable	20,000	22,500
Bonds payable	75,000	50,000
Common stock	100,000	100,000
Retained earnings	18,700	40,500
Totals	$231,200	$230,000

Bonds were issued during 1995 at face value, and plant and equipment were acquired for cash. Depreciation expense for the year was $50,000. A net loss of $21,800 was reported.

1. Prepare a statement of cash flows for 1995, using the indirect method in the operating activities section.

2. Explain briefly how Toppsie was able to increase its cash balance during a year it incurred a net loss.

■ REQUIRED

(LO 7) PROBLEM 14-2A STATEMENT OF CASH FLOWS USING A WORK SHEET— INDIRECT METHOD (APPENDIX 14A)

Refer to all of the facts in Problem 14-1A.

1. Using the format in Appendix 14A, prepare a statement of cash flows work sheet.

2. Prepare a statement of cash flows, using the indirect method in the operating activities section.

3. Explain briefly how Toppsie was able to increase its cash balance during a year it incurred a net loss.

■ REQUIRED

(LO 5) PROBLEM 14-3A STATEMENT OF CASH FLOWS—DIRECT METHOD

Wabash Corp. has just completed another very successful year as indicated by the following income statement:

	FOR THE YEAR ENDED DECEMBER 31, 1995
Sales revenue	$2,460,000
Cost of goods sold	1,400,000
Gross profit	$1,060,000
Operating expenses	460,000
Income before interest and taxes	$ 600,000
Interest expense	100,000
Income before taxes	$ 500,000
Income tax expense	150,000
Net income	$ 350,000

The following are comparative balance sheets:

	DECEMBER 31	
	1995	1994
Cash	$ 140,000	$ 210,000
Accounts receivable	60,000	145,000
Inventory	200,000	180,000
Prepayments	15,000	25,000
Total current assets	$ 415,000	$ 560,000
Land	$ 600,000	$ 700,000
Plant and equipment	850,000	600,000
Accumulated depreciation	(225,000)	(200,000)
Total long-term assets	$1,225,000	$1,100,000
Total assets	$1,640,000	$1,660,000

	DECEMBER 31	
	1995	**1994**
Accounts payable	$ 140,000	$ 120,000
Other accrued liabilities	50,000	55,000
Income taxes payable	80,000	115,000
Total current liabilities	$ 270,000	$ 290,000
Long-term bank loan payable	$ 200,000	$ 250,000
Common stock	$ 450,000	$ 400,000
Retained earnings	720,000	720,000
Total stockholders' equity	$1,170,000	$1,120,000
Total liabilities and stockholders' equity	$1,640,000	$1,660,000

Other information follows:

a. Dividends of $350,000 were declared and paid during the year.
b. Operating expenses include $25,000 of depreciation.
c. Land was sold for its book value and new plant and equipment was acquired for cash.
d. Part of the bank loan was repaid and additional common stock was issued for cash.

The president has asked you some questions about the year's results. She is very impressed with the profit margin of 14% (net income divided by sales revenue). She is bothered, however, by the decline in the company's cash balance during the year. One of the conditions of the existing bank loan is that the company always maintain a minimum cash balance of $100,000.

■ REQUIRED
1. Prepare a statement of cash flows for 1995, using the direct method in the operating activities section.
2. On the basis of your statement in requirement 1, draft a brief memo to the president to explain why cash decreased during such a profitable year. Include in your explanation any recommendations for improving the company's cash flow in future years.

(LO 6) PROBLEM 14-4A STATEMENT OF CASH FLOWS—INDIRECT METHOD
Refer to all of the facts in Problem 14-3A.

■ REQUIRED
1. Prepare a statement of cash flows for 1995, using the indirect method in the operating activities section.
2. On the basis of your statement in requirement 1, draft a brief memo to the president to explain why cash decreased during such a profitable year. Include in your explanation any recommendations for improving the company's cash flow in future years.

(LO 7) PROBLEM 14-5A STATEMENT OF CASH FLOWS USING A WORK SHEET—INDIRECT METHOD (APPENDIX 14A)
Refer to all of the facts in Problem 14-3A.

■ REQUIRED
1. Using the format in Appendix 14A, prepare a statement of cash flows work sheet.
2. Prepare a statement of cash flows, using the indirect method in the operating activities section.
3. On the basis of your statement in requirement 2, draft a brief memo to the president to explain why cash decreased during such a profitable year. Include in your explanation any recommendations for improving the company's cash flow in future years.

(LO 5) PROBLEM 14-6A STATEMENT OF CASH FLOWS—DIRECT METHOD

The income statement for Pluto, Inc., for 1995 follows:

	FOR THE YEAR ENDED DECEMBER 31, 1995
Sales revenue	$350,000
Cost of goods sold	150,000
Gross profit	$200,000
Operating expenses	250,000
Loss before interest and taxes	$(50,000)
Interest expense	10,000
Net loss	$(60,000)

Presented below are comparative balance sheets:

	DECEMBER 31	
	1995	1994
Cash	$ 25,000	$ 10,000
Accounts receivable	30,000	80,000
Inventory	100,000	100,000
Prepayments	36,000	35,000
Total current assets	$191,000	$225,000
Land	$300,000	$200,000
Plant and equipment	500,000	250,000
Accumulated depreciation	(90,000)	(50,000)
Total long-term assets	$710,000	$400,000
Total assets	$901,000	$625,000
Accounts payable	$ 50,000	$ 10,000
Other accrued liabilities	40,000	20,000
Interest payable	22,000	12,000
Total current liabilities	$112,000	$ 42,000
Long-term bank loan payable	$450,000	$100,000
Common stock	$300,000	$300,000
Retained earnings	39,000	183,000
Total stockholders' equity	$339,000	$483,000
Total liabilities and stockholders' equity	$901,000	$625,000

Other information follows:

a. Dividends of $84,000 were declared and paid during the year.

b. Operating expenses include $40,000 of depreciation.

c. Land and plant and equipment were issued for cash. Cash was received from additional bank loans.

The president has asked you some questions about the year's results. He is disturbed with the net loss of $60,000 for the year. He notes, however, that the cash position at the end of the year is improved. He is confused about what appear to be conflicting signals: "How could we have possibly added to our bank accounts during such a terrible year of operations?"

■ **REQUIRED**   **1.** Prepare a statement of cash flows for 1995, using the direct method in the operating activities section.

2. On the basis of your statement in requirement 1, draft a brief memo to the president to explain why cash increased during such an unprofitable year. Include in your memo your recommendations for improving the company's bottom line.

(LO 6) PROBLEM 14-7A STATEMENT OF CASH FLOWS—INDIRECT METHOD

Refer to all of the facts in Problem 14-6A.

■ **REQUIRED**   **1.** Prepare a statement of cash flows for 1995, using the indirect method in the operating activities section.

2. On the basis of your statement in requirement 1, draft a brief memo to the president to explain why cash increased during such an unprofitable year. Include in your memo your recommendations for improving the company's bottom line.

(LO 6) PROBLEM 14-8A YEAR-END BALANCE SHEET AND STATEMENT OF CASH FLOWS—INDIRECT METHOD

The balance sheet of Poodle Company at the end of 1994 is presented below along with certain other information for 1995:

	DECEMBER 31, 1994
Cash	$ 155,000
Accounts receivable	140,000
Total current assets	$ 295,000
Land	$ 100,000
Plant and equipment	700,000
Accumulated depreciation	(175,000)
Investments	125,000
Total long-term assets	$ 750,000
Total assets	$1,045,000
Current liabilities	$ 325,000
Bonds payable	$ 100,000
Common stock	$ 500,000
Retained earnings	120,000
Total stockholders' equity	$ 620,000
Total liabilities and stockholders' equity	$1,045,000

Other information follows:

a. Net income for 1995 was $50,000.

b. Included in operating expenses was $25,000 in depreciation.

c. Cash dividends of $40,000 were declared and paid.

d. An additional $50,000 of common stock was issued for cash.

e. Bonds payable of $100,000 were purchased for cash and retired at no gain or loss.

f. Cash purchases of plant and equipment during the year were $60,000.

g. An additional $200,000 of land was acquired in exchange for a long-term note payable.

h. Sales exceeded cash collections on account during the year by $15,000. All sales are on account.

i. The amount of current liabilities decreased by $20,000 during the year.

1. Prepare a statement of cash flows for 1995, using the indirect method in the operating activities section. Include a supplemental schedule for noncash activities.

2. Prepare a balance sheet at December 31, 1995.

3. What primary uses did Poodle make of the cash it generated from operating activities?

■ REQUIRED

ALTERNATE MULTI-CONCEPT PROBLEMS

(LO 5, 6) PROBLEM 14-9A STATEMENT OF CASH FLOWS—DIRECT AND INDIRECT METHODS

Slovakia Corp. is in the process of preparing its statement of cash flows for the year ended June 30, 1995. An income statement for the year and comparative balance sheets follow:

	FOR THE YEAR ENDED JUNE 30, 1995
Sales revenue	$400,000
Cost of goods sold	240,000
Gross profit	$160,000
General and administrative expenses	$ 40,000
Depreciation expense	80,000
Loss on sale of plant assets	10,000
Total expenses and losses	$130,000
Income before interest and taxes	$ 30,000
Interest expense	15,000
Income before taxes	$ 15,000
Income tax expense	5,000
Net income	$ 10,000

	JUNE 30	
	1995	1994
Cash	$ 25,000	$ 40,000
Accounts receivable	80,000	69,000
Inventory	75,000	50,000
Prepaid rent	2,000	18,000
Total current assets	$ 182,000	$ 177,000
Land	$ 60,000	$ 150,000
Plant and equipment	575,000	500,000
Accumulated depreciation	(310,000)	(250,000)
Total long-term assets	$ 325,000	$ 400,000
Total assets	$ 507,000	$ 577,000
Accounts payable	$ 145,000	$ 140,000
Other accrued liabilities	50,000	45,000
Income taxes payable	5,000	15,000
Total current liabilities	$ 200,000	$ 200,000
Long-term bank loan payable	$ 75,000	$ 150,000
Common stock	$ 100,000	$ 100,000
Retained earnings	132,000	127,000
Total stockholders' equity	$ 232,000	$ 227,000
Total liabilities and stockholders' equity	$ 507,000	$ 577,000

Dividends of $5,000 were declared and paid during the year. New plant assets were purchased for $125,000 in cash during the year. Also, land was sold for cash at its book value. Plant assets were sold during 1995 for $20,000 in cash. The original cost of the assets sold was $50,000, and their book value was $30,000. A portion of the bank loan was repaid.

■ REQUIRED

1. Prepare a statement of cash flows, using the direct method in the operating activities section.
2. Prepare a statement of cash flows, using the indirect method in the operating activities section.
3. Evaluate the following statement: "Whether a company uses the direct or the indirect method to report cash flows from operations is irrelevant because the amount of cash flow from operating activities is the same regardless of which method is used."

(LO 2, 5) PROBLEM 14-10A STATEMENT OF CASH FLOWS—DIRECT METHOD

Pyle Company has not yet prepared a formal statement of cash flows for 1995. Comparative balance sheets as of December 31, 1995 and 1994, and a statement of income and retained earnings for the year ended December 31, 1995, follow:

PYLE COMPANY
BALANCE SHEET
DECEMBER 31
(THOUSANDS OMITTED)

ASSETS	1995	1994
Current assets:		
Cash	$ 50	$ 75
U.S. Treasury bills (six month)	25	–0–
Accounts receivable	125	200
Inventory	525	500
Total current assets	$ 725	$ 775
Long-term assets:		
Land	$ 100	$ 80
Buildings and equipment	510	450
Accumulated depreciation	(190)	(150)
Patents (less amortization)	90	110
Total long-term assets	$ 510	$ 490
Total assets	$1,235	$1,265
LIABILITIES AND OWNERS' EQUITY		
Current liabilities:		
Accounts payable	$ 370	$ 330
Taxes payable	10	20
Notes payable	300	400
Total current liabilities	$ 680	$ 750
Term notes payable—due 1999	200	200
Total liabilities	$ 880	$ 950
Owners' equity:		
Common stock outstanding	$ 220	$ 200
Retained earnings	135	115
Total owners' equity	$ 355	$ 315
Total liabilities and owners' equity	$1,235	$1,265

PYLE COMPANY
STATEMENT OF INCOME AND RETAINED EARNINGS
YEAR ENDED DECEMBER 31, 1995
(THOUSANDS OMITTED)

Sales		$ 1,416
Less expenses and interest:		
Cost of goods sold	$ 990	
Salaries and benefits	195	
Heat, light, and power	70	
Depreciation	40	
Property taxes	2	
Patent amortization	20	
Miscellaneous expense	2	
Interest	45	1,364
Net income before income taxes		$ 52
Income taxes		12
Net income		$ 40
Retained earnings—January 1, 1995		115
		$ 155
Stock dividend distributed		20
Retained earnings—December 31, 1995		$ 135

■ REQUIRED

1. For purposes of a statement of cash flows, are the U.S. Treasury bills cash equivalents? If not, how should they be classified? Explain your answers.

2. Prepare a statement of cash flows, using the direct method in the operating activities section.

(CMA adapted)

CASES

READING AND INTERPRETING FINANCIAL STATEMENTS

(LO 2, 3) CASE 14-1 READING AND INTERPRETING BEN & JERRY'S STATEMENT OF CASH FLOWS

Refer to Ben & Jerry's statement of cash flows for 1992 and any other pertinent information in its annual report.

■ REQUIRED

1. According to a footnote in the annual report, how does the company define cash equivalents?

2. According to the statement of cash flows, did inventories increase or decrease during the most recent year? Explain your answer.

3. What are the major reasons for the difference between net income and net cash provided by operating activities?

4. Excluding operations, what was Ben & Jerry's largest source of cash during the most recent year? The largest use of cash?

5. What common type of cash outflow from financing activities is missing from Ben & Jerry's statement?

(LO 4) CASE 14-2 READING AND INTERPRETING HERMAN MILLER'S STATEMENT OF CASH FLOWS

Presented below is the first section of the statement of cash flows for Herman Miller, Inc., a manufacturer of office furniture, for the year ended May 31, 1992 (thousands omitted):

Net income (loss)	$(14,145)
Adjustments to reconcile net income (loss) to net cash provided by operating activities:	
Depreciation and amortization	$ 30,473
Restructuring charges	24,970
Provision for losses on accounts and notes receivable	11,588
Loss on sales of property and equipment	392
Stock grants earned	234
Other liabilities	19,285
Deferred taxes, noncurrent	(12,297)
Changes in current assets and liabilities	16,500
Total adjustments	$ 91,145
Net cash provided by operating activities	$ 77,000

■ REQUIRED

1. Which method, direct or indirect, does Herman Miller use in preparing this section of the statement? Explain.

2. On the basis of operations (i.e., making and selling office furniture), did Herman Miller have a good or bad year?

3. Provide an explanation for the add back of restructuring charges in the operating activities section.

MAKING FINANCIAL DECISIONS

(LO 1, 5) CASE 14-3 DIVIDEND DECISION AND THE STATEMENT OF CASH FLOWS— DIRECT METHOD

Bailey Corp. just completed the most profitable year in its 25-year history. Reported earnings of $1,020,000 on sales of $8,000,000 resulted in a very healthy profit margin of 12.75%. Each year before releasing the financial statements, the board of directors meets to decide on the amount of dividends to declare for the year. For each of the past nine years, the company has declared a dividend of $1 per share of common stock, which has been paid on January 15 of the following year.

Presented below are the income statement for the year and comparative balance sheets as of the end of the last two years.

	FOR THE YEAR ENDED DECEMBER 31, 1995
Sales revenue	$8,000,000
Cost of goods sold	4,500,000
Gross profit	$3,500,000
Operating expenses	1,450,000
Income before interest and taxes	$2,050,000
Interest expense	350,000
Income before taxes	$1,700,000
Income tax expense 40%	680,000
Net income	$1,020,000

	DECEMBER 31	
	1995	1994
Cash	$ 480,000	$ 450,000
Accounts receivable	250,000	200,000
Inventory	750,000	600,000
Prepayments	60,000	75,000
Total current assets	$ 1,540,000	$ 1,325,000
Land	$ 3,255,000	$ 2,200,000
Plant and equipment	4,200,000	2,500,000
Accumulated depreciation	(1,250,000)	(1,000,000)
Long-term investments	500,000	900,000
Patents	650,000	750,000
Total long-term assets	$ 7,355,000	$ 5,350,000
Total assets	$ 8,895,000	$ 6,675,000
Accounts payable	$ 350,000	$ 280,000
Other accrued liabilities	285,000	225,000
Income taxes payable	170,000	100,000
Dividends payable	–0–	200,000
Notes payable due within next year	200,000	–0–
Total current liabilities	$ 1,005,000	$ 805,000
Long-term notes payable	$ 300,000	$ 500,000
Bonds payable	2,200,000	1,500,000
Total long-term liabilities	$ 2,500,000	$ 2,000,000
Common stock, $10 par	$ 2,500,000	$ 2,000,000
Retained earnings	2,890,000	1,870,000
Total stockholders' equity	$ 5,390,000	$ 3,870,000
Total liabilities and stockholders' equity	$ 8,895,000	$ 6,675,000

Additional information follows:

a. All sales are on account as are all purchases.

b. Land was purchased through the issuance of bonds. Additional land (beyond the amount purchased through the issuance of bonds) was purchased for cash.

c. New plant and equipment were acquired during the year for cash. No plant assets were retired during the year. Depreciation expense is included in operating expenses.

d. Long-term investments were sold for cash during the year.

e. No new patents were acquired, and none were disposed of during the year. Amortization expense is included in operating expenses.

f. Notes payable due within the next year represents the amount reclassified from long term to short term.

g. Fifty thousand shares of common stock were issued during the year at par value.

As Bailey's controller, you have been asked to recommend to the board whether to declare a dividend this year, and if so, whether the precedent of paying a $1 per share dividend can be maintained. The president is eager to keep the dividend at $1 in view of the successful year just completed. He is also concerned, however, about the effect of a dividend on the company's cash position. He is particularly concerned about the large amount of notes payable that comes due next year. He further notes the aggressive growth pattern in recent years, as evidenced this year by large increases in land and plant and equipment.

■ REQUIRED

1. Using the format in Exhibit 14-14, convert the income statement from an accrual basis to a cash basis.

2. Prepare a statement of cash flows, using the direct method in the operating activities section.

3. What do you recommend to the board of directors concerning the declaration of a cash dividend? Should the $1 per share dividend be declared? Should a smaller amount be declared? Should no dividend be declared? Support your answer with any necessary computations. Include in your response your concerns, from a cash flow perspective, about the following year.

(LO 1, 6) CASE 14-4 EQUIPMENT REPLACEMENT DECISION AND CASH FLOWS FROM OPERATIONS

Auberge Company has been in operation for four years. The company is pleased with the continued improvement in net income but is concerned about a lack of cash available to replace existing equipment. Land, buildings, and equipment were purchased at the beginning of Year 1. No subsequent fixed asset purchases have been made, but the president believes that equipment will need to be replaced in the near future. The following information is available (all amounts are in millions of dollars):

YEAR OF OPERATION	YEAR 1	YEAR 2	YEAR 3	YEAR 4
Net income (loss)	$(10)	$(2)	$15	$20
Depreciation expense	30	25	15	14
Increase (decrease) in:				
Accounts Receivable	32	5	12	20
Inventories	26	8	5	9
Prepayments	0	0	10	5
Accounts payable	15	3	(5)	(4)

1. Compute the cash flow from operations for each of Auberge's first four years of operation.

2. Write a memo to the president explaining why the company is not generating sufficient cash from operations to pay for the replacement of equipment.

■ REQUIRED

ACCOUNTING AND ETHICS: WHAT WOULD YOU DO?

(LO 1, 6) CASE 14-5 LOAN DECISION AND THE STATEMENT OF CASH FLOWS— INDIRECT METHOD

Mega Enterprises is in the process of negotiating an extension of its existing loan agreements with a major bank. *The bank is particularly concerned with Mega's ability to generate sufficient cash flow from operating activities to meet the periodic principal and interest payments.* In conjunction with the negotiations, the controller prepared the following statement of cash flows to present to the bank:

MEGA ENTERPRISES
STATEMENT OF CASH FLOWS
FOR THE YEAR ENDED DECEMBER 31, 1995
(ALL AMOUNTS IN MILLIONS OF DOLLARS)

CASH FLOWS FROM OPERATING ACTIVITIES

Net income		$ 65
Adjustments to reconcile net income to net cash provided by operating activities:		
Depreciation and amortization		56
Increase in accounts receivable		(19)
Decrease in inventory		27
Decrease in accounts payable		(42)
Increase in other accrued liabilities		18
Net cash provided by operating activities		$ 105

CASH FLOWS FROM INVESTING ACTIVITIES

Acquisitions of other businesses		$ (234)
Acquisitions of plant and equipment		(125)
Sale of other businesses		300
Net cash used by investing activities		$ (59)

CASH FLOWS FROM FINANCING ACTIVITIES

Additional borrowings	$ 150
Repayments of borrowings	(180)
Cash dividends paid	(50)
Net cash used by financing activities	$ (80)
Net decrease in cash	$ (34)
Cash balance, January 1, 1995	42
Cash balance, December 31, 1995	$ 8

During 1995 Mega sold one of its businesses in California. A gain of $150 million was included in 1995 income as the difference between the proceeds from the sale of $450 million and the book value of the business of $300 million. The entry to record the sale is:

Cash	450	
California Properties		300
Gain on Sale of Business		150
To record sale of a business.		

■ REQUIRED

1. Comment on the presentation of the sale of the California properties on the statement of cash flows. Does the way in which the sale was reported violate generally accepted accounting principles? Regardless of whether it violates GAAP, does the way in which the transaction was reported on the statement result in a misstatement of the net decrease in cash for the period?

2. Prepare a revised statement of cash flows, with the proper presentation of the sale of the California business.

3. Has the controller acted in an unethical manner in reporting the sale on the statement of cash flows? Explain your answer.

(LO 2, 3) CASE 14-6 CASH EQUIVALENTS AND THE STATEMENT OF CASH FLOWS

In December 1995, Rangers, Inc., invested $100,000 of idle cash in U.S. Treasury notes. The notes mature on October 1, 1996, at which time Rangers expects to redeem them at face value of $100,000. The treasurer believes that the notes should be classified as cash equivalents because of the plans to hold them to maturity and receive face value. He would also like to avoid presentation of the purchase as an investing activity because the company has made sizable capital expenditures during the year. The treasurer realizes that the decision rests with you, as controller, as to the classification of the Treasury notes.

■ REQUIRED

1. According to generally accepted accounting principles, how should the investment in U.S. Treasury notes be classified for purposes of preparing a statement of cash flows? Explain your answer.

2. As controller for Rangers, what would you do in this situation? What would you tell the treasurer?

ANALYTICAL SOFTWARE CASE

To the Student: Your instructor may assign one or more parts of the analytical software case that is designed to accompany this chapter. This multi-part case gives you a chance to work with real financial statement data using software that stimulates, guides, and hones your analytical and problem-solving skills. It was created especially to support and strengthen your understanding of the chapter's Learning Objectives.

SOLUTION TO KEY TERMS QUIZ

1. Operating activities (p. 745)
2. Indirect method (p. 749)
3. Statement of cash flows (p. 741)
4. Cash equivalent (p. 744)
5. Investing activities (p. 746)
6. Direct method (p. 749)
7. Financing activities (p. 747)

Focus on Financial Results

The Boeing Company, headquartered in Seattle, Washington, is the largest aerospace firm in the United States and the world's leading manufacturer of commercial aircraft. During the early 1990s, Boeing was also the nation's largest exporter.

Due to cutbacks in demand for aircraft worldwide, the company laid off 20,000 workers in early 1993. It's an unfortunate fact of life in a cyclical industry like aerospace. But Boeing has kept itself financially strong. At the end of 1992, it had long-term

(Dollars in millions except per share data)	1993	1992
Sales and Other Operating Revenue	$ 25,438	$ 30,184
Net Earnings	1,244	1,554**
Earnings per Share	3.66	4.57**
Return on Average Equity	15%	19%**
Contractual Backlog	$ 73,528	$ 87,930
Research and Development	1,661	1,846
Capital Expenditures, net	1,317	2,160
Cash and Short-term Investments	3,108	3,614
Customer Financing	3,177	2,295
Long-term Debt	2,613	1,772
Cash Dividends	340	340

* Exclusive of earnings of $298 due to the adoption of Statement of Financial Accounting Standards No. 96.

**Exclusive of cumulative transition adjustment of $1,002 due to the adoption of Statement of Accounting Standards No. 106.

debt of only $1,772 million, compared to stockholders' equity of $8,056 million. This results in a ratio of long-term debt to total long-term debt and stockholders' equity of just 18%—the lowest of any major aerospace firm.

One of the most important items of financial information to analysts of Boeing is the company's backlog of orders. In 1991, the company's backlog amounted to $98 billion, more than three times 1991 sales. By 1992, that backlog had been whittled down to $88 billion, less than three times 1992 sales. As a result, the company has to cut back on production. During 1993, production rates were cut back significantly. For example, production of the Boeing 737 aircraft was cut from 14 to 10 during October 1993.

Chapter 15

Financial Statement Analysis

LEARNING OBJECTIVES

After studying this chapter, you should be able to

1. Explain the various limitations and considerations in financial statement analysis.
2. Use comparative financial statements to analyze a company over time (horizontal analysis).
3. Use common-size financial statements to compare various financial statement items (vertical analysis).
4. Compute and use various ratios to assess liquidity.
5. Compute and use various ratios to assess solvency.
6. Compute and use various ratios to assess profitability.

Linkages

A LOOK AT PREVIOUS CHAPTERS

In Chapter 2, we introduced a few key financial ratios and saw the way that investors and creditors use them to better understand a company's financial statements. In many of the subsequent chapters, we introduced ratios relevant to the particular topic being discussed.

A LOOK AT THIS CHAPTER

Ratio analysis is one important type of analysis used to interpret financial statements. In this chapter, we expand our discussion of ratio analysis and introduce other valuable techniques used by investors, creditors, and analysts in reaching informed decisions. We will find that ratios and other forms of analyses can provide additional insight beyond that available from merely reading the financial statements.

Precautions in Statement Analysis

Various groups have different purposes for analyzing a company's financial statements. For example, a banker is primarily interested in the likelihood that a loan will be repaid. Certain ratios, as we will see, indicate the ability to repay principal and interest. A stockholder, on the other hand, is concerned with a fair return on the amount invested in the company. Again, certain ratios are helpful in assessing the return to the stockholder. Management of a business is interested in the tools of financial statement analysis as well because the various outside groups normally judge management on the basis of its performance as measured by certain key ratios. Annual reports for publicly held corporations are required to include a section that reviews the past year with management's comments on its performance during the year as measured by selected ratios and other forms of analysis.

Before we turn our attention to various techniques commonly used in the financial analysis of a company, it is important to understand some of the limitations and other considerations in statement analysis.

Watch for Alternative Accounting Principles

LO 1

Explain the various limitations and considerations in financial statement analysis.

Every set of financial statements is based on various assumptions. For example, a cost-flow method must be assumed in valuing inventory and recognizing cost of goods sold. The accountant chooses FIFO, LIFO, or one of the other acceptable methods. The analyst or other user finds this type of information in the footnotes to the financial statements. The selection of a particular inventory valuation method has a significant effect on certain key ratios. Recognition of the acceptable alternatives is especially important in comparing two or more companies. Finally, as we saw in Chapter 12, *changes* in accounting methods, such as a change in the depreciation method, also make comparing results for a given company over time more difficult. Again, the reader must turn to the footnotes for information regarding these changes.

Take Care When Making Comparisons

Users of financial statements often place too much emphasis on summary indicators and key ratios, such as the current ratio and the earnings per share amount. No single ratio is capable of telling the user everything there is to know about a particular company. The calculation of various ratios for a company is only a starting point. One technique we discuss is the comparison of ratios for different periods of time. Has the ratio gone up or down from last year? What is the percentage of increase or decrease in the ratio over the last five years? Recognizing trends in ratios is important in analyzing any company.

The potential investor must also recognize the need to compare one company with others in the same industry. For example, a particular measure of performance may cause an investor to conclude that the company is not operating efficiently. Comparison with an industry standard, however, might indicate that the particular ratio is normal for companies in that industry. Various organizations publish summaries of selected ratios for a sample of companies in the United States. The ratios are usually organized by industry. Dun & Bradstreet's *Industry Norms and Key Business Ratios,* for example, is an annual review that organizes companies into five major industries and approximately 800 specific lines of business.

Although industry comparisons are useful, caution is necessary in interpreting the results of such analyses. Few companies in today's economy operate in a single industry. Exceptions exist (Wrigley is almost exclusively in the business of making and selling chewing gum), but most companies cross the boundaries of a single industry. Companies operating in more than one industry, known as *conglomerates,* present a special challenge to the analyst. Keep in mind also the point made earlier about alternative accounting methods. It is not unusual to find companies in the same industry using different inventory valuation techniques or depreciation methods.

One final point concerning the use of financial statements to make comparisons among companies is worth mentioning. Many corporate income statements contain nonoperating items, such as extraordinary items, cumulative effects from accounting changes, and gains and losses from discontinued operations. When these items exist, the reader must exercise extra caution in making comparisons. To assess the future prospects of a group of companies, it may be more meaningful to compare income statements *before* taking into account the effects on income from these items.

Understand the Possible Effects of Inflation

Inflation, or an increase in the level of prices, is another important consideration in analyzing financial statements. The statements, prepared to be used by outsiders, are based on historical costs and are not adjusted for the effects of increasing prices. For example, consider the following trend in a company's sales for the past three years:

	1995	1994	1993
Net sales	$121,000	$110,000	$100,000

As measured by the actual dollars of sales, it appears that sales have increased by 10% each year. Caution is necessary in concluding that the company is better off in each succeeding year because of the increase in sales *dollars.* Assume, for example, that 1993 sales of $100,000 are the result of selling 100,000 units at $1 each. Are 1994 sales of $110,000 the result of selling 110,000 units at $1 each or of selling 100,000 units at $1.10 each? Although on the surface it may seem unimportant which result accounts for the sales increase, the answer can have significant ramifications. If the company found it necessary to increase selling price to $1.10 in the face of increasing *costs,* it may be no better off than it was in 1993 in terms of gross profit. On the other hand, if the company is able to increase sales revenue by 10% primarily based on growth in unit sales, then its performance is usually considered stronger than if the increase is merely due to a price increase. The point to be made is one of caution: Published financial statements are stated in historical costs and therefore have not been adjusted for the effects of inflation.

Fortunately, inflation has been relatively subdued in the past several years. During the late 1970s, the FASB actually required a separate footnote in the financial statements to calculate the effects of inflation. The requirement was abandoned in the mid-1980s when inflation had subsided and the profession decided that the cost of providing inflation-adjusted information exceeded the benefits to the users.

Analysis of Comparative and Common-Size Statements

We are now ready to analyze a set of financial statements. We will begin by looking at the comparative statements of a company for a two-year period. The analysis of the statements over a series of years is often called **horizontal analysis.** We will then see how the statements can be recast in what are referred to as *common-size statements*. The analysis of common-size statements is called **vertical analysis.** Finally, we will consider the use of a variety of ratios to analyze a company.

Horizontal Analysis

LO 2

Use comparative financial statements to analyze a company over time (horizontal analysis).

Comparative balance sheets for a hypothetical entity, Henderson Company, are presented in Exhibit 15-1. The increase or decrease in each of the major accounts on the balance sheet is shown in both absolute dollars and as a percentage. The base year for computing the percentage increase or decrease in each account is the first year, 1994, and is normally shown on the right side. By reading across from right to left (thus, the term *horizontal analysis*), the analyst can quickly spot any unusual

EXHIBIT 15-1   Comparative Balance Sheets

HENDERSON COMPANY
COMPARATIVE BALANCE SHEETS
DECEMBER 31, 1995 AND 1994
(ALL AMOUNTS IN THOUSANDS OF DOLLARS)

	DECEMBER 31		INCREASE (DECREASE)	
	1995	1994	DOLLARS	PERCENT
Cash	$ 320	$ 1,350	$(1,030)	(76)%
Accounts receivable	5,500	4,500	1,000	22
Inventory	4,750	2,750	2,000	73
Prepaid insurance	150	200	(50)	(25)
Total current assets	$10,720	$ 8,800	$1,920	22
Land	2,000	2,000	–0–	–0–
Buildings and equipment	6,000	4,500	1,500	33
Accumulated depreciation	(1,850)	(1,500)	350	23
Total long-term assets	$ 6,150	$ 5,000	$1,150	23
Total assets	$16,870	$13,800	$3,070	22
Accounts payable	$ 4,250	$2,500	$1,750	70
Taxes payable	2,300	2,100	200	10
Notes payable	600	800	(200)	(25)
Current portion of bonds	100	100	–0–	–0–
Total current liabilities	$ 7,250	$ 5,500	$1,750	32
Bonds payable	700	800	(100)	(13)
Total liabilities	$ 7,950	$ 6,300	$1,650	26
Preferred stock, $5 par	500	500	–0–	–0–
Common stock, $1 par	1,000	1,000	–0–	–0–
Retained earnings	7,420	6,000	1,420	24
Total stockholders' equity	$ 8,920	$ 7,500	$1,420	19
Total liabilities and stockholders' equity	$16,870	$13,800	$3,070	22

Read from right to left

The base year is normally on the right

Note: Referenced amounts boldfaced for convenience.

EXHIBIT 15-2   Comparative Statements of Income and Retained Earnings

HENDERSON COMPANY
COMPARATIVE STATEMENTS OF INCOME AND RETAINED EARNINGS
FOR THE YEARS ENDED DECEMBER 31, 1995 AND 1994
(ALL AMOUNTS IN THOUSANDS OF DOLLARS)

	DECEMBER 31 1995	DECEMBER 31 1994	INCREASE (DECREASE) DOLLARS	INCREASE (DECREASE) PERCENT
Net sales	$24,000	$20,000	$ 4,000	20%
Cost of goods sold	18,000	14,000	4,000	29
Gross profit	$ 6,000	$ 6,000	$ –0–	–0–
Selling, general, and administrative expense	3,000	2,000	1,000	50
Operating income	$ 3,000	$ 4,000	$(1,000)	(25)
Interest expense	140	160	(20)	(13)
Income before tax	$ 2,860	$ 3,840	$ (980)	(26)
Income tax expense	1,140	1,540	(400)	(26)
Net income	$ 1,720	$ 2,300	$ (580)	(25)
Preferred dividends	50	50		
Income available to common	$ 1,670	$ 2,250		
Common dividends	250	250		
To retained earnings	$ 1,420	$ 2,000		
Retained earnings, 1/1	6,000	4,000		
Retained earnings, 12/31	$ 7,420	$ 6,000		

These three increases in revenue and expenses resulted in an operating income *decrease* of 25%.

Note: Referenced amounts boldfaced for convenience.

changes in accounts from the previous year. Three accounts stand out: Cash decreased by 76%, Inventory increased by 73%, and Accounts Payable increased by 70%. (These lines are boldfaced for convenience.) Individually, each of these large changes is a red flag. Taken together, however, the financial statement user would become alarmed that the business is deteriorating. Each of these large changes should be investigated further.

Exhibit 15-2 shows comparative statements of income and retained earnings for Henderson for 1995 and 1994. At first glance, the 20% increase in sales to $24 million appears promising, but management was not able to limit the increase in either cost of goods sold or selling, general, and administrative expense to 20%. The analysis indicates that cost of sales increased by 29% and selling, general, and administrative expense increased by 50%. The increases in these two expenses more than offset the increase in sales and resulted in a decrease in operating income of 25%.

Companies that experience sales growth often become lax about controlling expenses. Their managements sometimes forget that it is the bottom line that counts, not the top line. Perhaps the salespeople are given incentives to increase sales without considering the costs of the sales. Maybe management is spending too much on overhead, including its own salaries. The owners of the business will have to address these concerns if they want to get a reasonable return on their investment.

EXHIBIT 15-3 Quaker Oats Financial Summary

The Quaker Oats Company and Subsidiaries

Eleven-Year Selected Financial Data	Year Ended June 30	5-Year Compound Growth Rate	10-Year Compound Growth Rate	1993
	Financial Statistics(a)(b)			
	Current ratio			**1.0**
	Working capital			**$ (37.5)**
	Working capital turnover(c)			**87.4**
	Property, plant and equipment—net	5.9%	8.7%	**$ 1,228.2**
	Depreciation expense	8.0%	12.5%	**$ 129.9**
	Total assets	(0.5%)	7.3%	**$ 2,815.9**
	Long-term debt			**$ 632.6**
	Preferred stock (net of deferred compensation) and preference stock			**$ 11.4**
	Common shareholders' equity			**$ 551.1**
	Net cash provided by operating activities			**$ 558.2**
	Operating return on assets(d)			**21.1%**
	Gross profit as a percentage of sales			**50.1%**
	Advertising and merchandising as a percentage of sales			**25.7%**
	Research and development as a percentage of sales			**0.9%**
	Income from continuing operations before cumulative effect of accounting changes as a percentage of sales			**5.0%**
	Long-term debt ratio(e)			**52.9%**
	Total debt ratio(f)			**59.0%**
	Common dividends as a percentage of income available for common shares (excluding cumulative effect of accounting changes)			**48.9%**
	Number of common shareholders			**33,154**
	Number of employees worldwide			**20,200**
	Market price range of common stock —High			**$ 77**
	—Low			**$ 56 ¼**

(a)Income-related statistics exclude the results of businesses reported as discontinued operations. Balance sheet amounts and related statistics have not been restated for discontinued operations, other than Fisher-Price, due to materiality.
(b)Effective fiscal 1991, common shareholders' equity and number of employees worldwide were reduced as a result of the Fisher-Price spin-off (see Note 2).
(c)Net sales divided by average working capital.

Horizontal analysis can be extended to include more than two years of results. At a minimum, publicly held companies are required to include income statements and statements of cash flows for the three most recent years and balance sheets as of the end of the two most recent years. Many annual reports include, as supplementary information, financial summaries of operations for extended periods of time. As illustrated in Exhibit 15-3, for example, The Quaker Oats Company includes an 11-year summary of selected financial data, such as the current ratio, the gross profit ratio, and total assets. In addition, Quaker shows for selected items a 5-year and a 10-year compound growth rate. Note the trend over time in two of the ratios we discussed in earlier chapters: the current ratio and the gross profit ratio. The current ratio peaked at the end of 1989 at 1.8 and has declined steadily to 1.0 at the end of 1993. Conversely, Quaker's gross profit ratio has increased steadily over the 11-year period from a low of 38.4% in 1984 to a high of 50.1% in 1993.

Tracking items over a series of years, called *trend analysis*, can be a very powerful tool for the analyst. Advanced statistical techniques are available for analyzing trends in financial data and, most important, for projecting those trends to future periods. Some of the techniques, such as time series analysis, have been used extensively in forecasting sales trends.

FROM CONCEPT TO PRACTICE

READING BEN & JERRY'S ANNUAL REPORT

Where does Ben & Jerry's annual report provide a financial summary? How many years does it include? In terms of a trend over time, which item on the summary do you think is the most significant?

EXHIBIT 15-3   (continued)

Dollars in Millions (Except Per Share Data)

1992	1991	1990	1989	1988	1987	1986	1985	1984	1983
1.2	1.3	1.3	1.8	1.4	1.4	1.4	1.7	1.6	1.6
$ 168.7	$ 317.8	$ 342.8	$ 695.8	$ 417.5	$ 507.9	$ 296.8	$ 400.7	$ 316.8	$ 261.9
22.9	16.6	9.7	8.8	9.7	9.5	8.5	8.2	9.8	8.2
$1,273.3	$1,232.7	$1,154.1	$ 959.6	$ 922.5	$ 898.6	$ 691.0	$ 616.5	$ 650.1	$ 533.0
$ 129.7	$ 125.2	$ 103.5	$ 94.2	$ 88.3	$ 81.6	$ 59.1	$ 56.3	$ 57.4	$ 40.1
$3,039.9	$3,060.5	$3,377.4	$3,125.9	$2,886.1	$3,136.5	$1,944.5	$1,760.3	$1,726.5	$1,391.9
$ 688.7	$ 701.2	$ 740.3	$ 766.8	$ 299.1	$ 527.7	$ 160.9	$ 168.2	$ 200.1	$ 152.8
$ 7.9	$ 4.8	$ 1.8	—	—	—	—	$ 37.9	$ 38.5	$ 41.3
$ 842.1	$ 901.0	$1,017.5	$1,137.1	$1,251.1	$1,087.5	$ 831.7	$ 786.9	$ 720.1	$ 639.4
$ 581.3	$ 543.2	$ 460.0	$ 408.3	$ 320.8	$ 375.1	$ 266.9	$ 295.5	$ 263.6	$ 212.2
18.9%	18.8%	20.4%	14.4%	18.3%	22.1%	25.8%	24.5%	24.4%	27.1%
49.5%	48.3%	46.6%	45.6%	46.8%	45.8%	43.8%	40.2%	38.4%	40.5%
26.0%	25.6%	23.8%	23.4%	24.9%	22.9%	21.7%	19.4%	18.4%	18.6%
0.9%	0.8%	0.9%	0.8%	0.8%	0.8%	0.8%	0.7%	0.8%	0.8%
4.4%	4.3%	4.6%	3.1%	4.4%	4.0%	4.8%	4.4%	4.0%	4.5%
44.8%	43.6%	42.1%	40.3%	19.3%	32.7%	16.2%	16.9%	20.9%	18.3%
48.7%	47.4%	52.3%	44.2%	33.8%	50.2%	35.7%	28.9%	35.4%	32.9%
52.9%	58.9%	65.1%	46.9%	31.3%	25.9%	31.2%	33.0%	32.9%	75.8%
33,580	33,603	33,859	34,347	34,231	32,358	27,068	26,670	26,785	27,943
21,100	20,900	28,200	31,700	31,300	30,800	29,500	28,700	28,400	25,200
$ 75¼	$ 64⅞	$ 68⅛	$ 66¼	$ 57⅛	$ 57¾	$ 39¼	$ 26⅛	$ 16⅛	$ 12⅝
$ 50¼	$ 41¼	$ 45⅛	$ 42⅜	$ 31	$ 32⅜	$ 23½	$ 14¼	$ 10⅛	$ 8⅜

(d)Operating income divided by average identifiable assets of U.S. and Canadian and International Grocery Products.
(e)Long-term debt divided by long-term debt plus total shareholders' equity including preferred stock (net of related deferred compensation) and preference stock.
(f)Total debt divided by total debt plus total shareholders' equity including preferred stock (net of related deferred compensation) and preference stock.

Historically, attention has focused on the balance sheet and income statement in analyzing a company's position and results of operation. Only recently have analysts and other users begun to appreciate the value in incorporating the statement of cash flows into their analyses.

Comparative statements of cash flows for Henderson appear in Exhibit 15-4. Henderson's financing activities remained constant over the two-year period, as indicated in that section of the statements. Each year the company paid $200,000 on notes, another $100,000 to retire bonds, and $300,000 to stockholders in dividends. Cash outflow from investing activities slowed down somewhat in 1995, with the purchase of $1,500,000 in new buildings, compared with $2,000,000 the year before.

The most noticeable difference in Henderson's statements of cash flows between the two years is in the operating activities section. Operations generated almost $2 million less in cash in 1995 compared to 1994 ($1.07 million in 1995 versus $2.95 million in 1994). The decrease in net income, as presented in the exhibit, was partially responsible for this reduction in cash from operations. However, the increases in accounts receivable and inventories in 1995 had a significant impact on the decrease in cash generated from operating activities.

EXHIBIT 15-4   Comparative Statements of Cash Flow

HENDERSON COMPANY
COMPARATIVE STATEMENTS OF CASH FLOW
FOR THE YEARS ENDED DECEMBER 31, 1995 AND 1994
(ALL AMOUNTS IN THOUSANDS OF DOLLARS)

	1995	1994	INCREASE (DECREASE) DOLLARS	INCREASE (DECREASE) PERCENT
NET CASH FLOWS FROM OPERATING ACTIVITIES				
Net income	**$1,720**	**$2,300**	$ (580)	(25)%
Adjustments:				
Depreciation expense	350	300		
Changes in:				
Accounts receivable	**(1,000)**	**500**		
Inventory	**(2,000)**	**(300)**		
Prepaid insurance	50	50		
Accounts payable	1,750	(200)		
Taxes payable	200	300		
Net cash provided by operating activities [Unfavorable]	**$1,070** ←—	**$2,950**	$(1,880)	(64)%
NET CASH FLOWS FROM INVESTING ACTIVITIES				
Purchase of buildings	$(1,500)	$(2,000)	$ (500)	(25)%
NET CASH FLOWS FROM FINANCING ACTIVITIES				
Repayment of notes	$ (200)	$ (200)	–0–	–0–
Retirement of bonds	(100)	(100)	–0–	–0–
Cash dividends—preferred	(50)	(50)	–0–	–0–
Cash dividends—common	(250)	(250)	–0–	–0–
Net cash used by financing activities	$ (600)	$ (600)	–0–	–0–
Net increase (decrease) in cash	$(1,030)	$ 350		
Beginning cash balance	1,350	1,000		
Ending cash balance	$ 320	$ 1,350		
SUPPLEMENTAL INFORMATION				
Interest paid	$ 140	$ 160		
Income taxes paid	$ 940	$ 1,440		

Note: Referenced amounts boldfaced for convenience.

Vertical Analysis

LO   3

Use common-size financial statements to compare various financial statement items (vertical analysis).

Often it is easier to examine comparative financial statements if they have been standardized. *Common-size statements* recast all items on the statement as a percentage of a selected item on the statement. This excludes size as a relevant variable in the analysis. One could use this type of analysis to compare General Motors with the smaller Chrysler or IBM with the much smaller Apple Computer. It is also a convenient way to compare the same company from year to year.

Vertical analysis involves looking at the relative size and composition of various items on a particular financial statement. Common-size comparative balance sheets for Henderson Company are presented in Exhibit 15-5. Note that all asset accounts are stated as a percentage of total assets. Similarly, all liability and stockholders' equity accounts are stated as a percentage of the total of the right side of the balance sheet. The combination of the comparative balance sheets for the two years with the common-size feature allows the analyst to spot critical changes in the composition of the assets. We noted in Exhibit 15-1 that cash had decreased by 76% over the two years. The decrease of cash from 9.8% of total assets to only 1.9% is further highlighted in Exhibit 15-5.

One can also observe in the exhibit that total current assets have continued to represent just under two-thirds (63.5%) of the total assets. If cash has decreased significantly in terms of the percentage of total assets, what accounts have increased to maintain current assets at two-thirds of total assets? We can quickly determine from the data in Exhibit 15-5 that although inventory represented 19.9% of total assets at the end of 1994, the percentage is up to 28.1% at the end of 1995. This

EXHIBIT 15-5   Common-Size Comparative Balance Sheets

HENDERSON COMPANY
COMMON-SIZE COMPARATIVE BALANCE SHEETS
DECEMBER 31, 1995 AND 1994
(ALL AMOUNTS IN THOUSANDS OF DOLLARS)

	DECEMBER 31, 1995		DECEMBER 31, 1994	
	DOLLARS	PERCENT	DOLLARS	PERCENT
Cash	$ 320	1.9%	$ 1,350	9.8%
Accounts receivable	5,500	32.6	4,500	32.6
Inventory	4,750	28.1	2,750	19.9
Prepaid insurance	150	0.9	200	1.5
Total current assets	$10,720	63.5%	$ 8,800	63.8%
Land	2,000	11.9	2,000	14.5
Buildings and equipment, net	4,150	24.6	3,000	21.7
Total long-term assets	$ 6,150	36.5	$ 5,000	36.2
Total assets	$16,870	100.0%	$13,800	100.0%
Accounts payable	$ 4,250	25.2%	$ 2,500	18.1%
Taxes payable	2,300	13.6	2,100	15.2
Notes payable	600	3.6	800	5.8
Current portion of bonds	100	0.6	100	0.7
Total current liabilities	$ 7,250	43.0%	$ 5,500	39.8%
Bonds payable	700	4.1	800	5.8
Total liabilities	$ 7,950	47.1%	$ 6,300	45.6%
Preferred stock	500	3.0	500	3.6
Common stock	1,000	5.9	1,000	7.3
Retained earnings	7,420	44.0	6,000	43.5
Total stockholders' equity	$ 8,920	52.9%	$ 7,500	54.4%
Total liabilities and stockholders' equity	$16,870	100.0%	$13,800	100.0%

In **vertical analysis**, compare each line item as a percent of total (100%) to highlight company's overall condition.

Compare percentages across years to spot year-to-year trends.

Note: Referenced amounts boldfaced for convenience.

change in the relative composition of current assets between cash and inventory may have important implications. The change, for instance, may signal that the company is having trouble selling inventory.

Total current liabilities represent a slightly higher percentage of total liabilities and stockholders' equity at the end of 1995, compared to the end of 1994. The increase is balanced by a slight decrease in the relative percentages of long-term debt (the bonds) and of stockholders' equity. We will return later to further analysis of the composition of both the current and noncurrent accounts.

Common-size comparative income statements for Henderson are presented in Exhibit 15-6. The *base*, or benchmark, on which all other items in the income statement are compared is net sales. Again, observations from the comparative statements alone are further confirmed by examining the common-size statements. Although the **gross profit ratio**—gross profit as a percentage of sales—was 30% in 1994, the same ratio for 1995 is only 25%. Recall the earlier observation that although sales had increased by 20% from one year to the next, cost of goods sold increased by 29%.

In addition to the gross profit ratio, an important relationship from Exhibit 15-6 is the *ratio of net income to net sales* or **profit margin ratio.** The ratio is an overall indicator of management's ability to control expenses and reflects the amount of income for each dollar of sales. Some analysts prefer to look at income before tax, rather than final net income, because taxes are not typically an expense that can be controlled. Further, if the company does not earn a profit before tax, it will incur no tax expense. Note the decrease in Henderson's profit margin: from 11.5% in 1994 to 7.1% in 1995 (or from 19.2% to 11.9% on a before-tax basis).

EXHIBIT 15-6   Common-Size Comparative Income Statements

HENDERSON COMPANY
COMMON-SIZE COMPARATIVE INCOME STATEMENTS
FOR THE YEARS ENDED DECEMBER 31, 1995 AND 1994
(ALL AMOUNTS IN THOUSANDS OF DOLLARS)

	1995 DOLLARS	1995 PERCENT	1994 DOLLARS	1994 PERCENT	
Net sales	$24,000	100.0%	$20,000	100.0%	
Cost of goods sold	18,000	75.0	14,000	70.0	
Gross profit	$ 6,000	25.0%	$ 6,000	30.0%	← Gross profit as a percentage of sales is the **gross profit ratio.**
Selling, general, and administrative expense	3,000	12.5	2,000	10.0	
Operating income	$ 3,000	12.5%	$ 4,000	20.0%	
Interest expense	140	0.6	160	0.8	
Income before tax	$ 2,860	11.9%	$ 3,840	19.2%	
Income tax expense	1,140	4.8	1,540	7.7	
Net income	$ 1,720	7.1%	$ 2,300	11.5%	← The ratio of net income to net sales is the **profit margin ratio.**

Note: Referenced amounts boldfaced for convenience.

Liquidity Analysis and the Management of Working Capital

Two ratios were discussed in the last section: the *gross profit ratio* and the *profit margin ratio.* A ratio is simply the relationship, normally stated as a percentage, between two financial statement amounts. In this section, we consider a wide range of ratios used by management, analysts, and others for a variety of purposes. We classify the ratios in three main categories according to their use in performing (1) liquidity analysis, (2) solvency analysis, and (3) profitability analysis.

Liquidity is a relative measure of the nearness to cash of the assets and liabilities of a company. Nearness to cash deals with the length of time before cash is realized. Various ratios are used to measure liquidity, and they basically concern the company's ability to pay its debts as they come due. Recall the distinction between the current and long-term classifications on the balance sheet. Current assets are assets that will either be converted into cash or consumed within one year or the operating cycle, if the cycle is longer than one year. The operating cycle for a manufacturing company is the length of time between the purchase of raw materials and the eventual collection of any outstanding account receivable from the sale of the product. Current liabilities are a company's obligations that require the use of current assets or the creation of other current liabilities to satisfy them.

The nearness to cash of the current assets and liabilities is indicated by their placement on the balance sheet. Current assets are listed on the balance sheet in descending order of their nearness to cash. Liquidity is, of course, a matter of degree, with cash being the most liquid of all assets. With few exceptions, such as prepaid insurance, most current assets are convertible into cash. However, accounts receivable is closer to being converted into cash than is inventory. An account receivable need only be collected to be converted to cash. An item of inventory must first be sold and then, assuming that sales of inventory are on account, the account must be collected before cash is realized.

LO   **4**

Compute and use various ratios to assess liquidity.

Working Capital

Working capital is the excess of current assets over current liabilities at a point in time:

$$\text{Working Capital} = \text{Current Assets} - \text{Current Liabilities}$$

Reference to Henderson's comparative balance sheets in Exhibit 15-1 indicates the following:

	DECEMBER 31	
	1995	1994
Current assets	$10,720,000	$8,800,000
Current liabilities	7,250,000	5,500,000
Working capital	$ 3,470,000	$3,300,000

The management of working capital is an extremely important task for any business. A comparison of Henderson's working capital at the end of each of the two years indicates a slight increase in the degree of protection for short-term creditors of the company. Management must always strive for the ideal balance of current assets and current liabilities. The amount of working capital is limited in its informational value, however. For example, it tells us nothing about the composition of the current accounts. Also, the dollar amount of working capital can be used to compare other companies of different sizes in the same industry. Working capital of $3,470,000 may be adequate for Henderson Company, but it might signal impending bankruptcy for a company much larger than Henderson.

Current Ratio

The **current ratio** is one of the most widely used of all financial statement ratios and is calculated as follows:

$$\text{Current Ratio} = \frac{\text{Current Assets}}{\text{Current Liabilities}}$$

For Henderson Company, the ratio at each year-end is

DECEMBER 31	
1995	1994
$\frac{\$10,720,000}{\$7,250,000} = 1.48 \text{ to } 1$	$\frac{\$8,800,000}{\$5,500,000} = 1.60 \text{ to } 1$

At the end of 1995, Henderson had $1.48 of current assets for every $1 of current liabilities. Is this current ratio adequate? Or is it a sign of impending financial difficulties? There is no definitive answer to either of these questions. Some analysts use a general rule of thumb of 2:1 for the current ratio as a sign of short-term financial health. The answer depends first on the industry. Companies in certain industries have historically operated with current ratios much less than 2:1 (as we noted earlier in the chapter, Quaker Oats' current ratio has ranged from 1.6 to 1.0 over an 11-year period).

A second concern in interpreting the current ratio involves the composition of the current assets. Cash is usually the only acceptable means of payment for most liabilities. Therefore, it is important to consider the makeup, or *composition,* of the current assets. Refer to Exhibit 15-5 and Henderson's common-size balance sheets. Not only did the current ratio decline during 1995 but also the proportion of the total current assets made up by inventory increased, whereas the proportion made up by accounts receivable remained the same. Recall that accounts receivable is only one step removed from cash, whereas inventory requires both sale and collection of the subsequent account.

Acid-Test Ratio

The **acid-test** or **quick ratio** is a stricter test of a company's ability to pay its current debts as they are due. Specifically, it is intended to deal with the composition problem because it *excludes* inventories and prepaid assets from the numerator of the fraction:

$$\text{Acid-Test or Quick Ratio} = \frac{\text{Quick Assets}}{\text{Current Liabilities}}$$

where

Quick Assets = Cash + Marketable Securities + Current Receivables

Henderson's quick assets consist of only cash and accounts receivable, and its quick ratios are as follows:

DECEMBER 31

1995	1994

$$\frac{\$320,000 + \$5,500,000}{\$7,250,000} = 0.80 \text{ to } 1 \qquad \frac{\$1,350,000 + \$4,500,000}{\$5,500,000} = 1.06 \text{ to } 1$$

Does the quick ratio of less than 1:1 at the end of 1995 mean that Henderson will be unable to pay creditors on time? *For many companies, an acid-test ratio below 1 is not desirable, because it may signal the need to liquidate marketable securities to pay bills, regardless of the current trading price of the securities.* Although the quick ratio is a better indication of short-term debt-paying ability than the current ratio, it is still not perfect. For example, we would want to know the normal credit terms that Henderson extends to its customers, as well as the credit terms that the company receives from its suppliers.

Assume that Henderson requires its customers to pay their accounts within 30 days. On the other hand, assume that the normal credit terms extended by Henderson's suppliers allow payment anytime within 60 days. The relatively longer credit terms extended by Henderson's suppliers gives it some cushion in meeting its obligations. The due date of the $2,300,000 in taxes payable could also have a significant effect on the company's ability to remain in business.

Cash Flow from Operations to Current Liabilities

Two limitations exist with either the current ratio or the quick ratio as a measure of liquidity. First, almost all debts require the payment of cash. Thus, a ratio that focuses on cash is useful.[1] Second, both ratios focus on liquid assets at a *point in time*. Cash flow from operating activities, as reported on the statement of cash flows, can be used to indicate the flow of cash during the year to cover the debts due. The **cash flow from operations to current liabilities ratio** is computed as

$$\text{Cash Flow from Operations to Current Liabilities Ratio} = \frac{\text{Net Cash Provided by Operating Activities}}{\text{Average Current Liabilities}}$$

Note the use of *average* current liabilities in the denominator. This results in a denominator that is consistent with the numerator, which reports the cash flow over a period of time. Because we need to calculate the *average* current liabilities for both years, it is necessary to add the ending balance sheet for 1993 to the analysis. The balance sheet for Henderson on December 31, 1993, is given in Exhibit 15-7. The ratio for Henderson for each year is as follows:

DECEMBER 31

1995	1994

$$\frac{\$1,070,000}{(\$7,250,000 + \$5,500,000)/2} = 16.8\% \qquad \frac{\$2,950,000}{(\$5,500,000 + \$5,600,000)/2} = 53.2\%$$

Two factors are responsible for the large decrease in this ratio from 1994 to 1995. First, cash generated from operations during 1995 was less than half what it was during 1994 (the numerator). Second, average current liabilities were smaller in 1994 than in 1995 (the denominator). In examining the health of the company in terms of its liquidity, an analyst would concentrate on the reason for this.

[1] For a detailed discussion on the use of information contained in the statement of cash flows in performing ratio analysis, see Charles A. Carslaw and John R. Mills, "Developing Ratios for Effective Cash Flow Statement Analysis," *Journal of Accountancy* (November 1991), pp. 63–70.

EXHIBIT 15-7   Henderson's Balance Sheet

HENDERSON COMPANY
BALANCE SHEET
DECEMBER 31, 1993
(ALL AMOUNTS IN THOUSANDS OF DOLLARS)

Cash	$ 1,000
Accounts receivable	5,000
Inventory	2,450
Prepaid insurance	250
Total current assets	$ 8,700
Land	2,000
Buildings and equipment, net	1,300
Total long-term assets	$ 3,300
Total assets	$12,000
Accounts payable	$ 2,700
Taxes payable	1,800
Notes payable	1,000
Current portion of bonds	100
Total current liabilities	$ 5,600
Bonds payable	900
Total liabilities	$ 6,500
Preferred stock, $1 par	500
Common stock, $1 par	1,000
Retained earnings	4,000
Total stockholders' equity	$ 5,500
Total liabilities and stockholders' equity	$12,000

Accounts Receivable Analysis

The analysis of accounts receivable is an important component in the management of working capital. A company must be willing to extend credit terms that are liberal enough to attract and maintain customers, but at the same time, management must continually monitor the accounts to ensure their collection on a timely basis. One measure of the efficiency of the collection process is the **accounts receivable turnover ratio:**

$$\text{Accounts Receivable Turnover} = \frac{\text{Net Credit Sales}}{\text{Average Accounts Receivable}}$$

Note an important distinction between this ratio and either the current or quick ratio. Although both of those ratios measure liquidity at a point in time and all numbers come from the balance sheet, a turnover ratio is an *activity* ratio and consists of an activity (sales in this case) divided by a base to which it is naturally related (accounts receivable). Because an activity such as sales is for a period of time (a year in this case), the base should be stated as an average for that same period of time.

The accounts receivable turnover ratios for both years can now be calculated (we assume that all sales are on account):

1995	1994
$\dfrac{\$24,000,000}{(\$5,500,000 + \$4,500,000)/2} = 4.8$ times	$\dfrac{\$20,000,000}{(\$4,500,000 + \$5,000,000)/2} = 4.2$ times

Accounts turned over, on the average, 4.2 times in 1994, compared to 4.8 times in 1995. This means that the average number of times accounts were collected during the year was between four and five times. What does this mean about the average length of time that an account was outstanding? Another way to measure efficiency in the collection process is to calculate the **number of days' sales in receivables:**

$$\text{Number of Days' Sales in Receivables} = \frac{\text{Number of Days in the Period}}{\text{Accounts Receivable Turnover}}$$

For simplicity, we assume 360 days in a year:

1995	1994
$\dfrac{360 \text{ Days}}{4.8 \text{ Times}} = 75 \text{ Days}$	$\dfrac{360 \text{ Days}}{4.2 \text{ Times}} = 86 \text{ Days}$

The average number of days an account is outstanding, or the average collection period, is 75 days in 1995, down from 86 days in 1994. Is this acceptable? The answer depends on the company's credit policy. If Henderson's normal credit terms require payment within 60 days, further investigation is needed, even though the number of days outstanding has decreased from the previous year.

Management needs to be concerned with both the collectibility of an account as it ages as well as the cost of funds tied up in receivables. For example, a $1 million average receivable balance that requires an additional month to collect suggests that the company is forgoing $10,000 in lost profits if you assume that the money could be reinvested in the business to earn 1% per month, or 12% per year.

Inventory Analysis

A similar set of ratios can be calculated to analyze the efficiency in managing inventory. The **inventory turnover ratio** is

$$\text{Inventory Turnover Ratio} = \frac{\text{Cost of Goods Sold}}{\text{Average Inventory}}$$

The ratio for each of the two years follows:

1995	1994
$\dfrac{\$18,000,000}{(\$4,750,000 + \$2,750,000)/2}$	$\dfrac{\$14,000,000}{(\$2,750,000 + \$2,450,000)/2}$
$= 4.8$ times	$= 5.4$ times

Henderson was slightly more efficient in 1994 in moving its inventory. The number of "turns" each year varies widely for different industries. For example, a wholesaler of perishable fruits and vegetables may turn over inventory at least 50 times per year. An airplane manufacturer, however, may turn over its inventory once or twice a year. What does the number of turns per year tell us about the average length of time it takes to sell an item of inventory? The **number of days' sales in inventory** is an alternative measure of the company's efficiency in managing inventory. It is the number of days between the date an item of inventory is purchased and the date it is sold:

$$\text{Number of Days' Sales in Inventory} = \frac{\text{Number of Days in the Period}}{\text{Inventory Turnover}}$$

The number of days' sales in inventory for Henderson is

1995	1994
$\dfrac{360 \text{ Days}}{4.8 \text{ Times}} = 75 \text{ Days}$	$\dfrac{360 \text{ Days}}{5.4 \text{ Times}} = 67 \text{ Days}$

This measure can reveal a great deal about inventory management. For example, an unusually low turnover (and, of course, high number of days in inventory) may signal a large amount of obsolete inventory or problems in the sales department. Or, it may indicate that the company is pricing its products too high and the market is reacting by reducing demand for the company's products.

■ ACCOUNTING FOR YOUR DECISIONS   **You Are the Analyst**

What industries would you expect to have a very slow inventory turnover ratio? A fast ratio?

Cash Operating Cycle

The **cash to cash operating cycle** is the length of time between the purchase of merchandise for sale, assuming a retailer or wholesaler, and the eventual collection of the cash from the sale. One method to approximate the number of days in a company's operating cycle involves combining two measures:

$$\text{Cash to Cash Operating Cycle} = \text{Number of Days' Sales in Inventory} + \text{Number of Days' Sales in Receivables}$$

Henderson's operating cycle for 1995 and 1994 is

1995	1994
75 Days + 75 Days = 150 Days	67 Days + 86 Days = 153 Days

The average length of time between the purchase of inventory and the collection of cash from sale of the inventory was 150 days in 1995. Note that although the length of the operating cycle did not change significantly from 1994 to 1995, the composition did change: the increase in the average number of days in inventory was offset by the decrease in the average number of days in receivables.

Finally, the length of this cycle varies, depending on the type of business. The number of days' sales in inventory for a retailer or a wholesaler runs from the time products are purchased until they are sold. This same period for a manufacturer would be expanded to include the additional amount of time to transform raw material into a finished product.

Due to the perishable nature of their products and the steady inflow of cash from customers purchasing food and other necessities, grocery chains have high inventory turnovers and short cash-to-cash cycles. Firms in other segments, especially manufacturers, have relatively longer cycles.

Solvency Analysis

Solvency refers to a company's ability to remain in business over the long term. It is related to liquidity but differs in time. Although liquidity relates to the firm's ability to pay next year's debts as they are due, solvency has to do with the ability of the firm to stay financially healthy over the period of time that existing debt (short and long term) will be outstanding.

LO **5**

Compute and use various ratios to assess solvency.

Debt-to-Equity Ratio

Capital structure is the focal point in solvency analysis. This refers to the composition of the right side of the balance sheet and the mix between debt and stockholders' equity. The composition of debt and equity in the capital structure is an important determinant of the cost of capital to a company. We will have more to say later about the effects on profitability of the mix of debt and equity. For now, consider the **debt-to-equity ratio:**

$$\text{Debt-to-Equity Ratio} = \frac{\text{Total Liabilities}}{\text{Total Stockholders' Equity}}$$

Henderson's debt-to-equity ratio at each year-end is

1995	1994
$\dfrac{\$7,950,000}{\$8,920,000} = 0.89 \text{ to } 1$	$\dfrac{\$6,300,000}{\$7,500,000} = 0.84 \text{ to } 1$

The 1995 ratio indicates that for every $1 of capital that stockholders provided, creditors provided $.89. Variations of the debt-to-equity ratio are sometimes used to assess solvency. For example, an analyst might calculate the ratio of total liabilities to the sum of total liabilities and stockholders' equity. This results in a ratio that differs from the debt-to-equity ratio, but the objective of the measure is the same—to determine the degree to which the company relies on outsiders for funds.

What is an *acceptable* ratio of debt to equity? As with all ratios, the answer to this question depends on the company, the industry, and many other factors. You should not assume that the lower the debt-to-equity ratio, the better. Certainly taking on additional debt is risky. Many companies are able to benefit from borrowing money, however, by putting the cash raised to good uses in their businesses. Later in the chapter we discuss the concept of leverage, using borrowed money to benefit the company and its stockholders.

In the 1980s, investors and creditors tolerated a much higher debt-to-equity ratio than is considered prudent today. The savings and loan crisis in the 1980s prompted the federal government to enact regulations requiring financial institutions to have a lower proportion of debt-to-equity to avoid government penalties. By the mid-1990s, investors and creditors were demanding that all types of companies display lower debt-to-equity ratios before making investments or loans.

Times Interest Earned

The debt-to-equity ratio is a measure of the company's overall long-term financial health. Management must also be aware of its ability to meet current interest payments to creditors. The **times interest earned ratio** indicates the company's ability to meet current-year interest payments out of current-year earnings:

$$\text{Times Interest Earned} = \frac{\text{Net Income} + \text{Interest Expense} + \text{Income Tax Expense}}{\text{Interest Expense}}$$

Both interest expense and income tax expense are added back to net income in the numerator because interest is a deduction in arriving at the amount of income subject to tax. Stated slightly differently, if a company had just enough income to cover the payment of interest, tax expense would be zero. The greater the interest coverage, the better, as far as lenders are concerned. Bankers often place a greater importance on the times interest earned ratio than even earnings per share. The ratio for Henderson for each of the two years indicates a great deal of protection in this regard, as shown in the following ratios:

1995	1994
$\dfrac{\$1{,}720{,}000 + \$1{,}140{,}000 + \$140{,}000}{\$140{,}000}$	$\dfrac{\$2{,}300{,}000 + \$1{,}540{,}000 + \$160{,}000}{\$160{,}000}$
$= 21.4 \text{ to } 1$	$= 25 \text{ to } 1$

Debt Service Coverage

Two problems exist with the times interest earned ratio as a measure of the ability to pay creditors. First, the denominator of the fraction considers only *interest*. Management must also be concerned with the *principal* amount of loans maturing in the next year. The second problem deals with the difference between the cash and accrual bases of accounting. The numerator of the times interest earned ratio is not a measure of the *cash* available to repay loans. Keep in mind the various noncash adjustments, such as depreciation, which enter into the determination of net income. Also, recall that the denominator of the times interest earned ratio is a measure of interest expense, not interest payments. The **debt service coverage ratio** is a measure of the amount of cash generated from operating activities during the year that is available to repay interest due and any maturing principal amounts (that is, the amount available to "service" the debt):

$$\text{Debt Service Coverage Ratio} = \frac{\text{Cash Flow from Operations before Interest and Tax Payments}}{\text{Interest and Principal Payments}}$$

Some analysts use an alternative measure in the numerator of this ratio as well as for other purposes. The alternative is referred to as *EBITDA*, which stands for earnings before interest, taxes, depreciation, and amortization. Whether EBITDA is a good substitute for cash flow from operations before interest and tax payments depends on whether there were significant changes in current assets and current liabilities during the period. If significant changes in these accounts occurred during the period, cash flow from operations before interest and tax payments is a better measure of a company's ability to cover interest and debt payments than is EBITDA.

Cash flow from operations is available on the comparative statement of cash flows in Exhibit 15-4. As was the case with the times interest earned ratio, the net cash provided by operating activities is adjusted to reflect the amount available *before* paying interest and taxes.

Keep in mind that the income statement in Exhibit 15-2 reflects the *expense* for interest and taxes each year. The amounts of interest and taxes *paid* each year are shown as supplemental information at the bottom of the statement of cash flows in Exhibit 15-4 and are relevant in computing the debt service coverage ratio.

We must include any principal payments with interest paid in the denominator of the debt service coverage ratio. According to the financing activities section of the statements of cash flows in Exhibit 15-4, Henderson repaid $200,000 each year on the notes payable and $100,000 each year on the bonds. The debt service coverage ratio for the two years is calculated as follows:

1995

$$\frac{\$1,070,000 + \$140,000 + \$940,000}{\$140,000 + \$200,000 + \$100,000} = 4.89 \text{ times}$$

1994

$$\frac{\$2,950,000 + \$160,000 + \$1,440,000}{\$160,000 + \$200,000 + \$100,000} = 9.89 \text{ times}$$

As was the case with Henderson's times interest earned ratio, its debt service coverage ratio decreased during 1995. According to the calculations, however, Henderson still generated almost $5 of cash from operations during 1995 to "cover" every $1 of required interest and principal payments.

Cash Flow from Operations to Capital Expenditures Ratio

One final measure is useful in assessing the solvency of a business. The **cash flow from operations to capital expenditures ratio** measures a company's ability to finance its acquisitions of productive assets from operations. To the extent that a company is able to do this, it should rely less on external financing or additional contributions by the owners to replace and add to the existing capital base. The ratio is computed as

$$\frac{\text{Cash Flow from Operations}}{\text{to Capital Expenditures Ratio}} = \frac{\text{Cash Flow from Operations} - \text{Total Dividends Paid}}{\text{Cash Paid for Acquisitions}}$$

Note that the numerator of the ratio measures the cash flow *after* meeting all dividend payments.[2] The calculation of the ratios for Henderson is

1995	1994
$\dfrac{\$1,070,000 - \$300,000}{\$1,500,000} = 51.3\%$	$\dfrac{\$2,950,000 - \$300,000}{\$2,000,000} = 132.5\%$

Although the amount of capital expenditures was less in 1995 than in 1994, the company generated considerably less cash from operations in 1995 to cover these acquisitions. In fact, the ratio of less than 100% in 1995 indicates that Henderson was not able to finance all of its capital expenditures from operations *and* cover its dividend payments.

Profitability Analysis

Compute and use various ratios to assess profitability.

Liquidity analysis and solvency analysis deal with management's ability to repay short- and long-term creditors. Creditors are concerned with a company's profitability because a profitable company is more likely to be able to make principal and interest payments. Of course, stockholders care about a company's profitability because it affects the market price of the stock and the ability of the company to pay dividends. Various measures of **profitability** indicate how well management is using the resources at its disposal to earn a return on the funds invested by various groups.

Rate of Return on Assets

Before computing the rate of return, an important question must be answered: *Return to whom? Every return ratio is a measure of the relationship between the income earned by the company and the investment made in the company by various groups.* The broadest rate of return ratio is the **return on assets** ratio because it considers the investment made by *all* providers of capital, from short-term creditors to bondholders to stockholders. Therefore, the denominator, or base, for the return on assets ratio is average total assets—which of course is the same as average total liabilities and stockholders' equity.

The numerator of a return ratio will be some measure of the company's income for the period. The income selected for the numerator must match the investment or base in the denominator. For example, if average total assets is the base in the denominator, it is necessary to use an income number that is applicable to all providers of capital. Therefore, the income number used in the rate of return on assets is income *after* adding back interest expense. This adjustment considers creditors as one of the groups that have provided funds to the company. In other words, we want the amount of income before either creditors or stockholders have been given any distributions (that is, interest to creditors or dividends to stockholders). Interest

---

[2] Dividends paid are reported on the statement of cash flows in the financing activities section. The amount *paid* should be used for this calculation rather than the amount declared as it appears on the statement of retained earnings.

expense must be added back on a net-of-tax basis. Because net income is on an after-tax basis, for consistency purposes, interest must also be placed on a net, or after-tax, basis.

The rate of return on assets ratio is

$$\text{Rate of Return on Assets} = \frac{\text{Net Income} + \text{Interest Expense, Net of Tax}}{\text{Average Total Assets}}$$

If we assume a 40% tax rate (which *is* the actual ratio of income tax expense to income before tax for Henderson), its rates of return are as follows:

		1995		1994
Net income		$ 1,720,000		$ 2,300,000
Add back:				
Interest expense	$140,000		$160,000	
× (1 − tax rate)	0.6	84,000	0.6	96,000
Numerator		$ 1,804,000		$ 2,396,000
Assets, beginning of year		$13,800,000		$12,000,000
Assets, end of year		16,870,000		13,800,000
Total		$30,670,000		$25,800,000
Denominator:				
Average total assets		$15,335,000		$12,900,000
(total above divided by 2)				
Rate of return on assets		$ 1,804,000		$ 2,396,000
		$15,335,000		$12,900,000
		= 11.76%		= 18.57%

Components of Return on Assets

What caused Henderson's return on assets to decrease so dramatically from the previous year? The answer can be found by considering the two individual components that make up the return on assets. The first of these components is the **return on sales** and is calculated as follows:

$$\text{Return on Sales} = \frac{\text{Net Income} + \text{Interest Expense, Net of Tax}}{\text{Net Sales}}$$

The return on sales for Henderson for the two years follows:

1995	1994
$\dfrac{\$1,720,000 + \$84,000}{\$24,000,000} = 7.52\%$	$\dfrac{\$2,300,000 + \$96,000}{\$20,000,000} = 11.98\%$

The ratio for 1995 indicates that for every $1 of sales, the company was able to earn a profit, before the payment of interest, of between 7 and 8 cents, as compared to a return of almost 12 cents on the dollar in 1994.

The other component of the rate of return on assets is the **asset turnover ratio.** The ratio is similar to both the inventory turnover and the receivable turnover ratios because it is a measure of the relationship between some activity (net sales in this case) and some investment base (average total assets):

$$\text{Asset Turnover Ratio} = \frac{\text{Net Sales}}{\text{Average Total Assets}}$$

For Henderson, the ratio for each of the two years follows:

1995	1994
$\dfrac{\$24,000,000}{\$15,335,000} = 1.57$ times	$\dfrac{\$20,000,000}{\$12,900,000} = 1.55$ times

It now becomes evident that the explanation for the decrease in Henderson's return on assets lies in the drop in the return on sales because the turnover was almost the same. To summarize, note the relationship among the three ratios:

$$\text{Return on Assets} = \text{Return on Sales} \times \text{Asset Turnover}$$

For 1995 Henderson's return on assets consists of

$$\frac{\$1,804,000}{\$24,000,000} \times \frac{\$24,000,000}{\$15,335,000} = 7.52\% \times 1.57 = 11.8\%$$

Finally, notice that net sales cancels out of both ratios, leaving the net income adjusted for interest divided by average assets as the return on assets ratio.

Return on Common Stockholders' Equity

Reasoning similar to that used to calculate return on assets can be used to calculate the return on capital provided by the common stockholder. Because we are interested in the return to the common stockholder, our base is no longer average total assets but average common stockholders' equity. Similarly, the appropriate income figure for the numerator is net income less preferred dividends because we are interested in the return to the common stockholder after all claims have been settled. Income taxes and interest expense already have been deducted in arriving at net income, but preferred dividends have not been because dividends are a distribution of profits not an expense.

The **return on stockholders' equity** ratio is computed as

Return on Common Stockholders' Equity =
$$\frac{\text{Net Income} - \text{Preferred Dividends}}{\text{Average Common Stockholders' Equity}}$$

The average common stockholders' equity is calculated using information from Exhibits 15-1 and 15-7:

	ACCOUNT BALANCES AT DECEMBER 31		
	1995	1994	1993
Common stock, $1 par	$1,000,000	$1,000,000	$1,000,000
Retained earnings	7,420,000	6,000,000	4,000,000
Total common equity	$8,420,000	$7,000,000	$5,000,000

Average common equity for:
  1994: ($7,000,000 + $5,000,000)/2 = $6,000,000

  1995: ($8,420,000 + $7,000,000)/2 = $7,710,000

Net income less preferred dividends—or "income available to common," as it is called—can be found by referring to net income on the income statement and preferred dividends on the statement of retained earnings. Exhibit 15-2 presents a combined statement of income and retained earnings for the relevant amounts for the numerator. The return on equity for the two years is

1995	1994

$$\frac{\$1,720,000 - \$50,000}{\$7,710,000} = 21.66\% \qquad \frac{\$2,300,000 - \$50,000}{\$6,000,000} = 37.50\%$$

Even though Henderson's return on equity decreased significantly from one year to the next, most stockholders would be very happy to achieve these returns on their money. Very few investments offer much more than 10% return unless substantial risk is involved. This is particularly true in the low-interest-rate environment of the mid-1990s.

Return on Assets, Return on Equity, and Leverage

The return on assets for 1995 was 11.8%. But the return to the common stockholders was much higher: 21.7%. How do you explain this phenomenon? Why are the stockholders receiving a higher return on their money than all of the providers of money combined are getting? A partial answer to these questions can be found by reviewing the cost to Henderson of the various sources of capital.

Exhibit 15-1 indicates that notes, bonds, and preferred stock are the primary sources of capital other than common stock (accounts payable and taxes payable are *not* included because they represent interest-free loans to the company from suppliers and the government). These sources and the average amount of each outstanding during 1995 follow:

	ACCOUNT BALANCES AT DECEMBER 31		
	1995	1994	AVERAGE
Notes payable	$ 600,000	$ 800,000	$ 700,000
Current portion of bonds	100,000	100,000	100,000
Bonds payable—long-term	700,000	800,000	750,000
Total liabilities	$1,400,000	$1,700,000	$1,550,000
Preferred stock	$ 500,000	$ 500,000	$ 500,000

What was the cost to Henderson of each of these sources? The cost of the money provided by the preferred stockholders is clearly the amount of dividends of $50,000. The cost as a percentage is $50,000/$500,000, or 10%. The average cost of the borrowed money can be approximated by dividing the 1995 interest expense of $140,000 by the average of the notes payable and bonds payable of $1,550,000. The result is an average cost of these two sources of $140,000/$1,550,000, or approximately 9%.

The concept of **leverage** refers to the practice of using borrowed funds and amounts received from preferred stockholders in an attempt to earn an overall return that is higher than the cost of these funds. Recall the rate of return on assets for 1995: 11.8%. Because this return is on an after-tax basis, it is necessary for comparative purposes to convert the average cost of borrowed funds to an after-tax basis. Although we computed an average cost for borrowed money of 9%, the actual cost of the borrowed money is 5.4% [9% × (100% − 40%)] after taxes. Because dividends are *not* tax deductible, the cost of the money provided by preferred stockholders is 10%, as calculated earlier.

Has Henderson successfully employed favorable leverage? That is, has it been able to earn an overall rate of return on assets that is higher than the amounts that they must pay creditors and preferred stockholders? Henderson has been successful in using outside money: neither of the sources must be paid a rate in excess of the 11.8% overall rate on assets employed. Also keep in mind that Henderson has been able to borrow some amounts on an interest-free basis. As mentioned earlier, the accounts payable and taxes payable represent interest-free loans from suppliers and the government, although the loans are typically for a short period of time, such as 30 days.

In summary, the excess of the 21.7% return on equity over the 11.8% return on assets indicates that the Henderson management has been successful in employing leverage; that is, there is favorable leverage. Is it possible to be unsuccessful in this pursuit; that is, can there be unfavorable leverage? If the company must pay more for the amounts provided by creditors and preferred stockholders than they can earn overall, as indicated by the return on assets, there will, in fact, be unfavorable leverage. This may occur when interest requirements are high and net income is low. A company likely would have a high debt-to-equity ratio as well when there is unfavorable leverage.

Earnings per Share

Earnings per share is one of the most quoted statistics for publicly traded companies. Stockholders and potential investors want to know what their share of profits is, not just the total dollar amount. Presentation of profits on a per-share basis also allows the stockholder to relate earnings to what he or she paid for a share of stock or to the current trading price of a share of stock.

In simple situations, such as our Henderson Company example, earnings per share (EPS) is calculated as follows:

$$\text{Earnings per Share} = \frac{\text{Net Income} - \text{Preferred Dividends}}{\text{Weighted Average Number of Common Shares Outstanding}}$$

Because Henderson had 1,000,000 shares of common stock outstanding throughout both 1994 and 1995, its EPS for each of the two years is

1995	1994
$\dfrac{\$1,720,000 - \$50,000}{1,000,000 \text{ shares}} = \$1.67 \text{ per share}$	$\dfrac{\$2,300,000 - \$50,000}{1,000,000 \text{ shares}} = \$2.25 \text{ per share}$

A number of complications can arise in the computation of EPS, and the calculations can become exceedingly complex for a company with many different types of securities in its capital structure. Some of these complications, as well as the calculation of the weighted average number of shares, were discussed in Chapter 12; others are beyond the scope of this book and are discussed in more advanced accounting courses.

Price-Earnings Ratio

Earnings per share is an important ratio for an investor because of its relationship to dividends and market price. Stockholders hope to earn a return by either receiving periodic dividends or eventually selling the stock for more than they paid for it, or both. Although earnings are related to dividends and market price, the latter two are of primary interest to the stockholder.

We mentioned earlier the desire of investors to relate the earnings of the company to the market price of the stock. Now that we have stated Henderson's earnings on a per-share basis, we can calculate the **price-earnings** (or P/E) **ratio.** What market price is relevant? Should we use the market price that the investor paid for a share of stock, or should we use the current market price? Because earnings are based on the most recent evaluation of the company for accounting purposes, it seems logical to use current market price, which is based on the stock market's current assessment of the company. Therefore, the ratio is computed as follows:

$$\text{Price-Earnings Ratio} = \frac{\text{Current Market Price}}{\text{Earnings per Share}}$$

Assume that the current market price for Henderson's common stock is $15 per share at the end of 1995 and $18 per share at the end of 1994. The price-earnings ratio for each of the two years is

1995	1994
$\dfrac{\$15 \text{ per Share}}{\$1.67 \text{ per Share}} = 9 \text{ to } 1$	$\dfrac{\$18 \text{ per Share}}{\$2.25 \text{ per Share}} = 8 \text{ to } 1$

What is normal for a P/E ratio? As the Dow Jones Industrial Average approached 4000 in early 1994, the price-earnings ratio of the average company was about 20 times earnings, an historically high ratio. As is the case for all ratios, it is difficult to generalize as to what is good or bad. The P/E ratio compares the stock market's assessment of a company's performance with its success as reflected on the income statement. A relatively high P/E ratio may indicate that a stock is overpriced by the market; one that is relatively low could indicate that it is underpriced.

The P/E ratio is often thought to indicate the "quality" of a company's earnings. For example, assume that two companies have identical EPS ratios of $2 per share. Why should investors be willing to pay $20 per share (or 10 times earnings) for the stock of one company but only $14 per share for the stock of the other company?

Making financial decisions requires having the right tools at hand, including the annual reports of companies under consideration and recent stock market quotations, printed in most large newspapers.

First, we must realize that many factors in addition to the reported earnings of the company affect market prices. General economic conditions, the outlook for the particular industry, and pending lawsuits are just three examples of the various factors that can affect the trading price of a company's stock. The difference in P/E ratios for the two companies may reflect the market's assessment of the accounting practices of the companies, however. Assume that the company with a market price of $20 per share uses LIFO in valuing inventory and that the company trading at $14 per share uses FIFO. The difference in prices may indicate that investors believe that even though the companies have the same EPS, the LIFO company is "better off" because it will have a lower amount of taxes to pay. (Recall that in a period of inflation, the use of LIFO results in more cost of goods sold, less income, and therefore less income taxes.) Finally, aside from the way investors view the accounting practices of different companies, they also consider the fact that, to a large extent, earnings reflect the use of historical costs in assigning values to assets, as opposed to fair market values. Investors must consider the extent to which a company's assets are worth more than what was paid for them.

FROM CONCEPT TO PRACTICE

READING BEN & JERRY'S ANNUAL REPORT

Where does Ben & Jerry's annual report provide information on the market price of its stock? Based on the market price high for the fourth quarter of 1992, what was its P/E ratio?

ACCOUNTING FOR YOUR DECISIONS — **You Are the Investment Banker**

You are an adviser to a major tobacco company with large holdings in the food industry. It is common knowledge that food companies command a price/earnings ratio of 20 while tobacco companies typically carry a price/earnings ratio of about 8. Your client's combined P/E ratio is about 10. Would you suggest your client sell the tobacco business?

Dividend Ratios

Two ratios are used to evaluate a company's dividend policies: the **dividend payout ratio** and the **dividend yield ratio.** The dividend payout ratio is the ratio of the common dividends per share to the earnings per share:

$$\text{Dividend Payout Ratio} = \frac{\text{Common Dividends per Share}}{\text{Earnings per Share}}$$

	52 Weeks Hi	Lo	Stock	Sym	Div	Yld %	PE	Vol 100s	Hi	Lo	Close	Net Chg
	22⅝	8⅜	WheelPit	WHX		...	20	403	18½	18⅜	18⅜	– ¼
n	77¾	48	WheelPit pfA		3.25	4.9	...	26	66¾	66	66	–1
	16⅝	3¾	WheelPit wt			...	...	76	12½	11⅞	12¼	...
	73½	50⅝	Whirlpool	WHR	1.22	1.8	22	2385	69	67½	69	+1½
	17¾	12¾	Whitehall	WHT		...	dd	2	13¼	13¼	13¼	– ⅛
	17	12¾	WhitmanCp	WH	.30	2.0	20	1521	15½	15¼	15⅜	+ ⅛
	17⅞	12	Whittaker	WKR		...	10	55	15⅞	15⅝	15¾	– ⅛
	8⅝	5	WillcoxGbs	WG		...	18	427	7⅝	7⅜	7⅜	– ¼
	29¼	21⅞	WillmCoal un	WTU	2.16e	8.3	...	106	26	25¾	26	...
s	31⅞	22⅛	WilliamsCos	WMB	.84	3.3	12	3589	25½	25	25½	+ ½
	27⅞	25⅛	WilliamsCos pfA		2.21	8.6	...	62	25⅞	25½	25¾	+ ⅛
	18⅝	13⅞	WillCorroon	WCG	.62e	3.6	21	1055	17¼	16¾	17¼	+ ¾
	7⅜	6⅜	WilshireOil	WOC	.05r	.8	14	21	6⅝	6⅝	6⅝	...
	9¼	6⅛	Windmere	WND		...	13	227	8⅛	7⅞	7⅞	– ¼
	71	48¼	WinnDixie	WIN	1.44	2.6	17	542	54⅞	54⅜	54⅞	+ ⅜
	13⅞	5⅝	Winnebago	WGO		...	28	1926	13¾	12⅞	13¼	– ½

Each company's price-earnings ratio (here "PE") and the dividend yield ratio ("Yld %") are two of the statistics listed in daily stock quotations available from on-line services such as CompuServe and America Online as well as in most major newspapers.

Exhibit 15-2 indicates that Henderson paid $250,000 in common dividends each year, or with 1 million shares outstanding, $.25 per share. The two payout ratios are

1995	1994
$\dfrac{\$.25}{\$1.67} = 15.0\%$	$\dfrac{\$.25}{\$2.25} = 11.1\%$

Henderson management was faced with an important financial policy decision in 1995. Should the company maintain the same dividend of $.25 per share, even though EPS dropped significantly? Many companies prefer to maintain a level dividend pattern, hoping that a drop in earnings is only temporary.

PREPARING FOR OPPORTUNITY TO STRIKE, THIS MONEY MANAGER RELIES ON RATIOS

Name: Maceo Sloan
Profession: Money Manager
College Major: Business Administration

Virtually every investment firm uses financial ratios to a greater or lesser extent. "We use them a great deal in the process of analyzing companies for inclusion in our portfolios," says Maceo Sloan, CEO of Sloan Financial Group, an international financial services company based in Durham, N.C.

In the past few years, Mr. Sloan has built Sloan Financial Group into a huge enterprise with several divisions. The largest subsidiary is NCM Capital Management Group, which is an investment advisor that manages funds for institutional clients such as corporations, municipalities and unions. Total money under management: $3 billion in 1994, up from $600 million in 1991. Then there's New Africa Advisers, which provides investors access to African-related investment opportunities, particularly in post-apartheid South Africa.

Somehow, NCM Capital has to narrow down the world of stocks. One way to do that is to use computers to screen out companies that are unattractive based upon certain ratios. For example, a screen could filter out companies that are selling at more than 40 times earnings. Another variable might be that the stock have a minimum market capitalization of $200 million to insure liquidity.

One of the firm's big success stories was a company called Micron Technology. In 1991, the stock was selling at $30 per share. By 1994, the stock was selling in the mid $80s. A tipoff—the company had a high ratio of cash flow to earnings—$2.47 to $1. "Although the price-earnings ratio is 32, which may look rather high, the price-cash flow is actually much more modest than that," says Mr. Sloan, who holds an MBA from Georgia State University and a law degree from the North Carolina Central School of Law.

Another important ratio Mr. Sloan uses is return on equity, or ROE. "It's a judge of how good the management is," he says. "When you look at the return on equity number and compare to ROE for other firms in the same industry, you can tell whether the management team is reaching its potential for that industry."

Speaking of reaching one's potential, what advice would he give to college students seeking to follow in his footsteps? "It would probably be a motto that I've lived by all my life: luck is when opportunity meets preparation. Some people are very fortunate to get many opportunities, but it doesn't mean anything if you're not prepared."

EXHIBIT 15-8 Summary of Selected Financial Ratios

LIQUIDITY ANALYSIS

Working capital

$$\text{Current Assets} - \text{Current Liabilities}$$

Current ratio

$$\frac{\text{Current Assets}}{\text{Current Liabilities}}$$

Acid-test ratio (quick ratio)

$$\frac{\text{Cash} + \text{Marketable Securities} + \text{Short-term Receivables}}{\text{Current Liabilities}}$$

Cash flow from operations to current liabilities ratio

$$\frac{\text{Net Cash Provided by Operating Activities}}{\text{Average Current Liabilities}}$$

Accounts receivable turnover ratio

$$\frac{\text{Net Credit Sales}}{\text{Average Accounts Receivable}}$$

Number days' sales in receivables

$$\frac{\text{Numbers of Days in the Period}}{\text{Accounts Receivable Turnover}}$$

Inventory turnover ratio

$$\frac{\text{Cost of Goods Sold}}{\text{Average Inventory}}$$

Number days' sales in inventory

$$\frac{\text{Number of Days in the Period}}{\text{Inventory Turnover}}$$

Cash to cash operating cycle

$$\text{Number of Days' Sales in Inventory} +$$
$$\text{Number of Days' Sales in Receivables}$$

SOLVENCY ANALYSIS

Debt-to-equity ratio

$$\frac{\text{Total Liabilities}}{\text{Total Stockholders' Equity}}$$

Times interest earned ratio

$$\frac{\text{Net Income} + \text{Interest Expense} + \text{Income Tax Expense}}{\text{Interest Expense}}$$

Debt service coverage ratio

$$\frac{\text{Cash Flow from Operations, before Interest and Tax Payments}}{\text{Interest and Principal Payments}}$$

The second dividend ratio of interest to stockholders is the dividend yield ratio. It is calculated as

$$\text{Dividend Yield Ratio} = \frac{\text{Common Dividends per Share}}{\text{Market Price per Share}}$$

The yield to Henderson's stockholders would be

1995	1994
$\frac{\$.25}{\$15} = 1.7\%$	$\frac{\$.25}{\$18} = 1.4\%$

As we see, Henderson common stock does not provide a high yield to its investors. The relationship between the dividends and the market price indicates that investors buy the stock for reasons other than the periodic dividend return.

EXHIBIT 15-8 (continued)

Cash flow from operations to capital expenditures ratio	$$\frac{\text{Cash Flow from Operations} - \text{Total Dividends Paid}}{\text{Cash Paid for Acquisitions}}$$

PROFITABILITY ANALYSIS

Gross profit ratio	$$\frac{\text{Gross Profit}}{\text{Net Sales}}$$
Profit margin ratio	$$\frac{\text{Net Income}}{\text{Net Sales}}$$
Return on assets	$$\frac{\text{Net Income} + \text{Interest Expense, Net of Tax}}{\text{Average Total Assets}}$$
Return on sales	$$\frac{\text{Net Income} + \text{Interest Expense, Net of Tax}}{\text{Net Sales}}$$
Asset turnover ratio	$$\frac{\text{Net Sales}}{\text{Average Total Assets}}$$
Return on stockholders' equity	$$\frac{\text{Net Income} - \text{Preferred Dividends}}{\text{Average Common Stockholders' Equity}}$$
Earnings per share	$$\frac{\text{Net Income} - \text{Preferred Dividends}}{\text{Weighted Average Number of Common Shares Outstanding}}$$
Price-earnings ratio	$$\frac{\text{Current Market Price}}{\text{Earnings per Share}}$$
Dividend payout ratio	$$\frac{\text{Common Dividends per Share}}{\text{Earnings per Share}}$$
Dividend yield ratio	$$\frac{\text{Common Dividends per Share}}{\text{Market Price per Share}}$$

The dividend yield is very important to investors who depend on dividend checks to pay their living expenses. Utility stocks are popular among retirees because these shares have dividend yields as high as 5%. That is considered a good investment with relatively low risk and some opportunity for gains in the stock price. On the other hand, investors who want to put money into growing companies are willing to forgo dividends if it means the potential for greater price appreciation.

Summary of Selected Financial Ratios

We have now completed our review of the various ratios used to assess a company's liquidity, solvency, and profitability. For ease of reference, Exhibit 15-8 summarizes the ratios discussed in this chapter. Keep in mind that this list is not all-inclusive and that certain ratios used by analysts and others may be specific to a particular industry or type of business.

REVIEW PROBLEM

On the following pages are the comparative financial statements for Wm. Wrigley Jr. Company, the chewing gum manufacturer, as shown in its 1992 annual report.

■ REQUIRED

1. Compute the following ratios for the two years 1992 and 1991, either for each year or as of the end of each of the years, as appropriate. Beginning balances for 1991 are not available; that is, you do not have a balance sheet as of the end of 1990. Therefore, to be consistent, use year-end balances for both years where you would normally use average amounts for the year. To compute the return on assets ratio, you will need to find the tax rate. Use the relationship between income taxes and earnings before taxes and cumulative effects to find the rate for each year.

   a. Current ratio
   b. Quick ratio
   c. Cash flow from operations to current liabilities
   d. Number of days' sales in receivables
   e. Number of days' sales in inventory
   f. Debt-to-equity ratio
   g. Debt service coverage ratio
   h. Cash flow from operations to capital expenditures
   i. Rate of return on assets
   j. Return on common stockholders' equity

2. Comment on Wrigley's liquidity. Has it improved or declined over the two-year period?

3. Does Wrigley appear to be solvent to you? Does there appear to be anything unusual about its capital structure?

4. Comment on Wrigley's profitability. Would you buy stock in the company?

■ SOLUTION TO REVIEW PROBLEM

1. Ratios:

   a. 1992: \$448,639/\$149,490 = <u>3.00</u>
      1991: \$403,358/\$127,311 = <u>3.17</u>

   b. 1992: (\$84,144 + \$98,314 + \$95,939)/\$149,490 = <u>1.86</u>
      1991: (\$73,335 + \$71,575 + \$92,527)/\$127,311 = <u>1.87</u>

   c. 1992: \$189,268/\$149,490 = <u>1.27</u>
      1991: \$139,465/\$127,311 = <u>1.10</u>

   d. 1992: 360 days/[(\$1,286,921/\$95,939)] = 360/13.41 = <u>27 days</u>
      1991: 360 days/[(\$1,148,875/\$92,527)] = 360/12.42 = <u>29 days</u>

   e. 1992: 360 days/[(\$572,468/\$155,755)] = 360/3.68 = <u>98 days</u>
      1991: 360 days/[(\$507,795/\$155,506)] = 360/3.27 = <u>110 days</u>

STATEMENT OF CONSOLIDATED EARNINGS AND RETAINED EARNINGS

WM. WRIGLEY JR. COMPANY AND WHOLLY OWNED ASSOCIATED COMPANIES

YEAR ENDED DECEMBER 31	1992	1991	1990
	In thousands of dollars except for per share amounts		

EARNINGS

	1992	1991	1990
Revenues:			
Net sales	$1,286,921	1,148,875	1,110,639
Investment and other income	14,346	10,888	12,869
Total revenues	1,301,267	1,159,763	1,123,508
Costs and expenses:			
Cost of sales	572,468	507,795	508,957
Selling, distribution and general administrative	495,323	442,575	425,175
Interest	1,173	1,379	1,117
Total costs and expenses	1,068,964	951,749	935,249
Earnings before income taxes and cumulative effect of accounting changes	232,303	208,014	188,259
Income taxes	83,730	79,362	70,897
Earnings before cumulative effect of accounting changes	148,573	128,652	117,362
Cumulative effect of accounting changes for:			
Postretirement benefits — net of income tax effect	(10,143)	—	—
Income taxes	2,865	—	—
Net earnings	141,295	128,652	117,362

RETAINED EARNINGS

	1992	1991	1990
Retained earnings at beginning of the year	579,665	515,615	458,247
Dividends declared (per share: 1992—$.63; 1991—$.55; 1990—$.51)	(74,409)	(64,602)	(59,994)
Treasury stock retirement	(155,070)	—	—
Retained earnings at end of the year	$ 491,481	579,665	515,615

PER SHARE AMOUNTS

	1992	1991	1990
Earnings before cumulative effect of accounting changes	$ 1.27	1.09	1.00
Cumulative effect of accounting changes, net	(.06)	—	—
Net earnings per average share of common stock	$ 1.21	1.09	1.00
Dividends paid per share of common stock	$ .62	.55	.49

See accompanying accounting policies and notes.

STATEMENT OF
CONSOLIDATED CASH FLOWS

WM. WRIGLEY JR. COMPANY AND WHOLLY OWNED ASSOCIATED COMPANIES

YEAR ENDED DECEMBER 31	1992	1991	1990
	In thousands of dollars		
CASH FLOWS—OPERATING ACTIVITIES			
Net earnings	$141,295	128,652	117,362
Adjustments to reconcile net earnings to			
net cash flows from operating activities:			
Depreciation	29,806	28,695	26,860
Gain on sales of property, plant and equipment	(3,985)	(365)	(254)
(Increase) decrease in:			
Accounts receivable	(10,652)	(6,812)	(5,518)
Inventories	205	(7,924)	(22,371)
Other current assets	(115)	(1,198)	(5,328)
Other assets and deferred charges	(6,216)	(1,452)	(637)
Increase (decrease) in:			
Accounts payable	7,937	(5,444)	(4,079)
Accrued expenses	9,724	3,938	(293)
Income and other taxes payable	8,944	1,963	329
Deferred income taxes	(11,551)	(1,161)	787
Other noncurrent liabilities	23,876	573	2,438
Net cash flows—operating activities	189,268	139,465	109,296
CASH FLOWS—INVESTING ACTIVITIES			
Additions to property, plant and equipment	(66,682)	(45,235)	(45,463)
Proceeds from property retirements	7,983	4,671	4,606
Net (increase) decrease in short-term investments	(26,132)	4,355	9,491
Net cash flows—investing activities	(84,831)	(36,209)	(31,366)
CASH FLOWS—FINANCING ACTIVITIES			
Dividends paid	(72,511)	(64,609)	(58,060)
Common stock purchased	(17,579)	(3,318)	(8,200)
Net cash flows—financing activities	(90,090)	(67,927)	(66,260)
Effect of exchange rate changes on cash and cash equivalents	(3,538)	(385)	2,836
Net increase in cash and cash equivalents	10,809	34,944	14,506
Cash and cash equivalents at beginning of year	73,335	38,391	23,885
Cash and cash equivalents at end of year	$ 84,144	73,335	38,391
SUPPLEMENTAL CASH FLOW INFORMATION			
Income taxes paid	$ 78,938	79,935	69,734
Interest paid	$ 1,177	1,369	1,173
Interest and dividends received	$ 10,893	10,845	13,938

See accompanying accounting policies and notes.

CONSOLIDATED BALANCE SHEET

WM. WRIGLEY JR. COMPANY AND WHOLLY OWNED ASSOCIATED COMPANIES

As of December 31	1992	1991
	In thousands of dollars	
ASSETS		
Current assets:		
Cash and cash equivalents	$ 84,144	73,335
Short-term investments, at cost which approximates market	98,314	71,575
Accounts receivable		
(less allowance for doubtful accounts: **1992—$2,357**; 1991—$2,454)	95,939	92,527
Inventories—		
Finished goods	38,352	37,736
Raw materials and supplies	117,403	117,770
	155,755	155,506
Other current assets	10,270	10,415
Deferred income taxes - current	4,217	—
Total current assets	448,639	403,358
Marketable equity securities, at cost		
(market value: **1992—$29,501**; 1991—$28,553)	2,539	2,540
Other assets and deferred charges	24,115	17,790
Deferred income taxes—noncurrent	13,942	—
Property, plant and equipment, at cost:		
Land	17,010	16,629
Buildings and building equipment	166,342	157,044
Machinery and equipment	330,065	312,848
	513,417	486,521
Less accumulated depreciation	291,280	285,135
	222,137	201,386
Total assets	$711,372	625,074

As of December 31	1992	1991
	In thousands of dollars and shares	
LIABILITIES AND STOCKHOLDERS' EQUITY		
Current liabilities:		
Accounts payable	$ 53,761	48,034
Accrued expenses	50,912	43,224
Dividends payable	11,683	9,785
Income and other taxes payable	32,500	26,268
Deferred income taxes—current	634	—
Total current liabilities	149,490	127,311
Deferred income taxes—noncurrent	13,220	7,763
Other noncurrent liabilities	49,727	26,601
Stockholders' equity:		
Preferred stock—no par value Authorized: 2,000 shares Issued: None		
Common stock—no par value Common stock Authorized: 150,000 shares Issued: **1992—90,411 shares;** 1991—116,862 shares	12,121	15,582
Class B common stock—convertible Authorized: 45,000 shares Issued and outstanding: **1992—26,423 shares;** 1991—27,138 shares	3,457	3,618
Additional paid-in capital	1,568	2,504
Retained earnings	491,481	579,665
Foreign currency translation adjustment	(9,692)	5,719
Common stock in treasury, at cost (1991—26,582 shares)	—	(143,689)
Total stockholders' equity	498,935	463,399
Total liabilities and stockholders' equity	$711,372	625,074

See accompanying accounting policies and notes.

f. 1992: ($149,490 + $62,947)/$498,935 = $\underline{0.43}$

1991: ($127,311 + $34,364)/$463,399 = $\underline{0.35}$

g. 1992: ($189,268 + $78,938 + $1,177)/$1,177 = $\underline{229}$

1991: ($139,465 + $79,935 + $1,369)/$1,369 = $\underline{161}$

h. 1992: ($189,268 − $72,511)/$66,682 = $\underline{1.75}$

1991: ($139,465 − $64,609)/$45,235 = $\underline{1.65}$

i. 1992: [$141,295 + $1,173(1 − .36*)]/$711,372 = $\underline{20.0\%}$

1991: [$128,652 + $1,379(1 − .38*)]/$625,074 = $\underline{20.7\%}$

j. 1992: $141,295/($498,935†) = $\underline{28.3\%}$

1991: $128,652/($463,399†) = $\underline{27.8\%}$

* Tax rate for each of the two years is:
1992: $83,730/$232,303 = 0.36
1991: $79,362/$208,014 = 0.38

† In addition to its common stock, Wrigley has outstanding Class B common stock. Because this is a second class of stock (similar in many respects to preferred stock), the contributed capital attributable to it should be deducted from total stockholders' equity in the denominator. Similarly, any dividends paid on the Class B common stock should be deducted from net income in the numerator to find the return to the regular common stockholders. We have ignored the difficulties involved in determining these adjustments in our calculations of return on equity.

2. The current ratio decreased slightly during 1992, although the quick ratio was virtually unchanged. Although the current liabilities increased at the end of 1992, the cash generated from operations improved by almost $50,000,000. With a ratio of cash flow from operations to current liabilities of over 1:1 for each year, Wrigley appears to be quite liquid and should have no problems meeting debts.

3. Wrigley is extremely solvent. Its capital structure reveals that it does not rely in any significant way on long-term debt to finance its business. The amount of noncurrent liabilities is less than 10% of total liabilities and stockholders' equity at the end of each year. In fact, a majority of Wrigley's debt is in the form of interest-free current liabilities. Most revealing is the debt service coverage ratio of 229 times in 1992 and 161 times in 1991. The total interest expense at each year-end is insignificant.

4. The return on assets for 1992 is 20%, and the return on common stockholders' equity is 28.3%. These ratios together indicate a very profitable company. It should be noted that the company paid out over half of its 1992 earnings in dividends. Wrigley appears to be a very sound investment, but many other factors, including information on the current market price of the stock, should be considered before making a decision.

GUIDANCE ANSWERS TO ACCOUNTING FOR YOUR DECISIONS

YOU ARE THE ANALYST

One would expect a commercial aircraft company such as Boeing to have a slow inventory turnover ratio because it takes many months to assemble and sell aircraft. Another industry with a slow turnover ratio would be the wood products industry. On the other hand, one would expect a grocery company such as Safeway Stores to have a rapid inventory turnover. Another industry with a rapid inventory turnover would be the toy business.

YOU ARE THE INVESTMENT BANKER

The tobacco part of the business is dragging down the stock price for the entire company. If the food and tobacco companies are similar in size, the stock should be selling at a P/E ratio midway between the ratios for each of the two industries. Because of the increased concern over health issues related to smoking, investors fearing lawsuits are shying away from the company because of its tobacco interests. As the investment banker, you would advise your client to sell the tobacco segment of the business so that investors can achieve a higher price for their shares. Of course, that advice must be easier said than done, since two major tobacco companies with food interests—Philip Morris and RJR Nabisco—have not chosen to divest themselves of their tobacco holdings.

CHAPTER HIGHLIGHTS

1. **(LO 1)** A variety of parties, including management, creditors, stockholders, and others, perform financial statement analysis. Care must be exercised, however, in all types of financial analysis. For example, the existence of alternative accounting principles can make comparing different companies difficult. Published financial statements are not adjusted for the effects of inflation and thus comparisons over time must be made with caution.

2. **(LO 2)** Horizontal analysis uses comparative financial statements to examine the increases and decreases in items from one period to the next. The analysis can look at the change in items over an extended period of time. Many companies present a summary of selected financial items for a 5- or 10-year period.

3. **(LO 3)** Vertical analysis involves stating all items on a particular financial statement as a percentage of one item on the statement. For example, all expenses on a common-size income statement are stated as a percentage of net sales. This technique, along with horizontal analysis, can be useful in spotting problem areas within a company.

4. **(LO 4)** Ratios can be categorized according to their primary purpose. Liquidity ratios indicate the company's ability to pay its debts as they are due. The focus of liquidity analysis is on a company's current assets and current liabilities.

5. **(LO 5)** Solvency ratios deal with a company's long-term financial health, that is, its ability to repay long-term creditors. The right side of the balance sheet is informative in this respect, because it reports on the various sources of capital to the business.

6. **(LO 6)** Profitability ratios measure how well management has used the assets at its disposal to earn a return for the various providers of capital. Return on assets indicates the return to all providers; return on common stockholders' equity measures the return to the residual owners of the business. Certain other ratios are used to relate a company's performance according to the financial statements with its performance in the stock market.

KEY TERMS QUIZ

Because of the number of terms introduced in this chapter, there are two key term quizzes. For each quiz, select one of the following key terms in the chapter and fill in the appropriate blank to the left of each description. The solution appears at the end of the chapter.

Quiz 1:

Horizontal analysis

Gross profit ratio

Liquidity

Current ratio

Cash flow from operations to current
liabilities ratio

Number of days' sales in receivables

Cash to cash operating cycle

Vertical analysis

Profit margin ratio

Working capital

Acid-test or quick ratio

Accounts receivable turnover ratio

Inventory turnover ratio

Number of days' sales in inventory

_____

_____

_____

_____

_____

_____

_____

_____

_____

_____

_____

_____

_____

_____

1. A stricter test of liquidity than the current ratio that excludes inventory and prepayments from the numerator.

2. Current assets minus current liabilities.

3. The ratio of current assets to current liabilities.

4. A measure of the average age of accounts receivable.

5. A measure of the ability to pay current debts from operating cash flows.

6. A measure of the number of times accounts receivable are collected in a period.

7. A measure of how long it takes to sell inventory.

8. The length of time from the purchase of inventory to the collection of any receivable from the sale.

9. A measure of the number of times inventory is sold during a period.

10. Gross profit to net sales.

11. A comparison of various financial statement items within a single period with the use of common-size statements.

12. Net income to net sales.

13. The nearness to cash of the assets and liabilities.

14. A comparison of financial statement items over a period of time.

Quiz 2:

Solvency

Debt-to-equity ratio

Debt service coverage ratio

Profitability

Return on sales

Return on stockholders' equity

Earnings per share

Dividend payout ratio

Times interest earned ratio

Cash flow from operations to capital
expenditures ratio

Return on assets

Asset turnover ratio

Leverage

Price-earnings ratio

Dividend yield ratio

_____

_____

_____

1. A measure of a company's success in earning a return for the common stockholders.

2. The relationship between a company's performance according to the income statement as compared to its performance in the stock market.

3. The ability of a company to remain in business over the long term.

_____

_____

_____

_____

_____

_____

_____

_____

_____

_____

_____

4. A variation of the profit margin ratio; it measures earnings before payments to creditors.
5. A company's bottom line stated on a per-share basis.
6. The percentage of earnings paid out as dividends.
7. The ratio of total liabilities to total stockholders' equity.
8. A measure of the ability of a company to finance long-term asset acquisitions from cash from operations.
9. A measure of a company's success in earning a return for all providers of capital.
10. The relationship between net sales and total assets.
11. The relationship between dividends and market price of a company's stock.
12. The use of borrowed funds and amounts contributed by preferred stockholders to earn an overall return higher than the cost of these funds.
13. An income statement measure of the ability of a company to meet its interest payments.
14. A statement of cash flows measure of the ability of a company to meet its interest and principal payments.
15. How well management is using company resources to earn a return on the funds invested by the various groups.

ALTERNATE TERMS

ACID-TEST RATIO Quick ratio.

HORIZONTAL ANALYSIS Trend analysis.

NUMBER OF DAYS' SALES IN RECEIVABLES Average collection period.

PRICE-EARNINGS RATIO P/E ratio.

QUESTIONS

1. Two companies are in the same industry. Company A uses the LIFO method of inventory valuation and Company B uses FIFO. What difficulties does this present when comparing the two companies? Specifically, what financial statement ratios should be monitored in comparing the two companies?
2. You are told to compare the company's results for the year, as measured by various ratios, with one of the published surveys that arranges information by industry classification. What are some of the difficulties you may encounter when making comparisons using industry standards?
3. What types of problems does inflation cause in analyzing financial statements?
4. Distinguish between horizontal and vertical analysis. Why is the analysis of common-size statements called *vertical* analysis? Why is horizontal analysis sometimes called *trend* analysis?
5. A company experiences a 15% increase in sales over the previous year. However, gross profit actually decreased by 5% from the previous year. What are some of the possible causes for an increase in sales but a decline in gross profit?

6. A company's total current assets have increased by 5% over the prior year. Management is concerned, however, about the composition of the current assets. Why is the composition of current assets important?

7. Ratios were categorized in the chapter according to their use in performing three different types of analysis. What are the three types of ratios?

8. Describe the operating cycle for a manufacturing company. How would the cycle differ for a retailer?

9. What accounts for the order in which current assets are presented on a balance sheet?

10. A company has a current ratio of 1.25 but an acid-test or quick ratio of only 0.65. How can this difference in the two ratios be explained? What are some concerns that you would have about this company?

11. Explain the basic concept underlying all turnover ratios. Why is it advisable in computing a turnover ratio to use an average in the denominator (for example, average inventory)?

12. Sanders Company's accounts receivable turned over nine times during the year. The credit department extends terms of 2/10, net 30. Does the turnover ratio indicate any problems that management should investigate?

13. The turnover of inventory for Ace Company has slowed from 6.0 times per year to 4.5 times. What are some of the possible explanations for this decrease?

14. How does the operating cycle for a manufacturer differ from the operating cycle of a service company, for example, an airline?

15. What is the difference between liquidity analysis and solvency analysis?

16. Why is the debt service coverage ratio a better measure of solvency than the times interest earned ratio?

17. A friend tells you that the best way to assess solvency is by comparing total debt to total assets. Another friend says that solvency is measured by comparing total debt to total stockholders' equity. Which one is right?

18. A company is in the process of negotiating with a bank for an additional loan. Why will the bank be very interested in the company's debt service coverage ratio?

19. What is the rationale for deducting dividends when computing the ratio of cash flow from operations to capital expenditures?

20. The rate of return on assets ratio is computed by dividing net income and interest expense, net of tax, by average total assets. Why is the numerator net income and interest expense, net of tax, rather than just net income?

21. A company has a return on assets of 14% and a return on common stockholders' equity of 11%. The president of the company has asked you to explain the reason for this difference. What causes the difference? How is the concept of financial leverage involved?

22. What is meant by the "quality" of a company's earnings? Explain why the price-earnings ratio for a company may indicate the quality of earnings.

23. Some ratios are more useful for management, whereas others are better suited to the needs of outsiders, such as stockholders and bankers. What is an example of a ratio that is primarily suited to management use? What is one that is more suited to use by outsiders?

24. Service-oriented companies have different needs in analyzing financial statements as opposed to product-oriented companies. Why is this true? Give an example of a ratio that is meaningless to a service business.

EXERCISES

(LO 3) EXERCISE 15-1 COMMON-SIZE BALANCE SHEETS

Comparative balance sheets for Beagle Company for the past two years are as follows:

	DECEMBER 31	
	1995	1994
Cash	$ 16,000	$ 20,000
Accounts receivable	40,000	30,000
Inventory	30,000	50,000
Prepaid rent	18,000	12,000
Total current assets	$104,000	$112,000
Land	$150,000	$150,000
Plant and equipment	800,000	600,000
Accumulated depreciation	(130,000)	(60,000)
Total long-term assets	$820,000	$690,000
Total assets	$924,000	$802,000
Accounts payable	$ 24,000	$ 20,000
Income taxes payable	6,000	10,000
Short-term notes payable	70,000	50,000
Total current liabilities	$100,000	$ 80,000
Bonds payable	$150,000	$200,000
Common stock	$400,000	$300,000
Retained earnings	274,000	222,000
Total stockholders' equity	$674,000	$522,000
Total liabilities and stockholders' equity	$924,000	$802,000

■ REQUIRED

1. Using the format in Exhibit 15-5, prepare common-size comparative balance sheets for the two years for Beagle Company.

2. What observations can you make about the changes in the relative composition of Beagle's accounts from the common-size balance sheets? List at least five observations.

(LO 3) EXERCISE 15-2 COMMON-SIZE INCOME STATEMENTS

Income statements for Mariners Corp. for the past two years follow:

	(AMOUNTS IN THOUSANDS OF DOLLARS)	
	1995	1994
Sales revenue	$60,000	$50,000
Cost of goods sold	42,000	30,000
Gross profit	$18,000	$20,000
Selling and administrative expense	9,000	5,000
Operating income	$ 9,000	$15,000
Interest expense	2,000	2,000
Income before tax	$ 7,000	$13,000
Income tax expense	2,000	4,000
Net income	$ 5,000	$ 9,000

1. Using the format in Exhibit 15-6, prepare common-size comparative income statements for the two years for Mariners Corp.

2. What observations can you make about the common-size statements? List at least four observations.

■ REQUIRED

(LO 4) EXERCISE 15-3 EFFECT OF TRANSACTIONS ON WORKING CAPITAL, CURRENT RATIO, AND QUICK RATIO

The following account balances are taken from the records of South Bend, Inc.:

Cash	$ 50,000
Trading securities (short term)	60,000
Accounts receivable	80,000
Inventory	100,000
Prepaid insurance	10,000
Accounts payable	75,000
Taxes payable	25,000
Salaries and wages payable	40,000
Short-term loans payable	60,000

1. Compute the following for South Bend:

   a. Working capital

   b. Current ratio

   c. Acid-test or quick ratio

2. For each of the following transactions, indicate the effect each would have on working capital, the current ratio, and the quick ratio. Indicate an increase (I), a decrease (D), or no effect (NE). Consider each transaction independently; that is, assume that it is the *only* transaction that takes place.

■ REQUIRED

	EFFECT OF TRANSACTION ON:		
TRANSACTION	**WORKING CAPITAL**	**CURRENT RATIO**	**QUICK RATIO**
a. Purchased inventory on account for $20,000.			
b. Purchased inventory for cash, $15,000.			
c. Paid suppliers on account, $30,000.			
d. Received cash on account, $40,000.			
e. Paid insurance for next year, $20,000.			
f. Made sales on account, $60,000.			
g. Repaid short-term loans at bank, $25,000.			
h. Borrowed $40,000 at bank for 90 days.			
i. Declared and paid $45,000 cash dividend.			
j. Purchased $20,000 of trading securities (classified as current assets).			
k. Paid $30,000 in salaries.			
l. Accrued additional $15,000 in taxes.			

(LO 4) EXERCISE 15-4 ACCOUNTS RECEIVABLE ANALYSIS

The following account balances are taken from the records of the Faraway Travel Agency:

	DECEMBER 31		
	1995	**1994**	**1993**
Accounts receivable	$150,000	$100,000	$80,000
	1995	**1994**	
Net credit sales	$600,000	$540,000	

Faraway extends credit terms requiring full payment in 60 days, with no discount for early payment.

■ REQUIRED

1. Compute Faraway's accounts receivable turnover ratio for 1995 and 1994.

2. Compute the number of days' sales in receivables for 1995 and 1994. Assume 360 days in a year.

3. Comment on the efficiency of Faraway's collection efforts over the two-year period.

(LO 4) EXERCISE 15-5 INVENTORY ANALYSIS

The following account balances are taken from the records of Lewis, Inc., a wholesaler of fresh fruits and vegetables:

	DECEMBER 31		
	1995	**1994**	**1993**
Merchandise inventory	$ 200,000	$ 150,000	$120,000
	1995	**1994**	
Cost of goods sold	$7,100,000	$8,100,000	

■ REQUIRED

1. Compute Lewis' inventory turnover ratio for 1995 and 1994.

2. Compute the number of days' sales in inventory for 1995 and 1994. Assume 360 days in a year.

3. Comment on your answers in parts 1 and 2 relative to the company's management of inventory over the two years. What problems do you see in its inventory management?

(LO 5) EXERCISE 15-6 SOLVENCY ANALYSIS

The following information is available from the balance sheets at the ends of the two most recent years and the income statement for the most recent year of Western Company:

	DECEMBER 31	
	1995	**1994**
Accounts payable	$ 65,000	$ 50,000
Accrued liabilities	25,000	35,000
Taxes payable	60,000	45,000
Short-term notes payable	–0–	75,000
Bonds payable due within next year	200,000	200,000
Total current liabilities	$ 350,000	$ 405,000
Bonds payable	$ 600,000	$ 800,000
Common stock, $10 par	$1,000,000	$1,000,000
Retained earnings	650,000	500,000
Total stockholders' equity	$1,650,000	$1,500,000
Total liabilities and stockholders' equity	$2,600,000	$2,705,000

	1995
Sales revenue	$1,600,000
Cost of goods sold	950,000
Gross profit	$ 650,000
Selling and administrative expense	300,000
Operating income	$ 350,000
Interest expense	89,000
Income before tax	$ 261,000
Income tax expense	111,000
Net income	$ 150,000

Other Information

a. Short-term notes payable represents a 12-month loan that matured in November 1995. Interest of 12% was paid at maturity.

b. One million dollars of serial bonds had been issued 10 years earlier. The first series of $200,000 matures at the end of 1995, with interest of 8% payable annually.

c. Cash flow from operations was $185,000 in 1995. The amounts of interest and taxes paid during 1995 were $89,000 and $96,000, respectively.

1. Compute the following for Western Company:

    a. The debt-to-equity ratio at December 31, 1995, and December 31, 1994.

    b. The times interest earned ratio for 1995.

    c. The debt service coverage ratio for 1995.

2. Comment on Western's solvency at the end of 1995. Do the times interest earned ratio and the debt service coverage ratio differ in terms of their indication of Western's ability to pay its debts?

■ **REQUIRED**

(LO 6) EXERCISE 15-7 RETURN RATIOS AND LEVERAGE

The following selected data are taken from the financial statements of Elburn Company:

Sales revenue	$ 650,000
Cost of goods sold	400,000
Gross profit	$ 250,000
Selling and administrative expense	100,000
Operating income	$ 150,000
Interest expense	50,000
Income before tax	$ 100,000
Income tax expense (40%)	40,000
Net income	$ 60,000
Accounts payable	$ 45,000
Accrued liabilities	70,000
Income taxes payable	10,000
Interest payable	25,000
Short-term loans payable	150,000
Total current liabilities	$ 300,000
Long-term bonds payable	$ 500,000

Preferred stock, 10%, $100 par	$ 250,000
Common stock, no par	600,000
Retained earnings	350,000
Total stockholders' equity	$1,200,000
Total liabilities and stockholders' equity	$2,000,000

■ REQUIRED

1. Compute the following ratios for Elburn Company:

   a. Return on sales.

   b. Asset turnover (assume that total assets at the beginning of the year were $1,600,000).

   c. Return on assets.

   d. Return on common stockholders' equity (assume that the only changes in stockholders' equity during the year were from the net income for the year and dividends on the preferred stock).

2. Comment on Elburn's use of leverage. Has it successfully employed leverage? Explain your answer.

(LO 6) EXERCISE 15-8 RELATIONSHIPS AMONG RETURN ON ASSETS, RETURN ON SALES, AND ASSET TURNOVER

A company's return on assets is a function of its ability to turn over its investment (asset turnover) and earn a profit on each dollar of sales (return on sales). For each of the *independent* cases below, determine the missing amounts. (*Note:* Assume in each case that the company has no interest expense; that is, net income is used as the definition of income in all calculations.)

CASE 1

Net income	$ 10,000
Net sales	$ 80,000
Average total assets	$ 60,000
Return on assets	?

CASE 2

Net income	$ 25,000
Average total assets	$ 250,000
Return on sales	2%
Net sales	?

CASE 3

Average total assets	$ 80,000
Asset turnover	1.5 times
Return on sales	6%
Return on assets	?

CASE 4

Return on assets	10%
Net sales	$ 50,000
Asset turnover	1.25 times
Net income	?

CASE 5

Return on assets	15%
Net income	$ 20,000
Return on sales	5%
Average total assets	?

(LO 6) EXERCISE 15-9 EPS, P/E RATIO, AND DIVIDEND RATIOS

The stockholders' equity section of the balance sheet for Cooperstown Corp. at the end of 1995 appears as follows:

8%, $100 par, cumulative preferred stock, 200,000 shares authorized, 50,000 issued and outstanding	$ 5,000,000
Additional paid-in capital on preferred	2,500,000
Common stock, $5 par, 500,000 shares authorized, 400,000 issued and outstanding	2,000,000
Additional paid-in capital on common	18,000,000
Retained earnings	37,500,000
Total stockholders' equity	$65,000,000

Net income for the year was $1,300,000. Dividends were declared and paid on the preferred shares during the year and a quarterly dividend of $.40 per share was declared and paid each quarter on the common shares. The closing market price for the common shares on December 31, 1995, was $24.75 per share.

1. Compute the following ratios for the common stock:

   a. Earnings per share

   b. Price-earnings ratio

   c. Dividend payout ratio

   d. Dividend yield ratio

2. Assume that you are an investment adviser. What other information would you want to have before advising a client regarding the purchase of Cooperstown stock?

■ REQUIRED

(LO 6) EXERCISE 15-10 EARNINGS PER SHARE AND EXTRAORDINARY ITEMS

The stockholders' equity section of the balance sheet for Lahey Construction Company at the end of 1995 follows:

9%, $10 par, cumulative preferred stock, 500,000 shares authorized, 200,000 issued and outstanding	$ 2,000,000
Additional paid-in capital on preferred	7,500,000
Common stock, $1 par, 2,500,000 shares authorized, 1,500,000 issued and outstanding	1,500,000
Additional paid-in capital on common	21,000,000
Retained earnings	25,500,000
Total stockholders' equity	$57,500,000

The lower portion of the 1995 income statement indicates the following:

Net income before tax		$ 9,750,000
Income tax expense (40%)		(3,900,000)
Income before extraordinary items		$ 5,850,000
Extraordinary loss from flood	$ (6,200,000)	
Less: related tax effect (40%)	2,480,000	(3,720,000)
Net income		$ 2,130,000

Assume the number of shares outstanding did not change during the year.

■ REQUIRED

1. Compute earnings per share *before* extraordinary items.

2. Compute earnings per share *after* the extraordinary loss.

3. Which of the two EPS ratios is more useful to management? Explain your answer. Would your answer be different if the ratios were to be used by an outsider, for example, a potential stockholder? Why?

MULTI-CONCEPT EXERCISES

(LO 2, 4, 5) EXERCISE 15-11 HORIZONTAL ANALYSIS OF THE BALANCE SHEET, LIQUIDITY, SOLVENCY

Refer to the balance sheets for Beagle Company in Exercise 15-1.

■ REQUIRED

1. Using the format in Exhibit 15-1, prepare comparative balance sheets for Beagle Company, including columns for both the dollars and percentage increase or decrease in each item on the statement.

2. Identify the four items on the balance sheet that experienced the largest change from one year to the next. For each of these, explain where you would look to find additional information about the change.

3. For each of the two year-ends, compute the following ratios:

   a. Current ratio

   b. Acid-test ratio

   c. Debt-to-equity ratio

4. On the basis of your computations in part 3, does Beagle appear to be more or less liquid at the end of 1995 as compared to the end of 1994? More or less solvent? Explain your answers.

(LO 2, 6) EXERCISE 15-12 HORIZONTAL ANALYSIS OF THE INCOME STATEMENT, PROFITABILITY

Refer to the income statements for Mariners Corp. in Exercise 15-2.

■ REQUIRED

1. Using the format in Exhibit 15-2, prepare comparative income statements for Mariners Corp., including columns for both the dollars and percentage increase or decrease in each item on the statement.

2. Identify the two items on the income statement that experienced the largest change from one year to the next. For each of these, explain where you would look to find additional information about the change.

3. For each of the two years, compute the following ratios:

   a. Gross profit ratio

   b. Profit margin ratio

4. On the basis of your computations in part 3, does Mariners appear to be more or less profitable in 1995 compared to 1994? Explain your answer.

PROBLEMS

(LO 6) PROBLEM 15-1 GOALS FOR SALES AND RETURN ON ASSETS

The president of Stuart Corp. is reviewing the operating results of the year just completed with his vice presidents. Sales increased by 15% from the previous year to $60,000,000. Average total assets for the year were $40,000,000. Net income, after adding back interest expense, net of tax, was $5,000,000.

The president is happy with the performance over the past year but is never satisfied with the status quo. He has set two specific goals for next year: (1) a 20% growth in sales and (2) a return on assets of 15%.

In order to achieve the second goal, the president has stated his intention to increase the total asset base by 12.5% over the base for the year just completed.

■ REQUIRED

1. For the year just completed, compute the following ratios:

    a. Return on sales

    b. Asset turnover

    c. Return on assets

2. Compute the necessary asset turnover for next year to achieve the president's goal of a 20% increase in sales.

3. Calculate the income needed next year to achieve the goal of a 15% return on total assets. (*Note:* Assume that *income* is defined as net income plus interest, net of tax.)

4. Based on your answers to parts 2 and 3, comment on the reasonableness of the president's goals. What must the company focus on to attain these goals?

(LO 6) PROBLEM 15-2 GOALS FOR SALES AND INCOME GROWTH

Riverside Corp. is a major regional retailer. The chief executive officer (CEO) is concerned with the slow growth of both sales and net income and the subsequent effect on the trading price of the common stock. Selected financial data for the past three years follow.

RIVERSIDE CORP.
(IN MILLIONS)

	1995	1994	1993
1. Sales	$200.0	$192.5	$187.0
2. Net income	6.0	5.8	5.6
3. Dividends declared and paid	2.5	2.5	2.5
DECEMBER 31 BALANCES:			
4. Owners' equity	70.0	66.5	63.2
5. Debt	30.0	29.8	30.3
SELECTED YEAR-END FINANCIAL RATIOS			
Net income to sales	3.0%	3.0%	3.0%
Asset turnover	2 times	2 times	2 times
6. Return on owners' equity*	8.6%	8.7%	8.9%
7. Debt to total assets	30.0%	30.9%	32.4%

*Based on year-end balances in owners' equity.

The CEO believes that the price of the stock has been adversely affected by the downward trend of the return on equity, the relatively low dividend payout ratio, and the lack of dividend increases. To improve the price of the stock, she wants to improve the return on equity and dividends. She believes that the company should be able to meet these objectives by (1) increasing sales and net income at an annual rate of 10% a year and (2) establishing a new dividend policy that calls for a dividend payout of 50% of earnings or $3,000,000, whichever is larger.

The 10% annual sales increase will be accomplished through a new promotional program. The president believes that the present net income to sales ratio of 3% will be unchanged by the cost of this new program and any interest paid on new debt. She expects that the company can accomplish this sales and income growth while maintaining the current relationship of total assets to sales. Any capital needed to maintain this relationship that is not generated internally would be acquired through long-term debt financing. The CEO hopes that debt would not exceed 35% of total liabilities and owners' equity.

■ REQUIRED

1. Using the CEO's program, prepare a schedule that shows the appropriate data for the years 1996, 1997, and 1998 for the items numbered 1 through 7 on the preceding schedule.

2. Can the CEO meet all of her requirements if a 10% per year growth in income and sales is achieved? Explain your answer.

3. What alternative actions should the CEO consider to improve the return on equity and to support increased dividend payments?

4. Explain the reasons that the CEO might have for wanting to limit debt to 35% of total liabilities and owners' equity. (CMA adapted)

MULTI-CONCEPT PROBLEMS

(LO 4, 5, 6) PROBLEM 15-3 BASIC FINANCIAL RATIOS

The accounting staff of CCB Enterprises has completed the financial statements for the 1995 calendar year. The statement of income for the current year and the comparative statements of financial position for 1995 and 1994 follow.

CCB ENTERPRISES
STATEMENT OF INCOME
FOR THE YEAR ENDED DECEMBER 31, 1995
(THOUSANDS OMITTED)

Revenue:	
Net sales	$800,000
Other	60,000
Total revenue	$860,000
Expenses:	
Cost of goods sold	$540,000
Research and development	25,000
Selling and administrative	155,000
Interest	20,000
Total expenses	$740,000
Income before income taxes	$120,000
Income taxes	48,000
Net income	$ 72,000

CCB ENTERPRISES
COMPARATIVE STATEMENTS OF FINANCIAL POSITION
DECEMBER 31, 1995 AND 1994
(THOUSANDS OMITTED)

	1995	1994
ASSETS		
Current assets:		
Cash and short-term investments	$ 26,000	$ 21,000
Receivables, less allowance for doubtful accounts ($1,100 in 1995 and $1,400 in 1994)	48,000	50,000
Inventories, at lower of FIFO cost or market	65,000	62,000
Prepaid items and other current assets	5,000	3,000
Total current assets	$144,000	$136,000
Other assets:		
Investments, at cost	$106,000	$106,000
Deposits	10,000	8,000
Total other assets	$116,000	$114,000
Property, plant, and equipment		
Land	$ 12,000	$ 12,000
Buildings and equipment, less accumulated depreciation ($126,000 in 1995 and $122,000 in 1994)	268,000	248,000
Total property, plant, and equipment	$280,000	$260,000
Total assets	$540,000	$510,000
LIABILITIES AND STOCKHOLDERS' EQUITY		
Current liabilities:		
Short-term loans	$ 22,000	$ 24,000
Accounts payable	72,000	71,000
Salaries, wages, and other	26,000	27,000
Total current liabilities	$120,000	$122,000
Long-term debt:	160,000	171,000
Total liabilities	$280,000	$293,000
Stockholders' equity:		
Common stock, at par	$ 44,000	$ 42,000
Paid-in capital in excess of par	64,000	61,000
Total paid-in capital	$108,000	$103,000
Retained earnings	152,000	114,000
Total stockholders' equity	$260,000	$217,000
Total liabilities and stockholders' equity	$540,000	$510,000

I. Calculate the following financial ratios for 1995 for CCB Enterprises: ■ REQUIRED

a. Times interest earned

b. Return on total assets

    c. Return on common stockholders' equity

    d. Debt-equity ratio (at December 31, 1995)

    e. Current ratio (at December 31, 1995)

    f. Quick (acid-test) ratio (at December 31, 1995)

    g. Accounts receivable turnover ratio (assume that all sales are on credit)

    h. Number of days' sales in receivables

    i. Inventory turnover ratio (assume that all purchases are on credit)

    j. Number of days' sales in inventory

    k. Number of days in cash operating cycle

2. Prepare a few brief comments on the overall financial health of CCB Enterprises. For each comment, indicate any information not provided in the problem that you would need to fully evaluate the company's financial health.

(CMA adapted)

(LO 5, 6) PROBLEM 15-4 PROJECTED RESULTS TO MEET CORPORATE OBJECTIVES

Tablon, Inc., is a wholly owned subsidiary of Marbel Co. The philosophy of Marbel's management is to allow the subsidiaries to operate as independent units. Corporate control is exercised through the establishment of minimum objectives for each subsidiary accompanied by substantial rewards for success and penalties for failure. The time period for performance review is long enough for competent managers to display their abilities.

Each quarter the subsidiary is required to submit financial statements. The statements are accompanied by a letter from the subsidiary president explaining the results to date, a forecast for the remainder of the year, and the actions to be taken to achieve the objectives if the forecast indicates that the objectives will not be met.

Marbel management in conjunction with Tablon management had set the objectives listed below for the year ending May 31, 1996. These objectives are similar to those set in previous years.

Sales growth of 20%.

Return on stockholders' equity of 15%.

A long-term debt-to-equity ratio of not more than 1.0.

Payment of a cash dividend of 50% of net income, with a minimum payment of at least $400,000.

Tablon's controller has just completed the financial statements for the six months ended November 30, 1995, and the forecast for the year ending May 31, 1996. The statements are presented below.

After a cursory glance at the financial statements, Tablon's president concluded that all objectives would not be met. At a staff meeting of the Tablon management, the president asked the controller to review the projected results and recommend possible actions that could be taken during the remainder of the year so that Tablon would be more likely to meet the objectives.

TABLON, INC.
INCOME STATEMENT
(THOUSANDS OMITTED)

	YEAR ENDED MAY 31, 1995	SIX MONTHS ENDED NOVEMBER 30, 1995	FORECAST FOR YEAR ENDING MAY 31, 1996
Sales	$25,000	$15,000	$30,000
Cost of goods sold	$13,000	$ 8,000	$16,000
Selling expenses	5,000	3,500	7,000
Administrative expenses and interest	4,000	2,500	5,000
Income taxes (40%)	1,200	400	800
Total expenses and taxes	$23,200	$14,400	$28,800
Net income	$ 1,800	$ 600	$ 1,200
Dividends declared and paid	600	0	600
Income retained	$ 1,200	$ 600	$ 600

TABLON, INC.
STATEMENT OF FINANCIAL POSITION
(THOUSANDS OMITTED)

	MAY 31, 1995	NOVEMBER 30, 1995	FORECAST FOR MAY 31, 1996
ASSETS			
Cash	$ 400	$ 500	$ 500
Accounts receivable (net)	4,100	6,500	7,100
Inventory	7,000	8,500	8,600
Plant and equipment (net)	6,500	7,000	7,300
Total assets	$18,000	$22,500	$23,500
LIABILITIES AND EQUITIES			
Accounts payable	$ 3,000	$ 4,000	$ 4,000
Accrued taxes	300	200	200
Long-term borrowing	6,000	9,000	10,000
Common stock	5,000	5,000	5,000
Retained earnings	3,700	4,300	4,300
Total liabilities and equities	$18,000	$22,500	$23,500

■ REQUIRED

1. Calculate the projected results for each of the four objectives established for Tablon, Inc. State which results will not meet the objectives by year-end.

2. From the data presented, identify the factors that seem to contribute to the failure of Tablon, Inc., to meet all of its objectives.

3. Explain the possible actions that the controller could recommend in response to the president's request.   (CMA adapted)

(LO 4, 5, 6) PROBLEM 15-5 COMPARISON WITH INDUSTRY AVERAGES

Heartland, Inc., is a medium-size company that has been in business for 20 years. The industry has become very competitive in the last few years, and Heartland has decided that it must grow if it is going to survive. It has approached the bank for a sizable five-year loan, and the bank has requested its most recent financial statements as part of the loan package.

The industry in which Heartland operates consists of approximately 20 companies relatively equal in size. The trade association to which all of the competitors belong publishes an annual survey of the industry, including industry averages for selected ratios for the competitors. All companies voluntarily submit their statements to the association for this purpose.

Heartland's controller is aware that the bank has access to this survey and is very concerned about how the company fared this past year compared with the rest of the industry. The ratios included in the publication, and the averages for the past year, are as follows:

RATIO	INDUSTRY AVERAGE
Current ratio	1.23
Acid-test (quick) ratio	0.75
Accounts receivable turnover	33 times
Inventory turnover	29 times
Debt-to-equity ratio	0.53
Times interest earned	8.65 times
Return on sales	6.57%
Asset turnover	1.95 times
Return on assets	12.81%
Return on common stockholders' equity	17.67%

The financial statements to be submitted to the bank in connection with the loan follow:

HEARTLAND, INC.
STATEMENT OF INCOME AND RETAINED EARNINGS
FOR THE YEAR ENDED DECEMBER 31, 1995
(THOUSANDS OMITTED)

Sales revenue	$ 542,750
Cost of goods sold	(435,650)
Gross margin	$ 107,100
Selling, general, and administrative expense	$ (65,780)
Loss on sales of securities	(220)
Income before interest and taxes	$ 41,100
Interest expense	(9,275)
Income before taxes	$ 31,825
Income tax expense	(12,730)
Net income	$ 19,095
Retained earnings, January 1, 1995	58,485
	$ 77,580
Dividends paid on common stock	(12,000)
Retained earnings, December 31, 1995	$ 65,580

HEARTLAND, INC.
COMPARATIVE STATEMENTS OF FINANCIAL POSITION
(THOUSANDS OMITTED)

	DECEMBER 31, 1995	DECEMBER 31, 1994
ASSETS		
Current assets:		
Cash	$ 1,135	$ 750
Marketable securities	1,250	2,250
Accounts receivable, net of allowances	15,650	12,380
Inventories	12,680	15,870
Prepaid items	385	420
Total current assets	$ 31,100	$ 31,670
Long-term investments	$ 425	$ 425
Property, plant, and equipment:		
Land	$ 32,000	$ 32,000
Buildings and equipment, net of accumulated depreciation	216,000	206,000
Total property, plant, and equipment	$248,000	$238,000
Total assets	$279,525	$270,095
LIABILITIES AND STOCKHOLDERS' EQUITY		
Current liabilities:		
Short-term notes	$ 8,750	$ 12,750
Accounts payable	20,090	14,380
Salaries and wages payable	1,975	2,430
Income taxes payable	3,130	2,050
Total current liabilities	$ 33,945	$ 31,610
Long-term bonds payable	$ 80,000	$ 80,000
Stockholders' equity:		
Common stock, no par	$100,000	$100,000
Retained earnings	65,580	58,485
Total stockholders' equity	$165,580	$158,485
Total liabilities and stockholders' equity	$279,525	$270,095

1. Prepare a columnar report for the controller of Heartland, Inc., comparing the industry averages for the ratios published by the trade association with the comparable ratios for Heartland. For Heartland, compute the ratios as of December 31, 1995, or for the year ending December 31, 1995, whichever is appropriate.

2. Briefly evaluate Heartland's ratios relative to the industry.

3. Do you think that the bank will approve the loan? Explain your answer.

■ REQUIRED

ALTERNATE PROBLEMS

(LO 6) PROBLEM 15-1A GOALS FOR SALES AND RETURN ON ASSETS

The president of Samson Corp. is reviewing the operating results of the year just completed with her department managers. Sales increased by 12% from the previous year to $750,000. Average total assets for the year were $400,000. Net income, after adding back interest expense, net of tax, was $60,000.

The president is happy with the performance over the past year but is never satisfied with the status quo. She has set two specific goals for next year: (1) a 15% growth in sales and (2) a return on assets of 20%.

In order to achieve the second goal, the president has stated her intention to increase the total asset base by 10% over the base for the year just completed.

■ REQUIRED

1. For the year just completed, compute the following ratios:

  a. Return on sales

  b. Asset turnover

  c. Return on assets

2. Compute the necessary asset turnover for next year to achieve the president's goal of a 15% increase in sales.

3. Calculate the income needed next year to achieve the goal of a 20% return on total assets. (*Note:* Assume that *income* is defined as net income plus interest, net of tax.)

4. Based on your answers to parts 2 and 3, comment on the reasonableness of the president's goals. What must the company focus on to attain these goals?

(LO 6) PROBLEM 15-2A GOALS FOR SALES AND INCOME GROWTH

Oceanside Corp. is a major regional retailer. The chief executive officer (CEO) is concerned with the slow growth of both sales and net income and the subsequent effect on the trading price of the common stock. Selected financial data for the past three years follow.

OCEANSIDE CORP.
(IN MILLIONS)

	1995	1994	1993
1. Sales	$100.0	$96.7	$93.3
2. Net income	3.0	2.9	2.8
3. Dividends declared and paid	1.2	1.2	1.2
DECEMBER 31 BALANCES:			
4. Owners' equity	40.0	38.2	36.5
5. Debt	10.0	10.2	10.2
SELECTED YEAR-END FINANCIAL RATIOS			
Net income to sales	3.0%	3.0%	3.0%
Asset turnover	2 times	2 times	2 times
6. Return on owners' equity*	7.5%	7.6%	7.7%
7. Debt to total assets	20.0%	21.1%	21.8%

*Based on year-end balances in owners' equity.

The CEO believes that the price of the stock has been adversely affected by the downward trend of the return on equity, the relatively low dividend payout ratio, and the lack of dividend increases. To improve the price of the stock, he wants to improve the return on equity and dividends.

He believes that the company should be able to meet these objectives by (1) increasing sales and net income at an annual rate of 10% a year and (2) establishing a new dividend policy that calls for a dividend payout of 60% of earnings or $2,000,000, whichever is larger.

The 10% annual sales increase will be accomplished through a product enhancement program. The president believes that the present net income to sales ratio of 3% will be unchanged by the cost of this new program and any interest paid on new debt. He expects that the company can accomplish this sales and income growth while maintaining the current relationship of total assets to sales. Any capital needed to maintain this relationship that is not generated internally would be acquired through long-term debt financing. The CEO hopes that debt would not exceed 25% of total liabilities and owners' equity.

■ REQUIRED

1. Using the CEO's program, prepare a schedule that shows the appropriate data for the years 1996, 1997, and 1998 for the items numbered 1 through 7 on the preceding schedule.

2. Can the CEO meet all of his requirements if a 10% per year growth in income and sales is achieved? Explain your answers.

3. What alternative actions should the CEO consider to improve the return on equity and to support increased dividend payments?　　　(CMA adapted)

ALTERNATE MULTI-CONCEPT PROBLEMS

(LO 4, 5, 6) PROBLEM 15-3A BASIC FINANCIAL RATIOS

The accounting staff of SST Enterprises has completed the financial statements for the 1995 calendar year. The statement of income for the current year and the comparative statements of financial position for 1995 and 1994 follow.

SST ENTERPRISES
STATEMENT OF INCOME
YEAR ENDED DECEMBER 31, 1995
(THOUSANDS OMITTED)

Revenue:	
Net sales	$600,000
Other	45,000
Total revenue	$645,000
Expenses:	
Cost of goods sold	$405,000
Research and development	18,000
Selling and administrative	120,000
Interest	15,000
Total expenses	$558,000
Income before income taxes	$ 87,000
Income taxes	27,000
Net income	$ 60,000

SST ENTERPRISES
COMPARATIVE STATEMENTS OF FINANCIAL POSITION
DECEMBER 31, 1995 AND 1994
(THOUSANDS OMITTED)

	1995	1994
ASSETS		
Current assets:		
Cash and short-term investments	$ 27,000	$ 20,000
Receivables, less allowance for doubtful accounts ($1,100 in 1995 and $1,400 in 1994)	36,000	37,000
Inventories, at lower of FIFO cost or market	35,000	42,000
Prepaid items and other current assets	2,000	1,000
Total current assets	$100,000	$100,000
Property, plant, and equipment:		
Land	$ 9,000	$ 9,000
Buildings and equipment, less accumulated depreciation ($74,000 in 1995 and $62,000 in 1994)	191,000	186,000
Total property, plant, and equipment	$200,000	$195,000
Total assets	$300,000	$295,000
LIABILITIES AND STOCKHOLDERS' EQUITY		
Current liabilities:		
Short-term loans	$ 20,000	$ 15,000
Accounts payable	80,000	68,000
Salaries, wages, and other	5,000	7,000
Total current liabilities	$105,000	$ 90,000
Long-term debt	15,000	40,000
Total liabilities	$120,000	$130,000
Stockholders' equity:		
Common stock, at par	$ 50,000	$ 50,000
Paid-in capital in excess of par	25,000	25,000
Total paid-in capital	$ 75,000	$ 75,000
Retained earnings	105,000	90,000
Total stockholders' equity	$180,000	$165,000
Total liabilities and stockholders' equity	$300,000	$295,000

■ REQUIRED   1. Calculate the following financial ratios for 1995 for SST Enterprises:

   a. Times interest earned
   b. Return on total assets
   c. Return on common stockholders' equity
   d. Debt-equity ratio (at December 31, 1995)
   e. Current ratio (at December 31, 1995)
   f. Quick (acid-test) ratio (at December 31, 1995)
   g. Accounts receivable turnover ratio (assume that all sales are on credit)
   h. Number of days' sales in receivables
   i. Inventory turnover ratio (assume that all purchases are on credit)

j. Number of days' sales in inventory

k. Number of days in cash operating cycle

2. Prepare a few brief comments on the overall financial health of SST Enterprises. For each comment, indicate any information not provided in the problem that you would need to fully evaluate the company's financial health.

(CMA adapted)

(LO 5, 6) PROBLEM 15-4A PROJECTED RESULTS TO MEET CORPORATE OBJECTIVES

Grout, Inc., is a wholly owned subsidiary of Slait Co. The philosophy of Slait's management is to allow the subsidiaries to operate as independent units. Corporate control is exercised through the establishment of minimum objectives for each subsidiary accompanied by substantial rewards for success and penalties for failure. The time period for performance review is long enough for competent managers to display their abilities.

Each quarter the subsidiary is required to submit financial statements. The statements are accompanied by a letter from the subsidiary president explaining the results to date, a forecast for the remainder of the year, and the actions to be taken to achieve the objectives if the forecast indicates that the objectives will not be met.

Slait management in conjunction with Grout management had set the objectives listed below for the year ending September 30, 1996. These objectives are similar to those set in previous years.

Sales growth of 10%.

Return on stockholders' equity of 20%.

A long-term debt-to-equity ratio of not more than 1.0.

Payment of a cash dividend of 50% of net income, with a minimum payment of at least $500,000.

Grout's controller has just completed preparing the financial statements for the six months ended March 31, 1996, and the forecast for the year ending September 30, 1996. The statements are presented below.

After a cursory glance at the financial statements, Grout's president concluded that all objectives would not be met. At a staff meeting of the Grout management, the president asked the controller to review the projected results and recommend possible actions that could be taken during the remainder of the year so that Grout would be more likely to meet the objectives.

GROUT, INC.
INCOME STATEMENT
(THOUSANDS OMITTED)

	YEAR ENDED SEPTEMBER 30, 1995	SIX MONTHS ENDED MARCH 31, 1996	FORECAST FOR YEAR ENDING SEPTEMBER 30, 1996
Sales	$10,000	$6,000	$12,000
Cost of goods sold	$ 6,000	$4,000	$ 8,000
Selling expenses	1,500	900	1,800
Administrative expenses and interest	1,000	600	1,200
Income taxes (40%)	500	300	600
Total expenses and taxes	$ 9,000	$5,800	$11,600
Net income	$ 1,000	$ 200	$ 400
Dividends declared and paid	500	0	400
Income retained	$ 500	$ 200	$ 0

GROUT, INC.
STATEMENT OF FINANCIAL POSITION
(THOUSANDS OMITTED)

	SEPTEMBER 30, 1995	MARCH 31, 1996	FORECAST FOR SEPTEMBER 30, 1996
ASSETS			
Cash	$ 400	$ 500	$ 500
Accounts receivable (net)	2,100	3,400	2,600
Inventory	7,000	8,500	8,400
Plant and equipment (net)	2,800	2,500	3,200
Total assets	$12,300	$14,900	$14,700
LIABILITIES AND EQUITIES			
Accounts payable	$ 3,000	$ 4,000	$ 4,000
Accrued taxes	300	200	200
Long-term borrowing	4,000	5,500	5,500
Common stock	4,000	4,000	4,000
Retained earnings	1,000	1,200	1,000
Total liabilities and equities	$12,300	$14,900	$14,700

■ REQUIRED

1. Calculate the projected results for each of the four objectives established for Grout, Inc. State which results will not meet the objectives by year-end.

2. From the data presented, identify the factors that seem to contribute to the failure of Grout, Inc., to meet all of its objectives.

3. Explain the possible actions that the controller could recommend in response to the president's request. (CMA adapted)

(LO 4, 5, 6) PROBLEM 15-5A COMPARISON WITH INDUSTRY AVERAGES

Midwest, Inc., is a medium-size company that has been in business for 20 years. The industry has become very competitive in the last few years, and Midwest has decided that it must grow if it is going to survive. It has approached the bank for a sizable five-year loan, and the bank has requested its most recent financial statements as part of the loan package.

The industry in which Midwest operates consists of approximately 20 companies relatively equal in size. The trade association to which all of the competitors belong publishes an annual survey of the industry, including industry averages for selected ratios for the competitors. All companies voluntarily submit their statements to the association for this purpose.

Midwest's controller is aware that the bank has access to this survey and is very concerned about how the company fared this past year compared with the rest of the industry. The ratios included in the publication, and the averages for the past year, are as follows:

RATIO	INDUSTRY AVERAGE
Current ratio	1.20
Acid-test (quick) ratio	0.50
Inventory turnover	35 times
Debt-to-equity ratio	0.50
Times interest earned	25 times
Return on sales	3%
Asset turnover	3.5 times
Return on common stockholders' equity	20%

The financial statements to be submitted to the bank in connection with the loan follow:

MIDWEST, INC.
STATEMENT OF INCOME AND RETAINED EARNINGS
FOR THE YEAR ENDED DECEMBER 31, 1995
(THOUSANDS OMITTED)

Sales revenue	$ 420,500
Cost of goods sold	(300,000)
Gross margin	$ 120,500
Selling, general, and administrative expense	$ (85,000)
Income before interest and taxes	$ 35,500
Interest expense	(8,600)
Income before taxes	$ 26,900
Income tax expense	(12,000)
Net income	$ 14,900
Retained earnings, January 1, 1995	12,400
	$ 27,300
Dividends paid on common stock	(11,200)
Retained earnings, December 31, 1995	$ 16,100

MIDWEST, INC.
COMPARATIVE STATEMENTS OF FINANCIAL POSITION
(THOUSANDS OMITTED)

	DECEMBER 31, 1995	DECEMBER 31, 1994
ASSETS		
Current assets:		
Cash	$ 1,790	$ 2,600
Marketable securities	1,200	1,700
Accounts receivable, net of allowances	400	600
Inventories	8,700	7,400
Prepaid items	350	400
Total current assets	$ 12,440	$ 12,700
Long-term investments	$ 560	$ 400
Property, plant, and equipment:		
Land	$ 12,000	$ 12,000
Buildings and equipment, net of accumulated depreciation	87,000	82,900
Total property, plant, and equipment	$ 99,000	$ 94,900
Total assets	$112,000	$108,000
LIABILITIES AND STOCKHOLDERS' EQUITY		
Current liabilities:		
Short-term notes	$ 800	$ 600
Accounts payable	6,040	6,775
Salaries and wages payable	1,500	1,200
Income taxes payable	1,560	1,025
Total current liabilities	$ 9,900	$ 9,600
Long-term bonds payable	$ 36,000	$ 36,000

Stockholders' equity:		
Common stock, no par	$ 50,000	$ 50,000
Retained earnings	16,100	12,400
Total stockholders' equity	$ 66,100	$ 62,400
Total liabilities and stockholders' equity	$112,000	$108,000

■ REQUIRED

1. Prepare a columnar report for the controller of Midwest, Inc., comparing the industry averages for the ratios published by the trade association with the comparable ratios for Midwest. For Midwest, compute the ratios as of December 31, 1995, or for the year ending December 31, 1995, whichever is appropriate.

2. Briefly evaluate Midwest's ratios relative to the industry.

3. Do you think that the bank will approve the loan? Explain your answer.

CASES

READING AND INTERPRETING FINANCIAL STATEMENTS

(LO 2) CASE 15-1 HORIZONTAL ANALYSIS FOR BEN & JERRY'S

Refer to the comparative income statements for Ben & Jerry's included in its annual report.

■ REQUIRED

1. Prepare a work sheet with the following headings:

	INCREASE (DECREASE) FROM			
	1991 TO 1992		1990 TO 1991	
INCOME STATEMENT ACCOUNTS	DOLLARS	PERCENT	DOLLARS	PERCENT

2. Complete the work sheet using each of the account titles on Ben & Jerry's income statement. Round dollar amounts to the nearest one-tenth of $1 million and percentages to the nearest one-tenth of a percent. For example, the increase in net sales from 1990 to 1991 is $19,973,302. Record this increase on the work sheet as $20.0 million.

3. What observations can you make from this horizontal analysis? What is your overall analysis of operations? Has the company's operations improved over the three-year period?

(LO 3) CASE 15-2 VERTICAL ANALYSIS FOR BEN & JERRY'S

Refer to the financial statements for Ben & Jerry's included in its annual report.

■ REQUIRED

1. Using the format in Exhibit 15-6, prepare common-size comparative income statements for the years ended December 26, 1992, and December 28, 1991. Round dollar amounts to the nearest one-tenth of $1 million and percentages to the nearest one-tenth of a percent.

2. What changes do you detect in the income statement relationships from 1991 to 1992?

3. Using the format in Exhibit 15-5, prepare common-size comparative balance sheets at December 26, 1992, and December 28, 1991. Round dollar amounts to the nearest one-tenth of $1 million and percentages to the nearest one-tenth of a percent.

4. What observations can you make about the relative composition of Ben & Jerry's assets from the common-size statements? What observations can be made about the changes in the relative composition of liabilities and owners' equity accounts?

(LO 4, 5, 6) CASE 15-3 RATIO ANALYSIS FOR BEN & JERRY'S

Refer to the financial statements for Ben & Jerry's included in its annual report.

1. Compute the following ratios and other amounts for each of the two years, 1992 and 1991. Because only two years of data are given on the balance sheets, to be consistent, you should use year-end balances for each year in lieu of average balances. Assume a 40% tax rate and 360 days to a year. State any other necessary assumptions in making the calculations. Round all ratios to the nearest one-tenth of a percent.

■ **REQUIRED**

   a. Working capital

   b. Current ratio

   c. Acid-test ratio

   d. Cash flow from operations to current liabilities

   e. Number of days' sales in receivables

   f. Number of days' sales in inventory

   g. Debt-to-equity ratio

   h. Times interest earned

   i. Debt service coverage

   j. Cash flow from operations to capital expenditures

   k. Asset turnover

   l. Return on sales

   m. Return on assets

   n. Return on common stockholders' equity

2. What is your overall analysis of the financial health of Ben & Jerry's? What do you believe are the company's strengths and weaknesses?

MAKING FINANCIAL DECISIONS

(LO 4, 5, 6) CASE 15-4 ACQUISITION DECISION

Diversified Industries is a large conglomerate and is continually in the market for new acquisitions. The company has grown rapidly over the last 10 years through buyouts of medium-size companies. Diversified does not limit itself to companies in any one industry but looks for firms with a sound financial base and the ability to stand on their own financially.

The president of Diversified recently told a meeting of the company's officers: "I want to impress two points on all of you. First, we are not in the business of looking for bargains. Diversified has achieved success in the past by acquiring companies with the ability to be a permanent member of the corporate family. We don't want companies that may appear to be a bargain on paper but can't survive in the long run. Second, a new member of our family must be able to come in and make it on its own—the parent is not organized to be a funding agency for struggling subsidiaries."

Ron Dixon is the vice president of acquisitions for Diversified, a position he has held for five years. He is responsible for making recommendations to the board of directors on potential acquisitions. Because you are one of his assistants, he recently brought you a set of financials for a manufacturer, Heavy Duty Tractors. Dixon believes that Heavy Duty is a "can't-miss" opportunity for Diversified and asks you to confirm his hunch by performing basic financial statement analysis on the company. The most recent income statement and comparative balance sheets for the company follow.

HEAVY DUTY TRACTORS, INC.
STATEMENT OF INCOME AND RETAINED EARNINGS
FOR THE YEAR ENDED DECEMBER 31, 1995
(THOUSANDS OMITTED)

Sales revenue	$875,250
Cost of goods sold	542,750
Gross margin	$332,500
Selling, general, and administrative expenses	264,360
Operating income	$ 68,140
Interest expense	45,000
Net income before taxes and extraordinary items	$ 23,140
Income tax expense	9,250
Income before extraordinary items	$ 13,890
Extraordinary gain, less taxes of $6,000	9,000
Net income	$ 22,890
Retained earnings, January 1, 1995	169,820
	$192,710
Dividends paid on common stock	10,000
Retained earnings, December 31, 1995	$182,710

HEAVY DUTY TRACTORS, INC.
COMPARATIVE STATEMENTS OF FINANCIAL POSITION
(THOUSANDS OMITTED)

	DECEMBER 31, 1995	DECEMBER 31, 1994
ASSETS		
Current assets:		
Cash	$ 48,500	$ 24,980
Marketable securities	3,750	–0–
Accounts receivable, net of allowances	128,420	84,120
Inventories	135,850	96,780
Prepaid items	7,600	9,300
Total current assets	$324,120	$215,180
Long-term investments	$ 55,890	$ 55,890
Property, plant, and equipment:		
Land	$ 45,000	$ 45,000
Buildings and equipment, less accumulated depreciation of $385,000 in 1995 and $325,000 in 1994	545,000	605,000
Total property, plant, and equipment	$590,000	$650,000
Total assets	$970,010	$921,070

LIABILITIES AND STOCKHOLDERS' EQUITY

Current liabilities:

Short-term notes	$ 80,000	$ 60,000
Accounts payable	65,350	48,760
Salaries and wages payable	14,360	13,840
Income taxes payable	2,590	3,650
Total current liabilities	$162,300	$126,250
Long-term bonds payable, due 2002	$275,000	$275,000

Stockholders' equity:

Common stock, no par	$350,000	$350,000
Retained earnings	182,710	169,820
Total stockholders' equity	$532,710	$519,820
Total liabilities and stockholders' equity	$970,010	$921,070

1. How liquid is Heavy Duty Tractors? Support your answer with any ratios that you believe are necessary to justify your conclusion. Also indicate any other information that you would want to have in making a final determination on its liquidity.

2. In light of the president's comments, should you be concerned about the solvency of Heavy Duty Tractors? Support your answer with the necessary ratios. How does the maturity date of the outstanding debt affect your answer?

3. Has Heavy Duty demonstrated the ability to be a profitable member of the Diversified family? Support your answer with the necessary ratios.

4. What will you tell your boss? Should he recommend to the board of directors that Diversified put in a bid for Heavy Duty Tractors?

■ REQUIRED

(LO 3) CASE 15-5 PRICING DECISION

BPO's management believes that the company has been successful at increasing sales because it has not increased the selling price of the products, even though competition has increased prices and costs have increased. Price and cost relationships in Year 1 were established because they represented industry averages. The following income statements are available for BPO's first three years of operation:

	YEAR 3	YEAR 2	YEAR 1
Sales	$125,000	$110,000	$100,000
Cost of goods sold	62,000	49,000	40,000
Gross profit	$ 63,000	$ 61,000	$ 60,000
Operating expenses	53,000	49,000	45,000
Net income	$ 10,000	$ 12,000	$ 15,000

1. Using the format in Exhibit 15-6, prepare common-size comparative income statements for the three years.

2. Explain why net income has decreased when sales have increased.

3. Prepare an income statement for Year 4. Sales volume in units is expected to increase by 10% and costs are expected to increase by 8%.

4. Do you think BPO should raise its prices or maintain the same selling prices? Explain your answer.

■ REQUIRED

ACCOUNTING AND ETHICS: WHAT WOULD YOU DO?

(LO 4, 5) CASE 15-6 PROVISIONS IN A LOAN AGREEMENT

As controller of Midwest Construction Company, you are reviewing the financial statements for the year just ended with your assistant, Dave Jackson. As part of the review, he reminds you of an existing loan agreement with Southern National Bank. Midwest has agreed to the following conditions:

- The current ratio will be maintained at a minimum level of 1.5:1.0 at all times.
- The debt-to-equity ratio will not exceed .5:1.0 at any time.

Jackson has drawn up the following preliminary, condensed balance sheet for the year just ended:

MIDWEST CONSTRUCTION COMPANY
BALANCE SHEET
DECEMBER 31
(IN MILLIONS OF DOLLARS)

Current assets	$16	Current liabilities	$10
Long-term assets	64	Long-term debt	15
		Stockholders' equity	55
Total	$80	Total	$80

Jackson wants to discuss two items with you relative to these statements:

First, long-term debt currently includes a $5 million note payable to Eastern State Bank that is due in six months. The plan is to go to Eastern before the note is due and ask it to extend the maturity date of the note for five years. Jackson doesn't believe that Midwest needs to include the $5 million in current liabilities because the plan is to roll over the note.

Second, in December of this year, Midwest received a $2 million deposit from the state for a major road project. The contract calls for the work to be performed over the next 18 months. Jackson recorded the $2 million as revenue this year because the contract is with the state; there shouldn't be any question about being able to collect.

■ REQUIRED

1. Based on the balance sheet Jackson prepared, is Midwest in compliance with its loan agreement with Southern? Support your answer with any necessary computations.

2. What would you do with the two items in question? Do you see anything wrong with the way Jackson has handled each of them? Explain your answer.

3. Prepare a revised balance sheet based on your answer to part 2. Also, compute a revised current ratio and debt-to-equity ratio. Based on the revised ratios, is Midwest in compliance with its loan agreement?

(LO 4) CASE 15-7 INVENTORY TURNOVER

Garden Fresh, Inc., is a wholesaler of fresh fruits and vegetables. Each year it submits a set of financial ratios to a trade association. Even though the association doesn't publish the individual ratios for each company, the president of Garden Fresh thinks it is important for public relations that his company look as good as possible. Due to the nature of the fresh fruits and vegetables business, one of the major ratios tracked by the association is inventory turnover. Inventory stated at FIFO cost was as follows:

| | YEAR ENDING DECEMBER 31 | |
	1995	1994
Fruits	$10,000	$ 9,000
Vegetables	30,000	33,000
Total	$40,000	$42,000

Sales revenue for the year ending December 31, 1995 is $3,690,000. The company's gross profit ratio is normally 40%.

Based on these data, the president thinks the company should report an inventory turnover ratio of 90 times per year.

■ REQUIRED

1. Explain with the necessary calculations how the president came up with an inventory turnover ratio of 90 times.

2. Do you think the company should report a turnover ratio of 90 times? If not, explain why you disagree and explain, with calculations, what you think the ratio should be.

3. Assume you are the controller for Garden Fresh. What will you tell the president?

ANALYTICAL SOFTWARE CASE

To the Student: Your instructor may assign one or more parts of the analytical software case that is designed to accompany this chapter. This multi-part case gives you a chance to work with real financial statement data using software that stimulates, guides, and hones your analytical and problem-solving skills. It was created especially to support and strengthen your understanding of the chapter's Learning Objectives.

SOLUTION TO KEY TERMS QUIZ

Quiz 1:

1. Acid-test or quick ratio (p. 826)
2. Working capital (p. 825)
3. Current ratio (p. 826)
4. Number of days' sales in receivables (p. 829)
5. Cash flow from operations to current liabilities ratio (p. 827)
6. Accounts receivable turnover ratio (p. 828)
7. Number of days' sales in inventory (p. 830)
8. Cash to cash operating cycle (p. 830)
9. Inventory turnover ratio (p. 829)
10. Gross profit ratio (p. 824)
11. Vertical analysis (p. 818)
12. Profit margin ratio (p. 824)
13. Liquidity (p. 825)
14. Horizontal analysis (p. 817)

Quiz 2:

1. Return on stockholders' equity (p. 836)
2. Price-earnings ratio (p. 839)
3. Solvency (p. 831)
4. Return on sales (p. 835)
5. Earnings per share (p. 838)
6. Dividend payout ratio (p. 840)
7. Debt-to-equity ratio (p. 831)
8. Cash flow from operations to capital expenditures ratio (p. 833)
9. Return on assets (p. 834)
10. Asset turnover ratio (p. 835)
11. Dividend yield ratio (p. 840)
12. Leverage (p. 837)
13. Times interest earned ratio (p. 832)
14. Debt service coverage ratio (p. 833)
15. Profitability (p. 834)

INTEGRATIVE PROBLEM

FOR PART IV

COMPUTING AND COMPARING RATIOS FOR CONSOLIDATION IN U.S. AND BRITISH COMPANIES, PREPARING PROPOSAL ENTRY AND REVISED STATEMENTS TO REFLECT A CONSOLIDATION, AND RECOMMENDING FOR OR AGAINST THE PURCHASE.

The following condensed financial statements and additional information are available for Felknor, Inc. and Rimmer, Ltd., a British firm. Felknor is considering the acquisition of Rimmer but has asked your consulting firm for advice. The financial statements for Rimmer, Ltd. are presently stated in British pounds.

FELKNOR, INC.
BALANCE SHEET
AS OF DECEMBER 31, 1995
(IN MILLIONS OF DOLLARS)

Assets

Quick assets	$205
Other current assets	243
Total current assets	$448
Long-term assets	222
Total assets	$670

Liabilities

Current liabilities	$149
Long-term liabilities	63
Total liabilities	$212

Stockholders' equity

Common stock, $1 par	$ 10
Additional paid-in capital	140
Retained earnings	308
Total stockholders' equity	$458
Total liabilities and stockholders' equity	$670

FELKNOR, INC.
INCOME STATEMENT
FOR THE YEAR ENDED DECEMBER 31, 1995
(IN MILLIONS OF DOLLARS)

Net revenue	$130
Expenses:	
Cost of sales	57
Other expenses	50
Operating income	$ 23

Additional information for Felknor, Inc.:

1. Interest expense and income tax expense are not reflected on this income statement. Interest equals $1.4 million for 1995.

2. Income taxes amount to $6.5 million for 1995. The amount reflects a 30% rate of tax on income before taxes.

3. The market price of Felknor's common stock was $25 per share at the end of 1995.

RIMMER, LTD.
BALANCE SHEET
AS OF DECEMBER 31, 1995
(IN MILLIONS OF POUNDS £)

Assets

Quick assets	£19
Other current assets	17
Total current assets	£36
Long-term assets	52
Total assets	£88

Liabilities

Current liabilities	£18
Long-term liabilities	2
Total liabilities	20

Stockholders' equity

Common stock, $10 par	38
Additional paid-in capital	26.2
Retained earnings	3.8
Total stockholders' equity	£68
Total liabilities and stockholders' equity	£88

RIMMER, LTD.
INCOME STATEMENT
FOR THE YEAR ENDED DECEMBER 31, 1995
(IN MILLIONS OF POUNDS £)

Net revenue	£132
Expenses	
Cost of sales	94
Other expenses	31
Operating income	£ 7

Additional information for Rimmer, Ltd.:

1. This is Rimmer's first year of operation. Rimmer opened the facility at the beginning of 1995.

2. Interest expense and income tax expense are not reflected on this income statement. Interest equals £.7 million for 1995.

3. Income taxes amount to £2.5 million for 1995. This amount reflects a 40% rate of tax on income before taxes.

4. The market price of Rimmer's common stock was £10 per share at the end of 1995 (this was the equivalent of $16 per share in U.S. dollars).

5. Rimmer originally sold its stock at the beginning of 1995.

6. The following exchange rates are available:

	EXCHANGE RATE PER BRITISH POUND
Beginning of year	$1.5
End of year	1.6
Average for the year	1.5

The following industry-wide ratios are available for both Felknor and Rimmer:

	FELKNOR, INC.	RIMMER, LTD.
Current ratio	3.00	2.00
Acid-test ratio	1.50	1.00
Debt-to-equity ratio	0.30	0.65
Times interest earned	2 times	3 times
Return on assets	8.0%	15.0%
Return on stockholders' equity	10.0%	15.0%
Earnings per share	2.00	3.00
Price-earnings ratio	10.50	5.60

■ REQUIRED

1. For each of the industry-wide ratios listed above, compute the corresponding ratios for 1995 for:

a. Felknor, Inc., before the possible acquisition of Rimmer, Ltd.

b. Rimmer, Ltd., with all ratios based on British pounds.

2. Using the exchange rates provided, translate Rimmer's December 31, 1995 balance sheet and its 1995 income statement from British pounds into U.S. dollars.

3. For each of the industry-wide ratios, compute the corresponding ratios for 1995 for Rimmer, Ltd., with all ratios based on U.S. dollar amounts. Based on a comparison of these ratios to those calculated in part 1 (b), which of the ratios are affected by the translation process?

4. Assume that on December 31, 1995, Felknor, Inc. purchased all of the assets and assumed all of the liabilities of Rimmer, Ltd. for $110 million in cash. The fair values for all of Rimmer's assets and liabilities were equal to their book values on this date. Prepare the journal entry that would appear on Felknor's books to record the purchase of Rimmer.

5. Prepare a revised December 31, 1995 balance sheet and a revised 1995 income statement for Felknor to reflect the purchase of Rimmer.

6. For each of the industry-wide ratios, compute the corresponding ratios for 1995 for Felknor, Inc., assuming it purchases Rimmer, Ltd. on December 31, 1995. Based on a comparison of these ratios to those calculated in part 1(a), which of the ratios are improved and which of the ratios are adversely affected by the purchase of Rimmer?

7. As a consultant to Felknor, would you recommend that it purchase Rimmer? What other factors would be relevant to your recommendations? Explain your answers.

FINANCIAL STATEMENTS FOR BEN & JERRY'S HOMEMADE, INC.

These pages from the 1992 Annual Report of Ben & Jerry's Homemade, Inc., are your introduction to the company and its financial information. Use them to answer the questions posed in the Concept to Practice marginal boxes throughout the book.

Be sure to read the **Financial Funnies** running through the report; they are an easy way to learn about Ben & Jerry's in particular, financial statements generally, and the specialized terminology and statement relationships you've read about in Chapters 1–15. The Financial Funnies are not part of the formal financial statements, notes, management's discussion and analysis, or report of independent auditors—but they are an interesting and useful form of investor relations.

"From Concept to Practice" assignments, printed in the margins throughout the book, are based on the Ben & Jerry's annual report. For a convenient list of these assignments, see the **Index to "From Concept to Practice" Assignments** at the end of Appendix 1.

INTRO TO THE FINANCIAL STATEMENTS

One of our goals at Ben&Jerry's is to keep our Company friendly and accessible to small-scale individual investors. We have been told by some investors that our Annual Report serves them well in communicating the social part of our bottom line, but that they find the financial statements imposing and hard to understand.

What follows is our effort to explain some basic things about financial statements, why they are presented the way they are, and what they are designed to communicate. This information is not designed to comment on our financial statements in any way. The Management's Discussion and Analysis and the footnotes serve as Ben & Jerry's commentary on the financial statements. We invite you to read our Financial (not so very) Funnies and the separate financial statements and get in touch with our Investor Relations staff with any questions that occur to you.

FUN STUFF

In 1992, Ben & Jerry's has continued to seek and develop new and creative ways of addressing the three parts of our mission statement: Product, Social & Economic Missions.

7 1/2% of Ben & Jerry's '92 profit, or $917,000 went to Ben & Jerry's Foundation. The Foundation made awards to non-profit organizations & 1% for Peace, (a.k.a. Businesses for Social Responsibility).

Over 15,600 cows were needed to make the 5,600,000 gallons of cream and condensed skim milk used to make the ice cream produced in 1992.

In 1992 Ben & Jerry's donated 13,623 gallons of ice cream to various causes (9487 gallons in the state of Vermont). If you ate one 4-ounce serving per day, it would take you 1,194 years and 126 days to eat all of that ice cream.

Each farm that we buy milk from keeps an average of 75 cows and was responsible for the creation of over 275,000 gallons of ice cream.

Over 75,000 postcards were sent to Congress regarding children's issues and other national concerns following the 1992 Ben & Jerry's One World One Heart Festivals in Vermont, Newport, RI, Chicago and San Francisco.

Net sales in 1992 were $132 million, an increase of over 36% from the 1991 sales of $97 million.

In 1992, Ben&Jerry's recycled roughly 312,000 gallons of ice cream spillage by feeding it to 1500 pigs on Earl Mayo's farm in Stowe, Vermont. The pigs' favorite flavor was Cherry Garcia. They wouldn't touch Mint Chocolate Cookie.

MARKET INFORMATION

The Class A Common Stock is traded on the over-the-counter market under the symbol BJICA. The following table sets forth the high and low closing sales price for the Class A Common Stock on the NASDAQ National Market System for the period January 1, 1991 through March 31, 1993.

1992	High	Low
First Quarter	23	17 3/4
Second Quarter	27 1/2	16 1/2
Third Quarter	33	25
Fourth Quarter	31 3/4	26 1/4

1993	High	Low
First Quarter	32	22 1/4

1991	High	Low
First Quarter	9 5/8	7
Second Quarter	11 1/8	9
Third Quarter	16 1/2	9 5/8
Fourth Quarter	19 1/2	15 3/4

The Class B Common Stock is generally non-transferable and there is no trading market for the Class B Common Stock. The Class B Common Stock is freely convertible into Class A Common Stock on a share-for-share basis, and transferable thereafter.

The Company has never paid any cash dividends on the Class A Common Stock or the Class B Common Stock and the Company presently intends to reinvest earnings for use in its business and to finance future growth. Accordingly, the Board of Directors does not anticipate declaring any cash dividends in the foreseeable future.

As of April 30, 1993, there were approximately 9,132 holders of record of the Company's Class A Common Stock and 2,755 holders of record of the Company's Class B Common Stock.

Five Year Financial Highlights

(In thousands except per share data)

Summary of Operations:	Year Ended				
	12/26/92	12/28/91	12/29/90	12/30/89	12/31/88
Net sales	$ 131,969	$ 96,997	$ 77,024	$ 58,464	$ 47,561
Cost of sales	94,389	68,500	54,203	41,660	33,935
Gross profit	37,580	28,497	22,821	16,804	13,627
Selling, general and administrative expenses	26,243	21,264	17,639	13,009	10,655
Operating income	11,337	7,233	5,182	3,795	2,972
Other income (expense)—net	(23)	(729)	(709)	(362)	(274)
Income before taxes	11,314	6,504	4,473	3,433	2,698
Income taxes	4,639	2,765	1,864	1,380	1,079
Net income	6,675	3,739	2,609	2,053	1,618
Net income per common share[1]	$ 1.07	$ 0.67	$ 0.50	$ 0.40	$ 0.31
Weighted average common shares outstanding[1]	6,254,000	5,572,000	5,225,000	5,199,000	5,157,000

Balance Sheet Data:	Year Ended				
	12/26/92	12/28/91	12/29/90	12/30/89	12/31/88
Working capital	$ 18,053	$ 11,035	$ 8,202	$ 5,829	$ 5,614
Total assets	88,207	43,056	34,299	28,139	26,307
Long-term debt	2,641	2,787	8,948	9,328	9,670
Stockholders' equity[2]	66,760	26,269	16,101	13,405	11,245

[1] The per share amounts and average shares outstanding have been adjusted for the effects of all stock splits, including stock splits in the form of stock dividends.
[2] No cash dividends have been declared or paid by the Company on its capital stock since the Company's organization. The Company intends to reinvest earnings for use in its business and to finance future growth. Accordingly, the Board of Directors does not anticipate declaring any cash dividends in the foreseeable future.

MANAGEMENT'S DISCUSSION AND ANALYSIS OF FINANCIAL CONDITION AND RESULTS OF OPERATIONS

Results of Operations

The following table shows certain items as a percentage of net sales which are included in the Company's Statement of Income and the percentage increase (decrease) of such items as compared to the indicated prior period.

	Percentage of Net Sales Year Ended			Annual Increase (Decrease)		
	12/26/92	12/28/91	12/29/90	1992 Compared to 1991	1991 Compared to 1990	1990 Compared to 1989
Net sales	100.0 %	100.0 %	100.0 %	36.1 %	25.9 %	31.7 %
Cost of sales	71.5	70.6	70.4	37.8	26.4	30.1
Gross profit	28.5	29.4	29.6	31.9	24.9	35.8
Selling, general and administrative expenses	19.9	21.9	22.9	23.4	20.6	35.6
Operating income	8.6	7.5	6.7	56.7	39.6	36.5
Other income (expenses)	0.0	(0.8)	(0.9)	(96.9)	(2.8)	(95.9)
Income before income taxes	8.6	6.7	5.8	74.0	45.4	30.3
Federal and state income taxes	3.5	2.9	2.4	67.8	48.3	35.0
Net income	5.1 %	3.9 %	3.4 %	78.5	43.3	27.1 %

Sales

Net sales in 1992 increased 36% to $132 million from $97 million in 1991. This increase is due to a 40% increase in unit sales of packaged pints over the prior year. The increase in packaged pint sales is primarily due to the national introduction of frozen yogurt pints which commenced in January 1992 and accounted for 15% of total sales as compared with approximately 3% in 1991, as well as to a new flavor (Chocolate Chip Cookie Dough) introduced in March 1991 which accounted for 17% of total sales as compared to 12% of total sales in 1991. Additional growth in many target markets, especially on the West Coast, and also in non-target markets also contributed to the increase in pint sales. The increase in net sales was partially offset by loss of sales from Ben & Jerry's Light, a lower-fat version of its ice cream, which was discontinued as part of the national introduction of frozen yogurt.

Net sales of all packaged pints represented 83% of total net sales compared to 80% in 1991 and 78% in 1990. Net sales of ice cream packaged

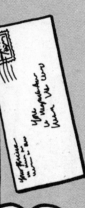

AAH, SMART DECISIONS ABOUT BEN & JERRY'S FINANCES – A REALLY IMPORTANT PART OF BEING SOCIALLY RESPONSIBLE – IMPORTANT FOR OUR EMPLOYEES AND OUR STOCKHOLDERS. REMEMBER, WE WOULDN'T BE AROUND TO BE SOCIALLY RESPONSIBLE IF WE DIDN'T MANAGE OUR MONEY RESPONSIBLY

LET'S TAKE A LOOK AT THE BALANCE SHEET & THE STATEMENT OF INCOME. THERE ARE OTHER FINANCIAL STATEMENTS, BUT WE'LL JUST TAKE THOSE TWO FOR NOW.

YOU GET A LETTER FROM A FRIEND AT THE END OF THE YEAR...

FRAN SMILED

in 2½ gallon containers increased 5% and represented 8% of total net sales compared to 10% in 1991 and 11% in 1990. Net sales of novelties increased 15% and represented 7% of total net sales in 1992 and 1991 as compared to 8% in 1990. The increase in novelties is primarily due to a promotion of these products in May and June 1992. Retail sales in the Company-owned scoop and gift shops increased approximately 5% in 1992 and were approximately 2% of total net sales in 1992 compared to 3% in 1991 and 1990.

Net sales in 1991 increased 26% to $97 million from $77 million in 1990. This increase in total net sales was primarily due to increased unit sales of the Company's super premium ice cream packaged in pints which increased 22%, primarily reflecting sales of the new flavor introductions, increased sales in certain regions of the country, especially on the West Coast, and also to an 8% price increase on packaged pints effective January 1, 1991. In addition, sales of ice cream packaged in 2½ gallon containers increased 11%, sales of novelties increased 14% and retail sales in the Company-owned scoop and gift shops increased approximately 8% in 1991.

The rate of growth in the Company's net sales slowed during the fourth quarter of 1992 as compared to the first three quarters of 1992, and the Company does not expect to achieve in 1993 the rate of growth in net sales and earnings experienced in the first three quarters of 1992.

Cost of Sales

Cost of sales in 1992 increased $25.9 million or 38% over 1991 while overall gross margins decreased from 29.4% of net sales to 28.5%. The lower gross margin percentage is primarily the result of higher manufacturing costs for having additional product produced for the Company by Edy's, a subsidiary of Dreyer's, at the Edy's plant in Fort Wayne, Indiana. In 1992, approximately 42% of the packaged pints manufactured by the Company were manufactured by Edy's as compared with approximately 32% in 1991. In addition, gross profit decreased due to costs associated with increasing the manufacturing capacity and adding pint manufacturing capability at the Company's plant in Springfield, Vermont, installing an interim pint line at the St. Albans Cooperative Creamery, and delays in the construction of the Company's new central distribution facility in Rockingham, Vermont.

Cost of sales in 1991 increased $14.3 million, or 26% over 1990, while overall gross margins slightly decreased from 29.6% to 29.4%. The slightly lower gross margin is primarily due to increased sales of higher cost products in the overall mix of total sales partially offset by the January 1, 1991 price increase on all packaged pints and slightly lower dairy costs.

Cost of sales in 1992 and 1991 would have been lower but for the Company's commitment, which began on May 1, 1991, to pay a certain minimum price for its dairy ingredients, other than yogurt cultures, which is based on the average price for dairy products in certain prior periods. This commitment is intended to foster the long-term supply of Vermont dairy products, free of chemical substances, against the marketplace background of a continuing trend of decreasing family dairy farms in Vermont. This commitment may continue to have some adverse impact on the Company's gross profit.

Selling, General and Administrative Expenses

Selling, general and administrative expenses increased 23% to $26.2 million from $21.3 million and decreased as a percentage of sales from 21.9% in 1991 to 19.9% in 1992. The dollar increase reflects higher selling, general administrative and legal costs and higher marketing expenditures for new product introductions – principally the national introduction of frozen yogurt. The decrease as a percentage of net sales is due to the sales growth outpacing that of the Company's sales and administrative support structure. Management expects to increase the Company's infrastructure to support the growth in net sales.

Selling, general and administrative expenses increased 21% to $21.3 million from $17.6 million and decreased as a percentage of sales to 21.9% in 1991 from 22.9% in 1990. The dollar increase is due to higher selling and general administrative and legal expenses. The decrease in selling, general and administrative expenses as a percentage of sales reflects principally the previous year's summer advertising and promotional campaign related to the national product introduction of Ben & Jerry's Light.

Other Income (Expenses) – Net

Other expense decreased $706,000 in 1992 as compared to 1991 due to lower interest costs and higher interest income. Interest expense decreased $555,000 due to the Company's redemption in September 1991 of its 9 1/2% convertible subordinated debentures. In addition, the Company did not borrow on its working capital line of credit in 1992 compared to average outstanding borrowings of $2.4 million in 1991. Interest income increased $248,000 due to interest earned on investments made with the proceeds of the Company's public stock offering in September 1992, pending their use in the Company's business.

Interest income decreased $149,000 in 1991 as compared to 1990 due to lower interest rates and reduced cash availability. Interest expense decreased $132,000 due to the Company's redemption of its $5.8 million outstanding 9 1/2% convertible debentures in September, 1991.

Income Taxes

Federal and state income taxes increased $1.9 million in 1992 as compared to 1991, reflecting higher pre-tax income slightly offset by a lower effective tax rate of 41.0% versus 42.5% in 1991. The lower effective tax rate reflected an increase in certain tax-exempt interest income and a lower overall state tax rate than in previous years as a result of a higher percentage of income being taxed at lower state rates.

Federal and state income taxes increased $900,000 in 1991 as compared to 1990, reflecting higher pre-tax income and a higher effective tax rate of 42.5% compared to 41.7% in 1990. The higher effective tax rate was caused by higher state taxes than in previous years.

Net Income

As a result of the foregoing, the Company's net income increased 78.5% to $6.7 million compared to $3.7 million in 1991 and $2.6 million in 1990. Net income as a percentage of net sales increased to 5.1% in 1992 from 3.9% in 1991 and 3.4% in 1990. Fully diluted net income per share, adjusted for the effect of all stock splits, increased 59.7% to $.67 in 1992 as compared to $.67 in 1991, and $.50 in 1990.

Seasonality

The Company typically experiences more demand for its products during the summer than during the winter.

Inflation

Inflation has not had a material effect on the Company's business to date. Management believes that the effects of inflation and changing prices have been successfully managed, with both margins and earnings being protected through a combination of pricing adjustments, cost control programs and productivity gains.

Other Matters

In February 1992, the Financial Accounting Standards Board ("FASB") issued Financial Accounting Standards ("FAS")No. 109 "Accounting for Income Taxes." The new accounting standard will be adopted in the first quarter of 1993. The cumulative effect through December 1992 of the change in accounting has been estimated to be approximately $100,000. The FASB issued FAS No. 106 "Employers' Accounting for Postretirement Benefits Other Than Pensions" in December 1990 and FAS No. 112 "Employers' Accounting for Postemployment Benefits" in November 1992. These standards are not applicable to the Company because the Company does not provide the type of benefits that are addressed by these standards.

Liquidity and Capital Resources

In September and October 1992 the Company issued 1,170,000 shares of Class A Common Stock in a $33.5 million public stock offering. Net proceeds of this offering will be used to build and equip a third manufacturing plant in St. Albans, Vermont and for working capital and general corporate purposes. As of December 26, 1992 the majority of these proceeds had been invested in short-term tax-free municipal securities and a significant portion of these short-term investments were classified for financial statement purposes as non-current assets reflecting their intended use in the future.

Inventories increased $8 million from $9 million at the end of 1991 to $17 million at December 26, 1992. This buildup reflects increased sales and management's decision to increase inventory levels to ensure demand is satisfied throughout 1993 and 1994 until the New Plant is up and running efficiently and also reflects the effect of a lower rate of sales growth in the fourth quarter of 1992. The levels of inventories at the end of 1992 represents approximately ten weeks as compared to six weeks at the end of 1991. Management plans to reduce this level of inventories over the first half of 1993 and expects to carry approximately six to eight weeks of inventory for the remainder of 1993.

Working capital at December 26, 1992 was approximately $18.1 million compared to $11.0 million at December 28, 1991. The increase was due primarily to the increase in inventories, partially offset by an increase in accounts payable and accrued expenses, both reflecting a buildup of inventory at year-end. Also contributing was accounts receivable, reflecting increased sales.

Net cash provided by operations was $3.9 million in 1992. Approximately $10.5 million was used for net additions to property, plant and equipment, $585,000 was used to repurchase the license rights for the Company's products in Canada and

$25.2 million, net, was invested in municipal debt instruments. Funds were provided by operations, the stock offering and from cash balances existing at December 28, 1991. The net result was a $650,000 increase in cash and cash equivalents at year-end 1992. There were no borrowings on the Company's working capital line of credit during 1992 compared with average outstanding borrowings of $2.4 million during 1991.

The Company's production capacity for packaged pints was constrained during the second and third quarters of 1992 and constraints on production capacity are expected to continue until the New Plant becomes fully operational. During 1992, the Company took steps to increase its available production capacity including the addition, in June 1992, of an interim pint manufacturing line in St. Albans, Vermont at the St. Albans Cooperative Creamery. The Company also increased the manufacturing capacity and added pint manufacturing capability to its 2½ gallon (bulk) line at its plant in Springfield, Vermont. This pint

manufacturing capability became available in September 1992. In addition, beginning in May 1992, the Company increased the amount of packaged pints being produced by Edy's Grand Ice Cream, Inc. under the manufacturing and warehouse agreement described in the next paragraph. Due to production constraints for the manufacture of packaged pints the Company started in April 1992 to limit each of its distributors to an allocation of product not exceeding specified amounts from time to time over the distributor's 1992 sales projections. These limits remained in place through October 1992 and the Company anticipates that it may have to maintain such allocation controls during periods of high demand for the Company's products until the New Plant is fully operational which is currently expected to occur sometime in 1994.

During the second quarter of 1989, the Company entered into a manufacturing and warehouse agreement with Edy's Grand Ice Cream, Inc. a subsidiary of Dreyer's Grand Ice Cream, Inc. to manufacture

product at Edy's plant in Fort Wayne, Indiana in accordance with specifications and quality control provided by the Company and using dairy products from Vermont. In September 1992 the Company amended this agreement to extend the period for an additional two years expiring December 1994. The agreement specifies certain minimum quantities which the Company is obligated to purchase, which represented approximately 7.4 million gallons or $51.8 million in future commitments at December 26, 1992. The agreement also specifies certain maximum quantities which the Company may manufacture. This agreement assists the Company in meeting its current and near-term expected product demand. Because per unit manufacturing costs are higher under this agreement than at the Company's plants, the Company expects this agreement to continue to have an adverse impact on its gross profit as a percentage of net sales through the expiration of the agreement.

In October 1992, the Company began construction of the New Plant in St. Albans, Vermont. The cost of building and equipping the New Plant is estimated to be approximately $25 million, of which $840,000 was spent in 1992. Construction is currently scheduled to be completed in 1994.

In addition to the above, the Company had other capital expenditures of approximately $9.7 million in 1992. Capital projects included the construction of the interim pint manufacturing line in St. Albans, Vermont (the assets of which are contemplated to be transferred to the New Plant), increasing 2 1/2 gallon (bulk) manufacturing capacity at the Springfield, Vermont plant and adding pint manufacturing capability to this line, and constructing and equipping a new central distribution facility in Rockingham, Vermont (which became operational in March 1993). Capital expenditures also include various manufacturing process improvements and other administrative capital needs.

The Company anticipates capital expenditures of approximately $6.0 million (excluding the cost of the New Plant) in 1993. These capital projects include upgrading the Waterbury and Springfield plants by installing process control equipment to the manufacturing facilities and expanding the Waterbury tours operation.

Management believes that internally generated funds, cash currently on hand (and investments held in marketable securities pending their use in the business), equipment lease financing and bank borrowings will be adequate to meet anticipated operating and capital requirements. Bank borrowings may include borrowings under an existing $9.0 million annual working capital line of credit with Marine Midland Bank, N.A., expiring April 30, 1993, subject to agreement at or before each advance as to amount, interest rate, maturity and other terms and conditions, or long-term debt that may be issued by the Company. The interest rate is currently stated at the bank's prime rate less .25%. As of March 19, 1993, there were no amounts outstanding under this line.

IMAGINE THAT AT MIDNIGHT ON THE LAST DAY OF THE FISCAL YEAR, FRAN THE SUPER CFO HOLLERS "STOP"... "STOP!"

1 MILLION 3, 1 MILLION 4, 1 MILLION 5,...

THEN SHE FLIES AROUND TO ALL THE SITES & COUNTS EVERYTHING ~ MONEY, TRUCKS FULL OF ICE CREAM, BILLS TO BE PAID, ETC. SHE WOULD COME UP WITH...

MIL

CONSOLIDATED BALANCE SHEET
ASSETS

	December 26, 1992	December 28, 1991
Current assets:		
Cash and cash equivalents	$ 7,356,133	$ 6,704,006
Accounts receivable, less allowance for doubtful accounts: $350,000 in 1992 and 1991	8,849,326	6,939,975
Income taxes receivable	306,193	
Inventories	17,089,857	8,999,666
Deferred income taxes	1,730,000	984,000
Prepaid expenses	208,996	107,325
Total current assets	35,540,505	23,734,972
Property, plant and equipment	39,312,513	28,496,080
Less accumulated depreciation	12,575,088	9,196,551
	26,737,425	19,299,529
Investments	25,200,000	
Other assets	728,885	21,598
	$ 88,206,815	$ 43,056,099

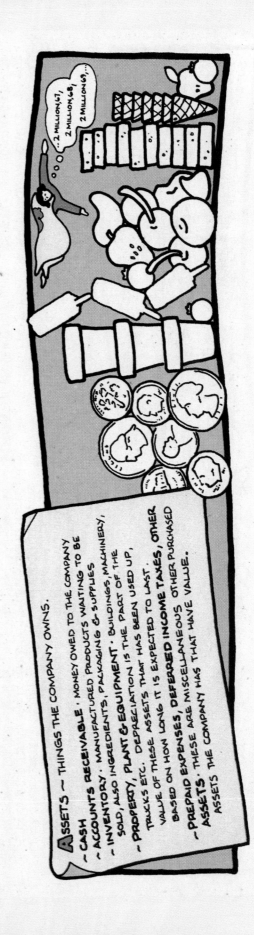

ASSETS — THINGS THE COMPANY OWNS.

~ CASH

~ ACCOUNTS RECEIVABLE ~ MONEY OWED TO THE COMPANY

~ INVENTORY ~ MANUFACTURED PRODUCTS WAITING TO BE SOLD, ALSO INGREDIENTS, PACKAGING & SUPPLIES

~ PROPERTY, PLANT & EQUIPMENT ~ BUILDINGS, MACHINERY, TRUCKS ETC. DEPRECIATION IS THE PART OF THE VALUE OF THESE ASSETS THAT HAS BEEN USED UP, BASED ON HOW LONG IT IS EXPECTED TO LAST.

~ PREPAID EXPENSES, DEFERRED INCOME TAXES, OTHER ASSETS ~ THESE ARE MISCELLANEOUS OTHER PURCHASED ASSETS THE COMPANY HAS THAT HAVE VALUE.

...2 MILLION, 47, 2 MILLION, 68, 2 MILLION, 69,...

LIABILITIES AND STOCKHOLDERS' EQUITY

	December 26, 1992	December 28, 1991
Current liabilities:		
Accounts payable and accrued expenses	$16,858,919	$11,951,308
Income taxes payable	628,098	233,853
Current portion of long-term debt and obligations under capital lease	17,487,017	514,905
Total current liabilities		12,700,066
Long-term debt and obligations under captial lease	2,640,982	2,786,659
Deferred income taxes	1,319,000	1,300,000
Commitments and contingencies		
Stockholders' equity:		
$1.20 noncumulative Class A preferred stock – $1.00 par value, redeemable at $12.00 per share; 900 shares authorized, issued and outstanding, aggregate preference on voluntary or involuntary liquidation – $9,000	900	900
Class A common stock – $.033 par value; authorized 10,000,000 shares; issued 6,239,575 shares at December 26, 1992 and 5,033,917 shares at December 28, 1991	206,327	166,541
Class B common stock – $.033 par value; authorized 3,000,000 shares; issued 962,008 shares at December 26, 1992 and 986,888 shares at December 28, 1991	31,746	32,565
Additional paid-in capital	47,941,134	14,261,484
Retained earnings	19,984,461	13,309,121
Unearned compensation	(38,014)	(134,588)
Treasury stock, at cost: 66,453 Class A and 1,092 Class B shares at December 26, 1992 and 66,419 Class A and 1,075 Class B shares at December 28, 1991	(1,366,738)	(1,366,649)
Total stockholders' equity	66,759,816	26,269,374
	$88,206,815	$43,056,099

See accompanying notes.

LIABILITIES ~ WHAT THE COMPANY OWES.

- **CURRENT LIABILITIES** – BILLS, PAYROLL DUE, TAXES & OTHER OBLIGATIONS THAT HAVE TO BE PAID WITHIN A YEAR.

- **LONG TERM DEBT & OBLIGATIONS UNDER CAPITAL LEASES** – LOANS OR AGREEMENTS TO PAY FOR USE OF EQUIPMENT A YEAR OR MORE FROM NOW.

- **OTHER LIABILITIES** – MISCELLANEOUS OTHER FINANCIAL COMMITMENTS.

STOCKHOLDERS' EQUITY

THIS IS CALLED THE "BOOK VALUE" OF THE OWNERS' STAKE IN THE COMPANY. IT INCLUDES PROCEEDS THE COMPANY RECEIVED FROM THE INITIAL AND SUBSEQUENT SALES OF STOCK TO THE PUBLIC, PLUS ACCUMULATED PROFITS, CALLED RETAINED EARNINGS.

THIS BOOK VALUE IS NOT THE SAME AS THE VALUE OF STOCK ON THE PUBLIC STOCK MARKET WHICH IS CALLED THE "MARKET VALUE". THE STOCK MARKET DETERMINES IN ITS OWN WAYS WHETHER THE COMPANY IS WORTH MORE THAN THE BOOK VALUE OF WHAT IT OWNS MINUS WHAT IT OWES. FOR EXAMPLE, A COMPANY'S STOCK PRICE CHANGES REGULARLY WITHOUT REGARD TO THE VALUE OF THE ASSETS & LIABILITIES IT USES TO RUN ITS BUSINESS.

CONSOLIDATED STATEMENT OF INCOME

		Years Ended	
	December 26, 1992	December 28, 1991	December 29, 1990
Net sales	$ 131,968,814	$ 96,997,339	$ 77,024,037
Cost of sales	94,389,391	68,500,402	54,202,387
Gross profit	37,579,423	28,496,937	22,821,650
Selling, general and administrative expenses	26,242,761	21,264,214	17,639,357
Operating income	11,336,662	7,232,723	5,182,293
Other income (expenses):			
Interest income	394,817	147,058	296,329
Interest expense	(181,577)	(736,248)	(868,736)
Other	(235,765)	(139,627)	(136,578)
	(22,525)	(728,817)	(708,985)
Income before income taxes	11,314,137	6,503,906	4,473,308
Income taxes	4,638,797	2,764,523	1,864,063
Net income	$ 6,675,340	$ 3,739,383	$ 2,609,245
Net income per common share	$ 1.07	$ 0.67	$ 0.50
Weighted average number of common shares outstanding	6,253,825	5,572,368	5,224,667

See accompanying notes.

28

STATEMENT OF INCOME

- NET SALES - THIS IS THE TOTAL SALES OF THE COMPANY MINUS THE VALUE OF PRODUCT DISCOUNTED OR RETURNED.
- COST OF SALES - WHAT IT COST TO MAKE & STORE THE PRODUCTS UNTIL THEY ARE SOLD. INCLUDES THE PACKAGING, LABOR COSTS, & THE COST TO RUN INGREDIENTS, & STORAGE MACHINERY.
- GROSS PROFIT - NET SALES MINUS COST OF SALES.
- SELLING & ADMINISTRATIVE EXPENSES - THESE ARE THE COSTS OF MARKETING & SELLING THE PRODUCT AFTER IT HAS BEEN MADE, PLUS ALL OF THE ADMINISTRATIVE COSTS TO RUN THE COMPANY.

- OPERATING INCOME - GROSS PROFIT MINUS SELLING, GENERAL & ADMINISTRATIVE EXPENSES. THIS MEASURES HOW MUCH A COMPANY EARNS (BEFORE TAXES) FROM THE CORE BUSINESS IT IS IN.
- INCOME BEFORE TAXES, INCOME TAXES & NET INCOME - INCOME TAXES ARE THE AMOUNT OF FEDERAL & STATE TAXES PAID OR DUE BASED ON THE COMPANY'S BOOK INCOME. SUBTRACTING THOSE TAXES FROM INCOME BEFORE TAXES RESULTS IN NET INCOME OR THE "BOTTOM LINE." CONTINUED → (REMEMBER, BEN&JERRY'S HAS TWO "BOTTOM LINES.")

CONSOLIDATED STATEMENT OF CASH FLOWS

Years Ended	12/26/92	12/28/91	12/29/90
Cash flows from operating activities:			
Net income	$ 6,675,340	$ 3,739,383	$ 2,609,245
Adjustments to reconcile net income to net cash provided			
by operating activities:			
Depreciation and amortization	3,455,720	2,980,826	2,320,666
Provision for doubtful accounts receivable		100,000	88,000
Deferred income taxes	(727,000)	(294,000)	91,000
Amortization of unearned compensation	96,574	77,162	
(Gain) Loss on disposition of assets	(14,232)	13,250	3,666
Stock awards	57,000	302,601	
Changes in assets and liabilities:			
Accounts receivable	(1,909,351)	(1,995,530)	(1,462,567)
Income tax receivable/payable	(540,046)	(98,441)	390,413
Inventories	(8,090,191)	1,083,476	(6,086,592)
Prepaid expenses	(101,671)	10,601	72,363
Other assets	93,656		
Accounts payable and accrued expenses	4,907,611	4,399,156	3,198,786
Net cash provided by operating activities	3,903,410	10,318,484	1,224,980
Cash flows from investing activities:			
Additions to property, plant and equipment	(10,447,007)	(4,034,124)	(2,597,635)
Proceeds from sale of property, plant and equipment	105,084	70,000	42,500
Increase in investments	(25,200,000)		
Changes in other assets	(836,657)		
Net cash used for investing activities	(36,378,580)	(3,964,124)	(2,555,135)
Cash flows from financing activities:			
Borrowings on short-term debt		8,900,000	
Repayments of short-term debt		(8,900,000)	
Repayments of long-term debt and capital leases	(534,231)	(439,002)	(348,731)
Net proceeds from issuance of common stock	33,661,528	95,325	81,763
Payment of bond redemption costs		(102,867)	
Net cash provided by (used for) financing activities	33,127,297	(446,544)	(266,968)
Increase (decrease) in cash and cash equivalents	652,127	5,907,816	(1,597,123)
Cash and cash equivalents at beginning of year	6,704,006	796,190	2,393,313
Cash and cash equivalents at end of year	$ 7,356,133	$6,704,006	$ 796,190

See accompanying notes.

CONSOLIDATED STATEMENT OF STOCKHOLDERS' EQUITY

	Preferred Stock Par Value	Common Stock Class A Par Value	Class B Par Value
Balance at December 30, 1989	$ 900	$131,909	$38,383
Net income			
Common Stock forfeited under restricted stock plan (306 Class A shares and 150 Class B shares)			
Common Stock issued under stock purchase plan (12,462 shares)		411	
Conversion of Class B shares to Class A shares (78,048 shares)		2,576	(2,576)
Conversion of subordinated debentures to Class A shares (644 shares)		21	
Balance at December 29, 1990	900	134,917	35,807
Net income			
Common stock issued under restricted stock plan (53,450 Class A shares)			
Amortization of unearned compensation			
Conversion of Class B shares to Class A shares (98,230 shares)		3,242	(3,242)
Conversion of subordinated debentures to Class A shares (847,804 shares)		27,976	
Common stock forfeited under restricted stock plan (40 Class A shares and 20 Class B shares)			
Common stock issued under stock purchase plan (12,292 Class A shares)		406	
Common stock contributed (89,624 Class A shares)			
Balance at December 28, 1991	900	166,541	32,565
Net income			
Common stock issued through public offering (1,170,000 Class A shares)		38,610	
Common stock issued under stock purchase plan (8,778 Class A shares)		291	
Common stock issued under restricted stock plan (2,000 Class A shares)		66	
Common stock forfeited under restricted stock plan (34 Class A shares and 17 Class B shares)			
Conversion of Class B to Class A shares (24,880 shares)		819	(819)
Amortization of unearned compensation			
Balance at December 26, 1992	$ 900	$ 206,327	$ 31,746

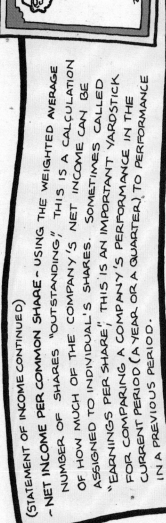

(STATEMENT OF INCOME CONTINUED)

~ NET INCOME PER COMMON SHARE ~ USING THE WEIGHTED AVERAGE NUMBER OF SHARES "OUTSTANDING," THIS IS A CALCULATION OF HOW MUCH OF THE COMPANY'S NET INCOME CAN BE ASSIGNED TO INDIVIDUAL'S SHARES. SOMETIMES CALLED "EARNINGS PER SHARE," THIS IS AN IMPORTANT YARDSTICK FOR COMPARING A COMPANY'S PERFORMANCE IN THE CURRENT PERIOD (A YEAR, OR A QUARTER) TO PERFORMANCE IN A PREVIOUS PERIOD.

	Additional Paid-in Capital	Retained Earnings	Unearned Compensation	Treasury Stock Class A Cost	Treasury Stock Class B Cost
	$6,302,851	$6,960,493	$ 0	($24,729)	($4,413)
	2,609,245			(534)	(264)
	82,149				
	4,978				
	6,389,978	9,569,738	0	(25,263)	(4,677)
	(53,450)	3,739,383	(211,750)	567,907	
	5,925,527		77,162		
	94,919			(71)	(35)
	1,904,510			(1,904,510)	
	14,261,484	13,309,121	(134,588)	(1,361,937)	(4,712)
	33,467,490	6,675,340			
	155,226			(59)	(30)
	56,934		96,574		
	$47,941,134	$19,984,461	$ (38,014)	$ (1,361,996)	$ (4,742)

See accompanying notes.

WOW AGAIN. I'M BEGINNING TO THINK I CAN FIGURE THIS OUT!

HERE'S THE TEST. FLIP THROUGH THE FINANCIAL STATEMENTS IN THIS ANNUAL REPORT & TAKE A HARD LOOK AT THEM. READ THE MANAGEMENT'S DISCUSSION & ANALYSIS & THE FOOTNOTES. GO AHEAD — YOU CAN DO IT. THEN THINK OF THE QUESTIONS YOU WANT TO ASK. CALL OR WRITE TO OUR INVESTOR RELATIONS STAFF. SEE IF YOU CAN STUMP 'EM. I DARE YOU.

OOH! WHAT A CHALLENGE. SEE YOU AT THE ANNUAL MEETING!

TO BE CONTINUED · NEXT YEAR.

31

NOTES TO CONSOLIDATED FINANCIAL STATEMENTS

1. SIGNIFICANT ACCOUNTING POLICIES

Business

Ben & Jerry's Homemade, Inc. (the Company) makes and sells super premium ice cream and other frozen dessert products through distributors and directly to retail outlets, including Company-owned and franchised ice cream parlors.

Principles of Consolidation

The consolidated financial statements include the accounts of the Company and all its wholly-owned subsidiaries. Intercompany accounts and transactions have been eliminated.

Fiscal Year

The Company's fiscal year is a fifty-two or fifty-three week period ending on the last Saturday in December.

Inventories

Inventories are stated at the lower of cost or market. Cost is determined by the first-in, first-out method.

Cash Equivalents and Investments

Cash equivalents represent highly liquid investments with maturities of three months or less at date of purchase. Investments representing bank certificates of deposit and tax-exempt debt instruments with a maturity of between three months and one year, are stated at aggregate amortized cost, which approximates market. Certain investments which have a maturity of less than three months have been classified as long-term to reflect their intended use to finance capital projects.

Concentration of Credit Risk

Financial instruments, which potentially subject the Company to concentration of risk, consist of cash, investments and trade receivables. The Company places its investments in highly rated financial institutions and investment grade short-term instruments, which limits the amount of credit exposure. The Company sells its products primarily to frozen food distribution companies. The Company performs ongoing credit evaluations of its customers and maintains reserves for potential credit losses. Historically, the Company has not experienced significant losses related to investments or trade receivables.

Property, Plant and Equipment

Property, plant and equipment are carried at cost. Depreciation, including amortization of leasehold improvements, is computed using the straight-line method over the estimated useful lives of the related assets. Amortization of assets under capital leases is computed on the straight-line method over the lease term and is included in depreciation expense in the accompanying financial statements.

Revenue Recognition – Franchising Operations

The Company recognizes initial franchise fees for individual stores as income when services required by the franchise agreement have been performed and the franchisee opens for business. Initial franchise fees relating to area franchise agreements are recognized in proportion to the stores for which the required mandatory services

have been substantially performed. Franchise fees recognized as income were $91,250, $95,500 and $117,416 in 1992, 1991 and 1990, respectively. These amounts have been included in net sales of the respective periods.

Income Taxes

Income tax expense is based on income for financial reporting purposes. Deferred income taxes are provided for timing differences between financial reporting and taxable income.

Earnings Per Share

Net income per common share is computed based on the weighted average number of shares of Class A and Class B Common Stock outstanding during the period, such shares having been adjusted for the effects of all stock splits, including stock splits in the form of stock dividends. Supplementary earnings per share, assuming conversions of the Company's 9.5% subordinated convertible debentures made during 1991 and 1990 had occurred at the beginning of the respective periods, were not materially different from the amounts presented.

Reclassifications

Certain amounts included in the financial statements for prior years have been reclassified to conform to the December 26, 1992 presentation.

2. INVENTORIES

Inventories consisted of the following:

	1992	1991
Ice cream and ingredients	$15,789,442	$ 8,247,887
Paper goods	484,446	291,715
Food, beverages, and gift items	815,969	460,064
	$17,089,857	$ 8,999,666

3. PROPERTY, PLANT AND EQUIPMENT

Property, plant and equipment consisted of the following:

	1992	1991	Estimated Useful Lives/ Lease Term
Land and improvements	$ 2,404,198	$ 2,398,684	15-25 years
Land under capital lease	846,458	481,868	
Buildings	12,229,708	9,794,344	25 years
Equipment and furniture	18,549,465	12,775,467	3-15 years
Equipment under capital lease	1,460,848	1,323,691	5 years
Leasehold improvements	2,008,768	1,051,738	3-10 years
Construction in progress	1,813,068	670,288	
	$ 39,312,513	$ 28,496,080	

Accumulated depreciation at December 26, 1992 and December 28, 1991, included accumulated amortization of assets under capital lease of $921,620 and $607,665 respectively. Assets acquired under capital leases totalled $501,747 in 1992, $1,012,034 in 1991 and $0 in 1990.

4. ACCOUNTS PAYABLE AND ACCRUED EXPENSES

Accounts payable and accrued expenses consisted of the following:

	1992	1991
Trade accounts payable	$10,874,041	$ 7,873,374
Accrued expenses	4,223,997	3,072,935
Accrued payroll and related costs	1,107,179	761,023
Other	653,702	243,976
	$16,858,919	$11,951,308

5: INCOME TAXES

The provisions for income taxes consisted of the following:

	1992	1991	1990
Federal – current	$ 4,181,088	$ 2,299,100	$ 1,348,249
– deferred	(617,950)	(194,000)	64,000
	3,563,138	2,105,100	1,412,249
State – current	1,184,709	759,423	424,814
– deferred	(109,050)	(100,000)	27,000
	1,075,659	659,423	451,814
	$ 4,638,797	$ 2,764,523	$ 1,864,063

Reconciliations of actual income tax expense to the amount computed by applying the U.S. Federal income tax rate (34%) to income before taxes are as follows:

	1992	1991	1990
Tax at statutory federal income tax rate	$ 3,846,807	$ 2,211,328	$ 1,520,925
Increases in taxes resulting from:			
State income taxes, net of federal benefit	709,935	435,219	298,197
Other, net	82,055	117,976	44,941
	$ 4,638,797	$ 2,764,523	$ 1,864,063

Deferred income taxes result from timing differences in the recognition of revenues and expenses for tax and financial reporting purposes. The sources of these differences and their tax effect in 1992, 1991 and 1990 are as follows:

	1992	1991	1990
Tax depreciation in excess of (less than) book	$ (139,000)	$ 175,000	$ 294,000
Contributions	26,000	67,000	30,000
Inventory tax basis in excess of book basis	(110,000)	(142,000)	(7,000)
Reserves for litigation and other claims	80,000	(360,000)	(80,000)
Vacation accrual	(102,000)	(12,000)	(49,000)
Other, net	(322,000)	(22,000)	(97,000)
	$ (727,000)	$ (294,000)	$ 91,000

Income taxes paid amounted to $5,905,843, $3,156,963 and $1,382,650, during 1992, 1991, and 1990, respectively.

In February 1992, the FASB issued Statement No. 109, "Accounting for Income Taxes," that becomes effective for fiscal years beginning after December 15, 1992. Under the new rules, deferred taxes are recognized using the liability method, whereby tax rates are applied to cumulative temporary differences based on when and how they are expected to affect the tax return. Deferred tax assets and liabilities are adjusted for tax rate changes. Under the rules presently applied (APB Opinion 11), deferred taxes are measured using the tax rates for the year in which timing differences arise. Deferred taxes are not adjusted for tax rate changes.

The Company will apply the new standard beginning in the first quarter of 1993. Application of the new rules will result in a cumulative adjustment through December 31, 1992 of approximately $100,000. The Company has determined that it will not restate prior year financial statements to reflect adoption of the new rules.

6. LONG-TERM DEBT AND OBLIGATIONS UNDER CAPITAL LEASE

	1992	1991
Industrial Revenue Bonds (IRB), payable in monthly installments of $12,500 plus interest at 75% of the prime rate (4.5% at December 26, 1992 and 4.875% at December 28, 1991) through June 2000; secured by all equipment, furniture and fixtures at the Waterbury plant location	1,077,893	1,244,623
Urban Development Action Grant, payable in quarterly installments of $22,130 including interest at 9% through April 2000; secured by property, plant and equipment at the Waterbury plant location subordinated to the IRB loan	467,661	511,593
Capital lease obligations	1,526,304	1,334,129
Vermont Industrial Development Authority loan payable in monthly installments of $1,849 including interest at 4% through December 2000; secured by all property, plant and equipment located at the Springfield Plant	197,222	211,219
	3,269,080	3,301,564
Less current portion	628,098	514,905
	$ 2,640,982	$ 2,786,659

Property, plant and equipment having a net book value of approximately $14,100,000 at December 26, 1992 was pledged as collateral for long-term debt.

In August 1991 the Company called for redemption of its $5,830,000 outstanding 9.5% convertible debentures. This resulted in redemption of $14,000 principal amount of debentures for cash and the issuance of 750,280 shares of Class A Common Stock. Prior to redemption, $756,000 and $5,000 of outstanding principal amount were converted into 97,524 and 644 Class A shares in 1991 and 1990, respectively.

The loan agreement in connection with the Industrial Revenue Bonds contains certain restrictive covenants requiring maintenance of working capital, current ratio and tangible net worth. At December 26, 1992, the Company was in compliance with the provisions of the loan agreement.

Long-term debt and obligations under capital lease at December 26, 1992 maturing in each of the next five years is as follows:

	Capital lease obligations	Long-term debt
1993	$ 523,543	$ 212,589
1994	277,446	217,653
1995	183,345	223,154
1996	363,285	230,549
1997	335,488	237,189
Thereafter	330,601	621,642
Total minimum payments	2,013,708	1,742,776
Less amounts representing interest	(487,404)	
Present value of minimum payments	$ 1,526,304	$ 1,742,776

Interest of approximately $68,000, $52,000 and $6,000 was capitalized in 1992, 1991 and 1990, respectively, as part of the acquisition cost of property, plant and equipment. Interest paid, net of interest capitalized, amounted to $188,528, $726,378 and $796,317 for 1992, 1991 and 1990, respectively.

The Company has available a $9,000,000 unsecured working capital line of credit agreement with a bank. Interest on borrowing is set at the bank's prime rate less .25%. The agreement expires April 30, 1993 and is expected to be extended. Borrowings are subject to agreement at or before each advance as to amount, maturity and other terms and conditions. No amounts were borrowed under this agreement during 1992 or 1990. Maximum amounts outstanding during 1991 were $7,600,000.

7. THE BEN & JERRY'S FOUNDATION, INC.

In October 1985, the Company issued Class A Preferred Stock to The Ben & Jerry's Foundation, Inc. (the Founda-

tion), a non-profit corporation qualified under section 501(c)(3) of the Internal Revenue Code. The primary purpose of the Foundation is to be the principal recipient of cash contributions from the Company which are then donated to various community organizations and other charitable institutions. Amounts accrued for contributions to the Foundation at the rate of approximately 7.5% of income before income taxes amounted to approximately $917,000, $528,000 and $363,000 for 1992, 1991 and 1990, respectively.

The Preferred Stock is entitled to vote as a separate class in certain business combinations, such that approval of two-thirds of the class is required for such business combinations. Two directors, including one of the founders of the Company, are members of the Board of Directors of the Foundation.

8. STOCK PLANS

The Company has an Employee Stock Purchase Plan, pursuant to which employees having six months of continuous

service may exercise six month options to purchase Class A Common Stock, through annual payroll withholdings of not less than 2% or more than 10% of their salary, at the lower of 85% of market value of the stock at the date of grant or date of purchase. At December 26, 1992, 53,620 shares had been issued under the plan and 246,380 shares were reserved for future issuance.

The Company has a Stock Option Plan under which options to purchase common stock may be granted to employees (including officers) and directors. The Plan provides that options are granted at market value as of the date of grant. At December 26, 1992, no options had been granted and an aggregate of 525,000 shares of Class A and Class B Common Stock were reserved for future issuance.

The Company has three restricted stock plans (the 1986, 1991 and 1992 Plans) which provide that employees, consultants or directors may be awarded shares of Class A Common Stock at the discretion of the Board of Directors or as otherwise specified in the plans. Shares

36

issued under the plans are vested or become vested over periods of up to five years. At December 26, 1992, a total of 73,900 shares had been awarded under these plans, of which 55,518 were fully vested. 76,100 shares were reserved for future awards. Unearned compensation on unvested shares is recorded as of the award date and is being amortized over the vesting period.

9. EMPLOYEE BENEFIT PLANS

The Company maintains profit sharing and savings plans for all eligible employees. Contributions to the profit sharing plan are allocated among all current full-time and regular part-time employees based upon length of service with the Company. The profit sharing plan is informal and discretionary. The savings plan is maintained in accordance with the provisions of Section 401(K) of the Internal Revenue Code and allows all employees with at least six months of service to make annual tax-deferred voluntary contributions up to fifteen percent of their salary. The Company may match the contribution up to two percent of the employee's gross annual salary.

Total contributions by the Company to the profit sharing and savings plans were approximately $815,000, $463,000, and $341,000 for 1992, 1991 and 1990, respectively.

10. COMMON STOCK

In June 1987, the Company's share-holders adopted an amendment to the Company's Articles of Association that authorized 3,000,000 shares of a new Class B Common Stock and redesignated the Company's existing Common Stock as Class A Common Stock. The Class B Common Stock has 10 votes per share on all matters, is generally non-transfer-able and is convertible into Class A Common Stock on a one-for-one basis.

In April 1991, the Company's Chair-man of the Board, who is a significant shareholder, gave the Company 89,624 shares of Class A Common Stock, having a market value of approximately $1,900,000, for no consideration. The effect of this transaction was to decrease total outstanding shares by 89,624 shares. Subsequently, 60,000 of these shares were reserved for delivery under the 1991 Restricted Stock Plan and the remaining shares were made available for issue for general corporate purposes.

On June 12, 1992, the Company issued a two-for-one stock split effected as a 100% stock dividend of one share of Class A Common Stock on each outstanding share of Class A Common Stock (2,498,667 Class A Shares) and a 100% stock dividend of one share of Class B Common Stock on each outstanding share of Class B Common Stock (480,044 Class B Shares). The dividends were payable to stockholders of record at the close of business on May 29, 1992. All share and per share information throughout these financial statements have been restated to reflect this transaction.

11. LEGAL MATTERS

The Company is subject to certain litigation and claims in the ordinary course of business which management believes are not material to the Company's business.

12. COMMITMENTS

In April 1989 the Company entered into a manufacturing and warehouse agreement with Edy's Grand Ice Cream, a subsidiary of Dreyer's Grand Ice Cream, Inc., to have product manufactured at Edy's plant in Fort Wayne, Indiana, for a period of three years. In September 1992 the Company amended this agree-ment to extend the period for an additional two years expiring in Decem-ber 1994. The agreement specifies minimum and maximum quantities which the Company is obligated to purchase. At December 26, 1992, the Company is obligated to purchase approximately 7,400,000 gallons through December 1994 which represents approximately $52,000,000 in future commitments.

At December 26, 1992, the Company has purchase commitments for certain ingredients approximating $8,000,000.

The Company leases certain prop-erty and equipment under operating leases. Minimum payments for operating leases having initial or remaining noncancellable terms in excess of one year are as follows:

1993	$ 267,051
1994	217,819
1995	152,972
1996	55,419

Rent expense for all operating leases amounted to approximately $310,000, $315,000 and $319,000 in 1992, 1991 and 1990, respectively.

The Company is in the process of building and equipping a third manufacturing plant in St. Albans, Vermont. Construction began in October 1992 and is expected to cost approximately $25,000,000. As of December 26, 1992, the Company has made commitments totalling $3,000,000 for construction costs, equipment and software related to the new facility.

13. SIGNIFICANT CUSTOMERS

The Company's most significant customer, Dreyer's Grand Ice Cream, Inc., accounted for 49% or $65.0 million of net sales in 1992, 44% or $42.3 million in 1991 and 40% or $31.2 million in 1990.

14. SELECTED QUARTERLY FINANCIAL INFORMATION (UNAUDITED)

	First Quarter	Second Quarter	Third Quarter	Fourth Quarter
1992				
Net Sales	$ 27,336,410	$ 35,820,845	$ 40,823,659	$ 27,987,900
Gross Profit	$ 8,214,868	$ 10,423,271	$ 11,472,225	$ 7,469,059
Operating Income	$ 2,016,976	$ 3,989,314	$ 3,833,242	$ 1,497,130
Net Income	$ 1,188,426	$ 2,300,085	$ 2,194,265	$ 992,564
Net Income Per Common Share*	$ .20	$ .39	$ .37	$ .14
1991				
Net Sales	$ 17,731,133	$ 25,700,499	$ 29,817,826	$ 23,747,881
Gross Profit	$ 5,108,854	$ 8,308,230	$ 8,640,858	$ 6,438,995
Operating Income	$ 1,016,159	$ 2,372,814	$ 2,741,944	$ 1,101,806
Net Income	$ 488,112	$ 1,157,170	$ 1,469,136	$ 624,965
Net Income Per Common Share*	$ .09	$ .22	$ .26	$ .11

*Net income per common share on a fully diluted basis assuming conversion of the Company's outstanding 9.5% subordinated convertible debentures was $.21 for the second quarter of 1991. The dilutive effect was not material in any other period presented.

REPORT OF
INDEPENDENT
AUDITORS

The Board of Directors and Stockholders
Ben & Jerry's Homemade, Inc.

We have audited the accompanying balance sheets of Ben & Jerry's Homemade, Inc. as of December 26, 1992 and December 28, 1991, and the related statements of income, stockholders' equity and cash flows for each of the three years in the period ended December 26, 1992. These financial statements are the responsibility of the Company's management. Our responsibility is to express an opinion on these financial statements based on our audits.

We conducted our audits in accordance with generally accepted auditing standards. Those standards require that we plan and perform the audit to obtain reasonable assurance about whether the financial statements are free of material misstatement. An audit includes examining, on a test basis, evidence supporting the amounts and disclosures in the financial statements. An audit also includes assessing the accounting principles used and significant estimates made by management, as well as evaluating the overall financial statement presentation. We believe that our audits provide a reasonable basis for our opinion.

In our opinion, the financial statements referred to above present fairly, in all material respects, the financial position of Ben & Jerry's Homemade, Inc. at December 26, 1992 and December 28, 1991, and the results of its operations and its cash flows for each of the three years in the period ended December 26, 1992 in conformity with generally accepted accounting principles.

Ernst + Young

ERNST & YOUNG

March 8, 1993

Index for "From Concept to Practice" Assignments Using Ben & Jerry's Annual Report

"From Concept to Practice" assignments, printed in the margins throughout the book, are based on the Ben & Jerry's annual report. This Index is a convenient list of these financial statement assignments, which can be used in conjunction with the chapter or as cumulative problems at key points in the course.

Chapter 1

Chapter 2

Chapter 3

Reading Ben & Jerry's **Statement of Cash Flows** p. 771
Did the disposal of assets during 1992 result in a gain or a loss? What is the amount?
Why is it deducted on the statement of cash flows?

Chapter 15

Reading Ben & Jerry's **Annual Report** p. 840
Where does Ben & Jerry's annual report provide information on the market price
of its stock? Based on the market price of high for the fourth quarter of 1992, what
was its P/E ratio?

Photo Credits

Chapter 1: page 2; Photo courtesy of Ben and Jerry's Homemade, Inc.; page 4: Photo courtesy of
Ben and Jerry's Homemade, Inc.; page 21: © The Stock Yard; page 27: Photo courtesy of Jeffrey
Laderman **Chapter 2:** page 52: © Rick Stewart; page 78: © Robert Gemin; page 87: Photo courtesy
of Rick Boettcher **Chapter 3** page 112: Cover image of Time Warner's 1993 annual report reprinted
by permission of Time Warner, Inc.; page 115: © Terry Vine, Tony Stone Images; page 119: © Don
Smetzer/Tony Stone Images; page 136: Photo courtesy of Krista Kaland **Chapter 4:** page 167: ©
Reuters/Bettmann; page 173: Photo courtesy of Boston Chicken; page 198: Photo courtesy of Steve
Ritzman **Chapter 5:** page 255: © Pattie McConville/The Image Bank; page 270: © Charles Gupton/
Tony Stone Images; page 279: Photo courtesy Steven Eldridge **Chapter 6:** page 312: © The Stock
Yard; page 322: © Charles Gupton/Tony Stone Images; page 336: © 1982, Philip M. Prosen/The
Image Bank; page 341: Photo courtesy of Michael La Tronica **Chapter 7:** page 370: Photo courtesy
of the Xerox Corporation; page 380: © Jay Fries/The Image Bank; page 402: © 1994 Matthew Mulbray
Chapter 8: page 422: Photo courtesy of Genentech, Inc.; page 427: © 1991 Michael Schneps/The
Image Bank; page 436: © Christian Bossu-Pica/Tony Stone Images; page 446: Photo courtesy of Ed
Meisen **Chapter 9:** page 472; Photo courtesy of Mattel, Inc.; page 483: Photo courtesy of the Tandy
Corporation; page 488: Photo courtesy of the Texas Lottery Commission, page 495: Photo courtesy
of Doris Nakamura **Chapter 10:** page 528: © Michael Newman/Photo Edit; page 531: Courtesy of
Southwestern Bell Telephone; page 532: © 1991, Bill Varie/The Image Bank; page 546: © Larry Dale
Gordon/The Image Bank; page 559: Photo courtesy of Kenneth Mabbs **Chapter 11:** page 582: Photo
courtesy of the Sears Merchandising Group; page 587: Courtesy of Ben and Jerry's Homemade, Inc.
Reprinted by permission; page 598: © Catherine Ursillo/Photo Researchers, Inc.; page 603: Photo
courtesy of Wayne Goldstein **Chapter 12:** page 630: Photo courtesy of General Electric 1992 annual
report; page 637: © AP/Wide World Photos; page 649: Photo courtesy of Randall Oliver **Chapter
13:** page 672: Photo courtesy of Whirlpool Corporation; page 711: Photo courtesy of Keith Ogata
Chapter 14: page 738: © Michael Salas/The Image Bank; page 774: © Stephen Johnson/Tony Stone
Images; page 776: Photo courtesy of Suzanne McGrath **Chapter 15:** page 814: Photo courtesy of the
Boeing Company; page 831: © Al Satterwhite/The Image Bank; page 839: © The Stock Yard; page
840: Reprinted by permission of the *Wall Street Journal*, 1994 Dow Jones & Company, Inc. All rights
reserved worldwide.; page 841: Photo courtesy of Maceo Sloan

Ben & Jerry's annual report material is reprinted by permission of Ben & Jerry's Homemade, Inc. All
rights reserved.

FEDERAL INCOME TAX CONSIDERATIONS
FOR BUSINESSES AND INDIVIDUALS

LEARNING OBJECTIVES

After studying this appendix, you should be able to:

1. Identify the choices that a taxable entity must make before filing a federal income tax return.

2. Identify and define the key components of the general framework for the income tax computation, without regard to the type of taxable entity.

3. Describe the general tax treatment of the following items for a corporate taxpayer: net capital gains, net capital losses, charitable contributions deductions, and the dividends received deduction.

4. Describe the corporate income tax rate schedule.

5. For individual taxpayers, provide examples of (1) deductions for adjusted gross income and (2) deductions from adjusted gross income, and describe the treatment of net capital gains and net capital losses.

6. Describe the individual income tax rate schedules, filing status, and any special tax rates applicable to specific types of income.

7. Explain the potential tax planning advantages of (1) a corporation increasing salary payments to family employees in family corporations and (2) a high-income individual investing in state or local bond obligations.

Our federal income tax system reflects an attempt by Congress to achieve a variety of objectives. Although it is a system designed primarily to raise revenue, it has also been used over the years to bring about economic, social, and political change. Unfortunately, this multipurpose function of the tax law complicates any attempt to simplify and explain the current provisions. Nonetheless, a basic understanding of these concepts is extremely important. For example, a corporation that incurs a $1,000 expenditure may in fact be spending only $660; as explained later, the company may keep the other $340 if the item is deductible against taxable sources of income. The purpose of this appendix is to (1) introduce the notion of tax authority, (2) offer an overview of basic tax concepts and choices affecting all taxpayers, (3) illustrate the basic formats for the corporate and individual tax computations, and (4) provide a brief introduction to tax planning.

Tax Authority

Our federal income tax laws are contained in Title 26 of the U.S. Code and are more commonly referred to as simply The Internal Revenue Code. The word *code* is a derivative of codification, the process of reworking and reorganizing laws into one cohesive set of authority. The last codification occurred in 1986, so our current tax law is generally referred to as the *Internal Revenue Code of 1986* (hereinafter referred to as the **Code**).

The Code is the primary source of *legislative authority,* in that Congress drafted and approved such laws. In some cases, the intent of Congress in enacting a particular provision may not be clear, and it may be necessary to consult other authorities. The two other primary sources of tax authority are *administrative authority* (regulatory interpretations of the Code, as issued by the Department of Treasury and the Internal Revenue Service, or IRS), and *judicial authority* (interpretations of Congressional authority as issued by the courts).

The following discussion is based on legislative authority, because our intent is to provide only a general overview of the basic rules of taxation. It is important to realize, however, that the Code cannot address every conceivable circumstance that may occur in daily business practice, and it may be necessary to consult both administrative and judicial authorities in an attempt to answer a particular tax question.

Initial Decisions in Filing the Federal Tax Return

LO ▮ I

Identify the choices that a taxable entity must make before filing a federal income tax return.

The Code provides taxpayers with a number of choices in reporting their income and expenses and paying their tax liabilities. When a taxpayer first begins a business, he or she must make three initial choices: (1) form of tax entity, (2) tax year, and (3) accounting method.

Choice of Tax Entity

The tax laws allow a taxpayer to choose one of four basic entity forms for reporting the results of business operations. These entities are (1) a sole proprietorship, (2) a partnership, (3) a regular C corporation, and (4) a special S corporation.

Sole Proprietorship   Taxpayers electing to organize their businesses as **sole proprietorships** report the results of their business operations each year as part of their personal individual tax return (Form 1040, as illustrated later in this chapter). The business results are reported on Schedule C, a special form that closely resembles an income statement. Sole proprietors must also report and pay social security taxes on the net income shown on the Schedule C, because they do not have employers to withhold (and match) such tax payments. This tax is referred to as the *self-employment tax* and is reported on a special form, Schedule SE.

Example I   Lana Mix owns and operates her own computer services business. During the year, her business revenues totaled $190,000, and her business expenses were $120,000. As a sole proprietor, Lana reports the revenue and expenses on Schedule C and transfers the net profit of $70,000 to her Form 1040 individual tax return. She also computes her self-employment tax liability on Schedule SE and adds the tax to her other taxes due on the Form 1040.

Partnership   When more than one owner is involved, a business may be organized as a **partnership.** For tax purposes, a partnership is a *tax-reporting entity,* not a tax-paying entity. The partnership must report the results of operations on a partnership tax return (Form 1065) and allocate the income among the different partners. Each partner then reports his or her share of the partnership income on his or her individual tax return (Form 1040).

Example 2   Lana Mix and Al Keim form LA Partnership. During the past year, the partnership had $190,000 of revenues and $120,000 in expenses. The partnership must file a Form 1065 with the government, reporting the $70,000 of net income and showing the allocation of income between Lana and Al. The partnership will not pay tax, however. Assuming that Lana and Al share profits equally, each must report a $35,000 share of the net income on their own personal income tax return.

Interestingly, a new type of entity known as a "limited liability company" has been approved by a number of states in recent years. Although usually cast as corporations for legal purposes, these entries are generally taxed as partnerships.

Regular C Corporation   A *corporation* is treated as a separate entity for tax purposes. Thus, a corporation reports its income and expenses on a separate corporation tax return (Form 1120, illustrated later in this chapter) and pays a tax on its income. Regular corporations are referred to as **C corporations** for tax purposes because they are described in Subchapter C of the Internal Revenue Code. One disadvantage of the corporate form of doing business is that the income is taxed twice if it is distributed to the business owners—that is, once at the corporate level as taxable income and once at the individual shareholder level as dividend income. (But see the tax planning discussion later in this appendix for a way that Lana and Al may minimize this double taxation.)

Example 3   Assume the same facts as those for Example 2, except that Lana and Al organize their business as LA Company, a C corporation. In this case, they must file a Form 1120 tax return and pay an income tax based on the $70,000 net income. In addition, any dividend distributions to Lana and Al are taxable on their individual tax returns. If the corporation decides to distribute dividends of $35,000 each to Lana and Al in the same year, the income is in effect taxed twice (once at the corporate level as taxable income and once at the individual level as taxable dividends).

S Corporation   Subchapter S of the Internal Revenue Code provides a special election whereby certain closely held corporate entities may elect to be taxed under a special set of rules as an **S corporation.** In general, such an election allows the corporation to avoid paying a tax at the corporate level by agreeing to allocate the income directly to the shareholders. In this respect, the tax scheme is similar to that of a partnership. The election allows the business owners to retain some of the tax and nontax advantages of the corporate form without the disadvantage of double taxation. This election is available only to corporations that meet certain requirements, the principal one of these being a limit of 35 shareholders.

Example 4   Assume the same facts as those for Example 3, except that Lana and Al elect to have LA Corporation taxed as an S corporation. In this case, no tax is imposed at the corporate level on the $70,000 income; rather, Lana and Al report their separate income shares on their individual income tax returns (in much the same manner as the partnership in Example 2).

Choice of Tax Year

All taxable entities, including individuals, must file a federal income tax return on an annual basis. A taxpayer may choose either a calendar year, a fiscal year, or a 52–53 week year. A *calendar year* is simply a tax year ending on December 31. A *fiscal year* is a tax year ending at the end of a month other than December; an example is a tax year ending each June 30.

A *52–53 week year* is a tax year ending on the same day of the week at the end of a particular month (or simply the same day of the week nearest the end of the month). Examples of 52–53 week years include a year ending on the Friday closest to December 31 and a year ending on the last Friday in December. In some years, the tax year will have 52 weeks, and in others it will have 53 weeks.

Once an accounting period has been selected, the taxpayer must continue to use that reporting period in future years, unless the IRS gives the taxpayer permission to change the period. Generally, the IRS grants permission to change accounting periods only when a valid business reason exists for the change.

Choice of Accounting Method

Generally, a taxpayer must use a method for reporting revenue and expenses that clearly reflects income, and the taxpayer must apply that method consistently. An *accounting method* is the basis on which the taxpayer regularly computes income. Although a few special methods are provided for individual items in the tax law (for example, inventory methods), as a practical matter, a taxpayer uses one of three basic overall methods of accounting: the cash method, the accrual method, or a hybrid method.

The Cash Method   Under the **cash method,** revenue is recognized when actually received and expenses when actually paid. This is the simplest accounting method, and it is used by the vast majority of individual taxpayers, who sometimes use their checkbook as their "accounting records" if the accrual method is not otherwise required. The cash method does not imply that income is recognized only when cash is received; the fair market value of property or services received must be reported as income on a "cash-equivalent" basis. Some assets, such as unsecured accounts receivable, are not considered to have a reasonably estimatable fair market value, however, and the income from such receivables is postponed until received under the cash basis.

Example 5   During the year, Bob Kravitz, a cash-basis taxpayer, sells inventory item A for $300 cash, inventory item B on credit through an ordinary accounts receivable for $400, and inventory item C for a used truck worth $275. Bob must report the $300 cash and $275 value of the truck as gross income during the year; however, the credit sale is not reported as income until it is actually collected in cash.

When a cash-basis taxpayer prepays an expense, the item is not deductible as an expense for tax purposes until the expense is "incurred" (that is, used up, under general accounting principles). In effect, a cash-basis taxpayer must both *incur* and *pay* a material expense item before the item is deductible.

Example 6   May East, a cash-basis, calendar-year taxpayer, borrows $10,000 to use in her business on October 1. The note, along with $600 interest, is due on April 1 of the following year. She may may not deduct any interest in the current year; even though three months of interest have been incurred at the end of the year, none has actually been paid.

The Accrual Method   Under the **accrual method,** revenues are recognized when they are earned and expenses are recognized when they are incurred. This is basically the same recognition principle used for financial accounting. There is one important exception, however; *unearned income is generally taxed when received for tax purposes.* This is a reflection of the **wherewithal-to-pay** principle: a taxpayer should pay tax when he or she is best able to pay and the IRS is best able to collect. Although this violates the matching principle discussed earlier in the text, it does improve the odds that the government receives its share of income as it is earned.

Example 7   Ace Company, an accrual-basis, calendar-year taxpayer, owns a commercial office building. On January 1, Ace leases the building to Tee Shirts. Tee prepays three years' rent, a total of $180,000. Even though Ace uses the accrual basis, it must recognize the entire $180,000 prepayment as taxable income in the current year.

Note that our discussion of accounting methods so far illustrates an interesting paradox on the treatment of prepaid expenses. Specifically, such items are taxed immediately as income to the recipient (even if on the accrual basis), yet the payment is not immediately deductible by the payor (even if on the cash basis). One of the frustrating aspects of studying the tax law is that there is no requirement that the tax law adhere to generally accepted accounting principles.

Example 8   Assume that Tee Shirt in Example 7 is a cash-basis taxpayer. Even though Tee Shirt paid the entire $180,000 rent at the beginning of the lease, only $60,000 ($180,000 × 12/36) is deductible during the current tax year. Again, an expense is deductible by a cash-basis taxpayer only when it is both *paid and incurred.*

The Hybrid Method   Taxpayers may also elect a *hybrid method* of accounting. As the name implies, a hybrid method is a combination of two or more acceptable methods of accounting. For example, the Internal Revenue Code requires the use of the accrual method for gross profit computations (sales less cost of goods sold); however, a taypayer using such a method may still elect the cash method for reporting expenses.

The General Framework for Determining the Income Tax Liability

Before examining the components of the corporate and individual tax formulas, it is important to understand the primary components of the tax formula for all entities. These are illustrated in Exhibit A2-1. Many tax principles associated with these components apply equally to all entities. A few of the more common principles are discussed in the following sections.

LO   2

Identify and define the key components of the general framework for the income tax computation, without regard to the type of taxable entity.

Gross Receipts

Gross receipts represents the broadest definition of income for tax purposes. In general, **gross receipts** represent total income flows received during the year other than loan proceeds. Any "cost of goods sold" may be deducted in determining gross receipts, however. Thus, a grocer who sells an item for $12 that originally cost $9 includes $3 in gross receipts.

Cost recoveries are also allowed on sales of noninventory items. For example, if B Corporation sells a machine used in its business for $10,000 at a time when it

EXHIBIT A2-1   General Framework for Income Tax Computation

Gross receipts	$ xx,xxx
Less: Statutory exclusions	(xx,xxx)
Gross income	$ xx,xxx
Less: Statutory deductions	(xx,xxx)
Taxable income	$ xx,xxx
Gross tax liability	$ xx,xxx
Less: Statutory tax credits	(xx,xxx)
Prepayments of tax liability	(xx,xxx)
Net tax liability (or refund due)	$ xx,xxx

has an adjusted basis (for example, cost less accumulated depreciation) of $6,000, only the $4,000 gain is included in gross receipts.

Statutory Exclusions

The Internal Revenue Code contains an all-inclusive definition of income. In general, for tax purposes **gross income** includes all income *from whatever source* unless the income is *specifically excludable* under the Code. In other words, income is presumed to be taxable unless a specific provision in the Code allows its excludability.

An **exclusion** is a statutory exemption from taxation. Over the years, Congress has enacted a number of exclusions. For example, interest on state or local bonds is excludable, because Congress did not want to impinge on a state or local government's ability to raise revenue. Another specific exclusion exempts gifts and inheritances received from federal income taxation.

Congress has also enacted a number of exclusions for certain fringe benefits received by employees on the job. For example, employer payments for health and accident coverage for an employee and his or her family members are excludable under the Code. The same is true for the first $5,000 of child or dependent care assistance payments received by an employee from his or her employer.

Example 9   Joy Rondos, an employee of Zee Company, received the following payments from her employer during the current year: $65,000 salary, $5,600 child care payments paid by the employer directly to the child care agency, $2,000 premiums on health insurance coverage paid by her employer, and a $4,000 cash bonus. Joy may exclude from income $5,000 of the child care payments and the entire $2,000 of health insurance payments made by her employer. The remaining amounts are taxable and are includable in gross income, because the Code has no provisions to allow their exclusion.

Gross Income

Gross income is simply gross receipts less all allowable statutory exclusions. Gross income also includes any gains (and some losses) realized on the sale of properties. In some cases, these gains or losses are termed *capital gains* or *capital losses* (for example, gains or losses on the sale of "capital assets") and are therefore eligible for special treatment under the tax law.

Capital assets include most investment properties (such as stocks and bonds) and all personal assets (such as those assets that are not used in a trade or business or an income-producing activity). Capital assets *never* include inventories, ordinary accounts or notes receivable, or properties used productively in a trade or business (for example, machinery, warehouse, and so on).

Example 10   Z Company's factory building is located on 20 acres of land. In addition, Z owns 10 acres of land on the other side of town that it is holding for its appreciation potential. The 10-acre plot of land is a capital asset, because it is held as an investment. The factory building and the related 20 acres of land are not capital assets, since both assets are used productively in the trade or business.

At the end of the tax year, all taxpayers must group all of their capital asset transactions into two summary categories: short-term gains and losses and long-term gains and losses. A *short-term gain or loss* occurs when the capital asset has been held one year or less; any capital asset held longer than one year at the time of sale generates a **long-term capital gain or loss.** These short-term and long-term gains and losses are then combined under special rules applicable to the type of tax entity, as explained later in this appendix. In general, a *net capital gain* may receive favorable treatment, whereas a *net capital loss* is subject to special limitations.

Before leaving the concept of capital gains and losses, it is important to mention briefly the tax treatment of gains and losses on the sale of business properties. Recall that earlier we stated that properties used productively in a trade or business are never capital assets. To encourage businesses to sell unproductive assets and buy productive ones, Congress enacted a special provision whereby business taxpayers obtain the "best of both tax worlds" on the sale of business properties held longer than one year.

Specifically, if the net gains from such sales exceed the net losses during the year, the net gain is treated as a capital gain (eligible for beneficial treatment for individuals, as explained below). On the other hand, if the net losses from such sales exceed the net gains during the year, the net loss is treated as a noncapital ordinary loss and is not subject to any of the special capital loss limits (also described below).

Example 11   Jane Eyre sells two business assets that she held more than one year. She sold asset A for a $40,000 gain and asset B for a $30,000 loss. Because the gains from business asset sales exceed the losses from such sales during the year, the net gain of $10,000 ($40,000 − $30,000) is treated as a long-term capital gain and is possibly eligible for a reduced rate of taxation (as explained later in this appendix).

Example 12   Assume the same facts as those for Example 11, except that asset B was sold for a $52,000 loss. Because the losses from business asset sales exceed the gains from such sales during the year, the net loss of $12,000 ($40,000 − $52,000) is treated as a fully deductible noncapital ordinary loss (and is not subject to the annual capital loss limits explained later in this chapter).

Deductions

Deductions are expenses and losses that are subtracted from gross income in determining taxable income. For federal income tax purposes, it is often said that "deductions are matters of legislative grace." In other words, *no item* is deductible unless the Code specifically provides for it as a deduction. It is interesting to note that, as explained earlier, Congress applies the *opposite* logic to income: All income is presumed to be taxable unless specifically excludable under the Code.

A taxpayer who wishes to deduct a specific expenditure must be able to identify a specific provision of the Code granting the deduction. Fortunately, Congress has simplified this search for authority by enacting two "umbrella" provisions in the Code that grant deductions for a variety of expenditures. These provisions allow deductions for (1) any expenses or losses incurred in carrying on a trade or business (Section 162 of the Code) and (2) any expenses associated with the production of income or the determination of a tax liability (Section 212 of the Code).

Example 13   Zero Company incurred $450 of advertising expenses in its hardware business during the year. This expense is deductible as a trade or business expense under the general grant of authority of Section 162 of the Code.

Example 14   Beth Jackson spent $185 to have the roof on her rental property repaired. This expenditure is deductible as an income-producing expense under the general grant of authority of Section 212 of the Code, because a rental property is not a "trade or business" covered by Section 162.

Any expenditure that does not fit into one of these umbrella provisions (generally, a personal expenditure) is presumed to be nondeductible unless a specific provision of the Code otherwise allows deductibility. As discussed later in this chapter, Congress has granted such authority for a number of personal expenditures generally referred to as *itemized deductions*.

Example 15   During the current year, Salamon Torres paid $12,000 in alimony and $6,000 of child support to his former spouse. Neither expenditure meets the deductibility requirements of either Section 162 or Section 212 of the Code. However, a separate provision in the Code specifically allows a deduction for alimony payments, so the $12,000 is deductible. The child support payments are not deductible because they are not allowed by a specific Code provision.

In many cases, items deductible for financial accounting purposes are also deductible for tax purposes. The Code does provide different treatments for a number of items, however. Three important differences are the tax treatments of depreciation, meal and entertainment expenses, and net operating losses.

Depreciation   In general, the tax deduction for depreciation (called a *cost recovery deduction* in the Code) is determined according to statutory recovery tables. The cost of the asset (unreduced for any salvage value) is multiplied by a table recovery factor for each year's cost recovery deduction.

Under the Modified Accelerated Cost Recovery System (**MACRS**), all assets acquired after 1986 are grouped into one of nine different statutory recovery classes as either *personalty* (property other than land or buildings) or *realty* (buildings). These classes are shown in Exhibit A2-2, along with the first-year recovery percentages for each class. In general, the recovery factors for the first four classes for personalty (3-, 5-, 7-, and 10-year classes) are based on the 200% declining-balance method with an assumed mid-year acquisition date for all assets in that class (declining-balance depreciation was discussed in Chapter 8). The next two classes for personalty (15- and 20-year classes) are based on the 150% declining-balance method, and the last two classes for realty (27.5- and 39-year classes) are based on straight-line recovery. In the case of realty, a building is classified as *residential realty* if at least 80% of the gross income from it is from dwelling units. Otherwise, the building is nonresidential (commercial) realty.

EXHIBIT A2-2   Summary of the MACRS Depreciation System

CLASS	COMMON ASSETS	YEAR I RECOVERY PERCENTAGE
3-year personalty	Assets with useful lives of less than 4 years	33.33
5-year personalty	Automobiles and computers	20.00
7-year personalty	Most machinery and equipment	14.29
10-year personalty	Assets with useful lives exceeding 16 years (e.g., greenhouses and fruit trees)	10.00
15-year personalty	Assets with useful lives exceeding 20 years (e.g., telephone distribution centers)	5.00
20-year personalty	Assets with useful lives exceeding 25 years (e.g., sewer pipes)	3.75
27.5-year realty	Residential realty (e.g., rental apartment buildings)	3.485*
39.0-year realty	Nonresidential realty (business buildings)	2.457*

*Assumes an acquisition in the first month of the taxable year

One other provision of the MACRS procedure is worth noting. A taxpayer who acquires depreciable business personalty during the year may elect to expense up to $17,500 of the cost in the year of acquisition. This is referred to as the **immediate expensing election** of Section 179 of the Code. (Qualifying acquisitions exceeding $200,000 during the year will reduce the $17,500 maximum dollar for dollar; the details of these computations are beyond the scope of this introduction.)

Example 16   August Corporation acquires $67,500 of machinery during the tax year that belongs in the 7-year MACRS class. August may elect to immediately deduct $17,500 of this cost, and the remaining $50,000 of the total acquisition cost is also eligible for a normal MACRS recovery deduction of $7,145 ($50,000 × .1429, the first year MACRS recovery factor for 7-year personalty from Exhibit A2-2).

Example 17   During January of the current year, T Company purchased a new business automobile for $10,000 and a new factory building for $100,000. Its total MACRS deduction (assuming that immediate expensing is not elected on the automobile) will be $4,457, computed as follows:

Automobile ($10,000 × .20 [5-year recovery])	$2,000
Factory ($100,000 × .02457 [39-year recovery])	2,457
Total MACRS deduction	$4,457

Meal and Entertainment Expenses   Meal and entertainment costs are deductible as legitimate business expenses for both financial accounting and tax purposes if incurred in a business setting, such as taking a client to lunch for business discussions. There is one difference for tax purposes, however: only 50% of the qualifying cost is deductible.

Example 18 R Company paid $2,000 for legitimate meal and entertainment expenses associated with customers during the year. On its tax return, R's deduction is limited to $1,000 ($2,000 × .50).

Net Operating Losses For financial accounting purposes, the results of one year's operations generally do not affect the results of operations in other years; under the time period assumption, each accounting period stands on its own. For tax purposes, Congress has provided a special **net operating loss** deduction by which large losses in one tax year may be used to offset incomes in other tax years. In this respect, a taxpayer is granted additional tax relief by being permitted to "average" the results of several years.

If a taxpayer's business operations produce a net loss, the net operating loss may be carried back 3 years and forward 15 years, or optionally, simply carried forward 15 years. A loss is "carried back" by filing an amended tax return with one additional deduction: the net operating loss deduction. If the loss is carried back, it is first carried to the third preceding year, then the second preceding year, and so on. Losses that are not completely used up at the end of the 15-year carryforward period are lost forever.

Example 19 Y Company incurs a $90,000 net operating loss in 1995. In 1992, Y reported taxable income of $50,000 and paid $7,500 in taxes. Y may now file an amended return for 1992 with an additional $90,000 deduction. Because the additional deduction eliminates the 1992 income, Y is entitled to a refund of the $7,500 taxes paid. In addition, Y has $40,000 of remaining net operating loss ($90,000 − $50,000) to carry over as a deduction in 1993. Any loss remaining after the 1993 carryback may be applied to 1994, and if any loss still remains, carried forward for 15 years beginning in 1996.

The option to forgo the 3-year carryback may be chosen by a taxpayer who expects to be in a higher tax bracket in the future, as compared to the previous 3 years. In Example 19, Y Company's tax rate for 1992 was only 15% ($7,500/$50,000). As explained later in this appendix, corporate tax rates can go as high as 34% or 35%. If Y expects to be in a 34% bracket after 1995, it may choose to forgo the 3-year carryback period and first deduct the $50,000 net operating loss on the 1996 tax return. In this case, the tax savings may be as high as $17,000 ($50,000 × .34) as opposed to $7,500 ($50,000 × .15).

Taxable Income and Gross Tax Liability

Taxable income is gross income less all allowable deductions. This amount is used to determine the gross tax liability from the appropriate tax rate schedules. The corporate and individual tax computations of taxable income and tax liability are illustrated in subsequent sections of this appendix.

Tax Credits and Prepayments of Tax Liability

Once the gross tax liability is determined, taxpayers may subtract two other items before the final net tax liability is determined. These items are allowable tax credits and prepayments of tax liability.

Tax Credits **Tax credits** represent dollar-for-dollar reductions in tax liability as provided by Congress in the Code. In this respect, credits are worth more than deductions, because they reduce the tax liability directly (as opposed to reducing income subject to tax). Over the years, Congress has enacted a number of business and personal tax credits as a means to provide tax relief and/or encourage certain types of expenditures. The most common business credits are for research expenses, rehabilitiation of old buildings, low-income housing investments, and wages of new employees from targeted high-unemployment groups. The most common individual credits are for dependent and child care expenses and for elderly taxpayers with little social security income. The details regarding these credits are beyond the scope of this introduction.

Example 20   Bumble Company is in the 34% tax bracket. A $100 deduction for Bumble will result in $34 of tax savings, because the deduction offsets $100 of income that would otherwise be subject to a 34% tax rate. On the other hand, a $100 credit will result in $100 of tax savings, because the credit is a direct offset to tax liability.

Prepayments of Tax Liability   Our tax system operates on a "pay-as-you-go basis," in that taxpayers must prepay their tax liabilities during the year that income is earned. This is accomplished through either withholdings of tax (for employees) or quarterly estimates of tax liability (for other taxpayers). These amounts reduce the gross tax liability in determining the net tax due (or refund due).

Computing the Corporate Income Tax: An Example

The best way to provide an overview of the corporate tax computation is to "walk through" a simple example that converts a company's financial accounting income statement into the corporate tax formula. Those computations that are unique to the tax formula are explained as part of the overview. The resulting tax computations are then transferred to a filled-in corporate tax return, Form 1120.

Exhibit A2-3 provides a financial accounting income statement of Kravitz Corporation. Additional information is provided as footnotes when more detail is needed for determining the corporate tax liability. This information in Exhibit A2-3 is rearranged in the form of the corporate income tax computation in Exhibit A2-4. The following discussion highlights those items that are subject to special tax treatment for corporations. Finally, the information from Exhibit A2-4 is used to prepare the corporate tax return, Form 1120, which is illustrated in Exhibit A2-5 on page A-41. Also illustrated in Exhibit A2-6 on page A-42, is the special Schedule M-1 of Form 1120, which is used to reconcile the differences between financial accounting income (before taxes) and taxable income (before special deductions).

LO 3

Describe the general tax treatment of the following items for a corporate taxpayer: net capital gains, net capital losses, charitable contributions deductions, and the dividends received deduction.

Gross Receipts for a Corporation

The gross receipts of a corporation include all sources of income. For Kravitz Corporation in Exhibit A2-4, this includes all inflows. Kravitz is permitted to deduct or recover the cost of goods sold in determining gross profit, and it is permitted to recover its costs on the two sales of security investments (capital assets).

Gross Dividends Received   Kravitz Corporation received $10,000 of dividends from a 10% interest in another corporation. The gross amount is always includable in gross income, even though Kravitz qualifies for a special *dividends received deduction*

EXHIBIT A2-3   Financial Accounting Income Statement for Kravitz Corporation

Sales revenue		$ 782,000
Cost of goods sold		(430,000)
Gross profit		352,000
Expenses of operations:		
Salaries and wages	$145,000	
Advertising expense	22,000	
Depreciation [a]	30,000	
Entertainment expenses [b]	6,000	
Repairs expense	13,000	
Contributions to charities	15,000	
Business interest paid	1,000	
Total expenses of operations		(232,000)
Income from operations		120,000
Other income and gains		
Dividend income [c]	$ 10,000	
Gain on sale of ABC Co. securities [d]	4,000	
Interest income (State of Ohio bonds) [e]	6,000	
Total other income and gains		20,000
Other expenses and losses:		
Loss on sale of DEF Co. securities [f]		(10,000)
Net income before taxes		$ 130,000
Less income tax expense [g]		(44,200)
Net income		$ 85,800

Notes:

[a] Depreciation, based on the straight-line method:

Machinery acquired 1/1/94 ($200,000 / 10)	$ 20,000
Building acquired 1/1/94 ($400,000 / 40)	10,000
Total depreciation deduction	$ 30,000

[b] Meals and entertainment expenses for customers.

[c] Dividend from 10% interest in GHI Corporation.

[d] Investment held for eight months on date of sale.

[e] Interest is exempt for federal income tax purposes.

[f] Investment held longer than two years on date of sale.

[g] Income tax liability estimated using 34% tax rate; actual quarterly estimates of income tax liability forwarded to the government totaled $28,000 (four quarterly payments of $7,000 each).

(described below). Full inclusion is required at this point in the computation to ensure that the contributions deduction limit (described below) is properly computed.

Capital Gains and Losses   As mentioned earlier, at the end of the tax year, a taxpayer must group all capital gain and loss transactions into short-term and long-term categories. The short-term and long-term results are then combined and the

EXHIBIT A2-4   Federal Income Tax Computation for Kravitz Corporation

Sales revenue		$ 782,000
Cost of goods sold		(430,000)
Gross profit		352,000
Gross dividend income (10% interest in GHI Co.)		10,000
Interest income—State of Ohio bonds		6,000
Capital gains and losses:		
Short-term gain on sale of ABC securities	$ 4,000	
Long-term loss on sale of DEF securities	(10,000)	
Net capital result [a]		–0–
Gross receipts		$ 368,000
Less exclusions (Interest income—Ohio bonds)		(6,000)
Gross income		$ 362,000
Deductions:		
Salaries and wages	$145,000	
Advertising expense	22,000	
Depreciation [b]	38,768	
Entertainment expenses ($6,000 × .50)	3,000	
Repairs expense	13,000	
Business interest paid	1,000	
Total expenses before charitable contributions		(222,768)
Taxable income before charitable contributions		$ 139,232
Contributions ($15,000, limited to $139,232 × .10) [c]		(13,923)
Taxable income before special deductions		$ 125,309
Special deductions:		
Dividends received deduction ($10,000 × .70)		(7,000)
Taxable income		$ 118,309
Gross tax liability:		
$50,000 × .15	$ 7,500	
$25,000 × .25	6,250	
$25,000 × .34	8,500	
$18,309 × .39	7,141	
Gross tax liability		$29,391
Less credits		(–0–)
Less prepayments of tax liability		(28,000)
Net tax liability (or refund due)		$ 1,391

Notes:

[a] A net capital loss is not deductible by a corporation;
however, the $6,000 net loss may be carried back 3 years
by filing amended tax returns.

[b] MACRS deductions for the two assets are as follows:

Machinery—7-year MACRS ($200,000 × .1429)		$ 28,580
Building—39-Year MACRS ($400,000 × .02547)		10,188
Total MACRS deduction		$ 38,768

[c] Limit is less than actual contributions of $15,000; the
$1,077 excess may be carried forward for 5 years.

net result enters income. For corporations, the results enter income under the following rules:

1. Net *gains* are included in income and are fully taxable.

2. Net *losses* may not offset noncapital gains income; rather, they may be carried back 3 years and forward 5 years to offset any capital gains in those years. All carrybacks and carryforwards are treated as *short-term* capital losses in the carryback or carryforward year.

In Exhibit A2-4, Kravitz Corporation incurred a $4,000 short-term capital gain on the sale of ABC stock (held 8 months) and a $10,000 long-term loss on the sale of DEF stock (held 2 years). Combining the short-term and long-term result yields a net long-term loss of $6,000 (long-term because the long-term result was larger than the short-term result). This loss cannot be deducted against ordinary (noncapital gains) income, so the net result in the tax formula is simply shown as $0.

Kravitz may carry the net capital loss back to the third prior year (as a short-term capital loss) and use it to offset any net capital gains reported in that year. This is accomplished by filing an amended tax return. Any loss that cannot be utilized within the 3 carryback years or 5 carryforward years is simply lost forever.

Example 21   Assume that Kravitz Corporation's federal income tax return filed 3 years ago included a $10,000 short-term capital gain, and that Kravitz's tax rate on that gain was 34%. Kravitz may now file an amended return for that year and include the $6,000 capital loss carryback from the current year. Kravitz is entitled to a refund of $2,040 ($6,000 × .34), since the $6,000 loss carryback offsets $6,000 of the gain originally reported in that prior year.

Exclusions for a Corporation

Kravitz Corporation qualifies for one exclusion in Exhibit A2-4, the exclusion for interest income on state and municipal bonds. The $6,000 of interest on the State of Ohio bonds is not subject to taxation and is subtracted in determining gross income.

Deductions for a Corporation

A comparison of Exhibit A2-3 and A2-4 indicates that the same amount is deductible for both accounting and tax purposes for several expenses incurred by Kravitz Corporation. However, three items are treated differently: depreciation, entertainment expenses, and charitable contributions.

Depreciation   Exhibit A2-3 discloses that Kravitz Corporation elected to use straight-line depreciation for financial accounting purposes, based on useful lives of 10 years for the machinery and 40 years for the building. For tax purposes, Kravitz uses the MACRS procedure for both assets and it is assumed that Kravitz does *not* elect Sec. 179 immediate expensing on the machine. The machinery is classifed as 7-year personalty for MACRS purposes, and the appropriate first-year recovery factor is .1429 (as disclosed in Exhibit A2-2). The building is 39-year nonresidential realty for MACRS purposes, and the appropriate first-year recovery factor (Exhibit A2-2) is .02547. The total deduction for depreciation for tax purposes ($38,768 in Exhibit A2-4) exceeds the financial accounting deduction ($30,000 in Exhibit A2-3) by $8,768.

Entertainment Expenses   As mentioned earlier in this appendix, only 50% of meals and entertainment expenses is deductible for tax purposes. Thus, only $3,000 is deducted in the tax formula (Exhibit A2-4), even though the entire $6,000 is treated as an expense for financial accounting purposes (Exhibit A2-3).

Charitable Contributions   The Code limits the charitable contribution deduction for tax purposes to 10% of an "intermediate" taxable income figure. This intermediate taxable income figure is gross income less all deductions other than the contributions deduction, any net operating loss or capital loss carryback deduction, and any dividends received deduction. Any nondeductible contribution may be carried forward for 5 years and is once again subject to the 10% limit.

In the case of Kravitz Corporation, this intermediate taxable income figure is $139,232. Therefore, only $13,923 ($139,232 × .10) of the $15,000 actual contributions made are deductible in the current year. The remaining $1,077 contributions may be carried forward to the following year and the 4 succeeding years as a potential deduction in those years (when combined with the actual contributions of those years).

Special Deductions for a Corporation

The Code provides for a number of *special deductions* that are not normally allowed for financial accounting purposes. For example, any net operating loss deduction carryback or carryover is treated as a special deduction for tax purposes.

Another important special deduction is the **dividends received deduction.** This deduction is designed to prevent double or even triple taxation of the same amount of income. For example, Corporation A may have a net income and distribute a dividend to shareholder Corporation B that in turn distributes a dividend to individual shareholder C. In this case, the same income is subject to three layers of taxation. The dividends received deduction lessens the tax bite by allowing Corporation B to deduct a percentage of the dividend it receives from Corporation A.

The dividends received deduction depends on the level of the recipient corporation's ownership in the dividend-paying corporation. The possible deductions based on the percentages of ownership in the paying corporation are as follows:

PERCENTAGE OF DIVIDEND-PAYING CORPORATION OWNED	DIVIDENDS RECEIVED DEDUCTION PERCENTAGE
Less than 20%	70
20% or more, but less than 80%	80
80% or more	100

Note that a corporation that owns at least 80% of the outstanding stock of another corporation receives a 100% dividends received deduction. This result makes sense, because the level of control means that the dividend payment is similar to "moving money from one's left pocket to the right pocket." Kravitz Corporation owns 10% of GHI's outstanding stock, so its dividends received deduction equals 70% of the $10,000 gross dividend, or $7,000.

Gross Tax Liability for a Corporation

Corporations are subject to a special tax rate schedule in the Code. This tax rate schedule may be summarized as follows:

LO   4

Describe the corporate income tax rate schedule.

CORPORATE TAX RATES

INCOME LEVEL	TAX RATE (PERCENTAGE)
$0 to $50,000	15
Over $50,000 to $75,000	25
Over $75,000 to $100,000	34
Over $100,000 to $335,000	39
Over $335,000 to $10,000,000	34
Over $10,000,000*	35

* Special computations are required when taxable income exceeds $15,000,000

In examining the corporate rate schedule, it may seem strange to you that the tax rates temporarily increase to 39% over a range of income and then drop back to 34%. This is a special computation to phase out the benefits of paying tax at the lower rates on the first $75,000 of taxable income, and is beyond the scope of our discussion.

Kravitz Corporation's taxable income is $118,309, and Exhibit A2-4 discloses that the gross tax liability is $29,391. This liability is reduced by $28,000 of quarterly estimates of tax liability already paid by Kravitz during the year. This leaves a final tax liability of $1,391, which must be paid when the tax return is filed.

Form 1120: The Corporate Income Tax Return

Exhibit A2-5 illustrates the front page of the corporate income tax return, *Form 1120,* using the information for Kravitz Corporation from Exhibit A2-4. Note that the form is not that user friendly, in that the charitable contributions deduction (line 19) is listed before other deductions that must be considered in determining the charitable deduction limit. Therefore, the deductions on lines 20 through 26 must also be subtracted from total income (line 11) before the charitable contributions limit can be computed. Also note that the special deductions (which included the dividends received deduction) are reported on line 29.

The corporate tax return is due 2½ months after the close of the tax year. If Kravitz Corporation is a calendar-year taxpayer, its return will be due by March 15 following the close of the tax year.

Exhibit A2-5 illustrates only the first page of the four-page Form 1120. Other portions of the tax return provide details of the summary totals on page 1 or request additional information. For example, Schedule L requires comparative beginning and ending balance sheets for the corporation. One very important part of the corporate tax return is *Schedule M-1,* illustrated in Exhibit A2-6.

We hesitate to show this part of the corporate tax return, because it has high potential to confuse the reader. We do want to stress the point, however, that the IRS needs a roadmap to reconcile the taxable income figure shown on the tax return with the net income shown on the financial statements, should it later audit the company. Schedule M-1 focuses directly on the differences between financial accounting and federal income tax treatments of certain income and expense items, and it can serve as a useful summary of the differences discussed thus far.

Note that Schedule M-1 begins on line 1 with the net income shown on the books ($85,800, per Exhibit A2-3) and works toward the taxable income before special deductions figure shown on line 28 of the Form 1120 ($125,309, per Exhibit A2-5). The first item of adjustment is the federal income tax expense deducted on the books ($44,200), because it is not deductible on the federal tax return. Other

EXHIBIT A2-5 Corporate Income Tax Return Form 1120

Form **1120**

Department of the Treasury
Internal Revenue Service

U.S. Corporation Income Tax Return

OMB No. 1545-0123

▶ **Instructions are separate. See page 1 for Paperwork Reduction Act Notice.**

A Check if a:
1 Consolidated return (attach Form 851) ☐
2 Personal holding co. (attach Sch. PH) ☐
3 Personal service corp. (as defined in Temporary Regs. sec. 1.441-4T— see instructions) ☐

Use IRS label. Other- wise, please print or type.

Name **KRAVITZ CORPORATION**

Number, street, and room or suite no. (If a P.O. box, see page 7 of instructions.) **1120 WIRELESS DRIVE**

City or town, state, and ZIP code **GREENLAND, IL 60115**

B Employer identification number **37-64402**

C Date incorporated **1-1-94**

D Total assets (see Specific Instructions) **$ 894,000**

E Check applicable boxes: (1) ☒ Initial return (2) ☐ Final return (3) ☐ Change of address

Income

1a	Gross receipts or sales **782,000** b Less returns and allowances **0** c Bal ▶	1c	**782,000**
2	Cost of goods sold (Schedule A, line 8)	2	**430,000**
3	Gross profit. Subtract line 2 from line 1c	3	**352,000**
4	Dividends (Schedule C, line 19)	4	**10,000**
5	Interest *(STATE OF OHIO BONDS —TAX EXEMPT— $6,000)*	5	**0**
6	Gross rents	6	**0**
7	Gross royalties	7	**0**
8	Capital gain net income (attach Schedule D (Form 1120)) *(NON DEDUCTIBLE $6000 LOSS)*	8	**0**
9	Net gain or (loss) from Form 4797, Part II, line 20 (attach Form 4797)	9	**0**
10	Other income (see instructions—attach schedule)	10	
11	**Total income.** Add lines 3 through 10 ▶	11	**362,000**

Deductions (See instructions for limitations on deductions.)

12	Compensation of officers (Schedule E, line 4)	12	**145,000**
13a	Salaries and wages _____ b Less employment credits _____ c Bal ▶	13c	
14	Repairs and maintenance	14	**13,000**
15	Bad debts	15	
16	Rents	16	
17	Taxes and licenses	17	
18	Interest	18	**1,000**
19	Charitable contributions (see instructions for 10% limitation) *($15,000 LIMITED TO $139,232×10)*	19	**13,923**
20	Depreciation (attach Form 4562) [20] **38,768**		
21	Less depreciation claimed on Schedule A and elsewhere on return [21a] **0**	21b	**38,768**
22	Depletion	22	
23	Advertising	23	**22,000**
24	Pension, profit-sharing, etc., plans	24	
25	Employee benefit programs	25	
26	Other deductions (attach schedule) *ENTERTAINMENT EXPENSES ($6000 X .50)*	26	**3,000**
27	**Total deductions.** Add lines 12 through 26 ▶	27	**236,691**
28	Taxable income before net operating loss deduction and special deductions. Subtract line 27 from line 11	28	**125,309**
29	**Less: a** Net operating loss deduction (see instructions) [29a]		
	b Special deductions (Schedule C, line 20) *($10,000 X .70)* [29b] **7,000**	29c	**7,000**

Tax and Payments

30	**Taxable income.** Subtract line 29c from line 28	30	**118,309**
31	**Total tax** (Schedule J, line 10)	31	**29,391**
32	**Payments: a** 1992 overpayment credited to 1993 [32a]		
b	1993 estimated tax payments [32b] **28,000**		
c	Less 1993 refund applied for on Form 4466 [32c] ( ) d Bal ▶ [32d] **28,000**		
e	Tax deposited with Form 7004 [32e]		
f	Credit from regulated investment companies (attach Form 2439) [32f]		
g	Credit for Federal tax on fuels (attach Form 4136). See instructions [32g]	32h	**28,000**
33	Estimated tax penalty (see instructions). Check if Form 2220 is attached ▶ ☐	33	
34	**Tax due.** If line 32h is smaller than the total of lines 31 and 33, enter amount owed	34	**1,391**
35	**Overpayment.** If line 32h is larger than the total of lines 31 and 33, enter amount overpaid	35	
36	Enter amount of line 35 you want: **Credited to 1994 estimated tax** ▶ Refunded ▶	36	

Please Sign Here

Under penalties of perjury, I declare that I have examined this return, including accompanying schedules and statements, and to the best of my knowledge and belief, it is true, correct, and complete. Declaration of preparer (other than taxpayer) is based on all information of which preparer has any knowledge.

▶ *Leonard R. Kravitz* | 3-15-95 | ▶ PRESIDENT
Signature of officer | Date | Title

Paid Preparer's Use Only

Preparer's signature ▶ | Date | Check if self-employed ☐ | Preparer's social security number

Firm's name (or yours if self-employed) and address ▶ | | E.I. No. ▶ | ZIP code ▶

Cat. No. 11450Q

EXHIBIT A2-6 Illustration of Schedule M–1, Form 1120

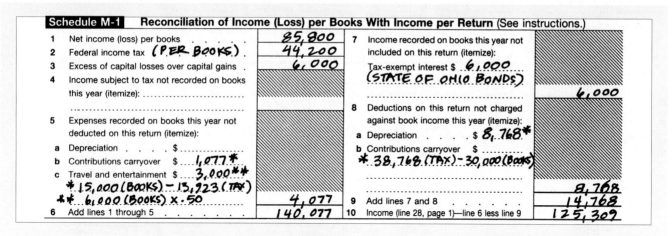

differences between book income and taxable income are then listed on lines 3 through 8 of Schedule M-1. A review of these items discloses each item of income or expense that was treated differently between the books and the tax return, with the exception of the dividends received deduction (which is deducted on the tax return *after* line 28 on Form 1120).

The Individual Income Tax Illustrated

The reporting procedures for individual taxpayers are quite different than the corporate procedures. For example, all deductions of individuals are further classified as either deductions *for* adjusted gross income or deductions *from* adjusted gross income. Also, individuals may deduct amounts for personal exemptions and certain personal expenditures as provided by Congress in the Code.

The best way to illustrate the individual tax computation is once again to walk through a comprehensive example. Exhibit A2-7 illustrates the individual tax computation for a hypothetical married couple, Allen and Ann Simpson. The following discussion highlights the major components of the individual tax formula disclosed in Exhibit A2-7.

Gross Receipts for Individuals

As is true with corporations, gross receipts include all sources of income received by the taxpayer during the year. The source of the payment is irrelevant; thus, lottery winnings would be part of gross receipts.

Exclusions for Individuals

As shown in Exhibit A2-7, the Simpsons qualify for one exclusion: interest income on state and local obligations. Note that none of the remaining sources of income qualify for exclusion because none are specifically exempted by Congress in the Code. For example, the lottery winnings are taxable because Congress has chosen not to exempt such earnings from taxation.

EXHIBIT A2-7   Illustration of the Individual Income Tax Computation

Facts: Allen and Ann Simpson are married taxpayers (both age 42) who elect to file a joint federal income tax return in 1994. They provide all of the support of their 12-year old son Sam and 8-year old daughter Pam.

Gross receipts:

Salaries ($40,000 Allen and $55,000 Ann)	$95,000	
Dividend income (JKL Corporation stock)	3,000	
Interest income (certificates of deposit)	5,000	
Interest income (State of Missouri bonds)	8,000	
Lottery winnings—Illinois lottery	4,000	
Gross receipts		$ 115,000

Exclusions *from* income:

Interest income (State of Missouri bonds)		(8,000)

Gross income $ 107,000

Deductions *for* adjusted gross income:

Alimony (paid by Allen to former spouse)	$ 4,000	
Loss on sale of GHI stock [a]	3,000	
Total deductions for adjusted gross income		(7,000)

Adjusted gross income $ 100,000

Deductions *from* adjusted gross income:

Personal exemption deductions ($2,450 × 4)		(9,800)

Larger of:

Standard deduction (joint return)	$ 6,350	

Total itemized deductions:

Medical expenses	$ –0–	
Interest on home mortgage	9,000	
Taxes (state and local)	11,000	
Charitable contributions	4,000	
Casualty and theft loss	–0–	
Miscellaneous itemized	–0–	
Total itemized deductions	$24,000	
Larger of standard or itemized		(24,000)

Taxable income $ 66,200

Gross tax liability (1994 joint return rates) $ 13,596

Less credits and prepayments:

Dependent care credit ($2,400 × .20)		(480)
Federal income tax prepayments (withholdings)		(13,000)

Net tax liability $ 116

[a] GHI stock was bought in 1990 for $12,000 and was sold in 1994 for $5,000. Of the $7,000 total long-term capital loss, a maximum of $3,000 may be deducted in 1994.

Gross Income for Individuals

Gross income, the excess of gross receipts over allowable exclusions, has special meaning for individual taxpayers. For example, the requirements to file a return and one of the tests for personal exemption deductions are both based on gross income levels. The details of these tests are beyond the scope of this introduction.

Deductions for an Individual's Adjusted Gross Income

LO 5

For individual taxpayers, provide examples of (1) deductions for adjusted gross income and (2) deductions from adjusted gross income, and describe the treatment of net capital gains and net capital losses.

Deductions for individual taxpayers are further classified into two categories for reporting purposes: deductions *for* adjusted gross income (AGI) and deductions *from* AGI. Sometimes these deductions are also referred to as *"above the line"* deductions (*for* AGI) and *"below the line"* deductions (*from* AGI).

Deductions for AGI are composed mainly of business-related expenditures, although over the years, Congress has added some personal expenditures, such as alimony and payments to individual retirement accounts, to the *for*-AGI category. In Exhibit A2-7, the Simpsons may deduct the $4,000 of alimony payments made to Allen's former spouse. Note that this expenditure is not deductible as a trade or business expense under Code Sec. 162 or as an income-producing expense under Sec. 212; however, Congress enacted a specific provision in the Code to allow a deduction for this otherwise nondeductible personal expenditure.

Another special *for*-AGI deduction for individual taxpayers is a limited deduction for net capital losses. Unlike corporate taxpayers, individuals may deduct a maximum of $3,000 of net capital losses in a year against other ordinary (noncapital gains) income shown on the tax return.

Thus, the Simpsons may deduct $3,000 of the total $7,000 long-term capital loss realized in 1994. The excess loss of $4,000 may be carried forward indefinitely as a long-term capital loss for possible deductibility in future years. (Recall that a corporation has a limited period for utilizing excess capital losses of the 3 preceding tax years and the following 5 tax years.)

What about any net capital gains of individuals? Both short-term and long-term capital gains realized by individuals are includable in gross income. Net long-term capital gains (but *not* short-term capital gains) are taxed, however, at a maximum rate of only 28% for individual taxpayers. Because the individual tax rates go as high as 39.6% (see the following discussion), this can result in some tax savings. Preferential rates are not available for corporate taxpayers, however.

Example 22   Assume that in 1995 the Simpsons (Exhibit A2-7) incurred a $10,000 net long-term capital gain. The unused long-term capital loss in 1994 of $4,000 ($7,000 total loss less $3,000 actually deducted) will be treated as a long-term capital loss incurred in 1995, which produces a final long-term capital result of a $6,000 gain ($10,000 − $4,000). If the Simpsons are in a tax bracket higher than 28%, they will pay a maximum tax rate of only 28% on this $6,000 long-term capital gain.

Adjusted Gross Income for Individuals

The concept of **adjusted gross income** has special meaning in the individual tax computation, in that this number serves as a key figure for different purposes in the Code. For example, certain itemized deductions are allowed only to the extent that they exceed a certain percentage of AGI. In Exhibit A2-7, the Simpsons have an AGI of $100,000.

Deductions from an Individual's Gross Income

The Code permits taxpayers to use two broad categories of **deductions from AGI** in arriving at taxable income. These are the personal exemptions deduction and the larger of the standard deduction or total itemized deductions.

Personal Exemptions Deduction   As part of our very first income tax laws, Congress granted a tax-free subsistence level of income as a **personal exemptions deduction** for every taxpayer, his or her spouse, and all family members who meet certain "dependency" tests in the Code. This amount has increased over the years and is currently established at $2,450 in 1994, with automatic annual increases for inflation.

Obviously, the $2,450 is an unrealistically low amount of subsistence in today's economy, but the deduction does provide some tax savings. The tax computation in Exhibit A2-7 assumes that the Simpsons qualify for four exemptions, one each for Allen and Ann and one each for their two children.

Larger of the Standard Deduction or Itemized Deductions   Over the years, Congress has granted a variety of personal deductions to individuals as deductions *from* AGI. These qualifying personal expenditures became known as **itemized deductions** because the taxpayer had to list the items individually on his or her return.

Exhibit A2-7 discloses the major categories of itemized deductions. These allowable deductions include primarily the following:

1. *Medical expenses,* but only to the extent that unreimbursed expenditures exceed 7.5% of adjusted gross income.
2. *Interest expense,* but only on qualified home mortgages and loans related to investments.
3. *Taxes paid,* limited generally to state and local income and property taxes.
4. *Charitable contributions,* generally cash and the fair market value of property given to qualified charities, but limited to 50% of adjusted gross income.
5. *Casualty and theft losses,* but only to the extent that unreimbursed losses exceed 10% of adjusted gross income.
6. *Miscellaneous itemized deductions,* such as tax return preparation fees, unreimbursed employee expenses, and investment expenses, but only to the extent that the total expenditures exceed 2% of adjusted gross income.

To simplify the tax calculation and reduce the administrative burden on the IRS, Congress instituted the concept of a standard deduction during World War II. A taxpayer was given the choice of either itemizing his or her personal deductions or simply subtracting the **standard deduction,** if this amount was larger than the itemized deduction. The standard deduction is currently fixed at an amount that depends on the taxpayer's filing status. The 1994 standard deduction for married taxpayers filing a joint return is $6,350. The deduction for single taxpayers is $3,800.

In Exhibit A2-7, the Simpsons have total itemized deductions of $24,000. Therefore, they elect to itemize their deductions, because this total exceeds the standard deduction for married taxpayers of $6,350.

Taxable Income for Individuals

Taxable income is the excess of adjusted gross income over the deductions from adjusted gross income. This figure is used to determine the gross tax liability of the taxpayer.

Gross Tax Liability for Individuals

LO 6

Describe the individual income tax rate schedules, filing status, and any special tax rates applicable to specific types of income.

The first step in determining the gross tax liability for an individual is to determine the appropriate *filing status.* The four basic filing statuses are (1) single, (2) married filing jointly, (3) married filing separately, and (4) head of household. The tax rate schedules for the two most common statuses are as follows:

SINGLE (UNMARRIED) TAX RATE SCHEDULE (1994)

IF TAXABLE INCOME IS OVER	BUT NOT OVER	THE TAX IS
$ –0–	$ 22,750	15% of taxable income
22,750	55,100	$3,412.50 plus 28% of the excess over $22,750
55,100	115,000	$12,470.50 plus 31% of the excess over $55,100
115,000	250,000	$31,039.50 plus 36% of the excess over $115,000
250,000	—	$79,639.50 plus 39.6% of the excess over $250,000

MARRIED FILING JOINTLY TAX RATE SCHEDULE (1994)

IF TAXABLE INCOME IS OVER	BUT NOT OVER	THE TAX IS
$ –0–	$ 38,000	15% of taxable income
38,000	91,850	$5,700.00 plus 28% of the excess over $38,000
91,850	140,000	$20,778.00 plus 31% of the excess over $91,850
140,000	250,000	$35,704.50 plus 36% of the excess over $140,000
250,000	—	$75,304.50 plus 39.6% of the excess over $250,000

The Simpsons have elected to file a joint return, in which all income and expenses of both spouses are combined on one tax return. Generally, this is more beneficial for a married couple than filing separate returns. (Interestingly, a married couple may *not* elect to file as single individuals, and this prohibition has led to the widely discussed "marriage penalty.") As a married couple, the Simpsons compute their gross tax liability with the tax rate schedule shown above. The Simpsons' income falls in the $38,000–$91,850 bracket, so their tax liability is computed as the sum of (1) $5,700 plus (2) 28% of $28,200 ($66,200 − $38,000), or a total tax liability of $13,596.

Credits and Prepayments for Individuals

As was true with corporate taxpayers, individuals may reduce their gross tax liabilities with allowable tax credits and income tax prepayments. In Exhibit A2-7, it is assumed that the Simpsons qualify for a $480 credit for childcare expenses (the details of this computation are beyond the scope of this discussion). Exhibit A2-7 assumes that $2,400 of expenses qualify for a 20% credit.

Individual taxpayers may also reduce their gross tax liability by any prepayments of income tax made during the year through withholdings by an employer or estimated tax payments. Exhibit A2-7 assumes that a total of $13,000 in income taxes were withheld from Allen and Ann's salaries during 1994.

Net Tax Liability for Individuals

Exhibit A2-7 discloses that the Simpsons owe net income taxes of $116 when they file their 1994 income tax return. Individuals must file their federal income tax returns within 3½ months of the end of the tax year. If the Simpsons use a calendar year (as most individuals do), the return is due by April 15, 1995.

Form 1040: The Individual Income Tax Return

Exhibit A2-8 illustrates a filled-in *Form 1040* for the Simpsons, using the data of Figure Exhibit A2-7. Note that the form closely follows the format of Exhibit A2-7 and that special schedules A and B are required.

Tax Planning

Tax planning may be loosely defined as structuring transactions to minimize the impact of taxes. Perhaps the most important key to successful tax planning is a thorough knowledge of the ins and outs of the federal income tax law and how it applies to the taxpayer. Obviously, the brief introduction to the tax law provided in this appendix may leave you a little short of this knowledge level. We can offer a few suggestions, however, based on our limited coverage of the tax laws.

LO **7**

Explain the potential tax planning advantages of (1) a corporation increasing salary payments to family employees in family corporations and (2) a high-income individual investing in state or local bond obligations.

Mitigating the Double Taxation of Family Corporations

Earlier we mentioned that one of the disadvantages of the corporate form is that income may be taxed twice, once when earned by the corporations and once when distributed as dividends to the shareholders (because such dividend payments are not deductible by the corporation). In many family corporations, however, the shareholders are also employees of the corporation, and any compensation paid to such employees is deductible by the corporation as salary expense. Thus, that portion of the corporate taxable income is taxed only once, at the shareholder level.

Example 23   Jill Wade owns 30% of her family's WXY Corporation and serves as the company's treasurer. WXY's taxable income for the current year is $100,000, after deducting Jill's salary of $40,000. Jill received dividends from WXY totaling $30,000 during the year. If WXY increases Jill's salary by $20,000 and reduces her dividends by the same amount, the corporation's deductions will increase by $20,000 and taxable income will be reduced to $80,000. This will save the corporation $6,800 in taxes ($20,000 × .34 tax rate). Jill will then report $60,000 salary and $10,000 dividends, the same total taxable gross income ($70,000) as before.

Of course, the IRS is aware of this planning strategy and will want to know if the $60,000 salary is a "reasonable" amount for the work that Jill performs. If it believes that this amount is overstated, the IRS has the power to reclassify the excessive salary as dividend income. But WXY Corporation may be able to justify the additional salary if the amount is comparable to amounts that similar companies pay in similar circumstances.

EXHIBIT A2-8 Individual Income Tax Return Form 1040

Form **1040**
Department of the Treasury—Internal Revenue Service
U.S. Individual Income Tax Return (M)

IRS Use Only—Do not write or staple in this space.

OMB No. 1545-0074

Label
(See instructions on page 12.)

Use the IRS label. Otherwise, please print or type.

Your first name and initial: ALLEN A. Last name: SIMPSON

Your social security number: 468 22 1042

If a joint return, spouse's first name and initial: ANN B. Last name: SIMPSON

Spouse's social security number: 492 11 6060

Home address (number and street). If you have a P.O. box, see page 12. Apt. no.

112 MAIN STREET

City, town or post office, state, and ZIP code. If you have a foreign address, see page 12.

RICHMOND, VA 23201

For Privacy Act and Paperwork Reduction Act Notice, see page 4.

Presidential Election Campaign
(See page 12.)

Do you want $3 to go to this fund? — Yes: X

If a joint return, does your spouse want $3 to go to this fund? — Yes: X

Note: Checking "Yes" will not change your tax or reduce your refund.

Filing Status
(See page 12.)

Check only one box.

1. Single
2. X Married filing joint return (even if only one had income)
3. Married filing separate return. Enter spouse's social security no. above and full name here. ▶
4. Head of household (with qualifying person). (See page 13.) If the qualifying person is a child but not your dependent, enter this child's name here. ▶
5. Qualifying widow(er) with dependent child (year spouse died ▶ 19   ). (See page 13.)

Exemptions
(See page 13.)

6a X Yourself. If your parent (or someone else) can claim you as a dependent on his or her tax return, **do not** check box 6a. But be sure to check the box on line 33b on page 2

b X Spouse

c Dependents:

(1) Name (first, initial, and last name)	(2) Check if under age 1	(3) If age 1 or older, dependent's social security number	(4) Dependent's relationship to you	(5) No. of months lived in your home in 1993
SAM		816 40 3522	SON	12
PAM		832 10 1165	DAUGHTER	12

If more than six dependents, see page 14.

No. of boxes checked on 6a and 6b: **2**

No. of your children on 6c who:
• lived with you: **2**
• didn't live with you due to divorce or separation (see page 15)

Dependents on 6c not entered above

d If your child didn't live with you but is claimed as your dependent under a pre-1985 agreement, check here ▶ ☐

e Total number of exemptions claimed

Add numbers entered on lines above ▶ **4**

Income

Attach Copy B of your Forms W-2, W-2G, and 1099-R here.

If you did not get a W-2, see page 10.

If you are attaching a check or money order, put it on top of any Forms W-2, W-2G, or 1099-R.

7	Wages, salaries, tips, etc. Attach Form(s) W-2	7	95,000
8a	Taxable interest income (see page 16). Attach Schedule B if over $400	8a	5,000
b	Tax-exempt interest (see page 17). DON'T include on line 8a 8b 8,000		
9	Dividend income. Attach Schedule B if over $400	9	3,000
10	Taxable refunds, credits, or offsets of state and local income taxes (see page 17)	10	
11	Alimony received	11	
12	Business income or (loss). Attach Schedule C or C-EZ	12	
13	Capital gain or (loss). Attach Schedule D	13	(3,000)
14	Capital gain distributions not reported on line 13 (see page 17)	14	
15	Other gains or (losses). Attach Form 4797	15	
16a	Total IRA distributions 16a b Taxable amount (see page 18)	16b	
17a	Total pensions and annuities 17a b Taxable amount (see page 18)	17b	
18	Rental real estate, royalties, partnerships, S corporations, trusts, etc. Attach Schedule E	18	
19	Farm income or (loss). Attach Schedule F	19	
20	Unemployment compensation (see page 19)	20	
21a	Social security benefits 21a b Taxable amount (see page 19)	21b	
22	Other income. List type and amount—see page 20 LOTTERY WINNINGS	22	4,000
23	Add the amounts in the far right column for lines 7 through 22. This is your **total income** ▶	23	104,000

Adjustments to Income
(See page 20.)

24a	Your IRA deduction (see page 20) 24a		
b	Spouse's IRA deduction (see page 20) 24b		
25	One-half of self-employment tax (see page 21) 25		
26	Self-employed health insurance deduction (see page 22) 26		
27	Keogh retirement plan and self-employed SEP deduction 27		
28	Penalty on early withdrawal of savings 28		
29	Alimony paid. Recipient's SSN ▶ 364 11 2023 29 4,000		
30	Add lines 24a through 29. These are your **total adjustments** ▶	30	4,000

Adjusted Gross Income

31 Subtract line 30 from line 23. This is your **adjusted gross income**. If this amount is less than $23,050 and a child lived with you, see page EIC-1 to find out if you can claim the "Earned Income Credit" on line 56 ▶ | 31 | 100,000

Cat. No. 11320B

Form **1040**

9

EXHIBIT A2-8 Individual Income Tax Return Form 1040, continued

Form 1040   Page **2**

Tax Compu-tation (See page 23.)	**32**	Amount from line 31 (adjusted gross income)	**32**	100,000
	33a	Check if: ☐ **You** were 65 or older, ☐ Blind; ☐ **Spouse** was 65 or older, ☐ Blind. Add the number of boxes checked above and enter the total here . . . . ▶ **33a**		
	b	If your parent (or someone else) can claim you as a dependent, check here . ▶ **33b** ☐		
	c	If you are married filing separately and your spouse itemizes deductions or you are a dual-status alien, see page 24 and check here . . . . ▶ **33c** ☐		
	34	Enter the larger of your: **Itemized deductions** from Schedule A, line 26, **OR** **Standard deduction** shown below for your filing status. **But if you checked any box on line 33a or b,** go to page 24 to find your standard deduction. If you checked **box 33c,** your standard deduction is zero. • Single—$3,700 • Head of household—$5,450 • Married filing jointly or Qualifying widow(er)—$6,200 • Married filing separately—$3,100	**34**	24,000
	35	Subtract line 34 from line 32	**35**	76,000
	36	If line 32 is $81,350 or less, multiply $2,350 by the total number of exemptions claimed on line 6e. If line 32 is over $81,350, see the worksheet on page 25 for the amount to enter .	**36**	9,800
If you want the IRS to figure your tax, see page 24.	**37**	**Taxable income.** Subtract line 36 from line 35. If line 36 is more than line 35, enter -0-	**37**	66,200
	38	Tax. Check if from a ☐ Tax Table, b ☐ Tax Rate Schedules, c ☐ Schedule D Tax Work-sheet, or d ☐ Form 8615 (see page 25). Amount from Form(s) 8814 ▶ e ____	**38**	13,596
	39	Additional taxes (see page 25). Check if from a ☐ Form 4970 b ☐ Form 4972 . .	**39**	
	40	Add lines 38 and 39 . . . . ▶	**40**	13,596
Credits (See page 25.)	**41**	Credit for child and dependent care expenses. Attach Form 2441	**41**	480
	42	Credit for the elderly or the disabled. Attach Schedule R . .	**42**	
	43	Foreign tax credit. Attach Form 1116	**43**	
	44	Other credits (see page 26). Check if from a ☐ Form 3800 b ☐ Form 8396 c ☐ Form 8801 d ☐ Form (specify) ____	**44**	
	45	Add lines 41 through 44	**45**	480
	46	Subtract line 45 from line 40. If line 45 is more than line 40, enter -0- . . . . . ▶	**46**	13,116
Other Taxes	**47**	Self-employment tax. Attach Schedule SE. Also, see line 25 .	**47**	
	48	Alternative minimum tax. Attach Form 6251	**48**	
	49	Recapture taxes (see page 26). Check if from a ☐ Form 4255 b ☐ Form 8611 c ☐ Form 8828	**49**	
	50	Social security and Medicare tax on tip income not reported to employer. Attach Form 4137	**50**	
	51	Tax on qualified retirement plans, including IRAs. If required, attach Form 5329 . . .	**51**	
	52	Advance earned income credit payments from Form W-2	**52**	
	53	Add lines 46 through 52. This is your **total tax** . . . . ▶	**53**	13,116
Payments Attach Forms W-2, W-2G, and 1099-R on the front.	**54**	Federal income tax withheld. If any is from Form(s) 1099, check ▶ ☐ [54] 13,000		
	55	1993 estimated tax payments and amount applied from 1992 return . [55]		
	56	**Earned income credit.** Attach Schedule EIC . . . . . [56]		
	57	Amount paid with Form 4868 (extension request) . . . . [57]		
	58a	Excess social security, Medicare, and RRTA tax withheld (see page 28) . [58a]		
	b	Deferral of additional 1993 taxes. Attach Form 8841 . . [58b]		
	59	Other payments (see page 28). Check if from a ☐ Form 2439 b ☐ Form 4136 [59]		
	60	Add lines 54 through 59. These are your **total payments** . . . . ▶	**60**	13,000
Refund or Amount You Owe	**61**	If line 60 is more than line 53, subtract line 53 from line 60. This is the amount you **OVERPAID.** ▶	**61**	
	62	Amount of line 61 you want **REFUNDED TO YOU.** . . . . ▶	**62**	
	63	Amount of line 61 you want **APPLIED TO YOUR 1994 ESTIMATED TAX** ▶ [63]		
	64	If line 53 is more than line 60, subtract line 60 from line 53. This is the **AMOUNT YOU OWE.** For details on how to pay, including what to write on your payment, see page 29 . . .	**64**	116
	65	Estimated tax penalty (see page 29). Also include on line 64 . . . [65]		

Sign Here Keep a copy of this return for your records.	Under penalties of perjury, I declare that I have examined this return and accompanying schedules and statements, and to the best of my knowledge and belief, they are true, correct, and complete. Declaration of preparer (other than taxpayer) is based on all information of which preparer has any knowledge.			
	▶ Your signature *Allen Simpson*	Date 4-15-95	Your occupation SALESPERSON	
	▶ Spouse's signature. If a joint return, BOTH must sign. *Ann Simpson*	Date 4-15-95	Spouse's occupation CPA	
Paid Preparer's Use Only	Preparer's signature ▶	Date	Check if self-employed ☐	Preparer's social security no.
	Firm's name (or yours if self-employed) and address ▶		E.I. No. ZIP code	

10

Measuring the Value of an Exclusion

Good tax planning takes advantage of exclusions provided in the Code wherever possible. The following examples relate to two exclusions mentioned earlier in this appendix.

First, investments in state or local obligations have become increasingly popular in recent years, as the spread between interest rates on these obligations and other types of obligations has narrowed. For example, assume that an individual is considering two possible investments: (1) a corporate bond that pays 7% annual (taxable) interest or (2) a state bond that pays 5% (tax-exempt) interest. Which one should the taxpayer choose?

The answer depends on the taxpayer's *marginal tax rate* (the tax rate applicable to the next dollar of taxable income). If taxpayer A is in the 36% tax bracket, the after-tax return on the corporate bond is 4.48%, or 7% times .64 (the portion of the interest income that the taxpayer can keep after paying 36% of the interest income to the government as federal income taxes).

On the other hand, if taxpayer B is in the 15% tax bracket, the after-tax return on the corporate bond will be 5.95%, or 7% times .85 (the interest income left after paying 15% to the government in taxes). Because the after-tax return on the state bond is 5% in either case, taxpayer A is better off investing in the state bond and taxpayer B is better off investing in the corporate bond.

As another illustration of the value of an exclusion, consider a taxpayer in the 36% tax bracket whose employer pays $6,400 of health insurance premiums for the employee during the year. As mentioned earlier, these payments are excludable. Does this mean that the exclusion is worth $6,400? No; actually, the exclusion is worth $10,000! The reason is that if the taxpayer had to pay the premiums, he or she would need $10,000 additional salary from the employer so that, after paying taxes at a 36% rate, $6,400 would be left to purchase the same health insurance coverage.

REVIEW PROBLEM (CORPORATE TAXATION)

The financial accounting income statement of Zee Corporation for the current year discloses the following:

Gross sales revenue		$ 640,500
Cost of goods sold		(322,400)
Gross profit		$ 318,100
Expenses of operations:		
Salaries and wages	$120,600	
Utilities	8,400	
Repairs	4,600	
Entertainment of customers	5,800	
Office expenses	2,300	
Depreciation expense (a)	16,000	
Contributions to charities	18,000	
Total expenses of operation		(175,700)

Income from operations	$ 142,400
Other income and gains:	
Dividend income (b)	20,000
Interest Income (c)	5,000
Other expenses and losses:	
Loss on sale of securities (d)	(15,000)
Net income before taxes	$ 152,400
Less income tax expense (e)	(51,816)
Net income	$ 100,584

(a) Depreciation, based on the straight-line method:

Factory building acquired in January (240,000/40)	6,000
Machinery acquired in January ($100,000/10)	10,000

(b) Total represents $10,000 dividend from Ace Corporation (a 12% ownership interest) and $10,000 dividend from Blue Corporation (a 30% ownership interest)

(c) Interest earned on State of Utah bond obligations

(d) Loss on shares (capital asset) held for 6 years as investment

(e) Estimated at 34% of financial net income (actual quarterly payments of federal income tax total $32,000)

■ REQUIRED

1. Determine Zee Corporation's taxable income for the current year, assuming that Zee uses the MACRS depreciation method and elects Sec. 179 immediate expensing on the machinery.

2. Determine Zee's net tax liability (or refund due), assuming that Zee made four quarterly estimated federal income tax payments of $8,000 each. Also assume that Zee qualifies for a special rehabilitation tax credit of $5,000.

■ SOLUTION TO REVIEW PROBLEM (CORPORATE TAXATION)

1. Gross sales revenue		$ 640,500
Cost of goods sold		(322,400)
Gross profit		$ 318,100
Gross dividend income		20,000
Interest income—Utah bonds		5,000
Capital loss on sale of investment (a)		0
Gross receipts		$ 343,100
Less exclusion (tax-exempt interest on bonds)		(5,000)
Gross income		$ 338,100
Deductions other than contributions:		
Salaries and wages	$120,600	
Utilities	8,400	
Repairs	4,600	
Entertainment of customers (b)	2,900	
Office expenses	2,300	
Depreciation expense (c)	35,402	
Total before contributions		174,202
Income before contributions and special deductions		$ 163,898
Contributions deduction (d)		(16,390)

Income before dividends received deduction	$ 147,508
Dividends received deduction (e)	(15,000)
Taxable income	$ 132,508

(a) Net capital loss is not deductible in the current year
(b) Only 50% of entertainment expenses are deductible
(c) Depreciation, based on MACRS:

Factory building—39-year MACRS ($240,000 × .02547)	$ 6,113
Machinery—Sec. 179 expense deduction (maximum)	17,500
Machinery—Non-Sec. 179 MACRS ($82,500 × .1429)	11,789
Total MACRS (tax depreciation deduction)	$ 35,402

(d) Contributions deduction limited to 10% of $163,898, since this is less than the $18,000 actual contributions
(e) The dividends received deduction is $7,000 for the Ace stock ($10,000 × .70), and $8,000 for the Blue stock ($10,000 × .80)

2. Gross tax liability:

$50,000 × .15	$ 7,500
25,000 × .25	6,250
25,000 × .34	8,500
32,508 × .39	12,678
Gross tax liability	$34,928
Less: Rehabilitation tax credit	(5,000)
Estimated tax payments	(32,000)
Refund due	$ 2,072

REVIEW PROBLEM (INDIVIDUAL TAXATION)

Ralph and Joan Prizler, both age 50, are married taxpayers who elect to file a joint income tax return for the current year. Ralph and Joan provide all of the support of their 15-year old daughter Laurie.

Ralph and Joan's personal records provide the following information for the current year:

Sources of Income:

Ralph's salary as a plumber	$56,000
Joan's salary as a university professor	62,000
Dividend income on IBM stock	1,200
Interest income on savings account	3,400
Interest income from State of Iowa bonds	4,200
Loss on sale of ABC stock (acquired 9 months ago)	(1,000)
Loss on sale of DEF stock (acquired 4 years ago)	(1,500)

Expenditures:

Federal income tax withholdings from salaries	$14,000
Alimony to Joan's former spouse	6,000
Interest on home mortgage	7,000
State income taxes paid during the year	8,600

Contributions to charities (all cash)	4,400
Personal utilities on residence	2,600
Personal groceries	6,600

In addition, Ralph and Joan incurred child care expenses that qualify for a $900 tax credit for the year.

1. Determine Ralph and Joan Prizler's taxable income for the current tax year, assuming that a joint income tax return is filed.

2. Determine Ralph and Joan Prizler's final federal income tax liability (or refund due) for the current tax year.

■ **REQUIRED**

■ **SOLUTION TO REVIEW PROBLEM (INDIVIDUAL TAXATION)**

1. Computation of taxable income:

Gross receipts:			
Salaries ($56,000 + $62,000)			$ 118,000
Dividend income (IBM stock)			1,200
Interest on savings account			3,400
Interest income on Iowa bonds			4,200
Gross receipts			$ 126,800
Less exclusions:			
Interest income on Iowa bonds (a)			(4,200)
Gross income			$ 122,600
Less deductions for adjusted gross income:			
Alimony paid to former spouse			(6,000)
Capital gains and losses:			
Short-term loss on ABC stock sale		(1,000)	
Long-term loss on DEF stock sale		(1,500)	
Net capital loss deduction (b)			(2,500)
Adjusted gross income			$ 114,100
Deductions from adjusted gross income:			
Personal exemption deduction (2,450 × 3) (c)			(7,350)
Itemized deductions:			
State income taxes		8,600	
Contributions to charities		4,400	
Interest on home mortgage		7,000	
Total itemized deductions (d)			(20,000)
Taxable income			$ 86,750

(a) Interest on state bonds is excludable

(b) Net capital loss is fully deductible, since the total loss is less than the $3,000 annual limitation

(c) Exemptions are for Ralph, Joan, and Laurie (a dependent)

(d) Ralph and Joan will elect to itemize, since the total allowable deductions ($20,000) exceed the $6,200 standard deduction for a married couple (Note: the utilities and the groceries are nondeductible personal expenses)

2. Computation of net tax liability:

Gross tax liability (e)	$ 19,350
Less: Child care credit	(900)
Income tax withholdings	(14,000)
Net tax liability	$ 4,450

The gross tax liability is computed using the married filing jointly rate schedules, and is computed as follows:

(e) $\$5,700 + [.28 \times (\$86,750 - \$38,000)] = \underline{\$19,350}$

APPENDIX HIGHLIGHTS

1. (LO 1) The four basic business entity forms for business tax reporting purposes are a sole proprietorship, a partnership, a regular "C" corporation, and a special "S" corporation.

2. (LO 1) A taxpayer may generally choose one of three basic reporting periods: a calendar year, a fiscal year, or a 52–53 week year. In addition, a taxpayer may choose one of three basic overall methods of accounting: the cash method, the accrual method, or a hybrid method.

3. (LO 2) Under the wherewithal-to-pay principle, unearned (prepaid) income is generally taxed when received (regardless of the taxpayer's overall accounting method) since this is the time that the taxpayer is best able to pay the tax and the IRS is best able to collect. But on the expense side, prepaid expenses are not deductible until the expense is in fact "incurred," even if the taxpayer uses the cash method.

4. (LO 2) Generally, all income is presumed to be taxable unless the item is specifically listed as an "exclusion" in the Code. Gains and losses on the sale of certain properties known as "capital assets" may be subject to special tax treatment.

5. (LO 2) An expenditure is not deductible for tax purposes unless expressly provided as a deduction in the Code. Generally, deductible expenses must be either (1) incurred in a trade or business, (2) incurred in an income-producing activity, or (3) allowed as a personal "itemized" deduction in the Code.

6. (LO 2) Under the MACRS cost recovery system, all properties are classified into one of nine categories (7 categories of personalty and 2 categories of realty). The immediate expensing election of Code Sec. 179 permits a taxpayer to elect to expense up to $17,500 of the cost of personalty acquired during the tax year.

7. (LO 2) The gross tax liability of a taxpayer may be reduced dollar for dollar by any allowable tax credits and prepayments of tax liability (for example, withholdings or estimated payments).

8. (LO 3) The net capital gains of a corporation are fully taxable, and the net capital losses are not deductible but may offset any capital gains in the preceeding 3 years or following 5 years. Utilization of unused losses in the 3 prior years requires the filing of amended tax returns.

9. (LO 3) Special rules apply for the corporate charitable contribution deduction and the dividends received deduction. The charitable contribution deduction for corporations is limited to 10% of an intermediate taxable income figure (that is, before considering the charitable contributions, any dividends received deduction, or any net operating loss or capital loss carryback). The dividends received deduction for a corporation is one of the following percentages of the gross dividend: 70% (if the interest owned in the payor corporation is less than 20%), 80% (if the interest owned is 20% or greater but less than 80%), or 100% (if the interest owned is 80% or greater).

10. **(LO 4)** Corporations are subject to a progressive tax rate schedule, with tax rates ranging from 15% to 39%. The tax liability is reported on Form 1120, which includes a Schedule M-1 reconciliation of book and taxable incomes.

11. **(LO 5)** For individual taxpayers, deductions are classified as either "for adjusted gross income (AGI)" or "from adjusted gross income (AGI)." Deductions for AGI are composed mainly of business expenses, net capital losses, and a few personal expenditures such as alimony and individual retirement accounts. The two primary deductions from AGI are the personal exemption deduction ($2,450 per exemption in 1994) and the larger of the standard deduction or total itemized (personal) deductions.

12. **(LO 5)** Net capital losses of individual taxpayers may offset a maximum of $3,000 of noncapital gains income in a year (with an unlimited carryover), and net long-term capital gains are never taxed at a rate exceeding 28%.

13. **(LO 6)** Individuals are subject to a progressive tax rate schedule, based on four filing statuses, with rates ranging from 15% to 39.6%. Individuals report their net tax liabilities on Form 1040.

14. **(LO 7)** Tax planning is the process of arranging one's transactions so that the impact of taxes is minimized. Strategies for corporations include paying salaries to family shareholder-employees, and strategies for high-income individuals include investing in tax-exempt securities.

KEY TERMS QUIZ

Select from the following key terms used in the appendix and fill in the appropriate blank to the left of each description. The solution appears at the end of the appendix.

Accrual method	Immediate expensing election
Adjusted gross income	Itemized deduction
C corporation	Long-term capital gain (loss)
Capital asset	MACRS
Cash method	Net operating loss
Code	Partnership
Deductions	Personal exemptions deduction
Deductions for AGI	S corporation
Deductions from AGI	Sole proprietorship
Dividends received deduction	Standard deduction
Exclusion	Tax credits
Gross income	Wherewithal-to-pay
Gross receipts	

_____ 1. Allowable dollar-for-dollar reductions in tax liability.

_____ 2. Alimony is an example of such a deduction.

_____ 3. The primary source of legislative authority as drafted by Congress.

_____ 4. The cost recovery (depreciation) system for assets acquired after 1986.

_____ 5. Automatic deductions for a taxpayer, his or her spouse, and any dependents.

_____ 6. An elective deduction for the first $17,500 cost of personalty acquired during the year.

_____ 7. Gross income less all deductions permitted for AGI (adjusted gross income).

_____ 8. A noncorporate joint-venture tax entity that does not pay income taxes at the entity level.

_____ 9. The tax entity used by a single individual who is in business by himself or herself.

_____ 10. Special properties, such as investments and personal properties, that qualify for special tax treatment.

_____ 11. The procedure that requires income to be recognized when earned and expenses when incurred.

_____ 12. An item of income specifically exempted from tax under the Code.

_____ 13. The broadest definition of income in the Code that includes all sources but cost recoveries.

_____ 14. Special deductions for personal expenditures that are expressly listed in the Code.

_____ 15. The procedure that requires income to be recognized when received and expenses when paid.

_____ 16. Gross receipts less all allowable exclusions.

_____ 17. A corporate tax entity that does not pay tax at the entity level; instead, the tax is paid by the shareholders.

_____ 18. A special corporate deduction expressed as a percentage of certain types of income in order to lessen multiple rounds of taxing the same income.

_____ 19. Gains and losses on sales of capital assets held longer than one year.

_____ 20. Statutory reductions in gross income for certain expenditures listed in the Code.

_____ 21. The guiding principle for taxing prepaid income when it is received, since this is the best time that the tax can be collected.

_____ 22. A flat reduction in adjusted gross income that is in lieu of itemized deductions.

_____ 23. A corporate tax entity that pays tax at the corporate level.

_____ 24. Personal exemption deductions and the larger of itemized deductions or the standard deduction are its two components.

_____ 25. An excess of business expenses over income that can offset income of other years for tax purposes.

SECONDARY TERMS

ACCOUNTING METHOD The overall reporting procedure used by a taxpayer to report income for tax purposes.

ADMINISTRATIVE AUTHORITY Tax authority represented by interpretations of the tax law, such as regulations, issued by the Department of Treasury and the Internal Revenue Service.

FILING STATUS A designation of the appropriate tax rate schedule to be used by a taxpayer in computing tax liability that depends on the marital status and the number of dependents of the taxpayer.

FORM 1040 The basic tax reporting form for individual taxpayers.

FORM 1120 The basic tax reporting form for corporate taxpayers.

HYBRID METHOD An accounting method that is a combination of two or more general methods of accounting, such as the cash and accrual method.

JUDICIAL AUTHORITY Tax authority represented by court decisions dealing with tax issues.

LEGISLATIVE AUTHORITY Tax authority represented by laws passed by Congress as part of the Internal Revenue Code.

RESIDENTIAL REALTY Real estate that produces at least 80% of its gross income from dwelling (noncommercial) units.

SCHEDULE M-1 The portion of the corporate income tax form 1120 that reconciles book (accounting) income with taxable (tax return) income.

QUESTIONS

1. What is meant by the expression "the Code"? Is the Code the sole authority for answering a tax question? Explain.

2. One of the disadvantages of choosing the corporate form of organization for tax purposes is the possibility of having the same income taxed twice. Why can double taxation occur with a regular C corporation?

3. What are the three possible tax years that a taxpayer may choose from when filing a first tax return?

4. Nancy Gain, a cash-basis taxpayer, owns a rental property. During the current year, a tenant gave her a used air conditioner (worth $300) in lieu of paying the December rent due (also $300). The tenant bought the air conditioner 5 years ago for $700. Does Nancy realize any gross income on this transaction? Explain.

5. "Deductions are matters of legislative grace." What does this statement mean as it relates to deductions for federal income tax purposes?

6. Give an example of a *capital asset*. What distinguishes a short-term capital asset from a long-term capital asset?

7. Zen Corporation paid $1,000 to entertain potential customers during the current year. How much (if any) of this expenditure is deductible?

8. Tau Corporation suffered a net operating loss during the current year. What choices does it have in carrying this loss deduction to other years? What factors will influence such a choice?

9. A taxpayer in the 30% tax bracket is given a choice between receiving a $100 tax deduction or a $40 tax credit. Which should the taxpayer choose? Explain.

10. Unlike corporations, individual taxpayers must separate deductions into one of two categories for tax reporting purposes. What are these two categories? Give an example of a deduction in each category.

EXERCISES

(LO 1) EXERCISE A2-1 TAX ENTITY CHOICE

For each of the following items, indicate which tax entity (or entities) is described. Use the following key:

SP—Sole proprietor   C—Regular C corporation
PS—Partnership   S—S corporation (by election)

_____ a. Income is generally not taxed at the entity level.
_____ b. Its earnings can be subject to double taxation.
_____ c. Tax is paid on income with individual tax return 1040.
_____ d. Income is generally subject to self-employment tax.

(LO 1) EXERCISE A2-2 AMOUNT REPORTABLE BY ACCOUNTING METHOD

Red pays Blue $24,000 on January 1, 1993, for 24 months rent on an office building owned by Blue. Assuming that both Red and Blue are calendar-year taxpayers, determine the amount reportable as rent income by Blue and deductible as rent expense by Red, assuming the following accounting methods:

	ACCOUNTING METHODS			
	CASH BASIS		ACCRUAL BASIS	
	1993	1994	1993	1994
Income reportable by Blue	_____	_____	_____	_____
Expense reportable by Red	_____	_____	_____	_____

(LO 2) EXERCISE A2-3 GENERAL FRAMEWORK FOR TAX LIABILITY COMPUTATION

Match the following terms to the descriptions given:

Credits   Gross receipts
Exclusions   Deductions
Prepayments of tax   Gross income

_____ a. Total income received during the year.
_____ b. Dollar-for-dollar reductions in tax liability.
_____ c. Statutory exemptions from taxation in determining gross income.
_____ d. Income tax withholdings from paychecks.
_____ e. Statutory reductions in gross income.
_____ f. Income after subtracting statutory exclusions.

(LO 2) EXERCISE A2-4 CLASSIFICATION OF ASSETS UNDER MACRS

What class life would the following assets be classified in under the MACRS procedure (the possible choices are 3, 5, 7, 10, 15, 20, 27.5, and 39 years; you may want to refer to Exhibit A2-2 for assistance)?

_____ a. Office furniture
_____ b. Factory warehouse
_____ c. Delivery automobile
_____ d. Residential apartment complex
_____ e. Drill punch machine

(LO 2) EXERCISE A2-5 DETERMINING MAXIMUM SEC. 179 DEDUCTION

Able Corporation bought a new business machine during the current year (the only item of personalty acquired during the year). Ignoring the regular MACRS deduction, what is Able's maximum Sec. 179 immediate expensing deduction for the machine, assuming that the cost of the machine was

_____ a. $160,000?   _____ c. $214,000?
_____ b. $203,000?   _____ d. $223,000?

(LO 3) EXERCISE A2-6 DETERMINING MAXIMUM CORPORATE CHARITABLE DEDUCTION

Deal Corporation has a current year net income before charitable contributions deduction of $100,000. What is the maximum charitable deduction, assuming that its contributions during the current year were

_____ a. $8,500?   _____ c. $10,600?
_____ b. $9,900?   _____ d. $15,000?

(LO 3) EXERCISE A2-7 DETERMINING THE DIVIDENDS RECEIVED DEDUCTION

Motley Corporation received $10,000 of dividends from each of three corporations (A, B, and C) during the tax year. How much of each dividend is taxable after considering any dividends received deduction, assuming that Motley owns the following percentage interests in each company:

_____ Corporation A (a 47% interest)
_____ Corporation B (a 90% interest)
_____ Corporation C (a 16% interest)

(LO 5) EXERCISE A2-8 CLASSIFYING DEDUCTIONS OF INDIVIDUALS

Indicate whether each of the following items is a deduction *for* adjusted gross income or a deduction *from* adjusted gross income for an individual taxpayer:

_____ a. Personal exemptions deduction
_____ b. Alimony paid to former spouse
_____ c. State and local income taxes paid
_____ d. Standard deduction (in lieu of itemized deductions)
_____ e. Short-term capital loss of $2,000

MULTI-CONCEPT EXERCISES

(LO 3, 5) EXERCISE A2-9 DETERMINE CAPITAL LOSS DEDUCTIONS

During the current year, Able incurred $3,000 of short-term capital gains, $1,000 of short-term capital losses, and $8,000 of long-term capital losses. Determine the maximum capital loss deduction for the current year (if any) and any capital loss carryover for Able, assuming that Able is a(n):

	INDIVIDUAL TAXPAYER	CORPORATE TAXPAYER
Maximum deduction	$ _____	$ _____
Loss carryover	$ _____	$ _____

(LO 3, 5) EXERCISE A2-10 TAX TREATMENT OF SPECIFIC ITEMS

For each of the following items, indicate whether the item is treated the same (S) or differently (D) for individual and corporate taxpayers for federal income tax purposes:

_____ a. Charitable contributions
_____ b. Net long-term capital gains
_____ c. Interest income on State of Kentucky bonds
_____ d. Advertising expense
_____ e. Dividend income from corporate investment
_____ f. Interest income on certificate of deposit

PROBLEMS

(LO 2) PROBLEM A2-1 DETERMINING MACRS DEDUCTION

Dee Corporation bought the two assets listed below in January of the current year. Determine Dee's maximum MACRS deduction for the year on the assets, assuming that Dee elects to expense immediately as much of the machinery cost as possible (refer to Exhibit A2-2 for the appropriate MACRS recovery factors):

Drill press machine (7-Year MACRS property)	$ 27,500
Factory warehouse	$100,000

(LO 3) PROBLEM A2-2 CORPORATE CAPITAL ASSET NETTING

During 1994 Bombay Corporation had the following capital gains and losses:

Short-term capital gains	$ 4,000
Short-term capital losses	2,000
Long-term capital gains	6,000
Long-term capital losses	13,000

How will these transactions affect Bombay's 1994 taxable income? Will the transactions affect other tax years?

(LO 3) PROBLEM A2-3 CORPORATE TAXABLE INCOME CALCULATION

Tredgar Corporation realized $180,000 gross profit on inventory sales during the year and received $20,000 dividends from its 30% interest in Z Company. Tredgar also incurred the following expenses during the year: $30,000 MACRS deductions, $40,000 salary expenses, $20,000 miscellaneous cash expenses, and $10,500 charitable contributions. Determine Tredgar's taxable income (but not tax liability) for the year.

(LO 4) PROBLEM A2-4 CORPORATE TAX LIABILITY COMPUTATION

Pleasant Corporation has $150,000 of taxable income during the current year. Pleasant qualifies for tax credits totaling $4,000, and it made quarterly payments of estimated income tax liability during the tax year totaling $24,000. Determine Pleasant's net tax liability owed (or refund due) for the current year.

(LO 5) PROBLEM A2-5 INDIVIDUAL CAPITAL ASSET NETTING

During 1993 Hal Rein's capital transactions netted a $7,000 short-term capital loss, of which the maximum amount was used to offset 1992 income. During 1994, Hal incurred $5,000 of short-term capital gains, $6,000 of short-term capital losses, $14,000 of long-term capital gains, and $3,000 of long-term capital losses. How will Hal report his capital transactions in 1994? Note any special treatments.

(LO 5) PROBLEM A2-6 INDIVIDUAL TAXABLE INCOME COMPUTATION

Melva Rhymes, a single taxpayer, received the following income during the current year: $40,000 salary, $20,000 interest on a savings account, and $12,000 interest on City of Chicago bonds. Her legitimate itemized deductions total $3,200. Determine Melva's taxable income for the year, assuming that she has no other dependents. Do not compute tax liability.

(LO 6) PROBLEM A2-7 INDIVIDUAL TAX LIABILITY COMPUTATION

Rick and Cheryl Boley file a joint return for the current year. Their taxable income is $62,000, and they qualify for a $2,000 child and dependent care credit. Assuming that they prepaid $13,000 of their taxes through income tax withholdings during the year, determine their final net tax liability (or refund due) for the year.

(LO 7) PROBLEM A2-8 INDIVIDUAL TAX PLANNING

Gloria Stenson expects to be in the 36% tax bracket during the upcoming tax year. She is considering two investments: (1) in a taxable corporate bond that pays 8% annual interest and (2) in a tax-exempt state bond that pays 5% interest. Which investment would provide the largest after-tax return? Explain.

MULTI-CONCEPT PROBLEMS

(LO 3, 4) PROBLEM A2-9 CORPORATE TAXABLE INCOME AND TAX LIABILITY

Blue Corporation's results for the current year included the following:

Gross profit on inventory sales	$300,000
Gross dividend income (10% interest)	20,000
Net long-term capital loss	(10,000)
MACRS deductions on assets	50,000
Salaries expenses	120,000
Miscellaneous cash expenses	50,000
Contributions	24,000

Determine Blue's taxable income, gross tax liability, and final amount due for the current year, assuming that Blue made estimated income tax payments during the year totaling $12,000.

(LO 5, 6) PROBLEM A2-10 INDIVIDUAL TAXABLE INCOME AND TAX LIABLITY

Michael and Brenda Irby file a joint return for the current year. Their income consists of $56,000 salaries, $4,000 interest on State of Utah bonds, a $4,000 short-term capital gain, a $9,000 short-term capital loss, and $4,000 dividends from Z Company. They provide all of the support for their 6-year-old daughter Jennifer. Their legitimate itemized deductions total $8,200. Assuming that their federal income tax withholdings for the year total $12,000, determine their gross tax liability and the final amount due (or refund due).

CASES

READING AND INTERPRETING FINANCIAL STATEMENTS

(LO 3) CASE A2-1 CLASSIFYING FINANCIAL STATEMENT ITEMS FOR INCOME TAX EXPENSE DEDUCTION

In examining a company's financial statements, it is not uncommon to notice a federal income tax expense deduction on the income statement that differs significantly from the federal income taxes actually paid by the company. In addition, a Deferred Income Taxes account sometimes shows up on the balance sheet. In trying to account for these differences, it is helpful to distinguish three types of items: (1) those that result in timing differences between books and tax return, (2) those that result in permanent differences between books and tax return, (3) and those that are treated the same for both books and tax return. Classify each of the following items as fitting in one of these three categories:

a. State bond interest income
b. Net loss on capital assets
c. Depreciation deduction
d. Gross sales revenue

e. Repairs expense
f. Dividend income
g. Charitable contributions
h. Salaries expense

MAKING FINANCIAL DECISIONS

(LO 7) CASE A2-2 TAX PLANNING STRATEGY

Sam Adams is a 60% shareholder in Z Corporation, which had taxable income during the current year of $110,000 after deducting Sam's salary of $60,000. The salary and $40,000 of dividends from Z were Sam's only sources of income during the year, and he is single and uses the standard deduction. Sam has been told by his accountant that he should increase his salary to $90,000 (and decrease dividends to $10,000) to save taxes. How much taxes would such an action save? Are there any risks in taking such action? Explain.

ACCOUNTING AND ETHICS: WHAT WOULD YOU DO?

(LO 4) CASE A2-3 THE "MARRIAGE PENALTY"

Sam Rule and Janis Abider are contemplating marriage in December of the current year. Each earns $62,000 from present jobs, and they normally elect the standard deduction on their single tax returns. Estimate the "marriage penalty" that will be imposed if Sam and Janis marry before the end of the year by comparing (1) the sum of their tax liabilities when filing as two single (unmarried) individuals and (2) their tax liability if they marry before the end of the year and file a joint return. Why do you believe that Congress has ignored the societal implications of this marriage penalty?

SOLUTION TO KEY TERMS QUIZ

1. Tax credits (p. A-34)
2. Deductions for AGI (p. A-44)
3. Code (p. A-26)
4. MACRS (p. A-32)
5. Personal exemptions (p. A-45)
6. Immediate expensing election (p. A-33)
7. Adjusted gross income (p. A-44)
8. Partnership (p. A-27)
9. Sole proprietorship (p. A-26)
10. Capital asset (p. A-31)
11. Accrual method (p. A-29)
12. Exclusion (p. A-30)
13. Gross receipts (p. A-29)
14. Itemized deduction (p. A-45)
15. Cash method (p. A-28)
16. Gross income (p. A-30)
17. S corporation (p. A-27)
18. Dividends received deduction (p. A-39)
19. Long-term capital gain (loss) (p. A-31)
20. Deductions (p. A-31)
21. Wherewithal-to-pay (p. A-29)
22. Standard deduction (p. A-45)
23. C corporation (p. A-27)
24. Deductions from AGI (p. A-45)
25. Net operating loss (p. A-34)

Appendix 3, by K. K. Raman, University of North Texas, is a complete study unit available to adopters. To obtain a copy or for more information, ask your Dryden Press sales representative or call 1-817-334-7782.

LEARNING OBJECTIVES

After studying this appendix, you should be able to:

1. Discuss the essential characteristic of government and nonprofit entities.

2. Identify the users of government and nonprofit financial statements and the objectives of financial reporting for these entities.

3. Identify the difference between the accounting equation for a business entity and the accounting equation for a government or nonprofit entity.

4. Use the statement of activities for a nonprofit organization to identify the four measures of performance.

5. Identify two differences between a business statement of cash flows and that of a nonprofit entity.

6. Identify the measurement focus in government accounting.

7. Identify the difference between a business balance sheet and the combined balance sheet for governments.

8. Use the operating statement to evaluate the performance of a government.

9. Read the budget and actual comparison statement for a government.

Outline of Topics

An Overview of Government and Nonprofit Activities
Objectives of Government and Nonprofit Financial Reporting
   User-Oriented Objectives
      Reporting Service Accomplishments
Financial Reporting for Nonprofit Organizations
   The Statement of Financial Position (Balance Sheet)
   Balance Sheet Categories
      Classification of Net Assets

GLOSSARY

ACCELERATED DEPRECIATION   A term that refers to several depreciation methods where a greater amount of depreciation is recorded in the early years of an asset's life and a lesser amount is recorded in the later years.

ACCOUNT   The record used to accumulate monetary amounts for each individual asset, liability, revenue, expense, and component of owners' equity.

ACCOUNTING   The process of identifying, measuring, and communicating economic information to various users.

ACCOUNTING CONTROL   A procedure concerned with the safeguarding of assets or the reliability of the financial statements.

ACCOUNTING SYSTEM   The methods and records used to accurately report an entity's transactions and to maintain accountability for its assets and liabilities.

ACCOUNTS PAYABLE   Amounts owed for the purchase of inventory, goods, or services acquired in the normal course of business.

ACCOUNTS RECEIVABLE TURNOVER   A measure of the number of times accounts receivable are collected in a period.

ACCRUAL   Cash has not yet been paid or received, but expense has been incurred or revenue earned.

ACCRUAL BASIS   A system of accounting in which revenues are recognized when earned and expenses when incurred.

ACCRUED ASSET   An asset resulting from the recognition of a revenue prior to the receipt of cash.

ACCRUED LIABILITY   A liability resulting from the recognition of an expense prior to the payment of cash.

ACCRUED PENSION COST   An account that represents the difference between the amount of pension recorded as an expense and the amount of the funding payment made to the pension fund.

ACCUMULATED BENEFIT OBLIGATION   A measure of the amount owed to employees for pensions if the employees retired at their existing salary levels.

ACID-TEST OR QUICK RATIO   A stricter test of liquidity than the current ratio that excludes inventory and prepayments from the numerator.

ACQUISITION COST   This amount includes all of the costs normally necessary to acquire an asset and prepare it for its intended use.

ADDITIONAL PAID-IN CAPITAL   The amount received for the issuance of stock in excess of the par value of the stock.

ADJUSTING ENTRIES   Journal entries made at the end of a period by a company using the accrual basis of accounting.

ADMINISTRATIVE CONTROL   A procedure concerned with efficient operation of the business and adherence to managerial policies.

AFFILIATE   A company in which another company owns enough of the stock to exercise significant influence.

AGING SCHEDULE   A form used to categorize the various individual accounts receivable according to the length of time each has been outstanding.

ALLOWANCE METHOD   A method of estimating bad debts on the basis of either the net credit sales of the period or the amount of accounts receivable at the end of the period.

AMERICAN ACCOUNTING ASSOCIATION   The professional organization for accounting educators.

AMERICAN INSTITUTE OF CERTIFIED PUBLIC ACCOUNTANTS   The professional organization for certified public accountants.

AMORTIZED COST METHOD   A method of accounting for investments in bonds in which the investment account is adjusted periodically to recognize the amortization of premium or discount.

ANNUITY   A series of payments of equal amount.

APPROPRIATION OF RETAINED EARNINGS   An account that indicates a company has designated a portion of the balance of Retained Earnings for a specific purpose.

ASSET   A future economic benefit.

ASSET TURNOVER RATIO   The relationship between net sales and total assets.

AUDIT COMMITTEE   A sub-set of the board of directors that acts as a direct contact between the stockholders and the independent accounting firm.

AUDITING   The process of examining the financial statements and underlying records of a company in order to render an opinion as to whether the statements are fairly presented.

AUTHORIZED SHARES   The maximum number of shares a corporation may issue as indicated in the corporate charter.

AVAILABLE-FOR-SALE SECURITIES   Stocks and bonds that are not classified as either held-to-maturity or trading securities.

BALANCE SHEET   The financial statement that summarizes the assets, liabilities, and owners' equity at a specific point in time.

BANK RECONCILIATION   A form used by the accountant to reconcile the balance shown on the bank statement for a particular account with the balance shown in the accounting records.

BANK STATEMENT   A detailed listing provided by the bank of all the activity for a particular account during the month.

BLIND RECEIVING REPORT   A form used by the receiving department to account for the quantity and condition of merchandise received from a supplier.

BOARD OF DIRECTORS   The group composed of key officers of a corporation and other outside members responsible for the general oversight of the affairs of the entity.

BOND   A certificate issued by corporations representing a promise to repay a certain amount of money and interest in the future.

BOND ISSUE PRICE   The total of the present value of the cash flows produced by a bond. It is calculated as the present value of the annuity of interest payments plus the present value of the principal.

BOOK VALUE   The original acquisition cost of an asset minus the amount of accumulated depreciation.

BOOK VALUE PER SHARE   Total stockholders' equity divided by the number of shares of common stock outstanding.

CALLABLE BONDS   Bonds that may be redeemed or retired before their specified due date.

CALLABLE STOCK   Allows the issuing firm to eliminate a class of stock by paying the stockholders a fixed amount.

CAPITAL EXPENDITURE   A cost that improves an operating asset and is added to the asset account.

CAPITAL LEASE   A lease that meets one or more of the four FASB criteria and is recorded as an asset by the lessee.

CAPITAL STOCK   A category on the balance sheet to indicate amounts contributed by the owners to a corporation.

CAPITALIZATION OF INTEREST   The process of adding the cost of interest on constructed assets to the cost of the asset rather than as an expense.

CARRYING VALUE   The face value of a bond plus the amount of unamortized premium or minus the amount of unamortized discount.

CASH BASIS   A system of accounting in which revenues are recognized when cash is received and expenses when cash is paid.

CASH EQUIVALENT   An item readily convertible to a known amount of cash and with an original maturity to the investor of three months or less.

CASH FLOW FROM OPERATIONS TO CAPITAL EXPENDITURES   A measure of the ability of a company to finance long-term asset acquisitions from cash from operations.

CASH FLOW FROM OPERATIONS TO CURRENT LIABILITIES   A measure of the ability to pay current debts from operating cash flows.

CASH TO CASH OPERATING CYCLE   The length of time from the purchase of inventory to the collection of any receivable from the sale.

CERTIFIED PUBLIC ACCOUNTANT   The professional designation for public accountants who have passed a rigorous exam and met certain requirements determined by the state.

CHANGE IN ACCOUNTING PRINCIPLE   An income statement item that occurs when a company changes from one accounting method to another method.

CHANGE IN ESTIMATE   A change in the life of an asset or in the expected residual value of the asset.

CHART OF ACCOUNTS   A numerical listing of all the accounts used by a company.

COMPARABILITY   The quality of accounting information that allows a user to analyze two or more companies and look for similarities and differences.

COMPENSATED ABSENCES   Absences from employment such as sick days and vacation days for which it is expected that employees will be paid.

COMPOUND INTEREST   Interest that is calculated on the principal and on previous amounts of interest.

COMPOUND JOURNAL ENTRY   A journal entry in which there are multiple debits or credits, or both.

COMPREHENSIVE INCOME   The amount that reflects the total change in stockholders' equity from all sources except investment or withdrawals by the owners of the company.

CONGLOMERATE   A combination of companies with operations in different industries.

CONSERVATISM   The practice of using the least optimistic estimate when two estimates of amounts are about equally likely.

CONSIGNMENT   A legal arrangement in which inventory owned by one company is turned over to another one for sale.

CONSISTENCY   The quality of accounting information that allows a user to compare two or more accounting periods for a single company.

CONSOLIDATED FINANCIAL STATEMENTS   Statements that report on the parent corporation and any separate legal entities called subsidiaries.

CONTINGENT ASSET   An amount that involves an existing condition dependent upon some future event where the company stands to gain.

CONTINGENT LIABILITY   A liability that involves an existing condition dependent upon some future event where the company stands to lose.

CONTRA ACCOUNT   An account with an opposite balance of a related account.

CONTROL ACCOUNT   The general ledger account that is supported by a subsidiary ledger.

CONTROLLER   The chief accounting officer for a company.

CONVERTIBLE STOCK   Allows preferred stock to be returned to the corporation in exchange for common stock.

CORPORATION   A form of entity organized under the laws of a particular state; ownership evidenced by shares of stock.

COST OF GOODS AVAILABLE FOR SALE   Beginning inventory plus cost of goods purchased.

COST OF GOODS SOLD   Cost of goods available for sale minus ending inventory.

COST PRINCIPLE   Assets are recorded at the cost to acquire them.

CREDIT   An entry on the right side of an account.

CREDIT CARD DRAFT   A multiple-copy document used by a company that accepts a credit card for a sale.

CREDIT MEMORANDA   Additions on a bank statement for such items as interest paid on the account and notes collected by the bank for the customer.

CREDITOR   Someone to whom a company has a debt.

CUMULATIVE EFFECT   The total effect of a change in accounting principle for all years prior to the current year.

CUMULATIVE STOCK   The holders of this stock have a right to dividends in arrears before the current year dividend is distributed.

CURRENT ASSET   An asset that is expected to be realized in cash or sold or consumed during the operating cycle or within one year if the cycle is shorter than one year.

CURRENT LIABILITY   An obligation that will be satisfied within the next operating cycle or within one year if the cycle is shorter than one year.

CURRENT MATURITIES OF LONG-TERM DEBT   The portion of a long-term liability that will be paid within one year of the balance sheet date.

CURRENT RATIO   The ratio of current assets to current liabilities.

CURRENT VALUE   The amount of cash, or its equivalent, that could be received by selling an asset currently.

DEBENTURE BONDS   Bonds that are backed by the general credit worthiness of the issuer and are not backed by specific collateral.

DEBIT   An entry on the left side of an account.

DEBIT MEMORANDA   Deductions on a bank statement for such items as NSF checks and various service charges.

DEBT-TO-EQUITY RATIO   The ratio of total liabilities to total stockholders' equity.

DEBT SECURITIES   Securities issued by corporations and governmental bodies as a form of borrowing.

DEBT SERVICE COVERAGE RATIO   A statement of cash flows measure of the ability of a company to meet its interest and principal payments.

DEBT TO TOTAL ASSETS RATIO   Total liabilities divided by total assets.

DEFERRAL   Cash has either been paid or received, but expense or revenue has not yet been recognized.

DEFERRED EXPENSE   An asset resulting from the payment of cash prior to the incurrence of expense.

DEFERRED REVENUE   A liability resulting from the receipt of cash prior to the recognition of revenue.

DEFERRED TAX   The account that is used to reconcile the difference between the amount recorded as income tax expense and the amount that is payable as income tax.

DEPOSIT-IN-TRANSIT   A deposit recorded on the books but not yet reflected on the bank statement.

DEPRECIATION   The allocation of the original acquisition cost of an asset to the periods benefited by the asset's use.

DIRECT METHOD   The approach to preparing the operating activities section of the statement of cash flows in which cash receipts and cash payments are reported.

DIRECT WRITE-OFF METHOD   The recognition of bad debts expense at the point an account is written off as uncollectible.

DISCONTINUED OPERATIONS   A category on the income statement that indicates that a major segment or division of the company has been sold or will be sold.

DISCOUNTED NOTE   An alternative name for a non-interest bearing promissory note.

DISCOUNTING   Process of selling a promissory note.

DISCOUNT ON BONDS   The excess of the face value of bonds over the issue price. It occurs when the market rate on the bonds exceeds the face rate.

DISCOUNT ON NOTES PAYABLE   A contra-liability account that represents interest deducted in advance on a loan or note.

DIVIDEND PAYOUT RATIO   The annual dividend amount divided by the annual net income.

DIVIDENDS   A distribution of the net income of a business to its owners.

DIVIDEND YIELD   The relationship between dividends and market price of a company's stock.

DOUBLE DECLINING BALANCE METHOD   A depreciation method where depreciation is recorded at twice the straight line rate but the depreciable balance is reduced in each period.

DOUBLE ENTRY SYSTEM   A system of accounting in which every transaction is recorded with equal debits and credits and the accounting equation is kept in balance.

EARNINGS PER SHARE   A number that represents the rights of the common stockholders to the income of the company and is calculated as net income minus preferred dividends divided by the number of shares of common stock outstanding.

ECONOMIC ENTITY CONCEPT   The assumption that requires that a single, identifiable unit be accounted for in all situations.

EFFECTIVE INTEREST METHOD OF AMORTIZATION   The process of transferring a portion of premium or discount to interest expense. This method transfers an amount such that it results in a constant effective interest rate.

EQUITY METHOD   A method of accounting for investments in which income is recognized as a proportionate share of the income of the investee.

EQUITY SECURITIES   Securities issued by corporations as a form of ownership in the business.

ESTIMATED LIABILITY   A contingent liability that is accrued and recorded on the balance sheet. Common examples are warranties, guarantees, and premium offers.

EVENT   A happening of consequence to an entity.

EXCHANGE RATE   A measure of the relative worth of two different currencies.

EXPENSES   Outflows or other using up of assets or incurrences of liabilities from delivering goods, rendering services, or carrying out other activities.

EXTERNAL EVENT   An event involving interaction between an entity and its environment.

EXTRAORDINARY ITEM   An item that is considered both unusual and infrequent and is presented in a separate category of the income statement.

FACE RATE OF INTEREST   The interest rate that is stated on the bond certificate. It is also called the nominal or coupon rate.

FACE VALUE   The principal amount of the bond as stated on the bond certificate.

FIFO   An inventory costing method that assigns the most recent costs to ending inventory.

FINANCIAL ACCOUNTING   The branch of accounting concerned with the preparation of general purpose financial statements for use by both management and outsiders.

FINANCIAL ACCOUNTING STANDARDS BOARD   The group in the private sector with authority to set accounting standards.

FINANCING ACTIVITIES   Activities of a business concerned with the raising and repayment of funds in the form of debt and equity.

FINISHED GOODS   The inventory of a manufacturer that is complete and ready for sale.

FOB DESTINATION POINT   Terms that require the seller to pay for the cost of shipping the merchandise to the buyer.

FOB SHIPPING POINT   Terms that require the buyer to pay the shipping costs.

FOREIGN CORRUPT PRACTICES ACT   Legislation intended to increase the accountability of management for accurate records and reliable financial statements.

FOREIGN CURRENCY TRANSACTION   A transaction in which a company agrees to receive or make payment in a foreign currency.

FOREIGN CURRENCY TRANSLATION   The process of restating the financial statements of a company from one currency to another.

FUNCTIONAL CURRENCY   The currency of the primary economic environment in which an entity operates.

FUNDING PAYMENT   A payment made by the employer to the pension fund or its trustee.

FUTURE VALUE OF AN ANNUITY   The amount that will be accumulated in the future when a series of payments is invested and accrues interest until the future time.

FUTURE VALUE OF A SINGLE AMOUNT   The amount that will be accumulated in the future when one amount is invested at the present time and accrues interest until the future time.

GAIN ON SALE OF ASSET   An amount that indicates the selling price of an asset exceeds the book value of the asset.

GAIN OR LOSS ON REDEMPTION   The difference between the carrying value and the redemption price at the time bonds are redeemed. This amount is recorded as an income statement account.

GENERAL JOURNAL   The journal used in lieu of a specialized journal.

GENERAL LEDGER   A book, file, diskette, magnetic tape, or other device containing all of a company's accounts.

GENERALLY ACCEPTED ACCOUNTING PRINCIPLES   The various methods, rules, practices, and other procedures that have evolved over time in response to the need to regulate the preparation of financial statements.

GOING CONCERN   The assumption that an entity is not in the process of liquidation and that it will continue indefinitely.

GOODWILL   The amount that indicates that the purchase price of a business exceeded the total fair market values of the identifiable net assets at the time the business was acquired.

GROSS METHOD   The recording of either a purchase or sale at the full amount, before deducting any discount for early payment.

GROSS PROFIT   The amount of net sales minus the amount of cost of sales.

GROSS PROFIT METHOD   A technique used to establish an estimate of the cost of inventory stolen, destroyed, or otherwise damaged, or the amount of inventory on hand at an interim date.

GROSS PROFIT PERCENTAGE   A ratio calculated as the gross profit divided by the net sales.

GROSS PROFIT RATIO   Gross profit divided by net sales.

GROSS WAGES   The amount of an employee's wages before deductions.

HELD-TO-MATURITY SECURITIES   Investments in bonds of other companies in which the investor has the positive intent and the ability to hold the securities to maturity.

HISTORICAL COST   The amount paid for an asset that is used as a basis for recognizing it on the balance sheet and carrying it on later balance sheets.

HORIZONTAL ANALYSIS   A comparison of financial statement items over a period of time.

HORIZONTAL COMBINATION   A combination of businesses that are in competition with each other.

INCOME BEFORE INCOME TAXES   A subtotal on the income statement calculated as operating income plus other income items, such as interest, and minus other expense items.

INCOME STATEMENT   A statement that summarizes revenues and expenses.

INDIRECT METHOD   The approach to preparing the operating activities section of the statement of cash flows in which net income is reconciled to net cash flow from operations.

INSTALLMENT METHOD   Method in which revenue is recognized at the time cash is collected. Used for various types of consumer items, such as automobiles and appliances.

INTANGIBLE ASSET   A long-term asset that has no physical properties, for example, patents, copyrights, and goodwill.

INTEREST   The difference between the principal amount of a promissory note and its maturity value.

INTEREST-BEARING NOTE   A promissory note in which the interest rate is explicitly stated.

INTERNAL AUDITING   The department in a company responsible for the review and appraisal of a company's accounting and administrative controls.

INTERNAL AUDIT STAFF   The department responsible for the monitoring and evaluation of the internal control system.

INTERNAL CONTROL STRUCTURE   The policies and procedures established to provide assurance that entity objectives are achieved.

INTERNAL CONTROL SYSTEM   Policies and procedures necessary to insure the safeguarding of an entity's assets, the reliability of its accounting records, and the accomplishment of overall company objectives.

INTERNAL EVENT   An event occurring entirely within an entity.

INVENTORY PROFIT   That portion of the gross profit due to holding inventory during a period of rising prices.

INVENTORY TURNOVER   A measure of the number of times inventory is sold during a period.

INVESTING ACTIVITIES   Activities of a business concerned with the acquisition and disposal of long-term assets.

INVOICE   The form sent by the seller to the buyer as evidence of a sale.

INVOICE APPROVAL FORM   A form used by the accounting department prior to payment to document the accuracy of all the information about a purchase.

ISSUED SHARES   The number of shares sold or distributed to stockholders.

JOURNAL   A chronological record of transactions, also known as the book of original entry.

JOURNALIZING   The act of recording journal entries.

LAND IMPROVEMENTS   Additions that are made to a piece of property such as paving a parking lot or landscaping. The costs are treated separately from land in order to record depreciation.

LEVERAGE   The use of borrowed funds and amounts contributed by preferred stockholders to earn an overall return higher than the cost of these funds.

LIABILITY   An obligation of a business.

LIFO   An inventory costing method that assigns the most recent costs to cost of goods sold expense.

LIFO CONFORMITY RULE   A requirement of the IRS that if LIFO is used on the tax return then it must also be used in reporting income to stockholders.

LIFO LIQUIDATION   The result of selling more units than are purchased during the period, which can have negative tax consequences if a company is using LIFO.

LIFO RESERVE   The excess of the value of a company's inventory stated at FIFO as compared to LIFO.

LIQUIDITY   The ability of a company to pay its debts as they come due.

LONG-TERM LIABILITY   An obligation that will not be satisfied within one year.

LOSS ON SALE OF ASSET   An amount that indicates the book value of an asset exceeds the selling price received upon disposal of the asset.

LOWER-OF-COST-OR-MARKET RULE   A conservative approach to valuing inventory which is an attempt to anticipate declines in the value of inventory prior to its actual sale.

MAKER   The party to a promissory note that agrees to repay the money at some future date.

MANAGEMENT ACCOUNTING   The branch of accounting concerned with providing management with information to facilitate the planning and control functions.

MARKET RATE OF INTEREST   The interest rate that bondholders could obtain by investing in other bonds that are similar to the issuing firm's bonds.

MARKET VALUE PER SHARE   The selling price of the stock as indicated by the most recent stock transactions on, for example, the stock exchange.

MATCHING PRINCIPLE   The association of revenue of a period with all of the costs necessary to generate that revenue.

MATERIALITY   The magnitude of an omission or misstatement in accounting information that will affect the judgment of someone relying on the information.

MATURITY DATE   The date that a promissory note is due.

MATURITY VALUE   The amount of cash to be paid by the maker to the payee on the maturity date of a promissory note.

MERCHANDISE INVENTORY   The type of inventory held for sale by wholesalers and retailers.

MINORITY INTEREST   The owners' equity of a subsidiary not attributable to the interest of the parent.

MONETARY UNIT   The yardstick used to measure amounts in financial statements; the dollar in the U.S.

MOVING AVERAGE METHOD   The name given to an average cost method when it is used with a perpetual inventory system.

MULTIPLE-STEP INCOME STATEMENT   An income statement that provides the reader with classifications of revenues and expenses as well as with important subtotals.

NET METHOD   The recording of either a purchase or sale at the full amount less the applicable discount for early payment.

NET PAY   The amount of an employee's paycheck after deductions.

NET SALES   Sales revenue less sales returns and allowances and sales discounts.

NONBUSINESS ENTITY   Organization operated for some purpose other than to earn a profit.

NON-INTEREST BEARING NOTE   A promissory note in which interest is not explicitly stated but is implicit in the agreement.

NOTE PAYABLE   A liability resulting from the signing of a promissory note.

NOTE RECEIVABLE   An asset resulting from the acceptance of a promissory note from another company.

NUMBER OF DAYS' SALES IN INVENTORY   A measure of how long it takes to sell inventory.

NUMBER OF DAYS' SALES IN RECEIVABLES   A measure of the average age of accounts receivable.

OPERATING ACTIVITIES   Activities of a business concerned with the acquisition and sale of products and services.

OPERATING CYCLE   The period of time between the purchase of inventory and the collection of any receivable from the sale of the inventory.

OPERATING INCOME   A subtotal on the income statement calculated as gross profit minus operating expenses.

OPERATING LEASE   A lease that does not meet any of the four FASB criteria and is not recorded by the lessee.

ORGANIZATION COSTS   Costs that are incurred at the initial formation of a corporation and are treated as an intangible asset.

OUTSTANDING CHECK   A check written by a company but not yet presented to the bank for payment.

OUTSTANDING SHARES   The number of shares issued less the number of shares held as treasury stock.

OWNERS' EQUITY   The owners' claim on the assets of an entity.

PARENT   An entity that controls another entity by ownership of a majority of the other company's common stock.

PARTICIPATING PREFERRED STOCK   Stock which has a provision that allows the stockholders to share in the distribution of an abnormally large dividend on a percentage basis.

PARTNERSHIP   A business owned by two or more individuals and with the characteristic of unlimited liability.

PARTNERSHIP AGREEMENT   A document that specifies how much each owner should invest, salary of each owner, and how profits are to be shared.

PAR VALUE   An arbitrary amount stated on the face of the stock certificate that represents the legal capital of the firm.

PAYEE   The party to a promissory note that will receive the money at some future date.

PENSION   An obligation to pay retired employees as compensation for service performed while employed.

PERCENTAGE-OF-COMPLETION METHOD   A method used by contractors to recognize revenue prior to the completion of a long-term contract.

PERIODIC SYSTEM   The system in which the inventory account is updated only at the end of the period.

PERMANENT DIFFERENCE   A difference between the accounting for tax purposes and the accounting for financial reporting purposes. This type of difference occurs when an item affects one set of calculations but never affects the other calculations.

PERPETUAL SYSTEM   The system in which the inventory account is increased at the time of each purchase of merchandise and decreased at the time of each sale.

PETTY CASH FUND   Money kept on hand to make minor disbursements of coin and currency rather than by writing checks.

POOLING-OF-INTERESTS METHOD   An accounting approach to recording a business combination that is sometimes used when shares of stock in the two companies are exchanged.

POSTING   The process of transferring amounts from a journal to the appropriate ledger accounts.

PREMIUM ON BONDS   The excess of the issue price over the face value of bonds. It occurs when the face rate on the bonds exceeds the market rate.

PRESENT VALUE OF AN ANNUITY   The amount needed at the present time to be equivalent to a series of payments and interest in the future.

PRESENT VALUE OF A SINGLE AMOUNT   The amount at the present time that is equivalent to one amount at a future time.

PRICE/EARNINGS RATIO   The relationship between a company's performance according to the income statement as compared to its performance in the stock market.

PRINCIPAL   The amount of cash received, or the fair value of the products or services received, by the maker when a promissory note is issued.

PRIOR PERIOD ADJUSTMENT   A correction that is not recorded on the income statement but is presented as an adjustment of the balance of the Retained Earnings account.

PRODUCTION METHOD   Method in which revenue is recognized at the time a commodity is produced rather than when it is sold.

PROFITABILITY   How well management is using company resources to earn a return on the funds invested by the various groups.

PROFIT MARGIN   Net income divided by net sales.

PROJECTED BENEFIT OBLIGATION   A measure of the amount owed to employees for pensions that incorporates an estimate of the future salary increases that employees will receive.

PROMISSORY NOTE   A written promise to repay a definite sum of money on demand or at a fixed or determinable date in the future.

PROPRIETORSHIP   A business owned by a single owner.

PURCHASE DISCOUNTS   The contra-purchases account used to record reductions in purchase price for early payment to the supplier.

PURCHASE METHOD   An accounting approach to recording a business combination that is used when one company uses cash, other assets, or debt to acquire the other company.

PURCHASE ORDER   The form sent by the purchasing department to the supplier.

PURCHASE REQUISITION FORM   The form used by a department to initiate a request for an order of merchandise.

PURCHASE RETURNS AND ALLOWANCES   The contra-purchases account used in a periodic inventory system when a refund is received from a supplier or a reduction given in the balance owed to the supplier.

PURCHASES   The account used in a periodic inventory system to record acquisitions of merchandise.

QUANTITY DISCOUNT   A reduction in selling price for buying a large number of units of a product.

RAW MATERIALS   The inventory of a manufacturer before the addition of any direct labor or manufacturing overhead.

RECOGNITION   The process of recording an item in the financial statements as an asset, liability, revenue, expense, or the like.

REFINANCING   The term used to indicate that a short-term liability has not been paid, but has been replaced by a long-term loan or obligation.

RELEVANCE   The capacity of information to make a difference in a decision.

RELIABILITY   The quality of accounting information that makes it dependable in representing the events that it purports to represent.

REPLACEMENT COST   The current cost of a unit of inventory.

REPORT OF MANAGEMENT   A written statement in the annual report indicating the responsibility of management for the financial statements.

RESEARCH AND DEVELOPMENT COSTS   Expenditures incurred in the discovery of new knowledge and the translation of research in a design or plan for a new product.

RETAIL INVENTORY METHOD   A technique used by retailers to convert the retail value of inventory to a cost basis.

RETAINED EARNINGS   The part of owners' equity that represents the income earned less dividends paid over the life of an entity.

RETIREMENT OF STOCK   When a corporation buys its stock back and does not intend to reissue the stock.

RETURN ON ASSETS   A measure of a company's success in earning a return for all providers of capital.

RETURN ON SALES   A variation of the profit margin ratio, which measures earnings before payments to creditors.

RETURN ON STOCKHOLDERS' EQUITY   Net income divided by average stockholders' equity.

REVENUES   Inflows or other enhancements of assets or settlements of liabilities from delivering or producing goods, rendering services, or other activities.

REVENUE EXPENDITURE   A cost that keeps an operating asset in its normal operating condition and is treated as an expense of the period.

REVENUE RECOGNITION PRINCIPLE   Revenues are recognized in the income statement when they are realized, or realizable, and earned.

SALES DISCOUNTS   The contra-revenue account used to record discounts given customers for early payment of their accounts.

SALES RETURNS AND ALLOWANCES   The contra-revenue account used to record both refunds to customers and reductions of their accounts.

SECURITIES AND EXCHANGE COMMISSION   The federal agency with ultimate authority to determine the rules in preparing statements for companies whose stock is sold to the public.

SERIAL BONDS   Bonds that do not all have the same due date. A portion of the bonds come due each time period.

SHARE OF STOCK   A certificate that acts as ownership in a corporation.

SIMPLE INTEREST   Interest that is earned or paid on the principal amount only.

SINGLE-STEP INCOME STATEMENT   An income statement in which all expenses are added together and subtracted from all revenues.

SOLE PROPRIETORSHIP   Form of organization with a single owner.

SOLVENCY   The ability of a company to remain in business over the long run.

SOURCE DOCUMENT   A piece of paper, such as a sales invoice, that is used as the evidence to record a transaction.

SPECIFIC IDENTIFICATION   An inventory costing method that relies on a matching of unit costs with the actual units sold.

STATEMENT OF CASH FLOWS   The financial statement that summarizes the cash receipts and cash payments of an entity during the period from operating, investing, and financing activities.

STATEMENT OF RETAINED EARNINGS   The statement that summarizes the income earned and dividends paid over the life of a business.

STATEMENT OF STOCKHOLDERS' EQUITY   A statement that indicates the differences between beginning and ending balances for all accounts in the stockholders' equity category.

STATUTORY CONSOLIDATION   A business combination in which a new entity is created to carry on the activities of the entities involved in the combination.

STATUTORY MERGER   A business combination in which only one of the two entities survives.

STOCK ACQUISITION   A business combination in which one company acquires a majority of the common stock of the other company.

STOCK DIVIDEND   When a corporation declares and issues additional shares of its own stock to existing stockholders.

STOCK SPLIT   When additional shares of stock are created and the par value of the stock is reduced.

STOCK SUBSCRIPTION   An agreement by an investor to purchase stock and pay for it at a later date.

STOCKHOLDER   One of the owners of a corporation.

STOCKHOLDERS' EQUITY   The owners' equity in a corporation.

STRAIGHT-LINE DEPRECIATION   A depreciation method where the same dollar amount of depreciation is recorded in each year of asset use.

STRAIGHT LINE METHOD OF AMORTIZATION   The process of transferring a portion of premium or discount to interest expense. This method transfers the same dollar amount each period.

SUBSIDIARY   A separate legal entity controlled by another entity.

SUBSIDIARY LEDGER   The detail for a number of individual items that collectively make up a single general ledger account.

SUM-OF-YEARS'-DIGIT METHOD   A depreciation method where depreciation is recorded as a function of the total of the digits of the asset's life.

TEMPORARY DIFFERENCE   A difference between the accounting for tax purposes and the accounting for financial reporting purposes. This type of difference affects both book and tax calculations but not in the same time period.

TERM   The length of time a promissory note is outstanding.

TIME PERIOD   Artificial segment on the calendar used as the basis for preparing financial statements.

TIME VALUE OF MONEY   The concept that indicates that people should prefer an immediate amount at the present time over an equal amount in the future.

TIMES INTEREST EARNED   An income statement measure of the ability of a company to meet its interest payments.

TRADE DISCOUNT   A reduction in selling price offered to a special class of customers.

TRADING SECURITIES   Stocks and bonds of other companies bought and held for the purpose of selling them in the near term to generate profits on appreciation in their price.

TRANSACTION   Any event, external or internal, that is recognized in a set of financial statements.

TRANSLATION ADJUSTMENT   The amount needed to balance the two sides of a balance sheet when financial statements are translated from one currency into another currency.

TRANSPORTATION-IN   The adjunct account used to record freight costs paid by the buyer.

TREASURER   The officer of an organization responsible for the safeguarding and efficient use of a company's liquid assets.

TREASURY STOCK   Stock that has been issued by the firm and then repurchased but not retired.

TRIAL BALANCE   A work sheet showing the balances in each account; used to prove the equality of debits and credits.

UNDERSTANDABILITY   The quality of accounting information that makes it comprehensible to those willing to spend the necessary time.

UNITS-OF-PRODUCTION METHOD   A depreciation method where depreciation is determined as a function of the number of units produced by the asset.

UNREALIZED GAIN/LOSS AVAILABLE FOR SALE   An account in the stockholders' equity category which reflects that the investment in certain securities was adjusted to market value.

VERTICAL ANALYSIS A comparison of various financial statement items within a single period with the use of common-size statements.

VERTICAL COMBINATION A combination of a company with either a supplier or a customer.

WEIGHTED AVERAGE COST An inventory costing method that assigns the same unit cost to all units available for sale during the period.

WEIGHTED AVERAGE SHARES The number of shares of stock weighted by the time period that the stock was outstanding.

WHOLLY-OWNED SUBSIDIARY A subsidiary in which the parent owns all of the common stock.

WORKING CAPITAL Current assets minus current liabilities.

WORK IN PROCESS The cost of unfinished products in a manufacturing company.

SUBJECT INDEX

COMPANY INDEX